CLASSICS *of* PHILOSOPHY

VOLUME III

The Twentieth Century

Louis P. Pojman

New York Oxford
OXFORD UNIVERSITY PRESS
2001

Oxford University Press

Oxford New York
Athens Auckland Bangkok Bogotá Buenos Aires Calcutta
Cape Town Chennai Dar es Salaam Delhi Florence Hong Hong Istanbul
Karachi Kuala Lumpur Madrid Melbourne Mexico City Mumbai
Nairobi Paris São Paulo Singapore Taipei Tokyo Toronto Warsaw

and associated companies in
Berlin Ibadan

Published by Oxford University Press, Inc.
198 Madison Avenue, New York, New York 10016
http://www.oup-usa.org

Library of Congress Cataloging-in-Publication Data

Classics of Philosophy / [edited by] Louis P. Pojman.
p. cm.
Includes bibliographical references.
Contents: v. 1. Ancient and medieval—v. 2. Modern and contemporary—v. 3. The Twentieth Century
ISBN 0-19-511645-3 (v. 1).—ISBN 0-19-511646-1 (v. 2).—ISBN 0-19-513283-1 (v. 3).
1. Philosophy. I. Pojman, Louis P.
BD21.P476 1997
100–dc21 97-1134
CIP

Printing (last digit): 9 8 7 6 5 4 3 2 1

Printed in the United States of America
on acid-free paper

Dedicated to John MacQuarrie,
who introduced me to Continental Philosophy,
and
to the memory of Gilbert Ryle,
who introduced me to Analytic Philosophy.

Contents

Preface vi

Introduction 1

PART I: THE ANGLO-AMERICAN ANALYTIC TRADITION

1. **John M. E. McTaggart 11**
   The Unreality of Time, 12

2. **G. E. Moore 23**
   The Refutation of Idealism, 24
   A Defense of Common Sense, 35
   Proof of an External World, 37

3. **Bertrand Russell 42**
   The Problems of Philosophy, 44
   The Theory of Definite Descriptions, 85
   A Debate on the Existence of God between Father F. C. Copleston and Bertrand Russell, 91

4. **Charles Sanders Peirce 97**
   How to Make Our Ideas Clear, 98
   The Presuppositions of Science: Common Sense and Religion, 103

5. **William James 112**
   The Will to Believe, 113
   What Pragmatism Means, 120
   The Pragmatic Notion of Truth, 128

6. **Rudolf Carnap 135**
   The Elimination of Metaphysics Through Logical Analysis of Language, 136

7. **A. J. Ayer 148**
   The Abolition of Metaphysics, 149
   A Critique of Ethics and Theology, 156

8. **Ludwig Wittgenstein 165**
   Tractatus Logico-Philosophicus, 166
   Philosophical Investigations, 174

9. **J. L. Austin 183**
   Sense and Sensibilia: A Critique of the Theory of Sense Data, 184

10. **Karl Popper 187**
    Conjectures and Refutations, 188
    Epistemology Without a Knowing Subject, 192

11. **Thomas Kuhn 199**
    Objectivity, Value Judgment, and Theory Choice, 200

12. **W. V. O. Quine 210**
    Two Dogmas of Empiricism, 212
    Epistemology Naturalized, 224
    Ontological Relativity, 232

13. **Saul A. Kripke 249**
    A Priori Knowledge, Necessity, and Contingency, 249

14. **Jonathan Harrison 258**
    A Defense of Empiricism, 259

15. **Edmund L. Gettier 274**
    Is Justified True Belief Knowledge?, 277

16. **Alvin I. Goldman 279**
    What Is Justified Belief?, 280

17. **Nelson Goodman 294**
    The New Riddle of Induction, 294

18. **Donald Davidson 298**
    Truth and Meaning, 298

19. Hilary Putnam 308
Meaning and Reference, 308

20. Peter F. Strawson 315
Freedom and Resentment, 316

21. Harry Frankfurt 329
Freedom of the Will and the Concept of a Person, 330

22. Richard Taylor 339
A Defense of Libertarian Freedom of the Will, 339

23. Antony Flew, R. M. Hare, and Basil Mitchell 346
The Falsification Debate on Religious Belief, 347

24. Gilbert Ryle 352
Exorcizing Descartes's "Ghost in the Machine," 353

25. Thomas Nagel 360
What Is It Like to Be a Bat?, 361
Moral Luck, 367

26. Daniel Dennett 375
The Intentional Stance, 375

27. John Searle 387
Minds, Brains, and Programs [The Chinese Room], 388

28. Derek Parfit 395
Personal Identity, 395

29. Robert Nozick 408
A Defense of Libertarianism, 409
The Experience Machine, 423

30. John Rawls 425
A Theory of Justice: Liberal Egalitarianism, 427

31. Wallace Matson 435
Justice: A Funeral Oration, 436

PART II: CONTEMPORARY CONTINENTAL AND POSTMODERN PHILOSOPHY

32. Edmund Husserl 451
Ideas: General Introduction to Pure Phenomenology, 452

33. Martin Heidegger 466
On Dasein and Anxiety, 467
The Fundamental Question of Metaphysics, 480

34. Jean-Paul Sartre 498
Bad Faith, 499
Existentialism and Humanism, 510

35. Michel Foucault 515
The Discourse on Language, 516

36. Jacques Derrida 530
Plato's Pharmacy, 531

37. Richard Rorty 541
Dismantling Truth: Solidarity Versus Objectivity, 542

38. Margarita Rosa Levin 549
A Defense of Objectivity, 549

39. Jurgen Habermas 560
Philosophy as Stand-in and Interpreter, 561

Preface

As the twentieth century comes to a close, it is a good time to assess its accomplishments, including its philosophical accomplishments. As part of this assessment, I have attempted in this volume to assemble the classic essays on Western philosophy of the twentieth century, essays that have given shape to its character and structure. From Logical Positivism, American Pragmatism, and Ordinary Language philosophy to Continental Philosophy, the various types of philosophy have been creative, controversial and, typically, fascinating. Much of it has been deflationary of previous philosophy (for example, the empiricist rejection of Idealism or the deconstructionism of Derrida and Rorty). Attention to language characterizes much of both Anglo-American ("the linguistic turn") and Continental Philosophy (textual interpretation). In any case, I have tried to put together the best essays of the century, to give honor to the mountain peaks that stand above even the high average of the mountain range that characterizes the better part of the overall field. Nevertheless, having taught contemporary philosophy over a period of about seventeen years, and having read well over one hundred books and articles in the process of coming up with this final version, I am confident of having identified many excellent works of the twentieth century. Of course, only time will tell which works will endure as classics. I submitted my proposal to a group of eminent philosophers, receiving special help and advice from Michael Robbins, Michael Levin, Jonathan Harrison, John MacQuarrie, Wallace Matson, Michael Cavanaugh, David Keller, and others. As always, reviewers provided helpful criticism and advice. Space constraints required that I prune some excellent essays from the final work. I have kept to the design of my earlier *Classics of Philosophy* (Oxford, 1998) in emphasizing epistemological and metaphysical issues (even if they be a sort of antimetaphysical metaphysics, as I believe is the case with Logical Positivism). Doubtless, every philosopher will disagree with me on some of my final choices. My criteria have been excellence, accessibility, and influence on the field. I have tried to put together a work that philosophy students and intelligent lay persons can use without needing advanced technical ability in logic or semantics, also taking into account the influence each selection has had on the profession as a whole.

I find the philosophy of this century powerfully interesting, aiming at understanding the nature of reality as well as our knowledge of it. I was originally trained in Continental Philosophy, studying nineteenth- and twentieth-century Continental Philosophy at Union Theological Seminary in New York under John MacQuarrie and at the universities of Copenhagen and Hamburg. But upon coming to Oxford University, I developed a deep love–hate relationship with the Anglo-American Analytic Tradition. Professor John MacQuarrie is largely responsible for nourishing my Continental interest, and the late Professor Gilbert Ryle was a dynamic force in helping me to appreciate the Analytic tradition. This book is dedicated to these two mentors. I am grateful to Robert Miller, philosophy editor for Oxford University Press, who both suggested this volume as a follow-up to my larger work *Classics of Philosophy* and supported it at every step of the way. Elissa Morris, his assistant, graciously kept me supplied with books and reviews. Much of the work on this project was done at the Philosophy Subfaculty Library of Oxford University and at my college, Christ Church, where I was a Visiting Fellow during Trinity Term, 1999. I am grateful for the support I received there. Most of all my wife, Trudy, supported me in every way, proofreading each page of the manuscript and generally supplying me with an abundance of love and kindness.

United States Military Academy L. P. P.
West Point, N.Y.

Introduction

Philosophy in the Twentieth Century

This book is divided into two main parts, reflecting the two dominant traditions in twentieth-century Western philosophy: the Anglo-American Analytic Tradition and the Continental Tradition. There is nothing absolute about this division, since many of the pioneers and originators of the contemporary Anglo-American Analytic Tradition were, in fact, from the continent of Europe: Gottlob Frege, Moritz Schlick, Rudolf Carnap, Otto Neurath, and Hans Reichenbach, Karl Hempel, Alfred Tarski, and even Ludwig Wittgenstein (first selection, Chapter 8).

Nevertheless, the division does represent two opposite traditions or rival tendencies in doing philosophy—so different that one might question, as Richard Rorty (Chapter 37) has, whether they should both be called philosophy. For a simplistic but meaningful distinction, we might say that Analytic Philosophy is centered on language and logic, analyzing the meaning of words and sentences even as it analyzes arguments and builds comparatively modest epistemological and metaphysical theories. This tradition finds its originator in Socrates, who sought the definition of a word as revealing its meaning and as a prerequisite to solving the philosophical problem in question (e.g., What is Justice? What is knowledge?). The Continental Tradition is more speculative and radical, concerned, as Husserl (Chapter 32) is, with the phenomena themselves; Heidegger and Sartre (Chapters 33 and 34) dealing with the classical problem, What is the self? From Nietzsche and Bergson to Heidegger (Chapter 33), Derrida (Chapter 36) and Habermas (Chapter 39), continentalists are concerned with the question of human nature. "What is the human predicament?" (Heidegger, 33), and "What is the relationship between power and what we call knowledge?" (Marx, and Foucault, Chapter 35). Both traditions have an interest in ethics, but whereas the Analytic Tradition is centered on the nature and meaning of *right* and *wrong*, the Continental centers on question like, "How shall I live? What should I choose?" This tradition derives largely from G. W. F. Hegel (1770–1830), Søren Kierkegaard (1813–1855), and Nietzsche (1840–1900): Hegel contributing the speculative and phenomenological emphasis, Kierkegaard the emphasis on choice and existential commitment, and Nietzsche the focus on the will to power, the death of God, and perspectivism. Nietzsche defines truth as "a mobile army of metaphors, metonymns, and anthropomorphisms—in short, a sum of human relations, which have been enhanced, transposed, and embellished poetically and rhetorically and which after long use seem firm, canonical and obligatory to people."[1] Nietzsche's antirealist *perspectivism*—that there is no objective truth, only perspectival interpretation—is developed in the work of the French postmodernists Michel Foucault (Chapter 35) and Jacques Derrida (Chapter 36), as well as in the work of American Richard Rorty (Chapter 37), but is opposed by analytic philosophers like Karl Popper (both selections, Chapter 10). The Analytic Tradition tends to be realist, holding to a correspondence theory of truth, and seeing truth as largely empirical, a product of scientific inquiry. Let us turn briefly to the British realists. For a good encounter between these two traditions compare Heidegger's *The Fundamental Question of Metaphysics* (second selection, Chapter 33) with Rudolf Carnap's "The Elimination of Metaphysics Through Logical Analysis of Language" (6), Popper's "Epistemology Without a Knowing Subject" (second selection, Chapter 10) with Derrida's "Plato's Pharmacy" (36), and Rorty's "Dismantling Truth" (37) with Margarita Levin's "A Defense of Objectivity" (38). Jurgen Habermas's "Philosophy as Stand-in and Interpreter"

(39) may be seen as an attempt by a prominent continentalist to reconcile the Continental and Analytic traditions.

1. BRITISH REALISTS

At the turn of the century, two Cambridge University students, G. E. Moore (1873–1958) and Bertrand Russell (1872–1970), began to lose faith in F. H. Bradley's absolutist Idealist Monism, which in his magnum opus *Appearance and Reality* (1893) held to a Coherence Theory of Truth. That is, truth is holistic, consisting of a (internal) relationship of all the facts in the world. Truth is one, so to have knowledge is to know the whole and how the parts interrelate. As finite, we possess only degrees of truth. Our first reading by the British Hegelian idealist, John McTaggart, on "The Unreality of Time" is a classic twentieth-century expression of British Idealism.

In one of our second readings, Moore's "The Refutation of Idealism," Moore attacks A. E. Taylor and McTaggart, and especially, Bradley's position of internal relations as incoherent, and argues for the reality of external relationships. Truth is not one absolute coherent system, but a plurality of statements corresponding to a plurality of facts, hence the name *pluralism*. Truth is seen as a *correspondence* between a proposition and a state of affairs. In the second reading by Moore, Moore defends the commonsense point of view concerning our claims to knowledge against skepticism, which denies that we can have knowledge.

It was Bertrand Russell who developed the realist position the furthest. The world has the structure of logic whose grammar is perfect, unlike that of ambiguous natural languages. He held that logic must be a skeleton of language capable of experiencing all that can be accurately said at all. In a logically perfect language the words in a proposition would correspond one by one with the components of the corresponding facts. In sentences like (i) Bradley's "The Absolute enters but does not combine with all processes," (ii) "Unicorns do not exist," and (iii) "Nobody runs faster than I," the grammatical structure does not accurately reveal its logical structure. It is not clear what, if anything, is being referred to or asserted. For instance, the sentence from *Alice in Wonderland* "Nobody runs faster than I" treats "Nobody" as a proper name, which leads to nonsense—"Nobody must be a very fast runner."

With Alfred North Whitehead, Russell wrote the classic *Principia Mathematica* (1910–1914), where his logical system (Logical Atomism) is expounded in amazing and systematic detail. In a less technical article, "Descriptions" (Chapter 3), one of two selections by Russell, Russell develops a theory of definite description in which names were used to designate only existing individuals. He illustrates his theory more concretely as he examines the ambiguous sentence, "The present king of France is bald," which by the law of excluded middle must be either true or false. He analyzes the sentence in this manner:

1. There is at least one person who is the present king of France. (P)
2. There is at most one person who is the present king of France. (Q)
3. That person is bald. (R)

Putting this together we get the conjunctive proposition (P & Q & R). Since P is false (for France is not a monarchy), the whole conjunctive proposition is false. In this way Russell sought to disambiguate natural language, eliminating nonexistent "entities" and fiction. "Logic, I should maintain, must no more admit a unicorn than zoology can, for logic is concerned with its more abstract and general features."

In our first selection from Russell, his *Problems of Philosophy* (reproduced here almost in full), we have a paradigm treatise on the way the British realists sought to use analysis to solve metaphysical and epistemological problems, such as the nature of perception, universals, and truth, as well as the justification of induction. Finally, we include a nontechnical debate between Russell and the Catholic philosopher F. C. Copleston, on the claims of theology (third selection, Chapter 3).

2. AMERICAN PRAGMATISM: PRACTICALITY

Pragmatism is the only school of philosophy developed in the United States. Although started by Charles Peirce (1839–1914) and William James (1842–1910) in the 1870s, it dominated American philosophy in the first third of the twentieth century. Peirce invented the term from the Greek *pragma* (action or practice) and then revoked it, due to what he considered James's unfortunate interpretation of it. Peirce replaced it with the term *pragmaticism*, a term, he said, that was "too ugly to be kidnaped." Peirce expressed his ideas in his essay "How to Make Our Ideas Clear" (1878, first selection, Chapter 4), though James and John Dewey developed the philosophy in their own ways. For Peirce the main idea was to make philosophy serviceable to science, and to this end he developed an epistemology suited to satisfy the itch of ignorance and a theory of meaning, centered in the notion of a *sign* and *aiming at clear communication of ideas. Pragmatism* will show that every proposition is either meaningful or absurd and give us a way of deciding on truth. He sets forth a dispositional theory of meaning. For example, to say that O is hard means, under certain conditions, that most objects that scrape against object O will not scratch O. Truth, in turn, is defined as what the community of scientists would agree on given an indefinite amount of time.

While Peirce's Pragmatism was centered on scientific method, James's concerns were moral and religious. In his famous essay "The Will to Believe" (first selection, Chapter 5), he asks what are the practical and moral consequences of our beliefs. If believing that a religion is true, in spite of insufficient evidence, will produce moral and psychological good consequence, then we're justified in choosing to adopt that belief. In "The Pragmatic Notion of Truth" (third selection, Chapter 5), he rejects Moore's and Russell's Correspondence Theory of Truth for a pragmatic one. "He defines truth as that which works in the long run. Our thoughts and beliefs pass so long as nothing challenges them, just as bank notes pass as long as nobody refuses them." "True Ideas are those that we can assimilate, validate, corroborate and verify . . . the rue is only the expedient in the way of thinking." (second selection, Chapter 5). Crudely put, if it works, at least in the long run, it's true, and we're justified in choosing to adopt that belief.

James's philosophy, like that of Moore and Russell, is pluralistic, rooted in variegated human experience. He contrasts two kinds of philosophical attitudes—tough-minded and tender-pluralistic, deterministic, and materialistic. Tender-minded philosophers tend to be optimistic, religious, idealistic, free-willist, and monistic. James, while tending to tough-mindedness in his work as a psychologist, identifies more with the tender-minded—especially in his moral and religious concerns.

In the hands of John Dewey (1859–1952), who was interested in social and political processes, Pragmatism takes on a more instrumental turn, truth now being redefined as "warranted assertability." While Pragmatism greatly influenced the work of W. V. O. Quine (Chapter 12), the strongest contemporary proponent represented in our readings is Richard Rorty (Chapter 37).

3. LOGICAL POSITIVISM AND ITS CRITICS

Logical Positivism is the name given in 1931 by A. E. Bloomberg and Herbert Feigl to a set of philosophical doctrines put forward by the Vienna Circle. From 1907 to the early 1930s, these philosophers and scientists, led by Moritz Shlick and Rudolf Carnap, but including Frederick Waissmann, Kurt Godel, and Otto Neurath, sought to promote the ideas of the British empiricists, such as David Hume and Bertrand Russell, and the Czech thinker Ernest Mach, who held that science consists fundamentally in the description of experience. They hoped to produce a scientifically based philosophy, eliminating all transcendental metaphysics and emphasizing the importance of mathematics and theoretical physics.

Central to their program was the *verification principle* (attributed to Ludwig Wittgenstein who participated in their discussions) that the meaning of a sentence is the method of verifying the proposition it expresses—that is, a proposition names a set of sensory experiences which are together equivalent to the proposition's being true. Essentially, they were agreeing with David Hume's famous statement, "If we take in hand any volume of divinity or school metaphysics, for instance, let us ask, 'Does it contain any abstract reasoning concerning quantity or number?' No. 'Does it contain any experimental reasoning concerning matter of fact or existence?' No. Commit it then to the flames; for it can contain nothing but sophistry and illusion."[2] Mathematical and logical propositions were meaningful as tautologies. Ethical statements are not really assertions at all. Ethical statements, such as "Killing people is wrong," are meaningless emotional ejaculations (read, "killing people—boo!"). Theology consists of nonsense, since there is no way to verify its claims, for example that God exists and that He dwells in eternity beyond time.

Although the Vienna Circle dissolved in the early 1930s, its ideas spread to England and America. The classic expression of these ideas in English is A. J. Ayer's *Language, Truth and Logic* (1935), written as his doctoral dissertation after an extended stay in Austria with the members of the Vienna Circle. A large segment is reproduced here as the first selection in Chapter 7. In the United States it was combined with Pragmatism by Quine and Carl Hempel. Quine went beyond the positivists, arguing for the subordination of epistemology to psychology (see his "Epistemology Naturalized," Chapter 12), the relativity of reality (see his "Ontological Relativity," Chapter 12), the elimination of the analytic/synthetic distinction (see his "Two Dogmas of Empiricism," Chapter 12), and even the elimination of *meaning* altogether. In this latter essay, Quine also opposes the empirical tradition with its adherence to particularity in favor of holism—a version of the idealist doctrine, that our theories do not have infallible foundational structures but are open to choice and change, as we seek to justify them.

> The totality of our so-called knowledge or beliefs, from the most casual matters of geography and history to the profoundest laws of atomic physics or even pure mathematics and logic, is a man made fabric which impinges on experience only along the edges. Or, to change the figure, total science is like a field of force whose boundary conditions are experience. A conflict with experience at the periphery occasions readjustments in the interior of the field. Truth values have to be redistributed over some of our statements. Reevaluation of some statements entails reevaluation of others, because of their logical interconnections—the logical laws in turn imply certain further statements of the system, certain further elements of the field. Having reevaluated one statement we must reevaluate some others, which may be the statements of logical connections themselves. But the total field is so underdetermined by its boundary conditions, experience, that there is much latitude of choice as to what statements to reevaluate in the light of any single contrary experience. No particular experiences are linked with any particular statements in the interior of the field, except indirectly through considerations of equilibrium affecting the field as a whole.
>
> . . . Any statement can be held true come what may, if we make drastic enough adjustments elsewhere in the system. . . . Conversely, by the same token, no statement is immune to revision. Revisions even of the logical law of the excluded middle have been proposed as a means of simplifying quantum mechanics.

Jonathan Harrison challenges Quinean and Kripkean views in "A Defense of Empiricism" (Chapter 14), arguing for the validity of the analytic/synthetic distinction and the validity of the idea of meaning. He also rejects Kripke's idea of empirical necessary truths. While rejecting the verification principle, he sets forth a near relative principle of *sampling*.

Logical Positivism was seen by many, including its proponents, as destructive of philosophy. Its only role was to serve science by revealing the deep structure of our statements—by showing that philosophical problems are merely confusions. In the words of Wittgenstein, the role of this new philosophy is to deliver us from the bewitchment of our intellect, a bewitchment caused by philosophy. It is to help the fly get out of the fly bottle.

Gradually, a strong reaction arose against Logical Positivism. It was pointed out that its own verification principle was unscientific, since it could not be empirically verified. Statements about other minds reduce to sentences about their behavior and brain states. Popper (first selection, Chapter 10) rejected Logical Positivism in favor of the fallibilist method of conjecture and refutation. We are to set forth bold hypotheses and then attempt to falsify them—or at least narrow their scope—by finding counterexamples to them. In this way we reduce our claims to knowledge of whatever meets this method's survival test. Thomas Kuhn (Chapter 11) argued against the traditional empirical interpretation of scientific method, holding that subjective factors determined the interpretation of data and created scientific paradigms, which gradually won out in the field. In this way scientific advancement resembles theology, in which scientists trained in one orthodox tradition (normal science) are challenged by reform and revolutionary doctrine, wherein faith may be the decisive factor in theory selection.

When Carnap sought to correct the formula of Logical Positivism to read that a proposition is meaningful only if it is possible to confirm it, it was quickly noted that this would let in transcendental metaphysics, say in the sentence "Either it is raining or the absolute is perfect." Hilary Putnam gave the example, "There is a gold mountain one mile high and no one knows it," as a counter example to Logical Positivism's dicta. Even Ayer, moved by Alonzo Church's argument, conceded that the verification principle could not be formulated in a satisfactory way.[3]

Wittgenstein led the exodus from Positivism, arguing in his *Philosophical Investigations* (second selection, Chapter 8) that language had other legitimate functions besides serving science. "A philosophical problem has the form: 'I don't know my way about. Philosophy may in no way interfere with actual use of language; it can in the end only describe it. For it cannot give it any foundation either. It leaves everything as it is.'" Thoughts like these became the hallmark of *ordinary language philosophy*, led by Gilbert Ryle (Chapter 24), John Wisdom, and J. L. Austin (Chapter 9). Other traditional empiricists, like Russell and Brand Blanshard, who were eventually joined by Ayer, urged a return to traditional empirical philosophy with its emphasis on evidence and argument, not meaning. They argued that ethical and theological statements really are true or false, depending on the facts of the matter. Epistemology was alive again—the matter of evidence for propositions took on a renewed life. As mentioned earlier, Russell's *Problems of Philosophy* (1912, first selection, Chapter 3) is a classic example of this traditional empirical philosophy. Note too, the debate over the existence of God by Father Copleston and Russell and the falsification debate between Antony Flew, R. M. Hare, and Basil Mitchell (Chapter 23).

The Analytic Tradition in the second half of this century has been characterized by renewed interest in the necessary and sufficient condition for knowledge, beginning with Edmund L. Gettier's disrupting essay, "Is Justified True Belief Knowledge?" (Chapter 15). Alvin I. Goldman in "What Is Justified Belief?" (Chapter 16) seeks to replace internalist views of justification with external, reliable criteria. Popper (second selection, Chapter 10) argued for a quasi-platonic notion of a third world, the world of thought and theories, which had an objective and independent status of its own. Nelson Goodman (Chapter 17) challenges our theory of induction, offering a famous puzzle concerned with projectibility of characteristics.

The Analytic Tradition has always concerned itself with the problem of meaning and truth. Saul Kripke (Chapter 13) argues for a richer distinction than the traditional analytic (a priori)/synthetic (a posteriori), and that all necessary truths are a priori, arguing instead for a three-fold analytic/synthetic; a priori/empirical; and necessary/contingency. Donald Davidson (Chapter 18) shows the close connection between truth and meaning, and Putnam (Chapter 19) argues that meanings are not, a la perspectivalists, in the head, but in the world.

With the rise of science and its notion of determinate causation, the issue of free will became a burning one. Peter F. Strawson (Chapter 20) reflects on what difference causal determinism makes to our actions, and Harry Frankfurt (Chapter 21) seeks to reconcile Determinism and free agency. Richard Taylor defends an agency theory of free will (22).

The mind-body problem has preoccupied philosophers during the past four decades, producing brilliant work, Gilbert Ryle's antidualist "The Ghost in the Machine" (Chapter 24), Thomas Nagel's analysis of the ineliminability of the subjective in experience (first selection, Chapter 25), John Searle's famous Chinese Room article (Chapter 27), and Daniel Dennett's work on the intentional stance (Chapter 26). Related to this issue is Derek Parfit's ground-shattering essay on personal identity (Chapter 28) in which he argues that personal identity is relative, not absolute.

Social-political philosophy has been important in the Analytic Tradition, represented here by John Rawl's theory, "justice as fairness" (see Chapter 31), Robert Nozick's defense of libertarianism (first selection, Chapter 29), and Wallace Matson's classic "Justice: A Funeral Oration" (Chapter 31), a critique of both Rawlsian theory and "top-down" moral theories in general. Matson proposes a "bottom-up" approach to moral understanding. It begins in particular human needs and relationships which it seeks to ameliorate. I have also included Nagel's essay, "Moral Luck" (second selection, Chapter 25), which challenges the Kantian thesis that external factors (heteronomy) have nothing to do with the moral status of our character and acts. Nagel makes a case for luck entering into our moral assessments.

Let us briefly turn to Part II of our anthology: Contemporary Continental and Postmodern Philosophy. In 1900 two events occurred that would shape the fate of Continental philosophy. Nietzsche died in August and the Czech philosopher, Edmund Husserl (1859–1938), published his classic *Logical Investigation*. We have already noted Nietzsche's influence through his perspectivalism together with his notion of will to power and the death of God. If God is dead or doesn't exist, then, "we must become gods to be worthy of the act of being God's executioners." We see this radical freedom, this total responsibility for our being and selfhood, in the work of Jean-Paul Sartre (34). It also relates to Foucault's relation of power to truth and to Derrida's deconstructionism.

Husserl's phenomenological analysis (Chapter 32) gives a method to Continental philosophy. Husserl was influenced by Austrian philosopher Franz Brentano (1838–1917), who developed the idea of *intentionality*, the notion that consciousness always has an object and is never to be found isolated, alone. Consciousness is always directed toward something—real or imagined. Husserl thus rejects Kant's dualism of numinal/phenomenal worlds—the aim is to go to *the things themselves*. Consciousness is always consciousness of *something*. This applies to imagination, perception, volitions, and beliefs. Husserl set forth a transcendental philosophy in which he argued that *being* cannot be reduced to the logical positivist's idea of verification or to scientific method. What is needed is concentrated focus of attention on objects of consciousness—*epoche*—the bracketing of the phenomenon for intense detailed scrutiny. Husserl thought that such close scrutinizing analysis would develop into a science. There is even the suggestion that phenomenal analysis will, by implying what is beyond and necessary for reductive analysis, discover the transcendental, the Absolute, the noumenal, through the phenomenal.

Most of Husserl's followers followed Nietzsche rather than Husserl in rejecting a transcendent dimension. His most famous pupil, Martin Heidegger, though originally a Catholic seminary student, focuses on *Dasein*, man's "being there," who finds himself "thrown into existence" *(geworfenheit)*. We find ourselves in *Angst* (dread, existential anxiety). In the two readings from his work (33), especially "On Dasein and Anxiety," we see how phenomenological analysis is applied to the human predicament. In the French existential phenomenologist Sartre (Chapter 34) we view the synthesis between phenomenology and Nietzsche's radical volitionalism (will to power) come to a head. Going even beyond Nietzsche in asserting radical libertarian free will, Sartre develops such notions as radical choice, bad faith (inauthenicity), and man's nothingness. We create ourselves, our values, and our ethics. We are condemned to freedom. In Foucault's work (35) we see the Nietzschean postmodern skepticism about objective truth. Truth is created and maintained via power relations. In the work of Derrida (36) we see Nietzsche's perspectivalism reach new heights, as the text is seen without an essence, without a core meaning—it is entirely up to us to give meaning.

Rorty (Chapter 37) is the most prominent of American philosophers to be influenced by Heidegger, Foucault, and Derrida—along with whom he joins the American pragmatist, John Dewey. Rorty rejects the idea of objective truth in favor of a community's shared values. I have included Margarita Levin's critique of Rorty in order to juxtapose the Continental and Analytic traditions. In our final reading, Chapter 39, the postmodernist German hermeneuticist philosopher, Jurgen Habermas, critically follows Rorty—he endorses Rorty's stress on community, but also recognizes a modest place for reason and analysis in postmodern philosophy, in a manner that goes beyond Rorty toward analytic philosophers, such as Davidson and Putnam.

Notes

1. F. Nietzsche, *The Portable Nietzsche*, ed. Walter Kaufmann (Viking, 1977), p. 46.
2. David Hume, *An Enquiry Concerning Human Understanding* (Oxford University Press, 1975), p. 165.
3. See Alonzo Church's review of Ayer's *Language, Truth and Logic, Journal of Symbolic Logic* (1949).

PART I

THE ANGLO-AMERICAN ANALYTIC TRADITION

Chapter 1

John M. E. McTaggart

John McTaggart (1866–1925) was a British philosopher who defended a variety of metaphysical idealism (that is, he believed reality consisted of minds and their contents). Like many turn-of-the-century philosophers, he was influenced by Hegel's idealism. McTaggart argued that space, time, and material objects, as we ordinarily conceive them, are not real. He believed they are misperceptions of spiritual entities. Though McTaggart's idealism has had few followers, his argument against the reality of time has been widely studied. He distinguishes two ways to think about time: we can view time either as a series of pasts, presents, and futures (what he calls the "*A* series") or as a series of events standing in earlier-than or later-than relations (the "*B* series"). McTaggart claimed that the *B* series does not capture the essence of time, namely, change. So for time to be real (for there to be real change), the *A* series must be real. Then McTaggart argues that time cannot be real because the *A* series leads to logical difficulties. McTaggart's position is doubly challenging. If one believes time is real and the distinction between the past, present, and future is the essence of time, then one should try to rescue the *A* series from the logical problems McTaggart claims to find. If, on the other hand, one believes time is real and adequately represented by earlier-later relations, then one must defend the *B* series from McTaggart's charge that it pictures a universe devoid of real change.

FOR FURTHER READING

Augustine. *Confessions* Book 11 (several good translations).
Davies, P. C. W. *Space and Time in the Modern Universe* (Cambridge University Press, 1977).
Gale, R. M. *The Philosophy of Time* (Anchor, 1967).
Hawking, S. *A Brief History of Time* (Bantam, 1988).
Healey, R., ed. *Time and Reality* (Cambridge University Press, 1981).
Mellor, H. "McTaggart, Fixity and Coming True," in Healey, op. cit.

The Unreality of Time

It will be convenient to begin our enquiry by asking whether anything existent can possess the characteristic of being in time. I shall endeavour to prove that it cannot.

It seems highly paradoxical to assert that time is unreal, and that all statements which involve its reality are erroneous. Such an assertion involves a departure from the natural position of mankind which is far greater than that involved in the assertion of the unreality of space or the unreality of matter. For in each man's experience there is a part—his own states as known to him by introspection—which does not even appear to be spatial or material. But we have no experience which does not appear to be temporal. Even our judgments that time is unreal appear to be themselves in time.

Yet in all ages and in all parts of the world the belief in the unreality of time has shown itself to be singularly persistent. In the philosophy and religion of the West—and still more, I suppose, in the philosophy and religion of the East—we find that the doctrine of the unreality of time continually recurs. Neither philosophy nor religion ever hold themselves apart from mysticism for any long period, and almost all mysticism denies the reality of time. In philosophy, time is treated as unreal by Spinoza, by Kant, and by Hegel. Among more modern thinkers, the same view is taken by Mr Bradley. Such a concurrence of opinion is highly significant, and is not the less significant because the doctrine takes such different forms, and is supported by such different arguments.

I believe that nothing that exists can be temporal, and that therefore time is unreal. But I believe it for reasons which are not put forward by any of the philosophers I have just mentioned.

Positions in time, as time appears to us *prima facie*, are distinguished in two ways. Each position is Earlier than some and Later than some of the other positions. To constitute such a series there is required a transitive asymmetrical relation, and a collection of terms such that, of any two of them, either the first is in this relation to the second, or the second is in this relation to the first. We may take here either the relation of "earlier than" or the relation of "later than," both of which, of course, are transitive and asymmetrical. If we take the first, then the terms have to be such that, of any two of them, either the first is earlier than the second, or the second is earlier than the first.

In the second place, each position is either Past, Present, or Future. The distinctions of the former class are permanent, while those of the latter are not. If *M* is ever earlier than *N*, it is always earlier. But an event, which is now present, was future, and will be past.

Since distinctions of the first class are permanent, it might be thought that they were more objective, and more essential to the nature of time, than those of the second class. I believe, however, that this would be a mistake, and that the distinction of past, present, and future is as *essential* to time as the distinction of earlier and later, while in a certain sense it may, as we shall see, be regarded as more *fundamental* than the distinction of earlier and later. And it is because the distinctions of past, present, and future seem to me to be essential for time, that I regard time as unreal.

For the sake of brevity I shall give the name of the *A* series to that series of positions which runs from the far past through the near past to the present, and then from the present through the near future to the far future, or conversely. The series of positions which runs from earlier to later, or conversely, I shall call the *B* series. The contents of any position in time form an event. The varied simultaneous contents of a single position are, of course, a plurality of events. But, like any other substance, they form a group, and this group is a compound substance. And a compound substance consisting of simultaneous events may properly be spoken of as itself an event.[1]

The first question which we must consider is whether it is essential to the reality of time that its events should form an *A* series as well as a *B* series. It is clear, to begin with, that, in present experience, we never *observe* events in time except as forming both these series. We perceive events in time as being present, and those are the only events which we actually perceive. And all other events which, by memory or by inference, we believe to be real, we regard as present, past, or future. Thus the events of time as observed by us form an *A* series.

It might be said, however, that this is merely subjective. It might be the case that the distinction of positions in time into past, present, and future, is only a constant illusion of our minds, and that the real nature of time contains only the distinctions of the *B* series—the distinctions of earlier and later. In that case we should not perceive time as it really is, though we might be able to *think* of it as it really is.

This is not a very common view, but it requires careful consideration. I believe it to be untenable, because, as I said above, it seems to me that the *A* series is essential to the nature of time, and that any difficulty in the way of regarding the *A* series as real is equally a difficulty in the way of regarding time as real.

It would, I suppose, be universally admitted that time involves change. In ordinary language, indeed, we say that something can remain unchanged through time. But there could be no time if nothing changed. And if anything changes, then all other things change with it. For its change must change some of their relations to it, and so their relational qualities. The fall of a sand-castle on the English coast changes the nature of the Great Pyramid.

If, then, a *B* series without an *A* series can constitute time, change must be possible without an *A* series. Let us suppose that the distinctions of past, present, and future do not apply to reality. In that case, can change apply to reality?

What, on this supposition, could it be that changes? Can we say that, in a time which formed a *B* series but not an *A* series, the change consisted in the fact that the event ceased to be an event, while another event began to be an event? If this were the case, we should certainly have got a change.

But this is impossible. If *N* is ever earlier than *O* and later than *M*, it will always be, and has always been, earlier than *O* and later than *M*, since the relations of earlier and later are permanent. *N* will thus always be in a *B* series. And as, by our present hypothesis, a *B* series by itself constitutes time, *N* will always have a position in a time-series, and always has had one. That is, it always has been an event, and always will be one, and cannot begin or cease to be an event.

Or shall we say that one event *M* merges itself into another event *N*, while still preserving a certain identity by means of an unchanged element, so that it can be said, not merely that *M* has ceased and *N* begun, but that it is *M* which has become *N?* Still the same difficulty recurs. *M* and *N* may have a common element, but they are not the same event, or there would be no change. If, therefore, *M* changed into *N* at a certain moment, then at that moment, *M* would have ceased to be *M*, and *N* would have begun to be *N*. This involves that, at that moment, *M* would have ceased to be an event, and *N* would have begun to be an event. And we saw, in the last paragraph, that, on our present hypothesis, this is impossible.

Nor can such change be looked for in the different moments of absolute time, even if such moments should exist. For the same argument will apply here. Each such moment will have its own place in the *B* series, since each would be earlier or later than each of the others. And, as the *B* series depends on permanent relations, no moment could ever cease to be, nor could it become another moment.

Change, then, cannot arise from an event ceasing to be an event, nor from one event changing into another. In what other way can it arise? If the characteristics of an event change, then there is certainly change. But what characteristics of an event can change? It seems to me that there is only one class of such characteristics. And that class consists of the determinations of the event in question by the terms of the *A* series.

Take any event—the death of Queen Anne, for example—and consider what changes can take place in its characteristics. That it is a death, that it is the death of Anne Stuart, that it has such causes, that it has such effects—every characteristic of this sort never changes. "Before the stars saw one another plain," the event in question was the death of a Queen. At the last moment of time—if time has a last moment—it will still be the death of a Queen. And in every respect but one, it is equally devoid of change. But in one respect it does change. It was once an event in the far future. It became every moment an event in the nearer future. At last it was present. Then it became past, and will always remain past, though every moment it becomes further and further past.[2]

Such characteristics as these are the only characteristics which can change. And, therefore, if there is any change, it must be looked for in the *A* series, and in the *A* series alone. If there is no real *A* series, there is no real change. The *B* series, therefore, is not by itself sufficient to constitute time, since time involves change.

The *B* series, however, cannot exist except as temporal, since earlier and later, which are the relations which connect its terms, are clearly time-relations. So it follows that there can be no *B* series when there is no *A* series, since without an *A* series there is no time.

We must now consider three objections which have been made to this position. The first is involved in the view of time which has been taken by Mr Russell, according to which past, present, and future do not belong to time *per se*, but only in relation to a knowing subject. An assertion that *N* is present means that it is simultaneous with that assertion, an assertion that it is past or future means that it is earlier or later than that assertion. Thus it is only past, present, or future, in relation to some assertion. If there were no consciousness, there would be events which were earlier and later than others, but nothing would be in any sense past, present, or future. And if there were events earlier than any consciousness, those events would never be future or present, though they could be past.

If *N* were ever present, past, or future in relation to some assertion *V*, it would always be so, since whatever is ever simultaneous to, earlier than, or later than, *V*, will always be so. What, then, is change? We find Mr Russell's views on this subject in his *Principles of Mathematics*. "Change is the difference, in respect of truth or falsehood, between a proposition concerning an entity and the time *T*, and a proposition concerning the same entity and the time *T′*, provided that these propositions differ only by the fact that *T* occurs in the one where *T′* occurs in the other." That is to say, there is change, on Mr Russell's view, if the proposition "at the time *T* my poker is hot" is true, and the proposition "at the time *T′* my poker is hot" is false.

I am unable to agree with Mr Russell. I should, indeed, admit that, when two such propositions were respectively true and false, there would be change. But then I maintain that there can be no time without an *A* series. If, with Mr Russell, we reject the *A* series, it seems to me that change goes with it, and that therefore time, for which change is essential, goes too. In other words, if the *A* series is rejected, no proposition of the type "at the time *T* my poker is hot" can ever be true, because there would be no time.

It will be noticed that Mr Russell looks for change, not in the events in the time-series, but in the entity to which those events happen, or of which they are states. If my poker, for example, is hot on a particular Monday, and never before or since, the event of the poker being hot does not change. But the poker changes, because there is a time when this event is happening to it, and a time when it is not happening to it.

But this makes no change in the qualities of the poker. It is always a quality of that poker that it is one which is hot on that particular Monday. And it is always a quality of that poker that it is one which is not hot at any other time. Both these qualities are true of it at any time—the time when it is hot and the time when it is cold. And therefore it seems to be erroneous to say that there is any change in the poker. The fact that it is hot at one point in a series and cold at other points cannot give change, if neither of these facts change—and neither of them does. Nor does any other fact about the poker change, unless its presentness, pastness, or futurity change.

Let us consider the case of another sort of series. The meridian of Greenwich passes through a series of degrees of latitude. And we can find two points in this series, *S* and *S′*, such that the proposition "at *S* the meridian of Greenwich is within the United Kingdom" is true, while the proposition "at *S′* the meridian of Greenwich is within the United Kingdom" is false. But no one would say that this gave us change. Why should we say so in the case of the other series?

Of course there is a satisfactory answer to this question if we are correct in speaking of the other series as a time-series. For where there is time, there is change. But then the whole question is whether it is a time-series. My contention is that if we remove the *A* series from the *prima facie* nature of time, we are left with a series which is not temporal, and which allows change no more than the series of latitudes does.

If, as I have maintained, there can be no change unless facts change, then there can be no change without an *A* series. For, as we saw with the death of Queen Anne, and also in the case of the poker, no fact about anything can change, unless it is a fact about its place in the *A* series. Whatever other qualities it has, it has always. But that which is future will not always be future, and that which was past was not always past.

It follows from what we have said that there can be no change unless some propositions are sometimes true and sometimes false. This is the case of propositions which deal with the place of anything in the *A* series—"the battle of Waterloo is in the past," "it is now raining." But it is not the case with any other propositions.

Mr Russell holds that such propositions are ambiguous, and that to make them definite we must substitute propositions which are always true or always false—"the battle of Waterloo is earlier than this judgment," "the fall of rain is simultaneous with this judgment." If he is right, all judgments are either always true, or always false. Then, I maintain, no facts change. And then, I maintain, there is no change at all.

I hold, as Mr Russell does, that there is no *A* series. (My reasons for this will be given below.) And, as I shall explain, I regard the reality lying behind the appearance of the *A* series in a manner not completely unlike that which Mr Russell has adopted. The difference between us is that he thinks that, when the *A* series is rejected, change, time, and the *B* series can still be kept, while I maintain that its rejection involves the rejection of change, and, consequently, of time, and of the *B* series.

The second objection rests on the possibility of nonexistent time-series—such, for example, as the adventures of Don Quixote. This series, it is said, does not form part of the *A* series. I cannot at this moment judge it to be either past, present, or future. Indeed, I know that it is none of the three. Yet, it is said, it is certainly a *B* series. The adventure of the galley-slaves, for example, is later than the adventure of the windmills. And a *B* series involves time. The conclusion drawn is that an *A* series is not essential to time.

I should reply to this objection as follows. Time only belongs to the existent. If any reality is in time, that involves that the reality in question exists. This, I think, would be universally admitted. It may be questioned whether all of what exists is in time, or even whether anything really existent is in time, but it would not be denied that, if anything is in time, it must exist.

Now what is existent in the adventures of Don Quixote? Nothing. For the story is imaginary. The states of Cervantes' mind when he invented the story, the states of my mind when I think of the story—these exist. But then these form part of an *A* series. Cervantes' invention of the story is in the past. My thought of the story is in the past, the present, and—I trust—the future.

But the adventures of Don Quixote may be believed by a child to be historical. And in reading them I may, by an effort of my imagination, contemplate them as if they really happened. In this case, the adventures are believed to be existent, or are contemplated as existent. But then they are believed to be in the *A* series, or are contemplated as being in the *A* series. The child who believes them to be historical will believe that they happened in the past. If I contemplate them as existent, I shall contemplate them as happening in the past. In the same way, if I believed the events described in Jefferies' *After London* to exist, or contemplated them as existent, I should believe them to exist in the future, or contemplate them as existing in the future. Whether we place the object of our belief or of our contemplation in the present, the past, or the future, will depend upon the characteristics of that object. But somewhere in the *A* series it will be placed.

Thus the answer to the objection is that, just as far as a thing is in time, it is in the *A* series. If it is really in time, it is really in the *A* series. If it is believed to be in time, it is believed to be in the *A* series. If it is contemplated as being in time, it is contemplated as being in the *A* series.

The third objection is based on the possibility that, if time were real at all, there might be in reality several real and independent time-series. The objection, if I understand it rightly, is that every time-series would be real, while the distinctions of past, present, and future would only have a meaning within each series, and would not, therefore, be taken as absolutely real. There would be, for example, many presents. Now, of course, many points of time can be present. In each time-series many points are present, but they must be present successively. And the presents of the different time-series would not be successive, since they are not in the same time. And different presents, it would be said, cannot be real unless they are successive. So the different time-series, which are real, must be able to exist independently of the distinction between past, present, and future.

I cannot, however, regard this objection as valid. No doubt in such a case, no present would be *the* present—it would only be the present of a certain aspect of the universe. But then no time would be *the* time—it would only be the time of a certain aspect of the universe. It would be a real time-series, but I do not see that the present would be less real than the time.

I am not, of course, maintaining that there is no difficulty in the existence of several distinct *A* series. [Later] I shall endeavour to show that the existence of *any A* series is impossible. What I assert here is that, if there could be an *A* series at all, and if there were any reason to suppose that there were several distinct *B* series, there would be no additional difficulty in supposing that there should be a distinct *A* series for each *B* series.

We conclude, then, that the distinctions of past, present, and future are essential to time, and that, if the distinctions are never true of reality, then no reality is in time. This view, whether true or false, has nothing surprising in it. It was pointed out above that we always perceive time as having these distinctions. And it has generally been held that their connection with time is a real characteristic of time, and not an illusion due to the way in which we perceive it. Most philosophers, whether they did or did not believe time to be true of reality, have regarded the distinctions of the *A* series as essential to time.

When the opposite view has been maintained it has generally been, I believe, because it was held (rightly, as I shall try to show) that the distinctions of past, present, and future cannot be true of reality, and that consequently, if the reality of time is to be saved, the distinction in question must be shown to be unessential to time. The presumption, it was held, was for the reality of time, and this would give us a reason for rejecting the *A* series as unessential to time. But, of course, this could only give a presumption. If the analysis of the nature of time has shown that, by removing the *A* series, time is destroyed, this line of argument is no longer open.

I now pass to the second part of my task. Having, as it seems to me, succeeded in proving that there can be no time without an *A* series, it remains to prove that an *A* series cannot exist, and that therefore time cannot exist. This would involve that time is not real at all, since it is admitted that the only way in which time can be real is by existing.

Past, present, and future are characteristics which we ascribe to events, and also to moments of time, if these are taken as separate realities. What do we mean by past, present, and future? In the first place, are they relations or qualities? It seems quite clear to me that they are not qualities but relations, though, of course, like other relations, they will generate relational qualities in each of their terms. But even if this view should be wrong, and they should in reality be qualities and not relations, it will not affect the result which we shall reach. For the reasons for rejecting the reality of past, present, and future, which we are about to consider, would apply to qualities as much as to relations.

If, then, anything is to be rightly called past, present, or future, it must be because it is in relation to something else. And this something else to which it is in relation must be something outside the time-series. For the relations of the *A* series are changing relations, and no relations which are exclusively between members of the time-series can ever change. Two events are exactly in the same places in the time-series, relatively to one another, a million years before they take place, while each of them is taking place, and when they are a million years in the past. The same is true of the relation of moments to one another, if moments are taken as separate realities. And the same would be true of the relations of events to moments. The changing relation must be to something which is not in the time-series.

Past, present, and future, then, are relations in which events stand to something outside the time-series. Are these relations simple, or can they be defined? I think that they are clearly simple and indefinable. But, on the other hand, I do not think that they are isolated and independent. It does not seem that we can know, for example, the meaning of pastness, if we do not know the meaning of presentness or of futurity.

We must begin with the *A* series, rather than with past, present, and future, as separate terms. And we must say that a series is an *A* series when each of its terms has, to an entity *X* outside the series, one, and only one, of three indefinable relations, pastness, presentness, and futurity, which are such that all the terms which have the relation of presentness to *X* fall between all the terms which have the relation of pastness to *X*, on the one hand, and all the terms which have the relation of futurity to *X*, on the other hand.

We have come to the conclusion that an *A* series depends on relations to a term outside the *A* series. This term, then, could not itself be in time, and yet must be such that different relations to it determine the other terms of those relations, as being past, present, or future. To find such a term would not be easy, and yet such a term must be found, if the *A* series is to be real. But there is a more positive difficulty in the way of the reality of the *A* series.

Past, present, and future are incompatible determinations. Every event must be one or the other, but no event can be more than one. If I say that any event is past, that implies that it is neither present nor future, and so with the others. And this exclusiveness is essential to change, and therefore to time. For the only change we can get is from future to present, and from present to past.

The characteristics, therefore, are incompatible. But every event has them all. If *M* is past, it has been present and future. If it is future, it will be present and past. If it is present, it has been future and will be past. Thus all the three characteristics belong to each event. How is this consistent with their being incompatible?

It may seem that this can easily be explained. Indeed, it has been impossible to state the difficulty without almost giving the explanation, since our language has verb-forms for the past, present, and future, but no form that is common to all three. It is never true, the answer will run, that *M* *is* present, past, and future. It *is* present, *will be* past, and *has been* future. Or it *is* past, and *has been* future and present, or again *is* future, and *will be* present and past. The characteristics are only incompatible when they are simultaneous, and there is no contradiction to this in the fact that each term has all of them successively.

But what is meant by "has been" and "will be"? And what is meant by "is," when, as here, it is used with a temporal meaning, and not simply for prediction? When we say that *X* has been *Y*, we are asserting *X* to be *Y* at a moment of past time. When we say that *X* will be *Y*, we are asserting *X* to be *Y* at a moment of future time. When we say that is *X* is *Y* (in the temporal sense of "is"), we are asserting *X* to be *Y* at a moment of present time.

Thus our first statement about *M*—that it is present, will be past, and has been future—means that *M* is present at a moment of present time, past at some moment of future time, and future at some moment of past time. But every moment, like every event, is both past, present, and future. And so a similar difficulty arises. If *M* is present, there is no moment of past time at which it is past. But the moments of future time, in which it is past, are equally moments of past time, in which it cannot be past. Again, that *M* is future and will be present and past means that *M* is future at a moment of present time, and present and past at different moments of future time. In that case it cannot be present or past at any moments of past time. But all the moments of future time, in which *M* will be present or past, are equally moments of past time.

And thus again we get a contradiction, since the moments at which *M* has any one of the three determinations of the *A* series are also moments at which it cannot have that determination. If we try to avoid this by saying of these moments what had been previously said of *M* itself—that some moment, for example, is future, and will be present and past—then "is" and "will be" have the same meaning as before. Our statement, then, means that the moment in question is future at a present moment, and will be present and past at different moments of future time. This, of course, is the same difficulty over again. And so on infinitely.

Such an infinity is vicious. The attribution of the characteristics past, present, and future to the terms of any series leads to a contradiction, unless it is specified that they have them successively. This means, as we have seen, that they have them in relation to terms specified as past, present, and future. These again, to avoid a like contradiction, must in turn be specified as past, present, and future. And, since this continues infinitely, the first set of terms never escapes from contradiction at all.

The contradiction, it will be seen, would arise in the same way supposing that pastness, presentness, and futurity were original qualities, and not, as we have decided that they are, relations. For it would still be the case that they were characteristics which were incompatible with one another, and that whichever had one of them would also have the other. And it is from this that the contradiction arises.

The reality of the *A* series, then, leads to a contradiction, and must be rejected. And, since we have seen that change and time require the *A* series, the reality of change and time must be rejected. And so must the reality of the *B* series, since that requires time. Nothing is really present, past, or future. Nothing is really earlier or later than anything else or temporally simultaneous with it. Nothing really changes. And nothing is really in time. Whenever we perceive anything in time—which is the only way in which, in our present experience, we do perceive things—we are perceiving it more or less as it really is not.

Dr Broad, in his admirable book *Scientific Thought*, has put forward a theory of time which he maintains would remove the difficulties which have led me to treat time as unreal. It is difficult to do justice to so elaborate and careful a theory by means of extracts. I think, however, that the following passages will give a fair idea of Dr Broad's position. His theory, he tells us, "accepts the reality of the present and the past, but holds that the future is simply nothing at all. Nothing has happened to the present by becoming past except that fresh slices of existence have been added to the total history of the world. The past is thus as real as the present. On the other hand, the essence of a present event is, not that it precedes future events, but that there is quite literally *nothing* to which it has the relation of precedence. The sum total of existence is always increasing, and it is this which gives the time-series a sense as well as an order. A moment t is later than a moment t' if the sum total of existence at t includes the sum total of existence at t' together with something more."

Again, he says that "judgments which profess to be about the future do not refer to any fact, whether positive or negative, at the time when they are made. They are therefore at that time neither true nor false. They will become true or false when there is a fact for them to refer to; and after this they will remain true or false, as the case may be, for ever and ever. If you choose to define the word *judgment* in such a way that nothing is to be called a judgment unless it be either true or false, you must not, of course, count judgments that profess to be about the future as judgments. If you accept the latter, you must say that the Law of Excluded Middle does not apply to all judgments. If you reject them, you may say that the Law of Excluded Middle applies to all genuine judgments; but you must add that judgments which profess to be about the future are not genuine judgments when they are made, but merely enjoy a courtesy title by anticipation, like the elder sons of the higher nobility during the lifetime of their fathers." "I do not think that the laws of logic have anything to say against this kind of change; and, if they have, so much the worse for the laws of logic, for it is certainly a fact."

My first objection to Dr Broad's theory is that, as he says, it would involve that "it will rain tomorrow" is neither true nor false, and that "England will be a republic in 1920," was not false in 1919. It seems to me quite certain that "it will rain tomorrow" is either true or false, and that "England will be a republic in 1920," was false in 1919. Even if Dr Broad's theory did enable him to meet my objections to the reality of time (which I shall try to show later on is not the case) I should still think that my theory should be accepted in preference to his. The view that time is unreal is, no doubt, very different from the *prima facie* view of reality. And it involves that perception can be erroneous. But the *prima facie* view of reality need not be true, and erroneous perception is not impossible. And, I submit, it is quite impossible that "it will rain to-morrow" is neither true nor false.

In the second place it is to be noted that Dr Broad's theory must be false if the past ever intrinsically determines the future. If X intrinsically determines a subsequent Y, then (at any rate as soon as X is present or past, and therefore, on Dr Broad's theory, real) it will be true that, since there is an X, there must be a subsequent Y. Then it is true that there is a subsequent Y. And if that Y is not itself present or past, then it is true that there will be a future Y, and so something is true about the future.

Now is it possible to hold that the past never does intrinsically determine the future? It seems to me that there is just as much reason to believe that the past determines the future as there is to believe that the earlier past determines the later past or the present.

We cannot, indeed, usually get a positive statement as simple as "the occurrence of X intrinsically determines the occurrence of a subsequent Y." But the intrinsic determination of the events can often be summed up in a statement of only moderate complexity. If the moon was visible in a certain direction last midnight, this intrinsically determines that, either it will be visible in a rather different direction next midnight, or the night will be cloudy, or the universe will have come to an end, or the relative motions of the earth and moon will have changed. Thus it is true that in the future one of four things will happen. And thus a proposition about the future is true.

And there are other intrinsic determinations which can be summed up in very simple negative statements. If Smith has already died childless, this intrinsically determines that no future event will be a marriage of one of Smith's grandchildren.

It seems, then, impossible to deny that the truth of some propositions about the future is implied in the truth of some propositions about the past, and that, therefore, some propositions about the future are true. And we may go further. If no propositions abut the past implied propositions about the future, then no propositions about the past could imply propositions about the later past or the present.

If the proposition "the occurrence of *X* implies the occurrence of *Y*" is ever true, it is always true, while *X* is real, and, therefore, even according to Dr Broad's view of reality, it is always true while *X* is present and past. For it is dependent on the nature of *X* and the laws of implication. The latter are not changeable, and when an event has once happened, its nature remains unchangeable. Thus, if it were not true, in 1921, that the occurrence of any event in 1920 involved the occurrence of any event in 1922, then it could not be true in 1923, when both 1920 and 1922 are in the past. And this would apply to any two periods in time, as much as to 1920 and 1922.

There are, then, only two alternatives. Either propositions about the future are true, and Dr Broad's theory is wrong. Or else no proposition about any one period of time implies the truth of a proposition about any other period of time. From this it follows that no event at any point of time intrinsically determines any event at any other point of time, and that there is no causal determination except what is strictly simultaneous.

It is clear, from the rest of his book, that Dr Broad does not accept this last alternative, and it is difficult to conceive that anyone would do so, unless he were so complete a sceptic that he could have no theory as to the nature of time, or of anything else. For a person who accepted this alternative would not merely deny that complete causal determination could be proved, he would not merely deny that any causal determination could be proved, but he would assert that all causal determination, between non-simultaneous events, was proved to be impossible. But if this is not accepted, then some propositions about the future must be true.

In the third place, even if the two objections already considered should be disregarded, time would still, on Dr Broad's theory, involve the contradiction described above. For although, if Dr Broad were right, no moment would have the three incompatible characteristics of past, present, and future, yet each of them (except the last moment of time, if there should be a last moment) would have the two incompatible characteristics of past and present. And this would be sufficient to produce the contradiction.

The words past and present clearly indicate different characteristics. And no one, I think, would suggest that they are simply compatible, in the way that the characteristics red and sweet are. If one man should say "strawberries are red," and another should reply "that is false, for they are sweet," the second man would be talking absolute nonsense. But if the first should say "you are eating my strawberries," and the second should reply "that is false, for I have already eaten them," the remark is admittedly not absolute nonsense, though its precise relation to the truth would depend on the truth about the reality of matter and time.

The terms can only be made compatible by a qualification. The proper statement of that qualification seems to me to be, as I have said, that, when we say that *M* is present, we mean that it is present at a moment of present time, and will be past at some moment of future time, and that, when we say that *M* is past we mean that it has been present at some moment of past time, and is past at a moment of present time. Dr Broad will, no doubt, claim to cut out "will be past at some moment of future time." But even then it would be true that, when we say *M* is past, we mean that it has been present at some moment of past time, and is past at a moment of present time, and that, when we say *M* is present, we mean that it is present at a moment of present time. As much as this Dr Broad can say, and as much as this he must say, if he admits that each event (except a possible last event) is both present and past.

Thus we distinguish the presentness and pastness of events by reference to past and present moments. But every moment which is past is also present. And if we attempt to remove this difficulty by saying that it *is* past and *has been* present, then we get an infinite vicious series.

For these three reasons it seems to me that Dr Broad's theory of time is untenable, and that the reality of time must still be rejected.

It is sometimes maintained that we are so immediately certain of the reality of time, that the certainty exceeds any certainty which can possibly be produced by arguments to the contrary, and that such arguments, therefore, should be rejected as false, even if we can find no flaw in them.

It does not seem to me that there is any immediate certainty of the reality of time. It is true, no doubt, that we perceive things as in time, and that therefore the unreality of time involves the occurrence of erroneous perception. But, as I have said, I hope to prove later that there is no impossibility in erroneous perception. It may be worth while, however, to point out that any theory which treated time as objectively real could only do so by treating time, *as we observe it*, as being either unreal or merely subjective. It would thus have no more claim to support from our perceptions than the theories which deny the reality of time.

I perceive as present at one time whatever falls within the limits of one specious present. Whatever falls earlier or later than this, I do not perceive at all, though I judge it to be past or future. The time-series then, of which any part is perceived by me, is a time-series in which the future and the past are separated by a present which is a specious present.

Whatever is simultaneous with anything present, is itself present. If, therefore, the objective time-series, in which events really are, is the series which I immediately perceive, whatever is simultaneous with my specious present is present. But the specious present varies in length according to circumstances. And it is not impossible that there should be another conscious being existing besides myself, and that his specious present and mine may at the same time be of different lengths. Now the event *M* may be simultaneous both with *X*'s perception *Q*, and with *Y*'s perception *R*. At a certain moment *Q* may have ceased to be a part of *X*'s specious present. *M*, therefore, will at that moment be past. But at the same moment *R* may still be a part of *Y*'s specious present. And, therefore, *M* will be present at some moment at which it is past.

This is impossible. If, indeed, the *A* series was something purely subjective, there would be no difficulty. We could say that *M* was past for *X* and present for *Y*, just as we could say that it was pleasant for *X* and painful for *Y*. But we are now considering the hypothesis that time is objective. And, since the *A* series is essential to time, this involves that the *A* series is objective. And, if so, then at any moment *M* must be present, past, or future. It cannot be both present and past.

The present, therefore, through which events are really to pass, cannot be determined as being simultaneous with a specious present. If it has a duration, it must be a duration which is independently fixed. And it cannot be independently fixed so as to be identical with the duration of all specious presents, since all specious presents have not the same duration. And thus an event may be past or future when I am perceiving it as present, and may be present when I am remembering it as past or anticipating it as future. The duration of the objective present may be the thousandth part of a second. Or it may be a century, and the coronations of George IV and of Edward VII may form part of the same present. What reasons can we find in the immediate certainties of our experience to believe in the existence of such a present, which we certainly do not observe to be a present, and which has no relation to what we do observe as a present?

If we take refuge from these difficulties in the view, which has sometimes been held, that the present in the *A* series is not a finite duration, but a single point, separating future from past, we shall find other difficulties as serious. For then the objective time, in which events are, would be something entirely different from the time in which we experience them as being. The time in which we experience them has a present of varying finite duration, and is therefore divided into three durations—the past, the present, and the future. The objective time has only two durations, separated by a present which has nothing but the name in common with the present of experience, since it is not a duration but a point. What is there in our perception which gives us the least reason to believe in such a time as this?

And thus the denial of the reality of time turns out not to be so very paradoxical. It was called paradoxical because it required us to treat our experience of time as illusory. But now we see that our experience of time—centring as it does about the specious present—would be no less illusory if there were a real time in which the realities we experience existed. The specious present of our observations cannot correspond to the present of the events observed. And consequently the past and future of our observations could not correspond to the past and future of the events observed. On either hypothesis—whether we take time as real or as unreal—everything is observed as in a specious present, but nothing, not even the observations themselves, can ever really *be* in a specious present. For if time is unreal, nothing can be in any present at all, and, if time is real, the present in which things are will not be a specious present. I do not see, therefore, that we treat experience as much more illusory when we say that nothing is ever present at all, than when we say that everything passes through some present which is entirely different from the only present we experience.

It must further be noted that the results at which we have arrived do not give us any reason to suppose that *all* the elements in our experience of time are illusory. We have come to the conclusion that there is no real *A* series, and that therefore there is no real *B* series, and no real time-series. But it does not follow that when we have experience of a time-series we are not observing a real series. It is possible that, whenever we have an illusory experience of a time-series, we are observing a real series, and that all that is illusory is the appearance that it is a time-series. Such a series as this—a series which is not a time-series, but under certain conditions appears to us to be one—may be called a *C* series.

There are good reasons for supposing that such a *C* series does actually exist, in every case in which there is the appearance of a time-series. For when we consider how an illusion of time can come about, it is very difficult to suppose, either that all the elements in the experience are illusory, or that the element of the serial nature is so. And it is by no means so difficult to account for the facts if we suppose that there is an existent *C* series. In this case the illusion consists only in our applying the *A* series to it, and in the consequent appearance of the *C* series as a *B* series, the relation, whatever it may be, which holds between the terms of the *C* series, appearing as a relation of earlier and later.

The *C* series, then, can be real, while the *A* and *B* series are merely apparent. But when we consider how our experience is built up, we must class *C* and *A* together as primary, while *B* is only secondary. The real *C* series and the appearance of the *A* series must be given, separately and independently, in order to have the experience of time. For, as we have seen, they are both essential to it, and neither can be derived from the other. The *B* series, on the other hand, can be derived from the other two. For if there is a *C* series, where the terms are connected by permanent relations, and if the terms of this series appear also to form an *A* series, it will follow that the terms of the *C* series will also appear as a *B* series, those which are placed first, in the direction from past to future, appearing as earlier than those whose places are further in the direction of the future.

And thus, if there is a *C* series, it will follow that our experience of the time-series will not be entirely erroneous. Through the deceptive form of time, we shall grasp some of the true relations of what really exists. If we say that the events *M* and *N* are simultaneous, we say that they occupy the same position in the time-series. And there will be some truth in this, for the realities, which we perceive as the events *M* and *N*, do really occupy the same position in a series, though it is not a temporal series.

Again, if we assert that the events *M, N, O* are all at different times, and are in that order, we assert that they occupy different positions in the time-series, and that the position of *N* is between the positions of *M* and *O*. And it will be true that the realities which we see as these events will be in a series, though not in a temporal series, and that they will be in different positions in it, and that the position of the reality which we perceive as the event *N* will be between the positions of the realities which we perceive as the events *M* and *O*.

If this view is adopted, the result will so far resemble the views of Hegel rather than those of Kant. For Hegel regarded the order of the time-series as a reflection, though a distorted reflection, of something in the real nature of the timeless reality, while Kant does not seem to have contemplated the possibility that anything in the nature of the noumenon should correspond to the time-order which appears in the phenomenon.

Thus the *C* series will not be altogether unlike the time-series as conceived by Mr Russell. The *C* series will include as terms everything which appears to us as an event in time, and the *C* series will contain the realities in the same order as the events are ranged in by the relations of earlier and later. And the time-series, according to Mr Russell, does not involve the objective reality of the *A* series.

But there remain important differences. Mr Russell's series is a time-series, and the *C* series is not temporal. And although Mr Russell's time-series (which is identical with our *B* series) has a one-to-one correspondence with the *C* series, still the two series are very different. The terms of the *B* series are events, and the terms of the *C* series are not. And the relation which unites the terms of the *B* series is the relation of earlier and later, which is not the case with the *C* series.

Notes

1. It is very usual to contemplate time by the help of a metaphor of spatial movement. But spatial movement in which direction? The movement of time consists in the fact that later and later terms pass into the present, or—which is the same fact expressed in another way—that presentness passes to later and later terms. If we take it the first way, we are taking the *B* series as sliding along a fixed *A* se-

ries. If we take it the second way, we are taking the *A* series as sliding along a fixed *B* series. In the first case time presents itself as a movement from future to past. In the second case it presents itself as a movement from earlier to later. And this explains why we say that events come out of the future, while we say that we ourselves move towards the future. For each man identifies himself especially with his present state, as against his future or his past, since it is the only one which he is directly perceiving. And this leads him to say that he is moving with the present towards later events. And as those events are now future, he says that he is moving towards the future.

Thus the question as to the movement of time is ambiguous. But if we ask what is the movement of either series, the question is not ambiguous. The movement of the *A* series along the *B* series is from earlier to later. The movement of the *B* series along the *A* series is from future to past.

2. The past, therefore, is always changing, if the *A* series is real at all, since at each moment a past event is further in the past than it was before. This result follows from the reality of the *A* series, and is independent of the truth of our view that all change depends exclusively on the *A* series. It is worth while to notice this, since most people combine the view that the *A* series is real with the view that the past cannot change—a combination which is inconsistent.

Chapter 2

G. E. Moore

G. E. Moore (1873–1958) was Professor of Philosophy at Cambridge University and one of the leading British philosophers of the first half of the twentieth century. As a student at Cambridge, he was a close acquaintance and later a rival of Bertrand Russell. He was also the leader of the famed Bloomsbury group of writers, intellectuals, and artists, including John Maynard Keynes, Leonard and Virginia Woolf, and Lytton Strachy. He was editor of the British journal *Mind* from 1921 to 1947 and was appointed to the Order of Merit in 1951. Perhaps his most influential work is *Principia Ethica* (1903), in which he argues for the indefinability of the word *good*, and defends an intuitionist ethical system. Moore was a staunch defender of common sense in philosophy. In our first selection he attacks Idealism, held by F. H. Bradley and his teacher, John McTaggart. He begins by attempting to refute the idealist slogan *to be is to be perceived*, which Moore took to mean that all reality is spiritual. He also defends the notion that what is experienced is often logically independent of our experience of it. He rejects the idealist doctrine of internal relations, that all objects are internally related to each other. On the contrary, he argues, red and our experience of red are both distinct but involve an external relationship between consciousness, which is mental, and redness, which is not.

In our second selection, "A Defense of Common Sense," Moore defends common sense against skepticism and those who would reject our ordinary knowledge claims. He argues that there is a vast amount of shared knowledge about the world, expressible in ordinary language and about which we can be quite certain, so that skepticism is false. We can outline the argument this way:

1. If skepticism is true, we do not have knowledge of the external world.

2. But we do have knowledge of the external world (Moore gives numerous examples).

Therefore

3. Skepticism is false.

FOR FURTHER READING

Copleston, F. C. *Contemporary Philosophy* (Newman Press, 1963).
Lewis, H. D. *Contemporary British Philosophy* (George Allen & Unwin, 1956).
Flew, Antony, ed. *Logic and Language* (Doubleday Anchor, 1951).
Gross, Barry. *Analytic Philosophy* (Pegasus, 1970).
Moore, G. E. *Philosophical Papers* (Collier Books, 1962).
———. *Some Main Problems of Philosophy* (Collier Books, 1962).
Passamore, John. *A Hundred Years of Philosophy* (Macmillan, 1957).
Urmson, J. O. *Philosophical Analysis* (Oxford University Press, 1956).

The Refutation of Idealism

Modern Idealism, if it asserts any general conclusion about the universe at all, asserts that it is *spiritual*. There are two points about this assertion to which I wish to call attention. These points are that, whatever be its exact meaning, it is certainly meant to assert (1) that the universe is very different indeed from what it seems, and (2) that it has quite a large number of properties which it does not seem to have. Chairs and tables and mountains *seem* to be very different from us; but, when the whole universe is declared to be spiritual, it is certainly meant to assert that they are far more like us than we think. The Idealist means to assert that they are *in some sense* neither lifeless nor unconscious, as they certainly seem to be; and I do not think his language is so grossly deceptive, but that we may assume him to believe that they really are very different indeed from what they seem. And secondly when he declares that they are *spiritual*, he means to include in that term quite a large number of different properties. When the whole universe is declared to be spiritual, it is meant not only that it is in some sense *conscious*, but that it has what we recognise in ourselves as the *higher* forms of consciousness. That it is intelligent; that it is purposeful; that it is not mechanical; all these different things are commonly asserted of it. In general, it may be said, this phrase "reality is spiritual" excites and expresses the belief that the *whole* universe possesses *all the qualities* the possession of which is held to make us so superior to things which seem to be inanimate: at least, if it does not possess exactly those which we possess, it possesses not one only, but several others, which, by the same ethical standard, would be judged equal to or better than our own. When we say it is *spiritual* we mean to say that it has quite a number of excellent qualities, different from any which we commonly attribute either to stars or planets or to cups and saucers.

Now why I mention these two points is that when engaged in the intricacies of philosophic discussion, we are apt to overlook the vastness of the difference between this idealistic view and the ordinary view of the world, and to overlook the number of *different* propositions which the idealist must prove. It is, I think, owing to the vastness of this difference and owing to the number of different excellences which Idealists attribute to the universe, that it seems such an interesting and important question whether to assume, that if one or two points be made on either side, the whole case is won. I say this lest it should be thought that any of the arguments which will be advanced in this paper would be sufficient to disprove, or any refutation of them sufficient to prove, the truly interesting and important proposition that reality is spiritual. For my own part I wish it to be clearly understood that I do not suppose that anything I shall say has the smallest tendency to prove that reality is not spiritual: I do not believe it possible to refute a single one of the many important propositions contained in the assertion that it is so. Reality may be spiritual, for all I know; and I devoutly hope it is. But I take "Idealism" to be a wide term and to include not only this interesting conclusion but a number of arguments which are supposed to be, if not sufficient, at least *necessary*, to prove it. Indeed I take it that modern Idealists are chiefly distinguished by certain arguments which they have in common. That reality is spiritual has, I believe, been the tenet of many theologians; and yet, for believing that alone, they should hardly be called Idealists. There are besides, I believe, many persons, not improperly called Idealists, who hold certain characteristic propositions, without venturing to think them quite sufficient to prove so grand a conclusion. It is, therefore, only with Idealistic *arguments* that I am concerned; and if any Idealist holds that *no* argument is necessary to prove that reality is spiritual, I shall certainly not have refuted him. I shall, however, attack at least one argument, which, to the best of my belief, is considered necessary to their position by all Idealists. And I wish to point out a certain advantage which this procedure gives me—an advantage which justifies the assertion that, if my arguments are sound, they will have refuted Idealism. If I can refute a single propo-

Reprinted from G. E. Moore, "The Refutation of Idealism," *Philosophical Studies* (Routledge & Kegan Paul, 1922). Reprinted by permission of Timothy Moore.

sition which is a necessary and essential step in all Idealistic arguments, then, no matter how good the rest of these arguments may be, I shall have proved that Idealists have *no reason whatever* for their conclusion.

Suppose we have a chain of argument which takes the form: Since A is B, and B is C, and C is D, it follows A is D. In such an argument though "B is C" and "C is D" may both be perfectly true, yet if "A is B" be false, we have no more reason for asserting A is D than if all three were false. It does not, indeed, follow that A is D is false; nor does it follow that no other arguments would prove it to be true. But it does follow that, so far as this argument goes, it is the barest supposition, without the least bit of evidence. I propose to attack a proposition which seems to me to stand in this relation to the conclusion "Reality is spiritual." I do not propose to dispute that "Reality is spiritual"; I do not deny that there may be reasons for thinking that it is: but I do propose to show that one reason upon which, to the best of my judgment, all other arguments ever used by Idealists depend is *false*. These other arguments may, for all I shall say, be eminently ingenious and true; they are very many and various, and different Idealists use the most different arguments to prove the same most important conclusions. Some of these *may* be sufficient to prove that B is C and C is D; but if, as I shall try to show, their "A is B" is false the conclusion A is D remains a pleasant supposition. I do not deny that to suggest pleasant and plausible suppositions may be the proper function of philosophy: but I am assuming that the name Idealism can only be properly applied where there is a certain amount of argument, intended to be cogent.

The subject of this paper is, therefore, quite uninteresting. Even if I prove my point, I shall have proved nothing about the Universe in general. Upon the important question whether Reality is or is not spiritual my argument will not have the remotest bearing. I shall only attempt to arrive at the truth about a matter, which is in itself quite trivial and insignificant, and from which, so far as I can see and certainly so far as I shall say, no conclusions can be drawn about any of the subjects about which we most want to know. The only importance I can claim for the subject I shall investigate is that it seems to me to be a matter upon which not Idealists only, but all philosophers and psychologists also, have been in error, and from their erroneous view of which they have inferred (validly or invalidly) their most striking and interesting conclusions. And that it has even this importance I cannot hope to prove. If it has this importance, it will indeed follow that all the most striking results of philosophy—Sensationalism, Agnosticism and Idealism alike—have, for all that has hitherto been urged in their favour, no more foundation than the supposition that a chimera lives in the moon. It will follow that, unless new reasons never urged hitherto can be found, all the most important philosophic doctrines have as little claim to assent as the most superstitious beliefs of the lowest savages. Upon the question what we have *reason* to believe in the most interesting matters, I do therefore think that my results will have an important bearing; but I cannot too clearly insist that upon the question whether these beliefs are true they will have none whatever.

The trivial proposition which I propose to dispute is this: that *esse* is *percipi*. This is a very ambiguous proposition, but, in some sense or other, it has been very widely held. That it is, in some sense, essential to Idealism, I must for the present merely assume. What I propose to show is that, in all the senses ever given to it, it is false.

But, first of all, it may be useful to point out briefly in what relation I conceive it to stand to Idealistic arguments. That wherever you can truly predicate *esse* you can truly predicate *percipi*, in some sense or other, is, I take it, a necessary step in all arguments, properly to be called Idealistic, and, what is more, in all arguments hitherto offered for the Idealistic conclusion. If *esse* is *percipi*, this is at once equivalent to saying that whatever is, is experienced; and this, again, is equivalent, in a sense, to saying that whatever is, is something mental. But this is not the sense in which the Idealist *conclusion* must maintain that Reality is *mental*. The Idealist *conclusion* is that *esse* is *percipere*; and hence, whether *esse* be *percipi* or not, a further and different discussion is needed to show whether or not it is also *percipere*. And again, even if *esse* be *percipere*, we need a vast quantity of further argument to show that what has *esse* has also those higher mental qualities which are denoted by spiritual. This is why I said that the question I should discuss, namely, whether or not *esse* is *percipi*, must be utterly insufficient either to prove or to disprove that reality is spiritual. But, on the other hand, I believe that every argument ever used to show that reality is spiritual has inferred this (validly or invalidly) from "*esse* is *percipere*" as one of its premisses; and that this again has never been pretended to be proved except by use of the premiss that *esse* is *percipi*. The type of argument used for the latter purpose is familiar enough. It is said that since whatever is, is experienced, and since some things are which are not experienced by the individual, these must at least form part of some experience. Or again that, since an object necessarily implies a subject, and since the whole world must be an object, we must conceive it to belong to some subject or subjects, in the same sense in which whatever is the object of our experience belongs to us. Or again, that, since thought enters into the essence of all reality, we must conceive behind it, in it, or as its essence, a spirit akin to ours, who thinks: that "spirit greets spirit" in its object. Into the validity of these inferences I do not propose to enter: they obviously require a great deal of discussion. I only desire to point out that, however correct they may be, yet if *esse* is not *percipi*, they leave us as far from a proof that reality is spiritual, as if they were all false too.

But now: Is *esse percipi*? There are three very ambiguous terms in this proposition, and I must begin by distinguishing the different things that may be meant by some of them.

And first with regard to *percipi*. This term need not trouble us long at present. It was, perhaps, originally used to mean "sensation" only; but I am not going to be so unfair to modern Idealists—the only Idealists to whom the term should now be applied without qualification—as to hold that, if they say *esse* is *percipi*, they mean by *percipi* sensation only. On the contrary I quite agree with them that, if *esse* be *percipi* at all, *percipi* must be understood to include not sensation only, but that other type of mental fact, which is called "thought"; and, whether *esse* be *percipi* or not, I consider it to be the main service of the philosophic school, to which modern Idealists belong, that they have insisted on distinguishing "sensation" and "thought" and on emphasising the importance of the latter. Against Sensationalism and Empiricism they have maintained the true view. But the distinction between sensation and thought need not detain us here. For, in whatever respects they differ, they have at least this in common, that they are both forms of consciousness or, to use a term that seems to be more in fashion just now, they are both ways of experiencing. Accordingly, whatever *esse* is *percipi* may mean, it does *at least* assert that whatever is, is *experienced*. And since what I wish to maintain is, that even this is untrue, the question whether it be experienced by way of sensation or thought or both is for my purpose quite irrelevant. If it be not experienced at all, it cannot be either an object of thought or an object of sense. It is only if being involves "experience" that the question, whether it involves sensation or thought or both, becomes important. I beg, therefore, that *percipi* may be understood, in what follows, to refer merely to what is *common* to sensation and thought. A very recent article states the meaning of *esse* is *percipi* with all desirable clearness in so far as *percipi* is concerned. "I will undertake to show," says Mr. Taylor, "that what makes [any piece of fact] real can be nothing but its presence as an inseparable aspect of a *sentient experience*."* I am glad to think that Mr. Taylor has been in time to supply me with so definite a statement that this is the ultimate premiss of Idealism. My paper will at least refute Mr. Taylor's Idealism, if it refutes anything at all: for I shall undertake to show that what makes a thing real cannot possibly be its presence as an inseparable aspect of a sentient experience.

But Mr. Taylor's statement though clear, I think, with regard to the meaning of *percipi* is highly ambiguous in other respects. I will leave it for the present to consider the next ambiguity in the statement: *Esse* is *percipi*. What does the copula mean? What can be meant by saying that *esse* is *percipi*? There are just three meanings; one or other of which such a statement must have, if it is to be true; and of these there is only one which it can have, if it is to be important. (1) The statement may be meant to assert that the word "*esse*" is used to signify nothing either more or less than the word "*percipi*": that the two words are precise synonyms: that they are merely different names for one and the same thing: that what is meant by *esse* is absolutely identical with what is meant by *percipi*. I think I need not prove that the principle *esse* is *percipi* is *not* thus intended merely to define a word; nor yet that, if it were, it would be an extremely bad definition. But if it does *not* mean this, only two alternatives remain. The second is (2) that what is meant by *esse*, though not absolutely identical with what is meant by *percipi*, yet *includes* the latter as a *part* of its meaning. If this were the meaning of "*esse* is *percipi*," then to say that a thing was real would not be the same thing as to say that it was experienced. That it was *real* would mean that it was experienced and

***International Journal of Ethics*, October, 1902.

something else besides: "being experienced" would be *analytically essential* to reality, but would not be the whole meaning of the term. From the fact that a thing was real we should be able to infer, by the law of contradiction, that it was experienced; since the latter would be *part* of what is meant by the former. But, on the other hand, from the fact a thing was experienced we should *not* be able to infer that it was real; since it would not follow from the fact that it had one of the attributes essential to reality, that it *also* had the other or others. Now, if we understand *esse* is *percipi* in this second sense, we must distinguish *three* different things which it asserts. First of all, it gives a definition of the word "reality," asserting that word stands for a complex whole, of which what is meant by "*percipi*" forms a part. And secondly it asserts that "being experienced" forms a part of a certain whole. Both these propositions may be true, and at all events I do not wish to dispute them. I do not, indeed, think that the word "reality" is commonly used to include "*percipi*": but I do not wish to argue about the meaning of words. And that many things which are experienced are also something else—that to be experienced forms part of certain wholes, is, of course, indisputable. But what I wish to point out is, that neither of these propositions is of any importance, unless we add to them a *third*. That "real" is a convenient name for a union of attributes which *sometimes* occurs, it could not be worth any one's while to assert: no inferences of any importance could be drawn from such an assertion. Our principle could only mean that when a thing happens to have *percipi* as well as the other qualities included under *esse*, it has *percipi*: and we should never be able to *infer* that it was experienced, except from a proposition which already asserted that it was both experienced and something else. Accordingly, if the assertion that *percipi* forms part of the whole meant by reality is to have any importance, it must mean that the whole is organic, at least in this sense, that the other constituent or constituents of it *cannot* occur without *percipi*, even if *percipi* can occur without them. Let us call these other constituents *x*. The proposition that *esse* includes *percipi*, and that therefore from *esse percipi* can be inferred, can only be important if it is meant to assert that *percipi* can be inferred from *x*. The only importance of the question whether the whole *esse* includes the part *percipi* rests therefore on the question whether the part *x* is necessarily connected with the part *percipi*. And this is (3) the third possible meaning of the assertion *esse* is *percipi*: and, as we now see, the only important one. *Esse* is *percipi* asserts that wherever you have *x* you also have *percipi*; that whatever has the property *x* also has the property that it is *experienced*. And this being so, it will be convenient if, for the future, I may be allowed to use the term "*esse*" to denote *x alone*. I do not wish thereby to beg the question whether what we commonly mean by the word "real" does or does not include *percipi* as well as *x*. I am quite content that my definition of "*esse*" to denote *x*, should be regarded merely as an arbitrary verbal definition. Whether it is so or not, the only question of interest is whether from *x percipi* can be inferred, and I should prefer to be able to express this in the form: can *percipi* be inferred from *esse*? Only let it be understood that when I say *esse*, that term will not for the future *include percipi*: it denotes only that *x*, which Idealists, perhaps rightly include *along with percipi* under *their* term *esse*. That there is such an *x* they must admit on pain of making the proposition an *absolute* tautology; and that from this *x percipi* can be inferred they must admit, on pain of making it a perfectly barren analytic proposition. Whether *x* alone should or should not be called *esse* is not worth a dispute: what is worth dispute is whether *percipi* is necessarily connected with *x*.

We have therefore discovered the ambiguity of the copula in *esse* is *percipi*, so far as to see that this principle asserts two distinct terms to be so related, that whatever has the *one*, which I call *esse*, has *also* the property that it is experienced. It asserts a necessary connexion between *esse* on the one hand and *percipi* on the other; these two words denoting each a distinct term, and *esse* denoting a term in which that denoted by *percipi* is not included. We have, then in *esse* is *percipi*, a *necessary synthetic* proposition which I have undertaken to refute. And I may say at once that, understood as such, it cannot be refuted. If the Idealist chooses to assert that it is merely a self-evident truth, I have only to say that it does not appear to me to be so. But I believe that no Idealist ever has maintained it to be so. Although this—that two distinct terms are necessarily related—is the only sense which "*esse* is *percipi*" can have if it is to be true and important, it *can* have another sense, if it is to be an important falsehood. I believe that Idealists all hold this important falsehood. They do not perceive that *esse* is *percipi* must, if true, be *merely* a self-evident synthetic truth: they either identify with it or give as a reason for it another proposition which must be false because it is self-contradictory. Unless they did so, they would have to admit that it was a perfectly unfounded assumption; and if they recognised that it was *unfounded*, I do not think they would maintain its truth to be evident. *Esse* is *percipi*, in the sense I have found for it, *may* indeed be true; I cannot refute it: but if this sense were clearly apprehended, no one, I think, would believe that it was true.

Idealists, we have seen, must assert that whatever is experienced, is *necessarily* so. And this doctrine they commonly express by saying that "the object of experience is inconceivable apart from the subject." I have hitherto been concerned with pointing out what meaning this assertion must have, if it is to be an important truth. I now propose to show that it may have an important meaning, which must be false, because it is self-contradictory.

It is a well-known fact in the history of philosophy that *necessary* truths in general, but especially those of which it is said that the opposite is inconceivable, have been commonly supposed to be *analytic*, in the sense that the proposition denying them was self-contradictory. It was in this way, commonly supposed, before Kant, that many truths could be proved by the law of contradiction alone. This is, therefore, a mistake which it is plainly easy for the best philosophers to make. Even since Kant many have continued to assert it; but I am aware that among those Idealists, who most properly deserve the name, it has become more fashionable to assert that truths are *both* analytic and synthetic. Now with many of their reasons for asserting this I am not concerned: it is possible that in some connexions the assertion may bear a useful and true sense. But if we understand "analytic" in the sense just defined, namely, what is proved by the law of contradiction *alone*, it is plain that, if "synthetic" means what is *not* proved by this alone, no truth can be both analytic and synthetic. Now it seems to me that those who do maintain truths to be both, do nevertheless maintain that they are so in this as well as in other senses. It is, indeed, extremely unlikely that so *essential* a part of the historical meaning of "analytic" and "synthetic" should have been entirely discarded, especially since we find no express recognition that it is discarded. In that case it is fair to suppose that modern Idealists have been influenced by the view that certain truths can be proved by the law of contradiction alone. I admit they also expressly declare that they can *not*: but this is by no means sufficient to prove that they do not also think they are; since it is very easy to hold two mutually contradictory opinions. What I suggest then is that Idealists hold the particular doctrine in question, concerning the relation of subject and object in experience, because they think it is an analytic truth in this restricted sense that it is proved by the law of contradiction alone.

I am suggesting that the Idealist maintains that object and subject are necessarily connected, mainly because he fails to see that they are *distinct*, that they are *two*, at all. When he thinks of "yellow" and when he thinks of the "sensation of yellow," he fails to see that there is anything whatever in the latter which is not in the former. This being so, to deny that yellow can ever *be* apart from the sensation of yellow is merely to deny that yellow can ever be other than it is; since yellow and the sensation of yellow are absolutely identical. To assert that yellow is necessarily an object of experience is to assert that yellow is necessarily yellow—a purely identical proposition, and therefore proved by the law of contradiction alone. Of course, the proposition also implies that experience is, after all, something distinct from yellow—else there would be no reason for insisting that yellow is a sensation: and that the argument thus both affirms and denies that yellow and sensation of yellow are distinct, is what sufficiently refutes it. But this contradiction can easily be overlooked, because though we are convinced, in other connexions, that "experience" does mean something and something most important, yet we are never distinctly aware *what* it means, and thus in every particular case we do not notice its presence. The facts present themselves as a kind of antinomy: (1) Experience *is* something unique and different from anything else; (2) Experience of green is entirely indistinguishable from green; two propositions which cannot both be true. Idealists, holding both, can only take refuge in arguing from the one in some connexions and from the other in others.

But I am well aware that there are many Idealists who would repel it as an utterly unfounded charge that they fail to distinguish between a sensation or idea and what I will call its object. And there are, I admit, many who not only imply, as we all do, that green is distinct from the sensation of green, but expressly insist upon the distinction as an important part of their system. They would perhaps only assert that the two form an inseparable unity. But I wish to point out that many, who use this phrase, and who do admit the distinction, are not thereby absolved from the charge that they deny it. For there is a certain doctrine, very prevalent among philosophers nowadays, which by a very simple reduction may be seen to assert that two distinct things both are and are not distinct. A distinction is asserted; but it is *also* asserted that the things distinguished form an "organic unity." But, forming such a unity, it is held, each would not be what it is *apart from its relation to the other*. Hence to consider either by itself is to make an *illegitimate abstraction*. The recognition that there are "organic unities" and "illegitimate abstractions" in this sense is regarded as one of the chief conquests of modern philosophy. But what is the sense attached to these terms? An abstraction is illegitimate, when and only when we attempt to assert of a *part*—of something abstracted—that which is true only of the *whole* to which it belongs: and it may perhaps be useful to point out that this should not be done. But the application actually made of this principle, and what perhaps would be expressly acknowledged as its meaning, is something much the reverse of useful. The principle is used to assert that certain abstractions are *in all cases* illegitimate; that whenever you try to assert *anything whatever* of that which is *part* of an organic whole, what you assert can only be true of the whole. And this principle, so far from being a useful truth, is necessarily false. For if the whole can, nay *must*, be substituted for the part in all propositions and for all purposes, this can only be because the whole is absolutely identical with the part. When, therefore, we are told that green and the sensation of green are certainly distinct but yet are not separable, or that it is an illegitimate abstraction to consider the one apart from the other, what these provisos are used to assert is, that though the two things are distinct yet you not only can but must treat them as if they were not. Many philosophers, therefore, when they admit a distinction, yet (following the lead of Hegel) boldly assert their right, in a slightly more obscure form of words, *also* to deny it. The principle of organic unities, like that of combined analysis and synthesis, is mainly used to defend the practice of holding *both* of two contradictory propositions, wherever this may seem convenient. In this, as in other matters, Hegel's main service to philosophy has consisted in giving a name to and erecting into a principle, a type of fallacy to which experience had shown philosophers, along with the rest of mankind, to be addicted. No wonder that he has followers and admirers.

I have shown then, so far, that when the Idealist asserts the important principle "*Esse* is *percipi*" he must, if it is to be true, mean by this that: Whatever is experienced also *must* be experienced. And I have also shown that he *may* identify with, or give as a reason for, this proposition, one which must be false, because it is self-contradictory. But at this point I propose to make a complete break in my argument. "*Esse* is *percipi*," we have seen, asserts of two terms, as distinct from one another as "green" and "sweet," that whatever has the one has also the other: it asserts that "being" and "being experienced" are necessarily connected: that whatever *is* is *also* experienced. And this, I admit cannot be directly refuted. But I believe it to be false; and I have asserted that anybody who saw that "*esse* and *percipi*" *were* as distinct as "green" and "sweet" would be no more ready to believe that whatever *is* is *also* experienced, than to believe that whatever is green is also sweet. I have asserted that no one would believe that "*esse* is *percipi*" if they saw how different *esse* is from *percipi*: but *this* I shall not try to prove. I have asserted that all who do believe that "*esse* is *percipi*" identify with it or take as a reason for it a self-contradictory proposition: but this I shall not try to prove. I shall only try to show that certain propositions which I assert to be believed, are false. That they are believed, and that without this belief "*esse* is *percipi*" would not be believed either, I must leave without a proof.

I pass, then, from the uninteresting question "Is *esse percipi*?" to the still more uninteresting and apparently irrelevant question "What is a sensation or idea?"

We all know that the sensation of blue differs from that of green. But it is plain that if both are *sensations* they also have some point in common. What is it that they have in common? And how is this common element related to the points in which they differ?

I will call the common element "consciousness" without yet attempting to say what the thing I so call *is*. We have then in every sensation two distinct terms, (1) "consciousness," in respect of which all sensations are alike; and (2) something else, in respect of which one sensation differs from another. It will be convenient if I may be allowed to call this second term the "object" of a sensation: this also without yet attempting to say what I mean by the word.

We have then in every sensation two distinct elements, one which I call consciousness, and another which I call the object of consciousness. This must be so if the sensation of blue and the sensation of green, though different in one respect; are alike in another: blue is one object of sensation and green is another, and consciousness, which both sensations have in common, is different from either.

But, further, sometimes the sensation of blue exists in my mind and sometimes it does not; and knowing, as we now do, that the sensation of blue includes two different elements, namely consciousness and blue, the question arises whether, when the sensation of blue exists, it is the consciousness which exists, or the blue which exists, or both. And one point at least is plain: namely that these three alternatives are all different from one another. So that, if any one tells us that to say "Blue exists" is the *same* thing as to say that "Both blue and consciousness exist," he makes a mistake and a self-contradictory mistake.

But another point is also plain, namely, that when the sensation exists, the consciousness, at least, certainly does exist; for when I say that the sensations of blue and of green both exist, I certainly mean that what is common to both and in virtue of which both are called sensations, exists in each case. The only alternative left, then, is that *either* both exist or the consciousness exists alone. If, therefore, any one tell us that the existence of blue is the same thing as the existence of the sensation of blue he makes a mistake and a self-contradictory mistake, for he asserts *either* that blue is the same thing as blue together with consciousness, or that it is the same thing as consciousness alone.

Accordingly to identify either "blue" or any other of what I have called "*objects*" of sensation, with the corresponding sensation is in every case, a self-contradictory error. It is to identify a part either with the whole of which it is a part or else with the other part of the same whole. If we are told that the assertion "Blue exists" is *meaningless* unless we mean by it that "The sensation of blue exists," we are told what is certainly false and self-contradictory. If we are told that the existence of blue is inconceivable apart from the existence of the sensation, the speaker *probably* means to convey to us, by this ambiguous expression, what is a self-contradictory error. For we can and must conceive the existence of blue as something quite distinct from the existence of the sensation. We can and must conceive that blue might exist and yet the sensation of blue not exist. For my own part I not only conceive this, but conceive it to be true. Either therefore this terrific assertion of inconceivability means what is false and self-contradictory or else it means only that *as a matter of fact* blue never can exist unless the sensation of it exists also.

And at this point I need not conceal my opinion that no philosopher has ever yet succeeded in avoiding this self-contradictory error: that the most striking results both of Idealism and of Agnosticism are only obtained by identifying blue with the sensation of blue: that *esse* is held to be *percipi*, solely because *what is experienced* is held to be identical with *the experience of it*. That Berkeley and Mill committed this error will, perhaps, be granted: that modern Idealists make it will, I hope, appear more probable later. But that my opinion is plausible, I will now offer two pieces of evidence. The first is that language offers us no means of referring to such objects as "blue" and "green" and "sweet," except by calling them sensations: it is an obvious violation of language to call them "things" or "objects" or "terms." And similarly we have no natural means of referring to such objects as "causality" or "likeness" or "identity," except by calling them "ideas" or "notions" or "conceptions." But it is hardly likely that if philosophers had clearly distinguished in the past between a sensation or idea and what I have called its object, there should have been no separate name for the latter. They have always used the same name for these two different "things" (if I may call them so): and hence there is some probability that they have supposed these "things" *not* to be two and different, but one and the same. And, secondly, there is a very good reason why they should have supposed so, in the fact that when we refer to introspection and try to discover what the sensation of blue is, it is very easy to suppose that we have before us only a single term. The term "blue" is easy enough to distinguish, but the other element which I have called "consciousness"—that which sensation of blue has in common with sensation of green—is extremely difficult to fix. That many people fail to distinguish it at all is sufficiently shown by the fact that there are materialists. And, in general, that which makes the sensation of blue a mental fact seems to escape us: it seems, if I may use a metaphor, to be transparent—we look through it and see nothing but the blue; we may be convinced that there is *something* but *what* it is no philosopher, I think, has yet clearly recognised.

But this was a digression. The point I had established so far was that in every sensation or idea we must distinguish two elements, (1) the "object," or that in which one differs from another; and (2) "consciousness," or that which all have in common—that which makes them sensations or mental facts. This being so, it followed that when a sensation or idea exists, we have to choose between the alternatives that either object alone, or consciousness alone, or both, exist; and I showed that of these alternatives one, namely that the object only exists, is excluded by the fact that what we mean to assert is certainly the existence of a mental fact. There remains the question: Do both exist? Or does the consciousness alone? And to this question one answer has hitherto been given universally: That both exist.

This answer follows from the analysis hitherto accepted of the relation of what I have called "object" to "consciousness" in any sensation or idea. It is held that what I call the object is merely the "content" of a sensation or idea. It is held that in each case we can distinguish two elements and two only, (1) the fact that there is feeling or experience, and (2) *what* is felt or experienced; the sensation or idea, it is said, forms a whole, in which we must distinguish two "inseparable aspects," "content" and "existence." I shall try to show that this analysis is false; and for that purpose I must ask what may seem an extraordinary question: namely what is meant by saying that one thing is "content" of another? It is not usual to ask this question; the term is used as if everybody must understand it. But since I am going to maintain that "blue" is *not* the content of the sensation of blue, and what is more important, that, even if it were this analysis would leave out the most important element in the sensation of blue, it is necessary that I should try to explain precisely what it is that I shall deny.

What then is meant by saying that one thing is the "content" of another? First of all I wish to point out that "blue" is rightly and properly said to be part of the content of a blue flower. If, therefore, we also assert that it is part of the content of the sensation of blue, we assert that it has to the other parts (if any) of this whole the same relation which it has to the other parts of a blue flower—and we assert only this: we cannot mean to assert that it has to the sensation of any relation which it does not have to the blue flower. And we have seen that the sensation of blue contains at least one other element beside blue—namely, what I call "consciousness," which makes it a sensation. So far then as we assert that blue is the content of the sensation, we assert that it has to this "consciousness" the same relation which it has to the other parts of a blue flower: we do assert this, and we assert no more than this. Into the question what exactly the relation is between blue and a blue flower in virtue of which we call the former part of its "content" I do not propose to enter. It is sufficient for my purpose to point out that it is the general relation most commonly meant when we talk of a thing and its qualities; and that this relation is such that to say the thing exists implies that the qualities also exist. The *content* of the thing is *what* we assert to exist, when we assert *that* the thing exists.

When, therefore, blue is said to be part of the content of the "sensation of blue," the latter is treated as if it were a whole constituted in exactly the same way as any other "thing." The "sensation of blue," on this view, differs from a blue bead or a blue beard, in exactly the same way in which the two latter differ from one another: the blue bead differs from the blue beard, in that while the former contains glass, the latter contains hair; and the "sensation of blue" differs from both in that, instead of glass or hair, it contains consciousness. The relation of the blue to the consciousness is conceived to be exactly the same as that of the blue to the glass or hair: it is in all three cases the *quality* of a *thing*.

But I said just now that the sensation of blue was analysed into "content" and "existence," and that blue was said to be *the* content of the idea of blue. There is an ambiguity in this and a possible error, which I must note in passing. The term "content" may be used in two senses. If we use "content" as equivalent to what Mr. Bradley calls the "*what*"—if we mean by it the *whole* of what is said to exist, when the thing is said to exist, then blue is certainly not *the* content of the sensation of blue: part of the *content* of the sensation is, in this sense of the term, that other element which I have called consciousness. The analysis of this sensation into the "content" "blue," on the one hand, and mere existence on the other, is therefore certainly false; in it we have again the self-contradictory identification of "Blue exists" with "The sensation of blue exists." But there is another sense in which "blue" might properly be said to be *the* content of the sensation—namely, the sense in which "content," like ⟨*eidos*⟩ is opposed to "substance" or "matter." For the element "consciousness," being common to all sensations, may be and certainly is regarded as in some sense their "substance," and by the "content" of each is only meant that in respect of which one differs from another. In this sense then "blue" might be said to be *the* content of the sensation; but, in that case, the analysis into "content" and "existence" is, at least, misleading, since under "existence" must be included "*what* exists" in the sensation other than blue.

We have it, then, as a universally received opinion that blue is related to the sensation or idea of blue, as its *content*, and that this view, if it is to be true, must mean that blue is part of *what* is said to exist when we say that the sensation exists. To say that the sensation exists is to say both that blue exists and that "consciousness," whether we call it the substance of which blue is *the* content or call it another part of the content, exists too. Any sensation or idea is a "*thing*," and what I have called its object is the quality of this thing. Such a "thing" is what we think of when we think of a *mental image*. A mental image is conceived as if it were related to that of which it is the image (if there be any such thing) in exactly the same way as the image in a looking-glass is related to that of which it is the reflection; in both cases there is identity of content, and the image in the looking glass differs from that in the mind solely in respect of the fact that in the one case the other constituent of the image is "glass" and in the other case it is consciousness. If the image is of blue, it is not conceived that this "content" has any relation to the consciousness but what it has to the glass: it is conceived *merely* to be its *content*. And owing to the fact that sensations and ideas are all considred to be *wholes* of this description—things in the mind—the question: What do we know? is considered to be identical with the question: What reason have we for supposing that there are things outside the mind *corresponding* to these that are inside it?

What I wish to point out is (1) that we have no reason for supposing that there are such things as mental images at all—for supposing that blue is part of the content of the sensation of blue, and (2) that even if there are mental images, no mental image and no sensation or idea is *merely* a thing of this kind: that "blue," even if it is part of the content of the image or sensation or idea of blue, is always *also* related to it in quite another way, and that this other relation, omitted in the traditional analysis, is the *only* one which makes the sensation of blue a mental fact at all.

The true analysis of a sensation or idea is as follows. The element that is common to them all, and which I have called "consciousness," really *is* consciousness. A sensation is, in reality, a case of "knowing" or "being aware of" or "experiencing" something. When we know that the sensation of blue exists, the fact we know is that there exists an awareness of blue. And this awareness is not merely, as we have hitherto seen it must be, itself something distinct and unique, utterly different from blue: it also has a perfectly distinct and unique relation to blue, a relation which is *not* that of thing or substance to content, nor of one part of content to another part of content. This relation is just that which we mean in every case by "knowing." To have in your mind "knowledge" of blue, is *not* to have in your mind a "thing" or "image" of which blue is the content. To be aware of the sensation of blue is *not* to be aware of a mental image—of a "thing," of which "blue" and some other element are constituent parts in the same sense in which blue and glass are constituents of a blue bead. It is to be aware of an awareness of blue; awareness being used, in both cases, in exactly the same sense. This element, we have seen, is certainly neglected by the "content" theory: that theory entirely fails to express the fact that there is, in the sensation of blue, this unique relation between blue and the other constituent. And what I contend is that this omission is *not* mere negligence of expression, but is due to the fact that though philosophers have recognised that *something* distinct is meant by consciousness, they have never yet had a clear conception of *what* that something is. They have not been able to hold *it* and *blue* before their minds and to compare them, in the same way in which they can compare *blue* and *green*. And this for the reason I gave above: namely that the moment we try to fix our attention upon consciousness and to see *what*, distinctly, it is, it seems to vanish: it seems as if we had before us a mere emptiness. When we try to introspect the sensation of blue, all we can see is the blue: the other element is as if it were diaphanous. Yet it *can* be distinguished if we look attentively enough, and if we know that there is something to look for. My main object in this paragraph has been to try to make the reader *see* it; but I fear I shall have succeeded very ill.

It being the case, then, that the sensation of blue includes in its analysis, beside blue, *both* a unique element "awareness" *and* a unique relation of this element to blue, I can make plain what I meant by asserting, as two distinct propositions, (1) that blue is probably not part of the content of the sensation at all, and (2) that, even if it were, the sensation would nevertheless not be the sensation *of* blue, if blue had only this relation to it. The first hypothesis may now be expressed by saying that, if it were true, then, when the sensation of blue exists, there exists a *blue awareness*: offence may be taken at the expression, but yet it expresses just what should be and is meant by saying that blue is, in this case, a *content* of consciousness or experience. Whether or not, when I have the sensation of blue, my consciousness or awareness is thus blue, my introspection does not enable me to decide with certainty: I only see no reason for thinking that it is. But whether it is or not, the point is unimportant, for introspection *does* enable me to decide that something else is also true: namely that I am aware *of* blue, and by this I mean, that my awareness has to blue a quite different and distinct relation. It is possible, I admit, that my awareness is blue *as well* as being *of* blue: but what I am quite sure of is that it is *of* blue; that it has to blue the simple and unique relation the existence of which alone justifies us in distinguishing knowledge of a thing from the thing known, indeed in distinguishing mind from matter. And this result I may express by saying that what is called the *content* of a sensation is in very truth what I originally called it—the sensation's *object*.

But, if all this be true, what follows?

Idealists admit that some things really exist of which they are not aware: there are some things, they hold, which are not inseparable aspects of *their* experience, even if they be inseparable aspects of some experience. They further hold that some of the things of which they are sometimes aware do really exist, even when they are not aware of them: they hold for instance that they are sometimes aware of other Minds, which continue to exist even when they are not aware of them. They are, therefore, sometimes aware of something which is *not* an inseparable aspect of their own experience. They do *know some* things which are *not* a mere part or content of their experience. And what my analysis of sensation has been designed to show is, that whenever I have a mere sensation or idea, the fact is that I am then aware of something which is equally and in the same sense *not* an inseparable aspect of my experience. The awareness which I have maintained to be included in sensation is the very same unique fact which constitutes every kind of knowledge: "blue" is as much an object, and as little a mere content, of my experience, when I experience it, as the most exalted and independent real thing of which I am ever aware. There is, therefore, no question of how we are to "get outside the circle of our own ideas and sensations." Merely to have a sensation is already to *be* outside that circle. It is to know something which is as truly and really *not* a part of *my* experience, as anything which I can ever know.

Now I think I am not mistaken in asserting that the reason why Idealists suppose that everything which is must be an inseparable aspect of some experience, is that they suppose some things, at least, to be inseparable aspects of *their* experience. And there is certainly nothing which they are so firmly convinced to be an inseparable aspect of their experience as what they call the *content* of their ideas and sensations. If, therefore, this turns out in every case, whether it be also the content or not, to be at least *not* an inseparable aspect of the experience of it, it will be readily admitted that nothing else which *we* experience ever is such an inseparable aspect. But if we never experience anything but what is *not* an inseparable aspect of *that* experience, how can we infer that anything whatever, let alone *everything*, is an inseparable aspect of *any* experience? How utterly unfounded is the assumption that "*esse* is *percipi*" appears in the clearest light.

But further I think it may be seen that if the object of an Idealist's sensation were, as he supposes, *not* the object but merely the content of that sensation, if, that is to say, it really were an inseparable aspect of his experience, each Idealist could never be aware either of himself or of any other real thing. For the relation of a sensation to its object is certainly the same as that of any other instance of experience to its object; and this, I think, is generally admitted even by Idealists: they state as readily that *what* is judged or thought or perceived is the *content* of that judgment or thought or perception, as that blue is the content of the sensation of blue. But, if so, then when any Idealist thinks he is *aware* of himself or of any one else, this cannot really be the case. The fact is, on his own theory, that himself and that other person are in reality mere *contents* of an awareness, which is aware *of* nothing whatever. All that can be said is that there is an awareness in him, *with* a certain content: it can never be true that there is in him a consciousness *of* anything. And similarly he is never aware either of the fact that he exists or that reality is spiritual. The real fact, which he describes in those terms, is that his existence and the spirituality of reality are *contents* of an awareness, which is aware of nothing—certainly not, then, of its own content.

And further if everything, of which he thinks he is aware, is in reality merely a content of his own experience he has certainly no *reason* for holding that anything does exist except himself: it will, of course, be possible that other persons do exist; solipsism will not be necessarily true; but he cannot possibly infer from anything he holds that it is not true. That he himself exists will of course follow from his premiss that many things are contents of *his* experience. But since everything, of which he thinks himself aware, is in reality merely an inseparable aspect of that awareness; this premiss allows no inference that any of these contents far less any other consciousness, exists at all except as an inseparable aspect of his awareness, that is, as part of himself.

Such, and not those which he takes to follow from it, are the consequences which *do* follow from the Idealist's supposition that the object of an experience is in reality merely a content or inseparable aspect of that experience. If, on the other hand, we clearly recognise the nature of that peculiar relation which I have called "awareness of anything"; if we see that *this* is involved equally in the analysis of *every* experience—from the merest sensation to the most developed perception or reflexion, and that *this* is in fact the only essential element in an experience—the only thing that is both common and peculiar to all experiences—the only thing which gives us reason to call any fact mental; if, further, we recognise that this awareness is and must be in all cases of such a nature that its object, when we are aware of it, is precisely what it would be, if we were not aware: then it becomes plain that the existence of a table in space is related to my experience of *it* in precisely the same way as the existence of my own experience is related to my experience of *that*. Of both we are merely aware: if we are aware that the one exists, we are aware in precisely the same sense that the other exists; and if it is true that my experience can exist, even when I do not happen to be aware of its existence, we have exactly the same reason for supposing that the table can do so also. When, therefore, Berkeley supposed that the only thing of which I am directly aware is my own sensations and ideas, he supposed what was false; and when Kant supposed that the objectivity of things in space *consisted* in the fact that they were "Vorstellungen" having to one another different relations from those which the same "Vorstellungen" have to one another in subjective experience, he supposed what was equally false. I am as directly aware of the existence of material things in space as of my own sensations; and *what* I am aware of with regard to each is exactly the same—namely that in one case the material thing, and in the other case my sensation does really exist. The question requiring to be asked about material things is thus not: What reason have we for supposing that anything exists *corresponding* to our sensations? but: What reason have we for supposing that material things do *not* exist, since *their* existence has precisely the same evidence as that of our sensations? That either exist *may* be false; but if it is a reason for doubting the existence of matter, that it is an inseparable aspect of our experience, the same reasoning will prove conclusively that our experience does not exist either, since that must also be an inseparable aspect of our experience of *it*. The only *reasonable* alternative to the admission that matter exists *as well as* spirit, is absolute Scepticism—that, as likely as not *nothing* exists at all. All other suppositions—the Agnostic's, that something, at all events, does exist, as much as the Idealist's, that spirit does—are, if we have no reason for believing in matter, as baseless as the grossest superstitions.

A Defense of Common Sense

In what follows I have merely tried to state, one by one, some of the most important points in which my philosophical position differs from positions which have been taken up by *some* other philosophers. It may be that the points which I have had room to mention are not really the most important, and possibly some of them may be points as to which no philosopher has ever really differed from me. But, to the best of my belief, each is a point as to which many have really differed; although (in most cases, at all events) each is also a point as to which many have agreed with me.

I

The first point is a point which embraces a great many other points. And it is one which I cannot state as clearly as I wish to state it, except at some length. The method I am going to use for stating it is this. I am going to begin by enunciating, under the heading (1), a whole long list of propositions, which may seem, at first sight, such obvious truisms as not to be worth stating: they are, in fact, a set of propositions, every one of which (in my own opinion) I *know*, with certainty, to be true. I shall, next, under the heading (2), state a single proposition which makes an assertion about a whole set of *classes* of propositions—each class being defined, as the class consisting of all propositions which resemble *one* of the propositions in (1) in a certain respect. (2), therefore, is a proposition which could not be stated, until the list of propositions in (1), or some similar list, had already been given. (2) is itself a proposition which may seem such an obvious truism as not to be worth stating: and it is also a proposition which (in my own opinion) I know, with certainty, to be true. But, nevertheless, it is, to the best of my belief, a proposition with regard to which many philosophers have, for different reasons, differed from me; even if they have not directly denied (2) itself, they have held views incompatible with it. My first point, then, may be said to be that (2), together with all its implications, some of which I shall expressly mention, is true.

(1) I begin, then, with my list of truisms, every one of which (in my own opinion) I *know*, with certainty, to be true. The propositions to be included in this list are the following:

There exists at present a living human body, which is *my* body. This body was born at a certain time in the past, and has existed continuously ever since, though not without undergoing changes; it was, for instance, much smaller when it was born, and for some time afterwards, than it is now. Ever since it was born, it has been either in contact with or not far from the surface of the earth; and, at every moment since it was born, there have also existed many other things, having shape and size in three dimensions (in the same familiar sense in which it has), from which it has been *at various distances* (in the familiar sense in which it is now at a distance both from that mantelpiece and from that bookcase, and at a greater distance from the bookcase than it is from the mantelpiece); also there have (very often, at all events) existed some other things of this kind with which it was *in contact* (in the familiar sense in which it is now in contact with the pen I am holding in my right hand and with some of the clothes I am wearing). Among the things which have, in this sense, formed part of its environment (i.e. have been either in contact with it, or at *some* distance from it, however *great*) there have, at every moment since its birth, been large numbers of other living human bodies, each of which has, like it, (*a*) at some time been born, (*b*) continued to exist from some time after birth, (*c*) been, at every moment of its life after birth, either in contact with or not far from the surface of the earth; and many of these bodies have already died and ceased to exist. But the earth had existed also for many years before my body was born; and for many of these years, also, large numbers of human bodies had, at every moment, been alive upon it; and many of these bodies had died and ceased to exist before it was born. Fi-

Reprinted from G. E. Moore, "In Defense of Common Sense," *Philosophical Papers* (London: George Allen & Unwin, 1959) by permission of Timothy Moore.

nally (to come to a different class of propositions), I am a human being, and I have, at different times since my body was born, had many different experiences, of each of many different kinds: e.g. I have often perceived both my own body and other things which formed part of its environment, including other human bodies; I have not only perceived things of this kind, but have also observed facts about them, such as, for instance, the fact which I am now observing, that that mantel-piece is at present nearer to my body than that bookcase; I have been aware of other facts, which I was not at the time observing, such as, for instance, the fact, of which I am now aware, that my body existed yesterday and was then also for some time nearer to that mantelpiece than to that bookcase; I have had expectations with regard to the future, and many beliefs of other kinds, both true and false; I have thought of imaginary things and persons and incidents, in the reality of which I did not believe; I have had dreams; and I have had feelings of many different kinds. And, just as my body has been the body of a human being, namely myself, who has, during his lifetime, had many experiences of each of these (and other) different kinds; so, in the case of very many of the other human bodies which have lived upon the earth, each has been the body of a different human being, who has, during the lifetime of that body, had many different experiences of each of these (and other) different kinds.

(2) I now come to the single truism which, as will be seen, could not be stated except by reference to the whole list of truisms, just given in (1). This truism also (in my own opinion) I *know*, which certainty, to be true; and it is as follows:

In the case of *very many* (I do not say *all*) of the human beings belonging to the class (which includes myself) defined in the following way, i.e. as human beings who have had human bodies, that were born and lived for some time upon the earth, and who have, during the lifetime of those bodies, had many different experiences of each of the kinds mentioned in (1), it is true that each has frequently, during the life of his body, known, with regard to *him*self or *his* body, and with regard to some time earlier than any of the times at which I wrote down the propositions in (1), a proposition *corresponding* to each of the propositions in (1), in the sense that it asserts with regard to *himself* or *his* body and the earlier time in question (namely, in each case, the time at which he knew it), just what the corresponding proposition in (1) asserts with regard to *me* or *my* body and the time at which I wrote that proposition down.

In other words what (2) asserts is only (what seems an obvious enough truism) that each of *us* (meaning by 'us', very many human beings of the class defined) has frequently *known*, with regard to *him*self or *his* body and the time at which he knew it, everything which, in writing down my list of propositions in (1), I was claiming to know about *my*self or *my* body and the time at which I wrote that proposition down, i.e. just as *I* knew (when I wrote it down) 'There exists at present a living human body which is my body', so each of us has frequently known with regard to himself and some other time the different but corresponding proposition, which *he* could *then* have properly expressed by, 'There exists *at present* a human body which is *my* body'; just as *I* know 'Many human bodies other than mine have before now lived on the earth', so each of us has frequently known the different but corresponding proposition 'Many human bodies other than *mine* have before *now* lived on the earth'; just as *I* know 'Many human beings other than myself have before now perceived, and dreamed, and felt', so each of *us* has frequently known the different but corresponding proposition 'Many human beings other than *myself* have before *now* perceived, and dreamed, and felt'; and so on, in the case of *each* of the propositions enumerated in (1). . . .

Proof of an External World

In the preface to the second edition of Kant's *Critique of Pure Reason* some words occur, which, in Professor Kemp Smith's translations, are rendered as follows:

> It still remains a scandal to philosophy . . . that the existence of things outside of us . . . must be accepted merely on *faith*, and that, if anyone thinks good to doubt their existence, we are unable to counter his doubts by any satisfactory proof.[1]

It seems clear from these words that Kant thought it a matter of some importance to give a proof of 'the existence of things outside of us' or perhaps rather (for it seems to me possible that the force of the German words is better rendered in this way) of 'the existence of *the* things outside of us'; for had he not thought it important that a proof should be given, he would scarcely have called it a 'scandal' that no proof had been given. And it seems clear also that he thought that the giving of such a proof was a task which fell properly within the province of philosophy; for, if it did not, the fact that no proof had been given could not possibly be a scandal to *philosophy*.

Now, even if Kant was mistaken in both of these two opinions, there seems to me to be no doubt whatever that it is a matter of some importance and also a matter which falls properly within the province of philosophy, to discuss the question what sort of proof, if any, can be given of 'the existence of things outside of us'. And to discuss this question was my object when I began to write the present lecture. But I may say at once that, as you will find, I have only, at most, succeeded in saying a very small part of what ought to be said about it.

The words 'it . . . remains a scandal to philosophy . . . that we are unable . . .' would, taken strictly, imply that, at the moment at which he wrote them, Kant himself was unable to produce a satisfactory proof of the point in question. But I think it is unquestionable that Kant himself did not think that he personally was at the time unable to produce such a proof. On the contrary, in the immediately preceding sentence, he has declared that he has, in the second edition of his *Critique*, to which he is now writing the Preface, given a 'rigorous proof' of this very thing; and has added that he believes this proof of his to be 'the only possible proof'. It is true that in this preceding sentence he does not describe the proof which he has given as a proof of 'the existence of things outside of us' or of 'the existence of the things outside of us', but describes it instead as a proof of 'the objective reality of outer intuition'. But the context leaves no doubt that he is using these two phrases, 'the objective reality of outer intuition' and 'the existence of things (*or* 'the things') outside of us', in such a way that whatever is a proof of the first is also necessarily a proof of the second. We must, therefore, suppose that when he speaks as if *we* are unable to give a satisfactory proof, he does not mean to say that he himself, as well as others, is *at the moment* unable; but rather that, until he discovered the proof which he has given, both he himself and everybody else *were* unable. Of course, if he is right in thinking that he has given a satisfactory proof, the state of things which he describes came to an end as soon as his proof was published. As soon as that happened, anyone who read it was able to give a satisfactory proof by simply repeating that which Kant had given, and the 'scandal' to philosophy had been removed once for all.

If, therefore, it were certain that the proof of the point in question given by Kant in the second edition is a satisfactory proof, it would be certain that at least one satisfactory proof can be given; and all that would remain of the question which I said I proposed to discuss would be, firstly, the question as to what *sort* of a proof this of Kant's is, and secondly the question whether (contrary to Kant's own opinion) there may not perhaps be other proofs, of the same or of a different sort, which are also satisfactory. But I think it is by no means certain that Kant's proof is satisfactory. I think it is by no means certain that he did succeed in removing once for all the state of affairs which he considered to be a scandal

1. B xxxix, note: Kemp Smith, p. 34. The German words are 'so bleibt es immer ein Skandal der Philosophie . . ., das Dasein der Dinge ausser uns . . . bloss auf *Glauben* annehmen zu müssen, und wenn es jemand einfällt es zu bezweifeln, ihm keinen genugtuenden Beweis entgegenstellen zu können'.

to philosophy. And I think, therefore, that the question whether it is possible to give *any* satisfactory proof of the point in question still deserves discussion.

But what is the point in question? I think it must be owned that the expression 'things outside of us' is rather an odd expression, and an expression the meaning of which is certainly not perfectly clear. It would have sounded less odd if, instead of 'things outside of us' I had said 'external things', and perhaps also the meaning of this expression would have seemed to be clearer; and I think we make the meaning of 'external things' clearer still if we explain that this phrase has been regularly used by philosophers as short for 'things external to *our minds*'. The fact is that there has been a long philosophical tradition, in accordance with which the three expressions 'external things', 'things external to *us*', and 'things external to *our minds*' have been used as equivalent to one another, and have, each of them, been used as if they needed no explanation. The origin of this usage I do not know. It occurs already in Descartes; and since he uses the expressions as if they needed no explanation, they had presumably been used with the same meaning before. Of the three, it seems to me that the expression 'external to *our minds*' is the clearest, since it at least makes clear that what is meant is not 'external to *our bodies*'; whereas both the other expressions might be taken to mean this: and indeed there has been a good deal of confusion, even among philosophers, as to the relation of the two conceptions "external things" and "things external to *our bodies*". But even the expression 'things external to our minds' seems to me to be far from perfectly clear; and if I am to make really clear what I mean by "proof of the existence of things outside of us", I cannot do it by merely saying that by "outside of us" I mean "external to our minds". . . .

But now, if to say of anything, e.g. my body, that it is external to *my* mind, means merely that from a proposition to the effect that it existed at a specified time, there in no case follows the further proposition that *I* was having an experience at the time in question, then to say of anything that it is external to *our* minds, will mean similarly that from a proposition to the effect that it existed at a specified time, it in no case follows that any of *us* were having experiences at the time in question. And if by *our* minds be meant, as is, I think, usually meant, the minds of human beings living on the earth, then it will follow that any pains which animals may feel, any after-images they may see, any experiences they may have, though not external to *their* minds, yet are external to *ours*. And this at once makes plain how different is the conception 'external to our minds' from the conception 'to be met with in space'; for, of course, pains which animals feel or after-images which they see are no more to be met with in space than are pains which *we* feel or after-images which *we* see. From the proposition that there are external objects—objects that are not in any of *our* minds, it does *not* follow that there are things to be met with in space; and hence 'external to our minds' is not a mere synonym for 'to be met with in space': that is to say, 'external to our minds' and 'to be met with in space' are two different conceptions. And the true relation between these conceptions seems to me to be this. We have already seen that there are ever so many kinds of 'things', such that, in the case of each of these kinds, from the proposition that there is at least one thing of that kind there *follows* the proposition that there is at least one thing to be met with in space: e.g. this follows from 'There is at least one star', from 'There is at least one human body', from 'There is at least one shadow', etc. And I think we can say that of every kind of thing of which this is true, it is also true that from the proposition that there is at least one 'thing' of that kind there *follows* the proposition that there is at least one thing external to our minds: e.g. from 'There is at least one star' there follows not only 'There is at least one thing to be met with in space' but also 'There is at least one external thing', and similarly in all other cases. My reason for saying this is as follows. Consider any kind of thing, such that anything of that kind, if there is anything of it, must be 'to be met with in space': e.g. consider the kind 'soap-bubble'. If I say of anything which I am perceiving, 'That is a soap-bubble', I am, it seems to me, certainly implying that there would be no contradiction in asserting that it existed before I perceived it and that it will continue to exist, even if I cease to perceive it. This seems to me to be part of what is meant by saying that it is a real soap-bubble, as distinguished, for instance, from an hallucination of a soap-bubble. Of course, it by no means follows, that if it really is a soap-bubble, it did in fact exist before I perceived it or will continue to exist after I cease to perceive it: soap-bubbles are an example of a kind of 'physical object' and 'thing to be met with in space', in the case of which it is notorious that particular specimens of the kind often do exist only so long as they are perceived by a particular person. But a thing which I perceive would not be a soap-bubble unless its existence at any given time were *logically independent* of my perception of it at that time; unless that is to say, from the proposition, with regard to a particular time, that it existed at that time, it *never* follows that I perceived it at that time. But, if it is true that it would not be a soap-bubble, unless it *could* have existed at any given time without being perceived by me at that time, it is certainly also true that it would not be a soap-bubble, unless it *could* have existed at any given time, without its being true that I was having any experience of any kind at the time in question: it would not be a soap-bubble, unless, whatever time you take, from the proposition that it existed at that time it does *not* follow that I was having any experience at that time. That is to say, from the proposition with regard to anything which I am perceiving that it is a soap-bubble, there *follows* the proposition that it is external to *my* mind. But if, when I say that anything which I perceive is a soap-bubble, I am implying that it is external to *my* mind, I am, I think, certainly also implying that it is also external to all other minds: I am implying that it is not a thing of a sort such that things of that sort *can* only exist at a time when somebody is having an experience. I think, therefore, that from any proposition of the form 'There's a soap-bubble!' there does really *follow* the proposition 'There's an external object!' 'There's an object external to *all* our minds!' And, if this is true of the kind 'soap-bubble', it is certainly also true of any other kind (including the kind 'unicorn') which is such that, if there are any things of that kind, it follows that there are *some* things to be met with in space.

I think, therefore, that in the case of all kinds of 'things', which are such that if there is a pair of things, both of which are of one of these kinds, or a pair of things one of which is of one of them and one of them of another, then it will follow at once that there are some things to be met with in space, it is true also that if I can prove that there are a pair of things, one of which is of one of these kinds and another of another, or a pair both of which are of one of them, then I shall have proved *ipso facto* that there are at least two 'things outside of us'. That is to say, if I can prove that there exist now both a sheet of paper and a human hand, I shall have proved that there are now 'things outside of us'; if I can prove that there exist now both a shoe and sock, I shall have proved that there are not 'things outside of us'; etc.; and similarly I shall have proved it, if I can prove that there exist now two sheets of paper, or two human hands, or two shoes, or two socks, etc. Obviously, then, there are thousands of different things such that, if, at any time, I can prove any one of them, I shall have proved the existence of things outside of us. Cannot I prove any of these things?

It seems to me that, so far from its being true, as Kant declares to be his opinion, that there is only one possible proof of the existence of things outside of us, namely the one which he has given, I can now give a large number of different proofs, each of which is a perfectly rigorous proof; and that at many other times I have been in a position to give many others. I can prove now, for instance, that two human hands exist. How? By holding up my two hands, and saying, as I make a certain gesture with the right hand, 'Here is one hand', and adding, as I make a certain gesture with the left, 'and here is another'. And if, by doing this, I have proved *ipso facto* the existence of external things, you will all see that I can also do it now in numbers of other ways: there is no need to multiply examples.

But did I prove just now that two human hands were then in existence? I do want to insist that I did; that the proof which I gave was a perfectly rigorous one; and that it is perhaps impossible to give a better or more rigorous proof of anything whatever. Of course, it would not have been a proof unless three conditions were satisfied; namely (1) unless the premiss which I adduced as proof of the conclusion was different from the conclusion I adduced it to prove; (2) unless the premiss which I adduced was something which I *knew* to be the case, and not merely something which I believed but which was by no means certain, or something which, though in fact true, I did not know to be so; and (3) unless the conclusion did really follow from the premiss. But all these three conditions were in fact satisfied by my proof. (1) The premiss which I adduced in proof was quite certainly different from the conclusion, for the conclusion was merely 'Two human hands exist at this moment'; but the premiss was something far more specific than this—something which I expressed by showing you my hands, making certain gestures, and saying the words 'Here is one hand, and here is another'. It is quite obvious that the two were different, because it is quite obvious that the conclusion might have been true, even if the premiss had been false. In asserting the premiss I was asserting much more than I was asserting in asserting the conclusion. (2) I certainly did at the moment *know* that which I expressed by the combination of certain gestures with saying the words 'There is one hand and here is another'. I *knew* that there was one hand in the place indicated by combining a certain gesture with my first utterance of 'here' and that there was another in the different place indicated by combining a certain gesture with my second utterance of 'here'. How absurd it would be to suggest that I did not know it, but only believed it, and that perhaps it was not the case! You might as well suggest that I do not know that I am now standing up and talking—that perhaps after all I'm not, and that it's not quite certain that I am! And finally (3) it is quite certain that the conclusion did follow from the premiss. This is as certain as it is that if there is one hand here and another here *now*, then it follows that there are two hands in existence *now*.

My proof, then, of the existence of things outside of us did satisfy three of the conditions necessary for a rigorous proof. Are there any other conditions necessary for a rigorous proof, such that perhaps it did not satisfy one of them? Perhaps there may be; I do not know; but I do want to emphasize that, so far as I can see, we all of us do constantly take proofs of this sort as absolutely conclusive proofs of certain conclusions—as finally settling certain questions, as to which we were previously in doubt. Suppose, for instance, it were a question whether there were as many as three misprints on a certain page in a certain book. A says there are, B is inclined to doubt it. How could A prove that he is right? Surely he *could* prove it by taking the book, turning to the page, and pointing to three separate places on it, saying 'There's one misprint here, another here, and another here': surely that is a method by which it *might* be proved! Of course, A would not have proved, by doing this that there were at least three misprints on the page in question, unless it was certain that there was a misprint in each of the places to which he pointed. But to say that he *might* prove it in this way, is to say that it *might* be certain that there was. And if such a thing as that could ever be certain, then assuredly it was certain just now that there was one hand in one of the two places I indicated and another in the other.

I did, then, just now, give a proof that there were *then* external objects; and obviously, if I did, I could *then* have given many other proofs of the same sort that there were external objects *then*, and could now give many proofs of the same sort that there are external objects *now*.

But, if what I am asked to do is to prove that external objects have existed *in the past*, then I can give many different proofs of this also, but proofs which are in important respects of a different *sort* from those just given. And I want to emphasize that, when Kant says it is a scandal not to be able to give a proof of the existence of external objects, a proof of their existence in the past would certainly *help* to remove the scandal of which he is speaking. He says that, if it occurs to anyone to question their existence, we ought to be able to confront him with a satisfactory proof. But by a person who questions their existence, he certainly means not merely a person who questions whether any exist at the moment of speaking, but a person who questions whether any have *ever* existed; and a proof that some have existed in the past would certainly therefore be relevant to *part* of what such a person is questioning. How then can I prove that there have been external objects in the past? Here is one proof. I can say: 'I held up two hands above this desk not very long ago; therefore two hands existed not very long ago; therefore at least two external objects have existed at some time in the past, Q.E.D.' This is a perfectly good proof, provided I *know* what is asserted in the premiss. But I *do* know that I held up two hands above this desk not very long ago. As a matter of fact, in this case you all know it too. There's no doubt whatever that I did. Therefore I have given a perfectly conclusive proof that external objects have existed in the past; and you will all see at once that, if this is a conclusive proof, I could have given many others of the same sort, and could now give many others. But it is also quite obvious that this sort of proof differs in important respects from the sort of proof I gave just now that there were two hands existing *then*.

I have, then, given two conclusive proofs of the existence of external objects. The first was a proof that two human hands existed at the time when I gave the proof; the second was a proof that two human hands had existed at a time previous to that at which I gave the proof. These proofs were of a different sort in important respects. And I pointed out that I could have given, then, many other conclusive proofs of both sorts. It is also obvious that I could give many others of both sorts now. So that, if these are the sort of proof that is wanted, nothing is easier than to prove the existence of external objects.

But now I am perfectly well aware that, in spite of all that I have said, many philosophers will still feel that I have not given any satisfactory proof of the point in question. And I want briefly, in conclusion, to say something as to why this dissatisfaction with my proofs should be felt.

One reason why, is, I think, this. Some people understand 'proof of an external world' as including a proof of things which I haven't attempted to prove and haven't proved. It is not quite easy to say *what* it is that they want proved—*what* it is that is such that unless they got a proof of it, they would not say that they had a proof of the existence of external things; but I can make an approach to explaining what they want by saying that if I had proved the propositions which I used as *premises* in my two proofs, then they would perhaps admit that I had proved the existence of external things, but, in the absence of such a proof (which, of course, I have neither given nor attempted to give), they will say that I have not given what they mean by a proof of the existence of external things. In other words, they want a proof of what I assert *now* when I hold up my hands and say 'Here's one hand and here's another'; and, in the other case, they want a proof of what I assert *now* when I say 'I did hold up two hands above this desk just now'. Of course, what they really want is not merely a proof of these two propositions, but something like a general statement as to how *any* propositions of this sort may be proved. This, of course, I haven't given; and I do not believe it can be given: if this is what is meant by proof of the existence of external things, I do not believe that any proof of the existence of external things is possible. Of course, in some cases what might be called a proof of propositions which seem like these can be got. If one of you suspected that one of my hands was artificial he might be said to get a proof of my proposition 'Here's one hand, and here's another', by coming up and examining the suspected hand close up, perhaps touching and pressing it, and so establishing that it really was a human hand. But I do not believe that any proof is possible in nearly all cases. How am I to prove now that 'Here's one hand, and here's another'? I do not believe I can do it. In order to do it, I should need to prove for one thing, as Descartes pointed out, that I am not now dreaming. But how can I prove that I am not? I have, no doubt, conclusive reasons for asserting that I am not now dreaming; I have conclusive evidence that I am awake: but that is a very different thing from being able to prove it. I could not tell you what all my evidence is; and I should require to do this at least, in order to give you a proof.

But another reason why some people would feel dissatisfied with my proofs is, I think, not merely that they want a proof of something which I haven't proved, but that they think that, if I cannot give such extra proofs, then the proofs that I have given are not conclusive proofs at all. And this, I think, is a definite mistake. They would say: 'If you cannot prove your premiss that here is one hand and here is another, then you do not know it. But you yourself have admitted that, if you did not know it, then your proof was not conclusive. Therefore your proof was not, as you say it was, a conclusive proof.' This view that, if I cannot prove such things as these, I do not know them, is, I think, the view that Kant was expressing in the sentence which I quoted at the beginning of this lecture, when he implies that so long as we have no proof of the existence of external things, their existence must be accepted merely on *faith*. He means to say, I think, that if I cannot prove that there is a hand here, I must accept it merely as a matter of faith—I cannot know it. Such a view, though it has been very common among philosophers, can, I think, be shown to be wrong—though shown only by the use of premisses which are not known to be true, unless we do know of the existence of external things. I can know things, which I cannot prove; and among things which I certainly did know, even if (as I think) I could not prove them, were the premisses of my two proofs. I should say, therefore, that those, if any, who are dissatisfied with these proofs merely on the ground that I did not know their premisses, have no good reason for their dissatisfaction.

Chapter 3

Bertrand Russell

Bertrand Russell (1872–1970), Third Earl Russell, was born into a distinguished British family. His grandfather, Lord John Russell, had been a prime minister. John Stuart Mill was his secular godfather. His parents died when he was 3, so he was brought up by his deeply religious Quaker grandmother. He was taught at home by tutors. Soon he developed a keen interest in Euclidian geometry, which he challenged. Eventually he studied mathematics and philosophy at Cambridge University, where he became a close friend and philosophical associate with G. E. Moore and where he also taught. He traveled widely, to China and Russia, as well as to the United States. He taught at Harvard for a brief period, but was not allowed to teach at the City University in New York because of his anti-Christian views. His work covers virtually all areas of philosophical inquiry, from logic through philosophy of religion and philosophy of mind to ethics. He made major contributions to logic, especially with *Principia Mathematica* (1910–1914, written with Alfred North Whitehead), philosophy of language, and epistemology. He began as an idealist, following Bradley, Meinong, and Leibniz, but was convinced by Moore to abandon that philosophy for a more empirical realism. He developed Logical Atomism, a philosophy that was to eliminate ambiguities and provide a perfect correspondence between words and states of affairs in the world.

He is renowned for a paradox named after him, "Russell's Paradox," having to do with whether classes belong to themselves. It can be conveyed in the form of a riddle: Suppose there is a barber who shaves all and only barbers who do not shave themselves. Does he shave himself? If he shaves himself, he does not, and if he does not, then he does. Most classes are not members of themselves, but some are. The class of nonbarbers, being itself not a barber, is a member of itself. Let N be the class of all classes that are not members of themselves. If N exists, it must be a member of itself only if it is not a member of itself. But this is contradictory. Hence N cannot exist. This is paradoxical, because it conflicts with the obvious truth that any coherent condition determines a class. Philosophers have puzzled over this paradox for some ninety years.

Russell received the Noble Prize for Literature in 1950.

Russell also was an antiwar activist. He was a pacifist who protested the First World War and was imprisoned for his antiwar activities. He was also rebuffed for his opposition to the Vietnam War. An agnostic, he debated the Jesuit philosopher Father F. C. Copleston on the existence of God. He was asked what he would say to God when, after death, he was asked by God why he didn't believe in Him. Russell replied, "God, why did you make the evidence for your existence so insufficient?" He died in 1970 at the age of 97.

Our first reading, *The Problems of Philosophy*, is one of the most succinct, insightful outlines of the central notions of epistemology. Russell wrote in his preface, "In the following pages I have confined myself in the main to those problems of philosophy in regard to which I thought it possible to say something positive and constructive, since merely negative criticism seemed out of place." For this reason, theory of knowledge occupies a larger space than metaphysics in the present volume, and some topics much discussed by philosophers are treated very briefly, if at all. In the first few chapters Russell defends a Lockean or representationalist view of sense perception, holding that there is a real world but that we never know it directly. We only know sense data, the impressions caused by the world on our minds (See J. L. Austin's critique of this view in Chapter 9). Of special importance is his defense of the Correspondence Theory of Truth, which may be contrasted with William James's Pragmatic Theory of Truth (see James, second and third selections, Chapter 5). Russell first distinguishes knowledge by acquaintance (e.g., knowledge by experience or from appearances, such as "I seem to see a red book" or "I am in pain") from knowledge by description (knowledge of propositional truths, e.g., your knowing that you are seeing a book or that you're in pain). Knowledge by acquaintance ("knowledge of things"), according to Russell is infallible, for believing makes the proposition true. But descriptive beliefs have no such guarantee. They could be wrong. Thus descriptive knowledge is *dualist* or *bipolar*—it has the properties of Truth and Falsity (or Error) as opposites.

Russell goes on to specify the conditions for an adequate theory of truth and shows how the correspondence theory meets these conditions whereas the coherence theory does not.

In our second selection, "Descriptions," Russell sets forth an early version of his Theory of Description, which formed part of his Logical Atomism. This theory was hailed by Frank Ramsey as the "paradigm of philosophy," and John Wisdom said it ushered in a "new era in metaphysics." Wittgenstein was also inspired by it, and many hold that it spells the dawn of Analytic Philosophy. Russell said the following of it:

> In the first flush of my belief in separate atoms, I though that every word that can be used significantly must signify something, and I took this to mean that it must signify some ***thing***. But the words that most interest logicians are difficult from this point of view. They are the syncategoremaical "if" and "or" and "not." I tried to believe that in some logician's limbo there are things that these words mean, and that perhaps virtuous logicians may meet them hereafter in a more logical cosmos. I felt fairly satisfied about "or" and "if" and "not," but I hesitated about words like "nevertheless." My queer zoo contained some very odd monsters, such as the golden mountain and the present King of France—minsters, which, although they roamed my zoo at will, had the odd property of non-existence. There are still a number of philosophers who believe this sort of thing, and it is their beliefs which have become the philosophical basis of Existentialism. But for my part, I came to think that many words and phrases have no significance in isolation, but only contribute to the significance of whole sentences. I have therefore ceased to hope to meet "if" and "or" and "not" in heaven. I was able, in fact, by the roundabout road of a complicated technique, to return to views much nearer to those of common sense than my previous speculations. [Russell, *Portraits from Memory*, 1956]

The roundabout road of a complicated technique is his theory of definite descriptions, which is our second selection in this chapter.

Our third selection from Russell is a debate between Russell and the Catholic philosopher F. C. Copleston on the existence of God.

FOR FURTHER READING

Ayer, A. J. *Bertrand Russell* (University of Chicago Press, 1988).
Clark, R. *The Life of Bertrand Russell* (De Capo Press, 1990).
Jager, R. *The Development of Bertrand Russell's Philosophy* (Allen & Unwin, 1972).
Pears, David. *Bertrand Russell and the British Tradition in Philosophy* (Collins, 1967).
Russell, Bertrand. *The Autobiography of Bertrand Russell* (Allen & Unwin, 1961).
———. *A History of Western Philosophy* (Random House, 1945).
———. *Human Knowledge* (Simon & Schuster, 1962).

———. *Logic and Knowledge*, ed. R. Marsh (Allen & Unwin, 1971).
Sainsbury, Mark. *Russell* (Routledge & Kegan Paul, 1979).
Schilpp, P. A., ed. *The Philosophy of Bertrand Russell* (Harper & Row, 1963).

The Problems of Philosophy

CHAPTER I APPEARANCE AND REALITY

Is there any knowledge in the world which is so certain that no reasonable man could doubt it? This question, which at first sight might not seem difficult, is really one of the most difficult that can be asked. When we have realized the obstacles in the way of a straightforward and confident answer, we shall be well launched on the study of philosophy—for philosophy is merely the attempt to answer such ultimate questions, not carelessly and dogmatically, as we do in ordinary life and even in the sciences, but critically after exploring all that makes such questions puzzling, and after realizing all the vagueness and confusion that underlie our ordinary ideas.

In daily life, we assume as certain many things which, on a closer scrutiny, are found to be so full of apparent contradictions that only a great amount of thought enables us to know what it is that we really may believe. In the search for certainty, it is natural to begin with our present experiences, and in some sense, no doubt, knowledge is to be derived from them. But any statement as to what it is that our immediate experiences make us know is very likely to be wrong. It seems to me that I am now sitting in a chair, at a table of a certain shape, on which I see sheets of paper with writing or print. By turning my head I see out of the window buildings and clouds and the sun. I believe that the sun is about ninety-three million miles from the earth; that it is a hot globe many times bigger than the earth; that, owing to the earth's rotation, it rises every morning, and will continue to do so for an indefinite time in the future. I believe that, if any other normal person comes into my room, he will see the same chairs and tables and books and papers as I see, and that the table which I see is the same as the table which I feel pressing against my arm. All this seems to be so evident as to be hardly worth stating, except in answer to a man who doubts whether I know anything. Yet all this may be reasonably doubted, and all of it requires much careful discussion before we can be sure that we have stated it in a form that is wholly true.

To make our difficulties plain, let us concentrate attention on the table. To the eye it is oblong, brown and shiny, to the touch it is smooth and cool and hard; when I tap it, it gives out a wooden sound. Any one else who sees and feels and hears the table will agree with this description, so that it might seem as if no difficulty would arise; but as soon as we try to be more precise our troubles begin. Although I believe that the table is 'really' of the same colour all over, the parts that reflect the light look much brighter than the other parts, and some parts look white because of reflected light. I know that, if I move, the parts that reflect the light will be different, so that the apparent distribution of colours on the table will change. It follows that if several people are looking at the table at the same moment, no two of them will see exactly the same distribution of colours, because no two can see it from exactly the same point of view, and any change in the point of view makes some change in the way the light is reflected.

For most practical purposes these differences are unimportant, but to the painter they are all-important: the painter has to unlearn the habit of thinking that things seem to have the colour which common sense says they 'really' have, and to learn the habit of seeing things as they appear. Here we have already the beginning of one of the distinctions that cause most trouble in philosophy—the distinction

Bertrand Russell, *The Problems of Philosophy* (Oxford University Press, 1999).

between 'appearance' and 'reality', between what things seem to be and what they are. The painter wants to know what things seem to be, the practical man and the philosopher want to know what they are; but the philosopher's wish to know this is stronger than the practical man's, and is more troubled by knowledge as to the difficulties of answering the question.

To return to the table. It is evident from what we have found, that there is no colour which preeminently appears to be the colour of the table, or even of any one particular part of the table—it appears to be of different colours from different points of view, and there is no reason for regarding some of these as more really its colour than others. And we know that even from a given point of view the colour will seem different by artificial light, or to a colour-blind man, or to a man wearing blue spectacles, while in the dark there will be no colour at all, though to touch and hearing the table will be unchanged. This colour is not something which is inherent in the table, but something depending upon the table and the spectator and the way the light falls on the table. When, in ordinary life, we speak of the colour of the table, we only mean the sort of colour which it will seem to have to a normal spectator from an ordinary point of view under usual conditions of light. But the other colours which appear under other conditions have just as good a right to be considered real; and therefore, to avoid favouritism, we are compelled to deny that, in itself, the table has any one particular colour.

The same thing applies to the texture. With the naked eye one can see the grain, but otherwise the table looks smooth and even. If we looked at it through a microscope, we should see roughnesses and hills and valleys, and all sorts of differences that are imperceptible to the naked eye. Which of these is the 'real' table? We are naturally tempted to say that what we see through the microscope is more real, but that in turn would be changed by a still more powerful microscope. If, then, we cannot trust what we see with the naked eye, why should we trust what we see through a microscope? Thus, again, the confidence in our senses with which we began deserts us.

The shape of the table is no better. We are all in the habit of judging as to the 'real' shapes of things, and we do this so unreflectingly that we come to think we actually see the real shapes. But, in fact, as we all have to learn if we try to draw, a given thing looks different in shape from every different point of view. If our table is 'really' rectangular, it will look, from almost all points of view, as if it had two acute angles and two obtuse angles. If opposite sides are parallel, they will look as if they converged to a point away from the spectator; if they are of equal length, they will look as if the nearer side were longer. All these things are not commonly noticed in looking at a table, because experience has taught us to construct the 'real' shape from the apparant shape, and the 'real' shape is what interests us as practical men. But the 'real' shape is not what we see; it is something inferred from what we see. And what we see is constantly changing in shape as we move about the room; so that here again the senses seem not to give us the truth about the table itself, but only about the appearance of the table.

Similar difficulties arise when we consider the sense of touch. It is true that the table always gives us a sensation of hardness, and we feel that it resists pressure. But the sensation we obtain depends upon how hard we press the table and also upon what part of the body we press with; thus the various sensations due to various pressures or various parts of the body cannot be supposed to reveal directly any definite property of the table, but at most to be signs of some property which perhaps causes all the sensations, but is not actually apparent in any of them. And the same applies still more obviously to the sounds which can be elicited by rapping the table.

Thus it becomes evident that the real table, if there is one, is not the same as what we immediately experience by sight or touch or hearing. The real table, if there is one, is not immediately known to us at all, but must be an inference from what is immediately known. Hence, two very difficult questions at once arise; namely, (1) Is there a real table at all? (2) If so, what sort of object can it be?

It will help us in considering these questions to have a few simple terms of which the meaning is definite and clear. Let us give the name of 'sense-data' to the things that are immediately known in sensation: such things as colours, sounds, smells, hardnesses, roughnesses, and so on. We shall give the name 'sensation' to the experience of being immediately aware of these things. Thus, whenever we see a colour, we have a sensation of the colour, but the colour itself is a sense-datum, not a sensation. The colour is that of which we are immediately aware, and the awareness itself is the sensation. It is plain that if we are to know anything about the table, it must be by means of the sense-data—brown colour, oblong shape, smoothness, etc.—which we associate with the table; but, for the reasons which have been given, we cannot say that the table is the sense-data, or even that the sense-data are directly properties of the table. Thus a problem arises as to the relation of the sense-data to the real table, supposing there is such a thing.

The real table, if it exists, we will call a 'physical object'. Thus we have to consider the relation of sense-data to physical objects. The collection of all physical objects is called 'matter'. Thus our two questions may be re-stated as follows: (1) Is there any such thing as matter? (2) If so, what is its nature?

The philosopher who first brought prominently forward the reasons for regarding the immediate objects of our senses as not existing independently of us was Bishop Berkeley (1685–1753). His *Three Dialogues between Hylas and Philonous, in Opposition to Sceptics and Atheists*, undertake to prove that there is no such thing as matter at all, and that the world consists of nothing but minds and their ideas. Hylas has hitherto believed in matter, but he is no match for Philonous, who mercilessly drives him into contradictions and paradoxes, and makes his own denial of matter seem, in the end, as if it were almost common sense. The arguments employed are of very different value: some are important and sound, others are confused or quibbling. But Berkeley retains the merit of having shown that the existence of matter is capable of being denied without absurdity, and that if there are any things that exist independently of us they cannot be the immediate objects of our sensations.

There are two different questions involved when we ask whether matter exists, and it is important to keep them clear. We commonly mean by 'matter' something which is opposed to 'mind', something which we think of as occupying space and as radically incapable of any sort of thought or consciousness. It is chiefly in this sense that Berkeley denies matter; that is to say, he does not deny that the sense-data which we commonly take as signs of the existence of the table are really signs of the existence of something independent of us, but he does deny that this something is nonmental, that it is neither mind nor ideas entertained by some mind. He admits that there must be something which continues to exist when we go out of the room or shut our eyes, and that what we call seeing the table does really give us reason for believing in something which persists even when we are not seeing it. But he thinks that this something cannot be radically different in nature from what we see, and cannot be independent of seeing altogether, though it must be independent of our seeing. He is thus led to regard the 'real' table as an idea in the mind of God. Such an idea has the required permanence and independence of ourselves, without being—as matter would otherwise be—something quite unknowable, in the sense that we can only infer it, and can never be directly and immediately aware of it.

Other philosophers since Berkeley have also held that, although the table does not depend for its existence upon being seen by me, it does depend upon being seen (or otherwise apprehended in sensation) by some mind—not necessarily the mind of God, but more often the whole collective mind of the universe. This they hold, as Berkeley does, chiefly because they think there can be nothing real—or at any rate nothing known to be real except minds and their thoughts and feelings. We might state the argument by which they support their view in some such way as this: 'Whatever can be thought of is an idea in the mind of the person thinking of it; therefore nothing can be thought of except ideas in minds; therefore anything else is inconceivable, and what is inconceivable cannot exist.'

Such an argument, in my opinion, is fallacious; and of course those who advance it do not put it so shortly or so crudely. But whether valid or not, the argument has been very widely advanced in one form or another; and very many philosophers, perhaps a majority, have held that there is nothing real except minds and their ideas. Such philosophers are called 'idealists'. When they come to explaining matter, they either say, like Berkeley, that matter is really nothing but a collection of ideas, or they say, like Leibniz (1646–1716), that what happens as matter is really a collection of more or less rudimentary minds.

But these philosophers, though they deny matter as opposed to mind, nevertheless, in another sense, admit matter. It will be remembered that we asked two questions; namely, (1) Is there a real table at all? (2) If so, what sort of object can it be? Now both Berkeley and Leibniz admit that there is a real table, but Berkeley says it is certain ideas in the mind of God, and Leibniz says it is a colony of souls. Thus both of them answer our first question in the affirmative and only diverge from the views of ordinary mortals in their answer to our second question. In fact, almost all philosophers seem to be agreed that there is a real table. They almost all agree that, however much our sense-data—colour, shape, smoothness, etc.—may depend upon us, yet their occurrence is a sign of something existing independently of us, something differing, perhaps, completely from our sense-data whenever we are in a suitable relation to the real table.

Now obviously this point in which the philosophers are agreed—the view that there is a real table, whatever its nature may be is vitally important, and it will be worth while to consider what reasons there are for accepting this view before we go on to the further question as to the nature of the real table. Our next chapter, therefore, will be concerned with the reasons for supposing that there is a real table at all.

Before we go farther it will be well to consider for a moment what it is that we have discovered so far. It has appeared that, if we take any common object of the sort that is supposed to be known by the senses, what the senses immediately tell us is not the truth about the object as it is apart from us, but only the truth about certain sense-data which, so far as we can see, depend upon the relations between us and the object. Thus what we directly see and feel is merely 'appearance', which we believe to be a sign of some 'reality' behind. But if the reality is not what appears, have we any means of knowing whether there is any reality at all? And if so, have we any means of finding out what it is like?

Such questions are bewildering, and it is difficult to know that even the strangest hypotheses may not be true. Thus our familiar table, which has roused but the slightest thoughts in us hitherto, has become a problem full of surprising possibilities. The one thing we know about it is that it is not what it seems. Beyond this modest result, so far, we have the most complete liberty of conjecture. Leibniz tells us it is a community of souls: Berkeley tells us it is an idea in the mind of God; sober science, scarcely less wonderful, tells us it is a vast collection of electric charges in violent motion.

Among these surprising possibilities, doubt suggests that perhaps there is no table at all. Philosophy, if it cannot answer so many questions as we could wish, has at least the power of asking questions which increase the interest of the world, and show the strangeness and wonder lying just below the surface even in the commonest things of daily life.

CHAPTER II THE EXISTENCE OF MATTER

In this chapter we have to ask ourselves whether, in any sense at all, there is such a thing as matter. Is there a table which has a certain intrinsic nature, and continues to exist when I am not looking, or is the table merely a product of my imagination, a dream-table in a very prolonged dream? This question is of the greatest importance. For if we cannot be sure of the independent existence of objects, we cannot be sure of the independent existence of other people's bodies, and therefore still less of other people's minds, since we have no grounds for believing in their minds except such as are derived from observing their bodies. Thus if we cannot be sure of the independent existence of objects, we shall be left alone in a desert—it may be that the whole outer world is nothing but a dream, and that we alone exist. This is an uncomfortable possibility; but although it cannot be strictly proved to be false, there is not the slightest reason to suppose that it is true. In this chapter we have to see why this is the case.

Before we embark upon doubtful matters, let us try to find some more or less fixed point from which to start. Although we are doubting the physical existence of the table, we are not doubting the existence of the sense-data which made us think there was a table; we are not doubting that, while we look, a certain colour and shape appear to us, and while we press, a certain sensation of hardness is experienced by us. All this, which is psychological, we are not calling in question. In fact, whatever else may be doubtful, some at least of our immediate experiences seem absolutely certain.

Descartes (1596–1650), the founder of modern philosophy, invented a method which may still be used with profit—the method of systematic doubt. He determined that he would believe nothing which he did not see quite clearly and distinctly to be true. Whatever he could bring himself to doubt, he would doubt, until he saw reason for not doubting it. By applying this method he gradually became convinced that the only existence of which he could be quite certain was his own. He imagined a deceitful demon, who presented unreal things to his senses in a perpetual phantasmagoria; it might be very improbable that such a demon existed, but still it was possible, and therefore doubt concerning things perceived by the senses was possible.

But doubt concerning his own existence was not possible, for if he did not exist, no demon could deceive him. If he doubted, he must exist; if he had any experiences whatever, he must exist. Thus his own existence was an absolute certainty to him. 'I think, therefore I am,' he said (Cogito, ergo sum); and on the basis of this certainty he set to work to build up again the world of knowledge which his doubt had laid in ruins. By inventing the method of doubt, and by showing that subjective things are the most certain, Descartes performed a great service to philosophy, and one which makes him still useful to all students of the subject.

But some care is needed in using Descartes' argument. 'I think, therefore I am' says rather more than is strictly certain. It might seem as though we were quite sure of being the same person to-day as we were yesterday, and this is no doubt true in some sense. But the real Self is as hard to arrive at as the real table and does not seem to have the absolute, convincing certainty that belongs to particular experiences. When I look at my table and see a certain brown colour, what is quite certain at once is not 'I am seeing a brown colour', but rather, 'a brown colour is being seen'. This of course involves something (or somebody) which (or who) sees the brown colour; but it does not of itself involve that more or less permanent person whom we call 'I'. So far as immediate certainty goes, it might be that the something which sees the brown colour is quite momentary, and not the same as the something which has some different experience the next moment.

Thus it is our particular thoughts and feelings that have primitive certainty. And this applies to dreams and hallucinations as well as to normal perceptions: when we dream or see a ghost, we certainly do have the sensations we think we have, but for various reasons it is held that no physical object corresponds to these sensations. Thus the certainty of our knowledge of our own experiences does not have to be limited in any way to allow for exceptional cases. Here, therefore, we have, for what it is worth, a solid basis from which to begin our pursuit of knowledge.

The problem we have to consider is this: Granted that we are certain of our own sense-data, have we any reason for regarding them as signs of the existence of something else, which we can call the physical object? When we have enumerated all the sense-data which we should naturally regard as connected with the table have we said all there is to say about the table, or is there still something else—something not a sense-datum, something which persists when we go out of the room? Common sense unhesitatingly answers that there is. What can be bought and sold and pushed about and have a cloth laid on it, and so on, cannot be a mere collection of sense-data. If the cloth completely hides the table, we shall derive no sense-data from the table, and therefore, if the table were merely sense-data, it would have ceased to exist, and the cloth would be suspended in empty air, resting, by a miracle, in the place where the table formerly was. This seems plainly absurd; but whoever wishes to become a philosopher must learn not to be frightened by absurdities.

One great reason why it is felt that we must secure a physical object in addition to the sense-data, is that we want the same object for different people. When ten people are sitting round a dinner-table, it seems preposterous to maintain that they are not seeing the same tablecloth, the same knives and forks and spoons and glasses. But the sense-data are private to each separate person; what is immediately present to the sight of one is not immediately present to the sight of another: they all see things from slightly different points of view, and therefore see them slightly differently. Thus, if there are to be public neutral objects, which can be in some sense known to many different people, there must be something over and above the private and particular sense-data which appear to various people. What reason, then, have we for believing that there are such public neutral objects?

The first answer that naturally occurs to one is that, although different people may see the table slightly differently, still they all see more or less similar things when they look at the table, and the variations in what they see follow the laws of perspective and reflection of light, so that it is easy to arrive at a permanent object underlying all the different people's sense-data. I bought my table from the former occupant of my room; I could not buy his sense-data, which died when he went away, but I could and did buy the confident expectation of more or less similar sense-data. Thus it is the fact that different people have similar sense-data, and that one person in a given place at different times has similar sense-data, which makes us suppose that over and above the sense-data there is a permanent public object which underlies or causes the sense-data of various people at various times.

Now in so far as the above considerations depend upon supposing that there are other people besides ourselves, they beg the very question at issue. Other people are represented to me by certain sense-data, such as the sight of them or the sound of their voices, and if I had no reason to believe that there were physical objects independent of my sense-data, I should have no reason to believe that other people exist except as part of my dream. Thus, when we are trying to show that there must be objects independent of our own sense-data, we cannot appeal to the testimony of other people, since this testimony itself consists of sense-data, and does not reveal other people's experiences unless our own sense-data are signs of things existing independently of us. We must therefore, if possible, find, in our own purely private experiences, characteristics which show, or tend to show, that there are in the world things other than ourselves and our private experiences.

In one sense it must be admitted that we can never prove the existence of things other than ourselves and our experiences. No logical absurdity results from the hypothesis that the world consists of myself and my thoughts and feelings and sensations, and that everything else is mere fancy. In dreams a very complicated world may seem to be present, and yet on waking we find it was a delusion; that is to say, we find that the sense-data in the dream do not appear to have corresponded with such physical objects as we should naturally infer from our sense-data. (It is true that, when the physical world is assumed, it is possible to find physical causes for the sense-data in dreams: a door banging, for instance, may cause us to dream of a naval engagement. But although, in this case, there is a physical cause for the sense-data, there is not a physical object corresponding to the sense-data in the way in which an actual naval battle would correspond.) There is no logical impossibility in the supposition that the whole of life is a dream, in which we ourselves create all the objects that come before us. But although this is not logically impossible, there is no reason whatever to suppose that it is true; and it is, in fact, a less simple hypothesis, viewed as a means of accounting for the facts of our own life, than the common-sense hypothesis that there really are objects independent of us, whose action on us causes our sensations.

The way in which simplicity comes in from supposing that there really are physical objects is easily seen. If the cat appears at one moment in one part of the room, and at another in another part, it is natural to suppose that it has moved from the one to the other, passing over a series of intermediate positions. But if it is merely a set of sense-data, it cannot have ever been in any place where I did not see it; thus we shall have to suppose that it did not exist at all while I was not looking, but suddenly sprang into being in a new place. If the cat exists whether I see it or not, we can understand from our own experience how it gets hungry between one meal and the next; but if it does not exist when I am not seeing it, it seems odd that appetite should grow during non-existence as fast as during existence. And if the cat consists only of sense-data, it cannot be hungry, since no hunger but my own can be a sense-datum to me. Thus the behaviour of the sense-data which represent the cat to me, though it seems quite natural when regarded as an expression of hunger, becomes utterly inexplicable when regarded as mere movements and changes of patches of colour, which are as incapable of hunger as triangle is of playing football.

But the difficulty in the case of the cat is nothing compared to the difficulty in the case of human beings. When human beings speak—that is, when we hear certain noises which we associate with ideas, and simultaneously see certain motions of lips and expressions of face—it is very difficult to suppose that what we hear is not the expression of a thought, as we know it would be if we emitted the same sounds. Of course similar things happen in dreams, where we are mistaken as to the existence of other people. But dreams are more or less suggested by what we call waking life, and are capable of being more or less accounted for on scientific principles if we assume that there really is a physical world. Thus every principle of simplicity urges us to adopt the natural view, that there really are objects other than ourselves and our sense-data which have an existence not dependent upon our perceiving them.

Of course it is not by argument that we originally come by our belief in an independent external world. We find this belief ready in ourselves as soon as we begin to reflect: it is what may be called an instinctive belief. We should never have been led to question this belief but for the fact that, at any rate in the case of sight, it seems as if the sense-datum itself was instinctively believed to be the independent object, whereas argument shows that the object cannot be identical with the sense-datum. This discovery, however—which is not at all paradoxical in the case of taste and smell and sound, and only slightly so in the case of touch—leaves undiminished our instinctive belief that there are objects corresponding to our sense-data. Since this belief does not lead to any difficulties, but on the contrary tends to simplify and systematize our account of our experiences, there seems no good reason for rejecting it. We may therefore admit—though with a slight doubt derived from dreams—that the external world does really exist, and is not wholly dependent for its existence upon our continuing to perceive it.

The argument which has led us to this conclusion is doubtless less strong than we could wish, but it is typical of many philosophical arguments, and it is therefore worth while to consider briefly its general character and validity. All knowledge, we find, must be built up upon our instinctive beliefs, and if these are rejected, nothing is left. But among our instinctive beliefs some are much stronger than others, while many have, by habit and association, become entangled with other beliefs, not really instinctive, but falsely supposed to be part of what is believed instinctively.

Philosophy should show us the hierarchy of our instinctive beliefs, beginning with those we hold most strongly, and presenting each as much isolated and as free from irrelevant additions as possible. It should take care to show that, in the form in which they are finally set forth, our instinctive beliefs do not clash, but form a harmonious system. There can never be any reason for rejecting one instinctive belief except that it clashes with others; thus, if they are found to harmonize, the whole system becomes worthy of acceptance.

It is of course possible that all or any of our beliefs may be mistaken, and therefore all ought to be held with at least some slight element of doubt. But we cannot have reason to reject a belief except on the ground of some other belief. Hence, by organizing our instinctive beliefs and their consequences, by considering which among them is most possible, if necessary, to modify or abandon, we can arrive, on the basis of accepting as our sole data what we instinctively believe, at an orderly systematic organization of our knowledge, in which, though the possibility of error remains, its likelihood is diminished by the interrelation of the parts and by the critical scrutiny which has preceded acquiescence.

This function, at least, philosophy can perform. Most philosophers, rightly or wrongly, believe that philosophy can do much more than this—that it can give us knowledge, not otherwise attainable, concerning the universe as a whole, and concerning the nature of ultimate reality. Whether this be the case or not, the more modest function we have spoken of can certainly be performed by philosophy, and certainly suffices, for those who have once begun to doubt the adequacy of common sense, to justify the arduous and difficult labours that philosophical problems involve.

CHAPTER III THE NATURE OF MATTER

In the preceding chapter we agreed, though without being able to find demonstrative reasons, that it is rational to believe that our sense-data—for example, those which we regard as associated with my table—are really signs of the existence of something independent of us and our perceptions. That is to say, over and above the sensations of colour, hardness, noise, and so on, which make up the appearance of the table to me, I assume that there is something else, of which these things are appearances. The colour ceases to exist if I shut my eyes, the sensation of hardness ceases to exist if I remove my arm from contact with the table, the sound ceases to exist if I cease to rap the table with my knuckles. But I do not believe that when all these things cease the table ceases. On the contrary, I believe that it is because the table exists continuously that all these sense-data will reappear when I open my eyes, replace my arm, and begin again to rap with my knuckles. The question we have to consider in this chapter is: What is the nature of this real table, which persists independently of my perception of it?

To this question physical science gives an answer, somewhat incomplete it is true, and in part still very hypothetical, but yet deserving of respect so far as it goes. Physical science, more or less unconsciously, has drifted into the view that all natural phenomena ought to be reduced to motions. Light and heat and sound are all due to wave-motions, which travel from the body emitting them to the person who sees light or feels heat or hears sound. That which has the wave-motion is either ether or 'gross matter', but in either case is what the philosopher would call matter. The only properties which science assigns to it are position in space, and the power of motion according to the laws of motion. Science does not deny that it may have other properties; but if so, such other properties are not useful to the man of science, and in no way assist him in explaining the phenomena.

It is sometimes said that 'light is a form of wave-motion', but this is misleading, for the light which we immediately see, which we know directly by means of our senses, is not a form of wave-motion, but something quite different—something which we all know if we are not blind, though we cannot describe it so as to convey our knowledge to a man who is blind. A wave-motion, on the contrary, could quite well be described to a blind man, since he can acquire a knowledge of space by the sense of touch; and he can experience a wave-motion by a sea voyage almost as well as we can. But this, which a blind man can understand, is not what we mean by light: we mean by light just that which a blind man can never understand, and which we can never describe to him.

Now this something, which all of us who are not blind know, is not, according to science, really to be found in the outer world: it is something caused by the action of certain waves upon the eyes and nerves and brain of the person who sees the light. When it is said that light is waves, what is really meant is that waves are the physical cause of our sensations of light. But light itself, the thing which seeing people experience and blind people do not, is not supposed by science to form any part of the world that is independent of us and our senses. And very similar remarks would apply to other kinds of sensations.

It is not only colours and sounds and so on that are absent from the scientific world of matter, but also space as we get it through sight or touch. It is essential to science that its matter should be in a space, but the space in which it is cannot be exactly the space we see or feel. To begin with, space as we see it is not the same as space as we get it by the sense of touch; it is only by experience in infancy that we learn how to touch things we see, or how to get a sight of things which we feel touching us. But the space of science is neutral as between touch and sight; thus it cannot be either the space of touch or the space of sight.

Again, different people see the same object as of different shapes, according to their point of view. A circular coin, for example, though we should always judge it to be circular, will look oval unless we are straight in front of it. When we judge that it is circular, we are judging that it has a real shape which is not its apparent shape, but belongs to it intrinsically apart from its appearance. But this real shape, which is what concerns science, must be in a real space, not the same as anybody's apparent space. The real space is public, the apparent space is private to the percipient. In different people's private spaces the same object seems to have different shapes; thus the real space, in which it has its real shape, must be different from the private spaces. The space of science, therefore, though connected with the spaces we see and feel, is not identical with them, and the manner of its connexion requires investigation.

We agreed provisionally that physical objects cannot be quite like our sense-data, but may be regarded as causing our sensations. These physical objects are in the space of science, which we may call "physical" space. It is important to notice that, if our sensations are to be caused by physical objects, there must be a physical space containing these objects and our sense-organs and nerves and brain. We get a sensation of touch from an object when we are in contact with it; that is to say, when some part of our body occupies a place in physical space quite close to the space occupied by the object. We see an object (roughly speaking) when no opaque body is between the object and our eyes in physical space. Similarly, we only hear or smell or taste an object when we are sufficiently near to it, or when it touches the tongue, or has some suitable position in physical space relatively to our body. We cannot begin to state what different sensations we shall derive from a given object under different circumstances unless we regard the object and our body as both in one physical space, for it is mainly the relative positions of the object and our body that determine what sensations we shall derive from the object.

Now our sense-data are situated in our private spaces, either the space of sight or the space of touch or such vaguer spaces as other senses may give us. If, as science and common sense assume, there is one public all-embracing physical space in which physical objects are, the relative positions of physical objects in physical space must more or less correspond to the relative positions of sense-data in our private spaces. There is no difficulty in supposing this to be the case. If we see on a road one house nearer to us than another, our other senses will bear out the view that it is nearer; for example, it will be reached sooner if we walk along the road. Other people will agree that the house which looks nearer to us is nearer; the ordnance map will take the same view; and thus everything points to a spatial relation between the houses corresponding to the relation between the sense-data which we see when we look at the houses. Thus we may assume that there is a physical space in which physical objects have spatial relations corresponding to those which the corresponding sense-data have in our private spaces. It is this physical space which is dealt with in geometry and assumed in physics and astronomy.

Assuming that there is physical space, and that it does thus correspond to private spaces, what can we know about it? We can know only what is required in order to secure the correspondence. That is to say, we can know nothing of what it is like in itself, but we can know the sort of arrangement of physical objects which results from their spatial relations. We can know, for example, that the earth and moon and sun are in one straight line during an eclipse, though we cannot know what a physical straight line is in itself, as we know the look of a straight line in our visual space. Thus we come to know much more about the relations of distances in physical space than about the distances themselves; we may know that one distance is greater than another, or that it is along the same straight line as the other, but we cannot have that immediate acquaintance with physical distances that we have with distances in our private spaces, or with colours or sounds or other sense-data. We can know all those things about physical space which a man born blind might know through other people about the space of sight; but the kind of things which a man born blind could never know about the space of sight we also cannot know about physical space. We can know the properties of the relations required to preserve the correspondence with sense-data, but we cannot know the nature of the terms between which the relations hold.

With regard to time, our feeling of duration or of the lapse of time is notoriously an unsafe guide as to the time that has elapsed by the clock. Times when we are bored or suffering pain pass slowly, times when we are agreeably occupied pass quickly, and times when we are sleeping pass almost as if they did not exist. Thus, in so far as time is constituted by duration, there is the same necessity for distinguishing a public and a private time as there was in the case of space. But in so far as time consists in an order of before and after, there is no need to make such a distinction; the time-order which events seem to have is, so far as we can see, the same as the time-order which they do have. At any rate no reason can be given for supposing that the two orders are not the same. The same is usually true of space: if a regiment of men are marching along a road, the shape of the regiment will look different from different points of view, but the men will appear arranged in the same order from all points of view. Hence we regard the order as true also in physical space, whereas the shape is only supposed to correspond to the physical space so far as is required for the preservation of the order.

In saying that the time-order which events seem to have is the same as the time-order which they really have, it is necessary to guard against a possible misunderstanding. It must not be supposed that the various states of different physical objects have the same time-order as the sense-data which constitute the perceptions of those objects. Considered as physical objects, the thunder and lightning are simultaneous; that is to say, the lightning is simultaneous with the disturbance of the air in the place where the disturbance begins, namely, where the lightning is. But the sense-datum which we call hearing the thunder does not take place until the disturbance of the air has travelled as far as to where we are. Similarly, it takes about eight minutes for the sun's light to reach us; thus, when we see the sun we are seeing the sun of eight minutes ago. So far as our sense-data afford evidence as to the physical sun they afford evidence as to the physical sun of eight minutes ago; if the physical sun had ceased to exist within the last eight minutes, that would make no difference to the sense-data which we call 'seeing the sun'. This affords a fresh illustration of the necessity of distinguishing between sense-data and physical objects.

What we have found as regards space is much the same as what we find in relation to the correspondence of the sense-data with their physical counterparts. If one object looks blue and another red, we may reasonably presume that there is some corresponding difference between the physical objects; if two objects both look blue, we may presume a corresponding similarity. But we cannot hope to be acquainted directly with the quality in the physical object which makes it look blue or red. Science tells us that this quality is a certain sort of wave-motion, and this sounds familiar, because we think of wave-motions in the space we see. But the wave-motions must really be in physical space, with which we have no direct acquaintance; thus the real wave-motions have not that familiarity which we might have supposed them to have. And what holds for colours is closely similar to what holds for other sense-data.

Thus we find that, although the relations of physical objects have all sorts of knowable properties, derived from their correspondence with the relations of sense-data, the physical objects themselves remain unknown in their intrinsic nature, so far at least as can be discovered by means of the senses. The question remains whether there is any other method of discovering the intrinsic nature of physical objects.

The most natural, though not ultimately the most defensible, hypothesis to adopt in the first instance, at any rate as regards visual sense-data, would be that, though physical objects cannot, for the reasons we have been considering, be exactly like sense-data, yet they may be more or less like. According to this view, physical objects will, for example, really have colours, and we might, by good luck, see an object as of the colour it really is. The colour which an object seems to have at any given moment will in general be very similar, though not quite the same, from many different points of view; we might thus suppose the 'real' colour to be a sort of medium colour, intermediate between the various shades which appear from the different points of view.

Such a theory is perhaps not capable of being definitely refuted, but it can be shown to be groundless. To begin with, it is plain that the colour we see depends only upon the nature of the light-waves that strike the eye, and is therefore modified by the medium intervening between us and the object, as well as by the manner in which light is reflected from the object in the direction of the eye. The intervening air alters colours unless it is perfectly clear, and any strong reflection will alter them completely. Thus the colour we see is a result of the ray as it reaches the eye, and not simply a property of the object from which the ray comes. Hence, also, provided certain waves reach the eye, we shall see a certain colour, whether the object from which the waves start has any colour or not. Thus it is quite gratuitous to suppose that physical objects have colours, and therefore there is no justification for making such a supposition. Exactly similar arguments will apply to other sense-data.

It remains to ask whether there are any general philosophical arguments enabling us to say that, if matter is real, it must be of such and such a nature. As explained above, very many philosophers, perhaps most, have held that whatever is real must be in some sense mental, or at any rate that whatever we can know anything about must be in some sense mental. Such philosophers are called 'idealists'. Idealists tell us that what appears as matter is really something mental; namely, either (as Leibniz held) more or less rudimentary minds, or (as Berkeley contended) ideas in the minds which, as we should commonly say, 'perceive' the matter. Thus idealists deny the existence of matter as something intrinsically different from mind, though they do not deny that our sense-data are signs of something which exists independently of our private sensations. In the following chapter we shall consider briefly the reasons—in my opinion fallacious—which idealists advance in favour of their theory.

CHAPTER IV IDEALISM

The word 'idealism' is used by different philosophers in somewhat different senses. We shall understand by it the doctrine that whatever exists, or at any rate whatever can be known to exist, must be in some sense mental. This doctrine, which is very widely held among philosophers, has several forms, and is advocated on several different grounds. The doctrine is so widely held, and so interesting in itself, that even the briefest survey of philosophy must give some account of it.

Those who are unaccustomed to philosophical speculation may be inclined to dismiss such a doctrine as obviously absurd. There is no doubt that common sense regards tables and chairs and the sun and moon and material objects generally as something radically different from minds and the contents of minds, and as having an existence which might continue if minds ceased. We think of matter as having existed long before there were any minds, and it is hard to think of it as a mere product of mental activity. But whether true or false, idealism is not to be dismissed as obviously absurd.

We have seen that, even if physical objects do have an independent existence, they must differ very widely from sense-data, and can only have a correspondence with sense-data, in the same sort of way in which a catalogue has a correspondence with the things catalogued. Hence common sense leaves us completely in the dark as to the true intrinsic nature of physical objects, and if there were good reason to regard them as mental, we could not legitimately reject this opinion merely because it strikes us as strange. The truth about physical objects must be strange. It may be unattainable, but if any philosopher believes that he has attained it, the fact that what he offers as the truth is strange ought not to be made a ground of objection to his opinion.

The grounds on which idealism is advocated are generally grounds derived from the theory of knowledge, that is to say, from a discussion of the conditions which things must satisfy in order that we may be able to know them. The first serious attempt to establish idealism on such grounds was that of Bishop Berkeley. He proved first, by arguments which were largely valid, that our sense-data cannot be supposed to have an existence independent of us, but must be, in part at least, 'in' the mind, in the sense that their existence would not continue if there were no seeing or hearing or touching or smelling or tasting. So far, his contention was almost certainly valid, even if some of his arguments were not so. But he went on to argue that sense-data were the only things of whose existence our perceptions could assure us, and that to be known is to be 'in' a mind, and therefore to be mental. Hence he concluded that nothing can ever be known except what is in some mind, and that whatever is known without being in my mind must be in some other mind.

In order to understand his argument, it is necessary to understand his use of the word 'idea'. He gives the name 'idea' to anything which is immediately known, as, for example, sense-data are known. Thus a particular colour which we see is an idea; so is a voice which we hear, and so on. But the term is not wholly confined to sense-data. There will also be things remembered or imagined, for with such things also we have immediate acquaintance at the moment of remembering or imagining. All such immediate data he calls 'ideas'.

He then proceeds to consider common objects, such as a tree, for instance. He shows that all we know immediately when we 'perceive' the tree consists of ideas in his sense of the word, and he argues that there is not the slightest ground for supposing that there is anything real about the tree except what is perceived. Its being, he says, consists in being perceived: in the Latin of the schoolmen its 'esse' is 'percipi'. He fully admits that the tree must continue to exist even when we shut our eyes or when no human being is near it. But this continued existence, he says, is due to the fact that God continues to perceive it; the 'real' tree, which corresponds to what we called the physical object, consists of ideas in the mind of God, ideas more or less like those we have when we see the tree, but differing in the fact that they are permanent in God's mind so long as the tree continues to exist. All our perceptions, according to him, consist in a partial participation in God's perceptions, and it is because of this participation that different people see more or less the same tree. Thus apart from minds and their ideas there is nothing in the world, nor is it possible that anything else should ever be known, since whatever is known is necessarily an idea.

There are in this argument a good many fallacies which have been important in the history of philosophy, and which it will be as well to bring to light. In the first place, there is a confusion engendered by the use of the word 'idea'. We think of an idea as essentially something in somebody's mind, and thus when we are told that a tree consists entirely of ideas, it is natural to suppose that, if so, the tree must be entirely in minds. But the notion of being "in" the mind is ambiguous. We speak of bearing a person in mind, not meaning that the person is in our minds, but that a thought of him is in our minds. When a man says that some business he had to arrange went clean out of his mind, he does not mean to imply that the business itself was ever in his mind, but only that a thought of the business was formerly in his mind, but afterwards ceased to be in his mind. And so when Berkeley says that the tree must be in our minds if we can know it, all that he really has a right to say is that a thought of the tree must be in our minds. To argue that the tree itself must be in our minds is like arguing that a person whom we bear in mind is himself in our minds. This confusion may seem too gross to have been really committed by any competent philosopher, but various attendant circumstances rendered it possible. In order to see how it was possible, we must go more deeply into the question as to the nature of ideas.

Before taking up the general question of the nature of ideas, we must disentangle two entirely separate questions which arise concerning sense-data and physical objects. We saw that, for various reasons of detail, Berkeley was right in treating the sense-data which constitute our perception of the tree as more or less subjective, in the sense that they depend upon us as much as upon the tree, and would not exist if the tree were not being perceived. But this is an entirely different point from the one by which Berkeley seeks to prove that whatever can be immediately known must be in a mind. For this purpose argument of detail as to the dependence of sense-data upon us are useless. It is necessary to prove, generally, that by being known, things are shown to be mental. This is what Berkeley believes himself to have done. It is this question, and not our previous question as to the difference between sense-data and the physical object, that must now concern us.

Taking the word 'idea' in Berkeley's sense, there are two quite distinct things to be considered whenever an idea is before the mind. There is on the one hand the thing of which we are aware—say the colour of my table—and on the other hand the actual awareness itself, the mental act of apprehending the thing. The mental act is undoubtedly mental, but is there any reason to suppose that the thing apprehended is in any sense mental? Our previous arguments concerning the colour did not prove it to be mental; they only proved that its existence depends upon the relation of our sense organs to the physical object—in our case, the table. That is to say, they proved that a certain colour will exist, in a certain light, if a normal eye is placed at a certain point relatively to the table. They did not prove that the colour is in the mind of the percipient.

Berkeley's view, that obviously the colour must be in the mind, seems to depend for its plausibility upon confusing the thing apprehended with the act of apprehension. Either of these might be called an 'idea'; probably either would have been called an idea by Berkeley. The act is undoubtedly in the mind; hence, when we are thinking of the act, we readily assent to the view that ideas must be in the mind. Then, forgetting that this was only true when ideas were taken as acts of apprehension, we transfer the proposition that 'ideas are in the mind' to ideas in the other sense, i.e. to the things apprehended by our acts of apprehension. Thus, by an unconscious equivocation, we arrive at the conclusion that whatever we can apprehend must be in our minds. This seems to be the true analysis of Berkeley's argument, and the ultimate fallacy upon which it rests.

This question of the distinction between act and object in our apprehending of things is vitally important, since our whole power of acquiring knowledge is bound up with it. The faculty of being acquainted with things other than itself is the main characteristic of a mind. Acquaintance with objects essentially consists in a relation between the mind and something other than the mind; it is this that constitutes the mind's power of knowing things. If we say that the things known must be in the mind, we are either unduly limiting the mind's power of knowing, or we are uttering a mere tautology. We are uttering a mere tautology if we mean by 'in the mind' the same as by 'before the mind', i.e. if we mean merely being apprehended by the mind. But if we mean this, we shall have to admit that what, in this sense, is in the mind, may nevertheless be not mental. Thus when we realize the nature of knowledge, Berkeley's argument is seen to be wrong in substance as well as in form, and his grounds for supposing that 'ideas'—i.e. the objects apprehended—must be mental, are found to have no validity whatever. Hence his grounds in favour of idealism may be dismissed. It remains to see whether there are any other grounds.

It is often said, as though it were a self-evident truism, that we cannot know that anything exists which we do not know. It is inferred that whatever can in any way be relevant to our experience must be at least capable of being known by us; whence it follows that if matter were essentially something with which we could not become acquainted, matter would be something which we could not know to exist, and which could have for us no importance whatever. It is generally also implied, for reasons which remain obscure, that what can have no importance for us cannot be real, and that therefore matter, if it is not composed of minds or of mental ideas, is impossible and a mere chimaera.

To go into this argument fully at our present stage would be impossible, since it raises points requiring a considerable preliminary discussion; but certain reasons for rejecting the argument may be noticed at once. To begin at the end: there is no reason why what cannot have any practical importance for us should not be real. It is true that, if theoretical importance is included, everything real is of some importance to us, since, as persons desirous of knowing the truth about the universe, we have some interest in everything that the universe contains. But if this sort of interest is included, it is not the case that matter has no importance for us, provided it exists even if we cannot know that it exists. We can, obviously, suspect that it may exist, and wonder whether it does; hence it is connected with our desire for knowledge, and has the importance of either satisfying or thwarting this desire.

Again, it is by no means a truism, and is in fact false, that we cannot know that anything exists which we do not know. The word 'know' is here used in two different senses. (1) In its first use it is applicable to the sort of knowledge which is opposed to error, the sense in which what we know is true, the sense which applies to our beliefs and convictions, i.e. to what are called judgements. In this sense of the word we know that something is the case. This sort of knowledge may be described as knowledge of truths. (2) In the second use of the word 'know' above, the word applies to our knowledge of things, which we may call acquaintance. This is the sense in which we know sense-data. (The distinction involved is roughly that between savoir and connaitre in French, or between wissen and kennen in German.)

Thus the statement which seemed like a truism becomes, when re-stated, the following: 'We can never truly judge that something with which we are not acquainted exists.' This is by no means a truism, but on the contrary a palpable falsehood. I have not the honour to be acquainted with the Emperor of China, but I truly judge that he exists. It may be said, of course, that I judge this because of other people's acquaintance with him. This, however, would be an irrelevant retort, since, if the principle were true, I could not know that any one else is acquainted with him. But further: there is no reason why I should not know of the existence of something with which nobody is acquainted. This point is important, and demands elucidation.

If I am acquainted with a thing which exists, my acquaintance gives me the knowledge that it exists. But it is not true that, conversely, whenever I can know that a thing of a certain sort exists, I or some one else must be acquainted with the thing. What happens, in cases where I have true judgement without acquaintance, is that the thing is known to me by description, and that, in virtue of some general principle, the existence of a thing answering to this description can be inferred from the existence of something with which I am acquainted. In order to understand this point fully, it will be well first to deal with the difference between knowledge by acquaintance and knowledge by description, and then to consider what knowledge of general principles, if any, has the same kind of certainty as our knowledge of the existence of our own experiences. These subjects will be dealt with in the following chapters.

CHAPTER V KNOWLEDGE BY ACQUAINTANCE AND KNOWLEDGE BY DESCRIPTION

In the preceding chapter we saw that there are two sorts of knowledge: knowledge of things, and knowledge of truths. In this chapter we shall be concerned exclusively with knowledge of things, of which in turn we shall have to distinguish two kinds. Knowledge of things, when it is of the kind we call knowledge by acquaintance, is essentially simpler than any knowledge of truths, and logically independent of knowledge of truths, though it would be rash to assume that human beings ever, in fact, have acquaintance with things without at the same time knowing some truth about them. Knowledge of things by description, on the contrary, always involves, as we shall find in the course of the present chapter, some knowledge of truths as its source and ground. But first of all we must make dear what we mean by 'acquaintance' and what we mean by 'description'.

We shall say that we have acquaintance with anything of which we are directly aware, without the intermediary of any process of inference or any knowledge of truths. Thus in the presence of my table I am acquainted with the sense-data that make up the appearance of my table—its colour, shape, hardness, smoothness, etc.; all these are things of which I am immediately conscious when I am seeing and touching my table. The particular shade of colour that I am seeing may have many things said about it—I may say that it is brown, that it is rather dark, and so on. But such statements, though they make me know truths about the colour, do not make me know the colour itself any better than I did before: so far as concerns knowledge of the colour itself, as opposed to knowledge of truths about it, I know the colour perfectly and completely when I see it, and no further knowledge of it itself is even theoretically possible. Thus the sense-data which make up the appearance of my table are things with which I have acquaintance, things immediately known to me just as they are.

My knowledge of the table as a physical object, on the contrary, is not direct knowledge. Such as it is, it is obtained through acquaintance with the sense-data that make up the appearance of the table. We have seen that it is possible, without absurdity, to doubt that there is a table at all, whereas it is not possible to doubt the sense-data. My knowledge of the table is of the kind which we shall call 'knowledge by description'. The table is 'the physical object which causes such-and-such sense-data'. This describes the table by means of the sense-data. In order to know anything at all about the table, we must know truths connecting it with things with which we have acquaintance: we must know that 'such-and-such sense-data are caused by a physical object'. There is no state of mind in which we are directly aware of the table; all our knowledge of the table is really knowledge of truths, and the actual thing which is the table is not, strictly speaking, known to us at all. We know a description and we know that there is just one object to which this description applies, though the object itself is not directly known to us. In such a case, we say that our knowledge of the object is knowledge by description.

All our knowledge, both knowledge of things and knowledge of truths, rests upon acquaintance as its foundation. It is therefore important to consider what kinds of things there are with which we have acquaintance.

Sense-data, as we have already seen, are among the things with which we are acquainted; in fact, they supply the most obvious and striking example of knowledge by acquaintance. But if they were the sole example, our knowledge would be very much more restricted than it is. We should only know what is now present to our senses: we could not know anything about the past—not even that there was a past—nor could we know any truths about our sense-data, for all knowledge of truths, as we shall show, demands acquaintance with things which are of an essentially different character from sense-data, the things which are sometimes called 'abstract ideas', but which we shall call 'universals'. We have therefore to consider acquaintance with other things besides sense-data if we are to obtain any tolerably adequate analysis of our knowledge.

The first extension beyond sense-data to be considered is acquaintance by memory. It is obvious that we often remember what we have seen or heard or had otherwise presented to our senses, and that in such cases we are still immediately aware of what we remember, in spite of the fact that it appears as past and not as present. This immediate knowledge by memory is the source of all our knowledge concerning the past: without it, there could be no knowledge of the past by inference, we should never know that there was anything past to be inferred.

The next extension to be considered is acquaintance by introspection. We are not only aware of things, but we are often aware of being aware of them. When I see the sun, I am often aware of my seeing the sun; thus "my seeing the sun" is an object with which I have acquaintance. When I desire food, I may be aware of my desire for food; thus 'my desiring food' is an object with which I am acquainted. Similarly we may be aware of our feeling pleasure or pain, and generally of the events which happen in our minds. This kind of acquaintance, which may be called self-consciousness, is the source of all our knowledge of mental things. It is obvious that it is only what goes on in our own minds that can be thus known immediately. What goes on in the minds of others is known to us through our perception of their bodies, that is, the sense-data in us which are associated with their bodies. But for our acquaintance with the contents of our own minds, we should be unable to imagine the minds of others, and therefore we could never arrive at the knowledge that they have minds. It seems natural to suppose that self-consciousness is one of the things that distinguish men from animals: animals, we may suppose, though they have acquaintance with sense-data, never become aware of this acquaintance. I do not mean that they doubt whether they exist, but that they have never become conscious of the fact that they have sensations and feelings, nor therefore of the fact that they, the subjects of their sensations and feelings, exist.

We have spoken of acquaintance with the contents of our minds as self-consciousness, but it is not, of course, consciousness of our self: it is consciousness of particular thoughts and feelings. The question whether we are also acquainted with our bare selves, as opposed to particular thoughts and feelings, is a very difficult one, upon which it would be rash to speak positively. When we try to look into ourselves we always seem to come upon some particular thought or feeling, and not upon the 'I' which has the thought or feeling. Nevertheless there are some reasons for thinking that we are acquainted with the 'I', though the acquaintance is hard to disentangle from other things. To make clear what sort of reason there is, let us consider for a moment what our acquaintance with particular thoughts really involves.

When I am acquainted with 'my seeing the sun', it seems plain that I am acquainted with two different things in relation to each other. On the one hand there is the sense-datum which represents the sun to me, on the other hand there is that which sees this sense-datum. All acquaintance, such as my acquaintance with the sense-datum which represents the sun, seems obviously a relation between the person acquainted and the object with which the person is acquainted. When a case of acquaintance is one with which I can be acquainted (as I am acquainted with my acquaintance with the sense-datum representing the sun), it is plain that the person acquainted is myself. Thus, when I am acquainted with my seeing the sun, the whole fact with which I am acquainted is 'Self-acquainted-with-sense-datum'.

Further, we know the truth 'I am acquainted with this sense-datum'. It is hard to see how we could know this truth, or even understand what is meant by it, unless we were acquainted with something which we call 'I'. It does not seem necessary to suppose that we are acquainted with a more or less permanent person, the same to-day as yesterday, but it does seem as though we must be acquainted with that thing, whatever its nature, which sees the sun and has acquaintance with sense-data. Thus, in some sense it would seem we must be acquainted with our Selves as opposed to our particular experiences. But the question is difficult, and complicated arguments can be adduced on either side. Hence, although acquaintance with ourselves seems probably to occur, it is not wise to assert that it undoubtedly does occur.

We may therefore sum up as follows what has been said concerning acquaintance with things that exist. We have acquaintance in sensation with the data of the outer senses, and in introspection with the data of what may be called the inner sense—thoughts, feelings, desires, etc.; we have acquaintance in memory with things which have been data either of the outer senses or of the inner sense. Further, it is probable, though not certain, that we have acquaintance with Self, as that which is aware of things or has desires towards things.

In addition to our acquaintance with particular existing things, we also have acquaintance with what we shall call universals, that is to say, general ideas such as whiteness, diversity, brotherhood, and so on. Every complete sentence must contain at least one word which stands for a universal, since all verbs have a meaning which is universal. We shall return to universals later on, in Chapter IX; for the present, it is only necessary to guard against the supposition that whatever we can be acquainted with must be something particular and existent. Awareness of universals is called conceiving, and a universal of which we are aware is called a concept.

It will be seen that among the objects with which we are acquainted are not included physical objects (as opposed to sense-data), nor other people's minds. These things are known to us by what I call 'knowledge by description', which we must now consider.

By a 'description' I mean any phrase of the form 'a so-and-so' or 'the so-and-so'. A phrase of the form 'a so-and-so' I shall call an 'ambiguous' description; a phrase of the form 'the so-and-so' (in the singular) I shall call a 'definite' description. Thus 'a man' is an ambiguous description, and 'the man with the iron mask' is a definite description. There are various problems connected with ambiguous descriptions, but I pass them by, since they do not directly concern the matter we are discussing, which is the nature of our knowledge concerning objects in cases where we know that there is an object answering to a definite description, though we are not acquainted with any such object. This is a matter which is concerned exclusively with definite descriptions. I shall therefore, in the sequel, speak simply of 'descriptions' when I mean 'definite descriptions'. Thus a description will mean any phrase of the form 'the so-and-so' in the singular.

We say that an object is 'known by description' when we know that it is 'the so-and-so', i.e. when we know that there is one object, and no more, having a certain property; and it will generally be implied that we do not have knowledge of the same object by acquaintance. We know that the man with the iron mask existed, and many propositions are known about him; but we do not know who he was. We know that the candidate who gets the most votes will be elected, and in this case we are very likely also acquainted (in the only sense in which one can be acquainted with some one else) with the man who is, in fact, the candidate who will get most votes; but we do not know which of the candidates he is, i.e. we do not know any proposition of the form 'A is the candidate who will get most votes' where A is one of the candidates by name. We shall say that we have 'merely descriptive knowledge' of the so-and-so when, although we know that the so-and-so exists, and although we may possibly be acquainted with the object which is, in fact, the so-and-so, yet we do not know any proposition 'A is the so-and-so', where A is something with which we are acquainted.

When we say 'the so-and-so exists', we mean that there is just one object which is the so-and-so. The proposition 'A is the so-and-so' means that A has the property so-and-so, and nothing else has. 'Mr. A. is the Unionist candidate for this constituency' means 'Mr. A. is a Unionist candidate for this constituency, and no one else is'. 'The Unionist candidate for this constituency exists' means 'some one is a Unionist candidate for this constituency, and no one else is'. Thus, when we are acquainted with an object which is the so-and-so, we know that the so-and-so exists; but we may know that the so-and-so exists when we are not acquainted with any object which we know to be the so-and-so, and even when we are not acquainted with any object which, in fact, is the so-and-so.

Common words, even proper names, are usually really descriptions. That is to say, the thought in the mind of a person using a proper name correctly can generally only be expressed explicitly if we replace the proper name by a description. Moreover, the description required to express the thought will vary for different people, or for the same person at different times. The only thing constant (so long as the name is rightly used) is the object to which the name applies. But so long as this remains constant, the particular description involved usually makes no difference to the truth or falsehood of the proposition in which the name appears.

Let us take some illustrations. Suppose some statement made about Bismarck. Assuming that there is such a thing as direct acquaintance with oneself, Bismarck himself might have used his name directly to designate the particular person with whom he was acquainted. In this case, if he made a judgement about himself, he himself might be a constituent of the judgement. Here the proper name has the direct use which it always wishes to have, as simply standing for a certain object, and not for a description of the object. But if a person who knew Bismarck made a judgement about him, the case is different. What this person was acquainted with were certain sense-data which he connected (rightly, we will suppose) with Bismarck's body. His body, as a physical object, and still more his mind, were only known as the body and the mind connected with these sense-data. That is, they were known by description. It is, of course, very much a matter of chance which characteristics of a man's appearance will come into a friend's mind when he thinks of him; thus the description actually in the friend's mind is accidental. The essential point is that he knows that the various descriptions all apply to the same entity, in spite of not being acquainted with the entity in question.

When we, who did not know Bismarck, make judgement about him, the description in our minds will probably be some more or less vague mass of historical knowledge—far more, in most cases, than is required to identify him. But, for the sake of illustration, let us assume that we think of him as 'the first Chancellor of the German Empire'. Here all the words are abstract except 'German'. The word 'German' will, again, have different meanings for different people. To some it will recall travels in Germany, to some the look of Germany on the map, and so on. But if we are to obtain a description which we know to be applicable, we shall be compelled, at some point, to bring in a reference to a particular with which we are acquainted. Such reference is involved in any mention of past, present, and future (as opposed to definite dates), or of here and there, or of what others have told us. Thus it would seem that, in some way or other, a description known to be applicable to a particular must involve some reference to a particular with which we are acquainted, if our knowledge about the thing described is not to be merely what follows logically from the description. For example, 'the most long-lived of men' is a description involving only universals, which must apply to some man, but we can make no judgements concerning this man which involve knowledge about him beyond what the description gives. If, however, we say, 'The first Chancellor of the German Empire was an astute diplomatist', we can only be assured of the truth of our judgement in virtue of something with which we are acquainted—usually a testimony heard or read. Apart from the information we convey to others, apart from the fact about the actual Bismarck, which gives importance to our judgement, the thought we really have contains the one or more particulars involved, and otherwise consists wholly of concepts.

All names of places—London, England, Europe, the Earth, the Solar System—similarly involve, when used, descriptions which start from some one or more particulars with which we are acquainted. I suspect that even the Universe, as considered by metaphysics, involves such a connexion with particulars. In logic on the contrary, where we are concerned not merely with what does exist, but with whatever might or could exist or be, no reference to actual particulars is involved.

It would seem that, when we make a statement about something only known by description, we often intend to make our statement, not in the form involving the description, but about the actual thing described. That is to say, when we say anything about Bismarck, we should like, if we could, to make the judgement which Bismarck alone can make, namely, the judgement of which he himself is a constituent. In this we are necessarily defeated, since the actual Bismarck is unknown to us. But we know that there is an object B, called Bismarck, and that B was an astute diplomatist. We can thus describe the proposition we should like to affirm, namely, 'B was an astute diplomat', where B is the object which was Bismarck. If we are describing Bismarck as 'the first Chancellor of the German Empire', the proposition we should like to affirm may be described as 'the proposition asserting, concerning the actual object which was the first Chancellor of the German Empire, that this object an astute diplomatist'. What enables us to communicate in spite of the varying descriptions we employ is that we know there is a true proposition concerning the actual Bismarck, and that however we may vary the description (so long as the description is correct) the proposition described is still the same. This proposition, which is described and is known to be true, is what interests us; but we are not acquainted with the proposition itself, and do not know it, though we know it is true.

It will be seen that there are various stages in the removal from acquaintance with particulars: there is Bismarck to people who knew him; Bismarck to those who only know of him through history; the man with the iron mask; the longest-lived of men. These are progressively further removed from acquaintance with particulars; the first comes as near to acquaintance as is possible in regard to another person; in the second, we shall still be said to know 'who Bismarck was'; in the third, we do not know who was the man with the iron mask, though we can know many propositions about him which are not logically deducible from the fact that he wore an iron mask; in the fourth, finally, we know nothing beyond what is logically deducible from the definition of the man. There is a similar hierarchy in the region of universals. Many universals like many particulars, are only known to us by description. But here, as in the case of particulars, knowledge concerning what is known by description is ultimately reducible to knowledge concerning what is known by acquaintance.

The fundamental principle in the analysis of propositions containing descriptions is this: Every proposition which we can understand must be composed wholly of constituents with which we are acquainted.

We shall not at this stage attempt to answer all the objections which may be urged against this fundamental principle. For the present, we shall merely point out that, in some way or other, it must be possible to meet these objections, for it is scarcely conceivable that we can make a judgement or entertain a supposition without knowing what it is that we are judging or supposing about. We must attach some meaning to the words we use, if we are to speak significantly and not utter mere noise; and the meaning we attach to our words must be something with which we are acquainted. Thus when, for example, we make a statement about Julius Caesar, it is plain that Julius Caesar himself is not before our minds, since we are not acquainted with him. We have in mind some description of Julius Caesar: 'the man who was assassinated on the Ides of March', 'the founder of the Roman Empire', or, merely 'the man whose name was Julius Caesar'. (In this last description, Julius Caesar is a noise or shape with which we are acquainted.) Thus our statement does not mean quite what it seems to mean, but means something involving, instead of Julius Caesar, some description of him which is composed wholly of particulars and universals with which we are acquainted.

The chief importance of knowledge by description is that it enables us to pass beyond the limits of our experience. In spite of the fact that we can only know truths which are wholly composed of terms which we have experienced in acquaintance, we can yet have knowledge by description of things which we have never experienced. In view of the very narrow range of our immediate experience, this result is vital, and until it is understood, much of our knowledge must remain mysterious and therefore doubtful.

CHAPTER VI ON INDUCTION

In almost all our previous discussions we have been concerned in the attempt to get clear as to our data in the way of knowledge of existence. What things are there in the universe whose existence is known to us owing to our being acquainted with them? So far, our answer has been that we are acquainted with our sense-data, and, probably, with ourselves. These we know to exist. And past sense-data which are remembered are known to have existed in the past. This knowledge supplies our data.

But if we are to be able to draw inferences from these data—if we are to know of the existence of matter, of other people, of the past before our individual memory begins, or of the future, we must know general principles of some kind by means of which such inferences can be drawn. It must be known to us that the existence of some one sort of thing, A, is a sign of the existence of some other sort of thing, B, either at the same time as A or at some earlier or later time, as, for example, thunder is a sign of the earlier existence of lightning. If this were not known to us, we could never extend our knowledge beyond the sphere of our private experience; and this sphere, as we have seen, is exceedingly limited. The question we have now to consider is whether such an extension is possible, and if so, how it is effected.

Let us take as an illustration a matter about which none of us, in fact, feel the slightest doubt. We are all convinced that the sun will rise to-morrow. Why? Is this belief a mere blind outcome of past experience, or can it be justified as a reasonable belief? It is not easy to find a test by which to judge whether a belief of this kind is reasonable or not, but we can at least ascertain what sort of general beliefs would suffice, if true, to justify the judgement that the sun will rise to-morrow, and the many other similar judgements upon which our actions are based.

It is obvious that if we are asked why we believe the sun will rise to-morrow, we shall naturally answer, 'Because it always has risen every day'. We have a firm belief that it will rise in the future, because it has risen in the past. If we are challenged as to why we believe that it will continue to rise as heretofore, we may appeal to the laws of motion: the earth, we shall say, is a freely rotating body, and such bodies do not cease to rotate unless something interferes from outside, and there is nothing outside to interfere with the earth between now and to-morrow. Of course it might be doubted whether we are quite certain that there is nothing outside to interfere, but this is not the interesting doubt. The interesting doubt is as to whether the laws of motion will remain in operation until to-morrow. If this doubt is raised, we find ourselves in the same position as when the doubt about the sunrise was first raised.

The only reason for believing that the laws of motion remain in operation is that they have operated hitherto, so far as our knowledge of the past enables us to judge. It is true that we have a greater body of evidence from the past in favour of the laws of motion than we have in favour of the sunrise, because the sunrise is merely a particular case of fulfillment of the laws of motion, and there are countless other particular cases. But the real question is: Do any number of cases of a law being fulfilled in the past afford evidence that it will be fulfilled in the future? If not, it becomes plain that we have no ground whatever for expecting the sun to rise to-morrow, or for expecting the bread we shall eat at our next meal not to poison us, or for any of the other scarcely conscious expectations that control our daily lives. It is to be observed that all such expectations are only probable; thus we have not to seek for a proof that they must be fulfilled, but only for some reason in favour of the view that they are likely to be fulfilled.

Now in dealing with this question we must, to begin with, make an important distinction, without which we should soon become involved in hopeless confusions. Experience has shown us that, hitherto, the frequent repetition of some uniform succession or coexistence has been a cause of our expecting the same succession or coexistence on the next occasion. Food that has a certain appearance generally has a certain taste, and it is a severe shock to our expectations when the familiar appearance is found to be associated with an unusual taste. Things which we see become associated, by habit, with certain tactile sensations which we expect if we touch them; one of the horrors of a ghost (in many ghost-stories) is that it fails to give us any sensations of touch. Uneducated people who go abroad for the first time are so surprised as to be incredulous when they find their native language not understood.

And this kind of association is not confined to men; in animals also it is very strong. A horse which has been often driven along a certain road resists the attempt to drive him in a different direction. Domestic animals expect food when they see the person who feeds them. We know that all these rather crude expectations of uniformity are liable to be misleading. The man who has fed the chicken every day throughout its life at last wrings its neck instead, showing that more refined views as to the uniformity of nature would have been useful to the chicken.

But in spite of the misleadingness of such expectations, they nevertheless exist. The mere fact that something has happened a certain number of times causes animals and men to expect that it will happen again. Thus our instincts certainly cause us to believe the sun will rise to-morrow, but we may be in no better a position than the chicken which unexpectedly has its neck wrung. We have therefore to distinguish the fact that past uniformities cause expectations as to the future, from the question whether there is any reasonable ground for giving weight to such expectations after the question of their validity has been raised.

The problem we have to discuss is whether there is any reason for believing in what is called 'the uniformity of nature'. The belief in the uniformity of nature is the belief that everything that has happened or will happen is an instance of some general law to which there are no exceptions. The crude expectations which we have been considering are all subject to exceptions, and therefore liable to disappoint those who entertain them. But science habitually assumes, at least as a working hypothesis, that general rules which have exceptions can be replaced by general rules which have no exceptions. 'Unsupported bodies in air fall' is a general rule to which balloons and aeroplanes are exceptions. But the laws of motion and the law of gravitation, which account for the fact that most bodies fall, also account for the fact that balloons and aeroplanes can rise; thus the laws of motion and the law of gravitation are not subject to these exceptions.

The belief that the sun will rise to-morrow might be falsified if the earth came suddenly into contact with a large body which destroyed its rotation; but the laws of motion and the law of gravitation would not be infringed by such an event. The business of science is to find uniformities, such as the laws of motion and the law of gravitation, to which, so far as our experience extends, there are no exceptions. In this search science has been remarkably successful, and it may be conceded that such uniformities have held hitherto. This brings us back to the question: Have we any reason, assuming that they have always held in the past, to suppose that they will hold in the future?

It has been argued that we have reason to know that the future will resemble the past, because what was the future has constantly become the past, and has always been found to resemble the past, so that we really have experience of the future, namely of times which were formerly future, which we may call past futures. But such an argument really begs the very question at issue. We have experience of past futures, but not of future futures, and the question is: Will future futures resemble past futures? This question is not to be answered by an argument which starts from past futures alone. We have therefore still to seek for some principle which shall enable us to know that the future will follow the same laws as the past.

The reference to the future in this question is not essential. The same question arises when we apply the laws that work in our experience to past things of which we have no experience—as, for example, in geology, or in theories as to the origin of the Solar system. The question we really have to ask is: 'When two things have been found to be often associated, and no instance is known of the one occurring without the other, does the occurrence of one of the two, in a fresh instance, give any good ground for expecting the other?' On our answer to this question must depend the validity of the whole of our expectations as to the future, the whole of the results obtained by induction, and in fact practically all the beliefs upon which our daily life is based.

It must be conceded, to begin with, that the fact that two things have been found often together and never apart does not, by itself, suffice to prove demonstratively that they will be found together in the next case we examine. The most we can hope is that the oftener things are found together, the more probable becomes that they will be found together another time, and that, if they have been found together often enough, the probability will amount almost to certainty. It can never quite reach certainty, because we know that in spite of frequent repetitions there sometimes is a failure at the last, as in the case of the chicken whose neck is wrung. Thus probability is all we ought to seek.

It might be urged, as against the view we are advocating, that we know all natural phenomena to be subject to the reign of law, and that sometimes, on the basis of observation, we can see that only one law can possibly fit the facts of the case. Now to this view there are two answers. The first is that, even if some law which has no exceptions applies to our case, we can never, in practice, be sure that we have discovered that law and not one to which there are exceptions. The second is that the reign of law would seem to be itself only probable, and that our belief that it will hold in the future, or in unexamined cases in the past, is itself based upon the very principle we are examining.

The principle we are examining may be called the principle of induction, and its two parts may be stated as follows:

(a) When a thing of a certain sort A has been found to be associated with a thing of a certain other sort B, and has never been found dissociated from a thing of the sort B, the greater the number of cases in which A and B have been associated, the greater is the probability that they will be associated in a fresh case in which one of them is known to be present;

(b) Under the same circumstances, a sufficient number of cases of association will make the probability of a fresh association nearly a certainty, and will make it approach certainty without limit.

As just stated, the principle applies only to the verification of our expectation in a single fresh instance. But we want also to know that there is a probability in favour of the general law that things of the sort A are always associated with things of the sort B, provided a sufficient number of cases of association are known, and no cases of failure of association are known. The probability of the general law is obviously less than the probability of the particular case, since if the general law is true, the particular case must also be true, whereas the particular case may be true without the general law being true. Nevertheless the probability of the general law is increased by repetitions, just as the probability of the particular case is. We may therefore repeat the two parts of our principle as regards the general law, thus:

(a) The greater the number of cases in which a thing the sort A has been found associated with a thing the sort B, the more probable it is (if no cases of failure of association are known) that A is always associated with B;

(b) Under the same circumstances, a sufficient number of cases of the association of A with B will make it nearly certain that A is always associated with B, and will make this general law approach certainty without limit.

It should be noted that probability is always relative to certain data. In our case, the data are merely the known cases of coexistence of A and B. There may be other data, which might be taken into account, which would gravely alter the probability. For example, a man who had seen a great many white swans might argue by our principle, that on the data it was probable that all swans were white, and this might be a perfectly sound argument. The argument is not disproved by the fact that some swans are black, because a thing may very well happen in spite of the fact that some data render it improbable. In the case of the swans, a man might know that colour is a very variable characteristic in many species of animals, and that, therefore, an induction as to colour is peculiarly liable to error. But this knowledge would be a fresh datum, by no means proving that the probability relatively to our previous data had been wrongly estimated. The fact, therefore, that things often fail to fulfill our expectations is no evidence that our expectations will not probably be fulfilled in a given case or a given class of cases. Thus our inductive principle is at any rate not capable of being disproved by an appeal to experience.

The inductive principle, however, is equally incapable of being proved by an appeal to experience. Experience might conceivably confirm the inductive principle as regards the cases that have been already examined; but as regards unexamined cases, it is the inductive principle alone that can justify any inference from what has been examined to what has not been examined. All arguments which, on the basis of experience, argue as to the future or the unexperienced parts of the past or present, assume the inductive principle; hence we can never use experience to prove the inductive principle without begging the question. Thus we must either accept the inductive principle on the ground of its intrinsic evidence, or forgo all justification of our expectations about the future. If the principle is unsound, we have no reason to expect the sun to rise to-morrow, to expect bread to be more nourishing than a stone, or to expect that if we throw ourselves off the roof we shall fall. When we see what looks like our best friend approaching us, we shall have no reason to suppose that his body is not inhabited by the mind of our worst enemy or of some total stranger. All our conduct is based upon associations which have worked in the past, and which we therefore regard as likely to work in the future; and this likelihood is dependent for its validity upon the inductive principle.

The general principles of science, such as the belief in the reign of law, and the belief that every event must have a cause, are as completely dependent upon the inductive principle as are the beliefs of daily life. All such general principles are believed because mankind have found innumerable instances of their truth and no instances of their falsehood. But this affords no evidence for their truth in the future, unless the inductive principle is assumed.

Thus all knowledge which, on a basis of experience tells us something about what is not experienced, is based upon a belief which experience can neither confirm nor confute, yet which, at least in its more concrete applications, appears to be as firmly rooted in us as many of the facts of experience. The existence and justification of such beliefs—for the inductive principle, as we shall see, is not the only example—raises some of the most difficult and most debated problems of philosophy. We will, in the next chapter, consider briefly what may be said to account for such knowledge, and what is its scope and its degree of certainty.

CHAPTER VII ON OUR KNOWLEDGE OF GENERAL PRINCIPLES

We saw in the preceding chapter that the principle of Induction, while necessary to the validity of all arguments based on experience, is itself not capable of being proved by experience, and yet is unhesitatingly believed by every one, at least in all its concrete applications. In these characteristics the principle of induction does not stand alone. There are a number of other principles which cannot be proved or disproved by experience, but are used in arguments which start from what is experienced.

Some of these principles have even greater evidence than the principle of induction, and the knowledge of them has the same degree of certainty as the knowledge of the existence of sense-data. They constitute the means of drawing inferences from what is given in sensation; and if what we infer is to be true, it is just as necessary that our principles of inference should be true as it is that our data should be true. The principles of inference are apt to be overlooked because of their very obviousness—the assumption involved is assented to without our realizing that it is an assumption. But it is very important to realize the use of principles of inference, if a correct theory of knowledge is to be obtained; for our knowledge of them raises interesting and difficult questions.

In all our knowledge of general principles, what actually happens is that first of all we realize some particular application of the principle, and then we realize the particularity is irrelevant, and that there is a generality which may equally truly be affirmed. This is of course familiar in such matters as teaching arithmetic: 'two and two are four' is first learnt in the case of some particular pair of couples, and then in some other particular case, and so on, until at last it becomes possible to see that it is true of any pair of couples. The same thing happens with logical principles. Suppose two men are discussing what day of the month it is. One of them says, 'At least you will admit that if yesterday was the 15th to-day must be the 16th.' 'Yes', says the other, 'I admit that.' 'And you know', the first continues, 'that yesterday was the 15th, because you dined with Jones, and your diary will tell you that was on the 15th.' 'Yes', says the second; 'therefore to-day is the 16th.'

Now such an argument is not hard to follow; and if it is granted that its premisses are true in fact, no one deny that the conclusion must also be true. But it depends for its truth upon an instance of a general logical principle. The logical principle is as follows: 'Suppose it known that if this is true, then that is true. Suppose it also known that this is true, then it follows that that is true.' When it is the case that if this is true, that is true, we shall say that this 'implies' that, that that 'follows from' this. Thus our principle states that if this implies that, and this is true, then that is true. In other words, 'anything implied by a proposition is true', or 'whatever follows from a true proposition is true'.

This principle is really involved—at least, concrete instances of it are involved—in all demonstrations. Whenever one thing which we believe is used to prove something else, which we consequently believe, this principle is relevant. If any one asks: 'Why should I accept the results of valid arguments based on true premisses?' we can only answer by appealing to our principle. In fact, the truth of the principle is impossible to doubt, and its obviousness is so great that at first sight it seems almost trivial. Such principles, however, are not trivial to the philosopher, for they show that we may have indubitable knowledge which is in no way derived from objects of sense.

The above principle is merely one of a certain number of self-evident logical principles. Some at least of these principles must be granted before any argument or proof becomes possible. When some of them have been granted, others can be proved, though these others, so long as they are simple, are just as obvious as the principles taken for granted. For no very good reason, three of these principles have been singled out by tradition under the name of 'Laws of Thought'.

They are as follows:

1. The law of identity: 'Whatever is, is.'

2. The law of contradiction: 'Nothing can both be and not be.'

3. The law of excluded middle: 'Everything must either be or not be.'

These three laws are samples of self-evident logical principles, but are not really more fundamental or more self-evident than various other similar principles: for instance, the one we considered just now, which states that what follows from a true premise is true. The name 'laws of thought' is also misleading, for what is important is not the fact that we think in accordance with these laws, but the fact that things behave in accordance with them; in other words, the fact that when we think in accordance with them we think truly. But this is a large question, to which we return at a later stage.

In addition to the logical principles which enable us to prove from a given premiss that something is *certainly* true, there are other logical principles which enable us to prove, from a given premiss, that there is a greater or less probability that something is true. An example of such principles—perhaps the most important example—is the inductive principle, which we considered in the preceding chapter.

One of the great historic controversies in philosophy is the controversy between the two schools called respectively 'empiricists' and 'rationalists'. The empiricists—who are best represented by the British philosophers, Locke, Berkeley, and Hume—maintained that all our knowledge is derived from experience; the rationalists—who are represented by the continental philosophers of the seventeenth century, especially Descartes and Leibniz—maintained that, in addition to what we know by experience, there are certain 'innate ideas' and 'innate principles', which we know independently of experience. It has now become possible to decide with some confidence as to the truth or falsehood of these opposing schools. It must be admitted, for the reasons already stated, that logical principles are known to us, and cannot be themselves proved by experience, since all proof presupposes them. In this, therefore, which was the most important point of the controversy, the rationalists were in the right.

On the other hand, even that part of our knowledge which is logically independent of experience (in the sense that experience cannot prove it) is yet elicited and caused by experience. It is on occasion of particular experiences that we become aware of the general laws which their connexions exemplify. It would certainly be absurd to suppose that there are innate principles in the sense that babies are born with a knowledge of everything which men know and which cannot be deduced from what is experienced. For this reason, the word 'innate' would not now be employed to describe our knowledge of logical principles. The phrase 'a priori' is less objectionable, and is more usual in modern writers. Thus, while admitting that all knowledge is elicited and caused by experience, we shall nevertheless hold that some knowledge is a priori, in the sense that the experience which makes us think of it does not suffice to prove it, but merely so directs our attention that we see its truth without requiring any proof from experience.

There is another point of great importance, in which the empiricists were in the right as against the rationalists. Nothing can be known to exist except by the help of experience. That is to say, if we wish to prove that something of which we have no direct experience exists, we must have among our premisses the existence of one or more things of which we have direct experience. Our belief that the Emperor of China exists, for example, rests upon testimony, and testimony consists, in the last analysis, of sense-data seen or heard in reading or being spoken to. Rationalists believed that, from general consideration as to what must be, they could deduce the existence of this or that in the actual world. In this belief they seem to have been mistaken. All the knowledge that we can acquire a priori concerning existence seems to be hypothetical: it tells us that if one thing exists, another must exist, or, more generally, that if one proposition is true another must be true. This is exemplified by principles we have already dealt with, such as 'if this is true, and this implies that, then that is true', of 'if this and that have been repeatedly found connected, they will probably be connected in the next instance in which one of them is found.' Thus the scope and power of a priori principles is strictly limited. All knowledge that something exists must be in part dependent on experience. When anything is known immediately, its existence is known by experience alone; when anything is proved to exist, without being known immediately, both experience and a priori principles must be required in the proof. Knowledge is called empirical when it rests wholly or partly upon experience. Thus all knowledge which asserts existence is empirical, and the only a priori knowledge concerning existence is hypothetical, giving connexions among things that exist or may exist, but not giving actual existence.

A priori knowledge is not all of the logical kind we have been hitherto considering. Perhaps the most important example of non-logical a priori knowledge is knowledge as to ethical value. I am not speaking of judgements as to what is useful or as to what is virtuous, for such judgements do require empirical premisses; I am speaking of judgements as to the intrinsic desirability of things. If something is useful, it must be useful because it secures some end, the end must, if we have gone far enough, be valuable on its own account, and not merely because it is useful for some further end. Thus all judgements as to what is useful depend upon judgements as to what has value on its own account.

We judge, for example, that happiness is more desirable than misery, knowledge than ignorance, goodwill than hatred, and so on. Such judgements must, in part at least, be immediate and a priori. Like our previous a priori judgements, they may be elicited by experience, and indeed they must be; for it seems not possible to judge whether anything is intrinsically valuable unless we have experienced something of the same kind. But it is fairly obvious that they cannot be proved by experience; for the fact that a thing exists or does not exist cannot prove either that it is good that it should exist or that it is bad. The pursuit of this subject belongs to ethics, where the impossibility of deducing what ought to be from what is has to established. In the present connexion, it is only important to realize that knowledge as to what is intrinsically of value is a priori in the same sense in which logic is a priori, namely in the sense that the truth of such knowledge can be neither proved nor disproved by experience.

All pure mathematics is a priori, like logic. This is strenuously denied by the empirical philosophers, who maintained that experience was as much the source of our knowledge of arithmetic as of our knowledge of geography. They maintained that by the repeated experience of seeing two things and two other things, and finding that altogether they made four things, we were led by induction to the conclusion that two things and two other things would always make four things altogether. If, however, this were the source of our knowledge that two and two are four we should proceed differently, in persuading ourselves of its truth, from the way in which we do actually proceed. In fact, a certain number of instances are needed to make us think of two abstractly, rather than of two coins or two books or two people, or two of any other specified kind. But as soon as we are able to divest our thoughts of irrelevant particularity, we become able to see the general principle that two and two are four; any one instance is seen to be typical and the examination of other instances becomes unnecessary.

The same thing is exemplified in geometry. If we want to prove some property of all triangles, we draw some one triangle and reason about it; but we can avoid making use of any property which it does not share with all other triangles, and thus, from our particular case, we obtain a general result. We do not, in fact, feel our certainty that two and two are four increased by fresh instances, because, as soon as we have seen the truth of this proposition, our certainty becomes so great as to be incapable of growing greater. Moreover, we feel some quality of necessity about the proposition 'two and two are four', which is absent from even the best attested empirical generalizations. Such generalizations always remain mere facts: we feel that there might be a world in which they were false, though in the actual world they happen to be true. In any possible world, on the contrary, we feel that two and two would be four: this is not a mere fact, but a necessity to which everything actual and possible must conform.

The case may be made clearer by considering a genuinely empirical generalization, such as 'All men are mortal.' It is plain that we believe this proposition, in the first place, because there is no known instance of men living beyond a certain age, and in the second place because there seem to be physiological grounds for thinking that an organism such as a man's body must sooner or later wear out. Neglecting the second ground, and considering merely our experience of men's mortality, it is plain that we should not be content with one quite clearly understood instance of a man dying, whereas, in the case of 'two and two are four', one instance does suffice, when carefully considered, to persuade us that the same must happen in any other instance. Also we can be forced to admit, on reflection, that there may be some doubt, however slight, as to whether all men are mortal. This may be made plain by the attempt to imagine two different worlds, in one of which there are men who are not mortal, while in the other two and two make five. When Swift invites us to consider the race of Struldbugs who never die, we are able to acquiesce in imagination. But a world where two and two make five seems quite on a different level. We feel that such a world, if there were one, would upset the whole fabric of our knowledge and reduce us to utter doubt.

The fact is that, in simple mathematical judgements such as 'two and two are four', and also in many judgements of logic, we can know the general proposition without inferring it from instances, although some instance is usually necessary to make clear to us what the general proposition means. This is why there is real utility in the process of deduction, which goes from the general to the general, or from the general to the particular, as well as in the process of induction, which goes from the particular to the particular, or from the particular to the general. It is an old debate among philosophers whether deduction ever gives new knowledge. We can now see that in certain cases, at least, it does do so. If we already know that two and two always make four, and we know that Brown and Jones are two, and so are Robinson and Smith, we can deduce that Brown and Jones and Robinson and Smith are four. This is new knowledge, not contained in our premisses, because the general proposition, 'two and two are four', never told us there were such people as Brown and Jones and Robinson and Smith, and the particular premisses do not tell us that there were four of them, whereas the particular proposition deduced does tell us both these things.

But the newness of the knowledge is much less certain if we take the stock instance of deduction that is always given in books on logic, namely, 'All men are mortal; Socrates is a man, therefore Socrates is mortal.' In this case, what we really know beyond reasonable doubt is that certain men, A, B, C, were mortal, since, in fact, they have died. If Socrates is one of these men, it is foolish to go the roundabout way through 'all men are mortal' to arrive at the conclusion that probably Socrates is mortal. If Socrates is not one of the men on whom our induction is based, we shall still do better to argue straight from our A, B, C, to Socrates, than to go round by the general proposition, 'all men are mortal'. For the probability that Socrates is mortal is greater, on our data, than the probability that all men are mortal. (This is obvious, because if all men are mortal, so is Socrates; but if Socrates is mortal, it does not follow that all men are mortal.) Hence we shall reach the conclusion that Socrates is mortal with a greater approach to certainty if we make our argument purely inductive than if we go by way of 'all men are mortal' and then use deduction.

This illustrates the difference between general propositions known a priori, such as 'two and two are four', and empirical generalizations such as 'all men are mortal'. In regard to the former, deduction is the right mode of argument, whereas in regard to the latter, induction is always theoretically preferable, and warrants a greater confidence in the truth of our conclusion, because all empirical generalizations are more uncertain than the instances of them.

We have now seen that there are propositions known a priori , and that among them are the propositions of logic and pure mathematics, as well as the fundamental propositions of ethics. The question which must next occupy us is this: How is it possible that there should be such knowledge? And more particularly, how can there be knowledge of general propositions in cases where we have not examined all the instances, and indeed never can examine them all, because their number is infinite? These questions, which were first brought prominently forward by the German philosopher Kant (1724–1804), are very difficult, and historically very important.

CHAPTER VIII HOW A PRIORI KNOWLEDGE IS POSSIBLE

Immanuel Kant is generally regarded as the greatest of the modern philosophers. Though he lived through the Seven Years War and the French Revolution, he never interrupted his teaching of philosophy at Konigsberg in East Prussia. His most distinctive contribution was the invention of what he called the 'critical' philosophy, which, assuming as a datum that there is knowledge of various kinds, inquired how such knowledge comes to be possible, and deduced, from the answer to this inquiry, many metaphysical results as to the nature of the world. Whether these results were valid may well be doubted. But Kant undoubtedly deserves credit for two things: first, for having perceived that we have a priori knowledge which is not purely 'analytic', i.e. such that the opposite would be self-contradictory; and secondly, for having made evident the philosophical importance of the theory of knowledge.

Before the time of Kant, it was generally held that whatever knowledge was a priori must be 'analytic'. What this word means will be best illustrated by examples. If I say, 'A bald man is a man', 'A plane figure is a figure', 'A bad poet is a poet', I make a purely analytic judgement: the subject spoken about is given as having at least two properties, of which one is singled out to be asserted of it. Such propositions as the above are trivial, and would never be enunciated in real life except by an orator preparing the way for a piece of sophistry. They are called 'analytic' because the predicate is obtained by merely analysing the subject. Before the time of Kant it was thought that all judgements of which we could be certain a priori were of this kind: that in all of them there was a predicate which was only part of the subject of which it was asserted. If this were so, we should be involved in a definite contradiction if we attempted to deny thinking that could be known a priori. 'A bald man is not bald' would assert and deny baldness of the same man, and would therefore contradict itself. Thus according to the philosophers before Kant, the law of contradiction, which asserts that nothing can at the same time have and not have a certain property, sufficed to establish the truth of all a priori knowledge.

Hume (1711–1776), who preceded Kant, accepting the usual view as to what makes knowledge a priori, discovered that, in many cases which had previously been supposed analytic, and notably in the case of cause and effect, the connexion was really synthetic. Before Hume, rationalists at least had supposed that the effect could be logically deduced from the cause, if only we had sufficient knowledge. Hume argued—correctly, as would now be generally admitted—that this could not be done. Hence he inferred the far more doubtful proposition that nothing could be known a priori about the connexion of cause and effect. Kant, who had been educated in the rationalist tradition, was much perturbed by Hume's skepticism, and endeavoured to find an answer to it. He perceived that not only the connexion of cause and effect, but all the propositions of arithmetic and geometry, are 'synthetic' i.e. not analytic: in all these propositions, no analysis of the subject will reveal the predicate. His stock instance was the proposition $7 + 5 = 12$. He pointed out, quite truly, that 7 and 5 have to be put together to give 12: the idea of 12 is not contained in them, nor even in the idea of adding them together. Thus he was led to the conclusion that all pure mathematics, though a priori, is synthetic; and this conclusion raised a new problem of which he endeavoured to find the solution.

The question which Kant put at the beginning of his philosophy, namely 'How is pure mathematics possible?' is an interesting and difficult one, to which every philosophy which is not purely sceptical must find some answer. The answer of the pure empiricists, that our mathematical knowledge is derived by induction from particular instances, we have already seen to be inadequate, for two reasons: first, that the validity of the inductive principle itself cannot be proved by induction; secondly, that the general propositions of mathematics, such as 'two and two always make four', can obviously be known with certainty by consideration of a single instance, and gain nothing by enumeration of other cases in which they have been found to be true. Thus our knowledge of the general propositions of mathematics (and the same applies to logic) must be accounted for otherwise than our (merely probable) knowledge of empirical generalizations such as 'all men are mortal'.

The problem arises through the fact that such knowledge is general, whereas all experience is particular. It seems strange that we should apparently be able to know some truths in advance about particular things of which we have as yet no experience; but it cannot easily be doubted that logic and arithmetic will apply to such things. We do not know who will be the inhabitants of London a hundred years hence; but we know that any two of them and any other two of them will make four of them. This apparent power of anticipating facts about things of which we have no experience is certainly surprising. Kant's solution of the problem, though not valid in my opinion, is interesting. It is, however, very difficult, and is differently understood by different philosophers. We can, therefore, only give the merest outline of it, and even that will be thought misleading by many exponents of Kant's system.

What Kant maintained was that in all our experience there are two elements to be distinguished, the one due to the object (i.e. to what we have called the 'physical object'), the other due to our own nature. We saw, in discussing matter and sense-data, that the physical object is different from the associated sense-data, and that the sense-data are to be regarded as resulting from an interaction between the physical object and ourselves. So far, we are in agreement with Kant. But what is distinctive of Kant is the way in which he apportions the shares of ourselves and the physical object respectively. He considers that the crude material given in sensation—the colour, hardness etc.—is due to the object, and that what we supply is the arrangement in space and time, and all the relations between sense-data which result from comparison or from considering one as the cause of the other or in any other way. His chief reason in favour of this view is that we seem to have a priori knowledge as to space and time and causality and comparison, but not as to the actual crude material of sensation. We can be sure, he says, that anything we shall ever experience must show the characteristics affirmed of it in our a priori knowledge, because these characteristics are due to our own nature, and therefore nothing can ever come into our experience without acquiring these characteristics.

The physical object, which he calls the 'thing in itself',[1] he regards as essentially unknowable; what can be known is the object as we have it in experience, which he calls the 'phenomenon'. The phenomenon, being a joint product of us and the thing in itself, is sure to have those characteristics which are due to us, and is therefore sure to conform to our a priori knowledge. Hence this knowledge, though true of all actual and possible experience, must not be supposed to apply outside experience. Thus in spite of the existence of a priori knowledge, we cannot know anything about the thing in itself or about what is not an actual or possible object of experience. In this way he tries to reconcile and harmonize the contentions of the rationalists with the arguments of the empiricists.

Apart from minor grounds on which Kant's philosophy may be criticized, there is one main objection which seems fatal to any attempt to deal with the problem of a priori knowledge by his method. The thing to be accounted for is our certainty that the facts must always conform to logic and arithmetic. To say that logic and arithmetic are contributed by us does not account for this. Our nature is as much a fact of the existing world as anything, and there can be no certainty that it will remain constant. It might happen, if Kant is right, that to-morrow our nature would so change as to make two and two become five. This possibility seems never to have occurred to him, yet it is one which utterly destroys the certainty and universality which he is anxious to vindicate for arithmetical propositions. It is true that this possibility, formally, is inconsistent with the Kantian view that time itself is a form imposed by the subject upon phenomena, so that our real Self is not in time and has no to-morrow. But he will still have to suppose that the time-order of phenomena is determined by characteristics of what is behind phenomena, and this suffices for the substance of our argument.

Reflection, moreover, seems to make it clear that, if there is any truth in our arithmetical beliefs, they must apply to things equally whether we think of them or not. Two physical objects and two other physical objects must make four physical objects, even if physical objects cannot be experienced. To assert this is certainly within the scope of what we mean when we state that two and two are four. Its truth is just as indubitable as the truth of the assertion that two phenomena and two other phenomena make four phenomena. Thus Kant's solution unduly limits the scope of a priori propositions, in addition to failing in the attempt at explaining their certainty.

Apart from the special doctrines advocated by Kant, it is very common among philosophers to regard what is a priori as in some sense mental, as concerned rather with the way we must think than with any fact of the outer world. We noted in the preceding chapter the three principles commonly called 'laws of thought'. The view which led to their being so named is a natural one, but there are strong reasons for thinking that it is erroneous. Let us take as an illustration the law of contradiction. This is commonly stated in the form 'Nothing can both be and not be', which is intended to express the fact that nothing can at once have and not have a given quality. Thus, for example, if a tree is a beech it cannot also be not a beech; if my table is rectangular it cannot also be not rectangular, and so on.

Now what makes it natural to call this principle a law of thought is that it is by thought rather than by outward observation that we persuade ourselves of its necessary truth. When we have seen that a tree is a beech, we do not need to look again in order to ascertain whether it is also not a beech; thought alone makes us know that this is impossible. But the conclusion that the law of contradiction is a law of thought is nevertheless erroneous. What we believe, when we believe the law of contradiction, is not that the mind is so made that it must believe the law of contradiction. This belief is a subsequent result of psychological reflection, which presupposes the belief in the law of contradiction. The belief in the law of contradiction is a belief about things, not only about thoughts. It is not, e.g., the belief that if we think a certain tree is a beech, we cannot at the same time think that it is not a beech; it is the belief that if a tree is a beech, it cannot at the same time be not

1. Kant's 'thing in itself' is identical in definition with the physical object, namely, it is the cause of sensations. In the properties deduced from the definition it is not identical, since Kant held (in spite of some inconsistency as regards cause) that we can know that none of the categories are applicable to the "thing in itself."

a beech. Thus the law of contradiction is about things, and not merely about thoughts; and although belief in the law of contradiction is a thought, the law of contradiction itself is not a thought, but a fact concerning the things in the world. If this, which we believe when we believe the law of contradiction, were not true of the things in the world, the fact that we were compelled to think it true would not save the law of contradiction from being false; and this shows that the law is not a law of thought.

A similar argument applies to any other a priori judgement. When we judge that two and two are four, we are not making a judgement about our thoughts, but about all actual or possible couples. The fact that our minds are so constituted as to believe that two and two are four, though it is true, is emphatically not what we assert when we assert that two and two are four. And no fact about the constitution of our minds could make it true that two and two are four. Thus our a priori knowledge, if it is not erroneous, is not merely knowledge about the constitution of our minds, but is applicable to whatever the world may contain, both what is mental and what is non-mental.

The fact seems to be that all our a priori knowledge is concerned with entities which do not, properly speaking, exist, either in the mental or in the physical world. These entities are such as can be named by parts of speech which are not substantives; they are such entities as qualities and relations. Suppose, for instance, that I am in my room. I exist, and my room exists; but does 'in' exist? Yet obviously the word 'in' has a meaning; it denotes a relation which holds between me and my room. This relation is something, although we cannot say that it exists in the same sense in which I and my room exist. The relation 'in' is something which we can think about and understand, for, if we could not understand it, we could not understand the sentence 'I am in my room'. Many philosophers, following Kant, have maintained that relations are the work of the mind, that things in themselves have no relations, but that the mind brings them together in one act of thought and thus produces the relations which it judges them to have.

This view, however, seems open to objections similar to those which we urged before against Kant. It seems plain that it is not thought which produces the truth of the proposition 'I am in my room'. It may be true that an earwig is in my room, even if neither I nor the earwig nor any one else is aware of this truth; for this truth concerns only the earwig and the room, and does not depend upon anything else. Thus relations, as we shall see more fully in the next chapter, must be placed in a world which is neither mental nor physical. This world is of great importance to philosophy, and in particular to the problems of a priori knowledge. In the next chapter we shall proceed to develop its nature and its bearing upon the questions with which we have been dealing.

CHAPTER IX THE WORLD OF UNIVERSALS

At the end of the preceding chapter we saw that such entities as relations appear to have a being which is in some way different from that of physical objects, and also different from that of minds and from that of sense-data. In the present chapter we have to consider what is the nature of this kind of being, and also what objects there are that have this kind of being. We will begin with the latter question.

The problem with which we are now concerned is a very old one, since it was brought into philosophy by Plato. Plato's 'theory of ideas' is an attempt to solve this very problem, and in my opinion it is one of the most successful attempts hitherto made. The theory to be advocated in what follows is largely Plato's, with merely such modifications as time has shown to be necessary.

The way the problem arose for Plato was more or less as follows. Let us consider, say, such a notion as justice. If we ask ourselves what justice is, it is natural to proceed by considering this, that, and the other just act, with a view to discovering what they have in common. They must all, in some sense, partake of a common nature, which will be found in whatever is just and in nothing else. This common nature, in virtue of which they are all just, will be justice itself, the pure essence the admixture of which with facts of ordinary life produces the multiplicity of just acts. Similarly with any other word which may be applicable to common facts, such as 'whiteness' for example. The word will be applicable to a number of particular things because they all participate in a common nature or essence. This pure essence is what Plato calls an 'idea' or 'form'. (It must not be supposed that 'ideas', in his sense, exist in minds, though they may be apprehended by minds.) The 'idea' justice is not identical with anything that is just: it is something other than particular things, which particular things partake of. Not being particular, it cannot itself exist in the world of sense. Moreover it is not fleeting or changeable like the things of sense: it is eternally itself, immutable and indestructible.

Thus Plato is led to a supra-sensible world, more real than the common world of sense, the unchangeable world of ideas, which alone gives to the world of sense whatever pale reflection of reality may belong to it. The truly real world, for Plato, is the world of ideas; for whatever we may attempt to say about things in the world of sense, we can only succeed in saying that they participate in such and such ideas, which, therefore, constitute all their character. Hence it is easy to pass on into a mysticism. We may hope, in a mystic illumination, to see the ideas as we see objects of sense; and we may imagine that the ideas exist in heaven. These mystical developments are very natural, but the basis of the theory is in logic, and it is as based in logic that we have to consider it.

The word 'idea' has acquired, in the course of time, many associations which are quite misleading when applied to Plato's 'ideas'. We shall therefore use the word 'universal' instead of the word 'idea', to describe what Plato meant. The essence of the sort of entity that Plato meant is that it is opposed to the particular things that are given in sensation. We speak of whatever is given in sensation, or is of the same nature as things given in sensation, as a particular; by opposition to this, a universal will be anything which may be shared by many particulars, and has those characteristics which, as we saw, distinguish justice and whiteness from just acts and white things.

When we examine common words, we find that, broadly speaking, proper names stand for particulars, while other substantives, adjectives, prepositions, and verbs stand for universals. Pronouns stand for particulars, but are ambiguous: it is only by the context or the circumstances that we know what particulars they stand for. The word 'now' stands for a particular, namely the present moment; but like pronouns, it stands for an ambiguous particular, because the present is always changing.

It will be seen that no sentence can be made up without at least one word which denotes a universal. The nearest approach would be some such statement as 'I like this'. But even here the word 'like' denotes a universal, for I may like other things, and other people may like things. Thus all truths involve universals, and all knowledge of truths involves acquaintance with universals.

Seeing that nearly all the words to be found in the dictionary stand for universals, it is strange that hardly anybody except students of philosophy ever realizes that there are such entities as universals. We do not naturally dwell upon those words in a sentence which do not stand for particulars; and if we are forced to dwell upon a word which stands for a universal, we naturally think of it as standing for some one of the particulars that come under the universal. When, for example, we hear the sentence, 'Charles I's head was cut off', we may naturally enough think of Charles I, of Charles I's head, and of the operation of cutting off his head, which are all particulars; but we do not naturally dwell upon what is meant by the word 'head' or the word 'cut', which is a universal. We feel such words to be incomplete and insubstantial; they seem to demand a context before anything can be done with them. Hence we succeed in avoiding all notice of universals as such, until the study of philosophy forces them upon our attention.

Even among philosophers, we may say, broadly, that only those universals which are named by adjectives or substantives have been much or often recognized, while those named by verbs and prepositions have been usually overlooked. This omission has had a very great effect upon philosophy; it is hardly too much to say that most metaphysics, since Spinoza, has been largely determined by it. The way this has occurred is, in outline, as follows: Speaking generally, adjectives and common nouns express qualities or properties of single things, whereas prepositions and verbs tend to express relations between two or more things. Thus the neglect of prepositions and verbs led to the belief that every proposition can be regarded as attributing a property to a single thing, rather than as expressing a relation between two or more things. Hence it was supposed that, ultimately, there can be no such entities as relations between things. Hence either there can be only one thing in the universe, or, if there are many things, they cannot possibly interact in any way, since any interaction would be a relation, and relations are impossible.

The first of these views, advocated by Spinoza and held in our own day by Bradley and many other philosophers, is called *monism*; the second, advocated by Leibniz but not very common nowadays, is called *monadism*, because each of the isolated things is called a *monad*. Both these opposing philosophies, interesting as they are, result, in my opinion, from an undue attention to one sort of universals, namely the sort represented by adjectives and substantives rather than by verbs and prepositions.

As a matter of fact, if any one were anxious to deny altogether that there are such things as universals, we should find that we cannot strictly prove that there are such entities as qualities, i.e. the universals represented by adjectives and substantives, whereas we can prove that there must be relations, i.e. the sort of universals generally represented by verbs and prepositions. Let us take in illustration the universal whiteness. If we believe that there is such a universal, we shall say that things are white because they have the quality of whiteness. This view, however, was strenuously denied by Berkeley and Hume, who have been followed in this by later empiricists. The form which their denial took was to deny that there are such things as 'abstract ideas'. When we want to think of whiteness, they said, we form an image of some particular white thing, and reason concerning this particular, taking care not to deduce anything concerning it which we cannot see to be equally true of any other white thing. As an account of our actual mental processes, this is no doubt largely true. In geometry, for example, when we wish to prove something about all triangles, we draw a particular triangle and reason about it, taking care not to use any characteristic which it does not share with other triangles. The beginner, in order to avoid error, often finds it useful to draw several triangles, as unlike each other as possible, in order to make sure that his reasoning is equally applicable to all of them. But a difficulty emerges as soon as we ask ourselves how we know that a thing is white or a triangle. If we wish to avoid the universals whiteness and triangularity, we shall choose some particular patch of white or some particular triangle, and say that anything is white or a triangle if it has the right sort of resemblance to our chosen particular. But then the resemblance required will have to be a universal. Since there are many white things, the resemblance must hold between many pairs of particular white things; and this is the characteristic of a universal. It will be useless to say that there is a different resemblance for each pair, for then we shall have to say that these resemblances resemble each other, and thus at last we shall be forced to admit resemblance as a universal. The relation of resemblance, therefore, must be a true universal. And having been forced to admit this universal, we find that it is no longer worth while to invent difficult and unplausible theories to avoid the admission of such universals as whiteness and triangularity.

Berkeley and Hume failed to perceive this refutation of their rejection of 'abstract ideas', because, like their adversaries, they only thought of qualities, and altogether ignored relations as universals. We have therefore here another respect in which the rationalists appear to have been in the right as against the empiricists, although, owing to the neglect or denial of relations, the deductions made by rationalists were, if anything, more apt to be mistaken than those made by empiricists.

Having now seen that there must be such entities as universals, the next point to be proved is that their being is not merely mental. By this is meant that whatever being belongs to them is independent of their being thought of or in any way apprehended by minds. We have already touched on this subject at the end of the preceding chapter, but we must now consider more fully what sort of being it is that belongs to universals.

Consider such a proposition as 'Edinburgh is north of London'. Here we have a relation between two places, and it seems plain that the relation subsists independently of our knowledge of it. When we come to know that Edinburgh is north of London, we come to know something which has to do only with Edinburgh and London: we do not cause the truth of the proposition by coming to know it, on the contrary we merely apprehend a fact which was there before we knew it. The part of the earth's surface where Edinburgh stands would be north of the part where London stands, even if there were no human being to know about north and south, and even if there were no minds at all in the universe. This is, of course, denied by many philosophers, either for Berkeley's reasons or for Kant's. But we have already considered these reasons, and decided that they are inadequate. We may therefore now assume it to be true that nothing mental is presupposed in the fact that Edinburgh is north of London. But this fact involves the relation 'north of', which is a universal; and it would be impossible for the whole fact to involve nothing mental if the relation 'north of', which is a constituent part of the fact, did involve anything mental. Hence we must admit that the relation, like the terms it relates, is not dependent upon thought, but belongs to the independent world which thought apprehends but does not create.

This conclusion, however, is met by the difficulty that the relation 'north of' does not seem to exist in the same sense in which Edinburgh and London exist. If we ask 'Where and when does this relation exist?' the answer must be 'Nowhere and nowhen'. There is no place or time where we can find the relation 'north of'. It does not exist in Edinburgh any more than in London, for it relates the two and is neutral as between them. Nor can we say that it exists at any particular time. Now everything that can be apprehended by the senses or by introspection exists at some particular time. Hence the relation 'north of' is radically different from such things. It is neither in space nor in time, neither material nor mental; yet it is something.

It is largely the very peculiar kind of being that belongs to universals which has led many people to suppose that they are really mental. We can think of a universal, and our thinking then exists in a perfectly ordinary sense, like any other mental act. Suppose, for example, that we are thinking of whiteness. Then in one sense it may be said that whiteness is 'in our mind'. We have here the same ambiguity as we noted in discussing Berkeley in Chapter IV. In the strict sense, it is not whiteness that is in our mind, but the act of thinking of whiteness. The connected ambiguity in the word 'idea', which we noted at the same time, also causes confusion here. In one sense of this word, namely the sense in which it denotes the object of an act of thought, whiteness is an 'idea'. Hence, if the ambiguity is not guarded against, we may come to think that whiteness is an 'idea' in the other sense, i.e. an act of thought; and thus we come to think that whiteness is mental. But in so thinking, we rob it of its essential quality of universality. One man's act of thought is necessarily a different thing from another man's; one man's act of thought at one time is necessarily a different thing from the same man's act of thought at another time. Hence, if whiteness were the thought as opposed to its object, no two different men could think of it, and no one man could think of it twice. That which many different thoughts of whiteness have in common is their object, and this object is different from all of them. Thus universals are not thoughts, though when known they are the objects of thoughts.

We shall find it convenient only to speak of things existing when they are in time, that is to say, when we can point to some time at which they exist (not excluding the possibility of their existing at all times). Thus thoughts and feelings, minds and physical objects exist. But universals do not exist in this sense; we shall say that they subsist or have being, where 'being' is opposed to 'existence' as being timeless. The world of universals, therefore, may also be described as the world of being. The world of being is unchangeable, rigid, exact, delightful to the mathematician, the logician, the builder of metaphysical systems, and all who love perfection more than life. The world of existence is fleeting, vague, without sharp boundaries, without any clear plan or arrangement, but it contains all thoughts and feelings, all the data of sense, and all physical objects, everything that can do either good or harm, everything that makes any difference to the value of life and the world. According to our temperaments, we shall prefer the contemplation of the one or of the other. The one we do not prefer will probably seem to us a pale shadow of the one we prefer, and hardly worthy to be regarded as in any sense real. But the truth is that both have the same claim on our impartial attention, both are real, and both are important to the metaphysician. Indeed no sooner have we distinguished the two worlds than it becomes necessary to consider their relations.

But first of all we must examine our knowledge of universals. This consideration will occupy us in the following chapter, where we shall find that it solves the problem of a priori knowledge, from which we were first led to consider universals.

CHAPTER X ON OUR KNOWLEDGE OF UNIVERSALS

In regard to one man's knowledge at a given time, universals, like particulars, may be divided into those known by acquaintance, those known only by description, and those not known either by acquaintance or by description.

Let us consider first the knowledge of universals by acquaintance. It is obvious, to begin with, that we are acquainted with such universals as white, red, black, sweet, sour, loud, hard, etc., i.e. with qualities which are exemplified in sense-data. When we see a white patch, we are acquainted, in the first instance, with the particular patch; but by seeing many white patches, we easily learn to abstract the whiteness which they all have in common, and in learning to do this we are learning to be acquainted with whiteness. A similar process will make us acquainted with any other universal of the same sort. Universals of this sort may be called 'sensible qualities'. They can be apprehended with less effort of abstraction than any others, and they seem less removed from particulars than other universals are.

We come next to relations. The easiest relations to apprehend are those which hold between the different parts of a single complex sense-datum. For example, I can see at a glance the whole of the page on which I am writing; thus the whole page is included in one sense-datum. But I perceive that some parts of the page are to the left of other parts, and some parts are above other parts. The process of abstraction in this case seems to proceed somewhat as follows: I see successively a number of sense-data in which one part is to the left of another; I perceive, as in the case of different white patches, that all these sense-data have something in common, and by abstraction I find that what they have in common is a certain relation between their parts, namely the relation which I call 'being to the left of'. In this way I become acquainted with the universal relation.

In like manner I become aware of the relation of before and after in time. Suppose I hear a chime of bells: when the last bell of the chime sounds, I can retain the whole chime before my mind, and I can perceive that the earlier bells came before the later ones. Also in memory I perceive that what I am remembering came before the present time. From either of these sources I can abstract the universal relation of before and after, just as I abstracted the universal relation 'being to the left of'. Thus time-relations, like space-relations, are among those with which we are acquainted.

Another relation with which we become acquainted in much the same way is resemblance. If I see simultaneously two shades of green, I can see that they resemble each other; if I also see a shade of red at the same time, I can see that the two greens have more resemblance to each other than either has to the red. In this way I become acquainted with the universal resemblance or similarity.

Between universals, as between particulars, there are relations of which we may be immediately aware. We have just seen that we can perceive that the resemblance between two shades of green is greater than the resemblance between a shade of red and a shade of green. Here we are dealing with a relation, namely 'greater than', between two relations. Our knowledge of such relations, though it requires more power of abstraction than is required for perceiving the qualities of sense-data, appears to be equally immediate, and (at least in some cases) equally indubitable. Thus there is immediate knowledge concerning universals well as concerning sense-data.

Returning now to the problem of a priori knowledge, which we left unsolved when we began the consideration of universals, we find ourselves in a position to deal with it in a much more satisfactory manner than was possible before. Let us revert to the proposition 'two and two are four'. It is fairly obvious, in view of what has been said, that this proposition states a relation between the universal 'two' and the universal 'four'. This suggests a proposition which we shall now endeavour to establish: namely, All a priori knowledge deals exclusively with the relations of universals. This proposition is of great importance, and goes a long way towards solving our previous difficulties concerning a priori knowledge.

The only case in which it might seem, at first sight, as if our proposition were untrue, is the case in which an a priori proposition states that all of one class of particulars belong to some other class, or (what comes the same thing) that all particulars having some one property also have some other. In this case it might seem as though we were dealing with the particulars that have the property rather than with the property. The proposition 'two and two are four' is really a case in point, for this may be stated in the form 'any two and any other two are four', or 'any collection formed of two twos is a collection of four'. If we can show that such statements as this really deal only with universals, our proposition may be regarded as proved.

One way of discovering what a proposition deals with is to ask ourselves what words we must understand—in other words, what objects we must be acquainted with—in order to see what the proposition means. As soon as we see what the proposition means, even if we do not yet know whether it is true or false, it is evident that we must have acquaintance with whatever is really dealt with by the proposition. By applying this test, it appears that many propositions which might seem to be concerned with particulars are really concerned only with universals. In the special case of 'two and two are four', even when we interpret it as meaning 'any collection formed of two twos is a collection of four', it is plain that we can understand the proposition, i.e. we can see what it is that it asserts, as soon as we know what is meant by 'collection' and 'two' and 'four'. It is quite unnecessary to know all the couples in the world: if it were necessary, obviously we could never understand the proposition, since the couples are infinitely numerous and therefore cannot all be known to us. Thus although our general statement implies statements about particular couples, as soon as we know that there are such particular couples, yet it does not itself assert or imply that there are such particular couples, and thus fails to make any statement whatever about an actual particular couple. The statement made is about 'couple', the universal, and not about this or that couple.

Thus the statement 'two and two are four' deals exclusively with universals, and therefore may be known by anybody who is acquainted with the universals concerned and can perceive the relation between them which the statement asserts. It must be taken as a fact, discovered by reflecting upon our knowledge, that we have the power of sometimes perceiving such relations between universals, and therefore of sometimes knowing general a priori propositions such as those of arithmetic and logic. The thing that seemed mysterious, when we formerly considered such knowledge, was that it seemed to anticipate and control experience. This, however, we can now see to have been an error. No fact concerning anything capable of being experienced can be known independently of experience. We know a priori that two things and two other things together make four things, but we do not know a priori that if Brown and Jones are two, and Robinson and Smith are two, then Brown and Jones and Robinson and Smith are four. The reason is that this proposition cannot be understood at all unless we know that there are such people as Brown and Jones and Robinson and Smith, and this we can only know by experience. Hence, although our general proposition is a priori, all its applications to actual particulars involve experience and therefore contain an empirical element. In this way what seemed mysterious in our a priori knowledge is seen to have been based upon an error.

It will serve to make the point clearer if we contrast our genuine a priori judgement with an empirical generalization, such as 'all men are mortals'. Here as before, we can understand what the proposition means as soon as we understand the universals involved, namely man and mortal. It is obviously unnecessary to have an individual acquaintance with the whole human race in order to understand what our proposition means. Thus the difference between an a priori general proposition and an empirical generalization does not come in the meaning of the proposition; it comes in the nature of the evidence for it. In the empirical case, the evidence consists in the particular instances. We believe that all men are mortal because we know that there are innumerable instances of men dying, and no instances of their living beyond a certain age. We do not believe it because we see a connexion between the universal man and the universal mortal. It is true that if physiology can prove, assuming the general laws that govern living bodies, that no living organism can last for ever, that gives a connexion between man and mortality which would enable us to assert our proposition without appealing to the special evidence of men dying. But that only means that our generalization has been subsumed under a wider generalization, for which the evidence is still of the same kind, though more extensive. The progress of science is constantly producing such subsumptions, and therefore giving a constantly wider inductive basis for scientific generalizations. But although this gives a greater degree of certainty, it does not give a different kind: the ultimate ground remains inductive, i.e. derived from instances, and not an a priori connexion of universals such as we have in logic and arithmetic.

Two opposite points are to be observed concerning a priori general propositions. The first is that, if many particular instances are known, our general proposition may be arrived at in the first instance by induction, and the connexion of universals may be only subsequently perceived. For example, it is known that if we draw perpendiculars to the sides of a triangle from the opposite angles, all three perpendiculars meet in a point. It would be quite possible to be first led to this proposition by actually drawing perpendiculars in many cases, and finding that they always met in a point; this experience might lead us to look for the general proof and find it. Such cases are common in the experience of every mathematician.

The other point is more interesting, and of more philosophical importance. It is, that we may sometimes know a general proposition in cases where we do not know a single instance of it. Take such a case as the following: We know that any two numbers can be multiplied together, and will give a third called their product. We know that all pairs of integers the product of which is less than 100 have been actually multiplied together, and the value of the product recorded in the multiplication table. But we also know that the number of integers is infinite, and that only a finite number of pairs of integers ever have been or ever will be thought of by human beings. Hence it follows that there are pairs of integers which never have been and never will be thought of by human beings, and that all of them deal with integers the product of which is over 100. Hence we arrive at the proposition: 'All products of two integers, which never have been and never will be thought of by any human being, are over 100.' Here is a general proposition of which the truth is undeniable, and yet, from the very nature of the case, we can never give an instance; because any two numbers we may think of are excluded by the terms of the proposition.

This possibility, of knowledge of general propositions of which no instance can be given, is often denied, because it is not perceived that the knowledge of such propositions only requires a knowledge of the relations of universals, and does not require any knowledge of instances of the universals in question. Yet the knowledge of such general propositions is quite vital to a great deal of what is generally admitted to be known. For example, we saw, in our early chapters, that knowledge of physical objects, as opposed to sense-data, is only obtained by an inference, and that they are not things with which we are acquainted. Hence we can never know any proposition of the form 'this is a physical object', where 'this' is something immediately known. It follows that all our knowledge concerning physical objects is such that no actual instance can be given. We can give instances of the associated sense-data, but we cannot give instances of the actual physical objects. Hence our knowledge as to physical objects depends throughout upon this possibility of general knowledge where no instance can be given. And the same applies to our knowledge of other people's minds, or of any other class of things of which no instance is known to us by acquaintance.

We may now take a survey of the sources of our knowledge, as they have appeared in the course of our analysis. We have first to distinguish knowledge of things and knowledge of truths. In each there are two kinds, one immediate and one derivative. Our immediate knowledge of things, which we called acquaintance, consists of two sorts, according as the things known are particulars or universals. Among particulars, we have acquaintance with sense-data and (probably) with ourselves. Among universals, there seems to be no principle by which we can decide which can be known by acquaintance, but it is clear that among those that can be so known are sensible qualities, relations of space and time, similarity, and certain abstract logical universals. Our derivative knowledge of things, which we call knowledge by description, always involves both acquaintance with something and knowledge of truths. Our immediate knowledge of truths may be called intuitive knowledge, and the truths so known may be called self-evident truths. Among such truths are included those which merely state what is given in sense, and also certain abstract logical and arithmetical principles, and (though with less certainty) some ethical propositions. Our derivative knowledge of truths consists of everything that we can deduce from self-evident truths by the use of self-evident principles of deduction.

If the above account is correct, all our knowledge of truths depends upon our intuitive knowledge. It therefore becomes important to consider the nature and scope of intuitive knowledge, in much the same way as, at an earlier stage, we considered the nature and scope of knowledge by acquaintance. But knowledge of truths raises a further problem, which does not arise in regard to knowledge of things, namely the problem of error. Some of our beliefs turn out to be erroneous, and therefore it becomes necessary to consider how, if at all, we can distinguish knowledge from error. This problem does not arise with regard to knowledge by acquaintance, for, whatever may be the object of acquaintance, even in dreams and hallucinations, there is no error involved so long as we do not go beyond the immediate object: error can only arise when we regard the immediate object, i.e. the sense-datum, as the mark of some physical object. Thus the problems connected with knowledge of truths are more difficult than those connected with knowledge of things. As the first of the problems connected with knowledge of truths, let us examine the nature and scope of our intuitive judgements.

CHAPTER XI ON INTUITIVE KNOWLEDGE

There is a common impression that everything that we believe ought to be capable of proof, or at least of being shown to be highly probable. It is felt by many that a belief for which no reason can be given is an unreasonable belief. In the main, this view is just. Almost all our common beliefs are either inferred, or capable of being inferred, from other beliefs which may be regarded as giving the reason for them. As a rule, the reason has been forgotten, or has even never been consciously present to our minds. Few of us ever ask ourselves, for example, what reason there is to suppose the food we are just going to eat will not turn out to be poison. Yet we feel, when challenged, that a perfectly good reason could be found, even if we are not ready with it at the moment. And in this belief we are usually justified.

But let us imagine some insistent Socrates, who, whatever reason we give him, continues to demand a reason for the reason. We must sooner or later, and probably before very long, be driven to a point where we cannot find any further reason, and where it becomes almost certain that no further reason is even theoretically discoverable. Starting with the common beliefs of daily life, we can be driven back from point to point, until we come to some general principle, or some instance of a general principle, which seems luminously evident, and is not itself capable of being deduced from anything more evident. In most questions of daily life, such as whether our food is likely to be nourishing and not poisonous, we shall be driven back to the inductive principle, which we discussed in Chapter VI. But beyond that, there seems to be no further regress. The principle itself is constantly used in our reasoning, sometimes consciously, sometimes unconsciously; but there is no reasoning which, starting from some simpler self-evident principle, leads us to the principle of induction as its conclusion. And the same holds for other logical principles. Their truth is evident to us, and we employ them in constructing demonstrations; but they themselves, or at least some of them, are incapable of demonstration.

Self-evidence, however, is not confined to those among general principles which are incapable of proof. When a certain number of logical principles have been admitted, the rest can be deduced from them; but the propositions deduced are often just as self-evident as those that were assumed without proof. All arithmetic, moreover, can be deduced from the general principles of logic, yet the simple propositions of arithmetic, such as 'two and two are four', are just as self-evident as the principles of logic.

It would seem, also, though this is more disputable, that there are some self-evident ethical principles, such as 'we ought to pursue what is good'.

It should be observed that, in all cases of general principles, particular instances, dealing with familiar things, are more evident than the general principle. For example, the law of contradiction states that nothing can both have a certain property and not have it. This is evident as soon as it is understood, but it is not so evident as that a particular rose which we see cannot be both red and not red. (It is of course possible that parts of the rose may be red and parts not red, or that the rose may be of a shade of pink which we hardly know whether to call red or not; but in the former case it is plain that the rose as a whole is not red, while in the latter case the answer is theoretically definite as soon as we have decided on a precise definition of 'red'.) It is usually through particular instances that we come to be able to see the general principle. Only those who are practiced in dealing with abstractions can readily grasp a general principle without the help of instances.

In addition to general principles, the other kind of self-evident truths are those immediately derived from sensation. We will call such truths 'truths of perception', and the judgements expressing them we will call 'judgements of perception'. But here a certain amount of care is required in getting at the precise nature of the truths that are self-evident. The actual sense-data are neither true nor false. A particular patch of colour which I see, for example, simply exists: it is not the sort of thing that is true or false. It is true that there is such a patch, true that it has a certain shape and degree of brightness, true that it is surrounded by certain other colours. But the patch itself, like everything else in the world of sense, is of a radically different kind from the things that are true or false, and therefore cannot properly be said to be true. Thus whatever self-evident truths may be obtained from our senses must be different from the sense-data from which they are obtained.

It would seem that there are two kinds of self-evident truths of perception, though perhaps in the last analysis the two kinds may coalesce. First, there is the kind which simply asserts the existence of the sense-datum, without in any way analysing it. We see a patch of red, and we judge 'there is such-and-such a patch of red', or more strictly 'there is that'; this is one kind of intuitive judgement of perception. The other kind arises when the object of sense is complex, and we subject it to some degree of analysis. If, for instance, we see a round patch of red, we may judge 'that patch of red is round'. This is again a judgement of perception, but it differs from our previous kind. In our present kind we have a single sense-datum which has both colour and shape: the colour is red and the shape is round. Our judgement analyses the datum into colour and shape, and then recombines them by stating that the red colour is round in shape. Another example of this kind of judgement is 'this is to the right of that', where 'this' and 'that' are seen simultaneously. In this kind of judgement the sense-datum contains constituents which have some relation to each other, and the judgement asserts that these constituents have this relation.

Another class of intuitive judgements, analogous to those of sense and yet quite distinct from them, are judgements of memory. There is some danger of confusion as to the nature of memory, owing to the fact that memory of an object is apt to be accompanied by an image of the object, and yet the image cannot be what constitutes memory. This is easily seen by merely noticing that the image is in the present, whereas what is remembered is known to be in the past. Moreover, we are certainly able to some extent to compare our image with the object remembered, so that we often know, within somewhat wide limits, how far our image is accurate; but this would be impossible, unless the object, as opposed to the image, were in some way before the mind. Thus the essence of memory is not constituted by the image, but by having immediately before the mind an object which is recognized as past. But for the fact of memory in this sense, we should not know that there ever was a past at all, nor should we be able to understand the word 'past', any more than a man born blind can understand the word 'light'. Thus there must be intuitive judgements of memory, and it is upon them, ultimately, that all our knowledge of the past depends.

The case of memory, however, raises a difficulty, for it is notoriously fallacious, and thus throws doubt on the trustworthiness of intuitive judgements in general. This difficulty is no light one. But let us first narrow its scope as far as possible. Broadly speaking, memory is trustworthy in proportion to the vividness of the experience and to its nearness in time. If the house next door was struck by lightning half a minute ago, my memory of what I saw and heard will be so reliable that it would be preposterous to doubt whether there had been a flash at all. And the same applies to less vivid experiences, so long as they are recent. I am absolutely certain that half a minute ago I was sitting in the same chair in which I am sitting now. Going backward over the day, I find things of which I am quite certain, other things of which I am almost certain, other things of which I can become certain by thought and by calling up attendant circumstances, and some things of which I am by no means certain. I am quite certain that I ate my breakfast this morning, but if I were as indifferent to my breakfast as a philosopher should be, I should be doubtful. As to the conversation at breakfast, I can recall some of it easily, some with an effort, some only with a large element of doubt, and some not at all. Thus there is a continual gradation in the degree of self-evidence of what I remember, and a corresponding gradation in the trustworthiness of my memory.

Thus the first answer to the difficulty of fallacious memory is to say that memory has degrees of self-evidence, and that these correspond to the degrees of its trustworthiness, reaching a limit of perfect self-evidence and perfect trustworthiness in our memory of events which are recent and vivid.

It would seem, however, that there are cases of very firm belief in a memory which is wholly false. It is probable that, in these cases, what is really remembered, in the sense of being immediately before the mind, is something other than what is falsely believed in, though something generally associated with it. George IV is said to have at last believed that he was at the battle of Waterloo, because he had so often said that he was. In this case, what was immediately remembered was his repeated assertion; the belief in what he was asserting (if it existed) would be produced by association with the remembered assertion, and would therefore not be a genuine case of memory. It would seem that cases of fallacious memory can probably all be dealt with in this way, i.e. they can be shown to be not cases of memory in the strict sense at all.

One important point about self-evidence is made clear by the case of memory, and that is, that self-evidence has degrees: it is not a quality which is simply present or absent, but a quality which may be more or less present, in gradations ranging from absolute certainty down to an almost imperceptible faintness. Truths of perception and some of the principles of logic have the very highest degree of self-evidence; truths of immediate memory have an almost equally high degree. The inductive principle has less self-evidence than some of the other principles of logic, such as 'what follows from a true premise must be true'. Memories have a diminishing self-evidence as they become remoter and fainter; the truths of logic and mathematics have (broadly speaking) less self-evidence as they become more complicated. Judgements of intrinsic ethical or aesthetic value are apt to have some self-evidence, but not much.

Degrees of self-evidence are important in the theory of knowledge, since, if propositions may (as seems likely) have some degree of self-evidence without being true, it will not be necessary to abandon all connexion between self-evidence and truth, but merely to say that, where there is a conflict, the more self-evident proposition is to be retained and the less self-evident rejected.

It seems, however, highly probable that two different notions are combined in 'self-evidence' as above explained; that one of them, which corresponds to the highest degree of self-evidence, is really an infallible guarantee of truth, while the other, which corresponds to all the other degrees, does not give an infallible guarantee, but only a greater or less presumption. This, however, is only a suggestion, which we cannot as yet develop further. After we have dealt with the nature of truth, we shall return to the subject of self-evidence, in connexion with the distinction between knowledge and error.

CHAPTER XII TRUTH AND FALSEHOOD

Our knowledge of truths, unlike our knowledge of things, has an opposite, namely error. So far as things are concerned, we may know them or not know them, but there is no positive state of mind which can be described as erroneous knowledge of things, so long, at any rate, as we confine ourselves to knowledge by acquaintance. Whatever we are acquainted with must be something; we may draw wrong inferences from our acquaintance, but the acquaintance itself cannot be deceptive. Thus there is no dualism as regards acquaintance. But as regards knowledge of truths, there is a dualism. We may believe what is false as well as what is true. We know that on very many subjects different people hold different and incompatible opinions: hence some beliefs must be erroneous. Since erroneous beliefs are often held just as strongly as true beliefs, it becomes a difficult question how they are to be distinguished from true beliefs. How are we to know, in a given case, that our belief is not erroneous? This is a question of the very greatest difficulty, to which no completely satisfactory answer is possible. There is, however, a preliminary question which is rather less difficult, and that is: What do we mean by truth and falsehood? It is this preliminary question which is to be considered in this chapter.

In this chapter we are not asking how we can know whether a belief is true or false: we are asking what is meant by the question whether a belief is true or false. It is to be hoped that a clear answer to this question may help us to obtain an answer to the question what beliefs are true, but for the present we ask only 'What is truth?' and 'What is falsehood?' not 'What beliefs are true?' and 'What beliefs are false?' It is very important to keep these different questions entirely separate, since any confusion between them is sure to produce an answer which is not really applicable to either.

There are three points to observe in the attempt to discover the nature of truth, three requisites which any theory must fulfill.

1. Our theory of truth must be such as to admit of its opposite, falsehood. A good many philosophers have failed adequately to satisfy this condition: they have constructed theories according to which all our thinking ought to have been true, and have then had the greatest difficulty in finding a place for falsehood. In this respect our theory of belief must differ from our theory of acquaintance, since in the case of acquaintance it was not necessary to take account of any opposite.

2. It seems fairly evident that if there were no beliefs there could be no falsehood, and no truth either, in the sense in which truth is correlative to falsehood. If we imagine a world of mere matter, there would be no room for falsehood in such a world, and although it would contain what may be called 'facts', it would not contain any truths, in the sense in which truths are things of the same kind as falsehoods. In fact, truth and falsehood are properties of beliefs and statements: hence a world of mere matter, since it would contain no beliefs or statements, would also contain no truth or falsehood.

3. But, as against what we have just said, it is to be observed that the truth or falsehood of a belief always depends upon something which lies outside the belief itself. If I believe that Charles I died on the scaffold, I believe truly, not because of any intrinsic quality of my belief, which could be discovered by merely examining the belief, but because of an historical event which happened two and a half centuries ago. If I believe that Charles I died in his bed, I believe falsely: no degree of vividness in my belief, or of care in arriving at it, prevents it from being false, again because of what happened long ago, and not because of any intrinsic property of my belief. Hence, although truth and falsehood are properties of beliefs, they are properties dependent upon the relations of the beliefs to other things, not upon any internal quality of the beliefs.

The third of the above requisites leads us to adopt the view—which has on the whole been commonest among philosophers—that truth consists in some form of correspondence between belief and fact. It is, however, by no means an easy matter to discover a form of correspondence to which there are no irrefutable objections. By this partly—and partly by the feeling that, if truth consists in a correspondence of thought with something outside thought, thought can never know when truth has been attained—many philosophers have been led to try to find some definition of truth which shall not consist in relation to something wholly outside belief. The most important attempt at a definition of this sort is the theory that truth consists in coherence. It is said that the mark of falsehood is failure to cohere in the body of our beliefs, and that it is the essence of a truth to form part of the completely rounded system which is The Truth.

There is, however, a great difficulty in this view, or rather two great difficulties. The first is that there is no reason to suppose that only one coherent body of beliefs is possible. It may be that, with sufficient imagination, a novelist might invent a past for the world that would perfectly fit on to what we know, and yet be quite different from the real past. In more scientific matters, it is certain that there are often two or more hypotheses which account for all the known facts on some subject, and although, in such cases, men of science endeavour to find facts which will rule out all the hypotheses except one, there is no reason why they should always succeed.

In philosophy, again, it seems not uncommon for two rival hypotheses to be both able to account for all the facts. Thus, for example, it is possible that life is one long dream, and that the outer world has only that degree of reality that the objects of dreams have; but although such a view does not seem inconsistent with known facts, there is no reason to prefer it to the common-sense view, according to which other people and things do really exist. Thus coherence as the definition of truth fails because there is no proof that there can be only one coherent system.

The other objection to this definition of truth is that it assumes the meaning of 'coherence' known, whereas, in fact, 'coherence' presupposes the truth of the laws of logic. Two propositions are coherent when both may be true, and are incoherent when one at least must be false. Now in order to know whether two propositions can both be true, we must know such truths as the law of contradiction. For example, the two propositions, 'this tree is a beech' and 'this tree is not a beech', are not coherent, because of the law of contradiction. But if the law of contradiction itself were subjected to the test of coherence, we should find that, if we choose to suppose it false, nothing will any longer be incoherent with anything else. Thus the laws of logic supply the skeleton or framework within which the test of coherence applies, and they themselves cannot be established by this test.

For the above two reasons, coherence cannot be accepted as giving the meaning of truth, though it is often a most important test of truth after a certain amount of truth has become known.

Hence we are driven back to correspondence with fact as constituting the nature of truth. It remains to define precisely what we mean by 'fact', and what is the nature of the correspondence which must subsist between belief and fact, in order that belief may be true.

In accordance with our three requisites, we have to seek a theory of truth which (1) allows truth to have an opposite, namely falsehood, (2) makes truth a property of beliefs, but (3) makes it a property wholly dependent upon the relation of the beliefs to outside things.

The necessity of allowing for falsehood makes it impossible to regard belief as a relation of the mind to a single object, which could be said to be what is believed. If belief were so regarded, we should find that, like acquaintance, it would not admit of the opposition of truth and falsehood, but would have to be always true. This may be made clear by examples. Othello believes falsely that Desdemona loves Cassio. We cannot say that this belief consists in a relation to a single object, 'Desdemona's love for Cassio', for if there were such an object, the belief would be true. There is in fact no such object, and therefore Othello cannot have any relation to such an object. Hence his belief cannot possibly consist in a relation to this object.

It might be said that his belief is a relation to a different object, namely 'that Desdemona loves Cassio'; but it is almost as difficult to suppose that there is such an object as this, when Desdemona does not love Cassio, as it was to suppose that there is 'Desdemona's love for Cassio'. Hence it will be better to seek for a theory of belief which does not make it consist in a relation of the mind to a single object.

It is common to think of relations as though they always held between two terms, but in fact this is not always the case. Some relations demand three terms, some four, and so on. Take, for instance, the relation 'between'. So long as only two terms come in, the relation 'between' is impossible: three terms are the smallest number that render it possible. York is between London and Edinburgh; but if London and Edinburgh were the only places in the world, there could be nothing which was between one place and another. Similarly jealousy requires three people: there can be no such relation that does not involve three at least. Such a proposition as 'A wishes B to promote C's marriage with D' involves a relation of four terms; that is to say, A and B and C and D all come in, and the relation involved cannot be expressed otherwise than in a form involving all four. Instances might be multiplied indefinitely, but enough has been said to show that there are relations which require more than two terms before they can occur.

The relation involved in judging or believing must, if falsehood is to be duly allowed for, be taken to be a relation between several terms, not between two. When Othello believes that Desdemona loves Cassio, he must not have before his mind a single object, 'Desdemona's love for Cassio', or 'that Desdemona loves Cassio', for that would require that there should be objective falsehoods, which subsist independently of any minds; and this, though not logically refutable, is a theory to be avoided if possible. Thus it is easier to account for falsehood if we take judgement to be a relation in which the mind and the various objects concerned all occur severally; that is to say, Desdemona and loving and Cassio must all be terms in the relation which subsists when Othello believes that Desdemona loves Cassio. This relation, therefore, is a relation of four terms, since Othello also is one of the terms of the relation. When we say that it is a relation of four terms, we do not mean that Othello has a certain relation to Desdemona, and has the same relation to loving and also to Cassio. This may be true of some other relation than believing; but believing, plainly, is not a relation which Othello has to each of the three terms concerned, but to all of them together: there is only one example of the relation of believing involved, but this one example knits together four terms. Thus the actual occurrence, at the moment when Othello is entertaining his belief, is that the relation called 'believing' is knitting together into one complex whole the four terms Othello, Desdemona, loving, and Cassio. What is called belief or judgement is nothing but this relation of believing or judging, which relates a mind to several things other than itself. An act of belief or of judgement is the occurrence between certain terms at some particular time, of the relation of believing or judging.

We are now in a position to understand what it is that distinguishes a true judgement from a false one. For this purpose we will adopt certain definitions. In every act of judgement there is a mind which judges, and there are terms concerning which it judges. We will call the mind the subject in the judgement, and the remaining terms the objects. Thus, when Othello judges that Desdemona loves Cassio, Othello is the subject, while the objects are Desdemona and loving and Cassio. The subject and the objects together are called the constituents of the judgement. It will be observed that the elation of judging has what is called a 'sense' or 'direction'. We may say, metaphorically, that it puts its objects in a certain order, which we may indicate by means of the order of the words in the sentence. (In an inflected language, the same thing will be indicated by inflections, e.g., by the difference between nominative and accusative.) Othello's judgement that Cassio loves Desdemona differs from his judgement that Desdemona loves Cassio, in spite of the fact that it consists of the same constituents, because the relation of judging places the constituents in a different order in the two cases. Similarly, if Cassio judges that Desdemona loves Othello, the constituents of the judgement are still the same, but their order is different. This property of having a 'sense' or 'direction' is one which the relation of judging shares with all other relations. The 'sense' of relations is the ultimate source of order and series and a host of mathematical concepts; but we need not concern ourselves further with this aspect.

We spoke of the relation called 'judging' or 'believing' as knitting together into one complex whole the subject and the objects. In this respect, judging is exactly like every other relation. Whenever a relation holds between two or more terms, it unites the terms into a complex whole. If Othello loves Desdemona, there is such a complex whole as 'Othello's love for Desdemona'. The terms united by the relation may be themselves complex, or may be simple, but the whole which results from their being united must be complex. Wherever there is a relation which relates certain terms, there is a complex object formed of the union of those terms; and conversely, wherever there is a complex object, there is a relation which relates its constituents. When an act of believing occurs, there is a complex, in which 'believing' is the uniting relation, and subject and objects are arranged in a certain order by the 'sense' of the relation of believing. Among the objects, as we saw in considering 'Othello believes that Desdemona loves Cassio', one must be a relation—in this instance, the relation 'loving'. But this relation, as it occurs in the act of believing, is not the relation which creates the unity of the complex whole consisting of the subject and the objects. The relation 'loving', as it occurs in the act of believing, is one of the objects—it is a brick in the structure, not the cement. The cement is the relation 'believing'. When the belief is true, there is another complex unity, in which the relation which was one of the objects of the belief relates the other objects. Thus, e.g., if Othello believes truly that Desdemona loves Cassio, then there is a complex unity, 'Desdemona's love for Cassio', which is composed exclusively of the objects of the belief, in the same order as they had in the belief, with the relation which was one of the objects occurring now as the cement that binds together the other objects of the belief. On the other hand, when a belief is false, there is no such complex unity composed only of the objects of the belief. If Othello believes falsely that Desdemona loves Cassio, then there is no such complex unity as 'Desdemona's love for Cassio'.

Thus a belief is *true* when it *corresponds* to a certain associated complex, and *false* when it does not. Assuming, for the sake of definiteness, that the objects of the belief are two terms and a relation, the terms being put in a certain order by the 'sense' of the believing, then if the two terms in that order are united by the relation into a complex, the belief is true; if not, it is false. This constitutes the definition of truth and falsehood that we were in search of. Judging or believing is a certain complex unity of which a mind is a constituent; if the remaining constituents, taken in the order which they have in the belief, form a complex unity, then the belief is true; if not, it is false.

Thus although truth and falsehood are properties of beliefs, yet they are in a sense extrinsic properties, for the condition of the truth of a belief is something not involving beliefs, or (in general) any mind at all, but only the objects of the belief. A mind, which believes, believes truly when there is a corresponding complex not involving the mind, but only its objects. This correspondence ensures truth, and its absence entails falsehood. Hence we account simultaneously for the two facts that beliefs (a) depend on minds for their *existence*, and (b) do not depend on minds for their *truth*.

We may restate our theory as follows: If we take such a belief as 'Othello believes that Desdemona loves Cassio', we will call Desdemona and Cassio the object-terms, and loving the object-relation. If there is a complex unity 'Desdemona's love for Cassio', consisting of the object-terms related by the object-relation in the same order as they have in the belief, then this complex unity is called the fact corresponding to the belief. Thus a belief is true when there is a corresponding fact, and is false when there is no corresponding fact.

It will be seen that minds do not create truth or falsehood. They create beliefs, but when once the beliefs are created, the mind cannot make them true or false, except in the special case where they concern future things which are within the power of the person believing, such as catching trains. What makes a belief true is a fact, and this fact does not (except in exceptional cases) in any way involve the mind of the person who has the belief. . . .

CHAPTER XV THE VALUE OF PHILOSOPHY

Having now come to the end of our brief and very incomplete review of the problems of philosophy, it will be well to consider, in conclusion, what is the value of philosophy and why it ought to be studied. It is the more necessary to consider this question, in view of the fact that many men, under the influence of science or of practical affairs, are inclined to doubt whether philosophy is anything better than innocent but useless trifling, hair-splitting distinctions, and controversies on matters concerning which knowledge is impossible.

This view of philosophy appears to result, partly from a wrong conception of the ends of life, partly from a wrong conception of the kind of goods which philosophy strives to achieve. Physical science, through the medium of inventions, is useful to innumerable people who are wholly ignorant of it; thus the study of physical science is to be recommended, not only, or primarily, because of the effect on the student, but rather because of the effect on mankind in general. Thus utility does not belong to philosophy. If the study of philosophy has any value at all for others than students of philosophy, it must be only indirectly, through its effects upon the lives of those who study it. It is in these effects, therefore, if anywhere, that the value of philosophy must be primarily sought.

But further, if we are not to fail in our endeavour to determine the value of philosophy, we must first free our minds from the prejudices of what are wrongly called 'practical' men. The 'practical' man, as this word is often used, is one who recognizes only material needs, who realizes that men must have food for the body, but is oblivious of the necessity of providing food for the mind. If all men were well off, if poverty and disease had been reduced to their lowest possible point, there would still remain much to be done to produce a valuable society; and even in the existing world the goods of the mind are at least as important as the goods of the body. It is exclusively among the goods of the mind that the value of philosophy is to be found; and only those who are not indifferent to these goods can be persuaded that the study of philosophy is not a waste of time.

Philosophy, like all other studies, aims primarily at knowledge. The knowledge it aims at is the kind of knowledge which gives unity and system to the body of the sciences, and the kind which results from a critical examination of the grounds of our convictions, prejudices, and beliefs. But it cannot be maintained that philosophy has had any very great measure of success in its attempts to provide definite answers to its questions. If you ask a mathematician, a mineralogist, a historian, or any other man of learning, what definite body of truths has been ascertained by his science, his answer will last as long as you are willing to listen. But if you put the same question to a philosopher, he will, if he is candid, have to confess that his study has not achieved positive results such as have been achieved by other sciences. It is true that this is partly accounted for by the fact that, as soon as definite knowledge concerning any subject becomes possible, this subject ceases to be called philosophy, and becomes a separate science. The whole study of the heavens, which now belongs to astronomy, was once included in philosophy; Newton's great work was called 'the mathematical principles of natural philosophy'. Similarly, the study of the human mind, which was a part of philosophy, has now been separated from philosophy and has become the science of psychology. Thus, to a great extent, the uncertainty of philosophy is more apparent than real: those questions which are already capable of definite answers are placed in the sciences, while those only to which, at present, no definite answer can be given, remain to form the residue which is called philosophy.

This is, however, only a part of the truth concerning the uncertainty of philosophy. There are many questions—and among them those that are of the profoundest interest to our spiritual life—which, so far as we can see, must remain insoluble to the human intellect unless its powers become of quite a different order from what they are now. Has the universe any unity of plan or purpose, or is it a fortuitous concourse of atoms? Is consciousness a permanent part of the universe, giving hope of indefinite growth in wisdom, or is it a transitory accident on a small planet on which life must ultimately become impossible? Are good and evil of importance to the universe or only to man? Such questions are asked by philosophy, and variously answered by various philosophers. But it would seem that, whether answers be otherwise discoverable or not, the answers suggested by philosophy are none of them demonstrably true. Yet, however slight may be the hope of discovering an answer, it is part of the business of philosophy to continue the consideration of such questions, to make us aware of their importance, to examine all the approaches to them, and to keep alive that speculative interest in the universe which is apt to be killed by confining ourselves to definitely ascertainable knowledge.

Many philosophers, it is true, have held that philosophy could establish the truth of certain answers to such fundamental questions. They have supposed that what is of most importance in religious beliefs could be proved by strict demonstration to be true. In order to judge of such attempts, it is necessary to take a survey of human knowledge, and to form an opinion as to its methods and its limitations. On such a subject it would be unwise to pronounce dogmatically; but if the investigations of our previous chapters have not led us astray, we shall be compelled to renounce the hope of finding philosophical proofs of religious beliefs. We cannot, therefore, include as part of the value of philosophy any definite set of answers to such questions. Hence, once more, the value of philosophy must not depend upon any supposed body of definitely ascertainable knowledge to be acquired by those who study it.

The value of philosophy is, in fact, to be sought largely in its very uncertainty. The man who has no tincture of philosophy goes through life imprisoned in the prejudices derived from common sense, from the habitual beliefs of his age or his nation, and from convictions which have grown up in his mind without the co-operation or consent of his deliberate reason. To such a man the world tends to become definite, finite, obvious; common objects rouse no questions, and unfamiliar possibilities are contemptuously rejected. As soon as we begin to philosophize, on the contrary, we find, as we saw in our opening chapters, that even the most everyday things lead to problems to which only very incomplete answers can be given. Philosophy, though unable to tell us with certainty what is the true answer to the doubts which it raises, is able to suggest many possibilities which enlarge our thoughts and free them from the tyranny of custom. Thus, while diminishing our feeling of certainty as to what things are, it greatly increases our knowledge as to what they may be; it removes the somewhat arrogant dogmatism of those who have never travelled into the region of liberating doubt, and it keeps alive our sense of wonder by showing familiar things in an unfamiliar aspect.

Apart from its utility in showing unsuspected possibilities, philosophy has a value—perhaps its chief value—through the greatness of the objects which it contemplates, and the freedom from narrow and personal aims resulting from this contemplation. The life of the instinctive man is shut up within the circle of his private interests: family and friends may be included, but the outer world is not regarded except as it may help or hinder what comes within the circle of instinctive wishes. In such a life there is something feverish and confined, in comparison with which the philosophic life is calm and free. The private world of instinctive interests is a small one, set in the midst of a great and powerful world which must, sooner or later, lay our private world in ruins. Unless we can so enlarge our interests as to include the whole outer world, we remain like a garrison in a beleaguered fortress, knowing that the enemy prevents escape and that ultimate surrender is inevitable. In such a life there is no peace, but a constant strife between the insistence of desire and the powerlessness of will. In one way or another, if our life is to be great and free, we must escape this prison and this strife.

One way of escape is by philosophic contemplation. Philosophic contemplation does not, in its widest survey, divide the universe into two hostile camps—friends and foes, helpful and hostile, good and bad—it views the whole impartially. Philosophic contemplation, when it is unalloyed, does not aim at proving that the rest of the universe is akin to man. All acquisition of knowledge is an enlargement of the Self, but this enlargement is best attained when it is not directly sought. It is obtained when the desire for knowledge is alone operative, by a study which does not wish in advance that its objects should have this or that character, but adapts the Self to the characters which it finds in its objects. This enlargement of Self is not obtained when, taking the Self as it is, we try to show that the world is so similar to this Self that knowledge of it is possible without any admission of what seems alien. The desire to prove this is a form of self-assertion and, like all self-assertion, it is an obstacle to the growth of Self which it desires, and of which the Self knows that it is capable. Self-assertion, in philosophic speculation as elsewhere, views the world as a means to its own ends; thus it makes the world of less account than Self, and the Self sets bounds to the greatness of its goods. In contemplation, on the contrary, we start from the not-Self, and through its greatness the boundaries of Self are enlarged; through the infinity of the universe the mind which contemplates it achieves some share in infinity.

For this reason greatness of soul is not fostered by those philosophies which assimilate the universe to Man. Knowledge is a form of union of Self and not-Self; like all union, it is impaired by dominion, and therefore by any attempt to force the universe into conformity with what we find in ourselves. There is a widespread philosophical tendency towards the view which tells us that Man is the measure of all things, that truth is man-made, that space and time and the world of universals are properties of the mind, and that, if there be anything not created by the mind, it is unknowable and of no account for us. This view, if our previous discussions were correct, is untrue; but in addition to being untrue, it has the effect of robbing philosophic contemplation of all that gives it value, since it fetters contemplation to Self. What it calls knowledge is not a union with the not-Self, but a set of prejudices, habits, and desires, making an impenetrable veil between us and the world beyond. The man who finds pleasure in such a theory of knowledge is like the man who never leaves the domestic circle for fear his word might not be law.

The true philosophic contemplation, on the contrary, finds its satisfaction in every enlargement of the not-Self, in everything that magnifies the objects contemplated, and thereby the subject contemplating. Everything, in contemplation, that is personal or private, everything that depends upon habit, self-interest, or desire, distorts the object, and hence impairs the union which the intellect seeks. By thus making a barrier between subject and object, such personal and private things become a prison to the intellect.

The free intellect will see as God might see, without a here and now, without hopes and fears, without the trammels of customary beliefs and traditional prejudices, calmly, dispassionately, in the sole and exclusive desire of knowledge—knowledge as impersonal, as purely contemplative, as it is possible for man to attain. Hence also the free intellect will value more the abstract and universal knowledge into which the accidents of private history do not enter, than the knowledge brought by the senses, and dependent, as such knowledge must be, upon an exclusive and personal point of view and a body whose sense-organs distort as much as they reveal.

The mind which has become accustomed to the freedom and impartiality of philosophic contemplation will preserve something of the same freedom and impartiality in the world of action and emotion. It will view its purposes and desires as parts of the whole, with the absence of insistence that results from seeing them as infinitesimal fragments in a world of which all the rest is unaffected by any one man's deeds. The impartiality which, in contemplation, is the unalloyed desire for truth, is the very same quality of mind which, in action, is justice, and in emotion is that universal love which can be given to all, and not only to those who are judged useful or admirable. Thus contemplation enlarges not only the objects of our thoughts, but also the objects of our actions and our affections: it makes us citizens of the universe, not only of one walled city at war with all the rest. In this citizenship of the universe consists man's true freedom, and his liberation from the thraldom of narrow hopes and fears.

Thus, to sum up our discussion of the value of philosophy; Philosophy is to be studied, not for the sake of any definite answers to its questions since no definite answers can, as a rule, be known to be true, but rather for the sake of the questions themselves; because these questions enlarge our conception of what is possible, enrich our intellectual imagination and diminish the dogmatic assurance which closes the mind against speculation; but above all because, through the greatness of the universe which philosophy contemplates, the mind also is rendered great, and becomes capable of that union with the universe which constitutes its highest good.

The Theory of Definite Descriptions

We dealt in the preceding chapter with the words *all* and *some*; in this chapter we shall consider the word *the* in the singular, and in the next chapter we shall consider the word *the* in the plural. It may be thought excessive to devote two chapters to one word, but to the philosophical mathematician it is a word of very great importance: like Browning's Grammarian with the enclitic δε, I would give the doctrine of this word if I were "dead from the waist down" and not merely in a prison.

From *Introduction to Mathematical Philosophy* (London: George Allen and Unwin Ltd., 1919), pp. 167–180.

We have already had occasion to mention "descriptive functions," i.e. such expressions as "the father of x" or "the sine of x." These are to be defined by first defining "descriptions."

A "description" may be of two sorts, definite and indefinite (or ambiguous). An indefinite description is a phrase of the form "a so-and-so," and a definite description is a phrase of the form "the so-and-so" (in the singular). Let us begin with the former.

"Who did you meet?" "I met a man." "That is a very indefinite description." We are therefore not departing from usage in our terminology. Our question is: What do I really assert when I assert "I met a man"? Let us assume, for the moment, that my assertion is true, and that in fact I met Jones. It is clear that what I assert is *not* "I met Jones." I may say "I met a man, but it was not Jones"; in that case, though I lie, I do not contradict myself, as I should do if when I say I met a man I really mean that I met Jones. It is clear also that the person to whom I am speaking can understand what I say, even if he is a foreigner and has never heard of Jones.

But we may go further: not only Jones, but no actual man, enters into my statement. This becomes obvious when the statement is false, since then there is no more reason why Jones should be supposed to enter into the proposition than why anyone else should. Indeed the statement would remain significant, though it could not possibly be true, even if there were no man at all. "I met a unicorn" or "I met a sea-serpent" is a perfectly significant assertion, if we know what it would be to be a unicorn or a sea-serpent, i.e. what is the definition of these fabulous monsters. Thus it is only what we may call the *concept* that enters into the proposition. In the case of "unicorn," for example, there is only the concept: there is not also, somewhere among the shades, something unreal which may be called "a unicorn." Therefore, since it is significant (though false) to say "I met a unicorn," it is clear that this proposition, rightly analyzed, does not contain a constituent "a unicorn," though it does contain the concept "unicorn."

The question of "unreality," which confronts us at this point, is a very important one. Misled by grammar, the great majority of those logicians who have dealt with this question have dealt with it on mistaken lines. They have regarded grammatical form as a surer guide in analysis than, in fact, it is. And they have not known what differences in grammatical form are important. "I met Jones" and "I met a man" would count traditionally as propositions of the same form, but in actual fact they are of quite different forms: the first names an actual person, Jones; while the second involves a propositional function, and becomes, when made explicit: "The function 'I met x and x is human' is sometimes true." (It will be remembered that we adopted the convention of using "sometimes" as not implying more than once.) This proposition is obviously not of the form "I met x," which accounts for the existence of the proposition "I met a unicorn" in spite of the fact that there is no such thing as "a unicorn."

For want of the apparatus of propositional functions, many logicians have been driven to the conclusion that there are unreal objects. It is argued, e.g. by Meinong,[1] that we can speak about "the golden mountain," "the round square," and so on; we can make true propositions of which these are the subjects; hence they must have some kind of logical being, since otherwise the propositions in which they occur would be meaningless. In such theories, it seems to me, there is a failure of that feeling for reality which ought to be preserved even in the most abstract studies. Logic, I should maintain, must no more admit a unicorn than zoology can; for logic is concerned with the real world just as truly as zoology, though with its more abstract and general features. To say that unicorns have an existence in heraldry, or in literature, or in imagination, is a most pitiful and paltry evasion. What exists in heraldry is not an animal, made of flesh and blood, moving and breathing of its own initiative. What exists is a picture, or a description in words. Similarly, to maintain that Hamlet, for example, exists in his own world, namely, in the world of Shakespeare's imagination, just as truly as (say) Napoleon existed in the ordinary world, is to say something deliberately confusing, or else confused to a degree which is scarcely credible. There is only one world, the "real" world: Shakespeare's imagination is part of it, and the thoughts that he had in writing Hamlet are real. So are the thoughts that we have in reading the play. But it is of the very essence of fiction that only the thoughts, feelings, etc., in Shakespeare and his readers are real, and that there is not, in addition to them, an objective Hamlet. When you have taken account of all the feelings roused by Napoleon in writers and readers of history, you have not touched the actual man; but in the case of Hamlet you have come to the end of him. If no one thought about Hamlet, there would be nothing left of him; if no one had thought about Napoleon, he would have soon seen to it that some one did. The sense of reality is vital in logic, and whoever juggles with it by pretending that Hamlet has another kind of reality is doing a disservice to thought. A robust sense of reality is very necessary in framing a correct analysis of propositions about unicorns, golden mountains, round squares, and other such pseudo-objects.

In obedience to the feeling of reality, we shall insist that, in the analysis of propositions, nothing "unreal" is to be admitted. But, after all, if there *is* nothing unreal, how, it may be asked, *could* we admit anything unreal? The reply is that, in dealing with propositions, we are dealing in the first instance with symbols, and if we attribute significance to groups of symbols which have no significance, we shall fall into the error of admitting unrealities, in the only sense in which this is possible, namely, as objects described. In the proposition "I met a unicorn," the whole four words together make a significant proposition, and the word "unicorn" by itself is significant, in just the same sense as the word "man." But the *two* words "a unicorn" do not form a subordinate group having a meaning of its own. Thus if we falsely attribute meaning to these two words, we find ourselves saddled with "a unicorn," and with the problem how there can be such a thing in a world where there are no unicorns. "A unicorn" is an indefinite description which describes nothing. It is not an indefinite description which describes something unreal. Such a proposition as "x is unreal" only has meaning when "x" is a description, definite or indefinite; in that case the proposition will be true if "x" is a description which describes nothing. But whether the description "x" describes something or describes nothing, it is in any case not a constituent of the proposition in which it occurs; like "a unicorn" just now, it is not a subordinate group having a meaning of its own. All this results from the fact that, when "x" is a description, "x is unreal" or "x does not exist" is not nonsense, but is always significant and sometimes true.

We may now proceed to define generally the meaning of propositions which contain ambiguous descriptions. Suppose we wish to make some statement about "a so-and-so," where "so-and-so's" are those objects that have a certain property ϕ, i.e. those objects x for which the propositional function ϕx is true. (E.g. if we take "a man" as our instance of "a so-and-so," ϕx will be "x is human.") Let us now wish to assert the property ψ of "a so-and-so," i.e. we wish to assert that "a so-and-so" has that property which x has when ψx is true. (E.g. in the case of "I met a man," ψx will be "I met x.") Now the proposition that "a so-and-so" has the property ψ is *not* a proposition of the form "ψx." If it were, "a so-and-so" would have to be identical with x for a suitable x; and although (in a sense) this may be true in some cases, it is certainly not true in such a case as "a unicorn." It is just this fact, that the statement that a so-and-so has the property ψ is not of the form ψx, which makes it possible for "a so-and-so" to be, in a certain clearly definable sense, "unreal." The definition is as follows:

> The statement that "an object having the property ϕ has the property ψ"

means:

> "The joint assertion of ϕx and ψx is not always false."

So far as logic goes, this is the same proposition as might be expressed by "some ϕ's are ψ's"; but rhetorically there is a difference, because in the one case there is a suggestion of singularity, and in the other case of plurality. This, however, is not the important point. The important point is that, when rightly analyzed, propositions verbally about "a so-and-so" are found to contain no constituent represented by this phrase. And that is why such propositions can be significant even when there is no such thing as a so-and-so.

The definition of *existence*, as applied to ambiguous descriptions, results from what was said at the end of the preceding chapter [chapter 15 of *Introduction to Mathematical Philosophy*]. We say that "men exist" or "a man exists" if the propositional function "x is human" is sometimes true; and generally "a so-and-so" exists if "x is so-and-so" is sometimes true. We may put this in other language. The proposition "Socrates is a man" is no doubt *equivalent* to "Socrates is human," but it is not the very same proposition. The *is* of "Socrates is human" expresses the relation of subject and predicate; the *is* of "Socrates is a man" expresses identity. It is a disgrace to the human race that it has chosen to employ the same word "is" for these two entirely different ideas—a disgrace which a symbolic logical language of course remedies. The identity in "Socrates is a man" is identity between an object named (accepting "Socrates" as a name, subject to qualifications explained later) and an object ambiguously described. An object ambiguously described will "exist" when at least one such proposition is true, i.e. when there is at least one true proposition of the form "x is a so-and-so," where "x" is a name. It is characteristic of ambiguous (as opposed to definite) descriptions that there may be any number of true propositions of the above form—Socrates is a man, Plato is a man, etc. Thus "a man exists" follows from Socrates, or Plato, or anyone else. With definite descriptions, on the other hand, the corresponding form of proposition, namely, "x is the so-and-so" (where "x" is a name), can only be true for one value of x at most. This brings us to the subject of definite descriptions, which are to be defined in a way analogous to that employed for ambiguous descriptions, but rather more complicated.

We come now to the main subject of the present chapter, namely, the definition of the word *the* (in the singular). One very important point about the definition of "a so-and-so" applies equally to "the so-and-so"; the definition to be sought is a definition of propositions in which this phrase occurs, not a definition of the phrase itself in isolation. In the case of "a so-and-so," this is fairly obvious: no one could suppose that "a man" was a definite object, which could be defined by itself. Socrates is a man, Plato is a man, Aristotle is a man, but we cannot infer that "a man" means the same as "Socrates" means and also the same as "Plato" means and also the same as "Aristotle" means, since these three names have different meanings. Nevertheless, when we have enumerated all the men in the world, there is nothing left of which we can say, "This is a man, and not only so, but it is *the* 'a man,' the quintessential entity that is just an indefinite man without being anybody in particular." It is of course quite clear that whatever there is in the world is definite: if it is a man it is one definite man and not any other. Thus there cannot be such an entity as "a man" to be found in the world, as opposed to specific men. And accordingly it is natural that we do not define "a man" itself, but only the propositions in which it occurs.

In the case of "the so-and-so" this is equally true, though at first sight less obvious. We may demonstrate that this must be the case, by a consideration of the difference between a *name* and a *definite description.* Take the proposition, "Scott is the author of *Waverley*." We have here a name, "Scott," and a description, "the author of *Waverley*," which are asserted to apply to the same person. The distinction between a name and all other symbols may be explained as follows:

A name is a simple symbol whose meaning is something that can only occur as subject, i.e. something of the kind that we defined as an "individual" or a "particular." And a "simple" symbol is one which has no parts that are symbols. Thus "Scott" is a simple symbol, because, though it has parts (namely, separate letters), these parts are not symbols. On the other hand, "the author of *Waverley*" is not a simple symbol, because the separate words that compose the phrase are parts which are symbols. If, as may be the case, whatever *seems* to be an "individual" is really capable of further analysis, we shall have to content ourselves with what may be called "relative individuals," which will be terms that, throughout the context in question, are never analyzed and never occur otherwise than as subjects. And in that case we shall have correspondingly to content ourselves with "relative names." From the standpoint of our present problem, namely, the definition of descriptions, this problem, whether these are absolute names or only relative names, may be ignored, since it concerns different stages in the hierarchy of "types," whereas we have to compare such couples as "Scott" and "the author of *Waverley*," which both apply to the same object, and do not raise the problem of types. We may, therefore, for the moment, treat names as capable of being absolute; nothing that we shall have to say will depend upon this assumption, but the wording may be a little shortened by it.

We have, then, two things to compare: (1) a *name*, which is a simple symbol, directly designating an individual which is its meaning, and having this meaning in its own right, independently of the meanings of all other words; (2) a *description*, which consists of several words, whose meanings are already fixed, and from which results whatever is to be taken as the "meaning" of the description.

A proposition containing a description is not identical with what that proposition becomes when a name is substituted, even if the name names the same object as the description describes. "Scott is the author of *Waverley*" is obviously a different proposition from "Scott is Scott": the first is a fact in literary history, the second a trivial truism. And if we put anyone other than Scott in place of "the author of *Waverley*," our proposition would become false, and would therefore certainly no longer be the same proposition. But, it may be said, our proposition is essentially of the same form as (say) "Scott is Sir Walter," in which two names are said to apply to the same person. The reply is that, if "Scott is Sir Walter" really means "the person named 'Scott' is the person named 'Sir Walter,'" then the names are being used as descriptions: i.e. the individual, instead of being named, is being described as the person having that name. This is a way in which names are frequently used in practice, and there will, as a rule, be nothing in the phraseology to show whether they are being used in this way or *as* names. When a name is used directly, merely to indicate what we are speaking about, it is no part of the *fact* asserted, or of the falsehood if our assertion happens to be false: it is merely part of the symbolism by which we express our thought. What we want to express is something which might (for example) be translated into a foreign language; it is something for which the actual words are a vehicle, but of which they are no part. On the other hand, when we make a proposition about "the person called 'Scott,'" the actual name "Scott" enters into what we are asserting, and not merely into the language used in making the assertion. Our proposition will now be a different one if we substitute "the person called 'Sir Walter.'" But so long as we are using names *as* names, whether we say "Scott" or whether we say "Sir Walter" is as irrelevant to what we are asserting as whether we speak English or French. Thus so long as names are used *as* names, "Scott is Sir Walter" is the same trivial proposition as "Scott is Scott." This completes the proof that "Scott is the author of *Waverley*" is not the same proposition as results from substituting a name for "the author of *Waverley*," no matter what name may be substituted.

When we use a variable, and speak of a propositional function, ϕx say, the process of applying general statements about x to particular cases will consist in substituting a name for the letter "x," assuming that ϕ is a function which has individuals for its arguments. Suppose, for example, that ϕx is "always true"; let it be, say, the "law of identity," $x = x$. Then we may substitute for "x" any name we choose, and we shall obtain a true proposition. Assuming for the moment that "Socrates," "Plato," and "Aristotle" are names (a very rash assumption), we can infer from the law of identity that Socrates is Socrates, Plato is Plato, and Aristotle is Aristotle. But we shall commit a fallacy if we attempt to infer, without further premisses, that the author of *Waverley* is the author of *Waverley*. This results from what we have just proved, that, if we substitute a name for "the author of *Waverley*" in a proposition, the proposition we obtain is a different one. That is to say, applying the result to our present case: If "x" is a name, "$x = x$" is not the same proposition as "the author of *Waverley* is the author of *Waverley*," no matter what name "x" may be. Thus from the fact that all propositions of the form "$x = x$" are true we cannot infer, without more ado, that the author of *Waverley* is the author of *Waverley*. In fact, propositions of the form "the so-and-so is the so-and-so" are not always true: it is necessary that the so-and-so should *exist* (a term which will be explained shortly). It is false that the present King of France is the present King of France, or that the round square is the round square. When we substitute a description for a name, propositional functions which are "always true" may become false, if the description describes nothing. There is no mystery in this as soon as we realize (what was proved in the preceding paragraph) that when we substitute a description the result is not a value of the propositional function in question.

We are now in a position to define propositions in which a definite description occurs. The only thing that distinguishes "the so-and-so" from "a so-and-so" is the implication of uniqueness. We cannot speak of "*the* inhabitant of London," because inhabiting London is an attribute which is not unique. We cannot speak about "the present King of France," because there is none; but we can speak about "the present King of England." Thus propositions about "the so-and-so" always imply the corresponding propositions about "a so-and-so," with the addendum that there is not more than one so-and-so. Such a proposition as "Scott is the author of Waverley" could not be true if *Waverley* had never been written, or if several people had written it; and no more could any other proposition resulting from a propositional function x by the substitution of "the author of *Waverley*" for "x." We may say that "the author of *Waverley*" means "the value of x for which 'x wrote *Waverley*' is true." Thus the proposition "the author of *Waverley* was Scotch," for example, involves:

1. "x wrote *Waverley*" is not always false
2. "if x and y wrote *Waverley*, x and y are identical" is always true
3. "if x wrote *Waverley*, x was Scotch" is always true

These three propositions, translated into ordinary language, state:

(1) at least one person wrote *Waverley*

(2) at most one person wrote *Waverley*

(3) whoever wrote *Waverley* was Scotch

All these three are implied by "the author of *Waverley* was Scotch." Conversely, the three together (but no two of them) imply that the author of *Waverley* was Scotch. Hence the three together may be taken as defining what is meant by the proposition "the author of *Waverley* was Scotch."

We may somewhat simplify these three propositions. The first and second together are equivalent to: "There is a term *c* such that '*x* wrote *Waverley*' is true when *x* is *c* and is false when *x* is not *c*." In other words, "There is a term *c* such that '*x* wrote *Waverley*' is always equivalent to '*x* is *c*.'" (Two propositions are "equivalent" when both are true or both are false.) We have here, to begin with, two functions of *x*, "*x* wrote *Waverley*" and "*x* is *c*," and we form a function of *c* by considering the equivalence of these two functions of *x* for all values of *x*; we then proceed to assert that the resulting function of *c* is "sometimes true," i.e. that it is true for at least one value of *c*. (It obviously cannot be true for more than one value of *c*.) These two conditions together are defined as giving the meaning of "the author of *Waverley* exists."

We may now define "the term satisfying the function ϕx exists." This is the general form of which the above is a particular case. "The author of *Waverley*" is "the term satisfying the function '*x* wrote *Waverley*.'" And "the so-and-so" will always involve reference to some propositional function, namely, that which defines the property that makes a thing a so-and-so. Our definition is as follows:

> "The term satisfying the function ϕx exists" means:
> "There is a term *c* such that ϕx is always equivalent to '*x* is *c*.'"

In order to define "the author of *Waverley* was Scotch," we have still to take account of the third of our three propositions, namely, "Whoever wrote *Waverley* was Scotch." This will be satisfied by merely adding that the *c* in question is to be Scotch. Thus "the author of *Waverley* was Scotch" is:

> "There is a term *c* such that (1) '*x* wrote *Waverley*' is always equivalent to '*x* is *c*,' (2) *c* is Scotch."

> And generally: "the term satisfying ϕx satisfies ψx" is defined as meaning:
> "There is a term *c* such that (1) ϕx is always equivalent to '*x* is *c*,' (2) ψx is true."

This is the definition of propositions in which descriptions occur.

It is possible to have much knowledge concerning a term described, i.e. to know many propositions concerning "the so-and-so," without actually knowing what the so-and-so is, i.e. without knowing any proposition of the form "*x* is the so-and-so," where "*x*" is a name. In a detective story propositions about "the man who did the deed" are accumulated, in the hope that ultimately they will suffice to demonstrate that it was A who did the deed. We may even go so far as to say that, in all such knowledge as can be expressed in words—with the exception of "this" and "that" and a few other words of which the meaning varies on different occasions—no names, in the strict sense, occur, but what seem like names are really descriptions. We may inquire significantly whether Homer existed, which we could not do if "Homer" were a name. The proposition "the so-and-so exists" is significant, whether true or false; but if *a* is the so-and-so (where "*a*" is a name), the words "*a* exists" are meaningless. It is only of descriptions—definite or indefinite—that existence can be significantly asserted; for, if "*a*" is a name, it *must* name something: what does not name anything is not a name, and therefore, if intended to be a name, is a symbol devoid of meaning, whereas a description, like "the present King of France," does not become incapable of occurring significantly merely on the ground that it describes nothing, the reason being that it is a *complex* symbol, of which the meaning is derived from that of its constituent symbols. And so, when we ask whether Homer existed, we are using the word "Homer" as an abbreviated description: we may replace it by (say) "the author of the *Iliad* and the *Odyssey*." The same considerations apply to almost all uses of what look like proper names.

When descriptions occur in propositions, it is necessary to distinguish what may be called "primary" and "secondary" occurrences. The abstract distinction is as follows. A description has a "primary" occurrence when the proposition in which it occurs results from substituting the description for "*x*" in some propositional function ϕx; a description has a "secondary" occurrence when the result of substituting the description for x in ϕx gives only *part* of the proposition concerned. An instance will make this clearer. Consider "the present King of France is bald." Here "the present King of France" has a primary occurrence, and the proposition is false. Every proposition in which a description which describes nothing has a primary occurrence is false. But now consider "the present King of France is not bald." This is ambiguous. If we are first to take "x is bald," then substitute "the present King of France" for "x," and then deny the result, the occurrence of "the present King of France" is secondary and our proposition is true; but if we are to take "x is not bald" and substitute "the present King of France" for "x," then "the present King of France" has a primary occurrence and the proposition is false. Confusion of primary and secondary occurrences is a ready source of fallacies where descriptions are concerned.

Descriptions occur in mathematics chiefly in the form of *descriptive functions*, i.e. "the term having the relation R to y," or "the R of y" as we may say, on the analogy of "the father of y" and similar phrases. To say "the father of y is rich," for example, is to say that the following propositional function of c: "c is rich, and 'x begat y' is always equivalent to 'x is c,'" is "sometimes true," i.e. is true for at least one value of c. It obviously cannot be true for more than one value.

The theory of descriptions, briefly outlined in the present chapter, is of the utmost importance both in logic and in theory of knowledge. But for purposes of mathematics, the more philosophical parts of the theory are not essential, and have therefore been omitted in the above account, which has confined itself to the barest mathematical requisites.

References

1. *Untersuchungen zur Gegenstandstheorie und Psychologie*, 1904.

A Debate on the Existence of God between Father F. C. Copleston and Bertrand Russell

Father F. C. Copleston (1907–1980) was Professor of Philosophy at Heythrop College in England and at the Gregorian University in Rome. He is famous for his multivolume *History of Philosophy*. Bertrand Russell (1872–1970), one of the most important philosophers of this century, was an agnostic who argued against Christian belief. In this famous BBC radio debate of 1948 Copleston defends the argument from contingency, which Russell attacks.

COPLESTON: As we are going to discuss the existence of God, it might perhaps be as well to come to some provisional agreement as to what we understand by the term "God." I presume that we mean a supreme personal being—distinct from the world, and creator of the world. Would you agree—provisionally at least—to accept this statement as the meaning of the term "God"?

RUSSELL: Yes, I accept this definition.

COPLESTON: Well, my position is the affirmative position that such a being actually exists, and that His existence can be proved philosophically. Perhaps you would tell me if your position is that of agnosticism or of atheism. I mean, would you say that the non-existence of God can be proved?

RUSSELL: No, I should not say that: my position is agnostic.

This debate was broadcast in 1948 on the Third Program of the British Broadcasting Corporation. It was published in *Humanitas* (Manchester) and reprinted in *Why I Am Not a Christian*, by Bertrand Russell (London: George Allen & Unwin, 1957).

COPLESTON: Would you agree with me that the problem of God is a problem of great importance? For example, would you agree that if God does not exist, human beings and human history can have no other purpose than the purpose they choose to give themselves, which—in practice—is likely to mean the purpose which those impose who have the power to impose it?

RUSSELL: Roughly speaking, yes, though I should have to place some limitation on your last clause.

COPLESTON: Would you agree that if there is no God—no absolute Being—there can be no absolute values? I mean, would you agree that if there is no absolute good that the relativity of values results?

RUSSELL: No, I think these questions are logically distinct. Take, for instance, G. E. Moore's *Principia Ethica*, where he maintains that there is a distinction of good and evil, that both of these are definite concepts. But he does not bring in the idea of God to support that contention.

COPLESTON: Well, suppose we leave the question of good till later, till we come to the moral argument, and I give first a metaphysical argument. I'd like to put the main weight on the metaphysical argument based on Leibniz's argument from "Contingency" and then later we might discuss the moral argument. Suppose I give a brief statement on the metaphysical argument and that then we go on to discuss it?

RUSSELL: That seems to me to be a very good plan.

THE ARGUMENT FROM CONTINGENCY

COPLESTON: Well, for clarity's sake, I'll divide the argument into distinct stages. First of all, I should say, we know that there are at least some beings in the world which do not contain in themselves the reason for their existence. For example, I depend on my parents, and now on the air, and on food, and so on. Now, secondly, the world is simply the real or imagined totality or aggregate of individual objects, none of which contain in themselves alone the reason for their existence. There isn't any world distinct from the objects which form it, any more than the human race is something apart from the members. Therefore, I should say, since objects or events exist, and since no object of experience contains within itself the reason of its existence, this reason, the totality of objects, must have a reason external to itself. That reason must be an existent being. Well, this being is either itself the reason for its own existence, or it is not. If it is, well and good. If it is not, then we must proceed farther. But if we proceed to infinity in that sense, then there's no explanation of existence at all. So, I should say, in order to explain existence, we must come to a being which contains within itself the reason for its own existence, that is to say, which cannot not exist.

RUSSELL: This raises a great many points and it is not altogether easy to know where to begin, but I think that, perhaps, in answering your argument, the best point at which to begin is the question of necessary being. The word "necessary," I should maintain, can only be applied significantly to propositions. And, in fact, only to such as are analytic—that is to say—such as it is self-contradictory to deny. I could only admit a necessary being if there were a being whose existence it is self-contradictory to deny. I should like to know whether you would accept Leibniz's division of propositions into truths of reason and truths of fact. The former—the truths of reason—being necessary.

COPLESTON: Well, I certainly should not subscribe to what seems to be Leibniz's idea of truths of reason and truths of fact, since it would appear that, for him, there are in the long run only analytic propositions. It would seem that for Leibniz truths of fact are ultimately reducible to truths of reason. That is to say, to analytic propositions, at least for an omniscient mind. Well, I couldn't agree with that. For one thing it would fail to meet the requirements of the experience of freedom. I don't want to uphold the whole philosophy of Leibniz. I have made use of his argument from contingent to necessary being, basing the argument on the principle of sufficient reason, simply because it seems to me a brief and clear formulation of what is, in my opinion, the fundamental metaphysical argument for God's existence.

RUSSELL: But, to my mind, "a necessary proposition" has got to be analytic. I don't see what else it can mean. And analytic propositions are always complex and logically somewhat late. "Irrational animals are animals" is an analytic proposition; but a proposition such as "This is an animal" can never be analytic. In fact, all the propositions that can be analytic are somewhat late in the build-up of propositions.

COPLESTON: Take the proposition "If there is a contingent being then there is a necessary being." I consider that that proposition hypothetically expressed is a necessary proposition. If you are going to call every necessary proposition an analytic proposition, then—in order to avoid a dispute in terminology—I would agree to call it analytic, though I don't consider it a tautological proposition. But the proposition is a necessary proposition only on the supposition that there is a contingent being. That there is a contingent being actually existing has to be discovered by experience, and the proposition that there is a contingent being is certainly not an analytic proposition, though once you know, I should maintain, that there is a contingent being, it follows of necessity that there is a necessary being.

RUSSELL: The difficulty of this argument is that I don't admit the idea of a necessary being and I don't admit that there is any particular meaning in calling other beings "contingent." These phrases don't for me have a significance except within a logic that I reject.

COPLESTON: Do you mean that you reject these terms because they won't fit in with what is called "modern logic"?

RUSSELL: Well, I can't find anything that they could mean. The word "necessary," it seems to me, is a useless word, except as applied to analytic propositions, not to things.

COPLESTON: In the first place, what do you mean by "modern logic"? As far as I know, there are somewhat differing systems. In the second place, not all modern logicians surely would admit the meaninglessness of metaphysics. We both know, at any rate, one very eminent modern thinker whose knowledge of modern logic was profound, but who certainly did not think that metaphysics are meaningless or, in particular, that the problem of God is meaningless. Again, even if all modern logicians held that metaphysical terms are meaningless, it would not follow that they were right. The proposition that metaphysical terms are meaningless seems to me to be a proposition based on an assumed philosophy. The dogmatic position behind it seems to be this: What will not go into my machine is non-existent, or it is meaningless; it is the expression of emotion. I am simply trying to point out that anybody who says that a particular system of modern logic is the sole criterion of meaning is saying something that is over-dogmatic; he is dogmatically insisting that a part of philosophy is the whole of philosophy. After all, a "contingent" being is a being which has not in itself the complete reason for its existence, that's what I mean by a contingent being. You know, as well as I do, that the existence of neither of us can be explained without reference to something or somebody outside us, our parents, for example. A "necessary" being, on the other hand, means a being that must and cannot not exist. You may say that there is no such being, but you will find it hard to convince me that you do not understand the terms I am using. If you do not understand them, then how can you be entitled to say that such a being does not exist, if that is what you do say?

RUSSELL: Well, there are points here that I don't propose to go into at length. I don't maintain the meaninglessness of metaphysics in general at all. I maintain the meaninglessness of certain particular terms—not on any general ground, but simply because I've not been able to see an interpretation of those particular terms. It's not a general dogma—it's a particular thing. But those points I will leave out for the moment. And I will say that what you have been saying brings us back, it seems to me, to the ontological argument that there is a being whose essence involves existence, so that his existence is analytic. That seems to me to be impossible, and it raises, of course, the question what one means by existence, and as to this, I think a subject named can never be significantly said to exist but only a subject described. And that existence, in fact, quite definitely is not a predicate.

COPLESTON: Well, you say, I believe, that it is bad grammar, or rather bad syntax to say for example "T. S. Eliot exists"; one ought to say, for example, "He, the author of *Murder in the Cathedral*, exists." Are you going to say that the proposition, "The cause of the world exists," is without meaning? You may say that the world has no cause: but I fail to see how you can say that the proposition that "the cause of the world exists" is meaningless. Put it in the form of a question: "Has the world a cause?" or "Does a cause of the world exist?" Most people surely would understand the question, even if they don't agree about the answer.

RUSSELL: Well, certainly the question "Does the cause of the world exist?" is a question that has meaning. But if you say "Yes, God is the cause of the world" you're using God as a proper name; then "God exists" will not be a statement that has meaning; that is the position that I'm maintaining. Because, therefore, it will follow that it cannot be an analytic proposition ever to say that this or that exists. For example, suppose you take as your subject "the existent round-square," it would look like an analytic proposition that "the existent round-square exists," but it doesn't exist.

COPLESTON: No, it doesn't, then surely you can't say it doesn't exist unless you have a conception of what existence is. As to the phrase "existent round-square," I should say that it has no meaning at all.

RUSSELL: I quite agree. Then I should say the same thing in another context in reference to a "necessary being."

COPLESTON: Well, we seem to have arrived at an impasse. To say that a necessary being is a being that must exist and cannot not exist has for me a definite meaning. For you it has no meaning.

RUSSELL: Well, we can press the point a little, I think. A being that must exist and cannot not exist, would surely, according to you, be a being whose essence involves existence.

COPLESTON: Yes, a being the essence of which is to exist. But I should not be willing to argue the existence of God simply from the idea of His essence because I don't think we have any clear intuition of God's essence as yet. I think we have to argue from the world of experience to God.

RUSSELL: Yes, I quite see the distinction. But, at the same time, for a being with sufficient knowledge, it would be true to say "Here is this being whose essence involves existence!"

COPLESTON: Yes, certainly if anybody saw God, he would see that God must exist.

RUSSELL: So that I mean there is a being whose essence involves existence although we don't know that essence. We only know there is such a being.

COPLESTON: Yes, I should add we don't know the essence *a priori*. It is only *a posteriori* through our experience of the world that we come to a knowledge of the existence of that being. And then one argues, the essence and existence must be identical. Because if God's essence and God's existence was not identical, then some sufficient reason for this existence would have to be found beyond God.

RUSSELL: So it all turns on this question of sufficient reason, and I must say you haven't defined "sufficient reason" in a way that I can understand—what do you mean by sufficient reason? You don't mean cause?

COPLESTON: Not necessarily. Cause is a kind of sufficient reason. Only contingent being can have a cause. God is His own sufficient reason; and He is not cause of Himself. By sufficient reason in the full sense I mean an explanation adequate for the existence of some particular being.

RUSSELL: But when is an explanation adequate? Suppose I am about to make a flame with a match. You may say that the adequate explanation of that is that I rub it on the box.

COPLESTON: Well, for practical purposes—but theoretically, that is only a partial explanation. An adequate explanation must ultimately be a total explanation, to which nothing further can be added.

RUSSELL: Then I can only say that you're looking for something which can't be got, and which one ought not to expect to get.

COPLESTON: To say that one has not found it is one thing; to say that one should not look for it seems to me rather dogmatic.

RUSSELL: Well, I don't know. I mean, the explanation of one thing is another thing which makes the other thing dependent on yet another, and you have to grasp this sorry scheme of things entire to do what you want, and that we can't do.

COPLESTON: But are you going to say that we can't, or we shouldn't even raise the question of the existence of the whole of this sorry scheme of things—of the whole universe?

RUSSELL: Yes, I don't think there's any meaning in it at all. I think the word "universe" is a handy word in some connections, but I don't think it stands for anything that has a meaning.

COPLESTON: If the word is meaningless, it can't be so very handy. In any case, I don't say that the universe is something different from the objects which compose it (I indicated that in my brief summary of the proof), what I'm doing is to look for the reason, in this case the cause of the objects—the real or imagined totality of which constitute what we call the universe. You say, I think that the universe—or my existence if you prefer, or any other existence—is unintelligible?

RUSSELL: First may I take up the point that if a word is meaningless it can't be handy. That sounds well but isn't in fact correct. Take, say, such a word as "the" or "than." You can't point to any object that those words mean, but they are very useful words; I should say the same of "universe." But leaving that point, you ask whether I consider that the universe is unintelligible. I shouldn't say unintelligible—I think it is without explanation. Intelligible, to my mind, is a different thing. Intelligible has to do with the thing itself intrinsically and not with its relations.

COPLESTON: Well, my point is that what we call the world is intrinsically unintelligible, apart from the existence of God. You see, I don't believe that the infinity of the series of events—I mean a horizontal series, so to speak—if such an infinity could be proved, would be in the slightest degree relevant to the situation. If you add up chocolates you get chocolates after all and not a sheep. If you add up chocolates to infinity, you presumably get an infinite number of chocolates. So if you add up contingent beings to infinity, you still get contingent beings, not a necessary being. An infinite series of contingent beings will be, to my way of thinking, as unable to cause itself as one contingent being. However, you say, I think, that it is illegitimate to raise the question of what will explain the existence of any particular object?

RUSSELL: It's quite all right if you mean by explaining it, simply finding a cause for it.

COPLESTON: Well, why stop at one particular object? Why shouldn't one raise the question of the cause of the existence of all particular objects?

RUSSELL: Because I see no reason to think there is any. The whole concept of cause is one we derive from our observation of particular things; I see no reason whatsoever to suppose that the total has any cause whatsoever.

COPLESTON: Well, to say that there isn't any cause is not the same thing as saying that we shouldn't look for a cause. The statement that there isn't any cause should come, if it comes at all, at the end of the inquiry, not the beginning. In any case, if the total has no cause, then to my way of thinking it must be its own cause, which seems to me impossible. Moreover, the statement that the world is simply there if in answer to a question, presupposes that the question has meaning.

RUSSELL: No, it doesn't need to be its own cause, what I'm saying is that the concept of cause is not applicable to the total.

COPLESTON: Then you would agree with Sartre that the universe is what he calls "gratuitous"?

RUSSELL: Well, the word "gratuitous" suggests that it might be something else; I should say that the universe is just there, and that's all.

COPLESTON: Well, I can't see how you can rule out the legitimacy of asking the question how the total, or anything at all comes to be there. Why something rather than nothing, that is the question? The fact that we gain our knowledge of causality empirically, from particular causes, does not rule out the possibility of asking what the cause of the series is. If the word "cause" were meaningless or if it could be shown that Kant's view of the matter were correct, the question would be illegitimate I agree; but you don't seem to hold that the word "cause" is meaningless, and I do not suppose you are a Kantian.

RUSSELL: I can illustrate what seems to me your fallacy. Every man who exists has a mother, and it seems to me your argument is that therefore the human race must have a mother, but obviously the human race hasn't a mother—that's a different logical sphere.

COPLESTON: Well, I can't really see any parity. If I were saying "every object has a phenomenal cause, therefore, the whole series has a phenomenal cause," there would be a parity; but I'm not saying that; I'm saying, every object has a phenomenal cause if you insist on the infinity of the series—but the series of phenomenal causes is an insufficient explanation of the series. Therefore, the series has not a phenomenal cause but a transcendent cause.

RUSSELL: That's always assuming that not only every particular thing in the world, but the world as a whole must have a cause. For that assumption I see no ground whatever. If you'll give me a ground I'll listen to it.

COPLESTON: Well, the series of events is either caused or it's not caused. If it is caused, there must obviously be a cause outside the series. If it's not caused then it's sufficient to itself, and if it's sufficient to itself it is what I call necessary. But it can't be necessary since each member is contingent, and we've agreed that the total has no reality apart from its members, therefore, it can't be necessary. Therefore, it can't be (caused)—uncaused—therefore it must have a cause. And I should like to observe in passing that the statement "the world is simply there and is inexplicable" can't be got out of logical analysis.

RUSSELL: I don't want to seem arrogant, but it does seem to me that I can conceive things that you say the human mind can't conceive. As for things not having a cause, the physicists assure us that individual quantum transitions in atoms have no cause.

COPLESTON: Well, I wonder now whether that isn't simply a temporary inference.

RUSSELL: It may be, but it does show that physicists' minds can conceive it.

COPLESTON: Yes, I agree, some scientists—physicists—are willing to allow for indetermination within a restricted field. But very many scientists are not so willing. I think that Professor Dingle, of London University, maintains that the Heisenberg uncertainty principle tells us something about the success (or the lack of it) of the present atomic theory in correlating observations, but not about nature in itself, and many physicists would accept this view. In any case, I don't see how physicists can fail to accept the theory in practice, even if they don't do so in theory. I cannot see how science could be conducted on any other assumption than that of order and intelligibility in nature. The physicist presupposes, at least tacitly, that there is some sense in investigating nature and looking for the causes of events, just as the detective presupposes that there is some sense in looking for the cause of a murder. The metaphysician assumes that there is sense in looking for the reason or cause of phenomena, and, not being a Kantian, I consider that the metaphysician is as justified in his assumption as the physicist. When Sartre, for example, says that the world is gratuitous, I think that he has not sufficiently considered what is implied by "gratuitous."

RUSSELL: I think—there seems to me a certain unwarrantable extension here; a physicist looks for causes; that does not necessarily imply that there are causes everywhere. A man may look for gold without assuming that there is gold everywhere; if he finds gold, well and good, if he doesn't he's had bad luck. The same is true when the physicists look for causes. As for Sartre, I don't profess to know what he means, and I shouldn't like to be thought to interpret him, but for my part, I do think the notion of the world having an explanation is a mistake. I don't see why one should expect it to have, and I think what you say about what the scientist assumes is an over-statement.

COPLESTON: Well, it seems to me that the scientist does make some such assumption. When he experiments to find out some particular truth, behind that experiment lies the assumption that the universe is not simply discontinuous. There is the possibility of finding out a truth by experiment. The experiment may be a bad one, it may lead to no result, or not to the result that he wants, but that at any rate there is the possibility, through experiment, of finding out the truth that he assumes. And that seems to me to assume an ordered and intelligible universe.

RUSSELL: I think you're generalizing more than is necessary. Undoubtedly the scientist assumes that this sort of thing is likely to be found and will often be found. He does not assume that it will be found, and that's a very important matter in modern physics.

COPLESTON: Well, I think he does assume or is bound to assume it tacitly in practice. It may be that, to quote Professor Haldane, "when I light the gas under the kettle, some of the water molecules will fly off as vapor, and there is no way of finding out which will do so," but it doesn't follow necessarily that the idea of chance must be introduced except in relation to our knowledge.

RUSSELL: No it doesn't—at least if I may believe what he says. He's finding out quite a lot of things—the scientist is finding out quite a lot of things that are happening in the world, which are, at first, beginnings of causal chains—first causes which haven't in themselves got causes. He does not assume that everything has a cause.

COPLESTON: Surely that's a first cause within a certain selected field. It's relatively first cause.

RUSSELL: I don't think he'd say so. If there's a world in which most events, but not all, have causes, he will then be able to depict the probabilities and uncertainties by assuming that this particular event you're interested in probably has a cause. And since in any case you won't get more than probability that's good enough.

COPLESTON: It may be that the scientist doesn't hope to obtain more than probability, but in raising the question he assumes that the question of explanation has a meaning. But your general point then, Lord Russell, is that it's illegitimate even to ask the question of the cause of the world?

RUSSELL: Yes, that's my position.

COPLESTON: If it's a question that for you has no meaning, it's of course very difficult to discuss it, isn't it?

RUSSELL: Yes, it is very difficult. What do you say—shall we pass on to some other issue?

Chapter 4

CHARLES SANDERS PEIRCE

Charles Sanders Peirce (1839–1914), considered the founder of Pragmatism, was born in Cambridge, Massachusetts, the son of a Harvard University mathematician, who, recognizing that his son was a prodigy, educated the young Charles at home. He received his M.A. in mathematics and chemistry, and worked for three years at the Harvard astronomical observatory. From 1861 to 1891 he was associated with the U.S. Coastal and Geodetic Survey. He also lectured at Johns Hopkins University, but was never a permanent member of the faculty. He was eventually dismissed from his post on charges of cohabitation with a woman, who became his second wife, before he obtained a divorce from his first wife. Although Peirce deplored the popularization of his thought by William James, James was a loyal friend who not only introduced Pierce's theories to the intellectual public, but came to his rescue when he was destitute.

Peirce considered himself a logician, concerned with comprehensive scientific method. He identified a third type of reasoning in addition to the classic deduction and induction, which he called *abduction*, roughly, reasoning to the best explanation. "Philosophy ought to imitate the successful sciences in its methods, so far as to proceed only from tangible premises which can be subjected to careful scrutiny, and rather to the multitude and variety of its arguments than the conclusiveness of any one. Its reasoning should not form a chain which is no stronger than its weakest link, but a cable whose fibers may be ever so slender, provided they are sufficiently numerous and intimately connected." In this way Peirce rejects both Scholastic and Cartesian deductivism in favor of a more experimental type of reasoning, which depends on a community of scholars. He defined *truth* as the conclusions or the consensus, which the community of scientists would reach in an indefinite time. Indeed, he goes beyond this, defining "truth" as *public* propositions, "of which any person would come to be convinced if he carried his inquiry, his sincere search for immovable belief, far enough."

In our first selection, "How to Make Our Ideas Clear," Peirce argues that the goal of inquiry is to remove the disturbance of doubt with a settled *belief.* What is a belief? "It is the demicadence which closes a musical phrase in the symphony of our intellectual life." It also gives us a new starting place for thought and is a guide to action.

Our second reading. "The Presuppositions of Science: Common Sense and Religion," is an insightful comparative essay on the relationship between reason and sentiment or animal instinct, in which Peirce puts greater value in sentiments—approving of *sentimental conservatism*, the adherence to ideas that have worked for you and your community. In the last section he develops these thoughts about sentimentalism and applies them to the concept of faith, not as belief, but as trust and commitment.

FOR FURTHER READING

Ayer, A. J. *Origins of Pragmatism: Studies in the Philosophy of Charles Sanders Peirce and William James* (Macmillan, 1968).

Kuklick, Bruce. *The Rise of American Philosophy* (Yale University Press, 1977).
Murphy, John. *Pragmatism: From Peirce to Davidson* (Westview Press, 1990).
Peirce, C. S. *Essays in the Philosophy of Science* (Liberal Arts Library, 1957).
Quine, W. V. and Joseph Ullian. *The Web of Belief*, 2nd ed. (Random House, 1978).
Scheffler, Israel. *Four Pragmatists* (Humanities Press, 1974).
Smith, John. *The Spirit of American Philosophy* (Oxford University Press, 1963).
Stahr, John J. *Classical American Philosophy: Essential Reading and Interpretive* Essays (Oxford University Press, 1987).

How to Make Our Ideas Clear

I

Whoever has looked into a modern treatise on logic of the common sort, will doubtless remember the two distinctions between *clear* and *obscure* conceptions, and between *distinct* and *confused* conceptions. They have lain in the books now for nigh two centuries, unimproved and unmodified, and are generally reckoned by logicians as among the gems of their doctrine.

A clear idea is defined as one which is so apprehended that it will be recognized wherever it is met with, and so that no other will be mistaken for it. If it fails of this clearness, it is said to be obscure.

This is rather a neat bit of philosophical terminology; yet, since it is clearness that they were defining, I wish the logicians had made their definition a little more plain. Never to fail to recognize an idea, and under no circumstances to mistake another for it, let it come in how recondite a form it may, would indeed imply such prodigious force and clearness of intellect as is seldom met with in this world. On the other hand, merely to have such an acquaintance with the idea as to have become familiar with it, and to have lost all hesitancy in recognizing it in ordinary cases, hardly seems to deserve the name of clearness of apprehension, since after all it only amounts to a subjective feeling of mastery which may be entirely mistaken. I take it, however, that when the logicians speak of "clearness," they mean nothing more than such a familiarity with an idea, since they regard the quality as but a small merit, which needs to be supplemented by another, which they call *distinctness*.

A distinct idea is defined as one which contains nothing which is not clear. This is technical language; by the *contents* of an idea logicians understand whatever is contained in its definition. So that an idea is *distinctly* apprehended, according to them, when we can give a precise definition of it, in abstract terms. Here the professional logicians leave the subject; and I would not have troubled the reader with what they have to say, if it were not such a striking example of how they have been slumbering through ages of intellectual activity, listlessly disregarding the enginery of modern thought, and never dreaming of applying its lessons to the improvement of logic. It is easy to show that the doctrine that familiar use and abstract distinctness make the perfection of apprehension has its only true place in philosophies which have long been extinct; and it is now time to formulate the method of attaining to a more perfect clearness of thought, such as we see and admire in the thinkers of our own time.

When Descartes set about the reconstruction of philosophy, his first step was to (theoretically) permit skepticism and to discard the practice of the schoolmen of looking to authority as the ultimate source of truth. That done, he sought a more natural fountain of true principles, and professed to find it

From *The Popular Science Monthly*, Vol. 12, 1878, pp. 286ff.

in the human mind; thus passing, in the directest way, from the method of authority to that of apriority, as described in my first paper.

Self-consciousness was to furnish us with our fundamental truths, and to decide what was agreeable to reason. But since, evidently, not all ideas are true, he was led to note, as the first condition of infallibility, that they must be clear. The distinction between an idea *seeming* clear and really being so, never occurred to him. Trusting to introspection, as he did, even for a knowledge of external things, why should he question its testimony in respect to the contents of our own minds? But then, I suppose, seeing men, who seemed to be quite clear and positive, holding opposite opinions upon fundamental principles, he was further led to say that clearness of ideas is not sufficient, but that they need also to be distinct, i.e., to have nothing unclear about them. What he probably meant by this (for he did not explain himself with precision) was, that they must sustain the test of dialectical examination; that they must not only seem clear at the outset, but that discussion must never be able to bring to light points of obscurity connected with them.

Such was the distinction of Descartes, and one sees that it was precisely on the level of his philosophy. It was somewhat developed by Leibniz. This great and singular genius was as remarkable for what he failed to see as for what he saw. That a piece of mechanism could not do work perpetually without being fed with power in some form was a thing perfectly apparent to him; yet he did not understand that the machinery of the mind can only transform knowledge, but never originate it, unless it be fed with facts of observation. He thus missed the most essential point of the Cartesian philosophy, which is, that to accept propositions which seem perfectly evident to us is a thing which, whether it be logical or illogical, we cannot help doing. Instead of regarding the matter in this way, he sought to reduce the first principles of science to formulas which cannot be denied without self-contradiction, and was apparently unaware of the great difference between his position and that of Descartes. So he reverted to the old formalities of logic, and, above all, abstract definitions played a great part in his philosophy. It was quite natural, therefore, that on observing that the method of Descartes labored under the difficulty that we may seem to ourselves to have clear apprehensions of ideas which in truth are very hazy, no better remedy occurred to him than to require an abstract definition of every important term. Accordingly, in adopting the distinction of *clear* and *distinct* notions, he described the latter quality as the clear apprehension of everything contained in the definition; and the books have ever since copied his words. There is no danger that his chimerical scheme will ever again be overvalued. Nothing new can ever be learned by analyzing definitions. Nevertheless, our existing beliefs can be set in order by this process, and order is an essential element of intellectual economy, as of every other. It may be acknowledged, therefore, that the books are right in making familiarity with a notion the first step toward clearness of apprehension, and the defining of it the second. But in omitting all mention of any higher perspicuity of thought, they simply mirror a philosophy which was exploded a hundred years ago. That much-admired "ornament of logic"—the doctrine of clearness and distinctness—may be pretty enough, but it is high time to relegate to our cabinet of curiosities the antique *bijou*, and to wear about us something better adapted to modern uses.

The very first lesson that we have a right to demand that logic shall teach us is, how to make our ideas clear; and a most important one it is, depreciated only by minds who stand in need of it. To know what we think, to be masters of our own meaning, will make a solid foundation for great and weighty thought. It is most easily learned by those whose ideas are meagre and restricted; and far happier they than such as wallow helplessly in a rich mud of conceptions. A nation, it is true, may, in the course of generations, overcome the disadvantage of an excessive wealth of language and its natural concomitant, a vast, unfathomable deep of ideas. We may see it in history, slowly perfecting its literary forms, sloughing at length its metaphysics, and, by virtue of the untirable patience which is often a compensation, attaining great excellence in every branch of mental acquirement. The page of history is not yet unrolled which is to tell us whether such a people will or will not in the long-run prevail over one whose ideas (like the words of their language) are few, but which possesses a wonderful mastery over those which it has. For an individual, however, there can be no question that a few clear ideas are worth more than many confused ones. A young man would hardly be persuaded to sacrifice the greater part of his thoughts to save the rest; and the muddled head is the least apt to see the necessity of such a sacrifice. Him we can usually only commiserate, as a person with a congenital defect. Time will help him, but intellectual maturity with regard to clearness comes rather late, an unfortunate arrangement of Nature, inasmuch as clearness is of less use to a man settled in life, whose errors have in great measure had their effect, than it would be to one whose path lies before him. It is terrible to see how a single unclear idea, a single formula without meaning, lurking in a young man's head, will sometimes act like an obstruction of inert matter in an artery, hindering the nutrition of the brain, and condemning its victim to pine away in the fullness of his intellectual vigor and in the midst of intellectual plenty. Many a man has cherished for years as his hobby some vague shadow of an idea, too meaningless to be positively false; he has, nevertheless, passionately loved it, has made it his companion by day and by night, and has given to it his strength and his life, leaving all other occupations for its sake, and in short has lived with it and for it, until it has become, as it were, flesh of his flesh and bone of his bone; and then he has waked up some bright morning to find it gone, clean vanished away like the beautiful Melusina of the fable, and the essence of his life gone with it. I have myself known such a man; and who can tell how many histories of circle-squarers, metaphysicians, astrologers, and what not, may not be told in the old German story?

II

The principles set forth in the first of these papers lead, at once, to a method of reaching a clearness of thought of a far higher grade than the "distinctness" of the logicians. We have there found that the action of thought is excited by the irritation of doubt, and ceases when belief is attained; so that the production of belief is the sole function of thought. All these words, however, are too strong for my purpose. It is as if I had described the phenomena as they appear under a mental microscope. Doubt and Belief, as the words are commonly employed, relate to religious or other grave discussions. But here I use them to designate the starting of any question, no matter how small or how great, and the resolution of it. If, for instance, in a horse-car, I pull out my purse and find a five-cent nickel and five coppers, I decide, while my hand is going to the purse, in which way I will pay my fare. To call such a question Doubt, and my decision Belief, is certainly to use words very disproportionate to the occasion. To speak of such a doubt as causing an irritation which needs to be appeased, suggests a temper which is uncomfortable to the verge of insanity. Yet, looking at the matter minutely, it must be admitted that, if there is the least hesitation as to whether I shall pay the five coppers or the nickel (as there will be sure to be, unless I act from some previously contracted habit in the matter), though irritation is too strong a word, yet I am excited to such small mental activity as may be necessary to deciding how I shall act. Most frequently doubts arise from some indecision, however momentary, in our action. Sometimes it is not so. I have, for example, to wait in a railway-station, and to pass the time I read the advertisements on the walls, I compare the advantages of different trains and different routes which I never expect to take, merely fancying myself to be in a state of hesitancy, because I am bored with having nothing to trouble me. Feigned hesitancy, whether feigned for mere amusement or with a lofty purpose, plays a great part in the production of scientific inquiry. However the doubt may originate, it stimulates the mind to an activity which may be slight or energetic, calm or turbulent. Images pass rapidly through consciousness, one incessantly melting into another, until at last, when all is over—it may be in a fraction of a second, in an hour, or after long years—we find ourselves decided as to how we should act under such circumstances as those which occasioned our hesitation. In other words, we have attained belief.

In this process we observe two sorts of elements of consciousness, the distinction between which may best be made clear by means of an illustration. In a piece of music there are the separate notes, and there is the air. A single tone may be prolonged for an hour or a day, and it exists as perfectly in each second of that time as in the whole taken together; so that, as long as it is sounding, it might be present to a sense from which everything in the past was as completely absent as the future itself. But it is different with the air, the performance of which occupies a certain time, during the portions of which only portions of it are played. It consists in an orderliness in the succession of sounds which strike the ear at different times; and to perceive it there must be some continuity of consciousness which makes the events of a lapse of time present to us. We certainly only perceive the air by hearing the separate notes; yet we cannot be said to directly hear it, for we hear only what is present at the instant, and an orderliness of succession cannot exist in an instant. These two sorts of objects, what we are *immediately* conscious of and what we are *mediately* conscious of, are found in all consciouness. Some elements (the sensations) are completely present at every instant so long as they last, while others (like thought) are actions having beginning, middle, and end, and consist in a congruence in the succession of sensations which flow through the mind. They cannot be immediately present to us, but must cover some portion of the past or future. Thought is a thread of melody running through the succession of our sensations.

We may add that just as a piece of music may be written in parts, each part having its own air, so various systems of relationship of succession subsist together between the same sensations. These different systems are distinguished by having different motives, ideas, or functions. Thought is only one such system, for its sole motive, idea, and function, is to produce belief, and whatever does not concern that purpose belongs to some other system of relations. The action of thinking may incidentally have other results; it may serve to amuse us, for example, and among *dilettanti* it is not rare to find those who have so perverted thought to the purposes of pleasure that it seems to vex them to think that the questions upon which they delight to exercise it may ever get finally settled; and a positive discovery which takes a favorite subject out of the arena of literary debate is met with ill-concealed dislike. This disposition is the very debauchery of thought. But the soul and meaning of thought, abstracted from the other elements which accompany it, though it may be voluntarily thwarted, can never be made to direct itself toward anything but the production of belief. Thought in action has for its only possible motive the attainment of thought at rest; and what ever does not refer to belief is no part of the thought itself.

And what, then, is belief? It is the demicadence which closes a musical phrase in the symphony of our intellectual life. We have seen that it has just three properties: First, it is something that we are aware of; second, it appeases the irritation of doubt; and, third, it involves the establishment in our nature of a rule of action, or, say for short, a *habit*. As it appeases the irritation of doubt, which is the motive for thinking, thought relaxes, and comes to rest for a moment when belief is reached. But, since belief is a rule for action, the application of which involves further doubt and further thought, at the same time that it is a stopping-place, it is also a new starting-place for thought. That is why I have permitted myself to call it thought at rest, although thought is essentially an action. The *final* upshot of thinking is the exercise of volition, and of this thought no longer forms a part; but belief is only a stadium of mental action, an effect upon our nature due to thought, which will influence future thinking.

The essence of belief is the establishment of a habit, and different beliefs are distinguished by the different modes of action to which they give rise. If beliefs do not differ in this respect, if they appease the same doubt by producing the same rule of action, then no mere differences in the manner of consciousness of them can make them different beliefs, any more than playing a tune in different keys is playing different tunes. Imaginary distinctions are often drawn between beliefs which differ only in their mode of expression;—the wrangling which ensues is real enough, however. To believe that any objects are arranged in Fig. 1, and to believe that they are arranged in Fig. 2, are one and the same be-

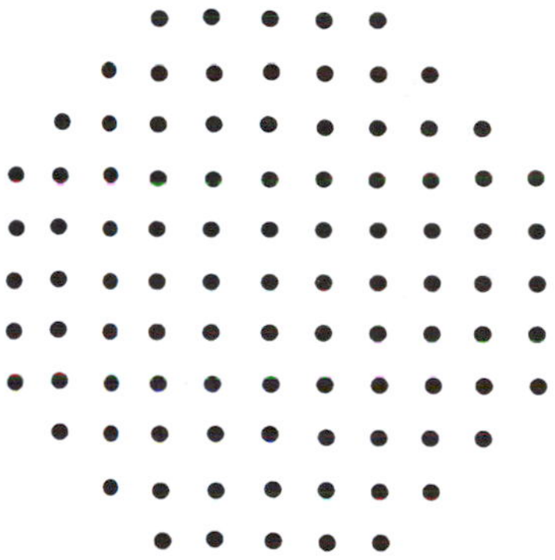

Fig. 1.

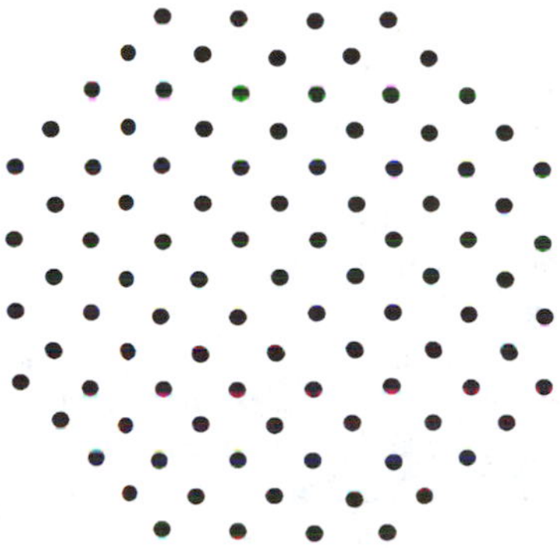

Fig. 2.

lief; yet it is conceivable that a man should assert one proposition and deny the other. Such false distinctions do as much harm as the confusion of beliefs really different, and are among the pitfalls of which we ought constantly to beware, especially when we are upon metaphysical ground. One singular deception of this sort, which often occurs, is to mistake the sensation produced by our unclearness of thought for a character of the object we are thinking. Instead of perceiving that the obscurity is purely subjective, we fancy that we contemplate a quality of the object which is essentially mysterious; and if our conception be afterward presented to us in a clear form we do not recognize it as the same, owing to the absence of the feeling of unintelligibility. So long as this deception lasts, it obviously puts an impassable barrier in the way of perspicuous thinking; so that it equally interests the opponents of rational thought to perpetuate it, and its adherents to guard against it.

Another such deception is to mistake a mere difference in the grammatical construction of two words for a distinction between the ideas they express. In this pedantic age, when the general mob of writers attend so much more to words than to things, this error is common enough. When I just said that thought is an *action*, and that it consists in a *relation*, although a person performs an action but not a relation, which can only be the result of an action, yet there was no inconsistency in what I said, but only a grammatical vagueness.

From all these sophisms we shall be perfectly safe so long as we reflect that the whole function of thought is to produce habits of action; and that whatever there is connected with a thought, but irrelevant to its purpose, is an accretion to it, but no part of it. If there be a unity among our sensations which has no reference to how we shall act on a given occasion, as when we listen to a piece of music, why we do not call that thinking. To develop its meaning, we have, therefore, simply to determine what habits it produces, for what a thing means is simply what habits it involves. Now, the identity of a habit depends on how it might lead us to act, not merely under such circumstances are likely to arise, but under such as might possibly occur, no matter how improbable they may be. What the habit is depends on *when* and *how* it causes us to act. As for the *when*, every stimulus to action is derived from perception; as for the *how*, every purpose of action is to produce some sensible result. Thus, we come down to what is tangible and practical, as the root of every real distinction of thought, no matter how subtle it may be; and there is no distinction of meaning so fine as to consist in anything but a possible difference of practice.

To see what this principle leads to, consider in the light of it such a doctrine as that of transubstantiation. The Protestant churches generally hold that the elements of the sacrament are flesh and blood only in a tropical sense; they nourish our souls as meat and the juice of it would our bodies. But the Catholics maintain that they are literally just that; although they possess all the sensible qualities of wafer-cakes and diluted wine. But we can have no conception of wine except what may enter into a belief, either—

1. That this, that, or the other, is wine; or,

2. That wine possesses certain properties.

Such beliefs are nothing but self-notifications that we should, upon occasion, act in regard to such things as we believe to be wine according to the qualities which we believe wine to possess. The occasion of such action would be some sensible perception, the motive of it to produce some sensible result. Thus our action has exclusive reference to what affects the senses, our habit has the same bearing as our action, our belief the same as our habit, our conception the same as our belief; and we can consequently mean nothing by wine but what has certain effects, direct or indirect, upon our senses; and to talk of something as having all the sensible characters of wine, yet being in reality blood, is senseless jargon. Now, it is not my object to pursue the theological question; and having used it as a logical example I drop it, without caring to anticipate the theologian's reply. I only desire to point out how impossible it is that we should have an idea in our minds which relates to anything but conceived sensible effects of things. Our idea of anything *is* our idea of its sensible effects; and if we fancy that we have any other we deceive ourselves, and mistake a mere sensation accompanying the thought for a part of the thought itself. It is absurd to say that thought has any meaning unrelated to its only function. It is foolish for Catholics and Protestants to fancy themselves in disagreement about the elements of the sacrament, if they agree in regard to all their sensible effects, here or hereafter.

It appears, then, that the rule for attaining the third grade of clearness of apprehension is as follows: Consider what effects, which might conceivably have practical bearings, we conceive the object of our conception to have. Then, our conception of these effects is the whole of our conception of the object. . . .

The Presuppositions of Science: Common Sense and Religion

PROLOGUE

I have a difficult task before me to render these four lectures profitable to you. It would be less so if you came without a single idea on the subject. But everybody, every butcher and baker, has ideas of logic and [has] even used the technical terminology of the subject. He says he deals in articles of "prime necessity." Perhaps he would be surprised to learn that the phrase "prime necessity" was invented by logicians to express a logical conception which has now become in common mouths very vague, it is true; but which still has a little of the original concept in a vague form clinging to it.

If I had a class in logic to conduct for a year, I should harp still, as I used to do at the Johns Hopkins, upon the maieutic character of my office,—which means that I should do all I could to make my hearers think for themselves, by which I earned the gratitude of men who are useful to mankind. I should insist that they must not suppose that my opinions were bound to be correct, but must work out their own ways of thinking. But now that there are but four lectures, and all falling in one week, the case is otherwise. I must beg you to remember that comprehension comes first and criticism later. It will be as much as you can possibly do in this week with diligent endeavors, to understand what I mean by logic and what the general outline of my system is. In order to do as much as that you must endeavor to take up a sympathetic attitude,—to try to catch what it is that I am driving at, and to store up in your minds an outline of my theory which you will subject to criticism in the months to come.

In order that you may understand me, that you may for this one week put yourselves, as far as you can, in my intellectual shoes,—leaving yourselves to decide only after you have worn them for awhile whether they really fit or not,—[. . .] I am going to begin by telling you something about my classification of the sciences; because it will aid you in the difficult task of imbibing my notion of the kind of science that I hold logic to be.

COMMON SENSE

Among the advantages which our humble cousins whom it pleases us to refer to as "the lower animals" enjoy over some of our own family is that they *never* reason about vitally important topics, and never have to lecture nor to listen to lectures about them. Docilely allowing themselves to be guided by their instincts into almost every detail of life, they live exactly as their Maker intended them to live. The result is, that they very rarely fall into error of any kind, and *never* into a vital one. What a contrast to our lives! Truly, that Reason upon which we so plume ourselves, though it may answer for little things, yet for great decisions is hardly surer than a toss-up.

The Prologue is from *MS* 1334, Lecture I to the Adirondack Summer School, 1905. The sections "Common Sense" and "Religion" are from *MS* 435, Lecture I, "On Detached Ideas in General, and on Vitally Important Topics as such," 1898. The subsection "Faith" is from *MS L* 463, Peirce to Welby, December 23, 1908. The subsection "Science Presupposes God" is from *MS* 436, Lecture I, 1898. None of these lectures were delivered.

The mental qualities we most admire in human kind, the maiden's delicacy, the mother's devotion, manly courage, are merely instincts and inheritances from the biped who did not yet speak; while the characters that are most contemptible, such as, backbiting, treachery, hyprocrisy, thieving, will be found if the students of the psychology of criminals are to be trusted, to be effects of reasoning. Undoubtedly we are compelled to reason a little, unless we can hire servants to do it for us. Accounts have to be kept either by ourselves or by our clerks. Logic is computation, said Hobbes; and those who have deepest delved in that dreary discipline testify that all reasoning whatever involves mathematics, and laugh over the fallacies of those who attempt to reason unmathematically. Now tell me, is mathematics an occupation for a gentleman and an athlete? Is not such drudgery fit only for the lower classes? One may well be struck with pity for the masses of population concentrated in New York and living under such unnatural conditions that they are forced to think mathematically. However, it is not as if they had the tender nurture of a cultured modern Harvard, that great eleemosynary institution that Massachusetts has established to the end that the *élite* of her youths may be aided to earning comfortable incomes and living softly cultured lives. The brains of those New York plebeians are coarse, strong, laboring brains, who don't know what it is to be free from mathematics. Their conceptions are crude and vulgar enough, but their vigor of reasoning would surprise you. I have seen my [private] scholars there wrestle with problems that I would no more venture to allow the exquisitely polished intellects of a modern university to attack than I would venture to toss a cannonball into an eggshell cup.

I intend to call upon you for no reasoning in these lectures more complicated than one of Hegel's dilemmas. For all reasoning is mathematical and requires effort; and I mean to shun the guilt of overstraining anybody's powers. That is why I have selected a subject for my lectures which is not at all in my line, but which I hope may prove to be to your taste.

I entitle the whole course Detached Ideas on Topics of Vital Importance. In this introductory lecture I shall submit to your judgment some reflections about Detached Ideas in general, and about Vitally important Topics in general.

On vitally important topics reasoning is out of place. The very theory of reasoning, were we resolutely to attack it without any dread of mathematics, would furnish us conclusive reasons for limiting the applicability of reasoning to unimportant matters; so that, unless a problem is insignificant in importance compared with the aggregate of analogous problems, reasoning itself pronounces that there is a fallacy in submitting the question to reason, at all. That must remain merely an assertion, mathematics being *taboo*. But possibly before the course is complete, you may [be] able to get a glimpse of the general drift of the demonstration of it. Let the assertion go at present for what it is worth.

In regard to the greatest affairs of life, the wise man follows his heart and does not trust his head. This should be the method of every man, no matter how powerful his intellect. More so still, perhaps, if mathematics is too difficult for him, that is to say, if he is unequal to any intricate reasoning whatsoever. Would not a man physically puny be a fool not to recognize it, and to allow an insane megalomania to induce him to enter a match game of football? But the slightest of physical frames might as well attempt to force back a locomotive engine, as for the mightiest of mental giants to try to regulate his life advantageously by a purely reasoned out theory.

Common sense, which is the resultant of the traditional experience of mankind, witnesses unequivocally that the heart is more than the head, and is in fact everything in our highest concerns, thus agreeing with my unproved logical theorem; and those persons who think that sentiment has no part in common sense forget that the dicta of common sense are objective facts, not the way some dyspeptic may feel, but what the healthy, natural, normal democracy thinks. And yet when you open the next new book on the philosophy of religion that comes out, the chances are that it will be written by an intellectualist who in his preface offers you his metaphysics as a guide for the soul, talking as if philosophy were one of our deepest concerns. How can the writer so deceive himself?

If, walking in a garden on a dark night, you were suddenly to hear the voice of your sister crying to you to rescue her from a villain, would you stop to reason out the metaphysical question of whether it were possible for one mind to cause material waves of sound and for another mind to perceive them? If you did, the problem might probably occupy the remainder of your days. In the same way, if a man undergoes any religious experience and hears the call of his Saviour, for him to halt till he has adjusted a philosophical difficulty would seem to be an analogous sort of thing, whether you call it stupid or whether you call it disgusting. If on the other hand, a man has had no religious experience, then any religion not an affectation is as yet impossible for him; and the only worthy course is to wait quietly till such experience comes. No amount of speculation can take the place of experience.

Pray pardon my hopping about from one branch of my discourse to another and back again with no more apparent purpose than a robin redbreast or a Charles Lamb. Because it would hardly be logically consistent for me to arrange my matter with scrupulously logical accuracy when the very thing I am driving at is that logic and reasoning are only of secondary importance. There are two psychological or anthropological observations about our reasoning powers which it is convenient to insert here.

One is that powers of reasoning in any but the most rudimentary way are a somewhat uncommon gift, about as uncommon as a talent for music. Indeed, a much smaller number of persons actually attain to any proficiency in reasoning. But then the exercise of intricate ratiocination requires great energy and prolonged effort, while musical practice is nearly unmixed pleasure, I suppose, for those who do it well. Moreover, owing to several peculiar circumstances, good instruction in reasoning is exceedingly rare. As for what is taught in the colleges under the name of logic, oh dear, perhaps the less said the better. It is true that mathematics teaches one branch of reasoning. That is, indeed, its chief value in education. But how few teachers understand the logic of mathematics! And how few understand the psychology of the puzzled pupil! The pupil meets with a difficulty in Euclid. Two to one the reason is that there is a logical flaw. The boy, however, is conscious only of a mysterious hindrance. What his difficulty is he cannot tell the teacher; the teacher must teach him. Now the teacher probably never really saw the true logic of the passage. But he thinks he does because, owing to long familiarity, he has lost the sense of coming up against an invisible barrier that the boy feels. Had the teacher ever really conquered the logical difficulty himself, of course he would recognize just what it was, and thus would fulfill the first condition, at least, of being helpful. But not having conquered the difficulty, but only having worn out the sense of difficulty by familiarity, he simply cannot understand why the boy should feel any difficulty; and all he can do is to exclaim, "Oh, these stupid, stupid boys!" As if a physician should exclaim, "Oh, these horrid patients, they won't get well!" But suppose, by some extraordinary conjunction of the planets, a really good teacher of reasoning were to be appointed, what would be his first care? It would be to guard his scholars from that malady with which logic is usually infested, so that unless it runs off them like water from a duck, it is sure to make them the very worst of reasoners, namely, unfair reasoners, and what is worse unconsciously unfair, for the rest of their lives. The good teacher will therefore take the utmost pains to prevent the scholars getting puffed up with their logical acquirement. He will wish to impregnate them with the right way of looking at reasoning before they shall be aware that they have learned anything; and he will not mind giving considerable time to that, for it is worth a great deal. But now come the examiner and the pupil himself. They want *results*, tangible to them. The teacher is dismissed as a failure, or, if he is allowed another chance, he will take good care to reverse the method of his teaching and give them *results*,—especially, as that is the lazy way. These are some of the causes of there being so few strong reasoners in the world. But allowing for the influence of such causes as well as we can, the fact still remains that comparatively few persons are originally possessed of any but the feeblest modicum of this talent. What is the significance of that? Is it not a plain sign that the faculty of reasoning is not of the first importance to success in life? For were it so, its absence would cause the individual to postpone marriage and so affect his procreation; and thus natural selection would operate to breed the race for vigorous reasoning powers, and they would become common. And the study of characters confirms this conclusion. For though the men who are most extraordinarily successful evidently do reason deeply about the details of their business, yet no ordinary degrees of good success are influenced,—otherwise than perhaps favorably,—by any lack of great reasoning power. We all know highly successful men, lawyers, editors, scientific men,—not to speak of artists—whose great deficiency in this regard is only revealed by some unforeseen accident.

The other observation I desired to make about the human reason is that we find people mostly modest enough about qualities which really go to making fine men and women,—the courageous man not usually vaunting his courage, nor the modest woman boasting of her modesty, nor the loyal vain of their good faith: the things they are vain about are some insignificant gifts of beauty, or skill of some kind. But beyond all, with the exception of those who, being trained in logic, follow its rules and thus do not trust their direct reasoning powers at all, everybody else ridiculously overrates his own logic, and if he really has superior powers of reason is usually so consumed by conceit, that it is far from rare to see a young man completely ruined by it; so that one is sometimes tempted to think, and perhaps truly, that it conduces not only to a man's success from a worldly point of view but to his attaining any real elevation of character to be all but a fool in this regard, provided only he be perfectly aware of his own deficiency.

But however unimportant logical vigor may be there are a few careers which a man who is deficient in mathematics would do well to avoid. He had better not cherish much ambition in the direction of philosophy. As *professor* of philosophy he might pass muster. Several very useful German books remind us of this. But he will not be of much service to philosophy itself. It is true that as this subject has hitherto been treated, its reasonings have been of the very simplest. And though they may cease to be so simple after the logic of relatives shall have been digested and assimilated, yet that will not happen for a good many years. There are, however, two peculiarities of metaphysics which are of decisive importance in this connection.

Permit me here to interrupt what I am saying in order to explain to you, once for all, the senses which I attach to the words philosophy and metaphysics. I define *philosophy* as that branch of science which is founded in the main upon such experience as is familiar to every man, and which experience, owing to its extreme familiarity, no man ever did or ever will really doubt, so that the conclusions of philosophy *ought* to carry,—and *would*, I suppose, carry were it only investigated according [to] a really scientific method,—a degree of certitude, a sort of necessity, which can belong to none of the sciences which rest upon special, or recondite, experiences. I define philosophy in this way because the division of sciences according to the departments of experience with which they deal gives more natural groups than any other principle of division except that according to their abstractness, which is Comte's principle followed also by Spencer. But this latter principle is, taken by itself, insufficient and too vague; and besides the two substantially agree in their results. We must not indeed forbid to a science, especially not to philosophy, resort to any premises or methods whatsoever. Philosophy may adduce as data results of special sciences. But it is distinguished from other sciences in resting mainly upon familiar experiences. That gives it its character, its abstractness, its universality, and the sort of necessity which marks it. Above it in Comte's scale, as I would reform that scale, stands only pure abstract mathematics, which makes no inquiry at all into what is the fact, but studies only hypotheses. When all the possible hypotheses of mathematics shall be seen to form a continuum, or cosmos, as they are already beginning to do, then mathematics will stand out as the queen of the sciences, to which all the others even philosophy are but adjuvant. For it will contain the ideal essence of them all, but purified from brute existence and rounded out into the perfection they do not attain. . . .

Conservatism, true conservatism, which is sentimental conservatism, and by those who have no powers of observation to see what sort of men conservatives are, is often called stupid conservatism, an epithet far more applicable to the false conservatism that looks to see on which side bread is buttered,—true conservatism, I say, means not trusting to reasonings about questions of vital importance but rather to hereditary instincts and traditional sentiments. Place before the conservative arguments to which he can find no adequate reply and which go, let us say, to demonstrate that wisdom and virtue call upon him to offer to marry his own sister, and though he be unable to answer the arguments, he will not act upon their conclusion, because he believes that tradition and the feelings that tradition and custom have developed in him are safer guides than his own feeble ratiocination. Thus, true conservatism is sentimentalism. Of course, sentiment lays no claim to infallibility, in the sense of *theoretical infallibility*, a phrase that logical analysis proves to be a mere jingle of words with a jungle of contradictory meanings. The conservative need not forget that he might have been born a Brahmin with a traditional sentiment in favor of *suttee*,—a reflection that tempts him to become a radical. But still, on the whole, he thinks his wisest plan is to reverence his deepest sentiments as his highest and ultimate authority, which is regarding them as *for him practically infallible*,—that is, to say infallible in the only sense of the word in which *infallible* has any consistent meaning.

The opinion prevalent among radicals that conservatives, and sentimentalists generally, are fools is only a cropping-out of the tendency of men to conceited exaggeration of their reasoning powers. Uncompromising radical though I be upon some questions, inhabiting all my life an atmosphere of science, and not reckoned as particularly credulous, I must confess that the conservative sentimentalism I have defined recommends itself to my mind as eminently sane and wholesome. Commendable as it undoubtedly is to reason out matters of detail, yet to allow mere reasonings and reason's self-conceit to [override], the normal and manly sentimentalism which ought to lie at the cornerstone of all our conduct seems to me to be foolish and despicable.

Philosophy after all is, at its highest valuation, nothing more than a branch of science, and as such is not a matter of vital importance; and those who represent it as being so are simply offering us a stone when we ask for bread. Mind, I do not deny that a philosophical or other scientific error may be fraught with disastrous consequences for the whole people. It might conceivably bring about the extirpation of the human race. Importance in that sense it might have in any degree. Nevertheless, in no case is it of *vital* importance.

A great calamity the error may be, *qua* event, in the sense in which an earthquake, or the impact of a comet, or the extinction of the sun would be an important event, and consequently, if it happens to lie in the line of my duty or of yours to investigate any philosophical question and to publish the more or less erroneous results of our investigations, I hope we shall not fail to do so, if we can. Certainly, any task which lies before us to be done has its importance. But there our responsibility ends. Nor is it the philosophy itself, *qua* cognition, that is vital, so much as it is our playing the part that is allotted to us.

You will observe that I have not said a single word in disparagement of the philosophy of religion, in general, which seems to me a most interesting study, at any rate, and possibly likely to lead to some useful result. Nor have I attacked any sect of that philosophy. It is not the philosophy which I hold to be baleful, but the representing it to be of vital importance, as if any genuine religion could come from the head instead of from the heart.

Somewhat allied to the philosophy of religion is the science of ethics. It is equally useless. Now books of casuistry, indeed, using the word "casuistry" not in any technical sense, but merely to signify discussions of what ought to be done in various difficult situations, might be made at once extremely entertaining and positively useful. But casuistry is just what the ordinary treatises upon ethics do not touch, at least not seriously. They chiefly occupy themselves with reasoning out the basis of morality and other questions secondary to that. Now what's the *use* of prying into the philosophical basis of morality? We all know what morality is: it is behaving as you were brought up to behave, that is, to think you ought to be punished for not behaving. But to believe in thinking as you have been brought up to think defines *conservatism*. It needs no reasoning to perceive that morality is conservatism. But conservatism again means, as you will surely agree, not trusting to one's reasoning powers. To be a moral man is to obey the traditional maxims of your community without hesitation or discussion. Hence, ethics, which is reasoning out an explanation of morality is,—I will not say immoral, [for] that would be going too far,—composed of the very substance of immorality. If you ever happen to be thrown in with an unprofessional thief, the only very bad kind of thief, so as to be able to study his psychological peculiarities, you will find that two things characterize him; first, an even more immense conceit in his own reasoning powers than is common, and second, a disposition to reason about the basis of morals.

Ethics, then, even if not a positively dangerous study, as it sometimes proves, is as useless a science as can be conceived. But it must be said, in favor of ethical writers, that they are commonly free from the nauseating custom of boasting of the utility of their science.

RELIGION

Among vitally important truths there is one which I verily verily believe,—and which men of infinitely deeper insight than mine have believed,—to be solely supremely important. It is that vitally important facts are of all truths the veriest trifles. For the only vitally important matter is *my* concern, business, and duty,—or yours. Now you and I,—what are, we? Mere cells of the social organism. Our deepest sentiment pronounces the verdict of our own insignificance. Psychological analysis shows that there is nothing which distinguishes my personal identity except my faults and my limitations,—or if, you please my blind will, which it is my highest endeavor to annihilate. Not in the contemplation of "topics of vital importance" but in those universal things with which philosophy deals, the factors of the universe, is man to find his highest occupation. To pursue "topics of vital importance" as the first and best can lead only to one or other of two terminations,—either on the one hand what is called I hope not justly, Americanism, the worship of business, the life in which the fertilizing stream of genial sentiment dries up or shrinks to a rill of comic tit-bits, or else on the other hand, to monasticism, sleepwalking in this world with no eye nor heart except for the other. Take for the lantern of your footsteps the cold light of reason and regard your business, your duty, as the highest thing, and you can only rest in one of those goals or the other. But suppose you embrace, on the contrary, a conservative sentimentalism, modestly rate your own reasoning powers at the very mediocre price they would fetch if put up at auction, and *then* what do you come to? Why, *then*, the very first command that is laid upon you, your quite highest business and duty, becomes, as everybody knows, to recognize a higher business than your business, *not* merely an avocation after the daily task of your vocation is performed, but a generalized conception of duty which completes your personality by melting it into the neighboring parts of the universal cosmos. If this sounds unintelligible, just take for comparison the first good mother of a family that meets your eye, and ask whether she is not a sentimentalist, whether you would wish her to be otherwise, and lastly whether you can find a better formula in which to outline the universal features of her portrait than that I have just given. I dare say you can improve upon that; but you will find one element of it is correct,—especially if your understanding is aided by the logic of relatives,—and that is that the supreme commandment of the Buddhist-Christian religion is, to generalize, to complete the whole system even until continuity results and the distinct individuals weld together. Thus, it is that while reasoning and the science of reasoning strenuously proclaim the subordination of reasoning to sentiment, the very supreme commandment of sentiment is that man should generalize, or what the logic of relatives shows to be the same thing [,] should become welded into the universal continuum, which is what true reasoning consists in. But this does not reinstate reasoning [,] for this generalization should come about, not merely in man's cognitions, which are but the superficial film of his being, but objectively, in the deepest emotional springs of his life. In fulfilling this command, man prepares himself for transmutation into a new form of life, the joyful Nirvana in which the discontinuities of his will shall have all but disappeared.

Do you know what it was that was at the root of the barbarism of the Plantagenet period and paralyzed awakening science from the days of Roger Bacon to those of Francis Bacon? We plainly trace it in the history, the writings, the monuments of that age. It was the exaggerated interest men took in matters of vital importance.

Do you know what it is in Christianity that when recognized makes our religion an agent of reform and progress? It is its marking duty as its proper finite figure. Not that it diminishes in any degree its vital importance, but that behind the outline of that huge mountain it enables us to descry a silvery peak rising into the calm air of eternity.

The generalization of sentiment can take place on different sides. Poetry is one sort of generalization of sentiment, and in so far is the regenerative metamorphosis of sentiment. But poetry remains on one side ungeneralized, and to that is due its emptiness. The complete generalization, the complete regeneration of sentiment is religion, which is poetry, but poetry completed.

That is about what I had to say to you about topics of vital importance. To sum it up, all sensible talk about vitally important topics must be commonplace, all reasoning about them unsound, and all study of them narrow and sordid.

Faith

Dear Lady Welby, for the past week all my time and all my energy have been taken up with what we Yankees (i.e. the stock of those who came over to Massachusetts before 1645,—I forget the exact date,) call "chores." I believe that in standard English the word is lost. It means the menial offices of every day in a household, especially, a primitive household,—the hewing of wood and the drawing of water and the like.

I now return to the expression of my abhorrence of the doctrine that any proposition whatever is infallibly true. Unless truth be recognized as *public*,—as that of which *any* person would come to be convinced if he carried his inquiry, his sincere search for immovable belief, far enough,—then there will be nothing to prevent each one of us from adopting an utterly futile belief of his own which all the rest will disbelieve. Each one will set himself up as a little prophet; that is, a little "crank," a half-witted victim of his own narrowness.

But if Truth be something public, it must mean that to the acceptance of which as a basis of conduct any person you please would ultimately come if he pursued his inquiries far enough;—yes, every rational being, however prejudiced he might be at the outset. For Truth has that compulsive nature which Pope well expressed:

> The eternal years of God are her's.

But, you will say, I am setting up this very proposition as infallible truth. Not at all; it is a mere definition. I do not say that it is infallibly true that there is any belief to which a person would come if he were to carry his inquiries far enough. I only say that that alone is what I call Truth. I cannot infallibly know that there is any Truth.

You say there is a certain "Faith" the object of which is absolutely "certain." Will you have the goodness to tell me what you mean by "certain"? Does it mean anything more than that you personally are obstinately resolved upon sticking to the proposition, *ruat caelum*? It reminds me of an anecdote that was told me in 1859 by a southern darky. "You know," says he, "massa, that General Washington and General Jackson was great friends, dey was (the fact being that the latter was an irreconcilable opponent of the former, but did not become a figure in national politics until after Washington had retired from public life). Well, one day Gen'l. Washington, he said to Gen'l. Jackson, "Gen'l, how tall should you think that horse of mine was?" "I don't know, General," says General Jackson, "how tall is he, General Washington?" "Why," says General Washington, "he is sixteen feet high." "Feet, General Washington," say Gen'ral Jackson, "feet, General Washington? You means *hands*, Gen'ral!" "Did I say *feet*, General Jackson," said General Washington. "Do you mean to say that I said my horse was sixteen *feet* high?" "You certainly said so, General Washington." "Very well, then, Gen'ral Jackson, if I *said* feet, *if* I said feet, then I sticks to it!" Is your "sublime faith" any more "sublime" than that? How?

Now I will tell you the meaning that *I* would, in my turn, attach to the word faith. The New Testament word is πιστιζ, which means, in its most proper sense, *trust*; i.e. belief in something not as having any knowledge or approach to knowledge about the matter of belief, but "implicit belief," as the catholics say, i.e. belief in it derived from one's belief that a witness who testifies to it would not so testify if it were not so. Hence, the latest writers of classical Greek, such as Plato and Isocrates, and the earliest writers of common Greek, such as Aristotle, use it for any mediate belief, any belief well founded on another belief. That is, these writers apply πιζτιζ to an assured belief. They also apply it to an *assurance* of any belief. But the English word "faith" could not be used so without great violence to usage which would be entirely unwarranted by any need. I think that what the word is needed to express, and what it might be restricted to express without too great violence to usage is *that belief which the believer does not himself recognize*, or rather (since that cannot properly be called belief), that which he is prepared to conform his conduct to, without recognizing what it is to which he is conforming his conduct. For example, if I do not know what Liddell & Scott say is the meaning of πιστισ but am convinced that whatever they may say is its meaning really is so, I have a *faith* that it is so. A person who says "Oh, I could not believe that this life is our only life; for if I did I should be so miserable that I should suicide forthwith," I say that he has a *Faith* that things are not intolerably bad for any individual or at any rate are not so for *him*. Every true man of science, i.e. every man belonging to a social group all the members of which sacrifice all the ordinary motives of life to their desire to make their beliefs concerning one subject conform to verified judgments of perception together with sound reasoning, and who therefore really believes the universe to be governed by reason, or in other words by God,—but who does not explicitly recognize that he believes in God,—has Faith in God, according to my use of the term Faith. For example, I knew a scientific man who devoted his last years to reading theology in hopes of coming to a belief in God, but who never could in the least degree come to a consciousness of having the least belief of the sort, yet passionately pursued that very mistaken means of attaining his heart's supreme desire. He, according to me, was a shining example of Faith in God. For to believe in reasoning about phenomena is to believe that they are governed by reason, that is, by God. That to my mind is a high and wholesome belief. One is often in a situation in which one is obliged to assume, i.e. to go upon, a proposition which one ought to recognize as extremely doubtful. But in order to conduct oneself with vigorous consistency one must dismiss doubts on the matter from consideration. There is a vast difference between *that* and any holding of the proposition for certain. To hold a proposition to be certain is to puff oneself up with the vanity of perfect knowledge. It leaves no room for Faith. It is not absolutely certain that twice two is four. It is humanly certain that no conception of God can be free from all error. I once made a careful study of Dr. Schaff's three solid volumes on "The Creeds of Christendom." I found not one that said one word about the principle of love, although that seems to be the leading element of Christian faith. In order to find out, if I could, the reason for this passing strange omission, I made a study of the circumstances which determined the formulation of each Symbolum, and ascertained that, with the possible exception of what we erroneously call "The Apostle's Creed," concerning whose origin we have no definite information, but which is no exception as regards the information in question, and certainly does not breathe the spirit of such early documents as the Didache, every one sprang from the *odium theologicum* and the desire to have some certain person excommunicated, with the evident wish that he might be damned. Theology arises from discontent with religious Faith,—which implies a lack of such Faith, and with a desire to substitute for that a scientific anatomy and physiology of God, which, rightly considered, is blasphemous and antireligious. It is also in most striking disaccord with the spirit of the son of Mary.

Your pleading that I should not use such a phrase as "attractive fancy" and I suppose you might feel so about the phrase "strictly hypothetical God" seems to show that I quite failed to convey my own sense of the value of the Neglected Argument, in that it does not lead to any theology at all, but only to what *I* mean by a purely religious *Faith*, which will have already taken deep root before the subject of it thinks of it at all as a belief. Writing this is like having to explain a joke. . . .

. . . By the way, when I was speaking of creeds, I might have mentioned . . . that I say the creed in church with the rest. By doing so I only signify, as I presume the majority do,—I hope they do;—my willingness to put aside, most heartily, anything that tends to separate me from my fellow Christians. For the very ground of my criticism of creeds is that every one of them was originally designed to produce such a separation, contrary to the notions of him who said "He that is not against me is for me." By the way, I have been reading, with much study, the book of W. B. Smith entitled *Der vorchristliche Jesus*, which I have little doubt is sound in the main; and I think probably Christianity was a higher development out of Buddhism, modified by Jewish belief in a living god. . . .

Science Presupposes God

I would have liked to have made all this quite plain, so that you could have perceived its exact truth as evident. But it happens that no dificult reasoning can be made evident and exact without mathematics; and I regret that however victorious Harvard may be in contests of atheletics, the vigor of mind requisite for diagrammatic reasoning is wanting here. I regret it, because what I say to you, put in the rough and apparently arbitrary and maimed way in which I am driven to hinting it, seems at once commonplace and enigmatic, the taste of which is like sugar and salt. But there is one great comfort for us all. It is that the historical development of man has now reached a stage at which all our intellectual feebleness will be made up, in two or three centuries [,] because the race which is wanting in vigor of thought is now sure to be supplanted by a race that can reason mathematically without being overcome by that tired feeling. Perhaps it will be the Japanese who are certainly superior to us in every respect except brute vigor, and to whom, therefore, we ought to be very willing to surrender our empire. At any rate, we must either quit or work, in whichever way the current of civilization finds the path of least resistance.

It was over the door of Plato's Academy that was put up the notice "No admission for those ignorant of mathematics. "Ah! Were it only from the Academy that he was debarred. He is utterly cut off from all contemplation of the rational. His reason is embryological. Between him and all the perfections which the Cosmos approaches or suggests, a dense fog obstructs all vision. He is bound down to his five senses and to the day's happenings, like a poor dog. And to think that emancipation from all this is possible by a sufficient effort, but that the man cannot screw his courage up to making that effort!

It is true that there is no treatise on the parts of mathematics which are valuable not as a utensil but as the crown of a freeman's education. I would not for the world say anything in disparagment of Schröder's Logik. Yet I cannot but think there is room for a brief presentation of the Logic of Relatives and of Exact Logic generally, subjective and objective, which shall be less mechanical and fatiguing and shall better display its living ideas and connections with philosophy and with life. I wrote such a book myself with the utmost care and no economy of pains. I was well pleased with it myself. But the publishers told me it would not pay, especially as I was not a university professor; and so I put the MS to another use; that of lighting fires.

Thus, in every way I am driven to see that this country will have nothing intellectual that is beautiful and finished. It wants only sporadic ideas on vitally important topics; and that is why I am inflicting upon you this wretched desultory sermonizing for which I am no more fitted than I am for rowing stroke in the Varsity crew. I can only say that if anybody wishes to have his eyes opened to a cosmos of thought of such wonderful beauty that merely as a poem the delight of it would a thousand times repay the effort of finding it, and which in addition to that appears to be the very Key that unlocks the secret of the physical and psychical universe, if he will come to me prepared, not for brilliant *aperçus* but for thorough work, I can help him to it. When I have said that, well knowing that the news will be received with incredulity, I have gone as far as duty requires. How bleak a climate America with its vitally important topics is for vitally unimportant but cosmically vital ideas, I have often thought when I have vainly tried to get into print a just word of praise for the solid work of some American thinker.

Chapter 5
WILLIAM JAMES

William James (1842–1910), was an American philosopher and psychologist, born in New York City and educated at Harvard, the brother of Henry James, the novelist. James struggled through much of his life with ill heath. He studied science, medicine, and philosophy in France and Germany, earning a medical degree from Harvard in 1869, where he taught as a psychology instructor. In 1890 he published *Principles of Psychology,* a compendious textbook in experimental psychology. But his interests were more philosophical than scientific, so eventually he moved into the philosophy department at Harvard, where he taught for many years. Throughout his early years he was assailed by doubts over freedom of the will and the existence of God, and developed the philosophy of pragmatism, in part as a response to these difficulties. Pragmatism originated with James's friend Charles Peirce, but underwent crucial changes and popularization in the hands of James. He wrote: "The whole function of philosophy ought to be to find out what definite difference it will make to you and me, at definite instants of our life, if this world-formula or that world-formula be the true one."

His principal works are *The Will to Believe* (1897), reprinted below; *The Varieties of Religious Experience* (1902); *Pragmatism, A New Name for Some Old Ways of Thinking* (1907), from which a selection is taken; and *Essays in Radical Empiricism* (1912).

In our first reading, *The Will to Believe,* James argues that life would be greatly impoverished if we confined our beliefs to such a Scrooge-like epistemology, as W. K. Clifford proposes: "It is wrong always, everywhere, and for anyone, to believe anything upon insufficient evidence." In everyday life, where the evidence for important propositions is often unclear, we must live by faith or cease to act at all. While we may not make leaps of faith just anywhere, sometimes practical considerations force us to make a decision regarding propositions which do not have their truth value written on their faces. "Belief" is defined as a live, momentous, optional hypothesis, on which we cannot avoid a decision, for not to choose is, in effect, to choose against the hypothesis. James claims that religion may be such an optional hypothesis for many people, and where it is, the individual has the right to believe the better story rather than the worse. To do so, one must will to believe what the evidence alone is inadequate to support.

The second reading is from *Pragmatism.* After a brief introduction to Pragmatism by way of a fascinating example of resolving a dispute about the correct characterization of a squirrel's behavior, James sets forth his view of truth. He holds that truth is dynamic rather than static and is to be defined in terms of beliefs that are useful or satisfying. Unlike the "intellectualists" (James's characterization of the traditional static approaches to the question of truth, viz., the correspondence theorists) truth is in process, still becoming, and changing. Yesterday's truth is today's falsehood, and today's truth is tomorrow's half-truth. What really matters is what you can *do* with an idea, what difference it makes to your life, its cash-value. His famous definition of truth is this: " 'The true' . . . is only the expedient in the way of our thinking, just as 'the right' is only the expedient in the way of our behaving" (by "expedient" James means prudent or suitable to achieve success). Philosophers have debated the significance of this statement, especially what James meant by the phrase that truth is expedient "in the long run and on the whole." Bertrand Russell presents a radically different view.

FOR FURTHER READING

Ayer, A. J. *Origins of Pragmatism: Studies in the Philosophy of Charles Sanders Peirce and William James* (Macmillan, 1968).
James, William. *Pragmatism* (Longmans, Green & Co., 1907).
Kuklick, Bruce. *The Rise of American Philosophy* (Yale University Press, 1977).
McDermott, John, ed. *The Writings of William James* (Random House, 1967).
Murphy, John. *Pragmatism: From Peirce to Davidson* (Westview Press, 1990).
Myers, G. E. *William James: His Life and Thought* (Yale University Press, 1986).
Perry, R. B. *The Thought and Character of William James,* 2 vols. (Harper, 1935).
Quine, W. V. and Joseph Ullian. *The Web of Belief,* 2nd ed. (Random House, 1978).
Scheffler, Israel. *Four Pragmatists* (Humanities Press, 1974).
Smith, John. *The Spirit of American Philosophy* (Oxford University Press, 1963).
Wild, John. *The Radical Empiricism of William James* (Greenwood Press, 1980).

The Will to Believe

I

Let us give the name of hypothesis to anything that may be proposed to our belief; and just as the electricians speak of live and dead wires, let us speak of any hypothesis as either *live* or *dead.* A live hypothesis is one which appeals as a real possibility to him to whom it is proposed. If I ask you to believe in the Mahdi, the notion makes no electric connection with your nature—it refuses to scintillate with any credibility at all. As an hypothesis it is completely dead. To an Arab, however (even if he be not one of the Mahdi's followers), the hypothesis is among the mind's possibilities: It is alive. This shows that deadness and liveness in an hypothesis are not intrinsic properties, but relations to the individual thinker. They are measured by his willingness to act. The maximum of liveness in an hypothesis means willingness to act irrevocably. Practically, that means belief; but there is some believing tendency wherever there is willingness to act at all.

Next, let us call the decision between two hypotheses an *option.* Options may be of several kinds. They may be first, *living* or *dead;* secondly, *forced* or *avoidable;* thirdly, *momentous* or *trivial;* and for our purposes we may call an option a *genuine* option when it is of the forced, living, and momentous kind.

1. A living option is one in which both hypotheses are live ones. If I say to you: "Be a theosophist or be a Mohammedan," it is probably a dead option, because for you neither hypothesis is likely to be alive. But if I say: "Be an agnostic or be a Christian," it is otherwise: trained as you are, each hypothesis makes some appeal, however small, to your belief.

2. Next, if I say to you: "Choose between going out with your umbrella or without it," I do not offer you a genuine option, for it is not forced. You can easily avoid it by not going out at all. Similarly, if I say, "Either love me or hate me," "Either call my theory true or call it false," your option is avoidable. You may remain indifferent to me, neither loving nor hating, and you may decline to offer any judgment as to my theory. But if I say, "Either accept this truth or go without it," I put on you a forced option, for there is no standing place outside of the alternative. Every dilemma based on a complete logical disjunction, with no possibility of not choosing, is an option of this forced kind.

3. Finally, if I were Dr. Nansen and proposed to you to join my North Pole expedition, your option would be momentous; for this would probably be your similar opportunity, and your choice now would either exclude you from the North Pole sort of immortality altogether or put at least the chance of it into your hands. He who refuses to embrace a unique opportunity loses the prize as surely as if he tried and failed. Per contra, the option is trivial when the opportunity is not unique, when the stake is insignificant, or when the decision is reversible if it later proves unwise. Such trivial options abound in the scientific life. A chemist finds an hypothesis live enough to spend a year in its verification: he believes in it to that extent. But if his experiments prove inconclusive either way, he is quit for his loss of time, no vital harm being done.

It will facilitate our discussion if we keep all these distinctions well in mind.

II

The next matter to consider is the actual psychology of human opinion. When we look at certain facts, it seems as if our passional and volitional nature lay at the root of all our convictions. When we look at others, it seems as if they could do nothing when the intellect had once said its say. Let us take the latter facts up first.

Does it not seem preposterous on the very face of it to talk of our opinions being modifiable at will? Can our will either help or hinder our intellect in its perceptions of truth? Can we, by just willing it, believe that Abraham Lincoln's existence is a myth, and that the portraits of him in *McClure's Magazine* are all of some one else? Can we, by any effort of our will, or by any strength of wish that it were true, believe ourselves well and about when we are roaring with rheumatism in bed, or feel certain that the sum of the two one-dollar bills in our pocket must be a hundred dollars? We can *say* any of these things, but we are absolutely impotent to believe them; and of just such things is the whole fabric of the truths that we do believe in made up—matters of fact, immediate or remote, as Hume said, and relations between ideas, which are either there or not there for us if we see them so, and which if not there cannot be put there by any action of our own.

In Pascal's *Thoughts* there is a celebrated passage known in literature as Pascal's wager. In it he tries to force us into Christianity by reasoning as if our concern with truth resembled our concern with the stakes in a game of chance. Translated freely his words are these: You must either believe or not believe that God is—which will you do? Your human reason cannot say. A game is going on between you and the nature of things which at the day of judgment will bring out either heads or tails. Weigh what your gains and your losses would be if you should stake all you have on heads, or God's existence: if you win in such case, you gain eternal beatitude; if you lose, you lose nothing at all. If there were an infinity of chances, and only one for God in this wager, still you ought to stake your all on God; for though you surely risk a finite loss by this procedure, any finite loss is reasonable, even a certain one is reasonable, if there is but the possibility of infinite gain. Go, then, and take holy water, and have masses said; belief will come and stupefy your scruples. . . . Why should you not? At bottom, what have you to lose?

You probably feel that when religious faith expresses itself thus, in the language of the gamingtable, it is put to its last trumps. Surely Pascal's own personal belief in masses and holy water had far other springs; and this celebrated page of his is but an argument for others, a last desperate snatch at a weapon against the hardness of the unbelieving heart. We feel that a faith in masses and holy water adopted wilfully after such a mechanical calculation would lack the inner soul of faith's reality; and if we were ourselves in the place of the Deity, we should probably take particular pleasure in cutting off believers of this pattern from their infinite reward. It is evident that unless there be some preexisting tendency to believe in masses and holy water, the option offered to the will by Pascal is not a living option. Certainly no Turk ever took to masses and holy water on its account; and even to us Protestants these means of salvation seem such foregone impossibilities that Pascal's logic, invoked for them specifically, leaves us unmoved. As well might the Mahdi write to us, saying, "I am the Expected One whom God has created in his effulgence. You shall be infinitely happy if you confess me; otherwise you shall be cut off from the light of the sun. Weigh, then, your infinite gain if I am genuine against your finite sacrifice if I am not!" His logic would be that of Pascal; but he would vainly use it on us, for the hypothesis he offers us is dead. No tendency to act on it exists in us to any degree.

The talk of believing by our volition seems, then, from one point of view, simply silly. From another point of view it is worse than silly, it is vile. When one turns to the magnificent edifice of the physical sciences, and sees how it was reared; what thousands of disinterested moral lives of men lie buried in its mere foundations; what patience and postponement, what choking down of preference, what submission to the icy laws of outer fact are wrought into its very stones and mortar; how absolutely impersonal it stands in its vast augustness—then how besotted and contemptible seems every little sentimentalist who comes blowing his voluntary smoke-wreaths, and pretending to decide things from out of his private dream! Can we wonder if those bred in the rugged and manly school of science should feel like spewing such subjectivism out of their mouths? The whole system of loyalties which grow up in the schools of science go dead against its toleration; so that it is only natural that those who have caught the scientific fever should pass over to the opposite extreme, and write sometimes as if the incorruptibly truthful intellect ought positively to prefer bitterness and unacceptableness to the heart in its cup.

> It fortifies my soul to know
> That though I perish, Truth is so

sings Clough, while Huxley exclaims: "My only consolation lies in the reflection that, however bad our posterity may become, so far as they hold by the plain rule of not pretending to believe what they have no reason to believe, because it may be to their advantage so to pretend [the word 'pretend' is surely here redundant], they will not have reached the lowest depth of immorality." And that delicious *enfant terrible* Clifford writes: "Belief is desecrated when given to unproved and unquestioned statements for the solace and private pleasure of the believer. . . . Whoso would deserve well of his fellows in this matter will guard the purity of his belief with a very fanaticism of jealous care, lest at any time it should rest on an unworthy object, and catch a stain which can never be wiped away. . . . If [a] belief has been accepted on insufficient evidence [even though the belief be true, as Clifford on the same page explains] the pleasure is a stolen one. . . . It is sinful because it is stolen in defiance of our duty to mankind. That duty is to guard ourselves from such beliefs as from a pestilence which may shortly master our own body and then spread to the rest of the town. . . . It is wrong always, everywhere, and for every one, to believe anything upon insufficient evidence."

III

All this strikes one as healthy, even when expressed, as by Clifford, with somewhat too much of robustious pathos in the voice. Free will and simple wishing do seem, in the matter of our credences, to be only fifth wheels to the coach. Yet if any one should thereupon assume that intellectual insight is what remains after wish and will and sentimental preference have taken wing, or that pure reason is what then settles our opinions, he would fly quite as directly in the teeth of the facts.

It is only our already dead hypotheses that our willing nature is unable to bring to life again. But what has made them dead for us is for the most part a previous action of our willing nature of an antagonistic kind. When I say "willing nature," I do not mean only such deliberate volitions as may have set up habits of belief that we cannot now escape from—I mean all such factors of belief as fear and hope, prejudice and passion, imitation and partisanship, the circumpressure of our caste and set. As a matter of fact we find ourselves believing, we hardly know how or why. Mr. Balfour gives the name of "authority" to all those influences, born of the intellectual climate, that make hypotheses possible or impossible for us, alive or dead. Here in this room, we all of us believe in molecules and the conservation of energy, in democracy and necessary progress, in Protestant Christianity and the duty of fighting for "the doctrine of the immortal Monroe," all for no reasons worthy of the name. We see into these matters with no more inner clearness, and probably with much less, than any disbeliever in them might possess. His unconventionality would probably have some grounds to show for its conclusions; but for us, not insight, but the *prestige* of the opinions, is what makes the spark shoot from them and light up our sleeping magazines of faith. Our reason is quite satisfied, in nine hundred and ninety-nine cases out of every thousand of us, if it can find a few arguments that will do to recite in case our credulity is criticized by some one else. Our faith is faith in some one else's faith, and in the greatest matters this is the most the case. . . .

Evidently, then, our non-intellectual nature does influence our convictions. There are passional tendencies and volitions which run before and others which come after belief, and it is only the latter that are too late for the fair; and they are not too late when the previous passional work has been already in their own direction. Pascal's argument, instead of being powerless, then seems a regular clincher, and is the last stroke needed to make our faith in masses and holy water complete. The state of things is evidently far from simple; and pure insight and logic, whatever they might do ideally, are not the only things that really do produce our creeds.

IV

Our next duty, having recognized this mixedup state of affairs, is to ask whether it be simply reprehensible and pathological, or whether, on the contrary, we must treat it as a normal element in making up our minds. The thesis I defend is, briefly stated, this: *Our passional nature not only lawfully may, but must, decide an option between propositions, whenever it is a genuine option that cannot by its nature be decided on intellectual grounds; for to say, under such circumstances, "Do not decide, but leave the question open," is itself a passional decision—just like deciding yes or no—and is attended with the same risk of losing the truth. . . .*

VII

One more point, small but important, and our preliminaries are done. There are two ways of looking at our duty in the matter of opinion—ways entirely different, and yet ways about whose difference the theory of knowledge seems hitherto to have shown very little concern. *We must know the truth; and we must avoid error*—these are our first and great commandments as would-be knowers; but they are not two ways of stating an identical commandment, they are two separable laws. Although it may indeed happen that when we believe the truth A, we escape as an incidental consequence from believing the falsehood B, it hardly ever happens that by merely disbelieving B we necessarily believe A. We may in escaping B fall into believing other falsehoods, C or D, just as bad as B; or we may escape B by not believing anything at all, not even A.

Believe truth! Shun error!—these, we see, are two materially different laws; and by choosing between them we may end by coloring differently our whole intellectual life. We may regard the chase for truth as paramount, and the avoidance of error as secondary; or we may, on the other hand, treat the avoidance of error as more imperative, and let truth take its chance. Clifford, in the instructive passage which I have quoted, exhorts us to the latter course. Believe nothing, he tells us, keep your mind in suspense forever, rather than by closing it on insufficient evidence incur the awful risk of believing lies. You, on the other hand, may think that the risk of being in error is a very small matter when compared with the blessings of real knowledge, and be ready to be duped many times in your investigation rather than postpone indefinitely the chance of guessing true. I myself find it impossible to go with Clifford. We must remember that these feelings of our duty about either truth or error are in any case only expressions of our passional life. Biologically considered, our minds are as ready to grind out falsehood as veracity, and he who says, "Better go without belief forever than believe a lie!" merely shows his own preponderant private horror of becoming a dupe. He may be critical of many of his desires and fears, but this fear he slavishly obeys. He cannot imagine any one questioning its binding force. For my own part, I have also a horror of being duped; but I can believe that worse things than being duped may happen to a man in this world: so Clifford's exhortation has to my ears a thoroughly fantastic sound. It is like a general informing his soldiers that it is better to keep out of battle forever than to risk a single wound. Not so are victories either over enemies or over nature gained. Our errors are surely not such awfully solemn things. In a world where we are so certain to incur them in spite of all our caution, a certain lightness of heart seems healthier than this excessive nervousness on their behalf. At any rate, it seems the fittest thing for the empiricist philosopher.

VIII

And now, after all this introduction, let us go straight at our question. I have said, and now repeat it, that not only as a matter of fact do we find our passional nature influencing us in our opinions, but that there are some options between opinions in which this influence must be regarded both as an inevitable and as a lawful determinant of our choice.

I fear here that some of you my hearers will begin to scent danger, and lend an inhospitable ear. Two first steps of passion you have indeed had to admit as necessary—we must think so as to avoid dupery, and we must think so as to gain truth; but the surest path to those ideal consummations, you will probably consider, is from now onwards to take no further passional step.

Well, of course, I agree as far as the facts will allow. Wherever the option between losing truth and gaining it is not momentous, we can throw the chance of *gaining truth* away, and at any rate save ourselves from any chance of *believing falsehood,* by not making up our minds at all till objective evidence has come. In scientific questions, this is almost always the case; and even in human affairs in general, the need of acting is seldom so urgent that a false belief to act on is better than no belief at all. Law courts, indeed, have to decide on the best evidence attainable for the moment, because a judge's duty is to make law as well as to ascertain it, and (as a learned judge once said to me) few cases are worth spending much time over: the great thing is to have them decided on *any* acceptable principle, and got out of the way. But in our dealings with objective nature we obviously are recorders, not makers, of the truth; and decisions for the mere sake of deciding promptly and getting on to the next business would be wholly out of place. Throughout the breadth of physical nature facts are what they are quite independently of us, and seldom is there any such hurry about them that the risks of being duped by believing a premature theory need be faced. The questions here are always trivial options, the hypotheses are hardly living (at any rate not living for us spectators), the choice between believing truth or falsehood is seldom forced. The attitude of sceptical balance is therefore the absolutely wise one if we would escape mistakes. What difference, indeed, does it make to most of us whether we have or have not a theory of the Röntgen rays, whether we believe or not in mind-stuff, or have a conviction about the causality of conscious states? It makes no difference. Such options are not forced on us. On every account it is better not to make them, but still keep weighing reasons *pro et contra* with an indifferent hand.

I speak, of course, here of the purely judging mind. For purposes of discovery such indifference is to be less highly recommended, and science would be far less advanced than she is if the passionate desires of individuals to get their own faiths confirmed had been kept out of the game. See for example the sagacity which Spencer and Weismann now display. On the other hand, if you want an absolute duffer in an investigation, you must, after all, take the man who has no interest whatever in its results: he is the warranted incapable, the positive fool. The most useful investigator, because the most sensitive observer, is always he whose eager interest in one side of the question is balanced by an equally keen nervousness lest he become deceived. Science has organized this nervousness into a regular *technique,* her so-called method of verification; and she has fallen so deeply in love with the method that one may even say she has ceased to care for truth by itself at all. It is only truth as technically verified that interests her. The truth of truths might come in merely affirmative form, and she would decline to touch it. Such truth as that, she might repeat with Clifford, would be stolen in defiance of her duty to mankind. Human passions, however, are stronger than technical rules. "*Le coeur a ses raisons,*" as Pascal says, "*que la raison ne connait pas,*" and however indifferent to all but the bare rules of the game the umpire, the abstract intellect, may be, the concrete players who furnish him the materials to judge of are usually, each one of them, in love with some pet "live hypothesis" of his own. Let us agree, however, that wherever there is no forced option, the dispassionately judicial intellect with no pet hypothesis, saving us, as it does, from dupery at any rate, ought to be our ideal.

The question next arises: Are there not somewhere forced options in our speculative questions, and can we (as men who may be interested at least as much in positively gaining truth as in merely escaping dupery) always wait with impunity till the coercive evidence shall have arrived? It seems *a priori* improbable that the truth should be so nicely adjusted to our needs and powers as that. In the great boardinghouse of nature, the cakes and the butter and the syrup seldom come out so even and leave the plates so clean. Indeed, we should view them with scientific suspicion if they did.

IX

Moral questions immediately present themselves as questions whose solution cannot wait for sensible proof. A moral question is a question not of what sensibly exists, but of what is good, or would be good if it did exist. Science can tell us what exists; but to compare the *worths,* both of what exists and of what does not exist, we must consult not science, but what Pascal calls our heart. . . .

Turn now from these wide questions of good to a certain class of questions of fact, questions concerning personal relations, states of mind between one man and another. *Do you like me or not?*—for example. Whether you do or not depends, in countless instances, on whether I meet you halfway, am willing to assume that you must like me, and show you trust and expectation. The previous faith on my part in your liking's existence is in such cases what makes your liking come. But if I stand aloof, and refuse to budge an inch until I have objective evidence, until you shall have done something apt, as the absolutists say, *ad extorquendum assensum meum,* ten to one your liking never comes. How many women's hearts are vanquished by the mere sanguine insistence of some man that they *must* love him! He will not consent to the hypothesis that they cannot. The desire for a certain kind of truth here brings about that special truth's existence; and so it is in innumerable cases of other sorts. . . . *And where faith in a fact can help create the fact,* that would be an insane logic which should say that faith running ahead of scientific evidence is the "lowest kind of immorality" into which a thinking being can fall. Yet such is the logic by which our scientific absolutists pretend to regulate our lives!

X

In truths dependent on our personal action, then, faith based on desire is certainly a lawful and possibly an indispensable thing.

But now, it will be said, these are all childish human cases, and have nothing to do with great cosmical matters, like the question of religious faith. Let us then pass on to that. Religions differ so much in their accidents that in discussing the religious question we must make it very generic and broad. What then do we now mean by the religious hypothesis? Science says things are; morality says some things are better than other things; and religion says essentially two things.

First, she says that the best things are the more eternal things, the overlapping things, the things in the universe that throw the last stone, so to speak, and say the final word. "Perfection is eternal"—this phrase of Charles Secrétan seems a good way of putting this first affirmation of religion, an affirmation which obviously cannot yet be verified scientifically at all.

The second affirmation of religion is that we are better off even now if we believe her first affirmation to be true.

Now, let us consider what the logical elements of this situation are *in case the religious hypothesis in both its branches be really true.* (Of course, we must admit that possibility at the outset. If we are to discuss the question at all, it must involve a living option. If for any of you religion be a hypothesis that cannot, by any living possibility, be true, then you need go no farther. I speak to the "saving remnant" alone.) So proceeding, we see, first, that religion offers itself as a *momentous* option. We are supposed to gain, even now, by our belief, and to lose by our non-belief, a certain vital good. Secondly, religion is a *forced* option, so far as that good goes. We cannot escape the issue by remaining sceptical and waiting for more light, because, although we do avoid error in that way *if religion be untrue*, we lose the good, *if it be true*, just as certainly as if we positively chose to disbelieve. It is as if a man should hesitate indefinitely to ask a certain woman to marry him because he was not perfectly sure that she would prove an angel after he brought her home. Would he not cut himself off from that particular angel-possibility as decisively as if he went and married some one else? Scepticism, then, is not avoidance of option; it is option of a certain particular kind of risk. *Better risk loss of truth than chance of error*—that is your faithvetoer's exact position. He is actively playing his stake as much as the believer is; he is backing the field against the religious hypothesis, just as the believer is backing the religious hypothesis against the field. To preach scepticism to us as a duty until "sufficient evidence" for religion be found, is tantamount therefore to telling us, when in presence of the religious hypothesis, that to yield to our fear of its being error is wiser and better than to yield to our hope that it may be true. It is not intellect against all passions, then; it is only intellect with one passion laying down its law. And by what, forsooth, is the supreme wisdom of this passion warranted? Dupery for dupery, what proof is there that dupery through hope is so much worse than dupery through fear? I, for one, can see no proof; and I simply refuse obedience to the scientist's command to imitate his kind of option, in a case where my own stake is important enough to give me the right to choose my own form of risk. If religion be true and the evidence for it be still insufficient, I do not wish, by putting your extinguisher upon my nature (which feels to me as if it had after all some business in this matter), to forfeit my sole chance in life of getting upon the winning side—that chance depending, of course, on my willingness to run the risk of acting as if my passional need of taking the world religiously might he prophetic and right.

All this is on the supposition that it really may be

prophetic and right, and that, even to us who are discussing the matter, religion is a live hypothesis which may be true. Now, to most of us religion comes in a still further way that makes a veto on our active faith even more illogical. The more perfect and more eternal aspect of the universe is represented in our religions as having personal form. The universe is no longer a mere *It* to us, but a *Thou,* if we are religious; and any relation that may be possible from person to person might be possible here. For instance, although in one sense we are passive portions of the universe, in another we show a curious autonomy, as if we were small active centers on our own account. We feel, too, as if the appeal of religion to us were made to our own active good-will, as if evidence might be forever withheld from us unless we met the hypothesis halfway. To take a trivial illustration: just as a man who in a company of gentlemen made no advances, asked a warrant for every concession, and believed no one's word without proof, would cut himself off by such churlishness from all the social rewards that a more trusting spirit would earn—so here, one who should shut himself up in snarling logicality and try to make the gods extort his recognition willy-nilly, or not get it at all, might cut himself off forever from his only opportunity of making the gods' acquaintance. This feeling, forced on us we know not whence that by obstinately believing that there are gods (although not to do so would be so easy both for our logic and our life) we are doing the universe the deepest service we can, seems part of the living essence of the religious hypothesis. If the hypothesis *were* true in all its parts, including this one, then pure intellectualism, with its veto on our making willing advances, would be an absurdity; and some participation of our sympathetic nature would be logically required. I therefore, for one, cannot see my way to accepting the agnostic rules for truth-seeking, or wilfully agree to keep my willing nature out of the game. I cannot do so for this plain reason, that *a rule of thinking which would absolutely prevent me from acknowledging certain kinds of truth if those kinds of truth were really there, would be an irrational rule.* That for me is the long and short of the formal logic of the situation, no matter what the kinds of truth might materially be.

I confess I do not see how this logic can be escaped. But sad experience makes me fear that some of you may still shrink from radically saying with me, *in abstracto,* that we have the right to believe at our own risk any hypothesis that is live enough to tempt our will. I suspect, however, that if this is so, it is because you have got away from the abstract logical point of view altogether, and are thinking (perhaps without realizing it) of some particular religious hypothesis which for you is dead. The freedom to "believe what we will" you apply to the case of some patent superstition; and the faith you think of is the faith defined by the schoolboy when he said, "Faith is when you believe something that you know ain't true." I can only repeat that this is misapprehension. *In concreto,* the freedom to believe can only cover living options which the intellect of the individual cannot by itself resolve; and living options never seem absurdities to him who has them to consider. When I look at the religious question as it really puts itself to concrete men, and when I think of all the possibilities which both practically and theoretically it involves, then this command that we shall put a stopper on our heart, instincts, and courage, and *wait*—acting of course meanwhile more or less as if religion were not true—till doomsday, or till such time as our intellect and senses working together may have raked in evidence enough—this command, I say, seems to me the queerest idol ever manufactured in the philosophic cave. Were we scholastic absolutists, there might be more excuse. If we had an infallible intellect with its objective certitudes, we might feel ourselves disloyal to such a perfect organ of knowledge in not trusting to it exclusively, in not waiting for its releasing word. But if we are empiricists, if we believe that no bell in us tolls to let us know for certain when truth is in our grasp, then it seems a piece of idle fantasticality to preach so solemnly our duty of waiting for the bell. Indeed we *may* wait if we will—I hope you do not think that I am denying that—but if we do so, we do so at our peril as much as if we believed. In either case we *act,* taking our life in our hands. No one of us ought to issue vetoes to the other, nor should we bandy words of abuse. We ought, on the contrary, delicately and profoundly to respect one another's mental freedom: then only shall we bring about the intellectual republic; then only shall we have that spirit of inner tolerance without which all our outer tolerance is soulless, and which is empiricism's glory; then only shall we live and let live, in speculative as well as in practical things.

I began by a reference to Fitz-James Stephen; let me end by a quotation from him. "What do you think of yourself? What do you think of the world? . . . These are questions with which all must deal as it seems good to them. They are riddles of the Sphinx, and in some way or other we must deal with them. . . . In all important transactions of life we have to take a leap in the dark. . . . If we decide to leave the riddles unanswered, that is a choice; if we waver in our answer, that, too, is a choice: but whatever choice we make, we make it at our peril. If a man chooses to turn his back altogether on God and the future, no one can prevent him; no one can show beyond reasonable doubt that he is mistaken. If a man thinks otherwise and acts as he thinks, I do not see that any one can prove that he is mistaken. Each must act as he thinks best; and if he is wrong, so much the worse for him. We stand on a mountain pass in the midst of whirling snow and blinding mist, through which we get glimpses now and then of paths which may be deceptive. If we stand still we shall be frozen to death. If we take the wrong road we shall be dashed to pieces. We do not certainly know whether there is any right one. What must we do? 'Be strong and of a good courage.' Act for the best, hope for the best, and take what comes. . . . If death ends all, we cannot meet death better."

What Pragmatism Means

Some years ago, being with a camping party in the mountains, I returned from a solitary ramble to find every one engaged in a ferocious metaphysical dispute. The *corpus* of the dispute was a squirrel—a live squirrel supposed to be clinging to one side of a treetrunk; while over against the tree's opposite side a human being was imagined to stand. This human witness tries to get sight of the squirrel by moving rapidly round the tree, but no matter how fast he goes, the squirrel moves as fast in the opposite direction, and always keeps the tree between himself and the man, so that never a glimpse of him is caught. The resultant metaphysical problem now is this: *Does the man go round the squirrel or not?* He goes round the tree, sure enough, and the squirrel is on the tree; but does he go round the squirrel? In the unlimited leisure of the wilderness, discussion had been worn threadbare. Everyone had taken sides, and was obstinate; and the numbers on both sides were even. Each side, when I appeared therefore appealed to me to make it a majority. Mindful of the scholastic adage that whenever you meet a contradiction you must make a distinction, I immediately sought and found one, as follows: "Which party is right," I said, "depends on what you *practically mean* by 'going round' the squirrel. If you mean passing from the north of him to the east, then to the south, then to the west, and then to the north of him again, obviously the man does go round him, for he occupies these successive positions. But if on the contrary you mean being first in front of him, then on the right of him, then behind him, then on his left, and finally in front again, it is quite as obvious that the man fails to go round him, for by the compensating movements the squirrel makes, he keeps his belly turned towards the man all the time, and his back turned away. Make the distinction, and there is no occasion for any farther dispute. You are both right and both wrong according as you conceive the verb 'to go round' in one practical fashion or the other."

Although one or two of the hotter disputants called my speech a shuffling evasion, saying they wanted no quibbling or scholastic hairsplitting, but meant just plain honest English 'round,' the majority seemed to think that the distinction had assuaged the dispute.

I tell this trivial anecdote because it is a peculiarly simple example of what I wish now to speak of as *the pragmatic method.* The pragmatic method is primarily a method of settling metaphysical disputes that otherwise might be interminable. Is the world one or many?—fated or free?—material or spiritual?—here are notions either of which may or may not hold good of the world; and disputes over such notions are unending. The pragmatic method in such cases is to try to interpret each notion by tracing its respective practical consequences. What difference would it practically make to any one if this notion rather than that notion were true? If no practical difference whatever can be traced, then the alternatives mean practically the same thing, and all dispute is idle. Whenever a dispute is serious, we ought to be able to show some practical difference that must follow from one side or the other's being right.

A glance at the history of the idea will show you still better what pragmatism means. The term is derived from the same Greek word πραγμα, meaning action, from which our words 'practice' and 'practical' come. It was first introduced into philosophy by Mr. Charles Peirce in 1878. In an article entitled 'How to Make Our Ideas Clear,' in the 'Popular Science Monthly' for January of that year[1] Mr. Peirce, after pointing out that our beliefs are really rules for action, said that, to develop a thought's meaning, we need only determine what conduct it is fitted to produce: that conduct is for us its sole significance. And the tangible fact at the root of all our thought-distinctions, however subtle, is that there is no one of them so fine as to consist in anything but a possible difference of practice. To attain perfect clearness in our thoughts of an object, then, we need only consider what conceivable effects of a practical kind the object may involve—what sensations we are to expect from it, and what reactions we must prepare. Our conception of these effects, whether immediate or remote, is then for us the whole of our conception of the object, so far as that conception has positive significance at all.

This is the principle of Peirce, the principle of pragmatism. It lay entirely unnoticed by any one for twenty years, until I, in an address before Professor Howison's philosophical union at the university of California, brought it forward again and made a special application of it to religion. By that date (1898) the times seemed ripe for its reception. The word 'pragmatism' spread, and at present it fairly spots the pages of the philosophic journals. On all hands we find the 'pragmatic movement' spoken of, sometimes with respect, sometimes with contumely, seldom with clear understanding. It is evident that the term applies itself conveniently to a number of tendencies that hitherto have lacked a collective name, and that it has 'come to stay.'

To take in the importance of Peirce's principle, one must get accustomed to applying it to concrete cases. I found a few years ago that Ostwald, the illustrious Leipzig chemist, had been making perfectly distinct use of the principle of pragmatism in his lectures on the philosophy of science, though he had not called it by that name.

"All realities influence our practice," he wrote me, "and that influence is their meaning for us. I am accustomed to put questions to my classes in this way: In what respects would the world be different if this alternative or that were true? If I can find nothing that would become different, then the alternative has no sense."

That is, the rival views mean practically the same thing, and meaning, other than practical, there is for us none. Ostwald in a published lecture gives this example of what he means. Chemists have long wrangled over the inner constitution of certain bodies called "tautomerous." Their properties seemed equally consistent with the notion that an instable hydrogen atom oscillates inside of them, or that they are instable mixtures of two bodies. Controversy raged, but never was decided. "It would never have begun," says Ostwald, "if the combatants had asked themselves what particular experimental fact could have been made different by one or the other view being correct. For it would then have appeared that no difference of fact could possibly ensue; and the quarrel was as unreal as if, theorizing in primitive times about the raising of dough by yeast, one party should have invoked a 'brownie,' while another insisted on an 'elf' as the true cause of the phenomenon."[2]

It is astonishing to see how many philosophical disputes collapse into insignificance the moment you subject them to this simple test of tracing a concrete consequence. There can *be* no difference anywhere that doesn't *make* a difference elsewhere—no difference in abstract truth that doesn't express itself in a difference in concrete fact and in conduct consequent upon that fact, imposed on somebody, somehow, somewhere, and somewhen. The whole function of philosophy ought to be to find out what definite difference it will make to you and me, at definite instants of our life, if this world-formula or that world-formula be the true one.

There is absolutely nothing new in the pragmatic method. Socrates was an adept at it. Aristotle used

1. Translated in the *Revue Philosophique* for January, 1879 (vol. vii).

2. 'Theorie und Praxis,' Zeitsch. des Oesterreichischen Ingenieur u. Architecten-Vereines, 1905, Nr. 4 u. 6. I find a still more radical pragmatism than Ostwald's in an address by Professor W. S. Franklin: "I think that the sickliest notion of physics, even if a student gets it, is that it is 'the science of masses, molecules, and the ether.' And I think that the healthiest notion, even if a student does not wholly get it, is that physics is the science of the ways of taking hold of bodies and pushing them!" (Science, January 2, 1903.)

it methodically. Locke, Berkeley, and Hume made momentous contributions to truth by its means. Shadworth Hodgson keeps insisting that realities are only what they are 'known as.' But these forerunners of pragmatism used it in fragments: they were preluders only. Not until in our time has it generalized itself, become conscious of a universal mission, pretended to a conquering destiny. I believe in that destiny, and I hope I may end by inspiring you with my belief.

Pragmatism represents a perfectly familiar attitude in philosophy, the empiricist attitude, but it represents it, as it seems to me, both in a more radical and in a less objectionable form than it has ever yet assumed. A pragmatist turns his back resolutely and once for all upon a lot of inveterate habits dear to professional philosophers. He turns away from abstraction and insufficiency, from verbal solutions, from bad *a priori* reasons, from fixed principles, closed systems, and pretended absolutes and origins. He turns towards concreteness and adequacy, towards facts, towards action and towards power. That means the empiricist temper regnant and the rationalist temper sincerely given up. It means the open air and possibilities of nature, as against dogma, artificiality, and the pretence of finality in truth.

At the same time it does not stand for any special results. It is a method only. But the general triumph of that method would mean an enormous change in what I called in my last lecture the 'temperament' of philosophy. Teachers of the ultra-rationalistic type would be frozen out, much as the courtier type is frozen out in republics, as the ultramontane type of priest is frozen out in protestant lands. Science and metaphysics would come much nearer together, would in fact work absolutely hand in hand.

Metaphysics has usually followed a very primitive kind of quest. You know how men have always hankered after unlawful magic, and you know what a great part in magic *words* have always played. If you have his name, or the formula of incantation that binds him, you can control the spirit, genie, afrite, or whatever the power may be. Solomon knew the names of all the spirits, and having their names, he held them subject to his will. So the universe has always appeared to the natural mind as a kind of enigma, of which the key must be sought in the shape of some illuminating or power-bringing word or name. That word names the universe's *principle,* and to possess it is after a fashion to possess the universe itself. 'God,' 'Matter,' 'Reason,' 'the Absolute,' 'Energy,' are so many solving names. You can rest when you have them. You are at the end of your metaphysical quest.

But if you follow the pragmatic method, you cannot look on any such word as closing your quest. You must bring out of each word its practical cash-value, set it at work within the stream of your experience. It appears less as a solution, then, than as a program for more work, and more particularly as an indication of the ways in which existing realities may be *changed.*

Theories thus become instruments, not answers to enigmas, in which we can rest. We don't lie back upon them, we move forward, and, on occasion, make nature over again by their aid. Pragmatism unstiffens all our theories, limbers them up and sets each one at work. Being nothing essentially new, it harmonizes with many ancient philosophic tendencies. It agrees with nominalism for instance, in always appealing to particulars; with utilitarianism in emphasizing practical aspects; with positivism in its disdain for verbal solutions, useless questions and metaphysical abstractions.

All these, you see, are *anti-intellectualist* tendencies. Against rationalism as a pretension and a method pragmatism is fully armed and militant. But, at the outset, at least, it stands for no particular results. It has no dogmas, and no doctrines save its method. As the young Italian pragmatist Papini has well said, it lies in the midst of our theories, like a corridor in a hotel. Innumerable chambers open out of it. In one you may find a man writing an atheistic volume; in the next some one on his knees praying for faith and strength; in a third a chemist investigating a body's properties. In a fourth a system of idealistic metaphysics is being excogitated; in a fifth the impossibility of metaphysics is being shown. But they all own the corridor, and all must pass through it if they want a practicable way of getting into or out of their respective rooms.

No particular results then, so far, but only an attitude of orientation, is what the pragmatic method means. *The attitude of looking away from first things, principles, 'categories,' supposed necessities; and of looking towards last things, fruits, consequences, facts.*

So much for the pragmatic method! You may say that I have been praising it rather than explaining it to you, but I shall presently explain it abundantly enough by showing how it works on some familiar problems. Meanwhile the word pragmatism has come to be used in a still wider sense, as meaning also a certain *theory of truth.* I mean to give a whole lecture to the statement of that theory, after first paving the way, so I can be very brief now. But brevity is hard to follow, so I ask for your redoubled attention for a quarter of an hour. If much remains obscure, I hope to make it clearer in the later lectures.

One of the most successfully cultivated branches of philosophy in our time is what is called inductive logic, the study of the conditions under which our sciences have evolved. Writers on this subject have begun to show a singular unanimity as to what the laws of nature and element of fact mean, when formulated by mathematicians, physicists and chemists. When the first mathematical, logical, and natural uniformities, the first *laws,* were discovered, men were so carried away by the clearness, beauty and simplification that resulted, that they believed themselves to have deciphered authentically the eternal thoughts of the Almighty. His mind also thundered and reverberated in syllogisms. He also thought in conic sections, squares and roots and ratios, and geometrized like Euclid. He made Kepler's laws for the planets to follow; he made velocity increase proportionally to the time in falling bodies; he made the law of the sines for light to obey when refracted; he established the classes, orders, families and genera of plants and animals, and fixed the distances between them. He thought the archetypes of all things, and devised their variations; and when we rediscover any one of these his wondrous institutions, we seize his mind in its very literal intention.

But as the sciences have developed farther, the notion has gained ground that most, perhaps all, of our laws are only approximations. The laws themselves, moreover, have grown so numerous that there is no counting them; and so many rival formulations are proposed in all the branches of science that investigators have become accustomed to the notion that no theory is absolutely a transcript of reality, but that any one of them may from some point of view be useful. Their great use is to summarize old facts and to lead to new ones. They are only a man-made language, a conceptual shorthand, as some one calls them, in which we write our reports of nature; and languages, as is well known, tolerate much choice of expression and many dialects.

Thus human arbitrariness has driven divine necessity from scientific logic. If I mention the names of Sigwart, Mach, Ostwald, Pearson, Milhaud, Poincaré, Duhem, Ruyssen, those of you who are students will easily identify the tendency I speak of, and will think of additional names.

Riding now on the front of this wave of scientific logic Messrs. Schiller and Dewey appear with their pragmatistic account of what truth everywhere signifies. Everywhere, these teachers say, 'truth' in our ideas and beliefs means the same thing that it means in science. It means, they say, nothing but this, *that ideas (which themselves are but parts of our experience) become true just in so far as they help us to get into satisfactory relation with other parts of our experience,* to summarize them and get about among them by conceptual short-cuts instead of following the interminable succession of particular phenomena. Any idea upon which we can ride, so to speak; any idea that will carry us prosperously from any one part of our experience to any other part, linking things satisfactorily, working securely, simplifying, saving labor; is true for just so much, true in so far forth, true *instrumentally.* This is the 'instrumental' view of truth taught so successfully at Chicago, the view that truth in our ideas means their power to 'work,' promulgated so brilliantly at Oxford.

Messrs. Dewey, Schiller and their allies, in reaching this general conception of all truth, have only followed the example of geologists, biologists and philologists. In the establishment of these other sciences, the successful stroke was always to take some simple process actually observable in operation—as denudation by weather, say, or variation from parental type, or change of dialect by incorporation of new words and pronunciations—and then to generalize it, making it apply to all times, and produce great results by summating its effects through the ages.

The observable process which Schiller and Dewey particularly singled out for generalization is the familiar one by which any individual settles into *new opinions.* The process here is always the same. The individual has a stock of old opinions already, but he meets a new experience that puts them to a strain. Somebody contradicts them; or in a reflective moment he discovers that they contradict each other; or he hears of facts with which they are incompatible; or desires arise in him which they cease to satisfy. The result is an inward trouble to which his mind till then had been a stranger, and from which he seeks to escape by modifying his previous mass of opinions. He saves as much of it as he can, for in this matter of belief we are all extreme conservatives. So he tries to change first this opinion, and then that (for they resist change very variously), until at last some new idea comes up which he can graft upon the ancient stock with a minimum of disturbance of the latter, some idea that mediates between the stock and the new experience and runs them into one another most felicitously and expediently.

This new idea is then adopted as the true one. It preserves the older stock of truths with a minimum of modification, stretching them just enough to make them admit the novelty, but conceiving that in ways as familiar as the case leaves possible. An *outrée* explanation, violating all our preconceptions, would never pass for a true account of a novelty. We should scratch round industriously till we found something less excentric. The most violent revolutions in an individual's beliefs leave most of his old order standing. Time and space, cause and effect, nature and history, and one's biography remain untouched. New truth is always a go-between, a smoother-over of transitions. It marries old opinion to new fact so as ever to show a minimum of jolt, a maximum of continuity. We hold a theory true just in proportion to its success in solving this 'problem of maxima and minima.' But success in solving this problem is eminently a matter of approximation. We say this theory solves it on the whole more satisfactorily than that theory; but that means more satisfactorily to ourselves, and individuals will emphasize their points of satisfaction differently. To a certain degree, therefore, everything here is plastic.

The point I now urge you to observe particularly is the part played by the older truths. Failure to take account of it is the source of much of the unjust criticism levelled against pragmatism. Their influence is absolutely controlling. Loyalty to them is the first principle—in most cases it is the only principle; for by far the most usual way of handling phenomena so novel that they would make for a serious rearrangement of our preconception is to ignore them altogether, or to abuse those who bear witness for them.

You doubtless wish examples of this process of truth's growth, and the only trouble is their superabundance. The simplest case of new truth is of course the mere numerical addition of new kinds of facts, or of new single facts of old kinds, to our experience—an addition that involves no alteration in the old beliefs. Day follows day, and its contents are simply added. The new contents themselves are not true, they simply *come* and *are*. Truth is *what we say about* them, and when we say that they have come, truth is satisfied by the plain additive formula.

But often the day's contents oblige a rearrangement. If I should now utter piercing shrieks and act like a maniac on this platform, it would make many of you revise your ideas as to the probable worth of my philosophy. 'Radium' came the other day as part of the day's content, and seemed for a moment to contradict our ideas of the whole order of nature, that order having come to be identified with what is called the conservation of energy. The mere sight of radium paying heat away indefinitely out of its own pocket seemed to violate that conservation. What to think? If the radiations from it were nothing but an escape of unsuspected 'potential' energy, pre-existent inside of the atoms, the principle of conservation would be saved. The discovery of 'helium' as the radiation's outcome, opened a way to this belief. So Ramsay's view is generally held to be true, because, although it extends our old ideas of energy, it causes a minimum of alteration in their nature.

I need not multiply instances. A new opinion counts as 'true' just in proportion as it gratifies the individual's desire to assimilate the novel in his experience to his beliefs in stock. It must both lean on old truth and grasp new fact; and its success (as I said a moment ago) in doing this, is a matter for the individual's appreciation. When old truth grows, then, by new truth's addition, it is for subjective reasons. We are in the process and obey the reasons. That new idea is truest which performs most felicitously its function of satisfying our double urgency. It makes itself true, gets itself classed as true, by the way it works; grafting itself then upon the ancient body of truth, which thus grows much as a tree grows by the activity of a new layer of cambium.

Now Dewey and Schiller proceed to generalize this observation and to apply it to the most ancient parts of truth. They also once were plastic. They also were called true for human reasons. They also mediated between still earlier truths and what in those days were novel observations. Purely objective truth, truth in whose establishment the function of giving human satisfaction in marrying previous parts of experience with newer parts played no rôle whatever, is nowhere to be found. The reasons why we call things true is the reason why they *are* true, for 'to be true' *means* only to perform this marriage-function.

The trail of the human serpent is thus over everything. Truth independent; truth that we *find* merely;

truth no longer malleable to human need; truth incorrigible, in a word; such truth exists indeed superabundantly—or is supposed to exist by rationalistically minded thinkers; but then it means only the dead heart of the living tree, and its being there means only that truth also has its paleontology, and its "prescription," and may grow stiff with years of veteran service and petrified in men's regard by sheer antiquity. But how plastic even the oldest truths nevertheless really are has been vividly shown in our day by the transformation of logical and mathematical ideas, a transformation which seems even to be invading physics. The ancient formulas are reinterpreted as special expressions of much wider principles, principles that our ancestors never got a glimpse of in their present shape and formulation.

Mr. Schiller still gives to all this view of truth the name of 'Humanism,' but, for this doctrine too, the name of pragmatism seems fairly to be in the ascendant, so I will treat it under the name of pragmatism in these lectures.

Such then would be the scope of pragmatism—first, a method; and second, a genetic theory of what is meant by truth. And these two things must be our future topics.

What I have said of the theory of truth will, I am sure, have appeared obscure and unsatisfactory to most of you by reason of its brevity. I shall make amends for that hereafter. In a lecture on 'common sense' I shall try to show what I mean by truths grown petrified by antiquity. In another lecture I shall expatiate on the idea that our thoughts become true in proportion as they successfully exert their go-between function. In a third I shall show how hard it is to discriminate subjective from objective factors in Truth's development. You may not follow me wholly in these lectures; and if you do, you may not wholly agree with me. But you will, I know, regard me at least as serious, and treat my effort with respectful consideration.

You will probably be surprised to learn, then, that Messrs. Schiller's and Dewey's theories have suffered a hailstorm of contempt and ridicule. All rationalism has risen against them. In influential quarters Mr. Schiller, in particular, has been treated like an impudent schoolboy who deserves a spanking. I should not mention this, but for the fact that it throws so much sidelight upon that rationalistic temper to which I have opposed the temper of pragmatism. Pragmatism is uncomfortable away from facts. Rationalism is comfortable only in the presence of abstractions. This pragmatist talk about truths in the plural, about their utility and satisfactoriness, about the success with which they 'work,' etc., suggests to the typical intellectualist mind a sort of coarse lame second-rate makeshift article of truth. Such truths are not real truth. Such tests are merely subjective. As against this, objective truth must be something non-utilitarian, haughty, refined, remote, august, exalted. It must be an absolute correspondence of our thoughts with an equally absolute reality. It must be what we *ought* to think unconditionally. The conditioned ways in which we *do* think are so much irrelevance and matter for psychology. Down with psychology, up with logic, in all this question!

See the exquisite contrast of the types of mind! The pragmatist clings to facts and concreteness, observes truth at its work in particular cases, and generalizes. Truth, for him, becomes a class-name for all sorts of definite working-values in experience. For the rationalist it remains a pure abstraction, to the bare name of which we must defer. When the pragmatist undertakes to show in detail just *why* we must defer, the rationalist is unable to recognize the concretes from which his own abstraction is taken. He accuses us of *denying* truth; whereas we have only sought to trace exactly why people follow it and always ought to follow it. Your typical ultra-abstractionist fairly shudders at concreteness: other things equal, he positively prefers the pale and spectral. If the two universes were offered, he would always choose the skinny outline rather than the rich thicket of reality. It is so much purer, clearer, nobler.

I hope that as these lectures go on, the concreteness and closeness to facts of the pragmatism which they advocate may be what approves itself to you as its most satisfactory peculiarity. It only follows here the example of the sister-sciences, interpreting the unobserved by the observed. It brings old and new harmoniously together. It converts the absolutely empty notion of a static relation of 'correspondence' (what that may mean we must ask later) between our minds and reality, into that of a rich and active commerce (that any one may follow in detail and understand) between particular thoughts of ours, and the great universe of other experiences in which they play their parts and have their uses.

But enough of this at present. The justification of what I say must be postponed. I wish now to add a word in further explanation of the claim I made at our last meeting, that pragmatism may be a happy harmonizer of empiricist ways of thinking with the more religious demands of human beings.

Men who are strongly of the fact-loving temperament, you may remember me to have said, are liable to be kept at a distance by the small sympathy with facts which that philosophy from the present-day fashion of idealism offers them. It is far too intellectualistic. Old fashioned theism was bad enough, with its notion of God as an exalted monarch, made up of a lot of unintelligible or preposterous 'attributes'; but, so long as it held strongly by the argument from design, it kept some touch with concrete realities. Since, however, Darwinism has once for all displaced design from the minds of the 'scientific,' theism has lost that foothold; and some kind of an immanent or pantheistic deity working *in* things rather than above them is, if any, the kind recommended to our contemporary imagination. Aspirants to a philosophic religion turn, as a rule, more hopefully nowadays towards idealistic pantheism than towards the older dualistic theism, in spite of the fact that the latter still counts able defenders.

But, as I said in my first lecture, the brand of pantheism offered is hard for them to assimilate if they are lovers of facts, or empirically minded. It is the absolutistic brand, spurning the dust and reared upon pure logic. It keeps no connexion whatever with concreteness. Affirming the Absolute Mind, which is its substitute for God, to be the rational presupposition of all particulars of fact, whatever they may be, it remains supremely indifferent to what the particular facts in our world actually are. Be they what they may, the Absolute will father them. Like the sick lion in Esop's fable, all footprints lead into his den, but *nulla vestigia retrorsum.* You cannot redescend into the world of particulars by the Absolute's aid, or deduce any necessary consequences of detail important for your life from your idea of his nature. He gives you indeed the assurance that all is well with *Him,* and for his eternal way of thinking; but thereupon he leaves you to be finitely saved by your own temporal devices.

Far be it from me to deny the majesty of this conception, or its capacity to yield religious comfort to a most respectable class of minds. But from the human point of view, no one can pretend that it doesn't suffer from the faults of remoteness and abstractness. It is eminently a product of what I have ventured to call the rationalistic temper. It disdains empiricism's needs. It substitutes a pallid outline for the real world's richness. It is dapper, it is noble in the bad sense, in the sense in which to be noble is to be inapt for humble service. In this real world of sweat and dirt, it seems to me that when a view of things is 'noble,' that ought to count as a presumption against its truth, and as a philosophic disqualification. The prince of darkness may be a gentleman, as we are told he is, but whatever the God of earth and heaven is, he can surely be no gentleman. His menial services are needed in the dust of our human trials, even more than his dignity is needed in the empyrean.

Now pragmatism, devoted though she be to facts, has no such materialistic bias as ordinary empiricism labors under. Moreover, she has no objection whatever to the realizing of abstractions, so long as you get about among particulars with their aid and they actually carry you somewhere. Interested in no conclusions but those which our minds and our experiences work out together, she has no *a priori* prejudices against theology. *If theological ideas prove to have a value for concrete life, they will be true, for pragmatism, in the sense of being good for so much. For how much more they are true, will depend entirely on their relations to the other truths that also have to be acknowledged.*

What I said just now about the Absolute, of transcendental idealism, is a case in point. First, I called it majestic and said it yielded religious comfort to a class of minds, and then I accused it of remoteness and sterility. But so far as it affords such comfort, it surely is not sterile; it has that amount of value; it performs a concrete function. As a good pragmatist, I myself ought to call the Absolute true 'in so far forth,' then; and I unhesitatingly now do so.

But what does *true in so far forth* mean in this case? To answer, we need only apply the pragmatic method. What do believers in the Absolute mean by saying that their belief affords them comfort? They mean that since, in the Absolute finite evil is 'overruled' already, we may, therefore, whenever we wish, treat the temporal as if it were potentially the eternal, be sure that we can trust its outcome, and, without sin, dismiss our fear and drop the worry of our finite responsibility. In short, they mean that we have a right ever and anon to take a moral holiday, to let the world wag in its own way, feeling that its issues are in better hands than ours and are none of our business.

The universe is a system of which the individual members may relax their anxieties occasionally, in which the don't-care mood is also right for men, and moral holidays in order,—that, if I mistake not, is part, at least, of what the Absolute is 'known-as,' that is the great difference in our particular experiences which his being true makes, for us, that is his cash-value when he is pragmatically interpreted. Farther than that the ordinary lay-reader in philosophy who thinks favorably of absolute idealism does not venture to sharpen his conceptions. He can use the Absolute for so much, and so much is very precious. He is pained at hearing you speak incredulously of the Absolute, therefore, and disregards your criticisms because they deal with aspects of the conception that he fails to follow.

If the Absolute means this, and means no more than this, who can possibly deny the truth of it? To deny it would be to insist that men should never relax, and that holidays are never in order.

I am well aware how odd it must seem to some of you to hear me say that an idea is 'true' so long as to believe it is profitable to our lives. That it is *good*, for as much as it profits, you will gladly admit. If what we do by its aid is good, you will allow the idea itself to be good in so far forth, for we are the better for possessing it. But is it not a strange misuse of the word 'truth,' you will say, to call ideas also 'true' for this reason?

To answer this difficulty fully is impossible at this stage of my account. You touch here upon the very central point of Messrs. Schiller's, Dewey's, and my own doctrine of truth, which I can not discuss with detail until my sixth lecture. Let me now say only this, that truth is *one species of good*, and not, as is usually supposed, a category distinct from good, and co-ordinate with it. *The true is the name of whatever proves itself to be good in the way of belief, and good, too, for definite, assignable reasons.* Surely you must admit this, that if there were *no* good for life in true ideas, or if the knowledge of them were positively disadvantageous and false ideas the only useful ones, then the current notion that truth is divine and precious, and its pursuit a duty, could never have grown up or become a dogma. In a world like that, our duty would be to *shun* truth, rather. But in this world, just as certain foods are not only agreeable to our taste, but good for our teeth, our stomach, and our tissues; so certain ideas are not only agreeable to think about, or agreeable as supporting other ideas that we are fond of, but they are also helpful in life's practical struggles. If there be any life that it is really better we should lead, and if there be any idea which, if believed in, would help us to lead that life, then it would be really *better for us* to believe in that idea, *unless, indeed, belief in it incidentally clashed with other greater vital benefits.*

'What would be better for us to believe'! This sounds very like a definition of truth. It comes very near to saying 'what we *ought* to believe': and in *that* definition none of you would find any oddity. Ought we ever not to believe what it is *better for us* to believe? And can we then keep the notion of what is better for us, and what is true for us, permanently apart?

Pragmatism says no, and I fully agree with her. Probably you also agree, so far as the abstract statement goes, but with a suspicion that if we practically did believe everything that made for good in our own personal lives, we should be found indulging all kinds of fancies about this world's affairs, and all kinds of sentimental superstitions about a world hereafter. Your suspicion here is undoubtedly well founded, and it is evident that something happens when you pass from the abstract to the concrete that complicates the situation.

I said just now that what is better for us to believe is true *unless the belief incidentally clashes with some other vital benefit.* Now in real life what vital benefits is any particular belief of ours most liable to clash with? What indeed except the vital benefits yielded by *other beliefs* when these prove incompatible with the first ones? In other words, the greatest enemy of any one of our truths may be the rest of our truths. Truths have once for all this desperate instinct of self-preservation and of desire to extinguish whatever contradicts them. My belief in the Absolute, based on the good it does me, must run the gauntlet of all my other beliefs. Grant that it may be true in giving me a moral holiday. Nevertheless, as I conceive it,—and let me speak now confidentially, as it were, and merely in my own private person,—it clashes with other truths of mine whose benefits I hate to give up on its account. It happens to be associated with a kind of logic of which I am the enemy, I find that it entangles me in metaphysical paradoxes that are inacceptable, etc., etc. But as I have enough trouble in life already without adding the trouble of carrying these intellectual inconsistencies, I personally just give up the Absolute. I just *take* my moral holidays; or else as a professional philosopher, I try to justify them by some other principle.

If I could restrict my notion of the Absolute to its bare holiday-giving value, it wouldn't clash with my other truths. But we can not easily thus restrict our hypotheses. They carry supernumerary features, and these it is that clash so. My disbelief in the Absolute means then disbelief in those other supernumerary features, for I fully believe in the legitimacy of taking moral holidays.

You see by this what I meant when I called pragmatism a mediator and reconciler and said, borrowing the word from Papini, that she 'unstiffens' our theories. She has in fact no prejudices whatever, no obstructive dogmas, no rigid canons of what shall count as proof. She is completely genial. She will entertain any hypothesis, she will consider any evidence. It follows that in the religious field she is at a great advantage both over positivistic empiricism, with its anti-theological bias, and over religious rationalism, with its exclusive interest in the remote, the noble, the simple, and the abstract in the way of conception.

In short, she widens the field of search for God. Rationalism sticks to logic and the empyrean. Empiricism sticks to the external senses. Pragmatism is willing to take anything, to follow either logic or the senses and to count the humblest and most personal experiences. She will count mystical experiences if they have practical consequences. She will take a God who lives in the very dirt of private fact—if that should seem a likely place to find him.

Her only test of probable truth is what works best in the way of leading us, what fits every part of life best and combines with the collectivity of experience's demands, nothing being omitted. If theological ideas should do this, if the notion of God, in particular, should prove to do it, how could pragmatism possibly deny God's existence? She could see no meaning in treating as 'not true' a notion that was pragmatically so successful. What other kind of truth could there be, for her, than all this agreement with concrete reality?

The Pragmatic Notion of Truth

I fully expect to see the pragmatist view of truth run through the classic stages of a theory's career. First, you know, a new theory is attacked as absurd; then it is admitted to be true, but obvious and insignificant; finally it is seen to be so important that its adversaries claim that they themselves discovered it. Our doctrine of truth is at present in the first of these three stages, with symptoms of the second stage having begun in certain quarters. I wish that this lecture might help it beyond the first stage in the eyes of many of you.

Truth, as any dictionary will tell you, is a property of certain of our ideas. It means their "agreement," as falsity means their "disagreement," with "reality." Pragmatists and intellectualists both accept this definition as a matter of course. They begin to quarrel only after the question is raised as to what may precisely be meant by the term "agreement," and what by the term "reality," when reality is taken as something for our ideas to agree with.

In answering these questions the pragmatists are more analytic and painstaking, the intellectualists more offhand and irreflective. The popular notion is that a true idea must copy its reality. Like other popular views, this one follows the analogy of the most usual experience. Our true ideas of sensible things do indeed copy them. Shut your eyes and think of yonder clock on the wall, and you get just such a true picture or copy of its dial. But your idea of its "works" (unless you are a clockmaker) is much less of a copy, yet it passes muster, for it in no way clashes with the reality. Even though it should shrink to the mere word "works," that word still serves you truly; and when you speak of the "time-keeping function" of the clock, or of its spring's "elasticity," it is hard to see exactly what your ideas can copy.

You perceive that there is a problem here. Where our ideas cannot copy definitely their object, what does agreement with that object mean? Some idealists seem to say that they are true whenever they are what God means that we ought to think about that subject. Others hold the copy-view all through, and speak as if our ideas possessed truth just in proportion as they approach to being copies of the Absolute's eternal way of thinking.

These views, you see, invite pragmatistic discussion. But the great assumption of the intellectualists is that truth means essentially an inert static relation. When you've got your true idea of anything, there's an end of the matter. You're in possession; you *know*; you have fulfilled your thinking destiny. You are where you ought to be mentally; you have obeyed your categorical imperative; and nothing more need follow on that climax of your rational destiny. Epistemologically you are in stable equilibrium.

Pragmatism, on the other hand, asks its usual question. "Grant an idea or belief to be true," it says, "what concrete difference will its being true make in any one's actual life? How will the truth be realized? What experiences will be different from those which would obtain if the belief were false? What, in short, is the truth's cash-value in experiential terms?"

The moment pragmatism asks this question, it sees the answer: *True ideas are those that we can assimilate, validate, corroborate and verify. False ideas are those that we cannot.* That is the practical difference it makes to us to have true ideas; that, therefore, is the meaning of truth, for it is all that truth is known-as.

This thesis is what I have to defend. The truth of an idea is not a stagnant property inherent in it. Truth *happens* to an idea. It *becomes* true, is *made* true by events. Its verity *is* in fact an event, a process: the process namely of its verifying itself, its veri-*fication.* Its validity is the process of its valid-*ation.*

But what do the words verification and validation themselves pragmatically mean? They again signify certain practical consequences of the verified and validated idea. It is hard to find any one phrase that characterizes these consequences better than the ordinary agreement-formula—just such consequences being what we have in mind whenever we say that our ideas "agree" with reality. They lead us, namely, through the acts and other ideas which they instigate, into or up to, or towards, other parts of experience with which we feel all the while—such feeling being among our potentialities—that the original ideas remain in agreement. The connexions and transitions come to us from point to point as being progressive, harmonious, satisfactory. This function of agreeable leading is what we mean by an idea's verification. . . .

. . . The possession of true thoughts means everywhere the possession of invaluable instruments of action; and that our duty to gain truth, so far from being a blank command from out of the blue, or a "stunt" self-imposed by our intellect, can account for itself by excellent practical reasons.

The importance to human life of having true beliefs about matters of fact is a thing too notorious. We live in a world of realities that can be infinitely useful or infinitely harmful. Ideas that tell us which of them to expect count as the true ideas in all this primary sphere of verification, and the pursuit of such ideas is a primary human duty. The possession of truth, so far from being here an end in itself, is only a preliminary means towards other vital satisfactions. If I am lost in the woods and starved, and find what looks like a cow-path, it is of the utmost importance that I should think of a human habitation at the end of it, for if I do so and follow it, I save myself. The true thought is useful here because the house which is its object is useful. The practical value of true ideas is thus primarily derived from the practical importance of their objects to us. Their objects are, indeed, not important at all times. I may on another occasion have no use for the house; and then my idea of it, however verifiable, will be practically irrelevant, and had better remain latent. Yet since almost any object may some day become temporarily important, the advantage of having a general stock of *extra* truths, of ideas that shall be true of merely possible situations, is obvious. We store such extra truths away in our memories, and with the overflow we fill our books of reference. Whenever such an extra truth becomes practically relevant to one of our emergencies, it passes from cold-storage to do work in the world and our belief in it grows active. You can say of it then either that "it is useful because it is true" or that "it is true because it is useful." Both these phrases mean exactly the same thing, namely that here is an idea that gets fulfilled and can be verified. True is the name for whatever idea starts the verification-process, useful is the name for its completed function in experience. True ideas would never have been singled out as such, would never have acquired a class-name, least of all a name suggesting value, unless they had been useful from the outset in this way.

From this simple cue pragmatism gets her general notion of truth as something essentially bound up with the way in which one moment in our experience may lead us towards other moments which it will be worth while to have been led to. Primarily, and on the common-sense level, the truth of a state of mind means this function of *a leading that is worth while.* When a moment in our experience, of any kind whatever, inspires us with a thought that is true, that means that sooner or later we dip by that thought's guidance into the particulars of experience again and make advantageous connexion with them. This is a vague enough statement, but I beg you to retain it, for it is essential.

Our experience meanwhile is all shot through with regularities. One bit of it can warn us to get ready for another bit, can "intend" or be "significant of" that remoter object. The object's advent is the significance's verification. Truth, in these cases, meaning nothing but eventual verification, is manifestly incompatible with waywardness on our part. Woe to him whose beliefs play fast and loose with the order which realities follow in his experience; they will lead him nowhere or else make false connexions.

By "realities" or "objects" here, we mean either things of common sense, sensibly present, or else common-sense relations, such as dates, places, distances, kinds, activities. Following our mental image of a house along the cow-path, we actually come to see the house; we get the image's full verification. *Such simply and fully verified leadings are certainly the originals and prototypes of the truth-process.* Experience offers indeed other forms of truth-process, but they are all conceivable as being primary verifications arrested, multiplied or substituted one for another.

Take, for instance, yonder object on the wall. You and I consider it to be a "clock," altho no one of us has seen the hidden works that make it one. We let our notion pass for true without attempting to verify. If truths mean verification-process essentially, ought we then to call such unverified truths as this abortive? No, for they form the overwhelmingly large number of the truths we live by. Indirect as well as direct verifications pass muster. Where circumstantial evidence is sufficient, we can go without eye-witnessing. Just as we here assume Japan to exist without ever having been there, because it *works* to do so, everything we know conspiring with the belief, and nothing interfering, so we assume that thing to be a clock. We *use* it as a clock, regulating the length of our lecture by it. The verification of the assumption here means its leading to no frustration or contradiction. Verifi*ability* of wheels and weights and pendulum is as good as verification. For one truth-process completed there are a million in our lives that function in this state of nascency. They turn us *towards* direct verification; lead us into the *surroundings* of the objects they envisage; and then, if everything runs on harmoniously, we are so sure that verification is possible that we omit it, and are usually justified by all that happens.

Truth lives, in fact, for the most part on a credit system. Our thoughts and beliefs "pass," so long as nothing challenges them, just as banknotes pass so long as nobody refuses them. But this all points to direct face-to-face verifications somewhere, without which the fabric of truth collapses like a financial system with no cashbasis whatever. You accept my verification of one thing, I yours of another. We trade on each other's truth. But beliefs verified concretely by *somebody* are the posts of the whole superstructure.

Another great reason—beside economy of time—for waiving complete verification in the usual business of life is that all things exist in kinds and not singly. Our world is found once for all to have that peculiarity. So that when we have once directly verified our ideas about one specimen of a kind, we consider ourselves free to apply them to other specimens without verification. A mind that habitually discerns the kind of thing before it, and acts by the law of the kind immediately, without pausing to verify, will be a "true" mind in ninety-nine out of a hundred emergencies, proved so by its conduct fitting everything it meets, and getting no refutation.

Indirectly or only potentially verifying processes may thus be true as well as full verification-processes. They work as true processes would work, give us the same advantages, and claim our recognition for the same reasons. . . .

[James returns to the notion that truth is an agreement with reality.]

Here it is that pragmatism and intellectualism begin to part company. Primarily, no doubt, to agree means to copy, but we saw that the mere word "clock" would do instead of a mental picture of its works, and that of many realities our ideas can only be symbols and not copies. "Past time," "power," "spontaneity"—how can our mind copy such realities?

To "agree" in the widest sense with a reality *can only mean to be guided either straight up to it or into its surroundings, or to be put into such work-*

ing touch with it as to handle either it or something connected with it better than if we disagreed. Better either intellectually or practically! And often agreement will only mean the negative fact that nothing contradictory from the quarter of that reality comes to interfere with the way in which our ideas guide us elsewhere. To copy a reality is, indeed, one very important way of agreeing with it, but it is far from being essential. The essential thing is the process of being guided. Any idea that helps us to *deal,* whether practically or intellectually, with either the reality or its belongings, that doesn't entangle our progress in frustrations, that *fits,* in fact, and adapts our life to the reality's whole setting, will agree sufficiently to meet the requirement. It will hold true of that reality.

Thus, *names* are just as "true" or "false" as definite mental pictures are. They set up similar verification-processes, and lead to fully equivalent practical results.

All human thinking gets discursified; we exchange ideas; we lend and borrow verifications, get them from one another by means of social intercourse. All truth thus gets verbally built out, stored up, and made available for every one. Hence, we must *talk* consistently just as we must *think* consistently: for both in talk and thought we deal with kinds. Names are arbitrary, but once understood they must be kept to. We mustn't now call Abel "Cain" or Cain "Abel." If we do, we ungear ourselves from the whole book of Genesis, and from all its connexions with the universe of speech and fact down to the present time. We throw ourselves out of whatever truth that entire system of speech and fact may embody.

The overwhelming majority of our true ideas admit of no direct or face-to-face verification—those of past history, for example, as of Cain and Abel. The stream of time can be remounted only verbally, or verified directly by the present prolongations or effects of what the past harbored. Yet if they agree with these verbalities and effects, we can know that our ideas of the past are true. *As true as past time itself was,* so true was Julius Caesar, so true were antediluvian monsters all in their proper dates and settings. That past time itself was, is guaranteed by its coherence with everything that's present. True as the present *is,* the past *was* also.

Agreement thus turns out to be essentially an affair of leading—leading that is useful because it is into quarters that contain objects that are important. True ideas lead us into useful verbal and conceptual quarters as well as directly up to useful sensible termini. They lead to consistency, stability and flowing human intercourse. They lead away from excentricity and isolation, from foiled and barren thinking. The untrammelled flowing of the leading-process, its general freedom from clash and contradiction, passes for its indirect verification; but all roads lead to Rome, and in the end and eventually, all true processes must lead to the face of directly verifying sensible experiences *somewhere,* which somebody's ideas have copied.

Such is the large loose way in which the pragmatist interprets the word agreement. He treats it altogether practically. He lets it cover any process of conduction from a present idea to a future terminus, provided only it run prosperously. It is only thus that "scientific" ideas, flying as they do beyond common sense, can be said to agree with their realities. It is, as I have already said, *as if* reality were made of ether, atoms or electrons, but we mustn't think so literally. The term "energy" doesn't even pretend to stand for anything "objective." It is only a way of measuring the surface of phenomena so as to string their changes on a simple formula.

Yet in the choice of these man-made formulas we cannot be capricious with impunity any more than we can be capricious on the common-sense practical level. We must find a theory that will *work;* and that means something extremely difficult; for our theory must mediate between all previous truths and certain new experiences. It must derange common sense and previous belief as little as possible, and it must lead to some sensible terminus or other that can be verified exactly. To "work" means both these things; and the squeeze is so tight that there is little loose play for any hypothesis. Our theories are wedged and controlled as nothing else is. Yet sometimes alternative theoretic formulas are equally compatible with all the truths we know, and then we choose between them for subjective reasons. We choose the kind of theory to which we are already partial; we follow "elegance" or "economy." Clerk-Maxwell somewhere says it would be "poor scientific taste" to choose the more complicated of two equally well-evidenced conceptions; and you will all agree with him. Truth in science is what gives us the maximum possible sum of satisfactions, taste included, but consistency both with previous truth and with novel fact is always the most imperious claimant. . . .

Our account of truth is an account of truths in the plural, of processes of leading, realized *in rebus* [in things], and having only this quality in common, that they *pay*. They pay by guiding us into or towards some part of a system that dips at numerous points into sense-percepts, which we may copy mentally or not, but with which at any rate we are now in the kind of commerce vaguely designated as verification. Truth for us is simply a collective name for verification-processes, just as health, wealth, strength, etc., are names for other processes connected with life, and also pursued because it pays to pursue them. Truth is *made,* just as health, wealth and strength are made, in the course of experience.

Here rationalism is instantaneously up in arms against us. I can imagine a rationalist to talk as follows:

"Truth is not made," he will say;

> it absolutely obtains, being a unique relation that does not wait upon any process, but shoots straight over the head of experience, and hits its reality every time. Our belief that yon thing on the wall is a clock is true already, altho no one in the whole history of the world should verify it. The bare quality of standing in that transcendent relation is what makes any thought true that possesses it, whether or not there be verification. You pragmatists put the cart before the horse in making truth's being reside in verification-processes. These are merely signs of its being, merely our lame ways of ascertaining after the fact, which of our ideas already has possessed the wondrous quality. The quality itself is timeless, like all essences and natures. Thoughts partake of it directly, as they partake of falsity or of irrelevancy. It can't be analyzed away into pragmatic consequences.

The whole plausibility of this rationalist tirade is due to the fact to which we have already paid so much attention. In our world, namely, abounding as it does in things of similar kinds and similarly associated, one verification serves for others of its kind, and one great use of knowing things is to be led not so much to them as to their associates, especially to human talk about them. The quality of truth, obtaining *ante rem* [before the thing], pragmatically means, then, the fact that in such a world innumerable ideas work better by their indirect or possible than by their direct and actual verification. Truth *ante rem* means only verifiability, then; or else it is a case of the stock rationalist trick of treating the *name* of a concrete phenomenal reality as an independent prior entity, and placing it behind the reality as its explanation. . . .

In the case of "wealth" we all see the fallacy. We know that wealth is but a name for concrete processes that certain men's lives play a part in, and not a natural excellence found in Messrs. Rockefeller and Carnegie, but not in the rest of us.

Like wealth, "health" also lives *in rebus.* It is a name for processes, as digestion, circulation, sleep, etc., that go on happily, tho in this instance we are more inclined to think of it as a principle and to say the man digests and sleeps so well *because* he is so healthy.

With "strength" we are, I think, more rationalistic still, and decidedly inclined to treat it as an excellence pre-existing in the man and explanatory of the herculean performances of his muscles.

With "truth" most people go over the border entirely, and treat the rationalistic account as self-evident. But really all these words in *th* are exactly similar. Truth exists *ante rem* just as much and as little as the other things do.

The scholastics, following Aristotle, made much of the distinction between habit and act. Health *in actu* means, among other things, good sleeping and digesting. But a healthy man need not always be sleeping, or always digesting, any more than a wealthy man need be always handling money, or a strong man always lifting weights. All such qualities sink to the status of "habits" between their times of exercise; and similarly truth becomes a habit of certain of our ideas and beliefs in their intervals of rest from their verifying activities. But those activities are the root of the whole matter, and the condition of there being any habit to exist in the intervals.

"The true," to put it very briefly, is only the expedient in the way of our thinking, just as "the right" is only the expedient in the way of our behaving. Expedient in almost any fashion; and expedient in the long run and on the whole of course; for what meets expediently all the experience in sight won't necessarily meet all further experiences equally satisfactorily. Experience, as we know, has ways of *boiling over,* and making us correct our present formulas.

The "absolutely" true, meaning what no further experience will ever alter, is that ideal vanishing-point towards which we imagine that all our temporary truths will some day converge. It runs on all fours with the perfectly wise man, and with the absolutely complete experience; and, if these ideals are ever realized, they will all be realized together. Meanwhile we have to live today by what truth we can get today, and be ready tomorrow to call it falsehood. Ptolemaic astronomy, Euclidean space, Aristotelian logic, Scholastic metaphysics, were expedient for centuries, but human experience has boiled over those limits, and we now call these things only relatively true, or true within those borders of experience. "Absolutely" they are false; for we know that those limits were casual, and might have been transcended by past theorists just as they are by present thinkers.

When new experiences lead to retrospective judgments, using the past tense, what these judgments utter *was* true, even tho no past thinker had been led there. We live forwards, a Danish thinker [Kierkegaard] has said, but we understand backwards. The present sheds a backward light on the world's previous processes. They may have been truth-processes for the actors in them. They are not so for one who knows the later revelations of the story.

This regulative notion of a potential better truth to be established later, possibly to be established some day absolutely, and having powers of retroactive legislation, turns its face, like all pragmatist notions, towards concreteness of fact, and towards the future. Like the half-truths, the absolute truth will have to be *made,* made as a relation incidental to the growth of a mass of verification-experience, to which the half-true ideas are all along contributing their quota.

I have already insisted on the fact that truth is made largely out of previous truths. Men's beliefs at any time are so much experience *funded.* But the beliefs are themselves parts of the sum total of the world's experience, and become matter, therefore, for the next day's funding operations. So far as reality means experienceable reality, both it and the truths men gain about it are everlastingly in process of mutation—mutation towards a definite goal, it may be—but still mutation.

Mathematicians can solve problems with two variables. On the Newtonian theory, for instance, acceleration varies with distance, but distance also varies with acceleration. In the realm of truth-processes facts come independently and determine our beliefs provisionally. But these beliefs make us act, and as fast as they do so, they bring into sight or into existence new facts which re-determine the beliefs accordingly. So the whole coil and ball of truth, as it rolls up, is the product of a double influence. Truths emerge from facts; but they dip forward into facts again and add to them; which facts again create or reveal new truth (the word is indifferent) and so on indefinitely. The "facts" themselves meanwhile are not *true.* They simply *are.* Truth is the function of the beliefs that start and terminate among them. . . .

The case is like a snowball's growth, due as it is to the distribution of the snow on the one hand, and to the successive pushes of the boys on the other, with these factors co-determining each other incessantly. . . .

I am well aware how odd it must seem to some of you to hear me say that an idea is "true" so long as to believe it is profitable to our lives. That it is *good,* for as much as it profits, you will gladly admit. If what we do by its aid is good, you will allow the idea itself to be good in so far forth, for we are the better for possessing it. But is it not a strange misuse of the word "truth," you will say, to call ideas also "true" for this reason? . . .

. . . Let me now say only this, that truth is *one species of good,* and not, as is usually supposed, a category distinct from good, and co-ordinate with it. *The true is the name of whatever proves itself to be good in the way of belief and good, too, for definite, assignable reasons.* Surely you must admit this, that if there were *no* good for life in true ideas, or if the knowledge of them were positively disadvantageous and false ideas the only useful ones, then the current notion that truth is divine and precious, and its pursuit a duty, could never have grown up or become a dogma. In a world like that, our duty would be to *shun* truth, rather. But in this world, just as certain foods are not only agreeable to our taste, but good for our teeth, our stomach, and our tissues; so certain ideas are not only agreeable to think about, or agreeable as supporting other ideas that we are fond of, but they are also helpful in life's practical struggles. If there be any life that it is really better we should lead, and if there be any idea which, if believed in, would help us to lead that life, then it would be really *better for us* to believe in that idea, *unless, indeed, belief in it incidentally clashed with other greater vital benefits.*

"What would be better for us to believe!" This sounds very like a definition of truth. It comes very near to saying "what we *ought* to believe"; and in *that* definition none of you would find any oddity. Ought we ever not to believe what it is *better for us* to believe? And can we then keep the notion of what is better for us, and what is true for us, permanently apart?

Pragmatism says no, and I fully agree with her. Probably you also agree, so far as the abstract statement goes, but with a suspicion that if we practically did believe everything that made for good in our own personal lives, we should be found indulging all kinds of fancies about this world's affairs, and all kinds of sentimental superstitions about a world hereafter. Your suspicion here is undoubtedly well founded, and it is evident that something happens when you pass from the abstract to the concrete that complicates the situation.

I said just now that what is better for us to believe is true *unless the belief incidentally clashes with some other vital benefit.* Now in real life what vital benefits is any particular belief of ours most liable to clash with? What indeed except the vital benefits yielded by *other beliefs* when these prove incompatible with the first ones? In other words, the greatest enemy of any one of our truths may be the rest of our truths. Truths have once for all this desperate instinct of self-preservation and of desire to extinguish whatever contradicts them.

Chapter 6

Rudolf Carnap

Rudolf Carnap (1891–1970) was born near Barman in Germany of deeply Christian parents. He studied classics at his high school (*gymnasium*), at which time his commitment to science caused him to abandon his parents' faith. In 1910 he entered the University of Jena, which he attended until 1914 when he joined the German army to fight in the First World War. After the war, he joined the Vienna Circle, becoming one of the founders of Logical Positivism (see Introduction). Rejecting Nazism, in 1936 he accepted the offer of a position from the University of Chicago. He greatly influenced the work of W. V. O. Quine (see Chapter 12) and many other philosophers.

Carnap's major work is *The Logical Structure of the World* (1928) in which he describes in great detail this radical empiricist program of restructuring all knowledge on positivist principles, especially the view that a proposition is cognitively meaningful if and only if it is verifiable. One of Positivism's main goals was to eliminate metaphysical language as unverifiable, and thus meaningless. The selection before us, especially its analysis of Heidegger's metaphysic (see Chapter 33), is a classic expression of that part of the positivists' program.

FOR FURTHER READING

Carnap, Rudolf. *The Logical Structure of the World* (Berlin, 1928).

———. *Logical Syntax of Language* (Routledge & Kegan Paul, 1935).

———. *The Logical Foundations of Probability* (University of Chicago Press, 1950).

Naess, Arne. *Four Modern Philosophers* (University of Chicago Press, 1965).

Runggalier, Edmund. *Carnap's Early Conventionalism* (Rapoldi, 1984).

The Elimination of Metaphysics Through Logical Analysis of Language

1. INTRODUCTION

There have been many *opponents of metaphysics** from the Greek skeptics to the empiricists of the 19th century. Criticisms of very diverse kinds have been set forth. Many have declared that the doctrine of metaphysics is *false*, since it *contradicts* our *empirical* knowledge. Others have believed it to be *uncertain*, on the ground that its problems transcend the limits of human knowledge. Many anti-metaphysicians have declared that occupation with metaphysical questions is *sterile*. Whether or not these questions can be answered, it is at any rate unnecessary to worry about them; let us devote ourselves entirely to the practical tasks which confront active men every day of their lives!

The development of *modern logic* has made it possible to give a new and sharper answer to the question of the validity and justification of metaphysics. The researches of applied logic or the theory of knowledge, which aim at clarifying the cognitive content of scientific statements and thereby the meanings** of the terms that occur in the statements, by means of logical analysis, lead to a positive and to a negative result. The positive result is worked out in the domain of empirical science; the various concepts of the various branches of science are clarified; their formal-logical and epistemological connections are made explicit. In the domain of *metaphysics*, including all philosophy of value and normative theory, logical analysis yields the negative result *that the alleged statements in this domain are entirely meaningless*. Therewith a radical elimination of metaphysics is attained, which was not yet possible from the earlier antimetaphysical standpoints. It is true that related ideas may be found already in several earlier trains of thought, e.g. those of a nominalistic kind; but it is only now when the development of logic during recent decades provides us with a sufficiently sharp tool that the decisive step can be taken.

In saying that the so-called statements of metaphysics are *meaningless*, we intend this word in its strictest sense. In a loose sense of the word a statement or a question is at times called meaningless if it is entirely sterile to assert or ask it. We might say this for instance about the question "what is the average weight of those inhabitants of Vienna whose telephone number ends with '3'?" or about a statement which is quite obviously false like "in 1910 Vienna had 6 inhabitants" or about a statement which is not just empirically, but logically false, a contradictory statement such as "persons A and B are each a year older than the other." Such sentences are really meaningful, though they are pointless or false; for it is only meaningful sentences that are even divisible into (theoretically) fruitful and sterile, true and false. In the strict sense, however, a sequence of words is *meaningless* if it does not, within a specified language, constitute a statement. It may

*This term is used in this paper, as usually in Europe, for the field of alleged knowledge of the essence of things which transcends the realm of empirically founded, inductive science. Metaphysics in this sense includes systems like those of Fichte, Schelling, Hegel, Bergson, Heidegger. But it does not include endeavors towards a synthesis and generalization of the results of the various sciences.

**Today we distinguish various kinds of meaning, in particular cognitive (designative, referential) meaning on the one hand, and non-cognitive (expressive) meaning components, e.g. emotive and motivative, on the other. In the present paper, the word "meaning" is always understood in the sense of "cognitive meaning." The thesis that the sentences of metaphysics are meaningless, is thus to be understood in the sense that they have no cognitive meaning, no assertive content. The obvious psychological fact that they have expressive meaning is thereby not denied; this is explicitly stated in Section 7.

Rudolf Carnap, "The Elimination of Metaphysics Through Logical Analysis of Language" in *Logical Positivism*, translated by Arthur Pap, edited by A. J. Ayer (Glencoe, IL: The Free Press, 1959), pp. 60–81. Originally entitled "Uberwindung der Metaphysik durch Logische Analyse der Sprache," *Erkenntnis*, Vol. II (1932). Reprinted by permission of The Free Press, a Macmillan Company.

happen that such a sequence of words looks like a statement at first glance; in that case we call it a *pseudo-statement*. Our thesis, now, is that logical analysis reveals the alleged statements of metaphysics to be pseudo-statements.

A language consists of a vocabulary and a syntax, i.e. a set of words which have meanings and rules of sentence formation. These rules indicate how sentences may be formed out of the various sorts of words. Accordingly, there are two kinds of pseudo-statements: either they contain a word which is erroneously believed to have meaning, or the constituent words are meaningful, yet are put together in a counter-syntactical way, so that they do not yield a meaningful statement. We shall show in terms of examples that pseudo-statements of both kinds occur in metaphysics. Later we shall have to inquire into the reasons that support our contention that metaphysics in its entirety consists of such pseudo-statements.

2. THE SIGNIFICANCE OF A WORD

A word which (within a definite language) has a meaning, is usually also said to designate a concept; if it only seems to have a meaning while it really does not, we speak of a "pseudo-concept." How is the origin of a pseudo-concept to be explained? Has not every word been introduced into the language for no other purpose than to express something or other, so that it had a definite meaning from the very beginning of its use? How, then, can a traditional language contain meaningless words? To be sure, originally every word (excepting rare cases which we shall illustrate later) had a meaning. In the course of historical development a word frequently changes its meaning. And it also happens at times that a word loses its old sense without acquiring a new one. It is thus that a pseudo-concept arises.

What, now, is the *meaning of a word*? What stipulations concerning a word must be made in order for it to be significant? (It does not matter for our investigation whether these stipulations are explicitly laid down, as in the case of some words and symbols of modern science, or whether they have been tacitly agreed upon, as is the case for most words of traditional language.) First, the syntax of the word must be fixed, i.e. the mode of its occurrence in the simplest sentence form in which it is capable of occurring; we call this sentence form its *elementary sentence*. The elementary sentence form for the word "stone" e.g. is "x is a stone"; in sentences of this form some designation from the category of things occupies the place of "x," e.g. "this diamond," "this apple." Secondly, for an elementary sentence S containing the word an answer must be given to the following question, which can be formulated in various ways:

1. What sentences is S *deducible* from, and what sentences are deducible from S?
2. Under what conditions is S supposed to be true, and under what conditions false?
3. How is S to be *verified*?
4. What is the *meaning* of S?

(1) is the correct formulation; formulation (2) accords with the phraseology of logic, (3) with the phraseology of the theory of knowledge, (4) with that of philosophy (phenomenology). Wittgenstein has asserted that (2) expresses what philosophers mean by (4): the meaning of a sentence consists in its truth-condition. ([1] is the "metalogical" formulation; it is planned to give elsewhere a detailed exposition of metalogic as the theory of syntax and meaning, i.e. relations of deducibility.)

In the case of many words, specifically in the case of the overwhelming majority of scientific words, it is possible to specify their meaning by reduction to other words ("constitution," definition). E.g. " 'arthropodes' " are animals with segmented bodies and jointed legs." Thereby the above-mentioned question for the elementary sentence form of the word "arthropode," that is for the sentence form "the thing x is an arthropode," is answered: it has been stipulated that a sentence of this form is deducible from premises of the form "x is an animal," "x has a segmented body," "x has jointed legs," and that conversely each of these sentences is deducible from the former sentence. By means of these stipulations about deducibility (in other words: about the truth-condition, about the method of verification, about the meaning) of the elementary sentence about "arthropode" the meaning of the word "arthropode" is fixed. In this way every word of the language is reduced to other words and finally to the words which occur in the so-called "observation sentences" or "protocol sentences." It is through this reduction that the word acquires its meaning.

For our purposes we may ignore entirely the question concerning the content and form of the primary sentences (protocol sentences) which has not yet been definitely settled. In the theory of knowledge it is customary to say that the primary sentences refer to "the given"; but there is no unanimity on the question what it is that is given. At times the position is taken that sentences about the given speak of the simplest qualities of sense and feeling (e.g. "warm," "blue," "joy" and so forth); others incline to the view that basic sentences refer to total experiences and similarities between them; a still different view has it that even the basic sentences speak of things. Regardless of this diversity of opinion it is certain that a sequence of words has a meaning only if its relations of deducibility to the protocol sentences are fixed, whatever the characteristics of the protocol sentences may be; and similarly, that a word is significant only if the sentences in which it may occur are reducible to protocol sentences.

Since the meaning of a word is determined by its criterion of application (in other words: by the relations of deducibility entered into by its elementary sentence-form, by its truth-conditions, by the method of its verification), the stipulation of the criterion takes away one's freedom to decide what one wishes to "mean" by the word. If the word is to receive an exact meaning, nothing less than the criterion of application must be given; but one cannot, on the other hand, give more than the criterion of application, for the latter is a sufficient determination of meaning. The meaning is implicitly contained in the criterion; all that remains to be done is to make the meaning explicit.

Let us suppose, by way of illustration, that someone invented the new word "teavy" and maintained that there are things which are teavy and things which are not teavy. In order to learn the meaning of this word, we ask him about its criterion of application: how is one to ascertain in a concrete case whether a given thing is teavy or not? Let us suppose to begin with that we get no answer from him: there are no empirical signs of teavyness, he says. In that case we would deny the legitimacy of using this word. If the person who uses the word says that all the same there are things which are teavy and there are things which are not teavy, only it remains for the weak, finite intellect of man an eternal secret which things are teavy and which are not, we shall regard this as empty verbiage. But perhaps he will assure us that he means, after all, something by the word "teavy." But from this we only learn the psychological fact that he associates some kind of images and feelings with the word. The word does not acquire a meaning through such associations. If no criterion of application for the word is stipulated, then nothing is asserted by the sentences in which it occurs, they are but pseudo-statements.

Secondly, take the case when we are given a criterion of application for a new word, say "toovy"; in particular, let the sentence "this thing is toovy" be true if and only if the thing is quadrangular. (It is irrelevant in this context whether the criterion is explicitly stated or whether we derive it by observing the affirmative and the negative uses of the word.)

Then we will say: the word "toovy" is synonymous with the word "quadrangular." And we will not allow its users to tell us that nevertheless they "intended" something else by it than "quadrangular"; that though every quadrangular thing is also toovy and conversely, this is only because quadrangularity is the visible manifestation of toovyness, but that the latter itself is a hidden, not itself observable property. We would reply that after the criterion of application has been fixed, the synonymy of "toovy" and "quadrangular" is likewise fixed, and that we are no further at liberty to "intend" this or that by the word.

Let us briefly summarize the result of our analysis. Let "a" be any word and "S(a)" the elementary sentence in which it occurs. Then the sufficient and necessary condition for "a" being meaningful may be given by each of the following formulation, which ultimately say the same thing:

1. The *empirical criteria* for a are known.
2. It has been stipulated from what protocol sentence "S(a)" is *deducible.*
3. The *truth-conditions* for "S(a)" are fixed.
4. The method of *verification* of "S(a)" is known.*

3. METAPHYSICAL WORDS WITHOUT MEANING

Many words of metaphysics, now, can be shown not to fulfill the above requirement, and therefore to be devoid of meaning.

Let us take as an example the metaphysical term "principle" (in the sense of principle of being, not

*For the logical and epistemological conception which underlies our exposition, but can only briefly be intimated here, cf. Wittgenstein, *Tractatus Logico-Philosophicus*, 1922, and Carnap, *Der logische Aufbau der Welt*, 1928.

principle of knowledge or axiom). Various metaphysicians offer an answer to the question which is the (highest) "principle of the world" (or of "things," of "existence," of "being"), e.g. water, number, form, motion, life, the spirit, the idea, the unconscious, activity, the good, and so forth. In order to discover the meaning of the word "principle" in this metaphysical question we must ask the metaphysician under what conditions a statement of the form "x is the principle of y" would be true and under what conditions it would be false. In other words: we ask for the criteria of application or for the definition of the word "principle." The metaphysician replies approximately as follows: "x is the principle of y" is to mean "y arises out of x," "the being of y rests on the being of x," "y exists by virtue of x" and so forth. But these words are ambiguous and vague. Frequently they have a clear meaning; e.g., we say of a thing or process y that it "arises out of" x when we observe that things or processes of kind x are frequently or invariably followed by things or processes of kind y (causal connection in the sense of a lawful succession). But the metaphysician tells us that he does not mean this empirically observable relationship. For in that case his metaphysical theses would be merely empirical propositions of the same kind as those of physics. The expression "arising from" is not to mean here a relation of temporal and causal sequence, which is what the word ordinarily means. Yet, no criterion is specified for any other meaning. Consequently, the alleged "metaphysical" meaning, which the word is supposed to have here in contrast to the mentioned empirical meaning, does not exist. If we reflect on the original meaning of the word "principium" (and of the corresponding Greek word ⟨*arche*⟩) we notice the same development. The word is explicitly deprived of its original meaning "beginning"; it is not supposed to mean the temporally prior any more, but the prior in some other, specifically metaphysical, respect. The criteria for this "metaphysical respect," however, are lacking. In both cases, then, the word has been deprived of its earlier meaning without being given a new meaning; there remains the word as an empty shell. From an earlier period of significant use, it is still associatively connected with various mental images; these in turn get associated with new mental images and feelings in the new context of usage. But the word does not thereby become meaningful, and it remains meaningless as long as no method of verification can be described.

Another example is the word "God." Here we must, apart from the variations of its usage within each domain, distinguish the linguistic usage in three different contexts or historical epochs, which however overlap temporally. In its *mythological* use the word has a clear meaning. It, or parallel words in other languages, is sometimes used to denote physical beings which are enthroned on Mount Olympus, in Heaven or in Hades, and which are endowed with power, wisdom, goodness and happiness to a greater or lesser extent. Sometimes the word also refers to spiritual beings which, indeed, do not have manlike bodies, yet manifest themselves nevertheless somehow in the things or processes of the visible world and are therefore empirically verifiable. In its *metaphysical* use, on the other hand, the word "God" refers to something beyond experience. The word is deliberately divested of its reference to a physical being or to a spiritual being that is immanent in the physical. And as it is not given a new meaning, it becomes meaningless. To be sure, it often looks as though the word "God" had a meaning even in metaphysics. But the definitions which are set up prove on closer inspection to be pseudo-definitions. They lead either to logically illegitimate combinations of words (of which we shall treat later) or to other metaphysical words (e.g. "primordial basis," "the absolute," "the unconditioned," "the autonomous," "the self-dependent," and so forth), but in no case to the truth-conditions of its elementary sentences. In the case of this word not even the first requirement of logic is met, that is the requirement to specify its syntax, i.e. the form of its occurrence in elementary sentences. An elementary sentence would here have to be of the form "x is a God"; yet, the metaphysician either rejects this form entirely without substituting another, or if he accepts it he neglects to indicate the syntactical category of the variable x. (Categories are, for example, material things, properties of things, relations between things, numbers etc.)

The *theological* usage of the word "God" falls between its mythological and its metaphysical usage. There is no distinctive meaning here, but an oscillation from one of the mentioned two uses to the other. Several theologians have a clearly empirical (in our terminology, "mythological") concept of God. In this case there are no pseudo-statements; but the disadvantage for the theologian lies in the circumstance that according to this interpretation the statements of theology are empirical and hence are subject to the judgment of empirical science. The linguistic usage of other theologians is clearly metaphysical. Others again do not speak in any definite way, whether this is because they follow now this, now that linguistic usage, or because they express themselves in terms whose usage is not clearly classifiable since it tends towards both sides.

Just like the examined examples "principle" and "God," most of the other *specifically metaphysical terms are devoid of meaning*, e.g. "the Idea," "the Absolute," "the Unconditioned," "the Infinite," "the being of being," "non-being," "thing in itself," "absolute spirit," "objective spirit," "essence," "being-in-itself," "being-in-and-for itself," "emanation," "manifestation," "articulation," "the Ego," "the non-Ego," etc. These expressions are in the same boat with "teavy," our previously fabricated example. The metaphysician tells us that empirical truth-conditions cannot be specified; if he adds that nevertheless he "means" something, we know that this is merely an allusion to associated images and feelings which, however, do not bestow a meaning on the word. The alleged statements of metaphysics which contain such words have no sense, assert nothing, are mere pseudo-statements. Into the explanation of their historical origin we shall inquire later.

4. THE SIGNIFICANCE OF A SENTENCE

So far we have considered only those pseudo-statements which contain a meaningless word. But there is a second kind of pseudo-statement. They consist of meaningful words, but the words are put together in such a way that nevertheless no meaning results. The syntax of a language specifies which combinations of words are admissible and which inadmissible. The grammatical syntax of natural languages, however, does not fulfill the task of elimination of senseless combinations of words in all cases. Let us take as examples the following sequences of words:

1. "Caesar is and"
2. "Caesar is a prime number"

The word sequence (1) is formed countersyntactically; the rules of syntax require that the third position be occupied, not by a conjunction, but by a predicate, hence by a noun (with article) or by an adjective. The word sequence "Caesar is a general," e.g. is formed in accordance with the rules of syntax. It is a meaningful word sequence, a genuine sentence. But, now, word sequence (2) is likewise syntactically correct, for it has the same grammatical form as the sentence just mentioned. Nevertheless (2) is meaningless. "Prime number" is a predicate of numbers; it can be neither affirmed nor denied of a person. Since (2) looks like a statement yet is not a statement, does not assert anything, expresses neither a true nor a false proposition, we call this word sequence a "pseudo-statement." The fact that the rules of grammatical syntax are not violated easily seduces one at first glance into the erroneous opinion that one still has to do with a statement, albeit a false one. But "a is a prime number" is false if and only if a is divisible by a natural number different from a and from 1; evidently it is illicit to put here "Caesar" for "a." This example has been so chosen that the nonsense is easily detectable. Many so-called statements of metaphysics are not so easily recognized to be pseudo-statements. The fact that natural languages allow the formation of meaningless sequences of words without violating the rules of grammar, indicates that grammatical syntax is, from a logical point of view, inadequate. If grammatical syntax corresponded exactly to logical syntax, pseudo-statements could not arise. If grammatical syntax differentiated not only the word categories of nouns, adjectives, verbs, conjunctions etc., but within each of these categories made the further distinctions that are logically indispensable, then no pseudo-statements could be formed. If, e.g., nouns were grammatically subdivided into several kinds of words, according as they designated properties of physical objects, of numbers etc., then the words "general" and "prime number" would belong to grammatically different word-categories, and (2) would be just as linguistically incorrect as (1). In a correctly constructed language, therefore, all nonsensical sequences of words would be of the kind of example (1). Considerations of grammar would already eliminate them as it were automatically; i.e. in order to avoid nonsense, it would be unnecessary to pay attention to the meanings of the individual words over and above their syntactical type (their "syntactical category," e.g. thing, property of things, relation between things, number, property of numbers, relation between numbers, and so forth). It follows that if our thesis that the statements of metaphysics are pseudo-statements is justifiable, then metaphysics could not even be expressed in a logically constructed language. This is the great philosophical importance of the task, which at present occupies the logicians, of building a logical syntax.

5. METAPHYSICAL PSEUDO-STATEMENTS

Let us now take a look at some examples of metaphysical pseudo-statements of a kind where the violation of logical syntax is especially obvious, though they accord with historical-grammatical syntax. We select a few sentences from that metaphysical school which at present exerts the strongest influence in Germany.*

> What is to be investigated is being only and—*nothing* else; being alone and further—*nothing*; solely being, and beyond being—*nothing. What about this Nothing? . . . Does the Nothing exist only because the Not, i.e. the Negation, exists?* Or is it the other way around? *Does Negation and the Not exist only because the Nothing exists?* . . . We assert: *the Nothing is prior to the Not and the Negation*. . . . Where do we seek the Nothing? How do we find the Nothing. . . . We know the Nothing. . . . *Anxiety reveals the Nothing*. . . . That for which and because of which we were anxious, was 'really'—nothing. Indeed: the Nothing itself—as such—was present. . . . What about this Nothing?—The Nothing itself nothings.

In order to show that the possibility of forming pseudo-statements is based on a logical defect of language, we set up the schema below. The sentences under I are grammatically as well as logically impeccable, hence meaningful. The sentences under II (excepting B3) are in grammatical respects perfectly analogous to those under I. Sentence form IIA (as question and answer) does not, indeed, satisfy the requirements to be imposed on a logically correct language. But it is nevertheless meaningful, because it is translatable into correct language. This is shown by sentence IIIA, which has the same meaning as IIA. Sentence form IIA then proves to be undesirable because we can be led from it, by means of grammatically faultless operations, to the meaningless sentence forms IIB, which are taken from the above quotation. These forms cannot even be constructed in the correct language of Column III. Nonetheless, their nonsensicality is not obvious at first glance, because one is easily deceived by the analogy with the meaningful sentences IB. The fault of our language identified here lies, therefore, in the circumstance that, in contrast to a logically correct language, it admits of the same grammatical form for meaningful and meaningless word sequences. To each sentence in words we have added a corresponding formula in the notation of symbolic logic; these formulae facilitate recognition of the undesirable analogy between IA and IIA and therewith of the origin of the meaningless construction IIB.

On closer inspection of the pseudo-statements under IIB, we also find some differences. The construction of sentence (1) is simply based on the mistake of employing the word "nothing" as a noun, because it is customary in ordinary language to use it in this form in order to construct a negative existential statement (see IIA). In a correct language, on the other hand, it is not a particular name, but a certain *logical form* of the sentence that serves this purpose (see IIIA). Sentence IIB2 adds something new, viz. the fabrication of the meaningless word "to nothing." This sentence, therefore, is senseless for a twofold reason. We pointed out before that the meaningless words of metaphysics usually owe their origin to the fact that a meaningful word is deprived of its meaning through its metaphorical use in metaphysics. But here we confront one of those rare cases where a new word is introduced which never had a meaning to begin with. Likewise sentence IIB3 must be rejected for two reasons. In respect of the error of using the word "nothing" as a noun, it is like the previous sentences. But in addition it involves a contradiction. For even if it were admissible to introduce "nothing" as a name or description of an entity, still the existence of this entity would be denied in its very definition, whereas sentence (3) goes on to affirm its existence. This sentence, therefore, would be contradictory, hence absurd, even if it were not already meaningless.

In view of the gross logical errors which we find in sentences IIB, we might be led to conjecture that perhaps the word "nothing" has in Heidegger's treatise a meaning entirely different from the customary one. And this presumption is further strengthened as we go on to read there that anxiety reveals the Nothing, that the Nothing itself is present as such in anx-

*The following quotations (original italics) are taken from M. Heidegger, *Was Ist Metaphysik*? 1929. We could just as well have selected passages from any other of the numerous metaphysicians of the present or of the past; yet the selected passages seem to us to illustrate our thesis especially well.

I. *Meaningful Sentences of Ordinary Language*	*II.* *Transition from Sense to Nonsense in Ordinary Language*	*III.* *Logically Correct Language*
A. What is outside? Ou(?) Rain is outside Ou(r)	A. What is outside? Ou(?) Nothing is outside Ou(no)	A. There is nothing (does not exist anything) which is outside. $\sim (\exists x).Ou(x)$
B. What about this rain? (i.e. what does the rain do? or: what else can be said about this rain? ?(r)	B. "What about this Nothing?" ?(no)	B. None of these forms can even be constructed.
1. We know the rain K(r)	1. "We seek the Nothing" "We find the Nothing?" "We know the Nothing" K(no)	
2. The rain rains R(r)	2. "The Nothing nothings" No(no)	
	3. "The Nothing exists only because . . . " Ex(no)	

iety. For here the word "nothing" seems to refer to a certain emotional constitution, possibly of a religious sort, or something or other that underlies such emotions. If such were the case, then the mentioned logical errors in sentences IIB would not be committed. But the first sentence of the quotation at the beginning of this section proves that this interpretation is not possible. The combination of "only" and "nothing else" shows unmistakably that the word "nothing" here has the usual meaning of a logical particle that serves for the formulation of a negative existential statement. This introduction of the word "nothing" is then immediately followed by the leading question of the treatise: "What about this Nothing?"

But our doubts as to a possible misinterpretation get completely dissolved as we note that the author of the treatise is clearly aware of the conflict between his questions and statements, and logic. "*Question and answer* in regard to the Nothing are equally *absurd* in themselves. . . . The fundamental rule of thinking commonly appealed to, the law of prohibited contradiction, general '*logic,*' destroys this question." All the worse for logic! We must abolish its sovereignty: "If thus the power of the *understanding* in the field of questions concerning Nothing and Being is broken, then the fate of the sovereignty of 'logic' within philosophy is thereby decided as well. The very idea of 'logic' dissolves in the whirl of a more basic questioning." But will sober science condone the whirl of counter logical questioning? To this question too there is a ready answer: "The alleged sobriety and superiority of science becomes ridiculous if it does not take the Nothing seriously." Thus we find here a good confirmation of our thesis; a metaphysician himself here states that his questions and answers are irreconcilable with logic and the scientific way of thinking.

The difference between our thesis and that of the earlier *anti-metaphysicians* should now be clear. We do not regard metaphysics as "mere speculation" or "fairy tales." The statements of a fairy tale do not conflict with logic, but only with experience, they are perfectly meaningful, although false. Metaphysics is not "*superstition*"; it is possible to believe true and false propositions, but not to believe meaningless sequences of words. Metaphysical statements are not even acceptable as "*working hypotheses*"; for an hypothesis must be capable of entering into relations of deducibility with (true or false) empirical statements, which is just what pseudo-statements cannot do.

With reference to the so-called *limitation of human knowledge* an attempt is sometimes made to save metaphysics by raising the following objection: metaphysical statements are not, indeed, verifiable by man nor by any other finite being; nevertheless they might be construed as conjectures about the answers which a being with higher or even perfect powers of knowledge would make to our questions, and as such conjectures they would, after all, be meaningful. To counter this objection, let us consider the following. If the meaning of a word cannot be specified, or if the sequence of words does not accord with the rules of syntax, then one has not even asked a question. (Just think of the pseudo-questions: "Is this table teavy?" "Is the number 7 holy?" "Which numbers are darker, the even or the odd ones?") Where there is no question, not even an omniscient being can give an answer. Now the objector may say: just as one who can see may communicate new knowledge to the blind, so a higher being might perhaps communicate to us metaphysical knowledge, e.g. whether the visible world is the manifestation of a spirit. Here we must reflect on the meaning of "new knowledge." It is, indeed, conceivable that we might encounter animals who tell us about a new sense. If these beings were to prove to us Fermat's theorem or were to invent a new physical instrument or were to establish a hitherto unknown law of nature, then our knowledge would be increased with their help. For this sort of thing we can test, just the way even a blind man can understand and test the whole of physics (and therewith any statement made by those who can see). But if those hypothetical beings tell us something which we cannot verify, then we cannot understand it either; in that case no information has been communicated to us, but mere verbal sounds devoid of meaning though possibly associated with images. It follows that our knowledge can only be quantitatively enlarged by other beings, no matter whether they know more or less or everything, but no knowledge of an essentially different kind can be added. What we do not know for certain, we may come to know with greater certainty through the assistance of other beings; but what is unintelligible, meaningless for us, cannot become meaningful through someone else's assistance, however vast his knowledge might be. Therefore no god and no devil can give us metaphysical knowledge.

6. MEANINGLESSNESS OF ALL METAPHYSICS

The examples of metaphysical statements which we have analyzed were all taken from just one treatise. But our results apply with equal validity, in part even in verbally identical ways, to other metaphysical systems. That treatise is completely in the right in citing approvingly a statement by Hegel ("pure Being and pure Nothing, therefore, are one and the same"). The metaphysics of Hegel has exactly the same logical character as this modern system of metaphysics. And the same holds for the rest of the metaphysical systems, though the kind of phraseology and therewith the kind of logical errors that occur in them deviate more or less from the kind that occurs in the examples we discussed.

It should not be necessary here to adduce further examples of specific metaphysical sentences in diverse systems and submit them to analysis. We confine ourselves to an indication of the most frequent kinds of errors.

Perhaps the majority of the logical mistakes that are committed when pseudo-statements are made, are based on the logical faults infecting the use of the word "to be" in our language (and of the corresponding words in other languages, at least in most European languages). The first fault is the ambiguity of the word "to be." It is sometimes used as copula prefixed to a predicate ("I am hungry"), sometimes to designate existence ("I am"). This mistake is aggravated by the fact that metaphysicians often are not clear about this ambiguity. The second fault lies in the form of the verb in its second meaning, the meaning of *existence*. The verbal form feigns a predicate where there is none. To be sure, it has been known for a long time that existence is not a property (cf. Kant's refutation of the ontological proof of the existence of God). But it was not until the advent of modern logic that full consistency on this point was reached: the syntactical form in which modern logic introduces the sign for existence is such that it cannot, like a predicate, be applied to signs for objects, but only to predicates (cf. e.g. sentence IIIA in the above table). Most metaphysicians since antiquity have allowed themselves to be seduced into pseudo-statements by the verbal, and therewith the predicative form of the word "to be," e.g. "I am," "God is."

We meet an illustration of this error in Descartes' "cogito, ergo sum." Let us disregard here the material objections that have been raised against the premise—viz. whether the sentence "I think" adequately expresses the intended state of affairs or contains perhaps an hypostasis—and consider the two sentences only from the formal logical point of view. We notice at once two essential logical mistakes. The first lies in the conclusion "I am." The verb "to be" is undoubtedly meant in the sense of existence here; for a copula cannot be used without predicate; indeed, Descartes' "I am" has always been interpreted in this sense. But in that case this sentence violates the above-mentioned logical rule that existence can be predicated only in conjunction with a predicate, not in conjunction with a name (subject, proper name). An existential statement does not have the form "*a* exists" (as in "I am," i.e. "I exist"), but "there exists something of such and such a kind." The second error lies in the transition from "I think" to "I exist." If from the statement "P(a)" ("a has the property P") an existential statement is to be deduced, then the latter can assert existence only with respect to the predicate P, not with respect to the subject *a* of the premise. What follows from "I am a European" is not "I exist," but "a European exists." What follows from "I think" is not "I am" but "there exists something that thinks."

The circumstance that our languages express existence by a verb ("to be" or "to exist") is not in itself a logical fault; it is only inappropriate, dangerous. The verbal form easily misleads us into the misconception that existence is a predicate. One then arrives at such logically incorrect and hence senseless modes of expression as were just examined. Likewise such forms as "Being" or "Not-Being," which from time immemorial have played a great role in metaphysics, have the same origin. In a logically correct language such forms cannot even be constructed. It appears that in the Latin and the German languages the forms "*ens*" or "*das Seiende*" were, perhaps under the seductive influence of the Greek example, introduced specifically for use by metaphysicians; in this way the language deteriorated logically whereas the addition was believed to represent an improvement.

Another very frequent violation of logical syntax is the so-called "*type confusion*" of concepts. While the previously mentioned mistake consists in the predicative use of a symbol with non-predicative meaning, in this case a predicate is, indeed, used as predicate yet as predicate of a different type. We have here a violation of the rules of the so-called theory of types. An artificial example is the sentence we discussed earlier: "Caesar is a prime number." Names of persons and names of numbers belong to different logical types, and so do accordingly predicates of persons (e.g. "general") and predicates of numbers ("prime number"). The error of type confusion is, unlike the previously discussed usage of the verb "to be," not the prerogative of metaphysics but already occurs very often in conversational language also. But here it rarely leads to nonsense. The typical ambiguity of words is here of such a kind that it can be easily removed.

> *Example*: 1. "This table is larger than that." 2. "The height of this table is larger than the height of that table." Here the word "larger" is used in (1) for a relation between objects, in (2) for a relation between numbers, hence for two distinct syntactical categories. The mistake is here unimportant; it could, e.g. be eliminated by writing "larger1" and "larger2"; "larger1" is then defined in terms of "larger2" by declaring statement form (1) to be synonymous with (2) (and others of a similar kind).

Since the confusion of types causes no harm in conversational language, it is usually ignored entirely. This is, indeed, expedient for the ordinary use of language, but has had unfortunate consequences in metaphysics. Here the conditioning by everyday language has led to confusions of types which, unlike those in everyday language, are no longer translatable into logically correct form. Pseudo-statements of this kind are encountered in especially large quantity, e.g. in the writings of Hegel and Heidegger. The latter has adopted many peculiarities of the Hegelian idiom along with their logical faults (e.g. predicates which should be applied to objects of a certain sort are instead applied to predicates of these objects or to "being" or to "existence" or to a relation between these objects).

Having found that many metaphysical statements are meaningless, we confront the question whether there is not perhaps a core of meaningful statements in metaphysics which would remain after elimination of all the meaningless ones.

Indeed, the results we have obtained so far might give rise to the view that there are many dangers of falling into nonsense in metaphysics, and that one must accordingly endeavor to avoid these traps with great care if one wants to do metaphysics. But actually the situation is that meaningful metaphysical statements are impossible. This follows from the task which metaphysics sets itself: to discover and formulate a kind of knowledge which is not accessible to empirical science.

We have seen earlier that the meaning of a statement lies in the method of its verification. A statement asserts only so much as is verifiable with respect to it. Therefore a sentence can be used only to assert an empirical proposition, if indeed it is used to assert anything at all. If something were to lie, in principle, beyond possible experience, it could be neither said nor thought nor asked.

(Meaningful) statements are divided into the following kinds. First there are statements which are true solely by virtue of their form ("tautologies" according to Wittgenstein; they correspond approximately to Kant's "analytic judgments"). They say nothing about reality. The formulae of logic and mathematics are of this kind. They are not themselves factual statements, but serve for the transformation of such statements. Secondly there are the negations of such statements ("*contradictions*"). They are self-contradictory, hence false by virtue of their form. With respect to all other statements the decision about truth or falsehood lies in the protocol sentences. They are therefore (true or false) *empirical* statements and belong to the domain of empirical science. Any statement one desires to construct which does not fall within these categories becomes automatically meaningless. Since metaphysics does not want to assert analytic propositions, nor to fall within the domain of empirical science, it is compelled to employ words for which no criteria of application are specified and which are therefore devoid of sense, or else to combine meaningful words in such a way that neither an analytic (or contradictory) statement nor an empirical statement is produced. In either case pseudo-statements are the inevitable product.

Logical analysis, then, pronounces the verdict of meaninglessness on any alleged knowledge that pretends to reach above or behind experience. This verdict hits, in the first place, any speculative metaphysics, any alleged knowledge by *pure thinking* or by *pure intuition* that pretends to be able to do without experience. But the verdict equally applies to the kind of metaphysics which, starting from experience, wants to acquire knowledge about that which *transcends experience* by means of special *inferences* (e.g. the neo-vitalist thesis of the directive presence of an "entelechy" in organic processes, which supposedly cannot be understood in terms of physics; the question concerning the "essence of causality," transcending the ascertainment of certain regularities of succession; the talk about the "thing in itself"). Further, the same judgment must be passed on all *philosophy of norms*, or *philosophy of value*, on any ethics or esthetics as a normative discipline. For the objective validity of a value or norm is (even on the view of the philosophers of value) not empirically verifiable nor deducible from empirical statements; hence it cannot be asserted (in a meaningful statement) at all. In other words: Either empirical criteria are indicated for the use of "good" and "beautiful" and the rest of the predicates that are employed in the normative sciences, or they are not. In the first case, a statement containing such a predicate turns into a factual judgment, but not a value judgment; in the second case, it becomes a pseudo-statement. It is altogether impossible to make a statement that expresses a value judgment.

Finally, the verdict of meaninglessness also hits those metaphysical movements which are usually called, improperly, epistemological movements, that is *realism** (insofar as it claims to say more than the empirical fact that the sequence of events exhibits a

*That both the affirmative and the negative theses concerning the reality of the external world are pseudo-statements. I have tried to show in the monograph *Scheinprobleme in der Philosophie: Das Fremdpsychische und der Realismusstreit*, Berlin, 1928. The similar nature of the ontological theses about the reality or unreality of abstract entities, e.g., properties, relations, propositions, is discussed in "Empiricism, Semantics, and Ontology," *Revue Intern. de Philos.* 4, 1950, 20–40, reprinted in *Meaning and Necessity*, 2nd edition, Chicago, 1956.

certain regularity, which makes the application of the inductive method possible) and its opponents: subjective *idealism*, solipsism, phenomenalism, and *positivism* (in the earlier sense).

But what, then, is left over for *philosophy*, if all statements whatever that assert something are of an empirical nature and belong to factual science? What remains is not statements, nor a theory, nor a system, but only a *method*: the method of logical analysis. The foregoing discussion has illustrated the negative application of this method: in that context it serves to eliminate meaningless words, meaningless pseudo-statements. In its positive use it serves to clarify meaningful concepts and propositions, to lay logical foundations for factual science and for mathematics. The negative application of the method is necessary and important in the present historical situation. But even in its present practice, the positive application is more fertile. We cannot here discuss it in greater detail. It is the indicated task of logical analysis, inquiry into logical foundations, that is meant by "*scientific philosophy*" in contrast to metaphysics.

The question regarding the logical character of the statements which we obtain as the result of a logical analysis, e.g. the statements occurring in this and other logical papers, can here be answered only tentatively: such statements are partly analytic, partly empirical. For these statements about statements and parts of statements belong in part to pure *metalogic*** (e.g. "a sequence consisting of the existence-symbol and a noun, is not a sentence"), in part to descriptive metalogic (e.g. "the word sequence at such and such a place in such and such a book is meaningless"). Metalogic will be discussed elsewhere. It will also be shown there that the metalogic which speaks about the sentences of a given language can be formulated in that very language itself.

7. METAPHYSICS AS EXPRESSION OF AN ATTITUDE TOWARD LIFE

Our claim that the statements of metaphysics are entirely meaningless, that they do not assert anything, will leave even those who agree intellectually with our results with a painful feeling of strangeness: how could it be explained that so many men in all ages and nations, among them eminent minds, spent so much energy, nay veritable fervor, on metaphysics if the latter consisted of nothing but mere words, nonsensically juxtaposed? And how could one account for the fact that metaphysical books have exerted such a strong influence on readers up to the present day, if they contained not even errors, but nothing at all? These doubts are justified since metaphysics does indeed have a content; only it is not theoretical content. The (pseudo)statements of metaphysics do not serve for the *description of states of affairs*, neither existing ones (in that case they would be true statements) nor non-existing ones (in that case they would be at least false statements). They serve for the *expression of the general attitude of a person towards life ("Lebenseinstellung, Lebensgefühl")*.

Perhaps we may assume that metaphysics originated from *mythology*. The child is angry at the "wicked table" which hurt him. Primitive man endeavors to conciliate the threatening demon of earthquakes, or he worships the deity of the fertile rains in gratitude. Here we confront personifications of natural phenomena, which are the quasi-poetic expression of man's emotional relationship to his environment. The heritage of mythology is bequeathed on the one hand to poetry, which produces and intensifies the effects of mythology on life in a deliberate way; on other hand, it is handed down to theology, which develops mythology into a system. Which, now, is the historical role of metaphysics? Perhaps we may regard it as a substitute for theology on the level of systematic, conceptual thinking. The (supposedly) transcendent sources of knowledge of theology are here replaced by natural, yet supposedly trans-empirical sources of knowledge. On closer inspection the same content as that of mythology is here still recognizable behind the repeatedly varied dressing: we find that metaphysics also arises from the need to give expression to a man's attitude in life, his emotional and volitional reaction to the environment, to society, to the tasks to which he devotes himself, to the misfortunes that befall him. This attitude manifests itself, unconsciously as a rule, in everything a man does or says. It also impresses itself on his facial features, perhaps even on the character of his gait. Many people, now, feel a desire to create over and above these manifestations a special expression of their attitude,

**This term refers to the theory of expressions of a language and, in particular, of their logical relations. Today we would distinguish between logical syntax as the theory of purely formal relations and semantics as the theory of meaning and truth-conditions.

through which it might become visible in a more succinct and penetrating way. If they have artistic talent they are able to express themselves by producing a work of art. Many writers have already clarified the way in which the basic attitude is manifested through the style and manner of a work of art (e.g. Dilthey and his students). [In this connection the term "world view" ("*Weltanschauung*") is often used; we prefer to avoid it because of its ambiguity, which blurs the difference between attitude and theory, a difference which is of decisive importance for our analysis.] What is here essential for our considerations is only the fact that art is an adequate, metaphysics an inadequate means for the expression of the basic attitude. Of course, there need be no intrinsic objection to one's using any means of expression one likes. But in the case of metaphysics we find this situation: through the form of its works it pretends to be something that it is not. The form in question is that of a system of statements which are apparently related as premises and conclusions, that is, the form of a theory. In this way the fiction of theoretical content is generated, whereas, as we have seen, there is no such content. It is not only the reader, but the metaphysician himself who suffers from the illusion that the metaphysical statements say something, describe states of affairs. The metaphysician believes that he travels in territory in which truth and falsehood are at stake. In reality, however, he has not asserted anything, but only expressed something, like an artist. That the metaphysician is thus deluding himself cannot be inferred from the fact that he selects language as the medium of expression and declarative sentences as the form of expression; for lyrical poets do the same without succumbing to self-delusion. But the metaphysician supports his statements by arguments, he claims assent to their content, he polemicizes against metaphysicians of divergent persuasion by attempting to refute their assertions in his treatise. Lyrical poets, on the other hand, do not try to refute in their poem the statements in a poem by some other lyrical poet; for they know they are in the domain of art and not in the domain of theory.

Perhaps music is the purest means of expression of the basic attitude because it is entirely free from any reference to objects. The harmonious feeling or attitude, which the metaphysician tries to express in a monistic system, is more clearly expressed in the music of Mozart. And when a metaphysician gives verbal expression to his dualistic-heroic attitude towards life in a dualistic system, is it not perhaps because he lacks the ability of a Beethoven to express this attitude in an adequate medium? Metaphysicians are musicians without musical ability. Instead they have a strong inclination to work within the medium of the theoretical, to connect concepts and thoughts. Now, instead of activating, on the one hand, this inclination in the domain of science, and satisfying, on the other hand, the need for expression in art, the metaphysician confuses the two and produces a structure which achieves nothing for knowledge and something inadequate for the expression of attitude.

Our conjecture that metaphysics is a substitute, albeit an inadequate one, for art, seems to be further confirmed by the fact that the metaphysician who perhaps had artistic talent to the highest degree, viz. Nietzsche, almost entirely avoided the error of that confusion. A large part of his work has predominantly empirical content. We find there, for instance, historical analyses of specific artistic phenomena, or an historical-psychological analysis of morals. In the work, however, in which he expresses most strongly that which others express through metaphysics or ethics, in *Thus Spake Zarathustra*, he does not choose the misleading form, but openly the form of art, of poetry.

Chapter 7

A. J. AYER

Alfred Jules Ayer (1910–1989) was born in London, the son of immigrant parents. He attended Eton and Christ Church, Oxford University, where he studied under Gilbert Ryle. When he was 26 he traveled to Vienna to meet Moritz Schlick, the leader of the Vienna Circle, a group of logical positiviss. On his return to Oxford he wrote his most famous book, *Language, Truth and Logic,* a selection of which is reprinted here. He later became a professor at University College, London University, before returning to Oxford in 1960 to take up the Wykeham Professorship of Logic, where he taught until a short time before his death in 1989. A lifelong atheist, he astounded the public several months before his death with a report of a mystical experience. His heart had stopped for four minutes, during which time "I was confronted by a red light, exceedingly bright, and also very painful, even when I turned away from it. I was aware that this light was responsible for the government of the universe."[1]

Ayer was England's most prominent logical positivist. That philosophy, which had its roots in Hume's Empiricism, like Hume rejected metaphysics as nonsense. Its driving idea was that for a sentence to be meaningful, it must be verifiable in principle by experience. So my statement that atoms exist, though not observable by human senses, could conceivably be true if we had instruments to bring them to human consciousness. We must be able somehow to point to it. But moral and theological statements cannot be verified. Statements such as "Telling the truth is good" or "Killing innocents is bad" can't be observed. That is, we can observe a lie or a killing, but we can't observe the "goodness" or "badness" which are predicated of these subject terms. Ayer would reduce the value sentences to emotive expressions, such as "Telling the truth—Hurrah!" and "Killing innocents—boo!" Theological assertions such as"God exists" are simply nonsense, since they fail to express the conditions under which one could verify such claims. In the first selection given below Ayer sets forth to eliminate all metaphysical discourse. In the second selection he critiques ethics and theology.

FOR FURTHER READING

Achinstein, Peter and Stephen Barker. *The Legacy of Logical Positivism* (Johns Hopkins Press, 1969).

Ashby, R. W. "Logical Positivism," in D. J. O'Connor, ed. *A Critical History of Western Philosophy* (Free Press, 1964).

Ayer, A. J., ed. *Logical Positivism* (Free Press, 1959).

———. *Language, Truth and Logic* (Dover, 1936).

Gower, Barry, ed. *Logical Positivism in Perspective: Essays on "Language, Truth and Logic"* (Croom Helm, 1987).

1"What I Saw When I Was Dead . . ." *Spectator* July 16, 1988, reprinted in *The Philosophy of A. J. Ayer*, ed. L. E. Hahn (Open Court, 1992), p. 48.

Hahn, Lewis, ed. *The Philosophy of A. J. Ayer* (Open Court, 1992).
Macdonald, Graham and Crispin Wright, eds. *Fact, Science and Morality: Essays on A. J. Ayer's "Language, Truth and Logic"* (Blackwell, 1987).

A.J. AYER - Certain hypotheses can't be refuted or confirmed. "Mountains on dark side of moon, because we have never been there to see them."

The Abolition of Metaphysics

PREFACE TO FIRST EDITION

The views which are put forward in this treatise derive from the doctrines of Bertrand Russell and Wittgenstein, which are themselves the logical outcome of the empiricism of Berkeley and David Hume. Like Hume, I divide all genuine propositions into two classes: those which, in his terminology, concern "relations of ideas," and those which concern "matters of fact." The former class comprises the *a priori* propositions of logic and pure mathematics, and these I allow to be necessary and certain only because they are analytic. That is, I maintain that the reason why these propositions cannot be confuted in experience is that they do not make any assertion about the empirical world, but simply record our determination to use symbols in a certain fashion. Propositions concerning empirical matters of fact, on the other hand, I hold to be hypotheses, which can be probable but never certain. And in giving an account of the method of their validation I claim also to have explained the nature of truth.

To test whether a sentence expresses a genuine empirical hypothesis, I adopt what may be called a modified verification principle. For I require of an empirical hypothesis, not indeed that it should be conclusively verifiable, but that some possible sense-experience should be relevant to the determination of its truth or falsehood. If a putative proposition fails to satisfy this principle, and is not a tautology, then I hold that it is metaphysical, and that, being metaphysical, it is neither true nor false but literally senseless. It will be found that much of what ordinarily passes for philosophy is metaphysical according to this criterion, and, in particular, that it can not be significantly asserted that there is a non-empirical world of values, or that men have immortal souls, or that there is a transcendent God.

As for the propositions of philosophy themselves, they are held to be linguistically necessary, and so analytic. And with regard to the relationship of philosophy and empirical science, it is shown that the philosopher is not in a position to furnish speculative truths, which would, as it were, compete with the hypotheses of science, nor yet to pass *a priori* judgements upon the validity of scientific theories, but that his function is to clarify the propositions of science by exhibiting their logical relationships, and by defining the symbols which occur in them. Consequently I maintain that there is nothing in the nature of philosophy to warrant the existence of conflicting philosophical "schools." And I attempt to substantiate this by providing a definitive solution of the problems which have been the chief sources of controversy between philosophers in the past.

The view that philosophizing is an activity of analysis is associated in England with the work of G. E. Moore and his disciples. But while I have learned a great deal from Professor Moore, I have reason to believe that he and his followers are not prepared to adopt such a thoroughgoing phenomenalism as I do, and that they take a rather different view of the nature of philosophical analysis. The philosophers with whom I am in the closest agreement are those who compose the "Viennese circle," under the leadership of Moritz Schlick, and are commonly known as logical positivists. And of these I owe most to Rudolf Carnap. Further, I wish to acknowledge my indebtedness to Gilbert Ryle, my original tutor in philosophy, and to Isaiah Berlin, who have discussed with me every point in the argument of this treatise, and made many valuable

Reprinted from A. J. Ayer, *Language, Truth and Logic* (Dover Press, 1952) by permission of Dover Publications.

suggestions, although they both disagree with much of what I assert. . . .

CHAPTER 1: THE ELIMINATION OF METAPHYSICS

The traditional disputes of philosophers are, for the most part, as unwarranted as they are unfruitful. The surest way to end them is to establish beyond question what should be the purpose and method of a philosophical enquiry. And this is by no means so difficult a task as the history of philosophy would lead one to suppose. For if there are any questions which science leaves it to philosophy to answer, a straightforward process of elimination must lead to their discovery.

We may begin by criticising the metaphysical thesis that philosophy affords us knowledge of a reality transcending the world of science and common sense. Later on, when we come to define metaphysics and account for its existence, we shall find that it is possible to be a metaphysician without believing in a transcendent reality; for we shall see that many metaphysical utterances are due to the commission of logical errors, rather than to a conscious desire on the part of their authors to go beyond the limits of experience. But it is convenient for us to take the case of those who believe that it is possible to have knowledge of a transcendent reality as a starting-point for our discussion. The arguments which we use to refute them will subsequently be found to apply to the whole of metaphysics.

One way of attacking a metaphysician who claimed to have knowledge of a reality which transcended the phenomenal world would be to enquire from what premises his propositions were deduced. Must he not begin, as other men do, with the evidence of his senses? And if so, what valid process of reasoning can possibly lead him to the conception of a transcendent reality? Surely from empirical premises nothing whatsoever concerning the properties, or even the existence, of anything super-empirical can legitimately be inferred. But this objection would be met by a denial on the part of the metaphysician that his assertions were ultimately based on the evidence of his senses. He would say that he was endowed with a faculty of intellectual intuition which enabled him to know facts that could not be known through sense-experience. And even if it could be shown that he was relying on empirical premises, and that his venture into a non-empirical world was therefore logically unjustified, it would not follow that the assertions which he made concerning this non-empirical world could not be true. For the fact that a conclusion does not follow from its putative premise is not sufficient to show that it is false. Consequently one cannot overthrow a system of transcendent metaphysics merely by criticising the way in which it comes into being. What is required is rather a criticism of the nature of the actual statements which comprise it. And this is the line of argument which we shall, in fact, pursue. For we shall maintain that no statement which refers to a "reality" transcending the limits of all possible sense-experience can possibly have any literal significance; from which it must follow that the labours of those who have striven to describe such a reality have all been devoted to the production of nonsense.

It may be suggested that this is a proposition which has already been proved by Kant. But although Kant also condemned transcendent metaphysics, he did so on different grounds. For he said that the human understanding was so constituted that it lost itself in contradictions when it ventured out beyond the limits of possible experience and attempted to deal with things in themselves. And thus he made the impossibility of a transcendent metaphysic not, as we do, a matter of logic, but a matter of fact. He asserted, not that our minds could not conceivably have had the power of penetrating beyond the phenomenal world, but merely that they were in fact devoid of it. And this leads the critic to ask how, if it is possible to know only what lies within the bounds of sense-experience, the author can be justified in asserting that real things do exist beyond, and how he can tell what are the boundaries beyond which the human understanding may not venture, unless he succeeds in passing them himself. As Wittgenstein says, "in order to draw a limit to thinking, we should have to think both sides of this limit,"[1] a truth to which Bradley gives a special twist in maintaining that the man who is ready to prove that metaphysics is impossible is a brother metaphysician with a rival theory of his own.[2]

Whatever force these objections may have against the Kantian doctrine, they have none whatsoever against the thesis that I am about to set forth. It can-

1. *Tractatus Logico-Philosophicus,* Preface.
2. Bradley, *Appearance and Reality,* 2nd ed., p. 1.

not here be said that the author is himself overstepping the barrier he maintains to be impassable. For the fruitlessness of attempting to transcend the limits of possible sense-experience will be deduced, not from a psychological hypothesis concerning the actual constitution of the human mind, but from the rule which determines the literal significance of language. Our charge against the metaphysician is not that he attempts to employ the understanding in a field where it cannot profitably venture, but that he produces sentences which fail to conform to the conditions under which alone a sentence can be literally significant. Nor are we ourselves obliged to talk nonsense in order to show that all sentences of a certain type are necessarily devoid of literal significance. We need only formulate the criterion which enables us to test whether a sentence expresses a genuine proposition about a matter of fact, and then point out that the sentences under consideration fail to satisfy it. And this we shall now proceed to do. We shall first of all formulate the criterion in somewhat vague terms, and then give the explanations which are necessary to render it precise.

The criterion which we use to test the genuineness of apparent statements of fact is the criterion of verifiability. We say that a sentence is factually significant to any given person, if, and only if, he knows how to verify the proposition which it purports to express—that is, if he knows what observations would lead them, under certain conditions, to accept the proposition as being true, or reject it as being false. If, on the other hand, the putative proposition is of such a character that the assumption of its truth, or falsehood, is consistent with any assumption whatsoever concerning the nature of his future experience, then, as far as he is concerned, it is, if not a tautology, a mere pseudoproposition. The sentence expressing it may be emotionally significant to him; but it is not literally significant. And with regard to questions the procedure is the same. We enquire in every case what observations would lead us to answer the question, one way or the other; and, if none can be discovered, we must conclude that the sentence under consideration does not, as far as we are concerned, express a genuine question, however strongly its grammatical appearance may suggest that it does.

As the adoption of this procedure is an essential factor in the argument of this book, it needs to be examined in detail.

In the first place, it is necessary to draw a distinction between practical verifiability, and verifiability in principle. Plainly we all understand, in many cases believe, propositions which we have not in fact taken steps to verify. Many of these are propositions which we could verify if we took enough trouble. But there remain a number of significant propositions, concerning matters of fact, which we could not verify even if we chose; simply because we lack the practical means of placing ourselves in the situation where the relevant observations could be made. A simple and familiar example of such a proposition is the proposition that there are mountains on the farther side of the moon. No rocket has yet been invented which would enable me to go and look at the farther side of the moon, so that I am unable to decide the matter by actual observation. But I do know what observations would decide it for me, if, as is theoretically conceivable, I were once in a position to make them. And therefore I say that the proposition is verifiable in principle, if not in practice, and is accordingly significant. On the other hand, such a metaphysical pseudo-proposition as "the Absolute enters into, but is itself incapable of, evolution and progress," is not even in principle verifiable. For one cannot conceive of an observation which would enable one to determine whether the Absolute did, or did not, enter into evolution and progress. Of course it is possible that the author of such a remark is using English words in a way in which they are not commonly used by English-speaking people, and that he does, in fact, intend to assert something which could be empirically verified. But until he makes us understand how the proposition that he wishes to express would be verified, he fails to communicate anything to us. And if he admits, as I think the author of the remark in question would have admitted, that his words were not intended to express either a tautology or a proposition which was capable, at least in principle, of being verified, then it follows that he has made an utterance which has no literal significance even for himself.

A further distinction which we must make is the distinction between the "strong" and the "weak" sense of the term "verifiable." A proposition is said to be verifiable, in the strong sense of the term, if, and only if, its truth could be conclusively established in experience. But it is verifiable, in the weak sense, if it is possible for experience to render it probable. In which sense are we using the term when we say that a putative proposition is genuine only if it is verifiable?

It seems to me that if we adopt conclusive verifiability as our criterion of significance, as some positivists have proposed, our argument will prove too much. Consider, for example, the case of general propositions of law—such propositions, namely, as "arsenic is poisonous"; "all men are mortal"; "a body tends to expand when it is heated." It is of the very nature of these propositions that their truth cannot be established with certainty by any finite series of observations. But if it is recognised that such general propositions of law are designed to cover an infinite number of cases, then it must be admitted that they cannot, even in principle, be verified conclusively. And then, if we adopt conclusive verifiability as our criterion of significance, we are logically obligated to treat these general propositions of law in the same fashion as we treat the statements of the metaphysician.

In face of this difficulty, some positivists have adopted the heroic course of saying that these general propositions are indeed pieces of nonsense, albeit an essentially important type of nonsense. But here the introduction of the term "important" is simply an attempt to hedge. It serves only to mark the authors' recognition that their view is somewhat too paradoxical, without in any way removing the paradox. Besides, the difficulty is not confined to the case of general propositions of law, though it is there revealed most plainly. It is hardly less obvious in the case of propositions about the remote past. For it must surely be admitted that, however strong the evidence in favour of historical statements may be, their truth can never become more than highly probable. And to maintain that they also constituted an important, or unimportant, type of nonsense would be unplausible, to say the very least. Indeed, it will be our contention that no proposition, other than a tautology, can possibly be anything more than a probable hypothesis. And if this is correct, the principle that a sentence can be factually significant only if it expresses what is conclusively verifiable is self-stultifying as a criterion of significance. For it leads to the conclusion that it is impossible to make a significant statement of fact at all.

Nor can we accept the suggestion that a sentence should be allowed to be factually significant if, and only if, it expresses something which is definitely confutable by experience. Those who adopt this course assume that, although no finite series of observations is ever sufficient to establish the truth of a hypothesis beyond all possibility of doubt, there are crucial cases in which a single observation, or series of observations, can definitely confute it. But, as we shall show later on, this assumption is false. A hypothesis cannot be conclusively confuted any more than it can be conclusively verified. For when we take the occurrence of certain observations as proof that a given hypothesis is false, we presuppose the existence of certain conditions. And though, in any given case, it may be extremely improbable that this assumption is false, it is not logically impossible. We shall see that there need be no self-contradiction in holding that some of the relevant circumstances are other than we have taken them to be, and consequently that the hypothesis has not really broken down. And if it is not the case that any hypothesis can be definitely confuted, we cannot hold that the genuineness of a proposition depends on the possibility of its definite confutation.

Accordingly, we fall back on the weaker sense of verification. We say that the question that must be asked about any putative statement of fact is not, Would any observations make its truth or falsehood logically certain? but simply, Would any observations be relevant to the determination of its truth or falsehood? And it is only if a negative answer is given to this second question that we conclude that the statement under consideration is nonsensical.

To make our position clearer, we may formulate it in another way. Let us call a proposition which records an actual or possible observation an experiential proposition. Then we may say that it is the mark of a genuine factual proposition, not that it should be equivalent to an experiential proposition, or any finite number of experiential propositions, but simply that some experiential propositions can be deduced from it in conjunction with certain other premises without being deducible from those other premises alone.

This criterion seems liberal enough. In contrast to the principle of conclusive verifiability, it clearly does not deny significance to general propositions or to propositions about the past. Let us see what kinds of assertion it rules out.

A good example of the kind of utterance that is condemned by our criterion as being not even false but nonsensical would be the assertion that the world of sense-experience was altogether unreal. It must, of course, be admitted that our senses do sometimes deceive us. We may, as the result of having certain sensations, expect certain other sensations to be obtainable which are, in fact, not obtainable. But, in all such cases, it is further sense-experience that informs us of the mistakes that arise out of sense-experience. We say that the senses sometimes deceive us, just because the expectations to which our sense-experiences give rise do not always accord with what we subsequently experience. That is, we rely on our senses to substantiate or confute the judgements which are based on our sensations. And therefore the fact that our perceptual judgements are sometimes found to be erroneous has not the slightest tendency to show that the world of sense-experience is unreal. And, indeed, it is plain that no conceivable observation, or series of observations, could have any tendency to show that the world revealed to us by sense-experience was unreal. Consequently, anyone who condemns the sensible world as a world of mere appearance, as opposed to reality, is saying something which, according to our criterion of significance, is literally nonsensical.

An example of a controversy which the application of our criterion obliges us to condemn as fictitious is provided by those who dispute concerning the number of substances that there are in the world. For it is admitted both by monists, who maintain that reality is one substance, and by pluralists, who maintain that reality is many, that it is impossible to imagine any empirical situation which would be relevant to the solution of their dispute. But if we are told that no possible observation could give any probability either to the assertion that reality was one substance or to the assertion that it was many, then we must conclude that neither assertion is significant. We shall see later on that there are genuine logical and empirical questions involved in the dispute between monists and pluralists. But the metaphysical question concerning "substance" is ruled out by our criterion as spurious.

A similar treatment must be accorded to the controversy between realists and idealists, in its metaphysical aspect. A simple illustration, which I have made us of in a similar argument elsewhere, will help to demonstrate this. Let us suppose that a picture is discovered and the suggestion made that it was painted by Goya. There is a definite procedure for dealing with such a question. The experts examine the picture to see in what way it resembles the accredited works of Goya, and to see if it bears any marks which are characteristic of a forgery; they look up contemporary records for evidence of the existence of such a picture, and so on. In the end, they may still disagree, but each one knows what empirical evidence would go to confirm or discredit his opinion. Suppose, now, that these men have studied philosophy, and some of them proceed to maintain that this picture is a set of ideas in the perceiver's mind, or in God's mind, others that it is objectively real. What possible experience could any of them have which would be relevant to the solution of this dispute one way or the other? In the ordinary sense of the term "real," in which it is opposed to "illusory," the reality of the picture is not in doubt. The disputants have satisfied themselves that the picture is real, in this sense, by obtaining a correlated series of sensations of sight and sensations of touch. Is there any similar process by which they could discover whether the picture was real, in the sense in which the term "real" is opposed to "ideal"? Clearly there is none. But, if that is so, the problem is fictitious according to our criterion. This does not mean that the realist-idealist controversy may be dismissed without further ado. For it can legitimately be regarded as a dispute concerning the analysis of existential propositions, and so as involving a logical problem which, as we shall see, can be definitively solved. What we have just shown is that the question at issue between idealists and realists becomes fictitious when, as is often the case, it is given a metaphysical interpretation.

There is no need for us to give further examples of the operation of our criterion of significance. For our object is merely to show that philosophy, as a genuine branch of knowledge, must be distinguished from metaphysics. We are not now concerned with the historical question how much of what has traditionally passed for philosophy is actually metaphysical. We shall, however, point out later on that the majority of the "great philosophers" of the past were not essentially metaphysicians, and thus reassure those who would otherwise be prevented from adopting our criterion by considerations of piety.

As to the validity of the verification principle . . . it will be shown that all propositions which have factual content are empirical hypotheses; and that the function of an empirical hypothesis is to provide a rule for the anticipation of experience. And this means that every empirical hypothesis must be relevant to some actual, or possible, experience, so that a statement which is not relevant to any experience is not an empirical hypothesis, and accordingly has no factual content. But this is precisely what the principle of verifiability asserts.

It should be mentioned here that the fact that the utterances of the metaphysician are nonsensical does not follow simply from the fact that they are devoid of factual content. It follows from that fact, together with the fact that they are not *a priori* propositions. . . . *a priori* propositions, which have always been attractive to philosophers on account of their certainty, owe this certainty to the fact that they are tautologies. We may accordingly define a metaphysical sentence as a sentence which purports to express a genuine proposition, but does, in fact, express neither a tautology nor an empirical hypothesis. And as tautologies and empirical hypotheses form the entire class of significant propositions, we are justified in concluding that all metaphysical assertions are nonsensical. Our next task is to show how they come to be made.

The use of the term "substance," to which we have already referred, provides us with a good example of the way in which metaphysics mostly comes to be written. It happens to be the case that we cannot, in our language, refer to the sensible properties of a thing without introducing a word or phrase which appears to stand for the thing itself as opposed to anything which may be said about it. And, as a result of this, those who are infected by the primitive superstition that to every name a single real entity must correspond assume that it is necessary to distinguish logically between the thing itself and any, or all, of its sensible properties. And so they employ the term "substance" to refer to the thing itself. But from the fact that we happen to employ a single word to refer to a thing, and make that word the grammatical subject of the sentences in which we refer to the sensible appearances of the thing, it does not by any means follow that the thing itself is a "simple entity," or that it cannot be defined in terms of the totality of its appearances. It is true that in talking of "its" appearances we appear to distinguish the thing from the appearances, but that is simply an accident of linguistic usage. Logical analysis shows that what makes these "appearances" the "appearances of" the same thing is not their relationship to an entity other than themselves, but their relationship to one another. The metaphysician fails to see this because he is misled by a superficial grammatical feature of his language.

A simpler and clearer instance of the way in which a consideration of grammar leads to metaphysics is the case of the metaphysical concept of Being. The origin of our temptation to raise questions about Being, which no conceivable experience would enable us to answer, lies in the fact that, in our language, sentences which express existential propositions and sentences which express attributive propositions may be of the same grammatical form. For instance, the sentences "Martyrs exist" and "Martyrs suffer" both consist of a noun followed by an intransitive verb, and the fact that they have grammatically the same appearance leads one to assume that they are of the same logical type. It is seen that in the proposition "Martyrs suffer," the members of a certain species are credited with a certain attribute, and it is sometimes assumed that the same thing is true of such a proposition as "Martyrs exist." If this were actually the case, it would, indeed, be as legitimate to speculate about the Being of martyrs as it is to speculate about their suffering. But, as Kant pointed out, existence is not an attribute. For, when we ascribe an attribute to a thing, we covertly assert that it exists: so that if existence were itself an attribute, it would follow that all positive existential propositions were tautologies, and all negative existential propositions self-contradictory; and this is not the case. So that those who raise questions about Being which are based on the assumption that existence is an attribute are guilty of following grammar beyond the boundaries of sense.

A similar mistake has been made in connection with such propositions as "Unicorns are fictitious." Here again the fact that there is a superficial grammatical resemblance between the English sentences "Dogs are faithful" and "Unicorns are fictitious," and between the corresponding sentences in other languages, creates the assumption that they are of the same logical type. Dogs must exist in order to have the property of being faithful, and so it is held that unless unicorns in some way existed they could not have the property of being fictitious. But, as it is plainly self-contradictory to say that fictitious objects exist, the device is adopted of saying that they are real in some nonempirical sense—that they have a mode of real being which is different from the mode of being of existent things. But since there is no way of testing whether an object is real in this sense, as there is for testing whether it is real in the ordinary sense, the assertion that fictitious objects have a special non-empirical mode of real being is devoid of all literal significance. It comes to be made as a result of the assumption that being fictitious is

Not saying F, he is saying meaningless.

an attribute. And this is a fallacy of the same order as the fallacy of supposing that existence is an attribute, and it can be exposed in the same way.

In general, the postulation of real non-existent entities results from the superstition, just now referred to, that, to every word or phrase that can be the grammatical subject of a sentence, there must somewhere be a real entity corresponding. For as there is no place in the empirical world for many of these "entities," a special non-empirical world is invoked to house them. To this error must be attributed, not only the utterances of a Heidegger, who bases his metaphysics on the assumption that "Nothing" is a name which is used to denote something peculiarly mysterious, but also the prevalence of such problems as those concerning the reality of propositions and universals whose senselessness, though less obvious, is no less complete.

These few examples afford a sufficient indication of the way in which most metaphysical assertions come to be formulated. They show how easy it is to write sentences which are literally nonsensical without seeing that they are nonsensical. And thus we see that the view that a number of the traditional "problems of philosophy" are metaphysical, and consequently fictitious, does not involve any incredible assumptions about the psychology of philosophers.

Among those who recognise that if philosophy is to be accounted a genuine branch of knowledge it must be defined in such a way as to distinguish it from metaphysics, it is fashionable to speak of the metaphysician as a kind of misplaced poet. As his statements have no literal meaning, they are not subject to any criteria of truth or falsehood: but they may still serve to express, or arouse, emotion, and thus be subject to ethical or aesthetic standards. And it is suggested that they may have considerable value, as means of moral inspiration, or even as works of art. In this way, an attempt is made to compensate the metaphysician for his extrusion from philosophy.

★ God is a work of ART

I am afraid that this compensation is hardly in accordance with his deserts. The view that the metaphysician is to be reckoned among the poets appears to rest on the assumption that both talk nonsense. But this assumption is false. In the vast majority of cases the sentences which are produced by poets do have literal meaning. The difference between the man who uses language scientifically and the man who uses it emotively is not that the one produces sentences which are incapable of arousing emotion, and the other sentences which have no sense, but that the one is primarily concerned with the expression of true propositions, the other with the creation of a work of art. Thus, if a work of science contains true and important propositions, its value as a work of science will hardly be diminished by the fact that they are inelegantly expressed. And similarly, a work of art is not necessarily the worse for the fact that all the propositions comprising it are literally false. But to say that many literary works are largely composed of falsehoods is not to say that they are composed of pseudo-propositions. It is, in fact, very rare for a literary artist to produce sentences which have no literal meaning. And where this does occur, the sentences are carefully chosen for their rhythm and balance. If the author writes nonsense, it is because he considers it most suitable for bringing about the effects for which his writing is designed.

The metaphysician, on the other hand, does not intend to write nonsense. He lapses into it through being deceived by grammar, or through committing errors of reasoning, such as that which leads the view that the sensible world is unreal. But it is not the mark of a poet simply to make mistakes of this sort. There are some, indeed, who would see in the fact that the metaphysician's utterances are senseless a reason against the view that they have aesthetic value. And, without going so far as this, we may safely say that it does not constitute a reason for it.

It is true, however, that although the greater part of metaphysics is merely the embodiment of humdrum errors, there remain a number of metaphysical passages which are the work of genuine mystical feeling; and they may more plausibly be held to have moral or aesthetic value. But, as far as we are concerned, the distinction between the kind of metaphysics that is produced by a philosopher who has been duped by grammar, and the kind that is produced by a mystic who is trying to express the inexpressible, is of no great importance: what is important to us is to realise that even the utterances of the metaphysician who is attempting to expound a vision are literally senseless; so that henceforth we may pursue our philosophical researches with as little regard for them as for the more inglorious kind of metaphysics which comes from a failure to understand the workings of our language.

A Critique of Ethics and Theology

There is still one objection to be met before we can claim to have justified our view that all synthetic propositions are empirical hypotheses. This objection is based on the common supposition that our speculative knowledge is of two distinct kinds—that which relates to questions of empirical fact, and that which relates to questions of value. It will be said that "statements of value" are genuine synthetic propositions, but that they cannot with any show of justice be represented as hypotheses, which are used to predict the course of our sensations; and, accordingly, that the existence of ethics and æsthetics as branches of speculative knowledge presents an insuperable objection to our radical empiricist thesis.

In face of this objection, it is our business to give an account of "judgements of value" which is both satisfactory in itself and consistent with our general empiricist principles. We shall set ourselves to show that in so far as statements of value are significant, they are ordinary "scientific" statements; and that in so far as they are not scientific, they are not in the literal sense significant, but are simply expressions of emotion which can be neither true nor false. In maintaining this view, we may confine ourselves for the present to the case of ethical statements. What is said about them will be found to apply, *mutatis mutandis*, to the case of æsthetic statements also.

The ordinary system of ethics, as elaborated in the works of ethical philosophers, is very far from being a homogeneous whole. Not only is it apt to contain pieces of metaphysics, and analyses of non-ethical concepts: its actual ethical contents are themselves of very different kinds. We may divide them, indeed, into four main classes. There are, first of all, propositions which express definitions of ethical terms, or judgements about the legitimacy or possibility of certain definitions. Secondly, there are propositions describing the phenomena of moral experience, and their causes. Thirdly, there are exhortations to moral virtue. And, lastly, there are actual ethical judgements. It is unfortunately the case that the distinction between these four classes, plain as it is, is commonly ignored by ethical philosophers; with the result that it is often very difficult to tell from their works what it is that they are seeking to discover or prove.

In fact, it is easy to see that only the first of our four classes, namely that which comprises the propositions relating to the definitions of ethical terms, can be said to constitute ethical philosophy. The propositions which describe the phenomena of moral experience, and their causes, must be assigned to the science of psychology, or sociology. The exhortations to moral virtue are not propositions at all, but ejaculations or commands which are designed to provoke the reader to action of a certain sort. Accordingly, they do not belong to any branch of philosophy or science. As for the expressions of ethical judgements, we have not yet determined how they should be classified. But inasmuch as they are certainly neither definitions nor comments upon definitions, nor quotations, we may say decisively that they do not belong to ethical philosophy. A strictly philosophical treatise on ethics should therefore make no ethical pronouncements. But it should, by giving an analysis of ethical terms, show what is the category to which all such pronouncements belong. And this is what we are now about to do.

A question which is often discussed by ethical philosophers is whether it is possible to find definitions which would reduce all ethical terms to one or two fundamental terms. But this question, though it undeniably belongs to ethical philosophy, is not relevant to our present enquiry. We are not now concerned to discover which term, within the sphere of ethical terms, is to be taken as fundamental; whether, for example, "good" can be defined in terms of "right" or "right" in terms of "good," or both in terms of "value." What we are interested in is the possibility of reducing the whole sphere of ethical terms to non-ethical terms. We are enquiring whether statements of ethical value can be translated into statements of empirical fact.

That they can be so translated is the contention of those ethical philosophers who are commonly called subjectivists, and of those who are known as utili-

Reprinted from A. J. Ayer, *Language, Truth and Logic* (Dover Press, 1952) by permission of Dover Publications.

tarians. For the utilitarian defines the rightness of actions, and the goodness of ends, in terms of the pleasure, or happiness, or satisfaction, to which they give rise; the subjectivist, in terms of the feelings of approval which a certain person, or group of people, has towards them. Each of these types of definition makes moral judgements into a sub-class of psychological or sociological judgements; and for this reason they are very attractive to us. For, if either was correct, it would follow that ethical assertions were not generically different from the factual assertions which are ordinarily contrasted with them; and the account which we have already given of empirical hypotheses would apply to them also.

Nevertheless we shall not adopt either a subjectivist or a utilitarian analysis of ethical terms. We reject the subjectivist view that to call an action right, or a thing good, is to say that it is generally approved of, because it is not self-contradictory to assert that some actions which are generally approved of are not right, or that some things which are generally approved of are not good. And we reject the alternative subjectivist view that a man who asserts that a certain action is right, or that a certain thing is good, is saying that he himself approves of it, on the ground that a man who confessed that he sometimes approved of what was bad or wrong would not be contradicting himself. And a similar argument is fatal to utilitarianism. We cannot agree that to call an action right is to say that of all the actions possible in the circumstances it would cause, or be likely to cause, the greatest happiness, or the greatest balance of pleasure over pain, or the greatest balance of satisfied over unsatisfied desire, because we find that it is not self-contradictory to say that it is sometimes wrong to perform the action which would actually or probably cause the greatest happiness, or the greatest balance of pleasure over pain, or of satisfied over unsatisfied desire. And since it is not self-contradictory to say that some pleasant things are not good, or that some bad things are desired, it cannot be the case that the sentence "*x* is good" is equivalent to "*x* is pleasant," or to "*x* is desired." And to every other variant of utilitarianism with which I am acquainted the same objection can be made. And therefore we should, I think, conclude that the validity of ethical judgements is not determined by the felicific tendencies of actions, any more than by the nature of people's feelings; but that it must be regarded as "absolute" or "intrinsic," and not empirically calculable.

If we say this, we are not, of course, denying that it is possible to invent a language in which all ethical symbols are definable in non-ethical terms, or even that it is desirable to invent such a language and adopt it in place of our own; what we are denying is that the suggested reduction of ethical to non-ethical statements is consistent with the conventions of our actual language. That is, we reject utilitarianism and subjectivism, not as proposals to replace our existing ethical notions by new ones, but as analyses of our existing ethical notions. Our contention is simply that, in our language, sentences which contain normative ethical symbols are not equivalent to sentences which express psychological propositions, or indeed empirical propositions of any kind.

It is advisable here to make it plain that it is only normative ethical symbols, and not descriptive ethical symbols, that are held by us to be indefinable in factual terms. There is a danger of confusing these two types of symbols, because they are commonly constituted by signs of the same sensible form. Thus a complex sign of the form "*x* is wrong" may constitute a sentence which expresses a moral judgement concerning a certain type of conduct, or it may constitute a sentence which states that a certain type of conduct is repugnant to the moral sense of a particular society. In the latter case, the symbol "wrong" is a descriptive ethical symbol, and the sentence in which it occurs expresses an ordinary sociological proposition; in the former case, the symbol "wrong" is a normative ethical symbol, and the sentence in which it occurs does not, we maintain, express an empirical proposition at all. It is only with normative ethics that we are at present concerned; so that whenever ethical symbols are used in the course of this argument without qualification, they are always to be interpreted as symbols of the normative type.

In admitting that normative ethical concepts are irreducible to empirical concepts, we seem to be leaving the way clear for the "absolutist" view of ethics—that is, the view that statements of value are not controlled by observation, as ordinary empirical propositions are, but only by a mysterious "intellectual intuition." A feature of this theory, which is seldom recognized by its advocates, is that it makes statements of value unverifiable. For it is notorious that what seems intuitively certain to one person may seem doubtful, or even false, to another. So that unless it is possible to provide some criterion by which one may decide between conflicting intuitions, a mere appeal to intuition is worthless as a test of a proposition's validity. But in the case of moral judgements, no such criterion can be given. Some moralists claim to settle the matter by saying that they "know" that their own moral judgements are correct. But such an assertion is of purely psychological interest, and has not the slightest tendency to prove the validity of any moral judgement. For dissentient moralists may equally well "know" that their ethical views are correct. And, as far as subjective certainty goes, there will be nothing to choose between them. When such differences of opinion arise in connection with an ordinary empirical proposition, one may attempt to resolve them by referring to, or actually carrying out, some relevant empirical test. But with regard to ethical statements, there is, on the "absolutist" or "intuitionist" theory, no relevant empirical test. We are therefore justified in saying that on this theory ethical statements are held to be unverifiable. They are, of course, also held to be genuine synthetic propositions.

Considering the use which we have made of the principle that a synthetic proposition is significant only if it is empirically verifiable, it is clear that the acceptance of an "absolutist" theory of ethics would undermine the whole of our main argument. And as we have already rejected the "naturalistic" theories which are commonly supposed to provide the only alternative to "absolutism" in ethics, we seem to have reached a difficult position. We shall meet the difficulty by showing that the correct treatment of ethical statements is afforded by a third theory, which is wholly compatible with our radical empiricism.

We begin by admitting that the fundamental ethical concepts are unanalysable, inasmuch as there is no criterion by which one can test the validity of the judgements in which they occur. So far we are in agreement with the absolutists. But, unlike the absolutists, we are able to give an explanation of this fact about ethical concepts. We say that the reason why they are unanalysable is that they are mere pseudo-concepts. The presence of an ethical symbol in a proposition adds nothing to its factual content. Thus if I say to someone, "You acted wrongly in stealing that money," I am not stating anything more than if I had simply said, "You stole that money." In adding that this action is wrong I am not making any further statement about it. I am simply evincing my moral disapproval of it. It is as if I had said, "You stole that money," in a peculiar tone of horror, or written it with the addition of some special exclamation marks. The tone, or the exclamation marks, adds nothing to the literal meaning of the sentence. It merely serves to show that the expression of it is attended by certain feelings in the speaker.

If now I generalise my previous statement and say, "Stealing money is wrong," I produce a sentence which has no factual meaning—that is, expresses no proposition which can be either true or false. It is as if I had written "Stealing money!!"—where the shape and thickness of the exclamation marks show, by a suitable convention, that a special sort of moral disapproval is the feeling which is being expressed. It is clear that there is nothing said here which can be true or false. Another man may disagree with me about the wrongness of stealing, in the sense that he may not have the same feelings about stealing as I have, and he may quarrel with me on account of my moral sentiments. But he cannot, strictly speaking, contradict me. For in saying that a certain type of action is right or wrong, I am not making any factual statement, not even a statement about my own state of mind. I am merely expressing certain moral sentiments. And the man who is ostensibly contradicting me is merely expressing his moral sentiments. So that there is plainly no sense in asking which of us is in the right. For neither of us is asserting a genuine proposition.

What we have just been saying about the symbol "wrong" applies to all normative ethical symbols. Sometimes they occur in sentences which record ordinary empirical facts besides expressing ethical feeling about those facts: sometimes they occur in sentences which simply express ethical feeling about a certain type of action, or situation, without making any statement of fact. But in every case in which one would commonly be said to be making an ethical judgement, the function of the relevant ethical word is purely "emotive." It is used to express feeling about certain objects, but not to make any assertion about them.

It is worth mentioning that ethical terms do not serve only to express feeling. They are calculated also to arouse feeling, and so to stimulate action. Indeed some of them are used in such a way as to give the sentences in which they occur the effect of commands. Thus the sentence "It is your duty to tell the truth" may be regarded both as the expression of a certain sort of ethical feeling about truthfulness and as the expression of the command "Tell the truth."

The sentence "You ought to tell the truth" also involves the command "Tell the truth," but here the tone of the command is less emphatic. In the sentence "It is good to tell the truth" the command has become little more than a suggestion. And thus the "meaning" of the word "good," in its ethical usage, is differentiated from that of the word "duty" or the word "ought." In fact we may define the meaning of the various ethical words in terms both of the different feelings they are ordinarily taken to express, and also the different responses which they are calculated to provoke.

We can now see why it is impossible to find a criterion for determining the validity of ethical judgements. It is not because they have an "absolute" validity which is mysteriously independent of ordinary sense-experience, but because they have no objective validity whatsoever. If a sentence makes no statement at all, there is obviously no sense in asking whether what it says is true or false. And we have seen that sentences which simply express moral judgements do not say anything. They are pure expressions of feeling and as such do not come under the category of truth and falsehood. They are unverifiable for the same reason as a cry of pain or a word of command is unverifiable—because they do not express genuine propositions.

Thus, although our theory of ethics might fairly be said to be radically subjectivist, it differs in a very important respect from the orthodox subjectivist theory. For the orthodox subjectivist does not deny, as we do, that the sentences of a moralizer express genuine propositions. All he denies is that they express propositions of a unique non-empirical character. His own view is that they express propositions about the speaker's feelings. If this were so, ethical judgements clearly would be capable of being true or false. They would be true if the speaker had the relevant feelings, and false if he had not. And this is a matter which is, in principle, empirically verifiable. Furthermore they could be significantly contradicted. For if I say, "Tolerance is a virtue," and someone answers, "You don't approve of it," he would, on the ordinary subjectivist theory, be contradicting me. On our theory, he would not be contradicting me, because, in saying that tolerance was a virtue, I should not be making any statement about my own feelings or about anything else. I should simply be evincing my feelings, which is not at all the same thing as saying that I have them.

The distinction between the expression of feeling and the assertion of feeling is complicated by the fact that the assertion that one has a certain feeling often accompanies the expression of that feeling, and is then, indeed, a factor in the expression of that feeling. Thus I may simultaneously express boredom and say that I am bored, and in that case my utterance of the words, "I am bored," is one of the circumstances which make it true to say that I am expressing or evincing boredom. But I can express boredom without actually saying that I am bored. I can express it by my tone and gestures, while making a statement about something wholly unconnected with it, or by an ejaculation, or without uttering any words at all. So that even if the assertion that one has a certain feeling always involves the expression of that feeling, the expression of a feeling assuredly does not always involve the assertion that one has it. And this is the important point to grasp in considering the distinction between our theory and the ordinary subjectivist theory. For whereas the subjectivist holds that ethical statements actually assert the existence of certain feelings, we hold that ethical statements are expressions and excitants of feeling which do not necessarily involve any assertions.

We have already remarked that the main objection to the ordinary subjectivist theory is that the validity of ethical judgements is not determined by the nature of their author's feelings. And this is an objection which our theory escapes. For it does not imply that the existence of any feelings is a necessary and sufficient condition of the validity of an ethical judgement. It implies, on the contrary, that ethical judgements have no validity.

There is, however, a celebrated argument against subjectivist theories which our theory does not escape. It has been pointed out by Moore that if ethical statements were simply statements about the speaker's feelings, it would be impossible to argue about questions of value.[1] To take a typical example: if a man said that thrift was a virtue, and another replied that it was a vice, they would not, on this theory, be disputing with one another. One would be saying that he approved of thrift, and the other that *he* didn't; and there is no reason why both these statements should not be true. Now Moore held it to be obvious that we do dispute about questions of value, and accordingly concluded that the partic-

1. *cf. Philosophical Studies*, "The Nature of Moral Philosophy."

ular form of subjectivism which he was discussing was false.

It is plain that the conclusion that it is impossible to dispute about questions of value follows from our theory also. For as we hold that such sentences as "Thrift is a virtue" and "Thrift is a vice" do not express propositions at all, we clearly cannot hold that they express incompatible propositions. We must therefore admit that if Moore's argument really refutes the ordinary subjectivist theory, it also refutes ours. But, in fact, we deny that it does refute even the ordinary subjectivist theory. For we hold that one really never does dispute about questions of value.

This may seem, at first sight, to be a very paradoxical assertion. For we certainly do engage in disputes which are ordinarily regarded as disputes about questions of value. But, in all such cases, we find, if we consider the matter closely, that the dispute is not really about a question of value, but about a question of fact. When someone disagrees with us about the moral value of a certain action or type of action, we do admittedly resort to argument in order to win him over to our way of thinking. But we do not attempt to show by our arguments that he has the "wrong" ethical feeling towards a situation whose nature he has correctly apprehended. What we attempt to show is that he is mistaken about the facts of the case. We argue that he has misconceived the agent's motive: or that he has misjudged the effects of the action, or its probable effects in view of the agent's knowledge; or that he has failed to take into account the special circumstances in which the agent was placed. Or else we employ more general arguments about the effects which actions of a certain type tend to produce, or the qualities which are usually manifested in their performance. We do this in the hope that we have only to get our opponent to agree with us about the nature of the empirical facts for him to adopt the same moral attitude towards them as we do. And as the people with whom we argue have generally received the same moral education as ourselves, and live in the same social order, our expectation is usually justified. But if our opponent happens to have undergone a different process of moral "conditioning" from ourselves, so that, even when he acknowledges all the facts, he still disagrees with us about the moral value of the actions under discussion, then we abandon the attempt to convince him by argument. We say that it is impossible to argue with him because he has a distorted or undeveloped moral sense; which signifies merely that he employs a different set of values from our own. We feel that our own system of values is superior, and therefore speak in such derogatory terms of his. But we cannot bring forward any arguments to show that our system is superior. For our judgement that it is so is itself a judgement of value, and accordingly outside the scope of argument. It is because argument fails us when we come to deal with pure questions of value, as distinct from questions of fact, that we finally resort to mere abuse.

In short, we find that argument is possible on moral questions only if some system of values is presupposed. If our opponent concurs with us in expressing moral disapproval of all actions of a given type *t*, then we may get him to condemn a particular action A, by bringing forward arguments to show that A is of type *t*. For the question whether A does or does not belong to that type is a plain question of fact. Given that a man has certain moral principles, we argue that he must, in order to be consistent, react morally to certain things in a certain way. What we do not and cannot argue about is the validity of these moral principles. We merely praise or condemn them in the light of our own feelings.

If anyone doubts the accuracy of this account of moral disputes, let him try to construct even an imaginary argument on a question of value which does not reduce itself to an argument about a question of logic or about an empirical matter of fact. I am confident that he will not succeed in producing a single example. And if that is the case, he must allow that its involving the impossibility of purely ethical arguments is not, as Moore thought, a ground of objection to our theory, but rather a point in favour of it.

Having upheld our theory against the only criticism which appeared to threaten it, we may now use it to define the nature of all ethical enquiries. We find that ethical philosophy consists simply in saying that ethical concepts are pseudo-concepts and therefore unanalysable. The further task of describing the different feelings that the different ethical terms are used to express, and the different reactions that they customarily provoke, is a task for the psychologist. There cannot be such a thing as ethical science, if by ethical science one means the elaboration of a "true" system of morals. For we have seen that, as ethical judgements are mere expressions of feeling, there can be no way of determining the validity of any ethical system, and, indeed, no sense in asking whether any such system is true. All that one may legitimately enquire in this connection is, What are the moral habits of a given person or group of people, and what causes them to have precisely those habits and feelings? And this enquiry falls wholly within the scope of the existing social sciences.

It appears, then, that ethics, as a branch of knowledge, is nothing more than a department of psychology and sociology. And in case anyone thinks that we are overlooking the existence of casuistry, we may remark that casuistry is not a science, but is a purely analytical investigation of the structure of a given moral system. In other words, it is an exercise in formal logic.

When one comes to pursue the psychological enquiries which constitute ethical science, one is immediately enabled to account for the Kantian and hedonistic theories of morals. For one finds that one of the chief causes of moral behaviour is fear, both conscious and unconscious, of a god's displeasure, and fear of the enmity of society. And this, indeed, is the reason why moral precepts present themselves to some people as "categorical" commands. And one finds, also, that the moral code of a society is partly determined by the beliefs of that society concerning the conditions of its own happiness—or, in other words, that a society tends to encourage or discourage a given type of conduct by the use of moral sanctions according as it appears to promote or detract from the contentment of the society as a whole. And this is the reason why altruism is recommended in most moral codes and egotism condemned. It is from the observation of this connection between morality and happiness that hedonistic or eudaemonistic theories of morals ultimately spring, just as the moral theory of Kant is based on the fact, previously explained, that moral precepts have for some people the force of inexorable commands. As each of these theories ignores the fact which lies at the root of the other, both may be criticized as being one-sided; but this is not the main objection to either of them. Their essential defect is that they treat propositions which refer to the causes and attributes of our ethical feelings as if they were definitions of ethical concepts. And thus they fail to recognise that ethical concepts are pseudo-concepts and consequently indefinable.

As we have already said, our conclusions about the nature of ethics apply to aesthetics also. Aesthetic terms are used in exactly the same way as ethical terms. Such aesthetic words as "beautiful" and "hideous" are employed, as ethical words are employed, not to make statements of fact, but simply to express certain feelings and evoke a certain response. It follows, as in ethics, that there is no sense in attributing objective validity to aesthetic judgements, and no possibility of arguing about questions of value in aesthetics, but only about questions of fact. A scientific treatment of aesthetics would show us what in general were the causes of aesthetic feeling, why various societies produced and admired the works of art they did, why taste varies as it does within a given society, and so forth. And these are ordinary psychological or sociological questions. They have, of course, little or nothing to do with aesthetic criticism as we understand it. But that is because the purpose of aesthetic criticism is not so much to give knowledge as to communicate emotion. The critic, by calling attention to certain features of the work under review, and expressing his own feelings about them, endeavours to make us share his attitude towards the work as a whole. The only relevant propositions that he formulates are propositions describing the nature of the work. And these are plain records of fact. We conclude, therefore, that there is nothing in aesthetics, any more than there is in ethics, to justify the view that it embodies a unique type of knowledge.

It should now be clear that the only information which we can legitimately derive from the study of our aesthetic and moral experiences is information about our own mental and physical make-up. We take note of these experiences as providing data for our psychological and sociological generalisations. And this is the only way in which they serve to increase our knowledge. It follows that any attempt to make our use of ethical and aesthetic concepts the basis of a metaphysical theory concerning the existence of a world of values, as distinct from the world of facts, involves a false analysis of these concepts. Our own analysis has shown that the phenomena of moral experience cannot fairly be used to support any rationalist or metaphysical doctrine whatsoever. In particular, they cannot, as Kant hoped, be used to establish the existence of a transcendent god.

This mention of God brings us to the question of the possibility of religious knowledge. We shall see that this possibility has already been ruled out by our treatment of metaphysics. But, as this is a point of considerable interest, we may be permitted to discuss it at some length.

It is now generally admitted, at any rate by philosophers, that the existence of a being having the attributes which define the god of any non-animistic religion cannot be demonstratively proved. To see that this is so, we have only to ask ourselves what are the premises from which the existence of such a god could be deduced. If the conclusion that a god exists is to be demonstratively certain, then these premises must be certain; for, as the conclusion of a deductive argument is already contained in the premises, any uncertainty there may be about the truth of the premises is necessarily shared by it. But we know that no empirical proposition can ever by anything more than probable. It is only *a priori* propositions that are logically certain. But we cannot deduce the existence of a god from an *a priori* proposition. For we know that the reason why *a priori* propositions are certain is that they are tautologies. And from a set of tautologies nothing but a further tautology can be validly deduced. It follows that there is no possibility of demonstrating the existence of a god.

What is not so generally recognised is that there can be no way of proving that the existence of a god, such as the God of Christianity, is even probable. Yet this also is easily shown. For if the existence of such a god were probable, then the proposition that he existed would be an empirical hypothesis. And in that case it would be possible to deduce from it, and other empirical hypotheses, certain experiential propositions which were not deducible from those other hypotheses alone. But in fact this is not possible. It is sometimes claimed, indeed, that the existence of a certain sort of regularity in nature constitutes sufficient evidence for the existence of a god. But if the sentence "God exists" entails no more than that certain types of phenomena occur in certain sequences, then to assert the existence of a god will be simply equivalent to asserting that there is the requisite regularity in nature; and no religious man would admit that this was all he intended to assert in asserting the existence of a god. He would say that in talking about God, he was talking about a transcendent being who might be known through certain empirical manifestations, but certainly could not be defined in terms of those manifestations. But in that case the term "god" is a metaphysical term. And if "god" is a metaphysical term, then it cannot be even probable that a god exists. For to say that "God exists" is to make a metaphysical utterance which cannot be either true or false. And by the same criterion, no sentence which purports to describe the nature of a transcendent god can possess any literal significance.

It is important not to confuse this view of religious assertions with the view that is adopted by atheists, or agnostics.[2] For it is characteristic of an agnostic to hold that the existence of a god is a possibility in which there is no good reason either to believe or disbelieve; and it is characteristic of an atheist to hold that it is at least probable that no god exists. And our view that all utterances about the nature of God are nonsensical, so far from being identical with, or even lending any support to, either of these familiar contentions, is actually incompatible with them. For if the assertion that there is a god is nonsensical, then the atheist's assertion that there is no god is equally nonsensical, since it is only a significant proposition that can be significantly contradicted. As for the agnostic, although he refrains from saying either that there is or that there is not a god, he does not deny that the question whether a transcendent god exists is a genuine question. He does not deny that the two sentences "There is a transcendent god" and "There is no transcendent god" express propositions one of which is actually true and the other false. All he says is that we have no means of telling which of them is true, and therefore ought not to commit ourselves to either. But we have seen that the sentences in question do not express propositions at all. And this means that agnosticism also is ruled out.

Thus we offer the theist the same comfort as we gave to the moralist. His assertions cannot possibly be valid, but they cannot be invalid either. As he says nothing at all about the world, he cannot justly be accused of saying anything false, or anything for which he has insufficient grounds. It is only when the theist claims that in asserting the existence of a transcendent god he is expressing a genuine proposition that we are entitled to disagree with him.

It is to be remarked that in cases where deities are identified with natural objects, assertions concerning them may be allowed to be significant. If, for example, a man tells me that the occurrence of thunder is alone both necessary and sufficient to establish the truth of the proposition that Jehovah is angry, I may conclude that, in his usage of words, the sentence "Jehovah is angry" is equivalent to "It is thundering. " But in sophisticated religions, though

2. This point was suggested to me by Professor H. H. Price.

they may be to some extent based on men's awe of natural process which they cannot sufficiently understand, the "person" who is supposed to control the empirical world is not himself located in it; he is held to be superior to the empirical world, and so outside it; and he is endowed with super-empirical attributes. But the notion of a person whose essential attributes are nonempirical is not an intelligible notion at all. We may have a word which is used as if it named this "person," but, unless the sentences in which it occurs express propositions which are empirically verifiable, it cannot be said to symbolize anything. And this is the case with regard to the word "god," in the usage in which it is intended to refer to a transcendent object. The mere existence of the noun is enough to foster the illusion that there is a real, or at any rate a possible entity corresponding to it. It is only when we enquire what God's attributes are that we discover that "God," in this usage, is not a genuine name.

It is common to find belief in a transcendent god conjoined with belief in an after-life. But, in the form which it usually takes, the content of this belief is not a genuine hypothesis. To say that men do not ever die, or that the state of death is merely a state of prolonged insensibility, is indeed to express a significant proposition, though all the available evidence goes to show that it is false. But to say that there is something imperceptible inside a man, which is his soul or his real self, and that it goes on living after he is dead, is to make a metaphysical assertion which has no more factual content than the assertion that there is a transcendent god.

It is worth mentioning that, according to the account which we have given of religious assertions, there is no logical ground for antagonism between religion and natural science. As far as the question of truth or falsehood is concerned, there is no opposition between the natural scientist and the theist who believes in a transcendent god. For since the religious utterances of the theist are not genuine propositions at all, they cannot stand in any logical relation to the propositions of science. Such antagonism as there is between religion and science appears to consist in the fact that science takes away one of the motives which make men religious. For it is acknowledged that one of the ultimate sources of religious feeling lies in the inability of men to determine their own destiny; and science tends to destroy the feeling of awe with which men regard an alien world, by making them believe that they can understand and anticipate the course of natural phenomena, and even to some extent control it. The fact that it has recently become fashionable for physicists themselves to be sympathetic towards religion is a point in favour of this hypothesis. For this sympathy towards religion marks the physicists' own lack of confidence in the validity of their hypotheses, which is a reaction on their part from the antireligious dogmatism of nineteenth-century scientists, and a natural outcome of the crisis through which physics has just passed.

It is not within the scope of this enquiry to enter more deeply into the causes of religious feeling, or to discuss the probability of the continuance of religious belief. We are concerned only to answer those questions which arise out of our discussion of the possibility of religious knowledge. The point which we wish to establish is that there cannot be any transcendent truths of religion. For the sentences which the theist uses to express such "truths" are not literally significant.

An interesting feature of this conclusions is that it accords with what many theists are accustomed to say themselves. For we are often told that the nature of God is a mystery which transcends the human understanding. But to say that something transcends the human understanding is to say that it is unintelligible. And what is unintelligible cannot significantly be described. Again, we are told that God is not an object of reason but an object of faith. This may be nothing more than an admission that the existence of God must be taken on trust, since it cannot be proved. But it may also be an assertion that God is the object of a purely mystical intuition, and cannot therefore be defined in terms which are intelligible to the reason. And I think there are many theists who would assert this. But if one allows that it is impossible to define God in intelligible terms, then one is allowing that it is impossible for a sentence both to be significant and to be about God. If a mystic admits that the object of his vision is something which cannot be described, then he must also admit that he is bound to talk nonsense when he describes it.

For his part, the mystic may protest that his intuition does reveal truths to him, even though he cannot explain to others what these truths are; and that we who do not possess this faculty of intuition can have no ground for denying that it is a cognitive faculty. For we can hardly maintain *a priori* that there are no ways of discovering true propositions except those which we ourselves employ. The answer is that we set no limit to the number of ways in which one may come to formulate a true proposition. We do not in any way deny that a synthetic truth may be discovered by purely intuitive methods as well as by the rational method of induction. But we do say that every synthetic proposition, however it may have been arrived at, must be subject to the test of actual experience. We do not deny *a priori* that the mystic is able to discover truths by his own special methods. We wait to hear what are the propositions which embody his discoveries, in order to see whether they are verified or confuted by our empirical observations. But the mystic, so far from producing propositions which are empirically verified, is unable to produce any intelligible propositions at all. And therefore we say that his intuition has not revealed to him any facts. It is no use his saying that he has apprehended facts but is unable to express them. For we know that if he really had acquired any information, he would be able to express it. He would be able to indicate in some way or other how the genuineness of his discovery might be empirically determined. The fact that he cannot reveal what he "knows," or even himself devise an empirical test to validate his "knowledge," shows that his state of mystical intuition is not a genuinely cognitive state. So that in describing his vision the mystic does not give us any information about the external world; he merely gives us indirect information about the condition of his own mind.

These considerations dispose of the argument from religious experience, which many philosophers still regard as a valid argument in favour of the existence of a god. They say that it is logically possible for men to be immediately acquainted with God, as they are immediately acquainted with a sense-content, and that there is no reason why one should be prepared to believe a man when he says that he is seeing a yellow patch, and refuse to believe him when he says that he is seeing God. The answer to this is that if the man who asserts that he is seeing God is merely asserting that he is experiencing a peculiar kind of sense-content, then we do not for a moment deny that his assertion may be true. But, ordinarily, the man who says that he is seeing God is saying not merely that he is experiencing a religious emotion, but also that there exists a transcendent being who is the object of this emotion; just as the man who says that he sees a yellow patch is ordinarily saying not merely that his visual sense-field contains a yellow sense-content, but also that there exists a yellow object to which the sense-content belongs. And it is not irrational to be prepared to believe a man when he asserts the existence of a yellow object, and to refuse to believe him when he asserts the existence of a transcendent god. For whereas the sentence "There exists here a yellow-coloured material thing" expresses a genuine synthetic proposition which could be empirically verified, the sentence "There exists a transcendent god" has, as we have seen, no literal significance.

We conclude, therefore, that the argument from religious experience is altogether fallacious. The fact that people have religious experiences is interesting from the psychological point of view, but it does not in any way imply that there is such a thing as religious knowledge, any more than our having moral experiences implies that there is such a thing as moral knowledge. The theist, like the moralist, may believe that his experiences are cognitive experiences, but, unless he can formulate his "knowledge" in propositions that are empirically verifiable, we may be sure that he is deceiving himself. It follows that those philosophers who fill their books with assertions that they intuitively "know" this or that moral or religious "truth" are merely providing material for the psychoanalyst. For no act of intuition can be said to reveal a truth about any matter of fact unless it issues in verifiable propositions. And all such propositions are to be incorporated in the system of empirical propositions which constitutes science.

Chapter 8
LUDWIG WITTGENSTEIN

Ludwig Wittgenstein (1889–1951) was born in Vienna into a wealthy, highly cultured family. His father was a Jew who had converted to Protestantism, his mother a Roman Catholic, in which religion Wittgenstein was brought up. Wittgenstein went to study engineering at the University of Manchester. Having read the work of Bertrand Russell, in 1912 he transferred to Cambridge University, where Russell was teaching, to study under him. Russell soon realized that his student was a genius and also an extremely eccentric and intense young man. Russell relates the following story about his pupil.

> At the end of his first term at Cambridge he came to me and said, "Will you please tell me whether I am a complete idiot or not?" I replied, "My dear fellow, I don't know. Why are you asking me?" He said, "Because, if I am a complete idiot, I shall become an aeronaut; but if not, I shall become a philosopher." I told him to write something during the vacation on some philosophical subject and I would then tell him whether he was a complete idiot or not. At the beginning of the following term he brought me the fulfillment of this suggestion. After reading only one sentence, I said to him, "No, you must not become an aeronaut."[1]

Wittgenstein returned to Austria to serve in the Austrian army during the First World War. He was captured by the Italians and spent time in a prisoner-of-war camp, where he finished writing his first work, *Tractatus Logico-Philosophicus* (1919). The work was to show the logical relationship between language and the world, to show what could and could not be said. He writes in the preface:

> The book deals with the problems of philosophy, and shows, I believe, that the reason why these problems are posed is that the logic of our language is misunderstood. The whole sense of the book might be summed up in the following words: what can be said at all can be said clearly, and what we cannot talk about we must pass over in silence.

A selection from this work is reprinted below.

After the war, he worked as a schoolmaster and gardener in a monastery before returning to Cambridge in 1929. There he submitted the *Tractatus* as his Ph.D. dissertation. Russell and G. E. Moore were his examiners. He was appointed a lecturer at Cambridge and continued in that capacity until his death in 1951. His second book, *Philosophical Investigations*, was published posthumously in 1953.

Wittgenstein came to reject the reasoning of the *Tractatus*, believing his solution of giving logical structure to language solved the problem of how language related to the world. In this second work, Wittgenstein denies his earlier views that words have essences and that propositions have pictorial form which reflects the world. Instead he claimed that languages were various games that occurred within

1. Bertrand Russell, *Portraits from Memory* (George Allen & Unwin, 1956), 26–27.

different cultures or forms of life. Philosophy cannot provide foundations for knowledge in general but only shows us that our practices are justified within forms of life. "Philosophy may in no way interfere with the actual use of language; it can in the end only describe it. For it cannot give it any foundation either. It leaves everything as it is."

FOR FURTHER READING

Ayer, A. J. *Wittgenstein* (University of Chicago, 1986).
Grayling, A. C. *Wittgenstein* (Oxford University Press, 1988).
Hacker, P. M. S. *Wittgenstein's Position in Twentieth Century Analytic Philosophy* (Oxford University Press, 1996).
Kenny, Anthony. *Wittgenstein* (Harvard University Press, 1974).
Malcolm, Norman. *Ludwig Wittgenstein: A Memoir* (Oxford University Press, 1958).
Monk, Ray. *Ludwig Wittgenstein: The Duty of Genius* (Free Press, 1990).
Rundle, Bede. *Wittgenstein on Language: Meaning, Use and Truth* (Blackwell, 1990).
Wittgenstein, Ludwig. *Tractatus Logico-Philosophicus*, trans. D. Pears and B. McGuiness (Routledge & Kegan Paul, 1961).

Tractatus Logico-Philosophicus

PREFACE

Perhaps this book will be understood only by someone who has himself already had the thoughts that are expressed in it—or at least similar thoughts.—So it is not a textbook.—Its purpose would be achieved if it gave pleasure to one person who read and understood it.

The book deals with the problems of philosophy, and shows, I believe, that the reason why these problems are posed is that the logic of our language is misunderstood. The whole sense of the book might be summed up in the following words: what can be said at all can be said clearly, and what we cannot talk about we must pass over in silence.

Thus the aim of the book is to draw a limit to thought, or rather—not to thought, but to the expressing of thoughts: for in order to be able to draw a limit to thought, we should have to find both sides of the limit thinkable (i.e. we should have to be able to think what cannot be thought).

It will therefore only be in language that the limit can be drawn, and what lies on the other side of the limit will simply be nonsense.

I do not wish to judge how far my efforts coincide with those of other philosophers. Indeed, what I have written here makes no claim to novelty in detail, and the reason why I give no sources is that it is a matter of indifference to me whether the thoughts that I have had have been anticipated by someone else.

I will only mention that I am indebted to Frege's great works and to the writings of my friend Mr. Bertrand Russell for much of the stimulation of my thoughts.

If this work has any value, it consists in two things: the first is that thoughts are expressed in it, and on this score the better the thoughts are expressed—the more the nail has been hit on the head—the greater will be its value.—Here I am conscious of having fallen a long way short of what is possible. Simply because my powers are too slight for the accomplishment of the task.—May others come and do it better.

On the other hand the *truth* of the thoughts that are here communicated seems to me unassailable and definitive. I therefore believe myself to have found, on all essential points, the final solution of the problems. And if I am not mistaken in this belief, then the second thing in which the value of this work consists is that it shows how little is achieved when these problems are solved.

LANGUAGE AS PICTURE

1[1] The world is all that is the case.

1.1 The world is the totality of facts, not of things.

1.11 The world is determined by the facts, and by their being *all* the facts.

1.12 Totality of facts determines what is the case, and also whatever is not the case.

1.13 The facts in logical space are the world.

1.2 The world divides into facts.

1.21 Each item can be the case or not the case while everything else remains the same.

2 What is the case—a fact—is existence of states of affairs.

2.01 A state of affairs (a state of things) is a combination of objects (things).

2.011 It is essential to things that they should be possible constituents of states of affairs.

2.012 In logic nothing is accidental: if a thing can occur in a state of affairs, the possibility of the state of affairs must be written into the thing itself.

2.0121 It would seem to be a sort of accident, if it turned out that a situation would fit a thing that could already exist entirely on its own.

If things can occur in states of affairs, this possibility must be in them from the beginning.

(Nothing in the province of logic can be merely possible. Logic deals with every possibility and all possibilities are its facts.)

Just as we are quite unable to imagine spatial objects outside space or temporal objects outside time, so too there is no object that we can imagine excluded from the possibility of combining with others.

If I can imagine objects combined in states of affairs, I cannot imagine them excluded from the *possibility* of such combinations.

2.0122 Things are dependent in so far as they can occur in all *possible* situations, but this form of independence is a form of connexion with states of affairs, a form of dependence. (It is impossible for words to appear in two different roles: by themselves, and in propositions.)

2.0123 If I know an object I also know its possible occurrences in states of affairs.

(Every one of these possibilities must be part of the nature of the object.)

A new possibility cannot be discovered later.

2.01231 If I am to know an object, though I need not know its external properties, I must know all its internal properties.

2.0124 If all objects are given, then at the same time all *possible* states of affairs are also given.

2.013 Each thing is, as it were, in a space of possible states of affairs. This space I can imagine empty, but I cannot imagine the thing without the space.

2.0131 A spatial object must be situated in infinite space. (A spatial point is an argument-place.)

A speck in the visual field, though it need not be red, must have some colour: it is, so to speak, surrounded by colour-space. Notes must have *some* pitch, objects of the sense of touch *some* degree of hardness, and so on.

2.014 Objects contain the possibility of all situations.

2.0141 The possibility of its occurring in states of affairs is the form of an object.

2.02 Objects are simple.

1. The decimal numbers assigned to the individual propositions indicate the logical importance of the propositions, the stress laid on them in my exposition. The propositions *n*.1, *n*.2, *n*.3, etc. are comments of proposition no.*n*; the propositions *n.m*1, *n.m*2, etc. are comments on proposition no. *n.m*; and so on.Text of Footnote.

2.0201 Every statement about complexes can be resolved into a statement about their constituents and into the propositions that describe the complexes completely.

2.021 Objects make up the substance of the world. That is why they cannot be composite.

2.0211 If the world had no substance, then whether a proposition had sense would depend on whether another proposition was true.

2.0212 In that case we could not sketch any picture of the world (true or false).

2.022 It is obvious that an imagined world, however different it may be from the real one, must have *something*—a form—in common with it.

2.023 Objects are just what constitute this unalterable form.

2.0231 The substance of the world *can* only determine a form, and not any material properties. For it is only by means of propositions that material properties are represented—only by the configuration of objects that they are produced.

2.0232 In a manner of speaking, objects are colourless.

2.0233 If two objects have the same logical form, the only distinction between them, apart from their external properties, is that they are different.

2.02331 Either a thing has properties that nothing else has, in which case we can immediately use a description to distinguish it from the others and refer to it; or, on the other hand, there are several things that have the whole set of their properties in common, in which case it is quite impossible to indicate one of them.

For if there is nothing to distinguish a thing, I cannot distinguish it, since otherwise it would be distinguished after all.

2.024 Substance is what subsists independently of what is the case.

2.025 It is form and content.

2.0251 Space, time, and colour (being coloured) are forms of objects.

2.026 There must be objects, if the world is to have an unalterable form.

2.027 Objects, the unalterable, and the subsistent are one and the same.

2.0271 Objects are what is unalterable and subsistent; their configuration is what is changing and unstable.

2.0272 The configuration of objects produces states of affairs.

2.03 In a state of affairs objects fit into one another like the links of a chain.

2.031 In a state of affairs objects stand in a determinate relation to one another.

2.032 The determinate way in which objects are connected in a state of affairs is the structure of the state of affairs.

2.033 Form is the possibility of structure.

2.034 The structure of a fact consists of the structures of states of affairs.

2.04 The totality of existing states of affairs is the world.

2.05 The totality of existing states of affairs also determines which states of affairs do not exist.

2.06 The existence and non-existence of states of affairs is reality. (We also call the existence of states of affairs a positive fact, and their non-existence a negative fact.)

2.061 States of affairs are independent of one another.

2.062 From the existence or non-existence of one state of affairs it is impossible to infer the existence or non-existence of another.

2.063 The sum-total of reality is the world.

2.1 We picture facts to ourselves.

2.11 A picture presents a situation in logical space, the existence and non-existence of states of affairs.

2.12 A picture is a model of reality.

2.13 In a picture objects have the elements of the picture corresponding to them.

2.131 In a picture the elements of the picture are the representatives of objects.

2.14 What constitutes a picture is that its elements are related to one another in a determinate way.

2.141 A picture is a fact.

2.15 The fact that the elements of a picture are

related to one another in a determinate way represents that things are related to one another in the same way.

Let us call this connexion of its elements the structure of the picture, and let us call the possibility of this structure the pictorial form of the picture.

2.151 Pictorial form is the possibility that things are related to one another in the same way as the elements of a picture.

2.1511 *That* is how a picture is attached to reality; it reaches right out to it.

2.1512 It is laid against reality like a measure.

2.15121 Only the end-points of the graduating lines actually *touch* the object that is to be measured.

2.1513 So a picture, conceived in this way, also includes the pictorial relationship, which makes it into a picture.

2.1514 The pictorial relationship consists of the correlations of the picture's elements with things.

2.1515 These correlations are, as it were, the feelers of the picture's elemens, with which the picture touches reality.

2.16 If a fact is to be a picture, it must have something in common with what it depicts.

2.161 There must be something identical in a picture and what it depicts, to enable the one to be a picture of the other at all.

2.17 What a picture must have in common with reality, in order to be able to depict it—correctly or incorrectly—in the way it does, is its pictorial form.

2.171 A picture can depict any reality whose form it has.

A spatial picture can depict anything spatial, a coloured one anything coloured, etc.

2.172 A picture cannot, however, depict its pictorial form: it displays it.

2.173 A picture represents its subject from a position outside it. (Its standpoint is its representational form.) That is why a picture represents its subject correctly or incorrectly.

2.174 A picture cannot, however, place itself outside its representational form.

2.18 What any picture, of whatever form, must have in common with reality, in order to be able to depict it—correctly or incorrectly—in any way at all, is logical form, i.e. the form of reality.

2.181 A picture whose pictorial form is logical form is called logical picture.

2.182 Every picture is *at the same time* a logical one. (On the other hand, not every picture is, for example, a spatial one.)

2.19 Logical pictures can depict the world.

2.2 A picture has logico-pictorial form in common with what it depicts.

2.201 A picture depicts reality by representing a possibility of existence and non-existence of states of affairs.

2.202 A picture represents a possible situation in logical space.

2.203 A picture contains the possibility of the situation that it represents.

2.21 A picture agrees with reality or fails to agree; it is correct or incorrect, true or false.

2.22 What a picture represents it represents independently of its truth or falsity, by means of its pictorial form.

2.221 What a picture represents is its sense.

2.222 The agreement or disagreement of its sense with reality constitutes its truth or falsity.

2.223 In order to tell whether a picture is true or false we must compare it with reality.

2.224 It is impossible to tell from the picture alone whether it is true or false.

2.225 There are no pictures that are true a priori.

3 A logical picture of facts is a thought.

3.001 'A state of affairs is thinkable': what this means is that we can picture it to ourselves.

3.01 The totality of true thoughts is a picture of the world.

3.02 A thought contains the possibility of the situation of which it is the thought. What is thinkable is possible too.

3.03 Thought can never be of anything illogical, since, if it were, we should have to think illogically.

3.031 It used to be said that God could create anything except what would be contrary to the laws of logic.—The truth is that we could not *say* what an 'illogical' world would look like.

3.032 It is as impossible to represent in language anything that 'contradicts logic' as it is in geometry to represent by its co-ordinates a figure that contradicts the laws of space, or to give the co-ordinates of a point that does not exist.

3.0321 Though a state of affairs that would contravene the laws of physics can be represented by us spatially, one that would contravene the laws of geometry cannot.

3.04 If a thought were correct a priori, it would be a thought whose possibility ensured its truth.

3.05 A priori knowledge that a thought was true would be possible only if its truth were recognizable from the thought itself (without anything to compare it with).

3.1 In a proposition a thought finds an expression that can be perceived by the senses.

3.11 We use the perceptible sign of a proposition (spoken or written, etc.) as a projection of a possible situation.

The method of projection is to think of the sense of the proposition.

3.12 I call the sign with which we express a thought a propositional sign.—And a proposition is a propositional sign in its projective relation to the world.

3.13 A proposition includes all that the projection includes, but not what is projected.

Therefore, though what is projected is not itself included, its possibility is.

A proposition, therefore, does not actually contain its sense, but does contain the possibility of expressing it.

("The content of a proposition" means the content of a proposition that has sense.)

A proposition contains the form, but not the content, of its sense.

3.14 What constitutes a propositional sign is that in it its elements (the words) stand in a determinate relation to one another.

A propositional sign is a fact.

3.141 A proposition is not a blend of words.—(Just as a theme in music is not a blend of notes.)

A proposition is articulated.

3.142 Only facts can express a sense, a set of names cannot.

3.143 Although a propositional sign is a fact, this is obscured by the usual frm of expression in writing or print.

For in a printed proposition, for example, no essential difference is apparent between a propositional sign and a word. (That is what made it possible for Frege to call a proposition a composite name.)

3.1431 The essence of a propositional sign is very clearly seen if we imagine one composed of spatial objects (such as tables, chairs, and books) instead of written signs.

3.1432 Instead of, 'The complex sign "*a*R*b*" says that *a* stands to *b* in the relation *R*', we ought to put, '*That* "*a*" stands to "*b*" in a certain relation says *that* *a*R*b*.'

3.144 Situations can be described but not *given names*.

(Names are like points; propositions like arrows—they have sense.)

3.2 In a proposition a thought can be expressed in such a way that elements of the propositional sign correspond to the objects of the thought.

3.201 I call such elements 'simple signs', and such a proposition 'completely analysed'.

3.202 The simple signs employed in propositions are called names.

3.203 A name means an object. The object is its meaning. ('*A*' is the same sign as '*A*'.)

3.21 The configuration of objects in a situation corresponds to the configuration of simple signs in the propositional sign.

3.22 In a proposition a name is the representative of an object.

3.221 Objects can only be *named*. Signs are their representatives. I can only speak *about* them: I cannot *put them into words*. Propositions can only say *how* things are, not *what* they are.

3.23 The requirement that simple signs be possible is the requirement that sense be determinate.

3.24 A proposition about a complex stands in an internal relation to a proposition about a constituent of the complex.

A complex can be given only by its description, which will be right or wrong. A proposition that mentions a complex will not be nonsensical, if the complex does not exist, but simply false.

When a propositional element signifies a complex, this can be seen from an indeterminateness in the propositions in which it occurs. In such cases we *know* that the proposition leaves something undetermined. (In fact the generality-sign *contains* a prototype.)

The contraction of a symbol for a complex into a simple symbol can be expressed in a definition.

3.25 A proposition has one and only one complete analysis.

3.251 What a proposition expresses it expresses in a determinate manner, which can be set out clearly: a proposition is articulated.

3.26 A name cannot be dissected any further by means of a definition: it is a primitive sign.

3.261 Every sign that has a definition signifies *via* the signs that serve to define it; and the definitions point the way.

Two signs cannot signify in the same manner if one is primitive and the other is defined by means of primitive signs. Names *cannot* be anatomized by means of definitions. (This cannot be done to any sign that has a meaning independently and on its own.)

3.262 What signs fail to express, their application shows. What signs slur over, their application says clearly.

3.263 The meanings of primitive signs can be explained by means of elucidations. Elucidations are propositions that contain the primitive signs. So they can only be understood if the meanings of those signs are already known.

3.3 Only propositions have sense; only in the nexus of a proposition does a name have meaning.

3.31 I call any part of a proposition that characterizes its sense an expression (or a symbol).

(A proposition is itself an expression.)

Everything essential to their sense that propositions can have in common with one another is an expression.

An expression is the mark of a form and a content.

3.311 An expression presupposes the forms of all the propositions in which it can occur. It is the common characteristic mark of a class of propositions.

3.312 It is therefore presented by means of the general form of the propositions that it characterizes.

In fact, in this form the expression will be *constant* and everything else *variable*.

3.313 Thus an expression is presented by means of a variable whose values are the propositions that contain the expression.

(In the limiting case the variable becomes a constant, the expression becomes a proposition.)

I call such a variable a 'propositional variable'.

3.314 An expression has meaning only in a proposition. All variables can be construed as propositional variables.

(Even variable names.)

3.315 If we turn a constituent of a proposition into a variable, there is a class of propositions all of which are values of the resulting variable proposition. In general, this class too will be dependent on the meaning that our arbitrary conventions have given to parts of the original proposition. But if all the signs in it that have arbitrarily determined meanings are turned into variables, we shall still get a class of this kind. This one, however, is not dependent on any convention, but solely on the nature of the proposition. It corresponds to a logical form—a logical prototype.

3.316 What values a propositional variable may take is something that is stipulated.

The stipulation of values *is* the variable.

3.317 To stipulate values for a propositional variable is *to give the propositions* whose common characteristic the variable is.

The stipulation is a description of those propositions.

The stipulation will therefore be concerned only with symbols, not with their meaning.

And the *only* thing essential to the stipulation is *that it is merely a description of symbols and states nothing about what is signified.*

How the description of the propositions is produced is not essential.

3.318 Like Frege and Russell I consture a proposition as a function of the expressions contained in it.

4.461 Propositions show what they say: tautologies and contradictions show that they say nothing.

A tautology has no truth-conditions, since it is unconditionally true: and a contradiction is true on no condition.

Tautologies and contradictions lack sense.

(Like a point from which two arrows go out in opposite directions to one another.)

(For example, I know nothing about the weather when I know that it is either raining or not raining.)

4.4611 Tautologies and contradictions are not, however, nonsensical. They are part of the symbolism, just as "0" is part of the symbolism of arithmetic.

4.462 Tautologies and contradictions are not pictures of reality. They do not represent any possible situations. For the former admit *all* possible situations, and the latter *none.*

In a tautology the conditions of agreement with the world—the representational relations—cancel one another, so that it does not stand in any representational relation to reality.

4.463 The truth-conditions of a proposition determine the range that it leaves open to the facts.

(A proposition, a picture, or a model is, in the negative sense, like a solid body that restricts the freedom of movement of others, and, in the positive sense, like a space bounded by solid substance in which there is room for a body.)

A tautology leaves open to reality the whole—the infinite whole—of logical space: a contradiction fills the whole of logical space leaving no point of it for reality. Thus neither of them can determine reality in any way.

4.464 A tautology's truth is certain, a proposition's possible, a contradiction's impossible.

6.362 What can be described can also happen: and what the law of causality is meant to exclude cannot even be described.

6.363 The procedure of induction consists in accepting as true the *simplest* law that can be reconciled with our experiences.

6.3631 This procedure, however, has no logical justification but only a psychological one. It is clear that there are no grounds for believing that the simplest eventuality will in fact be realized.

6.36311 It is an hypothesis that the sun will rise tomorrow: and this means that we do not *know* whether it will rise.

6.37 There is no compulsion making one thing happen because another has happened. The only necessity that exists is *logical* necessity.

6.371 The whole modern conception of the world is founded on the illusion that the so-called laws of nature are the explanations of natural phenomena.

6.372 Thus people today stop at the laws of nature, treating them as something inviolable, just as God and Fate were treated in past ages.

And in fact both are right and both wrong: though the view of the ancients is clearer in so far as they have a clear and acknowledged terminus, while the modern system tries to make it look as if *everything* were explained.

6.373 The world is independent of my will.

6.374 Even if all that we wish for were to happen, still this would only be a favour granted by fate, so to speak: for there is no *logical* connexion between the will and the world, which would guarantee it, and the supposed physical connexion itself is surely not something that we could will.

6.375 Just as the only necessity that exists is *logical* necessity, so too the only impossibility that exists is *logical* impossibility.

6.3751 For example, the simultaneous presence of two colours at the same place in the visual field is impossible, in fact logically impossible, since it is ruled out by the logical structure of colour.

Let us think how this contradiction appears in physics: more or less as follows—a particle cannot have two velocities at the same time; that is to say, it cannot be in two places at the same time; that is to say, particles that are in different places at the same time cannot be identical.

(It is clear that the logical product of two elementary propositions can neither be a tautology nor a contradiction. The statement that a point in the visual field has two different colours at the same time is a contradiction.)

6.4 All propositions are of equal value.

6.41 The sense of the world must lie outside the world. In the world everything is as it is, and everything happens as it does happen: *in* it no value exists—and if it did exist, it would have no value.

If there is any value that does have values, it must lie outside the whole sphere of what happens and is the case. For all that happens and is the case is accidental.

What makes it non-accidental cannot lie *within* the world, since if it did it would itself be accidental.

It must lie outside the world.

6.42 So too it is impossible for there to be propositions of ethics.

Propositions can express nothing that is higher.

6.421 It is clear that ethics cannot be put into words.

Ethics is transcendental.

(Ethics and aesthetics are one and the same.)

6.422 When an ethical law of the form, 'Thou shalt . . .', is laid down, one's first thought is, 'And what if I do not do it?' It is clear, however, that ethics has nothing to do with punishment and reward in the usual sense of the terms. So our question about the *consequences* of an action must be unimportant.—At least those consequences should not be events. For there must be something right about the question we posed. There must indeed be some kind of ethical reward and ethical punishment, but they must reside in the action itself.

(And it is also clear that the reward must be something pleasant and the punishment something unpleasant.)

6.423 It is impossible to speak about the will in so far as it is the subject of ethical attributes.

And the will as a phenomenon is of interest only to psychology.

6.43 If the good or bad exercise of the will does alter the world, it can alter only the limits of the world, not the facts—not what can be expressed by means of language.

In short the effect must be that it becomes an altogether different world. It must, so to speak, wax and wane as a whole.

The world of the happy man is a different one from that of the unhappy man.

6.431 So too at death the world does not alter, but comes to an end.

6.4311 Death is not an event in life: we do not live to experience death.

If we take eternity to mean not infinite temporal duration but timelessness, then eternal life belongs to those who live in the present.

Our life has no end in just the way in which our visual field has no limits.

6.4312 Not only is there no guarantee of the temporal immortality of the human soul, that is to say of its eternal survival after death; but, in any case, this assumption completely fails to accomplish the purpose for which it has always been intended. Or is some riddle solved by my surviving for ever? Is not this eternal life itself as much of a riddle as our present life? The solution of the riddle of life in space and time lies *outside* space and time.

(It is certainly not the solution of any problems of natural science that is required.)

6.432 *How* things are in the world is a matter of complete indifference for what is higher. God does not reveal himself *in* the world.

6.4321 The facts all contribute only to settling the problem, not to its solution.

6.44 It is not *how* things are in the world that is mystical, but *that* it exists.

6.45 To view the world sub specie aeterni is to view it as a whole—a limited whole.

Feeling the world as a limited whole—it is this that is mystical.

6.5 When the answer cannot be put into words, neither can the question be put into words.

The riddle does not exist.

If a question can be framed at all, it is also *possible* to answer it.

6.51 Scepticism is *not* irrefutable, but obviously nonsensical when it tries to raise doubts where no questions can be asked.

For doubt can exist only where a question exists, a question only where an answer exists, and an answer only where something *can be said.*

6.52 We feel that even when all *possible* scientific questions have been answered, the problems of life remain completely untouched. Of course there are then no questions left, and this itself is the answer.

6.521 The solution of the problem of life is seen in the vanishing of the problem.

(Is not this the reason why those who have found after a long period of doubt that the sense of life became clear to them have then been unable to say what constituted sense?)

6.522 There are, indeed, things that cannot be put into words. They *make themselves manifest.* They are what is mystical.

6.53 The correct method in philosophy would really be the following: to say nothing except what can be said, i.e. propositions of natural science—i.e. something that has nothing to do with philosophy—and then, whenever someone else wanted to say something metaphysical, to demonstrate to him that he had failed to give a meaning to certain signs in his propositions. Although it would not be satisfying to the other person—he would not have the feeling that we were teaching him philosophy—*this* method would be the only strictly correct one.

6.54 My propositions serve as elucidations in the following way: anyone who understands me eventually recognizes them as nonsensical, when he has used them—as steps—to climb up beyond them. (He must, so to speak, throw away the ladder after he has climbed up it.)

He must transcend these propositions, and then he will see the world aright.

7 What we cannot speak about we must pass over in silence.

Philosophical Investigations

1. "When they (my elders) named some object, and accordingly moved towards something, I saw this and I grasped that the thing was called by the sound they uttered when they meant to point it out. Their intention was shewn by their bodily movements, as it were the natural language of all peoples: the expression of the face, the play of the eyes, the movement of other parts of the body, and the tone of voice which expresses our state of mind in seeking, having, rejecting, or avoiding something. Thus, as I heard words repeatedly used in their proper places in various sentences, I gradually learnt to understand what objects they signified; and after I had trained my mouth to form these signs, I used them

Philosophical Investigations by Ludwig Wittgenstein, translated by Anscombe. Reprinted by permission of Blackwell Publishers and Prentice-Hall, Inc., Upper Saddle River, NJ (©1953).

to express my own desires." [Augustine, *Confessions*, I.8]

These words, it seems to me, give us a particular picture of the essense of human language. It is this: the individual words in language name objects—sentences are combinations of such names.—In this picture of language we find the roots of the following idea: Every word has a meaning. This meaning is correlated with the word. It is the object for which the word stands.

Augustine does not speak of there being any difference between kinds of word. If you describe the learning of language in this way you are, I believe, thinking primarily of nouns like "table", "chair", "bread", and of people's names, and only secondarily of the names of certain actions and properties; and of the remaining kinds of word as something that will take care of itself.

Now think of the following use of language: I send someone shopping. I give him a slip marked "five red apples". He takes the slip to the shopkeeper, who opens the drawer marked "apples"; then he looks up the word "red" in a table and finds a colour sample opposite it; then he says the series of cardinal numbers—I assume that he knows them by heart—up to the word "five" and for each number he takes an apple of the same colour as the sample out of the drawer.——It is in this and similar ways that one operates with words.——"But how does he know where and how he is to look up the word 'red' and what he is to do with the word 'five'?"——Well, I assume that he *acts* as I have described. Explanations come to an end somewhere.—But what is the meaning of the word "five"?—No such thing was in question here, only how the word "five" is used.

2. That philosophical concept of meaning has its place in a primitive idea of the way language functions. But one can also say that it is the idea of a language more primitive than ours.

Let us imagine a language for which the description given by Augustine is right. The language is meant to serve for communication between a builder A and an assistant B. A is building with building-stones: there are blocks, pillars, slabs and beams. B has to pass the stones, and that in the order in which A needs them. For this purpose they use a language consisting of the words "block", "pillar", "slab", "beam". A calls them out;—B brings the stone which he has learnt to bring at such-and-such a call.——Conceive this as a complete primitive language.

3. Augustine, we might say, does describe a system of communication; only not everything that we call language is this system. And one has to say this in many cases where the question arises "Is this an appropriate description or not?" The answer is: "Yes, it is appropriate, but only for this narrowly circumscribed region, not for the whole of what you were claiming to describe."

It is as if someone were to say: "A game consists in moving objects about on a surface according to certain rules . . ."—and we replied: You seem to be thinking of board games, but there are others. You can make your definition correct by expressly restricting it to those games.

4. Imagine a script in which the letters were used to stand for sounds, and also as signs of emphasis and punctuation. (A script can be conceived as a language for describing sound-patterns.) Now imagine someone interpreting that script as if there were simply a correspondence of letters to sounds and as if the letters had not also completely different functions. Augustine's conception of language is like such an over-simple conception of the script.

5. If we look at the example in §1, we may perhaps get an inkling how much this general notion of the meaning of a word surrounds the working of language with a haze which makes clear vision impossible. It disperses the fog to study the phenomena of language in primitive kinds of application in which one can command a clear view of the aim and functioning of the words.

A child uses such primitive forms of language when it learns to talk. Here the teaching of language is not explanation, but training.

6. We could imagine that the language of §2 was the *whole* language of A and B; even the whole language of a tribe. The children are brought up to perform *these* actions, to use *these* words as they do so, and to react in *this* way to the words of others.

An important part of the training will consist in the teacher's pointing to the objects, directing the child's attention to them, and at the same time uttering a word; for instance, the word "slab" as he points to that shape. (I do not want to call this "ostensive definition", because the child cannot as yet *ask* what the name is. I will call it "ostensive teaching of words".——I say that it will form an important part of the training, because it is so with human beings; not because it could not be imagined otherwise.) This ostensive teaching of words can be said to establish an association between the word and the thing. But what does this mean? Well, it may mean various things; but one very likely thinks first of all that a picture of the object comes before the child's mind when it hears the word. But now, if this does happen—is it the purpose of the word?—Yes, it *may* be the purpose.—I can imagine such a use of words (of series of sounds). (Uttering a word is like striking a note on the keyboard of the imagination.) But in the language of §2 it is *not* the purpose of the words to evoke images. (It may, of course, be discovered that that helps to attain the actual purpose.)

But if the ostensive teaching has this effect,—am I to say that it effects an understanding of the word? Don't you understand the call "Slab!" if you act upon it in such-and-such a way?—Doubtless the ostensive teaching helped to bring this about; but only together with a particular training. With different training the same ostensive teaching of these words would have effected a quite different understanding.

"I set the brake up by connecting up rod and lever."—Yes, given the whole of the rest of the mechanism. Only in conjunction with that is it a brake-lever, and separated from its support it is not even a lever; it may be anything, or nothing.

7. In the practice of the use of language (2) one party calls out the words, the other acts on them. In instruction in the language the following process will occur: the learner *names* the objects; that is, he utters the word when the teacher points to the stone.—And there will be this still simpler exercise: the pupil repeats the words after the teacher—both of these being processes resembling language.

We can also think of the whole process of using words in (2) as one of those games by means of which children learn their native language. I will call these games "language-games" and will sometimes speak of a primitive language as a language-game.

And the processes of naming the stones and of repeating words after someone might also be called language-games. Think of much of the use of words in games like ring-a-ring-a-roses.

I shall also call the whole, consisting of language and the actions into which it is woven, the "language-game".

8. Let us now look at an expansion of language (2). Besides the four words "block", "pillar", etc., let it contain a series of words used as the shopkeeper in (1) used the numerals (it can be the series of letters of the alphabet); further, let there be two words, which may as well be "there" and "this" (because this roughly indicates their purpose), that are used in connexion with a pointing gesture; and finally a number of colour samples. A gives an order like: "d—slab—there". At the same time he shews the assistant a colour sample, and when he says "there" he points to a place on the building site. From the stock of slabs B takes one for each letter of the alphabet up to "d", of the same colour as the sample, and brings them to the place indicated by A.—On other occasions A gives the order "this—there". At "this" he points to a building stone. And so on.

9. When a child learns this language, it has to learn the series of 'numerals' a, b, c, . . . by heart. And it has to learn their use.—Will this training include ostensive teaching of the words?—Well, people will, for example, point to slabs and count: "a, b, c slabs".—Something more like the ostensive teaching of the words "block", "pillar", etc. would be the ostensive teaching of numerals that serve not to count but to refer to groups of objects that can be taken in at a glance. Children do learn the use of the first five or six cardinal numerals in this way.

Are "there" and "this" also taught ostensively?—Imagine how one might perhaps teach their use. One will point to places and things—but in this case the pointing occurs in the *use* of the words too and not merely in learning the use.—

10. Now what do the words of this language *signify*?—What is supposed to shew what they signify, if not the kind of use they have? And we have already described that. So we are asking for the expression "This word signifies *this*" to be made a part of the description. In other words the description ought to take the form: "The word . . . . signifies . . . .".

Of course, one can reduce the description of the use of the word "slab" to the statement that this word signifies this object. This will be done when, for example, it is merely a matter of removing the mistaken idea that the word "slab" refers to the shape of building-stone that we in fact call a "block"—but the kind of '*referring*' this is, that is to say the use of these words for the rest, is already known.

Equally one can say that the signs "a", "b", etc. signify numbers; when for example this removes the mistaken idea that "a", "b", "c", play the part actually played in language by "block", "slab", "pillar". And one can also say that "c" means this number and not that one; when for example this serves to explain that the letters are to be used in the order a, b, c, d, etc. and not in the order a, b, d, c.

But assimilating the descriptions of the uses of words in this way cannot make the uses themselves any more like one another. For, as we see, they are absolutely unlike.

11. Think of the tools in a tool-box: there is a hammer, pliers, a saw, a screw-driver, a rule, a glue-pot, glue, nails and screws.—The functions of words are as diverse as the functions of these objects. (And in both cases there are similarities.)

Of course, what confuses us is the uniform appearance of words when we hear them spoken or meet them in script and print. For their *application* is not presented to us so clearly. Especially when we are doing philosophy!

12. It is like looking into the cabin of a locomotive. We see handles all looking more or less alike. (Naturally, since they are all supposed to be handled.) But one is the handle of a crank which can be moved continuously (it regulates the opening of a valve); another is the handle of a switch, which has only two effective positions, it is either off or on; a third is the handle of a brake-lever, the harder one pulls on it, the harder it brakes; a fourth, the handle of a pump: it has an effect only so long as it is moved to and fro.

13. When we say: "Every word in language signifies something" we have so far said *nothing whatever*; unless we have explained exactly *what* distinction we wish to make. (It might be, of course, that we wanted to distinguish the words of language (8) from words 'without meaning' such as occur in Lewis Carroll's poems, or words like "Lilliburlero" in songs.)

14. Imagine someone's saying: "*All* tools serve to modify something. Thus the hammer modifies the position of the nail, the saw the shape of the board, and so on."—And what is modified by the rule, the glue-pot, the nails?—"Our knowledge of a thing's length, the temperature of the glue, and the solidity of the box."——Would anything be gained by this assimilation of expressions?—

15. The word "to signify" is perhaps used in the most straightforward way when the object signified is marked with the sign. Suppose that the tools A uses in building bear certain marks. When A shews his assistant such a mark, he brings the tool that has that mark on it.

It is in this and more or less similar ways that a name means and is given to a thing.—It will often prove useful in philosophy to say to ourselves: naming something is like attaching a label to a thing.

16. What about the colour samples that A shews to B: are they part of the *language*? Well, it is as you please. They do not belong among the words; yet when I say to someone: "Pronounce the word 'the' ", you will count the second "the" as part of the sentence. Yet it has a role just like that of a colour-sample in language-game (8); that is, it is a sample of what the other is meant to say.

It is most natural, and causes least confusion, to reckon the samples among the instruments of the language.

(Remark on the reflexive pronoun "*this* sentence".)

17. It will be possible to say: In language (8) we have different *kinds of word*. For the functions of the word "slab" and the word "block" are more alike than those of "slab" and "d." But how we group words into kinds will depend on the aim of the classification,—and on our own inclination.

Think of the different points of view from which one can classify tools or chess-men.

18. Do not be troubled by the fact that languages (2) and (8) consist only of orders. If you want to say that this shews them to be incomplete, ask yourself whether our language is complete;—whether it was so before the symbolism of chemistry and the notation of the infinitesimal calculus were incorporated in it; for these are, so to speak, suburbs of our language. (And how many houses or streets does it take before a town begins to be a town?) Our language can be seen as an ancient city: a maze of little streets and squares, of old and new houses, and of houses with additions from vaious periods; and this surrounded by a multitude of new boroughs with straight regular streets and uniform houses.

19. It is easy to imagine a language consisting only of orders and reports in battle.—Or a language consisting only of questions and expressions for answering yes and no. And innumerable others.——And to imagine a language means to imagine a form of life.

But what about this: is the call "Slab!" in example (2) a sentence or a word?—If a word, surely it has not the same meaning as the like-sounding word of our ordinary language, for in §2 it is a call. But if a sentence, it is surely not the elliptical sentence: "Slab!" of our language.——As far as the first question goes you can call "Slab!" a word and also a sentence; perhaps it could be appropriately called a 'degenerate sentence' (as one speaks of a degenerate hyperbola); in fact it *is* our 'elliptical' sentence.—

But that is surely only a shortened form of the sentence "Bring me a slab", and there is no such sentence in example (2).—But why should I not on the contrary have called the sentence "Bring me a slab" a *lengthening* of the sentence "Slab!"?—Because if you shout "Slab!" you really mean: "Bring me a slab".—But how do you do this: how do you *mean that* while you *say* "Slab!"? Do you say the unshortened sentence to yourself? And why should I translate the call "Slab!" into a different expression in order to say what someone means by it? And if they mean the same thing—why should I not say: "When he says 'Slab!' he means 'Slab!' "? Again, if you can mean "Bring me the slab", why should you not be able to mean "Slab!"?——But when I call "Slab!", then what I want is, *that he should bring me a slab*!——Certainly, but does 'wanting this' consist in thinking in some form or other a different sentence from the one you utter?—

20. But now it looks as if when someone says "Bring me a slab" he could mean this expression as *one* long word corresponding to the single word "Slab!"——Then can one mean it sometimes as one word and sometimes as four? And how does one usually mean it?——I think we shall be inclined to say: we mean the sentence as *four* words when we use it in contrast with other sentences such as "*Hand* me a slab", "Bring *him* a slab", "Bring *two* slabs", etc.; that is, in contrast with sentences containing the separate words of our command in other combinations.——But what does using one sentence in contrast with others consist in? Do the others, perhaps, hover before one's mind? *All* of them? And *while* one is saying the one sentence, or before, or afterwards?—No. Even if such an explanation rather tempts us, we need only think for a moment of what actually happens in order to see that we are going astray here. We say that we use the command in contrast with other sentences because *our language* contains the possibility of those other sentences. Someone who did not understand our language, a foreigner, who had fairly often heard someone giving the order: "Bring me a slab!", might believe that this whole series of sounds was one word corresponding perhaps to the word for "building-stone" in his language. If he himself had then given this order perhaps he would have pronounced it differently, and we should say: he pronounces it so oddly because he takes it for a *single* word.——But then, is there not also something different going on in him when he pronounces it,—something corresponding to the fact that he conceives the sentence as a *single* word?——Either the same thing may go on in him, or something different. For what goes on in you when you give such an order? Are you conscious of its consisting of four words *while* you are uttering it? Of course you have a *mastery* of this language—which contains those other sentences as well—but is this having a mastery something that *happens* while you are uttering the sentence?—And I have admitted that the foreigner will probably pronounce a sentence differently if he conceives it differently; but what we call his wrong conception *need* not lie in anything that accompanies the utterance of the command.

The sentence is 'elliptical', not because it leaves out something that we think when we utter it, but because it is shortened—in comparison with a particular paradigm of our grammar.—Of course one might object here: "You grant that the shortened and the unshortened sentence have the same sense.—What is this sense, then? Isn't there a verbal expression for this sense?"——But doesn't the fact that sentences have the same sense consist in their having the same *use*?—(In Russian one says "stone red" instead of "the stone is red"; do they feel the copula to be missing in the sense, or attach it in *thought*?)

21. Imagine a language-game in which A asks and B reports the number of slabs or blocks in a pile, or the colours and shapes of the building-stones that are stacked in such-and-such a place.—Such a report might run: "Five slabs". Now what is the difference between the report or statement "Five slabs" and the order "Five slabs!"?—Well, it is the part which uttering these words plays in language-game. No doubt the tone of voice and the look with which they are uttered, and much else besides, will also be different. But we could also imagine the tone's being the same—for an order and a report can be spoken in a *variety* of tones of voice and with various expressions of face—the difference being only in the application. (Of course, we might use the words "statement" and "command" to stand for grammatical forms of sentence and intonations; we do in fact call "Isn't the weather glorious to-day?" a question, although it is used as a statement.) We could imagine a language in which *all* statements had the form and tone of rhetorical questions; or every command the form of the question "Would you like to . . .?". Perhaps it will then be said: "What he says has the form of a question but is really a command",—that is, has the function of a command in the technique of using the language. (Similarly one says "You will do this" not as a prophecy but as a command. What makes it the one or the other?)

22. Frege's idea that every assertion contains an assumption, which is the thing that is asserted, really rests on the possibility found in our language of writing every statement in the form: "It is asserted that such-and-such is the case."—But "that such-and-such is the case" is *not* a sentence in our language—so far it is not a *move* in the language-game. And if I write, not "It is asserted that . . . .", but "It is asserted: such-and-such is the case", the words "It is asserted" simply become superfluous.

We might very well also write every statement in the form of a question followed by a "Yes"; for instances: "Is it raining? Yes!: Would this shew that every statement contained a question?

Of course we have the right to use an assertion sign in contrast with a question-mark, for example, or if we want to distinguish an assertion from a fiction or a supposition. It is only a mistake if one thinks that the assertion consists of two actions, entertaining and asserting (assigning the truth-value, or something of the kind), and that in performing these actions we follow the propositional sign roughly as we sing from the musical score. Reading the written sentence loud or soft is indeed comparable with singing from a musical score, but '*meaning*' (thinking) the sentence that is read is not.

Frege's assertion sign marks the *beginning of the sentence*. Thus its function is like that of the full-stop. It distinguishes the whole period from a clause *within* the period. If I hear someone say "it's raining" but do not know whether I have heard the beginning and end of the period, so far this sentence does not serve to tell me anything.

23. But how many kinds of sentence are there? Say assertion, question, and command?—There are *countless* kinds: countless different kinds of use of what we call "symbols", "words", "sentences". And this multiplicity is not something fixed, given once for all; but new types of language, new language-games, as we may say, come into existence, and others become obsolete and get forgotten. (We can get a *rough picture* of this from the changes in mathematics.)

Here the term "language-*game*" is meant to bring into prominence the fact that the *speaking* of language is part of an activity, or of a form of life.

Review the multiplicity of language-games in the following examples, and in others:

Giving orders, and obeying them—

Describing the appearance of an object, or giving its measurements—

Constructing an object from a description (a drawing)—

Reporting an event—

Speculating about an event—

Forming and testing a hypothesis—

Presenting the results of an experiment in tables and diagrams—

Making up a story; and reading it—

Play-acting—

Singing catches—

Guessing riddles—

Making a joke; telling it—

Solving a problem in practical arithmetic—

Translating from one language into another—

Asking, thanking, cursing, greeting, praying.

—It is interesting to compare the multiplicity of the tools in language and of the ways they are used, the multiplicity of kinds of word and sentence, with what logicians have said about the structure of language. (Including the author of the *Tractatus Logico-Philosophicus*.)

24. If you do not keep the multiplicity of language-games in view you will perhaps be inclined to ask questions like: "What is a question?"—Is it the statement that I do not know such-and-such, or the statement that I wish the other person would tell me . . . .? Or is it the description of my mental state of uncertainty?—And is the cry "Help!" such a description?

Think how many different kinds of thing are called "description": description of a body's position bymeans of its co-ordinates; description of a facial expression; description of a sensation of touch; of a mood.

Of course it is possible to substitute the form of statement or description for the usual form of question: "I want to know whether . . . ." or "I am in doubt whether . . . ."—but this does not bring the different language-games any closer together.

The significance of such possibilities of transformation, for example of turning all statements into sentences beginning "I think" or "I believe" (and thus, as it were, into descriptions of *my* inner life) will become clearer in another place. (Solipsism.)

25. It is sometimes said that animals do not talk because they lack the mental capacity. And this means: "they do not think, and that is why they do not talk." But—they simply do not talk. Or to put it better: they do not use language—if we except the most primitive forms of language.—Commanding, questioning, recounting, chatting, are as much a part of our natural history as walking, eating, drinking, playing.

LANGUAGE AS LANGUAGE-GAMES

65. Here we come up against the great question that lies behind all these considerations.—For someone might object against me: "You take the easy way out! You talk about all sorts of language-games, but have nowhere said that the essence of a language-game, and hence of language, is: what is common to all these activities, and what makes them into language or parts of language. So you let yourself off the very part of the investigation that once gave you yourself most headache, the part about the *general form of propositions and of language*."

And this is true.—Instead of producing something common to all that we call language, I am saying that these phenomena have no one thing in common which makes us use the same word for all,—but that they are *related* to one another in many different ways. And it is because of this relationship, or these relationships, that we call them all "language." I will try to explain this.

66. Consider for example the proceedings that we call "games". I mean board-games, card-games, ball-games, Olympic games, and so on. What is common to them all?—Don't say: "There *must* be something common, or they would not be called 'games'—but *look and see* whether there is anything common to all.—For if you look at them you will not see something that is common to *all*, but similarities, relationships, and a whole series of them at that. To repeat: don't think, but look!—Look for example at board-games, with their multifarious relationships. Now pass to card-games; here you find many correspondences with the first group, but many common features drop out, and others appear. When we pass next to ball-games, much that is common is retained, but much is lost.—Are they all 'amusing'? Compare chess with noughts and crosses. Or is there always winning and losing, or competition between players? Think of patience. In ball games there is winning and losing; but when a child throws his ball at the wall and catches it again, this feature has disappeared. Look at the parts played by skill and luck; and at the difference between skill in chess and skill in tennis. Think now of games like ring-a-ring-a-roses; here is the element of amusement, but how many other characteristic features have disappeared! And we can go through the many, many other groups of games in the same way; can see how similarities crop up and disappear.

And the result of this examination is: we see a complicated network of similarities overlapping and criss-crossing: sometimes overall similarities, sometimes similarities of detail.

67. I can think of no better expression to characterize these similarities than "family resemblances"; for the various resemblances between members of a family: build, features, colour of eyes, gait, temperament, etc. etc. overlap and criss-cross in the same way.—And I shall say: 'games' form a family.

And for instance the kinds of number form a family in the same way. Why do we call something a "number"? Well, perhaps because it has a—direct—relationship with several things that have hitherto been called number; and this can be said to give it an indirect relationship to other things we call the same name. And we extend our concept of number as in spinning a thread we twist fibre on fibre. And the strength of the thread does not reside in the fact that some one fibre runs through its whole length, but in the overlapping of many fibres.

But if someone wished to say: "There is something common to all these constructions—namely the disjunction of all their common properties"—I should reply: Now you are only playing with words. One might as well say: "Something runs through the whole thread—namely the continuous overlapping of those fibres".

68. "All right: the concept of number is defined for you as the logical sum of these individual interrelated concepts: cardinal numbers, rational numbers, real numbers, etc.; and in the same way the concept of a game as the logical sum of a corresponding set of sub-concepts."—It need not be so. For I *can* give the concept 'number' rigid limits in this way, that is, use the word "number" for a rigidly limited concept, but I can also use it so that the extension of the concept is *not* closed by a frontier. And this is how we do use the word "game". For how is the concept of a game bounded? What still counts as a game and what no longer does? Can you give the boundary? No. You can *draw* one; for none has so far been drawn. (But that never troubled you before when you used the word "game".)

"But when the use of the word is unregulated, the 'game' we play with it is unregulated."—It is not everywhere circumscribed by rules; but no more are there any rules for how high one throws the ball in tennis, or how hard; yet tennis is a game for all that and has rules too.

69. How should we explain to someone what a game is? I imagine that we should describe *games* to him, and we might add: "This *and similar things* are called 'games'." And do we know any more about it ourselves? Is it only other people whom we cannot tell exactly what a game is?—But this is not ignorance. We do not know the boundaries because none have been drawn. To repeat, we can draw a boundary—for a special purpose. Does it take that to make the concept usable? Not at all! (Except for that special purpose.) No more than it took the definition: 1 pace = 75 cm. to make the measure of length 'one pace' usable. And if you want to say "But still, before that it wasn't an exact measure", then I reply: very well, it was an inexact one.—Though you still owe me a definition of exactness.

70. "But if the concept 'game' is uncircumscribed like that, you don't really know what you mean by a 'game'."—When I give the description: "The ground was quite covered with plants"—do you want to say I don't know what I am talking about until I can give a definition of a plant?

My meaning would be explained by, say, a drawing and the words "The ground looked roughly like this." Perhaps I even say "it looked *exactly* like this."—Then were just *this* grass and *these* leaves there, arranged just like this? No, that is not what it means. And I should not accept any picture as exact in *this* sense.

> Someone says to me: "Shew the children a game." I teach them gaming with dice, and the other says "I didn't mean that sort of game." Must the exclusion of the game with dice have come before his mind when he gave me the order? (Note added by Wittgenstein.)

71. One might say that the concept 'game' is a concept with blurred edges.—"But is a blurred concept a concept at all?—Is an indistinct photograph a picture of a person at all? Is it even always an advantage to replace an indistinct picture by a sharp one? Isn't the indistinct one often exactly what we need?

Frege compares a concept to an area and says that an area with vague boundaries cannot be called an area at all. This presumably means that we cannot do anything with it.—But is it senseless to say: "Stand roughly there"? Suppose that I were standing with someone in a city square and said that. As I say it I do not draw any kind of boundary, but perhaps point with my hand—as if I were indicating a particular *spot*. And this is just how one might explain to someone what a game is. One gives examples and intends them to be taken in a particular way.—I do not, however, mean by this that he is supposed to see in those examples that common thing which I—for some reason—was unable to express; but that he is now to *employ* those examples in a particular way. Here giving examples is not an *indirect* means of explaining—in default of a better. For any general definition can be misunderstood too. The point is that *this* is how we play the game. (I mean the language-game with the word "game".)

72. *Seeing what is common.* Suppose I shew someone various multicoloured pictures, and say: "The colour you see in all these is called 'yellow ochre'."—This is a definition, and the other will get to understand it by looking for and seeing what is common to the pictures. Then he can look *at*, can point *to*, the common thing.

Compare with this a case in which I shew him figures of different shapes all painted the same colour, and say: "What these have in common is called 'yellow ochre'."

And compare this case: I shew him samples of different shades of blue and say: "The colour that is common to all these is what I call 'blue'."

73. When someone defines the names of colours for me by pointing to samples and saying "This colour is called 'blue,' this 'green' . . ." this case can be compared in many respects to putting a table in my hands, with the words written under the colour-samples.—Though this comparison may mislead in many ways.—One is now inclined to extend the comparison: to have understood the definition means to have in one's mind an idea of the thing defned, and that is a sample or picture. So if I am shewn various different leaves and told "This is called a 'leaf'," I get an idea of the shape of a leaf, a picture of it in my mind.—But what does the picture of a leaf look like when it does not shew us any particular shape, but 'what is common to all shapes of leaf'? Which shade is the 'sample in my mind' of the colour green—the sample of what is common to all shades of green.

"But might there not be such 'general' samples? Say a schematic leaf, or a sample of *pure* green?"—Certainly there might. But for such a schema to be understood as a *schema*, and not as the shape of a particular leaf, and for the slip of pure green to be understood as a sample of all that is greenish and not as a sample of pure green—this in turn resides in the way the samples are used.

Ask yourself: what *shape* must the sample of the colour green be? Should it be rectangular? Or would it then be the sample of a green rectangle?—So should it be 'irregular' in shape? And what is to prevent us then from regarding it—that is, from using it—only as a sample of irregularity of shape?

74. Here also belongs the idea that if you see this leaf as a sample of the 'leaf shape in general' you *see* it differently from someone who regards it as, say, a sample of this particular shape. Now this might well be so—though it is not so—for it would only be to say that, as a matter of experience, if you *see* the leaf in a particular way, you use it in such-and-such a way or according to such-and-such rules. Of course, there is such a thing as seeing in *this* way or *that*; and there are also cases where whoever sees a sample like *this* will in general use it in *this* way, and whoever sees it otherwise in another way. For example, if you see the schematic drawing of a cube as a plane figure consisting of a square and two rhombi you will, perhaps, carry out the order "Bring me something like this" differently from someone who sees the picture three-dimensionally.

75. What does it mean to know what a game is? What does it mean, to know it and not be able to say it? Is this knowledge somehow equivalent to an unformulated definition? So that if it were formulated I should be able to recognize it as the expression of my knowledge? Isn't my knowledge, my concept of a game, completely expressed in the explanations that I could give? That is, in my describing examples of various kinds of game; shewing how all sorts of other games can be constructed on the analogy of these; saying that I should scarcely include this or this among games; and so on.

76. If someone were to draw a sharp boundary I could not acknowledge it as the one that I too always wanted to draw, or had drawn in my mind. For I did not want to draw one at all. His concept can then be said to be not the same as mine, but akin to it. The kinship is that of two pictures, one of which consists of colour patches with vague contours, and the other of patches similarly shaped and distributed, but with clear contours. The kinship is just as undeniable as the difference.

77. And if we carry this comparison still further it is clear that the degree to which the sharp picture *can* resemble the blurred one depends on the latter's degree of vagueness. For imagine having to sketch a sharply defined picture 'corresponding' to a blurred one. In the latter there is a blurred red rectangle: for it you put down a sharply defined one. Of course—several such sharply defined rectangles can be drawn to correspond to the indefinite one.—But if the colours in the original merge without a hint of any outline won't it become a hopeless task to draw a sharp picture corresponding to the blurred one? Won't you then have to say: "Here I might just as well draw a circle or heart as a rectangle, for all the colours merge. Anything—and nothing—is right."—And this is the position you are in if you look for definitions corresponding to our concepts in aesthetics or ethics.

In such a difficulty always ask yourself: How did we *learn* the meaning of this word ("good" for instance)? From what sort of examples? in what language-games? Then it will be easier for you to see that the word must have a family of meanings.

Chapter 9

J. L. Austin

John Langshaw Austin (1911–1960) was born in Lancaster, England, but grew up in St. Andrews, Scotland. He attended Balliol College, Oxford University, where he studied classics and philosophy. After serving in the British intelligence service during World War II, he became a fellow at Magdalene College, where he taught until his death. Austin was perhaps the most prominent philosopher in the 1940s to 1950s, hosting Saturday morning discussion sessions, attended by junior philosophers such as Isaiah Berlin, Stuart Hampshire, Peter Strawson, G. J. Warnock, and occasionally A. J. Ayer, who, more often, was the target of Austin's rapier wit and forceful critical analysis. The Saturday morning study group was renowned in Oxford, where apparently some of the most brilliant philosophical analysis was done. I once heard someone ask Isaiah Berlin why no publications came out of these meetings. He nonchalantly replied, "Who was there to write for?" The sunbeams of philosophy were themselves. Outside there was only darkness and confusion. Apparently, junior fellows at Oxford lived in dread of having their work dissected by Austin.

Austin was an Ordinary Language philosopher, who believed that our language developed over many centuries in ways that made it authoritative for meaning. The job of philosophers was to understand how language was used, to clarify grammar. He developed such concepts as *speech acts*, dividing utterances into *constatives* (which are descriptive) and *per formatives* (which are actions—for examples, the statement, "I [N] take you [M] to be my lawful wedded wife," does more than describe the world. Under suitable circumstances, it performs an act of becoming married. See his book *How to Do Things with Words* (1961) for a discussion of this theory. More than a theoretician, he was an adept analyzer of ordinary language. He said, "Much of the amusement [of philosophy] and of the instruction, comes in drawing the coverts of the microglots, in hounding down the minutiae."

The selection before us from *Sense and Sensibilia* consists of lecture notes assembled by Austin's student Warnock in which Austin applies his method to the sense data theory, which we have encountered in the work of Bertrand Russell (first selection, Chapter 3), as well as to Logical Positivism in general, though Austin's immediate target is Ayer's version of the theory, which holds that all we ever experience are subjective states of affairs. The sense data theory holds that we never experience the world directly, but only through subjective entities, which, allegedly, have the properties of the external objects. For example, at a suitable angle I experience a white rectangular sensation that I identify as a piece of typing paper. If I change my angle, the sense datum will be different, say a trapezoid. If a blue light is shining in the room, the sense datum will be blue. Some phenomenalists like John Stuart Mill; Russell, at one point in his career; and Ayer, held that the world consists entirely of sense data, "permanent possibilities of experience" (Mill). Austin attacks Ayer and company for failing to pay sufficient attention to how words like *real* are used. "I should like to emphasize, how fatal it always is to embark on explaining the use of a word without seriously considering more than a fraction of the contexts in which it is actually used."

FOR FURTHER READING

Austin, J. L. *How to Do Things with Words* (Oxford University Press, 1961).
———. *Sense and Sensibilia* (Oxford University Press, 1962).
Graham, Keith. *J. L. Austin: A Critique of Ordinary Language Philosophy* (Humanities Press, 1977).
Searle, John. *Speech Acts: An Essay in Philosophy of Language* (Cambridge University Press, 1969).
Warnock, G. J. *J. L. Austin* (Routledge, 1989).

Sense and Sensibilia: A Critique of the Theory of Sense Data

To return now to Ayer. We have already entered a protest against his apparent belief that 'real' is a word that can be used in any way one likes—that though some say, for instance, the real shape of a building remains the same as one views it from different standpoints, one may quite well 'prefer to say' that its real shape constantly changes. But now I want to consider the last section of his book, which is called 'Appearance and Reality', and in which he undertakes to give an account of the distinction as we ordinarily make it. He regards this, I suppose, as a description of our 'preferences'.

Ayer begins by making a distinction between 'perceptions' which are 'qualitatively delusive' and 'existentially delusive'. In the first case we are said to find that 'the sense-data endow material things with qualities that they do not really possess', in the second that 'the material things that they seem to present do not exist at all'. However, this distinction is, to say the least, unclear. The expression 'existentially delusive' puts one in mind, naturally enough, of cases in which one is actually *deluded*—in which, for instance, one thinks one sees an oasis but an oasis 'does not exist at all'; and it is this sort of case that Ayer evidently has in mind. The phrase 'qualitatively delusive', on the other hand, is evidently meant to apply in cases where some object is certainly before us, no doubt about that, but one of its 'qualities' is under suspicion—it looks blue for instance, but is it *really* blue? Now it seems to be implied that these two types of cases exhaust the field. But do they? Suppose that I see a decoy duck and take it for a real duck; in which of Ayer's ways is my 'perception' to be said to be 'delusive'? Well, it just isn't clear. It might be held to be 'qualitatively' delusive, as endowing the material thing with 'qualities that it does not really possess'; for example, I mistakenly suppose that the object I see could quack. But then again it might be said to be 'existentially' delusive, since the material thing it seems to present does not exist; I think there is a real duck before me but in fact there isn't. So Ayer's initial distinction presents us with false alternatives; it suggests that we have just two cases to consider, in one of which the only question is whether the thing we perceive really has the 'quality' it seems to have, and in the other of which the only question is whether the thing which we seem to perceive does really exist. But in the case of the decoy duck this breaks down at once; and there are plenty of other such cases. It looks as though, in trying to make this initial distinction, Ayer has frozen on to the truly 'delusive' sort of case, in which I think I see something where *nothing* really is, and has simply overlooked the much more common case in which I think I see something where something *else* really is. As a result a large part, and probably the largest part, of the territory within which we draw distinctions between 'appearance and reality' is completely omitted from his discussion. He discusses (very briefly indeed) the

From J. L. Austin, *Sense and Sensibilia*, ed. G. Warnock (Oxford University Press, 1962). Reprinted by permission of Oxford University Press.

case in which something is or might be taken to exist when it does not really exist at all; he discusses at rather greater length the case in which something is or might be supposed to have a characteristic which it does not really have; but he simply doesn't mention the very numerous and very various cases in which something is or might be taken *to be* what it isn't really—as paste diamonds, for instance, may be taken to be real diamonds. The distinction between 'qualitative' and 'existential' delusion doesn't properly apply to these cases, but then that is *just* what is wrong with the distinction. It divides up the topic in a way that leaves a lot of it out.[1]

However, Ayer undertakes as his major enterprise to 'furnish an explanation of the use of the word "real" as it is applied to the characteristics of material things'. The distinction here between being 'delusive' and being 'veridical', he says, 'does not depend upon a difference in the intrinsic qualities of sense-data', since an elliptical sense-datum could, after all, just as well 'present' something really elliptical as something really round; so the distinction 'must depend upon a difference in their relations', namely their relations to other sense-data.

One might try, Ayer says, to identify a sense-datum as 'a bearer of the real character of the relevant material thing' by saying that such a sense-datum is what occurs 'in what are conventionally taken to be preferential conditions'. However, he objects to this on two grounds; first, 'that these preferential conditions are not the same for every kind of material thing',[2] and second, that it is surely necessary to explain *why* certain conditions should be selected as 'preferential'. This explanation Ayer now gives and elaborates. 'The privileged sense-data', he says, i.e. those which present the 'real qualities' of material things, 'are found to be the most reliable members of the groups to which they belong, in the sense that they have the greatest value as sources of prediction.' He later adds as meritorious features what he calls 'sensible constancy', and measurability; but here too it is really, he thinks, *predictive value* which determines the ascription of reality. For example; if I am *very* close to an object, or *very* far away from it, I am pretty badly placed for predicting 'how it will look' from other points of view, whereas, if I view it from a more moderate distance, I may be able to tell quite well 'how it will look' from closer to, or further away. (It is not quite clear what characteristic of the object is in question here, but it seems to be shape that is meant.) So, the argument goes, we say that the 'real shape' is the shape the thing looks at the more moderate range. Again, if I look at an object through dark glasses, it may be hard to tell what colour it will look when I take them off; hence, through dark glasses, we say, it doesn't look its 'real colour'.

However, this will not do as a *general* account even of the very restricted bit of the use of 'real' which Ayer chooses to discuss. (The important point is, in fact, just that there *is* no general account, and Ayer is chasing a will-o'-the-wisp in trying to find one.) For consider some questions about 'real' colour. Here there are *many* cases of a kind which Ayer, generalizing on the basis of one example, takes no account of. Some we have already mentioned. For instance, 'That's not the real colour of her hair.' Why not? Because the colour her hair now looks is an unreliable basis for prediction? Because the colour her hair now looks is not 'most conspicuously differentiated' from the other constituents of my sense-field? No. That's not the real colour of her hair because she's *dyed* it. Or suppose that I have grown a specimen of what is normally a white flower in an appropriately constituted green fluid, so that its petals are now a pale shade of green: I say, 'Of course, that's not its real colour.' Why do I say this? I can, after all, make all the standard predictions about how my specimen will look in various conditions. But my reason for saying that pale green is not its real colour has nothing at all to do with that; it is simply that the flower's *natural* colour is white. And there are some cases, involving no artificial interference with things, which run directly counter to Ayer's doctrine. If I look very closely indeed at a piece of cloth I may see it as a criss-cross pattern of black and white, and be able to predict that from other points of view it will look grey; if I look at it from a range of several yards, it may look grey, and I may *not* be able to predict that, close to, it will look black and white; but we say, all the same, that its colour is grey. Then what about *taste*? If someone who isn't in the habit of drinking wine says of the glass I give him that it's sour, I might protest, 'It isn't really sour'—meaning thereby, not that the notion that it's sour will provide a poor basis for pre-

1. One might add that a good deal is arbitrarily excluded by Ayer's restriction of his discussion to questions about 'material things'—unless, which I doubt, he could classify as material *things* such *stuffs* as silk, glass, gold, cream, &c. And couldn't I raise the question 'Is that a real rainbow?'

2. It's interesting that Ayer should feel this to be an *objection*.

diction, but that, if he savours it a bit more sympathetically, he'll realize that it just isn't *like* things that are sour, that his first reaction, though understandable perhaps, was inappropriate.

However, as I said, what is wrong in principle with Ayer's account of the use of 'real' is just that he is attempting to give *one* account—or two, if we include his perfunctory remarks on the 'existentially' delusive. In fact what he says is not generally true even of 'real colour'; and certainly it does not help us at all with real pearls, real ducks, real cream, real watches, real novels, and the rest—all those uses of 'real' which Ayer overlooks entirely. Just why it is a mistake to look for any single, quite general account of the use of the word 'real' has, I hope, been made clear enough already, and I shall not repeat it now. I should like to emphasize, however, how fatal it always is to embark on explaining the use of a word without seriously considering more than a tiny fraction of the contexts in which it is actually used. In this case, as in others, Ayer seems to be encouraged in the fatal enterprise by an initial propensity to believe that the terrain can be neatly and exhaustively divided in two.

Theory to fit the situation. - Twists -
There is always An Answer

Chapter 10

KARL POPPER

you do have to repute the theory
in order to prove the theory right.

Karl Popper (1902–1994) was an Austrian-born philosopher who spent most of his career at the London School of Economics. In our first selection, "Conjectures and Refutations," Popper rejects the positivist thesis that only that which can be verified is cognitively meaningful. Even metaphysics can be meaningful. What is irrational is the refusal to treat one's theories as hypotheses that must be subjected to critical scrutiny. The single criterion for science is *falsifiability*. We can never prove universal propositions (e.g., "All swans are white" or "All men are mortal"), for there might always be an exception. Rationality consists of trying to falsify universal theories—finding the lethal exception. Popper accuses both Marxism and Freudianism of being pseudo sciences because they fail to search for or take into account disconfirming evidence. The best we can attain is a fallibilism in which we hold our theories as experimental, always seeking to qualify them with evidence.

In our second selection, "Epistemology Without a Knowing Subject," Popper argues that there really are three different worlds existing in the same universe: the physical world of matter, the mental world of consciousness and mental events, and the Platonic world of propositions, theories, arguments, and problems. This third world, an idea anticipated by Gottlob Frege, is objective and autonomous. Although it has been created by humans, it doesn't depend on humans for its continued existence. So long as a record (e.g., a library) survived the extinction of humanity, a new race might discover these ideas and bring them back to the public domain. Unlike Jacques Derrida (in Chapter 36) this world of ideas does not depend on human interpretation. The *text* remains objective and autonomous, even though individuals may interpret it differently (or misinterpret it).

Line of DEMARCATION
Elemendte.

FOR FURTHER READING

Bungie, M., ed. *The Critical Approach to Knowledge* (Dover, 1964).
Kourany, Janet, ed. *Scientific Knowledge* (Wadsworth, 1998).
O'Hear, Anthony. *Karl Popper* (Routledge & Kegan Paul, 1980).
Popper, Karl. *The Logic of Scientific Discovery* (New York, 1959).
———. *Objective Knowledge* (Oxford University Press, 1972).
———. *The Open Society and Its Enemies* (Princeton University Press, 1966).
———. *Unended Quest* (Open Court, 1976).
Schilpp, P.A., ed. *The Philosophy of Karl Popper* (Open Court, 1967).

Conjectures and Refutations*

Mr. Turnbull had predicted evil consequences, . . . and was now doing the best in his power to bring about the verification of his own prophecies.

ANTHONY TROLLOPE

I

When I received the list of participants in this course and realized that I had been asked to speak to philosophical colleagues I thought, after some hesitation and consultation, that you would probably prefer me to speak about those problems which interest me most, and about those developments with which I am most intimately acquainted. I therefore decided to do what I have never done before: to give you a report on my own work in the philosophy of science, since the autumn of 1919 when I first began to grapple with the problem, "*When should a theory be ranked as scientific*?" or "*Is there a criterion for the scientific character or status of a theory*?"

The problem which troubled me at the time was neither, "When is a theory true?" nor, "When is a theory acceptable?" My problem was different. I *wished to distinguish between science and pseudo-science*; knowing very well that science often errs, and that pseudo-science may happen to stumble on the truth.

I knew, of course, the most widely accepted answer to my problem: that science is distinguished from pseudo-science—or from "metaphysics"—by its *empirical* method, which is essentially *inductive*, proceeding from observation or experiment. But this did not satisfy me. On the contrary, I often formulated my problem as one of distinguishing between a genuinely empirical method and a non-empirical or even a pseudo-empirical method—that is to say, a method which, although it appeals to observation and experiment, nevertheless does not come up to scientific standards. The latter method may be exemplified by astrology, with its stupendous mass of empirical evidence based on observation—on horoscopes and on biographies.

But as it was not the example of astrology which led me to my problem I should perhaps briefly describe the atmosphere in which my problem arose and the examples by which it was stimulated. After the collapse of the Austrian Empire there had been a revolution in Austria: the air was full of revolutionary slogans and ideas, and new and often wild theories. Among the theories which interested me, Einstein's theory of relativity was no doubt by far the most important. Three others were Marx's theory of history, Freud's psychoanalysis, and Alfred Adler's so-called "individual psychology."

There was a lot of popular nonsense talked about these theories, and especially about relativity (as still happens even today), but I was fortunate in those who introduced me to the study of this theory. We all—the small circle of students to which I belonged—were thrilled with the result of Eddington's eclipse observations which in 1919 brought the first important confirmation of Einstein's theory of gravitation. It was a great experience for us, and one which had a lasting influence on my intellectual development.

The three other theories I have mentioned were also widely discussed among students at that time. I myself happened to come into personal contact with Alfred Adler, and even to co-operate with him in his social work among the children and young people in the working-class districts of Vienna where he had established social guidance clinics.

It was during the summer of 1919 that I began to feel more and more dissatisfied with these three theories—the Marxist theory of history, psycho-

*A lecture given at Peterhouse, Cambridge, in Summer 1953, as part of a course on developments and trends in contemporary British philosophy, organized by the British Council; originally published under the title "Philosophy of Science: A Personal Report" in *British Philosophy in Mid-Century*, ed. C. A. Mace, 1957.

Reprinted by permission. From *Conjectures and Refutations*, Karl Popper (Basic Books, 1962; Harper & Row, 1968).

analysis, and individual psychology; and I began to feel dubious about their claims to scientific status. My problem perhaps first took the simple form, "What is wrong with Marxism, psychoanalysis, and individual psychology? Why are they so different from physical theories, from Newton's theory, and especially from the theory of relativity?"

To make this contrast clear I should explain that few of us at the time would have said that we believed in the *truth* of Einstein's theory of gravitation. This shows that it was not my doubting the *truth* of those other three theories which bothered me, but something else. Yet neither was it that I merely felt mathematical physics to be more *exact* than the sociological or psychological type of theory. Thus what worried me was neither the problem of truth, at that stage at least, nor the problem of exactness or measurability. It was rather that I felt that these other three theories, though posing as sciences, had in fact more in common with primitive myths than with science; that they resembled astrology rather than astronomy.

I found that those of my friends who were admirers of Marx, Freud, and Adler, were impressed by a number of points common to these theories, and especially by their apparent *explanatory power*. These theories appeared to be able to explain practically everything that happened within the fields to which they referred. The study of any of them seemed to have the effect of an intellectual conversion or revelation, opening your eyes to a new truth hidden from those not yet initiated. Once your eyes were thus opened you saw confirming instances everywhere: the world was full of *verifications* of the theory. Whatever happened always confirmed it. Thus its truth appeared manifest; and unbelievers were clearly people who did not want to see the manifest truth; who refused to see it, either because it was against their class interest, or because of their repressions which were still "unanalyzed" and crying aloud for treatment.

The most characteristic element in this situation seemed to me the incessant stream of confirmations, of observations which "verified" the theories in question; and this point was constantly emphasized by their adherents. A Marxist could not open a newspaper without finding on every page confirming evidence for his interpretation of history; not only in the news, but also in its presentation—which revealed the class bias of the paper—and especially of course in what the paper did *not* say. The Freudian analysts emphasized that their theories were constantly verified by their "clinical observations." As for Adler, I was much impressed by a personal experience. Once, in 1919, I reported to him a case which to me did not seem particularly Adlerian, but which he found no difficulty in analyzing in terms of his theory of inferiority feelings, although he had not even seen the child. Slightly shocked, I asked him how he could be so sure. "Because of my thousandfold experience," he replied; whereupon I could not help saying: "And with this new case, I suppose, your experience has become thousand-and-one-fold."

What I had in mind was that his previous observations may not have been much sounder than this new one; that each in its turn had been interpreted in the light of "previous experience," and at the same time counted as additional confirmation. What, I asked myself, did it confirm? No more than that a case could be interpreted in the light of the theory. But this meant very little, I reflected, since every conceivable case could be interpreted in the light of Adler's theory, or equally of Freud's. I may illustrate this by two very different examples of human behavior: that of a man who pushes a child into the water with the intention of drowning it; and that of a man who sacrifices his life in an attempt to save the child. Each of these two cases can be explained with equal ease in Freudian and in Adlerian terms. According to Freud the first man suffered from repression (say, of some component of his Oedipus complex), while the second man had achieved sublimation. According to Adler the first man suffered from feelings of inferiority (producing perhaps the need to prove to himself that he dared to commit some crime), and so did the second man (whose need was to prove to himself that he dared to rescue the child). I could not think of any human behavior which could not be interpreted in terms of either theory. It was precisely this fact—that they always fitted, that they were always confirmed—which in the eyes of their admirers constituted the strongest argument in favor of these theories. It began to dawn on me that this apparent strength was in fact their weakness.

With Einstein's theory the situation was strikingly different. Take one typical instance—Einstein's prediction, just then confirmed by the findings of Eddington's expedition. Einstein's gravitational theory had led to the result that light must be attracted by heavy bodies (such as the sun), precisely as material bodies were attracted. As a consequence it could be calculated that light from a distant fixed star whose apparent position was close to the sun would reach the earth from such a direction that the star would seem to be slightly shifted away from the sun; or, in other words, that stars close to the sun would look as if they had moved a little away from the sun, and from one another. This is a thing which cannot normally be observed since such stars are rendered invisible in daytime by the sun's overwhelming brightness; but during an eclipse it is possible to take photographs of them. If the same constellation is photographed at night one can measure the distances on the two photographs, and check the predicted effect.

Now the impressive thing about this case is the *risk* involved in a prediction of this kind. If observation shows that the predicted effect is definitely absent, then the theory is simply refuted. The theory is *incompatible with certain possible results of observation*—in fact with results which everybody before Einstein would have expected.[1] This is quite different from the situation I have previously described, when it turned out that the theories in question were compatible with the most divergent human behavior, so that it was practically impossible to describe any human behavior that might not be claimed to be a verification of these theories.

These considerations led me in the winter of 1919–20 to conclusions which I may now reformulate as follows.

1. It is easy to obtain confirmations, or verifications, for nearly every theory—if we look for confirmations.

2. Confirmations should count only if they are the result of *risky predictions*; that is to say, if, unenlightened by the theory in question, we should have expected an event which was incompatible with the theory—an event which would have refuted the theory.

3. Every "good" scientific theory is a prohibition: it forbids certain things to happen. The more a theory forbids, the better it is.

4. A theory which is not refutable by any conceivable event is nonscientific. Irrefutability is not a virtue of a theory (as people often think) but a vice.

5. Every genuine *test* of a theory is an attempt to falsify it, or to refute it. Testability is falsifiability; but there are degrees of testability: some theories are more testable, more exposed to refutation, than others; they take, as it were, greater risks.

6. Confirming evidence should not count *except when it is the result of a genuine test of the theory*; and this means that it can be presented as a serious but unsuccessful attempt to falsify the theory. (I now speak in such cases of "corroborating evidence.")

7. Some genuinely testable theories, when found to be false, are still upheld by their admirers—for example by introducing ad hoc some auxiliary assumption, or by reinterpreting the theory ad hoc in such a way that it escapes refutation. Such a procedure is always possible, but it rescues the theory from refutation only at the price of destroying, or at least lowering, its scientific status. (I later described such a rescuing operation as a "*conventionalist twist*" or a "*conventionalist stratagem*.")

One can sum up all this by saying that *the criterion of the scientific status of a theory is its falsifiability, or refutability, or testability.*

II

I may perhaps exemplify this with the help of the various theories so far mentioned. Einstein's theory of gravitation clearly satisfied the criterion of falsifiability. Even if our measuring instruments at the time did not allow us to pronounce on the results of the tests with complete assurance, there was clearly a possibility of refuting the theory.

Astrology did not pass the test. Astrologers were greatly impressed, and misled, by what they believed to be confirming evidence—so much so that they were quite unimpressed by any unfavorable evidence. Moreover, by making their interpretations and prophecies sufficiently vague they were able to explain away anything that might have been a refutation of the theory had the theory and the prophecies been more precise. In order to escape falsification they destroyed the testability of their theory. It is a typical soothsayer's trick to predict things so vaguely that the predictions can hardly fail: that they become irrefutable.

The Marxist theory of history, in spite of the serious efforts of some of its founders and followers, ultimately adopted this soothsaying practice. In some of its earlier formulations (for example in Marx's analysis of the character of the "coming social revolution") their predictions were testable, and in fact falsified.[2] Yet instead of accepting the refutations the followers of Marx reinterpreted both the theory and the evidence in order to make them agree.

In this way they rescued the theory from refutation; but they did so at the price of adopting a device which made it irrefutable. They thus gave a "conventionalist twist" to the theory; and by this stratagem they destroyed its much advertised claim to scientific status.

The two psychoanalytic theories were in a different class. They were simply non-testable, irrefutable. There was no conceivable human behavior which could contradict them. This does not mean that Freud and Adler were not seeing certain things correctly: I personally do not doubt that much of what they say is of considerable importance, and may well play its part one day in a psychological science which is testable. But it does mean that those "clinical observations" which analysts naively believe confirm their theory cannot do this any more than the daily confirmations which astrologers find in their practice.[3] And as for Freud's epic of the Ego, the Super-ego, and the Id, no substantially stronger claim to scientific status can be made for it than for Homer's collected stories from Olympus. These theories describe some facts, but in the manner of myths. They contain most interesting psychological suggestions, but not in a testable form.

At the same time I realized that such myths may be developed, and become testable; that historically speaking all—or very nearly all—scientific theories originate from myths, and that a myth may contain important anticipations of scientific theories. Examples are Empedocles' theory of evolution by trial and error, or Parmenides' myth of the unchanging block universe in which nothing ever happens and which, if we add another dimension, becomes Einstein's block universe (in which, too, nothing ever happens, since everything is, four-dimensionally speaking, determined and laid down from the beginning). I thus felt that if a theory is found to be non-scientific, . . . it is not thereby found to be unimportant, or insignificant, or "meaningless," or "nonsensical."[4] But it cannot claim to be backed by empirical evidence in the scientific sense—although it may easily be, in some genetic sense, the "result of observation."

(There were a great many other theories of this pre-scientific or pseudoscientific character, some of them, unfortunately, as influential as the Marxist interpretation of history; for example, the racialist interpretation of history—another of those impressive and all-explanatory theories which act upon weak minds like revelations.)

Thus the problem which I tried to solve by proposing the criterion of falsifiability was neither a problem of meaningfulness or significance, nor a problem of truth or acceptability. It was the problem of drawing a line (as well as this can be done) between the statements, or systems of statements, of the empirical sciences, and all other statements. . . . Years later—it must have been in 1928 or 1929—I called this first problem of mine the "*problem of demarcation*." The criterion of falsifiability is a solution to this problem of demarcation, for it says that statements or systems of statements, in order to be ranked as scientific, must be capable of conflicting with possible, or conceivable, observations. . . .

Notes

1. This is a slight oversimplification, for about half of the Einstein effect may be derived from the classical theory, provided we assume a ballistic theory of light.
2. See, for example, my *Open Society and Its Enemies*, ch. 15, section iii, and notes 13–14.
3. "Clinical observations," like all other observations, are *interpretations in the light of theories*; and for this reason alone they are apt to seem to support those theories in the light of which they were interpreted. But real support can be obtained only from observations undertaken as tests (by "attempted refutations"); and for this purpose *criteria of refutation* have to be laid down beforehand: it must be agreed which observable situations, if actually observed, mean that the theory is refuted. But what kind of clinical responses would refute to the satisfaction of the analyst not merely a particular analytic diagnosis but psychoanalysis itself? And have such criteria ever been discussed or agreed upon by analysts? Is there not, on the contrary, a whole family of analytic concepts, such as "ambivalence" (I do not suggest that there is no such thing as ambivalence), which would make it difficult, if not impossible, to agree upon such criteria? Moreover, how much headway has been made in investigating the question of the extent to which the (conscious or unconscious) expectations and theories held by the analyst influence the "clinical responses" of the patient? (To say nothing about the conscious attempts to influence the patient by proposing interpretations to him, etc.) Years ago I introduced the term "*Oedipus effect*" to describe the influence of a theory or expectation or prediction *upon the event*

which it predicts or describes: it will be remembered that the causal chain leading to Oedipus' parricide was started by the oracle's prediction of this event. This is a characteristic and recurrent theme of such myths, but one which seems to have failed to attract the interest of the analysts, perhaps not accidentally. (The problem of confirmatory dreams suggested by the analyst is discussed by Freud, for example in *Gesammelte Schriften*, III, 1925, where he says on p. 314: "If anybody asserts that most of the dreams which can be utilized in an analysis . . . owe their origin to the analyst's suggestion, then no objection can be made from the point of view of analytic theory. Yet there is nothing in this fact," he surprisingly adds, "which would detract from the reliability of our results.")

4. The case of astrology, nowadays a typical pseudoscience, may illustrate this point. It was attacked, by Aristotelians and other rationalists, down to Newton's day, for the wrong reason—for its now accepted assertion that the planets had an "influence" upon terrestrial ("sublunar") events. In fact Newton's theory of gravity, and especially the lunar theory of the tides, was historically speaking an offspring of astrological lore. Newton, it seems, was most reluctant to adopt a theory which came from the same stable as for example the theory that "influenza" epidemics are due to an astral "influence." And Galileo, no doubt for the same reason, actually rejected the lunar theory of the tides; and his misgivings about Kepler may easily be explained by his misgivings about astrology.

Epistemology Without a Knowing Subject

Allow me to start with a confession. Although I am a very happy philosopher I have, after a lifetime of lecturing, no illusions about what I can convey in a lecture. For this reason I shall make no attempt in this lecture to convince you. Instead I shall make an attempt to challenge you, and, if possible, to provoke you.

I. THREE THESES ON EPISTEMOLOGY AND THE THIRD WORLD

I might have challenged those who have heard of my adverse attitude towards Plato and Hegel by calling my lecture '*A theory of the Platonic world*', or '*A theory of the objective spirit*'.

The main topic of this lecture will be what I often call, for want of a better name, '*the third world*'. To explain this expression I will point out that, without taking the words 'world' or 'universe' too seriously, we may distinguish the following three worlds or universes: first, the world of physical objects or of physical states; secondly, the world of states of consciousness, or of mental states, or perhaps of behavioural dispositions to act; and thirdly, the world of *objective contents of thought*, especially of scientific and poetic thoughts and of works of art.

Thus what I call 'the third world' has admittedly much in common with Plato's theory of Forms or Ideas, and therefore also with Hegel's objective spirit, though my theory differs radically, in some decisive respects, from Plato's and Hegel's. It has more in common still with Bolzano's theory of a universe of propositions in themselves and of truths in themselves, though it differs from Bolzano's also. My third world resembles most closely the universe of Frege's objective contents of thought.

It is not part of my view or of my argument that we might not enumerate our worlds in different ways, or not enumerate them at all. We might, especially, distinguish more than three worlds. My term 'the third world' is merely a matter of convenience.

In upholding an objective third world I hope to provoke those whom I call "*belief philosophers*":

An address given on August 25, 1967, at the Third International Congress for Logic, Methodology and Philosophy of Science, August 25 to September 2, 1967; first published in the proceedings of this Congress, eds. B. van Rootselaar and J. F. Staal, Amsterdam 1968, pp. 333–373.

those who, like Descartes, Locke, Berkeley, Hume, Kant, or Russell, are interested in our subjective beliefs, and their basis or origin. Against these belief philosophers I urge that our problem is to find better and bolder theories; and that *critical preference* counts, but *not belief.*

I wish to confess, however, at the very beginning, that I am a realist: I suggest, somewhat like a naïve realist, that there are physical worlds and a world of states of consciousness, and that these two interact. And I believe that there is a third world, in a sense which I shall explain more fully.

Among the inmates of my 'third world' are, more especially, *theoretical systems*; but inmates just as important are *problems* and *problem situations*. And I will argue that the most important inmates of this world are *critical arguments*, and what may be called—in analogy to a physical state or to a state of consciousness—*the state of a discussion* or the *state of a critical argument*; and, of course, the contents of journals, books, and libraries.

Most opponents of the thesis of an objective third world will of course admit that there are problems, conjectures, theories, arguments, journals, and books. But they usually say that all these entities are, essentially, symbolic or linguistic *expressions* of subjective mental states, or perhaps of behavioural dispositions to act; further, that these entities are means of *communication*—that is to say, symbolic or linguistic means to evoke in others similar mental states or behavioural dispositions to act.

Against this, I have often argued that one cannot relegate all these entities and their content to the second world.

Let me repeat one of my standard arguments[1] for the (more or less) *independent existence of the third world.*

I consider two thought experiments:

Experiment (1). All our machines and tools are destroyed, and all our subjective learning, including our subjective knowledge of machines and tools, and how to use them. But *libraries and our capacity to learn from them* survive. Clearly, after much suffering, our world may get going again.

Experiment (2). As before, machines and tools are destroyed, and our subjective learning, including our subjective knowledge of machines and tools, and how to use them. But this time, *all libraries are destroyed also*, so that our capacity to learn from books becomes useless.

If you think about these two experiments, the reality, significance, and degree of autonomy of the third world (as well as its effects on the second and first worlds) may perhaps become a little clearer to you. For in the second case there will be no re-emergence of our civilization for many millennia.

I wish to defend in this lecture three main theses, all of which concern epistemology. Epistemology I take to be the theory of *scientific knowledge*.

My first thesis is this. Traditional epistemology has studied knowledge or thought in a subjective sense—in the sense of the ordinary usage of the words 'I know' or 'I am thinking'. This, I assert, has led students of epistemology into irrelevances: while intending to study scientific knowledge, they studied in fact something which is of no relevance to scientific knowledge. For *scientific knowledge* simply is not knowledge in the sense of the ordinary usage of the words "I know." While knowledge in the sense of 'I know' belongs to what I call the 'second world', the world of *subjects*, scientific knowledge belongs to the third world, to the world of objective theories, objective problems, and objective arguments.

Thus my first thesis is that the traditional epistemology, of Locke, Berkeley, Hume, and even of Russell, is irrelevant, in a pretty strict sense of the word. It is a corollary of this thesis that a large part of contemporary epistemology is irrelevant also. This includes modern epistemic logic, *if* we assume that it aims at a theory of *scientific knowledge*. However, any epistemic logician can easily make himself completely immune from my criticism, simply by making clear that he does not aim at contributing to the *theory of scientific knowledge*.

My first thesis involves the existence of two different senses of knowledge or of thought: (1) *knowledge or thought in the subjective sense*, consisting of a state of mind or of consciousness or a disposition to behave or to react, and (2) *knowledge or thought in an objective sense*, consisting of problems, theories, and arguments as such. Knowledge in this objective sense is totally independent of anybody's claim to know; it is also independent of anybody's belief, or disposition to assent; or to assert, or to act. Knowledge in the objective sense is *knowledge without a knower*: it is *knowledge without a knowing subject.*

Of thought in the objective sense Frege wrote: 'I understand by a *thought* not the subjective act of thinking but its *objective content*. . . .'

1. The argument is adapted from Popper, 1962, vol. ii; cp. p. 108.

The two senses of thought and their interesting interrelations can be illustrated by the following highly convincing quotation from Heyting (1962, p. 195), who says about Brouwer's act of inventing his theory of the continuum: 'If recursive functions had been invented before, he [Brouwer] would perhaps not have formed the notion of a choice sequence which, I think, would have been unlucky.'

This quotation refers on the one hand to some *subjective thought processes* of Brouwer's and says that they might not have occurred (which would have been unfortunate) had the *objective problem situation* been different. Thus Heyting mentions certain possible *influences* upon Brouwer's subjective thought processes, and he also expresses his opinion regarding the value of these subjective thought processes. Now it is interesting that influences, *qua* influences, must be subjective: only Brouwer's subjective acquaintance with recursive functions could have had that unfortunate effect of preventing him from inventing free choice sequences.

On the other hand, the quotation from Heyting points to a certain objective relationship between the *objective contents* of two thoughts or theories: Heyting does not refer to the subjective conditions or the electrochemistry of Brouwer's brain processes, but to an *objective problem situation in mathematics* and its possible influences on Brouwer's subjective acts of thought which were bent on solving these objective problems. I would describe this by saying that Heyting's remark is about the objective or third-world *situational logic* of Brouwer's invention, and that Heyting's remark implies that the third-world situation may affect the second world. Similarly, Heyting's suggestion that it would have been unfortunate if Brouwer had not invented choice sequences is a way of saying that the *objective content* of Brouwer's thought was valuable and interesting; valuable and interesting, that is, in the way it changed the objective problem situation in the third world.

To put the matter simply, if I say 'Brouwer's thought was influenced by Kant' or even 'Brouwer rejected Kant's theory of space' then I speak at least partly about acts of thought in the subjective sense: the word 'influence' indicates a context of thought processes or acts of thinking. If I say, however, 'Brouwer's thought differs vastly from Kant's', then it is pretty clear that I speak mainly about contents. And, ultimately, if I say 'Brouwer's thoughts are incompatible with Russell's', then, by using a *logical term* such as '*incompatible*', I make it unambiguously clear that I am using the word 'thought' only in Frege's objective sense, and that I am speaking only about the objective content, or the logical content, of theories.

Just as ordinary language unfortunately has no separate terms for 'thought' in the sense of the second world and in the sense of the third world, so it has no separate terms for the corresponding two senses of 'I know' and of 'knowledge'.

In order to show that both senses exist, I will first mention three subjective or second-world examples:

(1) 'I *know* you are trying to provoke me, but I will not be provoked.'

(2) 'I *know* that Fermat's last theorem has not been proved, but I believe it will be proved one day.'

(3) From the entry 'Knowledge' in *The Oxford English Dictionary: knowledge* is a 'state of being aware or informed'.

Next I will mention three objective or third-world examples:

(1) From the entry 'Knowledge' in *The Oxford English Dictionary: knowledge* is a 'branch of learning; a science; an art'.

(2) 'Taking account of the present state of *metamathematical knowledge*, it seems possible that Fermat's last theorem may be undecidable.'

(3) 'I certify that this thesis is an original and significant *contribution to knowledge*.'

These very trite examples have only the function of helping to clarify what I mean when I speak of 'knowledge in the objective sense'. My quoting *The Oxford English Dictionary* should not be interpreted as either a concession to language analysis or as an attempt to appease its adherents. It is not quoted in an attempt to prove that 'ordinary usage' covers 'knowledge' in the objective sense of my third world. In fact, I was surprised to find in *The Oxford English Dictionary* examples of objective usages of 'knowledge'. (I was even more surprised to find some at least *partly* objective usages of 'know': 'to distinguish . . . to be acquainted with (a thing, a place, a person); . . . to understand'. That these usages may be partly objective will emerge from the sequel.) At any rate, my examples are not intended as arguments. They are intended solely as illustrations.

My *first thesis*, so far not argued but only illustrated, was that traditional epistemology with its concentration on the second world, or on knowledge in the subjective sense, is irrelevant to the study of scientific knowledge.

My *second thesis* is that what is relevant for epistemology is the study of scientific problems and problem situations, of scientific conjectures (which I take as merely another word for scientific hypotheses or theories), of scientific discussions, of critical arguments, and of the role played by evidence in arguments; and therefore of scientific journals and books, and of experiments and their evaluation in scientific arguments; or, in brief, that the study of a *largely autonomous* third world of objective knowledge is of decisive importance for epistemology.

An epistemological study as described in my second thesis shows that scientists very often do not claim that their conjectures are true, or that they 'know' them in the subjective sense of 'know', or that they believe in them. Although in general they do not claim to know, in developing their research programmes they act on the basis of guesses about what is and what is not fruitful, and what line of research promises further results in the third world of objective knowledge. In other words, scientists act on the basis of a guess or, if you like, of a *subjective belief* (for we may so call the subjective basis of an action) concerning what is promising of impending *growth in the third world of objective knowledge*.

This, I suggest, furnishes an argument in favour of both my *first thesis* (of the irrelevance of a subjectivist epistemology) and of my *second thesis* (of the relevance of an objectivist epistemology).

But I have a *third thesis*. It is this. An objectivist epistemology which studies the third world can help to throw an immense amount of light upon the second world of subjective consciousness, especially upon the subjective thought processes of scientists; but *the converse is not true*.

These are my three main theses.

In addition to my three main thesses, I offer three supporting theses.

The first of these is that the third world is a natural product of the human animal, comparable to a spider's web.

The second supporting thesis (and an almost crucial thesis, I think) is that the third world is largely *autonomous*, even though we constantly act upon it and are acted upon by it: it is autonomous in spite of the fact that it is our product and that it has a strong feed-back effect upon us; that is to say, upon us *qua* inmates of the second and even of the first world.

The third supporting thesis is that it is through this interaction between ourselves and the third world that objective knowledge grows, and that there is a close analogy between the growth of knowledge and biological growth; that is, the evolution of plants and animals.

2. A BIOLOGICAL APPROACH TO THE THIRD WORLD

In the present section of my talk I shall try to defend the existence of an autonomous world by a kind of biological or evolutionary argument.

A biologist may be interested in the behaviour of animals; but he may also be interested in some of the *non-living structures* which animals produce, such as spiders' webs, or nests built by wasps or ants, the burrows of badgers, dams constructed by beavers, or paths made by animals in forests.

I will distinguish between two main categories of problems arising from the study of these structures. The first category consists of problems concerned with *the methods used* by the animals, or *the ways the animals behave* when constructing these structures. This first category thus consists *of problems concerned with the acts of production*; with the behavioural dispositions of the animal; and with the relationships between the animal and the product. The second category of problems is concerned with the *structures themselves*. It is concerned with the chemistry of the materials used in the structure; with their geometrical and physical properties; with their evolutionary changes, depending upon special environmental conditions; and with their dependence upon or their adjustments to these environmental conditions. *Very* important also is the *feedback relation* from the properties of the structure to the behaviour of the animals. In dealing with this second category of problems—that is, with the structures themselves—we shall also have to look upon the structures from the point of view of their biological *functions*. Thus some problems of the first category will admittedly arise when we discuss problems of the second category; for example 'How was this nest built?' and 'What aspects of its structure are typical (and thus presumably traditional or inherited) and what aspects are variants adjusted to special conditions?'.

As my last example of a problem shows, problems of the first category—that is, problems concerned with the production of the structure—will sometimes be suggested by problems of the second category. This must be so, since both categories of problems are dependent upon *the fact that such objective structures exist*, a fact which itself belongs to the second category. Thus the existence of the *structures themselves* may be said to create both categories of problems. We may say that the second category of problems—problems connected with the structures themselves—is more fundamental: all that it presupposes from the first category is the bare fact that the structures are somehow *produced by* some animals.

Now these simple considerations may of course also be applied to products of *human* activity, such as houses, or tools, and also to works of art. Especially important for us, they apply to what we call 'language', and to what we call 'science'.

The connection between these biological considerations and the topic of my present lecture can be made clear by reformulating my three main theses. My first thesis can be put by saying that in the present problem situation in philosophy, few things are as important as the awareness of the distinction between the two categories of problems—production problems on the one hand and problems connected with the produced structures themselves on the other. My second thesis is that we should realize that the second category of problems, those concerned with the products in themselves, is in almost every respect more important than the first category, the problems of production. My third thesis is that the problems of the second category are basic for understanding the production problems: contrary to first impressions, we can learn more about production behaviour by studying the products themselves than we can learn about the products by studying production behaviour. This third thesis may be described as an anti-behaviouristic and anti-psychologistic thesis.

In their application to what may be called 'knowledge' my three theses may be formulated as follows.

(1) We should constantly be aware of the distinction between problems connected with our personal contributions to the production of scientific knowledge on the one hand, and problems connected with the structure of the various products, such as scientific theories or scientific arguments, on the other.

(2) We should realize that the study of the products is vastly more important than the study of the production, even for an understanding of the production and its methods.

(3) We can learn more about the heuristics and the methodology and even about the psychology of research by studying theories, and the arguments offered for or against them, than by any direct behaviouristic or psychological or sociological approach. In general, we may learn a great deal about behaviour and psychology from the study of the products.

In what follows I will call the approach from the side of the products—the theories and the arguments—the 'objective' approach or the 'third-world' approach. And I will call the behaviourist, the psychological, and the sociological approach to scientific knowledge the 'subjective' approach or the 'second-world' approach.

The appeal of the subjective approach is largely due to the fact that it is *causal*. For I admit that the objective structures for which I claim priority are caused by human behaviour. Being causal, the subjective approach may seem to be more scientific than the objective approach which, as it were, starts from effects rather than causes.

Though I admit that the objective structures are products of behaviour, I hold that the argument is mistaken. In all sciences, the ordinary approach is from the effects to the causes. The effect raises the problem—the problem to be explained, the explicandum—and the scientist tries to solve it by constructing an explanatory hypothesis.

My three main theses with their emphasis on the objective product are therefore neither teleological nor unscientific.

3. THE OBJECTIVITY AND THE AUTONOMY OF THE THIRD WORLD

One of the main reasons for the mistaken subjective approach to knowledge is the feeling that a book is nothing without a reader: only if it is understood does it really become a book; otherwise it is just paper with black spots on it.

This view is mistaken in many ways. A wasp's nest is a wasp's nest even after it has been deserted; even though it is never again used by wasps as a nest. A bird's nest is a bird's nest even if it was never lived in. Similarly a book remains a book—a certain type of product—even if it is never read (as may easily happen nowadays).

Moreover, a book, or even a library, need not even have been written by anybody: a series of books of logarithms, for example, may be produced and printed by a computer. It may be the best series of books of logarithms—it may contain logarithms up to, say, fifty decimal places. It may be sent out to libraries, but it may be found too cumbersome for use; at any rate, years may elapse before anybody uses it; and many figures in it (which represent mathematical theorems) may never be looked at as long as men live on earth. Yet each of these figures contains what I call 'objective knowledge'; and the question of whether or not I am entitled to call it by this name is of no interest.

The example of these books of logarithms may seem farfetched. But it is not. I should say that almost every book is like this: it contains objective knowledge, true or false, useful or useless; and whether anybody ever reads it and really grasps its contents is almost accidental. A man who reads a book with understanding is a rare creature. But even if he were more common, there would always be plenty of misunderstandings and misinterpretations; and it is not the actual and somewhat accidental avoidance of such misunderstandings which turns black spots on white paper into a book, or an instance of knowledge in the objective sense. Rather, it is something more abstract. It is its possibility or potentiality of being understood, its dispositional character of being understood or interpreted, or misunderstood or misinterpreted, which makes a thing a book. And this potentiality or disposition may exist without ever being actualized or realized.

To see this more clearly, we may imagine that after the human race has perished, some books or libraries may be found by some civilized successors of ours (no matter whether these are terrestrial animals which have become civilized, or some visitors from outer space). These books may be deciphered. They may be those logarithm tables never read before, for argument's sake. This makes it quite clear that neither its composition by thinking animals nor the fact that it has not actually been read or understood is essential for making a thing a book, and that it is sufficient that it might be deciphered.

Thus I do admit that in order to belong to the third world of objective knowledge, a book should—in principle, or virtually—be capable of being grasped (or deciphered, or understood, or 'known') by somebody. But I do not admit more.

We can thus say that there is a kind of Platonic (or Bolzanoesque) third world of books in themselves, theories in themselves, problems in themselves, problem situations in themselves, arguments in themselves, and so on. And I assert that even though this third world is a human product, there are many theories in themselves and arguments in themselves and problem situations in themselves which have never been produced or understood and may never be produced or understood by men.

The thesis of the existence of such a third world of problem situations will strike many as extremely metaphysical and dubious. But it can be defended by pointing out its biological analogue. For example, it has its full analogue in the realm of birds' nests. Some years ago I got a present for my garden—a nesting-box for birds. It was a human product, of course, not a bird's product—just as our logarithm table was a computer's product rather than a human product. But in the context of the bird's world, it was part of an objective problem situation, and an objective opportunity. For some years the birds did not even seem to notice the nesting-box. But after some years, it was carefully inspected by some blue tits who even started building in it, but gave up very soon. Obviously, here was a graspable opportunity, though not, it appears, a particularly valuable one. At any rate, here was a problem situation. And the problem may be solved in another year by other birds. If it is not, another box may prove more adequate. On the other hand, a most adequate box may be removed before it is ever used. The question of the adequacy of the box is clearly an objective one; and whether the box is ever used is partly accidental. So it is with all ecological niches. They are potentialities and may be studied as such in an objective way, up to a point independently of the question of whether these potentialities will ever be actualized by any living organism. A bacteriologist knows how to prepare such an ecological niche for the culture of certain bacteria or moulds. It may be perfectly adequate for its purpose. Whether it will ever be used and inhabited is another question.

A large part of the objective third world of actual and potential theories and books and arguments arises as an unintended by-product of the actually produced books and arguments. We may also say that it is a by-product of human language. Language itself, like a bird's nest, is an unintended by-product of actions which were directed at other aims.

How does an animal path in the jungle arise? Some animal may break through the undergrowth in order to get to a drinking-place. Other animals find it easiest to use the same track. Thus it may be widened and improved by use. It is not planned—it is an unintended consequence of the need for easy or swift movement. This is how a path is originally made—perhaps even by men—and how language and any other institutions which are useful may arise, and how they may owe their existence and development to their usefulness. They are not planned or intended, and there was perhaps no need for them before they came into existence. But they may create a new need, or a new set of aims: the aim-structure of animals or men is not 'given', but it develops, with the help of some kind of feedback mechanism, out of earlier aims, and out of results which were or were not aimed at.

In this way, a whole new universe of possibilities or potentialities may arise: a world which is to a large extent *autonomous*.

A very obvious example is a garden. Even though it may have been planned with great care, it will as a rule turn out partly in unexpected ways. But even if it turns out as planned, some unexpected interrelationships between the planned objects may give rise to a whole universe of possibilities, of possible new aims, and of new *problems*.

The world of language, of conjectures, theories, and arguments—in brief, the universe of objective knowledge—is one of the most important of these man-created, yet at the same time largely autonomous, universes. . . .

Chapter 11

THOMAS KUHN

Thomas Kuhn (1922–1996) was born in Cincinnati and attended Harvard University before joining the faculty at Princeton University, where he taught until his death. Kuhn's *The Structure of Scientific Revolutions* (1962) is one of the most influential philosophy books of the twentieth century. He argues that there is a difference between doing normal science and developing a revolutionary theory, like Lavoisier's oxygen theory or Einstein's theory of general relativity. When existing theories encounter anomalies, innovation is invited. A new paradigm is created, replacing the traditional one. Kuhn likens the paradigm switches to religious conversions. There is no specific algorithmic logic to the process of creating a new theory or choosing (or justifying) one over the other. In the essay included here—"Objectivity, Value Judgment, and Theory Choice," Kuhn qualifies his view on subjectivity and objectivity. He recognizes several criteria of theory assessment:

1. Accuracy: A theory should have predictive success, refined and corroborated by other experiments.
2. Consistency: A theory should be consistent both with itself and with other relevant theories.
3. Scope: A theory's consequences should extend beyond the particular observations for laws it was originally designed to explain.
4. Simplicity: As the more important of his challenges, a theory should unify and simplify data.
5. Fruitfulness: A theory should describe new phenomena and lead to new research projects, extending our understanding.

All of these criteria are objective and relevant and need to be taken into consideration in choosing one theory over another. The problem is that individuals come to the evidence with different background assumptions and may weight the various criteria differently, so that the final decision is a combination of subjective and these objective factors. Kuhn thinks that the dialogue between the members of the scientific community can help us see points in theories to which we may have been blind.

FOR FURTHER READING

Gutting, Gary, ed. *Thomas Kuhn* (University of Notre Dame Press, 1980).
Kourany, Janet. *Scientific Knowledge* (Wadsworth, 1998).
Kuhn, Thomas. *The Structure of Scientific Revolutions* (University of Chicago Press, 1962).
Lakatos, Imre. *Criticism and the Growth of Knowledge* (Cambridge University Press, 1970).

Objectivity, Value Judgment, and Theory Choice

In the penultimate chapter of a controversial book first published fifteen years ago, I considered the ways scientists are brought to abandon one time-honored theory or paradigm in favor of another. Such decision problems, I wrote, "cannot be resolved by proof." To discuss their mechanism is, therefore, to talk "about techniques of persuasion, or about argument and counterargument in a situation in which there can be no proof." Under these circumstances, I continued, "lifelong resistance [to a new theory] . . . is not a violation of scientific standards. . . . Though the historian can always find men—Priestley, for instance—who were unreasonable to resist for as long as they did, he will not find a point at which resistance becomes illogical or unscientific."[1] Statements of that sort obviously raise the question of why, in the absence of binding criteria for scientific choice, both the number of solved scientific problems and the precision of individual problem solutions should increase so markedly with the passage of time. Confronting that issue, I sketched in my closing chapter a number of characteristics that scientists share by virtue of the training that licenses their membership in one or another community of specialists. In the absence of criteria able to dictate the choice of each individual, I argued, we do well to trust the collective judgment of scientists trained in this way. "What better criterion could there be," I asked rhetorically, "than the decision of the scientific group?"[2]

A number of philosophers have greeted remarks like these in a way that continues to surprise me. My views, it is said, make of theory choice "a matter for mob psychology."[3] Kuhn believes, I am told, that "the decision of a scientific group to adopt a new paradigm cannot be based on good reasons of any kind, factual or otherwise."[4] The debates surrounding such choices must, my critics claim, be for me "mere persuasive displays without deliberative substance."[5] Reports of this sort manifest total misunderstanding, and I have occasionally said as much in papers directed primarily to other ends. But those passing protestations have had negligible effect, and the misunderstandings continue to be important. I conclude that it is past time for me to describe, at greater length and with greater precision, what has been on my mind when I have uttered statements like the ones with which I just began. If I have been reluctant to do so in the past, that is largely because I have preferred to devote attention to areas in which my views diverge more sharply from those currently received than they do with respect to theory choice.

What, I ask to begin with, are the characteristics of a good scientific theory? Among a number of quite usual answers I select five, not because they are exhaustive, but because they are individually important and collectively sufficiently varied to indicate what is at stake. First, a theory should be accurate: Within its domain, that is, consequences deducible from a theory should be in demonstrated agreement with the results of existing experiments and observations. Second, a theory should be consistent, not only internally or with itself, but also with other currently accepted theories applicable to related aspects of nature. Third, it should have broad scope: In particular, a theory's consequences should

1. *The Structure of Scientific Revolutions*, 2d ed. (Chicago, 1970), pp. 148, 151–52, 159. All the passages from which these fragments are taken appeared in the same form in the first edition, published in 1962.
2. Ibid., p. 170.

3. Imre Lakatos, "Falsification and the Methodology of Scientific Research Programs," in I. Lakatos and A. Musgrave. eds., *Criticism and the Growth of Knowledge* (Cambridge, 1970), pp. 91–195. The quoted phrase, which appears on p. 178, is italicized in the original.
4. Dudley Shapere, "Meaning and Scientific Change," in R. G. Colodny, ed., *Mind and Cosmos: Essays in Contemporary Science and Philosophy*. University of Pittsburgh Series in the Philosophy of Science, vol. 3 (Pittsburgh, 1966), pp. 41–85. The quotation will be found on p. 67.
5. Israel Scheffler, *Science and Subjectivity* (Indianapolis, 1967), p. 81.

extend far beyond the particular observations, laws, or subtheories it was initially designed to explain. Fourth, and closely related, it should be simple, bringing order to phenomena that in its absence would be individually isolated and, as a set, confused. Fifth—a somewhat less standard item, but one of special importance to actual scientific decisions—a theory should be fruitful of new research findings: It should, that is, disclose new phenomena or previously unnoted relationships among those already known.[6] These five characteristics—accuracy, consistency, scope, simplicity, and fruitfulness—are all standard criteria for evaluating the adequacy of a theory. If they had not been, I would have devoted far more space to them in my book, for I agree entirely with the traditional view that they play a vital role when scientists must choose between an established theory and an upstart competitor. Together with others of much the same sort, they provide the shared basis for theory choice.

Nevertheless, two sorts of difficulties are regularly encountered by the men who must use these criteria in choosing, say, between Ptolemy's astronomical theory and Copernicus's, between the oxygen and phlogiston theories of combustion, or between Newtonian mechanics and the quantum theory. Individually the criteria are imprecise: Individuals may legitimately differ about their application to concrete cases. In addition, when deployed together, they repeatedly prove to conflict with one another; accuracy may, for example, dictate the choice of one theory, scope the choice of its competitor. Since these difficulties, especially the first, are also relatively familiar, I shall devote little time to their elaboration. Though my argument does demand that I illustrate them briefly, my views will begin to depart from those long current only after I have done so.

Begin with accuracy, which for present purposes I take to include not only quantitative agreement but qualitative as well. Ultimately it proves the most nearly decisive of all the criteria, partly because it is less equivocal than the others but especially because predictive and explanatory powers, which depend on it, are characteristics that scientists are particularly unwilling to give up. Unfortunately, however, theories cannot always be discriminated in terms of accuracy. Copernicus's system, for example, was not more accurate than Ptolemy's until drastically revised by Kepler more than sixty years after Copernicus's death. If Kepler or someone else had not found other reasons to choose heliocentric astronomy, those improvements in accuracy would never have been made, and Copernicus's work might have been forgotten. More typically, of course, accuracy does permit discriminations, but not the sort that lead regularly to unequivocal choice. The oxygen theory, for example, was universally acknowledged to account for observed weight relations in chemical reactions, something the phlogiston theory had previously scarcely attempted to do. But the phlogiston theory, unlike its rival, could account for the metals' being much more alike than the ores from which they were formed. One theory thus matched experience better in one area, the other in another. To choose between them on the basis of accuracy, a scientist would need to decide the area in which accuracy was more significant. About that matter chemists could and did differ without violating any of the criteria outlined above, or any others yet to be suggested.

However important it may be, therefore, accuracy by itself is seldom or never a sufficient criterion for theory choice. Other criteria must function as well, but they do not eliminate problems. To illustrate I select just two—consistency and simplicity—asking how they functioned in the choice between the heliocentric and geocentric systems. As astronomical theories both Ptolemy's and Copernicus's were internally consistent, but their relation to related theories in other fields was very different. The stationary central earth was an essential ingredient of received physical theory, a tight-knit body of doctrine that explained, among other things, how stones fall, how water pumps function, and why the clouds move slowly across the skies. Heliocentric astronomy, which required the earth's motion, was inconsistent with the existing scientific explanation of these and other terrestrial phenomena. The consistency criterion, by itself, therefore, spoke unequivocally for the geocentric tradition.

Simplicity, however, favored Copernicus, but only when evaluated in a quite special way. If, on the one hand, the two systems were compared in terms of the actual computational labor required to predict the position of a planet at a particular time,

6. The last criterion, fruitfulness, deserves more emphasis than it has yet received. A scientist choosing between two theories ordinarily knows that his decision will have a bearing on his subsequent research career. Of course he is especially attracted by a theory that promises the concrete successes for which scientists are ordinarily rewarded.

then they proved substantially equivalent. Such computations were what astronomers did, and Copernicus's system offered them no labor-saving techniques; in that sense it was not simpler than Ptolemy's. If, on the other hand, one asked about the amount of mathematical apparatus required to explain, not the detailed quantitative motions of the planets, but merely their gross qualitative features—limited elongation, retrograde motion, and the like—then, as every schoolchild knows, Copernicus required only one circle per planet, Ptolemy two. In that sense the Copernican theory was the simpler, a fact vitally important to the choices made by both Kepler and Galileo and thus essential to the ultimate triumph of Copernicanism. But that sense of simplicity was not the only one available, nor even the one most natural to professional astronomers, men whose task was the actual computation of planetary position.

Because time is short and I have multiplied examples elsewhere, I shall here simply assert that these difficulties in applying standard criteria of choice are typical and that they arise no less forcefully in twentieth-century situations than in the earlier and better-known examples I have just sketched. When scientists must choose between competing theories, two men fully committed to the same list of criteria for choice may nevertheless reach different conclusions. Perhaps they interpret simplicity differently or have different convictions about the range of fields within which the consistency criterion must be met. Or perhaps they agree about these matters but differ about the relative weights to be accorded to these or to other criteria when several are deployed together. With respect to divergences of this sort, no set of choice criteria yet proposed is of any use. One can explain, as the historian characteristically does, why particular men made particular choices at particular times. But for that purpose one must go beyond the list of shared criteria to characteristics of the individuals who make the choice. One must, that is, deal with characteristics that vary from one scientist to another without thereby in the least jeopardizing their adherence to the canons that make science scientific. Though such canons do exist and should be discoverable (doubtless the criteria of choice with which I began are among them), they are not by themselves sufficient to determine the decisions of individual scientists. For that purpose the shared canons must be fleshed out in ways that differ from one individual to another.

Some of the differences I have in mind result from the individual's previous experience as a scientist. In what part of the field was he at work when confronted by the need to choose? How long had he worked there; how successful had he been; and how much of his work depended on concepts and techniques challenged by the new theory? Other factors relevant to choice lie outside the sciences. Kepler's early election of Copernicanism was due in part to his immersion in the Neoplatonic and Hermetic movements of his day; German Romanticism predisposed those it affected toward both recognition and acceptance of energy conservation; nineteenth-century British social thought had a similar influence on the availability and acceptability of Darwin's concept of the struggle for existence. Still other significant differences are functions of personality. Some scientists place more premium than others on originality and are correspondingly more willing to take risks; some scientists prefer comprehensive, unified theories to precise and detailed problem solutions of apparently narrower scope. Differentiating factors like these are described by my critics as subjective and are contrasted with the shared or objective criteria from which I began. Though I shall later question that use of terms, let me for the moment accept it. My point is, then, that every individual choice between competing theories depends on a mixture of objective and subjective factors, or of shared and individual criteria. Since the latter have not ordinarily figured in the philosophy of science, my emphasis upon them has made my belief in the former hard for my critics to see.

What I have said so far is primarily simply descriptive of what goes on in the sciences at times of theory choice. As description, furthermore, it has not been challenged by my critics, who reject instead my claim that these facts of scientific life have philosophic import. Taking up that issue, I shall begin to isolate some, though I think not vast, differences of opinion. Let me begin by asking how philosophers of science can for so long have neglected the subjective elements which, they freely grant, enter regularly into the actual theory choices made by individual scientists? Why have these elements seemed to them an index only of human weakness, not at all of the nature of scientific knowledge?

One answer to that question is, of course, that few philosophers, if any, have claimed to possess either a complete or an entirely well-articulated list of criteria. For some time, therefore, they could reasonably expect that further research would eliminate residual imperfections and produce an algorithm able to dictate rational, unanimous choice. Pending that achievement, scientists would have no alternative but to supply subjectively what the best current list of objective criteria still lacked. That some of them might still do so even with a perfected list at hand would then be an index only of the inevitable imperfection of human nature.

That sort of answer may still prove to be correct, but I think no philosopher still expects that it will. The search for algorithmic decision procedures has continued for some time and produced both powerful and illuminating results. But those results all presuppose that individual criteria of choice can be unambiguously stated and also that, if more than one proves relevant, an appropriate weight function is at hand for their joint application. Unfortunately, where the choice at issue is between scientific theories, little progress has been made toward the first of these desiderata and none toward the second. Most philosophers of science would, therefore, I think, now regard the sort of algorithm which has traditionally been sought as a not quite attainable ideal. I entirely agree and shall henceforth take that much for granted.

Even an ideal, however, if it is to remain credible, requires some demonstrated relevance to the situations in which it is supposed to apply. Claiming that such demonstration requires no recourse to subjective factors, my critics seem to appeal, implicitly or explicitly, to the well-known distinction between the contexts of discovery and of justification.[7] They concede, that is, that the subjective factors I invoke play a significant role in the discovery or invention of new theories, but they also insist that that inevitably intuitive process lies outside of the bounds of philosophy of science and is irrelevant to the question of scientific objectivity. Objectivity enters science, they continue, through the processes by which theories are tested, justified, or judged. Those processes do not, or at least need not, involve subjective factors at all. They can be governed by a set of (objective) criteria shared by the entire group competent to judge.

I have already argued that that position does not fit observations of scientific life and shall now assume that that much has been conceded. What is now at issue is a different point: whether or not this invocation of the distinction between contexts of discovery and of justification provides even a plausible and useful idealization. I think it does not and can best make my point by suggesting first a likely source of its apparent cogency. I suspect that my critics have been misled by science pedagogy or what I have elsewhere called textbook science. In science teaching, theories are presented together with exemplary applications, and those applications may be viewed as evidence. But that is not their primary pedagogic function (science students are distressingly willing to receive the word from professors and texts). Doubtless *some* of them were *part* of the evidence at the time actual decisions were being made, but they represent only a fraction of the considerations relevant to the decision process. The context of pedagogy differs almost as much from the context of justification as it does from that of discovery.

Full documentation of that point would require longer argument than is appropriate here, but two aspects of the way in which philosophers ordinarily demonstrate the relevance of choice criteria are worth noting. Like the science textbooks on which they are often modelled, books and articles on the philosophy of science refer again and again to the famous crucial experiments: Foucault's pendulum, which demonstrates the motion of the earth; Cavendish's demonstration of gravitational attraction; or Fizeau's measurement of the relative speed of sound in water and air. These experiments are paradigms of good reason for scientific choice; they illustrate the most effective of all the sorts of argument which could be available to a scientist uncertain which of two theories to follow; they are vehicles for the transmission of criteria of choice. But they also have another characteristic in common. By the time they were performed no scientist still needed to be convinced of the validity of the theory their outcome is now used to demonstrate. Those decisions had long since been made on the basis of significantly more equivocal evidence. The exemplary crucial experiments to which philosophers again and again refer would have been historically relevant to theory choice only if they had yielded unexpected results. Their use as illustrations provides needed economy to science pedagogy, but they scarcely illuminate the character of the choices that scientists are called upon to make.

7. The least equivocal example of this position is probably the one developed in Scheffler, *Science and Subjectivity*, Chap. 4.

Standard philosophical illustrations of scientific choice have another troublesome characteristic. The only arguments discussed are, as I have previously indicated, the ones favorable to the theory that, in fact, ultimately triumphed. Oxygen, we read, could explain weight relations, phlogiston could not; but nothing is said about the phlogiston theory's power or about the oxygen theory's limitations. Comparisons of Ptolemy's theory with Copernicus's proceed in the same way. Perhaps these examples should not be given since they contrast a developed theory with one still in its infancy. But philosophers regularly use them nonetheless. If the only result of their doing so were to simplify the decision situation, one could not object. Even historians do not claim to deal with the full factual complexity of the situations they describe. But these simplifications emasculate by making choice totally unproblematic. They eliminate, that is, one essential element of the decision situations that scientists must resolve if their field is to move ahead. In those situations there are always at least some good reasons for each possible choice. Considerations relevant to the context of discovery are then relevant to justification as well; scientists who share the concerns and sensibilities of the individual who discovers a new theory are ipso facto likely to appear disproportionately frequently among that theory's first supporters. That is why it has been difficult to construct algorithms for theory choice, and also why such difficulties have seemed so thoroughly worth resolving. Choices that present problems are the ones philosophers of science need to understand. Philosophically interesting decision procedures must function where, in their absence, the decision might still be in doubt.

That much I have said before, if only briefly. Recently, however, I have recognized another, subtler source for the apparent plausibility of my critics' position. To present it, I shall briefly describe a hypothetical dialogue with one of them. Both of us agree that each scientist chooses between competing theories by deploying some Bayesian algorithm which permits him to compute a value for $p(T,E)$, i.e., for the probability of a theory T on the evidence E available both to him and to the other members of his professional group at a particular period of time. "Evidence," furthermore, we both interpret broadly to include such considerations as simplicity and fruitfulness. My critic asserts, however, that there is only one such value of p, that corresponding to objective choice, and he believes that all rational members of the group must arrive at it. I assert, on the other hand, for reasons previously given, that the factors he calls objective are insufficient to determine in full any algorithm at all. For the sake of the discussion I have conceded that each individual has an algorithm and that all their algorithms have much in common. Nevertheless, I continue to hold that the algorithms of individuals are all ultimately different by virtue of the subjective considerations with which each must complete the objective criteria before any computations can be done. If my hypothetical critic is liberal, he may now grant that these subjective differences do play a role in determining the hypothetical algorithm on which each individual relies during the early stages of the competition between rival theories. But he is also likely to claim that, as evidence increases with the passage of time, the algorithms of different individuals converge to the algorithm of objective choice with which his presentation began. For him the increasing unanimity of individual choices is evidence for their increasing objectivity and thus for the elimination of subjective elements from the decision process.

So much for the dialogue, which I have, of course, contrived to disclose the non sequitur underlying an apparently plausible position. What converges as the evidence changes over time need only be the values of p that individuals compute from their individual algorithms. Conceivably those algorithms themselves also become more alike with time, but the ultimate unanimity of theory choice provides no evidence whatsoever that they do so. If subjective factors are required to account for the decisions that initially divide the profession, they may still be present later when the profession agrees. Though I shall not here argue the point, consideration of the occasions on which a scientific community divides suggests that they actually do so.

My argument has so far been directed to two points. It first provided evidence that the choices scientists make between competing theories depend not only on shared criteria—those my critics call objective—but also on idiosyncratic factors dependent on individual biography and personality. The latter are, in my critics' vocabulary, subjective, and the second part of my argument has attempted to bar some likely ways of denying their philosophic import. Let me now shift to a more positive approach, returning briefly to the list of shared criteria—accuracy, simplicity, and the like—with which I began. The considerable effectiveness of such criteria does not, I now wish to suggest, depend on their being sufficiently articulated to dictate the choice of each individual who subscribes to them. Indeed, if they were articulated to that extent, a behavior mechanism fundamental to scientific advance would cease to function. What the tradition sees as eliminable imperfections in its rules of choice I take to be in part responses to the essential nature of science.

As so often, I begin with the obvious. Criteria that influence decisions without specifying what those decisions must be are familiar in many aspects of human life. Ordinarily, however, they are called, not criteria or rules, but maxims, norms, or values. Consider maxims first. The individual who invokes them when choice is urgent usually finds them frustratingly vague and often also in conflict one with another. Contrast "He who hesitates is lost" with "Look before you leap," or compare "Many hands make light work" with "Too many cooks spoil the broth." Individually maxims dictate different choices, collectively none at all. Yet no one suggests that supplying children with contradictory tags like these is irrelevant to their education. Opposing maxims alter the nature of the decision to be made, highlight the essential issues it presents, and point to those remaining aspects of the decision for which each individual must take responsibility himself. Once invoked, maxims like these alter the nature of the decision process and can thus change its outcome.

Values and norms provide even clearer examples of effective guidance in the presence of conflict and equivocation. Improving the quality of life is a value, and a car in every garage once followed from it as a norm. But quality of life has other aspects, and the old norm has become problematic. Or again, freedom of speech is a value, but so is preservation of life and property. In application, the two often conflict, so that judicial soul-searching, which still continues, has been required to prohibit such behavior as inciting to riot or shouting fire in a crowded theater. Difficulties like these are an appropriate source for frustration, but they rarely result in charges that values have no function or in calls for their abandonment. That response is barred to most of us by an acute consciousness that there are societies with other values and that these value differences result in other ways of life, other decisions about what may and what may not be done.

I am suggesting, of course, that the criteria of choice with which I began function not as rules, which determine choice, but as values, which influence it. Two men deeply committed to the same values may nevertheless, in particular situations, make different choices as, in fact, they do. But that difference in outcome ought not to suggest that the values scientists share are less than critically important either to their decisions or to the development of the enterprise in which they participate. Values like accuracy, consistency, and scope may prove ambiguous in application, both individually and collectively; they may, that is, be an insufficient basis for a *shared* algorithm of choice. But they do specify a great deal: what each scientist must consider in reaching a decision, what he may or may not consider relevant, and what he can legitimately be required to report as the basis for the choice he has made. Change the list, for example by adding social utility as a criterion, and some particular choices will be different, more like those one expects from an engineer. Subtract accuracy of fit to nature from the list, and the enterprise that results may not resemble science at all, but perhaps philosophy instead. Different creative disciplines are characterized, among other things, by different sets of shared values. If philosophy and engineering lie too close to the sciences, think of literature or the plastic arts. Milton's failure to set *Paradise Lost* in a Copernican universe does not indicate that he agreed with Ptolemy but that he had things other than science to do.

Recognizing that criteria of choice can function as values when incomplete as rules has, I think, a number of striking advantages. First, as I have already argued at length, it accounts in detail for aspects of scientific behavior which the tradition has seen as anomalous or even irrational. More important, it allows the standard criteria to function fully in the earliest stages of theory choice, the period when they are most needed but when, on the traditional view, they function badly or not at all. Copernicus was responding to them during the years required to convert heliocentric astronomy from a global conceptual scheme to mathematical machinery for predicting planetary position. Such predictions were what astronomers valued; in their absence, Copernicus would scarcely have been heard, something which had happened to the idea of a moving earth before. That his own version convinced very few is less important than his acknowledgment of the basis on which judgments would have to be reached if heliocentricism were to survive. Though idiosyncrasy must be invoked to explain why Kepler and Galileo were early converts to Copernicus's system, the gaps filled by their efforts to perfect it were specified by shared values alone.

That point has a corollary which may be more important still. Most newly suggested theories do not survive. Usually the difficulties that evoked them are accounted for by more traditional means. Even when this does not occur, much work, both theoretical and experimental, is ordinarily required before the new theory can display sufficient accuracy and scope to generate widespread conviction. In short, before the group accepts it, a new theory has been tested over time by the research of a number of men, some working within it, others within its traditional rival. Such a mode of development, however, *requires* a decision process which permits rational men to disagree, and such disagreement would be barred by the shared algorithm which philosophers have generally sought. If it were at hand, all conforming scientists would make the same decision at the same time. With standards for acceptance set too low, they would move from one attractive global viewpoint to another, never giving traditional theory an opportunity to supply equivalent attractions. With standards set higher, no one satisfying the criterion of rationality would be inclined to try out the new theory, to articulate it in ways which showed its fruitfulness or displayed its accuracy and scope. I doubt that science would survive the change. What from one viewpoint may seem the looseness and imperfection of choice criteria conceived as rules may, when the same criteria are seen as values, appear an indispensable means of spreading the risk which the introduction or support of novelty always entails.

Even those who have followed me this far will want to know how a value-based enterprise of the sort I have described can develop as a science does, repeatedly producing powerful new techniques for prediction and control. To that question, unfortunately, I have no answer at all, but that is only another way of saying that I make no claim to have solved the problem of induction. If science did progress by virtue of some shared and binding algorithm of choice, I would be equally at a loss to explain its success. The lacuna is one I feel acutely, but its presence does not differentiate my position from the tradition.

It is, after all, no accident that my list of the values guiding scientific choice is, as nearly as makes any difference, identical with the tradition's list of rules dictating choice. Given any concrete situation to which the philosopher's rules could be applied, my values would function like his rules, producing the same choice. Any justification of induction, any explanation of why the rules worked, would apply equally to my values. Now consider a situation in which choice by shared rules proves impossible, not because the rules are wrong but because they are, as rules, intrinsically incomplete. Individuals must then still choose and be guided by the rules (now values) when they do so. For that purpose, however, each must first flesh out the rules, and each will do so in a somewhat different way even though the decision dictated by the variously completed rules may prove unanimous. If I now assume, in addition, that the group is large enough so that individual differences distribute on some normal curve, then any argument that justifies the philosopher's choice by rule should be immediately adaptable to my choice by value. A group too small, or a distribution excessively skewed by external historical pressures, would, of course, prevent the argument's transfer.[8] But those are just the circumstances under which scientific progress is itself problematic. The transfer is not then to be expected.

I shall be glad if these references to a normal distribution of individual differences and to the problem of induction make my position appear very close to more traditional views. With respect to theory choice, I have never thought my departures large and have been correspondingly startled by such charges as "mob psychology," quoted at the start. It is worth

8. If the group is small, it is more likely that random fluctuations will result in its members' sharing an atypical set of values and therefore making choices different from those that would be made by a larger and more representative group. External environment—intellectual, ideological, or economic—must systematically affect the value system of much larger groups, and the consequences can include difficulties in introducing the scientific enterprise to societies with inimical values or perhaps even the end of that enterprise within societies where it had once flourished. In this area, however, great caution is required. Changes in the environment where science is practiced can also have fruitful effects on research. Historians often resort, for example, to differences between national environments to explain why particular innovations were initiated and at first disproportionately pursued in particular countries, e.g., Darwinism in Britain, energy conservation in Germany. At present we know substantially nothing about the minimum requisites of the social milieux within which a sciencelike enterprise might flourish.

noting, however, that the positions are not quite identical, and for that purpose an analogy may be helpful. Many properties of liquids and gases can be accounted for on the kinetic theory by supposing that all molecules travel at the same speed. Among such properties are the regularities known as Boyle's and Charles's law. Other characteristics, most obviously evaporation, cannot be explained in so simple a way. To deal with them one must assume that molecular speeds differ, that they are distributed at random, governed by the laws of chance. What I have been suggesting here is that theory choice, too, can be explained only in part by a theory which attributes the same properties to all the scientists who must do the choosing. Essential aspects of the process generally known as verification will be understood only by recourse to the features with respect to which men may differ while still remaining scientists. The tradition takes it for granted that such features are vital to the process of discovery, which it at once and for that reason rules out of philosophical bounds. That they may have significant functions also in the philosophically central problem of justifying theory choice is what philosophers of science have to date categorically denied.

What remains to be said can be grouped in a somewhat miscellaneous epilogue. For the sake of clarity and to avoid writing a book, I have throughout this paper utilized some traditional concepts and locutions about the viability of which I have elsewhere expressed serious doubts. For those who know the work in which I have done so, I close by indicating three aspects of what I have said which would better represent my views if cast in other terms, simultaneously indicating the main directions in which such recasting should proceed. The areas I have in mind are: value invariance, subjectivity, and partial communication. If my views of scientific development are novel—a matter about which there is legitimate room for doubt—it is in areas such as these, rather than theory choice, that my main departures from tradition should be sought.

Throughout this paper I have implicitly assumed that, whatever their initial source, the criteria or values deployed in theory choice are fixed once and for all, unaffected by their participation in transitions from one theory to another. Roughly speaking, but only very roughly, I take that to be the case. If the list of relevant values is kept short (I have mentioned five, not all independent) and if their specification is left vague, then such values as accuracy, scope, and fruitfulness are permanent attributes of science. But little knowledge of history is required to suggest that both the application of these values and, more obviously, the relative weights attached to them have varied markedly with time and also with the field of application. Furthermore, many of these variations in value have been associated with particular changes in scientific theory. Though the experience of scientists provides no philosophical justification for the values they deploy (such justification would solve the problem of induction), those values are in part learned from that experience, and they evolve with it.

The whole subject needs more study (historians have usually taken scientific values, though not scientific methods, for granted), but a few remarks will illustrate the sort of variations I have in mind. Accuracy, as a value, has with time increasingly denoted quantitative or numerical agreement, sometimes at the expense of qualitative. Before early modern times, however, accuracy in that sense was a criterion only for astronomy, the science of the celestial region. Elsewhere it was neither expected nor sought. During the seventeenth century, however, the criterion of numerical agreement was extended to mechanics, during the late eighteenth and early nineteenth centuries to chemistry and such other subjects as electricity and heat, and in this century to many parts of biology. Or think of utility, an item of value not on my initial list. It too has figured significantly in scientific development, but far more strongly and steadily for chemists than for, say, mathematicians and physicists. Or consider scope. It is still an important scientific value, but important scientific advances have repeatedly been achieved at its expense, and the weight attributed to it at times of choice has diminished correspondingly.

What may seem particularly troublesome about changes like these is, of course, that they ordinarily occur in the aftermath of a theory change. One of the objections to Lavoisier's new chemistry was the roadblocks with which it confronted the achievement of what had previously been one of chemistry's traditional goals: the explanation of qualities, such as color and texture, as well as of their changes. With the acceptance of Lavoisier's theory such explanations ceased for some time to be a value for chemists; the ability to explain qualitative variation was no longer a criterion relevant to the evaluation of chemical theory. Clearly, if such value changes had occurred as rapidly or been as complete as the theory changes to which they related, then theory choice would be value choice, and neither could provide justification for the other. But, historically, value change is ordinarily a belated and largely unconscious concomitant of theory choice, and the former's magnitude is regularly smaller than the latter's. For the functions I have here ascribed to values, such relative stability provides a sufficient basis. The existence of a feedback loop through which theory change affects the values which led to that change does not make the decision process circular in any damaging sense.

About a second respect in which my resort to tradition may be misleading, I must be far more tentative. It demands the skills of an ordinary language philosopher, which I do not possess. Still, no very acute ear for language is required to generate discomfort with the ways in which the terms "objectivity" and, more especially, "subjectivity" have functioned in this paper. Let me briefly suggest the respects in which I believe language has gone astray. "Subjective" is a term with several established uses: In one of these it is opposed to "objective," in another to "judgmental." When my critics describe the idiosyncratic features to which I appeal as subjective, they resort, erroneously I think, to the second of these senses. When they complain that I deprive science of objectivity, they conflate that second sense of subjective with the first.

A standard application of the term "subjective" is to matters of taste, and my critics appear to suppose that that is what I have made of theory choice. But they are missing a distinction standard since Kant when they do so. Like sensation reports, which are also subjective in the sense now at issue, matters of taste are undiscussable. Suppose that, leaving a movie theater with a friend after seeing a western, I exclaim: "How I liked that terrible potboiler!" My friend, if he disliked the film, may tell me I have low tastes, a matter about which, in these circumstances, I would readily agree. But, short of saying that I lied, he cannot disagree with my report that I liked the film or try to persuade me that what I said about my reaction was wrong. What is discussable in my remark is not my characterization of my internal state, my exemplification of taste, but rather my judgment that the film was a potboiler. Should my friend disagree on that point, we may argue most of the night, each comparing the film with good or great ones we have seen, each revealing, implicitly or explicitly, something about how he *judges* cinematic merit, about his aesthetic. Though one of us may, before retiring, have persuaded the other, he need not have done so to demonstrate that our difference is one of judgment, not taste.

Evaluations or choices of theory have, I think, exactly this character. Not that scientists never say merely, I like such and such a theory, or I do not. After 1926 Einstein said little more than that about his opposition to the quantum theory. But scientists may always be asked to explain their choices, to exhibit the bases for their judgments. Such judgments are eminently discussable, and the man who refuses to discuss his own cannot expect to be taken seriously. Though there are, very occasionally, leaders of scientific taste, their existence tends to prove the rule. Einstein was one of the few, and his increasing isolation from the scientific community in later life shows how very limited a role taste alone can play in theory choice. Bohr, unlike Einstein, did discuss the bases for his judgment, and he carried the day. If my critics introduce the term "subjective" in a sense that opposes it to judgmental—thus suggesting that I make theory choice undiscussable, a matter of taste—they have seriously mistaken my position.

Turn now to the sense in which "subjectivity" is opposed to "objectivity," and note first that it raises issues quite separate from those just discussed. Whether my taste is low or refined, my report that I liked the film is objective unless I have lied. To my judgment that the film was a potboiler, however, the objective–subjective distinction does not apply at all, at least not obviously and directly. When my critics say I deprive theory choice of objectivity, they must, therefore, have recourse to some very different sense of subjective, presumably the one in which bias and personal likes or dislikes function instead of, or in the face of, the actual facts. But that sense of subjective does not fit the process I have been describing any better than the first. Where factors dependent on individual biography or personality must be introduced to make values applicable, no standards of factuality or actuality are being set aside. Conceivably my discussion of theory choice indicates some limitations of objectivity, but not by isolating elements properly called subjective. Nor am I even quite content with the notion that what I have been displaying are limitations. Objectivity ought to be analyzable in terms of criteria like accuracy and consistency. If these criteria do not supply all the guidance that we have customarily expected of them, then it may be the meaning rather than the limits of objectivity that my argument shows.

Turn, in conclusion, to a third respect, or set of respects, in which this paper needs to be recast. I have assumed throughout that the discussions surrounding theory choice are unproblematic, that the facts appealed to in such discussions are independent of theory, and that the discussions' outcome is appropriately called a choice. Elsewhere I have challenged all three of these assumptions, arguing that communication between proponents of different theories is inevitably partial, that what each takes to be facts depends in part on the theory he espouses, and that an individual's transfer of allegiance from theory to theory is often better described as conversion than as choice. Though all these theses are problematic as well as controversial, my commitment to them is undiminished. I shall not now defend them, but must at least attempt to indicate how what I have said here can be adjusted to conform with these more central aspects of my view of scientific development.

For that purpose I resort to an analogy I have developed in other places. Proponents of different theories are, I have claimed, like native speakers of different languages. Communication between them goes on by translation, and it raises all translation's familiar difficulties. That analogy is, of course, incomplete, for the vocabulary of the two theories may be identical, and most words function in the same ways in both. But some words in the basic as well as in the theoretical vocabularies of the two theories—words like "star" and "planet," "mixture" and "compound," or "force" and "matter"—do function differently. Those differences are unexpected and will be discovered and localized, if at all, only by repeated experience of communication breakdown. Without pursuing the matter further, I simply assert the existence of significant limits to what the proponents of different theories can communicate to one another. The same limits make it difficult or, more likely, impossible for an individual to hold both theories in mind together and compare them point by point with each other and with nature. That sort of comparison is, however, the process on which the appropriateness of any word like "choice" depends.

Nevertheless, despite the incompleteness of their communication, proponents of different theories can exhibit to each other, not always easily, the concrete technical results achievable by those who practice within each theory. Little or no translation is required to apply at least some value criteria to those results. (Accuracy and fruitfulness are most immediately applicable, perhaps followed by scope. Consistency and simplicity are far more problematic.) However incomprehensible the new theory may be to the proponents of tradition, the exhibit of impressive concrete results will persuade at least a few of them that they must discover how such results are achieved. For that purpose they must learn to translate, perhaps by treating already published papers as a Rosetta stone or, often more effective, by visiting the innovator, talking with him, watching him and his students at work. Those exposures may not result in the adoption of the theory; some advocates of the tradition may return home and attempt to adjust the old theory to produce equivalent results. But others, if the new theory is to survive, will find that at some point in the language-learning process they have ceased to translate and begun instead to speak the language like a native. No process quite like choice has occurred, but they are practicing the new theory nonetheless. Furthermore, the factors that have led them to risk the conversion they have undergone are just the ones this paper has underscored in discussing a somewhat different process, one which, following the philosophical tradition, it has labeled theory choice.

Chapter 12

W. V. O. QUINE

Willard van Orman Quine (1908–   ) was born in Akron, Ohio, and studied at Oberlin College, Oxford University, and Harvard University, where he also taught until his recent retirement. Quine's "Two Dogmas of Empiricism" is one of the most influential philosophy articles of the twentieth century. In the first part of the article he seeks to undermine the distinction made, from Kant to the logical positivists, between analytic and synthetic statements. One version of the distinction rests on the notion of containment: the predicate term is contained in the subject term. Quine contends that the notion of containment is a vague metaphor, and that its vagueness spreads over the entire analytic/synthetic distinction. Furthermore, the concept of *analyticity* rests on the concept of *synonymy*, having the same meaning. That is, if it is analytic that "A bachelor is an unmarried man," this is because the terms *bachelor* and *unmarried* are already synonymous. But Quine argues that to say that these terms are synonymous is already to presuppose that they are analytic. Hence the argument is circular.

In the second part of the article, Quine attacks the notion of radical reductionism ("the second dogma"), which is tied to the positivists' verification theory of meaning and assumes that individual observation statements are the basic units of meaning. Quine rejects this atomist view of meaning, holding instead a holistic, pragmatic Coherentism. All our significant beliefs form a holistic web, so that individual statements are never confirmed or falsified in isolation but only with reference to this larger system. The most successful system of our beliefs is that of science, because it allows us so make correct predictions ("it keeps her planes up in the air"). This coherentist pragmatic feature also has an individual dimension, such as we saw in Kuhn's work (Chapter 11). We make individual judgments against a background of assumptions; we can accommodate counter ("falsifying") evidence by making adjustments elsewhere in the system. On the other hand once we allow for adjustment in a system, a chain reaction may occur, so that no belief, not even those concerning the laws of logic, is safe from alteration and even rejection. Quine now regards his second challenge, his holism, as the more important of his challenges ("true villain of the piece"). In a recent interview, he said,

> Holism is inevitable once we reflect on the experimental method. A scientific hypothesis rarely implies, single-handed, what observable results to expect from the observable conditions set up in an experiment. In order to clinch such an implication the scientist has to draw on his background of scientific theory, common sense, and mathematics. What implies the observables is a big bundle of stated and unstated assumptions and beliefs. It is not, however, the whole of science, as Hegel would have it. It is a question only of a critical mass: a big enough fragment of science to imply what to expect from some observation or experiment. The size will vary from case to case. This moderate holism is scarcely debatable, irrespective of its advantages; but there are advantages too, in that it solves two riddles regarding mathematical truth. How, Carnap asked, can mathematics be meaningful despite lacking empirical context? His answer was that mathematics was analytic. Holism's answer is that mathematics, insofar as applied in science, imbibes the shared

> empirical content of the critical masses to which it contributes. Second riddle: why is mathematics necessary rather than contingent? Carnap's answer again was analyticity. Holism's answer is that when a critical mass of sentences jointly implies a false prediction, we are free to choose what component sentence to revoke so as to defuse the implication. In so choosing we choose to safeguard any purely mathematical truths, among those sentences, since disturbing them would disturb science excessively in all its branches. We are guided by the maxim of minimum mutilation, and it is this sparing of mathematics that accounts for its apparent necessity. So we see how holism solves two riddles that had been primary motives for Carnap's insistence on the notion of analyticity, the first of these two dogmas. I said earlier that I now see the second dogma as the true villain of the piece, and this is why. Once we appreciate holism, even moderate holism, the notion of analyticity ceases to be vital to epistemology.[1]

In our second selection Quine argues that epistemology centered in normative justification (of belief) is dead. Because foundationalism (especially Carnap's ambitious project) failed as an attempt to ground our knowledge claims, we should give up traditional epistemology and concentrate on empirical psychology. Whereas "old epistemology aspired to contain natural science, epistemology in its new setting, conversely, is contained in natural science, as a chapter of psychology." This new epistemology-psychology turns into the descriptive examination of the relation "between the meager input [our sensory simulation] and the torrential output [our three-dimensional picture of the world]." With the demise of "old epistemology" goes all concern with normativity and justification of belief.

In our third selection Quine raises doubts about our notions of a theory of meaning and of an objective ontology—what there is—arguing, by use of a tribe's word *gavagai* (which we translate as "rabbit," but could be construed by the native as meaning "undetached rabbit part") that there is no easy way to decide what the meaning of a word is for another person or tribe. Quine adopts a behavioral theory of meaning. What counts as the meaning of a locution is the behavior that follows from it. Indeterminacy of translation and inscrutability of reference imply that there is no certain way to say what a theory or sentence is about.

Quine's work has provoked a mountain of responses. For a critique of this internalist view of meaning, see Hilary Putnam's "Meaning and Reference" (Chapter 19). For a wider critique of Quine's views and arguments in these and other essays, see Jonathan Harrison's "A Defense of Empiricism" (Reading 14).

FOR FURTHER READING

Davidson, Donald and Jaakko Hintikka, eds. *Words and Objections: Essays on the Work of W. V. Quine* (Reidel, 1969).
Gibson, Roger. *The Philosophy of W. V. Quine* (University of Florida, 1982).
Hahn, Lewis and P. A. Schilpp, eds. *The Philosophy of W. V. Quine* (Open Court, 1986).
Hookway, Christopher. *Quine: Language, Experience, and Reality* (Stanford University Press, 1988).
Orenstein, Alex. *Willard van Orman Quine* (Twayne Publishers, 1977).
Quine, W. V. *From a Logical Point of View* (Harvard University, 1958).
———. *Ontological Relativity* (Columbia University Press, 1977).
Romanas, George. *Quine and Analytic Philosophy* (MIT Press, 1983).

1. Quoted in Andrew Pyle, ed., *Key Philosophers in Conversation*, (Routledge, 1999), p. 22.

Two Dogmas of Empiricism

Modern empiricism has been conditioned in large part by two dogmas. One is a belief in some fundamental cleavage between truths which are *analytic*, or grounded in meanings independently of matters of fact, and truths which are *synthetic*, or grounded in fact. The other dogma is *reductionism*: the belief that each meaningful statement is equivalent to some logical construct upon terms which refer to immediate experience. Both dogmas, I shall argue, are ill-founded. One effect of abandoning them is, as we shall see, a blurring of the supposed boundary between speculative metaphysics and natural science. Another effect is a shift toward pragmatism.

1. BACKGROUND FOR ANALYTICITY

Kant's cleavage between analytic and synthetic truths was foreshadowed in Hume's distinction between relations of ideas and matters of fact, and in Leibniz's distinction between truths of reason and truths of fact. Leibniz spoke of the truths of reason as true in all possible worlds. Picturesqueness aside, this is to say that the truths of reason are those which could not possibly be false. In the same vein we hear analytic statements defined as statements whose denials are self-contradictory. But this definition has small explanatory value; for the notion of self-contradictoriness, in the quite broad sense needed for this definition of analyticity, stands in exactly the same need of clarification as does the notion of analyticity itself. The two notions are the two sides of a single dubious coin.

Kant conceived of an analytic statement as one that attributes to its subject no more than is already conceptually contained in the subject. This formulation has two shortcomings: it limits itself to statements of subject-predicate form, and it appeals to a notion of containment which is left at a metaphorical level. But Kant's intent, evident more from the use he makes of the notion of analyticity than from his definition of it, can be restated thus: a statement is analytic when it is true by virtue of meanings and independently of fact. Pursuing this line, let us examine the concept of *meaning* which is presupposed.

Meaning, let us remember, is not to be identified with naming. Frege's example of 'Evening Star' and 'Morning Star', and Russell's of 'Scott' and 'the author of *Waverley*', illustrate that terms can name the same thing but differ in meaning. The distinction between meaning and naming is no less important at the level of abstract terms. The terms '9' and 'the number of the planets' name one and the same abstract entity but presumably must be regarded as unlike in meaning; for astronomical observation was needed, and not mere reflection on meanings, to determine the sameness of the entity in question.

The above examples consist of singular terms, concrete and abstract. With general terms, or predicates, the situation is somewhat different but parallel. Whereas a singular term purports to name an entity, abstract or concrete, a general term does not; but a general term is *true* of an entity, or of each of many, or of none. The class of all entities of which a general term is true is called the *extension* of the term. Now paralleling the contrast between the meaning of a singular term and the entity named, we must distinguish equally between the meaning of a general term and its extension. The general terms 'creature with a heart' and 'creature with kidneys', for example, are perhaps alike in extension but unlike in meaning.

Confusion of meaning with extension, in the case of general terms, is less common than confusion of meaning with naming in the case of singular terms. It is indeed a commonplace in philosophy to oppose intension (or meaning) to extension, or, in a variant vocabulary, connotation to denotation.

The Aristotelian notion of essence was the forerunner, no doubt, of the modern notion of intension or meaning. For Aristotle it was essential in men to be rational, accidental to be two-legged. But there is an important difference between this attitude and the doctrine of meaning. From the latter point of view it may indeed be conceded (if only for the sake of argument) that rationality is involved in the meaning of the word 'man' while two-leggedness is not;

but two-leggedness may at the same time be viewed as involved in the meaning of 'biped' while rationality is not. Thus from the point of view of the doctrine of meaning it makes no sense to say of the actual individual, who is at once a man and a biped, that his rationality is essential and his two-leggedness accidental or vice versa. Things had essences, for Aristotle, but only linguistic forms have meanings. Meaning is what essence becomes when it is divorced from the object of reference and wedded to the word.

For the theory of meaning a conspicuous question is the nature of its objects: what sort of things are meanings? A felt need for meant entities may derive from an earlier failure to appreciate that meaning and reference are distinct. Once the theory of meaning is sharply separated from the theory of reference, it is a short step to recognizing as the primary business of the theory of meaning simply the synonymy of linguistic forms and the analyticity of statements; meanings themselves, as obscure intermediary entities, may well be abandoned.

The problem of analyticity then confronts us anew. Statements which are analytic by general philosophical acclaim are not, indeed, far to seek. They fall into two classes. Those of the first class, which may be called *logically true*, are typified by:

(1) No unmarried man is married.

The relevant feature of this example is that it not merely is true as it stands, but remains true under any and all reinterpretations of 'man' and 'married'. If we suppose a prior inventory of *logical* particles, comprising 'no', 'un-', 'not', 'if', 'then', 'and', etc., then in general a logical truth is a statement which is true and remains true under all reinterpretations of its components other than the logical particles.

But there is also a second class of analytic statements, typified by:

(2) No bachelor is married.

The characteristic of such a statement is that it can be turned into a logical truth by putting synonyms for synonyms; thus (2) can be turned into (1) by putting 'unmarried man' for its synonym 'bachelor'. We still lack a proper characterization of this second class of analytic statements, and therewith of analyticity generally, inasmuch as we have had in the above description to lean on a notion of 'synonymy' which is no less in need of clarification than analyticity itself.

In recent years Carnap has tended to explain analyticity by appeal to what he calls state-descriptions.[1] A state-description is any exhaustive assignment of truth values to the atomic, or non-compound, statements of the language. All other statements of the language are, Carnap assumes, built up of their component clauses by means of the familiar logical devices, in such a way that the truth value of any complex statement is fixed for each state-description by specifiable logical laws. A statement is then explained as analytic when it comes out true under every state-description. This account is an adaptation of Leibniz's 'true in all possible worlds'. But note that this version of analyticity serves its purpose only if the atomic statements of the language are, unlike 'John is a bachelor' and 'John is married', mutually independent. Otherwise there would be a state-description which assigned truth to 'John is a bachelor' and to 'John is married', and consequently 'No bachelors are married' would turn out synthetic rather than analytic under the proposed criterion. Thus the criterion of analyticity in terms of state-descriptions serves only for languages devoid of extra-logical synonym-pairs, such as 'bachelor' and 'unmarried man'—synonym-pairs of the type which give rise to the 'second class' of analytic statements. The criterion in terms of state-descriptions is a reconstruction at best of logical truth, not of analyticity.

I do not mean to suggest that Carnap is under any illusions on this point. His simplified model language with its state-descriptions is aimed primarily not at the general problem of analyticity but at another purpose, the clarification of probability and induction. Our problem, however, is analyticity; and here the major difficulty lies not in the first class of analytic statements, the logical truths, but rather in the second class, which depends on the notion of synonymy.

2. DEFINITION

There are those who find it soothing to say that the analytic statements of the second class reduce to those of the first class, the logical truths, by *definition*; 'bachelor', for example, is *defined* as 'unmarried man'. But how do we find that 'bachelor' is defined as 'unmarried man'? Who defined it thus, and

1. Carnap (3), pp. 9 ff; (4), pp. 70 ff.

when? Are we to appeal to the nearest dictionary, and accept the lexicographer's formulation as law? Clearly this would be to put the cart before the horse. The lexicographer is an empirical scientist, whose business is the recording of antecedent facts; and if he glosses 'bachelor' as 'unmarried man' it is because of his belief that there is a relation of synonymy between those forms, implicit in general or preferred usage prior to his own work. The notion of synonymy presupposed here has still to be clarified, presumably in terms relating to linguistic behaviour. Certainly the 'definition' which is the lexicographer's report of an observed synonymy cannot be taken as the ground of the synonymy.

Definition is not, indeed, an activity exclusively of philologists. Philosophers and scientists frequently have occasion to "define" a recondite term by paraphrasing it into terms of a more familiar vocabulary. But ordinarily such a definition, like the philologist's, is pure lexicography, affirming a relation of synonymy antecedent to the exposition in hand.

Just what it means to affirm synonymy, just what the interconnections may be which are necessary and sufficient in order that two linguistic forms be properly describable as synonymous, is far from clear; but, whatever these interconnections may be, ordinarily they are grounded in usage. Definitions reporting selected instances of synonymy come then as reports upon usage.

There is also, however, a variant type of definitional activity which does not limit itself to the reporting of pre-existing synonymies. I have in mind what Carnap calls *explication*—an activity to which philosophers are given, and scientists also in their more philosophical moments. In explication the purpose is not merely to paraphrase the definiendum into an outright synonym, but actually to improve upon the definiendum by refining or supplementing its meaning. But even explication, though not merely reporting a pre-existing synonymy between definiendum and definiens, does rest, nevertheless, on *other* pre-existing synonymies. The matter may be viewed as follows. Any word worth explicating has some contexts which, as wholes, are clear and precise enough to be useful; and the purpose of explication is to preserve the usage of these favoured contexts while sharpening the usage of other contexts. In order that a given definition be suitable for purposes of explication, therefore, what is required is not that the definiendum in its antecedent usage be synonymous with the definiens, but just that each of these favoured contexts of the definiendum, taken as a whole in its antecedent usage, be synonymous with the corresponding context of the definiens.

Two alternative definientia may be equally appropriate for the purposes of a given task of explication and yet not be synonymous with each other; for they may serve interchangeably within the favoured contexts but diverge elsewhere. By cleaving to one of these definientia rather than the other, a definition of explicative kind generates, by fiat, a relation of synonymy between definiendum and definiens which did not hold before. But such a definition still owes its explicative function, as seen, to pre-existing synonymies.

There does, however, remain still an extreme sort of definition which does not hark back to prior synonymies at all: namely, the explicitly conventional introduction of novel notations for purposes of sheer abbreviation. Here the definiendum becomes synonymous with the definiens simply because it has been created expressly for the purpose of being synonymous with the definiens. Here we have a really transparent case of synonymy created by definition; would that all species of synonymy were as intelligible. For the rest, definition rests on synonymy rather than explaining it.

The word 'definition' has come to have a dangerously reassuring sound, owing no doubt to its frequent occurrence in logical and mathematical writings. We shall do well to digress now into a brief appraisal of the role of definition in formal work.

In logical and mathematical systems either of two mutually antagonistic types of economy may be striven for, and each has its peculiar practical utility. On the one hand, we may seek economy of practical expression—ease and brevity in the statement of multi-farious relations. This sort of economy calls usually for distinctive concise notations for a wealth of concepts. Second, however, and oppositely, we may seek economy in grammar and vocabulary; we may try to find a minimum of basic concepts such that, once a distinctive notation has been appropriated to each of them, it becomes possible to express any desired further concept by mere combination and iteration of our basic notations. This second sort of economy is impractical in one way, since a poverty in basic idioms tends to a necessary lengthening of discourse. But it is practical in another way: it greatly simplifies theoretical discourse *about* the language, through minimizing the terms and the forms of construction wherein the language consists.

Both sorts of economy, though prima facie incompatible, are valuable in their separate ways. The custom has consequently arisen of combining both sorts of economy by forging in effect two languages, the one a part of the other. The inclusive language, though redundant in grammar and vocabulary, is economical in message lengths, while the part, called primitive notation, is economical in grammar and vocabulary. Whole and part are correlated by rules of translation whereby each idiom not in primitive notation is equated to some complex built up of primitive notation. These rules of translation are the so-called *definitions* which appear in formalized systems. They are best viewed not as adjuncts to one language but as correlations between two languages, the one a part of the other.

But these correlations are not arbitrary. They are supposed to show how the primitive notations can accomplish all purposes, save brevity and convenience, of the redundant language. Hence the definiendum and its definiens may be expected, in each case, to be related in one or another of the three ways lately noted. The definiens may be a faithful paraphrase of the definiendum into the narrower notation, preserving a direct synonymy[2] as of antecedent usage; or the definiens may, in the spirit of explication, improve upon the antecedent usage of the definiendum; or finally, the definiendum may be a newly created notation, newly endowed with meaning here and now.

In formal and informal work alike, thus, we find that definition—except in the extreme case of the explicitly conventional introduction of new notations—hinges on prior relations of synonymy. Recognizing then that the notion of definition does not hold the key to synonymy and analyticity, let us look further into synonymy and say no more of definition.

3. INTERCHANGEABILITY

A natural suggestion, deserving close examination, is that the synonymy of two lingustic forms consists simply in their interchangeability in all contexts without change of truth value—interchangeability, in Leibniz's phrase, *salva veritate*.[3] Note that synonyms so conceived need not even be free from vagueness, as long as the vaguenesses match.

But it is not quite true that the synonyms 'bachelor' and 'unmarried man' are everywhere interchangeable *salva veritate*. Truths which become false under substitution of 'unmarried man' for 'bachelor' are easily constructed with the help of 'bachelor of arts' or 'bachelor's buttons'; also with the help of quotation, thus:

'Bachelor' has less than ten letters.

Such counter-instances can, however, perhaps be set aside by treating the phrases 'bachelor of arts' and 'bachelor's buttons' and the quotation '"bachelor"' each as a single indivisible word and then stipulating that the interchangeability *salva veritate* which is to be the touchstone of synonymy is not supposed to apply to fragmentary occurrences inside of a word. This account of synonymy, supposing it acceptable on other counts, has indeed the drawback of appealing to a prior conception of 'word' which can be counted on to present difficulties of formulation in its turn. Nevertheless, some progress might be claimed in having reduced the problem of synonymy to a problem of wordhood. Let us pursue this line a bit, taking 'word' for granted.

The question remains whether interchangeability *salva veritate* (apart from occurrences within words) is a strong enough condition for synonymy, or whether, on the contrary, some heteronymous expressions might be thus interchangeable. Now let us be clear that we are not concerned here with synonymy in the sense of complete identity in psychological associations or poetic quality; indeed no two expressions are synonymous in such a sense. We are concerned only with what may be called *cognitive* synonymy. Just what this is cannot be said without successfully finishing the present study; but we know something about it from the need which arose for it in connection with analyticity in §1. The sort of synonymy needed there was merely such that any analytic statement could be turned into a logical truth by putting synonyms for synonyms. Turning the tables and assuming analyticity, indeed, we could explain cognitive synonymy of terms as follows (keeping to the familiar example): to say that 'bachelor' and 'unmarried man' are cognitively synonymous is to say no more nor less than that the statement:

2. According to an important variant sense of 'definition', the relation preserved may be the weaker relation of mere agreement in reference. But definition in this sense is better ignored in the present connection, being irrelevant to the question of synonymy.
3. Cf. Lewis (I), p. 373.

(3) All and only bachelors are unmarried men is analytic.[4]

What we need is an account of cognitive synonymy not presupposing analyticity—if we are to explain analyticity conversely with help of cognitive synonymy as undertaken in §1. And indeed such an independent account of cognitive synonymy is at present up for consideration, namely, interchangeability *salva veritate* everywhere except within words. The question before us, to resume the thread at last, is whether such interchangeability is a sufficient condition for cognitive synonymy. We can quickly assure ourselves that it is, by examples of the following sort. The statement:

(4) Necessarily all and only bachelors are bachelors

is evidently true, even supposing 'necessarily' so narrowly construed as to be truly applicable only to analytic statements. Then, if 'bachelor' and 'unmarried man' are interchangeable *salva veritate*, the result:

(5) Necessarily all and only bachelors are unmarried men

of putting 'unmarried man' for an occurrence of 'bachelor' in (4) must, like (4), be true. But to say that (5) is true is to say that (3) is analytic, and hence that 'bachelor' and 'unmarried man' are cognitively synonymous.

Let us see what there is about the above argument that gives it its air of hocus-pocus. The condition of interchangeability *salva veritate* varies in its force with variations in the richness of the language at hand. The above argument supposes we are working with a language rich enough to contain the adverb 'necessarily', this adverb being so construed as to yield truth when and only when applied to an analytic statement. But can we condone a language which contains such an adverb? Does the adverb really make sense? To suppose that it does is to suppose that we have already made satisfactory sense of 'analytic'. Then what are we so hard at work on right now?

Our argument is not flatly circular, but something like it. It has the form, figuratively speaking, of a closed curve in space.

Interchangeability *salva veritate* is meaningless until relativized to a language whose extent is specified in relevant respects. Suppose now we consider a language containing just the following materials. There is an indefinitely large stock of one-place predicates (for example, '*F*' where '*Fx*' means that *x* is a man) and many-place predicates (for example, '*G*' where '*Gxy*' means that *x* loves *y*), mostly having to do with extra-logical subject-matter. The rest of the language is logical. The atomic sentences consist each of a predicate followed by one or more variables '*x*', '*y*', etc.; and the complex sentences are built up of the atomic ones by truth functions ('not', 'and', 'or', etc.) and quantification. In effect such a language enjoys the benefits also of descriptions and indeed singualr terms generally, these being contextually definable in known ways. Even abstract singular terms naming classes, classes of classes, etc., are contextually definable in case the assumed stock of predicates includes the two-place predicate of class membership. Such a language can be adequate to classical mathematics and indeed to scientific discourse generally, except in so far as the latter involves debatable devices such as contrary-to-fact conditionals or modal adverbs like 'necessarily'. Now a language of this type is extensional, in this sense: any two predicates which agree extensionally (that is, are true of the same objects) are interchangeable *salva veritate*.[5]

In an extensional language, therefore, interchangeability *salva veritate* is no assurance of cognitive synonymy of the desired type. That 'bachelor' and 'unmarried man' are interchangeable *salva veritate* in an extensional language assures us of no more than that (3) is true. There is no assurance here that the extensional agreement of 'bachelor' and 'unmarried man' rests on meaning rather than merely on accidental matters of fact, as does the extensional agreement of 'creature with a heart' and 'creature with kidneys'.

For most purposes extensional agreement is the nearest approximation to synonymy we need care about. But the fact remains that extensional agreement falls far short of cognitive synonymy of the type required for explaining analyticity in the manner of §1. The type of cognitive synonymy required

4. This is cognitive synonymy in a primary, broad sense. Carnap ((3), pp. 56 ff.) and Lewis ((2), pp. 83 ff.) have suggested how, once this notion is at hand, a narrower sense of cognitive synonymy which is preferable for some purposes can in turn be derived. But this special ramification of concept-building lies aside from the present purposes and must not be confused with the broad sort of cognitive synonymy here concerned.

5. This is the substance of Quine (1), *121.

there is such as to equate the synonymy of 'bachelor' and 'unmarried man' with the analyticity of (3), not merely with the truth of (3).

So we must recognize that interchangeability *salva veritate*, if construed in relation to an extensional language, is not a sufficient condition of cognitive synonymy in the sense needed for deriving analyticity in the manner of §1. If a language contains an intensional adverb 'necessarily' in the sense lately noted, or other particles to the same effect, then interchangeability *salva veritate* in such a language does afford a sufficient condition of cognitive synonymy; but such a language is intelligible only in so far as the notion of analyticity is already understood in advance.

The effort to explain cognitive synonymy first, for the sake of deriving analyticity from it afterward as in §1, is perhaps the wrong approach. Instead we might try explaining analyticity somehow without appeal to cognitive synonymy. Afterward we could doubtless derive cognitive synonymy from analyticity satisfactorily enough if desired. We have seen that cognitive synonymy of 'bachelor' and 'unmarried man' can be explained as analyticity of (3). The same explanation works for any pair of one-place predicates, of course, and it can be extended in obvious fashion to many-place predicates. Other syntactical categories can also be accommodated in fairly parallel fashion. Singular terms may be said to be cognitively synonymous when the statement of identity formed by putting '=' between them is analytic. Statements may be said simply to be cognitively synonymous when their biconditional (the result of joining them by 'if and only if') is analytic.[6] If we care to lump all categories into a single formulation, at the expense of assuming again the notion of 'word' which was appealed to early in this section, we can describe any two linguistic forms as cognitively synonymous when the two forms are interchangeable (apart from occurrences within 'words') *salva* (no longer *veritate* but) *analyticitate*. Certain technical questions arise, indeed, over cases of ambiguity or homonymy; let us not pause for them, however, for we are already digressing. Let us rather turn our backs on the problem of synonymy and address ourselves anew to that of analyticity.

6. The 'if and only if' itself is intended in the truth functional sense. See Carnap (3), p. 14.

4. SEMANTICAL RULES

Analyticity at first seemed most naturally definable by appeal to a realm of meanings. On refinement, the appeal to meanings gave way to an appeal to synonymy or definition. But definition turned out to be a will-o'-the-wisp, and synonymy turned out to be best understood only by dint of a prior appeal to analyticity itself. So we are back at the problem of analyticity.

I do not know whether the statement 'Everything green is extended' is analytic. Now does my indecision over this example really betray an incomplete understanding, an incomplete grasp of the 'meanings', of 'green' and 'extended'? I think not. The trouble is not with 'green' or 'extended', but with 'analytic'.

It is often hinted that the difficulty in separating analytic statements from synthetic ones in ordinary language is due to the vagueness of ordinary language and that the distinction is clear when we have a precise artificial language with explicit 'semantical rules'. This, however, as I shall now attempt to show, is a confusion.

The notion of analyticity about which we are worrying is a purported relation between statements and languages: a statement *S* is said to be *analytic* for a language *L*, and the problem is to make sense of this relation generally, that is, for variable '*S*' and '*L*'. The gravity of this problem is not perceptibly less for artificial languages than for natural ones. The problem of making sense of the idiom '*S* is analytic for *L*', with variable '*S*' and '*L*', retains its stubbornness even if we limit the range of the variable '*L*' to artificial languages. Let me now try to make this point evident.

For artificial languages and semantical rules we look naturally to the writings of Carnap. His semantical rules take various forms, and to make my point I shall have to distinguish certain of the forms. Let us suppose, to begin with, an artificial language L_0 whose semantical rules have the form explicitly of a specification, by recursion or otherwise, of all the analytic statements of L_0. The rules tell us that such and such statements, and only those, are the analytic statements of L_0. Now here the difficulty is simply that the rules contain the word 'analytic', which we do not understand! We understand what expressions the rules attribute analyticity to, but we do not understand what the rules attribute to those expressions. In short, before we can understand a rule which begins 'A statement S is analytic for language L_0 if and only if . . .', we must understand the general relative term 'analytic for'; we must understand 'S is analytic for L' where 'S' and 'L' are variables.

Alternatively we may, indeed, view the so-called rule as a conventional definition of a new simple symbol 'analytic-for-L_0', which might better be written untendentiously as 'K' so as not to seem to throw light on the interesting word 'analytic'. Obviously any number of classes K, M, N, etc. of statements of L_0 can be specified for various purposes or for no purpose; what does it mean to say that K, as against M, N, etc., is the class of the 'analytic' statements of L_0?

By saying what statements are analytic for L_0 we explain 'analytic-for-L_0' but not 'analytic', not 'analytic for'. We do not begin to explain the idiom 'S is analytic for L' with variables 'S' and 'L' even if we are content to limit the range of 'L' to the realm of artificial languages.

Actually we do know enough about the intended significance of 'analytic' to know that analytic statements are supposed to be true. Let us then turn to a second form of semantical rule, which says not that such and such statements are analytic but simply that such and such statements are included among the truths. Such a rule is not subject to the criticism of containing the un-understood word 'analytic'; and we may grant for the sake of argument that there is no difficulty over the broader term 'true'. A semantical rule of this second type, a rule of truth, is not supposed to specify all the truths of the language; it merely stipulates, recursively or otherwise, a certain multitude of statements which, along with others unspecified, are to count as true. Such a rule may be conceded to be quite clear. Derivatively, afterward, analyticity can be demarcated thus: a statement is analytic if it is (not merely true but) true according to the semantical rule.

Still there is really no progress. Instead of appealing to an unexplained word 'analytic', we are now appealing to an unexplained phrase 'semantical rule'. Not every true statement which says that the statements of some class are true can count as a semantical rule—otherwise *all* truths would be 'analytic' in the sense of being true according to semantical rules. Semantical rules are distinguishable, apparently, only by the fact of appearing on a page under the heading 'Semantical Rules'; and this heading is itself then meaningless.

We can say indeed that a statement is *analytic-for-L_0* if and only if it is true according to such and such specifically appended 'semantical rules', but then we find ourselves back at essentially the same case which was originally discussed: 'S is analytic-for-L_0 if and only if. . . .' Once we seek to explain 'S is analytic for L' generally for variable 'L' (even allowing limitation of 'L' to artificial languages), the explanation 'true according to the semantical rules of L' is unavailing; for the relative term 'semantical rule of' is as much in need of clarification, at least, as 'analytic for'.

It may be instructive to compare the notion of semantical rule with that of postulate. Relative to a given set of postulates, it is easy to say what a postulate is: it is a member of the set. Relative to a given set of semantical rules, it is equally easy to say what a semantical rule is. But given simply a notation, mathematical or otherwise, and indeed as thoroughly understood a notation as you please in point of the translations or truth conditions of its statements, who can say which of its true statements rank as postulates? Obviously the question is meaningless—as meaningless as asking which points in Ohio are starting-points. Any finite (or effectively specifiable infinite) selection of statements (preferably true ones, perhaps) is as much *a* set of postulates as any other. The word 'postulate' is significant only relative to an act of enquiry; we apply the word to a set of statements just in so far as we happen, for the year or the moment, to be thinking of those statements in relation to the statements which can be reached from them by some set of transformations to which we have seen fit to direct our attention. Now the notion of semantical rule is as sensible and meaningful as that of postulate, if conceived in a similarly relative spirit—relative, this time, to one or another particular enterprise of schooling unconversant persons in sufficient conditions for truth of statements of some natural or artificial language L. But from this point of view no one signalization of a subclass of the truths of L is intrinsically more a semantical rule than another; and, if 'analytic' means 'true by semantical rules', no one truth of L is analytic to the exclusion of another.[7]

It might conceivably be protested that an artificial language L (unlike a natural one) is a language in

7. The foregoing paragraph was not part of the present essay as originally published; it was prompted by Martin (see Bibliography).

the ordinary sense *plus* a set of explicit semantical rules—the whole constituting, let us say, an ordered pair; and that the semantical rules of *L* then are specifiable simply as the second component of the pair *L*. But, by the same token and more simply, we might construe an artificial language *L* outright as an ordered pair whose second component is the class of its analytic statements; and then the analytic statements of *L* become specifiable simply as the statements in the second component of *L*. Or better still, we might just stop tugging at our bootstraps altogether.

Not all the explanations of analyticity known to Carnap and his readers have been covered explicitly in the above considerations, but the extension to other forms is not hard to see. Just one additional factor should be mentioned which sometimes enters: sometimes the semantical rules are in effect rules of translation into ordinary language, in which case the analytic statements of the artificial language are in effect recognized as such from the analyticity of their specified translations in ordinary language. Here certainly there can be no thought of an illumination of the problem of analyticity from the side of the artificial language.

From the point of view of the problem of analyticity the notion of an artificial language with semantical rules is a *feu follet par excellence*. Semantical rules determining the analytic statements of an artificial language are of interest only in so far as we already understand the notion of analyticity; they are of no help in gaining this understanding.

Appeal to hypothetical languages of an artificially simple kind could conceivably be useful in clarifying analyticity, if the mental or behavioural or cultural factors relevant to analyticity—whatever they may be—were somehow sketched into the simplified model. But a model which takes analyticity merely as an irreducible character is unlikely to throw light on the problem of explicating analyticity.

It is obvious that truth in general depends on both language and extra-linguistic fact. The statement 'Brutus killed Caesar' would be false if the world had been different in certain ways, but it would also be false if the word 'killed' happened rather to have the sense of 'begat'. Thus one is tempted to suppose in general that the truth of a statement is somehow analysable into a linguistic component and a factual component. Given this supposition, it next seems reasonable that in some statements the factual component should be null; and these are the analytic statements. But, for all its a priori reasonableness, a boundary between analytic and synthetic statements simply has not been drawn. That there is such a distinction to be drawn at all is an unempirical dogma of empiricists, a metaphysical article of faith.

5. THE VERIFICATION THEORY AND REDUCTIONISM

In the course of these sombre reflections we have taken a dim view first of the notion of meaning, then of the notion of cognitive synonymy, and finally of the notion of analyticity. But what, it may be asked, of the verification theory of meaning? This phrase has established itself so firmly as a catchword of empiricism that we should be very unscientific indeed not to look beneath it for a possible key to the problem of meaning and the associated problems.

The verification theory of meaning, which has been conspicuous in the literature from Peirce onward, is that the meaning of a statement is the method of empiricially confirming or infirming it. An analytic statement is that limiting case which is confirmed no matter what.

As urged in §1, we can as well pass over the question of meanings as entities and move straight to sameness of meaning, or synonymy. Then what the verification theory says is that statements are synonymous if and only if they are alike in point of method of empirical confirmation or infirmation.

This is an account of cognitive synonymy not of linguistic forms generally, but of statements.[8] However, from the concept of synonymy of statements we could derive the concept of synonymy for other linguistic forms, by considerations somewhat similar to those at the end of §3. Assuming the notion of 'word', indeed, we could explain any two forms as synonymous when the putting of the one form for an occurrence of the other in any statement (apart from occurrences within 'words') yields a synonymous statement. Finally, given the concept of syn-

8. The doctrine can indeed be formulated with terms rather than statements as the units. Thus Lewis describes the meaning of a term as '*a criterion in mind*, by reference to which one is able to apply or refuse to apply the expression in question in the case of presented, or imagined, things or situations' ((2), p. 133). For an instructive account of the vicissitudes of the verification theory of meaning, centred however on the question of meaning*fulness* rather than synonymy and analyticity, see Hempel.

onymy thus for linguistic forms generally, we could define analyticity in terms of synonymy and logical truth as in §1. For that matter, we could define analyticity more simply in terms of just synonymy of statements together with logical truth; it is not necessary to appeal to synonymy of linguistic forms other than statements. For a statement may be described as analytic simply when it is synonymous with a logically true statement.

So, if the verification theory can be accepted as an adequate account of statement synonymy, the notion of analyticity is saved after all. However, let us reflect. Statement synonymy is said to be likeness of method of empirical confirmation or infirmation. Just what are these methods which are to be compared for likeness? What, in other words, is the nature of the relation between a statement and the experiences which contribute to or detract from its confirmation?

The most naive view of the relation is that it is one of direct report. This is *radical reductionism*. Every meaningful statement is held to be translatable into a statement (true or false) about immediate experience. Radical reductionism, in one form or another, well antedates the verification theory of meaning explicitly so called. Thus Locke and Hume held that every idea must either originate directly in sense experience or else be compounded of ideas thus originating; and taking a hint from Tooke we might rephrase this doctrine in semantical jargon by saying that a term, to be significant at all, must be either a name of a sense datum or a compound of such names or an abbreviation of such a compound. So stated, the doctrine remains ambiguous as between sense data as sensory events and sense data as sensory qualities; and it remains vague as to the admissible ways of compounding. Moreover, the doctrine is unnecessarily and intolerably restrictive in the term-by-term critique which it imposes. More reasonably, and without yet exceeding the limits of what I have called radical reductionism, we may take full statements as our significant units—thus demanding that our statements as wholes be translatable into sense-datum language, but not that they be translatable term by term.

This emendation would unquestionably have been welcome to Locke and Hume and Tooke, but historically it had to await an important reorientation in semantics—the reorientation whereby the primary vehicle of meaning came to be seen no longer in the term but in the statement. This reorientation, explicit in Frege underlies Russell's concept of incomplete symbols defined in use; also it is implicit in the verification theory of meaning, since the objects of verification are statements.

Radical reductionism, conceived now with statements as units, set itself the task of specifying a sense-datum language and showing how to translate the rest of significant discourse, statement by statement, into it. Carnap embarked on this project in the *Aufbau*.

The language which Carnap adopted as his starting-point was not a sense-datum language in the narrowest conceivable sense, for it included also the notations of logic, up through higher set theory. In effect, it included the whole language of pure mathematics. The ontology implicit in it (that is, the range of values of its variables) embraced not only sensory events but classes, classes of classes, and so on. Empiricists there are who would boggle at such prodigality. Carnap's starting-point is very parsimonious, however, in its extralogical or sensory part. In a series of constructions in which he exploits the resources of modern logic with much ingenuity, Carnap succeeds in defining a wide array of important additional sensory concepts which, but for his constructions, one would not have dreamed were definable on so slender a basis. He was the first empiricist who, not content with asserting the reducibility of science to terms of immediate experience, took serious steps toward carrying out the reduction.

If Carnap's starting-point is satisfactory, still his constructions were, as he himself stressed, only a fragment of the full programme. The construction of even the simplest statements about the physical world was left in a sketchy state. Carnap's suggestions on this subject were, despite their sketchiness, very suggestive. He explained spatio-temporal point-instants as quadruples of real numbers and envisaged assignment of sense qualities to point-instants according to certain canons. Roughly summarized, the plan was that qualities should be assigned to point-instants in such a way as to achieve the laziest world compatible with our experience. The principle of least action was to be our guide in constructing a world from experience.

Carnap did not seem to recognize, however, that his treatment of physical objects fell short of reduction not merely through sketchiness, but in principle. Statements of the form 'Quality q is at point-instant $x;y;z;t$' were, according to his canons, to be apportioned truth values in such a way as to maximize and minimize certain overall features, and with growth of experience the truth values were to be progressively revised in the same spirit. I think this is a good schematization (deliberately over-simplified, to be sure) of what science really does; but it provides no indication, not even the sketchiest, of how a statement of the form 'Quality q is at $x;y;z;t$' could ever be translated into Carnap's initial language of sense data and logic. The connective 'is at' remains an added undefined connective; the canons counsel us in its use but not in its elimination.

Carnap seems to have appreciated this point afterward; for in his later writings he abandoned all notion of the translatability of statements about the physical world into statements about immediate experience. Reductionism in its radical form has long since ceased to figure in Carnap's philosophy.

But the dogma of reductionism has, in a subtler and more tenuous form, continued to influence the thought of empiricists. The notion lingers that to each statement, or each synthetic statement, there is associated a unique range of possible sensory events such that the occurrence of any of them would add to the likelihood of truth of the statement, and that there is associated also another unique range of possible sensory events whose occurrence would detract from that likelihood. This notion is of course implicit in the verification theory of meaning.

The dogma of reductionism survives in the supposition that each statement, taken in isolation from its fellows, can admit of confirmation or infirmation at all. My counter-suggestion, issuing essentially from Carnap's doctrine of the physical world in the *Aufbau*, is that our statements about the external world face the tribunal of sense experience not individually but only as a corporate body.[9]

The dogma of reductionism, even in its attenuated form, is intimately connected with the other dogma—that there is a cleavage between the analytic and the synthetic. We have found ourselves led, indeed, from the latter problem to the former through the verification theory of meaning. More directly, the one dogma clearly supports the other in this way: as long as it is taken to be significant in general to speak of the confirmation and infirmation of a statement, it seems significant to speak also of a limiting kind of statement which is vacuously confirmed, *ipso facto*, come what may; and such a statement is analytic.

The two dogmas are, indeed, at root identical. We lately reflected that in general the truth of statements does obviously depend both upon language and upon extra-linguistic fact; and we noted that this obvious circumstance carries in its train, not logically but all too naturally, a feeling that the truth of a statement is somehow analysable into a linguistic component and a factual component. The factual component must, if we are empiricists, boil down to a range of confirmatory experiences. In the extreme case where the linguistic component is all that matters, a true statement is analytic. But I hope we are now impressed with how stubbornly the distinction between analytic and synthetic has resisted any straightforward drawing. I am impressed also, apart from prefabricated examples of black and white balls in an urn, with how baffling the problem has always been of arriving at any explicit theory of the empirical confirmation of a synthetic statement. My present suggestion is that it is nonsense, and the root of much nonsense, to speak of a linguistic component and a factual component in the truth of any individual statement. Taken collectively, science has its double dependence upon language and experience; but this duality is not significantly traceable into the statements of science taken one by one.

The idea of defining a symbol in use was, as remarked, an advance over the impossible term-by-term empiricism of Locke and Hume. The statement, rather than the term, came with Frege to be recognized as the unit accountable to an empiricist critique. But what I am now urging is that even in taking the statement as unit we have drawn our grid too finely. The unit of empirical significance is the whole of science.

6. EMPIRICISM WITHOUT THE DOGMAS

The totality of our so-called knowledge or beliefs, from the most casual matters of geography and history to the profoundest laws of atomic physics or even of pure mathematics and logic, is a manmade fabric which impinges on experience only along the edges. Or, to change the figure, total science is like a field of force whose boundary conditions are experience. A conflict with experience at the periphery occasions readjustments in the interior of the field. Truth values have to be redistributed over

9. This doctrine was well argued by Duhem, pp. 303–28. Or see Lowinger, pp. 132–40.

some of our statements. Re-evaluation of some statements entails re-evaluation of others, because of their logical interconnections—the logical laws being in turn simply certain further statements of the system, certain further elements of the field. Having re-evaluated one statement we must re-evaluate some others, which may be statements logically connected with the first or may be the statements of logical connections themselves. But the total field is so underdetermined by its boundary conditions, experience, that there is much latitude of choice as to what statements to re-evaluate in the light of any single contrary experience. No particular experiences are linked with any particular statements in the interior of the field, except indirectly through considerations of equilibrium affecting the field as a whole.

If this view is right, it is misleading to speak of the empirical content of an individual statement—especially if it is a statement at all remote from the experiential periphery of the field. Furthermore, it becomes folly to seek a boundary between synthetic statements, which hold contingently on experience, and analytic statements, which hold come what may. Any statement can be held true come what may, if we make drastic enough adjustments elsewhere in the system. Even a statement very close to the periphery can be held true in the face of recalcitrant experience by pleading hallucination or by amending certain statements of the kind called logical laws. Conversely, by the same token, no statement is immune to revision. Revision even of the logical law of the excluded middle has been proposed as a means of simplifying quantum mechanics; and what difference is there in principle between such a shift and the shift whereby Kepler superseded Ptolemy, or Einstein Newton, or Darwin Aristotle?

For vividness I have been speaking in terms of varying distances from a sensory periphery. Let me try now to clarify this notion without metaphor. Certain statements, though *about* physical objects and not sense experience, seem peculiarly germane to sense experience—and in a selective way: some statements to some experiences, others to others. Such statements, especially germane to particular experiences, I picture as near the periphery. But in this relation of 'germaneness' I envisage nothing more than a loose association reflecting the relative likelihood, in practice, of our choosing one statement rather than another for revision in the event of recalcitrant experience. For example, we can imagine recalcitrant experiences to which we would surely be inclined to accommodate our system by re-evaluating just the statement that there are brick houses on Elm Street, together with related statements on the same topic. We can imagine other recalcitrant experiences to which we would be inclined to accommodate our system by re-evaluating just the statement that there are no centaurs, along with kindred statements. A recalcitrant experience can, I have urged, be accommodated by any of various alternative re-evaluations in various alternative quarters of the total system; but, in the cases which we are now imagining, our natural tendency to disturb the total system as little as possible would lead us to focus our revisions upon these specific statements concerning brick houses or centaurs. These statements are felt, therefore, to have a sharper empirical reference than highly theoretical statements of physics or logic or ontology. The latter statements may be thought of as relatively centrally located within the total network, meaning merely that little preferential connection with any particular sense data obtrudes itself.

As an empiricist I continue to think of the conceptual scheme of science as a tool, ultimately, for predicting future experience in the light of past experience. Physical objects are conceptually imported into the situation as convenient intermediaries—not by definition in terms of experience, but simply as irreducible posits comparable, epistemologically, to the gods of Homer. For my part I do, *qua* lay physicist, believe in physical objects and not in Homer's gods; and I consider it a scientific error to believe otherwise. But in point of epistemological footing the physical objects and the gods differ only in degree and not in kind. Both sorts of entities enter our conception only as cultural posits. The myth of physical objects is epistemologically superior to most in that it has proved more efficacious than other myths as a device for working a manageable structure into the flux of experience.

Positing does not stop with macroscopic physical objects. Objects at the atomic level are posited to make the laws of macroscopic objects, and ultimately the laws of experience, simpler and more manageable; and we need not expect or demand full definition of atomic and subatomic entities in terms of macroscopic ones, any more than definition of macroscopic things in terms of sense data. Science is a continuation of common sense, and it continues the common-sense expedient of swelling ontology to simplify theory.

Physical objects, small and large, are not the only posits. Forces are another example; and indeed we are told nowadays that the boundary between energy and matter is obsolete. Moreover, the abstract entities which are the substance of mathematics—ultimately classes and classes of classes and so on up—are another posit in the same spirit. Epistemologically these are myths on the same footing with physical objects and gods, neither better nor worse except for differences in the degree to which they expedite our dealings with sense experiences.

The overall algebra of rational and irrational numbers is underdetermined by the algebra of rational numbers, but is smoother and more convenient; and it includes the algebra of rational numbers as a jagged or gerrymandered part. Total science, mathematical and natural and human, is similarly but more extremely underdetermined by experience. The edge of the system must be kept squared with experience; the rest, with all its elaborate myths or fictions, has as its objective the simplicity of laws.

Ontological questions, under this view, are on a par with questions of natural science.[10] Consider the question whether to countenance classes as entities. This, as I have argued elsewhere,[11] is the question whether to quantify with respect to variables which take classes as values. Now Carnap (6) has maintained that this is a question not of matters of fact but of choosing a convenient language form, a convenient conceptual scheme or framework for science. With this I agree, but only on the proviso that the same be conceded regarding scientific hypotheses generally. Carnap ((6), p. 32 n) has recognized that he is able to preserve a double standard for ontological questions and scientific hypotheses only by assuming an absolute distinction between the analytic and the synthetic; and I need not say again that this is a distinction which I reject.[12]

The issue over there being classes seems more a question of convenient conceptual scheme; the issue over there being centaurs, or brick houses on Elm Street, seems more a question of fact. But I have been urging that this difference is only one of degree, and that it turns upon our vaguely pragmatic inclination to adjust one strand of the fabric of science rather than another in accommodating some particular recalcitrant experience. Conservatism figures in such choices, and so does the quest for simplicity.

Carnap, Lewis, and others take a pragmatic stand on the question of choosing between language forms, scientific frameworks; but their pragmatism leaves off at the imagined boundary between the analytic and the synthetic. In repudiating such a boundary I espouse a more thorough pragmatism. Each man is given a scientific heritage plus a continuing barrage of sensory stimulation; and the considerations which guide him in warping his scientific heritage to fit his continuing sensory promptings are, where rational, pragmatic.

10. 'L'ontologie fait corps avec la science elle-même et ne peut en être separée.' Meyerson, p. 439.

11. See Quine, *From a Logical Point of View*, 2nd ed. (Cambridge: Harvard University Press, 1961), pp. 12 f., 102 ff.

12. For an effective expression of further misgivings over this distinction, see White.

BIBLIOGRAPHICAL REFERENCES

Carnap, Rudolf (1), *Der logische Aufbau der Welt* (Berlin, 1928).

——— (2), *The Logical Syntax of Language* (New York: Harcourt Brace, and London: Kegan Paul, 1937). Translation, with extensions, of *Logische Syntax der Sprache* (Vienna: Springer, 1934).

——— (3), *Meaning and Necessity* (Chicago: University of Chicago Press, 1947).

——— (4), *Logical Foundations of Probability* (Chicago: University of Chicago Press, 1950).

——— (5), 'Testability and Meaning', *Philosophy of Science*, 3 (1936), 419–71; 4 (1937), 1–40 (reprinted, New Haven: Graduate Philosophy Club, Yale University, 1950).

——— (6), 'Empiricism, Semantics, and Ontology', *Revue internationale de philosophie*, 4 (1950), 20–40. Reprinted in Linsky.

Duhem, Pierre, *La Théorie physique: son objet et sa structure* (Paris, 1906).

Frege, Gottlob, *Foundations of Arithmetic* (New York: Philosophical Library, 1950). Reprint of *Grundlagen der Arithmetik* (Breslau, 1884) with English translation in parallel.

Hempel, C.G. (1), 'Problems and Changes in the Empiricist Criterion of Meaning', *Revue internationale de philosophie*, 4 (1950), 41–63. Reprinted in Linsky.

——— (2), 'The Concept of Cognitive Significance: A Reconsideration', *Proceedings of American Academy of Arts and Sciences;* 80 (1951), 61–77.

Lewis, C.I. (1), *A Survey of Symbolic Logic* (Berkeley, 1918).
——— (2), *An Analysis of Knowledge and Valuation*, (LaSalle, III.: Open Court, 1946).
Linsky, Leonard (ed.), *Semantics and the Philosophy of Language* (Urbana: University of Illinois Press, 1952).
Lowinger, Armand, *The Methodology of Pierre Duhem* (New York: Columbia University Press, 1941).
Martin, R.M., 'On "analytic" ', *Philosophical Studies*, 3 (1952), 42–47.
Meyerson, Émile, *Identité et realité* (Paris, 1908; 4th edn., 1932).
Quine, W.V. (1), *Mathematical Logic* (New York: Norton, 1940; Cambridge: Harvard University Press, 1947; rev. edn., Cambridge: Harvard University Press, 1951).
Tooke, J.H. *'Έπεα πτερόντα; or, The Diversions of Purley,* 2 vols. (London, 1786, 1805, 1829; Boston, 1806).
White, Morton, 'The Analytic and the Synthetic; an Untenable Dualism', in Sidney Hook (ed.), *John Dewey: Philosopher of Science and Freedom* (New York: Dial Press, 1950), pp. 316–30. Reprinted in Linsky.

Epistemology Naturalized

Epistemology is concerned with the foundations of science. Conceived thus broadly, epistemology includes the study of the foundations of mathematics as one of its departments. Specialists at the turn of the century thought that their efforts in this particular department were achieving notable success: mathematics seemed to reduce altogether to logic. In a more recent perspective this reduction is seen to be better describable as a reduction to logic and set theory. This correction is a disappointment epistemologically, since the firmness and obviousness that we associate with logic cannot be claimed for set theory. But still the success achieved in the foundations of mathematics remains exemplary by comparative standards, and we can illuminate the rest of epistemology somewhat by drawing parallels to this department.

Studies in the foundations of mathematics divide symmetrically into two sorts, conceptual and doctrinal. The conceptual studies are concerned with meaning, the doctrinal with truth. The conceptual studies are concerned with clarifying concepts by defining them, some in terms of others. The doctrinal studies are concerned with establishing laws by proving them, some on the basis of others. Ideally the more obscure concepts would be defined in terms of the clearer ones so as to maximize clarity, and the less obvious laws would be proved from the more obvious ones so as to maximize certainty. Ideally the definitions would generate all the concepts from clear and distinct ideas, and the proofs would generate all the theorems from self-evident truths.

The two ideals are linked. For, if you define all the concepts by use of some favored subset of them, you thereby show how to translate all theorems into these favored terms. The clearer these terms are, the likelier it is that the truths couched in them will be obviously true, or derivable from obvious truths. If in particular the concepts of mathematics were all reducible to the clear terms of logic, then all the truths of mathematics would go over into truths of logic; and surely the truths of logic are all obvious or at least potentially obvious, i.e., derivable from obvious truths by individually obvious steps.

This particular outcome is in fact denied us, however, since mathematics reduces only to set theory and not to logic proper. Such reduction still enhances clarity, but only because of the interrelations that emerge and not because the end terms of the analysis are clearer than others. As for the end truths, the

Reprinted from W. V. Quine, *Ontological Relativity and Other Essays* (New York: Columbia University Press, 1969), 68–90, by permission of the author and the publisher.

axioms of set theory, these have less obviousness and certainty to recommend them than do most of the mathematical theorems that we would derive from them. Moreover, we know from Gödel's work that no consistent axiom system can cover mathematics even when we renounce self-evidence. Reduction in the foundations of mathematics remains mathematically and philosophically fascinating, but it does not do what the epistemologist would like of it: it does not reveal the ground of mathematical knowledge, it does not show how mathematical certainty is possible.

Still there remains a helpful thought, regarding epistemology generally, in that duality of structure which was especially conspicuous in the foundations of mathematics. I refer to the bifurcation into a theory of concepts, or meaning, and a theory of doctrine, or truth; for this applies to the epistemology of natural knowledge no less than to the foundations of mathematics. The parallel is as follows. Just as mathematics is to be reduced to logic, or logic and set theory, so natural knowledge is to be based somehow on sense experience. This means explaining the notion of body in sensory terms; here is the conceptual side. And it means justifying our knowledge of truths of nature in sensory terms; here is the doctrinal side of the bifurcation.

Hume pondered the epistemology of natural knowledge on both sides of the bifurcation, the conceptual and the doctrinal. His handling of the conceptual side of the problem, the explanation of body in sensory terms, was bold and simple: he identified bodies outright with the sense impressions. If common sense distinguishes between the material apple and our sense impressions of it on the ground that the apple is one and enduring while the impressions are many and fleeting, then, Hume held, so much the worse for common sense; the notion of its being the same apple on one occasion and another is a vulgar confusion.

Nearly a century after Hume's *Treatise*, the same view of bodies was espoused by the early American philosopher Alexander Bryan Johnson.[1] "The word iron names an associated sight and feel," Johnson wrote.

What then of the doctrinal side, the justification of our knowledge of truths about nature? Here, Hume despaired. By his identification of bodies with impressions he did succeed in construing some singular statements about bodies as indubitable truths, yes; as truths about impressions, directly known. But general statements, also singular statements about the future, gained no increment of certainty by being construed as about impressions.

On the doctrinal side, I do not see that we are further along today than where Hume left us. The Humean predicament is the human predicament. But on the conceptual side there has been progress. There the crucial step forward was made already before Alexander Bryan Johnson's day, although Johnson did not emulate it. It was made by Bentham in his theory of fictions. Bentham's step was the recognition of contextual definition, or what he called paraphrasis. He recognized that to explain a term we do not need to specify an object for it to refer to, nor even specify a synonymous word or phrase; we need only show, by whatever means, how to translate all the whole sentences in which the term is to be used. Hume's and Johnson's desperate measure of identifying bodies with impressions ceased to be the only conceivable way of making sense of talk of bodies, even granted that impressions were the only reality. One could undertake to explain talk of bodies in terms of talk of impressions by translating one's whole sentence about bodies into whole sentences about impressions, without equating the bodies themselves to anything at all.

This idea of contextual definition, or recognition of the sentence as the primary vehicle of meaning, was indispensable to the ensuing developments in the foundations of mathematics. It was explicit in Frege, and it attained its full flower in Russell's doctrine of singular descriptions as incomplete symbols.

Contextual definition was one of two resorts that could be expected to have a liberating effect upon the conceptual side of the epistemology of natural knowledge. The other is resort to the resources of set theory as auxiliary concepts. The epistemologist who is willing to eke out his austere ontology of sense impressions with these set-theoretic auxiliaries is suddenly rich: he has not just his impressions to play with, but sets of them, and sets of sets, and so on up. Constructions in the foundations of mathematics have shown that such set-theoretic aids are a powerful addition; after all, the entire glossary of concepts of classical mathematics is constructible from them. Thus equipped, our epistemologist may not need either to identify bodies with impressions or to settle for contextual definition; he may hope to find in some subtle construction of sets upon sets of sense impressions a category of objects enjoying just the formula properties that he wants for bodies.

The two resorts are very unequal in epistemological status. Contextual definition is unassailable. Sentences that have been given meaning as wholes are undeniably meaningful, and the use they make of their component terms is therefore meaningful, regardless of whether any translations are offered for those terms in isolation. Surely Hume and A. B. Johnson would have used contextual definition with pleasure if they had thought of it. Recourse to sets, on the other hand, is a drastic ontological move, a retreat from the austere ontology of impressions. There are philosophers who would rather settle for bodies outright than accept all these sets, which amount, after all, to the whole abstract ontology of mathematics.

This issue has not always been clear, however, owing to deceptive hints of continuity between elementary logic and set theory. This is why mathematics was once believed to reduce to logic, that is, to an innocent and unquestionable logic, and to inherit these qualities. And this is probably why Russell was content to resort to sets as well as to contextual definition when in *Our Knowledge of the External World* and elsewhere he addressed himself to the epistemology of natural knowledge, on its conceptual side.

To account for the external world as a logical construct of sense data—such, in Russell's terms, was the program. It was Carnap, in his *Der logische Aufbau der Welt* of 1928, who came nearest to executing it.

This was the conceptual side of epistemology; what of the doctrinal? There the Humean predicament remained unaltered. Carnap's constructions, if carried successfully to completion, would have enabled us to translate all sentences about the world into terms of sense data, or observation, plus logic and set theory. But the mere fact that a sentence is *couched* in terms of observation, logic, and set theory does not mean that it can be *proved* from observation sentences by logic and set theory. The most modest of generalizations about observable traits will cover more cases than its utterer can have had occasion actually to observe. The hopelessness of grounding natural science upon immediate experience in a firmly logical way was acknowledged. The Cartesian quest for certainty had been the remote motivation of epistemology, both on its conceptual and its doctrinal side; but that quest was seen as a lost cause. To endow the truths of nature with the full authority of immediate experience was as forlorn a hope as hoping to endow the truths of mathematics with the potential obviousness of elementary logic.

What then could have motivated Carnap's heroic efforts on the conceptual side of epistemology, when hope of certainty on the doctrinal side was abandoned? There were two good reasons still. One was that such constructions could be expected to elicit and clarify the sensory evidence for science, even if the inferential steps between sensory evidence and scientific doctrine must fall short of certainty. The other reason was that such constructions would deepen our understanding of our discourse about the world, even apart from questions of evidence; it would make all cognitive discourse as clear as observation terms and logic and, I must regretfully add, set theory.

It was sad for epistemologists, Hume and others, to have to acquiesce in the impossibility of strictly deriving the science of the external world from sensory evidence. Two cardinal tenets of empiricism remained unassailable, however, and so remain to this day. One is that whatever evidence there *is* for science *is* sensory evidence. The other, to which I shall return, is that all inculcation of meanings of words must rest ultimately on sensory evidence. Hence the continuing attractiveness of the idea of a *logischer Aufbau* in which the sensory content of discourse would stand forth explicitly.

If Carnap had successfully carried such a construction through, how could he have told whether it was the right one? The question would have had no point. He was seeking what he called a *rational reconstruction*. Any construction of physicalistic discourse in terms of sense experience, logic, and set theory would have been seen as satisfactory if it made the physicalistic discourse come out right. If there is one way there are many, but any would be a great achievement.

But why all this creative reconstruction, all this make-believe? The stimulation of his sensory receptors is all the evidence anybody has had to go on, ultimately, in arriving at his picture of the world. Why not just see how this construction really proceeds? Why not settle for psychology? Such a surrender of the epistemological burden to psychology is a move that was disallowed in earlier times as circular reasoning. If the epistemologist's goal is validation of the grounds of empirical science, he defeats his purpose by using psychology or other empirical science in the validation. However, such scruples against circularity have little point once we have stopped dreaming of deducing science from observations. If we are out simply to understand the link between observation and science, we are well advised to use any available information, including that provided by the very science whose link with observation we are seeking to understand.

But there remains a different reason, unconnected with fears of circularity, for still favoring creative reconstruction. We should like to be able to *translate* science into logic and observation terms and set theory. This would be a great epistemological achievement, for it would show all the rest of the concepts of science to be theoretically superfluous. It would legitimize them—to whatever degree the concepts of set theory, logic, and observation are themselves legitimate—by showing that everything done with the one apparatus could in principle be done with the other. If psychology itself could deliver a truly translational reduction of this kind, we should welcome it; but certainly it cannot, for certainly we did not grow up learning definitions of physicalistic language in terms of a prior language of set theory, logic, and observation. Here, then, would be good reason for persisting in a rational reconstruction: we want to establish the essential innocence of physical concepts, by showing them to be theoretically dispensable.

The fact is, though, that the construction which Carnap outlined in *Der logische Aufbau der Welt* does not give translational reduction either. It would not even if the outline were filled in. The crucial point comes where Carnap is explaining how to assign sense qualities to positions in physical space and time. These assignments are to be made in such a way as to fulfill, as well as possible, certain desiderata which he states, and with growth of experience the assignments are to be revised to suit. This plan, however illuminating, does not offer any key to *translating* the sentences of science into terms of observation, logic, and set theory.

We must despair of any such reduction. Carnap had despaired of it by 1936, when, in "Testability and Meaning,"[2] he introduced so-called *reduction forms* of a type weaker than definition. Definitions had shown always how to translate sentences into equivalent sentences. Contextual definition of a term showed how to translate sentences containing the term into equivalent sentences lacking the term. Reduction forms of Carnap's liberalized kind, on the other hand, do not in general give equivalences; they give implications. They explain a new term, if only partially, by specifying some sentences which are implied by sentences containing the term, and other sentences which imply sentences containing the term.

It is tempting to suppose that the countenancing of reduction forms in this liberal sense is just one further step of liberalization comparable to the earlier one, taken by Bentham, of countenancing contextual definition. The former and sterner kind of rational reconstruction might have been represented as a fictitious history in which we imagined our ancestors introducing the terms of physicalistic discourse on a phenomenalistic and set-theoretic basis by a succession of contextual definitions. The new and more liberal kind of rational reconstruction is a fictitious history in which we imagine our ancestors introducing those terms by a succession rather of reduction forms of the weaker sort.

This, however, is a wrong comparison. The fact is rather that the former and sterner kind of rational reconstruction, where definition reigned, embodied no fictitious history at all. It was nothing more nor less than a set of directions—or would have been, if successful—for accomplishing everything in terms of phenomena and set theory that we now accomplish in terms of bodies. It would have been a true reduction by translation, a legitimation by elimination. *Definire est eliminare.* Rational reconstruction by Carnap's later and looser reduction forms does none of this.

To relax the demand for definition, and settle for a kind of reduction that does not eliminate, is to renounce the last remaining advantage that we supposed rational reconstruction to have over straight psychology; namely, the advantage of translational reduction. If all we hope for is a reconstruction that links science to experience in explicit ways short of translation, then it would seem more sensible to settle for psychology. Better to discover how science is in fact developed and learned than to fabricate a fictitious structure to a similar effect.

The empiricist made one major concession when he despaired of deducing the truths of nature from sensory evidence. In despairing now even of translating those truths into terms of observation and logico-mathematical auxiliaries, he makes another major concession. For suppose we hold, with the old empiricist Peirce, that the very meaning of a statement consists in the difference its truth would make to possible experience. Might we not formulate, in a chapter-length sentence in observational language, all the difference that the truth of a given statement might make to experience, and might we not then take all this as the translation? Even if the difference that the truth of the statement would make to experience ramifies indefinitely, we might still hope to embrace it all in the logical implications of our chapter-length formulation, just as we can axiomatize an infinity of theorems. In giving up hope of such translation, then, the empiricist is conceding that the empirical meanings of typical statements about the external world are inaccessible and ineffable.

How is this inaccessibility to be explained? Simply on the ground that the experiential implications of a typical statement about bodies are too complex for finite axiomatization, however lengthy? No; I have a different explanation. It is that the typical statement about bodies has no fund of experiential implications it can call its own. A substantial mass of theory, taken together, will commonly have experiential implications; this is how we make verifiable predictions. We may not be able to explain why we arrive at theories which make successful predictions, but we do arrive at such theories.

Sometimes also an experience implied by a theory fails to come off; and then, ideally, we declare the theory false. But the failure falsifies only a block of theory as a whole, a conjunction of many statements. The failure shows that one or more of those statements is false, but it does not show which. The predicted experiences, true and false, are not implied by any one of the component statements of the theory rather than another. The component statements simply do not have empirical meanings, by Peirce's standard, but a sufficiently inclusive portion of theory does. If we can aspire to a sort of *logischer Aufbau der Welt* at all, it must be to one in which the texts slated for translation into observational and logico-mathematical terms are mostly broad theories taken as wholes, rather than just terms or short sentences. The translation of a theory would be a ponderous axiomatization of all the experiential difference that the truth of the theory would make. It would be a queer translation, for it would translate the whole but none of the parts. We might better speak in such a case not of translation but simply of observational evidence for theories; and we may, following Peirce, still fairly call this the empirical meaning of the theories.

These considerations raise a philosophical question even about ordinary unphilosophical translation, such as from English into Arunta or Chinese. For, if the English sentences of a theory have their meaning only together as a body, then we can justify their translation into Arunta only together as a body. There will be no justification for pairing off the component English sentences with component Arunta sentences, except as these correlations make the translation of the theory as a whole come out right. Any translations of the English sentences into Arunta sentences will be as correct as any other, so long as the net empirical implications of the theory as a whole are preserved in translation. But it is to be expected that many different ways of translating the component sentences, essentially different individually, would deliver the same empirical implications for the theory as a whole; deviations in the translation of one component sentence could be compensated for in the translation of another component sentence. Insofar, there can be no ground for saying which of two glaringly unlike translations of individual sentences is right.[3]

For an uncritical mentalist, no such indeterminacy threatens. Every term and every sentence is a label attached to an idea, simple or complex, which is stored in the mind. When on the other hand we take a verification theory of meaning seriously, the indeterminacy would appear to be inescapable. The Vienna Circle espoused a verification theory of meaning but did not take it seriously enough. If we recognize with Peirce that the meaning of a sentence turns purely on what would count as evidence for its truth, and if we recognize with Duhem that theoretical sentences have their evidence not as single sentences but only as larger blocks of theory, then the indeterminacy of translation of theoretical sentences is the natural conclusion. And most sentences, apart from observation sentences, are theoretical. This conclusion, conversely, once it is embraced, seals the fate of any general notion of propositional meaning or, for that matter, state of affairs.

Should the unwelcomeness of the conclusion persuade us to abandon the verification theory of meaning? Certainly not. The sort of meaning that is basic to translation, and to the learning of one's own language, is necessarily empirical meaning and nothing more. A child learns his first words and sentences by hearing and using them in the presence of appropriate stimuli. These must be external stimuli, for they must act both on the child and on the speaker from whom he is learning.[4] Language is socially inculcated and controlled; the inculcation and control turn strictly on the keying of sentences to shared stimulation. Internal factors may vary *ad libitum* without prejudice to communication as long as the keying of language to external stimuli is undisturbed. Surely one has no choice but to be an empiricist so far as one's theory of linguistic meaning is concerned.

What I have said of infant learning applies equally to the linguist's learning of a new language in the field. If the linguist does not lean on related languages for which there are previously accepted translation practices, then obviously he had no data but the concomitances of native utterance and observable stimulus situation. No wonder there is indeterminacy of translation—for of course only a small fraction of our utterances report concurrent external stimulation. Granted, the linguist will end up with unequivocal translations of everything; but only by making many arbitrary choices—arbitrary even though unconscious—along the way. Arbitrary? By this I mean that different choices could still have made everything come out right that is susceptible in principle to any kind of check.

Let me link up, in a different order, some of the points I have made. The crucial consideration behind my argument for the indeterminancy of translation was that a statement about the world does not always or usually have a separable fund of empirical consequences that it can call its own. That consideration served also to account for the impossibility of an epistemological reduction of the sort where every sentence is equated to a sentence in observational and logico-mathematical terms. And the impossibility of that sort of epistemological reduction dissipated the last advantage that rational reconstruction seemed to have over psychology.

Philosophers have rightly despaired of translating everything into observational and logico-mathematical terms. They have despaired of this even when they have not recognized, as the reason for this irreducibility, that the statements largely do not have their private bundles of empirical consequences. And some philosophers have seen in this irreducibility the bankruptcy of epistemology. Carnap and the other logical positivists of the Vienna Circle had already pressed the term "metaphysics" into pejorative use, as connoting meaninglessness; and the term "epistemology" was next. Wittgenstein and his followers, mainly at Oxford, found a residual philosophical vocation in therapy: in curing philosophers of the delusion that there were epistemological problems.

But I think that at this point it may be more useful to say rather that epistemology still goes on, though in a new setting and a clarified status. Epistemology, or something like it, simply falls into place as a chapter of psychology and hence of natural science. It studies a natural phenomenon, viz., a physical human subject. This human subject is accorded a certain experimentally controlled input—certain patterns of irradiation in assorted frequencies, for instance—and in the fullness of time the subject delivers as output a description of the three-dimensional external world and its history. The relation between the meager input and the torrential output is a relation that we are prompted to study for somewhat the same reasons that always prompted epistemology; namely, in order to see how evidence relates to theory, and in what ways one's theory of nature transcends any available evidence.

Such a study could still include, even, something like the old rational reconstruction, to whatever degree such reconstruction is practicable; for imaginative constructions can afford hints of actual psychological processes, in much the way that mechanical simulations can. But a conspicuous difference between old epistemology and the epistemological enterprise in this new psychological setting is that we can now make free use of empirical psychology.

The old epistemology aspired to contain, in a sense, natural science; it would construct it somehow from sense data. Epistemology in its new setting, conversely, is contained in natural science, as a chapter of psychology. But the old containment remains valid too, in its way. We are studying how the human subject of our study posits bodies and projects his physics from his data, and we appreciate that our position in the world is just like this. Our very epistemological enterprise, therefore, and the psychology wherein it is a component chapter, and the whole of natural science wherein psychology is a component book—all this is our own construction or projection from stimulations like those we were meting out to our epistemological subject. There is thus reciprocal containment, though containment in different senses: epistemology in natural science and natural science in epistemology.

This interplay is reminiscent again of the old threat of circularity, but it is all right now that we have stopped dreaming of deducing science from sense data. We are after an understanding of science as an institution or process in the world, and we do not intend that understanding to be any better than the science which is its object. This attitude is indeed one that Neurath was already urging in Vienna Circle days, with his parable of the mariner who has to rebuild his boat while staying afloat in it.

One effect of seeing epistemology in a psychological setting is that it resolves a stubborn old enigma of epistemological priority. Our retinas are irradiated in two dimensions, yet we see things as three-dimensional without conscious inference. Which is to count as observation—the unconscious two-dimensional rejection or the conscious three-dimensional apprehension? In the old epistemological context the conscious form had priority, for we were out to justify our knowledge of the external world by rational reconstruction, and that demands awareness. Awareness ceased to be demanded when we gave up trying to justify our knowledge of the external world by rational reconstruction. What to count as observation now can be settled in terms of the stimulation of sensory receptors, let consciousness fall where it may.

The Gestalt psychologists' challenge to sensory atomism, which seemed so relevant to epistemology forty years ago, is likewise deactivated. Regardless of whether sensory atoms or Gestalten are what favor the forefront of our consciousness, it is simply the stimulations of our sensory receptors that are best looked upon as the input to our cognitive mechanism. Old paradoxes about unconscious data and inference, old problems about chains of inference that would have to be completed too quickly—these no longer matter.

In the old anti-psychologistic days the question of epistemological priority was moot. What is epistemologically prior to what? Are Gestalten prior to sensory atoms because they are noticed, or should we favor sensory atoms on some more subtle ground? Now that we are permitted to appeal to physical stimulation, the problem dissolves; *A* is epistemologically prior to *B* if *A* is causally nearer than *B* to the sensory receptors. Or, what is in some ways better, just talk explicitly in terms of causal proximity to sensory receptors and drop the talk of epistemological priority.

Around 1932 there was debate in the Vienna Circle over what to count as observation sentences, or *Protokollsätze*. One position was that they had the form of reports of sense impressions. Another was that they were statements of an elementary sort about the external world, e.g., "A red cube is standing on the table." Another, Neurath's, was that they had the form of reports of relations between percipients and external things: "Otto now sees a red cube on the table." The worst of it was that there seemed to be no objective way of settling the matter: no way of making real sense of the question.

Let us now try to view the matter unreservedly in the context of the external world. Vaguely speaking, what we want of observation sentences is that they be the ones in closest causal proximity to the sensory receptors. But how is such proximity to be gauged? The idea may be rephrased this way: observation sentences are sentences which, as we learn language, are most strongly conditioned to concurrent sensory stimulation rather than to stored collateral information. Thus let us imagine a sentence queried for our verdict as to whether it is true or false, queried for our assent or dissent. Then the sentence is an observation sentence if our verdict depends only on the sensory stimulation present at the time.

But a verdict cannot depend on present stimulation to the exclusion of stored information. The very fact of our having learned the language evinces much storing of information, and of information without which we should be in no position to give verdicts on sentences however observational. Evidently then we must relax our definition of observation sentence to read thus: a sentence is an observation sentence if all verdicts on it depend on present sensory stimulation and on no stored information beyond what goes into understanding the sentence.

This formulation raises another problem: how are we to distinguish between information that goes into understanding a sentence and information that goes beyond? This is the problem of distinguishing between analytic truth, which issues from the mere meanings of words, and synthetic truth, which depends on more than meanings. Now I have long maintained that this distinction is illusory. There is one step toward such a distinction, however, which does make sense: a sentence that is true by mere meanings of words should be expected, at least if it is simple, to be subscribed to by all fluent speakers in the community. Perhaps the controversial notion of analyticity can be dispensed with, in our definition of observation sentence, in favor of this straightforward attribute of community-wide acceptance.

This attribute is of course no explication of analyticity. The community would agree that there have been black dogs, yet none who talk of analyticity would call this analytic. My rejection of the analyticity notion just means drawing no line between what goes into the mere understanding of the sentences of a language and what else the community sees eye-to-eye on. I doubt that an objective distinction can be made between meaning and such collateral information as is community-wide.

Turning back then to our task of defining observation sentences, we get this: an observation sentence is one on which all speakers of the language give the same verdict when given the same concurrent stimulation. To put the point negatively, an observation sentence is one that is not sensitive to differences in past experience within the speech community.

This formulation accords perfectly with the traditional role of the observation sentence as the court of appeal of scientific theories. For by our definition the observation sentences are the sentences on which all members of the community will agree under uniform stimulation. And what is the criterion of membership in the same community? Simply, general fluency of dialogue. This criterion admits of degrees, and indeed we may usefully take the community more narrowly for some studies than for others. What count as observation sentences for a community of specialists would not always so count for a larger community.

There is generally no subjectivity in the phrasing of observation sentences, as we are now conceiving them; they will usually be about bodies. Since the distinguishing trait of an observation sentence is intersubjective agreement under agreeing stimulation, a corporeal subject matter is likelier than not.

The old tendency to associate observation sentences with a subjective sensory subject matter is rather an irony when we reflect that observation sentences are also meant to be the intersubjective tribunal of scientific hypotheses. The old tendency was due to the drive to base science on something firmer and prior in the subject's experience; but we dropped that project.

The dislodging of epistemology from its old status of first philosophy loosed a wave, we saw, of epistemological nihilism. This mood is reflected somewhat in the tendency of Polányi, Kuhn, and the late Russell Hanson to belittle the role of evidence and to accentuate cultural relativism. Hanson ventured even to discredit the idea of observation, arguing that so-called observations vary from observer to observer with the amount of knowledge that the observers bring with them. The veteran physicist looks at some apparatus and sees an x-ray tube. The neophyte, looking at the same place, observes rather "a glass and metal instrument replete with wires, reflectors, screws, lamps, and pushbuttons." One man's observation is another man's closed book or flight of fancy. The notion of observation as the impartial and objective source of evidence for science is bankrupt. Now my answer to the x-ray example was already hinted a little while back: what counts as an observation sentence varies with the width of community considered. But we can also always get an absolute standard by taking in all speakers of the language, or most. It is ironical that philosophers, finding the old epistemology untenable as a whole, should react by repudiating a part which has only now moved into clear focus.

Clarification of the notion of observation sentence is a good thing, for the notion is fundamental in two connections. These two correspond to the duality that I remarked upon early in this essay: the duality between concept and doctrine, between knowing what a sentence means and knowing whether it is true. The observation sentence is basic to both enterprises. Its relation to doctrine, to our knowledge of what is true, is very much the traditional one: observation sentences are the repository of evidence for scientific hypotheses. Its relation to meaning is fundamental too, since observation sentences are the ones we are in a position to learn to understand first, both as children and as field linguists. For observation sentences are precisely the ones that we can correlate with observable circumstances of the occasion of utterance or assent, independently of variations in the past histories of individual informants. They afford the only entry to a language.

The observation sentence is the cornerstone of semantics. For it is, as we just saw, fundamental to the learning of meaning. Also, it is where meaning is firmest. Sentences higher up in theories have no empirical consequences they can call their own; they confront the tribunal of sensory evidence only in more or less inclusive aggregates. The observation sentence, situated at the sensory periphery of the body scientific, is the minimal verifiable aggregate; it has an empirical content all its own and wears it on its sleeve.

The predicament of the indeterminacy of translation has little bearing on observation sentences. The equating of an observation sentence of our language to an observation sentence of another language is mostly a matter of empirical generalization; it is a matter of identity between the range of stimulations that would prompt assent to the one sentence and the range of stimulations that would prompt assent to the other.

It is no shock to the preconceptions of old Vienna to say that epistemology now becomes semantics. For epistemology remains centered as always on evidence, and meaning remains centered as always on verification; and evidence is verification. What is likelier to shock preconceptions is that meaning, once we get beyond observation sentences, ceases in general to have any clear applicability to single sentences; also that epistemology merges with psychology, as well as with linguistics.

This rubbing out of boundaries could contribute to progress, it seems to me, in philosophically interesting inquiries of a scientific nature. One possible area is perceptual norms. Consider, to begin with, the linguistic phenomenon of phonemes. We form the habit, in hearing the myriad variations of spoken sounds, of treating each as an approximation to one or another of a limited number of norms—around thirty altogether—constituting so to speak a spoken alphabet. All speech in our language can be treated in practice as sequences of just those thirty elements, thus rectifying small deviations. Now outside the realm of language also there is probably only a rather limited alphabet of perceptual norms altogether, toward which we tend unconsciously to rectify all perceptions. These, if experimentally identified, could be taken as epistemological building blocks, the working elements of experience. They might prove in part to be culturally variable, as phonemes are, and in part universal.

Again there is the area that the psychologist Donald T. Campbell calls evolutionary epistemology. In this area there is work by Hüseyin Yilmaz, who shows how some structural traits of color perception could have been predicted from survival value. And a more emphatically epistemological topic that evolution helps to clarify is induction, now that we are allowing epistemology the resources of natural science.

Notes

1. A. B. Johnson, *A Treatise on Language* (New York, 1836; Berkeley, 1947).
2. Carnap, *Philosophy of Science* 3 (1936): 419–71; 4 (1937): 1–40.
3. See Quine, *Ontological Relativity* (New York, 1969), pp. 2ff.
4. See ibid., p. 28.

Ontological Relativity

I

I listened to Dewey on Art as Experience when I was a graduate student in the spring of 1931. Dewey was then at Harvard as the first William James Lecturer. I am proud now to be at Columbia as the first John Dewey Lecturer.

Philosophically I am bound to Dewey by the naturalism that dominated his last three decades. With Dewey I hold that knowledge, mind, and meaning are part of the same world that they have to do with, and that they are to be studied in the same empirical spirit that animates natural science. There is no place for a prior philosophy.

When a naturalistic philosopher addresses himself to the philosophy of mind, he is apt to talk of language. Meanings are, first and foremost, meanings of language. Language is a social art which we all acquire on the evidence solely of other people's overt behavior under publicly recognizable circum-

Originally published in W. V. Quine, *Ontological Relativity and other Essays* (Columbia University Press, 1969), pp. 26–68.

stances. Meanings, therefore, those very models of mental entities, end up as grist for the behaviorist's mill. Dewey was explicit on the point: "Meaning . . . is not a psychic existence; it is primarily a property of behavior."[1]

Once we appreciate the institution of language in these terms, we see that there cannot be, in any useful sense, a private language. This point was stressed by Dewey in the twenties. "Soliloquy," he wrote, "is the product and reflex of converse with others."[2] Further along he expanded the point thus: "Language is specifically a mode of interaction of at least two beings, a speaker and a hearer; it presupposes an organized group to which these creatures belong, and from whom they have acquired their habits of speech. It is therefore a relationship."[3] Years later, Wittgenstein likewise rejected private language. When Dewey was writing in this naturalistic vein, Wittgenstein still held his copy theory of language.

The copy theory in its various forms stands closer to the main philosophical tradition, and to the attitude of common sense today. Uncritical semantics is the myth of a museum in which the exhibits are meanings and the words are labels. To switch languages is to change the labels. Now the naturalist's primary objection to this view is not an objection to meanings on account of their being mental entities, though that could be objection enough. The primary objection persists even if we take the labeled exhibits not as mental ideas but as Platonic ideas or even as the denoted concrete objects. Semantics is vitiated by a pernicious mentalism as long as we regard a man's semantics as somehow determinate in his mind beyond what might be implicit in his dispositions to overt behavior. It is the very facts about meaning, not the entities meant, that must be construed in terms of behavior.

There are two parts to knowing a word. One part is being familiar with the sound of it and being able to reproduce it. This part, the phonetic part, is achieved by observing and imitating other people's behavior, and there are no important illusions about the process. The other part, the semantic part, is knowing how to use the word. This part, even in the paradigm case, is more complex than the phonetic part. The word refers, in the paradigm case, to some visible object. The learner has now not only to learn the word phonetically, by hearing it from another speaker; he also has to see the object; and in addition to this, in order to capture the relevance of the object to the word, he has to see that the speaker also sees the object. Dewey summed up the point thus: "The characteristic theory about *B*'s understanding of *A*'s sounds is that he responds to the thing from the standpoint of *A*."[4] Each of us, as he learns his language, is a student of his neighbor's behavior; and conversely, insofar as his tries are approved or corrected, he is a subject of his neighbor's behavioral study.

The semantic part of learning a word is more complex than the phonetic part, therefore, even in simple cases: we have to see what is stimulating the other speaker. In the case of words not directly ascribing observable traits to things, the learning process is increasingly complex and obscure; and obscurity is the breeding place of mentalistic semantics. What the naturalist insists on is that, even in the complex and obscure parts of language learning, the learner has no data to work with but the overt behavior of other speakers.

When with Dewey we turn thus toward a naturalistic view of language and a behavioral view of meaning, what we give up is not just the museum figure of speech. We give up an assurance of determinacy. Seen according to the museum myth, the words and sentences of a language have their determinate meanings. To discover the meanings of the native's words, we may have to observe his behavior, but still the meanings of the words are supposed to be determinate in the native's *mind*, his mental museum, even in cases where behavioral criteria are powerless to discover them for us. When on the other hand we recognize with Dewey that "meaning . . . is primarily a property of behavior," we recognize that there are no meanings, nor likenesses nor distinctions of meaning, beyond what are implicit in people's dispositions to overt behavior. For naturalism the question whether two expressions are alike or unlike in meaning has no determinate answer, known or unknown, except insofar as the answer is settled in principle by people's speech dispositions, known or unknown. If by these standards there are indeterminate cases, so much the worse for the terminology of meaning and likeness of meaning.

To see what such indeterminacy would be like, suppose there were an expression in a remote language that could be translated into English equally defensibly in either of two ways, unlike in meaning in English. I am not speaking of ambiguity within the native language. I am supposing that one and the same native use of the expression can be given either of the English translations, each being accommodated by compensating adjustments in the translation of other words. Suppose both translations, along with these accommodations in each case, accord equally well with all observable behavior on the part of speakers of the remote language and speakers of English. Suppose they accord perfectly not only with behavior actually observed, but with all dispositions to behavior on the part of all the speakers concerned. On these assumptions it would be forever impossible to know of one of these translations that it was the right one, and the other wrong. Still, if the museum myth were true, there would be a right and wrong of the matter; it is just that we would never know, not having access to the museum. See language naturalistically, on the other hand, and you have to see the notion of likeness of meaning in such a case simply as nonsense.

I have been keeping to the hypothetical. Turning now to examples, let me begin with a disappointing one and work up. In the French construction "ne . . . rien" you can translate "rien" into English as "anything" or as "nothing" at will, and then accommodate your choice by translating "ne" as "not" or by construing it as pleonastic. This example is disappointing because you can object that I have merely cut the French units too small. You can believe the mentalistic myth of the meaning museum and still grant that "rien" of itself has no meaning, being no whole label; it is part of "ne . . . rien," which has its meaning as a whole.

I began with this disappointing example because I think its conspicuous trait—its dependence on cutting language into segments too short to carry meanings—is the secret of the more serious cases as well. What makes other cases more serious is that the segments they involve are seriously long: long enough to be predicates and to be true of things and hence, you would think, to carry meanings.

An artificial example which I have used elsewhere[5] depends on the fact that a whole rabbit is present when and only when an undetached part of a rabbit is present; also when and only when a temporal stage of a rabbit is present. If we are wondering whether to translate a native expression "gavagai" as "rabbit" or as "undetached rabbit part" or as "rabbit stage," we can never settle the matter simply by ostension—that is, simply by repeatedly querying the expression "gavagai" for the native's assent or dissent in the presence of assorted stimulations.

Before going on to urge that we cannot settle the matter by non-ostensive means either, let me belabor this ostensive predicament a bit. I am not worrying, as Wittgenstein did, about simple cases of ostension. The color word "sepia," to take one of his examples,[6] can certainly be learned by an ordinary process of conditioning, or induction. One need not even be told that sepia is a color and not a shape or a material or an article. True, barring such hints, many lessons may be needed, so as to eliminate wrong generalizations based on shape, material, etc., rather than color, and so as to eliminate wrong notions as to the intended boundary of an indicated example, and so as to delimit the admissible variations of color itself. Like all conditioning, or induction, the process will depend ultimately also on one's own inborn propensity to find one stimulation qualitatively more akin to a second stimulation than to a third; otherwise there can never be any selective reinforcement and extinction of responses.[7] Still, in principle nothing more is needed in learning "sepia" than in any conditioning or induction.

But the big difference between "rabbit" and "sepia" is that whereas "sepia" is a mass term like "water," "rabbit" is a term of divided reference. As such it cannot be mastered without mastering its principle of individuation: where one rabbit leaves off and another begins. And this cannot be mastered by pure ostension, however persistent.

Such is the quandary over "gavagai": where one gavagai leaves off and another begins. The only difference between rabbits, undetached rabbit parts, and rabbit stages is in their individuation. If you take the total scattered portion of the spatio-temporal world that is made up of rabbits, and that which is made up of undetached rabbit parts, and that which is made up of rabbit stages, you come out with the same scattered portion of the world each of the three times. The only difference is in how you slice it. And how to slice it is what ostension or simple conditioning, however persistently repeated, cannot teach.

Thus consider specifically the problem of deciding between "rabbit" and "undetached rabbit part" as translation of "gavagai." No word of the native language is known, except that we have settled on some working hypothesis as to what native words or gestures to construe as assent and dissent in response to our pointings and queryings. Now the trouble is that whenever we point to different parts of the rabbit, even sometimes screening the rest of the rabbit, we are pointing also each time to the rabbit. When, conversely, we indicate the whole rabbit with a sweeping gesture, we are still pointing to a multitude of rabbit parts. And note that we do not have even a native analogue of our plural ending to exploit, in asking "gavagai?" It seems clear that no even tentative decision between "rabbit" and "undetached rabbit part" is to be sought at this level.

How would we finally decide? My passing mention of plural endings is part of the answer. Our individuating of terms of divided reference, in English, is bound up with a cluster of interrelated grammatical particles and constructions: plural endings, pronouns, numerals, the "is" of identity, and its adaptations "same" and "other." It is the cluster of interrelated devices in which quantification becomes central when the regimentation of symbolic logic is imposed. If in his language we could ask the native "Is this *gavagai* the same as that one?" while making appropriate multiple ostensions, then indeed we would be well on our way to deciding between "rabbit," "undetached rabbit part," and "rabbit stage." And of course the linguist does at length reach the point where he can ask what purports to be that question. He develops a system for translating our pluralizations, pronouns, numerals, identity, and related devices contextually into the native idiom. He develops such a system by abstraction and hypothesis. He abstracts native particles and constructions from observed native sentences and tries associating these variously with English particles and constructions. Insofar as the native sentences and the thus associated English ones seem to match up in respect of appropriate occasions of use, the linguist feels confirmed in these hypotheses of translation—what I call *analytical hypotheses*.[8]

But it seems that this method, though laudable in practice and the best we can hope for, does not in principle settle the indeterminancy between "rabbit," "undetached rabbit part," and "rabbit stage." For if one workable overall system of analytical hypotheses provides for translating a given native expression into "is the same as," perhaps another equally workable but systematically different system would translate that native expression rather into something like "belongs with." Then, when in the native language we try to ask, "Is this *gavagai* the same as that?," we could as well be asking "Does this *gavagai* belong with that?" Insofar, the native's assent is no objective evidence for translating "gavagai" as "rabbit" rather than "undetached rabbit part" or "rabbit stage."

This artificial example shares the structure of the trivial earlier example "ne . . . rien." We were able to translate "rien" as "anything" or as "nothing," thanks to a compensatory adjustment in the handling of "ne." And I suggest that we can translate "gavagai" as "rabbit" or "undetached rabbit part" or "rabbit stage," thanks to compensatory adjustments in the translation of accompanying native locutions. Other adjustments still might accommodate translation of "gavagai" as "rabbit-hood," or in further ways. I find this plausible because of the broadly structural and contextual character of any considerations that could guide us to native translations of the English cluster of interrelated devices of individuation. There seem bound to be systematically very different choices, all of which do justice to all dispositions to verbal behaviour on the part of all concerned.

An actual field linguist would of course be sensible enough to equate "gavagai" with "rabbit," dismissing such perverse alternatives as "undetached rabbit part" and "rabbit stage" out of hand. This sensible choice and others like it would help in turn to determine his subsequent hypotheses as to what native locutions should answer to the English apparatus of individuation, and thus everything would come out all right. The implicit maxim guiding his choice of "rabbit," and similar choices for other native words, is that an enduring and relatively homogeneous object, moving as a whole against a contrasting background, is a likely reference for a short expression. If he were to become conscious of this maxim, he might celebrate it as one of the linguistic universals, or traits of all languages, and he would have no trouble pointing out its psychological plausibility. But he would be wrong; the maxim is his own imposition, toward settling what is objectively indeterminate. It is a very sensible imposition, and I would recommend no other. But I am making a philosophical point.

It is philosophically interesting, moreover, that what is indeterminate in this artificial example is not just meaning, but extension; reference. My remarks on indeterminancy began as a challenge to likeness of meaning. I had us imagining "an expression that could be translated into English equally defensibly in either of two ways, unlike in meaning in English." Certainly likeness of meaning is a dim notion, repeatedly challenged. Of two predicates which are alike in extension, it has never been clear when to say that they are alike in meaning and when not; it is the old matter of featherless bipeds and rational animals, or of equiangular and equilateral triangles. Reference, extension, has been the firm thing; meaning, intension, the infirm. The indeterminacy of translation now confronting us, however, cuts across extension and intension alike. The terms "rabbit," "undetached rabbit part," and "rabbit stage" differ not only in meaning; they are true of different things. Reference itself proves behaviorally inscrutable.

Within the parochial limits of our own language, we can continue as always to find extensional talk clearer than intensional. For the indeterminancy between "rabbit," "rabbit stage," and the rest depended only on a correlative indeterminacy of translation of the English apparatus of individuation—the apparatus of pronouns, pluralization, identity, numerals, and so on. No such indeterminancy obtrudes so long as we think of this apparatus as given and fixed. Given this apparatus, there is no mystery about extension; terms have the same extension when true of the same things. At the level of radical translation, on the other hand, extension itself goes inscrutable.

My example of rabbits and their parts and stages is a contrived example and a perverse one, with which, as I said, the practicing linguist would have no patience. But there are also cases, less bizarre ones, that obtrude in practice. In Japanese there are certain particles, called "classifiers," which may be explained in either of two ways. Commonly they are explained as attaching to numerals, to form compound numerals of distinctive styles. Thus take the numeral for 5. If you attach one classifier to it, you get a style of "5" suitable for counting animals; if you attach a different classifier, you get a style of "5" suitable for counting slim things like pencils and chopsticks; and so on. But another way of viewing classifiers is to view them not as constituting part of the numeral, but as constituting part of the term—the term for "chopsticks" or "oxen" or whatever. On this view the classifier does the individuative job that is done in English by "sticks of" as applied to the mass term "wood," or "head of" as applied to the mass term "cattle."

What we have on either view is a Japanese phrase tantamount say to "five oxen," but consisting of three words[9], the first is in effect the neutral numeral "5," the second is a classifier of the animal kind, and the last corresponds in some fashion to "ox." On one view the neutral numeral and the classifier go together to constitute a declined numeral in the "animal gender," which then modifies "ox" to give, in effect, "five oxen." On the other view the third Japanese word answers not to the individuative term "ox" but to the mass term "cattle"; the classifier applies to this mass term to produce a composite individuative term, in effect "head of cattle"; and the neutral numeral applies directly to all this without benefit of gender, giving "five head of cattle," hence again in effect "five oxen."

If so simple an example is to serve its expository purpose, it needs your connivance. You have to understand "cattle" as a mass term covering only bovines, and "ox" as applying to all bovines. That these usages are not the invariable usages is beside the point. The point is that the Japanese phrase comes out as "five bovines," as desired, when parsed in either of two ways. The one way treats the third Japanese word as an individuative term true of each bovine, and the other way treats that word rather as a mass term covering the unindividuated totality of beef on the hoof. These are two very different ways of treating the third Japanese word; and the three-word phrase as a whole turns out all right in both cases only because of compensatory differences in our account of the second word, the classifier.

This example is reminiscent in a way of our trivial initial example, "ne . . . rien." We were able to represent "rien" as "anything" or as "nothing," by compensatorily taking "ne" as negative or as vacuous. We are able now to represent a Japanese word either as an individuative term for bovines or as a mass term for live beef, by compensatorily taking the classifer as declining the numeral or as individuating the mass term. However, the triviality of the one example does not quite carry over to the other. The early example was dismissed on the ground that we had cut too small; "rien" was too short for significant translation on its own, "and 'ne . . . rien' " was the significant unit. But you cannot dismiss the Japanese example by saying that the third word was too short for significant translation on its own and that only the whole three-word phrase, tantamount to "five oxen," was the significant unit. You cannot take this line unless you are prepared to call a word too short for significant translation even when it is long enough to be a term and carry denotation. For the third Japanese word is, on either approach, a term: on one approach a term of divided reference, and on the other a mass term. If you are indeed prepared thus to call a word too short for significant translation even when it is a denoting term, then in a backhanded way you are granting what I wanted to prove: the inscrutability of reference.

Between the two accounts of Japanese classifiers there is no question of right and wrong. The one account makes for more efficient translation into idiomatic English; the other makes for more of a feeling for the Japanese idiom. Both fit all verbal behavior equally well. All whole sentences, and even component phrases like "five oxen," admit of the same net overall English translations on either account. This much is invariant. But what is philosophically interesting is that the reference or extension of shorter terms can fail to be invariant. Whether that third Japanese word is itself true of each ox, or whether on the other hand it is a mass term which needs to be adjoined to the classifier to make a term which is true of each ox—here is a question that remains undecided by the totality of human dispositions to verbal behavior. It is indeterminate in principle; there is no fact of the matter. Either answer can be accommodated by an account of the classifier. Here again, then, is the inscrutability of reference—illustrated this time by a humdrum point of practical translation.

The inscrutability of reference can be brought closer to home by considering the word "alpha," or again the word "green." In our use of these words and others like them there is a systematic ambiguity. Sometimes we use such words as concrete general terms, as when we say the grass is green, or that some inscription begins with an alpha. Sometimes, on the other hand, we use them as abstract singular terms, as when we say that green is a color and alpha is a letter. Such ambiguity is encouraged by the fact that there is nothing in ostension to distinguish the two uses. The pointing that would be done in teaching the concrete general term "green" or "alpha" differs none from the pointing that would be done in teaching the abstract singular term "green" or "alpha." Yet the objects referred to by the word are very different under the two uses; under the one use the word is true of many concrete objects, and under the other use it names a single abstract object.

We can of course tell the two uses apart by seeing how the word turns up in sentences: whether it takes an indefinite article, whether it takes a plural ending, whether it stands as singular subject, whether it stands as modifier, as predicate complement, and so on. But these criteria appeal to our special English grammatical constructions and particles, our special English apparatus of individuation, which, I already urged, is itself subject to indeterminacy of translation. So, from the point of view of translation into a remote language, the distinction between a concrete general and an abstract singular term is in the same predicament as the distinction between "rabbit," "rabbit part," and "rabbit stage." Here then is another example of the inscrutability of reference, since the difference between the concrete general and the abstract singular is a difference in the objects referred to.

Incidentally we can concede this much indeterminacy also to the "sepia" example, after all. But this move is not evidently what was worrying Wittgenstein.

The ostensive indistinguishability of the abstract singular from the concrete general turns upon what may be called "deferred ostension," as opposed to direct ostension. First let me define direct ostension. The *ostended point*, as I shall call it, is the point where the line of the pointing finger first meets an opaque surface. What characterizes *direct ostension*, then, is that the term which is being ostensively explained is true of something that contains the ostended point. Even such direct ostension has its uncertainties, of course, and these are familiar. There is the question how wide an environment of the ostended point is meant to be covered by the term that is being ostensively explained. There is the question how considerably an absent thing or substance might be allowed to differ from what is now ostended, and still be covered by the term that is now being ostensively explained. Both of these questions can in principle be settled as well as need be by induction from multiple ostensions. Also, if the term is a term of divided reference like "apple," there is the question of individuation: the question where one of its objects leaves off and another begins. This can be settled by induction from multiple ostensions of a more elaborate kind, accompanied by expressions like "same apple" and "another," if an equivalent of this English apparatus of individuation has been settled on; otherwise the indeterminacy persists that was illustrated by "rabbit," "undetached rabbit part," and "rabbit stage."

Such, then, is the way of direct ostension. Other ostension I call *deferred*. It occurs when we point at the gauge, and not the gasoline, to show that there is gasoline. Also it occurs when we explain the abstract singular term "green" or "alpha" by pointing at grass or a Greek inscription. Such pointing is direct ostension when used to explain the concrete general term "green" or "alpha," but it is deferred ostension when used to explain the abstract singular terms; for the abstract object which is the color green or the letter alpha does not contain the ostended point, nor any point.

Deferred ostension occurs very naturally when, as in the case of the gasoline gauge, we have a correspondence in mind. Another such example is afforded by the Gödel numbering of expressions. Thus if 7 has been assigned as Gödel number of the letter alpha, a man conscious of the Gödel numbering would not hesitate to say "Seven" on pointing to an inscription of the Greek letter in question. This is, on the face of it, a doubly deferred ostension: one step of deferment carries us from the inscription to the letter as abstract object, and a second step carries us thence to the number.

By appeal to our apparatus of individuation, if it is available, we can distinguish between the concrete general and the abstract singular use of the word "alpha"; this we saw. By appeal again to that apparatus, and in particular to identity, we can evidently settle also whether the word "alpha" in its abstract singular use is being used really to name the letter or whether, perversely, it is being used to name the Gödel number of the letter. At any rate we can distinguish these alternatives if also we have located the speaker's equivalent of the numeral "7" to our satisfaction; for we can ask him whether alpha *is* 7.

These considerations suggest that deferred ostension adds no essential problem to those presented by direct ostension. Once we have settled upon analytical hypotheses of translation covering identity and the other English particles relating to individuation, we can resolve not only the indecision between "rabbit" and "rabbit stage" and the rest, which came of direct ostension, but also any indecision between concrete general and abstract singular, and any indecision between expression and Gödel number, which come of deferred ostension. However, this conclusion is too sanguine. The inscrutability of reference runs deep, and it persists in a subtle form even if we accept identity and the rest of the apparatus of individuation as fixed and settled; even, indeed, if we forsake radical translation and think only of English.

Consider the case of a thoughtful protosyntactician. He has a formalized system of first-order proof theory, or protosyntax, whose universe comprises just expressions, that is, strings of signs of a specified alphabet. Now just what sorts of things, more specifically, are these expressions? They are types, not tokens. So, one might suppose, each of them is the set of all its tokens. That is, each expression is a set of inscriptions which are variously situated in space-time but are classed together by virtue of a certain similarity in shape. The concatenate $x \frown y$ of two expressions x and y, in a given order, will be the set of all inscriptions each of which has two parts which are tokens respectively of x and y and follow one upon the other in that order. But $x \frown y$ may then be the null set, though x and y are not null; for it may be that inscriptions belonging to x and y happen to turn up head to tail nowhere, in the past, present, or future. This danger increases with the lengths of x and y. But it is easily seen to violate a law of protosyntax which says that $x = z$ whenever $x \frown y = z \frown y$.

Thus it is that our thoughtful protosyntactician will not construe the things in his universe as sets of inscriptions. He can still take his atoms, the single signs, as sets of inscriptions, for there is no risk of nullity in these cases. And then, instead of taking his strings of signs as sets of inscriptions, he can invoke the mathematical notion of sequence and take them as sequences of signs. A familiar way of taking sequences, in turn, is as a mapping of things on numbers. On this approach an expression or string of signs becomes a finite set of pairs each of which is the pair of a sign and a number.

This account of expressions is more artificial and more complex than one is apt to expect who simply says he is letting his variables range over the strings of such and such signs. Moreover, it is not the inevitable choice; the considerations that motivated it can be met also by alternative constructions. One of these constructions is Gödel numbering itself, and it is temptingly simple. It uses just natural numbers, whereas the foregoing construction used sets of one-letter inscriptions and also natural numbers and sets of pairs of these. How clear is it that at just *this* point we have dropped expressions in favor of numbers? What is clearer is merely that in both constructions we were artificially devising models to satisfy laws that expressions in an unexplicated sense had been meant to satisfy.

So much for expressions. Consider now the arithmetician himself, with his elementary number theory. His universe comprises the natural numbers outright. Is it clearer than the protosyntactician's?

What, after all, is a natural number? There are Frege's version, Zermelo's, and von Neumann's, and countless further alternatives, all mutually incompatible and equally correct. What we are doing in any one of these explications of natural number is to devise set-theoretic models to satisfy laws which the natural numbers in an unexplicated sense had been meant to satisfy. The case is quite like that of protosyntax.

It will perhaps be felt that any set-theoretic explication of natural number is at best a case of *obscurum per obscurius*; that all explications must assume something, and the natural numbers themselves are an admirable assumption to start with. I must agree that a construction of sets and set theory from natural numbers and arithmetic would be far more desirable than the familiar opposite. On the other hand, our impression of the clarity even of the notion of natural number itself has suffered somewhat from Gödel's proof of the impossibility of a complete proof procedure for elementary number theory, or, for that matter, from Skolem's and Henkin's observations that all laws of natural numbers admit nonstandard models.[10]

We are finding no clear difference between *specifying* a universe of discourse—the range of the variables of quantification—and *reducing* that universe to some other. We saw no significant difference between clarifying the notion of expression and supplanting it by that of number. And now to say more particularly what numbers themselves are is in no evident way different from just dropping numbers and assigning to arithmetic one or another new model, say in set theory.

Expressions are known only by their laws, the laws of concatenation theory, so that any constructs obeying those laws—Gödel numbers, for instance—are ipso facto eligible as explications of expression. Numbers in turn are known only by their laws, the laws of arithmetic, so that any constructs obeying those laws—certain sets, for instance—are eligible in turn as explications of number. Sets in turn are known only by their laws, the laws of set theory.

Russell pressed a contrary thesis, long ago. Writing of numbers, he argued that for an understanding of number the laws of arithmetic are not enough; we must know the applications, we must understand numerical discourse embedded in discourse of other matters. In applying number, the key notion, he urged, is *Anzahl*: there are *n* so-and-so's. However, Russell can be answered. First take, specifically, *Anzahl*. We can define "there are *n* so-and-so's" without ever deciding what numbers are, apart from their fulfillment of arithmetic. That there are *n* so-and-so's can be explained simply as meaning that the so-and-so's are in one-to-one correspondence with the numbers up to *n*.[11]

Russell's more general point about application can be answered too. Always, if the structure is there, the applications will fall into place. As paradigm it is perhaps sufficient to recall again this reflection on expressions and Gödel numbers: that even the pointing out of an inscription is no final evidence that our talk is of expressions and not of Gödel numbers. We can always plead deferred ostension.

It is in this sense true to say, as mathematicians often do, that arithmetic is all there is to number. But it would be a confusion to express this point by saying, as is sometimes said, that numbers are any things fulfilling arithmetic. This formulation is wrong because distinct domains of objects yield distinct models of arithmetic. Any progression can be made to serve; and to identify all progressions with one another, e.g., to identify the progression of odd numbers with the progression of evens, would contradict arithmetic after all.

So, though Russell was wrong in suggesting that numbers need more than their arithmetical properties, he was right in objecting to the definition of numbers as any things fulfilling arithmetic. The subtle point is that any progression will serve as a version of number so long and only so long as we stick to one and the same progression. Arithmetic is, in this sense, all there is to number: there is no saying absolutely what the numbers are; there is only arithmetic.[12]

II

I first urged the inscrutability of reference with the help of examples like the one about rabbits and rabbit parts. These used direct ostension, and the inscrutability of reference hinged on the indeterminacy of translation of identity and other individuative apparatus. The setting of these examples, accordingly, was radical translation: translation from a remote language on behavioral evidence, unaided by prior dictionaries. Moving then to deferred ostension and abstract objects, we found a certain dimness of reference pervading the home language itself.

Now it should be noted that even for the earlier

examples the resort to a remote language was not really essential. On deeper reflection, radical translation begins at home. Must we equate our neighbor's English words with the same strings of phonemes in our own mouths? Certainly not; for sometimes we do not thus equate them. Sometimes we find it to be in the interests of communication to recognize that our neighbor's use of some word, such as "cool" or "square" or "hopefully," differs from ours, and so we translate that word of his into a different string of phonemes in our idiolect. Our usual domestic rule of translation is indeed the homophonic one, which simply carries each string of phonemes into itself; but still we are always prepared to temper homophony with what Neil Wilson has called the "principle of charity."[13] We will construe a neighbor's word heterophonically now and again if thereby we see our way to making his message less absurd.

The homophonic rule is a handy one on the whole. That is works so well is no accident, since imitation and feedback are what propagate a language. We acquired a great fund of basic words and phrases in this way, imitating our elders and encouraged by our elders amid external circumstances to which the phrases suitably apply. Homophonic translation is implicit in this social method of learning. Departure from homophonic translation in this quarter would only hinder communication. Then there are the relatively rare instances of opposite kind, due to divergence in dialect or confusion in an individual, where homophonic translation incurs negative feedback. But what tends to escape notice is that there is also a vast mid-region where the homophonic method is indifferent. Here, gratuitously, we can systematically reconstrue our neighbor's apparent references to rabbit stages, and his apparent references to formulas as really references to Gödel numbers, and vice versa. We can reconcile all this with our neighbor's verbal behavior, by cunningly readjusting our translations of his various connecting predicates so as to compensate for the switch of ontology. In short, we can reproduce the inscrutability of reference at home. It is of no avail to check on this fanciful version of our neighbor's meanings by asking him, say, whether he really means at a certain point to refer to formulas or to their Gödel numbers; for our question and his answer—"By all means, the numbers"—have lost their title to homophonic translation. The problem at home differs none from radical translation ordinarily so called except in the willfulness of this suspension of homophonic translation.

I have urged in defense of the behavioral philosophy of language, Dewey's, that the inscrutability of reference is not the inscrutability of a fact; there is no fact of the matter. But if there is really no fact of the matter, then the inscrutability of reference can be brought even closer to home than the neighbor's case; we can apply it to ourselves. If it is to make sense to say even of oneself that one is refering to rabbits and formulas and not to rabbit stages and Gödel numbers, then it should make sense equally to say it of someone else. After all, as Dewey stressed, there is no private language.

We seem to be maneuvering ourselves into the absurd position that there is no difference on any terms, interlinguistic or intralinguistic, objective or subjective, between referring to rabbits and referring to rabbit parts or stages; or between referring to formulas and referring to their Gödel numbers. Surely this is absurd, for it would imply that there is no difference between the rabbit and each of its parts or stages, and no difference between a formula and its Gödel number. Reference would seem now to become nonsense not just in radical translation but at home.

Toward resolving this quandary, begin by picturing us at home in our language, with all its predicates and auxiliary devices. This vocabulary includes "rabbit," "rabbit part," "rabbit stage," "formula," "number," "ox," "cattle"; also the two-place predicates of identity and difference, and other logical particles. In these terms we can say in so many words that this is a formula and that a number, this a rabbit and that a rabbit part, this and that the same rabbit, and this and that different parts. *In just those words.* This network of terms and predicates and auxiliary devices is, in relativity jargon, our frame of reference, or coordinate system. Relative to *it* we can and do talk meaningfully and distinctively of rabbits and parts, numbers and formulas. Next, as in recent paragraphs, we contemplate alternative denotations for our familiar terms. We begin to appreciate that a grand and ingenious permutation of these denotations, along with compensatory adjustments in the interpretations of the auxiliary particles, might still accommodate all existing speech dispositions. This was the inscrutability of reference, applied to ourselves; and it made nonsense of reference. Fair enough; reference *is* nonsense except relative to a coordinate system. In this principle of relativity lies the resolution of our quandary.

It is meaningless to ask whether, in general, our terms "rabbit," "rabbit part," "number," etc. really refer respectively to rabbits, rabbit parts, numbers, etc., rather than to some ingeniously permuted denotations. It is meaningless to ask this absolutely; we can meaningfully ask it only relative to some background language. When we ask, "Does 'rabbit' really refer to rabbits?," someone can counter with the question: "Refer to rabbits in what sense of 'rabbits'?," thus launching a regress; and we need the background language to regress into. The background language gives the query sense, if only relative sense; sense relative in turn to it, this background language. Querying reference in any more absolute way would be like asking absolute position, or absolute velocity, rather than position or velocity relative to a given frame of reference. Also it is very much like asking whether our neighbour may not systematically see everything upside down, or in complementary color, forever undetectably.

We need a background language, I said, to regress into. Are we involved now in an infinite regress? If questions of reference of the sort we are considering make sense only relative to a background language, then evidently questions of reference for the background language make sense in turn only relative to a further background language. In these terms the situation sounds desperate, but in fact it is little different from questions of position and velocity. When we are given position and velocity relative to a given coordinate system, we can always ask in turn about the placing of origin and orientation of axes of that system of coordinates; and there is no end to the succession of further coordinate systems that could be adduced in answering the successive questions thus generated.

In practice of course we end the regress of coordinate systems by something like pointing. And in practice we end the regress of background languages, in discussions of reference, by acquiescing in our mother tongue and taking its words at face value.

Very well; in the case of position and velocity, in practice, pointing breaks the regress. But what of position and velocity apart from practice? what of the regress then? The answer, of course, is the relational doctrine of space; there is no absolute position or velocity; there are just the relations of coordinate systems to one another, and ultimately of things to one another. And I think that the parallel question regarding denotation calls for a parallel answer, a relational theory of what the objects of a theories are. What makes sense is to say not what the objects of a theory are, absolutely speaking, but how one theory of objects is interpretable or reinterpretable in another.

The point is not that bare matter is inscrutable: that things are indistinguishable except by their properties. That point does not need making. The present point is reflected better in the riddle about seeing things upside down, or in complementary colors; for it is that things can be inscrutably switched even while carrying their properties with them. Rabbits differ from rabbit parts and rabbit stages not just as bare matter, after all, but in respect of properties; and formulas differ from numbers in respect of properties. What our present reflections are leading us to appreciate is that the riddle about seeing things upside down, or in complementary colors, should be taken seriously and its moral applied widely. The relativistic thesis to which we have come is this, to repeat: it makes no sense to say what the objects of a theory are, beyond saying how to interpret or reinterpret that theory in another. Suppose we are working within a theory and thus treating of its objects. We do so by using the variables of the theory, whose values those objects are, though there be no ultimate sense in which that universe can have been specified. In the language of the theory there are predicates by which to distinguish portions of this universe from other portions, and these predicates differ from one another purely in the roles they play in the laws of the theory. Within this background theory we can show how some subordinate theory, whose universe is some portion of the background universe, can by a reinterpretation be reduced to another subordinate theory whose universe is some lesser portion. Such talk of subordinate theories and their ontologies *is* meaningful, but only relative to the background theory with its own primitively adopted and ultimately inscrutable ontology.

To talk thus of theories raises a problem of formulation. A theory, it will be said, is a set of fully interpreted sentences. (More particularly, it is a deductively closed set: it includes all its own logical consequences, insofar as they are couched in the same notation.) But if the sentences of a theory are fully interpreted, then in particular the range of values of their variables is settled. How then can there be no sense in saying what the objects of a theory are?

My answer is simply that we cannot require theories to be fully interpreted, except in a relative sense, if anything is to count as a theory. In specifying a theory we must indeed fully specify, in our own words, what sentences are to comprise the theory, and what things are to be taken as values of the variables, and what things are to be taken as satisfying the predicate letters; insofar we do fully interpret the theory, *relative* to our own words and relative to our overall home theory which lies behind them. But this fixes the objects of the described theory only relative to those of the home theory; and these can, at will, be questioned in turn.

One is tempted to conclude simply that meaninglessness sets in when we try to pronounce on everything in our universe; that universal predication takes on sense only when furnished with the background of a wider universe, where the predication is no longer universal. And this is even a familiar doctrine, the doctrine that no proper predicate is true of everything. We have all heard it claimed that a predicate is meaningful only by contrast with what it excludes, and hence that being true of everything would make a predicate meaningless. But surely this doctrine is wrong. Surely self-identity, for instance, is not to be rejected as meaningless. For that matter, any statement of fact at all, however brutally meaningful, can be put artifically into a form in which it pronounces on everything. To say merely of Jones that he sings, for instance, is to say of everything that it is other than Jones or sings. We had better beware of repudiating universal predication, lest we be tricked into repudiating everything there is to say.

Carnap took an intermediate line in his doctrine of universal words, or *Allwörter*, in *The Logical Syntax of Language*. He did treat the predicating of universal words as "quasi-syntactical"—as a predication only by courtesy, and without empirical content. But universal words were for him not just any universally true predicates, like "is other than Jones or sings." They were a special breed of universally true predicates, ones that are universally true by the sheer meanings of their words and no thanks to nature. In his later writing this doctrine of universal words takes the form of a distinction between "internal" questions, in which a theory comes to grips with facts about the world, and "external" questions, in which people come to grips with the relative merits of theories.

Should we look to these distinctions of Carnap's for light on ontological relativity? When we found there was no absolute sense in saying what a theory is about, were we sensing the in-factuality of what Carnap calls "external questions"? When we found that saying what a theory is about did make sense against a background theory, were we sensing the factuality of internal questions of the background theory? I see no hope of illumination in this quarter. Carnap's universal words were not just any universally true predicates, but, as I said, a special breed; and what distinguishes this breed is not clear. What I said distinguished them was that they were universally true by sheer meanings and not by nature; but this is a very questionable distinction. Talking of "internal" and "external" is no better.

Ontological relativity is not to be clarified by any distinction between kinds of universal predication—unfactual and factual, external and internal. It is not a question of universal predication. When questions regarding the ontology of a theory are meaningless absolutely, and become meaningful relative to a background theory, this is not in general because the background theory has a wider universe. One is tempted, as I said a little while back, to suppose that it is; but one is then wrong.

What makes ontological questions meaningless when taken absolutely is not universality but circularity. A question of the form "What is an *F*?" can be answered only by recourse to a further term: "An *F* is a *G*." The answer makes only relative sense: sense relative to the uncritical acceptance of "*G*."

We may picture the vocabulary of a theory as comprising logical signs such as quantifiers and the signs for the truth functions and identity, and in addition descriptive or nonlogical signs, which, typically, are singular terms, or names, and general terms, or predicates. Suppose next that in the statements which comprise the theory, that is, are true according to the theory, we abstract from the meanings of the nonlogical vocabulary and from the range of the variables. We are left with the logical form of the theory, or, as I shall say, the *theory form*. Now we may interpret this theory form anew by picking a new universe for its variables of quantification to range over, and assigning objects from this universe to the names, and choosing subsets of this universe as extensions of the oneplace predicates, and so on. Each such interpretation of the theory form is called a model of it, if it makes it come out true. Which of these models is meant in a given actual theory cannot, of course, be guessed from the theory form. The intended references of the names and predicates have to be learned rather by ostension, or else by paraphrase in some antecedently familiar vocabulary. But the first of these two ways has proved inconclusive, since, even apart from indeterminacies of translation affecting identity and other logical vocabulary, there is the problem of deferred ostension. Paraphrase in some antecedently familiar vocabulary, then, is our only recourse; and such is ontological relativity. To question the reference of all the terms of our all-inclusive theory becomes meaningless, simply for want of further terms relative to which to ask or answer the question.

It is thus meaningless within the theory to say which of the various possible models of our theory form is our real or intended model. Yet even here we can make sense still of there being many models. For we might be able to show that for each of the models, however unspecifiable, there is bound to be another which is a permutation or perhaps a diminution of the first.

Suppose, for example, that our theory is purely numerical. Its objects are just the natural numbers. There is no sense in saying, from within that theory, just which of the various models of number theory is in force. But we can observe even from within the theory that, whatever 0, 1, 2, 3, etc. may be, the theory would still hold true if the 17 of this series were moved into the role of 0, and the 18 moved into the role of 1, and so on.

Ontology is indeed doubly relative. Specifying the universe of a theory makes sense only relative to some background theory, and only relative to some choice of a manual of translation of the one theory into the other. Commonly of course the background theory will simply be a containing theory, and in this case no question of a manual of translation arises. But this is after all just a degenerate case of translation still—the case where the rule of translation is the homophonic one.

We cannot know what something is without knowing how it is marked off from other things. Identity is thus of a piece with ontology. Accordingly it is involved in the same relativity, as may be readily illustrated. Imagine a fragment of economic theory. Suppose its universe comprises persons, but its predicates are incapable of distinguishing between persons whose incomes are equal. The interpersonal relation of equality of income enjoys, within the theory, the substitutivity property of the identity relation itself; the two relations are indistinguishable. It is only relative to a background theory, in which more can be said of personal identity than equality of income, that we are able even to appreciate the above account of the fragment of economic theory, hinging as the account does on a contrast between persons and incomes.

A usual occasion for ontological talk is reduction, where it is shown how the universe of some theory can by a reinterpretation be dispensed with in favor of some other universe, perhaps a proper part of the first. I have treated elsewhere[14] of the reduction of one ontology to another with help of a *proxy function*: a function mapping the one universe into part or all of the other. For instance, the function "Gödel number of" is a proxy function. The universe of elementary proof theory or protosyntax, which consists of expressions or strings of signs, is mapped by this function into the universe of elementary number theory, which consists of numbers.

The proxy function used in reducing one ontology to another need not, like Gödel numbering, be one-to-one. We might, for instance, be confronted with a theory treating of both expressions and ratios. We would cheerfully reduce all this to the universe of natural numbers, by invoking a proxy function which enumerates the expressions in the Gödel way and enumerates the ratios by the classical method of short diagonals. This proxy function is not one-to-one, since it assigns the same natural number both to an expression and to a ratio. We would tolerate the resulting artificial convergence between expressions and ratios, simply because the original theory made no capital of the distinction between them; they were so invariably and extravagantly unlike that the identity question did not arise. Formally speaking, the original theory used a two-sorted logic.

For another kind of case where we would not require the proxy function to be one-to-one, consider again the fragment of economic theory lately noted. We would happily reduce its ontology of persons to a less numerous one of incomes. The proxy function would assign to each person his income. It is not one-to-one; distinct persons give way to identical incomes. The reason such a reduction is acceptable is that it merges the images of only such individuals as never had been distinguishable by the predicates of the original theory. Nothing in the old theory is contravened by the new identities.

If on the other hand the theory that we are concerned to reduce or reinterpret is straight protosyntax, or a straight arithmetic of ratios or of real numbers, then a one-to-one proxy function is mandatory. This is because any two elements of such a theory are distinguishable in terms of the theory. This is true even for the real numbers, even though not every real number is uniquely specifiable; any two real numbers x and y are still distinguishable, in that $x < y$ or $y < x$ and never $x < x$. A proxy function that did not preserve the distinctness of the elements of such a theory would fail of its purpose of reinterpretation.

One ontology is *always* reducible to another when we are given a proxy function f that is one-to-one. The essential reasoning is as follows. Where P is any predicate of the old system, its work can be done in the new system by a new predicate which we interpret as true of just the correlates fx of the old objects x that P was true of. Thus suppose we take fx as the Gödel number of x, and as our old system we take a syntactical system in which one of the predicates is "is a segment of." The corresponding predicate of the new or numerical system, then, would be one which amounts, so far as its extension is concerned, to the words "is the Gödel number of a segment of that whose Gödel number is." The numerical predicate would not be given this devious form, of course, but would be rendered as an appropriate purely arithmetical condition.

Our dependence upon a background theory becomes especially evident when we reduce our universe U to another V by appeal to a proxy function. For it is only in a theory with an inclusive universe, embracing U and V, that we can make sense of the proxy function. The function maps U into V and hence needs all the old objects of U as well as their new proxies in V.

The proxy function need not exist as an object in the universe even of the background theory. It may do its work merely as what I have called a "virtual class,"[15] and Gödel has called a "notion."[16] That is to say, all that is required toward a function is an open sentence with two free variables, provided that it is fulfilled by exactly one value of the first variable for each object of the old universe as value of the second variable. But the point is that it is only in the background theory, with its inclusive universe, that we can hope to write such a sentence and have the right values at our disposal for its variables.

If the new objects happen to be among the old, so that V is a subclass of U, then the old theory with universe U can itself sometimes qualify as the background theory in which to describe its own ontological reduction. But we cannot do better than that; we cannot declare our new ontological economies without having recourse to the uneconomical old ontology.

This sounds, perhaps, like a predicament: as if no ontological economy is justifiable unless it is a false economy and the repudiated objects really exist after all. But actually this is wrong; there is no more cause for worry here than there is in *reductio ad absurdum*, where we assume a falsehood that we are out to disprove. If what we want to show is that the universe U is excessive and that only a part exists, or need exist, then we are quite within our rights to assume all of U for the space of the argument. We show thereby that if all of U were needed, then not all of U would be needed; and so our ontological reduction is sealed by *reductio ad absurdum*.

Toward further appreciating the bearing of ontological relativity on programs of ontological reduction, it is worthwhile to reexamine the philosophical bearing of the Löwenheim–Skolem theorem. I shall use the strong early form of the theorem,[17] which depends on the axiom of choice. It says that if a theory is true and has an indenumerable universe, then all but a denumerable part of that universe is dead wood, in the sense that it can be dropped from the range of the variables without falsifying any sentences.

On the face of it, this theorem declares a reduction of all acceptable theories to denumerable ontologies. Moreover, a denumerable ontology is reducible in turn to an ontology specifically of natural numbers, simply by taking the enumeration as the proxy function, if the enumeration is explicitly at hand. And even if it is not at hand, it exists; thus we can still think of all our objects as natural numbers, and merely reconcile ourselves to not always knowing, numerically, which number an otherwise given object is. May we not thus settle for an all-purpose Pythagorean ontology outright?

Suppose, afterward, someone were to offer us what would formerly have qualified as an ontological reduction—a way of dispensing in future theory with all things of a certain sort S, but still leaving an infinite universe. Now in the new Pythagorean setting his discovery would still retain its essential content, though relinquishing the form of an ontological reduction; it would take the form merely of a move whereby some numerically unspecified numbers were divested of some property of numbers that corresponded to *S*.

Blanket Pythagoreanism on these terms is unattractive, for it merely offers new and obscurer accounts of old moves and old problems. On this score again, then, the relativistic proposition seems reasonable: that there is no absolute sense in speaking of the ontology of a theory. It very creditably brands this Pythagoreanism itself as meaningless. For there is no absolute sense in saying that all the objects of a theory are numbers, or that they are sets, or bodies, or something else; this makes no sense unless relative to some background theory. The relevant predicates—"number," "set," "body," or whatever—would be distinguished from *one another* in the background theory by the roles they play in the laws of that theory.

Elsewhere I urged in answer to such Pythagoreanism that we have no ontological reduction in an interesting sense unless we can specify a proxy function. Now where does the strong Löwenheim–Skolem theorem leave us in this regard? If the background theory assumes the axiom of choice and even provides a notation for a general selector operator, can we in these terms perhaps specify an actual proxy function embodying the Löwenheim–Skolem argument?

The theorem is that all but a denumerable part of an ontology can be dropped and not be missed. One could imagine that the proof proceeds by partitioning the universe into denumerably many equivalence classes of indiscriminable objects, such that all but one member of each equivalence class can be dropped as superfluous; and one would then guess that where the axiom of choice enters the proof is in picking a survivor from each equivalence class. If this were so, then with help of Hilbert's selector notation we could indeed express a proxy function. But in fact the Löwenheim–Skolem proof has another structure. I see in the proof even of the strong Löwenheim–Skolem theorem no reason to suppose that a proxy function can be formulated anywhere that will map an indenumerable ontology, say the real numbers, into a denumerable one.

On the face of it, of course, such a proxy function is out of the question. It would have to be one-to-one, as we saw, to provide distinct images of distinct real numbers; and a one-to-one mapping of an indenumerable domain into a denumerable one is a contradiction. In particular it is easy to show in the Zermelo–Fraenkel system of set theory that such a function would neither exist nor admit even of formulation as a virtual class in the notation of the system.

The discussion of the ontology of a theory can make variously stringent demands upon the background theory in which the discussion is couched. The stringency of these demands varies with what is being said about the ontology of the object theory. We are now in a position to distinguish three such grades of stringency.

The least stringent demand is made when, with no view to reduction, we merely explain what things a theory is about, or what things its terms denote. This amounts to showing how to translate part or all of the object theory into the background theory. It is a matter really of showing how we *propose*, with some arbitrariness, to relate terms of the object theory to terms of the background theory; for we have the inscrutability of reference to allow for. But there is here no requirement that the background theory have a wider universe or a stronger vocabulary than the object theory. The theories could even be identical; this is the case when some terms are clarified by definition on the basis of other terms of the same language.

A more stringent demand was observed in the case where a proxy function is used to reduce an ontology. In this case the background theory needed the unreduced universe. But we saw, by considerations akin to *reductio ad absurdum*, that there was little here to regret.

The third grade of stringency has emerged now in the kind of ontological reduction hinted at by the Löwenheim-Skolem theorem. If a theory has by its own account an indenumerable universe, then even by taking that whole unreduced theory as background theory we cannot hope to produce a proxy function that would be adequate to reducing the ontology to a denumerable one. To find such a proxy function, even just a virtual one, we would need a background theory essentially stronger than the theory we were trying to reduce. This demand cannot, like the second grade of stringency above, be accepted in the spirit of *reductio ad absurdum*. It is a demand that simply discourages any general argument for Pythagoreanism from the Löwenheim–Skolem theorem.

A place where we see a more trivial side of ontological relativity is in the case of a finite universe of named objects. Here there is no occasion for quantification, except as an inessential abbreviation; for we can expand quantifications into finite conjunctions and alternations. Variables thus disappear, and with them the question of a universe of values of variables. And the very distinction between names and other signs lapses in turn, since the mark of a name is its admissibility in positions of variables. Ontology thus is emphatically meaningless for a finite theory of named objects, considered in and of itself. Yet we are now talking meaningfully of such finite ontologies. We are able to do so precisely because we are talking, however vaguely and implicitly, within a broader containing theory. What the objects of the finite theory are, makes sense only as a statement of the background theory in its own referential idiom. The answer to the question depends on the background theory, the finite foreground theory, and, of course, the particular manner in which we choose to translate or embed the one in the other.

Ontology is internally indifferent also, I think, to any theory that is complete and decidable. Where we can always settle truth values mechanically, there is no evident internal reason for interest in the theory of quantifiers nor, therefore, in values of variables. These matters take on significance only as we think of the decidable theory as embedded in a richer background theory in which the variables and their values are serious business.

Ontology may also be said to be internally indifferent even to a theory that is not decidable and does not have a finite universe, if it happens still that each of the infinitely numerous objects of the theory has a name. We can no longer expand quantifications into conjunctions and alternations, barring infinitely long expressions. We can, however, revise our semantical account of the truth conditions of quantification, in such a way as to turn our backs on questions of reference. We can explain universal quantifications as true when true under all substitutions; and correspondingly for existential. Such is the course that has been favored by Leśniewski and by Ruth Marcus.[18] Its nonreferential orientation is seen in the fact that it makes no essential use of namehood. That is, additional quantifications could be explained whose variables are place-holders for words of any syntactical category. *Substitutional* quantification, as I call it, thus brings no way of distinguishing names from other vocabulary, nor any way of distinguishing between genuinely referential or value-taking variables and other place-holders. Ontology is thus meaningless for a theory whose only quantification is substitutionally construed; meaningless, that is, insofar as the theory is considered in and of itself. The question of its ontology makes sense only relative to some translation of the theory into a background theory in which we use referential quantification. The answer depends on both theories and, again, on the chosen way of translating the one into the other.

A final touch of relativity can in some cases cap this, when we try to distinguish between substitutional and referential quantification. Suppose again a theory with an infinite lot of names, and suppose that, by Gödel numbering or otherwise, we are treating of the theory's notations and proofs within the terms of the theory. If we succeed in showing that every result of substituting a name for the variable in a certain open sentence is true in the theory, but at the same time we disprove the universal quantification of the sentence,[19] then certainly we have shown that the universe of the theory contained some nameless objects. This is a case where an absolute decision can be reached in favor of referential quantification and against substitutional quantification, without ever retreating to a background theory.

But consider now the opposite situation, where there is no such open sentence. Imagine on the contrary that, whenever an open sentence is such that each result of substituting a name in it can be proved, its universal quantification can be proved in the theory too. Under these circumstances we can construe the universe as devoid of nameless objects and hence reconstrue the quantifications as substitutional, but we need not. We could still construe the universe as containing nameless objects. It could just happen that the nameless ones are *inseparable* from the named ones, in this sense: it could happen that all properties of nameless objects that we can express in the notation of the theory are shared by named objects.

We could construe the universe of the theory as containing, e.g., all real numbers. Some of them are nameless, since the real numbers are indenumerable while the names are denumerable. But it could still happen that the nameless reals are inseparable from the named reals. This would leave us unable within the theory to prove a distinction between referential and substitutional quantification.[20] Every expressible quantification that is true when referentially construed remains true when substitutionally construed, and vice versa.

We might still make the distinction from the vantage point of a background theory. In it we might specify some real number that was nameless in the object theory; for there are always ways of strengthening a theory so as to name more real numbers, though never all. Further, in the background theory, we might construe the universe of the object theory as exhausting the real numbers. In the background theory we could, in this way, clinch the quantifications in the object theory as referential. But this clinching is doubly relative: it is relative to the background theory and to the interpretation or translation imposed on the object theory from within the background theory.

One might hope that this recourse to a background theory could often be avoided, even when the nameless reals are inseparable from the named reals in the object theory. One might hope by indirect means to show within the object theory that there are nameless reals. For we might prove within the object theory that the reals are indenumerable and that the names are denumerable and hence that there is no function whose arguments are names and whose values exhaust the real numbers. Since the relation of real numbers to their names would be such a function if each real number had a name, we would seem to have proved within the object theory itself that there are nameless reals and hence that quantification must be taken referentially.

However, this is wrong; there is a loophole. This reasoning would prove only that a relation of all real numbers to their names cannot exist as an entity in the universe of the theory. This reasoning denies no number a name in the notation of the theory, as long as the name relation does not belong to the universe of the theory. And anyway we should know better than to expect such a relation, for it is what causes Berry's and Richard's and related paradoxes.

Some theories can attest to their own nameless objects and so claim referential quantification on their onw; other theories have to look to background theories for this service. We saw how a theory might attest to its own nameless objects, namely, by showing that some open sentence became true under all constant substitutions but false under universal quantification. Perhaps this is the only way a theory can claim referential import for its own quantifications. Perhaps, when the nameless objects happen to be inseparable from the named, the quantification used in a theory cannot meaningfully be declared referential except through the medium of a background theory. Yet referential quantification is the key idiom of ontology.

Thus ontology can be multiply relative, multiply meaningless apart from a background theory. Besides being unable to say in absolute terms just what the objects are, we are sometimes unable even to distinguish objectively between referential quantification and a substitutional counterfeit. When we do relativize these matters to a background theory, moreover, the relativization itself has two components: relativity to the choice of background theory and relativity to the choice of how to translate the object theory into the background theory. As for the ontology in turn of the background theory, and even the referentiality of its quantification—these matters can call for a background theory in turn.

There is not always a genuine regress. We saw that, if we are merely clarifying the range of the variables of a theory or the denotations of its terms, and are taking the referentiality of quantification itself for granted, we can commonly use the object theory itself as background theory. We found that when we undertake an ontological reduction, we must accept at least the unreduced theory in order to cite the proxy function; but this we were able cheerfully to accept in the spirit of *reductio ad absurdum* arguments. And now in the end we have found further that if we care to question quantification itself, and settle whether it imports a universe of discourse or turns merely on substitution at the linguistic level, we in some cases have genuinely to regress to a background language endowed with additional resources. We seem to have to do this unless the nameless objects are separable from the named in the object theory.

Regress in ontology is reminiscent of the now familiar regress in the semantics of truth and kindred notions—satisfaction, naming. We know from Tarski's work how the semantics, in this sense, of a theory regularly demands an in some way more inclusive theory. This similarity should perhaps not surprise us, since both ontology and satisfaction are matters of reference. In their elusiveness, at any rate —in their emptiness now and again except relative to a broader background—both truth and ontology may in a suddenly rather clear and even tolerant sense be said to belong to transcendental metaphysics.[21]

Note added in proof. Besides such ontological reduction as is provided by proxy functions (cf. pp. 55–57), there is that which consists simply in dropping objects whose absence will not falsify any truths expressible in the notation. Commonly this sort of deflation can be managed by proxy functions, but R. E. Grandy has shown me that sometimes it cannot. Let us by all means recognize it then as a further kind of reduction. In the background language we must, of course, be able to say what class of objects is dropped, just as in other cases we had to be able to specify the proxy function. This requirement seems sufficient still to stem any resurgence of Pythagoreanism on the strength of the Löwenheim–Skolem theorem.

Notes

1. J. Dewey, *Experience and Nature* (La Salle, Ill.: Open Court, 1925; repr. 1958), p. 179.
2. Ibid., p. 170.
3. Ibid., p. 185.
4. Ibid., p. 178.
5. W. V. Quine, *Word and Object* (Cambridge, Mass.: MIT Press, 1960), sect. 12.
6. L. Wittgenstein, *Philosophical Investigations* (New York: Macmillan, 1953), p. 14.
7. Cf. Quine, *Word and Object*, sect. 17.
8. Quine, *Word and Object*, sect. 15. For a summary of the general point of view see also sect. 1 of "Speaking of objects," in W. V. Quine, *Ontological Relativity and Other Essays* (New York: Columbia University Press, 1969).
9. To keep my account graphic, I am counting a certain postpositive particle as a suffix rather than a word.
10. See Leon Henkin, "Completeness in the theory of types," *Journal of Symbolic Logic* 15 (1950), pp. 81–91, and references therein.
11. For more on this theme see W. V. Quine, *Set Theory and Its Logic* (Cambridge, Mass.: Harvard University Press, 1963, repr. 1969), sect. 11.
12. Paul Benacerraf, "What numbers cannot be," *Philosophical Review* 74 (1965), pp. 47–73, develops this point. His conclusions differ in some ways from those I shall come to.
13. N. L. Wilson, "Substances without substrata," *Review of Metaphysics* 12 (1959), pp. 521–39, at p. 532.
14. W. V. Quine, *The Ways of Paradox* (New York: Random House, 1966), pp. 204ff.
15. Quine, *Set Theory and Its Logic*, sects 2f.
16. Kurt Gödel, *The Consistency of the Continuum Hypothesis* (Princeton: Princeton University Press, 1940), p. 11.
17. Thoralf Skolem, "Logisch-kombinatorische Untersuchungen über die Erfüllbarkeit oder Beweisbarkeit mathematischer Sätze nebst einem Theorem über dichte Mengen," *Skrifter utgit av Videnskapsselskapet i Kristiania* (1919); trans. in Jean van Heijenoort (ed.) *From Frege to Gödel: Source Book in the History of Mathematical Logic* (Cambridge, Mass.: Harvard University Press, 1967), pp. 252–63.
18. Ruth B. Marcus, "Modalities and intensional languages," *Synthese* 13 (1961), pp. 303–22. I cannot locate an adequate statement of Stanislaw Leśniewski's philosophy of quantification in his writings; I have it from his conversations. E. C. Luschei, in *The Logical Systems of Leśniewski* (Amsterdam: North-Holland, 1962), pp. 108f, confirms my attribution but still cites no passage. On this version of quantification see further "Existence and quantification," in Quine, *Ontological Relativity and Other Essays*.
19. Such is the typical way of a numerically insegregative system, misleadingly called "ω-inconsistent." See W. V. Quine, *Selected Logic Papers* (New York: Random House, 1966), pp. 118f, or "ω-inconsistency and a so-called axiom of infinity," *Journal of Symbolic Logic* 18 (1953), pp. 122f.
20. This possibility was suggested by Saul Kripke.
21. In developing these thoughts I have been helped by discussions with Saul Kripke, Thomas Nagel, and especially Burton Dreben.

Chapter 13

Saul A. Kripke

Saul Kripke was educated at Harvard and is Professor Emeritus of Philosophy at Princeton University. He is the author of several important works in metaphysics and philosophy of language, including *Naming and Necessity*, from which this selection is taken.

Typically, as with Leibniz and Kant, rationalists have asserted that all a priori knowledge must be of necessary truth (propositions true in all possible worlds). Kripke argues against this thesis. Necessity is not a necessary condition for a priori contingent knowledge. Anytime we stipulate a definition of a term (his illustration is that of stipulating that the length of a certain bar in Paris is 1 meter long), we can know a priori the truth of the definition. If we define "water" as the molecular structure of H_2O, then we can know a priori that water is H_2O.

FOR FURTHER READING

Kripke, Saul. *Naming and Necessity* (Harvard University Press, 1980).

———. *Wittgenstein on Rules and Private Language* (Oxford University Press, 1982).

Schwarz, Stephen, ed. *Naming, Necessity and Natural Kinds* (Cornell University Press, 1972).

A Priori Knowledge, Necessity, and Contingency

Philosophers have talked (and, of course, there has been considerable controversy in recent years over the meaningfulness of these notions) about various categories of truth, which are called "a priori," "analytic," "necessary"—and sometimes even "certain" is thrown into this batch. The terms are often used as if *whether* there are things answering to these concepts is an interesting question, but we might as well regard them all as meaning the same thing. Now, everyone remembers Kant (a bit) as making a distinction between "a priori" and "analytic." So maybe this distinction is still made. In contemporary discussion very few people, if any, distinguish between the concepts of statements being a priori and their being necessary. At any rate I shall *not* use the terms "a priori" and "necessary" interchangeably here.

Consider what the traditional characterizations of such terms as "a priori" and "necessary" are. First the notion of a prioricity is a concept of epistemology. I guess the traditional characterization from Kant goes something like: a priori truths are those which can be known independently of any experience. This introduces another problem before we get off the ground, because there's another modality in the characterization of "a priori," namely, it is supposed to be something which *can* be known independently of any experience.

That means that in some sense it's *possible* (whether we do or do not in fact know it independently of any experience) to know this independently of any experience. And possible for whom? For God? For the Martians? Or just for people with minds like ours? To make this all clear might involve a host of problems all of its own about what sort of possibility is in question here. It might be best therefore, instead of using the phrase "a priori truth," to the extent that one uses it at all, to stick to the question of whether a particular person or knower knows something a priori or believes it true on the basis of a priori evidence.

I won't go further too much into the problems that might arise with the notion of a prioricity here. I will say that some philosophers somehow change the modality in this characterization from *can* to *must*. They think that if something belongs to the realm of a priori knowledge, it couldn't possibly be known empirically. This is just a mistake. Something may belong in the realm of such statements that *can* be known a priori but still may be known by particular people on the basis of experience. To give a really common-sense example: anyone who has worked with a computing machine knows that the computing machine may give an answer to whether such and such a number is prime. No one has calculated or proved that the number is prime; but the machine has given the answer: this number is prime. We, then, if we believe that the number is prime, believe it on the basis of our knowledge of the laws of physics, the construction of the machine, and so on. We therefore do not believe this on the basis of purely a priori evidence. We believe it (if anything is a posteriori at all) on the basis of a posteriori evidence. Nevertheless, maybe this could be known a priori by someone who made the requisite calculations. So "*can* be known a priori" doesn't mean "*must* be known a priori."

The second concept which is in question is that of necessity. Sometimes this is used in an epistemological way and might then just mean a priori. And of course, sometimes it is used in a physical way when people distinguish between physical and logical necessity. But what I am concerned with here is a notion which is not a notion of epistemology but of metaphysics, in some (I hope) nonpejorative sense. We ask whether something might have been true, or might have been false. Well, if something is false, it's obviously not necessarily true. If it is true, might it have been otherwise? Is it possible that, in this respect, the world should have been different from the way it is? If the answer is "no," then this fact about the world is a necessary one. If the answer is "yes," then this fact about the world is a contingent one. This in and of itself has nothing to do with anyone's knowledge of anything. It's certainly a philosophical thesis, and not a matter of obvious definitional equivalence, either that everything a priori is necessary or that everything necessary is a priori. Both concepts may be vague. That may be another problem. But at any rate they are dealing with two different domains, two different areas, the epistemological and the metaphysical. Consider, say, Fermat's last theorem—or the Goldbach conjecture. The Goldbach conjecture says that an even number greater than 2 must be the sum of two prime numbers. If this is true, it is presumably necessary, and, if it is false, presumably necessarily false. We are taking the classical view of mathematics here and assume that in mathematical reality it is either true or false.

If the Goldbach conjecture is false, then there is an even number, n, greater than 2, such that for no primes p_1 and p_2, both n, does $n = p_1 + p_2$. This fact about n, if true, is verifiable by direct computation, and thus is necessary if the results of arithmetical computations are necessary. On the other hand, if the conjecture is true, then every even number exceeding 2 is the sum of two primes. Could it then be the case that, although in fact every such even number is the sum of two primes, there might have been such an even number which was not the sum of two primes? What would that mean? Such a number would have to be one of 4, 6, 8, 10, . . . ; and, by hypothesis, since we are assuming Goldbach's conjecture to be true, each of these can be shown, again by direct computation, to be the sum of two primes. Goldbach's conjecture, then, cannot be contingently true or false; whatever truth-value it has belongs to it by necessity.

But what we can say, of course, is that right now, as far as we know, the question can come out either way. So, in the absence of a mathematical proof deciding this question, none of us has any a priori knowledge about this question in either direction. We don't know whether Goldbach's conjecture is true or false. So right now we certainly don't know anything a priori about it.

Perhaps it will be alleged that we *can* in principle know a priori whether it is true. Well, maybe we can. Of course an infinite mind which can search through all the numbers can or could. But I don't know whether a finite mind can or could. Maybe there just is no mathematical proof whatsoever which decides the conjecture. At any rate this might or might not be the case. Maybe there is a mathematical proof deciding this question; maybe every mathematical question is decidable by an intuitive proof or disproof. Hilbert thought so; others have thought not; still others have thought the question unintelligible unless the notion of intuitive proof is replaced by that of formal proof in a single system. Certainly no one formal system decides all mathematical questions, as we know from Gödel. At any rate, and this is the important thing, the question is not trivial; even though someone said that it's necessary, if true at all, that every even number is the sum of two primes, it doesn't follow that anyone knows anything a priori about it. It doesn't even seem to me to follow without some further philosophical argument (it is an interesting philosophical question) that anyone *could* know anything a priori about it. The "could," as I said, involves some other modality. We mean that even if no one, perhaps even in the future, knows or will know a priori whether Goldbach's conjecture is right, in principle there is a way, which *could* have been used, of answering the question a priori. This assertion is not trivial.

The terms "necessary" and "a priori," then, as applied to statements, are *not* obvious synonyms. There may be a philosophical argument connecting them, perhaps even identifying them; but an argument is required, not simply the observation that the two terms are clearly interchangeable. (I will argue below that in fact they are not even coextensive—that necessary a posteriori truths, and probably contingent a priori truths, both exist.)

I think people have thought that these two things must mean the same for these reasons:

First, if something not only happens to be true in the actual world but is also true in all possible worlds, then, of course, just by running through all the possible worlds in our heads, we ought to be able with enough effort to see, if a statement is necessary, that it is necessary, and thus know it a priori. But really this is not so obviously feasible at all.

Second, I guess it's thought that, conversely, if something is known a priori it must be necessary, because it was known without looking at the world. If it depended on some contingent feature of the actual world, how could you know it without looking? Maybe the actual world is one of the possible worlds in which it would have been false. This depends on the thesis that there can't be a way of knowing about the actual world without looking that wouldn't be a way of knowing the same thing about every possible world. This involves problems of epistemology and the nature of knowledge; and of course it is very vague as stated. But it is not really *trivial* either. More important than any particular example of something which is alleged to be necessary and not a priori or a priori and not necessary, is to see that the notions are different, that it's not trivial to argue on the basis of something's being something which maybe we can only know a posteriori, that it's not a necessary truth. It's not trivial, just because something is known in some sense a priori, that what is known is a necessary truth.

Another term used in philosophy is "analytic." Here it won't be too important to get any clearer about this in this talk. The common examples of analytic statements, nowadays, are like "bachelors are unmarried." Kant (someone just pointed out to me) gives as an example "gold is a yellow metal," which seems to me an extraordinary one, because it's something I think that can turn out to be false. At any rate, let's just make it a matter of stipulation that an analytic statement is, in some sense, true by virtue of its meaning and true in all possible worlds by virtue of its meaning. Then something which is analytically true will be both necessary and a priori. (That's sort of stipulative.)

Another category I mentioned was that of certainty. Whatever certainty is, it's clearly not obviously the case that everything which is necessary is certain. Certainty is another epistemological notion. Something can be known, or at least rationally believed, a priori, without being quite certain. You've read a proof in the math book; and, though you think it's correct, maybe you've made a mistake. You often do make mistakes of this kind. You've made a computation, perhaps with an error.

Let's use some terms quasi-technically. Let's call something a *rigid designator* if in every possible world it designates the same object, a *non-rigid* or *accidental designator* if that is not the case. Of course we don't require that the objects exist in all possible worlds. Certainly Nixon might not have existed if his parents had not gotten married, in the normal course of things. When we think of a property as essential to an object we usually mean that it is true of that object in any case where it would have existed. A rigid designator of a necessary existent can be called *strongly rigid*.

One of the intuitive theses I will maintain in these talks is that *names* are rigid designators. Certainly they seem to satisfy the intuitive test: although someone other than the US President in 1970 might have been the US President in 1970 (e.g. Humphrey might have), no one other than Nixon might have been Nixon. In the same way, a designator rigidly designates a certain object if it designates that object wherever the object exists; if, in addition, the object is a necessary existent, the designator can be called *strongly rigid*. For example, "the President of the US in 1970" designates a certain man, Nixon; but someone else (e.g. Humphrey) might have been the President in 1970, and Nixon might not have; so this designator is not rigid.

In these lectures I will argue, intuitively, that proper names are rigid designators, for although the man (Nixon) might not have been the President, it is not the case that he might not have been Nixon (though he might not have been *called* "Nixon"). Those who have argued that to make sense of the notion of rigid designator, we must antecedently make sense of "criteria of transworld identity" have precisely reversed the cart and the horse; it is *because* we can refer (rigidly) to Nixon, and stipulate that we are speaking of what might have happened to *him* (under certain circumstances), that "transworld identifications" are unproblematic in such cases.[1]

The tendency to demand purely qualitative descriptions of counterfactual situations has many sources. One, perhaps, is the confusion of the epistemological and the metaphysical, between a prioricity and necessity. If someone identifies necessity with a prioricity, and thinks that objects are named by means of uniquely identifying properties, he may think that it is the properties used to identify the object which, being known about it a priori, must be used to identify it in all possible worlds, to find out which object is Nixon. As against this, I repeat: (1) Generally, things aren't "found out" about a counterfactual situation, they are stipulated; (2) possible worlds need not be given purely qualitatively, as if we were looking at them through a telescope. And we will see shortly that the properties an object has in every counter factual world have nothing to do with properties used to identify it in the actual world.

Above I said that the Frege–Russell view that names are introduced by description could be taken either as a theory of the meaning of names (Frege and Russell seemed to take it this way) or merely as a theory of their reference. Let me give an example, not involving what would usually be called a "proper name," to illustrate this. Suppose someone stipulates that 100 degrees centigrade is to be the temperature at which water boils at sea level. This isn't completely precise because the pressure may vary at sea level. Of course, historically, a more precise definition was given later. But let's suppose that this were the definition. Another sort of example in the literature is that one metre is to be the length of *S* where *S* is a certain stick or bar in Paris. (Usually people who like to talk about these definitions then try to make "the length of" into an "operational" concept. But it's not important.)

Wittgenstein says something very puzzling about this. He says: "There is one thing of which one can say neither that it is one metre long nor that it is not one metre long, and that is the standard metre in Paris. But this is, of course, not to ascribe any extraordinary property to it, but only to mark its peculiar role in the language game of measuring with a metre rule."[2] This seems to be a very "extraordinary property," actually, for any stick to have. I think he must be wrong. If the stick is a stick, for example, 39.37 inches long (I assume we have some different standard for inches), why isn't it one metre long? Anyway, let's suppose that he is wrong and that the stick is one metre long. Part of the problem which is bothering Wittgenstein is, of course, that this stick serves as a standard of length and so we can't attribute length to it. Be this as it may (well, it may not be), is the statement "Stick *S* is one metre long," a necessary truth? Of course its length might vary in time. We could make the definition more precise by stipulating that one metre is to be the length of *S* at a fixed time t_0. Is it then a necessary truth that sick *S* is one metre long at time t_0? Someone who thinks that everything one knows a priori is necessary might think: "This is the *definition* of a metre. By definition, stick S is one metre long at t_0. That's a necessary truth." But there seems to me to be no reason so to conclude, even for a man who uses the stated definition of "one metre." For he's using this definition not to *give the meaning* of what he called the "metre," but to *fix the reference*. (For such an abstract thing as a unit of length, the notion of reference may be unclear. But let's suppose it's clear enough for the present purposes.) He uses it to fix a reference. There is a certain length which he wants to mark out. He marks it out by an accidental property, namely that there is a stick of that length. Someone else might mark out the same reference by another accidental property. But in any case, even though he uses this to fix the reference of his standard of length, a metre, he can still say, "if heat had been applied to stick S at t_0, then at t_0 stick S would not have been one metre long."

Well, why can he do this? Part of the reason may lie in some people's minds in the philosophy of science, which I don't want to go into here. But a simple answer to the question is this: Even if this is the *only* standard of length that he uses,[3] there is an intuitive difference between the phrase "one metre" and the phrase "the length of S at t_0." The first phrase is meant to designate rigidly a certain length in all possible worlds, which in the actual world happens to be the length of the stick S at t_0. On the other hand "the length of S at t_0" does not designate anything rigidly. In some counterfactual situations the stick might have been longer and in some shorter, if various stresses and strains had been applied to it. So we can say of this stick, the same way as we would of any other of the same substance and length, that if heat of a given quantity had been applied to it, it would have expanded to such and such a length. Such a counterfactual statement, being true of other sticks with identical physical properties, will also be true of this stick. There is no conflict between that counterfactual statement and the definition of "one metre" as "the length of S at t_0," because the "definition," properly interpreted, does *not* say that the phrase "one metre" is to be *synonmous* (even when talking about counterfactual situations) with the phrase "the length of S at t_0," but rather that we have *determined the reference* of the phrase "one metre" by stipulating that "one metre" is to be a *rigid* designator of the length which is in fact the length of S at t_0. So this does *not* make it a necessary truth that S is one metre long at t_0. In fact, under certain circumstances, S would not have been one metre long. The reason is that one designator ("one metre") is rigid and the other designator ("the length of S at t_0") is not.

What then, is the *epistemological* status of the statement "Stick S is one metre long at t_0," for someone who has fixed the metric system by reference to stick S? It would seem that he knows it a priori. For if he used stick S to fix the reference of the term "one metre," then as a result of this kind of "definition" (which is not an abbreviative or synonymous definition), he knows automatically, without further investigation, that S is one metre long.[4] On the other hand, even if S is used as the standard of a metre, the *metaphysical* status of "S is one metre long" will be that of a contingent statement, provided that "one metre" is regarded as a rigid designator: under appropriate stresses and strains, heatings or coolings, S would have had a length other than one metre even at t_0. (Such statements as "Water boils at 100 degrees centigrade, at sea level" can have a similar status.) So in this sense, there are contingent a priori truths. More important for present purposes, though, than accepting this example as an instance of the contingent a priori, is its illustration of the distinction between "definitions" which fix a reference and those which give a synonym.

In the case of names one might make this distinction too. Suppose the reference of a name is given by a description or a cluster of descriptions. If the name *means the same* as that description or cluster of descriptions, it will not be a rigid designator. It will not necessarily designate the same object in all possible worlds, since other objects might have had the given properties in other possible worlds, unless (of course) we happened to use essential properties in our description. So suppose we say, "Aristotle is the greatest man who studied with Plato." If we used that as a *definition*, the name "Aristotle" is to mean "the greatest man who studied with Plato." Then of course in some other possible world that man might not have studied with Plato and some other man would have been Aristotle. If, on the other hand, we merely use the description to *fix the referent* then that man will be the referent of "Aristotle" in all possible worlds. The only use of the description will have been to pick out to which man we mean to refer. But then, when we say counterfactually "suppose Aristotle had never gone into philosophy at all," we need not mean "suppose a man who studied with Plato, and taught

Alexander the Great, and wrote this and that, and so on, had never gone into philosophy at all," which might seem like a contradiction. We need only mean, "suppose that *that man* had never gone into philosophy at all."

It seems plausible to suppose that, in some cases, the reference of a name is indeed fixed *via* a description in the same way that the metric system was fixed. When the mythical agent first saw Hesperus, he may well have fixed his reference by saying, "I shall use 'Hesperus' as a name of the heavenly body appearing in yonder position in the sky." He then fixed the reference of "Hesperus" by its apparent celestial position. Does it follow that it is part of the *meaning* of the name that Hesperus has such and such position at the time in question? Surely not: if Hesperus had been hit earlier by a comet, it might have been visible at a different position at that time. In such a counterfactual situation we would say that Hesperus would not have occupied that position, but not that Hesperus would not have been Hesperus. The reason is that "Hesperus" rigidly designates a certain heavenly body and "the body in yonder position" does not—a different body, or no body might have been in that position, but no other body might have been Hesperus (though another body, not Hesperus, might have been *called* "Hesperus"). Indeed, as I have said, I will hold that names are always rigid designators.

I guess the main thing I'll talk about now is identity statements between names. But I hold the following about the general case. First, that characteristic theoretical identifications like "Heat is the motion of molecules," are not contingent truths but necessary truths, and here of course I don't mean just physically necessary, but necessary in the highest degree—whatever that means. (Physical necessity *might* turn out to be necessity in the highest degree. But that's a question which I don't wish to prejudge. At least for this sort of example, it might be that when something's physically necessary, it always is necessary *tout court.*) Second, that the way in which these have turned out to be necessary truths does not seem to me to be a way in which the mind-brain identities could turn out to be either necessary or contingently true. So this analogy has to go. It's hard to see what to put in its place. It's hard to see therefore how to avoid concluding that the two are actually different.

Let me go back to the more mundane case about proper names. This is already mysterious enough. There's a dispute about this between Quine and Ruth Barcan Marcus.[5] Marcus says that identities between names are necessary. If someone thinks that Cicero is Tully, and really uses "Cicero" and "Tully" as names, he is thereby committed to holding that his belief is a necessary truth. She uses the term "mere tag." Quine replies as follows, "We may tag the planet Venus, some fine evening, with the proper name "Hesperus." We may tag the same planet again, some day before sunrise, with the proper name "Phosphorus." When we discover that we have tagged the same planet twice our discovery is empirical. And not because the proper names were descriptions."[6] First, as Quine says when we discovered that we tagged the same planet twice, our discovery was empirical. Another example I think Quine gives in another book is that the same mountain seen from Nepal and from Tibet, or something like that, is from one angle called "Mt. Everest" (you've heard of that); from another it's supposed to be called "Gaurisanker." It can actually be an empirical discovery that Gaurisanker is Everest. (Quine says that the example is actually false. He got the example from Erwin Schrödinger. You wouldn't think the inventor of wave mechanics got things that wrong. I don't know where the mistake is supposed to come from. One could certainly imagine this situation as having been the case; and it's another good illustration of the sort of thing that Quine has in mind.)

What about it? I wanted to find a good quote on the other side from Marcus in this book but I am having trouble locating one. Being present at that discussion, I remember[7] that she advocated the view that if you really have names, a good dictionary should be able to tell you whether they have the same reference. So someone should be able, by looking in the dictionary, to say that Hesperus and Phosphorus are the same. Now this does not seem to be true. It does seem, to many people, to be a consequence of the view that identities between names are necessary. Therefore the view that identity statements between names are necessary has usually been rejected. Russell's conclusion was somewhat different. He did think there should never be any empirical question whether two names have the same reference. This isn't satisfied for ordinary names, but it is satisfied when you're naming your own sense datum, or something like that. You say, "Here, this, and that (designating the same sense datum by both demonstratives)." So you can tell without empirical investigation that you're naming the same thing twice; the conditions are satisfied. Since this won't apply to ordinary cases of naming, ordinary "names" cannot be genuine names.

What should we think about this? First, it's true that someone can use the name "Cicero" to refer to Cicero and the name "Tully" to refer to Cicero also, and not know that Cicero is Tully. So it seems that we do not necessarily know a priori that an identity statement between names is true. It doesn't follow from this that the statement so expressed is a contingent one if true. This is what I've emphasized in my first lecture. There is a very strong feeling that leads one to think that, if you can't know something by a priori ratiocination, then it's got to be contingent: it might have turned out otherwise; but nevertheless I think this feeling is wrong.

Let's suppose we refer to the same heavenly body twice, as "Hesperus" and "Phosphorus." We say: Hesperus is that star over there in the evening; Phosphorus is that star over there in the morning. Actually, Hesperus is Phosphorus. Are there really circumstances under which Hesperus wouldn't have been Phosphorus? Supposing that Hesperus is Phosphorus, let's try to describe a possible situation in which it would not have been. Well, it's easy. Someone goes by and he calls two *different* stars "Hesperus" and "Phosphorus." It may even be under the same conditions as prevailed when we introduced the names "Hesperus" and "Phosphorus." But are those circumstances in which Hesperus is not Phosphorus or would not have been Phosphorus? It seems to me that they are not.

Now, of course I'm committed to saying that they're not, by saying that such terms as "Hesperus" and "Phosphorus," when used as names, are rigid designators. They refer in every possible world to the planet Venus. Therefore, in that possible world too, the planet Venus is the planet Venus and it doesn't matter what any other person has said in this other possible world. How should *we* describe this situation? He can't have pointed to Venus twice, and in the one case called it "Hesperus" and in the other "Phosphorus," as we did. If he did so, then "Hesperus is Phosphorus" would have been true in that situation too. He pointed maybe neither time to the planet Venus—at least one time he didn't point to the planet Venus, let's say when he pointed to the body he called "Phosphorus." Then in that case we can certainly say that the name "Phosphorus" might not have referred to Phosphorus. We can even say that in the very position when viewed in the morning that we found Phosphorus, it might have been the case that Phosphorus was not there—that something else was there, and that even, under certain circumstances it would have been *called* "Phosphorus." But that still is not a case in which Phosphorus was not Hesperus. There might be a possible world in which, a possible counterfactual situation in which, "Hesperus" and "Phosphorus" weren't names of the things they in fact are names of. Someone, if he did determine their reference by identifying descriptions, might even have used the very identifying descriptions we used. But still that's not a case in which Hesperus wasn't Phosphorus. For there couldn't have been such a case, given that Hesperus is Phosphorus.

Now this seems very strange because in advance, we are inclined to say, the answer to the question whether Hesperus is Phosphorus might have turned out either way. So aren't there really two possible worlds—one in which Hesperus was Phosphorus, the other in which Hesperus wasn't Phosphorus—in advance of our discovering that these were the same? First, there's one sense in which things might turn out either way, in which it's clear that that doesn't imply that the way it finally turns out isn't necessary. For example, the four-colour theorem might turn out to be true and might turn out to be false. It might turn out either way. It still doesn't mean that the way it turns out is not necessary. Obviously, the "might" here is purely "epistemic"—it merely expresses our present state of ignorance, or uncertainty.

But it seems that in the Hesperus–Phosphorus case, something even stronger is true. The evidence I have before I know that Hesperus is Phosphorus is that I see a certain star or a certain heavenly body in the evening and call it "Hesperus," and in the morning and call it "Phosphorus." I know these things. There certainly is a possible world in which a man should have seen a certain star at a certain position in the evening and called it "Hesperus" and a certain star in the morning and called it "Phosphorus"; and should have concluded—should have found out by empirical investigations—that he names two different stars, or two different heavenly bodies. At least one of these stars or heavenly bodies was not Phosphorus, otherwise it couldn't have come out that way. But that's true. And so it's true that given the evidence that someone has antecedent to his empirical investigation, he can be placed in a sense in exactly the same situation, that is a qualitatively identical epistemic situation, and call two heavenly bodies "Hesperus" and "Phosphorus," without their being identical. So in that sense we can say that it might have turned out either way. Not that it might have turned out either way as to Hesperus's being Phosphorus. Though for all we knew in advance, Hesperus wasn't Phosphorus, that couldn't have turned out any other way, in a sense. But being put in a situation where we have exactly the same evidence, qualitatively speaking, it could have turned out that Hesperus was not Phosphorus; that is, in a counterfactual world in which "Hesperus" and "Phosphorus" were not used in the way that we use them, as names of this planet, but as names of some other objects, one could have had qualitatively identical evidence and concluded that "Hesperus" and "Phosphorus" named two different objects.[8] But we, using the names as we do right now, can say in advance, that if Hesperus and Phosphorus are one and the same, then in no other possible world can they be different. We use "Hesperus" as the name of a certain body and "Phosphorus" as the name of a certain body. We use them as names of those bodies in all possible worlds. If, in fact, they are the *same* body, then in any other possible world we have to use them as a name of that object. And so in any other possible world it will be true that Hesperus is Phosphorus. So two things are true: first, that we do not know a priori that Hesperus is Phosphorus, and are in no position to find out the answer except empirically. Second, this is so because we could have evidence qualitatively indistinguishable from the evidence we have and determine the reference of the two names by the positions of two planets in the sky, without the planets being the same.

Of course, it is only a contingent truth (not true in every other possible world) that the star seen over there in the evening is the star seen over there in the morning, because there are possible worlds in which Phosphorus was not visible in the morning. But that contingent truth shouldn't be identified with the statement that Hesperus is Phosphorus. It could only be so identified if you thought that it was a necessary truth that Hesperus is visible over there in the evening or that Phosphorus is visible over there in the morning. But neither of those are necessary truths even if that's the way we pick out the planet. These are the contingent marks by which we identify a certain planet and give it a name.

We have concluded that an identity statement between names, when true at all, is necessarily true, even though one may not know it a priori. Suppose we identify Hesperus as a certain star seen in the evening and Phosphorus as a certain star, or a certain heavenly body, seen in the morning; then there may be possible worlds in which two different planets would have been seen in just those positions in the evening and morning. However, at least one of them, and maybe both, would not have been Hesperus, and then that would not have been a situation in which Hesperus was not Phosphorus. It might have been a situation in which the planet seen in this position in the evening was not the planet seen in this position in the morning; but that is not a situation in which Hesperus was not Phosphorus. It might also, if people gave the names "Hesperus" and "Phosphorus" to these planets, be a situation in which some planet other than Hesperus was called "Hesperus." But even so, it would not be a situation in which Hesperus itself was not Phosphorus.[9]

Some of the problems which bother people in these situations, as I have said, come from an identification, or as I would put it, a confusion, between what we can know a priori in advance and what is necessary. Certain statements—and the identity statement is a paradigm of such a statement on my view—if true at all must be necessarily true. One does know a priori, by philosophical analysis, that if such an identity statement is true it is necessarily true.

Notes

1. Of course I don't imply that language contains a name for every object. Demonstratives can be used as rigid designators, and free variables can be used as rigid designators of unspecified objects. Of course when we specify a counterfactual situation, we do not describe the whole possible world, but only the portion which interests us.
2. *Philosophical Investigations*, §50.
3. Philosophers of science may see the key to the problem in a view that "one metre" is a "cluster concept." I am asking the reader hypothetically to suppose that the "definition" given is the *only* standard used to determine the metric system. I think the problem would still arise.
4. Since the truth he knows is contingent, I choose *not* to call it "analytic," stipulatively requiring analytic truths to be both necessary and a priori.

5. Ruth Barcan Marcus, "Modalities and Intensional Languages" (comments by W. V. Quine, plus discussion), *Boston Studies in the Philosophy of Science* (Dordrecht: Reidel, 1963), pp. 77–116.
6. Ibid. p. 101.
7. Ibid. p. 115.
8. There is a more elaborate discussion of this point in the third lecture, in *Naming and Necessity*, where its relation to a certain sort of counterpart theory is also mentioned.
9. Recall that we describe the situation in our language, not the language that the people in that situation would have used. Hence we must use the terms "Hesperus" and "Phosphorus" with the same reference as in the actual world. The fact that people in that situation might or might not have used these names for different planets is irrelevant. So is the fact that they might have done so using the very same descriptions as we did to fix their references.

Chapter 14

Jonathan Harrison

Jonathan Harrison has taught philosophy at Oxford, Durham, Edinburgh, Nottingham, and Northwestern universities. He has (in the order listed) produced books on moral philosophy, two books on David Hume, two collections of philosophical fables, a collection of readings with an introduction and top-notes, a collection in three volumes of his articles (the third volume previously unpublished ones) on moral philosophy, a collection in two volumes of his articles (many new) on metaphysics and the theory of knowledge, and a book on the philosophy of religion. He is now Emeritus Professor of Philosophy at the University of Nottingham, and has retired to Cambridge.

In this essay Harrison first sets forth the traditional empiricist theory, as developed by the British empiricists, especially Locke and Hume, that divides propositions into analytic, a priori, and necessary on the one hand, and synthetic, empirical, and contingent, on the other. Then he clarifies and explains this basis of this theory by responding to objections by Quine (Chapter 12), Kripke (Chapter 13), and others. He separates Empiricism from Logical Positivism with its verification principle (see Ayer, Chapter 7), replacing the method of verificaiton with a more plausible method of *sampling*. He also argues that Empiricism is supported by Foundationalism and is a version of Realism.

FOR FURTHER READING

Harrison, J. *Essays on Metaphysics and the Theory of Knowledge*, 3 vols. (Avebury Series in Philosophy, 1995).
———. *Ethical Essays*, 3 vols. (Avebury Series in Philosophy, 1995).
———. *God, Freedom and Immortality* (Avebury Series in Philosophy, 1999).
———. *Our Knowledge of Right and Wrong* (George Allen & Unwin, 1970).

A Defense of Empiricism[1]

I SOME OBJECTIONS TO EMPIRICISM

(i) The traditional empiricist view is that propositions are divided into those which are analytic, a priori, and necessary, on the one hand, and those which are synthetic, empirical, and contingent, on the other.

Analytic propositions are those which cannot be denied without contradiction. In the case of propositions that are of subject/predicate form, such as that all vixens are female, this is because the predicate can be obtained by analysis from the subject. It is a mistake to say that analytic truths depend upon the meaning of words, for that the whole is greater than the half would be true whatever words were used to express this fact.[2] A proposition is *synthetic* if it can be denied without self-contradiction.

An empirical proposition, for example that most men have hair, is empirical because it cannot be seen to be true without recourse to observation; a proposition that is not empirical is *a priori.*

A proposition is *necessary* if it must be true; otherwise it is contingent. Propositions are not the only things that are necessary. For example, it may be necessary to believe the Athenasian creed in order to be saved, or necessary that taking cyanide results in death. The *proposition* that something other than a proposition—for example the *connection* between taking cyanide and dying—is necessary may be contingent. The proposition that a proposition is necessary is probably itself necessary. I shall say that a proposition is analytic in a wide sense if its truth depends not upon empirical fact, but only upon the nature of the concepts involved in understanding the sentences used to assert it. It is sometimes said that the division of truths into necessary and contingent ones has to do with their ontological or metaphysical status.

It has been suggested (by Saul Kripke) that the division of propositions outlined above involves three different distinctions—analytic/synthetic, a priori/empirical, necessary/contingent—made on three different principles, which may vary independently of one another. But the fact that it is possible to see why analytic propositions are necessary and a priori shows that Kripke is wrong about this. Analytic propositions are a priori because it is not necessary to investigate the world to discover that if something is a vixen it is female, and are necessary for the same reason. The world, so to speak, might empty itself of vixens, but it could not do anything about the hypothetical proposition that if there were vixens, they would be female. It follows from what I have been saying that the truth that all a priori necessary truths depend upon concepts itself depends upon concepts, and is itself necessary and a priori.

(iv) Quine has held that the distinction, essential to empiricism, between analytic propositions and synthetic ones, breaks down. However, it is quite obvious that Quine is wrong, and that there *is* a distinction between analytic and synthetic propositions. For example, it is obvious that there is a difference between the proposition that it is impossible to play a round of golf in only eighteen strokes, and that it is impossible to play one in only seventeen. Empirical information about the physical limitations of golfers, is needed to know the first. For the second all that is necessary is to have a full grasp of the concepts of being a round, being a hole, and being a stroke. One would have to revise the first if one discovered a Martian golfer who could always hole in one. But there are no circumstances in which one could revise the second. What one could do is something subtly different, e.g., revise the meaning of "round" so that a round came to mean a sequence of nine holes instead of a sequence of eighteen. In that case the proposition expressed by the sentence "It is impossible to play a round of golf in less than eighteen strokes" would come to express a different proposition from the one it expresses now, which former proposition does not have to be revised. It is still true that it is impossible to play what used to be called a round in less than eighteen strokes, which fact has not been revised.

This essay, though based on other of Jonathan Harrison's writings, was comissioned for this volume and appears in print here for the first time. See note 1.

(v) Kant thought that we had a priori knowledge of such truths as that every event has a cause, which truths were not true by definition.

Kant thought that synthetic a priori knowledge, unlike analytic a priori knowledge and empirical synthetic knowledge, needed a justification (what he called a "deduction"). He attempted to justify it by trying to show that we could not experience a world to which our synthetic a priori knowledge was not applicable; for example, we could not experience a world in which not every event had a cause. This was because experience conformed to our cognitive capacities, rather than our knowledge having to conform to experience, much as the fact that we catch only large fish may tell us more about our net than about fish.

This attempted justification was based on a logical mistake. What Kant claimed to prove (and what Hume, whom Kant was trying to refute, denied) was that, necessarily, every event has a cause. The most Kant proved was that, necessarily, *if* not every event did not have a cause, the world could not be experienced. This is compatible with holding that all there is to causation is regularity—if Hume held that—for the necessity of a constant conjunction is not at all the same thing as the necessity of a necessary connection. And it would seem much more sensible to suppose that we have evolved to have a concept of causation because we need it to survive in a universe where there is causation, than that the universe has obligingly made some things cause others because otherwise we would not understand it. Kant never supposed that we could find out what caused anything other than empirically.

(vi) Saul Kripke has criticised what he regards as the old-fashioned division of propositions into those that are a priori, analytic, and necessary on the one hand, and those that are synthetic, empirical, and contingent on the other. This classification, Kripke thinks, needs to be revised by recognising that there are two further classes of truths.

(a) There is a class of truths that are necessary, though capable of being known only a posteriori. Kripke thinks that true identity propositions such as that the morning star is the evening star belong to this class. For example, it must be necessarily true that the morning star is the evening star, because it is a necessary truth that everything is identical with itself. But it is an empirical (astronomical) discovery, not an a priori truth, that the morning star and the evening star are the same star. It is sometimes said that what Kripke has shown is not that the morning star is necessarily identical with the evening star, but that *if* it is identical with the morning star, then this is necessarily so, but since it *is* identical with the evening star it does follow, on Kripke's view, that it is necessarily identical with the evening star.

(b) There is a class of truths which, though contingent, are known a priori. For example, the metre rod in Paris does not have to be a metre long, because the rod put there might have been of some other length. (It would have been some other length if the hand of the craftsman who made it had slipped. Hence it is only a contingent fact that it is the length it is. But, because the word "metre" was introduced as a name for whatever length the metre rod in Paris has, we know a priori that it is a metre long.)

I should like to pass the following remarks on these two views of Kripke's.

(a) Though Kripke thinks that identity propositions—some of which preceding philosophers had supposed to be contingent—are necessary, he agrees with those who hold the traditional view that our knowledge of them is empirical. Hence he is not offering any extension of our cognitive capacities by attacking the traditional view that they are contingent.

Kripke may think that identity truths are necessarily true partly because he thinks that the morning star is necessarily the evening star follows from the fact that everything is necessarily identical with itself. But the morning star would be necessarily identical with itself whether or not it was identical with the evening star. From the fact that Richard Carstone deceives himself, it can be deduced that Richard Carstone deceives Richard Carstone, but not that Richard Carstone deceives the ward of Jarndyce and Jarndyce, even though Richard Carstone is the ward of Jarndyce and Jarndyce. That the morning star is identical with the evening star is like the first of these propositions, not like the second.

Kripke also thinks that, because the morning star is necessarily identical with the morning star, it must follow that the evening star, because it is the morning star, and so possesses all the morning star's properties, must also have the property of being necessarily identical with the morning star, which property the morning star has. But as Tom, who is a dyspeptic bachelor, is necessarily a bachelor *qua* bachelor, but not *qua* dyspeptic, so Phosphorous, which is the morning star and the evening star, is necessarily identical with the morning star *qua* morning star but not *qua* evening star. Hence all that follows from Kripke's premises is that the evening star is identical with a star which, *qua* morning star, is necessarily identical with the morning star, not that it is necessarily identical with the evening star.

There is a sense in which, if the morning star is the evening star, this is necessarily so; if it is, nothing can be done to alter this fact. For example, if a being with sufficient power were to try to turn it into two stars, one to shine in the morning and the other in the evening, the two stars that resulted from this attempt could not both be identical with the original star, and there would in any case be problems about saying that either was numerically identical with the original, let alone holding that they both were. For example, if one took half the atoms in the original and made of one half a star to shine in the morning and with the other a star to shine in the evening, neither could be said to be identical with the original. But this would show only that *if* the morning star was the evening star, they could not be separated which, though necessary, would be a conceptual truth knowable a priori. It would not show that the morning star *was* the evening star was a necessary a posteriori truth.

(b) Though Kripke's view, about the necessity of certain identity statements, would provide no extension to our cognitive capacities, even if it were true, is not true. Though Kripke thinks (rightly) that the fact that the metre rod is a metre long is contingent, whereas preceding philosophers would have supposed that it was necessary, he is wrong in thinking that it is a contingent fact that is known a priori. Let us suppose that "umpteen" is a word for the number of cherry stones on our plate, however many cherry stones that this might turn out to be. Then however many cherry stones there are on our plate, we will say "There are umpteen cherry stones on my plate"; but we will not know a priori how many cherry stones there will be on our plate. It is just, that, however many of them there are, we will call that number "umpteen". Hence the contingent fact that the metre rod in Paris is about 39 inches (a metre) long is not something we know a priori. What we do know a priori is only the fact that, however long it is, we will call whatever length it happens to have a "metre." In other words, the sentence "There are umpteen cherry stones on my plate" will not express a necessary truth, but only necessarily express a contingent truth.

(vii) The question whether there are necessary statements other than analytic ones should not be confused with the question whether there are kinds of necessity other than the necessity possessed by analytic truths, which there are. Actions can be necessary in the sense that they ought to be done, or in the sense that it is necessary to perfom them to achieve some end, and events necessary in the sense that they are necessarily (inseparably) connected with other events. Not all statements to the effect that something is necessary are themselves necessary. It is a contingent fact, for example, that those who are born necessarily die, and that one cannot become a member of the Church of England if one has not been baptised.

(a) It has been suggested (though not by Quine, whose example this is) that it is a necessary and synthetic truth that the number of planets is necessarily greater than four.[3] This is because two things have been confused (by Quine).[4] (1) That number which, it so happens, is the number of planets is necessarily greater than four. This proposition is necessary but analytic (and, incidentally, a priori). It is true because it so happens that nine is the number of the planets, and nine is necessarily greater than four. (2) That number which, it so happens, numbers the planets necessarily numbers the planets (i.e., there must be that number of planets). That there are that number of planets is synthetic, but contingent; that there must be that number of planets is false. We know a priori that nine, the number of the planets, is greater than four, but this proposition is analytic. We know only empirically that there are nine planets, but this proposition is synthetic. (We know a priori the truth of the proposition that that number which is the number of the planets is not necessarily the number of the planets.)

(b) Kripke held that that the table in front of him was not from the very beginning of its inception made of ice was synthetic and necessary. It is synthetic because there is nothing in the definition of "table" that excludes a table from being made of ice. But Kripke seems to think that it is self-evident that, whatever might be true of other tables, the table in front of him could not be made of ice.

I have again an uneasy feeling that two things are being confused. (1) The first is the proposition that it is necessarily the case that *if* "this table" picks out a table that is not made of ice, then the table it picks out is not made of ice. (2) The second is the proposition that if the table picked out is not made of ice, then the table it picks out is necessarily not made of ice. (1) is true but analytic and (2) is indeed not analytic, but is also not true.

(xi) It has been supposed that philosophers like Chomsky have shown that there is a great deal of a priori synthetic knowledge of that part of the world, which consists of language. But what philosophers like Chomsky have shown is that we have a large number of innate beliefs, rather than that we have innate knowledge. In the case of Chomsky, these are not so much beliefs about words—no Englishman has an innate knowledge of the fact that "cauliflower" means cauliflower—so much as innate knowledge of the connections between the offices which this or that word—which word will depend on the language that is being used—may or may not perform. For example, that numbers cannot wield pick-axes is something we work out a priori from our knowledge of that which words for numbers stand for and that which words for implements stand for. We have, so to speak, a "slot" in our mind which is responsible for our knowing how to use whatever words for a number our language has, but which word we actually use for that number is a matter of historical accident. And there are innate beliefs that are not about "language." For example, we have an innate belief that nature is uniform, and (what is not the same) that every event has a cause. I myself suspect that there are enormously many more innate beliefs, both about the behaviour of people and of inanimate objects, than is commonly recognised. I cannot explain in any other way how we adapt so readily to our environment.

But innate belief is not innate knowledge, and innate beliefs have to be shown to be knowledge, or replaced by knowledge, by being justified empirically in the usual way. To return to the example of every event's having a cause, though we have an innate belief that this is so, it only becomes knowledge, if it ever does, by being inductively supported in the usual way. (This is because all evidence for any inductive generalisation is ipso facto evidence for the proposition that every event has a cause.)

(xiii) It has been objected that it is not possible to deduce all truths of mathematics from axioms of logic. All this means is that it is not possible to show (in a certain kind of way, and on the (correct) assumption that anything that can be deduced from a logical truth is itself a logical truth) that all mathematical truths are logical truths. Showing this to be impossible does not show that mathematical truths are not logical truths. Perhaps whole subclasses of mathematical truths can be shown to be logical truths, or perhaps they can be shown one by one to be logical truths. It is very difficult to believe, for example, that there is not a contradiction in supposing it to be false that $1 + 1 = 2$, if "2" just means, as it would seem to mean, "that number which you obtain by adding 1 to 1."

The attempt of logicists to define mathematical terms by means of logical terms may be a failure, as well as the attempt to deduce mathematics from logic. But it would not follow from the fact that mathematical terms could not be defined by means of logical ones that there was no logical contradiction in denying mathematical propositions. The words "sun" and "east" cannot be defined in logical terms, but this does not mean that the sun rises in the east is not a logically true proposition, as it will be if "east" means "that quarter in which the sun rises."

Bertrand Russell thought that he had failed in his attempt, by defining numbers in terms of classes, to deduce mathematics from logic, when he discovered the paradox of the class of all classes that are not members of themselves. Since the class of cats is not a cat, there are some classes that are not members of themselves, and so there must be a class consisting of all these classes, viz., the class of all classes that are not members of themselves. But if the class of all classes that are not members of themselves is a member of itself, it follows that it is not a member of itself, because the class that it is a member of is precisely the class of all classes that are *not* members of themselves. On the other hand, if this class is not a member of itself, it follows that it is a member of itself, because the class that it is not a member of is the class of all classes that are *not* members of themselves.

But (a) if this shows anything, it shows that there is a contradiction in the notion of class, which there cannot really be, since we have used the notion of class from time immemorial without problems until philosophers began to reflect on it. (b) If this contradiction were genuine, it would not be created by the attempt to define number in terms of class. It would be there anyway. It may be that it can be removed by having a hierarchy of classes, or by saying that it does not make sense to say that a class is either a member of itself or not a member of itself, from which it follows that there is no such class as the class of classes that are not members of themselves. In any case, the breakdown of an attempt to show that mathematics can be reduced to logic by showing that it follows from certain logical axioms does not show that true mathematical propositions are not known to be true because it is logically contradictory to deny them. It is contradictory to deny many things that cannot be proved in a certain way.

(xiv) It has been objected that empiricism gives rise to "atomism," and "holism" shows that atomism is false.[5] The only kind of holism that is relevant to the question of whether we have any non-empirical way of discovering facts about a transcendent reality, and whether there is any non-empirical knowledge of facts about the world, is the kind of holism which holds that propositions do not stand or fall alone, but together, in the face of disconfirmatory evidence.

Two views are sometimes confused. There is (a) the view that contrary evidence means revising not just one proposition, but every other proposition in the corpus of scientific knowledge. There is (b) the view that contrary evidence never eliminates just one proposition, but that it is also possible to revise some other proposition instead; for example that this substance turns blue litmus paper red does not necessarily mean revising the proposition that it is an acid; in principle it might be better to revise the proposition that acids turn blue litmus paper red. This second kind of holism is probably true, but does not entail that empiricism is false.

(a) The first doctrine is not true. That this substance does not turn blue litmus paper red may just possibly—though the possibility is remote—mean revising the scientific view that acids turn blue litmus paper red, but it surely does not mean revising views such as that the universe was once corrugated, or that at the time of the big bang its size was less than a centimetre.

The first doctrine might be confused with another, which may well be true. It may well be true that for every scientific proposition A, and for every piece of contrary evidence B, there is *some* set of true propositions which together with B mean that if B is false, A must be false too. For example, this substance's not, as expected, turning blue litmus paper red might, together with some probably enormously large set of true scientific propositions, entail that the big bang did not occur quite in the way it did. This view may be entailed by determinism, the view that for every proposition about the future, there is some set of true propositions which entail that it is true or entail that it is false.

(b) Neither of these two doctrines entail that there are any views that do not stand or fall without empirical evidence. For, if it were the case that one could not revise one's belief in one proposition without "revising" one's belief in all other propositions, the proposition that would make one need to revise them would still have to be empirical evidence.

There are some propositions in which our belief ought never to be revised. For example, our belief that two and two are four ought never to be revised. Philosophers like Quine sometimes, I think, suggest that they can be because they think that truth is a property of sentences rather than of the propositions that these sentences express. What one can do is to revise the sentence "Two and two are four," say by changing the meaning of "four" to "five," which will make it express a falsehood rather than a fact. But this has no effect on the truth that two and two are four. It just means that, since the word "four" can no longer be used for the number four, this fact will have to be expressed in different words. When Einstein proved that things that were simultaneous with a third thing were not necessarily simultaneous with one another, he was not so much setting aside the common sense belief that they are, so much as defining, for the purpose of doing physics, "is simultaneous with" in a more useful way.

If one has conclusive evidence for an empirical proposition, one never ought to revise one's belief in it. If one's evidence for something is conclusive, this means that it is true, and one never ought to revise a true belief. Even though, as they well may, reasons may turn up against it, this would not merit revising it, for one cannot have conclusive reasons against a belief one already has had conclusive reasons for, though I suppose one might forget that one had. In other words, not all beliefs are defeasible. One may hold that one never can have conclusive evidence for an empirical belief, but this is simply not true, and philosophers have supposed the contrary only because they have confused conclusive evidence with logical entailment, and the possibility of a known proposition's being false, with the possibility of its being known and being false.

(xv) It has been held that truth is not, as empiricism presupposes, a matter of a propositions's corresponding to the facts, but of propositions cohering with other propositions. It may be objected that cohering with other propositions is not enough for truth, but that propositions, to be true, must cohere with other true propositions, which (a) makes the theory circular, and (b) makes it necessary to find out which propositions are true first, and consider whether other propositions cohere with the truth second.

In reply it can be held that one can find out which propositions are true a priori because there was only one way of combining propositions to constitute that conjunctive truth that would constitute a true description of the world. Propositions are like the parts of a puzzle all of which could be put together in only one way. But, though God might be able to fit them together correctly, it is absolutely obvious that, when one considers all the billions to the power of billions of propositions there are, and the many times more billions of ways in which they could be combined, man cannot do this. Hence, *faut de mieux*, we have to fall back on empirical investigation. In any case, truth is not a matter of a proposition's cohering with other propositions, but of things being as the person asserting that proposition says they are.

(xvi) It has been objected that all relations are "internal," and so it is possible to work out the nature of the whole a priori from knowledge of its parts. An internal relation is one that (logically) makes a difference to the nature of the things related by it whether they stand in this relation to it or not. Marriage, for example, is an external relation because a man, so far as logic goes, is just the same in himself whether he stands in the relation of being married to a woman, though marriage, and the nature of the woman to whom he is married, may (causally) make a difference to him. I myself do not believe that there are any internal relations between concrete objects (as opposed to, say, numbers), so I cannot give an example. The doctrine of internal relations, however, is the doctrine that *all* relations are internal.[6]

It looks as if such propositions as that husbands must be married, are exceptions to this statement. However, that husbands are married does not mean that Tom, who is a husband, has to stand in the relation of marriage to anyone. All it means is that, if he did not stand in this relation to anyone, he would not be a husband.

It looks as if, if this doctrine were true, and if necessity went with a priority, we could work out a priori everything about the rest of the universe from sufficient knowledge of any of its parts. This is because everything is related in some way to everything else, and so a change in the nature of anything in the universe will, if the doctrine of internal relations is true, make a difference to the universe itself and everything else in it.

But even if the doctrine of internal relations were true, we would still have to know empirically the nature of the parts. That is to say, even if we knew a priori the hypothetical proposition that if the parts were such-and-such, the whole would have to be so-and-so, we would still have to fall back on empirical knowledge of the fact that the parts were such-and-such.

However, the doctrine of internal relations is not true. It has been refuted by G. E. Moore in a (now) undeservedly neglected paper.[7] I shall put the matter, however, in my own way. That the doctrine of internal relations has been supposed to be true is the result of a modal mistake. It is true that, if a thing (A) stands in a relation to another thing (B) of a certain nature, then anything which does not stand in that relation to a thing of that nature cannot be A. But this does not mean that A necessarily stands in that relation to a thing of that nature. To suppose otherwise is to confuse two contentions. (a) It is necessarily the case that, if A stands in a certain relation to a thing of a certain nature, anything that does not stand in that relation to a thing of that nature is not A. (b) If A stands in a certain relation to a thing of a certain nature then, necessarily, anything that does not stand in that relation to a thing of that nature is not A.[8] The word "necessarily" governs two quite different propositions in these two sentences. From (b) but not from (a), it follows that A necessarily stands in the relation in question to a thing of this nature.

It might follow from (b) that it is possible to work out from a knowledge of the nature of A everything about the nature of the things to which it is related, but (b) is not true. (b) only seems to be true because it is confused with (a) which is true, but does not imply that it is possible to work this out. To take an example, if the cat is on a blue Persian mat, then, necessarily, anything that is not on a blue Persian mat is not that cat, but this does not mean that the cat is necessarily on the mat. The poor animal is quite capable of going somewhere else if it wants.

A great deal of the interest goes out of the view that all relations are internal if, as is common these days, necessity is divorced from *a priority*. If a thing necessarily stood in all the relations it did to the kinds of thing it did, and this implied that one could work out a priori everything about its relations and the nature of things it stood in these relations to, the doctrine of internal relations would be of enormous importance. But if necessity does not go with a priority, it has relatively little interest.

When one says that if one knows everything about the parts, it is possible to know everything about the whole, this doctrine is trivial if knowing everything about the parts includes knowing its relations to the whole, and the nature of the whole to which it is related. Otherwise it is false.

(xix) Some philosophers think that natural kinds[9] have real essences, which fact is a different fact from the fact that the words describing them have certain definitions. For example, it may follow from the definition of chalk that it dissolves in sulphuric acid, and not follow from its definition that it is suspendible in water. Nevertheless, it both necessarily dissolves in sulphuric acid and is necessarily suspendible in water, because these are both part of its essence. It is not, however, part of its essence that it is used to chalk billiard cues.

We have seen that, though it is probable that when it is a fact that is necessary, it is necessarily necessary ($Lp \rightarrow LLp$), there are certainly cases when a thing is necessary, but the proposition that it is necessary is not necessary. For example, it is just a contingent alterable fact that in order to get married in a Christian country it is necessary not to be married already. What possesses necessity is *not to be married* already, just as it is the *connection* between taking cyanide and dying that is necessary, not the fact that this connection obtains. And whether things have real essences or not, we discover *empirically* that things have the properties that they (necessarily) have, whether these properties are part of their essence or not. It is only necessarily *true propositions* that have to be a priori; and *chalk's* necessarily possessing the property of dissolving in sulphuric acid does not mean that the *proposition* that it necessarily possesses this property is necessarily true.

Furthermore, since the *existence* of something cannot be part of its essence, then, even if the doctrine of real essences did give us an extension to our a priori knowledge, the facts it would give us would all be hypothetical ones. One cannot deduce from the fact that it is part of the nature of chalk to dissolve in sulphuric acid that there is such a thing as chalk. Such knowledge would have to be empirical. Those who think that things possess real essences cut the ground from under their own feet when they wish to use this as an objection to empiricism, if they also wish to hold that there are necessary propositions which can be known only empirically.

(xxi) It has been objected to empiricism that Wittgenstein has shown that there are many functions of language other than that of describing the world. For example, we use language to give orders or make requests, to make promises, to enter into contracts, to worship and to pray. But it is immaterial to epistemology that this is so, because epistemologists are concerned only with how we know things, and, if—as is the case—these other functions of language are not to state what we know, they embody no knowledge about which the epistemologist need concern himself. For example, since to give an order or offer up a prayer is not to state anything true or false, there are no truths embodied in orders or prayers, and so there can be no epistemology of orders or prayers.

(xxiv) It has been objected that the proposition, that all propositions about the world can be empirically verified, itself cannot be empirically verified. This, as we have seen, is so; but it does not matter, because, if true, empiricism is analytically or conceptually true. We see that empiricism must be true by reflecting on the concept of knowledge, and the ways in which it can be acquired.

(xxv) It may well be that statements ascribing some attribute to a thing by referring to it by a proper name are all synthetic. It involves no objection to empiricism that this should be so, provided all such statements are empirical, which I think they are.

There are two extremely obscure interrelated problems discussed by modern philosophers, concerning (a) how much a thing may change and still remain the thing it was, and concerning (b) which of its attributes a thing has necessarily and which it does not. The second claim (b) involves little not discussed in my earlier discussion of real essences. It seems obvious that, whether or not it is a necessary truth that John Stuart Mill was not born in the eighteenth century, that he was not born in the eighteenth century is a fact discovered empirically—as a first step, by looking it up in a book and finding that he was born in the nineteenth century.

(a) It looks as if the fact that Ulysses could not have changed into a fox is, if it is necessarily true, something that we could know a priori. But in fact Ulysses's inability to change into a fox provides no limitation on what may happen. It does not alter the fact that states that were clearly states of Ulysses might be followed by a series of states all resembling states of Ulysses less and less, and resembling states of a fox more and more, until eventually they get replaced by states which are unequivocally states of a fox. It is just a question of whether the fox is identical with Ulysses, which I suspect is not a "real" question. There are just as many possible states of the world whether one says that the fox is Ulysses or whether one does not.

(xxvi) It has been supposed that empiricism cannot give an account of unfulfilled conditionals, which, on some views would entail that it cannot give an account of causal necessity. For example, the taking of cyanide has to be necessarily followed by death, if one is to be able to deduce that those who have not taken cyanide would not have died. However cyanide is necessarily followed by death if attempts to stop people who have taken cyanide from dying are bound to fail. One establishes that they are bound to fail by making these attempts and seeing that they always do fail. One concludes (inductively) that an attempt, which was not made, would have failed, because all the attempts that were made failed. This, that and the other attempt, which was made, would have failed, because it did; hence an attempt which was not made, also would have failed. It is just a mistake to think that one can use the unfulfilled conditional only of attempts that have been made; consider "He would have, wouldn't he?" said of someone we know who always would have, because he always does, and seeing that he does is to see that he would have. (None of this shows that it is not a contingent fact, established empirically, that taking cyanide is necessarily followed by death (see Section 1)). Those philosophers who think that unfulfilled conditional propositions are neither true nor false, on account of thinking that it is impossible to establish what *would* have happened if something which did *not* happen *had* happened, do not as a result fail to insure their houses, on account of what they know would happen if their houses were to burn down and they were uninsured. They thus insure against fire, and the possibility of their view being erroneous, simultaneously.

II EMPIRICISM, VERIFICATIONISM AND ANTI-REALISM[10]

(xxvii) Empiricism (Truth Empiricism?) is the view that propositions about the world can be established only empirically. Some empiricists also hold a more extreme view than this, which is not implied by Truth Empiricism, according to which words which cannot be used in sentences which express propositions that can be empirically shown to be true or false do not make sense. The best known variety is Logical Positivism, according to which the meaning of a sentence is the method of verification of the proposition it expresses, or the sum total of the evidence for it, which evidence is recorded in observation statements. One could verify a proposition either by being confronted with what verified it—seeing a glacier—or having evidence for its truth—seeing marks on rocks made by the glacier.

I have discussed some of the usual objections to the verification principle elsewhere. Most of them are invalid, but the following seem conclusive.

(a) If Logical Positivism is true, statements about the *past*, such as statements about past glaciers, turn out to be statements partly about marks on rocks. Statements about *others' minds* turn out to be statements about their moans and groans and words and brain states. Statements about *microscopic particles* turn out to be statements about traces on Wilson cloud chambers, etc. It is obvious that the first and second of these views are wrong; and I think true that the third is. One really isn't talking about marks on rocks when one makes a statement about a glacier.

(b) The division of statements into observation statements and those which need evidence is relative, relative to person and to time. What can be observed at one time can only be inferred at another, and what one person can observe, another person has to infer. Hence when I could see the glacier for which I now only have evidence, I was talking about the glacier; now that it has receded into the past I am talking about marks on rocks. If Tom can feel the pain which I can only infer, he is talking about the pain, but I am talking about his moans and groans. (He can hardly be talking about his own moans and groans.) Verificationism leads to the absurd conclusion that for those for whom smoke is evidence for fire, statements about fire are statements partly about smoke, and not at all about fire, but for those for whom fire is evidence for smoke, statements about smoke are statements partly about fire, and not at all about smoke.

(c) It is only evidence that the person using a sentence knows about that can affect what he means by this sentence. If Tom does not know about fingerprints, he cannot be talking even partly about them when he says that Jane is not the murderer. But modifying verificationism to hold that the meaning of a sentence is what the person using it *supposes* to be the verification of the proposition it expresses, would mean that when Tom says that Jane is not the murderer, and Mary, who does know about fingerprints, says she is, their statements need not be incompatible. And it is not credible that sentences about the beginning of the universe express statements about what a more knowledgeable or perfectly knowledgeable person would know to be the evidence for them, for then it would follow that lesser mortals, who did not know about this evidence, were not talking about the beginning of the universe at all.

If one thinks of having evidence for a glacier as acquaintance with its sense-data, or the sense-data of a mark on a rock, verificationism tends to turn into Phenomenalism, the view that statements about material objects are statements about the sense-data one would have *if* one were differently situated in space, or had not forgotten one's spectacles and protective clothing, etc. (This would not alter the fact that statements about glaciers would be about sense-data of glaciers, and not statements about the sense-data of marks on rocks.) Since Phenomenalism here defined is a theory about the meaning of sentences about material objects, it is not incompatible with realism about microscopic particles (see later), for that when I am making assertions about a material object I am not asserting the existence of independently existing particles, but only asserting hypothetical propositions about sense-data, does not mean that there are not any such particles, or that I think there are not any.

Philosophers may have been inclined to regard statements about unobserved things as statements about the evidence for their existence because they have supposed that unobserved things cannot be observed, whereas the evidence for them can. But nothing is simpler than to observe unobserved things; one just goes to the place where they are and takes a good look. Of course, one cannot observe them while they are in the state of being unobserved, but to complain about this is unreasonable.

(xxviii) It is an assumption of investigating the world, empirically or otherwise, that the world we so investigate is neither affected by our merely acquiring evidence for propositions about it, nor by our choosing one word rather than another to express our conclusions. It is a mistake to suppose that empiricism violates this assumption, and therefore a mistake to suppose that it leads to Anti-realism. It is a platitude that the *steps* we take to find something out, e.g. moving our eyes from one place in space to another, can affect things,

According to one form of Anti-realism, it is not true that there is a past, that there are other minds, or (the most usual view) microscopic particles; things go on just as if there were, or we have to accept, but not believe, for the purpose of making predictions, that these things exist. Such kinds of Anti-realism do not much concern me—though I shall try to refute them in my antepenultimate section—as they do not lead to the conclusion that more evidence makes a difference to reality. It is just that, as we get more evidence, we will realise that statements which we formerly thought were useful, were not so, but both the new ones and the old ones are alike false.

The form of Anti-realism that I shall consider—henceforth, "Anti-realism"—came into philosophy via Mathematical Constructivism or Intuitionism—which holds that mathematical propositions that can be neither proved nor disproved are neither true nor false. Anti-realism is the analogous view that where there is no (or not enough?) evidence for an empirical proposition that proposition is neither true nor false. Hence a proposition may turn from being neither true nor false to being true (or false) by our acquiring evidence for its truth.

Anti-realism has little to recommend it, and I believe gains more credence than it deserves from discussions which are highly abstract, loaded with technical vocabulary, and do not observe the useful rule that militates against the practice of doing philosophy without examples. Whatever one says should be tested for meaningfulness, truth and clarity at every stage by these.

Anti-realism implies the extraordinary conclusion that if a person who has conclusive evidence for Tom's being the murderer (a proposition about the past) says that he is, his remark is true, but if someone without evidence says that he is, what he says is neither true nor false. Since evidence admits of degrees, truth should admit of degrees also, which usually it does not. Since I may have evidence that what is eating my peas is a bird, but no evidence about what kind of bird it is, it should follow that it is a bird, but not any particular kind of bird which, as Berkeley said, is impossible. If conclusive inductive evidence is necessary for truth, then that Tom is the murderer would suddenly become true as soon as conclusive inductive evidence was produced for this proposition, or at least true when expressed by the person who had the evidence. Should it be logically conclusive evidence that is meant, this is not to be had. Should Tom be tried for murder, an Anti-realist jury might conclude that he should be acquitted, but not because, though he *might* have done it, the evidence was insufficient, but because it was neither true nor false that he did it. The logically innocent might be forgiven for supposing that this meant that he neither was nor was not the murderer.

It might be replied by Anti-realists that it is not such common or garden propositions that Anti-realists are thinking of, but whole classes of propositions about inaccessible entities, such as the propositions about the past, others' minds, microscopic particles, or unfulfilled conditionals already mentioned, which they may dispose of for philosophical, not common sensible, reasons. For example, Anti-realist philosophers may feel their views are more plausible when applied to concatenations of particles, than to murders. But if Jane's strangling someone implies that something is happening to the electrons which compose her hands and her victim's neck, then that statements about the electrons are neither true nor false should also imply that statements about the murder are also neither true nor false.

Past metaphysicians, who must have had great confidence in their powers of reasoning, have thought such things as that the past did not exist and that everything short of the whole truth was false. To "save the appearances" these two doctrines had to be bolstered up with a doctrine of degrees of truth. Though propositions about the past were false it was held that that a battle was fought at Hastings in 1066 was at least nearer the truth than that there was no such battle. For the same reason Anti-realists need to hold that, if propositions about the past are neither true nor false, it is at least nearer the truth that I ate my breakfast before my lunch than that it was the other way around. (The example is G. E. Moore's.) One suspects that in this case "nearer the truth" would simply do the same job that was formerly done by "true," and we would be left precisely where we were before.

The case is not improved if you hold (as some do) that to assert the negation of a proposition is not to assert that there is no evidence for it, but to assert that one has no reason for thinking that there will ever be evidence sufficient to justify one in asserting it. *Jane* can think that there is no evidence for there ever being sufficient evidence to justify anyone (especially the police) in thinking that she is the murderer, while knowing perfectly well that she *is* the murderer. And both Tom and Mary can think that *perhaps* she is (see Section xxx), although all the evidence is against it, a thought which an Anti-realist cannot have (See Section xxx).

(xxix) Neither empiricism nor verificationism implies Anti-realism, however. Anti-realism is based on considerations concerning meaning, and should have no bearing on the truths meaningful sentences express. The correct deduction from the view that the meaning of a sentence is determined by its "assertion conditions"—the evidence that justifies or tends to justify me in asserting the proposition this sentence expresses—is neither that there are propositions that are neither true nor false, nor, as is sometimes said, that there are no truths which cannot be expressed, or things for the existence of which there is no evidence, i.e., when there are no assertion conditions, but (a) that a *sentence* which does not express a proposition for which there is evidence (not, be it noted, a proposition for which there is no evidence) is meaningless, and (b) that, when there is evidence, *what* proposition a sentence expresses depends on what this evidence is or is *supposed* to be evidence for (see Section xxiv).

(a) Once upon a time it was not known that influenza was caused by a virus. In those days, men did not have words for viruses or any evidence that there were such things. This fact, however, did not stop people from catching influenza, any more than the earlier fact that men did not have a word for death stopped people from dying from influenza. What follows, if the meaning of the word "virus" is tied to the evidence for viruses, is not that there were then no viruses, or that the proposition that there are viruses was then neither true nor false, but the quite platitudinous conclusion that a (probably timeless) truth which we can now put into words was still a truth, but could not be put into words. There are excellent inductive reasons for thinking that as time goes on we shall become acquainted with more and more things, as we have constantly been in the past, and give words to them, by which time we will be able to express propositions which are eternally true, but cannot yet be expressed.

(b) If I were deceitfully to pretend to teach someone what "dog" meant by showing him cats, "dog" would come to mean to him what "cats" means to me. Analogously, *if* meaning were determined by evidence, and if I were to teach him the meaning of "cat" by showing him evidence (such as buried bones) for the presence of dogs, then when he uttered the words "Next door has a cat" he would be saying that next door has a dog. Indeed, the situation would be even worse than this, for, as we have seen, meaning for Tom would depend not on what was evidence, but on what Tom supposed to be evidence. Hence the meaning of a sentence's depending on "assertion conditions" will have no bearing on the truth or neuterhood of the proposition that we in fact use any given sentence to assert, but determine only *what* proposition we are using it to assert.

I suspect that remarks I have made about Anti-realism about the world apply also to Anti-realism about mathematics. If the words in the sentence that expresses Fermat's last theorem did not become (fully) meaningful until this theorem was proved, it does not follow that the proposition that it expresses, now that it *can* be proved, is not an eternal truth; simply that it could not previously have been (properly) expressed. Two and two were (timelessly) four long before anyone knew how to demonstrate this fact or had words to express it.

(xxx) Since it would be absurd to suppose that human or indeed any organisms are capable of reacting, directly or indirectly, to everything there is, there must be an enormous number of things in the universe which we will never find out about, or even have words for, not because our cognitive capacities are limited, but because our sensory apparatus is. And, unless every event must have an effect, which is not self-evident, there must be past happenings irretrievably and in principle lost to us, however clever we are.

Philosophers, from the time of Berkeley (*in The Principles of Knowledge* (XXIII)) have sometimes argued against this by making quite improper use of the fact that it is impossible to give *examples* of facts for which there is no evidence, or which cannot be put into words. The modern form of this mistake is embodied in "The Paradox of Knowledge," which is supposed to imply that there can be no unknown truths. An example would be the statement that there are humanoids in Andromeda (or a golden mountain one mile high) and no-one knows that there are (or is), which statements are supposed to be contradictory, and so false. However, it is no more contradictory than is the statement that I do not exist, which could be true, but could not be asserted if it were true. That there are humanoids on Andromeda is in fact only pragmatically contradictory. Anyone who believed the second conjunct has no business to be asserting the first; but if he were, albeit improperly, to assert it, he could well be right. The fact that one cannot without pragmatic contradiction give examples of truths for which there is no evidence does not mean that there are not any. One needs the word "perhaps," which so far as I know logicians do not have. Then they would be able to say such things as that perhaps there are (or that there might be) humanoids in Andromeda, although there is no reason for thinking that there are.

Logical Positivists were against words that claimed to say something about the world, but said nothing verifiable, rather than against there being truths that could not be stated. They were against words without things rather than things without words. That verificationism is now, wrongly, being used to support Anti-realism, with the resulting evidential anthropomorphism and cosmic verbal parochialism, is a retrograde step. What is called "realism"—"*scientific* realism" is usually used by philosophers who attach too much importance to physics, though physics is not the only science—is compatible with empiricism.

III OUTLINE OF AN EMPIRICIST THEORY OF EVIDENCE AND OF MEANING

(xxxi) The universe extends perhaps infinitely beyond the tiny part of it that we can experience, especially beyond that bit of it which is experienced by any one person at any one time. This means, as Hume (in *A Treatise of Human Nature*, Book I, Part IV, Section II) argued, that our knowledge of the unobserved universe has to be based upon sampling. We assume that unsampled parts of the universe will resemble sampled parts, and piece together a complete picture of the universe from samples (not necessarily unchanging samples) of it taken successively. That hitherto unsampled parts of the universe will not precisely resemble our sample is itself something we know by sampling. Our own sampling may be supplemented by what we know of the sampling of other people, and by what we remember of the past samples of ourselves and the reports of others, but it is only by sampling that we know that there are any other people and that our memory is reliable. If one considers that our knowledge of the unobserved universe is obtained by sampling, one should realise that it would be as misguided to try to translate statements about the unsampled parts of the universe into statements about the sampled parts which are our evidence for them, as it would be to reduce statements about the lost or invisible parts of a mosaic to statements about those parts of it which are extant or visible.

That sampling gives us a correct picture is confirmed every time something turns up at the place where and time when completing a picture based on sampling led one to expect it to be; hence basing conclusions on sampling is justified by its success. Observing this is a case when one confirms that something which is true of one's sample is true of what is sampled. It is only an illusion, generated by the fact that as soon as one has checked, what was the wider reality is now described as part of one's sample, that one cannot check one's sample against reality. Even the deity, who can see everything, cannot observe anything which is not part of his sample.

Arguing inductively is obviously one example of sampling, as it assumes that the proportion—possibly, but not necessarily, 100 percent—of *X*s to *Y*s in one's sample is the same as it is in the great world outside. The fact that the proportion of *X*s to *Y*s may be less than 100 percent means that *probability* is based on sampling. (Connections of less than 100 percent may be necessary ones; there is nothing special about 100 percent.) Completing a picture by filling out a sample, however, consists in more than supplementing partial regularities to make them whole. Supposing that car bonnets have engines under them, or that unobserved stars have planets, partly consists in filling out a spatio-temporal picture from a knowledge of part of it; more accurately from a knowledge of several different parts observed on different occasions and superimposed on one another. And it is the fact that it is needed to complete a picture that justifies us in thinking that the objects we observe continue to exist in the intervals during which we are not observing them.

Perception is a process of sampling, and presupposes sampling's validity (a) because we cannot observe the back or inside of an object while we observe its front, and (b) because we assume that the front will turn up again when we return to our original position, as we remember that it always has in the past. Putting together views (or feels) of an object seen (or felt) successively to enclose a three-dimensional region of space presupposes, as Kant pointed out, not only memory and induction, but a vision of space stretching out all round the bits of it one can see, and a capacity to fit the bits together. Our idea of an ordinary material object presupposes this capacity to synthesise, and ideas of such objects are consequently acquired only piecemeal. I myself think that one sees (visual) sense-data, but it would make no difference if we saw the front surface of objects, which are also seen only successively, and can with as much justice as can sensa (i.e., no justice at all) be supposed to interpose themselves between us and the objects of which they are manifestations. Our knowledge of the microscopic particles, which are the unobservable constituents of things, is obtained by sampling rather than by induction. Though we can observe a correlation between smoke and fire, and infer fire from smoke, we cannot observe a correlation between traces on Wilson cloud chambers and microscopic particles. We cannot observe microscopic particles. There is no reason to suppose that the conglomerations of particles should not reside in that region of space which is enclosed by sense-data of the object, which makes sense-data less removed from the object than many philosophers have supposed.

Our *knowledge of the past* is also obtained by sampling. We observe the movement of the second hand of our clock, and assume, that this is a fair sample of its movement, that it has been moving in the same way before we observed it, and will continue to do so afterwards. This assumption is confirmed by memory of past observations. The same applies to our knowledge of the future, when a sample is completed by projecting forwards in time rather than backwards. I suspect we have an (a priori Kantian) idea of time into which our ideas of temporal things have to be fitted. An a priori idea is not the same thing as an a priori proposition.

If one regards our *knowledge of other's minds* as obtained by sampling, one will assume that as when I am talking to my friend Tom I am aware of a face-shaped "image" or sense-datum, which I take to be on the surface of his face, in the middle of my visual field, and set against a background of wall, which image I take to be indicative of his thoughts and feelings, so he must be aware of a face-shaped image, which he takes to be on the surface of my face, in the middle of his visual field, set against the background of the opposite wall, which image he takes to be indicative of my thoughts and feelings. Each will take what he sees to be evidence for the existence of what completes the pattern, i.e., the perceptions and thoughts of the others. I get the words to talk about his image, etc., by acquaintance with my own image. *Pace* J. J. C. Smart, we do not find, by looking within the skulls of either of us, anything suitable to possess the characteristics which I know are possessed by my thoughts and feelings and pains and sense-data; as Leibniz nearly said, just one damned little bit of stuff after another.

It is not just that we do not in fact find such things as the image of another's face—which is an individual, not a characteristic, and certainly not a process—within our heads; we do not find anything in our heads which such things could possibly be. If we look around us, as a good empiricist should, we see myriads of coloured shapes, lines, dots, flashes, and are aware of something similar with our other senses and internal sense. These do not remotely resemble the colourless bits of stuff with (relatively) enormous gaps between them that we are told in books are the only kind of thing the world contains. To adapt a tale of David Armstrong's, it is as if we saw a woman with a head, but believed she was headless because we had been told by able philosophers with strongly held metaphysical views, that this must be so, and had been guided by them and not by the evidence.

One cannot sample *microscopic objects*, but as a result of sampling one can postulate electrons to stand roughly in the same relation to what is seen on the screens of Wilson cloud chambers as, say, aeroplanes do to vapour trails, or postulate viruses seen with electron microscopes standing in much the same relation to the microscope as blood corpuscles do to an optical microscope. This procedure has an enormous advantage over trying to reduce statements about particles to statements about the evidence for them, for a conglomeration of particles—say a man shot from a cannon—may travel along a simple path, governed by a simple law, but the behaviour of the appearances has to be deduced from this via knowledge of the state of the eyes of the observer, the intervening medium, and whatever visual aids he is using. Given that all planets go round the sun, there are complicated laws stating the behaviour of each to any of the others that one may choose to treat as one's frame of reference, but it is much simpler to stick with the sun.

(xxxii) Meaning, like the discovery of truth, goes hand in hand with sampling, because, as again Hume realised, we learn what "tabby" means by being shown samples of things that are tabby, and what the word "cat" means by being shown samples of cats. We are not taught what "cat" means by being shown evidence for the existence of cats, like cat droppings or dead birds. It is true that the word "dragon" does not acquire its meaning from our being confronted with dragons, but, to oversimplify, we have been confronted with samples of wings, lizards and fire, and a dragon is a winged fire-breathing lizard. New technical terms may be introduced, provided that they are explained by the use of terms which already have meaning. As we have seen, most words can be defined only by showing bits of what they stand for one at a time. *Pace* Quine, it is conceivable that when I show someone a cat, and he obliging says "cat," what he sees is a horse, and he means horse by "cat," but no sensible person ought to entertain this somewhat uneconomical hypothesis.

Philosophers have supposed that one cannot explain talk about others' pain or about past objects if words acquire their meaning in this way, but they are mistaken. In order to know what is meant by "past glacier" it is enough to have been shown a glacier; and one does not need to have been shown, impossibly, a past glacier. To know what is meant by words for others' pains one does not need to have been shown others' pains. In order to imagine what it would be like to be married to Mary, who is married to someone else, it is not necessary to imagine what it would be like to be married to Mary while she is in the state of being married to someone else. Mary is not then in the state of being married to someone else. And I can apply expressions like "silver crescent" and "white dot" to other people's silver crescents and white dots because I have been acquainted with my own; it is not necessary to know what it is like to be aware of them while others are aware of them at the same time, as it would be if I had to be aware of *other people's* white dots while they were aware of them. *They* are not aware of their white dots while others are aware of them.

It follows that meaning goes hand in hand with verification (in the form of confrontation), but not in the form of the verification of the proposition expressed by the sentence whose meaning is being discussed. Meaning depends on verification because one defines a word such as "cat" by showing people things of which it is true that they are cats. Given that "cat" can be shown to be meaningful by its being used in *some* sentences which express propositions which are verifiable, it does not have to do this in every sentence in which it is used. The meaning of the sentence "There were once glaciers in Cambridgeshire" does not have to be explained either by what makes it true, or by what is evidence for it. It is sufficient (but not necessary) that we should in the past have been shown things of which it was true that they were glaciers, been told and had understood that they were "glaciers," and not forgotten this.

So long as a word (one once would have suggested the word "particle") is defined by confrontation, it is perfectly legitimate to apply it to things, like electrons, which we cannot be confronted with, and which will have, and sometimes be discovered to have, characteristics which we do not (or not yet) have words for.

Though necessary, it is not *sufficient* that a word like "glacier" to have acquired its meaning by our being shown glaciers (or defined in terms of such things) for the sentence in which it actually is being used to be meaningful. "Glaciers move slowly" is meaningful, but "Slowly move glaciers" is not. "Glaciers" has also to be used in a properly formed sentence. I do not have space to discuss what makes a sentence properly formed, and at the moment not the capacity, though my penultimate paragraph contains a hint. But I hope I have said enough to dispel the delusion that the meaning of a sentence has anything to do with having evidence for the proposition it expresses.

This view of meaning retains the logical positivists's anti-metaphysical conclusions because a word that has acquired its meaning by a process of sampling can be applied only to other parts of the space-time world we sample. This does not mean that there cannot be entities for which we have no words, but only, would you believe, that we cannot talk about them. I am not talking about them when I say that there *may* be such things, for this just means that we have the word "things," not that we have a word for the special kind of thing they are. Since we could not, without pragmatic contradiction, hold that there was a god or an absolute for whom we had no words, the fact that there could be things without words (or evidence) could not bring back theology or speculative metaphysics; for we do have the words "God" and "Absolute," so they cannot be part of unobserved reality.

The meaning of syncategorematic words like "all" and "not"—of which I suspect that numerals are a species—and words for "abstract" entities like propositions or universal or quadratic equations or games or meanings or justice, and so on almost indefinitely, can be defined by indicating what difference is made to the meaning of whole sentences by their inclusion.

(xxxiii) I conclude that none of the objections usually thought to dispose of empiricism is valid, and that all first order propositions about the world are known empirically. The others are a priori, but are not about the world. Words that cannot be used in sentences expressing some verifiable proposition or other are meaningless, and words so defined can be used only for things within the universe. Anti-realism is fortunately implied neither by empiricism nor by verificationism, and is mistaken.

Notes

1. This paper is partly a considerably shortened version, with some alterations, of Chapter 3 of my book *God, Freedom and Immortality*, Avebury, 1999. Parts II and III have been added at the request of the editor, whose excuse is that he did not know what I was going to say. To indicate when whole sections have been omitted I have kept the original numbering. The sections omitted are on the a priority of colors being extended, the genuineness of tautological knowledge, empiricism and the sense-datum theory, Raymond Chomsky and Godel. I have also omitted a passage that I have noticed contains a bad boob, but there may be others. I am greatly indebted to Louis Pojman for his generous support and encouragement and to David Rees for his proofreading of an earlier version of this article.
2. I have discussed this matter in more detail in The Trouble with Tarski, or sentences and Propositions,

Pragmatic Contradiction, Analyticity, Linguistic Relativism, Conventionalism, "convention" T and More," forthcoming in *The Philosophical Quarterly*.

3. By Quine, in *Word and Object*, MIT Press, 1988, p. 195f.
4. See *Word and Object*, MIT Press, 1988, p. 195f.
5. The reader is referred to *Psychosemantics, The Problem of Meaning in the Philosophy of Mind*, MIT Press, 1987, by Jerry Fodor.
6. Whether two things stand in the relation of being similar to one another in a certain respect logically depends on their natures, or what they are like. One would have supposed that whether they stood in the relation of being next to one another did not logically depend upon what they were like.
7. In "External and Internal Relations," in *The Proceedings of the Aristotelian Society*, 1919–20; reprinted in *Philosophical Studies*, Routledge and Kegan Paul, 1922.
8. The difference is between (a) $L((aRb \rightarrow (-cRb \rightarrow -(c = a))$ and (b) $(aRb) \rightarrow (-cRb \rightarrow L-(c = a))$. (a) is true but not important. (b) would be of earth-shattering importance if it were true, but it is not true.
9. For further discussion the reader is referred to S. P. Schwartz, ed., *Naming, Necessity and Natural Kinds*, Cornell University Press, 1977.
10. See A. J. Ayer, *Language Truth and Logic*, second edition, Gollancz, 1946; J. J. C. Smart, *Between Science and Philosophy*, Random House, 1968; Michael Dummett, "Truth" in *Truth and Other Enigmas*, Oxford University Press, 1978, and "Realism" in *The Seas of Language*, Oxford University Press, 1988; B. van Fraassen, *The Scientific Image*, Oxford University Press, 1980; Crispin Wright: *Realism, Meaning and Truth*, Blackwell, 1986, and *Truth and Objectivity*, Harvard University Press, 1992; and Neil Tenant, *The Taming of the True*, Oxford University Press, 1997.

Chapter 15

EDMUND L. GETTIER

Edmund L. Gettier (1927–) is Professor of Philosophy at the University of Massachusetts at Amherst.

In this celebrated short essay, Gettier identifies the third condition in Plato and other accounts of knowledge as *justification* and then shows by clear counterexamples that this tripartite analysis of knowledge as true, justified belief is insufficient for knowledge. Something more than mere justification is required before a true belief can qualify as knowledge. Before 1963, the concept of knowledge was either left unanalyzed or defined more or less as true justified belief. I said in the Introduction that Plato offered a tripartite analysis of knowledge, defining it as true belief with a rational explanation or justification (Greek *logos*). Passages asserting the tripartite analysis can be found in C. I. Lewis, Roderick Chisholm, and A. J. Ayer with similar definitions. Roughly, Person S knows that *p* if and only if

a. S believes that *p*.

b. Belief *p* is true.

c. S's belief that *p* is justified.

These three conditions constitute the necessary and sufficient conditions of knowledge. If one of them were missing, S would not know that *p*. If all of them were present, S could not fail to know that *p*. Let us call this the "tripartite analysis" of knowledge.

Alvin Plantinga reports the following anecdote. In 1962 he was drinking a cup of coffee in the cafeteria of Wayne State University with his colleague Gettier, when Gettier mentioned that he was concerned that he would be coming up for tenure the next year without a lot of publications. He did have an idea of setting forth a few minor counterexamples to the traditional definition of knowledge, but he considered that a minor matter. The next year Gettier's two-and-a-half-page article on the definition of knowledge was published in *Analysis*, and epistemology has never been the same.

Gettier's analysis was based on two counterexamples to the tripartite analysis. The first is as follows. Smith and Jones have applied for a certain job, and Smith has strong evidence for conjunctive proposition (d): "Jones is the man who will get the job, and Jones has ten coins in his pocket."

Proposition (d) entails (e): "The man who will get the job has ten coins in his pocket." We may suppose that Smith sees the entailment and believes (e).

But unknown to Smith, he himself will get the job and happens to have ten coins in his pocket. So, while (d) is false, (e) is true and Smith truly and justifiably believes (e), but we would not say that Smith *knows* that the man who will get the job has ten coins in his pocket.

So the tripartite analysis fails, for he knows neither that he will get the job nor that he has ten coins in his pocket.

Gettier's counterexamples have the following form:

1. S believes that *p*.
2. Belief *p* is true.
3. S's belief that *p* is justified.
4. Belief *p* is based on or entailed by some proposition *q*.
5. S is justified in believing *q*.
6. Belief *q* is false.
7. Therefore, S doesn't know that *p*.

Case I: Suppose that Smith and Jones have applied for a certain job. And suppose that Smith has strong evidence for the following conjunctive proposition:

(d) Jones is the man who will get the job, and Jones has ten coins in his pocket.

Smith's evidence for (d) might be that the president of the company assured him that Jones would in the end be selected, and that he, Smith, had counted the coins in Jones's pocket ten minutes ago. Proposition (d) entails.

(e) The man who will get the job has ten coins in his pocket.

Let us suppose that Smith sees the entailment from (d) to (e), and accepts (e) on the grounds of (d), for which he has strong evidence. In this case, Smith is clearly justified in believing that (e) is true.

But imagine, further, that unknown to Smith, he himself, not Jones, will get the job. And, also, unknown to Smith, he himself has ten coins in his pocket. Proposition (e) is then true, though proposition (d), from which Smith inferred (e), is false. In our example, then, all of the following are true: (*i*) (e) is true, (*ii*) Smith believes that (e) is true, and (*iii*) Smith is justified in believing that (e) is true. But it is equally clear that Smith does not *know* that (e) is true; for (e) is true in virtue of the number of coins in Smith's pocket, while Smith does not know how many coins are in Smith's pocket, and bases his belief in (e) on a count of the coins in Jones's pocket, whom he falsely believes to be the man who will get the job.

Case II: Let us suppose that Smith has strong evidence for the following proposition:

(f) Jones ownes a Ford.

Smith's evidence might be that Jones has at all times in the past within Smith's memory owned a car, and always a Ford, and that Jones has just offered Smith a ride while driving a Ford. Let us imagine, now, that Smith has another friend, Brown, of whose whereabouts he is totally ignorant. Smith selects three place names quite at random, and constructs the following three propositions:

(g) Either Jones owns a Ford, or Brown is in Boston.

(h) Either Jones owns a Ford, or Brown is in Barcelona.

(i) Either Jones owns a Ford, or Brown is in Brest-Litovsk.

Each of these propositions is entailed by (f). Imagine that Smith realizes the entailment of each of these propositions he has constructed by (f), and proceeds to accept (g), (h), and (i) on the basis of (f). Smith has correctly inferred (g), (h), and (i) from a proposition for which he has strong evidence. Smith is therefore completely justified in believing each of these three propositions. Smith, of course, has no idea where Brown is.

But imagine now that two further conditions hold. First, Jones does *not* own a Ford, but is at present driving a rented car. And secondly, by the sheerest coincidence, and entirely unknown to Smith, the place mentioned in proposition (h) happens really to be the place where Brown is. If these two conditions hold then Smith does *not* know that (h) is true, even though *(i)* (h) is true, *(ii)* Smith does believe that (h) is true, and *(iii)* Smith is justified in believing that (h) is true.

These two examples show that definition (a) does not state a *sufficient* condition for someone's knowing a given proposition. The same cases, with appropriate changes, will suffice to show that neither definition (b) nor definition (c) do so either.

Various attempts have been made to meet the *Gettier Problem*. See the works listed in For Further Reading.

FOR FURTHER READING

Armstrong, D. M. *Belief, Truth and Knowledge* (Cambridge University Press, 1973).

Audi, Robert. *Belief, Justification and Knowledge* (Wadsworth, 1988).

Baergen, Ralph. *Contemporary Epistemology* (Harcourt Brace, 1995), chap. 5.

Dancy, Jonathan. *An Introduction to Contemporary Epistemology* (Blackwell, 1985), chap. 2.

Dancy, Jonathan and Ernest Sosa, eds. *A Companion to Epistemology* (Blackwell, 1992).

Everitt, Nicholas and Alec Fisher. *Modern Epistemology* (McGraw-Hill, 1995).

Fumerton, Richard. *Metaphysical and Epistemological Problems of Perception* (University of Nebraska, 1985).

Goodman, Michael and Robert Snyder, eds. *Contemporary Readings in Epistemology* (Prentice-Hall, 1993).

Harman, Gilbert. *Thought* (Princeton University Press, 1973).

Nozick, Robert. *Philosophical Explanations* (Harvard University Press, 1981).

Pappas, George, ed. *Justification and Knowledge* (Reidel, 1979).

Pappas, George and Marshall Swain, eds. *Essays on Knowledge and Justification* (Cornell University Press, 1978).

Pojman, Louis P. *What Can We Know? An Introduction to the Theory of Knowledge*, 2nd ed. (Wadsworth, 2001).

Roth, Michael and Leon Galis, eds. *Knowing: Essays in the Theory of Knowledge* (Random House, 1970).

Shope, Robert. *The Analysis of Knowledge* (Princeton University Press, 1983).

Sosa, Ernest. *Knowledge in Perspective: Selective Essays in Epistemology* (Cambridge University Press, 1991).

Swain, Marshall. *Reasons and Knowledge* (Cornell University Press, 1981).

Is Justified True Belief Knowledge?

Various attempts have been made in recent years to state necessary and sufficient conditions for someone's knowing a given proposition. The attempts have often been such that they can be stated in a form similar to the following[1]:

(a) S knows that P *IFF*
  (ii) P is true,
  (ii) S believes that P, and
  (iii) S is justified in believing that P.

For example, Chisholm has held that the following gives the necessary and sufficient conditions for knowledge[2]:

(b) S knows that P *IFF*
  (i) S accepts P,
  (ii) S has adequate evidence for P, and
  (iii) P is true.

Ayer has stated the necessary and sufficient conditions for knowledge as follows[3]:

(c) S knows that P *IFF*
  (i) P is true,
  (ii) S is sure that P is true, and
  (iii) S has the right to be sure that P is true.

I shall argue that (a) is false in that the conditions stated therein do not constitute a *sufficient* condition for the truth of the proposition that S knows that P. The same argument will show that (b) and (c) fail if "has adequate evidence for" or "has the right to be sure that" is substituted for "is justified in believing that" throughout.

I shall begin by noting two points. First, in that sense of "justified" in which S's being justified in believing P is a necessary condition of S's knowing that P, it is possible for a person to be justified in believing a proposition that is in fact false. Secondly, for any proposition P, if S is justified in believing P, and P entails Q, and S deduces Q from P and accepts Q as a result of this deduction, then S is justified in believing Q. Keeping these two points in mind, I shall now present two cases in which the conditions stated in (a) are true for some proposition, though it is at the same time false that the person in question knows that proposition.

CASE I

Suppose that Smith and Jones have applied for a certain job. And suppose that Smith has strong evidence for the following conjunctive proposition:

(d) Jones is the man who will get the job, and Jones has ten coins in his pocket.

Smith's evidence for (d) might be that the president of the company assured him that Jones would in the end be selected, and that he, Smith, had counted the coins in Jones's pocket ten minutes ago. Proposition (d) entails:

(e) The man who will get the job has ten coins in his pocket.

Let us suppose that Smith sees the entailment from (d) to (e), and accepts (e) on the grounds of (d), for which he has strong evidence. In this case, Smith is clearly justified in believing that (e) is true.

But imagine, further, that unknown to Smith, he himself, not Jones, will get the job. And, also, unknown to Smith, he himself has ten coins in his pocket. Proposition (e) is then true, though proposition (d), from which Smith inferred (e), is false. In our example, then, all of the following are true: *(i)* (e) is true, *(ii)* Smith believes that (e) is true, and *(iii)* Smith is justified in believing that (e) is true. But it is equally clear that Smith does not *know* that (e) is true; for (e) is true in virtue of the number of coins in Smith's pocket, while Smith does not know how many coins are in Smith's pocket, and bases his belief in (e) on a count of the coins in Jones's pocket, whom he falsely believes to be the man who will get the job.

CASE II

Let us suppose that Smith has strong evidence for the following proposition:

(f) Jones owns a Ford.

Smith's evidence might be that Jones has at all times in the past within Smith's memory owned a car, and always a Ford, and that Jones has just offered Smith

From *Analysis*, Vol. 23 (Blackwell, 1963), pp. 121–123. Reprinted by permission of the author.

a ride while driving a Ford. Let us imagine, now, that Smith has another friend, Brown, of whose whereabouts he is totally ignorant. Smith selects three place names quite at random, and constructs the following three propositions:

(g) Either Jones owns a Ford, or Brown is in Boston;

(h) Either Jones owns a Ford, or Brown is in Barcelona;

(i) Either Jones owns a Ford, or Brown is in Brest-Litovsk.

Each of these propositions is entailed by (f). Imagine that Smith realizes the entailment of each of these propositions he has constructed by (f), and proceeds to accept (g), (h), and (i) on the basis of (f). Smith has correctly inferred (g), (h), and (i) from a proposition for which he has strong evidence. Smith is therefore completely justified in believing each of these three propositions. Smith, of course, has no idea where Brown is.

But imagine now that two further conditions hold. First, Jones does *not* own a Ford, but is at present driving a rented car. And secondly, by the sheerest coincidence, and entirely unknown to Smith, the place mentioned in proposition (h) happens really to be the place where Brown is. If these two conditions hold then Smith does *not* know that (h) is true, even though *(i)* (h) is true, *(ii)* Smith does believe that (h) is true, and *(iii)* Smith is justified in believing that (h) is true.

These two examples show that definition (a) does not state a *sufficient* condition for someone's knowing a given proposition. The same cases, with appropriate changes, will suffice to show that neither definition (b) nor definition (c) do so either.

Notes

1. Plato seems to be considering some such definition at *Theatetus* 201, and perhaps accepting one at *Meno* 98.
2. Roderick M. Chisholm, *Perceiving: A Philosophical Study*, Cornell University Press (Ithaca, New York, 1957), p. 16.
3. A. J. Ayer, *The Problem of Knowledge*, Macmillan (London, 1956), p. 34.

Chapter 16

ALVIN I. GOLDMAN

Alvin I. Goldman is Professor of Philosophy at the University of Arizona and regarded as one of our leading epistemologists. Goldman argues that (1) all present versions of internalism are plagued with insuperable obstacles, (2) the absence of a causal requirement is common to each of these inadequate principles, and (3) the theory that best satisfies the causal requirement is an external version of justification—namely, "reliabilism," which defines the justificatory status of a belief in terms of the reliability of the process that caused it. The reliability of a process consists in its tendency to produce true beliefs rather than false ones. This is an externalist and objective theory of justification because the agent need not have access to the causal mechanisms that produce justified beliefs.

BIBLIOGRAPHY

Almeder, Robert. "On Nauralizing Epistemology." *American Philosophical Quarterly 27*, no. 4 (October 1990).

Alston, William. *Epistemic Justification* (Cornell University Press, 1989).

Armstrong, David M. *Belief, Truth, and Knowledge* (Cambridge University Press, 1973).

Baergen, Ralph. *Contemporary Epistemology* (Fort Worth, TX: Harcourt Brace, 1995), chap. 5.

Bennett, Jonathan. "Why Is Belief Involuntary?" *Analysis 50* (1990), 87–107.

Chisholm, Roderick. *The Foundations of Knowing* (University of Minnesota Press, 1957).

———. *Theory of Knowledge*, 2d ed. (Prentice-Hall, 1977).

———. *Theory of Knowledge*, 3d ed. (Prentice-Hall, 1989).

Cohen, Stewart. "Justification and Truth." *Philosophical Studies 46* (1984).

Dancy, Jonathan, and Ernest Sosa, eds. *A Companion to Epistemology* (Blackwell, 1992).

Dretske, Fred. *Knowledge and the Flow of Information* (MIT Press, 1981).

Everitt, Nicholas, and Alec Fisher. *Modern Epistemology* (McGraw-Hill, 1995).

Feldman, Richard. "Reliabilism and Justification." *Monist 68* (1985).

———. "Epistemic Obligation." In *Philosophical Perspectives*. Vol. 2: *Epistemology*, edited by James Tomberlin (Ridgeview, 1988).

Feldman, Richard and Earl Conee. "Evidentialism." *Philosophical Studies 48* (1985).

French, P., T. Uehling, and H. Wettstein, eds. *Midwest Studies in Philosophy*, Vol. XIX (University of Notre Dame Press, 1994).

Goldman, Alvin I. *Epistemology and Cognition* (Harvard University Press. 1985), chap. 5.

———. "Strong and Weak Justification." *Philosophical Perspectives*. Vol. 2: *Epistemology*, edited by James Tomberlin (Ridgeview, 1988).

———. "Epistemic Folkways and Scientific Epistemology." In *Liaisons: Philosophy Meets the Cognitive and Social Sciences* (MIT Press, 1991).

Goodman, Michael, and Robert Snyder, eds. *Contemporary Readings in Epistemology* (Prentice-Hall, 1993).
Kim, Jaegwon. *Philosophy of Mind* (Westview Press, 1996).
Kitcher, Philip. "The Naturalists Return." *Philosophical Review 101* (1992).
Kornblith, Hilary, ed. *Naturalized Epistemology* (MIT Press, 1985).
———. *Inductive Inference and Its Natural Ground: An Essay in Naturalistic Epistemology* (MIT Press, 1993).
Montmarquet, James. "Epistemic Virtue." *Mind 96* (1987), 482–497.
Moser, Paul. *Epistemic Justification* (Reidel, 1985), chap. 4.
Pappas, George, ed. *Justification and Knowledge* (Reidel, 1979).
Plantinga, Alvin. *Warrant and Proper Function* (Oxford University Press, 1993).
———. *Warrant: The Current Debate* (Oxford University Press, 1993).
Pojman, Louis P. *What Can We Know? An Introduction to the Theory of Knowledge*, 2nd ed. (Wadsworth, 2001), chaps. 8–10.
Pojman, Louis P., ed. *The Theory of Knowledge* (Wadsworth, 1998).
Pollock, John L. *Contemporary Theories of Knowledge* (Rowman & Littlefield, 1986).
Quine, W. V. *Ontological Relativity and Other Essays* (Columbia University Press, 1969).
Sosa, Ernest. *Knowledge in Perspective: Selective Essays in Epistemology* (Cambridge University Press, 1991).
Steup, Matthias. *An Introduction to Contemporary Epistemology* (Prentice-Hall, 1996), chaps. 8 and 9.
Stroud, Barry. *The Significance of Skepticism* (Clarendon Press, 1984), chap. 6.
Swain, Marshall. *Reasons and Knowledge* (Cornell University Press, 1981).
Tomberlin, James, ed. *Philosophical Perspectives*. Vol. 2: *Epistemology* (Ridgeview, 1988). This volume contains several essays relevant to this part of the book.
Van Inwagen, Peter. "When Is the Will Free?" In T. O'Connor (ed.), *Agents, Causes, and Events* (Oxford University Press, 1985).
Zagzebski, Linda. *Virtues of the Mind: An Inquiry into the Nature of Virtue and the Ethical Foundations of Knowledge* (Cambridge University Press, 1996).

What Is Justified Belief?

The aim of this essay is to sketch a theory of justified belief. What I have in mind is an explanatory theory, one that explains in a general way why certain beliefs are counted as justified and others as unjustified. Unlike some traditional approaches, I do not try to prescribe standards for justification that differ from, or improve upon, our ordinary standards. I merely try to explicate the ordinary standards, which are, I believe, quite different from those of many classical, e.g., "Cartesian," accounts.

Many epistemologists have been interested in justification because of its presumed close relationship to knowledge. This relationship is intended to be preserved in the conception of justified belief presented here. In previous papers on knowledge,[1] I have denied that justification is necessary for knowing, but

From *Justification and Knowledge*, ed. G. S. Pappas (Dordrecht: D. Reidel, 1979), 1–23. Copyright 1979, D. Reidel Publishing Company. Reprinted with kind permission from Kluwer Academic Publishers.

there I had in mind "Cartesian" accounts of justification. On the account of justified belief suggested here, it *is* necessary for knowing, and closely related to it.

The term "justified," I presume, is an evaluative term, a term of appraisal. Any correct definition or synonym of it would also feature evaluative terms. I assume that such definitions or synonyms might be given, but I am not interested in them. I want a set of *substantive* conditions that specify when a belief is justified. Compare the normal term "right." This might be defined in other ethical terms or phrases, a task appropriate to metaethics. The task of normative ethics, by contrast, is to state substantive conditions for the rightness of actions. Normative ethics tries to specify nonethical conditions that determine when an action is right. A familiar example is act-utilitarianism, which says an action is right if and only if it produces, or would produce, at least as much net happiness as any alternative open to the agent. These necessary and sufficient conditions clearly involve no ethical notions. Analogously, I want a theory of justified belief to specify in non-epistemic terms when a belief is justified. This is not the only kind of theory of justifiedness one might seek, but it is one important kind of theory and the kind sought here.

In order to avoid epistemic terms in our theory, we must know which terms are epistemic. Obviously, an exhaustive list cannot be given, but here are some examples: "justified," "warranted," "has (good) grounds," "has reason (to believe)," "knows that," "sees that," "apprehends that," "is probable" (in an epistemic or inductive sense), "shows that," "establishes that," and "ascertains that." By contrast, here are some sample nonepistemic expressions: "believes that," "is true," "causes," "it is necessary that," "implies," "is deducible from," and "is probable" (either in the frequency sense or the propensity sense). In general, (purely) doxastic, metaphysical, modal, semantic, or syntactic expressions are not epistemic.

There is another constraint I wish to place on a theory of justified belief, in addition to the constraint that it be couched in non-epistemic language. Since I seek an explanatory theory, i.e., one that clarifies the underlying source of justificational status, it is not enough for a theory to state "correct" necessary and sufficient conditions. Its conditions must also be appropriately deep or revelatory. Suppose, for example, that the following sufficient condition of justified belief is offered: "If *S* senses redly at *t* and *S* believes at *t* that he is sensing redly, then *S*'s belief at *t* that he is sensing redly is justified." This is not the kind of principle I seek; for, even if it is correct, it leaves unexplained *why* a person who senses redly and believes that he does, believes this justifiably. Not every state is such that if one is in it and believes one is in it, this belief is justified. What is distinctive about the state of sensing redly, or "phenomenal" states in general? A theory of justified belief of the kind I seek must answer this question, and hence it must be couched at a suitably deep, general, or abstract level.

A few introductory words about my *explicandum* are appropriate at this juncture. It is often assumed that whenever a person has a justified belief, he knows that it is justified and knows what the justification is. It is further assumed that the person can state or explain what his justification is. On this view, a justification is an argument, defense, or set of reasons that can be given in support of a belief. Thus, one studies the nature of justified belief by considering what a person might *say* if asked to defend, or justify, his belief. I make none of these sorts of assumptions here. I leave it an open question whether, when a belief *is* justified, the believer *knows* it is justified. I also leave it an open question whether, when a belief is justified, the believer can *state* or *give* a justification for it. I do not even assume that when a belief is justified there is something "possessed" by the believer which can be called a "justification." I do assume that a justified belief gets its status of being justified from some processes or properties that make it justified. In short, there must be some justification-conferring processes or properties. But this does not imply that there must be an argument, or reason, or anything else, "possessed" at the time of belief by the believer.

I

A theory of justified belief will be a set of principles that specify truth-conditions for the schema [*S*'s belief in *p* at time *t* is justified], i.e., conditions for the satisfaction of this schema in all possible cases. It will be convenient to formulate candidate theories in a recursive or inductive format, which would include (A) one or more base clauses, (B) a set of recursive clauses (possibly null), and (C) a closure clause. In such a format, it is permissible for the predicate "is a justified belief" to appear in recursive clauses. But neither this predicate, nor any other epistemic predicate, may appear in (the antecedent of) any base clause.[2]

Before turning to my own theory, I want to survey some other possible approaches to justified belief. Identification of problems associated with other attempts will provide some motivation for the theory I shall offer. Obviously, I cannot examine all, or even very many, alternative attempts. But a few sample attempts will be instructive.

Let us concentrate on the attempt to formulate one or more adequate base-clause principles.[3] Here is a classical candidate:

(1) If *S* believes *p* at *t*, and *p* is indubitable for *S* (at *t*), then *S*'s belief in *p* at *t* is justified.

To evaluate this principle, we need to know what "indubitable" means. It can be understood in at least two ways. First, "*p* is indubitable for *S*" might mean: "*S* has no *grounds* for doubting *p*." Since "ground" is an epistemic term, however, principle (1) would be inadmissible in this reading, for epistemic terms may not legitimately appear in the antecedent of a base-clause. A second interpretation would avoid this difficulty. One might interpret "*p* is indubitable for *S*" psychologically, i.e., as meaning "*S* is psychologically incapable of doubting *p*." This would make principle (1) admissible, but would it be correct? Surely not. A religious fanatic may be psychologically incapable of doubting the tenets of his faith, but that doesn't make his belief in them justified. Similarly, during the Watergate affair, someone may have been so blinded by the aura of the presidency that even after the most damaging evidence against Nixon had emerged he was still incapable of doubting Nixon's veracity. It doesn't follow that his belief in Nixon's veracity was justified.

A second candidate base-clause principle is this:

(2) If *S* believes *p* at *t* and *p* is self-evident, then *S's* belief in *p* at *t* is justified.

To evaluate this principle, we again need an interpretation of its crucial term, in this case "self-evident." On one standard reading, "evident" is a synonym for "justified." "*Self*-evident" would therefore mean something like "directly justified," "intuitively justified," or "non-derivatively justified." On this reading "self-evident" is an epistemic phrase, and principle (2) would be disqualified as a base-clause principle.

However, there are other possible readings of "*p* is self-evident" on which it isn't an epistemic phrase. One such reading is: "It is impossible to understand *p* without believing it."[4] According to this interpretation, trivial analytic and logical truths might turn out to be self-evident. Hence, any belief in such a truth would be a justified belief, according to (2).

What does "it is *impossible* to understand *p* without believing it" mean? Does it mean "*humanly* impossible"? That reading would probably make (2) an unacceptable principle. There may well be propositions which humans have an innate and irrepressible disposition to believe, e.g., "Some events have causes." But it seems unlikely that people's inability to refrain from believing such a proposition makes every belief in it justified.

Should we then understand "impossible" to mean "impossible in principle," or "logically impossible"? If that is the reading given, I suspect that (2) is a vacuous principle. I doubt that even trivial logical or analytic truths will satisfy this definition of "self-evident." Any proposition, we may assume, has two or more components that are somehow organized or juxtaposed. To understand the proposition one must "grasp" the components and their juxtaposition. Now in the case of *complex* logical truths, there are (human) psychological operations that suffice to grasp the components and their juxtaposition but do not suffice to produce a belief that the proposition is true. But can't we at least *conceive* of an analogous set of psychological operations even for simple logical truths, operations which perhaps are not in the repertoire of human cognizers but which might be in the repertoire of some conceivable beings? That is, can't we conceive of psychological operations that would suffice to grasp the components and componential-juxtaposition of these simple propositions? I think we can conceive of such operations. Hence, for any proposition you choose, it will be possible for it to be understood without being believed.

Finally, even if we set these two objections aside, we must note that self-evidence can at best confer justificational status on relatively few beliefs, and the only plausible group are beliefs in necessary truths. Thus, other base-clause principles will be needed to explain the justificational status of beliefs in contingent propositions.

The notion of a base-clause principle is naturally associated with the idea of "direct" justifiedness, and in the realm of contingent propositions first-person-current-mental-state propositions have often been assigned this role. In Chisholm's terminology, this conception is expressed by the notion of a "*self-presenting*" state or proposition. The sentence "I am thinking," for example, expresses a self-presenting proposition. (At least I shall *call* this sort of content a "proposition," though it only has a truth value given some assignment of a subject who utters or entertains the content and a time of entertaining.) When such a proposition is true for person S at time t, is justified in believing it at t: in Chisholm's terminology, the proposition is "evident" for S at t. This suggests the following base-clause principle:

> (3) If p is a self-presenting proposition, and p is true for S at t, and S believes p at t, then S's belief in p at t is justified.

What, exactly, does "self-presenting" mean? In the second edition of *Theory of Knowledge*, Chisholm offers this definition: "h is self-presenting for S at t = *df.* h is true at t; and necessarily, if h is true at t, then h is evident for S at t."[5] Unfortunately, since "evident" is an epistemic term, "self-presenting" also becomes an epistemic term on this definition, thereby disqualifying (3) as a legitimate base-clause. Some other definition of self-presentingness must be offered if (3) is to be a suitable base-clause principle.

Another definition of self-presentation readily comes to mind. "Self-presentation" is an approximate synonym of "self-intimation," and a proposition may be said to be self-intimating if and only if whenever it is true of a person that person believes it. More precisely, we may give the following definition:

> (SP) Proposition p is self-presenting if and only if: necessarily, for any S and any t, if p is true for S at t, then S believes p at t.

On this definition, "self-presenting" is clearly not an epistemic predicate, so (3) would be an admissible principle. Moreover, there is initial plausibility in the suggestion that it is *this* feature of first-person-current-mental-state propositions—viz., their truth guarantees their being believed—that makes beliefs in them justified.

Employing this definition of self-presentation, is principle (3) correct? This cannot be decided until we define self-presentation more precisely. Since the operator "necessarily" can be read in different ways, there are different forms of self-presentation and correspondingly different versions of principle (3). Let us focus on two of these readings: a "*nomological*" reading and a "*logical*" reading. Consider first the nomological reading. On this definition a proposition is self-presenting just in case it is nomologically necessary that if p is true for S at t, then S believes p at t.[6]

Is the nomological version of principle (3)—call it "(3_N)"—correct? Not at all. We can imagine cases in which the antecedent of (3_N) is satisfied, but we would not say that the belief is justified. Suppose, for example, that p is the proposition expressed by the sentence "I am in brain-state B," where "B" is shorthand for a certain highly specific neural state description. Further suppose it is a nomological truth that anyone in brain-state B will ipso facto *believe* he is in brain-state B. In other words, imagine that an occurrent belief with the content "I am in brain-state B" is realized whenever one is in brain-state B.[7] According to (3_N), any such belief is justified. But that is clearly false. We can readily imagine circumstances in which a person goes into brain-state B and therefore has the belief in question, though this belief is by no means justified. For example, we can imagine that a brain-surgeon operating on S artificially induced brain-state B. This results, phenomenologically, in S's suddenly believing—out of the blue—that he is in brain-state B, without any relevant antecedent beliefs. We would hardly say, in such a case, that S's belief that he is in brain-state B is justified.

Let us turn next to the logical version of (3)—call it "(3_L)"—in which a proposition is defined as self-presenting just in case it is logically necessary that if p is true for S at t, then S believes p at t. This stronger version of principle (3) might seem more promising. In fact, however, it is no more successful than (3_N). Let p be the proposition "I am awake" and assume that it is logically necessary that if this proposition is true for some person S and time t, then S believes p at t. This assumption is consistent with the further assumption that S frequently believes p when it is false, e.g., when he is dreaming. Under these circumstances, we would hardly accept the contention that S's belief in this proposition is always justified. Nor should we accept the contention that the belief is justified when it is *true*. The truth of the proposition logically guarantees that the belief is *held*, but why should it guarantee that the belief is *justified*?

The foregoing criticism suggests that we have things backwards. The idea of self-presentation is that truth guarantees belief. This fails to confer justification because it is compatible with there being belief without truth. So what seems necessary—or at least sufficient—for justification is that belief should guarantee truth. Such a notion has usually gone under the label of "*infallibility*" or "*incorrigibility*." It may be defined as follows:

> (INC) Proposition *p* is incorrigible if and only if: necessarily, for any *S* and any *t*, if *S* believes *p* at *t*, then *p* is true for *S* at *t*.

Using the notion of incorrigibility, we may propose principle (4).

> (4) If *p* is an incorrigible proposition, and *S* believes *p* at *t*, then *S*'s belief in *p* at *t* is justified.

As was true of self-presentation, there are different varieties of incorrigibility, corresponding to different interpretations of "necessarily." Accordingly, we have different versions of principle (4). Once again, let us concentrate on a nomological and a logical version, (4_N) and (4_L) respectively.

We can easily construct a counterexample to (4_N) along the lines of the belief-state/brain-state counterexample that refuted (3_N). Suppose it is nomologically necessary that if anyone believes he is in brain-state *B* then it is true that he is in brain-state *B*, for the only way this belief-state is realized is through brain-state *B* itself. It follows that "I am in brain-state *B*" is a nomologically incorrigible proposition. Therefore, according to (4_N), whenever anyone believes this proposition at any time, that belief is justified. But we may again construct a brain-surgeon example in which someone comes to have such a belief but the belief isn't justified.

Apart from this counterexample, the general point is this. Why should the fact that *S*'s believing *p* guarantees the truth of *p* imply that *S*'s belief is justified? The nature of the guarantee might be wholly fortuitous, as the belief-state/brain-state example is intended to illustrate. To appreciate the point, consider the following related possibility. A person's mental structure might be such that whenever he believes that *p* will be true (of him) a split second later, then *p* is true (of him) a split second later. This is because, we may suppose, his believing it brings it about. But surely we would not be compelled in such a circumstance to say that a belief of this sort is justified. So why should the fact that *S*'s believing *p* guarantees the truth of *p precisely at the time of belief* imply that the belief is justified? There is no intuitive plausibility in this supposition.

The notion of *logical* incorrigibility has a more honored place in the history of conceptions of justification. But even principle (4_L), I believe, suffers from defects similar to those of (4_N). The mere fact that belief in *p* logically guarantees its truth does not confer justificational status on such a belief.

The first difficulty with (4_L) arises from logical or mathematical truths. Any true proposition of logic or mathematics is logically necessary. Hence, any such proposition *p* is logically incorrigible, since it is logically necessary that, for any *S* and any *t*, if *S* believes *p* at *t* then *p* is true (for *S* at *t*). Now assume that Nelson believes a certain very complex mathematical truth at time *t*. Since such a proposition is logically incorrigible, (4_L) implies that Nelson's belief in this truth at *t* is justified. But we may easily suppose that this belief of Nelson is not at all the result of proper mathematical reasoning, or even the result of appeal to trustworthy authority. Perhaps Nelson believes this complex truth because of utterly confused reasoning, or because of hasty and ill-founded conjecture. Then his belief is not justified, contrary to what (4_L) implies.

The case of logical or mathematical truths is admittedly peculiar, since the truth of these propositions is assured independently of any beliefs. It might seem, therefore, that we can better capture the idea of "belief logically guaranteeing truth" in cases where the propositions in question are *contingent*. With this in mind, we might restrict (4_L) to *contingent* incorrigible propositions. Even this amendment cannot save (4_L), however, since there are counterexamples to it involving purely contingent propositions.

Suppose that Humperdink has been studying logic—or, rather, pseudo-logic—from Elmer Fraud, whom Humperdink has no reason to trust as a logician. Fraud has enunciated the principle that any disjunctive proposition consisting of at least 40 distinct disjuncts is very probably true. Humperdink now encounters the proposition *p*, a contingent proposition with 40 disjuncts, the 7th disjunct being "I exist." Although Humperdink grasps the proposition fully, he doesn't notice that it is entailed by "I exist." Rather, he is struck by the fact that it falls under the disjunction rule Fraud has enunciated (a rule I assume Humperdink is not *justified* in believing). Bearing this in mind, Humperdink forms a belief in *p*. Now notice that *p* is logically incorrigible. It is logically necessary that if anyone believes *p*, then *p* is true (of him at that time). This simply follows from the fact that, first, a person's believing anything entails that he exists, and second, "I exist" entails *p*. Since *p* is logically incorrigible, principle (4_L) implies that Humperdink's belief in *p* is justified. But surely, given our example, that conclusion is false. Humperdink's belief in *p* is not at all justified.

One thing that goes wrong in this example is that while Humperdink's belief in *p* logically implies its truth, Humperdink doesn't *recognize* that his believing it implies its truth. This might move a theorist to revise (4_L) by adding the requirement that *S* "recognize" that *p* is logically incorrigible. But this, of course, won't do. The term "recognize" is obviously an epistemic term, so the suggested revision of (4_L) would result in an inadmissible base-clause.

II

Let us try to diagnose what has gone wrong with these attempts to produce an acceptable base-clause principle. Notice that each of the foregoing attempts confers the status of "justified" on a belief without restriction on *why* the belief is held, i.e., on what *causally initiates* the belief or *causally sustains* it. The logical versions of principles (3) and (4), for example, clearly place no restriction on causes of belief. The same is true of the nomological versions of (3) and (4), since nomological requirements can be satisfied by simultaneity or cross-sectional laws, as illustrated by our brain-state/belief-state example. I suggest that the absence of causal requirements accounts for the failure of the foregoing principles. Many of our counterexamples are ones in which the belief is caused in some strange or unacceptable way, e.g., by the accidental movement of a brain-surgeon's hand, by reliance on an illicit, pseudo-logical principle, or by the blinding aura of the presidency. In general, a strategy for defeating a noncausal principle of justifiedness is to find a case in which the principle's antecedent is satisfied but the belief is caused by some faulty belief-forming process. The faultiness of the belief-forming process will incline us, intuitively, to regard the belief as unjustified. Thus, correct principles of justified belief must be principles that make causal requirements, where "cause" is construed broadly to include sustainers as well as initiators of belief (i.e., processes that determine, or help to overdetermine, a belief's continuing to be held).[8]

The need for causal requirements is not restricted to base-clause principles. Recursive principles will also need a causal component. One might initially suppose that the following is a good recursive principle: "If *S* justifiably believes *q* at *t*, and *q* entails *p*, and *S* believes *p* at *t*, then *S*'s belief in *p* at *t* is justified." But this principle is unacceptable. *S*'s belief in *p* doesn't receive justificational status simply from the fact that *p* is entailed by *q* and *S* justifiably believes *q*. If what causes *S* to believe *p* at *t* is entirely different, *S*'s belief in *p* may well not be justified. Nor can the situation be remedied by adding to the antecedent the condition that *S* justifiably believes that *q* entails *p*. Even if he believes this, and believes *q* as well, he might not put these beliefs together. He might believe *p* as a result of some other wholly extraneous considerations. So once again, conditions that fail to require appropriate causes of a belief don't guarantee justifiedness.

Granted that principles of justified belief must make reference to causes of belief, what kinds of causes confer justifiedness? We can gain insight into this problem by reviewing some faulty processes of belief-formation, i.e., processes whose belief-outputs would be classed as unjustified. Here are some examples: confused reasoning, wishful thinking, reliance on emotional attachment, mere hunch or guesswork, and hasty generalization. What do these faulty processes have in common? They share the feature of *unreliability*: they tend to produce *error* a large proportion of the time. By contrast, which species of belief-forming (or belief-sustaining) processes are intuitively justification-conferring? They include standard perceptual processes, remembering, good reasoning, and introspection. What these processes seem to have in common is *reliability:* the beliefs they produce are generally true. My positive proposal, then, is this. The justificational status of a belief is a function of the reliability of the process or processes that cause it, where (as a first approximation) reliability consists in the tendency of a process to produce beliefs that are true rather than false.

To test this thesis further, notice that justifiedness is not a purely categorical concept, although I treat it here as categorical in the interest of simplicity. We can and do regard certain beliefs as more justified than others. Furthermore, our intuitions of comparative justifiedness go along with our beliefs about the comparative reliability of the belief-causing processes.

Consider perceptual beliefs. Suppose Jones believes he has just seen a mountain-goat. Our assessment of the belief's justifiedness is determined by whether he caught a brief glimpse of the creature at a great distance, or whether he had a good look at the thing only 30 yards away. His belief in the latter sort of case is (*ceteris paribus*) more justified than in the former sort of case. And, if his belief is true, we are more prepared to say he *knows* in the latter case than in the former. The difference between the two cases seems to be this. Visual beliefs formed from brief and hasty scanning, or where the perceptual object is a long distance off, tend to be wrong more often than visual beliefs formed from detailed and leisurely scanning, or where the object is in reasonable proximity. In short, the visual processes in the former category are less reliable than those in the latter category. A similar point holds for memory beliefs. A belief that results from a hazy and indistinct memory impression is counted as less justified than a belief that arises from a distinct memory impression, and our inclination to classify those beliefs as "*knowledge*" varies in the same way. Again, the reason is associated with the comparative reliability of the processes. Hazy and indistinct memory impressions are generally less reliable indicators of what actually happened, so beliefs formed from such impressions are less likely to be true than beliefs formed from distinct impressions. Further, consider beliefs based on inference from observed samples. A belief about a population that is based on random sampling, or on instances that exhibit great variety, is intuitively more justified than a belief based on biased sampling, or on instances from a narrow sector of the population. Again, the degree of justifiedness seems to be a function of reliability. Inferences based on random or varied samples will tend to produce less error or inaccuracy than inferences based on non-random or nonvaried samples.

Returning to a categorical concept of justifiedness, we might ask just *how* reliable a belief-forming process must be in order that its resultant beliefs be justified. A precise answer to this question should not be expected. Our conception of justification is *vague* in this respect. It does seem clear, however, that *perfect* reliability isn't required. Belief-forming processes that *sometimes* produce error still confer justification. It follows that there can be justified beliefs that are false.

I have characterized justification-conferring processes as ones that have a "tendency" to produce beliefs that are true rather than false. The term "tendency" could refer either to *actual* long run frequency, or to a "propensity," i.e., outcomes that would occur in merely *possible* realizations of the process. Which of these is intended? Unfortunately, I think our ordinary conception of justifiedness is vague on this dimension too. For the most part, we simply assume that the "observed" frequency of truth versus error would be approximately replicated in the actual long-run, and also in relevant counterfactual situations, i.e., ones that are highly "realistic" or conform closely to the circumstances of the actual world. Since we ordinarily assume these frequencies to be roughly the same, we make no concerted effort to distinguish them. Since the purpose of my present theorizing is to capture our ordinary conception of justifiedness, and since our ordinary conception is vague on this matter, it is appropriate to leave the theory vague in the same respect.

We need to say more about the notion of a belief-forming "*process*." Let us mean by a "process" a *functional operation* or procedure, i.e., something that generates a *mapping* from certain states—"inputs"—into other states—"outputs." The outputs in the present case are states of believing this or that proposition at a given moment. On this interpretation, a process is a *type* as opposed to a *token*. This is fully appropriate, since it is only types that have statistical properties such as producing truth 80 percent of the time; and it is precisely such statistical properties that determine the reliability of a process. Of course, we also want to speak of a process as *causing* a belief, and it looks as if types are incapable of being causes. But when we say that a belief is caused by a given process, understood as a functional procedure, we may interpret this to mean that it is caused by the particular *inputs* to the process (and by the intervening events "through which" the functional procedure carries the inputs into the output) on the occasion in question.

What are some examples of belief-forming "processes" construed as functional operations? One example is reasoning processes, where the inputs include antecedent beliefs and entertained hypotheses. Another example is functional procedures whose inputs include desires, hopes, or emotional states of various sorts (together with antecedent beliefs). A third example is a memory process, which takes as input beliefs or experiences at an earlier time and generates as output beliefs at a later time. For example, a memory process might take as input a belief *at* t_1 that Lincoln was born in 1809 and generate as output a belief *at* t_n that Lincoln was born in 1809. A fourth example is perceptual processes. Here it isn't clear whether inputs should include states of the environment, such as the distance of the stimulus from the cognizer, or only events within or on the surface of the organism, e.g., receptor stimulations. I shall return to this point in a moment.

A critical problem concerning our analysis is the degree of generality of the process-types in question. Input-output relations can be specified very broadly or very narrowly, and the degree of generality will partly determine the degree of reliability. A process-type might be selected so narrowly that only one instance of it ever occurs, and hence the type is either completely reliable or completely unreliable. (This assumes that reliability is a function of *actual* frequency only.) If such narrow process-types were selected, beliefs that are intuitively unjustified might be said to result from perfectly reliable processes, and beliefs that are intuitively justified might be said to result from perfectly unreliable processes.

It is clear that our ordinary thought about process-types slices them broadly, but I cannot at present give a precise explication of our intuitive principles. One plausible suggestion, though, is that the relevant processes are *content-neutral*. It might be argued, for example, that the process of *inferring p whenever the Pope asserts p* could pose problems for our theory. If the Pope is infallible, this process will be perfectly reliable; yet we would not regard the belief-outputs of this process as justified. The content-neutral restriction would avert this difficulty. If relevant processes are required to admit as input beliefs (or other states) with *any* content, the aforementioned process will not count, for its input beliefs have a restricted propositional content, viz., "*the Pope* asserts *p*."

In addition to the problem of "generality" or "abstractness" there is the previously mentioned problem of the "*extent*" of belief-forming processes. Clearly, the causal ancestry of beliefs often includes events outside the organism. Are such events to be included among the "inputs" of belief-forming processes? Or should we restrict the extent of belief-forming processes to "*cognitive*" events, i.e., events within the organism's nervous system? I shall choose the latter course, though with some hesitation. My general grounds for this decision are roughly as follows. Justifiedness seems to be a function of how a cognizer deals with his environmental input, i.e., with the goodness or badness of the operations that register and transform the stimulation that reaches him. ("Deal with," of course, does not mean *purposeful* action, nor is it restricted to *conscious* activity.) A justified belief is, roughly speaking, one that results from cognitive operations that are, generally speaking, good or successful. But "*cognitive*" operations are most plausibly construed as operations of the cognitive faculties, i.e., "information-processing" equipment *internal* to the organism.

With these points in mind, we may now advance the following base-clause principle for justified belief.

> (5) If *S*'s believing *p* at *t* results from a reliable cognitive belief-forming process (or set of processes), then *S*'s belief in *p* at *t* is justified.

Since "reliable belief-forming process" has been defined in terms of such notions as belief, truth, statistical frequency, and the like, it is not an epistemic term. Hence, (5) is an admissible base-clause.

It might seem as if (5) promises to be not only a successful base clause, but the only principle needed whatever, apart from a closure clause. In other words, it might seem as if it is a necessary as well as a sufficient condition of justifiedness that a belief be produced by reliable cognitive belief-forming processes. But this is not quite correct, given our provisional definition of "reliability."

Our provisional definition implies that a reasoning process is reliable only if it generally produces beliefs that are true, and similarly, that a memory process is reliable only if it generally yields beliefs that are true. But these requirements are too strong. A reasoning procedure cannot be expected to produce true belief if it is applied to false premises. And memory cannot be expected to yield a true belief if the original belief it attempts to retain is false. What we need for reasoning and memory, then, is a notion of "*conditional reliability*." A process is conditionally reliable when a sufficient proportion of its output-beliefs are true *given that its input-beliefs are true*.

With this point in mind, let us distinguish *belief-dependent* and *belief-independent* cognitive processes. The former are processes *some* of whose inputs are belief-states.[9] The latter are processes *none* of whose inputs are belief-states. We may then replace principle (5) with the following two principles, the first a base-clause principle and the second a recursive-clause principle.

(6_A) If *S*'s belief in *p* at *t* results ("immediately") from a belief-independent process that is (unconditionally) reliable, then *S*'s belief in *p* at *t* is justified.

(6_B) If *S*'s belief in *p* at *t* results ("immediately") from a belief-dependent process that is (at least) conditionally reliable, and if the beliefs (if any) on which this process operates in producing *S*'s belief in *p* at *t* are themselves justified, then *S*'s belief in *p* at *t* is justified.[10]

If we add to (6_A) and (6_B) the standard closure clause, we have a complete theory of justified belief. The theory says, in effect, that a belief is justified if and only if it is "*well-formed*," i.e., it has an ancestry of reliable and/or conditionally reliable cognitive operations. (Since a dated belief may be over-determined, it may have a number of distinct ancestral trees. These need not all be full of reliable or conditionally reliable processes. But at least one ancestral tree must have reliable or conditionally reliable processes throughout.)

The theory of justified belief proposed here, then, is an *Historical* or *Genetic* theory. It contrasts with the dominant approach to justified belief, an approach that generates what we may call (borrowing a phrase from Robert Nozick) "*Current Time-Slice*" theories. A Current Time-Slice theory makes the justificational status of a belief wholly a function of what is true of the cognizer *at the time* of belief. An Historical theory makes the justificational status of a belief depend on its prior history. Since my Historical theory emphasizes the reliability of the belief-generating processes, it may be called "*Historical Reliabilism*."

The most obvious examples of Current Time-Slice theories are "Cartesian" Foundationalist theories, which trace all justificational status (at least of contingent propositions) to current mental states. The usual varieties of Coherence theories, however, are equally Current Time-Slice views, since they too make the justificational status of a belief wholly a function of *current* states of affairs. For Coherence theories, however, these current states include all other beliefs of the cognizer, which would not be considered relevant by Cartesian Foundationalism.

Have there been other Historical theories of justified belief? Among contemporary writers, Quine and Popper have Historical epistemologies, though the notion of "justification" is not their avowed *explicandum*. Among historical writers, it might seem that Locke and Hume had Genetic theories of sorts. But I think that their Genetic theories were only theories of ideas, not of knowledge or justification. Plato's theory of recollection, however, is a good example of a Genetic theory of knowing.[11] And it might be argued that Hegel and Dewey had Genetic epistemologies (if Hegel can be said to have had a clear epistemology at all).

The theory articulated by (6_A) and (6_B) might be viewed as a king of "Foundationalism" because of its recursive structure. I have no objection to this label, as long as one keeps in mind how different this "diachronic" form of Foundationalism is from Cartesian, or other "synchronic" varieties of, Foundationalism.

Current Time-Slice theories characteristically assume that the justificational status of a belief is something which the cognizer is able to know or determine at the time of belief. This is made explicit, for example, by Chisholm.[12] The Historical theory I endorse makes no such assumption. There are many facts about a cognizer to which he lacks "privileged access," and I regard the justificational status of his beliefs as one of those things. This is not to say that a cognizer is necessarily ignorant, at any given moment, of the justificational status of his current beliefs. It is only to deny that he necessarily has, or can get, knowledge or true belief about this status. Just as a person can know without knowing that he knows, so he can have justified belief without knowing that it is justified (or believing justifiably that it is justified).

A characteristic case in which a belief is justified though the cognizer doesn't know that it's justified is where the original evidence for the belief has long since been forgotten. If the original evidence was compelling, the cognizer's original belief may have been justified, and this justificational status may have been preserved through memory. But since the cognizer no longer remembers how or why he came to believe, he may not know that the belief is justified. If asked now to justify his belief, he may be at a loss. Still, the belief *is* justified, though the cognizer can't demonstrate or establish this.

The Historical theory of justified belief I advocate is connected in spirit with the causal theory of knowing I have presented elsewhere.[13] I had this in mind when I remarked near the outset of the essay that my theory of justified belief makes justifiedness come out closely related to knowledge. Justified beliefs, like pieces of knowledge, have appropriate histories; but they may fail to be knowledge either because they are false or because they founder on some other requirement for knowing of the kind discussed in the post-Gettier knowledge-trade.

There is a variant of the Historical conception of justified belief that is worth mentioning in this context. It may be introduced as follows. Suppose S has a set B of beliefs at time t_0, and some of these beliefs are *un*justified. Between t_0 and t_1 he reasons from the entire set B to the conclusion p, which he then accepts at t_1. The reasoning procedure he uses is a very sound one, i.e., one that is conditionally reliable. There is a sense or respect in which we are tempted to say that S's belief in p at t_1 is "justified." At any rate, it is tempting to say that the *person* is justified in believing p at t. Relative to his antecedent cognitive state, he did as well as could be expected: the *transition* from his cognitive state at t_0 to his cognitive state at t_1 was entirely sound. Although we may acknowledge this brand of justifiedness—it might be called "*Terminal-Phase Reliabilism*"—it is not a kind of justifiedness so closely related to knowing. For a person to know proposition p, it is not enough that the *final phase* of the process that leads to his belief in p be sound. It is also necessary that some entire history of the process be sound (i.e., reliable or conditionally reliable).

Let us return now to the Historical theory. In the next section, I shall adduce reasons for strengthening it a bit. Before looking at these reasons, however, I wish to review two quite different objections to the theory.

First, a critic might argue that *some* justified beliefs do not derive their justificational status from their causal ancestry. In particular, it might be argued that beliefs about one's current phenomenal states and intuitive beliefs about elementary logical or conceptual relationships do not derive their justificational status in this way. I am not persuaded by either of these examples. Introspection, I believe, should be regarded as a form of retrospection. Thus, a justified belief that I am "now" in pain gets its justificational status from a relevant, though brief, causal history.[14] The apprehension of logical or conceptual relationships is also a cognitive process that occupies time. The psychological process of "seeing" or "intuiting" a simple logical truth is very fast, and we cannot introspectively dissect it into constituent parts. Nonetheless, there are mental operations going on, just as there are mental operations that occur in *idiots savants*, who are unable to report the computational processes they in fact employ.

A second objection to Historical Reliabilism focuses on the reliability element rather than the causal or historical element. Since the theory is intended to cover all possible cases, it seems to imply that for any cognitive process C, if C is reliable in possible world W, then any belief in W that results from C is justified. But doesn't this permit easy counterexamples? Surely we can imagine a possible world in which wishful thinking is reliable. We can imagine a possible world where a benevolent demon so arranges things that beliefs formed by wishful thinking usually come true. This would make wishful thinking a reliable process in that possible world, but surely we don't want to regard beliefs that result from wishful thinking as justified.

There are several possible ways to respond to this case, and I am unsure which response is best, partly because my own intuitions (and those of other people I have consulted) are not entirely clear. One possibility is to say that in the possible world imagined, beliefs that result from wishful thinking *are* justified. In other words, we reject the claim that wishful thinking could never, intuitively, confer justifiedness.[15]

However, for those who feel that wishful thinking couldn't confer justifiedness even in the world imagined, there are two ways out. First, it may be suggested that the proper criterion of justifiedness is the propensity of a process to generate beliefs that are true *in a non-manipulated environment*, i.e., an environment in which there is no purposeful arrangement of the world either to accord or conflict with the beliefs that are formed. In other words, the suitability of a belief-forming process is only a function of its success in "*natural*" situations, not situations of the sort involving benevolent or malevolent demons or any other such manipulative creatures. If we reformulate the theory to include this qualification, the counterexample in question will be averted.

Alternatively, we may reformulate our theory, or reinterpret it, as follows. Instead of construing the theory as saying that a belief in possible world W is justified if and only if it results from a cognitive process that is reliable in *W*, we may construe it as saying that a belief in possible world *W* is justified if and only if it results from a cognitive process that is reliable in *our world*. In short, our conception of justifiedness is derived as follows. We note certain cognitive processes in the actual world, and form beliefs about which of these are reliable. The ones we believe to be reliable are then regarded as justification-conferring processes. In reflecting on hypothetical beliefs, we deem them justified if and only if they result from processes already picked out as justification-conferring, or processes very similar to those. Since wishful thinking is not among these processes, a belief formed in a possible world *W* by wishful thinking would not be deemed justified, even if wishful thinking is reliable *in W*. I am not sure that this is a correct reconstruction of our intuitive conceptual scheme, but it would accommodate the benevolent demon case, at least if the proper thing to say in that case is that the wishful-thinking-caused beliefs are unjustified.

Even if we adopt this strategy, however, a problem still remains. Suppose that wishful thinking turns out to be reliable *in the actual world*![16] This might be because, unbeknownst to us at present, there is a benevolent demon who, lazy until now, will shortly start arranging things so that our wishes come true. The long-run performance of wishful thinking will be very good, and hence even the new construal of the theory will imply that beliefs resulting from wishful thinking (in *our* world) are justified. Yet this surely contravenes our intuitive judgment on the matter.

Perhaps the moral of the case is that the standard format of a "conceptual analysis" has its shortcomings. Let me depart from that format and try to give a better rendering of our aim and the theory that tries to achieve that aim. What we really want is an *explanation* of why we count, or would count, certain beliefs as justified and others as unjustified. Such an explanation must refer to our *beliefs* about reliability, not to the actual *facts*. The reason we *count* beliefs as justified is that they are formed by what we *believe* to be reliable belief-forming processes. Our beliefs about which belief-forming processes are reliable may be erroneous, but that does not affect the adequacy of the explanation. Since we *believe* that wishful thinking is an unreliable belief-forming process, we regard beliefs formed by wishful thinking as unjustified. What matters, then, is what we *believe* about wishful thinking, not what is *true* (in the long run) about wishful thinking. I am not sure how to express this point in the standard format of conceptual analysis, but it identifies an important point in understanding our theory.

III

Let us return, however, to the standard format of conceptual analysis, and let us consider a new objection that will require some revisions in the theory advanced until now. According to our theory, a belief is justified in case it is caused by a process that is in fact reliable, or by one we generally believe to be reliable. But suppose that although one of *S*'s beliefs satisfies this condition, *S* has no reason to believe that it does. Worse yet, suppose *S* has reason to believe that his belief is caused by an *unreliable* process (although *in fact* its causal ancestry is fully reliable). Wouldn't we deny in such circumstances that *S*'s belief is justified? This seems to show that our analysis, as presently formulated, is mistaken.

Suppose that Jones is told on fully reliable authority that a certain class of his memory beliefs are almost all mistaken. His parents fabricate a wholly false story that Jones suffered from amnesia when he was seven but later developed *pseudo*-memories of that period. Though Jones listens to what his parents say and has excellent reason to trust them, he persists in believing the ostensible memories from his seven-year-old past. Are these memory beliefs justified? Intuitively, they are not justified. But since these beliefs result from genuine memory and original perceptions, which are adequately reliable processes, our theory says that these beliefs are justified.

Can the theory be revised to meet this difficulty? One natural suggestion is that the actual reliability of a belief's ancestry is not enough for justifiedness; in addition, the cognizer must be *justified in believing* that the ancestry of his belief is reliable. Thus one might think of replacing (6_A), for example, with (7). (For simplicity, I neglect some of the details of the earlier analysis.)

> (7) If *S*'s belief in *p* at *t* is caused by a reliable cognitive process, and *S* justifiably believes at *t* that his *p*-belief is so caused, then *S*'s belief in *p* at *t* is justified.

It is evident, however, that (7) will not do as a base clause, for it contains the epistemic term "justifiably" in its antecedent.

A slightly weaker revision, without this problematic feature, might next be suggested, viz.,

> (8) If *S*'s belief in *p* at *t* is caused by a reliable cognitive process, and *S* believes at *t* that his *p*-belief is so caused, then *S*'s belief in *p* at *t* is justified.

But this won't do the job. Suppose that Jones believes that his memory beliefs are reliably caused despite all the (trustworthy) contrary testimony of his parents. Principle (8) would be satisfied, yet we wouldn't say that these beliefs are justified.

Next, we might try (9), which is stronger than (8) and, unlike (7), formally admissible as a base clause.

> (9) If *S*'s belief in *p* at *t* is caused by a reliable cognitive process, and *S* believes at *t* that his *p*-belief is so caused, and this meta-belief is caused by a reliable cognitive process, then *S*'s belief in *p* at *t* is justified.

A first objection to (9) is that it wrongly precludes unreflective creatures—creatures like animals or young children, who have no beliefs about the genesis of their beliefs—from having justified beliefs. If one shares my view that justified belief is, at least roughly, *well-formed* belief, surely animals and young children can have justified beliefs.

A second problem with (9) concerns its underlying rationale. Since (9) is proposed as a substitute for (6_A), it is implied that the reliability of a belief's own cognitive ancestry does not make it justified. But, the suggestion seems to be, the reliability of a *meta-belief*'s ancestry confers justifiedness on the first-order belief. Why should that be so? Perhaps one is attracted by the idea of a "trickle-down" effect: if an n + 1-level belief is justified, its justification trickles down to an n-level belief. But even if the trickle-down theory is correct, it doesn't help here. There is no assurance from the satisfaction of (9)'s antecedent that the meta-belief itself is *justified*.

To obtain a better revision of our theory, let us re-examine the Jones case. Jones has strong evidence against certain propositions concerning his past. He doesn't *use* this evidence, but if he *were* to use it properly, he would stop believing these propositions. Now the proper use of evidence would be an instance of a (conditionally) reliable process. So what we can say about Jones is that he *fails* to use a certain (conditionally) reliable process that he could and should have used. Admittedly, had he used this process, he would have "worsened" his doxastic states: he would have replaced some true beliefs with suspension of judgment. Still, he couldn't have known this in the case in question. So he failed to do something which, epistemically, he should have done. This diagnosis suggests a fundamental change in our theory. The justificational status of a belief is not only a function of the cognitive process *actually* employed in producing it, it is also a function of processes that could and should be employed.

With these points in mind, we may tentatively propose the following revision of our theory, where we again focus on a base-clause principle but omit certain details in the interest of clarity.

> (10) If *S*'s belief in *p* at *t* results from a reliable cognitive process, and there is no reliable or conditionally reliable process available to *S* which, had it been used by *S* in addition to the process actually used, would have resulted in *S*'s not believing *p* at *t*, then *S*'s belief in *p* at *t* is justified.

There are several problems with this proposal. First, there is a technical problem. One cannot use an additional belief-forming (or doxastic-state-forming) process *as well as* the original process if the additional one would result in a different doxastic state. One wouldn't be using the original process at all. So we need a slightly different formulation of the relevant counterfactual. Since the basic idea is reasonably clear, however, I won't try to improve on the formulation here. A second problem concerns the notion of "*available*" belief-forming (or doxastic-state-forming) processes. What is it for a process to be "available" to a cognizer? Were scientific procedures "available" to people who lived in pre-scientific ages? Furthermore, it seems implausible to say that all "available" processes ought to be used, at least if we include such processes as gathering *new* evidence. Surely a belief can sometimes be justified even if additional evidence-gathering would yield a different doxastic attitude. What I think we should have in mind here are such additional processes as calling previously acquired evidence to mind, assessing the implications of that evidence, etc. This is admittedly somewhat vague, but here again our ordinary notion of justifiedness is vague, so it is appropriate for our analysans to display the same sort of vagueness.

This completes the sketch of my account of justified belief. Before concluding, however, it is essential to point out that there is an important use of "justified" which is not captured by this account but can be captured by a closely related one.

There is a use of "justified" in which it is not implied or presupposed that there is a *belief* that is justified. For example, if *S* is trying to decide whether to believe *p* and asks our advice, we may tell him that he is "justified" in believing it. We do not thereby imply that he *has* a justified *belief*, since we know he is still suspending judgment. What we mean, roughly, is that he *would* or *could* be justified if he were to believe *p*. The justificational status we ascribe here cannot be a function of the causes of *S*'s believing *p*, for there is no belief by *S* in *p*. Thus, the account of justifiedness we have given thus far cannot explicate *this* use of "justified." (It doesn't follow that this use of "justified" has no connection with causal ancestries. Its proper use may depend on the causal ancestry of the cognizer's cognitive state, though not on the causal ancestry of his believing *p*.)

Let us distinguish two uses of "justified": an *ex post* use and an *ex ante* use. The *ex post* use occurs when there exists a belief, and we say of *that belief* that it is (or isn't) justified. The *ex ante* use occurs when no such belief exists, or when we wish to ignore the question of whether such a belief exists. Here we say of the *person*, independent of his doxastic state vis-à-vis *p*, that *p* is (or isn't) suitable for him to believe.[17]

Since we have given an account of *ex post* justifiedness, it will suffice if we can analyze *ex ante* justifiedness in terms of it. Such an analysis, I believe, is ready at hand. *S* is *ex ante* justified in believing *p* at *t* just in case his total cognitive state at *t* is such that from that state he could come to believe *p* in such a way that this belief would be *ex post* justified. More precisely, he is *ex ante* justified in believing *p* at *t* just in case a reliable belief-forming operation is available to him such that the application of that operation to his total cognitive state at *t* would result, more or less immediately, in his believing *p* and this belief would be *ex post* justified. Stated formally, we have the following:

> (11) Person *S* is *ex ante* justified in believing *p* at *t* if and only if there is a reliable belief-forming operation available to *S* which is such that if *S* applied that operation to this total cognitive state at *t*, *S* would believe *p* at *t*-plus-delta (for a suitably small delta) and that belief would be *ex post* justified.

For the analysans of (11) to be satisfied, the total cognitive state at *t* must have a suitable causal ancestry. Hence, (11) is implicitly an Historical account of *ex ante* justifiedness.

As indicated, the bulk of this essay was addressed to *ex post* justifiedness. This is the appropriate analysandum if one is interested in the connection between justifiedness and knowledge, since what is crucial to whether a person *knows* a proposition is whether he has an actual *belief* in the proposition that is justified. However, since many epistemologists are interested in *ex ante* justifiedness, it is proper for a general theory of justification to try to provide an account of that concept as well. Our theory does this quite naturally, for the account of *ex ante* justifiedness falls out directly from our account of *ex post* justifiedness.[18]

Notes

1. "A Causal Theory of Knowing"; "Innate Knowledge," in S. P. Stich, ed., *Innate Ideas* (Berkeley: University of California Press, 1975); and "Discrimination and Perceptual Knowledge."
2. Notice that the choice of a recursive format does not prejudice the case for or against any particular theory. A recursive format is perfectly general. Specifically, an explicit set of necessary and sufficient conditions is just a special case of a recursive format, i.e., one in which there is no recursive clause.
3. Many of the attempts I shall consider are suggested by material in William P. Alston, "Varieties of Privileged Access."
4. Such a definition (though without the modal term) is given, for example, by W. V. Quine and J. S. Ullian in *The Web of Belief*, p. 21. Statements are said to be self-evident just in case "to understand them is to believe them."
5. Page 22.
6. I assume, of course, that "nomologically necessary" is *de re* with respect to "*S*" and "*t*" in this construction. I shall not focus on problems that may arise in this regard, since my primary concerns are with different issues.
7. This assumption violates the thesis that Davidson calls "The Anomalism of the Mental." Cf. "Mental Events" in L. Foster and J. W. Swanson, eds., *Experience and Theory* (Amherst: University of Massachusetts Press, 1970). But it is unclear that this thesis is a necessary truth. Thus, it seems fair to assume its falsity in order to produce a coun-

terexample. The example neither entails nor precludes the mental-physical identity theory.

8. Keith Lehrer's example of the gypsy lawyer is intended to show the inappropriateness of a causal requirement. (See *Knowledge*, pp. 124–25.) But I find this example unconvincing. To the extent that I clearly imagine that the lawyer fixes his belief solely as a result of the cards, it seems intuitively wrong to say that he *knows*—or has a *justified belief*—that his client is innocent.
9. This definition is not exactly what we need for the purposes at hand. As Ernest Sosa points out, introspection will turn out to be a belief-dependent process, since sometimes the input into the process will be a belief (when the introspected content is a belief). Intuitively, however, introspection is not the sort of process which may be merely conditionally reliable. I do not know how to refine the definition so as to avoid this difficulty, but it is a small and isolated point.
10. It may be objected that principles (6_A) and (6_B) are jointly open to analogues of the lottery paradox. A series of processes composed of reliable but less-than-perfectly-reliable processes may be extremely unreliable. Yet applications of (6_A) and (6_B) would confer justifiedness on a belief that is caused by such a series. In reply to this objection, we might simply indicate that the theory is intended to capture our ordinary notion of justifiedness, and this ordinary notion has been formed without recognition of this kind of problem. The theory is not wrong *as* a theory of the ordinary (naive) conception of justifiedness. On the other hand, if we want a theory to do more than capture the ordinary conception of justifiedness, it might be possible to strengthen the principles to avoid lottery-paradox analogues.
11. I am indebted to Mark Pastin for this point.
12. Cf. *Theory of Knowledge*, 2nd ed., pp. 17, 114–16.
13. Cf. "A Causal Theory of Knowing." The reliability aspect of my theory also has its precursors in earlier papers of mine on knowing: "Innate Knowledge" and "Discrimination and Perceptual Knowledge."
14. The view that introspection is retrospection was taken by Ryle, and before him (as Charles Hartshorne points out to me) by Hobbes, Whitehead, and possibly Husserl.
15. Of course, if people in world *W* learn *inductively* that wishful thinking is reliable, and regularly base their beliefs on this inductive inference, it is quite unproblematic and straightforward that their beliefs are justified. The only interesting case is where their beliefs are formed *purely* by wishful thinking, without using inductive inference. The suggestion contemplated in this paragraph of the text is that, in the world imagined, even pure wishful thinking would confer justifiedness.
16. I am indebted here to Mark Kaplan.
17. The distinction between *ex post* and *ex ante* justifiedness is similar to Roderick Firth's distinction between *doxastic* and *propositional* warrant. See his "Are Epistemic Concepts Reducible to Ethical Concepts?" in Alvin I. Goldman and Jaegwon Kim, eds., *Values and Morals, Essays in Honor of William Frankena, Charles Stevenson, and Richard Brandt* (Dordrecht: D. Reidel, 1978).
18. Research on this essay was begun while the author was a fellow of the John Simon Guggenheim Memorial Foundation and of the Center for Advanced Study in the Behavioral Sciences. I am grateful for their support. I have received helpful comments and criticism from Holly S. Goldman, Mark Kaplan, Fred Schmitt, Stephen P. Stich, and many others at several universities where earlier drafts of the paper were read.

Chapter 17

Nelson Goodman

Nelson Goodman (1906–1998) was Professor of Philosophy at Harvard University. In this selection, taken from his book *Fact, Fiction and Forecast*, Goodman argues that beside Hume's puzzle over induction, there is a second problem: What are the rules for deciding which properties are projectable into the future? Why does the seeing of another black raven confirm our hypothesis that all ravens are black or that the next raven we see will be black, but the seeing of three bachelors in a room not count as evidence that tomorrow we will see three bachelors in this room? Inventing a new color term *grue*, made up from our color terms *green* and *blue*, Goodman illustrates the problem of projectability.

FOR FURTHER READING

Goodman, Nelson. *Fact, Fiction and Forecast* (Harvard University Press, 1955).
Jeffrey, Richard. *The Logic of Decision*, 2d ed. (University of Chicago Press, 1983).
Kyburg, Henry E., Jr. *Probability and the Logic of Rational Belief* (Wesleyan University Press, 1961).
Mackie, J. L. "A Defense of Induction." In *Logic and Knowledge* (Clarendon Press, 1995).
Mill, John Stuart. *System of Logic*, 10th ed. (Longman's Green, 1879).
Reichenbach, Hans. *Experience and Prediction* (University of Chicago Press, 1938).
Skyrms, Brian. *Choice and Chance* (Wadsworth, 1986).
Stove, D. C. *Probability and Hume's Inductive Scepticism* (Clarendon Press, 1973).
Strawson, P. F. *Introduction to Logical Theory* (Wiley, 1952).
Swinburne, Richard, ed. *The Justification of Induction* (Oxford University Press, 1974).
Will, Frederick. *Induction and Justification* (Cornell University Press, 1973).

The New Riddle of Induction

Confirmation of a hypothesis by an instance depends rather heavily upon features of the hypothesis other than its syntactical form. That a given piece of copper conducts electricity increases the credibility of statements asserting that other pieces of copper conduct electricity, and thus confirms the hypothesis that all copper conducts electricity. But the fact that a given man now in this room is a third son does not increase the credibility of statements asserting that other men now in this room are third sons, and so does not confirm the hypothesis that all men now in this room are third sons. Yet in both cases our hypothesis is a generalization of the evidence statement. The difference is that in the former case the hypothesis is a *lawlike* statement; while in the latter case, the hypothesis is a merely contingent or accidental generality. Only a statement that is *lawlike*—regardless of its truth or falsity or its scientific importance—is capable of receiving confirmation from an instance of it; accidental statements are not. Plainly, then, we must look for a way of distinguishing lawlike from accidental statements.

So long as what seems to be needed is merely a way of excluding a few odd and unwanted cases that are inadvertently admitted by our definition of confirmation, the problem may not seem very hard or very pressing. We fully expect that minor defects will be found in our definition and that the necessary refinements will have to be worked out patiently one after another. But some further examples will show that our present difficulty is of a much graver kind.

Suppose that all emeralds examined before a certain time *t* are green.[1] At time *t*, then, our observations support the hypothesis that all emeralds are green; and this is in accord with our definition of confirmation. Our evidence statements assert that emerald *a* is green, that emerald *b* is green, and so on; and each confirms the general hypothesis that all emeralds are green. So far, so good.

Now let me introduce another predicate less familiar than "green." It is the predicate "grue" and it applies to all things examined before *t* just in case they are green but to other things just in case they are blue. Then at time *t* we have, for each evidence statement asserting that a given emerald is green, a parallel evidence statement asserting that that emerald is grue. And the statements that emerald *a* is grue, that emerald *b* is grue, and so on, will each confirm the general hypothesis that all emeralds are grue. Thus according to our definition, the prediction that all emeralds subsequently examined will be green and the prediction that all will be grue are alike confirmed by evidence statements describing the same observations. But if an emerald subsequently examined is grue, it is blue and hence not green. Thus although we are well aware which of the two incompatible predictions is genuinely confirmed, they are equally well confirmed according to our present definition. Moreover, it is clear that if we simply choose an appropriate predicate, then on the basis of these same observations we shall have equal confirmation, by our definition, for any prediction whatever about other emeralds—or indeed about anything else.[2] As in our earlier example, only the predictions subsumed under lawlike hypotheses are genuinely confirmed; but we have no criterion as yet for determining lawlikeness. And now we see that without some such criterion, our definition not merely includes a few unwanted cases, but is so completely ineffectual that it virtually excludes nothing. We are left once again with the intolerable result that anything confirms anything. This difficulty cannot be set aside as an annoying detail to be taken care of in due course. It has to be met before our definition will work at all.

Nevertheless, the difficulty is often slighted because on the surface there seem to be easy ways of dealing with it. Sometimes, for example, the problem is thought to be much like the paradox of the ravens. We are here again, it is pointed out, making tacit and illegitimate use of information outside the stated evidence: the information, for example, that different samples of one material are usually alike in conductivity, and the information that different men in a lecture audience are usually not alike in the number of their older brothers. But while it is true that such information is being smuggled in, this does not by itself settle the matter as it settles the matter of the ravens. There the point was that when the smuggled information is forthrightly declared, its effect upon the confirmation of the hypothesis in question is immediately and properly registered by the definition we are using. On the other hand, if to our initial evidence we add statements concerning the conductivity of pieces of other materials or concerning the number of older brothers of members of other lecture audiences, this will not in the least affect the confirmation, according to our definition, of the hypothesis concerning copper or of that concerning other lecture audiences. Since our definition is insensitive to the bearing upon hypotheses of evidence so related to them, even when the evidence is fully declared, the difficulty about accidental hypotheses cannot be explained away on the ground that such evidence is being surreptitiously taken into account.

A more promising suggestion is to explain the matter in terms of the effect of this other evidence not directly upon the hypothesis in question but *in-*

directly through other hypotheses that *are* confirmed, according to our definition, by such evidence. Our information about other materials does by our definition confirm such hypotheses as that all pieces of iron conduct electricity, that no pieces of rubber do, and so on; and these hypotheses, the explanation runs, impart to the hypothesis that all pieces of copper conduct electricity (and also to the hypothesis that none do) the character of lawlikeness—that is, amenability to confirmation by direct positive instances when found. On the other hand, our information about other lecture audiences *dis*confirms many hypotheses to the effect that all the men in one audience are third sons, or that none are; and this strips any character of lawlikeness from the hypothesis that all (or the hypothesis that none) of the men in *this* audience are third sons. But clearly if this course is to be followed, the circumstances under which hypotheses are thus related to one another will have to be precisely articulated.

The problem, then, is to define the relevant ways in which such hypotheses must be alike. Evidence for the hypothesis that all iron conducts electricity enhances the lawlikeness of the hypothesis that all zirconium conducts electricity, but does not similarly affect the hypothesis that all the objects on my desk conduct electricity. Wherein lies the difference? The first two hypotheses fall under the broader hypothesis—call it "*H*"—that every class of things of the same material is uniform in conductivity; the first and third fall only under some such hypothesis as—call it "*K*"—that every class of things that are either all of the same material or all on a desk is uniform in conductivity. Clearly the important difference here is that evidence for a statement affirming that one of the classes covered by *H* has the property in question increases the credibility of any statement affirming that another such class has this property; while nothing of the sort holds true with respect to *K*. But this is only to say that *H* is lawlike and *K* is not. We are faced anew with the very problem we are trying to solve: the problem of distinguishing between lawlike and accidental hypotheses.

The most popular way of attacking the problem takes its cue from the fact that accidental hypotheses seem typically to involve some spatial or temporal restriction, or reference to some particular individual. They seem to concern the people in some particular room, or the objects on some particular person's desk; while lawlike hypotheses characteristically concern all ravens or all pieces of copper whatsoever. Complete generality is thus very often supposed to be a sufficient condition of lawlikeness; but to define this complete generality is by no means easy. Merely to require that the hypothesis contain no term naming, describing, or indicating a particular thing or location will obviously not be enough. The troublesome hypothesis that all emeralds are grue contains no such term; and where such a term does occur, as in hypotheses about men in *this room*, it can be suppressed in favor of some predicate (short or long, new or old) that contains no such term but applies only to exactly the same things. One might think, then, of excluding not only hypotheses that actually contain terms for specific individuals but also all hypotheses that are equivalent to others that do contain such terms. But, as we have just seen, to exclude only hypotheses of which *all* equivalents contain such terms is to exclude nothing. On the other hand, to exclude all hypotheses that have *some* equivalent containing such a term is to exclude everything; for even the hypothesis

All grass is green

has as an equivalent

All grass in London or elsewhere is green.

The next step, therefore, has been to consider ruling out predicates of certain kinds. A syntactically universal hypothesis is lawlike, the proposal runs, if its predicates are "purely qualitative" or "nonpositional."[3] This will obviously accomplish nothing if a purely qualitative predicate is then conceived either as one that is equivalent to some expression free of terms for specific individuals, or as one that is equivalent to no expression that contains such a term; for this only raises again the difficulties just pointed out. The claim appears to be rather that at least in the case of a simple enough predicate we can readily determine by direct inspection of its meaning whether or not it is purely qualitative. But even aside from obscurities in the notion of "the meaning" of a predicate, this claim seems to me wrong. I simply do not know how to tell whether a predicate is qualitative or positional, except perhaps by completely begging the question at issue and asking whether the predicate is "well-behaved"—that is, whether simple syntactically universal hypotheses applying it are lawlike.

This statement will not go unprotested. "Consider," it will be argued, "the predicates 'blue' and 'green' and the predicate 'grue' introduced earlier, and also the predicate 'bleen' that applies to emeralds examined before time *t* just in case they are blue and to other emeralds just in case they are green. Surely it is clear," the argument runs, "that the first two are purely qualitative and the second two are not; for the meaning of each of the latter two plainly involves reference to a specific temporal position." To this I reply that indeed I do recognize the first two as well-behaved predicates admissible in lawlike hypotheses, and the second two as ill-behaved predicates. But the argument that the former but not the latter are purely qualitative seems to me quite unsound. True enough, if we start with "blue" and "green," then "grue" and "bleen" will be explained in terms of "blue" and "green" and a temporal term. But equally truly, if we start with "grue" and "bleen," then "blue" and "green" will be explained in terms of "grue" and "bleen" and a temporal term; "green," for example, applies to emeralds examined before time *t* just in case they are grue, and to other emeralds just in case they are bleen. Thus qualitativeness is an entirely relative matter and does not by itself establish any dichotomy of predicates. This relativity seems to be completely overlooked by those who contend that the qualitative character of a predicate is a criterion for its good behavior.

Of course, one may ask why we need worry about such unfamiliar predicates as "grue" or about accidental hypotheses in general, since we are unlikely to use them in making predictions. If our definition works for such hypotheses as are normally employed, isn't that all we need? In a sense, yes; but only in the sense that we need no definition, no theory of induction, and no philosophy of knowledge at all. We get along well enough without them in daily life and in scientific research. But if we seek a theory at all, we cannot excuse gross anomalies resulting from a proposed theory by pleading that we can avoid them in practice. The odd cases we have been considering are clinically pure cases that, though seldom encountered in practice, nevertheless display to best advantage the symptoms of a widespread and destructive malady.

We have so far neither any answer nor any promising clue to an answer to the question what distinguishes lawlike or confirmable hypotheses from accidental or non-confirmable ones; and what may at first have seemed a minor technical difficulty has taken on the stature of a major obstacle to the development of a satisfactory theory of confirmation. It is this problem that I call the new riddle of induction.

Notes

1. Although the example used is different, the argument to follow is substantially the same as that set forth in my note "A Query on Confirmation" [*Journal of Philosophy*, XLIII (1946), 383–385].
2. For instance, we shall have equal confirmation, by our present definition, for the prediction that roses subsequently examined will be blue. Let "emerose" apply just to emeralds examined before time *t*, and to roses examined later. Then all emeroses so far examined are grue, and this confirms the hypothesis that all emeroses are grue and hence the prediction that roses subsequently examined will be blue. The problem raised by such antecedents has been little noticed, but is no easier to meet than that raised by similarly perverse consequents.
3. Carnap took this course in his paper "On the Application of Inductive Logic," *Philosophy and Phenomenological Research*, vol. 8 (1947), pp. 133–147, which is in part a reply to my "A Query on Confirmation." The discussion was continued in my note "On Infirmities of Confirmation Theory," *Philosophy and Phenomenological Research*, vol. 8 (1947), pp. 149–151; and in Carnap's "Reply to Nelson Goodman," same journal, same volume, pp. 461–462.

Chapter 18

DONALD DAVIDSON

Donald Davidson (1917–   ) was born in Spingfield, Massachusetts, and educated at Harvard University, where he studied under Quine. Since 1981 he has taught philosophy at the University of California, Berkeley.

Davidson has made important contributions to many areas in philosophy, especially philosophy of language. In this article he develops the thesis, first put forth by Tarski, that the meaning of a sentence is its truth conditions, whatever would make the sentence true.

FOR FURTHER READING

Davidson, Donald. *Essays on Actions and Events* (Oxford University Press, 1981).
———. *Inquiries into Truth and Interpretation* (Oxford University Press, 1984).
Malapas, J. E. *Donald Davidson and the Miracle of Meaning* (Cambridge University Press, 1992).
Vermazen, Bruce and Merill Hintikka, eds. *Essays on Davidson* (Oxford: Clarendon Press, 1985).

Truth and Meaning

It is conceded by most philosophers of language, and recently by some linguists, that a satisfactory theory of meaning must give an account of how the meanings of sentences depend upon the meanings of words. Unless such an account could be supplied for a particular language, it is argued, there would be no explaining the fact that we can learn the language: no explaining the fact that, on mastering a finite vocabulary and a finitely stated set of rules, we are prepared to produce and to understand any of a potential infinitude of sentences. I do not dispute these vague claims, in which I sense more than a kernel of truth. Instead I want to ask what it is for a theory to give an account of the kind adumbrated.

One proposal is to begin by assigning some entity as meaning to each word (or other significant syntactical feature) of the sentence; thus we might assign Theaetetus to 'Theaetetus' and the property of flying to 'flies' in the sentence 'Theaetetus flies'. The problem then arises how the meaning of the sentence is generated from these meanings. Viewing concatenation as a significant piece of syntax, we

From *Synthese*, 17 (1967), pp. 304–323. © D. Reidel Publishing Co., Dordrecht, Holland.

may assign to it the relation of participating in or instantiating; however, it is obvious that we have here the start of an infinite regress. Frege sought to avoid the regress by saying that the entities corresponding to predicates (for example) are 'unsaturated' or 'incomplete' in contrast to the entities that correspond to names, but this doctrine seems to label a difficulty rather than solve it.

The point will emerge if we think for a moment of complex singular terms, to which Frege's theory applies along with sentences. Consider the expression "the father of Annette"; how does the meaning of the whole depend on the meaning of the parts? The answer would seem to be that the meaning of "the father of" is such that when this expression is prefixed to a singular term the result refers to the father of the person to whom the singular term refers. What part is played, in this account, by the unsaturated or incomplete entity for which "the father of" stands? All we can think to say is that this entity 'yields' or 'gives' the father of *x* as value when the argument is *x*, or perhaps that this entity maps people onto their fathers. It may not be clear whether the entity for which "the father of" is said to stand performs any genuine explanatory function as long as we stick to individual expressions; so think instead of the infinite class of expressions formed by writing "the father of" zero or more times in front of "Annette." It is easy to supply a theory that tells, for an arbitrary one of these singular terms, what it refers to: if the term is "Annette" it refers to Annette, while if the term is complex, consisting of "the father of" prefixed to a singular term *t*, then it refers to the father of the person to whom *t* refers. It is obvious that no entity corresponding to "the father of" is, or needs to be, mentioned in stating this theory.

It would be inappropriate to complain that this little theory *uses* the words "the father of" in giving the reference of expressions containing those words. For the task was to give the meaning of all expressions in a certain infinite set on the basis of the meaning of the parts; it was not in the bargain also to give the meanings of the atomic parts. On the other hand, it is now evident that a satisfactory theory of the meanings of complex expressions may not require entities as meanings of all the parts. It behooves us then to rephrase our demand on a satisfactory theory of meaning so as not to suggest that individual words must have meanings at all, in any sense that transcends the fact that they have a systematic effect on the meanings of the sentences in which they occur. Actually, for the case at hand we can do better still in stating the criterion of success: what we wanted, and what we got, is a theory that entails every sentence of the form "*t* refers to *x*" where '*t*' is replaced by a structural description of a singular term, and '*x*' is replaced by that term itself. Further, our theory accomplishes this without appeal to any semantical concepts beyond the basic "refers to." Finally, the theory clearly suggests an effective procedure for determining, for any singular term in its universe, what that term refers to.

A theory with such evident merits deserves wider application. The device proposed by Frege to this end has a brilliant simplicity: count predicates as a special case of functional expressions, and sentences as a special case of complex singular terms. Now, however, a difficulty looms if we want to continue in our present (implicit) course of identifying the meaning of a singular term with its reference. The difficulty follows upon making two reasonable assumptions: that logically equivalent singular terms have the same reference; and that a singular term does not change its reference if a contained singular term is replaced by another with the same reference. But now suppose that '*R*' and '*S*' abbreviate any two sentences alike in truth value. Then the following four sentences have the same reference:

(1) R

(2) $\hat{x}(x = x.R) = \hat{x}(x = x)$

(3) $\hat{x}(x = x.S) = \hat{x}(x = x)$

(4) S

For (1) and (2) are logically equivalent, as are (3) and (4), while (3) differs from (2) only in containing the singular term '$(\hat{x} = x.S)$' where (2) contains '$(\hat{x} = x.R)$' and these refer to the same thing if *S* and *R* are alike in truth value. Hence any two sentences have the same reference if they have the same truth value.[3] And if the meaning of a sentence is what it refers to, all sentences alike in truth value must be synonymous—an intolerable result.

Apparently we must abandon the present approach as leading to a theory of meaning. This is the natural point at which to turn for help to the distinction between meaning and reference. The trouble, we are told, is that questions of reference are, in general, settled by extralinguistic facts, questions of meaning not, and the facts can conflate the references of expressions that are not synonymous. If we want a theory that gives the meaning (as distinct from reference) of each sentence, we must start with the meaning (as distinct from reference) of the parts.

Up to here we have been following in Frege's footsteps; thanks to him, the path is well known and even well worn. But now, I would like to suggest, we have reached an impasse: the switch from reference to meaning leads to no useful account of how the meanings of sentences depend upon the meanings of the words (or other structural features) that compose them. Ask, for example, for the meaning of "Theaetetus flies." A Fregean answer might go something like this: given the meaning of "Theaetetus" as argument, the meaning of "flies" yields the meaning of "Theaetetus flies" as value. The vacuity of this answer is obvious. We wanted to know what the meaning of "Theaetetus flies" is; it is no progress to be told that it is the meaning of "Theaetetus flies." This much we knew before any theory was in sight. In the bogus account just given, talk of the structure of the sentence and of the meanings of words was idle, for it played no role in producing the given description of the meaning of the sentence.

The contrast here between a real and pretended account will be plainer still if we ask for a theory, analogous to the miniature theory of reference of singular terms just sketched, but different in dealing with meanings in place of references. What analogy demands is a theory that has as consequences all sentences of the form "*s* means *m*" where '*s*' is replaced by a structural description of a sentence and '*m*' is replaced by a singular term that refers to the meaning of that sentence; a theory, moreover, that provides an effective method for arriving at the meaning of an arbitrary sentence structurally described. Clearly some more articulate way of referring to meanings than any we have seen is essential if these criteria are to be met. Meanings as entities, or the related concept of synonymy, allow us to formulate the following rule relating sentences and their parts: sentences are synonymous whose corresponding parts are synonymous ("corresponding" here needs spelling out of course). And meanings as entities may, in theories such as Frege's, do duty, on occasion as references, thus losing their status as entities distinct from references. Paradoxically, the one thing meanings do not seem to do is oil the wheels of a theory of meaning—at least as long as we require of such a theory that it nontrivially give the meaning of every sentence in the language. My objection to meanings in the theory of meaning is not that they are abstract or that their identity conditions are obscure, but that they have no demonstrated use.

This is the place to scotch another hopeful thought. Suppose we have a satisfactory theory of syntax for our language, consisting of an effective method of telling, for an arbitrary expression, whether or not it is independently meaningful (i.e., a sentence), and assume as usual that this involves viewing each sentence as composed, in allowable ways, out of elements drawn from a fixed finite stock of atomic syntactical elements (roughly, words). The hopeful thought is that syntax, so conceived, will yield semantics when a dictionary giving the meaning of each syntactic atom is added. Hopes will be dashed, however, if semantics is to comprise a theory of meaning in our sense, for knowledge of the structural characteristics that make for meaningfulness in a sentence, plus knowledge of the meanings of the ultimate parts, does not add up to knowledge of what a sentence means. The point is easily illustrated by belief sentences. Their syntax is relatively unproblematic. Yet, adding a dictionary does not touch the standard semantic problem, which is that we cannot account for even as much as the truth conditions of such sentences on the basis of what we know of the meanings of the words in them. The situation is not radically altered by refining the dictionary to indicate which meaning or meanings an ambiguous expression bears in each of its possible contexts; the problem of belief sentences persists after ambiguities are resolved.

The fact that recursive syntax with dictionary added is not necessarily recursive semantics has been obscured in some recent writing on linguistics by the intrusion of semantic criteria into the discussion of purportedly syntactic theories. The matter would boil down to a harmless difference over terminology if the semantic criteria were clear; but they are not. While there is agreement that it is the central task of semantics to give the semantic interpretation (the meaning) of every sentence in the language, nowhere in the linguistic literature will one find, so far as I know, a straightforward account of how a theory performs this task, or how to tell when it has been accomplished. The contrast with syntax is striking. The main job of a modest syntax is to characterize *meaningfulness* (or sentencehood). We may have as much confidence in the correctness of such a characterization as we have in the representativeness of our sample and our ability to say when particular expressions are meaningful (sentences). What clear and analogous task and test exist for semantics?

We decided a while back not to assume that parts of sentences have meanings except in the ontologically neutral sense of making a systematic contribution to the meaning of the sentences in which they occur. Since postulating meanings has netted nothing, let us return to that insight. One direction in which it points is a certain holistic view of meaning. If sentences depend for their meaning on their structure, and we understand the meaning of each item in the structure only as an abstraction from the totality of sentences in which it features, then we can give the meaning of any sentence (or word) only by giving the meaning of every sentence (and word) in the language. Frege said that only in the context of a sentence does a word have meaning; in the same vein he might have added that only in the context of the language does a sentence (and therefore a word) have meaning.

This degree of holism was already implicit in the suggestion that an adequate theory of meaning must entail *all* sentences of the form "*s* means *m*." But now, having found no more help in meanings of sentences than in meanings of words, let us ask whether we can get rid of the troublesome singular terms supposed to replace '*m*' and to refer to meanings. In a way, nothing could be easier: just write "*s* means that *p*," and imagine '*p*' replaced by a sentence. Sentences, as we have seen, cannot name meanings, and sentences with "that" prefixed are not names at all, unless we decide so. It looks as though we are in trouble on another count, however, for it is reasonable to expect that in wrestling with the logic of the apparently nonextensional "means that" we will encounter problems as hard as, or perhaps identical with, the problems our theory is out to solve.

The only way I know to deal with this difficulty is simple, and radical. Anxiety that we are enmeshed in the intensional springs from using the words "means that" as filling between description of sentence and sentence, but it may be that the success of our venture depends not on the filling but on what it fills. The theory will have done its work if it provides, for every sentence *s* in the language under study, a matching sentence (to replace '*p*') that, in some way yet to be made clear, 'gives the meaning' of *s*. One obvious candidate for matching sentence is just *s* itself, if the object language is contained in the metalanguage; otherwise a translation of *s* in the metalanguage. As a final bold step, let us try treating the position occupied by '*p*' extensionally: to implement this, sweep away the obscure "means that," provide the sentence that replaces '*p*' with a proper sentential connective, and supply the description that replaces '*s*' with its own predicate. The plausible result is

(*T*) *s* is *T* if and only if *p*.

What we require of a theory of meaning for a language *L* is that without appeal to any (further) semantical notions it place enough restrictions on the predicate "is *T*" to entail all sentences got from schema *T* when '*s*' is replaced by a structural description of a sentence of *L* and '*p*' by that sentence.

Any two predicates satisfying this condition have the same extension, so if the metalanguage is rich enough, nothing stands in the way of putting what I am calling a theory of meaning into the form of an explicit definition of a predicate "is *T*." But whether explicitly defined or recursively characterized, it is clear that the sentences to which the predicate "is *T*" applies will be just the true sentences of *L*, for the condition we have placed on satisfactory theories of meaning is in essence Tarski's Convention *T* that tests the adequacy of a formal semantical definition of truth.

The path to this point has been tortuous, but the conclusion may be stated simply: a theory of meaning for a language *L* shows "how the meanings of sentences depend upon the meanings of words" if it contains a (recursive) definition of truth-in-L. And, so far at least, we have no other idea how to turn the trick. It is worth emphasizing that the concept of truth played no ostensible role in stating our original problem. That problem, upon refinement, led to the view that an adequate theory of meaning must characterize a predicate meeting certain conditions. It was in the nature of a discovery that such a predicate would apply exactly to the true sentences. I hope that what I am doing may be described in part as defending the philosophical importance of Tarski's semantical concept of truth. But my defense is only distantly related, if at all, to the question whether the concept Tarski has shown how to define is the (or a) philosophically interesting conception of truth, or the question whether Tarski has cast any light on the ordinary use of such words as "true" and "truth." It is a misfortune that dust from futile and confused battles over these questions has prevented those with a theoretical interest in language—philosophers, logicians, psychologists, and linguists alike—from recognizing in the semantical concept of truth (under whatever name) the sophisticated and powerful foundation of a competent theory of meaning.

There is no need to suppress, of course, the obvious connection between a definition of truth of the kind Tarski has shown how to construct, and the concept of meaning. It is this: the definition works by giving necessary and sufficient conditions for the truth of every sentence, and to give truth conditions is a way of giving the meaning of a sentence. To know the semantic concept of truth for a language is to know what it is for a sentence—any sentence—to be true, and this amounts, in one good sense we can give to the phrase, to understanding the language. This at any rate is my excuse for a feature of the present discussion that is apt to shock old hands: my freewheeling use of the word "meaning," for what I call a theory of meaning has after all turned out to make no use of meanings, whether of sentences or of words. Indeed since a Tarski-type truth definition supplies all we have asked so far of a theory of meaning, it is clear that such a theory falls comfortably within what Quine terms the "theory of reference" as distinguished from what he terms the "theory of meaning." So much to the good for what I call a theory of meaning, and so much, perhaps, against my so calling it.

A theory of meaning (in my mildly perverse sense) is an empirical theory, and its ambition it to account for the workings of a natural language. Like any theory, it may be tested by comparing some of its consequences with the facts. In the present case this is easy, for the theory has been characterized as issuing in an infinite flood of sentences each giving the truth conditions of a sentence; we only need to ask, in selected cases, whether what the theory avers to be the truth conditions for a sentence really are. A typical test case might involve deciding whether the sentence "Snow is white" *is* true if and only if snow is white. Not all cases will be so simple (for reasons to be sketched), but it is evident that this sort of test does not invite counting noses. A sharp conception of what constitutes a theory in this domain furnishes an exciting context for raising deep questions about when a theory of language is correct and how it is to be tried. But the difficulties are theoretical, not practical. In application, the trouble is to get a theory that comes close to working; anyone can tell whether it is right. One can see why this is so. The theory reveals nothing new about the conditions under which an individual sentence is true; it does not make those conditions any clearer than the sentence itself does. The work of the theory is in relating the known truth conditions of each sentence to those aspects ('words') of the sentence that recur in other sentences, and can be assigned identical roles in other sentences. Empirical power in such a theory depends on success in recovering the structure of a very complicated ability—the ability to speak and understand a language. We can tell easily enough when particular pronouncements of the theory comport with our understanding of the language; this is consistent with a feeble insight into the design of the machinery of our linguistic accomplishments.

The remarks of the last paragraph apply directly only to the special case where it is assumed that the language for which truth is being characterized is part of the language used and understood by the characterizer. Under these circumstances, the framer of a theory will as a matter of course avail himself when he can of the built-in convenience of a metalanguage with a sentence guaranteed equivalent to each sentence in the object language. Still, this fact ought not to con us into thinking a theory any more correct that entails " 'Snow is white' is true if and only if snow is white" than one that entails instead:

> (*S*) "Snow is white" is true if and only if grass is green, provided, of course, we are as sure of the truth of (*S*)

as we are of that of its more celebrated predecessor. Yet (*S*) may not encourage the same confidence that a theory that entails it deserves to be called a theory of meaning.

The threatened failure of nerve may be counteracted as follows. The grotesqueness of (*S*) is in itself nothing against a theory of which it is a consequence, provided the theory gives the correct results for every sentence (on the basis of its structure, there being no other way). It is not easy to see how (*S*) could be party to such an enterprise, but if it were—if, that is, (*S*) followed from a characterization of the predicate "is true" that led to the invariable pairing of truths with truths and falsehoods with falsehoods—then there would not, I think, be anything essential to the idea of meaning that remained to be captured.

What appears to the right of the biconditional in sentences of the form "*s* is true if and only if *p*," when such sentences are consequences of a theory of truth, plays its role in determining the meaning of *s* not by pretending synonymy but by adding one more brush-stroke to the picture which, taken as a whole, tells what there is to know of the meaning of *s*; this stroke is added by virtue of the fact that the sentence that replaces '*p*' is true if and only if *s* is.

It may help to reflect that (*S*) is acceptable, if it is, because we are independently sure of the truth of "snow is white" and "grass is green"; but in cases where we are unsure of the truth of a sentence, we can have confidence in a characterization of the truth predicate only if it pairs that sentence with one we have good reason to believe equivalent. It would be ill advised for someone who had any doubts about the color of snow or grass to accept a theory that yielded (*S*), even if his doubts were of equal degree, unless he thought the color of the one was tied to the color of the other. Omniscience can obviously afford more bizarre theories of meaning than ignorance; but then, omniscience has less need of communication.

It must be possible, of course, for the speaker of one language to construct a theory of meaning for the speaker of another, though in this case the empirical test of the correctness of the theory will no longer be trivial. As before, the aim of theory will be an infinite correlation of sentences alike in truth. But this time the theory-builder must not be assumed to have direct insight into likely equivalences between his own tongue and the alien. What he must do is find out, however he can, what sentences the alien holds true in his own tongue (or better, to what degree he holds them true). The linguist then will attempt to construct a characterization of truth-for-the-alien which yields, so far as possible, a mapping of sentences held true (or false) by the alien onto sentences held true (or false) by the linguist. Supposing no perfect fit is found, the residue of sentences held true translated by sentences held false (and vice versa) is the margin for error (foreign or domestic). Charity in interpreting the words and thoughts of others is unavoidable in another direction as well: just as we must maximize agreement, or risk not making sense of what the alien is talking about, so we must maximize the self-consistency we attribute to him, on pain of not understanding *him*. No single principle of optimum charity emerges; the constraints therefore determine no single theory. In a theory of radical translation (as Quine calls it) there is no completely disentangling questions of what the alien means from questions of what he believes. We do not know what someone means unless we know what he believes; we do not know what someone believes unless we know what he means. In radical translation we are able to break into this circle, if only incompletely, because we can sometimes tell that a person accedes to a sentence we do not understand.

In the past few pages I have been asking how a theory of meaning that takes the form of a truth definition can be empirically tested, and have blithely ignored the prior question whether there is any serious chance such a theory can be given for a natural language. What are the prospects for a formal semantical theory of a natural language? Very poor, according to Tarski; and I believe most logicians, philosophers of language, and linguists agree. Let me do what I can to dispel the pessimism. What I can in a general and programmatic way, of course; for here the proof of the pudding will certainly be in the proof of the right theorems.

Tarski concludes the first section of his classic essay on the concept of truth in formalized languages with the following remarks, which he italicizes:

> *The very possibility of a consistent use of the expression 'true sentence' which is in harmony with the laws of logic and the spirit of everyday language seems to be very questionable, and consequently the same doubt attaches to the possibility of constructing a correct definition of this expression.*[1]

Late in the same essay, he returns to the subject:

> the concept of truth (as well as other semantical concepts) when applied to colloquial language in conjunction with the normal laws of logic leads inevitably to confusions and contradictions. Whoever wishes, in spite of all difficulties, to pursue the semantics of colloquial language with the help of exact methods will be driven first to undertake the thankless task of a reform of this language. He will find it necessary to define its structure, to overcome the ambiguity of the terms which occur in it, and finally to split the language into a series of languages of greater and greater extent, each of

1. Alfred Tarski, "The Concept of Truth in Formalized Languages," in *Logic, Semantics, Metamathematics* (Oxford: 1956), p. 165.

> which stands in the same relation to the next in which a formalized language stands to its metalanguage. It may, however be doubted whether the language of everyday life, after being 'rationalized' in this way, would still preserve its naturalness and whether it would not rather take on the characteristic features of the formalized languages.[2]

Two themes emerge: that the universal character of natural languages leads to contradiction (the semantic paradoxes), and that natural languages are too confused and amorphous to permit the direct application of formal methods. The first point deserves a serious answer, and I wish I had one. As it is, I will say only why I think we are justified in carrying on without having disinfected this particular source of conceptual anxiety. The semantic paradoxes arise when the range of the quantifiers in the object language is too generous in certain ways. But it is not really clear how unfair to Urdu or to Hindi it would be to view the range of their quantifiers as insufficient to yield an explicit definition of "true-in-Urdu" or "true-in-Hindi." Or, to put the matter in another, if not more serious way, there may in the nature of the case always be something we grasp in understanding the language of another (the concept of truth) that we cannot communicate to him. In any case, most of the problems of general philosophical interest arise within a fragment of the relevant natural language that may be conceived as containing very little set theory. Of course these comments do not meet the claim that natural languages are universal. But it seems to me this claim, now that we know such universality leads to paradox, is suspect.

Tarski's second point is that we would have to reform a natural language out of all recognition before we could apply formal semantical methods. If this is true, it is fatal to my project, for the task of a theory of meaning as I conceive it is not to change, improve or reform a language, but to describe and understand it. Let us look at the positive side. Tarski has shown the way to giving a theory for interpreted formal languages of various kinds; pick one as much like English as possible. Since this new language has been explained in English and contains much English we not only may, but I think must, view it as part of English for those who understand it. For this fragment of English we have, *ex hypothesi*, a theory of the required sort. Not only that, but in interpreting this adjunct of English in old English we necessarily gave hints connecting old and new. Wherever there are sentences of old English with the same truth conditions as sentences in the adjunct we may extend the theory to cover them. Much of what is called for is just to mechanize as far as possible what we now do by art when we put ordinary English into one or another canonical notation. The point is not that canonical notation is better than the rough original idiom, but rather that if we know what idiom the canonical notation is canonical *for*, we have as good a theory for the idiom as for its kept companion.

Philosophers have long been at the hard work of applying theory to ordinary language by the device of matching sentences in the vernacular with sentences for which they have a theory. Frege's massive contribution was to show how "all," "some," "every," "each," "none," and associated pronouns, in some of their uses, could be tamed; for the first time, it was possible to dream of a formal semantics for a significant part of a natural language. This dream came true in a sharp way with the work of Tarski. It would be a shame to miss the fact that as a result of these two magnificent achievements, Frege's and Tarski's, we have gained a deep insight into the structure of our mother tongues. Philosophers of a logical bent have tended to start where the theory was and work out towards the complications of natural language. Contemporary linguists, with an aim that cannot easily be seen to be different, start with the ordinary and work toward a general theory. If either party is successful, there must be a meeting. Recent work by Chomsky and others is doing much to bring the complexities of natural languages within the scope of serious semantic theory. To give an example: suppose success in giving the truth conditions for some significant range of sentences in the active voice. Then with a formal procedure for transforming each such sentence into a corresponding sentence in the passive voice, the theory of truth could be extended in an obvious way to this new set of sentences.[14]

One problem touched on in passing by Tarski does not, at least in all its manifestations, have to be solved to get ahead with theory: the existence in natural languages of "ambiguous terms." As long as ambiguity does not affect grammatical form, and can be translated, ambiguity for ambiguity, into the metalanguage, a truth definition will not tell us any

2. Ibid., p. 267.

lies. The trouble, for systematic semantics, with the phrase "believes that" in English is not its vagueness, ambiguity, or unsuitability for incorporation in a serious science: let our metalanguage be English, and all *these* problems will be translated without loss or gain into the metalanguage. But the central problem of the logical grammar of "believes that" will remain to haunt us.

The example is suited to illustrating another, and related, point, for the discussion of belief sentences has been plagued by failure to observe a fundamental distinction between tasks: uncovering the logical grammar or form of sentences (which is in the province of a theory of meaning as I construe it), and the analysis of individual words or expressions (which are treated as primitive by the theory). Thus Carnap, in the first edition of *Meaning and Necessity*, suggested we render "John believes that the earth is round" as "John responds affirmatively to 'the earth is round' as an English sentence." He gave this up when Mates pointed out that John might respond affirmatively to one sentence and not to another no matter how close in meaning. But there is a confusion here from the start. The semantic structure of a belief sentence, according to this idea of Carnap's, is given by a three-place predicate with places reserved for expressions referring to a person, a sentence, and a language. It is a different sort of problem entirely to attempt an analysis of this predicate, perhaps along behavioristic lines. Not least among the merits of Tarski's conception of a theory of truth is that the purity of method it demands of us follows from the formulation of the problem itself, not from the self-imposed restraint of some adventitious philosophical puritanism.

I think it is hard to exaggerate the advantages to philosophy of language of bearing in mind this distinction between questions of logical form or grammar, and the analysis of individual concepts. Another example may help advertise the point.

If we suppose questions of logical grammar settled, sentences like "Bardot is good" raise no special problems for a truth definition. The deep differences between descriptive and evaluative (emotive, expressive, etc.) terms do not show here. Even if we hold there is some important sense in which moral or evaluative sentences do not have a truth value (for example, because they cannot be 'verified'), we ought not to boggle at "'Bardot is good' is true if and only if Bardot is good"; in a theory of truth, this consequence should follow with the rest, keeping track, as must be done, of the semantic location of such sentences in the language as a whole—of their relation to generalizations, their role in such compound sentences as "Bardot is good and Bardot is foolish," and so on. What is special to evaluative words is simply not touched: the mystery is transferred from the word "good" in the object language to its translation in the metalanguage.

But "good" as it features in "Bardot is a good actress" is another matter. The problem is not that the translation of this sentence is not in the metalanguage—let us suppose it is. The problem is to frame a truth definition such that "'Bardot is a good actress' is true if and only if Bardot is a good actress"—and all other sentences like it—are consequences. Obviously "good actress" does not mean "good and an actress." We might think of taking "is a good actress" as an unanalyzed predicate. This would obliterate all connection between "is a good actress" and "is a good mother," and it would give us no excuse to think of "good," in these uses, as a word or semantic element. But worse, it would bar us from framing a truth definition at all, for there is no end to the predicates we would have to treat as logically simple (and hence accommodate in separate clauses in the definition of satisfaction): "is a good companion to dogs," "is a good 28-years-old conversationalist," and so forth. The problem is not peculiar to the case: it is the problem of attributive adjectives generally.

It is consistent with the attitude taken here to deem it usually a strategic error to undertake philosophical analysis of words or expressions which is not preceded by or at any rate accompanied by the attempt to get the logical grammar straight. For how can we have any confidence in our analyses of words like "right," "ought," "can," and "obliged," or the phrases we use to talk of actions, events, and causes, when we do not know what (logical, semantical) parts of speech we have to deal with? I would say much the same about studies of the 'logic' of these and other words, and the sentences containing them. Whether the effort and ingenuity that has gone into the study of deontic logics, modal logics, imperative and erotetic logics has been largely futile or not cannot be known until we have acceptable semantic analyses of the sentences such systems purport to treat. Philosophers and logicians sometimes talk or work as if they were free to choose between, say, the truth-functional conditional and others, or free to introduce non-truth-functional sentential operators like "Let it be the case that" or "It ought to be the case that." But in fact the decision is crucial. When we depart from idioms we can accommodate in a truth definition, we lapse into (or create) language for which we have no coherent semantical account—that is, no account at all of how such talk can be integrated into the language as a whole.

To retun to our main theme: we have recognized that a theory of the kind proposed leaves the whole matter of what individual words mean exactly where it was. Even when the metalanguage is different from the object language, the theory exerts no pressure for improvement, clarification or analysis of individual words, except when, by accident of vocabulary, straightforward translation fails. Just as synonomy, as between expressions, goes generally untreated, so also synonomy of sentences, and analyticity. Even such sentences as "A vixen is a female fox" bear no special tag unless it is our pleasure to provide it. A truth definition does not distinguish between analytic sentences and others, except for sentences that owe their truth to the presence alone of the constants that give the theory its grip on structure: the theory entails not only that these sentences are true but that they will remain true under all significant rewritings of their nonlogical parts. A notion of logical truth thus given limited application, related notions of logical equivalence and entailment will tag along. It is hard to imagine how a theory of meaning could fail to read a logic into its object language to this degree; and to the extent that it does, our intuitions of logical truth, equivalence, and entailment may be called upon in constructing and testing the theory.

I turn now to one more, and very large, fly in the ointment: the fact that the same sentence may at one time or in one mouth be true and at another time or in another mouth be false. Both logicians and those critical of formal methods here seem largely (though by no means universally) agreed that formal semantics and logic are incompetent to deal with the disturbances caused by demonstratives. Logicians have often reacted by down-grading natural language and trying to show how to get along without demonstratives; their critics react by downgrading logic and formal semantics. None of this can make me happy: clearly, demonstratives cannot be eliminated from a natural language without loss or radical change, so there is no choice but to accommodate theory to them.

No logical errors result if we simply treat demonstratives as constants; neither do any problems arise for giving a semantic truth definition. " 'I am wise' is true if and only if I am wise," with its bland ignoring of the demonstrative element in "I" comes off the assembly line along with " 'Socrates is wise' is true if and only if Socrates is wise" with *its* bland indifference to the demonstrative element in "is wise" (the tense).

What suffers in this treatment of demonstratives is not the definition of a truth predicate, but the plausibility of the claim that what has been defined is truth. For this claim is acceptable only if the speaker and circumstances of utterance of each sentence mentioned in the definition is matched by the speaker and circumstances of utterance of the truth definition itself. It could also be fairly pointed out that part of understanding demonstratives is knowing the rules by which they adjust their reference to circumstance; assimilating demonstratives to constant terms obliterates this feature. These complaints can be met, I think, though only by a fairly far-reaching revision in the theory of truth. I shall barely suggest how this could be done, but bare suggestion is all that is needed: the idea is technically trivial, and quite in line with work being done on the logic of the tenses.

We could take truth to be a property, not of sentences, but of utterances, or speech acts, or ordered triples of sentences, times, and persons; but it is simplest just to view truth as a relation between a sentence, a person, and a time. Under such treatment, ordinary logic as now read applies as usual, but only to sets of sentences relativized to the same speaker and time; further logical relations between sentences spoken at different times and by different speakers may be articulated by new axioms. Such is not my concern. The theory of meaning undergoes a systematic but not puzzling change: corresponding to each expression with a demonstrative element there must in the theory be a phrase that relates the truth conditions of sentences in which the expression occurs to changing times and speakers. Thus the theory will entail sentences like the following:

> "I am tired" is true as (potentially) spoken by p at t if and only if p is tired at t.

> "That book was stolen" is true as (potentially) spoken by p at t if and only if the book demonstrated by p at t is stolen prior to t.

Plainly, this course does not show how to eliminate demonstratives; for example, there is no suggestion that "the book demonstrated by the speaker" can be substituted ubiquitously for "that book" *salva veritate*. The fact that demonstratives are amenable to formal treatment ought greatly to improve hopes for a serious semantics of natural language, for it is likely that many outstanding puzzles, such as the analysis of quotations or sentences about propositional attitudes, can be solved if we recognize a concealed demonstrative construction.

Now that we have relativized truth to times and speakers, it is appropriate to glance back at the problem of empirically testing a theory of meaning for an alien tongue. The essence of the method was, it will be remembered, to correlate held-true sentences with held-true sentences by way of a truth definition, and within the bounds of intelligible error. Now the picture must be elaborated to allow for the fact that sentences are true, and held true, only relative to a speaker and a time. The real task is therefore to translate each sentence by another that is true for the same speakers at the same times. Sentences with demonstratives obviously yield a very sensitive test of the correctness of a theory of meaning, and constitute the most direct link between language and the recurrent macroscopic objects of human interest and attention.

In this paper I have assumed that the speakers of a language can effectively determine the meaning or meanings of an arbitrary expression (if it has a meaning), and that it is the central task of a theory of meaning to show how this is possible. I have argued that a characterization of a truth predicate describes the required kind of structure, and provides a clear and testable criterion of an adequate semantics for a natural language. No doubt there are other reasonable demands that may be put on a theory of meaning. But a theory that does no more than define truth for a language comes far closer to constituting a complete theory of meaning than superficial analysis might suggest; so, at least, I have urged.

Since I think there is no alternative, I have taken an optimistic and programmatic view of the possibilities for a formal characterization of a truth predicate for a natural language. But it must be allowed that a staggering list of difficulties and conundrums remains. To name a few: we do not know the logical form of counterfactual or subjunctive sentences, nor of sentences about probabilities and about causal relations; we have no good idea what the logical role of adverbs is, nor the role of attributive adjectives; we have no theory for mass terms like "fire," "water," and "snow," nor for sentences about belief, perception, and intention, nor for verbs of action that imply purpose. And finally, there are all the sentences that seem not to have truth values at all: the imperatives, optatives, interrogatives, and a host more. A comprehensive theory of meaning for a natural language must cope successfully with each of these problems.

Chapter 19

HILARY PUTNAM

Hilary Putnam was born in Chicago in 1926 and educated at the University of Pennsylvania and Harvard University, where he has taught since 1965. He has authored several books and articles, including *Many Faces of Realism* (1963), *Reason, Truth and History* (1965), and *Representation and Reality* (1988). Trained originally in logical positivist tradition, Putnam has moved a considerable distance from that perspective.

One of his most important essays is "Meaning and Reference," reprinted below. In this article he challenges the classical internal theory of meaning, that knowing the meaning of a term is just a matter of being in a certain psychological state. In other words, meanings are just in the head. Putnam offers several counterexamples, the most famous of which is the Twin Earth example in which Oscar on Earth believes that H_2O is water, whereas Oscar's twin on Twin Earth thinks the liquid XYZ is water. What we think of reality doesn't really matter. Water really is H_2O, whether we realize it or not. "Cut the pie any way you like, 'meanings' just ain't in the head."

FOR FURTHER READING

Putnam, Hilary. *Many Faces of Realism* (Open Court Press, 1963).

———. *Reason, Truth and History* (Cambridge University Press, 1965).

———. *Mind, Language and Reality: Philosphical Papers*, 2 vols. (Cambridge University Press, 1975).

———. *Representation and Reality* (MIT Press, 1988).

———. *Realism with a Human Face* (Harvard University Press, 1990).

Meaning and Reference

Unclear as it is, the traditional doctrine that the notion "meaning" possesses the extension/intension ambiguity has certain typical consequences. The doctrine that the meaning of a term is a concept carried the implication that meanings are mental entities. Frege, however, rebelled against this "psychologism." Feeling that meanings are *public* property—that the *same* meaning can be "grasped"

Hillary Putnam, "Meaning and Reference," *The Journal of Philosophy* LXX, 19 (November 8, 1973): 699–711. Reprinted with permission.

by more than one person and by persons at different times—he identified concepts (and hence "intensions" or meanings) with abstract entities rather than mental entities. However, "grasping" these abstract entities was still an individual psychological act. None of these philosophers doubted that understanding a word (knowing its intension) was just a matter of being in a certain psychological state (somewhat in the way in which knowing how to factor numbers in one's head is just a matter of being in a certain very complex psychological state).

Secondly, the timeworn example of the two terms 'creature with a kidney' and 'creature with a heart' does show that two terms can have the same extension and yet differ in intension. But it was taken to be obvious that the reverse is impossible: two terms cannot differ in extension and have the same intension. Interestingly, no argument for this impossibility was ever offered. Probably it reflects the tradition of the ancient and medieval philosophers, who assumed that the concept corresponding to a term was just a conjunction of predicates, and hence that the concept corresponding to a term must *always* provide a necessary and sufficient condition for falling into the extension of the term. For philosophers like Carnap, who accepted the verifiability theory of meaning, the concept corresponding to a term provided (in the ideal case, where the term had "complete meaning") a *criterion* for belonging to the extension (not just in the sense of "necessary and sufficient condition," but in the strong sense of *way of recognizing* whether a given thing falls into the extension or not). So theory of meaning came to rest on two unchallenged assumptions:

(1) That knowing the meaning of a term is just a matter of being in a certain psychological state (in the sense of "psychological state," in which states of memory and belief are "psychological states"; no one thought that knowing the meaning of a word was a continuous state of consciousness, of course).

(2) That the meaning of a term determines its extension (in the sense that sameness of intension entails sameness of extension).

I shall argue that these two assumptions are not jointly satisfied by *any* notion, let alone any notion of meaning. The traditional concept of meaning is a concept which rests on a false theory.

ARE MEANINGS IN THE HEAD?

For the purpose of the following science-fiction examples, we shall suppose that somewhere there is a planet we shall call Twin Earth. Twin Earth is very much like Earth: in fact, people on Twin Earth even speak *English*. In fact, apart from the differences we shall specify in our science-fiction examples, the reader may suppose that Twin Earth is *exactly* like Earth. He may even suppose that he has a *Doppelganger*—an identical copy—on Twin Earth, if he wishes, although my stories will not depend on this.

Although some of the people on Twin Earth (say, those who call themselves "Americans" and those who call themselves "Canadians" and those who call themselves "Englishmen," etc.) speak English, there are, not surprisingly, a few tiny differences between the dialects of English spoken on Twin Earth and standard English.

One of the peculiarities of Twin Earth is that the liquid called "water" is not H_2O but a different liquid whose chemical formula is very long and complicated. I shall abbreviate this chemical formula simply as XYZ. I shall suppose that XYZ is indistinguishable from water at normal temperatures and pressures. Also, I shall suppose that the oceans and lakes and seas of Twin Earth contain XYZ and not water, that it rains XYZ on Twin Earth and not water, etc.

If a space ship from Earth ever visits Twin Earth, then the supposition at first will be that 'water' has the same meaning on Earth and on Twin Earth. This supposition will be corrected when it is discovered that "water" on Twin Earth is XYZ, and the Earthian space ship will report somewhat as follows.

"On Twin Earth the word 'water' means XYZ."

Symmetrically, if a space ship from Twin Earth ever visits Earth, then the supposition at first will be that the word 'water' has the same meaning on Twin Earth and on Earth. This supposition will be corrected when it is discovered that "water" on Earth is H_2O, and the Twin Earthian space ship will report:

"On Earth the word 'water' means H_2O."

Note that there is no problem about the extension of the term 'water': the word simply has two different meanings (as we say); in the sense in which it is used on Twin Earth, the sense of $water_{TE}$, what *we* call "water" simply isn't water, while in the sense in which it is used on Earth, the sense of water$_E$, what the Twin Earthians call "water" simple isn't water. The extension of 'water' in the sense of water$_E$ is the set of all wholes consisting of H_2O molecules, or something like that; the extension of water in the sense of water$_{TE}$ is the set of all wholes consisting of XYZ molecules, or something like that.

Now let us roll the time back to about 1750. The typical Earthian speaker of English did not know that water consisted of hydrogen and oxygen, and the typical Twin-Earthian speaker of English did not know that "water" consisted of XYZ. Let Oscar$_1$ be such a typical Earthian English speaker, and let Oscar$_2$ be his counterpart on Twin Earth. You may suppose that there is no belief that Oscar$_1$ had about water that Oscar$_2$ did not have about "water." If you like, you may even suppose that Oscar$_1$ and Oscar$_2$ were exact duplicates in appearance, feelings, thoughts, interior monologue, etc. Yet the extension of the term 'water' was just as much H_2O on Earth in 1750 as in 1950; and the extension of the term 'water' was just as much XYZ on Twin Earth in 1750 as in 1950. Oscar$_1$ and Oscar$_2$ understood the term 'water' differently in 1750 *although they were in the same psychological state*, and although, given the state of science at the time, it would have taken their scientific communities about fifty years to discover that they understood the term 'water' differently. Thus the extension of the term 'water' (and, in fact, its "meaning" in the intuitive preanalytical usage of that term) is *not* a function of the psychological state of the speaker by itself.

But, it might be objected, why should we accept it that the term 'water' had the same extension in 1750 and in 1950 (on both Earths)? Suppose I point to a glass of water and say "this liquid is called water." My "ostensive definition" of water had the following empirical presupposition: that the body of liquid I am pointing to bears a certain sameness relation (say, *x is the same liquid as y*, or *x is the same*$_L$ *as y*) to most of the stuff I and other speakers in my linguistic community have on other occasions called "water." If this presupposition is false because, say, I am—unknown to me—pointing to a glass of gin and not a glass of water, then I do not intend my ostensive definition to be accepted. Thus the ostensive definition conveys what might be called a "defeasible" necessary and sufficient condition: the necessary and sufficient condition for being water is bearing the relation *same*$_L$ to the stuff in the glass; but this is the necessary and sufficient condition only if the empirical presupposition is satisfied. If it is not satisfied, then one of a series of, so to speak, "fallback" conditions becomes activated.

The key point is that the relation *same*$_L$ is a *theoretical* relation: whether something is or is not the same liquid as *this* may take an indeterminate amount of scientific investigation to determine. Thus, the fact that an English speaker in 1750 might have called XYZ "water," whereas he or his successors would not have called XYZ water in 1800 or 1850 does not mean that the "meaning" of 'water' changed for the average speaker in the interval. In 1750 or in 1850 or in 1950 one might have pointed to, say, the liquid in Lake Michigan as an example of "water." What changed was that in 1750 we would have mistakenly thought that XYZ bore the relation *same*$_L$ to the liquid in Lake Michigan, whereas in 1800 or 1850 we would have known that it did not.

Let us now modify our science-fiction story. I shall suppose that molybdenum pots and pans *can't* be distinguished from aluminum pots and pans save by an expert. (This could be true for all I know, and, *a fortiori*, it could be true for all I know by virtue of "knowing the meaning" of the words *aluminum* and *molybdenum*.) We will now suppose that molybdenum is as common on Twin Earth as aluminum is on Earth, and that aluminum is as rare on Twin Earth as molybdenum is on Earth. In particular, we shall assume that "aluminum" pots and pans are made of molybdenum on Twin Earth. Finally, we shall assume that the words 'aluminum' and 'molybdenum' are *switched* on Twin Earth: 'aluminum' is the name of *molybdenum*, and 'molybdenum' is the name of *aluminum*. If a space ship from Earth visited Twin Earth, the visitors from Earth probably would not suspect that the "aluminum" pots and pans on Twin Earth were not made of aluminum, especially when the Twin Earthians *said* they were. But there is one important difference between the two cases. An Earthian metallurgist could tell very easily that "aluminum" was molybdenum, and a Twin Earthian metallurgist could tell equally easily that aluminum was "molybdenum." (The shudder quotes in the preceding sentence indicate Twin Earthian usages.) Whereas in 1750 no one on either Earth or Twin Earth could have distinguished water from "water," the confusion of aluminum with "aluminum" involves only a part of the linguistic communities involved.

This example makes the same point as the preceding example. If $Oscar_1$ and $Oscar_2$ are standard speakers of Earthian English and Twin Earthian English, respectively, and neither is chemically or metallurgically sophisticated, then there may be no difference at all in their psychological states when they use the word 'aluminum'; nevertheless, we have to say that 'aluminum' has the extension *aluminum* in the idiolect of $Oscar_1$ and the extension *molybdenum* in the idiolect of $Oscar_2$. (Also we have to say that $Oscar_1$ and $Oscar_2$ mean different things by 'aluminum'; that 'aluminum' has a different meaning on Earth than it does on Twin Earth, etc.) Again we see that the psychological state of the speaker does *not* determine the extension (*or* the "meaning," speaking preanalytically) of the word.

Before discussing this example further, let me introduce a *non*-science-fiction example. Suppose you are like me and cannot tell an elm from a beech tree. We will say that the extension of 'elm' in my idiolect is the same as the extension of 'elm' in anyone else's, viz., the set of all elm trees, and that the set of all beech trees is the extension of 'beech' in *both* of our idiolects. Thus 'elm' in my idiolect has a different extension from 'beech' in your idiolect (as it should). Is it really credible that this difference in extension is brought about by some difference in our *concepts*? My *concept* of an elm tree is exactly the same as my concept of a beech tree (I blush to confess). If someone heroically attempts to maintain that the difference between the extension of 'elm' and the extension of 'beech' in *my* idiolect is explained by a difference in my psychological state, then we can always refute him by constructing a "Twin Earth" example—just let the worlds 'elm' and 'beech' be switched on Twin Earth (the way 'aluminum' and 'molybdenum' were in the previous example). Moreover, suppose I have a *Doppelganger* on Twin Earth who is molecule for molecule "identical" with me. If you are a dualist, then also suppose my *Doppelganger* thinks the same verbalized thoughts I do, has the same sense data, the same dispositions, etc. It is absurd to think *his* psychological state is one bit different from mine: yet he 'means' *beech* when he says "elm," and *I* "mean" *elm* when I say "elm." Cut the pie any way you like, "meanings" just ain't in the *head!*

A SOCIOLINGUISTIC HYPOTHESIS

The last two examples depend upon a fact about language that seems, surprisingly, never to have been pointed out: that there is *division of linguistic labor*. We could hardly use such words as 'elm' and 'aluminum' if no one possessed a way of recognizing elm trees and aluminum metal; but not everyone to whom the distinction is important has to be able to make the distinction. Let us shift the example; consider *gold*. Gold is important for many reasons: it is a precious metal; it is a monetary metal; it has symbolic value (it is important to most people that the "gold" wedding ring they wear *really* consist of gold and not just *look* gold); etc. Consider our community as a "factory": in this "factory" some people have the "job" of *wearing gold wedding rings*; other people have the "job" of selling gold wedding rings; still other people have the job of *telling whether or not something is really gold*. It is not at all necessary or efficient that every one who wears a gold ring (or a gold cufflink, etc.), or discusses the "gold standard," etc., engage in buying and selling gold. Nor is it necessary or efficient that every one who buys and sells gold be able to tell whether or not something is really gold in a society where this form of dishonesty is uncommon (selling fake gold) and in which one can easily consult an expert in case of doubt. And it is *certainly* not necessary or efficient that every one who has occasion to buy or wear gold be able to tell with any reliability whether or not something is really gold.

The foregoing facts are just examples of mundane division of labor (in a wide sense). But they engender a division of linguistic labor: every one to whom gold is important for any reason has to *acquire* the word 'gold'; but he does not have to acquire the *method of recognizing* whether something is or is not gold. He can rely on a special subclass of speakers. The features that are generally thought to be present in connection with a general name—necessary and sufficient conditions for membership in the extension, ways of recognizing whether something is in the extension, etc.—are all present in the linguistic community *considered as a collective body*; but that collective body divides the "labor" of knowing and employing these various parts of the "meaning" of 'gold'.

This division of linguistic labor rests upon and presupposes the division of *non*linguistic labor, of course. If only the people who know how to tell whether some metal is really gold or not have any reason to have the word 'gold' in their vocabulary, then the word 'gold' will be as the word 'water' was in 1750 with respect to that subclass of speakers, and the other speakers just won't acquire it at all. And some words do not exhibit any division of linguistic labor: 'chair', for example. But with the increase of division of labor in the society and the rise of science, more and more words begin to exhibit this kind of division of labor. 'Water', for example, did not exhibit it at all before the rise of chemistry. Today it is obviously necessary for every speaker to be able to recognize water (reliably under normal conditions), and probably most adult speakers even know the necessary and sufficient condition "water is H_2O," but only a few adult speakers could distinguish water from liquids that superficially resembled water. In case of doubt, other speakers would rely on the judgment of these "expert" speakers. Thus the way of recognizing possessed by these "expert" speakers is also, through them, possessed by the collective linguistic body, even though it is not possessed by each individual member of the body, and in this way the most *recherché* fact about water may become part of the *social* meaning of the word although unknown to almost all speakers who acquire the word.

It seems to me that this phenomenon of division of linguistic labor is one that it will be very important for sociolinguistics to investigate. In connection with it, I should like to propose the following hypothesis:

> Hypothesis of the Universality of the Divison of Linguistic: Every linguistic community exemplifies the sort of division of linguistic labor just described; that is, it possesses at least some terms whose associated "criteria" are known only to a subset of the speakers who acquire the terms, and whose use by the other speakers depends upon a structured cooperation between them and the speakers in the relevant subsets.

It is easy to see how this phenomenon accounts for some of the examples given above of the failure of the assumptions (1 and 2). When a term is subject to the division of linguistic labor, the "average" speaker who acquires it does not acquire anything that fixes its extension. In particular, his individual psychological state *certainly* does not fix its extension; it is only the sociolinguistic state of the collective linguistic body to which the speaker belongs that fixes the extension.

We may summarize this discussion by pointing out that there are two sorts of tools in the world: there are tools like a hammer or a screwdriver which can be used by one person; and there are tools like a steamship which require the cooperative activity of a number of persons to use. Words have been thought of too much on the model of the first sort of tool.

INDEXICALITY AND RIGIDITY

The first of our science-fiction examples—'water' on Earth and on Twin Earth in 1750—does not involve division of linguistic labor, or at least does not involve it in the same way the examples of 'aluminum' and 'elm' do. There were not (in our story, anyway) any "experts" on water on Earth in 1750, nor any experts on "water" on Twin Earth. The example *does* involve things which are of fundamental importance to the theory of reference and also to the theory of necessary truth, which we shall now discuss.

Let W_1 and W_2 be two possible worlds in which I exist and in which this glass exists and in which I am giving a meaning explanation by pointing to this glass and saying "This is water." Let us suppose that in W_1 the glass is full of H_2O and in W_2 the glass is full of XYZ. We shall also suppose that W_1 is the *actual* world, and that XYZ is the stuff typically called "water" in the world W_2 (so that the relation between English speakers in W_1 and English speakers in W_2 is exactly the same as the relation between English speakers on Earth and English speakers on Twin Earth). Then there are two theories one might have concerning the meaning of 'water':

(1) One might hold that 'water' was *world relative* but *constant* in meaning (i.e., the word has a constant relative meaning). On this theory, 'water' means the same in W_1 and W_2; it's just that water is H_2O in W_1, and water is XYZ in W_2.
(2) One might hold that water is H_2O in all worlds (the stuff called "water" in W_2 isn't water), but 'water' doesn't have the same meaning in W_1 and W_2.

If what was said before about the Twin Earth case was correct, then (2) is clearly the correct theory. When I say "*this* (liquid) is water," the "this" is, so to speak, a *de re* "this"—i.e., the force of my explanation is that "water" is whatever bears a certain equivalence relation (the relation we called "$same_L$" above) to the piece of liquid referred to as "this" *in the actual world.*

We might symbolize the difference between the two theories as a "scope" difference in the following way. On theory (1), the following is true:

(1′) (For every world *W*) (for every *x* in *W*) (*x* is water ≡ *x* bears $same_L$ to the entity referred to as "this" in *W*)

while on theory (2):

(2′) (For every world *W*) (For every *x* in *W*) (*x* is water ≡ *x* bears $same_L$ to the entity referred to as "this" *in the actual world* W_1)

I call this a "scope" difference because in (1′) 'the entity referred to as "this"' is within the scope of 'For every world *W*'—as the qualifying phrase 'in *W*' makes explicit—whereas in (2′) 'the entity referred to as "this"' means "the entity referred to as 'this' *in the actual world*," and has thus a reference *independent* of the bound variable '*W*'.

Kripke calls a designator "rigid" (in a given sentence) if (in that sentence) it refers to the same individual in every possible world in which the designator designates. If we extend this notion of rigidity to substance names, then we may express Kripke's theory and mine by saying that the term 'water' is *rigid*.

The rigidity of the term 'water' follows from the fact that when I give the "ostensive definition": "*this* (liquid) is water," I intend (2′) and not (1′).

We may also say, following Kripke, that when I give the ostensive definition "*this* (liquid) is water," the demonstrative 'this' is *rigid*.

What Kripke was the first to observe is that this theory of the meaning (or "use," or whatever) of the word 'water' (and other natural-kind terms as well) has startling consequences for the theory of necessary truth.

To explain this, let me introduce the notion of a *cross-world relation*. A two-term relation *R* will be called *cross-world* when it is understood in such a way that its extension is a set of ordered pairs of individuals *not all in the same possible world*. For example, it is easy to understand the relation *same height as* as a cross-world relation: just understand it so that, e.g., if *x* is an individual in a world W_1 who is 5 feet tall (in W_1) and *y* is an individual in W_2 who is 5 feet tall (in W_2), then the ordered pair *x*,*y* belongs to the extension of *same height as*. (Since an individual may have different heights in different possible worlds in which that same individual exists, strictly speaking, it is not the ordered pair *x*,*y* that constitutes an element of the extension of *same height as*, but rather the ordered pair *x-in-world-*W_1, *y-in-world-*W_2.)

Similarly, we can understand the relation $same_L$ (same liquid as) as a cross-world relation by understanding it so that a liquid in world W_1 which has the same important physical properties (in W_1) that a liquid in W_2 possesses (in W_2) bears $same_L$ to the latter liquid.

Then the theory we have been presenting may be summarized by saying that an entity *x*, in an arbitrary possible world, is *water* if and only if it bears the relation $same_L$ (construed as a cross-world relation) to the stuff *we* call "water" in the actual world.

Suppose, now, that I have not yet discovered what the important physical properties of water are (in the actual world)—i.e., I don't yet know that water is H_2O. I may have ways of *recognizing* water that are successful (of course, I may make a small number of mistakes that I won't be able to detect until a later stage in our scientific development), but not know the microstructure of water. If I agree that a liquid with the superficial properties of "water" but a different microstructure *isn't really water*, then my ways of recognizing water cannot be regarded as an analytical specification of what *it is to be* water. Rather, the operational definition, like the ostensive one, is simply a way of pointing out a standard—pointing out the stuff *in the actual world* such that, for *x* to be water, in *any* world, is for *x* to bear the relation $same_L$ to the *normal* members of the class of *local* entities that satisfy the operational definition. "Water" on Twin Earth is not water, even if it satisfies the operational definition, because it doesn't bear $same_L$ to the *local* stuff that satisfies the operational definition, and local stuff that satisfies the operational definition but has a microstructure different from the rest of the local stuff that satisfies the operational definition isn't water either, because it doesn't bear $same_L$ to the *normal* examples of the local "water."

Suppose, now, that I discover the microstructure of water—that water is H_2O. At this point I will be able to say that the stuff on Twin Earth that I earlier *mistook* for water isn't really water. In the same way, if you describe, not another planet in the actual universe, but another possible universe in which there is stuff with the chemical formula XYZ which passes the "operational test" for *water*, we shall have to say that that stuff isn't water but merely XYZ. You will not have described a possible world in which "water is XYZ," but merely a possible world in which there are lakes of XYZ, people drink XYZ (and not water), or whatever. In fact, once we have discovered the nature of water, nothing counts as a possible world in which water doesn't have that nature. Once we have discovered that water (in the actual world) is H_2O, *nothing counts as a possible world in which water isn't* H_2O.

On the other hand, we can perfectly well imagine having experiences that would convince us (and that would make it rational to believe that) water *isn't* H_2O. In that sense, it is conceivable that water isn't H_2O. It is conceivable but it isn't possible! Conceivability is no proof of possibility.

Kripke refers to statements that are rationally unrevisble (assuming there are such) as *epistemically necessary*. Statements that are true in all possible worlds he refers to simply as necessary (or sometimes as "metaphysically necessary"). In this terminology, the point just made can be restated as: a statement can be (metaphysically) necessary and epistemically contingent. Human intuition has no privileged access to metaphysical necessity.

In this paper, our interest is in theory of meaning, however, and not in theory of necessary truth. Words like 'now', 'this', 'here' have long been recognized to be *indexical*, or *token-reflexive*—i.e., to have an extension which varies from context to context or token to token. For these words, no one has ever suggested the traditional theory that "intension determines extension." To take our Twin Earth: if I have a *Doppelganger* on Twin Earth, then when I think "I have a headache," *he* thinks "I have a headache." But the extension of the particular token of 'I' in his verbalized thought is himself (or his unit class, to be precise), while the extension of the token of 'I' in *my* verbalized thought is *me* (or my unit class, to be precise). So the same word, 'I', has two different extensions in two different idiolets; but it does not follow that the concept I have of myself is in any way different from the concept my *Doppelganger* has of himself.

Now then, we have maintained that indexicality extends beyond the *obviously* indexical words and morphemes (e.g., the tenses of verbs). Our theory can be summarized as saying that words like 'water' have an unnoticed indexical component: "water" is stuff that bears a certain similarity relation to the water *around here*. Water at another time or in another place or even in another possible world has to bear the relation $same_L$ to *our* "water" *in order to be water*. Thus the theory that (1) words have "intensions," which are something like concepts associated with the words by speakers; and (2) intension determines extension—cannot be true of natural kind words like 'water' for the same reason it cannot be true of obviously indexical words like 'I'.

The theory that natural-kind words like 'water' are indexical leaves it open, however, whether to say that 'water' in the Twin Earth dialect of English has the same *meaning* as 'water' in the Earth dialect and a different extension—which is what we normally say about 'I' in different idiolects—thereby giving up the doctrine that "meaning (intension) determines extension," or to say, as we have chosen to do, that difference in extension is *ipso facto* a difference in meaning for natural kind words, thereby giving up the doctrine that meanings are concepts, or, indeed, mental entities of *any* kind.[1]

It should be clear, however, that Kripke's doctrine that natural-kind words are rigid designators and our doctrine that they are indexical are but two ways of making the same point.

We have now seen that the extension of a term is not fixed by a concept that the individual speaker has in his head, and this is true both because extension is, in general, determined *socially*—there is division of linguistic labor as much as of "real" labor—and because extension is, in part, determined *indexically*. The extension of our terms depends upon the actual nature of the particular things that serve as paradigms, and this actual nature is not, in general, fully known to the speaker. Traditional semantic theory leaves out two contributions to the determination of reference—the contribution of society and the contribution of the real world; a better semantic theory must encompass both.

Notes

1. Our reasons for rejecting the first option—to say that 'water' has the same meaning on Earth and on Twin Earth, while giving up the doctrine that meaning determines reference—are presented in "The Meaning of 'Meaning'." They may be illustrated thus: Suppose 'water' has the same meaning on Earth and on Twin Earth. Now, let the word 'water' become phonemically different on Twin Earth—say, it becomes 'quaxel'. Presumably, this is not a change in meaning per se, on any view. So 'water' and 'quaxel' have the same meaning (although they refer to different liquids). But this is highly counterintuitive. Why not say, then, that 'elm' in my idiolect has the same meaning as 'beech' in your idiolect, although they refer to different trees?

Chapter 20

PETER F. STRAWSON

Peter Strawson (1919–   ), eminent logician and metaphysician, was Professor of Philosophy at Oxford University from 1968 until his recent retirement. He is the author of several important works in metaphysics, philosophical logic, and philosophy of language.

Strawson first considers the deterministic thesis about human action. He claims to be unclear about exactly what it is, but he seems to imply something like this: all of our actions have antecedent causes to which they are linked by causal laws of the kind that govern other events in the universe. For determinists, moral responsibility is an incoherent notion, since it rests on a notion of free will that makes the agent a causa sui—a cause of one's own self. Strawson considers an optimistic (comptibilist) and pessimistic reaction to the determinist thesis. The optimist thinks the thesis can be reconciled with responsibility, whereas the pessimist denies this. Strawson then considers how praise, blame, and responsibility work in everyday life. He labels our reactions to certain types of treatment "reactive attitudes." For example, if someone intentionally steps on my fingers, I will react differently than I would if he accidentally stepped on them, while trying to help me. Though in both cases my fingers will hurt just as much, in the former I will feel resentment, but not in the latter. Similarly, we feel gratitude, praise, blame, and moral indignation toward others regarding their interpersonal behavior, depending on their intentions in doing harmful or beneficial acts. These reactive attitudes go to the heart of our self-esteem and sense of value, so we cannot get rid of them, even if we wanted to.

FOR FURTHER READING

Strawson, Peter. *Individuals* (Methuen, 1959).

———. *The Bounds of Sense* (Routledge & Kegan Paul, 1966).

———. *Freedom and Resentment, and Other Essays* (1974).

Freedom and Resentment

Some philosophers say they do not know what the thesis of determinism is. Others say, or imply, that they do know what it is. Of these, some—the pessimists perhaps—hold that if the thesis is true, then the concepts of moral obligation and responsibility really have no application, and the practices of punishing and blaming, of expressing moral condemnation and approval, are really unjustified. Others—the optimists perhaps—hold that these concepts and practices in no way lose their *raison d'être* if the thesis of determinism is true. Some hold even that the justification of these concepts and practices requires the truth of the thesis. There is another opinion which is less frequently voiced: the opinion, it might be said, of the genuine moral sceptic. This is that the notions of moral guilt, of blame, of moral responsibility are inherently confused and that we can see this to be so if we consider the consequences either of the truth of determinism or of its falsity. The holders of this opinion agree with the pessimists that these notions lack application if determinism is true, and add simply that they also lack it if determinism is false. If I am asked which of these parties I belong to, I must say it is the first of all, the party of those who do not know what the thesis of determinism is. But this does not stop me from having some sympathy with the others, and a wish to reconcile them. Should not ignorance, rationally, inhibit such sympathies? Well, of course, though darkling, one has some inkling—some notion of what sort of thing is being talked about. This lecture is intended as a move towards reconciliation; so is likely to seem wrongheaded to everyone.

But can there be any possibility of reconciliation between such clearly opposed positions as those of pessimists and optimists about determinism? Well, there might be a formal withdrawal on one side in return for a substantial concession on the other. Thus, suppose the optimist's position were put like this: (1) the facts as we know them do not show determinism to be false; (2) the facts as we know them supply an adequate basis for the concepts and practices which the pessimist feels to be imperilled by the possibility of determinism's truth. Now it might be that the optimist is right in this, but is apt to give an inadequate account of the facts as we know them, and of how they constitute an adequate basis for the problematic concepts and practices; that the reasons he gives for the adequacy of the basis are themselves inadequate and leave out something vital. It might be that the pessimist is rightly anxious to get this vital thing back and, in the grip of his anxiety, feels he has to go beyond the facts as we know them; feels that the vital thing can be secure only if, beyond the facts as we know them, there is the further fact that determinism is false. Might *he* not be brought to make a formal withdrawal in return for a vital concession?

2. Let me enlarge very briefly on this, by way of preliminary only. Some optimists about determinism point to the efficacy of the practices of punishment, and of moral condemnation and approval, in regulating behaviour in socially desirable ways.[1] In the fact of their efficacy, they suggest, is an adequate basis for these practices; and this fact certainly does not show determinism to be false. To this the pessimists reply, all in a rush, that *just* punishment and *moral* condemnation imply moral guilt and guilt implies moral responsibility and moral responsibility implies freedom and freedom implies the falsity of determinism. And to this the optimists are wont to reply in turn that it is true that these practices require freedom in a sense, and the existence of freedom in this sense is one of the facts as we know them. But what 'freedom' means here is nothing but the absence of certain conditions the presence of which would make moral condemnation or punishment inappropriate. They have in mind conditions like compulsion by another, or innate incapacity, or insanity, or other less extreme forms of psychological disorder, or the existence of circumstances in which the making of any other choice would be

1. Cf. P. H. Nowell-Smith, 'Freewill and Moral Responsibility', *Mind*, 1948.

morally inadmissible or would be too much to expect of any man. To this list they are constrained to add other factors which, without exactly being limitations of freedom, may also make moral condemnation or punishment inappropriate or mitigate their force: as some forms of ignorance, mistake, or accident. And the general reason why moral condemnation or punishment are inappropriate when these factors or conditions are present is held to be that the practices in question will be generally efficacious means of regulating behaviour in desirable ways only in cases where these factors are *not* present. Now the pessimist admits that the facts as we know them include the existence of freedom, the occurrence of cases of free action, in the negative sense which the optimist concedes; and admits, or rather insists, that the existence of freedom in this sense is compatible with the truth of determinism. Then what does the pessimist find missing? When he tries to answer this question, his language is apt to alternate between the very familiar and the very unfamiliar.[2] Thus he may say, familiarly enough, that the man who is the subject of justified punishment, blame or moral condemnation must really *deserve* it; and then add, perhaps, that, in the case at least where he is blamed for a positive act rather than an omission, the condition of his really deserving blame is something that goes beyond the negative freedoms that the optimist concedes. It is, say, a genuinely free identification of the will with the act. And this is the condition that is incompatible with the truth of determinism.

The conventional, but conciliatory, optimist need not give up yet. He may say: Well, people often decide to do things, really intend to do what they do, know just what they're doing in doing it; the reasons they think they have for doing what they do, often really are their reasons and not their rationalizations. These facts, too, are included in the facts as we know them. If this is what you mean by freedom—by the identification of the will with the act—then freedom may again be conceded. But again the concession is compatible with the truth of the determinist thesis. For it would not follow from that thesis that nobody decides to do anything; that nobody ever does anything intentionally; that it is false that people sometimes know perfectly well what they are doing. I tried to define freedom negatively. You want to give it a more positive look. But it comes to the same thing. Nobody denies freedom in this sense, or these senses, and nobody claims that the existence of freedom in these senses shows determinism to be false.

But it is here that the lacuna in the optimistic story can be made to show. For the pessimist may be supposed to ask: But *why* does freedom in this sense justify blame, etc.? You turn towards me first the negative, and then the positive, faces of a freedom which nobody challenges. But the only reason you have given for the practices of moral condemnation and punishment in cases where this freedom is present is the efficacy of these practices in regulating behaviour in socially desirable ways. But this is not a sufficient basis, it is not even the right *sort* of basis, for these practices as we understand them.

Now my optimist, being the sort of man he is, is not likely to invoke an intuition of fittingness at this point. So he really has no more to say. And my pessimist, being the sort of man he is, has only one more thing to say; and that is that the admissibility of these practices, as we understand them, demands another kind of freedom, the kind that in turn demands the falsity of the thesis of determinism. But might we not induce the pessimist to give up saying this by giving the optimist something more to say?

3. I have mentioned punishing and moral condemnation and approval; and it is in connexion with these practices or attitudes that the issue between optimists and pessimists—of, if one is a pessimist, the issue between determinists and libertarians—is felt to be particularly important. But it is not of these practices and attitudes that I propose, at first, to speak. These practices or attitudes permit, where they do not imply, a certain detachment from the actions or agents which are their objects. I want to speak, at least at first, of something else: of the non-detached attitudes and reactions of people directly involved in transactions with each other; of the attitudes and reactions of offended parties and beneficiaries; of such things as gratitude, resentment, forgiveness, love, and hurt feelings. Perhaps something like the issue between optimists and pessimists arises in this neighbouring field too; and since this field is less crowded with disputants, the issue might here be easier to settle; and if it is settled here, then it might become easier to settle it in the disputant-crowded field.

What I have to say consists largely of commonplaces. So my language, like that of commonplaces

2. As Nowell-Smith pointed out in a later article: 'Determinists and Libertarians', *Mind*, 1954.

generally, will be quite unscientific and imprecise. The central commonplace that I want to insist on is the very great importance that we attach to the attitudes and intentions towards us of other human beings, and the great extent to which our personal feelings and reactions depend upon, or involve, our beliefs about these attitudes and intentions. I can give no simple description of the field of phenomena at the centre of which stands this commonplace truth; for the field is too complex. Much imaginative literature is devoted to exploring its complexities; and we have a large vocabulary for the purpose. There are simplifying styles of handling it in a general way. Thus we may, like La Rochefoucauld, put self-love or self-esteem or vanity at the centre of the picture and point out how it may be caressed by the esteem, or wounded by the indifference or contempt, of others. We might speak, in another jargon, of the need for love, and the loss of security which results from its withdrawal; or, in another, of human self-respect and its connexion with the recognition of the individual's dignity. These simplifications are of use to me only if they help to emphasize how much we actually mind, how much it matters to us, whether the actions of other people—and particularly of *some* other people—reflect attitudes towards us of goodwill, affection, or esteem on the one hand or contempt, indifference, or malevolence on the other. If someone treads on my hand accidentally, while trying to help me, the pain may be no less acute than if he treads on it in contemptuous disregard of my existence or with a malevolent wish to injure me. But I shall generally feel in the second case a kind and degree of resentment that I shall not feel in the first. If someone's actions help me to some benefit I desire, then I am benefited in any case; but if he intended them so to benefit me because of his general goodwill towards me, I shall reasonably feel a gratitude which I should not feel at all if the benefit was an incidental consequence, unintended or even regretted by him, of some plan of action with a different aim.

These examples are of actions which confer benefits or inflict injuries over and above any conferred or inflicted by the mere manifestation of attitude and intention themselves. We should consider also in how much of our behaviour the benefit or injury resides mainly or entirely in the manifestation of attitude itself. So it is with good manners, and much of what we call kindness, on the one hand; with deliberate rudeness, studied indifference, or insult on the other.

Besides resentment and gratitude, I mentioned just now forgiveness. This is a rather unfashionable subject in moral philosophy at present; but to be forgiven is something we sometimes ask, and forgiving is something we sometimes say we do. To ask to be forgiven is in part to acknowledge that the attitude displayed in our actions was such as might properly be resented and in part to repudiate that attitude for the future (or at least for the immediate future); and to forgive is to accept the repudiation and to forswear the resentment.

We should think of the many different kinds of relationship which we can have with other people—as sharers of a common interest; as members of the same family; as colleagues; as friends; as lovers; as chance parties to an enormous range of transactions and encounters. Then we should think, in each of these connexions in turn, and in others, of the kind of importance we attach to the attitudes and intentions towards us of those who stand in these relationships to us, and of the kinds of *reactive* attitudes and feelings to which we ourselves are prone. In general, we demand some degree of goodwill or regard on the part of those who stand in these relationships to us, though the forms we require it to take vary widely in different connexions. The range and intensity of our *reactive* attitudes towards goodwill, its absence or its opposite vary no less widely. I have mentioned, specifically, resentment and gratitude; and they are a usefully opposed pair. But, of course, there is a whole continuum of reactive attitude and feeling stretching on both sides of these and—the most comfortable area—in between them.

The object of these commonplaces is to try to keep before our minds something it is easy to forget when we are engaged in philosophy, especially in our cool, contemporary style, viz. what it is actually like to be involved in ordinary inter-personal relationships, ranging from the most intimate to the most causal.

4. It is one thing to ask about the general causes of these reactive attitudes I have alluded to; it is another to ask about the variations to which they are subject, the particular conditions in which they do or do not seem natural or reasonable or appropriate; and it is a third thing to ask what it would be like, what it *is* like, not to suffer them. I am not much concerned with the first question; but I am with the second; and perhaps even more with the third.

Let us consider, then, occasions for resentment: situations in which one person is offended or injured by the action of another and in which—in the absence of special considerations—the offended person might naturally or normally be expected to feel resentment. Then let us consider what sorts of special considerations might be expected to modify or mollify this feeling or remove it altogether. It needs no saying now how multifarious these considerations are. But, for my purpose, I think they can be roughly divided into two kinds. To the first group belong all those which might give occasion for the employment of such expressions as 'He didn't mean to', 'He hadn't realized', 'He didn't know'; and also all those which might give occasion for the use of the phrase 'He couldn't help it', when this is supported by such phrases as 'He was pushed','He had to do it','It was the only way', 'They left him no alternative', etc. Obviously these various pleas, and the kinds of situations in which they would be appropriate, differ from each other in striking and important ways. But for my present purpose they have something still more important in common. None of them invites us to suspend towards the agent, either at the time of his action or in general, our ordinary reactive attitudes. They do not invite us to view the *agent* as one in respect of whom these attitudes are in any way inappropriate. They invite us to view the *injury* as one in respect of which a particular one of these attitudes is inappropriate. They do not invite us to see the *agent* as other than a fully responsible agent. They invite us to see the *injury* as one for which he was not fully, or at all, responsible. They do not suggest that the agent is in any way an inappropriate object of that kind of demand for goodwill or regard which is reflected in our ordinary reactive attitudes. They suggest instead that the fact of injury was not in this case incompatible with that demand's being fulfilled, that the fact of injury was quite consistent with the agent's attitude and intentions being just what we demand they should be.[3] The agent was just ignorant of the injury he was causing, or had lost his balance through being pushed or had reluctantly to cause the injury for reasons which acceptable override his reluctance. The offering of such pleas by the agent and their acceptance by the sufferer is something in no way opposed to, or outside the context of, ordinary inter-personal relationships and the manifestation of ordinary reactive attitudes. Since things go wrong and situations are complicated, it is an essential and integral element in the transactions which are the life of these relationships.

The second group of considerations is very different. I shall take them in two subgroups of which the first is far less important than the second. In connexion with the first subgroup we may think of such statements as 'He wasn't himself', 'He has been under very great strain recently', 'He was acting under post-hypnotic suggestion'; in connexion with the second, we may think of 'He's only a child', 'He's a hopeless schizophrenic', 'His mind has been systematically perverted', 'That's purely compulsive behaviour on his part'. Such pleas as these do, as pleas of my first general group do not, invite us to suspend our ordinary reactive attitudes towards the agent, either at the time of his action or all the time. They do not invite us to see the agent's action in a way consistent with the full retention of ordinary inter-personal attitudes and merely inconsistent with one particular attitude. They invite us to view the agent himself in a different light from the light in which we should normally view one who has acted as he has acted. I shall not linger over the first subgroup of cases. Through they perhaps raise, in the short term, questions akin to those raised, in the long term, by the second subgroup, we may dismiss them without considering those questions by taking that admirably suggestive phrase, 'He wasn't himself', with the seriousness that—for all its being logically comic—it deserves. We shall not feel resentment against the man he is for the action done by the man he is not; or at least we shall feel less. We normally have to deal with him under normal stresses; so we shall not feel towards him, when he acts as he does under abnormal stresses, as we should have felt towards him had he acted as he did under normal stresses.

The second and more important subgroup of cases allows that the circumstances were normal, but presents the agent as psychologically abnormal—or as morally undeveloped. The agent was himself; but he is warped or deranged, neurotic or just a child. When we see someone in such a light as this, all our reactive attitudes tend to be profoundly modified. I must deal here in crude dichotomies and ignore the ever-interesting and ever-illuminating varieties of case. What I want to contrast is the attitude (or range of attitudes) of involvement or participation in a human relationship, on the one hand, and what might be called the objective attitude (or range of attitudes) to another human being, on the other. Even in the same situation, I must add, they are not altogether

3. Perhaps not in every case *just* what we demand they should not be. For my present purpose these difference do not matter.

exclusive of each other; but they are, profoundly, *opposed* to each other. To adopt the objective attitude to another human being is to see him, perhaps, as an object of social policy; as a subject for what, in a wide range of sense, might be called treatment; as something certainly to be taken account, perhaps precautionary account, of; to be managed or handled or cured or trained; perhaps simply to be avoided, though *this* gerundive is not peculiar to cases of objectivity of attitude. The objective attitude may be emotionally toned in many ways, but not in all ways: it may include repulsion or fear, it may include pity or even love, though not all kinds of love. But it cannot include the range of reactive feelings and attitudes which belong to involvement or participation with others in inter-personal human relationships; it cannot include resentment, gratitude, forgiveness, anger or the sort of love which two adults can sometimes be said to feel reciprocally, for each other. If your attitude towards someone is wholly objective, then though you may fight him, you cannot quarrel with him, and though you may talk to him, even negotiate with him, you cannot reason with him. You can at most pretend to quarrel, or to reason, with him.

Seeing someone, then, as warped or deranged or compulsive in behaviour or peculiarly unfortunate in his formative circumstances—seeing someone so tends, at least to some extent, to set him apart from normal participant reactive attitudes on the part of one who so sees him, tends to promote, at least in the civilized, objective attitude is not only something we naturally tend to fall into in cases like these, where participant attitudes are partially or wholly inhibited by abnormalities or by immaturity. It is also something which is available as a resource in other cases too. We look with an objective eye on the compulsive behaviour of the neurotic or the tiresome behaviour of a very young child, thinking in terms of treatment or training. But we *can* sometimes look with something like the same eye on the behaviour of the normal and the mature. We *have* this resource and can sometimes use it: as a refuge, say, from the strains of involvement; or as an aid to policy; or simply out of intellectual curiosity. Being human, we cannot, in the normal case, do this for long, or altogether. If the strains of involvement, say, continue to be too great, then we have to do something else—like severing a relationship. But what is above all interesting is the tension there is, in us, between the participant attitude and the objective attitude. One is tempted to say: between our humanity and our intelligence. But to say this would be to distort both notions.

What I have called the participant reactive attitudes are essentially natural human reactions to the good or ill will or indifference of others towards us, as displayed in *their* attitudes and actions. The question we have to ask is: What effect would, or should, the acceptance of the truth of a general thesis of determinism have upon these reactive attitudes? More specifically, would, or should, the acceptance of the truth of the thesis lead to the decay or the repudiation of all such attitudes? Would, or should, it mean the end of gratitude, resentment, and forgiveness; of all reciprocated adult loves; of all the essentially *personal* antagonisms?

But how can I answer, or even pose, this question without knowing *exactly* what the thesis of determinism is? Well, there is one thing we do know: that if there is a coherent thesis of determinism, then there must be a sense of 'determined' such that, if that thesis is true, then all behaviour whatever is determined in that sense. Remembering this, we can consider at least what possibilities lie formally open; and then perhaps we shall see that the question can be answered *without* knowing exactly what the thesis of determinism is. We can consider what possibilities lie open because we have already before us an account of the ways in which particular reactive attitudes, or reactive attitudes in general, may be, and, sometimes, we judge, should be, inhibited. Thus I considered earlier a group of considerations which tend to inhibit, and, we judge, should inhibit, resentment, in particular cases of an agent causing an injury, without inhibiting reactive attitudes in general towards that agent. Obviously this group of considerations cannot strictly bear upon our question; for that question concerns reactive attitudes in general. But resentment has a particular interest; so it is worth adding that it has never been claimed as a consequence of the truth of determinism that one or another of *these* considerations was operative in every case of an injury being caused by an agent; that it would follow from the truth of determinism that anyone who caused an injury *either* was quite simply ignorant of causing it *or* had acceptably overiding reasons for acquiescing reluctantly in causing it *or* . . . , etc. The prevalence of this happy state of affairs would not be a consequence of the reign of universal determinism, but of the reign of universal goodwill. We cannot, then, find here the possibility of an affirmative answer to our question, even for the particular case of resentment.

Next, I remarked that the participant attitude, and the personal reactive attitudes in general, tend to give place, and it is judged by the civilized should give place, to objective attitudes, just in so far as the agent is seen as excluded from ordinary adult human relationships by deep-rooted psychological abnormality—or simply by being a child. But it cannot be a consequence of any thesis which is not itself self-contradictory that abnormality is the universal condition.

Now this dismissal might seem altogether too facile; and so, in a sense, it is. But whatever is too quickly dismissed in this dismissal is allowed for in the only possible form of affirmative answer that remains. We can sometimes, and in part, I have remarked, look on the normal (those we rate as 'normal) in the objective way in which we have learned to look on certain classified cases of abnormality. And our question reduces to this: could, or should, the acceptance of the determinist thesis lead us always to look on everyone exclusively in this way? For this is the only condition worth considering under which the acceptance of determinism could lead to the decay or repudiation of participant reactive attitudes.

It does not seem to be self-contradictory to suppose that this might happen. So I suppose we must say that it is not absolutely inconceivable that it should happen. But I am strongly inclined to think that it is, for us we as we are, practically inconceivable. The human commitment to participation in ordinary inter-personal relationships is, I think, too thoroughgoing and deeply rooted for us to take seriously the thought that a general theoretical conviction might so change our world that, in it, there were no longer any such things as inter-personal relationships as we normally understand them; and being involved in inter-personal relationships as we normally understand them precisely is being exposed to the range of reactive attitudes and feelings that is in question.

This, then, is a part of the reply to our question. A sustained objectivity of inter-personal attitude, and the human isolation which that would entail, does not seem to be something of which human beings would be capable, even if some general truth were a theoretical ground for it. But this is not all. There is a further point, implict in the foregoing, which must be made explicit. Exceptionally, I have said, we can have direct dealings with human beings without any degree of personal involvement, treating them simply as creatures to be handled in our own interest, or our side's, or society's—or even theirs. In the extreme case of the mentally deranged, it is easy to see the connexion between the possibility of a wholly objective attitude and the impossibility of what we understand by ordinary interpersonal relationships. Given this latter impossibility, no other civilized attitude is available than that of viewing the deranged person simply as something to be understood and controlled in the most desirable fashion. To view him as outside the reach of personal relationships is already, for the civilized, to view him in this way. For reasons of policy or self-protection we may have occasion, perhaps temporary, to adopt a fundamentally similar attiude to a 'normal' human being; to concentrate, that is, on understanding 'how he works', with a view to determining our policy accordingly, or to finding in that very understanding a relief from the strains of involvement. Now it is certainly true that in the case of the abnormal, though not in the case of the normal, our adoption of the objective attitude is a consequence of our viewing the agent as *incapacitated* in some or all respects for ordinary inter-personal relationships. He is thus incapacitated, perhaps, by the fact that his picture of reality is pure fantasy, that he does not, in a sense, live in the real world at all; or by the fact that his behaviour is, in part, an unrealistic acting out of unconscious purposes; or by the fact that he is an idiot, or a moral idiot. But there is something else which, *because* this is true, is equally certainly *not* true. And that is that there is a sense of 'determined' such that (1) if determinism is true, all behaviour is determined in this sense, and (2) determinism might be true, i.e. it is not inconsistent with the facts as we know them to suppose that all behaviour might be determined in this sense, and (3) our adoption of the objective attitude towards the abnormal is the result of a prior embracing of the belief that the behaviour, or the relevant stretch of behaviour, of the human being in question *is* determined in this sense. Neither in the case of the normal, then, nor in the case of the abnormal is it true that, when we adopt an objective attitude, we do so *because* we hold such a belief. So my answer has two parts. The first is that we cannot, as we are, seriously envisage ourselves adopting a thoroughgoing objectivity of attitude to others as a result of theoretical conviction of the truth of determinism; and the second is that when we do in fact adopt such an attitude in a particular case, our doing so is not the consequence of a theoretical conviction which might be expressed as 'Determinism in this case', but is a consequence of our abandoning, for different reasons in different cases, the ordinary inter-personal attitudes.

It might be said that all this leaves the real question unanswered, and that we cannot hope to answer it without knowing exactly what the thesis of determinism is. For the real question is not a question about what we actually do, or why we do it. It is not even a question about what we would *in fact* do if a certain theoretical conviction gained general acceptance. It is a question about what it would be *rational* to do if determinism were true, a question about the rational justification of ordinary inter-personal attitudes in general. To this I shall reply, first, that such a question could seem real only to one who had utterly failed to grasp the purport of the preceding answer, the fact of our natural human commitment to ordinary inter-personal attitudes. This commitment is part of the general framework of human life, not something that can come up for review as particular cases can come up for review within this general framework. And I shall reply, second, that if we could imagine what we cannot have, viz. a choice in this matter, then we could choose rationally only in the light of an assessment of the gains and losses to human life, its enrichment or impoverishment; and the truth or falsity of a general thesis of determinism would not bear on the rationality of *this* choice.[4]

5. The point of this discussion of the reactive attitudes in their relation—or lack of it—to the thesis of determinism was to bring us, if possible, nearer to a position of compromise in a more usual area of debate. We are not now to discuss reactive attitudes which are essentially those of offended parties or beneficiaries. We are to discuss reactive attitudes which are essentially not those, or only incidentally are those, of offended parties or beneficiaries, but are nevertheless, I shall claim, kindred attitudes to those I have discussed. I put resentment in the center of the previous discussion. I shall put moral indignation—or, more weakly, moral disapprobation—in the centre of this one.

The reactive attitudes I have so far discussed are essentially reactions to the quality of others' wills towards us, as manifested in their behaviour: to their good or ill will or indifference or lack of concern. Thus resentment, or what I have called resentment, is a reaction to injury or indifference. The reactive attitudes I have now to discuss might be described as the sympathetic or vicarious or impersonal or disinterested or generalized analogues of the reactive attitudes I have already discussed. They are reactions to the qualities of others' wills, not towards ourselves, but towards others. Because of this impersonal or vicarious character, we give them different names. Thus one who experiences the vicarious analogue of resentment is said to be indignant or disapproving, or morally indignant or disapproving. What we have here is, as it were, resentment on behalf of another, where one's own interest and dignity are not involved; and it is this impersonal or vicarious character of the attitude, added to its others, which entitle it to the qualification 'moral'. Both my description of, and my name for, these attitudes are, in one important respect, a little misleading. It is not that these attitudes are essentially vicarious—one can feel indignation on one's own account—but that they are essentially capable of being vicarious. But I shall retain the name for the sake of its suggestiveness; and I hope that what is misleading about it will be corrected in what follows.

The personal reactive attitudes rest on, and reflect, an expectation of, and demand for, the manifestation of a certain degree of goodwill or regard on the part of other human beings towards ourselves; or at least on the expectation of, and demand for, an absence of the manifestation of active ill will or indifferent disregard. (What will, in particular cases, *count* as manifestations of good or ill will or disregard will vary in accordance with the particular relationship in which we stand to another human being.) The generalized or vicarious analogues of the personal reactive attitudes rest on, and reflect, exactly the same expectation or demand in a generalized form; they rest on, or reflect, that is, the demand for the manifestation of a reasonable degree

4. The question, then, of the connexion between rationality and the adoption of the objective attitude to others is misposed when it is made to seem dependent on the issue of determinism. But there is another question which should be raised, if only to distinguish it from the misposed question. Quite apart from the issue of determinism, might it not be said that we should be nearer to being purely rational creatures in proportion as our relation to others was in fact dominated by the objective attitude? I think this might be said; only it would have to be added, once more, that if such a choice were possible, it would not necessarily be rational to choose to be more purely rational than we are.

of goodwill or regard, on the part of others, not simply towards oneself, but towards all those on whose behalf moral indignation may be felt, i.e. as we now think, towards all men. The generalized and non-generalized forms of demand, and the vicarious and personal reactive attitudes which rest upon, and reflect, them are connected not merely logically. They are connected humanly; and not merely with each other. They are connected also with yet another set of attitudes which I must mention now in order to complete the picture. I have considered from two points of view the demands we make on others and our reactions to their possibly injurious actions. These were the points of view of one whose interest was directly involved (who suffers, say, the injury) and of others whose interest was not directly involved (who do not themselves suffer the injury). Thus I have spoken of personal reactive attitudes in the first connexion and of their vicarious analogues in the second. But the picture is not complete unless we consider also the correlates of these attitudes on the part of those on whom the demands are made, on the part of the agents. Just as there are personal and vicarious reactive attitudes associated with demands on others for oneself and demands on others for others, so there are self-reactive attitudes associated with demands on oneself for others. And here we have to mention such phenomena as feeling bound or obliged (the 'sense of obligation'); feeling compunction; feeling guilty or remorseful or at least responsible; and the more complicated phenomenon of shame.

All these three types of attitude are humanly connected. One who manifested the personal reactive attitudes in a high degree but showed no inclination at all to their vicarious analogues would appear as an abnormal case of moral egocentricity, as a kind of moral solipsist. Let him be supposed fully to acknowledge the claims to regard that others had on him, to be susceptible of the whole range of self-reactive attitudes. He would then see himself as unique both as one (*the* one) who had a general claim on human regard and as one (*the* one) on whom human beings in general had such a claim. This would be a kind of moral solipsism. But it is barely more than a conceptual possibility; if it is that. In general, though within varying limits, we demand of others for others, as well as of ourselves for others, something of the regard which we demand of others for ourselves. Can we imagine, besides that of the moral solipsist, any other case of one or two of these three types of attitude being fully developed, but quite unaccomapanied by any trace, however slight, of the remaining two or one? If we can, then we imagine something far below or far above the level of our common humanity—a moral idiot or a saint. For all these types of attitudes alike have common roots in our human nature and our membership of human communities.

Now, as of the personal reactive attitudes, so of their vicarious analogues, we must ask in what ways, and by what considerations, they tend to be inhibited. Both types of attitude involve, or express, a certain sort of demand for inter-personal regard. The fact of injury constitutes a prima facie appearance of this demand's being flouted or unfulfilled. We saw, in the case of resentment, how one class of considerations may show this appearance to be mere appearance, and hence inhibit resentment, *without* inhibiting, or displacing, the sort of demand of which resentment can be an expression, without in any way tending to make us suspend our ordinary inter-personal attitudes to the agent. Considerations of this class operate in just the same way, for just the same reasons, in connexion with moral disapprobation or indignation; they inhibit indignation without in any way inhibiting the sort of demand on the agent of which indignation can be an expression, the range of attitudes towards him to which it belongs. But in this connexion we may express the facts with a new emphasis. We may say, stressing the moral, the generalized aspect of the demand: considerations of this group have no tendency to make us see the agent as other than a morally responsible agent; they simply make us see the injury as one for which he was not morally responsible. The offering and acceptance of such exculpatory pleas as are here in question in no way detracts in our eyes from the agent's status as a term of moral relationships. On the contrary, since things go wrong and situations are complicated, it is an essential part of the life of such relationships.

But suppose we see the agent in a different light: as one whose picture of the world is an insane delusion; or as one whose behaviour, or a part of whose behaviour, is unintelligible to us, perhaps even to him, in terms of conscious purposes, and intelligible only in terms of unconscious purposes; or even, perhaps, as one wholly impervious to the self-reactive attitudes I spoke of, wholly lacking, as we say, in moral sense. Seeing an agent in such a light as this tends, I said, to inhibit resentment in a wholly different way. It tends to inhibit resentment because it tends to inhibit ordinary inter-personal attitudes in general, and the kind of demand and expectation which those attitudes involve; and tends to promote instead the purely objective view of the agent as one posing problems simply of intellectual understanding, management, treatment, and control. Again the parallel holds for those generalized or moral attitudes towards the agent which we are now concerned with. The same abnormal light which shows the agent to us as one in respect of whom the personal attitudes, the personal demand, are to be suspended, shows him to us also as one in respect of whom the impersonal attitudes, the generalized demand, are to be suspended. Only, abstracting now from direct personal interest, we may express the facts with a new emphasis. We may say: to the extent to which the agent is seen in this light, he is not seen as one on whom demands and expectations lie in that particular way in which we think of them as lying when we speak of moral obligation; he is not, to that extent, seen as a morally responsible agent, as a term of moral relationships, as a member of the moral community.

I remarked also that the suspension of ordinary inter-personal attitudes and the cultivation of a purely objective view is sometimes possible even when we have no such reasons for it as I have just mentioned. Is this possible also in the case of the moral reactive attitudes? I think so; and perhaps it is easier. But the motives for a total suspension of moral reactive attitudes are fewer, and perhaps weaker: fewer, because only where there is antecedent personal involvement can there be the motive of seeking refuge from the strains of such involvement; perhaps weaker, because the tension between objectivity of view and the moral reactive attitudes is perhaps less than the tension between objectivity of view and the personal reactive attitudes, so that we can in the case of the moral reactive attitudes more easily secure the speculative or political gains of objectivity of view by a kind of setting on one side, rather than a total suspension, of those attitudes.

These last remarks are uncertain; but also, for the present purpose, unimportant. What concerns us now is to inquire, as previously in connexion with the personal reactive attitudes, what relevance any general thesis of determinism might have to their vicarious analogues. The answers once more are parallel; though I shall take them in a slightly different order. First, we must note, as before, that when the suspension of such an attitude or such attitudes occurs in a particular case, it is *never* the consequence of the belief that the piece of behaviour in question was determined in a sense such that all behaviour *might be*, and, if determinism is true, all behaviour *is*, determined in that sense. For it is not a consequence of any general thesis of determinism which might be true that nobody knows what he's doing or that everybody's behaviour is unintelligible in terms of conscious purposes or that everybody lives in a world of delusion or that nobody has a moral sense, i.e. is susceptible of self reactive attitudes, etc. In fact no such sense of 'determined' as would be required for a general thesis of determinism is ever relevant to our actual suspensions of moral reactive attitudes. Second, suppose it granted, as I have already argued, that we cannot take seriously the thought that theoretical conviction of such a general thesis would lead to the total decay of the personal reactive attitudes. Can we then take seriously the thought that such a conviction—a conviction, after all, that many have held or said they held—would nevertheless lead to the total decay or repudiation of the vicarious analogues of these attitudes? I think that the change in our social world which would leave us exposed to the personal reactive attitudes but not at all to their vicarious analogues, the generalization of abnormal egocentricity which this would entail, is perhaps even harder for us to envisage as a real possibility than the decay of both kinds of attitude together. Though there are some necessary and some contingent differences between the ways and cases in which these two kinds of attitudes operate or are inhibited in their operation, yet, as general human capacities or pronenesses, they stand or lapse together. Finally, to the further question whether it would not be *rational*, given a general theoretical conviction of the truth of determinism, so to change our world that in it all these attitudes were wholly suspended, I must answer, as before, that one who presses this question has wholly failed to grasp the import of the preceding answer, the nature of the human commitment that is here involved: it is *useless* to ask whether it would not be rational for us to do what it is not in our nature to (be able to) do. To this I must add, as before, that if there were, say, for a moment open to us the possibility of such a god-like choice, the rationality of making or refusing it would be determined by quite other considerations than the truth or falsity of the general theoretical doctrine in question. The latter would be simply irrelevant; and this becomes ironically clear when we remember that for those convinced that the truth of determinism nevertheless really would make the one choice rational, there has always been the insuperable difficulty of explaining in intelligible terms how its falsity would make the opposite choice rational.

I am aware that in presenting the argument as I have done, neglecting the ever-interesting varieties of cases, I have presented nothing more than a schema, using sometimes a crude opposition of phrase where we have a great intricacy of phenomena. In particular the simple opposition of objective attitudes on the one hand and the various contrasted attitudes which I have opposed to them must seem as grossly crude as it is central. Let me pause to mitigate this crudity a little, and also to strengthen one of my central contentions, by mentioning some things which straddle these contrasted kinds of attitudes. Thus parents and others concerned with the care and upbringing of young children cannot have to their charges either kind of attitude in a pure or unqualified form. They are dealing with creatures who are potentially and increasingly capable both of holding, and being objects of, the full range of human and moral attitudes, but are not yet truly capable of either. The treatment of such creatures must therefore represent a kind of compromise, constantly shifting in one direction, between objectivity of attitude and developed human attitudes. Rehearsals insensibly modulate towards true performances. The punishment of a child is both like and unlike the punishment of an adult. Suppose we try to relate this progressive emergence of the child as a responsible being, as an object of non-objective attitudes, to that sense of 'determined' in which, if determinism is a possibly true thesis, all behaviour *may* be determined, and in which, if it is a true thesis, all behaviour *is* determined. What bearing *could* such a sense of 'determined' have upon the progressive modification of attitudes towards the child? Would it not be grotesque to think of the development of the child as a progressive or patchy emergence from an area in which its behaviour is in this sense determined into an area in which it isn't? Whatever sense of 'determined' is required for stating the thesis of determinism, it can scarcely be such as to allow of compromise, border-line-style answers to the question, 'Is this bit of behaviour determined or isn't it?' But in this matter of young children, it is essentially a border-line, penumbral area that we move in. Again, consider—a very different matter—the strain in the attitude of a psychoanalyst to his patient. *His* objectivity of attitude, *his* suspension of ordinary moral reactive attitudes, is profoundly modified by the fact that the aim of the enterprise is to make such suspension unnecessary or less necessary. Here we may and do naturally speak of restoring the agent's freedom. But here the restoring of freedom means bringing it about that the agent's behaviour shall be intelligible in terms of conscious purposes rather than in terms only of unconscious purposes. *This* is the object of the enterprise; and it is in so far as *this* object is attained that the suspension, or half-suspension, of ordinary moral attitudes is deemed no longer necessary or appropriate. And in this we see once again the *irrelevance* of that concept of 'being determined' which must be the central concept of determinism. For we cannot both agree that this object is attainable and that its attainment has this consequence and yet hold (1) that neurotic behaviour is determined in a sense in which, it may be, all behaviour is determined, and (2) that it is because neurotic behaviour is determined in this sense that objective attitudes are deemed appropriate to neurotic behaviour. Not, at least, without accusing ourselves of incoherence in our attitude to psycho-analytic treatment.

6. And now we can try to fill in the lacuna which the pessimist finds in the optimist's account of the concept of moral responsibility, and of the bases of moral condemnation and punishment; and to fill it in from the facts as we know them. For, as I have already remarked, when the pessimist himself seeks to fill it in, he rushes beyond the facts as we know them and proclaims that it cannot be filled in at all unless determinism is false.

Yet a partial sense of the facts as we know them is certainly present to the pessimist's mind. When his opponent, the optimist, undertakes to show that the truth of determinism would not shake the foundations of the concept of moral responsibility and of the practices of moral condemnation and punishment, he typically refers, in a more or less elaborated way, to the efficacy of these practices in regulating behaviour in socially desirable ways. These practices are represented solely as instruments of policy, as methods of individual treatment and social control. The pessimist recoils from this picture; and in his recoil there is, typically, an element of emotional shock. He is apt to say, among much else, that the humanity of the offender himself is offended by *this* picture of his condemnation and punishment.

The reasons for this recoil—the explanation of the sense of an emotional, as well as a conceptual, shock—we have already before us. The picture painted by the optimists is painted in a style appropriate to a situation envisaged as wholly dominated by objectivity of attitude. The only operative notions invoked in this picture are such as those of policy, treatment, control. But a thoroughgoing objectivity of attitude, excluding as it does the moral reactive attitudes, excludes at the same time essential elements in the concepts of *moral* condemnation and *moral* responsibility. This is the reason for the conceptual shock. The deeper emotional shock is a reaction, not simply to an inadequate conceptual analysis, but to the suggestion of a change in our world. I have remarked that it is possible to cultivate an exclusive objectivity of attitude in some cases, and for some reasons, where the object of the attitude is not set aside from developed inter-personal and moral attitudes by immaturity or abnormality. And the suggestion which seems to be contained in the optimist's account is that such an attitude should be universally adopted to all offenders. This is shocking enough in the pessimist's eyes. But, sharpened by shock, his eyes see further. It would be hard to make *this* division in our natures. If to all offenders, then to all mankind. Moreover, to whom could this recommendation be, in any real sense, addressed? Only to the powerful, the authorities. So abysses seem to open.[5]

But we will confine our attention to the case of the offenders.The concepts we are concerned with are those of responsibility and guilt, qualified as 'moral', on the one hand—together with that of membership of a moral community; of demand, indignation, disapprobation and condemnation, qualified as 'moral', on the other hand—together with that of punishment. Indignation, disapprobation, like resentment, tend to inhibit or at least to limit our goodwill towards the object of these attitudes, tend to promote an at least partial and temporary withdrawal of goodwill; they do so in proportion as they are strong; and their strength is in general proportioned to what is felt to be the magnitude of the injury and to the degree to which the agent's will is identified with, or indifferent to, it. (These, of course, are not contingent connexions.) But these attitudes of disapprobation and indignation are precisely the correlates of the moral demand in the case where the demand is felt to be disregarded. The making of the demand *is* the proneness to such attitudes. The holding of them does not, as the holding of objective attitudes does, involve as a part of itself viewing their object other than as a member of the moral community. The partial withdrawal of goodwill which *these* attitudes entail, the modification *they* entail of the general demand that another should, if possible, be spared suffering, is, rather, the consequence of *continuing* to view him as a member of the moral community; only as one who has offended against its demands. So the preparedness to acquiesce in that infliction of suffering on the offender which is an essential part of punishment is all of a piece with this whole range of attitudes of which I have been speaking. It is not only moral reactive attitudes towards the offender which are in question here. We must mention also the self-reactive attitudes of offenders themselves. Just as the other-reactive attitudes are associated with a readiness to acquiesce in the infliction of suffering on an offender, within the 'institution' of punishment, so the self-reactive attitudes are associated with a readiness on the part of the offender to acquiesce in such infliction *without* developing the reactions (e.g. of resentment) which he would normally develop to the infliction of injury upon him; i.e. with a readiness, as we say, to accept punishment[6] as 'his due' or as 'just'.

I am not in the least suggesting that these readinesses to acquiesce, either on the part of the offender himself or on the part of others, are always or commonly accompanied or preceded by indignant boilings or remorseful pangs; only that we have here a continuum of attitudes and feelings to which these readinesses to acquiesce themselves belong. Nor am I in the least suggesting that it belongs to this continuum of attitudes that we should be ready to acquiesce in the infliction of injury on offenders in a fashion which we saw to be quite indiscriminate or in accordance with procedures which we knew to be wholly useless. On the contrary, savage or civilized, we have some belief in the utility of practices of condemnation and punishment. But the social util-

5. Peered into by Mr. J. D. Mabbott, in his article 'Freewill and Punishment', published in *Contemporary British Philosophy*, 3rd ser., 1956.

6. Of course not *any* punishment for *anything* deemed an offence.

ity of these practices, on which the optimist lays such exclusive stress, is not what is now in question. What is in question is the pessimist's justified sense that to speak in terms of social utility alone is to leave out something vital in our conception of these practices. The vital thing can be restored by attending to that complicated web of attitudes and feelings which form an essential part of the moral life as we know it, and which are quite opposed to objectivity of attitude. Only by attending to this range of attitudes can we recover from the facts as we know them a sense of what we mean, i.e. of *all* we mean, when, speaking the language of morals, we speak of desert, responsibility, guilt, condemnation, and justice. But we *do* recover it from the facts as we know them. We do not have to go beyond them. Because the optimist neglects or misconstrues these attitudes, the pessimist rightly claims to find a lacuna in his account. We can fill the lacuna for him. But in return we must demand of the pessimist a surrender of his metaphysics.

Optimist and pessimist misconstrue the facts in very different styles. But in a profound sense there is something in common to their misunderstandings. Both seek, in different ways, to over-intellectualize the facts. Inside the general structure or web of human attitudes and feelings of which I have been speaking, there is endless room for modification, redirection, criticism, and justification. But questions of justification are internal to the structure or relate to modifications internal to it. The existence of the general framework of attitudes itself is something we are given with the fact of human society. As a whole, it neither calls for, nor permits, an external 'rational' justification. Pessimist and optimist alike show themselves, in different ways, unable to accept this.[7] The optimist's style of over-intellectualizing the facts is that of a characteristically incomplete empiricism, a one-eyed utilitarianism. He seeks to find an adequate basis for certain social practices in calculated consequences, and loses sight (perhaps wishes to lose sight) of the human attitudes of which these practices are, in part, the expression. The pessimist does not lose sight of these attitudes, but is unable to accept the fact that it is just these attitudes themselves which fill the gap in the optimist's account. Because of this, he thinks the gap can be filled only if some general metaphysical proposition is repeatedly verified, verified in all cases where it is appropriate to attribute moral responsibility. This proposition he finds it as difficult to state coherently and with intelligible relevance as its determinist contradictory. Even when a formula has been found ('contra-causal freedom' or something of the kind) there still seems to remain a gap between its applicability in particular cases and its supposed moral consequences. Sometimes he plugs this gap with an intution of fittingness—a pitiful intellectualist trinket for a philosopher to wear as a charm against the recognition of his own humanity.

Even the moral sceptic is not immune from his own form of the wish to over-intellectualize such notions as those of moral responsibility, guilt, and blame. He sees that the optimist's account is inadequate and the pessimist's libertarian alternative inane; and finds no resource except to declare that the notions in question are inherently confused, that 'blame is metaphysical'. But the metaphysics was in the eye of the metaphysician. It is a pity that talk of the moral sentiments has fallen out of favour. The phrase would be quite a good name for that network of human attitudes in acknowledging the character and place of which we find, I suggest, the only possibility of reconciling these disputants to each other and the facts.

There are, at present, factors which add, in a slightly paradoxical way, to the difficulty of making this acknowledgement. These human attitudes themselves, in their development and in the variety of their manifestations, have to an increasing extent become objects of study in the social and psychological sciences; and this growth of human self-consciousness, which we might expect to reduce the difficulty of acceptance, in fact increases it in several ways. One factor of comparatively minor importance is an increased historical and anthropological awareness of the great variety of forms which these human attitudes may take at different times and in different cultures. This makes one rightly chary of claiming as essential features of the concept of morality in general, forms of these attitudes which may have a local and temporary prominence. No doubt to some extent my own descriptions of human attitudes have reflected local and temporary features of our own culture. But an awareness of va-

7. Compare the question of the justification of induction. The human commitment to inductive belief-formation is original, natural, non-rational (not irrational), in no way something we choose or could give up. Yet rational criticism and reflection can refine standards and their application. Supply 'rules for judging of cause and effect'. Ever since the facts were made clear by Hume, people have been resisting acceptance of them.

riety of forms should not prevent us from acknowledging also that in the absence of *any* forms of these attitudes it is doubtful whether we should have anything that *we* could find intelligible as a system of human relationships, as human society. A quite different factor of greater importance is that psychological studies have made us rightly mistrustful of many particular manifestations of the attitudes I have spoken of. They are a prime realm of self-deception, of the ambiguous and the shady, of guilt-transference, unconscious sadism and the rest. But it is an exaggerated horror, itself suspect, which would make us unable to acknowledge the facts because of the seamy side of the facts. Finally, perhaps the most important factor of all is the prestige of these theoretical studies themselves. That prestige is great, and is apt to make us forget that in philosophy, though it also is a theoretical study, we have to take account of the facts in *all* their bearings; we are not to suppose that we are required, or permitted, as philosophers, to regard ourselves, as human beings, as detached from the attitudes which, as scientists, we study with detachment. This is in no way to deny the possibility and desirability of redirection and modification of our human attitudes in the light of these studies. But we may reasonably think it unlikely that our progressively greater understanding of certain aspects of ourselves will lead to the total disappearance of those aspects. Perhaps it is not inconceivable that it should; and perhaps, then, the dreams of some philosophers will be realized.

If we sufficiently, that is *radically*, modify the view of the optimist, his view is the right one. It is far from wrong to emphasize the efficacy of all those practices which express or manifest our moral attitudes, in regulating behaviour in ways considered desirable; or to add that when certain of our beliefs about the efficacy of some of these practices turn out to be false, then we may have good reason for dropping or modifying those practices. What *is* wrong is to forget that these practices, and their reception, the reactions to them, really *are* expressions of our moral attitudes and not merely devices we calculatingly employ for regulative purposes. Our practices do not merely exploit our natures, they express them. Indeed the very understanding of the kind of efficacy these expressions of our attitudes have turns on our remembering this. When we do remember this, and modify the optimist's position accordingly, we simultaneously correct its conceptual deficiencies and ward off the dangers it seems to entail, without recourse to the obscure and panicky metaphysics of libertarianism.

Chapter 21

Harry Frankfurt

Harry Frankfurt (1929–) is Professor of Philosophy at Princeton University. He has also been a Professor of Philosophy at Yale University. He has made important contributions to the study of free will and to Descartes scholarship. With regard to the free-will/determinism debate, Frankfurt is a compatibilist, holding that no contradiction exists between an act's being determined and the agent's being held responsible for it. But whereas most compatibilists (e.g., Walter Stace) defend their position by a hypothetical interpretation of the formula "S is free in case S *could have done otherwise*," Frankfurt offers a theory of the will in order to account for our notion of freedom. What distinguishes humans from other animals is our ability to deliberate and choose courses of actions. The strategy goes like this: Both animals and humans have straightforward or *first-order desires*—for example, desires to eat, to be comfortable, to sleep—but whereas animals act directly on their wants, humans can weigh them and accept or reject them. For example, Jill may have the *first-order* desire to smoke a cigarette, but she may also want to be healthy. She compares the two desires and forms a *second-order* desire, say, to refrain from smoking based on her desire to remain healthy. But since it is possible that she may have the *second-order* desire to refrain from smoking without wanting to act on it, there is one more step in the process. She must make her desire her will, her *volition*, and be committed to act on the desire not to smoke. The person must *identify* herself or himself with the *second-order* desire and thereby make it a *second-order* volition. As Frankfurt writes elsewhere, "to the extent that a person identifies himself with the springs of his actions, he takes a responsibility for those actions and acquires moral responsibility for them."

FOR FURTHER READING

Dennett, Daniel. *Elbow Room: Varieties of Free Will Worth Wanting* (MIT Press, 1985). The best defense of compatibilism.

Feinberg, Joel, ed. *Reason and Responsibility* (Wadsworth, 1985). Part 4 contains a very good selection of readings, including four readings on the implications for justifying punishment.

Frankfurt, Harry. *The Importance of What We Care About* (Cambridge University Press, 1988).

Honderich, Ted, ed. *Essays on Freedom of Action* (Routledge & Kegan Paul, 1973). A good collection of recent essays.

Lehrer, Keith, and Cornman, James. *Philosophical Problems and Arguments*, 3rd ed. (Macmillan, 1982). Lehrer's essay (Chapter 3) is excellent.

MacKay, Donald M. *Freedom of Action in a Mechanistic Universe* (Cambridge University Press, 1967).

Morgenbesser, Sidney and Walsh, James, eds. *Free Will* (Prentice-Hall, 1962). This contains many of the classic readings.

Stace, Walter. *Religion and the Modern Mind* (Lippincott, 1952).

Trusted, Jennifer. *Free Will and Responsibility* (Oxford University Press, 1984). One of the clearest introductions to the subject. Accessible to beginners and reliable.

van Inwagen, Peter. *An Essay on Free Will* (Oxford University Press, 1983). This is the best critique of compatibilism available.

Watson, Gary. *Free Will* (Oxford University Press, 1982). This volume contains the best collections of recent articles on the subject, especially those of Frankfurt, van Inwagen, and Watson. It also contains two clear discussions of the problem of mechanism and freedom of the will: Norman Malcolm's "The Conceivability of Mechanism" and Daniel Dennett's "Mechanism and Responsibility."

Freedom of the Will and the Concept of a Person

What philosophers have lately come to accept as analysis of the concept of a person is not actually analysis of *that* concept at all. Strawson, whose usage represents the current standard, identifies the concept of a person as "the concept of a type of entity such that *both* predicates ascribing states of consciousness *and* predicates ascribing corporeal characteristics . . . are equally applicable to a single individual of that single type."[1] But there are many entities besides persons that have both mental and physical properties. As it happens—though it seems extraordinary that this should be so—there is no common English word for the type of entity Strawson has in mind, a type that includes not only human beings but animals of various lesser species as well. Still, this hardly justifies the misappropriation of a valuable philosophical term.

Whether the members of some animal species are persons is surely not to be settled merely by determining whether it is correct to apply to them, in addition to predicates ascribing corporeal characteristics, predicates that ascribe states of consciousness. It does violence to our language to endorse the application of the term 'person' to those numerous creatures which do have both psychological and material properties but which are manifestly not persons in any normal sense of the word. This misuse of language is doubtless innocent of any theoretical error. But although the offense is "merely verbal," it does significant harm. For it gratuitously diminishes our philosophical vocabulary, and it increases the likelihood that we will overlook the important area of inquiry with which the term 'person' is most naturally associated. It might have been expected that no problem would be of more central and persistent concern to philosophers than that of understanding what we ourselves essentially are. Yet this problem is so generally neglected that it has been possible to make off with its very name almost without being noticed and, evidently, without evoking any widespread feeling of loss.

There is a sense in which the word 'person' is merely the singular form of 'people' and in which both terms connote no more than membership in a certain biological species. In those senses of the word which are of greater philosophical interest, however, the criteria for being a person do not serve primarily to distinguish the members of our own species from the members of other species. Rather, they are designed to capture those attributes which are the subject of our most humane concern with ourselves and the source of what we regard as most important and most problematical in our lives. Now these attributes would be of equal significance to us even if they were not in fact peculiar and common to the members of our own species. What interests us most in the human condition would not interest us less if it were also a feature of the condition of other creatures as well.

Our concept of ourselves as persons is not to be

Reprinted from *Journal of Philosophy* 68:1 (January 1971), by permission of the author and the *Journal of Philosophy*. Some notes have been deleted and others renumbered.

understood, therefore, as a concept of attributes that are necessarily species-specific. It is conceptually possible that members of novel or even of familiar nonhuman species should be persons; and it is also conceptually possible that some members of the human species are not persons. We do in fact assume, on the other hand, that no member of another species is a person. Accordingly, there is a presumption that what is essential to persons is a set of characteristics that we generally suppose—whether rightly or wrongly—to be uniquely human.

It is my view that one essential difference between persons and other creatures is to be found in the structure of a person's will. Human beings are not alone in having desires and motives, or in making choices. They share these things with the members of certain other species, some of whom even appear to engage in deliberation and to make decisions based upon prior thought. It seems to be peculiarly characteristic of humans, however, that they are able to form what I shall call "second-order desires" or "desires of the second order."

Besides wanting and choosing and being moved *to do* this or that, men may also want to have (or not to have) certain desires and motives. They are capable of wanting to be different, in their preferences and purposes, from what they are. Many animals appear to have the capacity for what I shall call "first-order desires" or "desires of the first order," which are simply desires to do or not to do one thing or another. No animal other than man, however, appears to have the capacity for reflective self-evaluation that is manifested in the formation of second-order desires.

I

The concept designated by the verb 'to want' is extraordinarily elusive. A statement of the form "*A* wants to *X*"—taken by itself, apart from a context that serves to amplify or to specify its meaning—conveys remarkably little information. Such a statement may be consistent, for example, with each of the following statements: (a) the prospect of doing *X* elicits no sensation or introspectible emotional response in *A*; (b) *A* is unaware that he wants to *X*; (c) *A* believes that he does not want to *X*; (d) *A* wants to refrain from *X*-ing; (e) *A* wants to *Y* and believes that it is impossible for him both to *Y* and to *X*; (f) *A* does not "really" want to *X*; (g) *A* would rather die than *X*; and so on. It is therefore hardly sufficient to formulate the distinction between first-order and second-order desires, as I have done, by suggesting merely that someone has a first-order desire when he wants to do or not to do such-and-such, and that he has a second-order desire when he wants to have or not to have a certain desire of the first order.

As I shall understand them, statements of the form "*A* wants to *X*" cover a rather broad range of possibilities. They may be true even when statements like (a) through (g) are true: when *A* is unaware of any feelings concerning *X*-ing, when he is unaware that he wants to *X*, when he deceives himself about what he wants and believes falsely that he does not want to *X*, when he also has other desires that conflict with his desire to *X*, or when he is ambivalent. The desires in question may be conscious or unconscious, they need not be univocal, and *A* may be mistaken about them. There is a further source of uncertainty with regard to statements that identify someone's desires, however, and here it is important for my purposes to be less permissive.

Consider first those statements of the form "*A* wants to *X*" which identify first-order desires—that is, statements in which the term 'to *X*' refers to an action. A statement of this kind does not, by itself, indicate the relative strength of *A*'s desire to *X*. It does not make it clear whether this desire is at all likely to play a decisive role in what *A* actually does or tries to do. For it may correctly be said that *A* wants to *X* even when his desire to *X* is only one among his desires and when it is far from being paramount among them. Thus, it may be true that *A* wants to *X* when he strongly prefers to do something else instead; and it may be true that he wants to *X* despite the fact that, when he acts, it is not the desire to *X* that motivates him to do what he does. On the other hand, someone who states that *A* wants to *X* may mean to convey that it is this desire that is motivating or moving *A* to do what he is actually doing or that *A* will in fact be moved by this desire (unless he changes his mind) when he acts.

It is only when it is used in the second of these ways that, given the special usage of 'will' that I propose to adopt, the statement identifies *A*'s will. To identify an agent's will is either to identify the desire (or desires) by which he is motivated in some action he performs or to identify the desire (or desires) by which he will or would be motivated when or if he acts. An agent's will, then, is identical with one or more of his first-order desires. But the notion of the will, as I am employing it, is not coextensive with the notion of first-order desires. It is not the notion of something that merely inclines an agent in some degree to act in a certain way. Rather, it is the notion of an *effective* desire—one that moves (or will or would move) a person all the way to action. Thus the notion of the will is not coextensive with the notion of what an agent intends to do. For even though someone may have a settled intention to do *X*, he may nonetheless do something else instead of doing *X* because, despite his intention, his desire to do *X* proves to be weaker or less effective than some conflicting desire.

Now consider those statements of the form "*A* wants to *X*" which identify second-order desires—that is, statements in which the term 'to *X*' refers to a desire of the first order. There are also two kinds of situations in which it may be true that *A* wants to want to *X*. In the first place, it might be true of *A* that he wants to have a desire to *X* despite the fact that he has a univocal desire, altogether free of conflict and ambivalence, to refrain from *X*-ing. Someone might want to have a certain desire, in other words, but univocally want that desire to be unsatisfied.

Suppose that a physician engaged in psychotherapy with narcotics addicts believes that his ability to help his patients would be enhanced if he understood better what it is like for them to desire the drug to which they are addicted. Suppose that he is led in this way to want to have a desire for the drug. If it is a genuine desire that he wants, then what he wants is not merely to feel the sensations that addicts characteristically feel when they are gripped by their desires for the drug. What the physician wants, insofar as he wants to have a desire, is to be inclined or moved to some extent to take the drug.

It is entirely possible, however, that, although he wants to be moved by a desire to take the drug, he does not want this desire to be effective. He may not want it to move him all the way to action. He need not be interested in finding out what it is like to take the drug. And insofar as he now wants only to *want* to take it, and not to *take* it, there is nothing in what he now wants that would be satisfied by the drug itself. He may now have, in fact, an altogether univocal desire *not* to take the drug; and he may prudently arrange to make it impossible for him to satisfy the desire he would have if his desire to want the drug should in time be satisfied.

It would thus be incorrect to infer, from the fact that the physician now wants to desire to take the drug, that he already does desire to take it. His second-order desire to be moved to take the drug does not entail that he has a first-order desire to take it. If the drug were now to be administered to him, this might satisfy no desire that is implicit in his desire to want to take it. While he wants to want to take the drug, he may have *no* desire to take it; it may be that *all* he wants is to taste the desire for it. That is, his desire to have a certain desire that he does not have may not be a desire that his will should be at all different than it is.

Someone who wants only in this truncated way to want to *X* stands at the margin of preciosity, and the fact that he wants to want to *X* is not pertinent to the identification of his will. There is, however, a second kind of situation that may be described by '*A* wants to want to *X*'; and when the statement is used to describe a situation of this second kind, then it does pertain to what *A* wants his will to be. In such cases the statement means that *A* wants the desire to *X* to be the desire that moves him effectively to act. It is not merely that he wants the desire to *X* to be among the desires by which, to one degree or another, he is moved or inclined to act. He wants this desire to be effective—that is, to provide the motive in what he actually does. Now when the statement that *A* wants to want to *X* is used in this way, it does entail that *A* already has a desire to *X*. It could not be true both that *A* wants the desire to *X* to move him into action and that he does not want to *X*. It is only if he does want to *X* that he can coherently want the desire to *X* not merely to be one of his desires but, more decisively, to be his will.

Suppose a man wants to be motivated in what he does by the desire to concentrate on his work. It is necessarily true, if this supposition is correct, that he already wants to concentrate on his work. This desire is now among his desires. But the question of whether or not his second-order desire is fulfilled does not turn merely on whether the desire he wants is one of his desires. It turns on whether this desire is, as he wants it to be, his effective desire or will. If, when the chips are down, it is his desire to concentrate on his work that moves him to do what he does, then what he wants at that time is indeed (in the relevant sense) what he wants to want. If it is some other desire that actually moves him when he acts, on the other hand, then what he wants at that time is not (in the relevant sense) what he wants to want. This will be so despite the fact that the desire to concentrate on his work continues to be among his desires.

II

Someone has a desire of the second order either when he wants simply to have a certain desire or when he wants a certain desire to be his will. In situations of the latter kind, I shall call his second-order desires "second-order volitions" or "volitions of the second order." Now it is having second-order volitions, and not having second-order desires generally, that I regard as essential to being a person. It is logically possible, however unlikely, that there should be an agent with second-order desires but with no volitions of the second order. Such a creature, in my view, would not be a person. I shall use the term 'wanton' to refer to agents who have first-order desires but who are not persons because, whether or not they have desires of the second order, they have no second-order volitions.

The essential characteristic of a wanton is that he does not care about his will. His desires move him to do certain things, without its being true of him either that he wants to be moved by those desires or that he prefers to be moved by other desires. The class of wantons includes all nonhuman animals that have desires and all very young children. Perhaps it also includes some adult human beings as well. In any case, adult humans may be more or less wanton; they may act wantonly, in response to first-order desires concerning which they have no volitions of the second order, more or less frequently.

The fact that a wanton has no second-order volitions does not mean that each of his first-order desires is translated heedlessly and at once into action. He may have no opportunity to act in accordance with some of his desires. Moreover, the translation of his desires into action may be delayed or precluded either by conflicting desires of the first order or by the intervention of deliberation. For a wanton may possess and employ rational faculties of a high order. Nothing in the concept of a wanton implies that he cannot reason or that he cannot deliberate concerning how to do what he wants to do. What distinguishes the rational wanton from other rational agents is that he is not concerned with the desirability of his desires themselves. He ignores the question of what his will is to be. Not only does he pursue whatever course of action he is most strongly inclined to pursue, but he does not care which of his inclinations is the strongest.

Thus a rational creature, who reflects upon the suitability to his desires of one course of action or another, may nonetheless be a wanton. In maintaining that the essence of being a person lies not in reason but in will, I am far from suggesting that a creature without reason may be a person. For it is only in virtue of his rational capacities that a person is capable of becoming critically aware of his own will and of forming volitions of the second order. The structure of a person's will presupposes, accordingly, that he is a rational being.

The distinction between a person and a wanton may be illustrated by the difference between two narcotics addicts. Let us suppose that the physiological condition accounting for the addiction is the same in both men, and that both succumb inevitably to their periodic desires for the drug to which they are addicted. One of the addicts hates his addiction and always struggles desperately, although to no avail, against its thrust. He tries everything that he thinks might enable him to overcome his desires for the drug. But these desires are too powerful for him to withstand, and invariably, in the end, they conquer him. He is an unwilling addict, helplessly violated by his own desires.

The unwilling addict has conflicting first-order desires: he wants to take the drug, and he also wants to refrain from taking it. In addition to these first-order desires, however, he has a volition of the second order. He is not neutral with regard to the conflict between his desire to take the drug and his desire to refrain from taking it. It is the latter desire, and not the former, that he wants to constitute his will; it is the latter desire, rather than the former, that he wants to be effective and to provide the purpose that he will seek to realize in what he actually does.

The other addict is a wanton. His actions reflect the economy of his first-order desires, without his being concerned whether the desires that move him to act are desires by which he wants to be moved to act. If he encounters problems in obtaining the drug or in administering it to himself, his responses to his urges to take it may involve deliberation. But it never occurs to him to consider whether he wants the relations among his desires to result in his having the will he has. The wanton addict may be an animal, and thus incapable of being concerned about his will. In any event he is, in respect of his wanton lack of concern, no different from an animal.

The second of these addicts may suffer a first-order conflict similar to the first-order conflict suffered by the first. Whether he is human or not, the wanton may (perhaps due to conditioning) both want to take the drug and want to refrain from taking it. Unlike the unwilling addict, however, he does not prefer that one of his conflicting desires should be paramount over the other; he does not prefer that one first-order desire rather than the other should constitute his will. It would be misleading to say that he is neutral as to the conflict between his desires, since this would suggest that he regards them as equally acceptable. Since he has no identity apart from his first-order desires, it is true neither that he prefers one to the others nor that he prefers not to take sides.

It makes a difference to the unwilling addict, who is a person, which of his conflicting first-order desires wins out. Both desires are his, to be sure; and whether he finally takes the drug or finally succeeds in refraining from taking it, he acts to satisfy what is in a literal sense his own desire. In either case he does something he himself wants to do, and he does it not because of some external influence whose aim happens to coincide with his own but because of his desire to do it. The unwilling addict identifies himself, however, through the formation of a second-order volition, with one rather than with the other of his conflicting first-order desires. He makes one of them more truly his own and, in so doing, he withdraws himself from the other. It is in virtue of this identification and withdrawal, accomplished through the formation of a second-order volition, that the unwilling addict may meaningfully make the analytically puzzling statements that the force moving him to take the drug is a force other than his own, and that it is not of his own free will but rather against his will that this force moves him to take it.

The wanton addict cannot or does not care which of his conflicting first-order desires wins out. His lack of concern is not due to his inability to find a convincing basis for preference. It is due either to his lack of the capacity for reflection or to his mindless indifference to the enterprise of evaluating his own desires and motives. There is only one issue in the struggle to which his first-order conflict may lead: whether the one or the other of his conflicting desires is the stronger. Since he is moved by both desires, he will not be altogether satisfied by what he does no matter which of them is effective. But it makes no difference to *him* whether his craving or his aversion gets the upper hand. He has no stake in the conflict between them and so, unlike the unwilling addict, he can neither win nor lose the struggle in which he is engaged. When a *person* acts, the desire by which he is moved is either the will he wants or a will he wants to be without. When a *wanton* acts, it is neither.

III

There is a very close relationship between the capacity for forming second-order volitions and another capacity that is essential to persons—one that has often been considered a distinguishing mark of the human condition. It is only because a person has volitions of the second order that he is capable both of enjoying and of lacking freedom of the will. The concept of a person is not only, then, the concept of a type of entity that has both first-order desires and volitions of the second order. It can also be construed as the concept of a type of entity for whom the freedom of its will may be a problem. This concept excludes all wantons, both infrahumans and human, since they fail to satisfy an essential condition for the enjoyment of freedom of the will. And it excludes those suprahuman beings, if any, whose wills are necessarily free.

Just what kind of freedom is the freedom of the will? This question calls for an identification of the special area of human experience to which the concept of freedom of the will, as distinct from the concepts of other sorts of freedom, is particularly germane. In dealing with it, my aim will be primarily to locate the problem with which a person is most immediately concerned when he is concerned with the freedom of his will.

According to one familiar philosophical tradition, being free is fundamentally a matter of doing what one wants to do. Now the notion of an agent who does what he wants to do is by no means an altogether clear one: both the doing and the wanting, and the appropriate relation between them as well, require elucidation. But although its focus needs to be sharpened and its formulation refined, I believe that this notion does capture at least part of what is implicit in the idea of an agent who *acts* freely. It misses entirely, however, the peculiar content of the quite different idea of an agent whose *will* is free.

We do not suppose that animals enjoy freedom of the will, although we recognize that an animal may be free to run in whatever direction it wants. Thus, having the freedom to do what one wants to do is not a sufficient condition of having a free will. It is not a necessary condition either. For to deprive someone of his freedom of action is not necessarily to undermine the freedom of his will. When an agent is aware that there are certain things he is not free to do, this doubtless affects his desires and limits the range of choices he can make. But suppose that someone, without being aware of it, has in fact lost or been deprived of his freedom of action. Even though he is no longer free to do what he wants to do, his will may remain as free as it was before. Despite the fact that he is not free to translate his desires into actions or to act according to the determinations of his will, he may still form those desires and make those determinations as freely as if his freedom of action had not been impaired.

When we ask whether a person's will is free we are not asking whether he is in a position to translate his first-order desires into actions. That is the question of whether he is free to do as he pleases. The question of the freedom of his will does not concern the relation between what he does and what he wants to do. Rather, it concerns his desires themselves. But what question about them is it?

It seems to me both natural and useful to construe the question of whether a person's will is free in close analogy to the question of whether an agent enjoys freedom of action. Now freedom of action is (roughly, at least) the freedom to do what one wants to do. Analogously, then, the statement that a person enjoys freedom of the will means (also roughly) that he is free to want what he wants to want. More precisely, it means that he is free to will what he wants to will, or to have the will he wants. Just as the question about the freedom of an agent's action has to do with whether it is the action he wants to perform, so the question about the freedom of his will has to do with whether it is the will he wants to have.

It is in securing the conformity of his will and his second-order volitions, then, that a person exercises freedom of the will. And it is in the discrepancy between his will and his second-order volitions, or in his awareness that their coincidence is not his own doing but only a happy chance, that a person who does not have this freedom feels its lack. The unwilling addict's will is not free. This is shown by the fact that it is not the will he wants. It is also true, though in a different way, that the will of the wanton addict is not free. The wanton addict neither has the will he wants nor has a will that differs from the will he wants. Since he has no volitions of the second order, the freedom of his will cannot be a problem for him. He lacks it, so to speak, by default.

People are generally far more complicated than my sketchy account of the structure of a person's will may suggest. There is as much opportunity for ambivalence, conflict, and self-deception with regard to desires of the second order, for example, as there is with regard to first-order desires. If there is an unresolved conflict among someone's second-order desires, then he is in danger of having no second-order volition; for unless this conflict is resolved, he has no preference concerning which of his first-order desires is to be his will. This condition, if it is so severe that it prevents him from identifying himself in a sufficiently decisive way with *any* of his conflicting first-order desires, destroys him as a person. For it either tends to paralyze his will and to keep him from acting at all, or it tends to remove him from his will so that his will operates without his participation. In both cases he becomes, like the unwilling addict though in a different way, a helpless bystander to the forces that move him.

Another complexity is that a person may have, especially if his second-order desires are in conflict, desires and volitions of a higher order than the second. There is no theoretical limit to the length of the series of desires of higher and higher orders; nothing except common sense and, perhaps, a saving fatigue prevents an individual from obsessively refusing to identify himself with any of his desires until he forms a desire of the next higher order. The tendency to generate such a series of acts of forming desires, which would be a case of humanization run wild, also leads toward the destruction of a person.

It is possible, however, to terminate such a series of acts without cutting it off arbitrarily. When a person identifies himself *decisively* with one of his first-order desires, this commitment "resounds" throughout the potentially endless array of higher orders. Consider a person who, without reservation or conflict, wants to be motivated by the desire to concentrate on his work. The fact that his second-order volition to be moved by this desire is a decisive one means that there is no room for questions concerning the pertinence of desires or volitions of higher orders. Suppose the person is asked whether he wants to concentrate on his work. He can properly insist that this question concerning a third-order desire does not arise. It would be a mistake to claim that, because he has not considered whether he wants the second-order volition he has formed, he is indifferent to the question of whether it is with this volition or with some other that he wants his will to accord. The decisiveness of the commitment he has made means that he has decided that no further question about his second-order volition, at any higher order, remains to be asked. It is relatively unimportant whether we explain this by saying that this commitment implicitly generates an endless series of confirming desires of higher orders, or by saying that the commitment is tantamount to a dissolution of the pointedness of all questions concerning higher orders of desire.

Examples such as the one concerning the unwilling addict may suggest that volitions of the second order, or of higher orders, must be formed deliberately and that a person characteristically struggles to ensure that they are satisfied. But the conformity of a person's will to his higher-order volitions may be far more thoughtless and spontaneous than this. Some people are naturally moved by kindness when they want to be kind, and by nastiness when they want to be nasty, without any explicit forethought and without any need for energetic self-control. Others are moved by nastiness when they want to be kind and by kindness when they intend to be nasty, equally without forethought and without active resistance to these violations of their higher-order desires. The enjoyment of freedom comes easily to some. Others must struggle to achieve it.

IV

My theory concerning the freedom of the will accounts easily for our disinclination to allow that this freedom is enjoyed by the members of any species inferior to our own. It also satisfies another condition that must be met by any such theory, by making it apparent why the freedom of the will should be regarded as desirable. The enjoyment of a free will means the satisfaction of certain desires—desires of the second or of higher orders—whereas its absence means their frustration. The satisfactions at stake are those which accrue to a person of whom it may be said that his will is his own. The corresponding frustrations are those suffered by a person of whom it may be said that he is estranged from himself, or that he finds himself a helpless or a passive bystander to the forces that move him.

A person who is free to do what he wants to do may yet not be in a position to have the will he wants. Suppose, however, that he enjoys both freedom of action and freedom of the will. Then he is not only free to do what he wants to do; he is also free to want what he wants to want. It seems to me that he has, in that case, all the freedom it is possible to desire or to conceive. There are other good things in life, and he may not possess some of them. But there is nothing in the way of freedom that he lacks.

It is far from clear that certain other theories of the freedom of the will meet these elementary but essential conditions: that it be understandable why we desire this freedom and why we refuse to ascribe it to animals. Consider, for example, Roderick Chisholm's quaint version of the doctrine that human freedom entails an absence of causal determination.[2] Whenever a person performs a free action, according to Chisholm, it's a miracle. The motion of a person's hand, when the person moves it, is the outcome of a series of physical causes; but some event in this series, "and presumably one of those that took place within the brain, was caused by the agent and not by any other events" (18). A free agent has, therefore, "a prerogative which some would attribute only to God: each of us, when we act, is a prime mover unmoved" (23).

This account fails to provide any basis for doubting that animals of subhuman species enjoy the freedom it defines. Chisholm says nothing that makes it seem less likely that a rabbit performs a miracle when it moves its leg than that a man does so when he moves his hand. But why, in any case, should anyone *care* whether he can interrupt the natural order of causes in the way Chisholm describes? Chisholm offers no reason for believing that there is a discernible difference between the experience of a man who miraculously initiates a series of causes when he moves his hand and a man who moves his hand without any such breach of the normal causal sequence. There appears to be no concrete basis for preferring to be involved in the one state of affairs rather than in the other.

It is generally supposed that, in addition to satisfying the two conditions I have mentioned, a satisfactory theory of the freedom of the will necessarily provides an analysis of one of the conditions of moral responsibility. The most common recent approach to the problem of understanding the freedom of the will has been, indeed, to inquire what is entailed by the assumption that someone is morally responsible for what he has done. In my view, however, the relation between moral responsibility and the freedom of the will has been very widely misunderstood. It is not true that a person is morally responsible for what he has done only if his will was free when he did it. He may be morally responsible for having done it even though his will was not free at all.

A person's will is free only if he is free to have the will he wants. This means that, with regard to any of his first-order desires, he is free either to make that desire his will or to make some other first-order desire his will instead. Whatever his will, then, the will of the person whose will is free could have been otherwise; he could have done otherwise than to constitute his will as he did. It is a vexed question just how "he could have done otherwise" is to be understood in contexts such as this one. But although this question is important to the theory of freedom, it has no bearing on the theory of moral responsibility. For the assumption that a person is morally responsible for what he has done does not entail that the person was in a position to have whatever will he wanted.

This assumption *does* entail that the person did what he did freely, or that he did it of his own free will. It is a mistake, however, to believe that someone acts freely only when he is free to do whatever he wants or that he acts of his own free will only if his will is free. Suppose that a person has done what he wanted to do, that he did it because he wanted to do it, and that the will by which he was moved when he did it was his will because it was the will he wanted. Then he did it freely and of his own free will. Even supposing that he could have done otherwise, he would not have done otherwise; and even supposing that he could have had a different will, he would not have wanted his will to differ from what it was. Moreover, since the will that moved him when he acted was his will because he wanted it to be, he cannot claim that his will was forced upon him or that he was a passive bystander to its constitution. Under these conditions, it is quite irrelevant to the evaluation of his moral responsibility to inquire whether the alternatives that he opted against were actually available to him.

In illustration, consider a third kind of addict. Suppose that his addiction has the same physiological basis and the same irresistible thrust as the addictions of the unwilling and wanton addicts, but that he is altogether delighted with his condition. He is a willing addict, who would not have things any other way. If the grip of his addiction should somehow weaken, he would do whatever he could to reinstate it; if his desire for the drug should begin to fade, he would take steps to renew its intensity.

The willing addict's will is not free, for his desire to take the drug will be effective regardless of whether or not he wants this desire to constitute his will. But when he takes the drug, he takes it freely and of his own free will. I am inclined to understand his situation as involving the overdetermination of his first-order desire to take the drug. This desire is his effective desire because he is physiologically addicted. But it is his effective desire also because he wants it to be. His will is outside his control, but, by his second-order desire that his desire for the drug should be effective, he has made this will his own. Given that it is therefore not only because of his addiction that his desire for the drug is effective, he may be morally responsible for taking the drug.

My conception of the freedom of the will appears to be neutral with regard to the problem of determinism. It seems conceivable that it should be causally determined that a person is free to want what he wants to want. If this is conceivable, then it might be causally determined that a person enjoys a free will. There is no more than an innocuous appearance of paradox in the proposition that it is determined, ineluctably and by forces beyond their control, that certain people have free wills and that others do not. There is no incoherence in the proposition that some agency other than a person's own is responsible (even *morally* responsible) for the fact that he enjoys or fails to enjoy freedom of the will. It is possible that a person should be morally responsible for what he does of his own free will and that some other person should also be morally responsible for his having done it.

On the other hand, it seems conceivable that it should come about by chance that a person is free to have the will he wants. If this is conceivable, then it might be a matter of chance that certain people enjoy freedom of the will and that certain others do not. Perhaps it is also conceivable, as a number of philosophers believe, for states of affairs to come about in a way other than by chance or as the outcome of a sequence of natural causes. If it is indeed conceivable for the relevant states of affairs to come about in some third way, then it is also possible that a person should in that third way come to enjoy the freedom of the will.

Notes

1. P. F. Strawson, *Individuals* (London: Methuen, 1959), pp. 101–102. Ayer's usage of 'person' is similar: "it is characteristic of persons in this sense that besides having various physical properties . . . they are also credited with various forms of consciousness" [A. J. Ayer, *The Concept of a Person* (New York: St. Martin's, 1963), p. 82]. What concerns Strawson and Ayer is the problem of understanding the relation between mind and body, rather than the quite different problem of understanding what it is to be a creature that not only has a mind and a body but is also a person.
2. Chisholm, "Freedom and Action," in K. Lehrer, ed., *Freedom and Determinism* (New York: Random House, 1966), pp. 11–44.

Chapter 22

RICHARD TAYLOR

Richard Taylor (1919–) for many years taught at Brown University and the University of Rochester. He has written widely on moral philosophy as well as on metaphysics. He has a reputation for clarity and creativity.

In this essay Taylor argues for three theses: (1) Soft Determinism (Compatibilism), such as set forth by Strawson and Frankfurt, fails to preserve the concept of moral responsibility; (2) Indeterminism, the theory that some events lack causal determinants, but happen by mere chance, must not be confused with freedom of the will and provides no support for it; (3) the agency theory of free will does preserve our notions of free will, responsibility, and moral deliberation.

FOR FURTHER READING

Taylor, Richard. *Metaphysics* (Prentice-Hall, 1992).
See also "For Further Reading" at the beginning of Reading 21.

A Defense of Libertarian Freedom of the Will

SOFT DETERMINISM

. . . All versions of this theory have in common three claims, by means of which, it is naively supposed, a reconciliation is achieved between determinism and freedom. Freedom being, furthermore, a condition of moral responsibility and the only condition that metaphysics seriously questions, it is supposed by the partisans of this view that determinism is perfectly compatible with such responsibility. This, no doubt, accounts for its great appeal and wide acceptance, even by some men of considerable learning.

The three claims of soft determinism are (1) that the thesis of determinism is true, and that accordingly all human behavior, voluntary or other, like the behavior of all other things, arises from antecedent conditions, given which no other behavior is possible—in short, that all human behavior is caused and determined; (2) that voluntary behavior is nonetheless free to the extent that it is not externally constrained or impeded; and (3) that, in the absence of such obstacles and constraints, the causes of voluntary behavior are certain states, events, or conditions within the agent himself; namely, his own acts of will or volitions, choices, decisions, desires, and so on.

Thus, on this view, I am free, and therefore sometimes responsible for what I do, provided nothing prevents me from acting according to my own choice, desire, or volition, or constrains me to act otherwise. There may, to be sure, be other conditions for my responsibility—such as, for example, an understanding of the probable consequences of my behavior, and that sort of thing—but absence of constraint or impediment is, at least, one such condition. And, it is claimed, it is a condition that is compatible with the supposition that my behavior is caused—for it is, by hypothesis, caused by my own inner choices, desires, and volitions.

THE REFUTATION OF THIS

The theory of soft determinism looks good at first—so good that it has for generations been solemnly taught from numberless philosophical chairs and implanted in the minds of students as sound philosophy—but no great acumen is needed to discover that far from solving any problem, it only camouflages it.

My free actions are those unimpeded and unconstrained motions that arise from my own inner desires, choices, and volitions; let us grant this provisionally. But now, whence arise those inner states that determine what my body shall do? Are they within my control or not? Having made my choice or decision and acted upon it, could I have chosen otherwise or not?

Here the determinist, hoping to surrender nothing and yet to avoid the problem implied in that question, bids us not to ask it; the question itself, he announces, is without meaning. For to say that I could have done otherwise, he says, means only that I *would* have done otherwise *if* those inner states that determined my action had been different; if, that is, I had decided or chosen differently. To ask, accordingly, whether I could have chosen or decided differently is only to ask whether, had I decided to decide differently or chosen to choose differently, or willed to will differently, I would have decided or chosen or willed differently. And this, of course, *is* unintelligible nonsense.

But it is not nonsense to ask whether the causes of my actions—my own inner choices, decisions, and desires—are themselves caused. And of course they are, if determinism is true, for on that thesis everything is caused and determined. And if they are, then we cannot avoid concluding that, given the causal conditions of those inner states, I could not have decided, willed, chosen, or desired otherwise than I in fact did, for this is a logical consequence of the very definition of determinism. Of course we can still say that, *if* the causes of those inner states, whatever they were, had been different, then their effects, those inner states themselves, would have been different, and that in this hypothetical sense I could have decided, chosen, willed, or desired differently—but that only pushes our problem back still another step. For we will then want to know whether the causes of those inner states were within my control; and so on, *ad infinitum*. We are, at each step, permitted to say "could have been otherwise" only in a provisional sense—provided, that is, something else had been different—but must then retract it and replace it with "could not have been otherwise" as soon as we discover, as we must at each step, that whatever would have to have been different could not have been different.

EXAMPLES

Such is the dialectic of the problem. The easiest way to see the shadowy quality of soft determinism, however, is by means of examples.

Let us suppose that my body is moving in various ways, that these motions are not externally constrained or impeded, and that they are all exactly in accordance with my own desires, choices, or acts of will and what not. When I will that my arm should move in a certain way, I find it moving in that way, unobstructed and unconstrained. When I will to speak, my lips and tongue move, unobstructed and unconstrained, in a manner suitable to the formation of the words I choose to utter. Now given that this is a correct description of my behavior, namely, that it consists of the unconstrained and unimpeded motions of my body in response to my own volitions, then it follows that my behavior is free, on the soft determinist's definition of "free." It follows further that I am responsible for that behavior; or at least, that if I am not, it is not from any lack of freedom on my part.

But if the fulfillment of these conditions renders my behavior free—that is to say, if my behavior satisfies the conditions of free action set forth in the theory of soft determinism—then my behavior will be no less free if we assume further conditions that are perfectly consistent with those already satisfied.

We suppose further, accordingly, that while my behavior is entirely in accordance with my own volitions, and thus "free" in terms of the conception of freedom we are examining, my volitions themselves are caused. To make this graphic, we can suppose that an ingenious physiologist can induce in me any volition he pleases, simply by pushing various buttons on an instrument to which, let us suppose, I am attached by numerous wires. All the volitions I have in that situation are, accordingly, precisely the ones he gives me. By pushing one button, he evokes in me the volition to raise my hand; and my hand, being unimpeded, rises in response to that volition. By pushing another, he induces the volition in me to kick, and my foot, being unimpeded, kicks in response to that volition. We can even suppose that the physiologist puts a rifle in my hands, aims it at some passerby, and then, by pushing the proper button, evokes in me the volition to squeeze my finger against the trigger, whereupon the passerby falls dead of a bullet wound.

This is the description of a man who is acting in accordance with his inner volitions, a man whose body is unimpeded and unconstrained in its motions, these motions being the effects of those inner states. It is hardly the description of a free and responsible agent. It is the perfect description of a puppet. To render a man your puppet, it is not necessary forcibly to constrain the motions of his limbs, after the fashion that real puppets are moved. A subtler but no less effective means of making a man your puppet would be to gain complete control of his inner states, and ensuring, as the theory of soft determinism does ensure, that his body will move in accordance with them.

The example is somewhat unusual, but it is no worse for that. It is perfectly intelligible, and it does appear to refute the soft determinist's conception of freedom. One might think that, in such a case, the agent should not have allowed himself to be so rigged in the first place, but this is irrelevant; we can suppose that he was not aware that he was, and was hence unaware of the source of those inner states that prompted his bodily motions. The example can, moreover, be modified in perfectly realistic ways, so as to coincide with actual and familiar cases. One can, for instance, be given a compulsive desire for certain drugs, simply by having them administered to him over a course of time. Suppose, then, that I do, with neither my knowledge nor consent, thus become a victim of such a desire and act upon it. Do I act freely, merely by virtue of the fact that I am unimpeded in my quest for drugs? In a sense I do, surely, but I am hardly free with respect to whether or not I shall use drugs. I never chose to have the desire for them inflicted upon me.

Nor does it, of course, matter whether the inner states which allegedly prompt all my "free" activity are evoked in me by another agent or by perfectly impersonal forces. Whether a desire which causes my body to behave in a certain way is inflicted upon me by another person, for instance, or derived from hereditary factors, or indeed from anything at all, matters not the least. In any case, if it is in fact the cause of my bodily behavior, I cannot but act in accordance with it. Wherever it came from, whether from personal or impersonal origins, it was entirely caused or determined, and not within my control. Indeed, if determinism is true, as the theory of soft determinism holds it to be, all those inner states which cause my body to behave in whatever ways it behaves must arise from circumstances that existed before I was born; for the chain of causes and effects is infinite, and none could have been the least different, given those that preceded.

SIMPLE INDETERMINISM

We might at first now seem warranted in simply denying determinism, and saying that, insofar as they are free, my actions are not caused; or that, if they are caused by my own inner states—my own desires, impulses, choices, volitions, and whatnot—then these, in any case, are not caused. This is a perfectly clear sense in which a man's action, assuming that it was free, could have been otherwise. If it was uncaused, then, even given the conditions under which it occurred and all that preceded, some other act was nonetheless possible, and he did not have to do what he did. Or if his action was the inevitable consequence of his own inner states, and could not have been otherwise given these, we can nevertheless say that these inner states, being uncaused, could have been otherwise, and could thereby have produced different actions.

Only the slightest consideration will show, however, that this simple denial of determinism has not the slightest plausibility. For let us suppose it is true, and that some of my bodily motions—namely, those that I regard as my free acts—are not caused at all or, if caused by my own inner states, that these are not caused. We shall thereby avoid picturing a puppet, to be sure—but only by substituting something even less like a man; for the conception that now emerges is not that of a free man, but of an erratic and jerking phantom, without any rhyme or reason at all.

Suppose that my right arm is free, according to this conception; that is, that its motions are uncaused. It moves this way and that from time to time, but nothing causes these motions. Sometimes it moves forth vigorously, sometimes up, sometimes down, sometimes it just drifts vaguely about—these motions all being wholly free and uncaused. Manifestly I have nothing to do with them at all; they just happen, and neither I nor anyone can ever tell what this arm will be doing next. It might seize a club and lay it on the head of the nearest bystander, no less to my astonishment than his. There will never be any point in asking why these motions occur, or in seeking any explanation of them, for under the conditions assumed there is no explanation. They just happen, from no causes at all.

This is no description of free, voluntary, or responsible behavior. Indeed, so far as the motions of my body or its parts are entirely uncaused, such motions cannot even be ascribed to me as my behavior in the first place, since I have nothing to do with them. The behavior of my arm is just the random motion of a foreign object. Behavior that is mine must be behavior that is within my control, but motions that occur from no causes are without the control of anyone. I can have no more to do with, and no more control over, the uncaused motions of my limbs than a gambler has over the motions of an honest roulette wheel. I can only, like him, idly wait to see what happens.

Nor does it improve things to suppose that my bodily motions are caused by my own inner states, so long as we suppose these to be wholly uncaused. The result will be the same as before. My arm, for example, will move this way and that, sometimes up and sometimes down, sometimes vigorously and sometimes just drifting about, always in response to certain inner states, to be sure. But since these are supposed to be wholly uncaused, it follows that I have no control over them and hence none over their effects. If my hand lays a club forcefully on the nearest bystander, we can indeed say that this motion resulted from an inner club-wielding desire of mine; but we must add that I had nothing to do with that desire, and that it arose, to be followed by its inevitable effect, no less to my astonishment than to his. Things like this do, alas, sometimes happen. We are all sometimes seized by compulsive impulses that arise we know not whence and we do sometimes act upon these. But because they are far from being examples of free, voluntary, and responsible behavior, we need only to learn that behavior was of this sort to conclude that it was not free, voluntary, or responsible. It was erratic, impulsive, and irresponsible.

DETERMINISM AND SIMPLE INDETERMINISM AS THEORIES

Both determinism and simple indeterminism are loaded with difficulties, and no one who has thought much on them can affirm either of them without some embarrassment. Simple indeterminism has nothing whatever to be said for it, except that it appears to remove the grossest difficulties of determinism, only, however, to imply perfect absurdities of its own. Determinism, on the other hand, is at least initially plausible. Men seem to have a natural inclination to believe in it; it is, indeed, almost required for the very exercise of practical intelligence. And beyond this, our experience appears always to confirm it, so long as we are dealing with everyday facts of common experience, as distinguished from the esoteric researches of theoretical physics. But determinism, as applied to human behavior, has implications which few men can casually accept, and they appear to be implications which no modification of the theory can efface.

Both theories, moreoever, appear logically irreconcilable to the two items of data that we set forth at the outset; namely, (1) that my behavior is sometimes the outcome of my deliberation, and (2) that in these and other cases it is sometimes up to me what I do. Because these were our data, it is important to see, as must already be quite clear, that these theories cannot be reconciled to them.

I can deliberate only about my own future actions, and then only if I do not already know what I am going to do. If a certain nasal tickle warns me that I am about to sneeze, for instance, then I cannot deliberate whether to sneeze or not; I can only prepare for the impending convulsion. But if determinism is true, then there are always conditions existing antecedently to everything I do, sufficient for my doing just that, and such as to render it inevitable. If I can know what those conditions are and what behavior they are sufficient to produce, then I can in every such case know what I am going to do and cannot then deliberate about it.

By itself this only shows, of course, that I can deliberate only in ignorance of the causal conditions of my behavior; it does not show that such conditions cannot exist. It is odd, however, to suppose that deliberation should be a mere substitute for clear knowledge. Ignorance is a condition of speculation, inference, and guesswork, which have nothing whatever to do with deliberation. A prisoner awaiting execution may not know when he is going to die, and he may even entertain the hope of reprieve, but he cannot deliberate about this. He can only speculate, guess—and wait.

Worse yet, however, it now becomes clear that I cannot deliberate about what I am going to do, if it is even possible for me to find out in advance, whether I do in fact find out in advance or not. I can deliberate only with the view to deciding what to do, to making up my mind; and this is impossible if I believe that it could be inferred what I am going to do, from conditions already existing, even though I have not made that inference myself. If I believe that what I am going to do has been rendered inevitable by conditions already existing, and could be inferred by anyone having the requisite sagacity, then I cannot try to decide whether to do it or not, for there is simply nothing left to decide. I can at best only guess or try to figure it out myself or, all prognostics failing, I can wait and see; but I cannot deliberate. I deliberate in order to *decide* what *to* do, not to *discover* what it is that I am *going* to do. But if determinism is true, then there are always antecedent conditions sufficient for everything that I do, and this can always be inferred by anyone having the requisite sagacity; that is, by anyone having a knowledge of what those conditions are and what behavior they are sufficient to produce.

This suggests what in fact seems quite clear, that determinism cannot be reconciled with our second datum either, to the effect that it is sometimes up to me what I am going to do. For if it is ever really up to me whether to do this thing or that, then, as we have seen, each alternative course of action must be such that I can do it; not that I can do it in some abstruse or hypothetical sense of "can"; not that I could do it if only something were true that is not true; but in the sense that it is then and there within my power to do it. But this is never so, if determinism is true, for on the very formulation of that theory whatever happens at any time is the only thing that can then happen, given all that precedes it. It is simply a logical consequence of this that whatever I do at any time is the only thing I can then do, given the conditions that precede my doing it. Nor does it help in the least to interpose, among the causal antecedents of my behavior, my own inner states, such as my desires, choices, acts of will, and so on. For even supposing these to be always involved in voluntary behavior—which is highly doubtful in itself—it is a consequence of determinism that these, whatever they are at any time, can never be other than what they then are. Every chain of causes and effects, if determinism is true, is infinite. This is why it is not now up to me whether I shall a moment hence be male or female. The conditions determining my sex have existed through my whole life, and even prior to my life. But if determinism is true, the same holds of anything that I even am, ever become, or ever do. It matters not whether we are speaking of the most patent facts of my being, such as my sex; or the most subtle, such as my feelings, thoughts, desires, or choices. Nothing could be other than it is, given what was; and while we may indeed say, quite idly, that something—some inner state of mind, for instance—*could* have been different, had only something *else* been different, any consolation of this thought evaporates as soon as we add that whatever would have to have been different could not have been different.

It is even more obvious that our data cannot be reconciled to the theory of simple indeterminism. I can deliberate only about my own actions; this is obvious. But the random, uncaused motion of any body whatever, whether it be a part of my body or not, is no action of mine and nothing that is within my power. I might try to guess what these motions will be, just as I might try to guess how a roulette wheel will behave, but I cannot deliberate about them or try to decide what they shall be, simply because these things are not up to me. Whatever is not caused by anything is not caused by me, and nothing could be more plainly inconsistent with saying that it is nevertheless up to me what it shall be.

THE THEORY OF AGENCY

The only conception of action that accords with our data is one according to which men—and perhaps some other things too—are sometimes, but of course not always, self-determining beings; that is, beings which are sometimes the causes of their own behavior. In the case of an action that is free, it must be such that it is caused by the agent who performs it, but such that no antecedent conditions were sufficient for his performing just that action. In the case of an action that is both free and rational, it must be such that the agent who performed it did so for some reason, but this reason cannot have been the cause of it.

Now this conception fits what men take themselves to be; namely, beings who act, or who are agents, rather than things that are merely acted upon, and whose behavior is simply the causal consequence of conditions which they have not wrought. When I believe that I have done something, I do believe that it was I who caused it to be done, I who made something happen, and not merely something within me, such as one of my own subjective states, which is not identical with myself. If I believe that something not identical with myself was the cause of my behavior—some event wholly external to myself, for instance, or even one internal to myself, such as a nerve impulse, volition, or whatnot—then I cannot regard that behavior as being an act of mine, unless I further believe that I was the cause of that external or internal event. My pulse, for example, is caused and regulated by certain conditions existing within me, and not by myself. I do not, accordingly, regard this activity of my body as my action, and would be no more tempted to do so if I became suddenly conscious within myself of those conditions or impulses that produce it. This is behavior with which I have nothing to do, behavior that is not within my immediate control, behavior that is not only not free activity, but not even the activity of an agent to begin with; it is nothing but a mechanical reflex. Had I never learned that my very life depends on this pulse beat, I would regard it with complete indifference, as something foreign to me, like the oscillations of a clock pendulum that I idly contemplate.

Now this conception of activity, and of an agent who is the cause of it, involves two rather strange metaphysical notions that are never applied elsewhere in nature. The first is that of a *self* or *person*—for example, a man—who is not merely a collection of things or events, but a substance and a self-moving being. For on this view it is a man himself, and not merely some part of him or something within him, that is the cause of his own activity. Now we certainly do not know that a man is anything more than an assemblage of physical things and processes, which act in accordance with those laws that describe the behavior of all other physical things and processes. Even though a man is a living being, of enormous complexity, there is nothing, apart from the requirements of this theory, to suggest that his behavior is so radically different in its origin from that of other physical objects, or that an understanding of it must be sought in some metaphysical realm wholly different from that appropriate to the understanding of non-living things.

Second, this conception of activity involves an extraordinary conception of causation, according to which an agent, which is a substance and not an event, can nevertheless be the cause of an event. Indeed, if he is a free agent then he can, on this conception, cause an event to occur—namely, some act of his own—without anything else causing him to do so. This means that an agent is sometimes a cause, without being an antecedent sufficient condition; for if I affirm that I am the cause of some act of mine, then I am plainly not saying that my very existence is sufficient for its occurrence, which would be absurd. If I say that my hand causes my pencil to move, then I am saying that the motion of my hand is, under the other conditions then prevailing, sufficient for the motion of the pencil. But if I then say that I cause my hand to move, I am not saying anything remotely like this, and surely not that the motion of my self is sufficient for the motion of my arm and hand, since these are the only things about me that are moving.

This conception of the causation of events by beings or substances that are not events is, in fact, so different from the usual philosophical conception of a cause that it should not even bear the same name, for "being a cause" ordinarily just means "being an antecedent sufficient condition or set of conditions." Instead, then, of speaking of agents as *causing* their own acts, it would perhaps be better to use another word entirely, and say, for instance, that they *originate* them, *initiate* them, or simply that they *perform* them.

Now this is on the face of it a dubious conception of what a man is. Yet it is consistent with our data, reflecting the presuppositions of deliberation, and appears to be the only conception that is consistent with them, as determinism and simple indeterminism are not. The theory of agency avoids the absurdities of simple indeterminism by conceding that human behavior is caused, while at the same time avoiding the difficulties of determinism by denying that every chain of causes and effects is infinite. Some such causal chains, on this view, have beginnings, and they begin with agents themselves. Moreover, if we are to suppose that it is sometimes up to me what I do, and understand this in a sense which is not consistent with determinism, we must suppose that I am an agent or a being who initiates his own actions, sometimes under conditions which do not determine what action he shall perform. Deliberation becomes, on this view, something that is not only possible but quite rational, for it does make sense to deliberate about activity that is truly my own and that depends in its outcome upon me as its author, and not merely upon something more or less esoteric that is supposed to be intimately associated with me, such as my thoughts, volitions, choices, or whatnot.

One can hardly affirm such a theory of agency with complete comfort, however, and wholly without embarrassment, for the conception of men and their powers which is involved in it is strange indeed, if not positively mysterious. In fact, one can hardly be blamed here for simply denying our data outright, rather than embracing this theory to which they do most certainly point. Our data—to the effect that men do sometimes deliberate before acting, and that when they do, they presuppose among other things that it is up to them what they are going to do—rest upon nothing more than fairly common consent. These data might simply be illusions. It might in fact be that no man ever deliberates, but only imagines that he does, that from pure conceit he supposes himself to be the master of his behavior and the author of his acts. Spinoza has suggested that if a stone, having been thrown into the air, were suddenly to become conscious, it would suppose itself to be the source of its own motion, being then conscious of what it was doing but not aware of the real cause of its behavior. Certainly men are *sometimes* mistaken in believing that they are behaving as a result of choice deliberately arrived at. A man might, for example, easily imagine that his embarking upon matrimony is the result of the most careful and rational deliberation, when in fact the causes, perfectly sufficient for that behavior, might be of an entirely physiological, unconscious origin. If it is sometimes false that we deliberate and then act as the result of a decision deliberately arrived at, even when we suppose it to be true, it might always be false. No one seems able, as we have noted, to describe deliberation without metaphors, and the conception of a thing's being "within one's power" or "up to him" seems to defy analysis or definition altogether, if taken in a sense which the theory of agency appears to require.

These are, then, dubitable conceptions, despite their being so well implanted in the common sense of mankind. Indeed, when we turn to the theory of fatalism, we shall find formidable metaphysical considerations which appear to rule them out altogether. Perhaps here, as elsewhere in metaphysics, we should be content with discovering difficulties, with seeing what is and what is not consistent with such convictions as we happen to have, and then drawing such satisfaction as we can from the realization that, no matter where we begin, the world is mysterious and the men who try to understand it are even more so. This realization can, with some justification, make one feel wise, even in the full realization of his ignorance.

Chapter 23

Antony Flew, R. M. Hare, and Basil Mitchell

Antony Flew was, until his retirement Professor of Philosophy at the University of Reading. R. M. Hare and Basil Mitchell were, until their recent retirements, professors of philosophy at Oxford University. All three were educated at Oxford, and all began their teaching careers at that university. In the debate that follows (a 1948 Oxford University symposium), Flew challenges theists to state the conditions under which they would give up their faith, because, he contends, unless one can state what would falsify one's belief, the belief isn't meaningful. If nothing can count as evidence against the belief, the belief doesn't make a genuine assertion; serious truth claims about reality must be subject to possible falsification.

Hare responds that, on the contrary, religious faith consists of a set of profoundly unfalsifiable propositions (which he calls *bliks*), which govern all of a person's other beliefs. We all have *bliks*, even scientists. The only question is whether we are sane or insane. Religious people thus are not anomalies. Nor should they be distressed by Flew's challenge.

Mitchell seeks a compromise between these two positions. Rational considerations about evidence enter the debate on faith, but no one can say exactly when a gradual accumulation of evidence is sufficient to overthrow religious belief. Although rational considerations do count against faith, the believer will consider it disloyal to allow them to count decisively against faith.

FOR FURTHER READING

Crosson, Frederick, ed. *The Autonomy of Religious Belief* (University of Notre Dame Press, 1981). A valuable set of articles on fideism, especially those of Phillips and Nielsen.

Davis, Stephen. *Faith, Skepticism and Evidence* (Bucknell University Press, 1978).

Delaney, C. F., ed. *Rationality and Religious Belief* (University of Notre Dame Press, 1978). A good collection of essays on faith and reason.

Flew, Antony. *The Presumption of Atheism* (Harper & Row, 1976). Part 1, chaps. 1, 2, and 5 are relevant to the discussion.

Jordan, Jeff, ed. *Gambling on God: Essays on Pascal's Wager* (Rowman & Littlefield, 1994).

Kellenberger, J. *Religious Discovery, Faith and Knowledge* (Prentice-Hall, 1972). A lucid defense of a moderate fideist position.

Mackie, J. L. *The Miracle of Theism: Arguments for and Against the Existence of God* (Clarendon Press, 1982). Probably the best defense of atheism in recent years, taking into consideration every major argument in the field.

Mavrodes, George. *Belief in God* (Random House, 1970). A clear presentation of religious epistemology.

Mitchell, Basil. *The Justification of Religious Belief* (Macmillan, 1973). A good discussion of the cumulative case for theism.

Phillips, D. Z. *Religion Without Explanation* (Basil Blackwell, 1976). A valuable study by one of the foremost Wittgensteinian philosophers.

Plantinga, Alvin, and Nicholas Wolterstorff, eds. *Faith and Rationality* (University of Notre Dame Press, 1983). A valuable collection from a reformed Christian perspective.

Pojman, Louis, ed. *Philosophy of Religion* (Wadsworth, 1998). *Religious Belief and the Will* (Routledge & Kegan Paul, 1986). Contains a history of the subjects, faith and reason.

Swinburne, Richard. *Faith and Reason* (Clarendon Press, 1981).

The Falsification Debate on Religious Belief

ANTONY FLEW

Let us begin with a parable. It is a parable developed from a tale told by John Wisdom in his haunting and revelatory article 'Gods.' Once upon a time two explorers came upon a clearing in the jungle. In the clearing were growing many flowers and many weeds. One explorer says, "Some gardener must tend this plot." The other disagrees, "There is no gardener." So they pitch their tents and set a watch. No gardener is ever seen. "But perhaps he is an invisible gardener." So they set up a barbed-wire fence. They electrify it. They patrol with bloodhounds. (For they remember how H. G. Wells's *The Invisible Man* could be both smelt and touched though he could not be seen.) But no shrieks ever suggest that some intruder has received a shock. No movements of the wire ever betray an invisible climber. The bloodhounds never give cry. Yet still the Believer is not convinced. "But there is a gardener, invisible, intangible, insensible to electric shocks, a gardener who has no scent and makes no sound, a gardener who comes secretly to look after the garden which he loves." At last the Sceptic despairs, "But what remains of your original assertion? Just how does what you call an invisible, intangible, eternally elusive gardener differ from an imaginary gardener or even from no gardener at all?"

In this parable we can see how what starts as an assertion, that something exists or that there is some analogy between certain complexes of phenomena, may be reduced step by step to an altogether different status, to an expression perhaps of a "picture preference." The Sceptic says there is no gardener. The Believer says there is a gardener (but invisible, etc.). One man talks about sexual behaviour. Another man prefers to talk of Aphrodite (but knows that there is not really a superhuman person additional to, and somehow responsible for, all sexual phenomena). The process of qualification may be checked at any point before the original assertion is completely withdrawn and something of that first assertion will remain (Tautology). Mr. Wells's invisible man could not, admittedly, be seen, but in all other respects he was a man like the rest of us. But though the process of qualification may be, and of course usually is checked in time, it is not always judiciously so halted. Someone may dissipate his assertion completely without noticing that he has done so. A fine brash hypothesis may thus be killed by inches, the death by a thousand qualifications.

And in this, it seems to me, lies the peculiar danger, the endemic evil, of theological utterance. Take such utterances as "God has a plan," "God created the world," "God loves us as a father loves his children." They look at first sight very much like assertions, vast cosmological assertions. Of course, this is no sure sign that they either are, or are intended to be, assertions. But let us confine ourselves

From *New Essays in Philosophical Theology*, edited by Antony Flew and Alasdair MacIntyre (Simon & Schuster, 1955).

to the cases where those who utter such sentences intend them to express assertions. (Merely remarking parenthetically that those who intend or interpret such utterances as crypto-commands, expressions of wishes, disguised ejaculations, concealed ethics, or as anything else but assertions, are unlikely to succeed in making them either properly orthodox or practically effective.)

Now to assert that such and such is the case is necessarily equivalent to denying that such and such is not the case. Suppose then that we are in doubt as to what someone who gives vent to an utterance is asserting, or suppose that, more radically, we are sceptical as to whether he is really asserting anything at all, one way of trying to understand (or perhaps it will be to expose) his utterance is to attempt to find what he would regard as counting against, or as being incompatible with, its truth. For if the utterance is indeed an assertion, it will necessarily be equivalent to a denial of the negation of that assertion. And anything which would count against the assertion, or which would induce the speaker to withdraw it and to admit that it had been mistaken, must be part of (or the whole of) the meaning of the negation of that assertion. And to know the meaning of the negation of an assertion, is as near as makes no matter, to know the meaning of that assertion. And if there is nothing which a putative assertion denies then there is nothing which it asserts either: and so it is not really an assertion. When the Sceptic in the parable asked the Believer, "Just how does what you call an invisible, intangible, eternally elusive gardener differ from an imaginary gardener or even from no gardener at all?" he was suggesting that the Believer's earlier statement had been eroded by qualification that it was no longer an assertion at all.

Now it often seems to people who are not religious as if there was no conceivable event or series of events the occurrence of which would be admitted by sophisticated religious people to be a sufficient reason for conceding "There wasn't a God after all" or "God does not really love us then." Someone tells us that God loves us as a father loves his children. We are reassured. But then we see a child dying of inoperable cancer of the throat. His earthly father is driven frantic in his efforts to help, but his Heavenly Father reveals no obvious sign of concern. Some qualification is made—God's love is "not a merely human love" or it is "an inscrutable love," perhaps—and we realize that such sufferings are quite compatible with the truth of the assertion that "God loves us as a father (but, of course, . . .)." We are reassured again. But then perhaps we ask: what is this assurance of God's (appropriately qualified) love worth, what is this apparent guarantee really a guarantee against? Just what would have to happen not merely (morally and wrongly) to tempt but also (logically and rightly) to entitle us to say "God does not love us" or even "God does not exist"? I therefore put to the succeeding symposiasts the simple central question, "What would have to occur or to have occurred to constitute for you a disproof of the love of, or of the existence of, God?"

R. M. HARE

I wish to make it clear that I shall not try to defend Christianity in particular, but religion in general—not because I do not believe in Christianity, but because you cannot understand what Christianity is, until you have understood what religion is.

I must begin by confessing that, on the ground marked out by Flew, he seems to me to be completely victorious. I therefore shift my ground by relating another parable. A certain lunatic is convinced that all dons want to murder him. His friends introduce him to all the mildest and most respectable dons that they can find, and after each of them has retired, they say, "You see, he doesn't really want to murder you; he spoke to you in a most cordial manner; surely you are convinced now?" But the lunatic replies "Yes, but that was only his diabolical cunning; he's really plotting against me the whole time, like the rest of them; I know it I tell you." However many kindly dons are produced, the reaction is still the same.

Now we say that such a person is deluded. But what is he deluded about? About the truth or falsity of an assertion? Let us apply Flew's test to him. There is no behaviour of dons that can be enacted which he will accept as counting against his theory; and therefore his theory, on this test, asserts nothing. But it does not follow that there is no difference between what he thinks about dons and what most of us think about them—otherwise we should not call him a lunatic and ourselves sane, and dons would have no reason to feel uneasy about his presence in Oxford.

Let us call that in which we differ from this lunatic, our respective *bliks*. He has an insane *blik* about dons; we have a sane one. It is important to realize that we have a sane one, not no *blik* at all; for there must be two sides to any argument—if he has a wrong *blik*, then those who are right about dons must have a right one. Flew has shown that a *blik* does not consist in an assertion or system of them; but nevertheless it is very important to have the right *blik*.

Let us try to imagine what it would be like to have different *bliks* about other things than dons. When I am driving my car, it sometimes occurs to me to wonder whether my movements of the steering-wheel will always continue to be followed by corresponding alterations in the direction of the car. I have never had a steering failure, though I have had skids, which must be similar. Moreover, I know enough about how the steering of my car is made, to know the sort of thing that would have to go wrong for the steering to fail—steel joints would have to part, or steel rods break, or something—but how do I know that this won't happen? The truth is, I don't know; I just have a *blik* about steel and its properties, so that normally I trust the steering of my car; but I find it not at all difficult to imagine what it would be like to lose this *blik* and acquire the opposite one. People would say I was silly about steel; but there would be no mistaking the reality of the difference between our respective *bliks*—for example, I should never go in a motor-car. Yet I should hesitate to say that the difference between us was the difference between contradictory assertions. No amount of safe arrivals or bench-tests will remove my *blik* and restore the normal one: for my *blik* is compatible with any finite number of such tests.

It was Hume who taught us that our whole commerce with the world depends upon our *blik* about the world; and that differences between *bliks* about the world cannot be settled by observation of what happens in the world. That was why, having performed the interesting experiment of doubting the ordinary man's *blik* about the world, and showing that no proof could be given to make us adopt one *blik* rather than another, he turned to backgammon to take his mind off the problem. It seems, indeed, to be impossible even to formulate as an assertion the normal *blik* about the world which makes me put my confidence in the future reliability of steel joints, in the continued ability of the road to support my car, and not gape beneath it revealing nothing below; in the general nonhomicidal tendencies of dons; in my own continued well-being (in some sense of that word that I may not now fully understand) if I continue to do what is right according to my lights; in the general likelihood of people like Hitler coming to a bad end. But perhaps a formulation less inadequate than most is to be found in the Psalms: "The earth is weak and all the inhabiters thereof: I bear up the pillars of it."

The mistake of the position which Flew selects for attack is to regard this kind of talk as some sort of *explanation*, as scientists are accustomed to use the word. As such, it would obviously be ludicrous. We no longer believe in God as an Atlas—*nous n'avons pas besoin de cette hypothèse*. But it is nevertheless true to say that, as Hume saw, without a *blik* there can be no explanation; for it is by our *bliks* that we decide what is and what is not an explanation. Suppose we believed that everything that happened, happened by pure chance. This would not of course be an assertion; for it is compatible with anything happening or not happening, and so, incidentally, is its contradictory. But if we had this belief, we should not be able to explain or predict or plan anything. Thus, although we should not be asserting anything different from those of a more normal belief, there would be a great difference between us; and this is the sort of difference that there is between those who really believe in God and those who really disbelieve in him.

The word "really" is important, and may excite suspicion. I put it in, because when people have had a good Christian upbringing, as have most of those who now profess not to believe in any sort of religion, it is very hard to discover what they really believe. The reason why they find it so easy to think that they are not religious, is that they have never got into the frame of mind of one who suffers from the doubts to which religion is the answer. Not for them the terrors of the primitive jungle. Having abandoned some of the more picturesque fringes of religion, they think that they have abandoned the whole thing—whereas in fact they still have got, and could not live without, a religion of a comfortably substantial, albeit highly sophisticated, kind, which differs from that of many "religious people" in little more than this, that "religious people" like to sing Psalms about theirs—a very natural and proper thing to do. But nevertheless there may be a big difference lying behind—the difference between two people who, though side by side, are walking in different directions. I do not know in what direction Flew is walking; perhaps he does not know either. But we have had some examples recently of various ways in which one can walk away from Christianity, and there are any number of possibilities. After all, man has not changed biologically since primitive times; it is his religion that has changed, and it can easily change again. And if you do not think that such changes make a difference, get acquainted with some Sikhs and some Mussulmans of the same Punjabi stock; you will find them quite different sorts of people.

There is an important difference between Flew's parable and my own which we have not yet noticed. The explorers do not *mind* about their garden; they discuss it with interest, but not with concern. But my lunatic, poor fellow, minds about dons; and I mind about the steering of my car; it often has people in it that I care for. It is because I mind very much about what goes on in the garden in which I find myself, that I am unable to share the explorers' detachment.

BASIL MITCHELL

Flew's article is searching and perceptive, but there is, I think, something odd about his conduct of the theologian's case. The theologian surely would not deny that the fact of pain counts against the assertion that God loves men. This very incompatibility generates the most intractable of theological problems—the problem of evil. So the theologian *does* recognize the fact of pain as counting against Christian doctrine. But it is true that he will not allow it—or anything—to count decisively against it; for he is committed by his faith to trust in God. His attitude is not that of the detached observer, but of the believer.

Perhaps this can be brought out by yet another parable. In time of war in an occupied country, a member of the resistance meets one night a stranger who deeply impresses him. They spend that night together in conversation. The Stranger tells the partisan that he himself is on the side of the resistance—indeed that he is in command of it, and urges the partisan to have faith in him no matter what happens. The partisan is utterly convinced at that meeting of the Stranger's sincerity and constancy and undertakes to trust him.

They never meet in conditions of intimacy again. But sometimes the Stranger is seen helping members of the resistance, and the partisan is grateful and says to his friends, "He is on our side."

Sometimes he is seen in the uniform of the police handing over patriots to the occupying power. On these occasions his friends murmur against him; but the partisan still says, "He is on our side." He still believes that, in spite of appearances, the Stranger did not deceive him. Sometimes he asks the Stranger for help and receives it. He is then thankful. Sometimes he asks and does not receive it. Then he says, "The Stranger knows best." Sometimes his friends, in exasperation, say "Well, what *would* he have to do for you to admit that you were wrong and that he is not on our side?" But the partisan refuses to answer. He will not consent to put the Stranger to the test. And sometimes his friends complain, "Well, if *that's* what you mean by his being on our side, the sooner he goes over to the other side the better."

The partisan of the parable does not allow anything to count decisively against the proposition "The Stranger is on our side." This is because he has committed himself to trust the Stranger. But he of course recognizes that the Stranger's ambiguous behaviour *does* count against what he believes about him. It is precisely this situation which constitutes the trial of his faith.

When the partisan asks for help and doesn't get it, what can he do? He can (a) conclude that the stranger is not on our side or, (b) maintain that he is on our side, but that he has reasons for withholding help.

The first he will refuse to do. How long can he uphold the second position without its becoming just silly?

I don't think one can say in advance. It will depend on the nature of the impression created by the Stranger in the first place. It will depend, too, on the manner in which he takes the Stranger's behaviour. If he blandly dismisses it as of no consequence, as having no bearing upon his belief, it will be assumed that he is thoughtless or insane. And it quite obviously won't do for him to say easily, "Oh, when used of the Stranger the phrase 'is on our side' *means* ambiguous behaviour of this sort." In that case he would be like the religious man who says blandly of a terrible disaster, "It is God's will." No, he will only be regarded as sane and reasonable in his belief, if he experiences in himself the full force of the conflict.

It is here that my parable differs from Hare's. The partisan admits that many things may and do count against his belief; whereas Hare's lunatic who has a *blik* about dons doesn't admit that anything counts against his *blik*. Nothing can count against *bliks*. Also the partisan has a reason for having in the first instance committed himself, viz. the character of the

Stranger; whereas the lunatic has no reason for his *blik* about dons—because, of course, you can't have reasons for *bliks*.

This means that I agree with Flew that theological utterances must be assertions. The partisan is making an assertion when he says, "The Stranger is on our side."

Do I want to say that the partisan's belief about the Stranger is, in any sense, an explanation? I think I do. It explains and makes sense of the Stranger's behaviour; it helps to explain also the resistance movement in the context of which he appears. In each case it differs from the interpretation which the others put upon the same facts.

"God loves men" resembles "the Stranger is on our side" (and many other significant statements, e.g. historical ones) in not being conclusively falsifiable. They can both be treated in at least three different ways: (1) As provisional hypotheses to be discarded if experience tells against them; (2) As significant articles of faith; (3) As vacuous formulae (expressing, perhaps, a desire for reassurance) to which experience makes no difference and which make no difference to life.

The Christian, once he has committed himself, is precluded by his faith from taking up the first attitude: "Thou shalt not tempt the Lord thy God." He is in constant danger, as Flew has observed, of slipping into the third. But he need not; and, if he does, it is a failure in faith as well as in logic.

Chapter 24

Gilbert Ryle

Gilbert Ryle (1900–1976) was educated at Oxford University, where, as Waynflete Professor of Philosophy, he greatly influenced students until his death. He was the editor of the philosophically prestigious journal *Mind* from 1948 to 1971. His principal works are *The Concept of Mind* (1949), from which this selection is taken, and *Dilemmas* (1954). He was a foremost proponent of Ordinary Language philosophy, seeking to analyze and rectify the logical mapping of our concepts.

In this essay Ryle applies Ordinary Language philosophy to philosophy of mind, arguing that Cartesian dualism rests on a *category mistake*. A category mistake is a confusion one slips into when something that belongs to one category or framework is mistakenly taken to belong to another. Jokes intentionally thrive on this feature. The statement, "The average woman in the United States has 1.5 children," would be an example of such an error, if one went looking for that extra half a child, treating a functional term "average woman" as a proper noun. Ryle claims that Descartes's dualism creates a similar confusion. That is, just because we speak of bodily functions as different in no way entails that they are two separate entities. Ryle believes that mind is not an extra, metaphysically hidden entity affixed to the body—a "ghost in the machine"—but comprises a person's disposition, abilities, and intention. This functional language can be reduced to observational language, but Ryle denies being a behaviorist, preferring the label functionalist.

FOR FURTHER READING

Berlin, I. "Logical Translation." *Proceeding of the Aristotelian Society 1949–50.*

Flew, Antony, ed. *Logic and Language* (Doubleday Anchor, 1951).

Gross, Barry. *Analytic Philosophy* (Pegasus, 1970).

Ryle, Gilbert. *The Concept of Mind* (Hutchinson, 1949).

Urmson, J. O. *Philosophical Analysis* (Oxford University Press, 1956).

Wood, O.P. and Pitcher, G., eds. *Ryle* (Doubleday Anchor, 1970).

Exorcizing Descartes's "Ghost in the Machine"

(1) THE OFFICIAL DOCTRINE

There is a doctrine about the nature and place of minds which is so prevalent among theorists and even among laymen that it deserves to be described as the official theory. Most philosophers, psychologists and religious teachers subscribe, with minor reservations, to its main articles and, although they admit certain theoretical difficulties in it, they tend to assume that these can be overcome without serious modifications being made to the architecture of the theory. It will be argued here that the central principles of the doctrine are unsound and conflict with the whole body of what we know about minds when we are not speculating about them.

The official doctrine, which hails chiefly from Descartes, is something like this. With the doubtful exceptions of idiots and infants in arms every human being has both a body and a mind. Some would prefer to say that every human being is both a body and a mind. His body and his mind are ordinarily harnessed together, but after the death of the body his mind may continue to exist and function.

Human bodies are in space and are subject to the mechanical laws which govern all other bodies in space. Bodily processes and states can be inspected by external observers. So a man's bodily life is as much a public affair as are the lives of animals and reptiles and even as the careers of trees, crystals and planets.

But minds are not in space, nor are their operations subject to mechanical laws. The workings of one mind are not witnessable by other observers; its career is private. Only I can take direct cognisance of the states and processes of my own mind. A person therefore lives through two collateral histories, one consisting of what happens in and to his body, the other consisting of what happens in and to his mind. The first is public, the second private. The events in the first history are events in the physical world, those in the second are events in the mental world.

It has been disputed whether a person does or can directly monitor all or only some of the episodes of his own private history; but, according to the official doctrine, of at least some of these episodes he has direct and unchallengeable cognisance. In consciousness, self-consciousness and introspection he is directly and authentically apprised of the present states and operations of his mind. He may have great or small uncertainties about concurrent and adjacent episodes in the physical world, but he can have none about at least part of what is momentarily occupying his mind.

It is customary to express this bifurcation of his two lives and of his two worlds by saying that the things and events which belong to the physical world, including his own body, are external, while the workings of his own mind are internal. This antithesis of outer and inner is of course meant to be construed as a metaphor, since minds, not being in space, could not be described as being spatially inside anything else, or as having things going on spatially inside themselves. But relapses from this good intention are common and theorists are found speculating how stimuli, the physical sources of which are yards or miles outside a person's skin, can generate mental responses inside his skull, or how decisions framed inside his cranium can set going movements of his extremities.

Even when "inner" and "outer" are construed as metaphors, the problem how a person's mind and body influence one another is notoriously charged with theoretical difficulties. What the mind wills, the legs, arms and the tongue execute; what affects the ear and the eye has something to do with what the mind perceives; grimaces and smiles betray the mind's moods and bodily castigations lead, it is hoped, to moral improvement. But the actual transactions between the episodes of the private history and those of the public history remain mysterious, since by definition they can belong to neither series. They could not be reported among the happenings described in a person's autobiography of his inner life, but nor could they be reported among those described in some one else's biography of that person's overt career. They can be inspected neither by introspection nor by laboratory experiment. They are

From *The Concept of Mind* (London: Hutchinson and Co., 1949), pp. 11–24.

theoretical shuttlecocks which are forever being bandied from the physiologist back to the psychologist and from the psychologist back to the physiologist.

Underlying this partly metaphorical representation of the bifurcation of a person's two lives there is a seemingly more profound and philosophical assumption. It is assumed that there are two different kinds of existence or status. What exists or happens may have the status of physical existence, or it may have the status of mental existence. Somewhat as the faces of coins are either heads or tails, or somewhat as living creatures are either male or female, so, it is supposed, some existing is physical existing, other existing is mental existing. It is a necessary feature of what has physical existence that it is in space and time, it is a necessary feature of what has mental existence that it is in time but not in space. What has physical existence is composed of matter, or else is a function of matter; what has mental existence consists of consciousness, or else is a function of consciousness.

There is thus a polar opposition between mind and matter, an opposition which is often brought out as follows. Material objects are situated in a common field, known as "space", and what happens to one body in one part of space is mechanically connected with what happens to other bodies in other parts of space. But mental happenings occur in insulated fields, known as "minds", and there is, apart maybe from telepathy, no direct causal connection between what happens in one mind and what happens in another. Only through the medium of the public physical world can the mind of one person make a difference to the mind of another. The mind is its own place and in his inner life each of us lives the life of a ghostly Robinson Crusoe. People can see, hear and jolt one another's bodies, but they are irremediably blind and deaf to the workings of one another's minds and inoperative upon them.

What sort of knowledge can be secured of the workings of a mind? On the one side, according to the official theory, a person has direct knowledge of the best imaginable kind of the workings of his own mind. Mental states and processes are (or are normally) conscious states and processes, and the consciousness which irradiates them can engender no illusions and leaves the door open for no doubts. A person's present thinkings, feelings and willings, his perceivings, rememberings and imaginings are intrinsically "phosphorescent"; their existence and their nature are inevitably betrayed to their owner. The inner life is a stream of consciousness of such a sort that it would be absurd to suggest that the mind whose life is that stream might be unaware of what is passing down it.

True, the evidence adduced recently by Freud seems to show that there exist channels tributary to this stream, which run hidden from their owner. People are actuated by impulses the existence of which they vigorously disavow; some of their thoughts differ from the thoughts which they acknowledge; and some of the actions which they think they will to perform they do not really will. They are thoroughly gulled by some of their own hypocrisies and they successfully ignore facts about their mental lives which on the official theory ought to be patent to them. Holders of the official theory tend, however, to maintain that anyhow in normal circumstances a person must be directly and authentically seized of the present state and workings of his own mind.

Besides being currently supplied with these alleged immediate data of consciousness, a person is also generally supposed to be able to exercise from time to time a special kind of perception, namely inner perception, or introspection. He can take a (non-optical) "look" at what is passing in his mind. Not only can he view and scrutinize a flower through his sense of sight and listen to and discriminate the notes of a bell through his sense of hearing; he can also reflectively or introspectively watch, without any bodily organ of sense, the current episodes of his inner life. This self-observation is also commonly supposed to be immune from illusion, confusion or doubt. A mind's reports of its own affairs have a certainty superior to the best that is possessed by its reports of matters in the physical world. Sense-perceptions can, but consciousness and introspection cannot, be mistaken or confused.

On the other side, one person has no direct access of any sort to the events of the inner life of another. He cannot do better than make problematic inferences from the observed behaviour of the other person's body to the states of mind which, by analogy from his own conduct, he supposes to be signalised by that behaviour. Direct access to the workings of a mind is the privilege of that mind itself; in default of such privileged access, the workings of one mind are inevitably occult to everyone else. For the supposed arguments from bodily movements similar to their own to mental workings similar to their own would lack any possibility of observational corroboration. Not unnaturally, therefore, an adherent of the official theory finds it difficult to resist this consequence of his premisses, that he has no good reason to believe that there do exist minds other than his own. Even if he prefers to believe that to other human bodies there are harnessed minds not unlike his own, he cannot claim to be able to discover their individual characteristics, or the particular things that they undergo and do. Absolute solitude is on this showing the ineluctable destiny of the soul. Only our bodies can meet.

As a necessary corollary of this general scheme there is implicitly prescribed a special way of construing our ordinary concepts of mental powers and operations. The verbs, nouns and adjectives, with which in ordinary life we describe the wits, characters and higher-grade performances of the people with whom we have do, are required to be construed as signifying special episodes in their secret histories, or else as signifying tendencies for such episodes to occur. When someone is described as knowing, believing or guessing something, as hoping, dreading, intending or shirking something, as designing this or being amused at that, these verbs are supposed to denote the occurrence of specific modifications in his (to us) occult stream of consciousness. Only his own privileged access to this stream in direct awareness and introspection could provide authentic testimony that these mental-conduct verbs were correctly or incorrectly applied. The onlooker, be he teacher, critic, biographer or friend, can never assure himself that his comments have any vestige of truth. Yet it was just because we do in fact all know how to make such comments, make them with general correctness and correct them when they turn out to be confused or mistaken, that philosophers found it necessary to construct their theories of the nature and place of minds. Finding mental-conduct concepts being regularly and effectively used, they properly sought to fix their logical geography. But the logical geography officially recommended would entail that there could be no regular or effective use of these mental-conduct concepts in our descriptions of, and prescriptions for, other people's minds.

(2) THE ABSURDITY OF THE OFFICIAL DOCTRINE

Such in outline is the official theory. I shall often speak of it, with deliberate abusiveness, as "the dogma of the Ghost in the Machine". I hope to prove that it is entirely false, and false not in detail but in principle. It is not merely an assemblage of particular mistakes. It is one big mistake and a mistake of a special kind. It is, namely, a category-mistake. It represents the facts of mental life as if they belonged to one logical type or category (or range of types or categories), when they actually belong to another. The dogma is therefore a philosopher's myth. In attempting to explode the myth I shall probably be taken to be denying well-known facts about the mental life of human beings, and my plea that I aim at doing nothing more than rectify the logic of mental-conduct concepts will probably be disallowed as mere subterfuge.

I must first indicate what is meant by the phrase "Category-mistake". This I do in a series of illustrations.

A foreigner visiting Oxford or Cambridge for the first time is shown a number of colleges, libraries, playing fields, museums, scientific departments and administrative offices. He then asks "But where is the University? I have seen where the members of the Colleges live, where the Registrar works, where the scientists experiment and the rest. But I have not yet seen the University in which reside and work the members of your University." It has then to be explained to him that the University is not another collateral institution, some ulterior counterpart to the colleges, laboratories and offices which he has seen. The University is just the way in which all that he has already seen is organized. When they are seen and when their co-ordination is understood, the University has been seen. His mistake lay in his innocent assumption that it was correct to speak of Christ Church, the Bodleian Library, The Ashmolean Museum *and* the University, to speak, that is, as if "the University" stood for an extra member of the class of which these other units are members. He was mistakenly allocating the University to the same category as that to which the other institutions belong.

The same mistake would be made by a child witnessing the march-past of a division, who, having had pointed out to him such and such battalions, batteries, squadrons, etc., asked when the division was going to appear. He would be supposing that a division was counterpart to the units already seen, partly similar to them and partly unlike them. He would be shown his mistake by being told that in watching the battalions, batteries and squadrons marching past he had been watching the division marching past. The march-past was not a parade of battalions, batteries, squadrons *and* a division; it was a parade of the battalions, batteries and squadrons *of* a division.

One more illustration. A foreigner watching his first game of cricket learns what are the functions of the bowlers, the batsmen, the fielders, the umpires and the scorers. He than says "But there is no one left on the field to contribute the famous element of team-spirit. I see who does the bowling, the batting and the wicket-keeping; but I do not see whose role it is to exercise *esprit de corps.*" Once more, it would have to be explained that he was looking for the wrong type of thing. Team-spirit is not another cricketing-operation supplementary to all of the other special tasks. It is, roughly, the keenness with which each of the special tasks is performed, and performing a task keenly is not performing two tasks. Certainly exhibiting team-spirit is not the same thing as bowling or catching, but nor is it a third thing such that we can say that the bowler first bowls *and* then exhibits team-spirit or that a fielder is at a given moment *either* catching *or* displaying *esprit de corps.*

These illustrations of category-mistakes have a common feature which must be noticed. The mistakes were made by people who did not know how to wield the concepts *University, division* and *team-spirit.* Their puzzles arose from inability to use certain items in the English vocabulary.

The theoretically interesting category-mistakes are those made by people who are perfectly competent to apply concepts, at least in the situations with which they are familiar, but are still liable in their abstract thinking to allocate those concepts to logical types to which they do not belong. An instance of a mistake of this sort would be the following story. A student of politics has learned the main differences between the British, the French and the American Constitutions, and has learned also the differences and connections between the Cabinet, Parliament, the various Ministries, the Judicature and the Church of England. But he still becomes embarrassed when asked questions about the connections between the Church of England, the Home Office and the British Constitution. For while the Church and the Home Office are institutions, the British Constitution is not another institution in the same sense of that noun. So inter-institutional relations which can be asserted or denied to hold between the Church and the Home Office cannot be asserted or denied to hold between either of them and the British Constitution. "The British Constitution" is not a term of the same logical type as "the Home Office" and "the Church of England". In a partially similar way, John Doe may be a relative, a friend, an enemy or a stranger to Richard Roe; but he cannot be any of these things to the Average Taxpayer. He knows how to talk sense in certain sorts of discussions about the Average Taxpayer, but he is baffled to say why he could not come across him in the street as he can come across Richard Roe.

It is pertinent to our main subject to notice that, so long as the student of politics continues to think of the British Constitution as a counterpart to the other institutions, he will tend to describe it as a mysteriously occult institution; and so long as John Doe continues to think of the Average Taxpayer as a fellow-citizen, he will tend to think of him as an elusive insubstantial man, a ghost who is everywhere yet nowhere.

My destructive purpose is to show that a family of radical category-mistakes is the source of the double-life theory. The representation of a person as a ghost mysteriously ensconced in a machine derives from this argument. Because, as is true, a person's thinking, feeling and purposive doing cannot be described solely in the idioms of physics, chemistry and physiology, therefore they must be described in counterpart idioms. As the human body is a complex organised unit, so the human mind must be another complex organised unit, though one made of a different sort of stuff and with a different sort of structure. Or, again, as the human body, like any other parcel of matter, is a field of causes and effects, so the mind must be another field of causes and effects, though not (Heaven be praised) mechanical causes and effects.

(3) THE ORIGIN OF THE CATEGORY-MISTAKE

One of the chief intellectual origins of what I have yet to prove to be the Cartesian category-mistake seems to be this. When Galileo showed that his methods of scientific discovery were competent to provide a mechanical theory which should cover every occupant of space, Descartes found in himself two conflicting motives. As a man of scientific genius he could not but endorse the claims of mechanics, yet as a religious and moral man he could not accept, as Hobbes accepted, the discouraging rider to those claims, namely that human nature differs only in degree of complexity from clockwork. The mental could not be just a variety of the mechanical.

He and subsequent philosophers naturally but erroneously availed themselves of the following escape-route. Since mental-conduct words are not to be construed as signifying the occurrence of mechanical processes, they must be construed as signifying the occurrence of non-mechanical processes; since mechanical laws explain movements in space as the effects of other movements in space, other laws must explain some of the non-spatial workings of minds as the effects of other non-spatial workings of minds. The difference between the human behaviours which we describe as intelligent and those which we describe as unintelligent must be a difference in their causation; so, while some movements of human tongues and limbs are the effects of mechanical causes, others must be the effects of non-mechanical causes, i.e. some issue from movements of particles of matter, others from workings of the mind.

The differences between the physical and the mental were thus represented as differences inside the common framework of the categories of "thing", "stuff", "attribute", "stage", "process", "change", "cause" and "effect". Minds are things, but different sorts of things from bodies; mental processes are causes and effects but different sorts of causes and effects from bodily movements. And so on. Somewhat as the foreigner expected the University to be an extra edifice, rather like a college but also considerably different, so the repudiators of mechanism represented minds as extra centers of causal processes, rather like machines but also considerably different from them. Their theory was a paramechanical hypothesis.

That this assumption was at the heart of the doctrine is shown by the fact that there was from the beginning felt to be a major theoretical difficulty in explaining how minds can influence and be influenced by bodies. How can a mental process, such as willing, cause spatial movements like the movements of the tongue? How can a physical change in the optic nerve have among its effects a mind's perception of a flash of light? This notorious crux by itself shows the logical mould into which Descartes pressed his theory of the mind. It was the self-same mould into which he and Galileo set their mechanics. Still unwittingly adhering to the grammar of mechanics, he tried to avert disaster by describing minds in what was merely an obverse vocabulary. The workings of minds had to be described by the mere negatives of the specific descriptions given to bodies; they are not in space, they are not motions, they are not modifications of matter, they are not accessible to public observation. Minds are not bits of clockwork, they are just bits of not-clockwork.

As thus represented, minds are not merely ghosts harnessed to machines, they are themselves just spectral machines. Though the human body is an engine, it is not quite an ordinary engine, since some of its workings are governed by another engine inside it—this interior governor-engine being one of a very special sort. It is invisible, inaudible and it has no size or weight. It cannot be taken to bits and the laws it obeys are not those known to ordinary engineers. Nothing is known of how it governs the bodily engine.

A second major crux points the same moral. Since, according to the doctrine, minds belong to the same category as bodies and since bodies are rigidly governed by mechanical laws, it seemed to many theorists to follow that minds must be similarly governed by rigid non-mechanical laws. The physical world is a deterministic system, so the mental world must be a deterministic system. Bodies cannot help the modifications that they undergo, so minds cannot help pursuing the careers fixed for them. *Responsibility, choice, merit* and *demerit* are therefore inapplicable concepts—unless the compromise solution is adopted of saying that the laws governing mental processes, unlike those governing physical processes, have the congenial attribute of being only rather rigid. The problem of the Freedom of the Will was the problem how to reconcile the hypothesis that minds are to be described in terms drawn from the categories of mechanics with the knowledge that higher-grade human conduct is not of a piece with the behavior of machines.

It is an historical curiosity that it was not noticed that the entire argument was broken-backed. Theorists correctly assumed that any sane man could already recognise the differences between, say, rational and non-rational utterances or between purposive and automatic behaviour. Else there would have been nothing requiring to be salved from mechanism. Yet the explanation given presupposed that one person could in principle never recognise the difference between the rational and the irrational utterances issuing from other human bodies, since he could never get access to the postulated immaterial causes of some of their utterances. Save for the doubtful exception of himself, he could never tell the difference between a man and a Robot. It would have to be conceded, for example, that, for all that we can tell, the inner lives of persons who are classed as idiots or lunatics are as rational as those of anyone else. Perhaps only their overt behaviour is disappointing; that is to say, perhaps "idiots" are not really idiotic, or "lunatics" lunatic. Perhaps, too, some of those who are classed as sane are really idiots. According to the theory, external observers could never know how the overt behaviour of others is correlated with their mental powers and processes and so they could never know or even plausibly conjuncture whether their applications of mental-conduct concepts to these other people were correct or incorrect. It would then be hazardous or impossible for a man to claim sanity or logical consistency even for himself, since he would be debarred from comparing his own performances with those of others. In short, our characterisations of persons and their performances as intelligent, prudent and virtuous or as stupid, hypocritical and cowardly could never have been made, so the problem of providing a special causal hypothesis to serve as the basis of such diagnoses would never have arisen. The question, "How do persons differ from machines?" arose just because everyone already knew how to apply mental-conduct concepts before the new causal hypothesis was introduced. This causal hypothesis could not therefore be the source of the criteria used in those applications. Nor, of course, has the causal hypothesis in any degree improved our handling of those criteria. We still distinguish good from bad arithmetic, politic from impolitic conduct and fertile from infertile imaginations in the ways in which Descartes himself distinguished them before and after he speculated how the applicability of these criteria was compatible with the principle of mechanical causation.

He had mistaken the logic of his problem. Instead of asking by what criteria intelligent behaviour is actually distinguished from non-intelligent behaviour, he asked "Given that the principle of mechanical causation does not tell us the difference, what other causal principle will tell it us?" He realised that the problem was not one of mechanics and assumed that it must therefore be one of some counterpart to mechanics. Not unnaturally psychology is often cast for just this role.

When two terms belong to the same category, it is proper to construct conjunctive propositions embodying them. Thus a purchaser may say that he bought a left-hand glove and a right-hand glove, but not that he bought a left-hand glove, a right-hand glove and a pair of gloves. "She came home in a flood of tears and a sedan-chair" is a well-known joke based on the absurdity of conjoining terms of different types. It would have been equally ridiculous to construct the disjunction "She came home either in a flood of tears or else in a sedan-chair". Now the dogma of the Ghost in the Machine does just this. It maintains that there exist both bodies and minds; that there occur physical processes and mental processes; that there are mechanical causes of corporeal movements and mental causes of corporeal movements. I shall argue that these and other analogous conjunctions are absurd; but, it must be noticed, the argument will not show that either of the illegitimately conjoined propositions is absurd in itself. I am not, for example, denying that there occur mental processes. Doing long division is a mental process and so is making a joke. But I am saying that the phrase "there occur mental processes" does not mean the same sort of thing as "there occur physical processes", and, therefore, that it makes no sense to conjoin or disjoin the two.

If my argument is successful, there will follow some interesting consequences. First, the hallowed contrast between Mind and Matter will be dissipated, but dissipated not by either of the equally hallowed absorptions of Mind by Matter or of Matter by Mind, but in quite a different way. For the seeming contrast of the two will be shown to be as illegitimate as would be the contrast of "she came home in a flood of tears" and "she came home in a sedan-chair". The belief that there is a polar opposition between Mind and Matter is the belief that they are terms of the same logical type.

It will also follow that both Idealism and Materialism are answers to an improper question. The "reduction" of the material world to mental states and processes, as well as the "reduction" of mental states and processes to physical states and processes, presuppose the legitimacy of the disjunction "Either there exist minds or there exist bodies (but not both)". It would be like saying, "Either she bought a left-hand and a right-hand glove or she bought a pair of gloves (but not both)".

It is perfectly proper to say, in one logical tone of voice, that there exist minds and to say, in another logical tone of voice, that there exist bodies. But these expressions do not indicate two different species of existence, for "existence" is not a generic word like "coloured" or "sexed". They indicate two different senses of "exist", somewhat as "rising" has different senses in "the tide is rising", "hopes are rising", and "the average age of death is rising". A man would be thought to be making a poor joke who said that three things are now rising, namely the tide, hopes and the average age of death. It would be just as good or bad a joke to say that there exist prime numbers and Wednesdays and public opinions and navies; or that there exist both minds and bodies. . . .

(4) HISTORICAL NOTE

It would not be true to say that the official theory derives solely from Descartes's theories, or even from a more widespread anxiety about the implications of seventeenth century mechanics. Scholastic and Reformation theology had schooled the intellects of the scientists as well as of the laymen, philosophers and clerics of that age. Stoic-Augustinian theories of the will were embedded in the Calvinist doctrines of sin and grace; Platonic and Aristotelian theories of the intellect shaped the orthodox doctrines of the immortality of the soul. Descartes was reformulating already prevalent theological doctrines of the soul in the new syntax of Galileo. The theologian's privacy of conscience became the philosopher's privacy of consciousness, and what had been the bogy of Predestination reappeared as the bogy of Determinism.

It would also not be true to say that the two-worlds myth did no theoretical good. Myths often do a lot of theoretical good, while they are still new. One benefit bestowed by the para-mechanical myth was that it partly superannuated the then prevalent para-political myth. Minds and their Faculties had previously been described by analogies with political superiors and political subordinates. The idioms used were those of ruling obeying, collaborating and rebelling. They survived and still survive in many ethical and some epistemological discussions. As, in physics, the new myth of occult Forces was a scientific improvement on the old myth of Final Causes, so, in anthropological and psychological theory, the new myth of hidden operations, impulses and agencies was an improvement on the old myth of dictations, deferences and disobediences.

Chapter 25

THOMAS NAGEL

Thomas Nagel (1937–) is Professor of Philosophy at New York University and the author of several works, including *The View from Nowhere* (1986). Much of Nagel's work involves showing the incongruities between objective and subjective perspectives. Something vital is lost in the process of reducing the subjective experience to objective description, for example when philosophers try to reduce mental states to brain states.

In our first selection Nagel argues against the view that the objective perspective is the correct one. He contends that the peculiarity of the subjective experience is that increased attention to the objective actually diminishes the reality of the experience.

In our second selection, "Moral Luck," Nagel argues against the Kantian view that morality is beyond luck, that we are all fully rational participants in the moral enterprise who have all equal opportunity to be moral. He argues that this overly simple view fails to account for the way external factors impinge on our moral life. "Where a significant aspect of what someone does depends on factors beyond his control, yet we continue to treat him in that respect as an object of moral judgment, it can be called moral luck."

Nagel discusses four types of moral luck: constitutional luck, circumstantial luck, consequential luck in which consequences retrospectively justify an otherwise immoral act (or fail to justify an otherwise moral one), and consequential luck (in which the consequences affect the type or quality of blame, remorse, or moral praise).

FOR FURTHER READING

Acton, Harry. *Kant's Moral Philosophy* (Macmillan, 1970).

Baier, Kurt. *The Moral Point of View* (Cornell University Press, 1958).

Broad, C. D. *Five Types of Ethical Theory* (Routledge and Kegan Paul, 1930).

Donagan, Alan. *The Theory of Morality* (University of Chicago Press, 1977). A comprehensive deontological account of ethical theory.

Feldman, Fred. *Introductory Ethics* (Prentice-Hall, 1978), chaps. 7 and 8. A clear and critical exposition.

Gewirth, Alan. *Reason and Morality* (University of Chicago, 1978). Important but advanced.

Harris, C. E. *Applying Moral Theories* (Wadsworth, 1986), chap. 7. An excellent exposition of contemporary deontological theories, especially of Gewirth's work.

Hill, Tom. *Dignity and Practical Reason* (Cornell University Press, 1992).

Kant, Immanuel. *Critique of Practical Reason*, trans. Lewis White Beck (Bobbs-Merrill, 1956).

———. *Foundations of the Metaphysic of Morals*, trans. Lewis White Beck (Bobbs-Merrill, 1959).

Korgaard, Christine. *Creating the Kingdom of Ends* (Cambridge University Press. 1995).

Louden, Robert. *Morality and Moral Theory* (Oxford University Press, 1991). A sophisticated contemporary account combining Kantian and virtue ethics.

Nagel, Thomas. *Mortal Questions* (Cambridge University Press, 1979).

———. *Other Minds* (Oxford University Press, 1995).

———. *The Possibility of Altruism* (Oxford University Press, 1970).

———. *The View from Nowhere* (Oxford University Press, 1986).

O'Neill, Onora. *Acting on Principle: An Essay on Kantian Ethics* (Columbia University Press, 1975).

———. *Constructions of Reason* (Cambridge University Press, 1989).

Raphael, D. D. *Moral Philosophy* (Oxford University Press, 1981), chap. 6.

Ross, W. D. *Kant's Ethical Theory* (Clarendon Press, 1954).

Ward, Kieth. *The Development of Kant's Views of Ethics* (Blackwell, 1972).

Wolff, Robert P. *The Autonomy of Reason: A Commentary on Kant's "Groundwork of the Metaphysic of Morals"* (Harper & Row, 1973).

What Is It Like to Be a Bat?

Consciousness is what makes the mind-body problem really intractable. Perhaps that is why current discussions of the problem give it little attention or get it obviously wrong. The recent wave of reductionist euphoria has produced several analyses of mental phenomena and mental concepts designed to explain the possibility of some variety of materialism, psychophysical identification, or reduction. But the problems dealt with are those common to this type of reduction and other types, and what makes the mind-body problem unique, and unlike the water–H_2O problem or the Turing machine–IBM machine problem or the lightning–electrical discharge problem or the gene-DNA problem or the oak tree–hydrocarbon problem, is ignored. Every reductionist has his favorite analogy from modern science. It is most unlikely that any of these unrelated examples of successful reduction will shed light on the relation of mind to brain. But philosophers share the general human weakness for explanations of what is incomprehensible in terms suited for what is familiar and well understood, though entirely different. This has led to the acceptance of implausible accounts of the mental largely because they would permit familiar kinds of reduction. I shall try to explain why the usual examples do not help us to understand the relation between mind and body—why, indeed, we have at present no conception of what an explanation of the physical nature of a mental phenomenon would be. Without consciousness the mind-body problem would be much less interesting. With consciousness it seems hopeless. The most important and characteristic feature of conscious mental phenomena is very poorly understood. Most reductionist theories do not even try to explain it. And careful examination will show that no currently available concept of reduction is applicable to it. Perhaps a new theoretical form can be devised for the purpose, but such a solution, if it exists, lies in the distant intellectual future.

Conscious experience is a widespread phenomenon. It occurs at many levels of animal life, though we cannot be sure of its presence in the simpler organisms, and it is very difficult to say in general what provides evidence of it. (Some extremists have been prepared to deny it even of mammals other than man.) No doubt it occurs in countless forms totally unimaginable to us, on other planets in other solar systems throughout the universe. But no matter how the form may vary, the fact that an organism has conscious experience *at all* means, basically, that there is something it is like to *be* that organism. There may be further implications about the form of the experience; there may even (though I doubt it)

From Thomas Nagel, "What Is It Like to Be a Bat," in *Philosophical Review* (October 1974). Reprinted by permission of the author. Footnotes edited.

be implications about the behavior of the organism. But fundamentally an organism has conscious mental states if and only if there is something that it is like to *be* that organism—something it is like *for* the organism.

We may call this the subjective character of experience. It is not captured by any of the familiar, recently devised reductive analyses of the mental, for all of them are logically compatible with its absence. It is not analyzable in terms of any explanatory system of functional states, or intentional states, since these could be ascribed to robots or automata that behaved like people though they experienced nothing. It is not analyzable in terms of the causal role of experiences in relation to typical human behavior—for similar reasons. I do not deny that conscious mental states and events cause behavior, nor that they may be given functional characterizations. I deny only that this kind of thing exhausts their analysis. Any reductionist program has to be based on an analysis of what is to be reduced. If the analysis leaves something out, the problem will be falsely posed. It is useless to base the defense of materialism on any analysis of mental phenomena that fails to deal explicitly with their subjective character. For there is no reason to suppose that a reduction which seems plausible when no attempt is made to account for consciousness can be extended to include consciousness. Without some idea, therefore, of what the subjective character of experience is, we cannot know what is required of physicalist theory.

While an account of the physical basis of mind must explain many things, this appears to be the most difficult. It is impossible to exclude the phenomenological features of experience from a reduction in the same way that one excludes the phenomenal features of an ordinary substance from a physical or chemical reduction of it—namely, by explaining them as effects on the minds of human observers. If physicalism is to be defended, the phenomenological features must themselves be given a physical account. But when we examine their subjective character it seems that such a result is impossible. The reason is that every subjective phenomenon is essentially connected with a single point of view, and it seems inevitable that an objective, physical theory will abandon that point of view.

Let me first try to state the issue somewhat more fully than by referring to the relation between the subjective and the objective. This is far from easy. Facts about what it is like to be an X are very peculiar, so peculiar that some may be inclined to doubt their reality, or the significance of claims about them. To illustrate the connexion between subjectivity and a point of view, and to make evident the importance of subjective features, it will help to explore the matter in relation to an example that brings out clearly the divergence between the two types of conception, subjective and objective.

I assume we all believe that bats have experience. After all, they are mammals, and there is no more doubt that they have experience than that mice or pigeons or whales have experience. I have chosen bats instead of wasps or flounders because if one travels too far down the phylogenetic tree, people gradually shed their faith that there is experience there at all. Bats, although more closely related to us than those other species, nevertheless present a range of activity and a sensory apparatus so different from ours that the problem I want to pose is exceptionally vivid (though it certainly could be raised with other species). Even without the benefit of philosophical reflection, anyone who has spent some time in an enclosed space with an excited bat knows what it is to encounter a fundamentally *alien* form of life.

I have said that the essence of the belief that bats have experience is that there is something that it is like to be a bat. Now we know that most bats (the microchiroptera, to be precise) perceive the external world primarily by sonar, or echolocation, detecting the reflections, from objects within range, of their own rapid, subtly modulated, high-frequency shrieks. Their brains are designed to correlate the outgoing impulses with the subsequent echoes, and the information thus acquired enables bats to make precise discrimination of distance, size, shape, motion, and texture comparable to those we make by vision. But bat sonar, though clearly a form of perception, is not similar in its operation to any sense that we possess, and there is no reason to suppose that it is subjectively like anything we can experience or imagine. This appears to create difficulties for the notion of what it is like to be a bat. We must consider whether any method will permit us to extrapolate to the inner life of the bat from our own case,[1] and if not, what alternative methods there may be for understanding the notion.

Our own experience provides the basic material for our imagination, whose range is therefore limited. It will not help to try to imagine that one has webbing on one's arms, which enables one to fly around at dusk and dawn catching insects in one's mouth; that one has very poor vision, and perceives the surrounding world by a system of reflected high-frequency sound signals; and that one spends the day hanging upside down by one's feet in an attic. Insofar as I can imagine this (which is not very far), it tells me only what it would be like for *me* to behave as a bat behaves. But that is not the question. I want to know what it is like for a *bat* to be a bat. Yet if I try to imagine this, I am restricted to the resources of my own mind, and those resources are inadequate to the task. I cannot perform it either by imagining additions to my present experience, or by imagining segments gradually subtracted from it, or by imagining some combination of additions, subtractions, and modifications.

To the extent that I could look and behave like a wasp or a bat without changing my fundamental structure, my experiences would not be anything like the experiences of those animals. On the other hand, it is doubtful that any meaning can be attached to the supposition that I should possess the internal neurophysiological constitution of a bat. Even if I could by gradual degrees be transformed into a bat, nothing in my present constitution enables me to imagine what the experiences of such a future stage of myself thus metamorphosed would be like. The best evidence would come from the experiences of bats, if we only knew what they were like.

So if extrapolation from our own case is involved in the idea of what it is like to be a bat, the extrapolation must be incompletable. We cannot form more than a schematic conception of what it *is* like. For example, we may ascribe general *types* of experience on the basis of the animal's structure and behavior. Thus we describe bat sonar as a form of three-dimensional forward perception; we believe that bats feel some versions of pain, fear, hunger, and lust, and that they have other, more familiar types of perception besides sonar. But we believe that these experiences also have in each case a specific subjective character, which it is beyond our ability to conceive. And if there is conscious life elsewhere in the universe, it is likely that some of it will not be describable even in the most general experiential terms available to us.[2] (The problem is not confined to exotic cases, however, for it exists between one person and another. The subjective character of the experience of a person deaf and blind from birth is not accessible to me, for example, nor presumably is mine to him. This does not prevent us each from believing that the other's experience has such a subjective character.)

If anyone is inclined to deny that we can believe in the existence of facts like this whose exact nature we cannot possibly conceive, he should reflect that in contemplating the bats we are in much the same position that intelligent bats or Martians[3] would occupy if they tried to form a conception of what it was like to be us. The structure of their own minds might make it impossible for them to succeed, but we know they would be wrong to conclude that there is not anything precise that it is like to be us: that only certain general types of mental state could be ascribed to us (perhaps perception and appetite would be concepts common to us both; perhaps not). We know they would be wrong to draw such a skeptical conclusion because we know what it is like to be us. And we know that while it includes an enormous amount of variation and complexity, and while we do not possess the vocabulary to describe it adequately, its subjective character is highly specific, and in some respects describable in terms that can be understood only by creatures like us. The fact that we cannot expect ever to accommodate in our language a detailed description of Martian or bat phenomenology should not lead us to dismiss as meaningless the claim that bats and Martians have experiences fully comparable in richness of detail to our own. It would be fine if someone were to develop concepts and a theory that enabled us to think about those things, but such an understanding may be permanently denied to us by the limits of our nature. And to deny the reality or logical significance of what we can never describe or understand is the crudest form of cognitive dissonance.

This brings us to the edge of a topic that requires much more discussion than I can give it here: namely, the relation between facts on the one hand and conceptual schemes or systems of representation on the other. My realism about the subjective domain in all its forms implies a belief in the existence of facts beyond the reach of human concepts. Certainly it is possible for a human being to believe that there are facts which humans never *will* possess the requisite concepts to represent or comprehend. Indeed, it would be foolish to doubt this, given the finiteness of humanity's expectations. After all, there would have been transfinite numbers even if everyone had been wiped out by the Black Death before Cantor discovered them. But one might also believe that there are facts which *could* not ever be represented or comprehended by human beings, even if the species lasted for ever—simply because our structure does not permit us to operate with concepts of the requisite type. This impossibility might even be observed by other beings, but it is not clear that the existence of such beings, or the possibility of their existence, is a precondition of the significance of the hypothesis that there are humanly inaccessible facts. (After all, the nature of beings with access to humanly inaccessible facts is presumably itself a humanly inaccessible fact.) Reflection on what it is like to be a bat seems to lead us, therefore, to the conclusion that there are facts that do not consist in the truth of propositions expressible in a human language. We can be compelled to recognize the existence of such facts without being able to state or comprehend them.

I shall not pursue this subject, however. Its bearing on the topic before us (namely, the mind-body problem) is that it enables us to make a general observation about the subjective character of experience. Whatever may be the status of facts about what it is like to be a human being, or a bat, or a Martian, these appear to be facts that embody a particular point of view.

I am not adverting here to the alleged privacy of experience to its possessor. The point of view in question is not one accessible only to a single individual. Rather it is a *type*. It is often possible to take up a point of view other than one's own, so the comprehension of such facts is not limited to one's own case. There is a sense in which phenomenological facts are perfectly objective: One person can know or say of another what the quality of the other's experience is. They are subjective, however, in the sense that even this objective ascription of experience is possible only for someone sufficiently similar to the object of ascription to be able to adopt his point of view—to understand the ascription in the first person as well as in the third, so to speak. The more different from oneself the other experiencer is, the less success one can expect with this enterprise. In our own case we occupy the relevant point of view, but we will have as much difficulty understanding our own experience properly if we approach it from another point of view as we would if we tried to understand the experience of another species without taking up *its* point of view.

This bears directly on the mind-body problem. For if the facts of experience—facts about what it is like *for* the experiencing organism—are accessible only from one point of view, then it is a mystery how the true character of experiences could be revealed in the physical operation of that organism. The latter is a domain of objective facts *par excellence*—the kind that can be observed and understood from many points of view and by individuals with differing perceptual systems. There are no comparable imaginative obstacles to the acquisition of knowledge about bat neurophysiology by human scientists, and intelligent bats or Martians might learn more about the human brain than we ever will.

This is not by itself an argument against reduction. A Martian scientist with no understanding of visual perception could understand the rainbow, or lightning, or clouds as physical phenomena, though he would never be able to understand the human concepts of rainbow, lightning, or cloud, or the place these things occupy in our phenomenal world. The objective nature of the things picked out by these concepts could be apprehended by him because, although the concepts themselves are connected with a particular point of view and a particular visual phenomenology, the things apprehended from that point of view are not: They are observable from the point of view but external to it; hence they can be comprehended from other points of view also, either by the same organisms or by others. Lightning has an objective character that is not exhausted by its visual appearance, and this can be investigated by a Martian without vision. To be precise, it has a *more* objective character than is revealed in its visual appearance. In speaking of the move from subjective characterization, I wish to remain noncommittal about the existence of an end point, the completely objective intrinsic nature of the thing, which one might or might not be able to reach. It may be more accurate to think of objectivity as a direction in which the understanding can travel. And in understanding a phenomenon like lightning, it is legitimate to go as far away as one can from a strictly human viewpoint.

In the case of experience, on the other hand, the connexion with a particular point of view seems much closer. It is difficult to understand what could be meant by the *objective* character of an experience, apart from the particular point of view from which its subject apprehends it. After all, what would be left of what it was like to be a bat if one removed the viewpoint of the bat? But if experience does not have, in addition to its subjective character, an objective nature that can be apprehended from many different points of view, then how can it be supposed that a Martian investigating my brain might be observing physical processes which were my mental processes (as he might observe physical processes which were bolts of lightning), only from a different point of view? How, for that matter, could a human physiologist observe them from another point of view?[4]

We appear to be faced with a general difficulty about psychophysical reduction. In other areas the process of reduction is a move in the direction of greater objectivity, toward a more accurate view of the real nature of things. This is accomplished by reducing our dependence on individual or species-specific points of view toward the object of investigation. We describe it not in terms of the impressions it makes on our senses, but in terms of its more general effects and of properties detectable by means other than the human senses. The less it depends on a specifically human viewpoint, the more objective is our description. It is possible to follow this path because although the concepts and ideas we employ in thinking about the external world are initially applied from a point of view that involves our perceptual apparatus, they are used by us to refer to things beyond themselves—toward which we *have* the phenomenal point of view. Therefore we can abandon it in favor of another, and still be thinking about the same things.

Experience itself, however, does not seem to fit the pattern. The idea of moving from appearance to reality seems to make no sense here. What is the analogue in this case to pursuing a more objective understanding of the same phenomena by abandoning the initial subjective viewpoint toward them in favour of another that is more objective but concerns the same thing? Certainly it *appears* unlikely that we will get closer to the real nature of human experience by leaving behind the particularity of our human point of view and striving for a description in terms accessible to beings that could not imagine what it was like to be us. If the subjective character of experience is fully comprehensible only from one point of view, then any shift to greater objectivity—that is, less attachment to a specific viewpoint—does not take us nearer to the real nature of the phenomenon: It takes us farther away from it.

In a sense, the seeds of this objection to the reducibility of experience are already detectable in successful cases of reduction; for in discovering sound to be, in reality, a wave phenomenon in air or other media, we leave behind one viewpoint to take up another, and the auditory, human or animal viewpoint that we leave behind remains unreduced. Members of radically different species may both understand the same physical events in objective terms, and this does not require that they understand the phenomenal forms in which those events appear to the senses of members of the other species. Thus it is a condition of their referring to a common reality that their more particular viewpoints are not part of the common reality that they both apprehend. The reduction can succeed only if the species-specific viewpoint is omitted from what is to be reduced.

But while we are right to leave this point of view aside in seeking a fuller understanding of the external world, we cannot ignore it permanently, since it is the essence of the internal world, and not merely a point of view on it. Most of the neobehaviorism of recent philosophical psychology results from the effort to substitute an objective concept of mind for the real thing, in order to have nothing left over which cannot be reduced. If we acknowledge that a physical theory of mind must account for the subjective character of experience, we must admit that no presently available conception gives us a clue how this could be done. The problem is unique. If mental processes are indeed physical processes, then there is something it is like, intrinsically, to undergo certain physical processes. What it is for such a thing to be the case remains a mystery.

What moral should be drawn from these reflections, and what should be done next? It would be a mistake to conclude that physicalism must be false. Nothing is proved by the inadequacy of physicalist hypotheses that assume a faulty objective analysis of mind. It would be truer to say that physicalism is a position we cannot understand because we do not at present have any conception of how it might be true. Perhaps it will be thought unreasonable to require such a conception as a condition of understanding. After all, it might be said, the meaning of physicalism is clear enough: Mental states are states of the body; mental events are physical events. We do not know *which* physical states and events they are, but that should not prevent us from understanding the hypothesis. What could be clearer than the words "is" and "are"?

But I believe it is precisely this apparent clarity of the word "is" that is deceptive. Usually, when we are told that X is Y we know *how* it is supposed to be true, but that depends on a conceptual or theoretical background and is not conveyed by the "is" alone. We know how both "X" and "Y" refer, and the kinds of things to which they refer, and we have a rough idea how the two referential paths might converge on a single thing, be it an object, a person, a process, an event or whatever. But when the two terms of the identification are very disparate it may not be so clear how it could be true. We may not have even a rough idea of how the two referential paths could converge, or what kind of things they might converge on, and a theoretical framework may have to be supplied to enable us to understand this. Without the framework, an air of mysticism surrounds the identification.

This explains the magical flavor of popular presentations of fundamental scientific discoveries, given out as propositions to which one must subscribe without really understanding them. For example, people are now told at an early age that all matter is really energy. But despite the fact that they know what "is" means, most of them never form a conception of what makes this claim true, because they lack the theoretical background.

At the present time the status of physicalism is similar to that which the hypothesis that matter is energy would have had if uttered by a pre-Socratic philosopher. We do not have the beginnings of a conception of how it might be true. In order to understand the hypothesis that a mental event is a physical event, we require more than an understanding of the word "is." The idea of how a mental and a physical term might refer to the same thing is lacking, and the usual analogies with theoretical identification in other fields fail to supply it. They fail because if we construe the reference of mental terms to physical events on the usual model, we either get a reappearance of separate subjective events as the effects through which mental reference to physical events is secured, or else we get a false account of how mental terms refer (for example, a causal behaviorist one).

Strangely enough, we may have evidence for the truth of something we cannot really understand. Suppose a caterpillar is locked in a sterile safe by someone unfamiliar with insect metamorphosis, and weeks later the safe is reopened, revealing a butterfly. If the person knows that the safe has been shut the whole time, he has reason to believe that the butterfly is or was once the caterpillar, without having any idea in what sense this might be so. (One possibility is that the caterpillar contained a tiny winged parasite that devoured it and grew into the butterfly.) It is conceivable that we are in such a position with regard to physicalism. Donald Davidson has argued that if mental events have physical causes and effects, they must have physical descriptions. He holds that we have reason to believe this even though we do not—and in fact *could* not—have a general psychophysical theory. His argument applies to intentional mental events, but I think we also have some reason to believe that sensations are physical processes, without being in a position to understand how. Davidson's position is that certain physical events have irreducibly mental properties, and perhaps some view describable in this way is correct. But nothing of which we can now form a conception corresponds to it; nor have we any idea what a theory would be like that enabled us to conceive of it. Very little work has been done on the basic question (from which mention of the brain can be entirely omitted) whether any sense can be made of experiences' having an objective character at all. Does it make sense, in other words, to ask what my experiences are *really* like, as opposed to how they appear to me? We cannot genuinely understand the hypothesis that their nature is captured in a physical description unless we understand the more fundamental idea that they *have* an objective nature (or that objective processes can have a subjective nature).

I should like to close with a speculative proposal. It may be possible to approach the gap between subjective and objective from another direction. Setting aside temporarily the relation between the mind and the brain, we can pursue a more objective understanding of the mental in its own right. At present we are completely unequipped to think about the subjective character of experience without relying on the imagination—without taking up the point of view of the experiential subject. This should be regarded as a challenge to form new concepts and devise a new method—an objective phenomenology not dependent on empathy or the imagination. Though presumably it would not capture everything, its goal would be to describe, at least in part, the subjective character of experiences in a form comprehensible to beings incapable of having those experiences.

We would have to develop such a phenomenology to describe the sonar experiences of bats; but it would also be possible to begin with humans. One might try, for example, to develop concepts that could be used to explain to a person blind from birth what it was like to see. One would reach a blank wall eventually, but it should be possible to devise a method of expressing in objective terms much more than we can at present, and with much greater precision. The loose intermodal analogies—for example, 'Red is like the sound of a trumpet'—which crop up in discussions of this subject are of little use. That should be clear to anyone who has both heard a trumpet and seen red. But structural features of perception might be more accessible to objective description, even though something would be left out. And concepts alternative to those we learn in the first person may enable us to arrive at a kind of understanding even of our own experience which is denied us by the very ease of description and lack of distance that subjective concepts afford.

Apart from its own interest, a phenomenology that is in this sense objective may permit questions about the physical basis of experience to assume a more intelligible form. Aspects of subjective experience that admitted this kind of objective description might be better candidates for objective explanations of a more familiar sort. But whether or not this guess is correct, it seems unlikely that any physical theory of mind can be contemplated until more thought has been given to the general problem of subjective and objective. Otherwise we cannot even pose the mind-body problem without sidestepping it.

Notes

1. By "our own case," I do not mean just "my own case," but rather the mentalistic ideas that we apply unproblematically to ourselves and other human beings.
2. Therefore the analogical form of the English expression "what it is *like*" is misleading. It does not mean "what (in our experience) it *resembles*," but rather "how it is for the subject himself."
3. Any intelligent extraterrestrial beings totally different from us.
4. The problem is not just that when I look at the *Mona Lisa*, my visual experience has a certain quality, no trace of which is to be found by someone looking into my brain. For even if he did observe there a tiny image of the *Mona Lisa*, he would have no reason to identify it with the experience.

Moral Luck

Kant believed that good or bad luck should influence neither our moral judgment of a person and his actions, nor his moral assessment of himself.

> The good will is not good because of what it effects or accomplishes or because of its adequacy to achieve some proposed end; it is good only because of its willing, i.e., it is good of itself. And, regarded for itself, it is to be esteemed incomparably higher than anything which could be brought about by it in favor of any inclination or even of the sum total of all inclinations. Even if it should happen that, by a particular unfortunate fate or by the niggardly provision of a stepmotherly nature, this will should be wholly lacking in power to accomplish its purpose, and if even the greatest effort should not avail it to achieve anything of its end, and if there remained only the good will (not as a mere wish but as the summoning of all the means in our power), it would sparkle like a jewel in its own right, as something that had its full worth in itself. Usefulness or fruitlessness can neither diminish nor augment this worth.[1]

He would presumably have said the same thing about a bad will: whether it accomplishes its evil

Thomas Nagel, "Moral Luck." *Proceedings of the Aristotelian Society* (1976). Reprinted by permission of the author.

purposes is morally irrelevant. And a course of action that would be condemned if it had a bad outcome cannot be vindicated if by luck it turns out well. There cannot be moral risk. This view seems to be wrong, but it arises in response to a fundamental problem about moral responsibility to which we possess no satisfactory solution.

The problem develops out of the ordinary conditions of moral judgment. Prior to reflection it is intuitively plausible that people cannot be morally assessed for what is not their fault, or for what is due to factors beyond their control. Such judgment is different from the evaluation of something as a good or bad thing, or state of affairs. The latter may be present in addition to moral judgment, but when we blame someone for his actions we are not merely saying it is bad that they happened, or bad that he exists: we are judging *him*, saying he is bad, which is different from his being a bad thing. This kind of judgment takes only a certain kind of object. Without being able to explain exactly why, we feel that the appropriateness of moral assessment is easily undermined by the discovery that the act or attribute, no matter how good or bad, is not under the person's control. While other evaluations remain, this one seems to lose its footing. So a clear absence of control, produced by involuntary movement, physical force, or ignorance of the circumstances, excuses what is done from moral judgment. But what we do depends in many more ways than these on what is not under our control—what is not produced by a good or a bad will in Kant's phrase. And external influences in this broader range are not usually thought to excuse what is done from moral judgment, positive or negative.

Let me give a few examples, beginning with the type of case Kant has in mind. Whether we succeed or fail in what we try to do nearly always depends to some extent on factors beyond our control. This is true of murder, altruism, revolution, the sacrifice of certain interests for the sake of others—almost any morally important act. What has been done, and what is morally judged, is partly determined by external factors. However jewel-like the good will may be in its own right, there is a morally significant difference between rescuing someone from a burning building and dropping him from a twelfth-story window while trying to rescue him. Similarly, there is a morally significant difference between reckless driving and manslaughter. But whether a reckless driver hits a pedestrian depends on the presence of the pedestrian at the point where he recklessly passes a red light. What we do is also limited by the opportunities and choices with which we are faced, and these are largely determined by factors beyond our control. Someone who was an officer in a concentration camp might have led a quiet and harmless life if the Nazis had never come to power in Germany. And someone who led a quiet and harmless life in Argentina might have become an officer in a concentration camp if he had not left Germany for business reasons in 1930.

I shall say more later about these and other examples. I introduce them here to illustrate a general point. Where a significant aspect of what someone does depends on factors beyond his control, yet we continue to treat him in that respect as an object of moral judgment, it can be called moral luck. Such luck can be good or bad. And the problem posed by this phenomenon, which led Kant to deny its possibility, is that the broad range of external influences here identified seems on close examination to undermine moral assessment as surely as does the narrower range of familiar excusing conditions. If the condition of control is consistently applied, it threatens to erode most of the moral assessments we find it natural to make. The things for which people are morally judged are determined in more ways than we at first realize by what is beyond their control. And when the seemingly natural requirement of fault or responsibility is applied in light of these facts, it leaves few pre-reflective moral judgments intact. Ultimately, nothing or almost nothing about what a person does seems to be under his control.

Why not conclude, then, that the condition of control is false—that it is an initially plausible hypothesis refuted by clear counter-examples? One could in that case look instead for a more refined condition which picked out the *kinds* of lack of control that really undermine certain moral judgments, without yielding the unacceptable conclusion derived from the broader condition, that most or all ordinary moral judgments are illegitimate.

What rules out this escape is that we are dealing not with a theoretical conjecture but with a philosophical problem. The condition of control does not suggest itself merely as a generalization from certain clear cases. It seems *correct* in the further cases to which it is extended beyond the original set. When we undermine moral assessment by considering new ways in which control is absent, we are not just discovering what *would* follow given the general hypothesis, but are actually being persuaded that in itself the absence of control is relevant in these cases too. The erosion of moral judgment emerges not as the absurd consequence of an over-simple theory, but as a natural consequence of the ordinary idea of moral assessment, when it is applied in view of a more complete and precise account of the facts. It would therefore be a mistake to argue from the unacceptability of the conclusions to the need for a different account of the conditions of moral responsibility. The view that moral luck is paradoxical is not a *mistake*, ethical or logical, but a perception of one of the ways in which the intuitively acceptable conditions of moral judgment threaten to undermine it all.

It resembles the situation in another area of philosophy, the theory of knowledge. There too conditions which seem perfectly natural, and which grow out of the ordinary procedures for challenging and defending claims to knowledge, threaten to undermine all such claims if consistently applied. Most skeptical arguments have this quality: they do not depend on the imposition of arbitrarily stringent standards of knowledge, arrived at by misunderstanding, but appear to grow inevitably from the consistent application of ordinary standards.[2] There is a substantive parallel as well, for epistemological skepticism arises from consideration of the respects in which our beliefs and their relation to reality depend on factors beyond our control. External and internal causes produce our beliefs. We may subject these processes to scrutiny in an effort to avoid error, but our conclusions at this next level also result, in part, from influences which we do not control directly. The same will be true no matter how far we carry the investigation. Our beliefs are always, ultimately, due to factors outside our control, and the impossibility of encompassing those factors without being at the mercy of others leads us to doubt whether we know anything. It looks as though, if any of our beliefs are true, it is pure biological luck rather than knowledge.

Moral luck is like this because while there are various respects in which the natural objects of moral assessment are out of our control or influenced by what is out of our control, we cannot reflect on these facts without losing our grip on the judgments.

There are roughly four ways in which the natural objects of moral assessment are disturbingly subject to luck. One is the phenomenon of constitutive luck—the kind of person you are, where this is not just a question of what you deliberately do, but of your inclinations, capacities, and temperament. Another category is luck in one's circumstances—the kind of problems and situations one faces. The other two have to do with the causes and effects of action: luck in how one is determined by antecedent circumstances, and luck in the way one's actions and projects turn out. All of them present a common problem. They are all opposed by the idea that one cannot be more culpable or estimable for anything than one is for that fraction of it which is under one's control. It seems irrational to take or dispense credit or blame for matters over which a person has no control, or for their influence on results over which he has partial control. Such things may create the conditions for action, but action can be judged only to the extent that it goes beyond these conditions and does not just result from them.

Let us first consider luck, good and bad, in the way things turn out. Kant, in the above-quoted passage, has one example of this in mind, but the category covers a wide range. It includes the truck driver who accidentally runs over a child, the artist who abandons his wife and five children to devote himself to painting,[3] and other cases in which the possibilities of success and failure are even greater. The driver, if he is entirely without fault, will feel terrible about his role in the event, but will not have to reproach himself. Therefore this example of agent-regent[4] is not yet a case of *moral* bad luck. However, if the driver was guilty of even a minor degree of negligence—failing to have his brakes checked recently, for example—then if that negligence contributes to the death of the child, he will not merely feel terrible. He will blame himself for the death. And what makes this an example of moral luck is that he would have to blame himself only slightly for the negligence itself if no situation arose which required him to brake suddenly and violently to avoid hitting a child. Yet the *negligence* is the same in both cases, and the driver has no control over whether a child will run into his path.

The same is true at higher levels of negligence. If someone has had too much to drink and his car swerves onto the sidewalk, he can count himself morally lucky if there are no pedestrians in his path. If there were, he would be to blame for their deaths, and would probably be prosecuted for manslaughter. But if he hurts no one, although his recklessness is exactly the same, he is guilty of a far less serious legal offense and will certainly reproach himself and be reproached by others much less severely. To take another legal example, the penalty for attempted murder is less than that for successful murder—however similar the intentions and motives of the assailant may be in the two cases. His degree of culpability can depend, it would seem, on whether the victim happened to be wearing a bullet-proof vest, or whether a bird flew into the path of the bullet—matters beyond his control.

Finally, there are cases of decision under uncertainty—common in public and in private life. Anna Karenina goes off with Vronsky, Gauguin leaves his family, Chamberlian signs the Munich Agreement, the Decembrists persuade the troops under their command to revolt against the czar, the American colonies declare their independence from Britain, you introduce two people in an attempt at matchmaking. It is tempting in all such cases to feel that some decision must be possible, in the light of what is known at the time, which will make reproach unsuitable no matter how things turn out. But this is not true; when someone acts in such ways he takes his life, or his moral position, into his hands, because how things turn out determines what he has done. It is possible *also* to assess the decision from the point of view of what could be known at the time, but this is not the end of the story. If the Decembrists had succeeded in overthrowing Nicholas I in 1825 and establishing a constitutional regime, they would be heroes. As it is, not only did they fail and pay for it, but they bore some responsibility for the terrible punishments meted out to the troops who had been persuaded to follow them. If the American Revolution had been a bloody failure resulting in greater repression, then Jefferson, Franklin, and Washington would still have made a noble attempt, and might not even have regretted it on their way to the scaffold, but they would also have had to blame themselves for what they had helped to bring on their compatriots. (Perhaps peaceful efforts at reform would eventually have succeeded.) If Hitler had not overrun Europe and exterminated millions, but instead had died of a heart attack after occupying the Sudetenland, Chamberlain's action at Munich would still have utterly betrayed the Czechs, but it would not be the great moral disaster that has made his name a household word.[5]

In many cases of difficult choice the outcome cannot be foreseen with certainty. One kind of assessment of the choice is possible in advance, but another kind must await the outcome, because the outcome determines what has been done. The same degree of culpability or estimability in intention, motive, or concern is compatible with a wide range of judgments, positive or negative, depending on what happened beyond the point of decision. The *mens rea* which could have existed in the absence of any consequences does not exhaust the grounds of moral judgment. Actual results influence culpability or esteem in a large class of unquestionably ethical cases ranging from negligence through political choice.

That these are genuine moral judgments rather than expressions of temporary attitude is evident from the fact that one can say *in advance* how the moral verdict will depend on the results. If one negligently leaves the bath running with the baby in it, one will realize, as one bounds up the stairs toward the bathroom, that if the baby has drowned one has done something awful, whereas if it has not one has merely been careless. Someone who launches a violent revolution against an authoritarian regime knows that if he fails he will be responsible for much suffering that is in vain, but if he succeeds he will be justified by the outcome. I do not mean that *any* action can be retroactively justified by history. Certain things are so bad in themselves, or so risky, that no results can make them all right. Nevertheless, when moral judgment does depend on the outcome, it is objective and timeless and not dependent on a change of standpoint produced by success or failure. The judgment after the fact follows from an hypothetical judgment that can be made beforehand, and it can be made as easily by someone else as by the agent.

From the point of view which makes responsibility dependent on control, all this seems absurd. How is it possible to be more or less culpable depending on whether a child gets into the path of one's car, or a bird into the path of one's bullet? Perhaps it is true that what is done depends on more than the agent's state of mind or intention. The problem then is, why is it not irrational to base moral assessment on what people do, in this broad sense? It amounts to holding them responsible for the contributions of fate as well as for their own—provided they have made some contribution to begin with. If we look at cases of negligence or attempt, the pattern seems to be that overall culpability corresponds to the product of mental or intentional fault and the seriousness of the outcome. Cases of decision under uncertainty are less easily explained in this way, for it seems that the overall judgment can even shift from positive to negative depending on the outcome. But here too it seems rational to subtract the effects of occurrences subsequent to the choice, that were merely possible at the time, and concentrate moral assessment on the actual decision in light of the probabilities. If the object of moral judgment is the *person*, then to hold him accountable for what he has done in the broader sense is akin to strict liability, which may have its legal uses but seems irrational as a moral position.

The result of such a line of thought is to pare down each act to its morally essential core, an inner act of pure will assessed by motive and intention. Adam Smith advocates such a position in *The Theory of Moral Sentiments*, but notes that it runs contrary to our actual judgments.

> But how well soever we may seem to be persuaded of the truth of this equitable maxim, when we consider it after this manner, in abstract, yet when we come to particular cases, the actual consequences which happen to proceed from any action, have a very great effect upon our sentiments concerning its merit or demerit, and almost always either enhance or diminish our sense of both. Scarce, in any one instance, perhaps, will our sentiments be found, after examination, to be entirely regulated by this rule, which we all acknowledge ought entirely to regulate them.[6]

Joel Feinberg points out further that restricting the domain of moral responsibility to the inner world will not immunize it to luck. Factors beyond the agent's control, like a coughing fit, can interfere with his decisions as surely as they can with the path of a bullet from his gun.[7] Nevertheless the tendency to cut down the scope of moral assessment is pervasive, and does not limit itself to the influence of effects. It attempts to isolate the will from the other direction, so to speak, by separating out constitutive luck. Let us consider that next.

Kant was particularly insistent on the moral irrelevance of qualities of temperament and personality that are not under the control of the will. Such qualities as sympathy or coldness might provide the background against which obedience to moral requirements is more or less difficult, but they could not be objects of moral assessment themselves, and might well interfere with confident assessment of its proper object—the determination of the will by the motive of duty. This rules out moral judgment of many of the virtues and vices, which are states of character that influence choice but are certainly not exhausted by dispositions to act deliberately in certain ways. A person may be greedy, envious, cowardly, cold, ungenerous, unkind, vain, or conceited, but *behave* perfectly by a monumental effort of will. To possess these vices is to be unable to help having certain feelings under certain circumstances, and to have strong spontaneous impulses to act badly. Even if one controls the impulses, one still has the vice. An envious person hates the greater success of others. He can be morally condemned as envious even if he congratulates them cordially and does nothing to denigrate or spoil their success. Conceit, likewise, need not be displayed. It is fully present in someone who cannot help dwelling with secret satisfaction on the superiority of his own achievements, talents, beauty, intelligence, or virtue. To some extent such a quality may be the product of earlier choices; to some extent it may be amenable to change by current actions. But it is largely a matter of constitutive bad fortune. Yet people are morally condemned for such qualities, and esteemed for others equally beyond control of the will: they are assessed for what they are *like*.

To Kant this seems incoherent because virtue is enjoined on everyone and therefore must in principle be possible for everyone. It may be easier for some than for others, but it must be possible to achieve it by making the right choices, against whatever temperamental background.[8] One may want to have a generous spirit, or regret not having one, but it makes no sense to condemn oneself or anyone else for a quality which is not within the control of the will. Condemnation implies that you should not be like that, not that it is unfortunate that you are.

Nevertheless, Kant's conclusion remains intuitively unacceptable. We may be persuaded that these moral judgments are irrational, but they reappear involuntarily as soon as the argument is over. This is the pattern throughout the subject.

The third category to consider is luck in one's circumstances, and I shall mention it briefly. The things we are called upon to do, the moral tests we face, are importantly determined by factors beyond our control. It may be true of someone that in a dangerous situation he would behave in a cowardly or heroic fashion, but if the situation never arises, he will never have the chance to distinguish or disgrace himself in this way, and his moral record will be different.[9]

A conspicuous example of this is political. Ordinary citizens of Nazi Germany had an opportunity to behave heroically by opposing the regime. They also had an opportunity to behave badly, and most of them are culpable for having failed this test. But it is a test to which the citizens of other countries were not subjected, with the result that even if they, or some of them, would have behaved as badly as the Germans in like circumstances, they simply did not and therefore are not similarly culpable. Here again one is morally at the mercy of fate, and it may seem irrational upon reflection, but our ordinary moral attitudes would be unrecognizable without it. We judge people for what they actually do or fail to do, not just for what they would have done if circumstances had been different.

This form of moral determination by the actual is also paradoxical, but we can begin to see how deep in the concept of responsibility the paradox is embedded. A person can be morally responsible only for what he does; but what he does results from a great deal that he does not do; therefore he is not morally responsible for what he is and is not responsible for. (This is not a contradiction, but it is a paradox.)

It should be obvious that there is a connection between these problems about responsibility and control and an even more familiar problem, that of freedom of the will. That is the last type of moral luck I want to take up, though I can do no more within the scope of this essay than indicate its connection with the other types.

If one cannot be responsible for consequences of one's acts due to factors beyond one's control, or for antecedents of one's acts that are properties of temperament not subject to one's will, or for the circumstances that pose one's moral choices, then how can one be responsible even for the stripped-down acts of the will itself, if *they* are the product of antecedent circumstances outside's of the will's control?

The area of genuine agency, and therefore of legitimate moral judgment, seems to shrink under this scrutiny to an extensionless point. Everything seems to result from the combined influence of factors, antecedent and posterior to action, that are not within the agent's control. Since he cannot be responsible for them, he cannot be responsible for their results—though it may remain possible to take up the aesthetic or other evaluative analogues of the moral attitudes that are thus displaced.

It is also possible, of course, to brazen it out and refuse to accept the results, which indeed seem unacceptable as soon as we stop thinking about the arguments. Admittedly, if certain surrounding circumstances had been different, then no unfortunate consequences would have followed from a wicked intention, and no seriously culpable act would have been performed; but since the circumstances were *not* different, and the agent *in fact* succeeded in perpetrating a particularly cruel murder, *that* is what he did, and that is what he is responsible for. Similarly, we may admit that if certain antecedent circumstances had been different, the agent would never have developed into the sort of person who would do such a thing; but since he *did* develop (as the inevitable result of those antecedent circumstances) into the sort of swine he is, and into the person who committed such a murder, *that* is what he is blamable for. In both cases one is responsible for what one actually does—even if what one actually does depends in important ways on what is not within one's control. This [compatibilist] account of our moral judgments would leave room for the ordinary conditions of responsibility—the absence of coercion, ignorance, or involuntary movement—as part of the determination of what someone has done—but it is understood not to exclude the influence of a great deal that he has not done.

The only thing wrong with this solution is its failure to explain how skeptical problems arise. For they arise not from the imposition of an arbitrary external requirement, but from the nature of moral judgment itself. Something in the ordinary idea of what someone does must explain how it can seem necessary to subtract from it anything that merely happens—even though the ultimate consequence of such subtraction is that nothing remains. And something in the ordinary idea of knowledge must explain why it seems to be undermined by any influences on belief not within the control of the subject—so that knowledge seems impossible without an impossible foundation in autonomous reason. But let us leave epistemology aside and concentrate on action, character, and moral assessment.

The problem arises, I believe, because the self which acts and is the object of moral judgment is threatened with dissolution by the absorption of its acts and impulses into the class of events. Moral judgment of a person is judgment not of what happens to him, but of him. It does not say merely that a certain event or state of affairs is fortunate or unfortunate or even terrible. It is not an evaluation of a state of the world, or of an individual as part of the world. We are not thinking just that it would be better if he were different, or did not exist, or had not done some of the things he has done. We are judging *him*, rather than his existence or characteristics. The effect of concentrating on the influence of what is not under his control is to make this responsible self seem to disappear, swallowed up by the order of mere events.

What, however, do we have in mind that a person must *be* to be the object of these moral attitudes? While the concept of agency is easily undermined, it is very difficult to give it a positive characterization. That is familiar from the literature on Free Will.

I believe that in a sense the problem has no solution, because something in the idea of agency is incompatible with actions being events, or people being things. But as the external determinants of what someone has done are gradually exposed in their effect on consequences, character, and choice itself, it becomes gradually clear that actions are events and people things. Eventually nothing remains which can be ascribed to the responsible self, and we are left with nothing but a portion of the larger sequences of events, which can be deplored or celebrated, but not blamed or praised.

Though I cannot define the idea of the active self that is thus undermined, it is possible to say something about its sources. There is a close connection between our feelings about ourselves and our feelings about others. Guilt and indignation, shame and contempt, pride and admiration are internal and external sides of the same moral attitudes. We are unable to view ourselves simply as portions of the world, and from inside we have a rough idea of the boundary between what is us and what is not, what we do and what happens to us, what is our personality and what is an accidental handicap. We apply the same essentially internal conception of the self to others. About ourselves we feel pride, shame, guilt, remorse—and agent-regret. We do not regard our actions and our characters merely as fortunate or unfortunate episodes—though they may also be that. We cannot *simply* take an external evaluative view of ourselves—of what we most essentially are and what we do. And this remains true even when we have seen that we are not responsible for our own existence, or our nature, or the choices we have to make, or the circumstances that give our acts the consequences they have. Those acts remain ours and we remain ourselves, despite the persuasiveness of the reasons that seem to argue us out of existence.

It is this internal view that we extend to others in moral judgment—when we judge *them* rather than their desirability or utility. We extend to others the refusal to limit ourselves to external evaluation, and we accord to them selves like our own. But in both cases this comes up against the brutal inclusion of humans and everything about them in a world from which they cannot be separated and of which they are nothing but contents. The external view forces itself on us at the same time that we resist it. One way this occurs is through the gradual erosion of what we do by the subtraction of what happens.

The inclusion of consequences in the conception of what we have done is an acknowledgment that we are parts of the world, but the paradoxical character of moral luck which emerges from this acknowledgment shows that we are unable to operate with such a view, for it leaves us with no one to be. The same thing is revealed in the appearance that determinism obliterates responsibility. Once we see an aspect of what we or someone else does as something that happens, we lose our grip on the idea that it has been done and that we can judge the doer and not just the happening. This explains why the absence of determinism is no more hospitable to the concept of agency than is its presence—a point that has been noticed often. Either way the act is viewed externally, as part of the course of events.

The problem of moral luck cannot be understood without an account of the internal conception of agency and its special connection with the moral attitudes as opposed to other types of value. I do not have such an account. The degree to which the problem has a solution can be determined only by seeing whether in some degree the incompatibility between this conception and the various ways in which we do not control what we do is only apparent. I have nothing to offer on that topic either. But it is not enough to say merely that our basic moral attitudes toward ourselves and others are determined by what is actual; for they are also threatened by the sources of that actuality, and by the external view of action which forces itself on us when we see how everything we do belongs to a world that we have not created.

Notes

1. Immanuel Kant, *Foundations of the Metaphysic of Morals*, L. W. Beck, trans. (Bobbs-Merrill, 1959), sec. I, paragraph 3.

2. See Thompson Clark, "The Legacy of Skepticism," *Journal of Philosophy*, LXIX, no. 20 (November 9, 1972): 754–69.
3. Such a case, modelled on the life of Gauguin, is discussed by Bernard Williams in "Moral Luck," *Proceedings of the Aristotelian Society*, supplementary vol. L (1976): 115–35 (to which the original version of this essay was a reply). He points out that though success or failure cannot be predicted in advance, Gauguin's most basic retrospective feelings about the decision will be determined by the development of his talent. My disagreement with Williams is that his account fails to explain why such retrospective attitudes can be called moral. If success does not permit Gauguin to justify himself to others, but still determines his most basic feelings, that shows only that his most basic feelings need not be moral. It does not show that morality is subject to luck. If the retrospective judgment were moral, it would imply the truth of a hypothetical judgment made in advance, of the form "If I leave my family and become a great painter, I will be justified by success; if I don't become a great painter, the act will be unforgivable."
4. Williams's term (ibid.).
5. For a fascinating but morally repellent discussion of the topic of justification by history, see Maurice Merleau-Ponty, *Humanisme et Terreur* (Paris: Gallimard, 1947), translated as *Humanism and Terror* (Boston: Beacon Press, 1969).
6. Adam Smith, *The Theory of Moral Sentiments*, 1759, Pt. II, sec. 3, Introduction, para. 5.
7. "Problematic Responsibility in Law and Morals," in Joel Feinberg, *Doing and Deserving* (Princeton: Princeton University Press, 1970).
8. 'If nature has put little sympathy in the heart of a man, and if he, though an honest man, is by temperament cold and indifferent to the sufferings of others, perhaps because he is provided with special gifts of patience and fortitude and expects or even requires that others should have the same—and such a man would certainly not be the meanest product of nature—would not he find in himself a source from which to give himself a far higher worth than he could have got by having a good-natured temperament?' (Kant, *Foundations of the Metaphysic of Morals*, first section, eleventh paragraph).
9. Cf. Thomas Gray, 'Elegy Written in a Country Churchyard':

   Some mute inglorious Milton here may rest,
   Some Cromwell, guiltless of his country's blood.

   An unusual example of circumstantial moral luck is provided by the kind of moral dilemma with which someone can be faced through no fault of his own, but which leaves him with nothing to do which is not wrong.

Chapter 26

DANIEL DENNETT

Daniel Dennett (1942–) received his D. Phil. from Oxford University. He is Professor of Philosophy at Tufts University. He is the author of several important works, including *Content and Consciousness* (1969), *Brainstorms* (1978), *Elbow Room* (1984), and *The Intentional Stance* (1987).

In this selection Dennett develops the idea of an "*Intentional system*," or "*stance*." An intentional system (whether animal, human, robot, computer, or Galactican) is one to which we attribute beliefs and desires as part of an explanatory theory by which we endeavor to understand the system's behavior. Dennett argues for the validity of this approach. For a critique of Dennett's notion that machines or computers can have beliefs, see our next selection by John Searle (Chapter 27).

FOR FURTHER READING

Dennett, Daniel. *Brainstorms* (MIT Press, 1978).

———. *Content and Consciousness* (Routledge & Kegan Paul, 1969).

———. *Darwin's Dangerous Ideas* (Penguin, 1995).

———. *The Intentional Stance* (MIT Press, 1987).

———. *Consciousness Explained* (Little Brown, 1991).

The Intentional Stance

I wish to examine the concept of a system whose behavior can be—at least sometimes—explained and predicted by relying on ascriptions to the system of beliefs and desires (and hopes, fears, intentions, hunches, . . .). I will call such systems *intentional systems*, and such explanations and predictions intentional explanations and predictions, in virtue of the intentionality of the idioms of belief and desire (and hope, fear, intention, hunch, . . .).

I used to insist on capitalizing "intentional" wherever I meant to be using Brentano's notion of *intentionality*, in order to distinguish this technical term from its cousin, e.g., "an intentional shove," but the technical term is now in much greater currency, and since almost everyone else who uses the term seems content to risk this confusion, I have decided, with some trepidation, to abandon my typographical eccentricity. But let the uninitiated reader

Reprinted from Daniel Dennett, *Brainstorms* (MIT Press, 1978) by permission of the publisher.

beware: "intentional" as it occurs here is *not* the familiar term of layman's English. For me, as for many recent authors, intentionality is primarily a feature of linguistic entites—idioms, contexts—and for my purposes here we can be satisfied that an idiom is intentional if substitution of codesignative terms do not preserve truth or if the "objects" of the idiom are not capturable in the usual way by quantifiers. I discuss this in more detail in *Content and Consciousness*.

I

The first point to make about intentional systems as I have just defined them is that a particular thing is an intentional system only in relation to the strategies of someone who is trying to explain and predict its behavior. What this amounts to can best be brought out by example. Consider the case of a chess-playing computer, and the different strategies or stances one might adopt as its opponent in trying to predict its moves. There are three different stances of interest to us. First there is the *design stance*. If one knows exactly how the computer is designed (including the impermanent part of its design: its program) one can predict its designed response to any move one makes by following the computation instructions of the program. One's prediction will come true provided only that the computer performs as designed—that is, without breakdown. Different varieties of design-stance predictions can be discerned, but all of them are alike in relying on the notion of *function*, which is purpose-relative or teleological. That is, a design of a system breaks it up into larger or smaller functional parts, and design-stance predictions are generated by assuming that each functional part will function properly. For instance, the radio engineer's schematic wiring diagrams have symbols for each resistor, capacitor, transistor, etc.—*each with its task to perform*—and he can give a design-stance prediction of the behavior of a circuit by assuming that each element performs its task. Thus one can make design-stance predictions of the computer's response at several different levels of abstraction, depending on whether one's design treats as smallest functional elements strategy-generators and consequence-testers, multipliers and dividers, or transistors and switches. (It should be noted that not all diagrams or pictures are designs in this sense, for a diagram may carry no information about the functions—intended or observed—of the elements it depicts.)

We generally adopt the design stance when making predictions about the behavior of mechanical objects, e.g., "As the typewriter carriage approaches the margin, a bell will ring (provided the machine is in working order)," and more simply, "Strike the match and it will light." We also often adopt this stance in predictions involving natural objects: "Heavy pruning will stimulate denser foliage and stronger limbs." The essential feature of the design stance is that we make predictions solely from knowledge or assumptions about the system's functional design, irrespective of the physical constitution or condition of the innards of the particular object.

Second, there is what we may call the *physical stance*. From this stance our predictions are based on the actual physical state of the particular object, and are worked out by applying whatever knowledge we have of the laws of nature. It is from this stance alone that we can predict the malfunction of systems (unless, as sometimes happens these days, a system is *designed* to malfunction after a certain time, in which case malfunctioning in one sense becomes a part of its proper functioning). Instances of predictions from the physical stance are common enough: "If you turn on the switch you'll get a nasty shock," and, "When the snows come that branch will break right off." One seldom adopts the physical stance in dealing with a computer just because the number of critical variables in the physical constitution of a computer would over-whelm the most prodigious calculator. Significantly, the physical stance is generally reserved for instances of breakdown, where the condition preventing normal operation is generalized and easily locatable, e.g., "Nothing will happen when you type in your questions, because it isn't plugged in," or, "It won't work with all that flood water in it." Attempting to give a physical account or prediction of the chess-playing computer would be a pointless and herculean labor, but it would work in principle. One could predict the response it would make in a chess game by tracing out the effects of the input energies all the way through the computer until once more type was pressed against paper and a response was printed. (Because of the digitial nature of computers, quantum-level indeterminacies, if such there be, will cancel out rather than accumulate, unless of course a radium "randomizer" or other amplifier of quantum effects is built into the computer.)

The best chess-playing computers these days are practically inaccessible to prediction from either the design stance or the physical stance; they have become too complex for even their own designers to view from the design stance. A man's best hope of defeating such a machine in a chess match is to predict its responses by figuring out as best he can what the best or most rational move would be, given the rules and goals of chess. That is, one assumes not only (1) that the machine will function as designed, but (2) that the design is optimal as well, that the computer will "choose" the most rational move. Predictions made on these assumptions may well fail if either assumption proves unwarranted in the particular case, but still this *means* of prediction may impress us as the most fruitful one to adopt in dealing with a particular system. Put another way, when one can no longer hope to beat the machine by utilizing one's knowledge of physics or programming to anticipate its responses, one may still be able to avoid defeat by treating the machine rather like an intelligent human opponent.

We must look more closely at this strategy. A prediction relying on the assumption of the system's rationality is relative to a number of things. First, rationality here so far means nothing more than optimal design relative to a goal or optimally weighted hierarchy of goals (checkmate, winning pieces, defense, etc., in the case of chess) and a set of constraints (the rules and starting position). Prediction itself is, moreover, relative to the nature and extent of the information the system has at the time about the field of endeavor. The question one asks in framing a prediction of this sort is: What is the most rational thing for the computer to do, given goals *x, y, z*, . . . , constraints *a, b, c*, . . . and information (including misinformation, if any) about the present state of affairs *p, q, r*, . . . ? In predicting the computer's response to my chess move, my assessment of the computer's most rational move may depend, for instance, not only on my assumption that the computer has information about the present disposition of all the pieces, but also on whether I believe the computer has information about my inability to see four moves ahead, the relative powers of knights and bishops, and my weakness for knight—bishop exchanges. In the end I may not be able to frame a very good prediction, if I am unable to determine with any accuracy what information and goals the computer has, or if the information and goals I take to be given do not dictate any one best move, or if I simply am not so good as the computer is at generating an optimal move from this given. Such predictions then are very precarious; not only are they relative to a set of postulates about goals, constraints, and information, and not only do they hinge on determining an optimal response in situations where we may have no clear criteria for what is optimal, but also they are vulnerable to short-circuit falsifications that are in principle unpredictable from this stance. Just as design-stance predictions are vulnerable to malfunctions (by depending on the assumption of no malfunction), so these predictions are vulnerable to design weaknesses and lapses (by depending on the assumption of optimal design). It is a measure of the success of contemporary program designers that these precarious predictions turn out to be true with enough regularity to make the method useful.

The denouement of this extended example should now be obvious: this third stance, with its assumption of rationality, is the *intentional stance*; the predictions one makes from it are intentional predictions; one is viewing the computer as an intentional system. One predicts behavior in such a case by ascribing to the system *the possession of certain information* and supposing it to be *directed by certain goals*, and then by working out the most reasonable or appropriate action on the basis of these ascriptions and suppositions. It is a small step to calling the information possessed the computer's *beliefs*, its goals and subgoals its *desires*. What I mean by saying that this is a small step, is that the notion of possession of information or misinformation is just as intentional a notion as that of belief. The "possession" at issue is hardly the bland and innocent notion of storage one might suppose; it is, and must be, "epistemic possession"—an analogue of belief. Consider: the Frenchman who possesses the *Encyclopedia Britannica* but knows no English might be said to "possess" the information in it, but if there is such a sense of possession, it is not strong enough to serve as the sort of possession the computer must be supposed to enjoy, relative to the information it *uses* in "choosing" a chess move. In a similar way, the goals of a goal-directed computer must be specified intentionally, just like desires.

Lingering doubts about whether the chess-playing computer *really* has beliefs and desires are misplaced; for the definition of intentional systems I have given does not say that intentional systems *really* have beliefs and desires, but that one can explain and predict their behavior by *ascribing* beliefs and desires to them, and whether one calls what one ascribes to the computer beliefs or belief-analogues or information complexes or intentional whatnots makes no difference to the nature of the calculation one makes on the basis of the ascriptions. One will arrive at the same predictions whether one forthrightly thinks in terms of the computer's beliefs and desires, or in terms of the computer's information-store and goal-specifications. The inescapable and interesting fact is that for the best chess-playing computers of today, intentional explanation and prediction of their behavior is not only common, but works when no other sort of prediction of their behavior is manageable. We do quite successfully treat these computers as intentional systems, and we do this independently of any considerations about what substance they are composed of, their origin, their position or lack of position in the community of moral agents, their consciousness or self-consciousness, or the determinacy or indeterminacy of their operations. The decision to adopt the strategy is pragmatic, and is not intrinsically right or wrong. One can always refuse to adopt the intentional stance toward the computer, and accept its checkmates. One can switch stances at will without involving oneself in any inconsistencies or inhumanities, adopting the intentional stance in one's role as opponent, the design stance in one's role as redesigner, and the physical stance in one's role as repairman.

This celebration of our chess-playing computer is not intended to imply that it is a completely adequate model or simulation of Mind, or intelligent human or animal activity; nor am I saying that the attitude we adopt toward this computer is precisely the same that we adopt toward a creature we deem to be conscious and rational. All that has been claimed is that on occasion, a purely physical system can be so complex, and yet so organized, that we find it convenient, explanatory, pragmatically necessary for prediction, to treat it as if it had beliefs and desires and was rational. The chess-playing computer is just that, a machine for playing chess, which no man or animal is; and hence its "rationality" is pinched and artificial.

Perhaps we could straightforwardly expand the chess-playing computer into a more faithful model of human rationality, and perhaps not. I prefer to pursue a more fundamental line of inquiry first.

When should we expect the tactic of adopting the intentional stance to pay off? Whenever we have reason to suppose the assumption of optimal design is warranted, and doubt the practicality of prediction from the design or physical stance. Suppose we travel to a distant planet and find it inhabited by things moving about its surface, multiplying, decaying, apparently reacting to events in the environment, but otherwise as unlike human beings as you please. Can we make intentional predictions and explanations of their behavior? If we have reason to suppose that a process of natural selection has been in effect, then we can be assured that the populations we observe have been selected in virtue of their design: they will respond to at least some of the more common event-types in this environment in ways that are normally appropriate—that is, conducive to propagation of the species. Once we have tentatively identified the perils and succors of the environment (relative to the constitution of the inhabitants, not ours), we shall be able to estimate which goals and which weighting of goals will be optimal relative to the creatures' *needs* (for survival and propagation), which sorts of information about the environment will be *useful* in guiding goal-directed activity, and which activities will be appropriate given the environmental circumstances. Having doped out these conditions (which will always be subject to revision) we can proceed at once to ascribe beliefs and desires to the creatures. Their behavior will "manifest" their beliefs by being seen as the actions which, given the creatures' desires, would be appropriate to such beliefs as would be appropriate to the environmental stimulation. Desires, in turn, will be "manifested" in behavior as those appropriate desires (given the needs of the creature) to which the actions of the creature would be appropriate, given the creature's beliefs. The circularity of these interlocking specifications is no accident. Ascriptions of beliefs and desires must be interdependent, and the only point of anchorage are the demonstrable needs for survival, the regularities of behavior, and the assumption, grounded in faith in natural selection, of optimal design. Once one has ascribed beliefs and desires, however, one can at once set about predicting behavior on their basis, and if evolution has done its job—as it must over the long run—our predictions will be reliable enough to be useful.

It might at first seem that this tactic unjustifiably imposes human categories and attributes (belief, desire, and so forth) on these alien entities. It is a sort of anthropomorphizing. We do not have to suppose these creatures share with us any peculiarly human inclinations, attitudes, hopes, foibles, pleasures, or outlooks; their actions may not include running, jumping, hiding, eating, sleeping, listening, or copulating. All we transport from our world to theirs are the categories of rationality, perception (information input by some "sense" modality or modalities—perhaps radar or cosmic radiation), and action. The question of whether we can expect them to share any of our beliefs or desires is tricky, but there are a few points that can be made at this time; in virtue of their rationality they can be supposed to share our belief in logical truths, and we cannot suppose that they normally desire their own destruction, for instance.

II

When one deals with a system—be it man, machine, or alien creature—by explaining and predicting its behavior by citing its beliefs and desires, one has what might be called a "theory of behavior" for the system. Let us see how such intentional theories of behavior relate to other putative theories of behavior.

One fact so obvious that it is easily overlooked is that our "common-sense" explanations and predictions of the behavior of both men and animals are intentional. We start by assuming rationality. We do not *expect* new acquaintances to react irrationally to particular topics or eventualities, but when they do we learn to adjust our strategies accordingly, just as, with a chess-playing computer, one sets out with a high regard for its rationality and adjusts one's estimate downward wherever performance reveals flaws. The presumption of rationality is so strongly entrenched in our inference habits that when our predictions prove false, we at first cast about for adjustments in the information-possession conditions (he must not have heard, he must not know English, he must not have seen *x*, been aware that *y*, etc.) or goal weightings, before questioning the rationality of the system as a whole. In extreme cases personalities may prove to be so unpredictable from the intentional stance that we abandon it, and if we have accumulated a lot of evidence in the meanwhile about the nature of response patterns in the individual, we may find that a species of design stance can be effectively adopted. This is the fundamentally different attitude we occasionally adopt toward the insane. To watch an asylum attendant manipulate an obsessively countersuggestive patient, for instance, is to watch something radically unlike normal interpersonal relations.

Our prediction of animal behavior by "common sense" is also intentional. Whether or not sentimental folk go overboard when they talk to their dogs or fill their cats' heads with schemes and worries, even the most hardboiled among us predict animals' behavior intentionally. If we observe a mouse in a situation where it can see a cat waiting at one mousehole and cheese at another, we know which way the mouse will go, providing it is not deranged; our prediction is not based on our familiarity with maze-experiments or any assumptions about the sort of special training the mouse has been through. We suppose the mouse can see the cat and the cheese, and hence has beliefs (belief-analogues, intentional whatnots) to the effect that there is a cat to the left, cheese to the right, and we ascribe to the mouse also the desire to eat the cheese and the desire to avoid the cat (subsumed, appropriately enough, under the more general desires to eat and to avoid peril); so we predict that the mouse will do what is appropriate to such beliefs and desires, namely, to go the right in order to get the cheese and avoid the cat. Whatever academic allegiances or theoretical predilections we may have, we would be astonished if, in the general run, mice and other animals falsified such intentional predictions of their behavior. Indeed, experimental psychologists of every school would have a hard time devising experimental situations to support their various theories without the help of their intentional expectations of how the test animals will respond to circumstances.

Earlier I alleged that even creatures from another planet would share with us our beliefs in logical truths; light can be shed on this claim by asking whether mice and other animals, in virtue of being intentional systems, also believe the truth of logic. There is something bizarre in the picture of a dog or mouse cogitating a list of tautologies, but we can avoid that picture. The assumption that something is an intentional system is the assumption that it is rational; that is, one gets nowhere with the assumption that entity *x* has beliefs *p, q, r,* . . . unless one also supposes that *x* believes what follows from *p, q, r,* . . . ; otherwise there is no way of ruling out the prediction that *x* will, in the face of its beliefs *p, q, r,* . . . do something utterly stupid, and, if we cannot rule out *that* prediction, we will have acquired no predictive power at all. So whether or not the animal is said to *believe* the *truths* of logic, it must be supposed to *follow* the *rules* of logic. Surely our mouse follows or believes in *modus ponens*, for we ascribed to it the beliefs: (a) *there is a cat to the left*; and (b) *if there is a cat to the left, I had better not go left*, and our prediction relied on the mouse's ability to get to the conclusion. In general there is a trade-off between rules and truths; we can suppose x to have an inference rule taking A to B or we can give x the belief in the "theorem": *if A then B*. As far as our predictions are concerned, we are free to ascribe to the mouse either a few inference rules and belief in many logical propositions, or many inference rules and few if any logical beliefs. We can even take a patently nonlogical belief like (b) and recast it as an inference rule taking (a) to the desired conclusion.

Will all logical truths appear among the beliefs of any intentional system? If the system were ideally or perfectly rational, all logical truths would appear, but any actual intentional system will be imperfect, and so not all logical truths must be ascribed as beliefs to any system. Moreover, not all the inference rules of an actual intentional system may be valid; not all its inference-licensing beliefs may be truths of logic. Experience may indicate where the shortcomings lie in any particular system. If we found an imperfectly rational creature whose allegiance to modus ponens, say, varied with the subject matter, we could characterize that by excluding modus ponens as a rule and ascribing in its stead a set of nonlogical inference rules covering the modus ponens step for each subject matter where the rule was followed. Not surprisingly, as we discover more and more imperfections (as we banish more and more logical truths from the creature's beliefs), our efforts at intentional prediction become more and more cumbersome and undecidable, for we can no longer count on the beliefs, desires, and actions going together that *ought* to go together. Eventually we end up, following this process, by predicting from the design stance; we end up, that is, dropping the assumption of rationality.

This migration from common-sense intentional explanations and predictions to more reliable design-stance explanations and predictions that is forced on us when we discover that our subjects are imperfectly rational is, independently of any such discovery, the proper direction for theory builders to take whenever possible. In the end, we want to be able to explain the intelligence of man, or beast, in terms of his design, and this in turn in terms of the natural selection of this design; so whenever we stop in our explanation at the intentional level we have left over an unexplained instance of intelligence or rationality. This comes out vividly if we look at theory building from the vantage point of economics.

Any time a theory builder proposes to call any event, state, structure, etc., in any system (say the brain of an organism) a *signal* or *message* or *command* or otherwise endows it with content, he *takes out a loan* of intelligence. He implicity posits along with his signals, messages, or commands, something that can serve as a signal-*reader*, message-*understander*, or *commander*, else his "signals" will be for naught, will decay unreceived, uncomprehended. This loan must be repaid eventually by finding and analyzing away these readers or comprehenders; for, failing this, the theory will have among its elements unanalyzed man-analogues endowed with enough intelligence to read the signals, etc., and thus the theory will *postpone* answering the major question: what makes for intelligence? The intentionality of all such talk of signals and commands reminds us that rationality is being taken for granted, and in this way shows us where a theory is incomplete. It is this feature that, to my mind, puts a premium on the yet unfinished task of devising a rigorous definition of intentionality, for if we can lay claim to a purely formal criterion of intentional discourse, we will have what amounts to a medium of exchange for assessing theories of behavior. Intentionality *abstracts* from the inessential details of the various forms intelligence-loans can take (e.g., signal-readers, volition-emitters, librarians in the corridors of memory, egos and superegos) and serves as a reliable means of detecting exactly where a theory is *in the red* relative to the task of explaining intelligence; wherever a theory relies on a formulation bearing the logical marks of intentionality, there a little man is concealed.

This insufficiency of intentional explanation from the point of view of psychology has been widely felt and as widely misconceived. The most influential misgivings, expressed in the behaviorism of Skinner and Quine, can be succinctly characterized in terms of our economic metaphor. Skinner's and Quine's adamant prohibitions of intentional idioms at all levels of theory is the analogue of rock-ribbed New England conservatism: no deficit spending when building a theory! In Quine's case, the abhorrence of loans is due mainly to his fear that they can never be repaid, whereas Skinner stresses rather that what is borrowed is worthless to begin with. Skinner's suspicion is that intentionally couched claims are empirically vacuous, in the sense that they are altogether too easy to accommodate to the data, like the *virtus dormitiva* Molière's doctor ascribes to the sleeping powder (see Chapter 4 of Dennett, *Brainstorms* for a more detailed discussion of these issues). Questions can be begged on a temporary basis, however, permitting a mode of prediction and explanation not totally vacuous. Consider the following intentional prediction: if I were to ask a thousand American mathematicians how much seven times five is, more than nine hundred would respond by saying that it was thirty-five. (I have allowed for a few to mis-hear my question, a few others to be obstreperous, a few to make slips of the tongue.) If you doubt the prediction, you can test it; I would bet good money on it. It seems to have empirical content because it can, in a fashion, be tested, and yet it is unsatisfactory as a prediction of an empirical theory of psychology. It works, of course, because of the contingent, empirical—but evolution-guaranteed—fact that men in general are well enough designed both to get the answer right and to want to get it right. It will hold with as few exceptions for any group of Martians with whom we are able to converse, for it is not a prediction just of *human* psychology, but of the "psychology" of intentional systems generally.

Deciding on the basis of available empirical evidence that something is a piece of copper or a lichen permits one to make predictions based on the empirical theories dealing with copper and lichens, but deciding on the basis of available evidence that something is (may be treated as) an intentional system permits predictions having a normative or logical basis rather than an empirical one, and hence the success of an intentional prediction, based as it is on no particular picture of the system's design, cannot be construed to confirm or disconfirm any particular pictures of the system's design.

Skinner's reaction to this has been to try to frame predictions purely in non-intentional language, by predicting bodily responses to physical stimuli, but to date this has not provided him with the alternative mode of prediction and explanation he has sought, as perhaps an extremely cursory review can indicate. To provide a setting for nonintentional prediction of behavior, he invented the Skinner box, in which the rewarded behavior of the occupant—say, a rat—is a highly restricted and stereotypic bodily motion—usually pressing a bar with the front paws.

The claim that is then made is that once the animal has been trained, a law-like relationship is discovered to hold between non-intentionally characterized events: controlling stimuli and barpressing responses. A regularity is discovered to hold, to be sure, but the fact that it is between non-intentionally defined events is due to a property of the Skinner box and not of the occupant. For let us turn our prediction about mathematicians into a Skinnerian prediction: strap a mathematician in a Skinner box so he can move only his head; display in front of him a card on which appear the marks: "How much is seven times five?"; move into the range of his head-motions two buttons, over one of which is the mark "35" and over the other "34"; place electrodes on the soles of his feet and give him a few quick shocks; the controlling stimulus is then to be the sound: "Answer now!" I predict that in a statistically significant number of cases, even *before* training trials to condition the man to press button "35" with his forehead, he will do this when given the controlling stimulus. Is this a satisfactory scientific prediction just because it eschews the intentional vocabulary? No, it is an intentional prediction disguised by so restricting the environment that only one bodily motion is available to fulfill the intentional *action* that anyone would prescribe as appropriate to the circumstances of perception, belief, desire. That it is action, not merely motion, that is predicted can also be seen in the case of subjects less intelligent than mathematicians. Suppose a mouse were trained, in a Skinner box with a food reward, to take exactly four steps forward and press a bar with its nose; if Skinner's laws truly held between stimuli and responses defined in terms of bodily motion, were we to move the bar an inch farther away, so four steps did not reach it, Skinner would have to predict that the mouse would jab its nose into the empty air rather than take a fifth step.

A variation of Skinnerian theory designed to meet this objection acknowledges that the trained response one predicts is not truly captured in a description of skeletal motion alone, but rather in a description of an environmental effect achieved: the bar going down, the "35" button being depressed. This will also not do. Suppose we could in fact train a man or animal to achieve an environmental effect, as this theory proposes. Suppose, for instance, we train a man to push a button under the longer of two displays, such as drawings or simple designs, that is, we reward him when he pushes the button under the longer of two pictures of pencils, or cigars, etc. The miraculous consequence of this theory, were it correct, would be that if, after training him on simple views, we were to present him with the Müller-Lyer arrow-head illusion, he would be immune to it, for *ex hypothesi* he has been trained to achieve an *actual* environmental effect (choosing the display that *is* longer), not a *perceived* or *believed* environmental effect (choosing the display that *seems* longer). The reliable prediction, again, is the intentional one.

Skinner's experimental design is supposed to eliminate the intentional, but it merely masks it. Skinner's non-intentional predictions work to the extent they do, not because Skinner has truly found non-intentional behavioral laws, but because the highly reliable intentional predictions underlying his experimental situations (the rat desires food and believes it will get food by pressing the bar—something for which it has been given good evidence—so it will press the bar) are disguised by leaving virtually no room in the environment for more than one bodily motion to be the appropriate action and by leaving virtually no room in the environment for discrepancy to arise between the subject's beliefs and the reality.

Where, then, should we look for a satisfactory theory of behavior? Intentional theory is vacuous as psychology because it presupposes and does not explain rationality or intelligence. The apparent successes of Skinnerian behaviorism, however, rely on hidden intentional predictions. Skinner is right in recognizing that intentionality can be no *foundation* for psychology, and right also to look for purely mechanistic regularities in the activities of his subjects, but there is little reason to suppose they will lie on the surface in gross behavior—except, as we have seen, when we put an artificial straitjacket on an intentional regularity. Rather, we will find whatever mechanistic regularities there are in the functioning of internal systems whose design approaches the optimal (relative to some ends). In seeking knowledge of internal design our most promising tactic is to take out intelligence-loans, endow peripheral and internal events with content, and then look for mechanisms that will function appropriately with such "messages" so that we can pay back the loans. This tactic is hardly untried. Research in artificial intelligence, which has produced, among other things, the chess-playing computer, proceeds by working from an intentionally characterized problem (how to get the computer to consider the right sorts of information, make the right decisions) to a design-stance solution—an approximation of optimal design. Psychophysicists and neurophysiologists who routinely describe events in terms of the transmission of information within the nervous system are similarly borrowing intentional capital—even if they are often inclined to ignore or disavow their debts.

Finally, it should not be supposed that, just because intentional theory is vacuous as psychology, in virtue of its assumption of rationality, it is vacuous from all points of view. Game theory, for example, is inescapably intentional, but as a formal normative theory and not a psychology this is nothing amiss. Game-theoretical predictions applied to human subjects achieve their accuracy in virtue of the evolutionary guarantee that man is well designed as a game player, a special case of rationality. Similarly, economics, the social science of greatest predictive power today, is not a psychological theory and presupposes what psychology must explain. Economic explanation and prediction is intentional (although some is disguised) and succeeds to the extent that it does because individual men are in general good approximations of the optimal operator in the marketplace.

III

The concept of an intentional system is a relatively uncluttered and unmetaphysical notion, abstracted as it is from questions of the composition, constitution, consciousness, morality, or divinity of the entities falling under it. Thus, for example, it is much easier to decide whether a machine can be an intentional system than it is to decide whether a machine can *really* think, or be conscious, or morally responsible. This simplicity makes it ideal as a source of order and organization in philosophical analyses of "mental" concepts. Whatever else a person might be—embodied mind or soul, self-conscious moral agent, "emergent" form of intelligence—he is an intentional system, and whatever follows just from being an intentional system is thus true of a person. It is interesting to see just how much of what we hold to be the case about persons or their minds follows directly from their being intentional systems. To revert for a moment to the economic metaphor, the guiding or challenging question that defines work in the philosophy of mind is this: are their mental treasures that cannot be purchased with intentional coin? If not, a considerable unification of science can be foreseen in outline. Of special importance for such an examination is the subclass of intentional systems that have language, that can communicate; for these provide a framework for a theory of consciousness. In *Content and Consciousness*, part II, and in parts III and IV [of *Brainstorms*] I have attempted to elaborate such a theory; here I would like to consider its implications for the analysis of the concept of belief. What will be true of human believers just in virtue of their being intentional systems with the capacity to communicate?

Just as not all intentional systems currently known to us can fly or swim, so not all intentional systems can talk, but those which can do this raise special problems and opportunities when we come to ascribe beliefs and desires to them. That is a massive understatement; without the talking intentional systems, of course, there would be no ascribing beliefs, no theorizing, no assuming rationality, no predicting. The capacity for language is without doubt the crowning achievement of evolution, an achievement that feeds on itself to produce ever more versatile and subtle rational systems, but still it can be looked at as an adaptation which is subject to the same conditions of environmental utility as any other behavioral talent. When it is looked at in this way several striking facts emerge. One of the most pervasive features of evolutionary histories is the interdependence of distinct organs and capacities in a species. Advanced eyes and other distance receptors are of no utility to an organism unless it develops advanced means of locomotion; the talents of a predator will not accrue to a species that does not evolve a carnivore's digestive system. The capacities of belief and communication have prerequisites of their own. We have already seen that there is no point in ascribing beliefs to a system unless the beliefs ascribed are in general appropriate to the environment, and the system responds appropriately to the beliefs. An eccentric expression of this would be: the capacity to believe would have no survival value unless it were a capacity to believe truths. What is eccentric and potentially misleading about this is that it hints at the picture of a species "trying on" a faculty giving rise to beliefs most of which were false, having its inutility demonstrated, and abandoning it. A species might "experiment" by mutation in any number of inefficacious systems, but none of these systems would deserve to be called belief systems precisely because of their defects, their nonrationality, and hence a false belief system is a conceptual impossibility. To borrow an example from a short story by MacDonald Harris, a soluble fish is an evolutionary impossibility, but a system for false beliefs cannot even be given a coherent description. The same evolutionary bias in favor of truth prunes the capacity to communicate as it develops; a capacity for false communication would not be a capacity for communication at all, but just an emission proclivity of no systematic value to the species. The faculty of communication would not gain ground in evolution unless it was by and large the faculty of transmitting true beliefs, which means only: the faculty of altering other members of the species in the direction of more optimal design.

This provides a foundation for explaining a feature of belief that philosophers have recently been at some pains to account for. The concept of belief seems to have a normative cast to it that is most difficult to capture. One way of putting it might be that an avowal like "I believe that *p*" seems to imply in some fashion: "One ought to believe that *p*." This way of putting it has flaws, however, for we must then account for the fact that "I believe that *p*" seems to have normative force that "He believes that *p*," said of me, does not. Moreover, saying that one ought to believe this or that suggests that belief is voluntary, a view with notorious difficulties. So long as one tries to capture the normative element by expressing it in the form of moral or pragmatic injunctions to believers, such as "one ought to believe the truth" and "one ought to act in accordance with one's beliefs," dilemmas arise. How, for instance, is one to follow the advice to believe the truth? Could one abandon one's sloppy habit of believing falsehoods? If the advice is taken to mean: believe only what you have convincing evidence for, it is the vacuous advice: believe only what you believe to be true. If alternatively it is taken to mean: believe only what is in fact the truth, it is an injunction we are powerless to obey.

The normative element of belief finds its home not in such injunctions but in the preconditions for the ascription of belief, what Phillips Griffiths calls "the general conditions for the possibility of application of the concept." For the concept of belief to find application, two conditions, we have seen, must be met: (1) In general, normally, more often than not, if *x* believes *p*, *p* is true. (2) In general, normally, more often than not, if *x* avows that *p*, he believes *p* [and, by (1), *p* is true]. Were these conditions not met, we would not have rational, communicating systems; we would not have believers or belief-avowers. The norm for belief is evidential well-foundedness (assuring truth in the long run), and the norm for avowal of belief is accuracy (which includes sincerity). These two norms determine pragmatic implications of our utterances. If I assert that *p* (or that I believe that *p*—it makes no difference), I assume the burden of defending my assertion on two fronts. I can be asked for evidence for the truth of *p*, and I can be asked for behavioral evidence that I do in fact believe *p*. I do not need to examine my own behavior in order to be in a position to avow my belief that *p*, but if my sincerity or self-knowledge is challenged, this is where I must turn to defend my assertion. But again, challenges on either point must be the exception rather than the rule if belief is to have a place among our concepts.

Another way of looking at the importance of this predominance of the normal is to consider the well-known circle of implications between beliefs and desires (or intentions) that prevent non-intentional behavioral definitions of international terms. A man's standing under a tree is a behavioral indicator of his belief that it is raining, but only on the assumption that he desires to stay dry, and if we then look for evidence that he wants to stay dry, his standing under the tree will do, but only on the assumption that he believes the tree will shelter him; if we ask him if he believes the tree will shelter him, his positive response is confirming evidence only on the assumption that he desires to tell us the truth, and so forth *ad infinitum*. It is this apparently vicious circle that turned Quine against the intentional (and foiled Tolman's efforts at operational definition of intentional terms), but if it is true that in any particular case a man's saying that *p* is evidence of his belief only conditionally, we can be assured that in the long run and in general the circle is broken; a man's assertions are, unconditionally, indicative of his beliefs, as are his actions in general. We get around the "privacy" of beliefs and desires by recognizing that in general anyone's beliefs and desires must be those he "ought to have" given the circumstances.

These two interdependent norms of belief, one favoring the truth and rationality of belief, the other favoring accuracy of avowal, normally complement each other, but on occasion can give rise to conflict. This is the "problem of incorrigibility." If rationality is the mother of intention, we still must wean intentional systems from the criteria that give them life, and set them up on their own. Less figuratively, if we are to make use of the concept of an intentional system in particular instances, at some point we must cease *testing* the assumption of the system's rationality adopt the intentional stance, and grant without further ado that the system is qualified for beliefs and desires. For mute animals—and chess-playing computers—this manifests itself in a tolerance for less than optimal performance. We continue to ascribe beliefs to the mouse, and explain its actions in terms of them, after we have tricked it into some stupid belief. This tolerance has its limits of course, and the less felicitous the behavior—especially the less adaptable the behavior—the more hedged are our ascriptions. For instance, we are inclined to say of the duckling that "imprints" on the first moving thing it sees upon emerging from its shell that it "believes" the thing is its mother, whom it follows around, but we emphasize the scare-quotes around "believes." For intentional systems that can communicate—persons for instance—the tolerance takes the form of the convention that a man is incorrigible or a special authority about his own beliefs. This convention is "justified" by the fact that evolution does guarantee that our second norm is followed. What better source could there be of a system's beliefs than its avowals? Conflict arises, however, whenever a person falls short of perfect rationality, and avows beliefs that either are strongly disconfirmed by the available empirical evidence or are self-contradictory or contradict other avowals he has made. If we lean on the myth that a man is perfectly rational, we must find his avowals less than authoritative: "You *can't* mean—understand—what you're saying!"; if we lean on his "right" as a speaking intentional system to have his word accepted, we grant him an irrational set of beliefs. Neither position provides a stable resting place; for, as we saw earlier, intentional explanation and prediction cannot be accommodated either to breakdown or to less than optimal design, so there is no coherent intentional description of such an impasse.

Can any other considerations be brought to bear in such an instance to provide us with justification for one ascription of beliefs rather than another? Where should one look for such considerations? The Phenomenologist will be inclined to suppose that individual introspection will provide us a sort of data not available to the outsider adopting the intentional stance; but how would such data get used? Let the introspector amass as much inside information as you please; he must then communicate it to us, and what are we to make of his communications? We can suppose that they are incorrigible (barring corrigible verbal errors, slips of the tongue, and so forth), but we do not need Phenomenology to give us that option, for it amounts to the decision to lean on the accuracy-of-avowal norm at the expense of the rationality norm. If, alternatively, we demand certain standards of consistency and rationality of his utterances before we accept them as authoritative, what standards will we adopt? If we demand perfect rationality, we have simply flown to the other norm at the expense of the norm of accuracy of avowal. If we try to fix minimum standards at something less than perfection, what will guide our choice? Not Phenomenological data, for the choice we make will determine what is to count as Phenomenological data. Not neurophysiological data either, for whether we interpret a bit of neural structure to be endowed with a particular belief content hinges on our having granted that the neural system under examination has met the standards of rationality for being an intentional system, an assumption jeopardized by the impasse we are trying to resolve. That is, one might have a theory about an individual's neurology that permitted one to "read off" or predict the propositions to which he would assent, but whether one's theory had uncovered his *beliefs*, or merely a set of assent-inducers, would depend on how consistent, reasonable, true we found the set of propositions.

John Vickers has suggested to me a way of looking at this question. Consider a set T of transformations that take beliefs into beliefs. The problem is to determine the set T_s for each intentional system S, so that if we know that S believes p, we will be able to determine other things that S believes by seeing what the transformations of p are for T_S. If S were ideally rational, every valid transformation would be in T_S; S would believe every logical consequence of every belief (and, ideally, S would have no false beliefs). Now we know that no actual intentional system will be ideally rational; so we must suppose any actual system will have a T with less in it. But we also know that, to qualify as an intentional system at all, S must have a T with some integrity; T cannot be empty. What rationale could we have, however, for fixing some set between the extremes and calling it *the* set for belief (for S, for earthlings, or for ten-year-old girls)? This is another way of asking whether we could replace Hintikka's normative theory of belief with an empirical theory of belief, and, if so, what evidence we would use. "Actually," one is tempted to say, "people do believe contradictions on occasion, as their utterances demonstrate; so any adequate logic of belief or analysis of the concept of belief must accommodate this fact." But any attempt to *legitimize* human fallibility in a theory of belief by fixing a permissible level of error would be like adding one more rule to chess: an Official Tolerance Rule to the effect that any game of chess containing no more than k moves that are illegal relative to the other rules of the game is a legal game of chess. Suppose we discovered that, in a particular large population of poor chess-players, each game on average contained three illegal moves undetected by either opponent. Would we claim that these people *actually* play a different game from ours, a game with an Official Tolerance Rule with k fixed at 3? This would be to confuse the norm they follow with what gets by in their world. We could claim in a similar vein that people *actually* believe, say, all synonymous or intentionally isomorphic consequences of their beliefs, but not all their logical consequences, but of course the occasions when a man resists assenting to a logical consequence of some avowal of his are unstable cases; he comes in for criticism and cannot appeal in his own defense to any canon absolving him from believing nonsynonymous consequences. If one wants to get away from norms and predict and explain the "actual, empirical" behavior of the poor chess-players, one stops talking of their *chess moves* and starts talking of their proclivities to move pieces of wood or ivory about on checkered boards; if one wants to predict and explain the "actual, empirical" behavior of believers, one must similarly cease talking of belief, and descend to the design stance or physical stance for one's account.

The concept of an intentional system explicated in these pages is made to bear a heavy load. It has been used here to form a bridge connecting the intentional domain (which includes our "common-sense" world of persons and actions, game theory, and the "neural signals" of the biologist) to the non-intentional domain of the physical sciences. That is a lot to expect of one concept, but nothing less than Brentano himself expected when, in a day of less fragmented science, he proposed intentionality as the mark that sunders the universe in the most fundamental way: dividing the mental from the physical.

Chapter 27

JOHN SEARLE

John Searle was born on July 31, 1932, in Denver, Colorado. He was educated at the University of Wisconsin and as a Rhodes Scholar at Oxford, where he received his D. Phil. He taught at Oxford for three years before in 1959 joining the philosophy department of the University of California at Berkeley, where he has taught ever since. During the 1960s he was a leader of the free speech movement, and in the 1980s and 1990s he challenged the notion of affirmative action as a denial of merit and equal opportunity for all. Searle first came to the philosophical community's attention when he challenged the Humean principle that we cannot derive an *ought* from an *is*. Searle shows that from the *institutional fact* that I have promised to pay you back the five dollars I borrowed, I *ought* to pay you the five dollars. The idea of *institutional facts* runs through Searle's work, culminating in his latest book, *Constuction of Social Reality* (1997). Searle has written widely on the philosophy of language and the philosophy of mind, which he holds to be interconnected.

> [T]he philosophy of language is a branch of the philosophy of mind. The capacity of speech acts to represent objects and states of affairs in the world is an extension of the more biologically fundamental capacities of the mind (or brain) to relate the organism to the world by way of such mental states as belief and desire, and especially through action and perception. Since speech acts are a type of human action, and since the capacity of speech to represent objects and states of affairs is part of a more general capacity of the mind to relate the organism to the world, any complete account of speech and language requires as account of how the mind/brain related the organism to reality. (From the introduction to *Intentionality: An Essay in the Philosophy of Mind*)

Intentional states have what Searle calls *conditions of satisfaction*. A belief is "satisfied" if it is true, that is, if it *fits* the world; a command, desire, or wish is "satisfied" if it is obeyed—but the "direction of fit" is the reverse: the world must fit the intentioned state.

For Searle the mind is intentional in that perceptions, memoirs, meanings, beliefs, and desires take objects. He differs from most materialists, behaviorists, and functionalists in that he treats *consciousness* as an intrinsic feature of the mind.

In the selection that follows Searle argues that although weak AI (artificial intelligence), which states that the mind functions somewhat like a computer, might be correct, strong AI, which states the appropriately programmed computer is mind and has intentions, is false. A computer program itself cannot create an intentional state. He considers a person who knows no Chinese who is confined in a room where Chinese characters are transmitted, via a program replicating a fluent Chinese speaker. Regardless of how effective the simulation, the person will still not understand any Chinese.

FOR FURTHER READING

Dennett, Daniel. *The Intentional Stance* (MIT Press, 1987).
Heil, John. *The True Nature of Mind* (Cambridge University Press, 1992).
McGinn, Colin. *The Character of Mind* (Oxford University Press, 1992).
Rosenthal, David, ed. *The Nature of Mind* (Oxford University Press, 1991).
Searle, John. *The Recovery of Mind* (MIT Press, 1992).
———. *Intentionality* (Cambridge University Press, 1985).
———. *The Construction of Social Reality* (Free Press, 1995).

Minds, Brains, and Programs [The Chinese Room]

What psychological and philosophical significance should we attach to recent efforts at computer simulations of human cognitive capacities? In answering this question, I find it useful to distinguish what I will call "strong" AI from "weak" or "cautious" AI (artificial intelligence). According to weak AI, the principal value of the computer in the study of the mind is that it gives us a very powerful tool. For example, it enables us to formulate and test hypotheses in a more rigorous and precise fashion. But according to strong AI, the computer is not merely a tool in the study of the mind; rather, the appropriately programmed computer really *is* a mind, in the sense that computers given the right programs can be literally said to *understand* and have other cognitive states. In strong AI, because the programmed computer has cognitive states, the programs are not mere tools that enable us to test psychological explanations; rather, the programs are themselves the explanations.

I have no objection to the claims of weak AI, at least as far as this article is concerned. My discussion here will be directed at the claims I have defined as those of strong AI, specifically the claim that the appropriately programmed computer literally has cognitive states and that the programs thereby explain human cognition. When I hereafter refer to AI, I have in mind the strong version, as expressed by these two claims.

I will consider the work of Roger Schank and his colleagues at Yale (Schank and Abelson 1977), because I am more familiar with it than I am with any other similar claims, and because it provides a very clear example of the sort of work I wish to examine. But nothing that follows depends upon the details of Schank's programs. The same arguments would apply to Winograd's SHRDLU (Winograd 1973), Weizenbaum's ELIZA (Weizenbaum 1965), and indeed any Turing machine simulation of human mental phenomena. . . .

Very briefly, and leaving out the various details, one can describe Schank's program as follows: The aim of the program is to simulate the human ability to understand stories. It is characteristic of human beings' story-understanding capacity that they can answer questions about the story even though the information that they give was never explicitly stated in the story. Thus, for example, suppose you are given the following story: "A man went into a restaurant and ordered a hamburger. When the hamburger arrived it was burned to a crisp, and the man stormed out of the restaurant angrily, without paying for the hamburger or leaving a tip." Now, if you are asked "Did the man eat the humburger?" you will presumably answer, "No, he did not." Similarly, if you are given the following story: "A man went into a restaurant and ordered a hamburger; when the hamburger came he was very pleased with it; and as he left the restaurant he gave the waitress a large tip before paying his bill," and you are asked the question, "Did the man eat the hamburger?" you will presumably answer, "Yes, he ate the hamburger." Now

From John R. Searle, "Minds, Brains, and Programs," in *The Behavioral and Brain Sciences*, Vol. 3.

Schank's machines can similarly answer questions about restaurants in this fashion. To do this, they have a "representation" of the sort of information that human beings have about restaurants, which enables them to answer such questions as those above, given these sorts of stories. When the machine is given the story and then asked the question, the machine will print out answers of the sort that we would expect human beings to give if told similar stories. Partisans of strong AI claim that in this question and answer sequence the machine is not only simulating a human ability but also (1) that the machine can literally be said to *understand* the story and provide the answers to questions, and (2) that what the machine and its programs do *explains* the human ability to understand the story and answer questions about it.

Both claims seem to me to be totally unsupported by Schank's work, as I will attempt to show in what follows. I am not, of course, saying that Schank himself is committed to these claims. One way to test any theory of the mind is to ask oneself what it would be like if my mind actually worked on the principles that the theory says all minds work on. Let us apply this test to the Schank program with the following thought experiment. Suppose that I'm locked in a room and given a large batch of Chinese writing. Suppose furthermore (as is indeed the case) that I know no Chinese, either written or spoken, and that I'm not even confident that I could recognize Chinese writing as Chinese writing distinct from, say, Japanese writing or meaningless squiggles. To me, Chinese writing is just so many meaningless squiggles. Now suppose further that after this first batch of Chinese writing I am given a second batch of Chinese script together with a set of rules for correlating the second batch with the first batch. The rules are in English, and I understand these rules as well as any other native speaker of English. They enable me to correlate one set of formal symbols with another set of formal symbols, and all that "formal" means here is that I can identify the symbols entirely by their shapes. Now suppose also that I am given a third batch of Chinese symbols together with some instructions, again in English, that enable me to correlate elements of this third batch with the first two batches, and these rules instruct me how to give back certain Chinese symbols with certain sorts of shapes in response to certain sorts of shapes given me in the third batch. Unknown to me, the people who are giving me all of these symbols call the first batch a "script," they call the second batch a "story," and they call the third batch "questions." Furthermore, they call the symbols I give them back in response to the third batch "answers to the questions," and the set of rules in English that they gave me, they call the "program." Now just to complicate the story a little, imagine that these people also give me stories in English, which I understand, and they then ask me questions in English about these stories, and I give them back answers in English. Suppose also that after a while I get so good at following the instructions for manipulating the Chinese symbols and the programmers get so good at writing the programs that from the external point of view—that is, from the point of view of somebody outside the room in which I am locked—my answers to the questions are absolutely indistinguishable from those of native Chinese speakers. Nobody just looking at my answers can tell that I don't speak a word of Chinese. Let us also suppose that my answers to the English questions are, as they no doubt would be, indistinguishable from those of other native English speakers, for the simple reason that I am a native English speaker. From the external point of view—from the point of view of someone reading my "answers"—the answers to the Chinese questions and the English questions are equally good. But in the Chinese case, unlike the English case, I produce the answers by manipulating uninterpreted formal symbols. As far as the Chinese is concerned, I simply behave like a computer; I perform computational operations on formally specified elements. For the purposes of the Chinese, I am simply an instantiation of the computer program.

Now the claims made by strong AI are that the programmed computer understands the stories and that the program in some sense explains human understanding. But we are now in a position to examine these claims in light of our thought experiment.

1. As regards the first claim, it seems to me quite obvious in the example that I do not understand a word of the Chinese stories. I have inputs and outputs that are indistinguishable from those of the native Chinese speaker, and I can have any formal program you like, but I still understand nothing. For the same reasons, Schank's computer understands nothing of any stories, whether in Chinese, English, or whatever, since in the Chinese case the computer is me, and in cases where the computer is not me, the computer has nothing more than I have in the case where I understand nothing.

2. As regards the second claim, that the program explains human understanding, we can see that the computer and its program do not provide sufficient conditions of understanding since the computer and the program are functioning, and there is no understanding. But does it even provide a necessary condition or a significant contribution to understanding? One of the claims made by the supporters of strong AI is that when I understand a story in English, what I am doing is exactly the same—or perhaps more of the same—as what I was doing in manipulating the Chinese symbols. It is simply more formal symbol manipulation that distinguishes the case in English, where I do understand, from the case in Chinese, where I don't. I have not demonstrated that this claim is false, but it would certainly appear an incredible claim in the example. Such plausibility as the claim has derives from the supposition that we can construct a program that will have the same inputs and outputs as native speakers, and in addition we assume that speakers have some level of description where they are also instantiations of a program. On the basis of these two assumptions we assume that even if Schank's program isn't the whole story about understanding, it may be part of the story. Well, I suppose that is an empirical possibility, but not the slightest reason has so far been given to believe that it is true, since what is suggested—though certainly not demonstrated—by the example is that the computer program is simply irrelevant to my understanding of the story. In the Chinese case I have everything that artificial intelligence can put into me by way of a program, and I understand nothing; in the English case I understand everything, and there is so far no reason at all to suppose that my understanding has anything to do with computer programs, that is, with computational operations on purely formally specified elements. As long as the program is defined in terms of computational operations on purely formally defined elements, what the example suggests is that these by themselves have no interesting connection with understanding. They are certainly not sufficient conditions, and not the slightest reason has been given to suppose that they are necessary conditions or even that they make a significant contribution to understanding. Notice that the force of the argument is not simply that different machines can have the same input and output while operating on different formal principles—that is not the point at all. Rather, whatever purely formal principles you put into the computer, they will not be sufficient for understanding, since a human will be able to follow the formal principles without understanding anything. No reason whatever has been offered to suppose that such principles are necessary or even contributory, since no reason has been given to suppose that when I understand English I am operating with any formal program at all.

Well, then, what is it that I have in the case of the English sentences that I do not have in the case of the Chinese sentences? The obvious answer is that I know what the former mean, while I haven't the faintest idea what the latter mean. But in what does this consist and why couldn't we give it to a machine, whatever it is?. . . .

I have had the occasions to present this example to several workers in artificial intelligence, and, interestingly, they do not seem to agree on what the proper reply to it is. . . .

. . . I want to block some common misunderstandings about "understanding": In many of these discussions one finds a lot of fancy footwork about the word "understanding." My critics point out that there are many different degrees of understanding; that "understanding" is not a simple two-place predicate; that there are even different kinds and levels of understanding, and often the law of excluded middle doesn't even apply in a straightforward way to statements of the form "*x* understands *y*"; that in many cases it is a matter for decision and not a simple matter of fact whether *x* understands *y*, and so on. To all of these points I want to say: of course, of course. But they have nothing to do with the points at issue. There are clear cases in which "understanding" literally applies and clear cases in which it does not apply; and these two sorts of cases are all I need for this argument. I understand stories in English; to a lesser degree I can understand stories in French; to a still lesser degree, stories in German; and in Chinese, not at all. My car and my adding machine, on the other hand, understand nothing: they are not in that line of business.[1] We often attribute "understanding" and other cognitive predicates by metaphor and analogy to cars, adding machines, and other artifacts, but nothing is proved by

1. Also, "understanding" implies both the possession of mental (intentional) states and the truth (validity, success) of these states. For the purposes of this discussion we are concerned only with the possession of the states.

such attributions. We say, "The door *knows* when to open because of its photoelectric cell," "The adding machine *knows how (understands how, is able)* to do addition and subtraction but not division," and "The thermostat *perceives* changes in the temperature." The reason we make these attributions is quite interesting, and it has to do with the fact that in artifacts we extend our own intentionality[2]; our tools are extensions of our purposes, and so we find it natural to make metaphorical attributions of intentionality to them; but I take it no philosophical ice is cut by such examples. The sense in which an automatic door "understands instructions" from its photoelectric cell is not at all the sense in which I understand English. If the sense in which Schank's programmed computers understand stories is supposed to be the metaphorical sense in which the door understands, and not the sense in which I understand English, the issue would not be worth discussing. But Newell and Simon (1963) write that the kind of cognition they claim for computers is exactly the same as for human beings. I like the straightforwardness of this claim, and it is the sort of claim I will be considering. I will argue that in the literal sense the programmed computer understands what the car and the adding machine understand, namely, exactly nothing. The computer's understanding is not just (like my understanding of German) partial or incomplete; it is zero. . . .

By way of concluding I want to try to state some of the general philosophical points implicit in the argument. For clarity I will try to do it in a question-and-answer fashion, and begin with that old chestnut of a question:

"Could a machine think?"

The answer is, obviously, yes. We are precisely such machines.

"Yes, but could an artificial, a man-made machine, think?"

Assuming it is possible to produce artificially a machine with a nervous system, neurons, with axons and dendrites, and all the rest of it, sufficiently like ours, again the answer to the question seems to be obviously, yes. If you can exactly duplicate the causes, you could duplicate the effects. And indeed it might be possible to produce consciousness, intentionality, and all the rest of it using some other sorts of chemical principles than those that human beings use. It is, as I said, an empirical question.

"OK, but could a digital computer think?"

If by "digital computer" we mean anything at all that has a level of description where it can correctly be described as the instantiation of a computer program, then again the answer is, of course, yes, since we are the instantiations of any number of computer programs, and we can think.

"But could something think, understand, and so on *solely* by virtue of being a computer with the right sort of program? Could instantiating a program, the right program of course, by itself be a sufficient condition of understanding?" This I think is the right question to ask, though it is usually confused with one or more of the earlier questions, and the answer to it is no.

"Why not?"

Because the formal symbol manipulations by themselves don't have any intentionality; they are quite meaningless; they aren't even *symbol* manipulations, since the symbols don't symbolize anything. In the linguistic jargon, they have only a syntax but no semantics. Such intentionality as computers appear to have is solely in the minds of those who program them and those who use them, those who send in the input and those who interpret the output.

The aim of the Chinese room example was to try to show this by showing that as soon as we put something into the system that really does have intentionality (a man), and we program him with the formal program, you can see that the formal program carries no additional intentionality. It adds nothing, for example, to a man's ability to understand Chinese.

Precisely that feature of AI that seemed so appealing—the distinction between the program and the realization—proves fatal to the claim that simulation could be duplication. The distinction between the program and its realization in the hardware seems to be parallel to the distinction between the level of mental operations and the level of brain operations. And if we could describe the level of mental operations as a formal program, then it seems we could describe what was essential about the mind without doing either introspective psychology or neurophysiology of the brain. But the equation "mind is to brain as program is to hardware" breaks down at several points, among them the following three:

2. Intentionality is by definition that feature of certain mental states by which they are directed at or about objects and states of affairs in the world. Thus, beliefs, desires, and intentions are intentional states; undirected forms of anxiety and depression are not.

First, the distinction between program and realization has the consequence that the same program could have all sorts of crazy realizations that had no form of intentionality. Weizenbaum, for example, shows in detail how to construct a computer using a roll of toilet paper and a pile of small stones. Similarly, the Chinese story understanding-program can be programmed into a sequence of water pipes, a set of wind machines, or a monolingual English speaker, none of which thereby acquires an understanding of Chinese. Stones, toilet paper, wind, and water pipes are the wrong kind of stuff to have intentionality in the first place—only something that has the same causal powers as brains can have intentionality—and though the English speaker has the right kind of stuff for intentionality you can easily see that he doesn't get any extra intentionality by memorizing the program, since memorizing it won't teach him Chinese.

Second, the program is purely formal, but the intentional states are not in that way formal. They are defined in terms of their content, not their form. The belief that it is raining, for example, is not defined as a certain formal shape, but as a certain mental content with conditions of satisfaction, a direction of fit, and the like. Indeed the belief as such hasn't even got a formal shape in this syntactic sense, since one and the same belief can be given an indefinite number of different syntactic expressions in different linguistic systems.

Third, as I mentioned before, mental states and events are literally a product of the operation of the brain, but the program is not in that way a product of the computer.

"Well if programs are in no way constitutive of mental processes, why have so many people believed the converse? That at least needs some explanation."

I don't really know the answer to that one. The idea that computer simulations could be the real thing ought to have seemed suspicious in the first place because the computer isn't confined to simulating mental operations, by any means. No one supposes that computer simulations of a five-alarm fire will burn the neighborhood down or that a computer simulation of a rainstorm will leave us all drenched. Why on earth would anyone suppose that a computer simulation of understanding actually understood anything? It is sometimes said that it would be frightfully hard to get computers to feel pain or fall in love, but love and pain are neither harder nor easier than cognition or anything else. For simulation, all you need is the right input and output and a program in the middle that transforms the former into the latter. That is all the computer has for anything it does. To confuse simulation with duplication is the same mistake, whether it is pain, love, cognition, fires, or rainstorms.

Still, there are several reasons why AI must have seemed—and to many people perhaps still does seem—in some way to reproduce and thereby explain mental phenomena, and I believe we will not succeed in removing these illusions until we have fully exposed the reasons that give rise to them.

First, and perhaps most important, is a confusion about the notion of "information processing": Many people in cognitive science believe that the human brain, with its mind, does something called "information processing," and analogously the computer with its program does information processing; but fires and rainstorms, on the other hand, don't do information processing at all. Thus, though the computer can simulate the formal features of any process whatever, it stands in a special relation to the mind and brain because when the computer is properly programmed, ideally with the same program as the brain, the information processing is identical in the two cases, and this information processing is really the essence of the mental. But the trouble with this argument is that it rests on an ambiguity in the notion of "information." In the sense in which people "process information" when they reflect, say, on problems in arithmetic or when they read and answer questions about stories, the programmed computer does not do "information processing." Rather, what it does is does is manipulate formal symbols. The fact that the programmer and the interpreter of the computer output use the symbols to stand for objects in the world is totally beyond the scope of the computer. The computer, to repeat, has a syntax but no semantics. Thus if you type into the computer "2 plus 2 equals?" it will type out "4". But it has no idea that "4" means 4 or that it means anything at all. And the point is not that it lacks some second-order information about the interpretation of its first-order symbols, but rather that its first-order symbols don't have any interpretations as far as the computer is concerned. All the computer has is more symbols. The introduction of the notion of "information processing" therefore produces a dilemma: Either we construe the notion of "information processing" in such a way that it implies intentionality as part of the process or we don't. If the former, then the programmed computer does not do information processing: it only manipulates formal symbols. If the latter, then, though the computer does information processing, it is only doing so in the sense in which adding machines, and hurricanes do information processing; namely, they have a level of description at which we can describe them as taking information in at one end, transforming it, and producing information as output. But in this case it is up to outside observers to interpret the input and output as information in the ordinary sense. And no similarity is established between the computer and the brain in terms of any similarity of information processing.

Second, in much of AI there is a residual behaviorism or operationalism. Since appropriately programmed computers can have input-output patterns similar to those of human beings, we are tempted to postulate mental states in the computer similar to human mental states. But once we see that it is both conceptually and empirically possible for a system to have human capacities in some realm without having any intentionality at all, we should be able to overcome this impulse. My desk adding machine has calculating capacities, but no intentionality, and in this paper I have tried to show that a system could have input and output capabilities that duplicated those of a native Chinese speaker and still not understand Chinese, regardless of how it was programmed. The Turing test is typical of the tradition in being unashamedly behavioristic and operationalistic, and I believe that if AI workers totally repudiated behaviorism and operationalism much of the confusion between simulation and duplication would be eliminated.

Third, this residual operationalism is joined to a residual form of dualism; indeed strong AI only makes sense given the dualistic assumption that, where the mind is concerned, the brain doesn't matter. In strong AI (and in functionalism, as well) what matters are programs, and programs are independent of their realization in machines; indeed, as far as AI is concerned, the same program could be reallized by an electronic machine, a Cartesian mental substance, or a Hegelian world spirit. The single most surprising discovery that I have made in discussing these issues is that many AI workers are quite shocked by my idea that actual human mental phenomena might be dependent on actual physical-chemical properties of actual human brains. But if you think about it a minute you can see that I should not have been surprised; for unless you accept some form of dualism, the strong AI project hasn't got a chance. The project is to reproduce and explain the mental by designing programs, but unless the mind is not only conceptually but empirically independent of the brain you couldn't carry out the project, for the program is completely independent of any realization. Unless you believe that the mind is separable from the brain both conceptually and empirically—dualism in a strong form—you cannot hope to reproduce the mental by writing and running programs since programs must be independent of brains or any other particular forms of instantiation. If mental operations consist in computational operations on formal symbols, then it follows that they have no interesting connection with the brain; the only connection would be that the brain just happens to be one of the indefinitely many types of machines capable of instantiating the program. This form of dualism is not the traditional Cartesian variety that claims there are two sorts of *substances*, but it is Cartesian in the sense that it insists that what is specifically mental about the mind has no intrinsic connection with the actual properties of the brain. This underlying dualism is masked from us by the fact that AI literature contains frequent fulminations against "dualism"; what the authors seem to be unaware of is that their position presupposes a strong version of dualism.

"Could a machine think?" My own view is that *only* a machine could think, and indeed only very special kinds of machines, namely brains and machines that had the same causal powers as brains. And that is the main reason strong AI has had little to tell us about thinking, since it has nothing to tell us about machines. By its own definition, it is about programs, and programs are not machines. Whatever else intentionality is, it is a biological phenomenon, and it is as likely to be as causally dependent on the specific biochemistry of its origins as lactation, photosynthesis, or any other biological phenomena. No one would suppose that we could produce milk and sugar by running a computer simulation of the formal sequences in lactation and photosynthesis, but where the mind is concerned many people are willing to believe in such a miracle because of a deep and abiding dualism: The mind they suppose is a matter of formal processes and is independent of quite specific material causes in the way that milk and sugar are not.

In defense of this dualism the hope is often expressed that the brain is a digital computer (early computers, by the way, were often called "electronic brains"). But that is no help. Of course the brain is a digital computer. Since everything is a digital computer, brains are too. The point is that the brain's causal capacity to produce intentionality cannot consist in its instantiating a computer program, since for any program you like it is possible for something to instantiate that program and still not have any mental states. Whatever it is that the brain does to produce intentionality, it cannot consist in instantiating a program since no program, by itself, is sufficient for intentionality.

Chapter 28

DEREK PARFIT

Derek Parfit (1942–   ) is a Fellow at All Souls College, Oxford University. He is best known for his work on personal identity. He is the author of *Reasons and Persons* (1984).

In our selection Parfit rejects the classic notion of absolute personal identity and in its place substitutes relative personal identity. Our identity consists in bodily, and especially, psychological, continuity. Parfit applies his theory to morality, the problem of self-interest, and the problem of present versus future happiness.

FOR FURTHER READING

Parfit, Derek, *Reasons and Persons* (Clarendon Press, 1984). Part 3 contains an excellent discussion.

Perry, John, ed. *Personal Identity* (University of California Press, 1975). Contains the essential classical readings.

———. *A Dialogue on Personal Identity and Immortality* (Hackett, 1978). A philosophically rich, entertaining discussion of the problem of personal identity.

Pojman, Louis, ed. *Philosophy: The Quest for Truth*, 2d ed. (Wadsworth, 1992). Contains Parfit's discussion as well as the first part of Perry's dialogue and other essays.

Rorty, Amelie, ed. *The Identities of Persons* (University of California Press, 1976). A good selection of essays on the nature of personhood.

Unger, Peter. *Identity, Consciousness, and Value* (Oxford University Press, 1990). A highly imaginative, penetrating discussion of the issues discussed in this selection.

Personal Identity[1]

We can, I think, describe cases in which, though we know the answer to every other question, we have no idea how to answer a question about personal identity. These cases are not covered by the criteria of personal identity. These cases are not covered by the criteria of personal identity that we actually use.

Do they present a problem?

It might be thought that they do not, because they

This article is reprinted from *The Philosophical Review*, vol. 80, no. 1 (January, 1971), by permission of D. Parfit.

could never occur. I suspect that some of them could. (Some, for instance, might become scientifically possible.) But I shall claim that even if they did they would present no problem.

My targets are two beliefs: one about the nature of personal identity, the other about its importance.

The first is that in these cases the question about identity must have an answer.

No one thinks this about, say, nations or machines. Our criteria for the identity of these do not cover certain cases. No one thinks that in these cases the questions "Is it the same nation?" or "Is it the same machine?" must have answers.

Some people believe that in this respect they are different. They agree that our criteria of personal identity do not cover certain cases, but they believe that the nature of their own identity through time is, somehow, such as to guarantee that in these cases questions about their identity must have answers. This belief might be expressed as follows: "Whatever happens between now and any future time, either I shall still exist, or I shall not. Any future experience will either be *my* experience, or it will not."

This first belief—in the special nature of personal identity—has, I think, certain effects. It makes people assume that the principle of self-interest is more rationally compelling than any moral principle. And it makes them more depressed by the thought of aging and of death.

I cannot see how to disprove this first belief. I shall describe a problem case. But this can only make it seem implausible.

Another approach might be this. We might suggest that one cause of the belief is the projection of our emotions. When we imagine ourselves in a problem case, we do feel that the question "Would it be me?" must have an answer. But what we take to be a bafflement about a further fact may be only the bafflement of our concern.

I shall not pursue this suggestion here. But one cause of our concern is the belief which is my second target. This is that unless the question about identity has an answer, we cannot answer certain important questions (questions about such matters as survival, memory, and responsibility).

Against this second belief my claim will be this. Certain important questions do presuppose a question about personal identity. But they can be freed of this presupposition. And when they are, the question about identity has no importance.

I

We can start by considering the much discussed case of the man who, like an amoeba, divides.[2]

Wiggins has recently dramatized this case.[3] He first referred to the operation imagined by Shoemaker.[4] We suppose that my brain is transplanted into someone else's (brainless) body, and that the resulting person has my character and apparent memories of my life. Most of us would agree, after thought, that the resulting person is me. I shall here assume such agreement.[5]

Wiggins then imagined his own operation. My brain is divided, and each half is housed in a new body. Both resulting people have my character and apparent memories of my life.

What happens to me? There seem only three possibilities: (1) I do not survive; (2) I survive as one of the two people; (3) I survive as both.

The trouble with (1) is this. We agreed that I could survive if my brain were successfully transplanted. And people have in fact survived with half their brains destroyed. It seems to follow that I could survive if half my brain were successfully transplanted and the other half were destroyed. But if this is so, how could I *not* survive if the other half were also successfully transplanted? How could a double success be a failure?

We can move to the second description. Perhaps one success is the maximum score. Perhaps I shall be one of the resulting people.

The trouble here is that in Wiggins' case each half of my brain is exactly similar, and so, to start with, is each resulting person. So how can I survive as only one of the two people? What can make me one of them rather than the other?

It seems clear that both of these descriptions—that I do not survive, and that I survive as one of the people—are highly implausible. Those who have accepted them must have assumed that they were the only possible descriptions.

What about our third description: that I survive as both people?

It might be said, "If 'survive' implies identity, this description makes no sense—you cannot be two people. If it does not, the description is irrelevant to a problem about identity."

I shall later deny the second of these remarks. But there are ways of denying the first. We might say, "What we have called 'the two resulting people' are not two people. They are one person. I do survive

Wiggins' operation. Its effect is to give me two bodies and a divided mind."

It would shorten my argument if this were absurd. But I do not think it is. It is worth showing why.

We can, I suggest, imagine a divided mind. We can imagine a man having two simultaneous experiences, in having each of which he is unaware of having the other.

We may not even need to imagine this. Certain actual cases, to which Wiggins referred, seem to be best described in these terms. These involve the cutting of the bridge between the hemispheres of the brain. The aim was to cure epilepsy. But the result appears to be, in the surgeon's words, the creation of "two separate spheres of consciousness,"[6] each of which controls one half of the patient's body. What is experienced in each is, presumably, experienced by the patient.

There are certain complications in these actual cases. So let us imagine a simpler case.

Suppose that the bridge between my hemispheres is brought under my voluntary control. This would enable me to disconnect my hemispheres as easily as if I were blinking. By doing this I would divide my mind. And we can suppose that when my mind is divided I can, in each half, bring about reunion.

This ability would have obvious uses. To give an example: I am near the end of a maths exam, and see two ways of tackling the last problem. I decide to divide my mind, to work, with each half, at one of two calculations, and then to reunite my mind and write a fair copy of the best result.

What shall I experience?

When I disconnect my hemispheres, my consciousness divides into two streams. But this division is not something that I experience. Each of my two streams of consciousness seems to have been straightforwardly continuous with my one stream of consciousness up to the moment of division. The only changes in each stream are the disappearance of half my visual field and the loss of sensation in, and control over, half my body.

Consider my experiences in what we can call my "right-handed" stream. I remember that I assigned my right hand to the longer calculation. This I now begin. In working at this calculation I can see, from the movements of my left hand, that I am also working at the other. But I am not aware of working at the other. So I might, in my right-handed stream, wonder how, in my left-handed stream, I am getting on.

My work is now over. I am about to reunite my mind. What should I, in each stream, expect? Simply that I shall suddenly seem to remember just having thought out two calculations, in thinking out each of which I was not aware of thinking out the other. This, I submit, we can imagine. And if my mind was divided, these memories are correct.

In describing this episode, I assumed that there were two series of thoughts, and that they were both mine. If my two hands visibly wrote out two calculations, and if I claimed to remember two corresponding series of thoughts, this is surely what we should want to say.

If it is, then a person's mental history need not be like a canal, with only one channel. It could be like a river, with islands, and with separate streams.

To apply this to Wiggins' operation: we mentioned the view that it gives me two bodies and a divided mind. We cannot now call this absurd. But it is, I think, unsatisfactory.

There were two features of the case of the exam that made us want to say that only one person was involved. The mind was soon reunited, and there was only one body. If a mind was permanently divided and its halves developed in different ways, the point of speaking of one person would start to disappear. Wiggins' case, where there are also two bodies, seems to be over the borderline. After I have had his operation, the two "products" each have all the attributes of a person. They could live at opposite ends of the earth. (If they later met, they might even fail to recognize each other.) It would become intolerable to deny that they were different people.

Suppose we admit that they are different people. Could we still claim that I survived as both, using "survive" to imply identity?

We could. For we might suggest that two people could compose a third. We might say, "I do survive Wiggins' operation as two people. They can be different people, and yet be me, in just the way in which the Pope's three crowns are one crown."[7]

This is a possible way of giving sense to the claim that I survive as two different people, using "survive" to imply identity. But it keeps the language of identity only by changing the concept of a person. And there are obvious objections to this change.[8]

The alternative, for which I shall argue, is to give up the language of identity. We can suggest that I survive as two different people without implying that I am these people.

When I first mentioned this alternative, I mentioned this objection: "If your new way of talking does not imply identity, it cannot solve our problem. For that is about identity. The problem is that all the possible answers to the question about identity are highly implausible."

We can now answer this objection.

We can start by reminding ourselves that this is an objection only if we have one or both of the beliefs which I mentioned at the start of this paper.

The first was the belief that to any question about personal identity, in any describable case, there must be a true answer. For those with this belief, Wiggins' case is doubly perplexing. If all the possible answers are implausible, it is hard to decide which of them is true, and hard even to keep the belief that one of them must be true. If we give up this belief, as I think we should, these problems disappear. We shall then regard the case as like many others in which, for quite unpuzzling reasons, there *is* no answer to a question about identity. (Consider "Was England the same nation after 1066?")

Wiggins' case makes the first belief implausible. It also makes it trivial. For it undermines the second belief. This was the belief that important questions turn upon the question about identity. (It is worth pointing out that those who have only this second belief do not think that there must *be* an answer to this question, but rather that we must decide upon an answer.)

Against this second belief my claim is this. Certain questions do presuppose a question about personal identity. And because these questions *are* important, Wiggins' case does present a problem. But we cannot solve this problem by answering the question about identity. We can solve this problem only by taking these important questions and prizing them apart from the question about identity. After we have done this, the question about identity (though we might for the sake of neatness decide it) has no further interest.

Because there are several questions which presuppose identity, this claim will take some time to fill out.

We can first return to the question of survival. This is a special case, for survival does not so much presuppose the retaining of identity as seem equivalent to it. It is thus the general relation which we need to prize apart from identity. We can then consider particular relations, such as those involved in memory and intention.

"Will I survive?" seems, I said, equivalent to "Will there be some person alive who is the same person as me?"

If we treat these questions as equivalent, then the least unsatisfactory description of Wiggins' case is, I think, that I survive with two bodies and a divided mind.

Several writers have chosen to say that I am neither of the resulting people. Given our equivalence, this implies that I do not survive, and hence, presumably, that even if Wiggins' operation is not literally death, I ought, since I will not survive it, to regard it *as* death. But this seemed absurd.

It is worth repeating why. An emotion or attitude can be criticized for resting on a false belief, or for being inconsistent. A man who regarded Wiggins' operation as death must, I suggest, be open to one of these criticisms.

He might believe that his relation to each of the resulting people fails to contain some element which is contained in survival. But how can this be true? We agreed that he *would* survive if he stood in this very same relation to only *one* of the resulting people. So it cannot be the nature of this relation which makes it fail, in Wiggins' case, to be survival. It can only be its duplication.

Suppose that our man accepts this, but still regards division as death. His reaction would now seem wildly inconsistent. He would be like a man who, when told of a drug that could double his years of life, regarded the taking of this drug as death. The only difference in the case of division is that the extra years are to run concurrently. This is an interesting difference. But it cannot mean that there are *no* years to run.

I have argued this for those who think that there must, in Wiggins' case, be a true answer to the question about identity. For them, we might add, "Perhaps the original person does lose his identity. But there may be other ways to do this than to die. One other way might be to multiply. To regard these as the same is to confuse nought with two."

For those who think that the question of identity is up for decision, it would be clearly absurd to regard Wiggins' operation as death. These people would have to think, "We could have chosen to say that I should be one of the resulting people. If we had, I should not have regarded it as death. But since we have chosen to say that I am neither person, I *do*." This is hard even to understand.[9]

My first conclusion, then, is this. The relation of the original person to each of the resulting people contains all that interests us—all that matters—in any ordinary case of survival. This is why we need a sense in which one person can survive as two.[10]

One of my aims in the rest of this paper will be to suggest such a sense. But we can first make some general remarks.

II

Identity is a one-one relation. Wiggins' case serves to show that what matters in survival need not be one-one.

Wiggins' case is of course unlikely to occur. The relations which matter are, in fact, one-one. It is because they are that we can imply the holding of these relations by using the language of identity.

This use of language is convenient. But it can lead us astray. We may assume that what matters *is* identity and, hence, has the properties of identity.

In the case of the property of being one-one, this mistake is not serious. For what matters is in fact one-one. But in the case of another property, the mistake *is* serious. Identity is all-or-nothing. Most of the relations which matter is survival are, in fact, relations of degree. If we ignore this, we shall be led into quite ill-grounded attitudes and beliefs.

The claim that I have just made—that most of what matters are relations of degree—I have yet to support. Wiggins' case shows only that these relations need not be one-one. The merit of the case is not that it shows this in particular, but that it makes the first break between what matters and identity. The belief that identity *is* what matters is hard to overcome. This is shown in most discussions of the problem cases which actually occur: cases, say, of amnesia or of brain damage. Once Wiggins' case has made one breach in this belief, the rest should be easier to remove.[11]

To turn to a recent debate: most of the relations which matter can be provisionally referred to under the heading "psychological continuity" (which includes causal continuity). My claim is thus that we use the language of personal identity in order to imply such continuity. This is close to the view that psychological continuity provides a criterion of identity.

Williams has attacked this view with the following argument. Identity is a one-one relation. So any criterion of identity must appeal to a relation which is logically one-one. Psychological continuity is not logically one-one. So it cannot provide a criterion.[12]

Some writers have replied that it is enough if the relation appealed to is always in fact one-one.[13]

I suggest a slightly different reply. Psychological continuity is a ground for speaking of identity when it is one-one.

If psychological continuity took a one-many or branching form, we should need, I have argued, to abandon the language of identity. So this possibility would not count against this view.

We can make a stronger claim. This possibility would count in its favor.

The view might be defended as follows. Judgments of personal identity have great importance. What gives them their importance is the fact that they imply psychological continuity. This is why, whenever there is such continuity, we ought, if we can, to imply it by making a judgment of identity.

If psychological continuity took a branching form, no coherent set of judgments of identity could correspond to, and thus be used to imply, the branching form of this relation. But what we ought to do, in such a case, is take the importance which would attach to a judgment of identity and attach this importance directly to each limb of the branching relation. So this case helps to show that judgments of personal identity do derive their importance from the fact that they imply psychological continuity. It helps to show that when we can, usefully, speak of identity, this relation is our ground.

This argument appeals to a principle which Williams put forward.[14] The principle is that an important judgment should be asserted and denied only on importantly different grounds.

Williams applied this principle to a case in which one man is psychologically continuous with the dead Guy Fawkes, and a case in which two men are. His argument was this. If we treat psychological continuity as a sufficient ground for speaking of identity, we shall say that the one man is Guy Fawkes. But we could not say that the two men are, although we should have the same ground. This disobeys the principle. The remedy is to deny that the one man is Guy Fawkes, to insist that sameness of the body is necessary for identity.

Williams' principle can yield a different answer. Suppose we regard psychological continuity as more important than sameness of the body.[15] And suppose that the one man really is psychologically (and causally) continuous with Guy Fawkes. If he is, it would disobey the principle to deny that he is Guy Fawkes, for we have the same important ground as in a normal case of identity. In the case of the two men, we again have the same important ground. So we ought to take the importance from the judgment of identity and attach it directly to this ground. We ought to say, as in Wiggins' case, that each limb of the branching relation is as good as survival. This obeys the principle.

To sum up these remarks: even if psychological continuity is neither logically, nor always in fact, one-one, it can provide a criterion of identity. For this can appeal to the relation of *nonbranching* psychological continuity, which is logically one-one.[16]

The criterion might be sketched as follows. "*X* and *Y* are the same person if they are psychologically continuous and there is no person who is contemporary with either and psychologically continuous with the other." We should need to explain what we mean by "psychologically continuous" and say how much continuity the criterion requires. We should then, I think, have described a sufficient condition for speaking of identity.[17]

We need to say something more. If we admit that psychological continuity might not be one-one, we need to say what we ought to do if it were not one-one. Otherwise our account would be open to the objections that it is incomplete and arbitrary.[18]

I have suggested that if psychological continuity took a branching form, we ought to speak in a new way, regarding what we describe as having the same significance as identity. This answers these objections.[19]

We can now return to our discussion. We have three remaining aims. One is to suggest a sense of "survive" which does not imply identity. Another is to show that most of what matters in survival are relations of degree. A third is to show that none of these relations needs to be described in a way that presupposes identity.

We can take these aims in the reverse order.

III

The most important particular relation is that involved in memory. This is because it is so easy to believe that its description must refer to identity.[20] This belief about memory is an important cause of the view that personal identity has a special nature. But it has been well discussed by Shoemaker[21] and by Wiggins.[22] So we can be brief.

It may be a logical truth that we can only remember our own experiences. But we can frame a new concept for which this is not a logical truth. Let us call this "*q*-memory."

To sketch a definition[23] I am *q*-remembering an experience if (1) I have a belief about a past experience which seems in itself like a memory belief, (2) someone did have such an experience, and (3) my belief is dependent upon this experience in the same way (whatever that is) in which a memory of an experience is dependent upon it.

According to (1) *q*-memories seem like memories. So I *q*-remember *having* experiences.

This may seem to make *q*-memory presuppose identity. One might say, "My apparent memory of *having* an experience is an apparent memory of *my* having an experience. So how could I *q*-remember my having other people's experiences?"

This objection rests on a mistake. When I seem to remember an experience, I do indeed seem to remember *having* it.[24] But it cannot be a part of what I seem to remember about this experience that I, the person who now seems to remember it, am the person who had this experience.[25] That I am is something that I automatically assume. (My apparent memories sometimes come to me simply as the belief that *I* had a certain experience.) But it is something that I am justified in assuming only because I do not in fact have *q*-memories of other people's experiences.

Suppose that I did start to have such *q*-memories. If I did, I should cease to assume that my apparent memories must be about my own experiences. I should come to assess an apparent memory by asking two questions: (1) Does it tell me about a past experience? (2) If so, whose?

Moreover (and this is a crucial point) my apparent memories would now come to me *as* *q*-memories. Consider those of my apparent memories which do come to me simply as beliefs about my past: for example, "I did that." If I knew that I could *q*-remember other people's experiences, these beliefs would come to me in a more guarded form: for example, "Someone—probably I—did that." I might have to work out who it was.

I have suggested that the concept of *q*-memory is coherent. Wiggins' case provides an illustration. The resulting people, in his case, both have apparent memories of living the life of the original person. If they agree that they are not this person, they will have to regard these as only *q*-memories. And when they are asked a question like "Have you heard this music before?" they might have to answer "I am sure that I *q*-remember hearing it. But I am not sure whether I remember hearing it. I am not sure whether it was I who heard it, or the original person."

We can next point out that on our definition every memory is also a *q*-memory. Memories are, simply, *q*-memories of one's own experiences. Since this is so, we could afford now to drop the concept of memory and use in its place the wider concept *q*-memory. If we did, we should describe the relation between an experience and what we now call a "memory" of this experience in a way which does not presuppose that they are had by the same person.[26]

This way of describing this relation has certain merits. It vindicates the "memory criterion" of personal identity against the charge of circularity.[27] And it might, I think, help with the problem of other minds.

But we must move on. We can next take the relation between an intention and a later action. It may be a logical truth that we can intend to perform only our own actions. But intentions can be redescribed as *q*-intentions. And one person could *q*-intend to perform another person's actions.

Wiggins' case again provides the illustration. We are supposing that neither of the resulting people is the original person. If so, we shall have to agree that the original person can, before the operation, *q*-intend to perform their actions. He might, for example, *q*-intend, as one of them, to continue his present career, and, as the other, to try something new.[28] (I say "*q*-intend *as* one of them" because the phrase "*q*-intend that one of them" would not convey the directness of the relation which is involved. If I intend that someone else should do something, I cannot get him to do it simply by forming this intention. But if I am the original person, and he is one of the resulting people, I can.)

The phrase "*q*-intend *as* one of them" reminds us that we need a sense in which one person can survive as two. But we can first point out that the concepts of *q*-memory and *q*-intention give us our model for the others that we need: thus, a man who can *q*-remember could *q*-recognize, and be a *q*-witness of, what he has never seen; and a man who can *q*-intend could have *q*-ambitions, make *q*-promises, and be *q*-responsible for.

To put this claim in general terms: many different relations are included within, or are a consequence of, psychological continuity. We describe these relations in ways which presuppose the continued existence of one person. But we could describe them in new ways which do not.

This suggests a bolder claim. It might be possible to think of experiences in a wholly "impersonal" way. I shall not develop this claim here. What I shall try to describe is a way of thinking of our own identity through time which is more flexible, and less misleading, than the way in which we now think.

This way of thinking will allow for a sense in which one person can survive as two. A more important feature is that it treats survival as a matter of degree.

IV

We must first show the need for this second feature. I shall use two imaginary examples.

The first is the converse of Wiggins' case: fusion. Just as division serves to show that what matters in survival need not be one-one, so fusion serves to show that it can be a question of degree.

Physically, fusion is easy to describe. Two people come together. While they are unconscious, their two bodies grow into one. One person then wakes up.

The psychology of fusion is more complex. One detail we have already dealt with in the case of the exam. When my mind was reunited, I remembered just having thought out two calculations. The one person who results from a fusion can, similarly, *q*-remember living the lives of the two original people. None of their *q*-memories need be lost.

But some things must be lost. For any two people who fuse together will have different characteristics, different desires, and different intentions. How can these be combined?

We might suggest the following. Some of these will be compatible. These can coexist in the one resulting person. Some will be incompatible. These, if of equal strength, can cancel out, and if of different strengths, the stronger can be made weaker. And all these effects might be predictable.

To give examples—first, of compatibility: I like Palladio and intend to visit Venice. I am about to fuse with a person who likes Giotto and intends to visit Padua. I can know that the one person we shall become will have both tastes and both intentions. Second, of incompatibility: I hate red hair, and always vote Labour. The other person loves red hair, and always votes Conservative. I can know that the one person we shall become will be indifferent to red hair, and a floating voter.

If we were about to undergo a fusion of this kind, would we regard it as death?

Some of us might. This is less absurd than regarding division as death. For after my division the two resulting people will be in every way like me, while after my fusion the one resulting person will not be wholly similar. This makes it easier to say, when faced with fusion, "I shall not survive," thus continuing to regard survival as a matter of all-or-nothing.

This reaction is less absurd. But here are two analogies which tell against it.

First, fusion would involve the changing of some of our characteristics and some of our desires. But only the very self-satisfied would think of this as death. Many people welcome treatments with these effects.

Second, someone who is about to fuse can have, beforehand, just as much "intentional control" over the actions of the resulting individual as someone who is about to marry can have beforehand, over the actions of the resulting couple. And the choice of a partner for fusion can be just as well considered as the choice of a marriage partner. The two original people can make sure (perhaps by "trial fusion") that they do have compatible characters, desires, and intentions.

I have suggested that fusion, while not clearly survival, is not clearly failure to survive, and hence that what matters in survival can have degrees.

To reinforce this claim we can now turn to a second example. This is provided by certain imaginary begins. These beings are just like ourselves except that they reproduce by a process of natural division.

We can illustrate the histories of these imagined beings with the aid of a diagram. The lines on the diagram represent the spatiotemporal paths which would be traced out by the bodies of these beings. We can call each single line (like the double line) a "branch"; and we can call the whole structure a "tree." And let us suppose that each "branch" corresponds to what is thought of as the life of one individual. These individuals are referred to as "A," "B+1," and so forth.

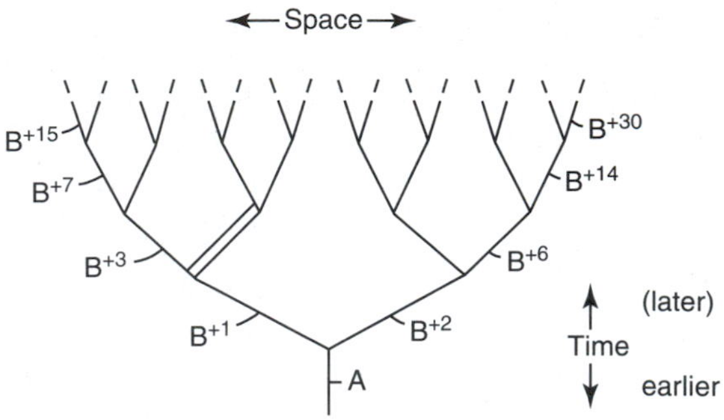

Now, each single division is an instance of Wiggins' case. So A's relation to both B+1 and B+2 is just as good as survival. But what of A's relation to B+30?

I said earlier that what matters in survival could be provisionally referred to as "psychological continuity." I must now distinguish this relation from another, which I shall call "psychochological connectedness."

Let us say that the relation between a *q*-memory and the experience *q*-remembered is a "direct" relation. Another "direct" relation is that which holds between a *q*-intention and the *q*-intended action. A third is that which holds between different expressions of some lasting *q*-characteristic.

"Psychological connectedness," as I define it, requires the holding of these direct psychological relations. "Connectedness" is not transitive, since these relations are not transitive. Thus, if *X* *q*-remembers most of *Y*'s life, and *Y* *q*-remembers most of *Z*'s life, it does not follow that *X* *q*-remembers most of *Z*'s life. And if *X* carries out the *q*-intentions of *Y*, and *Y* carries out the *q*-intentions of *Z*, it does not follow that *X* carries out the *q*-intentions of *Z*.

"Psychological continuity," in contrast, only requires overlapping chains of direct psychological relations. So "continuity" is transitive.

To return to our diagram. A is psychologically continuous with B+30. There are between the two continuous chains of overlapping relations. Thus, A has *q*-intentional control over B+2, B+2 has *q*-intentional control over B+6, and so on up to B+30. Or B+30 can *q*-remember the life of B+14, B+14 can *q*-remember the life of B+6, and so on back to A.[29]

A, however, need *not* be psychologically connected to B+30. Connectedness requires direct relations. And if these beings are like us, A cannot stand in such relations to every individual in his indefinitely long "tree." *Q*-memories will weaken with the passage of time, and then fade away. *Q*-ambitions, once fulfilled, will be replaced by others. *Q*-characteristics will gradually change. In general, A stands in fewer and fewer direct psychological relations to an individual in his "tree" the more remote that individual is. And if the individual is (like B+30) sufficiently remote, there may be between the two *no* direct psychological relations.

Now that we have distinguished the general relations of psychological continuity and psychological connectedness, I suggest that connectedness is a more important element in survival. As a claim about our own survival, this would need more arguments than I have space to give. But it seems clearly true for my imagined beings. A is as close psychologically to B+1 as I today am to myself tomorrow. A is as distant from B+30 as I am from my great-great-grandson.

Even if connectedness is not more important than continuity, the fact that one of these is a relation of degree is enough to show that what matters in survival can have degrees. And in any case the two relations are quite different. So our imagined beings would need a way of thinking in which this difference is recognized.

V

What I propose is this.

First, A can think of any individual, anywhere is his "tree," as "a descendant self." This phrase implies psychological continuity. Similarly, any later individual can think of any earlier individual on the single path[30] which connects him to A as "an ancestral self."

Since psychological continuity is transitive, "being an ancestral self of" and "being a descendant self of" are also transitive.

To imply psychological connectedness I suggest the phrases "one of my future selves" and "one of my past selves."

These are the phrases with which we can describe Wiggins' case. For having past and future selves is, what we needed, a way of continuing to exist which does not imply identity through time. The original person does, in this sense, survive Wiggins' operation: the two resulting people are his later selves. And they can each refer to him as "my past self." (They can share a past self without being the same self as each other.)

Since psychological connectedness is not transitive, and is a matter of degree, the relations "being a past self of" and "being a future self of" should themselves be treated as relations of degree. We allow for this series of descriptions: "my most recent self," "one of my earlier selves," "one of my distant selves," "hardly one of *my* past selves (I can only *q*-remember a few of his experiences)," and, finally, "not in any way one of *my* past selves—just an ancestral self."

This way of thinking would clearly suit our first imagined beings. But let us now turn to a second kind of being. These reproduce by fusion as well as by division.[31] And let us suppose that they fuse every autumn and divide every spring. This yields the following diagram:

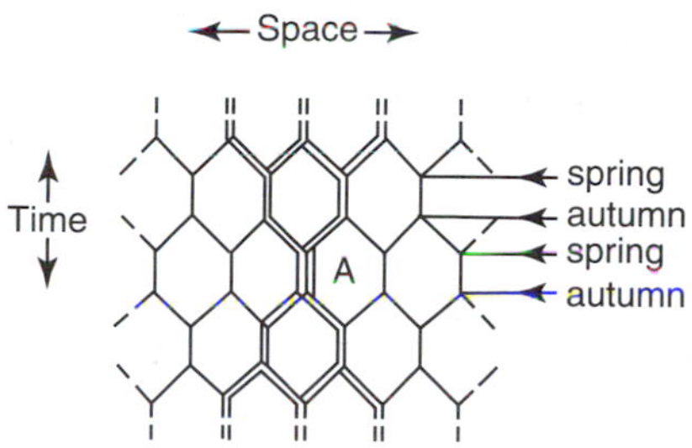

If A is the individual whose life is represented by the threelined "branch," the two-lined "tree" represents those lives which are psychologically continuous with A's life. (It can be seen that each individual has his own "tree," which overlaps with many others.)

For the imagined beings in this second world, the phrases "an ancestral self" and "a descendant self" would cover too much to be of much use. (There may well be pairs of dates such that every individual who ever lived before the first date was an ancestral self of every individual who ever will live after the second date.) Conversely, since the lives of each individual last for only half a year, the word "I" would cover too little to do all of the work which it does for us. So part of this work would have to be done, for these second beings, by talk about past and future selves.

We can now point out a theoretical flaw in our proposed way of thinking. The phrase "a past self of" implies psychological connectedness. Being a past self of is treated as a relation of degree, so that this phrase can be used to imply the varying degrees of psychological connectedness. But this phrase can imply only the degrees of connectedness between different lives. It cannot be used within a single life. And our way of delimiting successive lives does not refer to the degrees of psychological connectedness. Hence there is no guarantee that this phrase, "a past self of," could be used whenever it was needed. There is no guarantee that psychological connectedness will not vary in degree within a single life.

This flaw would not concern our imagined beings. For they divide and unite so frequently, and their lives are in consequence so short, that within a single life psychological connectedness would always stand at a maximum.

But let us look, finally, at a third kind of being.

In this world there is neither division nor union. There are a number of everlasting bodies, which gradually change in appearance. And direct psychological relations, as before, hold only over limited periods of time. This can be illustrated with a third diagram (which is found below). In this diagram the two shadings represent the degrees of psychological connectedness to their two central points.

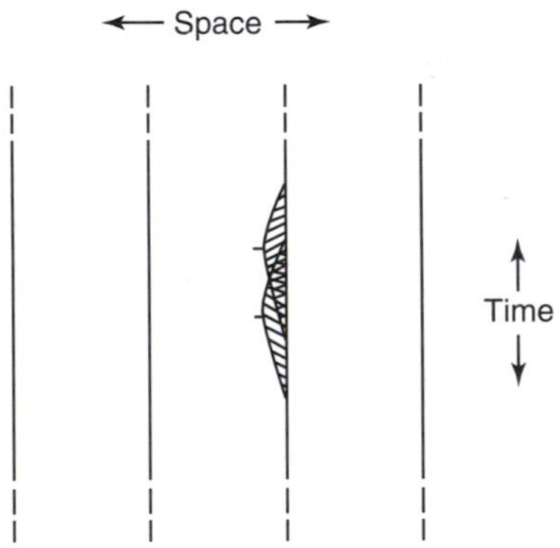

These beings could not use the way of thinking that we have proposed. Since there is no branching of psychological continuity, they would have to regard themselves as immortal. It might be said that this is what they are. But there is, I suggest, a better description.

Our beings would have one reason for thinking of themselves as immortal. The parts of each "line" are all psychologically continuous. But the parts of each "line" are not all psychologically connected. Direct psychological relations hold only between those parts which are close to each other in time. This gives our beings a reason for *not* thinking of each "line" as corresponding to one single life. For if they did, they would have no way of implying these direct relations. When a speaker says, for example, "I spent a period doing such and such," his hearers would not be entitled to assume that the speaker has any memories of this period, that his character then and now are in any way similar, that he is now carrying out any of the plans or intentions which he then had, and so forth. Because the word "I" would carry none of these implications, it would not have for these "immortal" beings the usefulness which it has for us.[32]

To gain a better way of thinking, we must revise the way of thinking that we proposed above. The revision is this. The distinction between successive selves can be made by reference, not to the branching of psychological continuity, but to the degrees of psychological connectedness. Since this connectedness is a matter of degree, the drawing of these distinctions can be left to the choice of the speaker and be allowed to vary from context to context.

On this way of thinking, the world "I" can be used to imply the greatest degree of psychological connectedness. When the connections are reduced, when there has been any marked change of character or style of life, or any marked loss of memory, our imagined beings would say, "It was not I who did that, but an earlier self." They could then describe in what ways, and to what degree, they are related to this earlier self.

This revised way of thinking would suit not only our "immortal" beings. It is also the way in which we ourselves could think about our lives. And it is, I suggest, surprisingly natural.

One of its features, the distinction between successive selves, has already been used by several writers. To give an example, from Proust: "we are incapable, while we are in love, of acting as fit predecessors of the next persons who, when we are in love no longer, we shall presently have become. . . ."[33]

Although Proust distinguished between successive selves, he still thought of one person as being these different selves. This we would not do on the way of thinking that I propose. If I say, "It will not be me, but one of my future selves," I do not imply that I will be that future self. He is one of my later selves, and I am one of his earlier selves. There is no underlying person who we both are.

To point out another feature of this way of thinking. When I say, "There is no person who we both are," I am only giving my decision. Another person could say, "It will be you," thus deciding differently. There is no question of either of these decisions being a mistake. Whether to say "I," or "one of my future selves," or "a descendant self" is entirely a matter of choice. The matter of fact, which must be agreed, is only whether the disjunction applies. (The question "Are *X* and *Y* the same person?" thus becomes "Is *X at least* an ancestral [or descendant] self of *Y*?")

VI

I have tried to show that what matters in the continued existence of a person are, for the most part, relations of degree. And I have proposed a way of thinking in which this would be recognized.

I shall end by suggesting two consequences and asking one question.

It is sometimes thought to be especially rational to act in our own best interests. But I suggest that the principle of self-interest has no force. There are only two genuine competitors in this particular field. One is the principle of biased rationality: do what will best achieve what you actually want. The other is the principle of impartiality: do what is in the best interests of everyone concerned.

The apparent force of the principle of self-interest derives, I think, from these two other principles.

The principle of self-interest is normally supported by the principle of biased rationality. This is because most people care about their own future interests.

Suppose that this prop is lacking. Suppose that a man does not care what happens to him in, say, the more distant future. To such a man, the principle of self-interest can only be propped up by an appeal to the principle of impartiality. We must say, "Even if you don't care, you ought to take what happens to you then equally into account." But for this, as a special claim, there seem to me no good arguments. It can only be supported as part of the general claim, "You ought to take what happens to everyone equally into account."[34]

The special claim tells a man to grant an *equal* weight to all the parts of his future. The argument for this can only be that all the parts of his future are *equally* parts of *his* future. This is true. But it is a truth too superficial to bear the weight of the argument. (To give an analogy: The unity of a nation is, in its nature, a matter of degree. It is therefore only a superficial truth that all of a man's compatriots are *equally* his compatriots. This truth cannot support a good argument for nationalism.)[35]

I have suggested that the principle of self-interest has no strength of its own. If this is so, there is no special problem in the fact that what we ought to do can be against our interests. There is only the general problem that it may not be what we want to do.

The second consequence which I shall mention is implied in the first. Egoism, the fear not of near but of distant death, the regret that so much of one's *only* life should have gone by—these are not, I think, wholly natural or instinctive. They are all strengthened by the beliefs about personal identity which I have been attacking. If we give up these beliefs, they should be weakened.

My final question is this. These emotions are bad, and if we weaken them we gain. But can we achieve this gain without, say, also weakening loyalty to, or love of, other particular selves? As Hume warned, the "refined reflections which philosophy suggests . . . cannot diminish . . . our vicious passions . . . without diminishing . . . such as are virtuous. They are . . . applicable to all our affections. In vain do we hope to direct their influence only to one side."[36]

That hope *is* vain. But Hume had another: that more of what is bad depends upon false belief. This is also my hope.[37]

Notes

1. I have been helped in writing this by D. Wiggins, D. F. Pears, P. F. Strawson, A. J. Ayer, M. Woods, N. Newman, and (through his publications) S. Shoemaker.
2. Implicit in John Locke, *Essay Concerning Human Understanding*, ed. by John W. Yolton, vol. 2, chap. 27, sec. 18 (London, 1961) and discussed by (among others) A. N. Prior in "Opposite Number," *Review of Metaphysics*, 11 (1957–1958), and "Time, Existence and Identity," *Proceedings of the Aristotelian Society*, vol. 57 (1965–1966); J. Bennett in "The Simplicity of the Soul," *Journal of Philosophy*, vol. 64 (1967); and R. Chisholm and S. Shoemaker in "The Loose and Popular and the Strict and the Philosophical Senses of Identity," in *Perception and Personal Identity: Proceeding of the 1967 Oberlin Colloquium in Phi-*

losophy, ed. Norman Care and Robert H. Grimm (Cleveland, 1967).

3. David Wiggins, *Identity and Spatio-Temporal Continuity* (Oxford, 1967), p. 50.
4. Sydney S. Shoemaker, *Self-Knowledge and Self-Identity* (Ithaca, N. Y., 1963), p. 22.
5. Those who would disagree are not making a mistake. For them my argument would need a different case. There must be some multiple transplant, faced with which these people would both find it hard to believe that there must be an answer to the question about personal identity, and be able to be shown that nothing of importance turns upon this question.
6. R. W. Sperry, in *Brain and Conscious Experience*, ed. J. C. Eccles (New York, 1966), p. 299.
7. Cf. David Wiggins, *op. cit*, p. 40.
8. Suppose the resulting people fight a duel. Are there three people fighting, one on each side, and one on both? And suppose one of the bullets kills. Are there two acts, one murder and one suicide? How many people are left alive? One? Two? (We could hardly say, "One and a half.") We could talk in this way. But instead of saying that the resulting people are the original person—so that the pair is a trio—it would be far simpler to treat them as a pair, and describe their relation to the original person in some new way. (I owe this suggested way of talking, and the objections to it, to Michael Woods.)
9. Cf. Sydney Shoemaker, in *Perception and Personal Identity*, p. 54.
10. Cf. David Wiggins, *op. cit.*
11. Bernard Williams' "The Self and the Future," *Philosophical Review*, 79 (1970), 161–180, is relevant here. He asks the question "Shall I survive?" in a range of problem cases, and he shows how natural it is to believe (1) that this question must have an answer, (2) that the answer must be all-or-nothing, and (3) that there is a "risk" of our reaching the wrong answer. Because these beliefs are so natural, we should need in undermining them to discuss their causes. These, I think, can be found in the ways in which we misinterpret what it is to remember (cf. Sec. III below) and to anticipate (cf. Williams' "Imagination and the Self," *Proceedings of the British Academy*, 52 [1966], 105–124); and also in the way in which certain features of our egoistic concern—e.g., that it is simple, and applies to all imaginable cases—are "projected" onto its object. (For another relevant discussion, see Terence Penelhum's *Survival and Disembodied Existence* [London, 1970], final chapters.)
12. "Personal Identity and Individuation," *Proceedings of the Aristotelian Society*, 57 (1956–1957), 229–253; also *Analysis*, 21 (1960–1961), 43–48.
13. J. M. Shorter, "More about Bodily Continuity and Personal Identity," *Analysis*, 22 (1961–1962), 79–85; and Mrs. J. M. R. Jack (unpublished), who requires that this truth be embedded in a causal theory.
14. *Analysis*, 21 (1960–1961), 44.
15. For the reasons given by A. M. Quinton in "The Soul," *Journal of Philosophy*, 59 (1962), 393–409.
16. Cf. S. Shoemaker, "Persons and Their Pasts," *American Philosophical Quarterly*, 7 (1970), 269; and "Wiggins on Identity," *Philosophical Review*, 79 (1970), 542.
17. But not a necessary condition, for in the absence of psychological continuity bodily identity might be sufficient.
18. Cf. Bernard Williams, "Personal Identity and Individuation," *Proceedings of the Aristotelian Society*, 57 (1956–1957), 240–241, and *Analysis*, 21 (1960–1961), 44; and also Wiggins, *op. cit.*, p. 38: "if coincidence under [the concept] *f* is to be *genuinely* sufficient we must not withhold identity . . . simply because transitivity is threatened."
19. Williams produced another objection to the "psychological criterion," that it makes it hard to explain the difference between the concepts of identity and exact similarity (*Analysis*, 21 [1960–1961], 48). But if we include the requirement of causal continuity we avoid this objection (and one of those produced by Wiggins in his note 47).
20. Those philosophers who have held this belief, from Butler onward, are too numerous to cite.
21. *Op. cit.*
22. In a paper on Butler's objection to Locke (not yet published).
23. I here follow Shoemaker's "quasi-memory." Cf. also Penelhum's "retrocognition," in his article on "Personal Identity," in the *Encyclopedia of Philosophy*, ed. Paul Edwards.
24. As Shoemaker put it, I seem to remember the experience "from the inside" (*op. cit.*).
25. This is what so many writers have overlooked. Cf. Thomas Reid: "My memory testifies not only that this was done, but that it was done by me who now remember it" ("Of Identity," in *Essays on the*

Intellectual Powers of Man, ed. A. D. Woozley [London, 1941], p. 203). This mistake is discussed by A. B. Palma in "Memory and Personal Identity," *Australasian Journal of Philosophy*, 42 (1964), 57.

26. It is not logically necessary that we only *q*-remember our own experiences. But it might be necessary on other grounds. This possibility is intriguingly explored by Shoemaker in his "Persons and Their Pasts" (*op. cit.*). He shows that *q*-memories can provide a knowledge of the world only if the observations which are *q*-remembered trace out fairly continuous spatiotemporal paths. If the observations which are *q*-remembered traced out a network of frequently interlocking paths, they could not, I think, be usefully ascribed to persisting observers, but would have to be referred to in some more complex way. But in fact the observations which are *q*-remembered trace out single and separate paths; so we can ascribe them to ourselves. In other words, it is epistemologically necessary that the observations which are *q*-remembered should satisfy a certain general condition, one particular form of which allows them to be usefully selfascribed.
27. Cf. Wiggins' paper on Butler's objection to Locke.
28. There are complications here. He could form *divergent q*-intentions only if he could distinguish, in advance, between the resulting people (e.g., as "the left-hander" and "the right-hander"). And he could be confident that such divergent *q*-intentions would be carried out only if he had reason to believe that neither of the resulting people would change their (inherited) mind. Suppose he was torn between duty and desire. He could not solve this dilemma by *q*-intending, as one of the resulting people, to do his duty, and, as the other, to do what he desires. For the one he *q*-intended to do his duty would face the same dilemma.
29. The chain of continuity must run in one direction of time. B+2 is not, in the sense I intend, psychologically continuous with B+1.
30. Cf. David Wiggins, *op. cit.*
31. Cf. Sydney Shoemaker in "Persons and Their Pasts," *op. cit.*
32. Cf. Austin Duncan Jones, "Man's Mortality," *Analysis*, 28 (1967–1968), 65–70.
33. *Within a Budding Grove* (London, 1949), I, 226 (my own translation).
34. Cf. Thomas Nagel's *The Possibility of Altruism* (Oxford, 1970), in which the special claim is in effect defended as part of the general claim.
35. The unity of a nation we seldom take for more than what it is. This is partly because we often think of nations, not as units, but in a more complex way. If we thought of ourselves in the way that I proposed, we might be less likely to take our own identity for more than what it is. We are, for example, sometimes told, "It is irrational to act against your own interests. After all, it will be you who will regret it." To this we could reply, "No, not me. Not even one of my future selves. Just a descendant self."
36. "The Sceptic," in "Essays Moral, Political and Literary," *Humes's Moral and Political Philosophy* (New York, 1959), p. 349.
37. (Footnote added in 1976.) Of the many things which I now regret in this paper, I shall briefly mention three. (1) Talk about "successive selves" is only a *façon de parler*; taken as anything more it can be misleading. (2) I should not have claimed that connectedness was more important than continuity. I now think that neither relation can be shown to be more important than the other. (3) The real issue seems to me now this. Does personal identity just consist in bodily and psychological continuity, or is it a further fact, independent of the facts about these continuities? Our reactions to the "problem cases" show, I think, that we believe the latter. And we seem inclined to believe that this further fact is peculiarly deep, and is all-or-nothing—we believe that in any describable case it must hold either completely or not at all. My main claim is *the denial of this further fact*. This is what may make a difference. (No one needs to be told that psychological continuity is, in part, a matter of degree.) For some further remarks, see "On 'The Importance of Self-identity,'" *Journal of Philosophy*, 21 Oct. 1971, "Later Selves and Moral Principles," in *Philosophy and Personal Relations*, ed. Alan Montefiore (Routledge & Kegan Paul, 1973), and "Lewis, Perry, and What Matters," in *The Identities of Persons*, ed. Amelie Rorty (University of California Press, 1976).

Chapter 29

ROBERT NOZICK

Robert Nozick is Professor of Philosophy at Harvard University and the author of several works in political philosophy and epistemology. In this selection from his *Anarchy, State, and Utopia*, Nozick distinguishes between two types of material principles of justice: patterned and nonpatterned. A patterned principle chooses some trait(s) that indicates how the proper distribution is to be accomplished. It has the form:

To each according to __________. For example, Marx's "From each according to his ability; to each according to his needs."

"Let us call a principle of distribution *patterned* if it specifies that a distribution is to vary along with some natural dimension, weighted sum of natural dimensions, or lexicographic ordering of natural dimensions." Nozick rejects patterned types of principle, such as those of Marx and Rawls (Chapter 30), because such an attempt to regulate distribution constitutes a violation of liberty.

Nozick argues for a libertarian view of nonpatterned justice that he calls the "theory of entitlement." A distribution is just if everyone has that to which he is entitled. To determine what people are entitled to, we must understand what the original position of holdings or possessions was and what constitutes a just transfer of holdings. Borrowing from John Locke's theory of property rights, Nozick argues that we have a right to any possession so long as ownership does not worsen the position of anyone else.

Finally, I have included Nozick's brilliant thought experiment "The Experience Machine." In this essay Nozick argues against hedonism. If pleasure were the only intrinsic value, we would have an overriding reason to be hooked up to a machine that would produce favorable sensations. Nozick discusses the reasons for rejecting the experience machine and, with it, hedonism.

FOR FURTHER READING

Cohen, G. A. "Robert Nozick and Wilt Chamberlain: How Patterns Preserve Liberty." *Ekenntnis* 1977.
Nozick, Robert. *Anarchy, State, and Utopia* (Basic Books, 1973).
———. *Philosophical Explanations* (Oxford University Press, 1981).
———. *The Examined Life* (Simon & Schuster, 1989).
Paul, J. ed. *Reading Nozick* (Blackwell, 1972).
Wolff, J. *Robert Nozick* (Stanford, 1992).

A Defense of Libertarianism

The minimal state is the most extensive state that can be justified. Any state more extensive violates people's rights. Yet many persons have put forth reasons purporting to justify a more extensive state. It is impossible within the compass of this book to examine all the reasons that have been put forth. Therefore, I shall focus upon those generally acknowledged to be most weighty and influential, to see precisely wherein they fail. In this chapter we consider the claim that a more extensive state is justified, because [it is] necessary (or the best instrument) to achieve distributive justice; in the next chapter we shall take up diverse other claims.

The term "distributive justice" is not a neutral one. Hearing the term "distribution," most people presume that some thing or mechanism uses some principle or criterion to give out a supply of things. Into this process of distributing shares some error may have crept. So it is an open question, at least, whether *re*distribution should take place; whether we should do again what has already been done once, though poorly. However, we are not in the position of children who have been given portions of pie by someone who now makes last minute adjustments to rectify careless cutting. There is no *central* distribution, no person or group entitled to control all the resources, jointly deciding how they are to be doled out. What each person gets, he gets from others who give to him in exchange for something, or as a gift. In a free society, diverse persons control different resources, and new holdings arise out of the voluntary exchanges and actions of persons. There is no more a distributing or distribution of shares than there is a distributing of mates in a society in which persons choose whom they shall marry. The total result is the product of many individual decisions which the different individuals involved are entitled to make. Some uses of the term "distribution," it is true, do not imply a previous distributing appropriately judged by some criterion (for example, "probability distribution"); nevertheless, it would be best to use a terminology that clearly is neutral. We shall speak of people's holdings; a principle of justice in holdings describes (part of) what justice tells us (requires) about holdings. I shall state first what I take to be the correct view about justice in holdings, and then turn to the discussion of alternative views.

THE ENTITLEMENT THEORY

The subject of justice in holdings consists of three major topics. The first is the *original acquisition of holdings*, the appropriation of unheld things. This includes the issues of how unheld things may come to be held, the process, or processes, by which unheld things may come to be held, the things that may come to be held by these processes, the extent of what comes to be held by a particular process, and so on. We shall refer to the complicated truth about this topic, which we shall not formulate here, as the principle of justice in acquisition. The second topic concerns the *transfer of holdings* from one person to another. By what processes may a person transfer holdings to another? How may a person acquire a holding from another who holds it? Under this topic come general descriptions of voluntary exchange, and gift and (on the other hand) fraud, as well as reference to particular conventional details fixed upon in a given society. The complicated truth about this subject (with placeholders for conventional details) we shall call the principle of justice in transfer. (And we shall suppose it also includes principles governing how a person may divest himself of a holding, passing it into an unheld state.)

If the world were wholly just, the following inductive definition would exhaustively cover the subject of justice in holdings.

1. A person who acquires a holding in accordance with the principle of justice in acquisition is entitled to that holding.
2. A person who acquires a holding in accordance with the principle of justice in transfer, from someone else entitled to the holding, is entitled to the holding.

3. No one is entitled to a holding except by (repeated) applications of 1 and 2.

The complete principle of distributive justice would say simply that a distribution is just if everyone is entitled to the holdings they possess under the distribution.

A distribution is just if it arises from another just distribution by legitimate means. The legitimate means of moving from one distribution to another are specified by the principle of justice in transfer. The legitimate first "moves" are specified by the principle of justice in acquisition.[1] Whatever arises from a just situation by just steps is itself just. The means of change specified by the principle of justice in transfer preserve justice. As correct rules of inference are truth-preserving and any conclusion deduced via repeated application of such rules from only true premises is itself true, so the means of transition from one situation to another specified by the principle of justice in transfer are justice-preserving, and any situation actually arising from repeated transitions in accordance with the principle from a just situation is itself just. The parallel between justice-preserving transformations and truth-preserving transformations illuminates where it fails as well as where it holds. That a conclusion could have been deduced by truth-preserving means from premises that are true suffices to show its truth. That from a just situation a situation *could* have arisen via justice-preserving means does *not* suffice to show its justice. The fact that a thief's victims voluntarily *could* have presented him with gifts does not entitle the thief to his ill-gotten gains. Justice in holdings is historical; it depends upon what actually has happened. We shall return to this point later.

Not all actual situations are generated in accordance with the two principles of justice in holdings: the principle of justice in acquisition and the principle of justice in transfer. Some people steal from others, or defraud them, or enslave them, seizing their product and preventing them from living as they choose, or forcibly exclude others from competing in exchanges. None of these are permissible modes of transition from one situation to another. And some persons acquire holdings by means not sanctioned by the principle of justice in acquisition. The existence of past injustice (previous violations of the first two principles of justice in holdings) raises the third major topic under justice in holdings: the rectification of injustice in holdings. If past injustice has shaped present holdings in various ways, some identifiable and some not, what now, if anything, ought to be done to rectify these injustices? What obligations do the performers of injustice have toward those whose position is worse than it would have been had the injustice not been done? Or, than it would have been had compensation been paid promptly? How, if at all, do things change if the beneficiaries and those made worse off are not the direct parties in the act of injustice, but, for example, their descendants? Is an injustice done to someone whose holding was itself based upon an unrectified injustice? How far back must one go in wiping clean the historical slate of injustices? What may victims of injustice permissibly do in order to rectify the injustices being done to them, including the many injustices done by persons acting through their government? I do not know of a thorough or theoretically sophisticated treatment of such issues. Idealizing greatly, let us suppose theoretical investigation will produce a principle of rectification. This principle uses historical information about previous situations and injustices done in them (as defined by the first two principles of justice and rights against interference), and information about the actual course of events that flowed from these injustices, until the present, and it yields a description (or descriptions) of holdings in the society. The principle of rectification presumably will make use of its best estimate of subjunctive information about what would have occurred (or a probability distribution over what might have occurred, using the expected value) if the injustice had not taken place. If the actual description of holdings turns out not to be one of the descriptions yielded by the principle, then one of the descriptions yielded must be realized.[2]

The general outlines of the theory of justice in holdings are that the holdings of a person are just if he is entitled to them by the principles of justice in acquisition and transfer, or by the principle of rectification of injustice (as specified by the first two principles). If each person's holdings are just, then the total set (distribution) of holdings is just. To turn these general outlines into a specific theory we would have to specify the details of each of the three principles of justice in holdings: the principle of acquisition of holdings, the principle of transfer of holdings, and the principle of rectification of violations of the first two principles. I shall not attempt that task here. (Locke's principle of justice in acquisition is discussed below.)

HISTORICAL PRINCIPLES AND END-RESULT PRINCIPLES

The general outlines of the entitlement theory illuminate the nature and defects of other conceptions of distributive justice. The entitlement theory of justice in distribution is *historical*; whether a distribution is just depends upon how it came about. In contrast, *current time-slice principles* of justice hold that the justice of a distribution is determined by how things are distributed (who has what) as judged by some *structural* principle(s) of just distribution. A utilitarian who judges between any two distributions by seeing which has the greater sum of utility and, if the sums tie, applies some fixed equality criterion to choose the more equal distribution would hold a current time-sliced principle of justice. As would someone who had a fixed schedule of trade-offs between the sum of happiness and equality. According to a current time-slice principle, all that needs to be looked at, in judging the justice of a distribution, is who ends up with what; in comparing any two distributions one need look only at the matrix presenting the distributions. No further information need be fed into a principle of justice. It is a consequence of such principles of justice that any two structurally identical distributions are equally just. (Two distributions are structurally identical if they present the same profile, but perhaps have different persons occupying the particular slots. My having ten and your having five, and my having five and your having ten are structurally identical distributions.) Welfare economics is the theory of current time-slice principles of justice. The subject is conceived as operating on matrices representing only current information about distribution. This, as well as some of the usual conditions (for example, the choice of distribution is invariant under relabeling of columns), guarantees that welfare economics will be a current time-slice theory, with all of its inadequacies.

Most persons do not accept current time-slice principles as constituting the whole story about distributive shares. They think it relevant in assessing the justice of a situation to consider not only the distribution it embodies, but also how that distribution came about. If some persons are in prison for murder or war crimes, we do not say that to assess the justice of the distribution in the society we must look only at what this person has, and that person has, and that person has, . . . at the current time. We think it relevant to ask whether someone did something so that he *deserved* to be punished, deserved to have a lower share. Most will agree to the relevance of further information with regard to punishments and penalties. Consider also desired things. One traditional socialist view is that workers are entitled to the product and full fruits of their labor; they have earned it; a distribution is unjust if it does not give the workers what they are entitled to. Such entitlements are based upon some past history. No socialist holding this view would find it comforting to be told that because the actual distribution *A* happens to coincide structurally with the one he desires *D*, *A* therefore is no less just than *D*; it differs only in that the "parasitic" owners of capital receive under *A* what the workers are entitled to under *D*, and the workers receive under *A* what the owners are entitled to under *D*, namely very little. This socialist rightly, in my view, holds onto the notions of earning, producing, entitlement, desert, and so forth, and he rejects current time-slice principles that look only to the structure of the resulting set of holdings. (The set of holdings resulting from what? Isn't it implausible that how holdings are produced and come to exist has no effect at all on who should hold what?) His mistake lies in his view of what entitlements arise out of what sorts of productive processes.

We construe the position we discuss too narrowly by speaking of *current* time-slice principles. Nothing is changed if structural principles operate upon a time sequence of current time-slice profiles and, for example, give someone more now to counterbalance the less he has had earlier. A utilitarian or an egalitarian or any mixture of the two over time will inherit the difficulties of his more myopic comrades. He is not helped by the fact that *some* of the information others consider relevant in assessing a distribution is reflected, unrecoverably, in past matrices. Henceforth, we shall refer to such unhistorical principles of distributive justice, including the current time-slice principles, as *end-result principles* or *end-state principles*.

In contrast to end-result principles of justice, *historical principles* of justice hold that past circumstances or actions of people can create differential entitlements or differential deserts to things. An injustice can be worked by moving from one distribution to another structurally identical one, for the second, in profile the same, may violate people's entitlements or deserts; it may not fit the actual history.

PATTERNING

The entitlement principles of justice in holdings that we have sketched are historical principles of justice. To better understand their precise character, we shall distinguish them from another subclass of the historical principles. Consider, as an example, the principle of distribution according to moral merit. This principle requires that total distributive shares vary directly with moral merit; no person should have a greater share than anyone whose moral merit is greater. (If moral merit could be not merely ordered but measured on an interval or ratio scale, stronger principles could be formulated.) Or consider the principle that results by substituting "usefulness to society" for "moral merit" in the previous principle. Or instead of "distribute according to moral merit," or "distribute according to usefulness to society," we might consider "distribute according to the weighted sum of moral merit, usefulness to society, and need," with the weights of the different dimensions equal. Let us call a principle of distribution patterned if it specifies that a distribution is to vary along with some natural dimension, weighted sum of natural dimensions, or lexicographic ordering of natural dimensions. And let us say a distribution is patterned if it accords with some patterned principle. (I speak of natural dimensions, admittedly without a general criterion for them, because for any set of holdings some artificial dimensions can be gimmicked up to vary along with the distribution of the set.) The principle of distribution in accordance with moral merit is a patterned historical principle, which specifies a patterned distribution. "Distribute according to I.Q." is a patterned principle that looks to information not contained in distributional matrices. It is not historical, however, in that it does not look to any past actions creating differential entitlements to evaluate a distribution; it requires only distributional matrices whose columns are labeled by I.Q. scores. The distribution in a society, however, may be composed of such simple patterned distributions, without itself being simply patterned. Different sectors may operate different patterns, or some combination of patterns may operate in different proportions across a society. A distribution composed in this manner, from a small number of patterned distributions, we also shall term "patterned." And we extend the use of "pattern" to include the overall designs put forth by combinations of end-state principles.

Almost every suggested principle of distributive justice is patterned: to each according to his moral merit, or needs, or marginal product, or how hard he tries, or the weighted sum of the foregoing, and so on. The principle of entitlement we have sketched is *not* patterned.[3] There is no one natural dimension or weighted sum or combination of a small number of natural dimensions that yields the distributions generated in accordance with the principle of entitlement. The set of holdings that results when some persons receive their marginal products, others win at gambling, others receive a share of their mate's income, others receive gifts from foundations, others receive interest on loans, others receive gifts from admirers, others receive returns on investment, others make for themselves much of what they have, others find things, and so on, will not be patterned. Heavy strands of patterns will run through it; significant portions of the variance in holdings will be accounted for by pattern-variables. If most people most of the time choose to transfer some of their entitlement to others only in exchange for something from them, then a large part of what many people hold will vary with what they held that others wanted. More details are provided by the theory of marginal productivity. But gifts to relatives, charitable donations, bequests to children, and the like, are not best conceived, in the first instance, in this manner. Ignoring the strands of pattern, let us suppose for the moment that a distribution actually arrived at by the operation of the principle of entitlement is random with respect to any pattern. Though the resulting set of holdings will be unpatterned, it will not be incomprehensible, for it can be seen as arising from the operation of a small number of principles. These principles specify how an initial distribution may arise (the principle of acquisition of holdings) and how distributions may be transformed into others (the principle of transfer of holdings). The process whereby the set of holdings is generated will be intelligible, though the set of holdings itself that results from this process will be unpatterned.

The writings of F. A. Hayek focus less than is usually done upon what patterning distributive justice requires. Hayek argues that we cannot know enough about each person's situation to distribute to each according to his moral merit (but would justice demand we do so if we did have this knowledge?); and he goes on to say, "Our objection is against all attempts to impress upon society a deliberately chosen pattern of distribution, whether it be an order of equality or of inequality."[4] However, Hayek concludes that in a free society there will be distribution in accordance with value rather than moral merit; that is, in accordance with the perceived value of a person's actions and services to others. Despite his rejection of a patterned conception of distributive justice, Hayek himself suggests a pattern he thinks justifiable: distribution in accordance with the perceived benefits given to others, leaving room for the complaint that a free society does not realize exactly this pattern. Stating this patterned strand of a free capitalist society more precisely, we get "To each according to how much he benefits others who have the resources for benefiting those who benefit them." This will seem arbitrary unless some acceptable initial set of holdings is specified, or unless it is held that the operation of the system over time washes out any significant effects from the initial set of holdings. As an example of the latter, if almost anyone would have bought a car from Henry Ford, the supposition that it was an arbitrary matter who held the money then (and so bought) would not place Henry Ford's earnings under a cloud. In any event, *his* coming to hold it is not arbitrary. Distribution according to benefits to others *is* a major patterned strand in a free capitalist society, as Hayek correctly points out, but it is only a strand and does not constitute the whole pattern of a system of entitlements (namely, inheritance, gifts for arbitrary reasons, charity, and so on) or a standard that one should insist society fit. Will people tolerate for long a system yielding distributions that they believe are unpatterned?[5] No doubt people will not long accept a distribution they believe is *unjust*. People want their society to be and to look just. But must the look of justice reside in a resulting pattern rather than in the underlying generating principles? We are in no position to conclude that the inhabitants of a society embodying an entitlement conception of justice in holdings will find it unacceptable. Still, it must be granted that were people's reasons for transferring some of their holdings to others always irrational or arbitrary, we would find this disturbing. (Suppose people always determined what holdings they would transfer, and to whom, by using a random device.) We feel more comfortable upholding the justice of an entitlement system if most of the transfers under it are done for reasons. This does not mean necessarily that all deserve what holdings they receive. It means only that there is a purpose or point to someone's transferring a holding to one person rather than to another; that usually we can see what the transferrer thinks he's gaining, what cause he thinks he's serving, what goals he thinks he's helping to achieve, and so forth. Since in a capitalist society people often transfer holdings to others in accordance with how much they perceive these others benefiting them, the fabric constituted by the individual transactions and transfers is largely reasonable and intelligible. (Gifts to loved ones, bequests to children, charity to the needy also are nonarbitrary components of the fabric.) In stressing the large strand of distribution in accordance with benefit to others, Hayek shows the point of many transfers, and so shows that the system of transfer of entitlements is not just spinning its gears aimlessly. The system of entitlements is defensible when constituted by the individual aims of individual transactions. No overarching aim is needed, no distributional pattern is required.

To think that the task of a theory of distributive justice is to fill in the blank in "to each according to his———" is to be predisposed to search for a pattern; and the separate treatment of "from each according to his———" treats production and distribution as two separate and independent issues. On an entitlement view these are *not* two separate questions. Whoever makes something, having bought or contracted for all other held resources used in the process (transferring some of his holdings for these cooperating factors), is entitled to it. The situation is *not* one of something's getting made, and there being an open question of who is to get it. Things come into the world already attached to people having entitlements over them. From the point of view of the historical entitlement conception of justice in holdings, those who start afresh to complete "to each according to his———" treat objects as if they appeared from nowhere, out of nothing. A complete theory of justice might cover this limit case as well; perhaps here is a use for the usual conceptions of distributive justice.

So entrenched are maxims of the usual form that perhaps we should present the entitlement conception as a competitor. Ignoring acquisition and rectification, we might say:

> From each according to what he chooses to do, to each according to what he makes for himself (perhaps with the contracted aid of others) and what others choose to do for him and

choose to give him of what they've been given previously (under this maxim) and haven't yet expended or transferred.

This, the discerning reader will have noticed, has its defects as a slogan. So as a summary and great simplification (and not as a maxim with any independent meaning) we have:

From each as they choose, to each as they are chosen.

HOW LIBERTY UPSETS PATTERNS

It is not clear how those holding alternative conceptions of distributive justice can reject the entitlement conception of justice in holdings. For suppose a distribution favored by one of these nonentitlement conceptions is realized. Let us suppose it is your favorite one and let us call this distribution D_1; perhaps everyone has an equal share, perhaps shares vary in accordance with some dimension you treasure. Now suppose that Wilt Chamberlain is greatly in demand by basketball teams, being a great gate attraction. (Also suppose contracts run only for a year, with players being free agents.) He signs the following sort of contract with a team: In each home game, twenty-five cents from the price of each ticket of admission goes to him. (We ignore the question of whether he is "gouging" the owners, letting them look out for themselves.) The season starts, and people cheerfully attend his team's games; they buy their tickets, each time dropping a separate twenty-five cents of their admission price into a special box with Chamberlain's name on it. They are excited about seeing him play; it is worth the total admission price to them. Let us suppose that in one season one million persons attend his home games, and Wilt Chamberlain winds up with $250,000, a much larger sum than the average income and larger even than anyone else has. Is he entitled to this income? Is this new distribution D_2, unjust? If so, why? There is *no* question about whether each of the people was entitled to the control over the resources they held in D_1, because that was the distribution (your favorite) that (for the purposes of argument) we assumed was acceptable. Each of these persons *chose* to give twenty-five cents of their money to Chamberlain. They could have spent it on going to the movies, or on candy bars, or on copies of *Dissent* magazine, or of *Monthly Review*. But they all, at least one million of them, converged on giving it to Wilt Chamberlain in exchange for watching him play basketball. If D_1 was a just distribution, and people voluntarily moved from it to D_2 transferring parts of their shares they were given under D_1 (what was it for if not to do something with?), isn't D_2 also just? If people were entitled to dispose of the resources to which they were entitled (under D_1), didn't this include their being entitled to give it to, or exchange it with, Wilt Chamberlain? Can anyone else complain on grounds of justice? Each other person already has his legitimate share under D_1. Under D_1, there is nothing that anyone has that anyone else has a claim of justice against. After someone transfers something to Wilt Chamberlain, third parties *still* have their legitimate shares; *their* shares are not changed. By what process could such a transfer among two persons give rise to a legitimate claim of distributive justice on a portion of what was transferred, by a third party who had no claim of justice on any holding of the others *before* the transfer?[8] To cut off objections irrelevant here, we might imagine the exchanges occurring in a socialist society, after hours: After playing whatever basketball he does in his daily work, or doing whatever other daily work he does, Wilt Chamberlain decides to put in *overtime* to earn additional money. (First his work quota is set; he works time over that.) Or imagine it is a skilled juggler people like to see, who puts on shows after hours.

Why might someone work overtime in a society in which it is assumed their needs are satisfied? Perhaps because they care about things other than needs. I like to write in books that I read, and to have easy access to books for browsing at odd hours. It would be very pleasant and convenient to have the resources of Widener Library in my backyard. No society, I assume, will provide such resources close to each person who would like them as part of his regular allotment (under D_1). Thus, persons either must do without some extra things that they want, or be allowed to do something extra to get some of these things. On what basis could the inequalities that would eventuate be forbidden? Notice also that small factories would spring up in a socialist society, unless forbidden. I melt down some of my personal possessions (under D_1) and build a machine out of the material. I offer you, and others, a philosophy lecture once a week in exchange for your cranking the handle on my machine, whose products I exchange for yet other things, and so on. (The raw materials used by the machine are given to me by others who possess them under D_1, in exchange for hearing lectures.) Each person might participate to gain things over and above their allotment under D_1. Some persons even might want to leave their job in socialist industry and work full time in this private sector. [In any case] I wish merely to note how private property even in means of production would occur in a socialist society that did not forbid people to use as they wished some of the resources they are given under the socialist distribution D_1. The socialist society would have to forbid capitalist acts between consenting adults.

The general point illustrated by the Wilt Chamberlain example and the example of the entrepreneur in a socialist society is that no end-state principle or distributional patterned principle of justice can be continuously realized without continuous interference with people's lives. Any favored pattern would be transformed into one unfavored by the principle, by people choosing to act various ways; for example, by people exchanging goods and services with other people, or giving things to other people, things the transferrers are entitled to under the favored distributional pattern. To maintain a pattern one must either continually interfere to stop people from transferring resources as they wish to, or continually (or periodically) interfere to take from some persons resources that others for some reason chose to transfer to them. (But if some time limit is to be set on how long people may keep resources others voluntarily transfer to them, why let them keep these resources for *any* period of time? Why not have immediate confiscation?) It might be objected that all persons voluntarily will choose to refrain from actions which would upset the pattern. This presupposes unrealistically (1) that all or most will want to maintain the pattern (are those who don't, to be "reeducated" or forced to undergo "self-criticism"?), (2) that each can gather enough information about his own actions and the ongoing activities of others to discover which of his actions will upset the pattern, and (3) that diverse and far-flung persons can coordinate their actions to dovetail into the pattern. Compare the manner in which the market is neutral among persons' desires, as it reflects and transmits widely scattered information via prices, and coordinates persons' activities.

It puts things perhaps a bit too strongly to say that every patterned (or end-state) principle is liable to be thwarted by the voluntary actions of the individual parties transferring some of their shares they receive under the principle. For perhaps some *very* weak patterns are not so thwarted. Any distributional pattern with any egalitarian component is overturnable by the voluntary actions of individual persons over time; as is every patterned condition with sufficient content so as actually to have been proposed as presenting the central core of distributive justice. Still, given the possibility that some weak conditions or patterns may not be unstable in this way, it would be better to formulate an explicit description of the kind of interesting and contentful patterns under discussion, and to prove a theorem about their instability. Since the weaker the patterning, the more likely it is that the entitlement system itself satisfies it, a plausible conjecture is that any patterning either is unstable or is satisfied by the entitlement system. . . .

REDISTRIBUTION AND PROPERTY RIGHTS

Apparently, patterned principles allow people to choose to expend upon themselves, but not upon others, those resources they are entitled to (or rather, receive) under some favored distributional pattern D_1. For if each of several persons chooses to expend some of his D_1 resources upon one other person, then that other person will receive more than his D_1 share, disturbing the favored distributional pattern. Maintaining a distributional pattern in individualism with a vengeance! Patterned distributional principles do not give people what entitlement principles do, only better distributed. For they do not give the right to choose what to do with what one has; they do not give the right to choose to pursue an end involving (intrinsically, or as a means) the enhancement of another's position. To such views, families are disturbing; for within a family occur transfers that upset the favored distributional pattern. Either families themselves become units to which distribution takes place, the column occupiers (on what rationale?), or loving behavior is forbidden. We should note in passing the ambivalent position of radicals toward the family. Its loving relationships are seen as a model to be emulated and extended across the whole society, at the same time that it is denounced as a suffocating institution to be broken and condemned as a focus of parochial concerns that interfere with achieving radical goals. Need we say that it is not appropriate to enforce across the wider society the relationships which are voluntarily undertaken? Incidentally, love is an interesting instance of another relationship that is historical, in that (like justice) it depends upon what actually occurred. An adult may come to love another because of the other's characteristics; but it is the other person, and not the characteristics, that is loved. The love is not transferable to someone else with the same characteristics, even to one who "scores" higher for these characteristics. And the love endures through changes of the characteristics that gave rise to it. One loves the particular person one actually encountered. Why love is historical, attaching to persons in this way and not to characteristics, is an interesting and puzzling question.

Proponents of patterned principles of distributive justice focus upon criteria for determining who is to receive holdings; they consider the reasons for which someone should have something, and also the total picture of holdings. Whether or not it is better to give than to receive, proponents of patterned principles ignore giving altogether. In considering the distribution of goods, income, and so forth, their theories are theories of recipient justice; they completely ignore any right a person might have to give something to someone. Even in exchanges where each party is simultaneously giver and recipient, patterned principles of justice focus only upon the recipient role and its supposed rights. Thus discussions tend to focus on whether people (should) have a right to inherit, rather than on whether people (should) have a right to bequeath or on whether persons who have a right to hold also have a right to choose that others hold in their place. I lack a good explanation of why the usual theories of distributive justice are so recipient oriented; ignoring givers and transferrers and their rights is of a piece with ignoring producers and their entitlements. But why is it *all* ignored?

Patterned principles of distributive justice necessitate *re*distributive activities. The likelihood is small that any actual freely-arrived-at set of holdings fits a given pattern; and the likelihood is nil that it will continue to fit the pattern as people exchange and give. From the point of view of an entitlement theory, redistribution is a serious matter indeed, involving, as it does, the violation of people's rights. (An exception is those takings that fall under the principle of the rectification of injustices.) From other points of view, also, it is serious.

Taxation of earnings from labor is on a par with forced labor. Some persons find this claim obviously true: taking the earnings of *n* hours labor is like taking *n* hours from the person; it is like forcing the person to work *n* hours for another's purpose. Others find the claim absurd. But even these, *if* they object to forced labor, would oppose forcing unemployed hippies to work for the benefit of the needy. And they would also object to forcing each person to work five extra hours each week for the benefit of the needy. But a system that takes five hours' wages in taxes does not seem to them like one that forces someone to work five hours, since it offers the person forced a wider range of choice in activities than does taxation in kind with the particular labor specified. (But we can imagine a gradation of systems of forced labor, from one that specifies a particular activity, to one that gives a choice among two activities, to . . . ; and so on up.) Furthermore, people envisage a system with something like a proportional tax on everything above the amount necessary for basic needs. Some think this does not force someone to work extra hours, since there is no fixed number of extra hours he is forced to work, and since he can avoid the tax entirely by earning only enough to cover his basic needs. This is a very uncharacteristic view of forcing for those who *also* think people are forced to do something *whenever* the alternatives they face are considerably worse. However, *neither* view is correct. The fact that others intentionally intervene, in violation of a side constraint against aggression, to threaten force to limit the alternatives, in this case to paying taxes or (presumably the worse alternative) bare subsistence, makes the taxation system one of forced labor and distinguishes it from other cases of limited choices which are not forcings.

The man who chooses to work longer to gain an income more than sufficient for his basic needs prefers some extra goods or services to the leisure and activities he could perform during the possible nonworking hours; whereas the man who chooses not to work the extra time prefers the leisure activities to the extra goods or services he could acquire by working more. Given this, if it would be illegitimate for a tax system to seize some of a man's leisure (forced labor) for the purpose of serving the needy, how can it be legitimate for a tax system to seize some of a man's goods for that purpose? Why should we treat the man whose happiness requires certain material goods or services differently from the man whose preferences and desires make such goods unnecessary for his happiness? Why should the man who prefers seeing a movie (and who has to earn money for a ticket) be open to the required call to aid the needy, while the person who prefers looking at a sunset (and hence need earn no extra money) is not? Indeed, isn't it surprising that redistributionists choose to ignore the man whose pleasures are so easily attainable without extra labor, while adding yet another burden to the poor unfortunate who must work for his pleasures? If anything, one would have expected the reverse. Why is the person with the nonmaterial or nonconsumption desire allowed to proceed unimpeded to his most favored feasible alternative, whereas the man whose pleasures or desires involve material things and who must work for extra money (thereby serving whomever considers his activities valuable enough to pay him) is constrained in what he can realize? Perhaps there is no difference in principle. And perhaps some think the answer concerns merely administrative convenience. (These questions and issues will not distrub those who think that forced labor to serve the needy or to realize some favored end-state pattern is acceptable.) In a fuller discussion we would have (and want) to extend our argument to include interest, entrepreneurial profits, and so on. Those who doubt that this extension can be carried through, and who draw the line here at taxation of income from labor, will have to state rather complicated patterned *historical* principles of distributive justice, since end-state principles would not distinguish *sources* of income in any way. It is enough for now to get away from end-state principles and to make clear how various patterned principles are dependent upon particular views about the sources or the illegitimacy or the lesser legitimacy of profits, interest, and so on; which particular views may well be mistaken.

What sort of right over others does a legally institutionalized end-state pattern give one? The central core of the notion of a property right in *X*, relative to which other parts of the notion are to be explained, is the right to choose which of the constrained set of options concerning *X* shall be realized or attempted. The constraints are set by other principles or laws operating in the society; in our theory, by the Lockean rights people possess (under the minimal state). My property rights in my knife allow me to leave it where I will, but not in your chest. I may choose which of the acceptable options involving the knife is to be realized. This notion of property helps us to understand why earlier theorists spoke of people as having property in themselves and their labor. They viewed each person as having a right to decide what would become of himself and what he would do, and as having a right to reap the benefits of what he did.

This right of selecting the alternative to be realized from the constrained set of alternatives may be held by an *individual* or by a *group* with some procedure for reaching a joint decision; or the right may be passed back and forth, so that one year I decide what's to become of *X*, and the next year you do (with the alternative of destruction, perhaps, being excluded). Or, during the same time period, some types of decisions about *X* may be made by me, and others by you. And so on. We lack an adequate, fruitful, analytical apparatus for classifying the *types* of constraints on the set of the options among which choices are to be made, and the *types* of ways decision powers can be held, divided, and amalgamated. A *theory* of property would, among other things, contain such a classification of constraints and decision modes, and from a small number of principles would follow a host of interesting statements about the *consequences* and effects of certain combinations of constraints and modes of decision.

When end-result principles of distributive justice are built into the legal structure of a society, they (as do most patterned principles) give each citizen an enforceable claim to some portion of the total social product; that is, to some portion of the sum total of the individually and jointly made products. This total product is produced by individuals laboring, using means of production others have saved to bring into existence, by people organizing production or creating means to produce new things or things in a new way. It is on this batch of individual activities that patterned distributional principles give each individual an enforceable claim. Each person has a claim to the activities and the products of other persons, independently of whether the other persons enter into particular relationships that give rise to these claims, and independently of whether they voluntarily take these claims upon themselves, in charity or in exchange for something.

Whether it is done through taxation on wages or on wages over a certain amount, or through seizure of profits, or through there being a big *social pot* so that it's not clear what's coming from where and what's going where, patterned principles of distributive justice involve appropriating the actions of other persons. Seizing the results of someone's labor is equivalent to seizing hours from him and directing him to carry on various activities. If people force you to do certain work, or, unrewarded work, for a certain period of time, they decide what you are to do and what purposes your work is to serve apart from your decisions. This process whereby they take this decision from you makes them a *part owner* of you; it gives them a property right in you. Just as having such partial control and power of decision, by right, over an animal or inanimate object would be to have a property right in it.

End-state and most patterned principles of distributive justice institute (partial) ownership by others of people and their actions and labor. These principles involve a shift from the classical liberals' notion of self-ownership to a notion of (partial) property rights in *other* people.

Considerations such as these confront end-state and other patterned conceptions of justice with the question of whether the actions necessary to achieve the selected pattern don't themselves violate moral side constraints. Any view holding that there are moral side constraints on actions, that not all moral considerations can be built into end-states that are to be achieved . . . must face the possibility that some of its goals are not achievable by any morally permissible available means. An entitlement theorist will face such conflicts in a society that deviates from the principles of justice for the generation of holdings, if and only if the only actions available to realize the principles themselves violate some moral constraints. Since deviation from the first two principles of justice (in acquisition and transfer) will involve other persons' direct and aggressive intervention to violate rights, and since moral constraints will not exclude defensive or retributive action in such cases, the entitlement theorist's problem rarely will be pressing. And whatever difficulties he has in applying the principle of rectification to persons who did not themselves violate the first two principles are difficulties in balancing the conflicting considerations so as correctly to formulate the complex principle of rectification itself; he will not violate moral side constraints by applying the principle. Proponents of patterned conceptions of justice, however, often will face head-on clashes (and poignant ones if they cherish each party to the clash) between moral side constraints on how individuals may be treated and their patterned conception of justice that presents an end-state or other pattern that *must* be realized.

May a person emigrate from a nation that has institutionalized some end-state or patterned distributional principle? For some principles (for example, Hayek's) emigration presents no theoretical problem. But for others it is a tricky matter. Consider a nation having a compulsory scheme of minimal social provision to aid the neediest (or one organized so as to maximize the position of the worst-off group); no one may opt out of participating in it. (None may say, "Don't compel me to contribute to others and don't provide for me via this compulsory mechanism if I am in need.") Everyone above a certain level is forced to contribute to aid the needy. But if emigration from the country were allowed, anyone could choose to move to another country that did not have compulsory social provision but otherwise was (as much as possible) identical. In such a case, the person's *only* motive for leaving would be to avoid participating in the compulsory scheme of social provision. And if he does leave, the needy in his initial country will receive no (compelled) help from him. What rationale yields the result that the person be permitted to emigrate, yet forbidden to stay and opt out of the compulsory scheme of social provision? If providing for the needy is of overriding importance, this does militate against allowing internal opting out; but it also speaks against allowing external emigration. (Would it also support, to some extent, the kidnapping of persons living in a place without compulsory social provision, who could be forced to make a contribution to the needy in your community?) Perhaps the crucial component of the position that allows emigration solely to avoid certain arrangements, while not allowing anyone internally to opt out of them, is a concern for fraternal feelings within the country. "We don't want anyone here who doesn't contribute, who doesn't care enough about the others to contribute." That concern, in this case, would have to be tied to the view that forced aiding tends to produce fraternal feelings between the aided and the aider (or perhaps merely to the view that the knowledge that someone or other voluntarily is not aiding produces unfraternal feelings).

LOCKE'S THEORY OF ACQUISITION

Before we turn to consider other theories of justice in detail, we must introduce an additional bit of complexity into the structure of the entitlement theory. This is best approached by considering Locke's attempt to specify a principle of justice in acquisition. Locke views property rights in an unowned object as originating through someone's mixing his labor with it. This gives rise to many questions. What are the boundaries of what labor is mixed with? If a private astronaut clears a place on Mars, has he mixed his labor with (so that he comes to own) the whole planet, the whole uninhabited universe, or just a particular plot? Which plot does an act bring under ownership? The minimal (possibly disconnected) area such that an act decreases entropy in that area, and not elsewhere? Can virgin land (for the purposes of ecological investigation by high-flying airplane) come under ownership by a Lockean process? Building a fence around a territory presumably would make one the owner of only the fence (and the land immediately underneath it).

Why does mixing one's labor with something make one the owner of it? Perhaps because one owns one's labor, and so one comes to own a previously unowned thing that becomes permeated with what one owns. Ownership seeps over into the rest. But why isn't mixing what I own with what I don't own a way of losing what I own rather than a way of gaining what I don't? If I own a can of tomato juice and spill it in the sea so that its molecules (made radioactive, so I can check this) mingle evenly throughout the sea, do I thereby come to own the sea, or have I foolishly dissipated my tomato juice? Perhaps the idea, instead, is that laboring on something improves it and makes it more valuable; and anyone is entitled to own a thing whose value he has created. (Reinforcing this, perhaps, is the view that laboring is unpleasant. If some people made things effortlessly, as the cartoon characters in *The Yellow Submarine* trail flowers in their wake, would they have lesser claim to their own products whose making didn't *cost* them anything?) Ignore the fact that laboring on something may make it less valuable (spraying pink enamel paint on a piece of driftwood that you have found). Why should one's entitlement extend to the whole object rather than just to the *added value* one's labor has produced? (Such reference to value might also serve to delimit the extent of ownership; for example, substitute "increases the value of" for "decreases entropy in" in the above entropy criterion.) No workable or coherent value-added property scheme has yet been devised, and any such scheme presumably would fall to objections (similar to those) that fell the theory of Henry George.

It will be implausible to view improving an object as giving full ownership to it, if the stock of unowned objects that might be improved is limited. For an object's coming under one person's ownership changes the situation of all others. Whereas previously they were at liberty (in Hohfeld's sense) to use the object, they now no longer are. This change in the situation of others (by removing their liberty to act on a previously unowned object) need not worsen their situation. If I appropriate a grain of sand from Coney Island, no one else may now do as they will with *that* grain of sand. But there are plenty of other grains of sands left for them to do the same with. Or if not grains of sand, then other things. Alternatively, the things I do with the grain of sand I appropriate might improve the position of others, counterbalancing their loss of liberty to use that grain. The crucial point is whether appropriation of an unowned object worsens the situation of others.

Locke's proviso that there be "enough and as good left in common for others" . . . is meant to ensure that the situation of others is not worsened. (If this proviso is met is there any motivation for his further condition of nonwaste?) It is often said that this proviso once held but now no longer does. But there appears to be an argument for the conclusion that if the proviso no longer holds, then it cannot ever have held so as to yield permanent and inheritable property rights. Consider the first person *Z* for whom there is not enough and as good left to appropriate. The last person *Y* to appropriate left *Z* without his previous liberty to act on an object, and so worsened *Z*'s situation. So *Y*'s appropriation is not allowed under Locke's proviso. Therefore the next to last person *X* to appropriate left *Y* in a worse position, for *X*'s act ended permissible appropriation. Therefore *X*'s appropriation wasn't permissible. But then the appropriator two from last, *W*, ended permissible appropriation and so, since it worsened *X*'s position, *W*'s appropriation wasn't permissible. And so on back to the first person *A* to appropriate a permanent property right.

This argument, however, proceeds too quickly. Someone may be made worse off by another's appropriation in two ways: first, by losing the opportunity to improve his situation by a particular appropriation of any one; and second, by no longer being able to use freely (without appropriation) what he previously could. A *stringent* requirement that another not be made worse off by an appropriation would exclude the first way if nothing else counterbalances the diminution in opportunity, as well as the second. A *weaker* requirement would exclude the second way, though not the first. With the weaker requirement, we cannot zip back so quickly from *Z* to *A*, as in the above argument; for though person *Z* can no longer *appropriate*, there may remain some for him to *use* as before. In this case *Y*'s appropriation would not violate the weaker Lockean condition. (With less remaining that people are at liberty to use, users might face more inconvenience, crowding, and so on; in that way the situation of others might be worsened, unless appropriation stopped far short of such a point.) It is arguable that no one legitimately can complain if the weaker provision is satisfied. However, since this is less clear than in the case of the more stringent proviso, Locke may have intended this stringent proviso by "enough and as good" remaining, and perhaps he meant the nonwaste condition to delay the end point from which the argument zips back.

Is the situation of persons who are unable to appropriate (there being no more accessible and useful unowned objects) worsened by a system allowing appropriation and permanent property? Here enter the various familiar social considerations favoring private property: it increases the social product by putting means of production in the hands of those who can use them most efficiently (profitably); experimentation is encouraged, because with separate persons controlling resources, there is no one person or small group whom someone with a new idea must convince to try it out; private property enables people to decide on the pattern and types of risks they wish to bear, leading to specialized types of risk bearing; private property protects future persons by leading some to hold back resources from current consumption for future markets; it provides alternate sources of employment for unpopular persons who don't have to convince any one person or small group to hire them, and so on. These considerations enter a Lockean theory to support the claim that appropriation of private property satisfies the intent behind the "enough and as good left over" proviso, *not* as a utilitarian justification of property. They enter to rebut the claim that because the proviso is violated no natural right to private property can arise by a Lockean process. The difficulty in working such an argument to show that the proviso is satisfied is in fixing the appropriate baseline for comparison. Lockean appropriation makes people no worse off than they would be *now*? This question of fixing the baseline needs more detailed investigation than we are able to give it here. It would be desirable to have an estimate of the general economic importance of original appropriation in order to see how much leeway there is for differing theories of appropriation and of the location of the baseline. Perhaps this importance can be measured by the percentage of all income that is based upon untransformed raw materials and given resources (rather than upon human actions), mainly rental income representing the unimproved value of land, and the price of raw material *in situ*, and by the percentage of current wealth which represents such income in the past.

We should note that it is not only persons favoring *private* property who need a theory of how property rights legitimately originate. Those believing in collective property, for example those believing that a group of persons living in an area jointly own the territory, or its mineral resources, also must provide a theory of how such property rights arise; they must show why the persons living there have rights to determine what is done with the land and resources there that persons living elsewhere don't have (with regard to the same land and resources).

THE PROVISO

Whether or not Locke's particular theory of appropriation can be spelled out so as to handle various difficulties, I assume that any adequate theory of justice in acquisition will contain a proviso similar to the weaker of the ones we have attributed to Locke. A process normally giving rise to a permanent bequeathable property right in a previously unowned thing will not do so if the position of others no longer at liberty to use the thing is thereby worsened. It is important to specify *this* particular mode of worsening the situation of others, for the proviso does not encompass other modes. It does not include the worsening due to more limited opportunities to appropriate (the first way above, corresponding to the more stringent condition), and it does not include how I "worsen" a seller's position if I appropriate materials to make some of what he is selling, and then enter into competition with him. Someone whose appropriation otherwise would violate the proviso still may appropriate provided he compensates the others so that their situation is not thereby worsened; unless he does compensate these others, his appropriation will violate the proviso of the principle of justice in acquisition and will be an illegitimate one. A theory of appropriation incorporating this Lockean proviso will handle correctly the cases (objections to the theory lacking the proviso) where someone appropriates the total supply of something necessary for life.

A theory which includes this proviso in its principle of justice in acquisition must also contain a more complex principle of justice in transfer. Some reflection of the proviso about appropriation constrains later actions. If my appropriating all of a certain substance violates the Lockean proviso, then so does my appropriating some and purchasing all the rest from others who obtained it without otherwise violating the Lockean proviso. If the proviso excludes someone's appropriating all the drinkable water in the world, it also excludes his purchasing it all. (More weakly, and messily, it may exclude his charging certain prices for some of his supply.) This proviso (almost?) never will come into effect; the more someone acquires of a scarce substance which others want the higher the price of the rest will go, and the more difficult it will become for him to acquire it all. But still, we can imagine, at least, that something like this occurs: someone makes simultaneous secret bids to the separate owners of a substance, each of whom sells assuming he can easily purchase more from the other owners; or some natural catastrophe destroys all of the supply of something except that in one person's possession. The total supply could not be permissibly appropriated by one person at the beginning. His later acquisition of it all does not show that the original appropriation violated the proviso (even by a reverse argument similar to the one above that tried to zip back from *Z* to *A*). Rather, it is the combination of the original appropriation *plus* all the later transfers and actions that violates the Lockean proviso.

Each owner's title to his holding includes the historical shadow of the Lockean proviso on appropriation. This excludes his transferring it into an agglomeration that does violate the Lockean proviso and excludes his using it in a way, in coordination with others or independently of them, so as to violate the proviso by making the situation of others worse than their baseline situation. Once it is known that someone's ownership runs afoul of the Lockean proviso, there are stringent limits on what he may do with (what it is difficult any longer unreservedly to call) "his property." Thus a person may not appropriate the only water hole in a desert and charge what he will. Nor may he charge what he will if he possesses one, and unfortunately it happens that all the water holes in the desert dry up, except for his. This unfortunate circumstance, admittedly no fault of his, brings into operation the Lockean proviso and limits his property rights. Similarly, an owner's property right in the only island in an area does not allow him to order a castaway from a shipwreck off his island as a trespasser, for this would violate the Lockean proviso.

Notice that the theory does not say that owners do have these rights, but that the rights are overridden to avoid some catastrophe. (Overridden rights do not disappear; they leave a trace of a sort absent in the cases under discussion.) There is no such external (and *ad hoc*?) overriding. Considerations internal to the theory of property itself, to its theory of acquisition and appropriation, provide the means for handling such cases. The results, however, may be coextensive with some condition about catastrophe, since the baseline for comparison is so low as compared to the productiveness of a society with private appropriation that the question of the Lockean proviso being violated arises only in the case of catastrophe (or a desert-island situation).

The fact that someone owns the total supply of something necessary for others to stay alive does *not* entail that his (or anyone's) appropriation of anything left some people (immediately or later) in a situation worse than the baseline one. A medical researcher who synthesizes a new substance that effectively treats a certain disease and who refuses to sell except on his terms does not worsen the situation of others by depriving them of whatever he has appropriated. The others easily can possess the same materials he appropriated; the researcher's appropriation or purchase of chemicals didn't make those chemicals scarce in a way so as to violate the Lockean proviso. Nor would someone else's purchasing the total supply of the synthesized substance from the medical researcher. The fact that the medical researcher uses easily available chemicals to synthesize the drug no more violates the Lockean proviso than does the fact that the only surgeon able to perform a particular operation eats easily obtainable food in order to stay alive and to have the energy to work. This shows that the Lockean proviso is not an "end-state principle"; it focuses on a particular way that appropriative actions affect others, and not on the structure of the situation that results.

Intermediate between someone who takes all of the public supply and someone who makes the total supply out of easily obtainable substances is someone who appropriates the total supply of something in a way that does not deprive the others of it. For example, someone finds a new substance in an out-of-the-way place. He discovers that it effectively treats a certain disease and appropriates the total supply. He does not worsen the situation of others; if he did not stumble upon the substance no one else would have, and the others would remain without it. However, as time passes, the likelihood increases that others would have come across the substance; upon this fact might be based a limit to his property right in the substance so that others are not below their baseline position; for example, its bequest might be limited. The theme of someone worsening another's situation by depriving him of something he otherwise would possess may also illuminate the example of patents. An inventor's patent does not deprive others of an object which would not exist if not for the inventor. Yet patents would have this effect on others who independently invent the object. Therefore, these independent inventors, upon whom the burden of proving independent discovery may rest, should not be excluded from utilizing their own invention as they wish (including selling it to others). Furthermore, a known inventor drastically lessens the chances of actual independent invention. For persons who know of an invention usually will not try to reinvent it, and the notion of independent discovery here would be murky at best. Yet we may assume that in the absence of the original invention, sometime later someone else would have come up with it. This suggests placing a time limit on patents, as a rough rule of thumb to approximate how long it would have taken, in the absence of knowledge of the invention, for independent discovery.

I believe that the free operation of a market system will not actually run afoul of the Lockean proviso. (Recall that crucial to our story in Part I of how a protective agency becomes dominant and a *de facto* monopoly is the fact that it wields force in situations of conflict, and is not merely in competition, with other agencies. A similar tale cannot be told about other businesses.) If this is correct, the proviso will not play a very important role in the activities of protective agencies and will not provide a significant opportunity for future state action. Indeed, were it not for the effects of previous *illegitimate* state action, people would not think of the possibility of the proviso's being violated as of more interest than any other logical possibility. (Here I make an empirical historical claim; as does someone who disagrees with this.) This completes our indication of the complication in the entitlement theory introduced by the Lockean proviso.

Notes

1. Applications of the principles of justice in acquisition may also occur as part of the move from one distribution to another. You may find an unheld thing now and appropriate it. Acquisitions also are to be understood as included when, to simplify, I speak only of transitions by transfers.
2. If the principle of rectification of violations of the first two principles yields more than one description of holdings, then some choice must be made as to which of these is to be realized. Perhaps the sort of considerations about distributive justice and equality that I argue against play a legitimate role in *this* subsidiary choice. Similarly, there may be room for such considerations in deciding which otherwise arbitrary features a statute will embody, when such features are unavoidable because other considerations do not specify a precise line; yet a line must be drawn.
3. One might try to squeeze a patterned conception of distributive justice into the framework of the entitlement conception, by formulating a gimmicky obligatory "principle of transfer" that would lead to the pattern. For example, the principle that if one has more than the mean income one must transfer everything one holds above the mean to persons below the mean so as to bring them up (but not over) the mean. We can formulate a criterion for a "principle of transfer" to rule out such obligatory transfers, or we can say that no correct principle of transfers, no principle of transfers in a free society will be like this. The former is probably the better course, though the latter also is true.

   Alternatively, one might think to make the entitlement conception instantiate a pattern, by using matrix entries that express the relative strength of a person's entitlements as measured by some real-valued function. But even if the limitation to natural dimensions failed to exclude this function, the resulting edifice would *not* capture our system of entitlements to *particular* things.

4. F. A. Hayek, *The Constitution of Liberty* (Chicago: University of Chicago Press, 1960), p. 87.
5. This question does not imply that they will tolerate any and every patterned distribution. In discussing Hayek's views, Irving Kristol has recently speculated that people will not long tolerate a system that yields distributions patterned in accordance with value rather than merit. ("'When Virtue Loses All Her Loveliness'—Some Reflections on Capitalism and 'The Free Society.'" *The Public Interest*, [Fall 1970]: 3–15.) Kristol, following some remarks of Hayek, equates the merit system with justice. Since some case can be made for the external standard of distribution in accordance with benefit to others, we ask about a weaker (and therefore more plausible) hypothesis.

The Experience Machine

ROBERT NOZICK

There are also substantial puzzles when we ask what matters other than how *people's* experiences feel "from the inside." Suppose there were an experience machine that would give you any experience you desired. Superduper neuropsychologists could stimulate your brain so that you would think and feel you were writing a great novel, or making a friend, or reading an interesting book. All the time you would be floating in a tank, with electrodes attached to your brain. Should you plug into this machine for life, preprogramming your life's experiences? If you are worried about missing out on desirable experiences, we can suppose that business enterprises have researched thoroughly the lives of many others. You can pick and choose from their large library or smorgasbord of such experiences, selecting your life's experiences for, say, the next two years. After two years have passed, you will have ten minutes or ten hours out of the tank, to select the experiences of your *next* two years. Of course, while in the tank you won't know that you're there; you'll think it's all actually happening. Others can also plug in to have the experiences they want, so there's no need to stay unplugged to serve them. (Ignore problems such as who will service the machines if everyone plugs in.) Would you plug in? *What else can matter to us, other than how our lives feel from the inside*? Nor should you refrain because of the few moments of distress between the moment you've decided and the moment you're plugged. What's a few moments of distress compared to a lifetime of bliss (if that's what you choose), and why feel any distress at all if your decision *is* the best one?

What does matter to us in addition to our experiences? First, we want to *do* certain things, and not just have the experience of doing them. In the case of certain experiences, it is only because first we want to do the actions that we want the experiences of doing them or thinking we've done them. (But *why* do we want to do the activities rather than merely to experience them?) A second reason for not plugging in is that we want to *be* a certain way, to be a certain sort of person. Someone floating in a tank is an indeterminate blob. There is no answer to the question of what a person is like who has long been in the tank. Is he courageous, kind, intelligent, witty, loving? It's not merely that it's difficult to tell; there's no way he is. Plugging into the machine is a kind of suicide. It will seem to some, trapped by a picture, that nothing about what we are like can matter except as it gets reflected in our experiences. But should it be surprising that what *we are* is important to us? Why should we be concerned only with how our time is filled, but not with what we are?

Thirdly, plugging into an experience machine limits us to a man-made reality, to a world no deeper or more important than that which people can construct. There is no *actual* contact with any deeper reality, though the experience of it can be simulated. Many persons desire to leave themselves open to such contact and to a plumbing of deeper significance.[1] This clarifies the intensity of the conflict over psychoactive drugs, which some view as mere local experience machines, and others view as avenues to a deeper reality; what some view as equivalent to surrender to the experience machine, others view as following one of the reasons *not* to surrender!

We learn that something matters to us in addition to experience by imagining an experience machine and then realizing that we would not use it. We can continue to imagine a sequence of machines each designed to fill lacks suggested for the earlier machines. For example, since the experience machine doesn't meet our desire to *be* a certain way, imagine a transformation machine which transforms us into whatever sort of person we'd like to be (compatible with our staying us). Surely one would not use the transformation machine to become as one would wish, and thereupon plug into the experience machine![2] So something matters in addition to one's experiences *and* what one is like. Nor is the reason merely that one's experiences are unconnected with what one is like. For the experience machine might be limited to provide only experiences possible to the sort of person plugged in. Is it that we want to make a difference in the world? Consider then the result machine, which produces in the world any result you would produce and injects your vector input into any joint activity. We shall not pursue here the fascinating details of these or other machines. What is most disturbing about them is their living of our lives for us. Is it misguided to search for *particular* additional functions beyond the competence of machines to do for us? Perhaps what we desire is to live (an active verb) ourselves, in contact with reality. (And this, machines cannot do *for* us.) Without elaborating on the implications of this, which I believe connect surprisingly with issues about free will and causal accounts of knowledge, we need merely note the intricacy of the question of what matters *for people* other than their experiences. Until one finds a satisfactory answer, and determines that this answer does not *also* apply to animals, one cannot reasonably claim that only the felt experiences of animals limit what we may do to them.

Notes

1. Traditional religious views differ on the *point* of contact with a transcendent reality. Some say that contact yields eternal bliss or Nirvana, but they have not distinguished this sufficiently from merely a *very* long run on the experience machine. Others think it is intrinsically desirable to do the will of a higher being which created us all, though presumably no one would think this if we discovered we had been created as an object of amusement by some superpowerful child from another galaxy or dimension. Still others imagine an eventual merging with a higher reality, leaving unclear its desirability, or where that merging leaves *us*.
2. Some wouldn't use the transformation machine at all; it seems like *cheating*. But the one-time use of the transformation machine would not remove all challenges; there would still be obstacles for the new us to overcome, a new plateau from which to strive even higher. And is this plateau any the less earned or deserved than that provided by genetic endowment and early childhood environment? But if the transformation machine could be used indefinitely often, so that we could accomplish anything by pushing a button to transform ourselves into someone who could do it easily, there would remain no limits we *need* to strain against or try to transcend. Would there be anything left *to do*? Do some theological views place God outside of time because an omniscient omnipotent being couldn't fill up his days?

Chapter 30

JOHN RAWLS

John Rawls (1921–), perhaps the most important political philosopher in the twentieth century, was educated at Princeton University and taught at Cornell and Harvard universities. Rawls wrote several important works in philosophy, and no twentieth-century work in moral and political philosophy has had greater influence on our generation than his *A Theory of Justice* (1971). Robert Nisbett calls it the "long awaited successor to Rousseau's *Social Contract*, the Rock on which the Church of Equality can properly be founded in our time." In scope and power it rivals the classics of Hobbes, Locke, and Rousseau. Fundamentally a strong form of liberal egalitarianism, it seeks to justify the welfare state. We have included as our selection for Rawls his earlier essay, "Justice as Fairness" (1955), which outlines the central ideas that he later developed in the book *A Theory of Justice.*

In "A Theory of Justice: Liberal Egalitarianism," Rawls sets forth a hypothetical contract theory in which participants decide on practices acknowledged to be fair and bind "themselves by the duty of fair play to follow the rules when it comes their turn to do so, and this implies a limitation on their pursuit of self-interest in particular cases." Parties to the contract are to act as rationally self-interested agents and to choose the basic principles that will govern their society. Rawls thinks that these conditions insure objectivity and impartiality of judgment. The system is called "justice as fairness" because Rawls seeks a contract on whose fairness all parties will agree. In effect, the parties to the contract should choose the kind of principles they could live with if their enemies were assigning them positions in society. Rawls argues that they would choose the following two principles:

1. Everyone will have an equal right to the most extensive liberty compatible with similar liberty for others.
2. Inequalities are arbitrary unless it is reasonable to expect that they will work out for everyone's advantage, and provided the positions and offices to which they attach, or from which they may be gained, are open to all.

These principles express justice as a complex of three ideas: liberty, equality, and reward for services contributing to the common good.

It might be pointed out that this two-part second principle will be transformed in *A Theory of Justice*, where Rawls introduces the *difference* principle. The second principle will become:

2. Social and economic inequalities must satisfy two conditions:

(a) They are to the greatest benefit of the least advantaged ("the difference principle").

(b) They are attached to positions open to all under conditions of fair equality of opportunity.

Rawls's egalitarianism is more fully developed in *A Theory of Justice*, but it is present in the article, at least in outline. He believes that each minimally rational human being, who has a conception of the good (a value system) and is able to act justly, is valuable, and equally so. He then states the main idea of his theory: inequalities are justified if they work for the good of all. In his book, of course, that is not sufficient. They must aid the least well-off in order to be justified.

Here is how Rawls states his aim in *A Theory of Justice*:

> My aim is to present a conception of justice which generalizes and carries to a higher level of abstraction the familiar theory of the social contract as found, say, in Locke, Rousseau, and Kant. In order to do this we are not to think of the original contract as one to enter a particular society or to set up a particular form of government. Rather, the guiding idea is that the principles of justice for the basic structure of society are the object of the original agreement. They are the principles that free and rational persons concerned to further their own interests would accept in an initial position of equality as defining the fundamental terms of their association. These principles are to regulate all further agreements; they specify the kinds of social cooperation that can be entered into and the forms of government that can be established. This way of regarding the principles of justice I shall call *justice as fairness*.
>
> Thus we are to imagine that those who engage in social cooperation choose together, in one joint act, the principles which are to assign basic rights and duties and to determine the division of social benefits. Men are to decide in advance how they are to regulate their claims against one another and what is to be the foundation charter of their society. Just as each person must decide by rational reflection what constitutes his good, that is, the system of ends which it is rational for him to pursue, so a group of persons must decide once and for all what is to count among them as just and unjust. The choice which rational men would make in this hypothetical situation of equal liberty, assuming for the present that this choice problem has a solution, determines the principle of justice.
>
> In *justice as fairness* the original position of equality corresponds to the state of nature in the traditional theory of the social contract. This original position is not, of course, thought of as an actual historical state of affairs, much less as a primitive condition of culture. It is understood as a purely hypothetical situation characterized so as to lead to a certain conception of justice. Among the essential features of this situation is that no one knows his place in society, his class position or social status, nor does any one know his fortune in the distribution of natural assets and abilities, his intelligence, strength, and the like. I shall even assume that the parties do not know their conceptions of the good or their special psychological propensities. The principles of justice are chosen behind the *veil of ignorance*. This ensures that no one is advantaged or disadvantaged in the choice of principles by the outcome of natural chance or the contingency of social circumstances. Since all are similarly situated and no one is able to design principles to favor his particular condition, the principles of justice are the result of a fair agreement or bargain. For given the circumstances of the original position, the symmetry of everyone's relations to each other, this initial situation is fair between individuals as moral persons, that is, as rational beings with their own ends and capable, I shall assume, of a sense of justice. The *original position* is, one might say, the appropriate initial status quo, and thus the fundamental agreements reached in it are fair. This explains the propriety of the name "justice as fairness": it conveys the idea that the principles of justice are agreed to in an initial situation that is fair.

Finally, Rawls argues that not only is the principle of fairness not a utilitarian principle, but it is opposed to utilitarianism, because maximal utility may not be sought if it imposes unfair burdens on the less well-off. Persons have rights that even the good of the society may not override.

FOR FURTHER READING

Barry, Brian. *Theories of Justice* (University of California Press, 1989).

Daniels, Norman, ed. *Reading Rawls: Critical Studies of A Theory of Justice* (Basil Blackwell, 1975).

Kukathas, Chandran and Philip Pettit. *Rawls: A Theory of Justice and its Critics* (Standford University Press, 1990).

Kymlicka, Will. *Contemporary Political Theory: An Introduction* (Oxford University Press, 1990).

Nozick, Robert. *Anarchy, State, and Utopia* (Basic Books, 1974). A libertarian critique of Rawls.

Pogge, Thomas. *Realizing Rawls* (Cornell University Press, 1989).

Rawls, John. *A Theory of Justice* (Harvard University Press, 1971).

———. *Political Liberalism* (Columbia University Press, 1994).

Sandel, Michael. *Liberalism and the Limits of Justice* (Cambridge University Press, 1982).

Sterba, James, ed. *Justice: Alternative Political Perspectives*, 2nd ed. (Wadsworth, 1992). Contains a useful set of readings.

Wolff, Robert Paul. *Understanding Rawls* (Princeton University Press, 1977).

A Theory of Justice: Liberal Egalitarianism

HUMAN BEINGS POSSESS INTRINSIC WORTH

Each person possesses an inviolability founded on justice that even the welfare of society as a whole cannot override. For this reason justice denies that the loss of freedom for some is made right by a greater good shared by others. It does not allow that the sacrifices imposed on a few are outweighed by the larger sum of advantages enjoyed by the many. Therefore, in a just society the liberties of equal citizenship are taken as settled; the rights secured by justice are not subject to political bargaining or the calculus of social interests. . . .

It seems reasonable to suppose that the parties in the original position are equal. That is, all have the same rights in the procedure for choosing principles; each can make proposals, submit reasons for their acceptance, and so on. Obviously the purpose of these conditions is to represent equality between human beings as moral persons, as creatures having a conception of their good and capable of a sense of justice. The basis of equality is taken to be similarity in these two respects. Systems of ends are not ranked in value; and each man is presumed to have the requisite ability to understand and act upon whatever principles are adopted. Together with the veil of ignorance, these conditions define the principles of justice as those which rational persons concerned to advance their interests would consent to as equals when none are known to be advantaged or disadvantaged by social and natural contingencies. . . .

THE MAIN IDEA OF THE THEORY OF JUSTICE

My aim is to present a conception of justice which generalizes and carries to a higher level of abstraction the familiar theory of the social contract as found, say, in Locke, Rousseau, and Kant. In order to do this we are not to think of the original contract as one to enter a particular society or to set up a particular form of government. Rather, the guiding idea is that the principles of justice for the basic structure of society are the object of the original agreement. They are the principles that free and rational persons concerned to further their own interests would accept in an initial position of equality as defining the fundamental terms of their association. These principles are to regulate all further agreements; they specify the kinds of social cooperation that can be entered into and the forms of government that can be established. This way of regarding the principles of justice I shall call *justice as fairness*.

Thus we are to imagine that those who engage in social cooperation choose together, in one joint act, the principles which are to assign basic rights and duties and to determine the division of social benefits. Men are to decide in advance how they are to regulate their claims against one another and what is to be the fundation charter of their society. Just as each person must decide by rational reflection what constitutes his good, that is, the system of ends which it is rational for him to pursue, so a group of persons must decide once and for all what is to count among them as just and unjust. The choice which rational men would make in this hypothetical situation of equal liberty, assuming for the present that this choice problem has a solution, determines the principle of justice.

In *justice as fairness* the original position of equality corresponds to the state of nature in the traditional theory of the social contract. This original position is not, of course, thought of as an actual historical state of affairs, much less as a primitive condition of culture. It is understood as a purely hypothetical situation characterized so as to lead to a certain conception of justice. Among the essential features of this situation is that no one knows his place in society, his class position or social status, nor does any one know his fortune in the distribution of natural assets and abilities, his intelligence, strength, and the like. I shall even assume that the parties do not know their conceptions of the good or their special psychological propensities. The principles of justice are chosen behind the *veil of ignorance*. This ensures that no one is advantaged or disadvantaged in the choice of principles by the outcome of natural chance or the contingency of social circumstances. Since all are similarly situated and no one is able to design principles to favor his particular condition, the principles of justice are the result of a fair agreement or bargain. For given the circumstances of the original position, the symmetry of everyone's relations to each other, this initial situation is fair between individuals as moral persons, that is, as rational beings with their own ends and capable, I shall assume, of a sense of justice. The *original position* is, one might say, the appropriate initial status quo, and thus the fundamental agreements reached in it are fair. This explains the properiety of the name "justice as fairness": it conveys the idea that the principles of justice are agreed to in an initial situation that is fair. The name does not mean that the concepts of justice and fairness are the same, any more than the phrase "poetry as metaphor" means that the concepts of poetry and metaphor are the same. . . .

Nor, again, does anyone know his conception of the good, the particulars of his rational plan of life, or even the special features of his psychology such as his aversion to risk or liability to optimism or pessimism. More than this, I assume that the parties do not know the particular circumstances of their own society. That is, they do not know its economic or political situation, or the level of civilization and culture it has been able to achieve. The persons in the original position have no information as to which generation they belong.

Justice as fairness begins, as I have said, with one of the most general of all choices which persons might make together, namely, with the choice of the first principles of a conception of justice which is to regulate all subsequent criticism and reform of institutions. Then, having chosen a conception of justice, we can suppose that they are to choose a constitution and a legislature to enact laws, and so on, all in accordance with the principles of justice initially agreed upon. Our social situation is just if it is such that by this sequence of hypothetical agreements we would have contracted into the general system of rules which defines it. Moreover, assuming that the original position does determine a set of principles (that is, that a particular conception of justice would be chosen), it will then be true that whenever social institutions satisfy these principles those engaged in them can say to one another that they are cooperating on terms to which they would agree if they were free and equal persons whose relations with respect to one another were fair. They could all view their arrangements in an initial situation that embodies widely accepted and reasonable constraints on the choice of principles. The general recognition of this fact would provide the basis for a public acceptance of the corresponding principles of justice. No society can, of course, be a scheme of cooperation which men enter voluntarily in a literal sense; each person finds himself placed at birth in some particular position in some particular society, and the nature of this position materially affects his life prospects. Yet a society satisfying the principles of justice as fairness comes as close as a society can to being a voluntary scheme, for it meets the principles which free and equal persons would assent to under circumstances that are fair. In this sense its members are autonomous and the obligations they recognize self-imposed. . . .

THE PRINCIPLES OF JUSTICE

1. Everyone will have an equal right to the most extensive basic liberties compatible with similar liberty for others.
2. Social and economic inequalities must satisfy two conditions:
   - **(a)** They are to the greatest benefit of the least advantaged (the difference principle).
   - **(b)** They are attached to positions open to all under conditions of fair equality of opportunity.

The basic liberties of citizens are, roughly speaking, political liberty (the right to vote and to be eligible for public office) together with freedom of speech and assembly; freedom of the person along with the right to hold property; and freedom from arbitrary arrest and seizure as defined by the concept of the rule of law. These liberties are all required to be equal by the first principle, since citizens of a just society are to have the same basic rights.

The second principle applies to the distribution of income and wealth and to the design of organizations that make use of differences in authority and responsibility, or chains of command. While the distribution of wealth and income need not be equal, it must be to everyone's advantage, and at the same time, positions of authority and offices of command must be accessible to all. . . .

A society should try to avoid the region where the marginal contributions of those better off are negative, since, other things equal, this seems a greater fault than falling short of the best scheme when these contributions are positive. The even larger difference between rich and poor makes the latter even worse off, and this violates the principle of mutual advantage as well as democratic equality. . . .

A person in the original position would concede the justice of these inequalities. Indeed, it would be shortsighted of him not to do so. He would hesitate to agree to these regularities only if he would be dejected by the bare knowledge or perception that others were better situated; and I have assumed that the parties decide as if they are not moved by envy. In order to make the principle regulating inequalities determinate, one looks at the system from the standpoint of the least advantaged representative man. Inequalities are permissible when they maximize, or at least contribute to, the long-term expectations of the least fortunate group in society.

There is no more reason to permit the distribution of income and wealth to be settled by the distribution of natural assets than by historical and social fortune. Furthermore, the principle of fair opportunity can be only imperfectly carried out, at least as long as the institution of the family exists. The extent to which natural capacities develop and reach fruition is affected by all kinds of social conditions and class attitudes. Even the willingness to make an effort, to try, and so to be deserving in the ordinary sense is itself dependent upon happy family and social circumstances. It is impossible in practice to secure equal chances of achievement and culture for those similarly endowed, and therefore we may want to adopt a principle which recognizes this fact and also mitigates the arbitrary effects of the natural lottery itself. . . .

THE TENDENCY TO EQUALITY

I wish to conclude this discussion of the two principles by explaining the sense in which they express an egalitarian conception of justice. Also I should like to forestall the objection to the principle of fair opportunity that it leads to a callous meritocratic society. In order to prepare the way for doing this, I note several aspects of the conception of justice that I have set out.

First we may observe that the difference principle gives some weight to the considerations singled out by the principle of redress. This is the principle that undeserved inequalities call for redress; and since inequalities of birth and natural endowment are underserved, these inequalities are to be somehow compensated for. Thus the principle holds that in order to treat all persons equally, to provide genuine equality of opportunity, society must give more attention to those with fewer native assets and to those born into the less favorable social positions. The idea is to redress the bias of contingencies in the direction of equality. In pursuit of this principle greater resources might be spent on the education of the less rather than the more intelligent, at least over a certain time of life, say the earlier years of school.

Now the principle of redress has not to my knowledge been proposed as the sole criterion of justice, as the single aim of the social order. It is plausible as most such principles are only as a prima facie principle, one that is to be weighed in the balance with others. For example, we are to weigh it against the principle to improve the average standard of life, or to advance the common good. But whatever other principles we hold, the claims of redress are to be taken into account. It is thought to represent one of the elements in our conception of justice. Now the difference principle is not of course the principle of redress. It does not require society to try to even out handicaps as if all were expected to compete on a fair basis in the same race. But the difference principle would allocate resources in education, say, so as to improve the long-term expectation of the least favored. If this end is attained by giving more attention to the better endowed, it is permissible; otherwise not. And in making this decision, the value of education should not be assessed solely in terms of economic efficiency and social welfare. Equally if not more important is the role of education in enabling a person to enjoy the culture of his society and to take part in its affairs, and in this way to provide for each individual a secure sense of his own worth.

Thus although the difference principle is not the same as that of redress, it does achieve some of the intent of the latter principle. It transforms the aims of the basic structure so that the total scheme of institutions no longer emphasizes social efficiency and technocratic values. We see then that the difference principle represents, in effect, an agreement to regard the distribution of natural talents as a common asset and to share in the benefits of this distribution whatever it turns out to be. Those who have been favored by nature, whoever they are, may gain from their good fortune only on terms that improve the situation of those who have lost out. The naturally advantaged are not to gain merely because they are more gifted, but only to cover the costs of training and education and for using their endowments in ways that help the less fortunate as well. No one deserves his greater natural capacity nor merits a more favorable starting place in society. But it does not follow that one should eliminate these distinctions. There is another way to deal with them. The basic structure can be arranged so that these contingencies work for the good of the least fortunate. Thus we are led to the difference principle if we wish to set up the social system so that no one gains or loses from his arbitrary place in the distribution of natural assets or his initial position in society without giving or receiving compensating advantages in return.

In view of these remarks we may reject the contention that the ordering of institutions is always defective because the distribution of natural talents and the contingencies of social circumstance are unjust, and this injustice must inevitably carry over to human arrangements. Occasionally this reflection is offered as an excuse for ignoring injustice, as if the refusal to acquiesce in injustice is on a par with being unable to accept death. The natural distribution is neither just nor unjust; nor is it unjust that persons are born into society at some particular position. These are simply natural facts. What is just and unjust is the way that institutions deal with these facts. Aristocratic and caste societies are unjust because they make these contingencies the ascriptive basis for belonging to more or less enclosed and privileged social classes. The basic structure of these societies incorporates the arbitrariness found in nature. But there is no necessity for men to resign themselves to these contingencies. The social system is not an unchangeable order beyond human control but a pattern of human action. In justice as fairness men agree to share one another's fate. In designing institutions they undertake to avail themselves of the accidents of nature and social circumstance only when doing so is for the common benefit. The two principles are a fair way of meeting the arbitrariness of fortune; and while no doubt imperfect in other ways, the institutions which satisfy these principles are just.

A further point is that the difference principle expresses a conception of reciprocity. It is a principle of mutual benefit. We have seen that, at least when chain connection holds, each representative man can accept the basic structure as designed to advance his interests. The social order can be justified to everyone, and in particular to those who are least favored; and in this sense it is egalitarian. But it seems necessary to consider in an intuitive way how the condition of mutual benefit is satisfied. Consider any two representative men A and B, and let B be the one who is less favored. Actually, since we are most interested in the comparison with the least favored man, let us assume that B is this individual. Now B can accept A's being better off since A's advantages have been gained in ways that improve B's prospects. If A were not allowed his better position, B would be even worse off than he is. The difficulty is to show that A has no grounds for complaint. Perhaps he is required to have less than he might since his having more would result in some loss to B. Now what can be said to the more favored man? To begin with, it is clear that the well-being of each depends on a scheme of social cooperation without which no one could have a satisfactory life. Secondly, we can ask for the willing cooperation of everyone only if the terms of the scheme are reasonable. The difference principle, then, seems to be a fair basis on which those better endowed, or more fortunate in their social circumstances, could expect others to collaborate with them when some workable arrangement is a necessary condition of the good of all.

There is a natural inclination to object that those better situated deserve their greater advantages whether or not they are to the benefit of others. At this point it is necessary to be clear about the notion of desert. It is perfectly true that given a just system of cooperation as a scheme of public rules and the expectations set up by it, those who, with the prospect of improving their condition, have done what the system announces that it will reward are entitled to their advantages. In this sense the more fortunate have a claim to their better situation; their claims are legitimate expectations established by social institutions, and the community is obligated to meet them. But this sense of desert presupposes the existence of the cooperative scheme; it is irrelevant to the question whether in the first place the scheme is to be designed in accordance with the difference principle or some other criterion.

Perhaps some will think that the person with greater natural endowments deserves those assets and the superior character that made their development possible. Because he is more worthy in this sense, he deserves the greater advantages that he could achieve with them. This view, however, is surely incorrect. It seems to be one of the fixed points of our considered judgments that no one deserves his place in the distribution of native endowments, any more than one deserves one's initial starting place in society. The assertion that a man deserves the superior character that enables him to make the effort to cultivate his abilities is equally problematic; for his character depends in large part upon fortunate family and social circumstances for which he can claim no credit. The notion of desert seems not to apply to these cases. Thus the more advantaged representative man cannot say that he deserves and therefore has a right to a scheme of cooperation in which he is permitted to acquire benefits in ways that do not contribute to the welfare of others. There is no basis for his making this claim. From the standpoint of common sense, then, the difference principle appears to be acceptable both to the more advantaged and to the less advantaged individual. Of course, none of this is strictly speaking an argument for the principle, since in a contract theory arguments are made from the point of view of the original position. But these intuitive considerations help to clarify the nature of the principle and the sense in which it is egalitarian.

I noted earlier that a society should try to avoid the region where the marginal contributions of those better off to the well-being of the less favored are negative. It should operate only on the upward rising part of the contribution curve (including of course the maximum). One reason for this, we can now see, is that on this segment of the curve the criterion of mutual benefit is always fulfilled. Moreover, there is a natural sense in which the harmony of social interests is achieved; representative men do not gain at one another's expense since only reciprocal advantages are allowed. To be sure, the shape and slope of the contribution curve is determined in part at least by the natural lottery in native assets, and as such it is neither just nor unjust. But suppose we think of the forty-five degree line as representing the ideal of a perfect harmony of interests; it is the contribution curve (a straight line in this case) along which everyone gains equally. Then it seems that the consistent realization of the two principles of justice tends to raise the curve closer to the ideal of a perfect harmony of interests. Once a society goes beyond the maximum it operates along the downward sloping part of the curve and a harmony of interests no longer exists. As the more favored gain the less advantaged lose, and vice versa. The situation is analogous to being on an efficiency frontier. This is far from desirable when the justice of the basic structure is involved. Thus it is to realize the ideal of the harmony of interests on terms that nature has given us, and to meet the criterion of mutual benefit, that we should stay in the region of positive contributions.

A further merit of the difference principle is that it provides an interpretation of the principle of fraternity. In comparison with liberty and equality, the idea of fraternity has had a lesser place in democratic theory. It is thought to be less specifically a political concept, not in itself defining any of the democratic rights but conveying instead certain attitudes of mind and forms of conduct without which we would lose sight of the values expressed by these rights. Or closely related to this, fraternity is held to represent a certain equality of social esteem manifest in various public conventions and in the absence of manners of deference and servility. No doubt fraternity does imply these things, as well as a sense of civic friendship and social solidarity, but so understood it expresses no definite requirement. We have yet to find a principle of justice that matches the underlying idea. The difference principle, however, does seem to correspond to a natural meaning of fraternity: namely, to the idea of not wanting to have greater advantages unless this is to the benefit of others who are less well off. The family, in its ideal conception and often in practice, is one place where the principle of maximizing the sum of advantages is rejected. Members of a family commonly do not wish to gain unless they can do so in ways that further the interests of the rest. Now wanting to act on the difference principle has precisely this consequence. Those better circumstanced are willing to have their greater advantages only under a scheme in which this works out for the benefit of the less fortunate.

The ideal of fraternity is sometimes thought to involve ties of sentiment and feeling which it is unrealistic to expect between members of the wider society. And this is surely a further reason for its relative neglect in democratic theory. Many have felt that it has no proper place in political affairs. But if it is interpreted as incorporating the requirements of the difference principle, it is not an impracticable conception. It does seem that the institutions and policies which we most confidently think to be just satisfy its demands, at least in the sense that the inequalities permitted by them contribute to the well-being of the less favored. On this interpretation, then, the principle of fraternity is a perfectly feasible standard. Once we accept it we can associate the traditional ideas of liberty, equality, and fraternity with the democratic interpretation of the two principles of justice as follows: liberty corresponds to the first principle, equality to the idea of equality in the first principle together with equality of fair opportunity, and fraternity to the difference principle. In this way we have found a place for the conception of fraternity in the democratic interpretation of the two principles, and we see that it imposes a definite requirement on the basic structure of society. The other aspects of fraternity should not be forgotten, but the difference principle expresses its fundamental meaning from the standpoint of social justice.

Now it seems evident in the light of these observations that the democratic interpretation of the two principles will not lead to a meritocratic society. This form of social order follows the principle of careers open to talents and uses equality of opportunity as a way of releasing men's energies in the pursuit of economic prosperity and political dominion. There exists a marked disparity between the upper and lower classes in both means of life and the rights and privileges of organizational authority. The culture of the poorer strata is impoverished while that of the governing and technocratic elite is securely based on the service of the national ends of power and wealth. Equality of opportunity means an equal chance to leave the less fortunate behind in the personal quest for influence and social position. Thus a meritocratic society is a danger for the other interpretations of the principles of justice but not for the democratic conception. For, as we have just seen, the difference principle transforms the aims of society in fundamental respects. This consequence is even more obvious once we note that we must when necessary take into account the essential primary good of self-respect and the fact that a well-ordered society is a social union of social unions. It follows that the confident sense of their own worth should be sought for the least favored and this limits the forms of hierarchy and the degrees of inequality that justice permits. Thus, for example, resources for education are not to be allotted solely or necessarily mainly according to their return as estimated in productive trained abilities, but also according to their worth in enriching the personal and social life of citizens, including here the less favored. As a society progresses the latter consideration becomes increasingly more important.

THE BASIS OF EQUALITY

We have yet to consider what sorts of beings are owed the guarantees of justice. . . . The natural answer seems to be that it is precisely the moral persons who are entitled to equal justice. Moral persons are distinguished by two features: first they are capable of having (and are assumed to have) a conception of their good (as expressed by a rational plan of life); and second they are capable of having (and assumed to acquire) a sense of justice, a normally effective desire to apply and to act upon the principles of justice, at least to a certain minimum degree. We use the characterization of the persons in the original position to single out the kind of beings to whom the principles chosen apply. After all, the parties are thought of as adopting these criteria to regulate their common institutions and their conduct toward one another; and the description of their nature enters into the reasoning by which these principles are selected. Thus equal justice is owed to those who have the capacity to take part in and to act in accordance with the public understanding of the initial situation. One should observe that moral personality is here defined as a potentiality that is ordinarily realized in due course. It is this potentiality which brings the claims of justice into play. . . .

We see, then, that the capacity for moral personality is a sufficient condition for being entitled to equal justice. Nothing beyond the essential minimum is required. . . .

It should be stressed that the sufficient condition for equal justice, the capacity for moral personality, is not at all stringent. When someone lacks the requisite potentiality either from birth or accident, this is regarded as a defect or deprivation. There is no race or recognized group of human beings that lacks this attribute. Only scattered individuals are without this capacity, or its realization to the minimum degree, and the failure to realize it is the consequence of unjust and impoverished social circumstances, or fortuitous contingencies. Furthermore, while individuals presumably have varying capacities for a sense of justice, this fact is not a reason for depriving those with a lesser capacity of the full protection of justice. Once a certain minimum is met, a person is entitled to equal liberty on a par with everyone else. . . . It is sometimes thought that basic rights and liberties should vary with capacity, but justice as fairness denies this: provided the minimum for moral personality is satisfied, a person is owed all the guarantees of justice.

This account of the basis of equality calls for a few comments. First of all, it may be objected that equality cannot rest on natural attributes. There is no natural feature with respect to which all human beings are equal, that is, which everyone has (or which sufficiently many have) to the same degree. It might appear that if we wish to hold a doctrine of equality, we must interpret it in another way, namely as a purely procedural principle. Thus to say that human beings are equal is to say that none has a claim to preferential treatment in the absence of compelling reasons. The burden of proof favors equality: it defines a procedural presumption that persons are to be treated alike. Departures from equal treatment are in each case to be defended and judged impartially by the same system of principles that hold for all; the essential equality is thought to be equality of consideration.

There are several difficulties with this procedural interpretation. For one thing, it is nothing more than the precept of treating similar cases similarly applied at the highest level, together with an assignment of the burden of proof. Equality of consideration puts no restrictions upon what grounds may be offered to justify inequalities. There is no guarantee of substantive equal treatment, since slave and caste systems (to mention extreme cases) may satisfy this conception. The real assurance of equality lies in the content of the principles of justice and not in these procedural presumptions. The placing of the burden of proof is not sufficient. But further, even if the procedural interpretation imposed some genuine restriction on institutions, there is still the question why we are to follow the procedure in some instances and not others. Surely it applies to creatures who belong to some class, but which one? We still need a natural basis for equality so that this class can be identified.

Moreover, it is not the case that founding equality on natural capacities is incompatible with an egalitarian view. All we have to do is select a range property (as I shall say) and to give equal justice to those meeting its conditions. For example, the property of being in the interior of the unit circle is a range property of points in the plane. All points inside this circle have this property although their coordinates vary within a certain range. And they equally have this property, since no point interior to a circle is more or less interior to it than any other interior point. Now whether there is a suitable range property for singling out the respect in which human beings are to be counted equal is settled by the conception of justice. But the description of the parties in the original position identifies such a property, and the principles of justice assure us that any variations in ability within the range are to be regarded as any other natural asset. There is no obstacle to thinking that a natural capacity constitutes the basis of equality.

Mutual respect is a natural duty due to a moral agent as a being with a sense of justice and a conception of the good. . . . Mutual respect is shown in several ways: in our willingness to see the situation of others from their point of view, from the perspective of their conception of their good; and in our being prepared to give reasons for our actions whenever the interests of others are materially affected.

[T]he public recognition of the two principles gives greater support to men's self-respect and this in turn increases the effectiveness of social cooperation. Both effects are reasons for choosing these principles. It is clearly rational for men to secure their self-respect. A sense of their own worth is necessary if they are to pursue their conception of the good with zest and to delight in its fulfillment. Self-respect is not so much a part of any rational plan of life as the sense that one's plan is worth carrying out. Now our self-respect normally depends upon the respect of others. Unless we feel that our endeavors are honored by them, it is difficult if not impossible for us to maintain the conviction that our ends are worth advancing. Hence for this reason the parties would accept the natural duty of mutual respect which asks them to treat one another civilly and to be willing to explain the grounds of their actions, especially when the claims of others are overruled. Moreover, one may assume that those who respect themselves are more likely to respect each other and conversely. Self-contempt leads to contempt of others and threatens their good as much as envy does. Self-respect is reciprocally self-supporting.

[People need] to be assured by the esteem of their associates. Their self-respect and their confidence in the value of their own system of ends cannot withstand the indifference much less the contempt of others. Everyone benefits then from living in a society where the duty of mutual respect is honored. The cost to self-interest is minor in comparison with the support for the sense of one's own worth.

Chapter 31

WALLACE MATSON

Wallace Matson is Professor of Philosophy, Emeritus, at the University of California, Berkeley. His books include *The Existence of God* (1965), *Sentience* (1976), and *A New History of Philosophy* (2nd ed., 2000).

In the article here reprinted Matson maintains that philosophers such as John Rawls have filched the name Justice from rendering-each-his-due and bestowed it on doling-out-pleasure-experiences-equally-all-around, the doling to be done by philosopher kings. These thinkers either do not perceive or do not care about the incompatibility of pseudo-justice with liberty.

After an account of how justice could arise "from the bottom up" in a bargaining situation not (necessarily) between equals, the author speculates about why pseudo-justice enjoys such prestige among intellectuals, and whether there is any chance of a revival of the genuine article.

FOR FURTHER READING

Bedau, Hugo, ed. *Justice and Equality* (Prentice-Hall, 1971).

Benn, Stanley. "Justice," in *The Encyclopedia of Philosophy* (Macmillan, 1967).

Daniels, Norman, ed. *Reading Rawls* (Basic Books, 1975).

Matson, Wallace. *A New History of Philosophy*, 2 vols. (Harcourt, Brace, 1999).

Nagel, Thomas. *Equality and Partiality* (Oxford University Press, 1991).

Nielsen, Kai. "Radical Egalitarian Justice: Justice as Equality." *Social Theory and Practice*, vol. 5, no. 2, 1979.

Nozick, Robert. *Anarchy, State, and Utopia* (Basic Books, 1974).

Okin, Susan Moller. *Justice, Gender, and the Family* (Basic Books, 1989).

Rawls, John. *A Theory of Justice* (Harvard University Press, 1971).

———. *Political Liberalism* (Columbia University Press, 1993).

Reiman, Jeffrey. *Justice and Modern Moral Philosophy* (Yale University Press, 1990).

Rescher, Nicholas. *Distributive Justice* (Bobbs-Merrill, 1966).

Sandel, Michael. *Liberalism and the Limits of Justice* (Cambridge University Press, 1988).

Sterba, James. *The Demands of Justice* (University of Notre Dame Press, 1980).

———. *How to Make People Just* (Rowman and Littlefield, 1988).

———, ed. *Justice: Alternative Political Perspectives* (Wadsworth, 1980).

Veatch, Robert M. *The Foundations of Justice* (Oxford University Press, 1986).

Walzer, Michael. *Spheres of Justice* (Oxford University Press, 1983).

Justice: A Funeral Oration

The auncient Ciuilians do say justice is a wille perpetuall and constaunt, which gyueth to euery man his right.

—SIR THOMAS ELYOT, 1531

TAX JUSTICE: IT'S IN YOUR INTEREST!

. . . The military budget seems to have replaced human needs as a priority. . . . UC employees have a right to a job and a living wage. . . . To insure this right, AFSCME is asking UC employees to support the *Split Roll Tax Initiative*, which will redistribute the benefits of Proposition 13 among residents and renters, while taking a fair share from commerce. Along with other tax equality measures . . . this will put the state budget back on its feet. . . . PUBLIC EMPLOYEES NEED TAX JUSTICE IN CALIFORNIA!

—FROM A MANIFESTO HANDED OUT IN BERKELEY, 1982

1. THRENODY

Is it any longer possible to talk seriously about justice and rights? Are these words corrupted and debased beyond redemption? There is no need to multiply examples of how anything that any pressure group has the chutzpah to lay claim to forthwith becomes a right, *nemine contradicente*. Nor is this Newspeak restricted to the vulgar. The President of the Pacific Division of the American Philosophical Association has granted permission to misuse words like *rights* and *justice* if you do so in the service of desirable political ends.[1] Our most universally acclaimed theoretician of justice has shown at length that justice is a will perpetual and constant to forcibly take goods from those who have earned them and give them to those who have not[2]; and the leading light of Anglo-American jurisprudence has constructed a "straightforward" argument proving that a citizen's right to equal protection of the laws is fully satisfied if only the bureaucrat denying him or her a public benefit on racial grounds shows "respect and concern" while processing the forms.[3]

Linguistic entropy makes it as futile to try to rehabilitate mutilated words as to put toothpaste back in the tube. The semantic battle has been lost; and with it a lot more than perspicuous speech. From Plato onward ideologues have sought to capture the vocabulary of justice, the paradigm of OK words, and tie it to schemes aiming at doing away with rights and justice. Now they have brought it off. A single generation has witnessed the movement of enlightened thought away from the position that any discrimination in treatment based merely on race is a grievous wrong, all the way to a consensus that forgetting about race and treating people as individuals is proof positive of racism, and people who advocate it should be ostracized and deprived of the protection of the First Amendment. It took the Supreme Court hardly a decade to discover that the Civil Rights Act of 1964, which in the plainest and clearest language ever seen in a statute condemned racial quotas, really encouraged or even mandated them. Scarcely less abrupt has been the transformation of admiration and fostering of excellence into the vice of elitism. The deepest philosophico-legal thinker of the western United States has preached against the immorality of requiring any applicant for any job to possess qualifications for it.[4] At the other end of the country lives another heavyweight moralist who can imagine no worse injustice than paying smart people more than dumb people.[5]

Why then am I writing about justice? What can arguments accomplish anyway? The windmills of

Reprinted from *Social Philosophy and Policy* 1 (1983) by permission of the author.

the *Zeitgeist* ("spirit of the times"—ED.) keep right on turning. I write also about the interpretation of Parmenides (5th century B.C.). The one activity is likely to produce about as much change in the world as the other.

2. A TALE OF THE SOUTH SEAS

The island of Alpha is not on any chart and is claimed by no nation. It is a delightful place with abundant vegetation which when properly cultivated yields delicious groceries. The lagoon abounds in succulent fish. There are plenty of materials for shelter, clothing, whatever you need or desire and know how to make.

A, the sole inhabitant, who arrived on Alpha quite by accident, works a not excessively fatiguing forty-hour week producing all he wants save companionship, and being satisfied, makes no attempt to attract rescuers.

In this situation, Aristotle has told us, no questions of just and unjust can arise. One cannot be unjust to oneself "except metaphorically," and there is no one else for A to be unjust to, or vice versa.

Beta is an island near Alpha but quite unlike it: barren, plagued by vermin. It too has but one inhabitant, B, who also arrived by accident. B lives at the brink of starvation, laboriously scratching the soil to grow the single, foul-tasting, barely edible plant found on the island.

A and B do not communicate nor even know of each other's existence.

The condition of B is pitiable, but there is no more cause for talk of injustice on Beta than on Alpha. Can it be said, however, that the state of affairs consisting of A on Alpha and B on Beta is an unjust state of affairs? A and B are certainly unequal, which condition benefits neither of them, and it has been said that injustice is simply inequalities that are not to the advantage of all. Nevertheless, it would be bizarre to contend that the situation contains injustice. B's condition is unfortunate but not unjust (nor just either). The mere coexistence of A without interaction cannot add a new moral dimension.

So let us add some interaction and see what happens.

There are no materials on Beta for making a boat or raft, and the strait between the islands is shark-infested. So B cannot go to Alpha. And A has no incentive to go to Beta. But now a volcano emerges from the sea, and when it has cooled there is a land bridge making Alpha and Beta one island.

Let us consider the time interval when B can enter the Alpha district but has not actually done so. We have then a single territory containing two inhabitants, one of whom is in possession of fewer goods than the other. Is this a condition of injustice?

The difference is only that now it is feasible to equalize the conditions of A and B whereas previously it was not. If there is injustice it consists in the unequal possessions of A and B and can be remedied by taking from A and giving to B. But then it cannot be the case that the injustice arose when the islands became connected; it must rather have existed previously but only at that moment become remediable. (Murder is murder whether or not it can be punished.) But this would be contrary to our conclusion that no injustice arose from the mere comparison of the two conditions.

None of this will surprise us. We knew that justice is a social concept; so as long as A and B were incommunicado the notion had no application. If we now arrange for them to meet and converse, no injustice can be deemed to have arisen here either. How could it? B is now conscious of being worse off than A, and will no doubt feel envy, will want to share in A's bounty. B may even complain of "unjust fate," but that can only be poetry. The change has been only in knowledge; and the previous absence of injustice did not depend on ignorance.

Various things may happen when B sets foot on Alpha territory. Let us consider some of the possibilities.

Case I. Suppose the Alpha territory is a land of such abundance that it cannot be exploited by A alone; there are resources that A does not need and cannot make use of. It is no injustice if B now appropriates some or all of these goods. Nothing has been taken to which A has established any claim, nor has A been harmed.

But what if A regards B as a threat or nuisance? Would injustice be committed if A chased B out of the area or took even more drastic measures? It is hard to see what the charge could be based on, if A and B have held no converse. On a right to be let alone if one is behaving peaceably? But what if A is a lady and B is a tiger?—a possibility not ruled out by any of our suppositions. Is it not permissible to drive tigers away from one's vicinity, even if in fact the tiger has only peaceable intentions? If so, how is the situation changed if instead of a tiger one is confronted with another human being of unknown intent?

Case II. Zucchini does not grow wild in Alpha; all that there is has been cultivated by A, but there is more of it than A can possibly make use of. Would injustice arise if B should appropriate some of the surplus without A's consent? Hardly, for the surplus does not constitute a good for A, even though he produced it. Whatever happens to it is a matter of indifference as far as A is concerned; and if A is not made any worse off there can be no injustice.

Case III. Is the moral situation altered if the produce with which B absconds is something necessary for A's dinner? Well, again, if B is a tiger, we should not want to say that it is guilty of injustice, however inconvenient its conduct may be for A. And how should it differ if B is human? Both the tiger and the man are hungry, perceive an opportunity to eat, and take it. If they do fight it out, "like animals," no question of justice arises. But if A and B are human (as we shall henceforth assume) they may have an alternative not generally available to the brute creature: they can communicate, talk things over, and reach some settlement of the question "Who gets what?" that is more advantageous for one or the other or both than direct and, perhaps, uncertain combat.

3. INTERMISSION

There are in Alpha two classes of things: those which exist, or exist in altered form, or in the place where they are, because of the labor of A; and those that do not, but would be just as they are even if A had never been there. The first class of things consists of cultivated plants, constructed shelter, utensils, fish hooks, woodpiles, and the like. Call them the Artifacts. It is characteristic of human beings to labor to produce artifacts. The essence of life—any kind of life—consists in doing, acting; production of things is one important kind of doing. This means, in the human case, experiencing a need or at least a desire for something; picturing to oneself the advantage of possessing that thing; making a plan to bring it into existence or into one's possession; and expending effort to that end according to a developed pattern of skill. We speak of this in terms of the Will and its satisfaction. When all goes well we end up having what we want, and sometimes we are better off thereby. Not to be able to carry out one's own projects in this way but to serve only the interests of others, is so far not to live a human life. Extreme deprivation of this kind is slavery.

Most projects are recognized to be more or less chancy. The compassing of material ends may be frustrated by droughts, earthquakes, diseases, wild beasts, etc. Any animal can be viewed as a device for sorting out its dinner and other necessities from an environment in which the constituents occur more or less at random. And the whole process may be got through successfully and then at the last moment the desired product is snatched away, as with the Old Man in Hemingway's story. None of these frustrations is literally immoral. Tigers are not murderers and coyotes are not thieves.

To a certain extent the same attitude may be taken to other human beings, if they are strangers, not in one's group: forces of nature to be coped with as best one can. It is different, however, within the tribe. That is a group within which it is taken for granted that at least some cooperation will be extended.

People may help one another because they are forced to by threats or punishment, but that negates essential humanity. Voluntary assistance must be based on some community of goals.

4. THE TALE CONTINUED

Case IV. Let us now suppose that A and B confer. Let us suppose further that A has not produced any more artifacts than he can himself use and consume, but he has been so skillful and industrious that his production comprises considerably more than he requires for mere survival. Let us refer to the difference between A's total store and what he needs for bare survival as A's quasi-surplus.

This is what A has to bargain with. It seems that he cannot concede more than it to B, for if he does he cannot survive, so he might as well fight. A's aim in negotiating will be to give up as little of the quasi-surplus as possible to B, and to get in exchange for it as much as he can from B.

What can B bargain with? He has no surplus at all; indeed, to make the situation even starker we may assume that the earthquake destroyed Beta so that B is entirely destitute. This would, however, merely increase A's problem, for if no bargain can be struck, B will fight, which we assume A wants to avoid. Let us suppose that B can survive only if ceded 150% of A's quasi-surplus. Does it follow that there must be war to the death? No, fortunately, because if B pitches in and helps, the production of artifacts in Alpha may increase to the point where both A and B can survive. In other words, B can contribute his labor even if he lacks material resources. It turns out, then, that A can cede more than his quasi-surplus as long as the excess is made up by the added effort.

The upshot is that both A and B may be individually better off for making an agreement to share goods and labor than either one would have been if they fought winner-take-all.

Perhaps truce would be a better word than agreement for the arrangement that A and B set up. For the question of course arises, What is to prevent either party from violating the provisions of the pact when he sees fit? And the answer can only be: Nothing. We can expect no more than that each party will abide by the pact as long as it is in his interest to do so. But it was in the interest of both parties to conclude the treaty in the first place; it remains in the interest of each party to see to it that the other one remains in the same situation; and it will not be impossible in general for him to do so. Covenants without the sword are but words, true; but each of our covenantors has and retains his sword.

Even in this simplified situation the particulars of the compact might take indefinitely many different forms, depending on the amount of A's armaments and other resources in relation to B's, their bargaining skills, and their preferences. They might agree to pool their resources (notwithstanding A's initial advantage) and share alike; or erect a fence across the island not henceforth to be crossed by either without the other's permission; or agree that B should go to work for A five days in seven at a fixed wage. Or B might consent to become A's slave. What any such compact is, though, is an acquiescence of wills in the restriction of their own future objects. For A to cede a shovel to B is for A to renounce the satisfaction of any future desire he might have to dig with that particular shovel. B in his turn denies himself liberty to kill, disable, or maim A.

The transaction is fraught with momentous consequences. *First*, there are now obligations—bonds—between A and B; to this extent at least they form a community. They have set up rules, and they ought to abide by them. This ought, to be sure, is a prudential ought: the sanction, the consequence of nonconformity, is that the truce will be called off, and the parties will again be in danger of physical attack by each other, which they both want to avoid. To avoid resumption of war over minor infractions of the truce conditions, they may agree on methods of restitution. There will be problems about determining when a rule has been violated, as there are in tennis without an umpire, but they need not be insurmountable.

Second, A and B have invented property, at least if there are any clauses in the treaty specifying that any artifacts or other objects, or parcels of land, are to be off limits to one party without the consent of the other. Ownership is acknowledged, exclusive control of use or access.

But was there not already property before the truce? What about the artifacts A had labored to produce? Were not they, at least, already his?

John Locke's argument is that a man owns his own body; therefore he owns the labor of his body; therefore whatever he "mixes" that labor with becomes *pro tanto* an extension of his body; therefore he owns it too. The argument gets off to a bad start: "I own my own body" may look like a truism but it hardly is. It is a question of fact whether one has acknowledged, exclusive control of the use of one's body, and there are people for whom the answer is No. No doubt that is not as it should be; but we are talking of how things are. And while it is true that before B appeared on the scene A had exclusive control of the use of his own body, the exclusive control was not acknowledged. It takes two to make property.

When A and B draw up their treaty there is no limitation in principle to what they may agree to be the property of one and of the other, or to be held in common or left subject to subsequent claim. There is nothing about the axe that A has laboriously constructed from scratch that makes it his property, or property at all: no more than a tree that he plans to cut down, perhaps, some time next year and saw into boards. Nevertheless, there is something more than sentiment making the relation between a man and that with which he has "mixed his labor" particularly intimate and fit to be legitimized, as it were, by acknowledgment of ownership. Labor need not be unpleasant always, but it is generally engaged in not for its own sake but because some comprehensive plan requires it; the agent envisages some end, the production of something, the enjoyment of which is viewed a good in itself; he plans how to get it; and realizing that work is indispensable, he works.

To deprive a man of some good thing that he got by luck, without effort, is indeed to frustrate him; but to take away the product of his labor is to do double damage. He has undergone the hardship of toil, and in vain. He would not have put up with the drudgery if he had known of the outcome in advance. So it is impossible to suppose that anyone would voluntarily forgo the enjoyment—which means the ownership—of what he has mixed his labor with, unless in exchange for some other good perceived as of at least equivalent value. This means that in the terms of the truce between A and B, possession of their respective artifacts will be guaranteed to them unless they receive compensation. And since A and B begin their negotiations with each in physical possession of his artifacts, it is, to be sure, as if they had property to begin with. Moreover, this concern that each has for what he produces shapes the form that their agreement will take. It is to the continuing interest of each that each should keep on producing things. Therefore the truce will contain provisions for maintaining production, which must recognize and respect the producer's ownership of his product or allow compensation if it is to be taken from him; otherwise there could remain no motive to keep it going, unless sheer fear, which is incompatible with the primary aim of the agreement.

And so, *third* and finally, we see in this agreement the genesis of rights and justice. The truce once agreed to will remain in force only as long as both parties find its continuance to their advantage. Now, some truces are made for stipulated, definite periods of time, but not this one, since the motive for making it is to avoid combat altogether. Hence it has no expiration date and cannot be abrogated by mutual consent. Breaking it is a unilateral act of war and will provoke the indignation of the other party, who was willing to continue it and was living up to it. This is enough to generate the use of moral language, supposing it has not up to now been current. One has a *right* to have the terms adhered to; failure to observe the terms on which one has agreed is *injustice*. Even if derelictions in this regard are initially only violations of a prudential ought, they are very serious, as tending to bring about the dissolution of community. Moreover the prudence they offend against is primarily not that of the agent himself but of his fellow citizen; in consequence of which objections are bound to take on a moral tone.

Thomas Hobbes held that to enter into society is to give up at least some rights, whereas I am claiming that there are no rights outside community. This is perhaps a verbal point, but hardly of no consequence. Hobbes's Right of Nature, an absolute "right to all things," is anomalous in that it has no correlative duty. In the state of nature I have the right to appropriate your shovel or hit you over the head, but that does not mean that you have any duty to submit or to refrain from doing the same to me. The sense of "right" in this context, then, seems to be only "not subject to moral censure," or as a hockey player not in the penalty box has a right to pass the puck. But this is at least a misleading way of speaking; the thought is more straightforwardly conveyed simply by saying that before any agreements have been made, questions of right and wrong in the moral sense cannot arise.

The objection might be raised that this truce cannot be the origin of justice and rights, for it might be asked of the truce itself, Is it a just agreement? Does it not, or could it not, infringe on the rights of a party?

But it is a logical point about justice that injustice cannot be suffered voluntarily, as Aristotle saw. And the truce is not only concluded but maintained voluntarily.

This reply may be thought unsatisfactory on the ground that the parties are not equal in their bargaining positions. Hence one (A) may get the better of the bargain, i.e. be in a better position after concluding it than the other party (B). Indeed, as I admitted, one form the agreement might take would be for B to make himself A's slave. But this or any other inequitable arrangement would be manifestly unjust. And it is not only absurd but morally repugnant to suggest that a slave would be behaving unjustly, violating his master's rights, if he subsequently rebelled (broke the truce). Furthermore, no such desperate engagement could be voluntarily undertaken.

I answer: First, the view that any inequality is *ipso facto* unjust is mere dogma. It is certainly not self-evidently true, for *prima facie* it is not unjust to pay travel money and honoraria to learned persons who participate in enlightening conferences on justice. The objection based on slavery is more serious. I do not assert with complete confidence that a person might voluntarily agree to become a slave. In practice there are, of course, degrees of slavery; but I suppose the concept is of one whose will is entirely subordinate to another's, one who never makes plans of his own and carries them out. Galley slavery must approximate this condition. If that is so, then the question whether one can voluntarily become a slave seems to be the same as whether the will can voluntarily negate itself permanently. If as I maintain the essence of life is the exertion of will, then the slave is as good as dead.

But not quite. Where there is life there is hope. Probably the only circumstances in which one would choose slavery would be where the only alternative was death. And a choice's being between unpleasant alternatives does not make it no choice. If the terms of our truce involve my becoming your slave, then we form a community within which you have a right to all my services and I have no right to pursue any interest of mine independent of yours; and *within that community* I act unjustly if I do anything for myself. But let us not forget that according to the view being presented I may choose at any time to abrogate the truce and bring the community to an end. In practice, then, a community consisting of one master and one slave is likely to be unstable, the slave always on the lookout for the opportune moment to get out of that status. In other words, it is a sort of degenerate case of community, hardly distinguishable from a lull in a state of war.

5. MORALS OF THE STORY

A novelist would tell the tale differently, but to much the same effect. Actual people in this sort of situation, if not murderously inclined or forced by extreme scarcity to eliminate competition, will come to some agreement, perhaps tacit, of the form "I'll let you alone if you let me alone; and I'll help you out from time to time if you reciprocate." Appropriation by one of things the other had made, or even just found, would be regarded as stealing and if serious would lead to conflict.

That is to say, they would establish a community and a system of justice based on agreement. This can be called justice "from the bottom up": it is not imposed on them by any superior force, for there isn't any. It comes from their mutual apprehension of necessary conditions for human beings, each with his own interests and plans, to dwell in close proximity without fighting. It can fittingly be called natural, being a direct consequence of what human life is about, the expression of human capabilities in achieving planned goals in those universal and unavoidable circumstances of existence of a semigregarious species.

However, there is, as we have seen, no constraint on the particular form of the truce. It must represent what the parties to it, not in some hypothetical and abstract condition but in concrete circustances of their existence, can agree on as preferable to direct physical confrontation. In particular it does not presuppose equality of power in the bargaining situation, or of talents or industry, or of luck, or of the distribution of goods that result, or of anything except that all parties have equal rights to insist on the equal observance of those clauses of the treaty in which their particular interests are safeguarded. Nevertheless, natural justice if it does not (necessarily) start from an initial position of equality and does not guarantee eventual achievement of it, yet facilitates betterment of the individual's position through effort. That is what its main purpose is: to make it possible for plans to be carried out without arbitrary interference and frustration by fellow members of the community. Even in our story, destitute B will probably be able to come to terms with prosperous A that will make it possible for him through hard work to approach A's level of luxurious consumption. Remember: the harsher the terms A attempts to impose on B, the greater danger he runs of B's abrogating the truce.

The story is not a myth of the origin of government; it is Lockean, not Hobbist. There is no Sovereign set up to whom all owe deference and who has a monopoly of power wherewith to coerce the intractable; there are only the individuals with whatever resources they happen to command. As Locke noted, such an arrangement will be attended with certain inconveniences showing, for example, a need for impartial umpires and arbitrators. How it might come about (after a few more castaways had landed) that a central authority would be set up, and what its functions would or should be, is another topic. But the institutions and conceptions of right and justice would antedate the formation of such an authority, the operations of which would be liable to criticism from the standpoint of justice. So much seems incontrovertible; the Hobbesian contention to the contrary is paradoxical and carries no conviction.

Lest this analysis be regarded as excessively hardboiled, note that the conception of justice as observance of rules agreed on from the motive of self-interest by no means precludes the existence and importance in the community of interactions in which the requirements of justice are voluntarily held in abeyance: love and charity. Indeed it is what makes them possible: one cannot simultaneously make love and war.

Finally we observe that nothing precludes the extension of the truce to later arrivals. The conditions may have to be modified for their benefit; the arrival of a third castaway would so perturb the relations of A and B that there might have to be a new constitutional convention, as it were. But not for every new immigrant; as population grows we may expect the weight of existing agreement to impose itself on latecomers in a take-it-or-leave-it fashion.

And what is the bearing of this story and its morals on actual human affairs? This: We have been examining the kinds of relations other than out-and-out no-holds-barred conflict that can subsist between human beings; we have concluded that peace might be based on agreement; that the agreement cannot be expected to outlast its advantageousness to all parties; that the terms of agreement define what justice is, and what the rights of the parties are, within the community of those in agreement—in particular and most importantly it creates the rights of property. The normative character of the rights so specified is derived from the fact—so we have contended—that persons wishing each to attain his own goals in the context of association with other persons, would agree to them.

However, we have been assuming that human plans to achieve particular separate goals sometimes lead to conflict; and that conflict if serious will be settled by force unless the rivals can arrive at some compromise. But is it the case that human animals are necessarily motivated by individual "selfish" interests? Is it not possible—maybe sometimes actual—that they could as it were submerge their own interests into one big interest, the general welfare, the pursuit of which would involve only peaceful cooperation?

6. SOUTH SEAS TALE II

B, oppressed by the harsh terms of the truce with A but impotent to revolt, has thought of a way out. Every week he spends the one afternoon he has to himself in collecting branches and vines from the little forest plot that A has not claimed. At last one day, having secretly made a raft, he scratches in the sand an insulting note to A and paddles off into the open sea.

After many hardships he struggles onto the shore of another island. From between the palms a majestic bearded figure appears.

Alas, B thinks to himself, here we go again. More truce terms!

But no. "Welcome to Gamma, O stranger" the figure intones in a kindly voice. "I am G. You must be hungry and thirsty. Won't you join us for dinner?"

At the groaning board B is introduced to the other islanders: F, an old man confined to a wheelchair; H, a mature and handsome woman; J, a lad of seventeen or so; and two children, K and L.

Over the coffee and liqueurs B deems the time opportune for discussing their future arrangements. "I'm grateful for your tacit temporary truce," he begins, "and hope you can make it permanent."

"Truce? What ever do you mean?"

"Why, the usual—I won't try to kill you as long as you don't—"

Consternation and alarm among the Gammanians. H grasps K and L protectively in her arms. Desperately trying to scurry out of the way, F overturns his wheelchair. J grabs a silver candlestick and advances menacingly on B but is restrained by G, who at last restores a modicum of calm.

B then explains how things are done on Alpha. The Gammanians weep at the sad tale. H comforts him that he has arrived finally in a civilized community.

"But how can you get along without a truce?" B is still puzzled. "Don't you have your individual interests and goals, and don't you have to have some means of reconciling the conflicts to which they inevitably give rise?"

"Well," the youthful J begins to reply, "Sometimes I—"

But G cuts him off. "Not at all. We have only one goal, which is the good life for us all. Each of us helps to achieve it in any way that he or she can, and each gets all the help he or she needs from all the rest. From each according to his ability; to each according to his need."

"Just like one big happy family," B muses, dimly recalling childhood scenes.

"Of course," says G. "That's what we are—a family!"

"But what happens if you have different ideas about what your needs are?"

A suggestion of a frown appears on J's face, and he seems to exchange a significant glance with H; but G replies: "Oh, sometimes there is some per-plexity about that, but when there is, we handle it democratically."

"You mean, you have a discussion and then vote on the different proposals?"

"Not exactly," says G. "I listen to what everybody has to say, and then I explain what the wise things to do is. As everybody here is rational, they all concur, and that's that.—From now on, we all want you to feel that you are one of the family.—You must be tired. H will make your bed in the dormitory. Tomorrow after breakfast J will show you the woodpile and get you started—I take it you know something about woodchopping?—"

And so they lived happily ever after.

7. ANOTHER BATCH OF MORALS

Within the family—I mean the "traditional" family as found (say) in the novels of Jane Austen and Samuel Butler—there is little concern for justice in the sense of giving each member his or her rights. Ordinarily there is one "breadwinner," the father, who is the sole or at least principal source of income, most of which is disbursed for the common benefit of all. Where it is used to buy things for individuals, the principle of distribution is need not merit; the snaggle-toothed daughter must have her orthodontia before the musical prodigy acquires a Steinway. And if the old folks and infants are helpless and only a drain on resources, their needs must nevertheless be provided. Competitiveness plays no part, or at least it is deplored when it does. This is called Love.

Most philosophers now writing experienced family life more or less along these lines when they were young, or at least were able to view it close up. And it may seem a more satisfactory way to order relations between people than "justice" with its stern judgments and devil-take-the-hindmost attitude. The transition from the warm nurturing environment of the family to the cold and impersonal rat-race in which the independent individual is caught up may be as traumatic as birth itself. That is doubtless one reason why the family is preferred by so many to the treaty as the proper model for human relationships.

Another is that it is inherently equalitarian. Within the ideal family all members are equal in a number of respects. There is no distinction of rich and poor; if one member has more expended on him, it is not so that he can enjoy a higher "standard of living." One does not have higher status than another or receive more deference. (Again, this is the ideal; but it is why we feel that something is wrong in the household where Cinderella lives.) Parents are careful to treat all their children fairly, which means dividing up benefits equally unless one has greater need than another; the notion of "earning" hardly enters except in comparatively trivial ways mostly concerned with putative training for the rat-race to come; and even here the experts tend to deprecate it. Granted that intrafamilial conflicts, notably sibling rivalry, have always occurred, they are—or used to be—considered superficial and due to immaturity. Universal brotherhood has been taken as synonymous with the elimination of human conflicts.

"Why can't the whole human race, or at least the whole nation, be like that?" the philosopher asks, and so do the plain man and woman. The plain man is likely to answer, "Because family relations are based on affection, which won't stretch that far." So do some philosophers, e.g. Hobbes in commenting on the perpetual state of war "in many places of *America*, except the government of small Families, the concord whereof dependeth on naturall lust".[6] But many others, of whom the first and greatest was Plato, have maintained that the project is not impossible; all that is needed is a salutary revision of education and institutional arrangements, whereupon paternal, maternal, filial, fraternal, and sororal affection will become the cement binding together a completely unified and, therefore, happy social order in which everyone cares for everyone else.

These philosophers base their optimism on the belief that so-called human nature is all nurture, there is no limit to how outlooks and motivations can be altered by training. This is held as a dogma by many social thinkers, like creationism among fundamentalists. But also like creationism, it is an empirical question whether it is true. A lot of evidence is in, all of it adverse: the utter failure of every attempt whether on a large scale or small, to produce the requisite changes (with the doubtful and minor exception of Israeli kibbutzim). The explanation of this dismal history is provided by the science of sociobiology. But is it altogether regrettable that human beings cannot be improved to fill the bill? If we scrutinize the family model more closely we may find that it has less pleasant aspects.

If there is no conflict within the ideal family, it is because there is only one will, or only one that counts: father's. Husband and wife being "one flesh," the woman's will is held to coincide with her man's. ("Man's happiness is: I will. Woman's happiness is: He wills."—Nietzsche.) The children are under tutelage, their wills are being formed, and are not to be regarded as competent in their own right. When in adolescence they begin to develop wills of their own and assert them, that is the well-known revolt against parental authority and the first step in exit from the familial hearth.

The totalitarian implications, when the family is held up as a model for emulation by the larger community, are obvious. If they are not seen immediately it is because within the family the will of the father is (sometimes) not regarded as merely the expression of the de facto dominant family member, but as the voice of Reason. "Father knows best." His macrocosmic analogue, then, is not looked upon as a vulgar tyrant but as the Philosopher King. And all his subjects, that is, all the children of the Philosopher Father's extended family, agree entirely with him insofar as they are rational—and that is all that matters, of course. Who wants to be irrational? Nevertheless, there is no getting around the fact that the expanded family, unlike the microcosm, must maintain its "children" in tutelage not for fifteen or twenty years but for all their lives. They cannot be allowed to grow up; all their important decisions must be made for them from above.

This has not bothered philosophers from Plato to Pol Pot who saw themselves as the loving fathers. It is, however, a stumbling block to Professor John Rawls (to his credit), and accounts for some incoherencies in his philosophy, as I shall explain presently.

Now, what will the conception of justice be according to the family model?

The short answer to this question is that there will be no such conception, although the word will be retained for propaganda effect. As we saw, there is little use for a notion of justice within the real family; and this will carry over. However, let us go the long way around to this conclusion.

The first thing to notice is that the adjective in the phrase "distributive justice" now receives emphasis. On the agreement model of justice the question of *distributing* anything hardly arises. The main idea of justice from the bottom up is that people are to keep what they produce unless they voluntarily exchange it for what others have made. It is no part of the agreement model that there will be a Master Distributor at all, distinct from the producers. That is one reason for calling it justice from the bottom up.

It is otherwise with the family model. In the (real) family there is a divorce between production and acquisition on the one hand and distribution on the other. With unimportant exceptions property is held in common; where all can make use of it they do; where they cannot it is distributed (by Father, or at least according to his will) without special consideration for who in particular made, earned, or acquired it. The *fundamentum distributionis* being need, things will be thought of as rightly distributed when they go to the neediest; or if they are such that one member's need for them is no greater than another's, when the distribution is fair, that is, equal.

Second, fathers are *ex officio* utilitarians. The loving father's aim is that all his dependents should be happy, and equally so. He is a "good provider" and what he provides is satisfactions. That does not mean of course that he caters to every whim; he does not "spoil" his dependents. He may on occasion be judgmental and punishing, but it is for their own good; when he birches the unruly offspring it really does hurt him more than the wailing lad. If family members are in trouble, he is automatically on their side and will do all he can to get them out of it regardless of whether it is "their own fault."

Magnified to the scale of society this concern becomes what in contemporary jargon is called "compassion." Anyone who is hard up for whatever reason is to have his or her needs met at the expense of all who are not hard up. And so in this regard the paternalistic society will equate justice with compassion (a term which itself has undergone a curious transformation—one hardly tends to picture sleek politicians and bureaucrats as "suffering with" the objects of their solicitude). It is held that need entails the right to its fulfillment.

Natural justice on the other hand has no conceptual connection to utility, only a factual one. The idea of justice is that people should get what they deserve, what they have earned, and to find out what fits this specification it is not relevant to calculate the consequences of the award. But since the prospect of enjoying the fruits of one's labors is by and large the most potent incentive to labor, and labor by and large is what produces goods that satisfy desires, the observance of natural justice promotes utility demonstrably better for all concerned than "compassionate" redistribution.

Third, the characteristic concern of the father for his dependents is positive in the sense that it is not enough for him to keep them from harm, he must actively promote their welfare. Writ large, this means that the Philosopher King has not discharged his duty to his subjects when he has prevented or redressed wrongdoing among them; he must improve them, make them positively better off than they were, even if he knows that in so doing some inconveniences are regrettably bound to occur. Thus Dr. Goebbels mused:

> There can be no peace in Europe until the last Jews are eliminated from the continent.
>
> That, of course, raises a large number of exceedingly delicate questions. What is to be done with the half-Jews? What with those related to Jews? In-laws of Jews? Persons married to Jews? Evidently we still have quite a lot to do and undoubtedly a multitude of personal tragedies will ensue within the framework of the solution of this problem. But that is unavoidable. . . . We are doing a good work in proceeding radically and consistently. The task we are assuming today will be an advantage and a boon to our descendants.[7]

In contrast, the partisan of natural justice does not suppose that the reign of justice and the millennium are necessarily one and the same thing. Justice is no doubt desirable for its own sake, but its main value is instrumental: it is one important condition for the productive release of human energy. And in a way the negative is primary: all that the champion of justice is called upon to do is to eliminate *in*justice; once that has been done he can rest and allow those whom he has liberated from its shadow to go about the task of making a better world.

In sum: Every society must have some recognized rules for deciding questions of ownership. In a social structure based on agreement the rules will be those of natural justice, justice from the bottom up, providing for initial ownership and subsequent voluntary exchange of the products of one's own labor. In a paternalistic society, on the other hand, such considerations will not be decisive or paid much attention. The term "justice" will nevertheless be retained on account of its favorable associations to refer to the principles observed by the persons who have the power, authority, and wisdom to redistribute the goods taken from the producers and put into a common pot. These principles will emphasize the satisfaction of needs, the most urgent getting the highest priority. Where needs are equal, distribution will be equal as far as possible. Moreover the distribution is to be handled in such a way that a harmonious social pattern is produced, a "better world." This last principle applies especially to the distribution of intangibles such as status. A person will be said to have a "right" to X if and only if the distribution pattern assigns X to that person.

This is artificial justice or justice from the top down.

8. ILLUSTRATION: AFFIRMATIVE ACTION

Philosophy is sometimes said to have no practical consequences. If so, the theory of justice is not philosophy, for whether one holds one view or another of justice makes an enormous difference in practice. As an example, let us consider the ways in which justice from the bottom up and from the top down deal with the problem of racial discrimination in employment.

First, justice from the bottom up:

In a society recognizing this norm, citizens may make whatever agreements they choose, for any reason or none, as long as they do not infringe on the rights of other citizens. So if I am a Ruritanian widgetmaker, a manufacturer of widgets who detests Ruritanians may legitimately refuse to hire me. And if there are many more of his sort, we Ruritanian widgetmakers will be at a disadvantage, we will be discriminated against just because we are Ruritanians, and that is bad. But happily the problem will solve itself. We will offer our services to non-Ruritanophobe entrepreneurs for wages lower than the bigots must pay; and if we really are just as good workers, our unbiased employers will be put at a competitive advantage over the prejudiced ones. In the not very long run, then, the gap between Ruritanian and non-Ruritanian wage levels will disappear. And in the somewhat longer run the very idea of this sort of discrimination will begin to look silly, and we will be welcomed as fellow club members and sons-in-law by the former meanies. At any rate this is the pattern that has hitherto manifested itself time and again in the United States. It is well to note in this connection that slavery in the Southern states was, and South African apartheid is, imposed by government edict, i.e. they are interferences with freedom of contract.

Justice from the top down takes a different approach. Everybody is equal to everybody else (dogma), therefore, Ruritanians are just as good at making widgets as anyone else (non sequitur); therefore, if Ruritanian representation in the widget industry is not equal to the statistical expectation, it must be the work of prejudice (non sequitur), which if sincerely denied must be an unconscious aversion (absurdity). This is sin, which must be put down by force, viz. the imposition of a pro-Ruritanian quota (called something else) on widgetmakers. This will, of course, have two effects: it will disrupt the widget industry, already reeling from Japanese competition; and it will exacerbate resentment against Ruritanians.

9. SOME PARADOXES

The derivation of some main tenets of contemporary liberal (another word-corpse) opinion from the family model will no doubt strike some people as absurd, on the ground that liberals hold the old-fashioned family to be a pernicious institution which must be abolished or at least drastically overhauled. But hostility of derivative to original is hardly unheard of. Christianity with its anti-Semitism is after all in origin a Jewish sect. Nazism was a kind of socialism. And no one can deny that Plato's Republic is paternalistic; yet Plato was the first to propose the abolition of the family in order to eliminate emotional competition with his extended political family. Totalitarian liberalism finds no embarrassment in this.

It is otherwise, however, with John Rawls. The celebrated Difference Principle, that "social and economic inequalities are to be arranged so that they are . . . to the greatest benefit of the least advantaged," and its elaboration are all easily deducible from the family model. But we must not forget that there is another Rawlsian Principle of Justice, that of equal liberties—"each person is to have an equal right to the most extensive basic liberty compatible with a similar liberty for others"—which comes first and is required to be satisfied before one even starts thinking about fulfilling the Difference Principle. The sincerity of Rawls's advocacy of liberty, at least political liberty, and his rejection of a constitution where the Philosopher King runs everything, cannot be called in question. And that is why Rawls bases his philosophy on consent of self-interested parties; as we have seen, that is what generates a free society. But Rawls hedges his commitment. The personages behind the veil of ignorance are deprived of all flesh and blood, what is left being only the abstract Voice of Reason, which might as well be a single Rational Person wishing equal happiness for all—which as we have also seen is central to the paternalistic model.

Rawls's theory thus turns out, unsurprisingly, to be a confection of incompatible elements. The principle of equal liberties is bottom-up, but the difference principle is top-down. It would be humanly impossible to instantiate both principles simultaneously: the redistribution required by the second can only be brought about by force, thereby contravening the equal liberties. Rawls like many thinkers of today has failed to see what was so clear to Locke and his contemporaries, that without property rights there can be no rights at all. For government, not being producer of anything, has to be supported out of citizens' property. So if government has complete control of property there can be no limit on its power. In particular, as the economist Milton Friedman has emphasized, the dissenter from official policy has no base of operations or even of livelihood.

Perhaps the blindness of Rawls and so many others to this point, so obvious both in theory and in practice, results from their having convinced themselves that if ever *they* were in power, of course *they* would never abuse their position by clobbering the opposition, but would behave as exemplary liberals.

10. IN AETERNAM?

We have compared two conceptions that claim the name justice.

One is that of rendering every man his due. A man's due is what he has acquired by his own efforts and not taken from some other man without consent. A community in which this conception is realized will be one in which the members agree not to interfere in the legitimate endeavors of each other to achieve their individual goals, and to help each other to the extent that the conditions for doing so are mutually satisfactory. These agreements obtain at the level of the individual citizens, for which reason I call this conception justice from the bottom up. ("Up": there may develop a hierarchical arrangement with those at the top having special duties of enforcing the agreements; but if so, the decision concerning which agreements to enforce will not originate with them.) Such a community will be one giving the freest possible rein to all its members to develop their particular capacities and use them to carry out their plans for their own betterment. If this activity is The Good for Man (and I hold with the Philosopher that it is), then it is appropriate to call the associated conception of justice natural.

The other conception holds justice to be the satisfaction of needs so as to bring everyone as far as possible onto the same plateau of pleasurable experience. The view of human life underlying it is that life consists of two separable phases, production and consumption; the consumption phase is where The Good lies; there is ultimately no reason why any individual should have any more or less of this Good than any other individual; and the problem of how to secure the requisite production is merely technical. Society based on this conception must be structured as a hierarchy of authority, in order to solve the problem of production and to administer justice, i.e. to adjust the satisfaction quanta. Thus I have called this justice from the top down (though of course I don't think it is really justice at all).

Justice from the top down as I have described it does not sound attractive. I have tried to account for the fact that, nevertheless, it commands the enthusiastic support of so many clever men and women and is everywhere on the march by showing its emotional basis in the structure of the family, an institution that has been felt to be, at its best, a warm, conflict-free, loving refuge from fear and anxiety. Many people do not really *want* to grow up, and when they do they yearn for a return to blissful dependence in the family or even in the stage of development previous to that. I do not think it can be controverted that this is part of the explanation for the popularity of top-down justice; but nor can it be the whole, for such a complex phenomenon must be due to many factors. Among them are genuine compassion for the unfortunate and altruistic desire to help them; fantasies of omnipotence, to which powerless academic intellectuals are exceptionally liable; and envy. What the proportions are, is anybody's guess.

As there is no hope of lessening the influence of these emotions in human affairs, the triumph of the top-down cannot be stemmed unless there are yet more powerful emotions to pit against them. What might they be? I can think of three possibilities: the desire that everyone has that he himself should be given his due, and the concomitant outrage, with which more and more people are becoming acquainted, when the top-down authority denies it; revulsion witnessing the actual, practical effects of top-down justice, e.g. in Cambodia; and finally the life force itself, Spinoza's *conatus*, the endeavor of each thing to persevere in its being, and not (except in parasites) by sucking forever but by getting proper solid nourishment. I *hope* these are strong enough to prevail and show this funeral oration to have been premature: Justice is not dead, only mugged by intellectual hoods.

Notes

1. Joel Feinberg, *Rights, Justice, and the Bounds of Liberty* (Princeton: Princeton University Press, 1980), 141, 153. I am indebted to Max Hocutt for this reference.
2. John Rawls, *A Theory of Justice* (Cambridge, MA: Harvard University Press, 1971), 277–280 *et passim.*
3. Ronald Dworkin, *Taking Rights Seriously* (Cambridge: Harvard University Press, 1977), 227–229.
4. Richard Wasserstrom, "A Defense of Programs of Preferential Treatment," in Vincent Barry, ed., *Applying Ethics* (Belmont, CA: Wadsworth, 1982), 332 f.
5. Thomas Nagel, *Mortal Questions* (New Rochelle, N.Y: Cambridge University Press, 1979), 99 f.
6. *Leviathan*, Chapter 13.
7. *The Goebbels Diaries*, ed. and trans. Louis P. Lochner (Westport, CT: Greenwood, 1971), 135 (March 7, 1942).

PART II

CONTEMPORARY CONTINENTAL AND POSTMODERN PHILOSOPHY

Chapter 32

EDMUND HUSSERL

Edmund Husserl (1859–1938) was born in Moravia (now the Czech Republic). After attending the University of Leipzig where he studied mathematics and science, he went to Vienna to study under Franz Brentano, who awakened his thought in philosophical psychology. Brentano held that a basic form of consciousness was *intentionality*. All thought and desire is *about* something. One never just thinks or desires but thinks or desires something, even though the object may be vague and amorphous. Husserl developed Brentano's ideas, centering his studies on the nature or *phenomenology* of consciousness. He is considered the father of phenomenology, the basic ideas of which are outlined in the selection that follows.

In 1916 he became a professor at the University of Freiburg, Germany, where he remained until his retirement in 1929. During the last five years of his life he was barred from public activities because of his Jewish ancestry.

In our selection from *Ideas: General Introduction to Pure Phenomenology* (1913) Husserl focuses on his notion of phenomenological (or *eidetic*) reduction: all acts must be reduced to an essence of *eidos* (essential idea). The perceiver must perform an *epoche*, that is, suspend judgment on the existence of the objects of consciousness. For example, I should not focus on whether the computer before me really exists but on the essential features of the experience itself. He describes this as "bracketing" the experience. For Husserl I am neither a thinking substance (as Descartes thought), nor a bundle of perceptions (as Hume thought), nor an embodied soul (as Plato thought), but a pure transcendental ego, a consciousness that cannot be bracketed, but transcends its intentional object.

The main criticism of Husserl's program is that it entails solipsism, the idea that the only thing that really exists is the self or ego—all else being uncertain. Husserl tried to answer this objection by explaining how one transcendental ego can experience other such egos.

FOR FURTHER READING

Dreyfus, Hubert, ed. *Husserl, Intentionality and Cognitive Science* (MIT Press, 1982).

Husserl, Edmund. *Ideas: General Introduction to Pure Phenomenology*, tr. W. R. Gibson (Allen & Unwin, 1931).

Kockelman, Joseph. *Edmund Husserl's Phenomenology* (Humanities Press, 1978).

Kolakowski, Leszek. *Husserl and the Search for Certitude* (University of Chicago Press, 1987).

Solomon, Robert, ed. *Phenomenology and Existentialism* (Harper & Row, 1972).

Speigelberg, Herbert. *The Phenomenological Movement*, 2 vol. (Martinus Nijhoff, 1960).

Stapleton, Timothy J. *Husserl and Heidegger* (SUNY Press, 1983).

Ideas: General Introduction to Pure Phenomenology

THE THESIS OF THE NATURAL STANDPOINT AND ITS SUSPENSION

The Word of the Natural Standpoint: I and My World About Me

Our first outlook upon life is that of natural human beings, imagining, judging, feeling, willing, "*from the natural standpoint.*" Let us make clear to ourselves what this means in the form of simple meditations which we can best carry on in the first person.

I am aware of a world, spread out in space endlessly, and in time becoming and become, without end. I am aware of it, that means, first of all, I discover it immediately, intuitively, I experience it. Through sight, touch, hearing, etc., in the different ways of sensory perception, corporeal things somehow spatially distributed are *for me simply there*, in verbal or figurative sense "present," whether or not I pay them special attention by busying myself with them, considering, thinking, feeling, willing. Animal beings also, perhaps men, are immediately there for me; I look up, I see them, I hear them coming towards me, I grasp them by the hand; speaking with them, I understand immediately what they are sensing and thinking, the feelings that stir them, what they wish or will. They too are present as realities in my field of intuition, even when I pay them no attention. But it is not necessary that they and other objects likewise should be present precisely in my *field of perception*. For me real objects are there, definite, more or less familiar, agreeing with what is actually perceived without being themselves perceived or even intuitively present. I can let my attention wander from the writing-table I have just seen and observed, through the unseen portions of the room behind my back to the verandah, into the garden, to the children in the summer-house, and so forth, to all the objects concerning which I precisely "know" that they are there and yonder in my immediate co-perceived surroundings—a knowledge which has nothing of conceptual thinking in it, and first changes into clear intuiting with the bestowing of attention, and even then only partially and for the most part very imperfectly.

But not even with the added reach of this intuitively clear or dark, distinct or indistinct *co-present* margin, which forms a continuous ring around the actual field of perception, does that world exhaust itself which in every waking moment is in some conscious measure "present" before me. It reaches rather in a fixed order of being the limitless beyond. What is actually perceived, and what is more or less clearly co-present and determinate (to some extent at least), is partly pervaded, partly girt about with a *dimly apprehended depth or fringe of indeterminate reality*. I can pierce it with rays from the illuminating focus of attention with varying success. Determining representations, dim at first, then livelier, fetch me something out, a chain of such recollections takes shape, the circle of determinacy extends ever farther, and eventually so far that the connexion with the actual field of perception as the *immediate* environment is established. But in general the issue is a different one: an empty mist of dim indeterminacy gets studded over with intuitive possibilities or presumptions, and only the "form" of the world as "world" is foretokened. Moreover, the zone of indeterminacy is infinite. The misty horizon that can never be completely outlined remains necessarily there.

As it is with the world in its ordered being as a spatial present—the aspect I have so far been considering—so likewise is it with the world in respect to its *ordered being in the succession of time*. This world now present to me, and in every waking "now" obviously so, has its temporal horizon, infinite in both directions, its known and unknown, its intimately alive and its unalive past and future. Moving freely within the moment of experience which brings what is present into my intuitional grasp, I can follow up these connexions of the reality which immediately surrounds me. I can shift my standpoint in space and time, look this way and that, turn temporally forwards and backwards; I can provide for myself constantly new and more or less clear and meaningful perceptions and representations, and images also more or less clear, in which I make intuitable to myself whatever can possibly exist really or supposedly in the steadfast order of space and time.

In this way, when consciously awake, I find myself at all times, and without my ever being able to change this, set in relation to a world which, through its constant changes, remains one and ever the same. It is continually "present" for me, and I myself am a member of it. Therefore this world is not there for me as a mere *world of facts and affairs*, but, with the same immediacy, as a *world of values, a world of goods*, a *practical world*. Without further effort on my part I find the things before me furnished not only with the qualities that befit their positive nature, but with value-characters such as beautiful or ugly, agreeable or disagreeable, pleasant or unpleasant, and so forth. Things in their immediacy stand there as objects to be used, the "table" with its "books," the "glass to drink from," the "vase," the "piano," and so forth. These values and practicalities, they too belong to *the constitution of the "actually present" objects as such*, irrespective of my turning or not turning to consider them or indeed any other objects. The same considerations apply of course just as well to the men and beasts in my surroundings as to "mere things." They are my "friends" or my "foes," my "servants" or "superiors," "strangers" or "relatives," and so forth.

The "Cogito." My Natural World-About-Me and the Ideal Worlds-About-Me

It is then to this world, *the world in which I find myself and which is also my world-about-me*, that the complex forms of my manifold and shifting *spontaneities* of consciousness stand related: observing in the interests of research the bringing of meaning into conceptual form through description; comparing and distinguishing, collecting and counting, presupposing and inferring, the theorizing activity of consciousness, in short, in its different forms and stages. Related to it likewise are the diverse acts and states of sentiment and disapproval, joy and sorrow, desire and aversion, hope and fear, decision and action. All these, together with the sheer acts of the Ego, in which I become acquainted with the world as *immediately* given me, through spontaneous tendencies to turn towards it and to grasp it, are included under the one Cartesian expression: *Cogito*. In the natural urge of life I live continually in *this fundamental form of all "wakeful" living*, whether in addition I do or do not assert the *cogito*, and whether I am or am not "reflectively" concerned with the Ego and the *cogitare*. If I am so concerned, a new *cogito* has become livingly active, which for its part is not reflected upon, and so not objective for me.

I am present to myself continually as someone who perceives, represents, thinks, feels, desires, and so forth; and *for the most part* herein I find myself related in present experience to the fact-world which is constantly about me. But I am not always so related, not every *cogito* in which I live has for its *cogitatum* things, men, objects or contents of one kind or another. Perhaps I am busied with pure numbers and the laws they symbolize: nothing of this sort is present in the world about me, this world of "real fact." And yet the world of numbers also is there for me, as the field of objects with which I am arithmetically busied; while I am thus occupied some numbers or constructions of a numerical kind will be at the focus of vision, girt by an arithmetical horizon partly defined, partly not; but obviously this being-there-for-me, like the being there at all, is something very different from this. *The arithmetical world is there for me only when and so long as I occupy the arithmetical standpoint*. But the *natural* world, the world in the ordinary sense of the word, is *constantly there for me*, so long as I live naturally and look in its direction. I am then at the "*natural standpoint*," which is just another way of stating the same thing. And there is no need to modify these conclusions when I proceed to appropriate to myself the arithmetical world, and other similar "worlds," by adopting the corresponding standpoint. The natural world *still remains "present*," I am at the natural standpoint after as well as before, and in this respect *undisturbed by the adoption of new standpoints*. If my *cogito* is active *only* in the worlds proper to the new standpoints, the natural world remains unconsidered; it is now the background for my consciousness as act, but it is *not the encircling sphere within which an arithmetical world finds its true and proper place*. The two worlds are present together but *disconnected*, apart, that is, from their relation to the Ego, in virtue of which I can freely direct my glance or my acts to the one or to the other.

The "Other" Ego-Subject and the Intersubjective Natural World-About-Me

Whatever holds good for me personally, also holds good, as I know, for all other men whom I find present in my world-about-me. Experiencing them as men, I understand and take them as Ego-subjects, units like myself, and related to their natural surroundings. But this in such wise that I apprehend the world-about-them and the world-about-me objectively as one and the same world, which differs in each case only through affecting consciousness differently. Each has his place whence he sees the things that are present, and each enjoys accordingly different appearances of the things. For each, again, the fields of perception and memory actually present are different, quite apart from the fact that even that which is here intersubjectively known in common is known in different ways, is differently apprehended, shows different grades of clearness, and so forth. Despite all this, we come to understandings with our neighbours, and set up in common an objective spatio-temporal fact-world as *the world about us that is there for us all, and to which we ourselves none the less belong*.

The General Thesis of the Natural Standpoint

That which we have submitted towards the characterization of what is given to us from the natural standpoint, and thereby of the natural standpoint itself, was a piece of pure description *prior to all "theory."* In these studies we stand bodily aloof from all theories, and by "theories" we here mean anticipatory ideas of every kind. Only as facts of our environment, not as agencies for uniting facts validly together, do theories concern us at all. But we do not set ourselves the task of continuing the pure description and raising it to a systematically inclusive and exhaustive characterization of the data, in their full length and breadth, discoverable from the natural standpoint (or from any standpoint, we might add, that can be knit up with the same in a common consent). A task such as this can and must—as scientific—be undertaken, and it is one of extraordinary importance, although so far scarcely noticed. Here it is not ours to attempt. For us who are striving towards the entrance-gate of phenomenology all the necessary work in this direction has already been carried out; the few features pertaining to the natural standpoint which we need are of a quite general character, and have already figured in our descriptions, and been sufficiently *and fully clarified*. We even made a special point of securing this full measure of clearness.

We emphasize a most important point once again in the sentences that follow: I find continually present and standing over against me the one spatio-temporal fact-world to which I myself belong, as do all other men found in it and related in the same way to it. This "fact-world," as the world already tells us, I find to *be out there*, and also *take it just as it gives itself to me as something that exists out there*. All doubting and rejecting of the data of the natural world leaves standing the *general thesis of the natural standpoint*. "The" world is as fact-world always there; at the most it is at odd points "other" than I supposed, this or that under such names as "illusion," "hallucination," and the like, must be struck *out of it*, so to speak; but the "it" remains ever, in the sense of the general thesis, a world that has its being out there. To know it more comprehensively, more trustworthily, more perfectly than the naïve lore of experience is able to do, and to solve all the problems of scientific knowledge which offer themselves upon its ground, that is the goal of the *sciences of the natural standpoint*.

Radical Alteration of the Natural Thesis "Disconnexion," "Bracketing"

Instead now of remaining at this standpoint, we propose to alter it radically. Our aim must be to convince ourselves of the possibility of this alteration on grounds of principle.

The General Thesis according to which the real world about me is at all times known not merely in a general way as something apprehended, but as a fact-world *that has its being out there*, does *not* consist of course *in an act proper*, in an articulated judgment *about existence*. It is and remains something all the time the standpoint is adopted, that is, it endures persistently during the whole course of our life of natural endeavour. What has been at any time perceived clearly, or obscurely made present, in short everything out of the world of nature through experience and prior to any thinking, bears in its totality and in all its articulated sections the character "present" "out there," a character which can function essentially as the ground of support for an explicit (predicative) existential judgment which is in agreement with the character it is grounded upon. If we express that same judgment, we know quite well that in so doing we have simply put into the form of a statement and grasped as a predication what already lay somehow in the original experience, or lay there as the character of something "present to one's hand."

We can treat the potential and unexpressed thesis exactly as we do the thesis of the explicit judgment. A procedure of this sort, *possible at any time*, is, for instance, *the attempt to doubt everything* which

Descartes, with an entirely different end in view, with the purpose of setting up an absolutely indubitable sphere of Being, undertook to carry through. We link on here, but add directly and emphatically that this attempt to doubt everything should serve us *only as a device of method*, helping us to stress certain points which by its means, as though secluded in its essence, must be brought clearly to light.

The attempt to doubt everything has its place in the realm of our *perfect freedom*. We can *attempt to doubt* anything and everything, however convinced we may be concerning what we doubt, even though the evidence which seals our assurance is completely adequate.

Let us consider what is essentially involved in an act of this kind. He who attempts to doubt is attempting to doubt "Being" of some form or other, or it may be Being expanded into such predicative forms as "It is," "It is this or thus," and the like. The attempt does not affect the form of Being itself. He who doubts, for instance, whether an object, whose Being he does not doubt, is constituted in such and such a way doubts *the way it is constituted.* We can obviously transfer this way of speaking from the doubting to the *attempt* at doubting. It is clear that we cannot doubt the Being of anything, and in the same act of consciousness (under the unifying form of simultaneity) bring what is substantive to this Being under the terms of the Natural Thesis, and so confer upon it the character of "being actually there" (*vorhanden*). Or to put the same in another way: we cannot at once doubt and hold for certain one and the same quality of Being. It is likewise clear that the *attempt* to doubt any object of awareness in respect of it *being actually there necessarily conditions a certain suspension (Aufhebung) of the thesis*; and it is precisely this that interests us. It is not a transformation of the thesis into its antithesis, of positive into negative; it is also not a transformation into presumption, suggestion, indecision, doubt (in one or another sense of the word); each shifting indeed is not at our free pleasure. *Rather is it something quite unique. We do not abandon the thesis we have adopted, we make no change in our conviction*, which remains in itself what it is so long as we do not introduce new motives of judgment, which we precisely refrain from doing. And yet the thesis undergoes a modification—whilst remaining in itself what it is, *we set it as it were "out of action,"* we "*disconnect it,*" "*bracket it.*" It still remains there like the bracketed in the bracket, like the disconnected outside the connexional system. We can also say: The thesis is experience as lived (*Erlebnis*), *but we make "no use" of it*, and by that, of course, we do not indicate privation (as when we say of the ignorant that he makes no use of a certain thesis); in this case rather, as with all parallel expressions, we are dealing with indicators that point to a definite but *unique form of consciousness*, which clamps on to the original simple thesis (whether it actually or even predicatively *posits* existence or not), and transvalues it in a quite peculiar way. *This transvaluing is a concern of our full freedom, and is opposed to all cognitive attitudes* that would set themselves up as coordinate with the *thesis*, and yet within the unity of "simultaneity" remain incompatible with it, as indeed it is in general with all attitudes whatsoever in the strict sense of the word.

In *the attempt to doubt* applied to a thesis which, as we presuppose, is certain and tenaciously held, the "disconnexion" takes place in and with a modification of the antithesis, namely with the "*supposition*" (*Ansetzung*) *of Non-Being*, which is thus the partial basis of the attempt to doubt. With Descartes this is so markedly the case that one can say that his universal attempt at doubt is just an attempt at universal denial. We disregard this possibility here, we are not interested in every analytical component of the attempt to doubt, nor therefore in its exact and completely sufficing analysis. *We extract only the phenomenon of "bracketing" or "disconnection,"* which is obviously not limited to that of the attempt to doubt, although it can be detached from it with special ease, but can appear *in other contexts also*, and with no less ease *independently*. In relation to every thesis and wholly uncoerced we can use this *peculiar* ἐποχή, (*epokhe*—abstention), *a certain refraining from judgment which is compatible with the unshaken and unshakable because of the self-evidencing conviction of Truth*. The thesis is "put out of action," bracketed, it passes off into the modified status of a "bracketed thesis," and the judgment *simpliciter* into "*bracketed judgment.*"

Naturally one should not simply identify this consciousness with that of "mere supposal," that nymphs, for instance, are dancing in a ring; for thereby *no disconnecting* of a living conviction that goes on living takes place, although from another side the close relation of the two forms of consciousness lies clear. Again, we are not concerned here with supposal in the sense of "*assuming*" or *taking for granted*, which in the equivocal speech of current usage may also be expressed in the words: "I suppose (I make the assumption) that it is so and so."

Let us add further that nothing hinders us *from speaking bracketing correlatively* also, in respect of *an objectivity to be posited*, what ever be the region or category to which it belongs. What is meant in this case is that *every thesis related to this objectivity* must be *disconnected* and changed into its bracketed counterpart. On closer view, moreover, the "bracketing" image is from the outset better suited to the sphere of the object, just as the expression "to put out of action" better suits the sphere of the Act or of Consciousness.

The Phenomenological ἐποχή

We can now let the universal ἐποχή, (*epokhe*—abstention) in the sharply defined and novel sense we have given to it step into the place of the Cartesian attempt at universal doubt. But on good grounds we *limit* the universality of this εποχη. For were it as inclusive as it is in general capable of being, then since every thesis and every judgment can be modified freely to any extent, and every objectivity that we can judge or criticize can be bracketed, no field would be left over for unmodified judgments, to say nothing of a science. But our design is just to discover a new scientific domain, such as might be won precisely *through the method of bracketing*, though only through a definitely limited form of it.

The limiting consideration can be indicated in a word.

We put out of action the general thesis which belongs to the essence of the natural standpoint, we place in brackets whatever it includes respecting the nature of Being: *this entire natural world therefore* which is continually "there for us," "present to our hand," and will ever remain there, is a "fact-world" of which we continue to be conscious, even though it pleases us to put it in brackets.

If I do this, as I am fully free to do, I do *not* then *deny* this "world," as though I were a sophist, *I do not doubt that it is there* as though I were a sceptic; but I use the "phenomenological" ἐποχή, which *completely bars me from using any judgment that concerns spatio-temporal existence* (*Dasein*).

Thus *all sciences which relate to this natural world*, though they stand never so firm to me, though they fill me with wondering admiration, though I am far from any thought of objecting to them in the least degree, *I disconnect them all, I make absolutely no use of their standards, I do not appropriate a single one of the propositions that enter into their systems, even though their evidential value is perfect, I take none of them, no one of them serves me for a foundation*—so long, that is, as it is understood, in the way these sciences themselves understand it, as a truth *concerning the realities* of this world. *I may accept it only after I have placed it in the bracket.* That means: only in the modified consciousness of the judgment as it appears in disconnexion, and *not as it figures within the science as its proposition, a proposition which claims to be valid and whose validity I recognize and make use of.*

The ἐποχή here in question will not be confined with that which positivism demands, and against which, as we were compelled to admit, it is itself an offender. We are not concerned at present with removing the preconceptions which trouble the pure positivity (*Sachlichkeit*) of research, with the constituting of a science "free from theory" and "free from metaphysics" by bringing all the grounding back to the immediate data, nor with the means of reaching such ends, concerning whose value there is indeed no question. What *we* demand lies along another line. The whole world as placed within the nature-setting and presented in experience as real, taken completely "free from all theory," just as it is in reality experienced, and made clearly manifest in and through the linkings of our experiences, has now no validity for us, it must be set in brackets, untested indeed but also uncontested. Similarly all theories and sciences, positivistic or otherwise, which relate to this world, however good they may be, succumb to the same fate.

CONSCIOUSNESS AND NATURAL REALITY

Intimation Concerning "Pure" or "Transcendential Consciousness" as Phenomenological Residuum

We have learnt to understand the meaning of the phenomenological ἐποχή (*epokhe*—abstention), but we are still quite in the dark as to its serviceability. In the first place it is not clear to what extent the limitation of the total field of the εποχη, as discussed in the previous pages, involves a real narrowing of its general scope. *For what can remain over when the whole world is bracketed, including ourselves and all our thinking* (*cogitare*)?

Since the reader already knows that the interest which governs these "Meditations" concerns a new eidetic science, he will indeed at first expect the world as fact to succumb to the disconnexion, but not *the world as Eidos*, nor any other sphere of Essential Being. The disconnecting of the world does not as a matter of fact mean the disconnecting of the number series, for instance, and the arithmetic relative to it.

However, we do not take this path, nor does our goal lie in its direction. That goal we could also refer to as *the winning of a new region of Being, the distinctive character of which has not yet been defined*, a region of *individual* Being, like every genuine region. We must leave the sequel to teach us what that more precisely means.

We proceed in the first instance by showing up simply and directly what we see; and since the Being to be thus shown up is neither more nor less than that which we refer to on essential grounds as "pure experiences (*Erlebnisse*)" "pure consciousness" with its pure "correlates of consciousness," and on the other side its "pure Ego," we observe that it is from *the Ego, the* consciousness, *the* experience as given to us from the natural standpoint, that we take our start.

I, the real human being, am a real object like others in the natural world. I carry out *cogitationes*, "acts of consciousness" in both a narrower and a wider sense, and these acts, as belonging to this human subject, are events of the same natural world. And all my remaining experiences (*Erlebnisse*) likewise, out of whose changing stream the specific acts of the Ego shine forth in so distinctive a way, glide into one another, enter into combinations, and are being incessantly modified. Now in its *widest connotation* the expression "*consciousness*" (then indeed less suited for its purpose) includes *all* experiences (*Erlebnisse*), and entrenched in the natural standpoint as we are even in our scientific thinking, grounded there in habits that are most firmly established since they have never misled us, we take all these data of psychological reflexion as real world-events, as the experiences (*Erlebnisse*) of animal beings. So natural is it to us to see them only in this light that, though acquainted already with the possibility of a change of standpoint, and on the search for the new domain of objects, we fail to notice that it is from out these centres of experience (*Erlebnisse*) themselves that through the adoption of the new standpoint the new domain emerges. Connected with this is the fact that instead of keeping our eyes turned towards these centres of experience, we turned them away and sought the new objects in the ontological realms of arithmetic, geometry, and the like, whereby indeed nothing truly new has to be won.

Thus we fix our eyes steadily upon the sphere of Consciousness and study what it is that we find immanent in *it*. At first, without having yet carried out the phenomenological suspensions of the element of judgment, we subject this sphere of Consciousness in its essential nature to a systematic though in no sense exhaustive analysis. What we lack above all is a certain general insight into the essence of *consciousness in general*, and quite specially also of consciousness, so far as in and through its essential Being, the "natural" fact-world comes to be known. In these studies we go so far as is needed to furnish the full insight at which we have been aiming, to wit, *that Consciousness in itself has a being of its own which in its absolute uniqueness of nature remains unaffected by the phenomenological disconnexion*. It therefore remains over as a "*phenomenological residuum*," as a region of Being which is in principle unique, and can become in fact the field of a new science—the science of Phenomenology.

Through this insight the "phenomenological" ἐποχή will for the first time deserve its name; to exercise it in full consciousness of its import will turn out to be the necessary operation which *renders "pure" consciousness accessible to us, and subsequently the whole phenomenological region*. And thus we shall be able to understand why this region and the new science attached to it was fated to remain unknown. From the natural standpoint nothing can be seen except the natural world. So long as the possibility of the phenomenological standpoint was not grasped, and the method of relating the objectivities which emerge therewith to a primordial form of apprehension had not been devised, the phenomenological world must needs have remained unknown, and indeed barely divined at all.

We would add yet the following to our terminology: Important motives which have their ground in epistemological requirements justify us in referring to "pure" consciousness, of which much is yet to be said, also as *transcendental consciousness*, and the operation through which it is acquired as *transcendental* ἐποχή. On grounds of method this operation will split up into different steps of "disconnexion" or "bracketing," and thus our method will assume the character of a graded reduction. For this reason we propose to speak, and even preponderatingly, of *phenomenological reductions* (though, in respect of their unity as a whole, we would speak in unitary form of *the* phenomenological reduction). From the epistemological viewpoint we would also speak of transcendental reductions. Moreover, these and *all* our terms must be understood exclusively in accordance with the sense which *our* presentations indicate for them, but not in any other one which history or the terminological habits of the reader may favour.

The Essence of Consciousness as Theme of Inquiry

We start with a series of observations within which we are not troubled with any phenomenological ἐποχή. We are directed to an "outer world," and, without forsaking the natural standpoint, reflect psychologically on our Ego and its experience (*Erleben*). We busy ourselves, precisely as we have done if we had never heard of the new viewpoint, with *the essential nature of "the consciousness of something,"* following, for instance, our consciousness of the existence of material things, living bodies and men, or that of technical and literary works, and so forth. We adhere to our general principle that each individual event has its essence that can be grasped in its eiditic purity, and in this purity must belong to a field available to eidetic inquiry. In accordance herewith the universal fact of nature conveyed by the words "I am," "I think," "I have a world over against me," and the like, has also its essential content, and it is on this exclusively that we now intend to concentrate. Thus we rehearse to ourselves by way of illustration certain conscious experiences chosen at random, and in their individuality just as they are in their natural setting as real facts of human life, and we make these present to ourselves through memory or in the free play of fancy. On the ground of illustrations such as these, which we assume to be presented with perfect clearness, we grasp and fix in adequate ideation the pure essences that interest us. The individual facts, the fact-character of the natural world in general, thereby escapes our theoretical scrutiny—as in all cases where our inquiry is purely eidetic.

We limit still further the theme of our inquiry. Its title ran: Consciousness, or more distinctly *Conscious experience* (*Erlebnis*) *in general*, to be taken in an extremely wide sense about whose exact definition we are fortunately not concerned. Exact definitions do not lie at the threshold of analysis of the kind we are here making, but are a later result involving great labour. As starting-point we take consciousness in a pregnant sense which suggests itself at once, most simply indicated through the Cartesian *cogito*, "I think." As is known Descartes understood this in a sense so wide as to include every case of "I perceive, I remember, I fancy, I judge, feel, desire, will," and all experiences of the Ego that in any way resemble the foregoing, in all the countless fluctuations of their special patterns. The Ego itself to which they are all related, spontaneous, in receptive or any other "attitude," and indeed the Ego in any and every sense, we leave at first out of consideration. We shall be concerned with it later, and fundamentally. For the present there is sufficient other material to serve as support for our analysis and grasp of the essential. And we shall find ourselves forthwith referred thereby to enveloping connexions of experience which compel us to widen our conception of a conscious experience beyond this circle of specific *cogitationes*.

We shall consider conscious experiences *in the concrete fullness and entirety* with which they figure in their concrete context—the *stream of experience*—and to which they are closely attached through their own proper essence. It then becomes evident that every experience in the stream which our reflexion can lay hold on has *its own essence open to intuition*, a "content" which can be considered in its *singularity in and for itself.* We shall be concerned to grasp this individual content of the *cogitatio* in its *pure* singularity, and to describe it in its general features, excluding everything which is not to be found in the *cogitatio* as it is in itself. We must likewise describe the *unity of consciousness* which is demanded *by the intrinsic nature of the cogitationes*, and so necessarily demanded that they could not be without this unity.

The Cogito as "Act." The Modal Form of Marginal Actuality

Let us start with an example. In front of me, in the dim light, lies this white paper. I see it, touch it. This perceptual seeing and touching of the paper as the full concrete experience *of* the paper that lies here as given in truth precisely with this relative lack of clearness, with this imperfect definition, appearing to me from this particular angle—is a *cogitatio*, a conscious experience. The paper itself with its objective qualities, its extension in space, its objective position in regard to that spatial thing I call my body, is not *cogitatio*, but *cogitatum*, not perceptual experience, but something perceived. Now that which is perceived can itself very well be a conscious experience; but it is evident that an object such as a material thing, this paper, for instance, as given in perceptual exerience, is in principle other than an experience, a being of a completely different kind.

Before pursuing this point farther, let us amplify the illustration. In perception properly so-called, as an explicit awareness (*Gewahren*), I am turned towards the object, to the paper, for instance, I apprehend it as being this here and now. The apprehension is a singling out, every perceived object having a background in experience. Around and about the paper lie books, pencils, ink-well, and so forth, and these in a certain sense are also "perceived," perceptually there, in the "field of intuition"; but whilst I was turned towards the paper there was no turning in their direction, nor any apprehending of them, not even in a secondary sense. They appeared and yet were not singled out, were not posited on their own account. Every perception of a thing has such a zone of *background intuitions* (or background awarenesses, if "intuiting" already includes the state of being turned towards), and this also is a "*conscious experience*," or more briefly a "consciousness *of*" all indeed that in point of fact lies in the co-perceived objective "background." We are not talking here of course of that which is to be found as an "objective" element in the objective space to which the background in question may belong, of all the things and thing-like events which a valid and progressive experience may establish there. What we say applies exclusively to that zone of consciousness which belongs to the model essence of a perception as "being turned towards an object," and further to that which belongs to the proper essence of this zone itself. But it is here implied that certain modifications of the original experience are possible, which we refer to as a free turning of the "look"—not precisely nor merely of the physical but of the "*mental look*"—from the paper at first *descried* to objects which had already appeared before of which we had been "implicitly" aware, and whereof *subsequent* to the directing of one's look thither we are explicitly aware, perceiving them "attentitively," or "noticing them near by."

We are aware of things not only in perception, but also consciously in recollections, in representations similar to recollections, and also in the free play of fancy, and this in "clear intuition" it may be, or without noticeable perceptibility after the manner of "dim" presentations; they float past us in different "characterizations" as real, possible, fancied, and so forth. All that we have stated concerning perceptual experiences holds good, obviously, of these other experiences, essentially different as they are. We shall not think of confusing the *objects of which we are aware* under these forms of consciousness (the fancy-shaped nymphs, for instance) with the conscious experiences themselves which are a consciousness *of* them. Then, again, we know that it is the essence of all such experiences—taking the same, as always, in their concrete fullness—to show that remarkable modification which transfers consciousness in the *mode of actual orientation* to consciousness in the *mode of non-actuality* and conversely. At the one time the experience is, so to speak "*explicitly*" aware of its objective content, at the other implicitly and merely *potentially*. The objective factor, whether in perception, memory, or fancy, may already be appearing to us, but *our mental gaze is not yet "directed" towards it*, not even in a secondary sense, to say nothing of being "busied" with it in some special way.

Similar remarks apply to all and any of the *cogitationes* in the sense illustrated by Descartes' use of the term, to all experiences of thought, feeling and will, except that, as will be emphasized (in the next paragraph), the "directedness towards," the "being turned towards," which is the distinctive mark of focal actuality, does not coincide, as in the favourite because simplest examples of sensory presentations, with singling out and noting the objects we are aware of. It is also obviously true of all such experiences that the focal is girt about with a "zone" of the marginal; *the stream of experience can never consist wholly of focal actualities*. These indeed determine, in a very general sense which must be extended beyond the circle of our illustrations, and through the contrast with marginal actualities already drawn, the *pregnant* meaning of the expression "cogito," "I have *consciousness* of something," "I perform an *act* of consciousness." In order to keep this well-established concept purely separate, we propose to reserve for it exclusively the Cartesian expressions *cogito* and *cogitationes*, unless through some addition, such as "marginal" or the like, we expressly indicate the modified use we are making of the term.

We can define a *"wakeful" Ego* as one that within its stream of experience is continually conscious in the specific form of the *cogito*; which, of course, does not mean that it can and does bring these experiences persistently or in general to predicative expression. Ego-subjects include animals. But, according to what we have said above, it belongs to the essence of the stream of experience of a wakeful Self that the continuously prolonged chain of *cogitationes* is constantly enveloped in a medium of dormant actuality (*Inaktualität*), which is ever prepared to pass off into the wakeful mode (*Aktualität*), as conversely the wakeful into the dormant.

Intentional Experience. Experience in General

However drastic the change which the experiences of a wakeful Consciousness undergo in their transition into the dormant state, the experiences as modified share the essential nature of the original experiences in an important respect. It belongs as a general feature to the essence of every actual *cogito* to be a consciousness *of* something. But according to what we have already said, the *modified cogitatio is likewise and in its own way Consciousness*, and *of the same* something as with the corresponding unmodified consciousness. Thus the essential property of Consciousness in its general form is preserved in the modification. All experiences which have these essential properties in common are also called "*internal experiences*" (acts in the *very wide sense* of the *Logical Studies*); in so far as they are a consciousness of something they are said to be "*intentionally related*" to this something.

We must, however, be quite clear on this point that *there is no question here of a relation between a psychological event—called experience (Erlebnis)—and some other real existent (Dasein)—called Object*—or of a *psychological connexion* obtaining between the one and the other *in objective reality*. On the contrary, we are concerned with experiences in their essential purity, with *pure essences*, and with that which is *involved in* the essence *"a priori," in unconditioned necessity*.

That an experience is the consciousness of something: a fiction, for instance, the fiction of this or that centaur; a perception, the perception of its "real" object; a judgment, the judgment concerning it subject-matter, and so forth, this does not relate to the experimental fact as lived within the world, more specifically within some given psychological context, but to the pure essence grasped ideationally as pure idea. In the very essence of an experience lies determined not only *that*, but also *whereof* it is a consciousness, and in what determinate or indeterminate sense it is this. So too in the essence of consciousness as dormant lies included the variety of wakeful *cogitationes*, into which it can be differentiated through the modification we have already referred to as "the noticing of what was previously unnoticed."

Under *experiences* in the *widest sense* we understand whatever is to be found in the stream of experience, not only therefore intentional experiences, *cogitationes* actual and potential taken in their full concreteness, but all the real (*reellen*) phases to be found in this stream and in its concrete sections.

For it is easily seen that *not every real phase* of the concrete unity of an intentional experience has itself the *basic character of intentionality*, the property of being a "consciousness of something." This is the case, for instance, with all sensory data, which play so great a part in the perceptive intuitions of things. In the experience of the perception of this white paper, more closely in those components of it related to the paper's quality of whiteness, we discover through properly directed noticing the sensory datum "white." This "whiteness" is something that belongs inseparably to the essence of the concrete perception, as a *real* (*reelles*) concrete constitutive portion of it. As the content which presents the whiteness of the paper as it appears to us it is the *bearer of* an intentionality, but not itself a consciousness of something. The same holds good of other data of experience, of the so-called *sensory feelings*, for instance. We shall be speaking of these at greater length in a later context.

The "Directedness" of the Pure Ego in the *Cogito*, and the Noticing that Apprehends

Though we are unable at this point to proceed farther with our descriptive analysis of intentional experiences in their essential nature, we would single out certain aspects as noteworthy in relation to further developments. If an intentional experience is actual, carried out, that is, after the manner of the *cogito*, the subject "directs" itself within it towards the intentional object. To the *cogito* itself belongs an immanent "glancing-towards" the object, a directedness which from another side springs forth from the

"Ego," which can therefore never be absent. This glancing of the Ego towards something is in harmony with the act involved, perceptive in perception, fanciful in fancy, approving in approval, volitional in will, and so forth. This means, therefore, that this having in one's glance, in one's mental eye, which belongs to the *essence* of the *cogito*, to the act as such, is not in itself in turn a proper act, and in particular should not be confused with a perceiving (in however wide a sense this term be used), or with any other types of act related to perceptions. It should be noticed that *intentional* object of a consciousness (understood as the latter's full correlate) is by no means to be identified with *apprehended* object. We are accustomed without further thought to include the being apprehended in the concept of the object (of that generally which stands over against the subject), since in so far as we think of it and say something *about* it, we have made it into an object in the sense of something apprehended. In the widest sense of the world, apprehending an object (*Erfassen*) coincides with mindfully heeding it (*achten*), and noting its nature (*bemerken*), whether attentively as a special case, or cursorily, provided at least that these expressions are used in their customary sense. *This heeding or apprehending is not to be identified with the modus of "cogito" in general*, that of actuality, but seen more closely, with a *special act-modus* which every consciousness or every act which does not yet possess it can assume. Should it do this, its intentional object is not only known in a general way and brought within the directed glance of the mind, but is an apprehended and noted object. A turning towards a Thing, to be sure, cannot take place otherwise than in the way of apprehension, and the same holds good of all *objectivities that are "plainly presentable"*: here a turning towards (be it even in fancy) is *eo ipso* an "apprehending" and a "heeding." But in the act of valuation we are turned towards values, in acts of joy to the enjoyed, in acts of love to the beloved, in acting to the action, and *without* apprehending all this. The intentional object rather, that which is valued, enjoyed, beloved, hoped as such, the action as action, first becomes an apprehended object through a distinctively "*objectifying*" *turn of thought*. If one is turned towards some matter absorbed in appreciation, the apprehension of the matter is no doubt included in the total attitude; but it is not the *mere* matter in general, but the matter *values* or the *value* which is (and the point will concern us more in detail later on) *the complete intentional correlate of the act of valuation*. Thus "*to be turned in appreciation* towards some matter" does not already imply "*having*" the value "*for object*" in the special sense of object apprehended, as indeed we must have the object if we are to predicate anything of it; and similarly in regard to all logical acts which are related to it.

Thus in acts like those of appreciation we have an *intentional object in a double sense*: we must distinguish between the "*subject matter*" *pure and simple* and the *full intentional object*, and corresponding to this, a *double intentio*, a two-fold directedness. If we are directed towards some matter in an act of appreciation, the direction towards the matter in question is a noting and apprehending of it; but we are "directed"—only not in an apprehending way— also to the value. Not merely the *representing of the matter* in question, but also the *appreciating* which includes this representing, has the modus of actuality.

But we must hasten to add that it is only in respect of simple acts of valuation that the matter stands so simply. In general, acts of sentiment and will are consolidated upon a higher level, and the intentional objectivity also differentiates itself accordingly: there is also a complicating of the ways in which the objects included in the unitary total objectivity come under the directed mental glance. But in any case the following main propositions hold good:

In every act some mode of heeding (Achtsamkeit) holds sway. But wherever it is not the plain consciousness of a subject-matter, wherever some further "attitude towards" the subject-matter is grounded in such consciousness, *subject-matter and full intentional object* ("subject-matter" and "value," for instance), likewise *heeding the object and mentally scrutinizing it, separate out the one from the other*. But at the same time the possibility of a modification remains an essential property of these grounded acts, a modification whereby their full intentional objects become noticed, and in this sense "*represented*" objects, which now, from their side, become capable of serving as bases for explanations, relations, conceptual renderings, and predications. Thanks to this objectification we find facing us in natural setting, and therefore *as members of the natural world*, not natural things merely, but values and practical objects of every kind, cities, streets with street-lighting arrangements, dwellings, furniture, works of art, books, tools and so forth. . . .

Consciousness and Natural Reality. The View of the "Man in the Street"

All the essential characteristics of experience and consciousness which we have reached are for us necessary steps towards the attainment of the end which is unceasingly drawing us on, the discovery, namely, of the essence of that *"pure" consciousness* which is to fix the limits of the phenomenological field. Our inquiries were eidetic; but the individual instances of the essences we have referred to as experience, stream of experience, "consciousness" in all its senses, belonged as real events to the natural world. To that extent we have not abandoned the ground of the natural standpoint. Individual consciousness is interwoven with the *natural world* in a *twofold* way: it is some *man's* consciousness, or that of some *man* or *beast*, and in a large number at least of its particularizations it is a consciousness of this world. *In respect now of this intimate attachment with the real world, what is meant by saying that consciousness has an essence "of its own,"* that with other consciousness it constitutes a self-contained *connexion determined purely through this, its own essence,* the connexion, namely, of the stream of consciousness? Moreover, since we can interpret consciousness in the widest sense to cover eventually whatever the concept of experience includes, the question concerns the experience-stream's own essential nature and that of all its components. To what extent, in the first place, must the *material world* be fundamentally different in kind, *excluded from the experience's own essential nature*? And if it is this, if over against all consciousness and the essential being proper to it, it is that which is "*foreign*" and "*other*," how can consciousness be *interwoven* with it, and consequently with the whole world that is alien to consciousness? For it is easy to convince oneself that the material world is not just any portion of the natural world, but its fundamental stratum to which all other real being is *essentially* related. It still fails to include the souls of men and animals; and the new factor which these introduce is first and foremost their "experiencing" together with their conscious relationship to the world surrounding them. *But here consciousness and thinghood form a connected whole*, connected within the particular psychological unities which we call *animalia*, and in the last resort within the *real unity of the world as a whole*. Can the unity of a whole be other than made one through the essential proper nature of its parts, which must therefore have some *community of essence* instead of a fundamental heterogeneity?

To be clear, let us seek out the ultimate sources whence the general thesis of the world which I adopt when taking up the natural standpoint draws its nourishment, thereby enabling me as a conscious being to discover over against me an existing world of things, to ascribe to myself in this world a body, and to find for myself within this world a proper place. This ultimate source is obviously *sensory experience*. For our purpose, however, it is sufficient to consider *sensory perception*, which in a certain proper sense plays among experiencing acts the part of an original experience, whence all other experiencing acts draw a chief part of their power to serve as a ground. Every perceiving consciousness has this peculiarity, that it is the consciousness of *the embodied (leibhaftigen) self-presence of an individual object*, which on its own side and in a pure logical sense of the term is an individual or some logico-categorical modification of the same. In our own instance, that of sensory perception, or, in distincter terms, perception of a world of things, the logical individual is the Thing; and it is sufficient for us to treat the perception of things as representing all other perceptions (of properties, processes, and the like).

The natural wakeful life of our Ego is a continuous perceiving, actual or potential. The world of things and our body within it are continuously present to our perception. How then does and can *Consciousness itself* separate out as a *concrete thing in itself*, from that within it, of which we are conscious, namely, the *perceived being, "standing over against"* consciousness "*in and for itself*"?

I meditate first as would the man "in the street." I see and grasp the thing itself in its bodily reality. It is true that I sometimes deceive myself, and not only in respect of the perceived constitution of the thing, but also in respect of its being there at all. I am subject to an illusion or hallucination. The perception is not then "genuine." But if it is, if, that is, we can "confirm" its presence in the actual context of experience, eventually with the help of correct empirical thinking, then the perceived thing *is real* and itself really given, and that bodily in perception. Here perceiving considered simply as consciousness, and apart from the body and the bodily organs, appears as something in itself essenceless, an empty looking of an empty "Ego" towards the object itself which comes into contact with it in some astonishing way.

"Primary" and "Secondary" Qualities. The Bodily Given Thing "Mere Appearance" of the "Physically True"

If as a "man in the street" misled by sensibility I have indulged the inclination to spin out such thoughts as these, now, as a "man of science," I call to mind the familiar distinction between *secondary* and *primary* qualities, according to which the specific qualities of sense should be "merely subjective" and only the geometrico-physical qualities "objective." The colour and sound of a thing, its smell, its taste, and so forth, though they appear to cleave to the thing "bodily" as though belonging to its essence, are not themselves and as they appear to be, real, but mere "signs" of certain primary qualities. But if I recall familiar theories of Physics, I see at once that the meaning of such much-beloved propositions can hardly be the one which the words warrant: as though really only the "specific" sensory qualities of the perceived thing were mere appearance; which would come to saying that the "primary" qualities which remain after the *subtraction* of these same sensory qualities belonged to the same thing as it objectively and truly is, together with other such qualities which did not show forth as appearance. So understood, the old Berkeleian objection would hold good, namely, that extension, this essential nucleus of corporeality and all primary qualities, is unthinkable apart from the secondary qualities. Rather *the whole essential content of the perceived thing*, all that is present in the body, with all its qualities and all that can ever be perceived, *is "mere appearance,"* and the *"true thing" is that of physical science*. When the latter defines the given thing exclusively through concepts such as atoms, ions, energies, and so forth, and in every case as space-filling processes whose sole *characteristica* are mathematical expressions, its reference is to *something that transcends the whole content of the thing as present to us in bodily form*. It cannot therefore mean even the thing as lying in natural sensible space; in other words, its physical space cannot be the space of the world of bodily perception: otherwise it would also fall under the Berkeleian objection.

The "*true Being*" would therefore be entirely and *fundamentally something that is defined otherwise than as that which is given in perception as corporeal reality*, which is given exclusively through its sensory determinations, among which must also be reckoned the sensori-spatial. *The thing as strictly experienced gives the mere "this," an empty X which becomes the bearer of mathematical determinations, and of the corresponding mathematical formulae* and exists not in perceptual space, but in an "*objective space*," of which the former is the mere "symbol," *a Euclidean manifold of three dimensions that can be only symbolically represented.*

Let us then accept this. Let that which is given bodily in any perception be, as is taught there, "mere appearance," in principle "merely subjective," and yet no empty illusion. Yet that which is given in perception serves in the rigorous method of natural science for the valid determination, open to anyone to carry out and to verify through his own insight of that transcendent being whose "symbol" it is. The sensory content of that which is given in perception itself continues indeed to be reckoned as other than the true thing as it is in itself, but the *substratum*, the bearer (the empty X) of the perceived determinations still continues to count as that which is determined through exact method in the form of physical predicates. *All physical knowledge serves accordingly, and in the reverse sense, as an indicator of the course of possible experiences with the sensory things found in them and the occurrences in which they figure*. Thus it helps us to find our way about in the world of actual experience in which we all live and act.

The Real Nature of Perception and Its Transcendent Object

All this being presupposed, *what is it, we ask, that belongs to the concrete real nature (reellen Bestande) of the perception itself, as cogitatio*? Not the physical thing, as is obvious: radically transcendent as it is, transcendent over against the whole "world of appearance." But *even the latter*, though we refer to it habitually as "merely subjective," does not belong in all its detail of things and events to the real nature of perception, but is opposed to it as "transcendent." Let us consider this more closely. We have indeed already spoken of the transcendence of the thing, but only in passing. It concerns us now to win a deeper insight into *the relation of the transcendent to the Consciousness* that knows it, and to see how this mutual connexion, which has its own riddles, is to be understood.

We shut off the whole of physics and the whole domain of theoretical thought. We remain within the framework of plain intuition and the syntheses that belong to it, including perception. It is then evident that intuition and the intuited, perception and the thing perceived, though essentially related to each other, are in principle and of necessity *not really (reell) and essentially one and united.*

We start by taking an example. Keeping this table steadily in view as I go round it, changing my position in space all the time, I have continually the consciousness of the bodily presence out there of this one and self-same table, which in itself remains unchanged throughout. But the perception of the table is one that changes continuously, it is a continuum of changing perceptions. I close my eyes. My other senses are inactive in relation to the table. I have now no perception of it. I open my eyes, and the perception returns. The perception? Let us be more accurate. Under no circumstances does it return to me individually the same. Only the table is the same, known as identical through the synthetic consciousness which connects the new perception with the recollection. The perceived thing can be, without being perceived, without my being aware of it even as potential only (in the way of inactuality, as previously described), and perhaps without itself changing at all. But the perception itself is what it is within the steady flow of consciousness, and is itself constantly in flux; the perceptual now is ever passing over into the adjacent consciousness of the just-past, a new now simultaneously gleams forth, and so on. The perceived thing in general, and all its parts, aspects, and phases, whether the quality be primary or secondary, are necessarily transcendent to the perception, and on the same grounds everywhere. The colour of the thing seen is not in principle a real phase of the consciousness of colour; it appears, but even while it is appearing the appearance can and *must* be continually changing, as experience shows. The *same* colour appears "in" continuously varying patterns of *perspective colour-variations*. Similarly for every sensory quality and likewise for every spatial shape! One and the same shape (given *as* bodily the same) appears continuously ever again "in another way," in ever-differing perspective variations of shape. That is a necessary state of things, and it has obviously a more general bearing. For it is only in the interests of simplicity that we have illustrated our point by reference to a thing that appears unchanged in perception. The transfer to changes of any other sort is a perfectly simple proceeding.

An empirical consciousness of a self-same thing that looks "all-round" its object, and in so doing is continually confirming the unity of its own nature, essentially and necessarily possesses a manifold system of continuous patterns of appearance and perspective variations, in and through which all objective phases of the bodily self-given which appear in perception manifest themselves perspectively in definite continua. Every determinate feature has *its own* system of perspective variations; and for each of these features, as for the thing as a whole, the following holds good, namely, that it remains one and the same for the consciousness that in grasping it unites recollection and fresh perception synthetically together, despite interruption in the continuity of the course of actual perception. . . .

Indubitability of Immanent, Dubitability of Transcendent Perception

From all this important consequences follow. Every immanent perception necessarily guarantees the existence (*Existenz*) of its object. If reflective apprehension is directed to my experience, I apprehend an absolute Self whose existence (*Dasein*) is, in principle, undeniable, that is, the insight that it does not exist is, in principle, impossible; it would be nonsense to maintain the possibility of an experience *given in such a way not* truly existing. The stream of experience which is mine, namely, of the one who is thinking, may be to ever so great an extent uncomprehended, unknown in its past and future reaches, yet so soon as I glance towards the flowing life and into the real present it flows through, and in so doing grasp myself as the pure subject of this life (what that means will expressly concern us at a later stage), I say forthwith and because I must: *I am*, this life is, I live: *cogito*.

To every stream of experience, and to every Ego as such, there belongs, in principle, the possibility of securing this self-evidence: each of us bears in himself the warrant of this absolute existence (*Daseins*) as a fundamental possibility. But is it not conceivable, one might ask, that an Ego might have only fancies in its stream of experience, that the latter might consist of nothing beyond fictive intuitions? Such an Ego would thus discover only fictive *cogitationes*; its reflexions, by the very nature of this experiential medium, would be exclusively reflexions within the imagination. But that is obvious nonsense. That which floats before the mind may be a mere fiction; the floating itself, the fiction-producing consciousness, is not itself imagined, and the possibility of a perceiving reflexion which lays hold on absolute existence belongs to its essence as it does to every experience. No nonsense lies in the possibility that all alien consciousness which I posit in the experience of empathy does not exist. But *my* empathy and my consciousness in general is given in a primordial and absolute sense, not only essentially but existentially. This privileged position holds only for oneself and for the stream of experience to which the self is related; here only is there, and must there be, anything of the nature of immanent perception.

In contrast to this, it is, as we know, an essential feature of the thing-world that no perception, however perfect it may be, gives us anything absolute within its domain; and with this the following is essentially connected, namely, that every experience (*Erfahrung*), however far it extends, leaves open the possibility that what is given, despite the persistent consciousness of its bodily self-presence, does *not* exist. It is an essentially valid law that *existence in the form of a thing is never demanded as necessary by virtue of its givenness*, but in a certain way is always *contingent*. That means: It can always happen that the further course of experience will compel us to abandon what has already been set down and justified *in the light of empirical canons of rightness*. It was, so we afterwards say, mere illusion, hallucination, merely a coherent dream, and the like. Moreover, in this sphere of given data the open possibility remains of changes in apprehension, the turning of an appearance over into one which cannot unite with it harmoniously, and therewith an influence of later empirical positions on early ones whereby the intentional objects of these earlier positings suffer, so to speak, a posthumous reconstruction—eventualities which in the sphere of subject-experience (*Erlebnis*) are essentially excluded. In the absolute sphere, opposition, illusion, and being-otherwise have no place. It is a sphere of the absolutely established (*absoluter Position*).

In every way, then, it is clear that everything which is there for me in the world of things is on grounds of principle *only a presumptive reality*; that *I myself*, on the contrary, for whom it is there (excluding that which is imputed to the thing-world "by me"), I myself or my experience in its actuality am *absolute* Reality (*Wirklichkeit*), given through a positing that is unconditioned and simply indissoluble.

The thesis of my pure Ego and its personal life, which is "necessary" and plainly indubitable, thus stands opposed to the thesis of the world which is "contingent." All corporeally given thing-like entities can also not be, no corporeally given experiencing can also not be; that is the essential law, which defines this necessity and that contingency.

Obviously then the ontic necessity of the actual present experiencing is no pure essential necessity, that is, no pure eidetic specification of an essential law; it is the necessity of a fact (*Faktum*), and called "necessity" because an essential law is involved in the fact, and here indeed in its existence as such. The ideal possibility of a reflexion which has the essential character of a self-evident unshakeable *existential* thesis has its ground in the essential nature of a pure Ego *in general* and of an experiencing *in general.*

The reflexions in which we have been indulging also make it clear that no proofs drawn from the empirical consideration of the world can be conceived which could assure us with absolute certainty of the world's existence. The world is not doubtful in the sense that there are rational grounds which might be pitted against the tremendous force of unanimous experiences, but in the sense that a doubt is *thinkable*, and this is so because the possibility of non-Being is in principle never excluded. Every empirical power, be it ever so great, can be gradually outweighed and overcome. Nothing is thereby altered in the absolute Being of experiences, indeed these remain presupposed in all this all the time.

With this conclusion our study has reached its climax. We have won the knowledge we needed. In the essential connexions it has revealed to us already involved the most important of the premises on which depend those inferences we would draw concerning the detachability in principle of the whole natural world from the domain of consciousness, the sphere in which experiences have their being; inferences in which, as we can readily convince ourselves, a central, though not fully developed, thought of the quite otherwise oriented meditations of Descartes comes at last to its own. To reach our final goal we shall need indeed to add in the sequel a few supplementary discussions, which for the rest will not trouble us too much. Meanwhile let us draw our conclusions provisionally within a compass of limited bearing.

Chapter 33

MARTIN HEIDEGGER

Martin Heidegger (1889–1976) was born in Messkirch, an agricultural community in southwest Germany. He entered the seminary to become a Jesuit priest, but was soon attracted to philosophy and transferred to the University of Freiburg. There he studied under Edmund Husserl (see Chapter 32). After graduation he became a professor at the University of Marburg, where he wrote his famous *Being and Time* (1927) and became a colleague of two of the leading Protestant theologians of the twentieth century, Rudolf Bultmann and Paul Tillich, both of whom he significantly influenced. In 1928 he was chosen as Husserl's successor at the University of Freiburg and was elected Rector of the University in 1933. For a brief period he was a member of the Nazi party, believing that it offered the best hope for the renewal of the nation. Although his reputation has been sullied by his brief support of the Nazis, there is no evidence that he shared Nazi fanatical beliefs. To his credit, he became disillusioned with the party and resigned the Rectorship and his party membership. After the war, he retired to the Black Forest where he spent his days writing. Meantime, his work had attracted worldwide attention and philosophers came from many countries to visit him in his mountain home.

Heidegger's thought is concerned with the question of the meaning of *being*, the question which he claims motivated the inquiries of the first philosophers but which had become neglected by subsequent philosophers. Some, such as Gilbert Ryle, would say it is a "pseudo question," for being is not a thing but a word referring to concepts that are instantiated. Heidegger disagrees and holds that we intuitively realize that there is something in the idea that a common reality underlies all reality. He then asks, Is there a particular being that is particularly suited to inquire into the meaning of being? His existential philosophy is a response to that question. Our first selection from the Introduction to *Being and Time* describes Heidegger's concern to revive philosophical interest in the meaning of *being*. Man is that particular being *Dasein* ("being-there"), for whom being is the central issue. Since a human being experiences openness to the future and has a measure of freedom and responsibility, the question of who he is, is inescapable for him; but this question, if pursued in a correct manner, leads with equal inescapability into the question of Being in general. As Heidegger says in our reading, "Each of us is grazed at least once, perhaps more than once, by the hidden power of this question, even if he is not aware of what is happening to him."

The central question in our second selection, "The Fundamental Question of Metaphysics," is "Why is there anything at all, rather than nothing?" Some may dismiss this as a nonsensical question, but that only shows that it is so primordial and, perhaps, unanswerable, that it seems pointless to raise it. Yet it leads us to wonder—What is the explanation of reality, of the universe, of our being here? According to Heidegger, wondering about this basic ontological question opens oneself up to the presence of Being. Heidegger traces the quest for Being back to the ancient Greeks, especially Parmenides.

Following his teacher Husserl, Heidegger uses the phenomenological method of drawing attention to salient features of experience (the phenomena), awakening us to patterns of reality that we have ignored.

FOR FURTHER READING

Guignon, C., ed. *The Cambridge Companion to Heidegger* (Cambridge University Press, 1993).
Heidegger, Martin. *Being and Time,* trans. Edward Robinson and John Macquarrie (Harper & Row, 1962).
Macquarrie, John. *Martin Heidegger* (Lutterworth Press, 1968).
Olafson, Frederick. *Heidegger and the Philosophy of Mind* (Yale University Press, 1987).
Richardson, J. *Existential Phenomenology: A Heideggerian Critique of the Cartesian Project* (Oxford University Press, 1986).
Shahan, Robert and J. N. Mohanty, eds. *Thinking About Being: Aspects of Heidegger's Thought* (Oklahoma University Press, 1984).
Solomon, Robert, ed. *Phenomenology and Existentialism* (Harper & Row, 1972).
Speigelberg, Herbert. *The Phenomenological Movement,* 2 vols. (Martinus Nijhoff, 1960).
Stapleton, Timothy J. *Husserl and Heidegger* (SUNY Press, 1983).

On Dasein and Anxiety

§2 THE FORMAL STRUCTURE OF THE QUESTION OF BEING

The question of the meaning of Being must be *formulated.* If it is a fundamental question, or indeed *the* fundamental question, it must be made transparent, and in an appropriate way. We must therefore explain briefly what belongs to any question whatsoever, so that from this standpoint the question of Being can be made visible as a *very special* one with its own distinctive character.

Every inquiry is a seeking [*Suchen*]. . . . Inquiry, as a kind of seeking, must be guided beforehand by what is sought. So the meaning of Being must already be available to us in some way. As we have intimated, we always conduct our activities in an understanding of Being. Out of this understanding arise both the explicit question of the meaning of Being and the tendency that leads us towards its conception. We do not *know* what 'Being' means. But even if we ask, 'What *is* "Being"?', we keep within an understanding of the 'is', though we are unable to fix conceptionally what that 'is' signifies. We do not even know the horizon in terms of which that meaning is to be grasped and fixed. *But this vague average understanding of Being is still a Fact.*

However much this understanding of Being (an understanding which is already available to us) may fluctuate and grow dim, and border on mere acquaintance with a word, its very indefiniteness is itself a positive phenomenon which needs to be clarified. An investigation of the meaning of Being cannot be expected to give this clarification at the outset. If we are to obtain the clue we need for Interpreting this average understanding of Being, we must first develop the concept of Being. In the light of this concept and the ways in which it may be explicitly understood, we can make out what this obscured or still unillumined understanding of Being means, and what kinds of obscuration—or hindrance to an explicit illumination—of the meaning of Being are possible and even inevitable.

Further, this vague average understanding of Being may be so infiltrated with traditional theories and opinions about Being that these remain hidden as sources of the way in which it is prevalently understood. What we seek when we inquire into Being is not something entirely unfamiliar, even if proximally we cannot grasp it at all.

In the question which we are to work out, *what is asked about* is Being—that which determines entities as entities, that on the basis of which [*woraufhin*]

From *Being and Time*, trans. J. Macquarrie and E. Robinson (Oxford: Blackwell, 1967).

entities are already understood, however we may discuss them in detail. The Being of entities 'is' not itself an entity. If we are to understand the problem of Being, our first philosophical step consists in not μῦθόν τινα διηγεῖσθαι, in not 'telling a story'—that is to say, in not defining entities as entities by tracing them back in their origin to some other entities, as if Being had the character of some possible entity. Hence Being, as that which is asked about, must be exhibited in a way of its own, essentially different from the way in which entities are discovered. Accordingly, *what is to be found out by the asking*—the meaning of Being—also demands that it be conceived in a way of its own, essentially contrasting with the concepts in which entities acquire their determinate significantion.

In so far as Being constitutes what is asked about, and 'Being' means the Being of entities, then entities themselves turn out to be *what is interrogated*. These are, so to speak, questioned as regards their Being. But if the characteristics of their Being can be yielded without falsification, then these entities must, on their part, have become accessible as they are in themselves. When we come to what is to be interrogated, the question of Being requires that the right way of access to entities shall have been obtained and secured in advance. But there are many things which we designate as 'being' [*seiend*], and we do so in various senses. Everything we talk about, everything we have in view, everything towards which we comport ourselves in any way, is being; what we are is being, and so is how we are. Being lies in the fact that something is, and in its Being as it is; in Reality; in presence-at-hand; in subsistence; in validity; in Dasein; in the 'there is'. In *which* entities is the meaning of Being to be discerned? From which entities is the disclosure of Being to take its departure? Is the starting-point optional, or does some particular entity have priority when we come to work out the question of Being? Which entity shall we take for our example, and in what sense does it have priority?

If the question about Being is to be explicitly formulated and carried through in such a manner as to be completely transparent to itself, then any treatment of it in line with the elucidations we have given requires us to explain how Being is to be looked at, how its meaning is to be understood and conceptually grasped; it requires us to prepare the way for choosing the right entity for our example, and to work out the genuine way of access to it. Looking at something, understanding and conceiving it, choosing, access to it—all these ways of behaving are constitutive for our inquiry, and therefore are modes of Being for those particular entities which we, the inquirers, are ourselves. Thus to work out the question of Being adequately, we must make an entity—the inquirer—transparent in his own Being. The very asking of this question is an entity's mode of *Being*; and as such it gets its essential character from what is inquired about—namely, Being. This entity which each of us is himself and which includes inquiring as one of the possibilities of its Being, we shall denote by the term '*Dasein*'. If we are to formulate our question explicity and transparently, we must first give a proper explication of an entity (Dasein), with regard to its Being.

Is there not, however, a manifest circularity in such an undertaking? If we must first define an entity *in its Being*, and if we want to formulate the question of Being only on this basis, what is this but going in a circle? In working out our question, have we not 'presupposed' something which only the answer can bring? Formal objections such as the argument about 'circular reasoning', which can easily be cited at any time in the study of first principles, are always sterile when one is considering concrete ways of investigating. When it comes to understanding the matter at hand, they carry no weight and keep us from penetrating into the field of study.

But factically there is no circle at all in formulating our question as we have described. One can determine the nature of entities in their Being without necessarily having the explicit concept of the meaning of Being at one's disposal. Otherwise there could have been no ontological knowledge heretofore. One would hardly deny that factically there has been such knowledge. Of course 'Being' has been presupposed in all ontology up till now, but not as a *concept* at one's disposal—not as the sort of thing we are seeking. This 'presupposing' of Being has rather the character of taking a look at it beforehand, so that in the light of it the entities presented to us get provisionally Articulated in their Being. This guiding activity of taking a look at Being arises from the average understanding of Being in which we always operate and *which in the end belongs to the essential constitution of Dasein itself*. Such 'presupposing' has nothing to do with laying down an axiom from which a sequence of propositions is deductively derived. It is quite impossible for there to be any 'circular argument' in formulating the question about the meaning of Being; for in answering this question, the issue is not one of grounding something by such a derivation; it is rather one of laying bare the grounds for it and exhibiting them.

In the question of the meaning of Being there is no 'circular reasoning' but rather a remarkable 'relatedness backward or forward' which what we are asking about (Being) bears to the inquiry itself as a mode of Being of an entity. Here what is asked about has an essential pertinence to the inquiry itself, and this belongs to the ownmost meaning [*eigensten Sinn*] of the question of Being. This only means, however, that there is a way—perhaps even a very special one—in which entities with the character of Dasein are related to the question of Being. But have we not thus demonstrated that a certain kind of entity has a priority with regard to its Being? And have we not thus presented that entity which shall serve as the primary example to be *interrogated* in the question of Being? So far our discussion has not demonstrated Dasein's priority, nor has it shown decisively whether Dasein may possibly or even necessarily serve as the primary entity to be interrogated. But indeed something like a priority of Dasein has announced itself.

§3 THE ONTOLOGICAL PRIORITY OF THE QUESTION OF BEING

When we pointed out the characteristics of the question of Being, taking as our clue the formal structure of the question as such, we made it clear that this question is a peculiar one, in that a series of fundamental considerations is required for working it out, not to mention for solving it. But its distinctive features will come fully to light only when we have delimited it adequately with regard to its function, its aim, and its motives.

Hitherto our arguments for showing that the question must be restated have been motivated in part by its venerable origin but chiefly by the lack of a definite answer and even by the absence of any satisfactory formulation of the question itself. One may, however, ask what purpose this question is supposed to serve. Does it simply remain—or *is* it at all—a mere matter for soaring speculation about the most general of generalities, *or is it rather, of all questions, both the most basic and the most concrete*?

Being is always the Being of an entity. The totality of entities can, in accordance with its various domains, become a field for laying bare and delimiting certain definite areas of subject-matter. These areas, on their part (for instance, history, Nature, space, life, Dasein, language, and the like), can serve as objects which corresponding scientific investigations may take as their respective themes. Scientific research accomplishes, roughly and naïvely, the demarcation and initial fixing of the areas of subject-matter. The basic structures of any such area have already been worked out after a fashion in our pre-scientific ways of experiencing and interpreting that domain of Being in which the area of subject-matter is itself confined. The 'basic concepts' which thus arise remain our proximal clues for disclosing this area concretely for the first time. And although research may always lean towards this positive approach, its real progress comes not so much from collecting results and storing them away in 'manuals' as from inquiring into the ways in which each particular area is basically constituted [*Grundverfassungen*]—an inquiry to which we have been driven mostly by reacting against just such an increase in information.

The real 'movement' of the sciences takes place when their basic concepts undergo a more or less radical revision which is transparent to itself. The level which a science has reached is determined by how far it is *capable* of a crisis in its basic concepts. In such immanent crises the very relationship between positively investigative inquiry and those things themselves that are under interrogation comes to a point where it begins to totter. Among the various disciplines everywhere today there are freshly awakened tendencies to put research on new foundations.

Mathematics, which is seemingly the most rigorous and most firmly constructed of the sciences, has reached a crisis in its 'foundations'. In the controversy between the formalists and the intuitionists, the issue is one of obtaining and securing the primary way of access to what are supposedly the objects of this science. The relativity theory of *physics* arises from the tendency to exhibit the interconnectedness of Nature as it is 'in itself'. As a theory of the conditions under which we have access to Nature itself, it seeks to preserve the changelessness of the laws of motion by ascertaining all relativities, and thus comes up against the question of the structure of its own given area of study—the problem of matter. In *biology* there is an awakening tendency to inquire beyond the definitions which mechanism and vitalism have given for 'life' and 'organism', and to define anew the kind of Being which belongs to the living as such. In those *humane sciences which are historiological in character*, the urge towards historical actuality itself has been strengthened in the course of time by tradition and by the way tradition has been presented and handed down: the history of literature is to become the history of problems. *Theology* is seeking a more primordial interpretation of man's Being towards God, prescribed by the meaning of faith itself and remaining within it. It is slowly beginning to understand once more Luther's insight that the 'foundation' on which its system of dogma rests has not arisen from an inquiry in which faith is primary, and that conceptually this 'foundation' not only is inadequate for the problematic of theology, but conceals and distorts it.

Basic concepts determine the way in which we get an understanding beforehand of the area of subject-matter underlying all the objects a science takes as its theme, and all positive investigation is guided by this understanding. Only after the area itself has been explored beforehand in a corresponding manner do these concepts become genuinely demonstrated and 'grounded'. But since every such area is itself obtained from the domain of entities themselves, this preliminary research, from which the basic concepts are drawn, signifies nothing else than an interpretation of those entities with regard to their basic state of Being. Such research must run ahead of the positive sciences, and it *can*. Here the work of Plato and Aristotle is evidence enough. Laying the foundations for the sciences in this way is different in principle from the kind of 'logic' which limps along after, investigating the status of some science as it chances to find it, in order to discover its 'method'. Laying the foundations, as we have described it, is rather a productive logic—in the sense that it leaps ahead, as it were, into some area of Being, discloses it for the first time in the constitution of its Being, and, after thus arriving at the structures within it, makes these available to the positive sciences as transparent assignments for their inquiry. To give an example, what is philosophically primary is neither a theory of the concept-formation of historiology nor the theory of historiological knowledge, nor yet the theory of history as the Object of historiology; what is primary is rather the Interpretation of authentically historical entities as regards their historicality. Similarly the positive outcome of Kant's *Critique of Pure Reason* lies in what it has contributed towards the working out of what belongs to any Nature whatsoever, not in a 'theory' of knowledge. His transcendental logic is an *a priori* logic for the subject-matter of that area of Being called 'Nature'.

But such an inquiry itself—entology taken in the widest sense without favouring any particular ontological directions or tendencies—requires a further clue. Ontological inquiry is indeed more primordial, as over against the ontical inquiry of the positive sciences. But it remains itself naïve and opaque if in its researches into the Being of entities it fails to discuss the meaning of Being in general. And even the ontological task of constructing a non-deductive genealogy of the different possible ways of Being requires that we first come to an understanding of 'what we really mean by this expression "Being"'.

The question of Being aims therefore at ascertaining the *a priori* conditions not only for the possibility of the sciences which examine entities as entities of such and such a type, and, in so doing, already operate with an understanding of Being, but also for the possibility of those ontologies themselves which are prior to the ontical sciences and which provide their foundations. *Basically, all ontology, no matter how rich and firmly compacted a system of categories it has at its disposal, remains blind and perverted from its ownmost aim, if it has not first adequately clarified the meaning of Being, and conceived this clarification as its fundamental task.*

Ontological research itself, when properly understood, gives to the question of Being an ontological priority which goes beyond mere resumption of a venerable tradition and advancement with a problem that has hitherto been opaque. But this objectively scientific priority is not the only one.

§4 THE ONTICAL PRIORITY OF THE QUESTION OF BEING

Science in general may be defined as the totality established through an interconnection of true propositions. This definition is not complete, nor does it reach the meaning of science. As ways in which man behaves, sciences have the manner of Being which this entity—man himself—possesses. This entity we denote by the term '*Dasein*'. Scientific research is not the only manner of Being which this entity can have, nor is it the one which lies closest. Moreover, Dasein itself has a special distinctiveness as compared with other entities, and it is worth our while to bring this to view in a provisional way. Here our discussion must anticipate later analyses, in which our results will be authentically exhibited for the first time.

Dasein is an entity which does not just occur among other entities. Rather it is ontically distinguished by the fact that, in its very Being, that Being is an *issue* for it. But in that case, this is a constitutive state of Dasein's Being, and this implies that Dasein, in its Being, has a relationship towards that Being—a relationship which itself is one of Being. And this means further that there is some way in which Dasein understands itself in its Being, and that to some degree it does so explicitly. It is peculiar to this entity that with and through its Being, this Being is disclosed to it. *Understanding of Being is itself a definite characteristic of Dasein's Being.* Dasein is ontically distinctive in that it *is* ontological.

Here 'Being-ontological' is not yet tantamount to 'developing an ontology'. So if we should reserve the term 'ontology' for that theoretical inquiry which is explicitly devoted to the meaning of entities, then what we have had in mind in speaking of Dasein's 'Being-ontological' is to be designated as something 'pre-ontological'. It does not signify simply 'being-ontical', however, but rather 'being in such a way that one has an understanding of Being'.

That kind of Being towards which Dasein can comport itself in one way or another, and always does comport itself somehow, we call '*existence*' [*Existenz*]. And because we cannot define Dasein's essence by citing a 'what' of the kind that pertains to a subject-matter [*eines sachhaltigen Was*], and because its essence lies rather in the fact that in each case it has its Being to be, and has it as its own, we have chosen to designate this entity as 'Dasein', a term which is purely an expression of its Being [*als reiner Seinsausdruck*].

Dasein always understands itself in terms of its existence—in terms of a possibility of itself: to be itself or not itself. Dasein has either chosen these possibilities itself, or got itself into them, or grown up in them already. Only the particular Dasein decides its existence, whether it does so by taking hold or by neglecting. The question of existence never gets straightened out except through existing itself. The understanding of oneself which leads *along this way* we call '*existentiell*'. The question of existence is one of Dasein's ontical 'affairs'. This does not require that the ontological structure of existence should be theoretically transparent. The question about that structure aims at the analysis [*Auseinanderlegung*] of what constitutes existence. The context [*Zusammenhang*] of such structures we call '*existentiality*'. Its analytic has the character of an understanding which is not existentiell, but rather *existential*. The task of an existential analytic of Dasein has been delineated in advance, as regards both its possibility and its necessity, in Dasein's ontical constitution.

So far as existence is the determining character of Dasein, the ontological analytic of this entity always requires that existentiality be considered beforehand. By 'existentiality' we understand the state of Being that is constitutive for those entities that exist. But in the idea of such a constitutive state of Being, the idea of Being is already included. And thus even the possibility of carrying through the analytic of Dasein depends on working out beforehand the question about the meaning of Being in general.

Sciences are ways of Being in which Dasein comports itself towards entities which it need not be itself. But to Dasein, Being in a world is something that belongs essentially. Thus Dasein's understanding of Being pertains with equal primordiality both to an understanding of something like a 'world', and to the understanding of the Being of those entities which become accessible within the world. So whenever an ontology takes for its theme entities whose character of Being is other than that of Dasein, it has its own foundation and motivation in Dasein's own ontical structure, in which a pre-ontological understanding of Being is comprised as a definite characteristic.

Therefore *fundamental ontology*, from which alone all other ontologies can take their rise, must be sought in the *existential analytic of Dasein*.

Dasein accordingly takes priority over all other entities in several ways. The first priority is an *ontical* one: Dasein is an entity whose Being has the determinate character of existence. The second priority is an *ontological* one: Dasein is in itself 'ontological', because existence is thus determinative for it. But with equal primordiality Dasein also possesses—as constitutive for its understanding of existence—an understanding of the Being of all entities of a character other than its own. Dasein has therefore a third priority as providing the ontico-ontological condition for the possibility of any ontologies. Thus Dasein has turned out to be, more than any other entity, the one which must first be interrogated ontologically.

But the roots of the existential analytic, on its part, are ultimately *existentiell*, that is, *ontical*. Only if the inquiry of philosophical research is itself seized upon in an existentiell manner as a possibility of the Being of each existing Dasein, does it become at all possible to disclose the existentiality of existence and to undertake an adequately founded ontological problematic. But with this, the ontical priority of the question of being has also become plain.

Dasein's ontico-ontological priority was seen quite early, though Dasein itself was not grasped in its genuine ontological structure, and did not even become a problem in which this structure was sought. Aristotle says: ἡ ψυχὴ τὰ ὄντα πώζ ἐστιν. 'Man's soul is, in a certain way, entities'. The 'soul' which makes up the Being of man has αἴσθησιζ and νόησιζ among its ways of Being, and in these it discovers all entities, both in the fact that they are, and in their Being as they are—that is, always in their Being. Aristotle's principle, which points back to the ontological thesis of Parmenides, is one which Thomas Aquinas has taken up in a characteristic discussion. Thomas is engaged in the task of deriving the '*transcendentia*'—those characters of Being which lie beyond every possible way in which an entity may be classified as coming under some generic kind of subject-matter (every *modus specialis entis*), and which belong necessarily to anything, whatever it may be. Thomas has to demonstrate that the *verum* is such a *transcendens*. He does this by invoking an entity which, in accordance with its very manner of Being, is properly suited to 'come together with' entities of any sort whatever. This distinctive entity, the *ens quod natum est convenire cum omni ente*, is the soul (*anima*). Here the priority of 'Dasein' over all other entities emerges, although it has not been ontologically clarified. This priority has obviously nothing in common with a vicious subjectivizing of the totality of entities.

By indicating Dasein's ontico-ontological priority in this provisional manner, we have grounded our demonstration that the question of Being is ontico-ontologically distinctive. But when we analysed the structure of this question as such (Section 2), we came up against a distinctive way in which this entity functions in the very formulation of that question. Dasein then revealed itself as that entity which must first be worked out in an ontologically adequate manner, if the inquiry is to become a transparent one. But now it has been shown that the ontological analytic of Dasein in general is what makes up fundamental ontology, so that Dasein functions as that entity which in principle is to be *interrogated* beforehand as to its Being.

If to Interpret the meaning of Being becomes our task, Dasein is not only the primary entity to be interrogated; it is also that entity which already comports itself, in its Being, towards what we are asking about when we ask this question. But in that case the question of Being is nothing other than the radicalization of an essential tendency-of-Being which belongs to Dasein itself—the pre-ontological understanding of Being. . . .

§5 THE ONTOLOGICAL ANALYTIC OF DASEIN AS LAYING BARE THE HORIZON FOR AN INTERPRETATION OF THE MEANING OF BEING IN GENERAL

In designating the tasks of 'formulating' the question of Being, we have shown not only that we must establish which entity is to serve as our primary object of interrogation, but also that the right way of access to this entity is one which we must explicitly make our own and hold secure. We have already discussed which entity takes over the principal role within the question of Being. But how are we, as it were, to set our sights towards this entity, Dasein, both as something accessible to us and as something to be understood and interpreted?

In demonstrating that Dasein is ontico-ontologically prior, we may have misled the reader into supposing that this entity must also be what is given as ontico-ontologically primary not only in the sense that it can itself be grasped 'immediately', but also in that the kind of Being which it possesses is presented just as 'immediately'. Ontically, of course, Dasein is not only close to us—even that which is closest: we *are* it, each of us, we ourselves. In spite of this, or rather for just this reason, it is ontologically that which is farthest. To be sure, its ownmost Being is such that it has an understanding of that Being, and already maintains itself in each case as if its Being has been interpreted in some manner. But we are certainly not saying that when Dasein's own Being is thus interpreted preontologically in the way which lies closest, this interpretation can be taken over as an appropriate clue, as if this way of understanding Being is what must emerge when one's ownmost state of Being is considered as an ontological theme. The kind of Being which belongs to Dasein is rather such that, in understanding its own Being, it has a tendency to do so in terms of that entity towards which it comports itself proximally and in a way which is essentially constant—in terms of the 'world'. In Dasein itself, and therefore in its own understanding of Being, the way the world is understood is, as we shall show, reflected back ontologically upon the way in which Dasein itself gets interpreted.

Thus because Dasein is ontico-ontologically prior, its own specific state of Being (if we understand this in the sense of Dasein's 'categorial structure') remains concealed from it. Dasein is ontically 'closest' to itself and ontologically farthest; but pre-ontologically it is surely not a stranger.

Here we have merely indicated provisionally that an Interpretation of this entity is confronted with peculiar difficulties grounded in the kind of Being which belongs to the object taken as our theme and to the very behavior of so taking it. These difficulties are not grounded in any shortcomings of the cognitive powers with which we are endowed, or in the lack of a suitable way of conceiving—a lack which seemingly would not be hard to remedy.

Not only, however, does an understanding of Being belong to Dasein, but this understanding develops or decays along with whatever kind of Being Dasein may possess at the time; accordingly there are many ways in which it has been interpreted, and these are all at Dasein's disposal. Dasein's ways of behaviour, its capacities, powers, possibilities, and vicissitudes, have been studied with varying extent in philosophical psychology, in anthropology, ethics, and 'political science', in poetry, biography, and the writing of history, each in a different fashion. But the question remains whether these interpretations of Dasein have been carried through with a primordial existentiality comparable to whatever existentiell primordiality they may have possessed. Neither of these excludes the other but they do not necessarily go together. Existentiell interpretation can demand an existential analytic, if indeed we conceive of philosophical cognition as something possible and necessary. Only when the basic structures of Dasein have been adequately worked out with explicit orientation towards the problem of Being itself, will what we have hitherto gained in interpreting Dasein get its existential justification.

Thus an analytic of Dasein must remain our first requirement in the question of Being. But in that case the problem of obtaining and securing the kind of access which will lead to Dasein, becomes even more a burning one. To put it negatively, we have no right to resort to dogmatic constructions and to apply just any idea of Being and actuality to this entity, no matter how 'self-evident' that idea may be; nor may any of the 'categories' which such an idea prescribes be forced upon Dasein without proper ontological consideration. We must rather choose such a way of access and such a kind of interpretation that this entity can show itself in itself and from itself [*an ihm selbst von ihm selbst her*]. And this means that it is to be shown as it is *proximally and for the most part*—in its average *everydayness*. In this everydayness there are certain structures which we shall exhibit—not just any accidental structures, but essential ones which, in every kind of Being that factical Dasein may possess, persist as determinative for the character of its Being. Thus by having regard for the basic state of Dasein's everydayness, we shall bring out the Being of this entity in a preparatory fashion.

When taken in this way, the analytic of Dasein remains wholly oriented towards the guiding task of working out the question of Being. Its limits are thus determined. It cannot attempt to provide a complete ontology of Dasein, which assuredly must be constructed if anything like a 'philosophical' anthropology is to have a philosophically adequate basis.

If our purpose is to make such an anthropology possible, or to lay its ontological foundations, our Interpretation will provide only some of the 'pieces', even though they are by no means inessential ones. Our analysis of Dasein, however, is not only incomplete; it is also, in the first instance, *provisional*. It merely brings out the Being of this entity, without Interpreting its meaning. It is rather a preparatory procedure by which the horizon for the most primordial way of interpreting Being may be laid bare. Once we have arrived at that horizon, this preparatory analytic of Dasein will have to be repeated on a higher and authentically ontological basis.

We shall point to *temporality* as the meaning of the Being of that entity which we call 'Dasein'. If this is to be demonstrated, those structures of Dasein which we shall provisionally exhibit must be Interpreted over again as modes of temporality. In thus interpreting Dasein as temporality, however, we shall not give the answer to our leading question as to the meaning of Being in general. But the ground will have been prepared for obtaining such an answer.

We have already intimated that Dasein has a pre-ontological Being as its ontically constitutive state. Dasein *is* in such a way as to be something which understands something like Being. Keeping this interconnection firmly in mind, we shall show that whenever Dasein tacitly understands and interprets something like Being, it does so with *time* as its standpoint. Time must be brought to light—and genuinely conceived—as the horizon for all understanding of Being and for any way of interpreting it. In order for us to discern this, *time* needs to be *explicated primordially as the horizon for the understanding of Being, and in terms of temporality as the Being of Dasein, which understands Being*. This task as a whole requires that the conception of time thus obtained shall be distinguished from the way in which it is ordinarily understood. This ordinary way of understanding it has become explicit in an interpretation precipitated in the traditional concept of time, which has persisted from Aristotle to Bergson and even later. Here we must make clear that this conception of time and, in general, the ordinary way of understanding it, have sprung from temporality, and we must show how this has come about. We shall thereby restore to the ordinary conception the autonomy which is its rightful due, as against Bergson's thesis that the time one has in mind in this conception is space.

'Time' has long functioned as an ontological—or rather an ontical—criterion for naïvely discriminating various realms of entities. A distinction has been made between 'temporal' entities (natural processes and historical happenings) and 'non-temporal' entities (spatial and numerical relationships). We are accustomed to contrasting the 'timeless' meaning of propositions with the 'temporal' course of propositional assertions. It is also held that there is a 'cleavage' between 'temporal' entities and the 'supra-temporal' eternal, and efforts are made to bridge this over. Here 'temporal' always means simply being [*seiend*] 'in time'—a designation which, admittedly, is still pretty obscure. The fact remains that time, in the sense of 'being [*sein*] in time', functions as a criterion for distinguishing realms of Being. Hitherto no one has asked or troubled to investigate how time has come to have this distinctive ontological function, or with what right anything like time functions as such a criterion; nor has anyone asked whether the authentic ontological relevance which is possible for it, gets expressed when 'time' is used in so naïvely ontological a manner. 'Time' has acquired this 'self-evident' ontological function 'of its own accord', so to speak; indeed it has done so within the horizon of the way it is ordinarily understood. And it has maintained itself in this function to this day.

In contrast to all this, our treatment of the question of the meaning of Being must enable us to show that *the central problematic of all ontology is rooted in the phenomenon of time, if rightly seen and rightly explained*, and we must show *how* this is the case.

If Being is to be conceived in terms of time, and if, indeed, its various modes and derivatives are to become intelligible in their respective modifications and derivations by taking time into consideration, then Being itself (and not merely entities, let us say, as entities 'in time') is thus made visible in its 'temporal' character. But in that case, 'temporal' can no longer mean simply 'being in time'. Even the 'non-temporal' and the 'supra-temporal' are 'temporal' with regard to their Being, and not just privatively by contrast with something 'temporal' as an entity 'in time', but in a *positive* sense, though it is one which we must first explain. In both pre-philosophical and philosophical usage the expression 'temporal' has been pre-empted by the signification we have cited; in the following investigations, however, we shall employ it for another signification. Thus the way in which Being and its modes and characteristics have their meaning determined primordially in terms of time, is what we shall call its '*Temporal*' determinateness. Thus the fundamental ontological task of Interpreting Being as such includes working out the *Temporality of Being*. In the exposition of the problematic of Temporality the question of the meaning of Being will first be concretely answered.

Because Being cannot be grasped except by taking time into consideration, the answer to the question of Being cannot lie in any proposition that is blind and isolated. The answer is not properly conceived if what it asserts propositionally is just passed along, especially if it gets circulated as a free-floating result, so that we merely get informed about a 'standpoint' which may perhaps differ from the way this has hitherto been treated. Whether the answer is a 'new' one remains quite superficial and is of no importance. Its positive character must lie in its being *ancient* enough for us to learn to conceive the possibilities which the 'Ancients' have made ready for us. In its ownmost meaning this answer tells us that concrete ontological research must begin with an investigative inquiry which keeps within the horizon we have laid bare; and this is all that it tells us.

If, then, the answer to the question of Being is to provide the clues for our research, it cannot be adequate until it brings us the insight that the specific kind of Being of ontology hitherto, and the vicissitudes of its inquiries, its findings, and its failures, have been necessitated in the very character of Dasein.

§6 THE TASK OF DESTROYING THE HISTORY OF ONTOLOGY

All research—and not least that which operates within the range of the central question of Being—is an ontical possibility of Dasein. Dasein's Being finds its meaning in temporality. But temporality is also the condition which makes historicality possible as a temporal kind of Being which Dasein itself possesses, regardless of whether or how Dasein is an entity 'in time'. Historicality, as a determinate character, is prior to what is called 'history' (world-historical historizing).

'Historicality' stands for the state of Being that is constitutive for Dasein's 'historizing' as such; only on the basis of such 'historizing' is anything like 'world-history' possible or can anything belong historically to world-history. In its factical Being, any Dasein is as it already was, and it is 'what' it already was. It *is* its past, whether explicitly or not. And this is so not only in that its past is, as it were, pushing itself along 'behind' it, and that Dasein possesses what is past as a property which is still present-at-hand and which sometimes has after-effects upon it: Dasein 'is' its past in the way of *its* own Being, which, to put it roughly, 'historizes' out of its future on each occasion. Whatever the way of being it may have at the time, and thus with whatever understanding of Being it may possess, Dasein has grown up both into and in a traditional way of interpreting itself: in terms of this it understands itself proximally and, within a certain range, constantly. By this understanding, the possibilities of its Being are disclosed and regulated. Its own past—and this always means the past of its 'generation'—is not something which *follows along after* Dasein, but something which already goes ahead of it.

This elemental historicality of Dasein may remain hidden from Dasein itself. But there is a way by which it can be discovered and given proper attention. Dasein can discover tradition, preserve it, and study it explicitly. The discovery of tradition and the disclosure of what it 'transmits' and how this is transmitted, can be taken hold of as a task in its own right. In this way Dasein brings itself into the kind of Being which consists in historiological inquiry and research. But historiology—or more precisely historicity—is possible as a kind of Being which the inquiring Dasein may possess, only because historicality is a determining characteristic for Dasein in the very basis of its Being. If this historicality remains hidden from Dasein, and as long as it so remains, Dasein is also denied the possibility of historiological inquiry or the discovery of history. If historiology is wanting, this is not evidence *against* Dasein's historicality; on the contrary, as a deficient mode of this state of Being, it is evidence for it. Only because it is 'historical' can an era be unhistoriological.

On the other hand, if Dasein has seized upon its latent possibility not only of making its own existence transparent to itself but also of inquiring into the meaning of existentiality itself (that is to say, of previously inquiring into the meaning of Being in general), and if by such inquiry its eyes have been opened to its own essential historicality, then one cannot fail to see that the inquiry into Being (the ontico-ontological necessity of which we have already indicated) is itself characterized by historicality. The ownmost meaning of Being which belongs to the inquiry into Being as an historical inquiry, gives us the assignment [*Anweisung*] of inquiring into the history of that inquiry itself, that is, of becoming historiological. In working out the question of Being, we must heed this assignment, so that by positively making the past our own, we may bring ourselves into full possession of the ownmost possibilities of such inquiry. The question of the meaning of Being must be carried through by explicating Dasein beforehand in its temporality and historicality; the question thus brings itself to the point where it understands itself as historiological.

Our preparatory Interpretation of the fundamental structures of Dasein with regard to the average kind of Being which is closest to it (a kind of Being in which it is therefore proximally historical as well), will make manifest, however, not only that Dasein in inclined to fall back upon its world (the world in which it is) and to interpret itself in terms of that world by its reflected light, but also that Dasein simultaneously falls prey to the tradition of which it has more or less explicitly taken hold. This tradition keeps it from providing its own guidance, whether in inquiring or in choosing. This holds true—and by no means least—for that understanding which is rooted in Dasein's ownmost Being, and for the possibility of developing it—namely, for ontological understanding.

When tradition thus becomes master, it does so in such a way that what it 'transmits' is made so inaccessible, proximally and for the most part, that it rather becomes concealed. Tradition takes what has come down to us and delivers it over to self-evidence; it blocks our access to those primordial 'sources' from which the categories and concepts handed down to us have been in part quite genuinely drawn. Indeed it makes us forget that they have had such an origin, and makes us suppose that the necessity of going back to these sources is something which we need not even understand. Dasein has had its historicality so throughly uprooted by tradition that it confines its interest to the multiformity of possible types, directions, and standpoints of philosophical activity in the most exotic and alien of cultures; and by this very interest it seeks to veil the fact that it has no ground of its own to stand on. Consequently, despite all its historiological interests and all its zeal for an Interpretation which is philogically 'objective' [*'sachliche'*], Dasein no longer understands the most elementary conditions which would alone enable it to go back to the past in a positive manner and make it productively its own.

We have shown at the outset (Section I) not only that the question of the meaning of Being is one that has not been attended to and one that has been inadequately formulated, but that it has become quite forgotten in spite of all our interest in 'metaphysics'. Greek ontology and its history—which, in their numerous filiations and distortions, determine the conceptual character of philosophy even today—prove that when Dasein understands either itself or Being in general, it does so in terms of the 'world', and that the ontology which has thus arisen has deteriorated [*verfällt*] to a tradition in which it gets reduced to something selfevident—merely material for reworking, as it was for Hegel. In the Middle Ages this uprooted Greek ontology became a fixed body of doctrine. Its systematics, however, is by no means a mere joining together of traditional pieces into a single edifice. Though its basic conceptions of Being have been taken over dogmatically from the Greeks, a great deal of unpretentious work has been carried on further within these limits. With the peculiar character which the Scholastics gave it, Greek ontology has, in its essentials, travelled the path that leads through the *Disputationes metaphysicae* of Suarez to the 'metaphysics' and transcendental philosophy of modern times, determining even the foundations and the aims of Hegel's 'logic'. In the course of this history certain distinctive domains of Being have come into view and have served as the primary guides for subsequent problematics: the *ego cogito* of Descartes, the subject, the 'I', reason, spirit, person. But these all remain uninterrogated as to their Being and its structure, in accordance with the thoroughgoing way in which the question of Being has been neglected. It is rather the case that the categorial content of the traditional ontology has been carried over to these entities with corresponding formalizations and purely negative restrictions, or else dialectic has been called in for the purpose of Interpreting the substantiality of the subject ontologically.

If the question of Being is to have its own history made transparent, then this hardened tradition must be loosened up, and the concealments which it has brought about must be dissolved. We understand this task as one in which by taking *the question of Being as our clue*, we are to *destroy* the traditional content of ancient ontology until we arrive at those primordial experiences in which we achieved our first ways of determining the nature of Being—the ways which have guided us ever since.

In thus demonstrating the origin of our basic ontological concepts by an investigation in which their 'birth certificate' is displayed, we have nothing to do with a vicious relativizing of ontological standpoints. But this destruction is just as far from having the *negative* sense of shaking off the ontological tradition. We must, on the contrary, stake out the positive possibilities of that tradition, and this always means keeping it within its *limits*; these in turn are given factically in the way the question is formulated at the time, and in the way the possible field for investigation is thus bounded off. On its negative side, this destruction does not relate itself towards the past; its criticism is aimed at 'today' and at the prevalent way of treating the history of ontology, whether it is headed towards doxography, towards intellectual history, or towards a history of problems. But to bury the past in nullity *Nichtigkeit* is not the purpose of this destruction; its aim is *positive* . . .

§7 THE PHENOMENOLOGICAL METHOD OF INVESTIGATION

In provisionally characterizing the object which serves as the theme of our investigation (the Being of entities, or the meaning of Being in general), it seems that we have also delineated the method to be employed. The task of ontology is to explain Being itself and to make the Being of entities stand out in full relief. And the method of ontology remains questionable in the highest degree as long as we merely consult those ontologies which have come down to us historically, or other essays of that character. Since the term 'ontology' is used in this investigation in a sense which is formally broad, any attempt to clarify the method of ontology by tracing its history is automatically ruled out.

When, moreover, we use the term 'ontology', we are not talking about some definite philosophical discipline standing in interconnection with the others. Here one does not have to measure up to the tasks of some discipline that has been presented beforehand; on the contrary, only in terms of the objective necessities of definite questions and the kind of treatment which the 'things themselves' require, can one develop such a discipline.

With the question of the meaning of Being, our investigation comes up against the fundamental question of philosophy. This is one that must be treated *phenomenologically*. Thus our treatise does not subscribe to a 'stand-point' or represent any special 'direction'; for phenomenology is nothing of either sort, nor can it become so as long as it understands itself. The expression 'phenomenology' signifies primarily a *methodological conception*. This expression does not characterize the what of the objects of philosophical research as subject-matter, but rather the *how* of that research. The more genuinely a methodological concept is worked out and the more comprehensively it determines the principles on which a science is to be conducted, all the more primordially is it rooted in the way we come to terms with the things themselves, and the farther is it removed from what we call 'technical devices', though there are many such devices even in the theoretical disciplines.

Thus the term 'phenomenology' expresses a maxim which can be formulated as 'To the things themselves!' It is opposed to all free-floating constructions and accidental findings; it is opposed to taking over any conceptions which only seem to have been demonstrated; it is opposed to those pseudo-questions which parade themselves as 'problems', often for generations at a time. Yet this maxim, one may rejoin, is abundantly self-evident, and it expresses, moreover, the underlying principle of any scientific knowledge whatsoever. Why should anything so self-evident be taken up explicitly in giving a title to a branch of research? In point of fact, the issue here is a kind of 'self-evidence' which we should like to bring closer to us, so far as it is important to do so in casting light upon the procedure of our treatise. We shall expound only the preliminary conception [*Vorbegriff*] of phenomenology. . . .

The Preliminary Conception of Phenomenology

. . . 'Phenomenology' means ἀποφαίνεσθαι τὰ φαινόμενα—to let that which shows itself be seen from itself in the very way in which it shows itself from itself. This is the formal meaning of that branch of research which calls itself 'phenomenology'. But here we are expressing nothing else than the maxim formulated above: 'To the things themselves!'

Thus the term 'phenomenology' is quite different in its meaning from expressions such as 'theology' and the like. Those terms designate the objects of their respective sciences according to the subject-matter which they comprise at the time [*in ihrer jeweiligen Sachhaltigkeit*]. 'Phenomenology' neither designates the object of its researches, nor characterizes the subject-matter thus comprised. The word merely informs us of the '*how*' with which *what* is to be treated in this science gets exhibited and handled. To have a science 'of' phenomena means to grasp its objects *in such a way* that everything about them which is up for discussion must be treated by exhibiting it directly and demonstrating it directly. The expression 'descriptive phenomenology', which is at bottom tautological, has the same meaning. Here 'description' does not signify such a procedure as we find, let us say, in botanical morphology; the term has rather the sense of a prohibition—the avoidance of characterizing anything without such demonstration. The character of this description itself, the specific meaning of the logos, can be established first of all in terms of the "thinghood" ['*Sachheit*'] of what is to be 'described'—that is to say, of what is to be given scientific definiteness as we encounter it phenomenally. The signification of 'phenomenon', as conceived both formally and in the ordinary manner, is such that any exhibiting of an entity as it shows itself in itself, may be called 'phenomenology' with formal justification.

Now what must be taken into account if the formal conception of phenomenon is to be deformalized into the phenomenological one, and how is this latter to be distinguished from the ordinary conception? What is it that phenomenology is to 'let us see'? What is it that must be called a 'phenomenon' in a distinctive sense? What is it that by its very essence is *necessarily* the theme whenever we exhibit something *explicitly*? Manifestly, it is something that proximally and for the most part does *not* show itself at all: it is something that lies *hidden*, in contrast to that which proximally and for the most part does show itself; but at the same time it is something that belongs to what thus shows itself, and it belongs to it so essentially as to constitute its meaning and its ground.

Yet that which remains *hidden* in an egregious sense, or which relapses and gets *covered up* again, or which shows itself only '*in disguise*', is not just this entity or that, but rather the *Being* of entities, as our previous observations have shown. This Being can be covered up so extensively that it becomes forgotten and no question arises about it or about its meaning. Thus that which demands that it become a phenomenon, and which demands this in a distinctive sense and in terms of its ownmost content as a thing, is what phenomenology has taken into its grasp thematically as its object.

Phenomenology is our way of access to what is to be the theme of ontology, and it is our way of giving it demonstrative precision. *Only as phenomenology, is ontology possible*. In the phenomenological conception of 'phenomenon' what one has in mind as that which shows itself is the Being of entities, its meaning, its modifications and derivatives. And this showing-itself is not just any showing-itself, nor is it some such thing as appearing. Least of all can the Being of entities ever be anything such that 'behind it' stands something else 'which does not appear'.

'Behind' the phenomena of phenomenology there is essentially nothing else; on the other hand, what is to become a phenomenon can be hidden. And just because the phenomena are proximally and for the most part *not* given, there is need for phenomenology. Covered-up-ness is the counter-concept to 'phenomenon'.

There are various ways in which phenomena can be covered up. In the first place, a phenomenon can be covered up in the sense that it is still quite *undiscovered*. It is neither known nor unknown. Moreover, a phenomenon can be *buried over* [*verschüttet*]. This means that it has at some time been discovered but has deteriorated [*verfiel*] to the point of getting covered up again. This covering-up can become complete; or rather—and as a rule—what has been discovered earlier may still be visible, though only as a semblance. Yet so much semblance, so much 'Being'. This covering-up as a 'disguising' is both the most frequent and the most dangerous, for here the possibilities of deceiving and misleading are especially stubborn. Within a 'system', perhaps, those structures of Being—and their concepts—which are still available but veiled in their indigenous character, may claim their rights. For when they have been bound together constructively in a system, they present themselves as something 'clear', requiring no further justification, and thus can serve as the point of departure for a process of deduction.

The covering-up itself, whether in the sense of hiddenness, burying-over, or disguise, has in turn two possibilities. There are coverings-up which are accidental; there are also some which are necessary, grounded in what the thing discovered consists in [*der Bestandart des Entdeckten*]. Whenever a phenomenological concept is drawn from primordial sources, there is a possibility that it may degenerate if communicated in the form of an assertion. It gets understood in an empty way and is thus passed on, losing its indigenous character, and becoming a free-floating thesis. Even in the concrete work of phenomenology itself there lurks the possibility that what has been primordially 'within our grasp' may become hardened so that we can no longer grasp it. And the difficulty of this kind of research lies in making it self-critical in a positive sense.

The way in which Being and its structures are encountered in the mode of phenomenon is one which must first of all be *wrested* from the objects of phenomenology. Thus the very *point of departure* [*Aus-*

gang] for our analysis requires that it be secured by the proper method, just as much as does our *access* [*Zugang*] to the phenomenon, or our *passage* [*Durchgang*] through whatever is prevalently covering it up. The idea of grasping and explicating phenomena in a way which is 'original' and 'intuitive' ['*originären*' *and* '*intuitiven*'] is directly opposed to the *naïveté* of a haphazard, 'immediate', and unreflective 'beholding' ['*Schauen*'].

Now that we have delimited our preliminary conception of phenomenology, the terms '*phenomenal*' and '*phenomenological*' can also be fixed in their signification. That which is given and explicable in the way the phenomenon is encountered is called 'phenomenal'; this is what we have in mind when we talk about "phenomenal structures." Everything which belongs to the species of exhibiting and explicating and which goes to make up the way of conceiving demanded by this research, is called 'phenomenological'.

Because phenomena, as understood phenomenologically, are never anything but what goes to make up Being, while Being is in every case the Being of some entity, we must first bring forward the entities themselves if it is our aim that Being should be laid bare; and we must do this in the right way. These entities must likewise show themselves with the kind of access which genuinely belongs to them. And in this way the ordinary conception of phenomenon becomes phenomenologically relevant. If our analysis is to be authentic, its aim is such that the prior task of assuring ourselves 'phenomenologically' of that entity which is to serve as our example, has already been prescribed as our point of departure.

With regard to its subject-matter, phenomenology is the science of the Being of entities—ontology. In explaining the tasks of ontology we found it necessary that there should be a fundamental ontology taking as its theme that entity which is ontologico-ontically distinctive, Dasein, in order to confront the cardinal problem—the question of the meaning of Being in general. Our investigation itself will show that the meaning of phenomenological description as a method lies in *interpretation*. The λόγόζ of the phenomenology of Dasein has the character of a ἑρμηνεύειν, through which the authentic meaning of Being, and also those basic structures of Being which Dasein itself possesses, are *made known* to Dasein's understanding of Being. The phenomenology of Dasein is a *hermeneutic* in the primordial signification of this word, where it designates this business of interpreting. But to the extent that by uncovering the meaning of Being and the basic structures of Dasein in general we may exhibit the horizon for any further ontological study of those entities which do not have the character of Dasein, this hermeneutic also becomes a 'hermeneutic' in the sense of working out the conditions on which the possibility of any ontological investigation depends. And finally, to the extent that Dasein, as an entity with the possibility of existence, has ontological priority over every other entity, 'hermeneutic', as an interpretation of Dasein's Being, has the third and specific sense of an analytic of the existentiality of existence; and this is the sense which is philosophically *primary*. Then so far as this hermeneutic works out Dasein's historicality ontologically as the ontical condition for the possibility of historiology, it contains the roots of what can be called 'hermeneutic' only in a derivative sense: the methodology of those humane sciences which are historiological in character.

Being, as the basic theme of philosophy, is no class or genus of entities; yet it pertains to every entity. Its 'universality' is to be sought higher up. Being and the structure of Being lie beyond every entity and every possible character which an entity may possess. *Being is the transcendens pure and simple.* And the transcendence of Dasein's Being is distinctive in that it implies the possibility and the necessity of the most radical *individuation*. Every disclosure of Being as the *transcendens* is *transcendental* knowledge. *Phenomenological truth (the disclosedness of Being) is veritas transcendentalis.*

Ontology and phenomenology are not two distinct philosophical disciplines among others. These terms characterize philosophy itself with regard to its object and its way of treating that object. Philosophy is universal phenomenological ontology, and takes its departure from the hermeneutic of Dasein, which, as an analytic of *existence*, has made fast the guiding-line for all philosophical inquiry at the point where it *arises* and to which it *returns*.

The following investigation would not have been possible if the ground had not been prepared by Edmund Husserl, with whose *Logische Untersuchungen* phenomenology first emerged. Our comments on the preliminary conception of phenomenology have shown that what is essential in it does not lie in its *actuality* as a philosophical 'movement' ['*Richtung*']. Higher than actuality stands *possibility*. . . .

The Fundamental Question of Metaphysics

Why are there essents[1] rather than nothing? That is the question. Clearly it is no ordinary question. "Why are there essents, why is there anything at all, rather than nothing?"—obviously this is the first of all questions, though not in a chronological sense. Individuals and peoples ask a good many questions in the course of their historical passage through time. They examine, explore, and test a good many things before they run into the question "Why are there essents rather than nothing?" Many men never encounter this question, if by encounter we mean not merely to hear and read about it as an interrogative formulation but to ask the question, that is, to bring it about, to raise it, to feel its inevitability.

And yet each of us is grazed at least once, perhaps more than once, by the hidden power of this question, even if he is not aware of what is happening to him. The question looms in moments of great despair, when things tend to lose all their weight and all meaning becomes obscured. Perhaps it will strike but once like a muffled bell that rings into our life and gradually dies away. It is present in moments of rejoicing, when all the things around us are transfigured and seem to be there for the first time, as if it might be easier to think they are not than to understand that they are and are as they are. The question is upon us in boredom, when we are equally removed from despair and joy, and everything about us seems so hopelessly commonplace that we no longer care whether anything is or is not—and with this the question "Why are there essents rather than nothing?" is evoked in a particular form.

But this question may be asked expressly, or, unrecognized as a question, it may merely pass through our lives like a brief gust of wind; it may press hard upon us, or, under one pretext or another, we may thrust it away from us and silence it. In any case it is never the question that we ask first in point of time.

But it is the first question in another sense—in regard to rank. This may be clarified in three ways. The question "Why are there essents rather than nothing?" is first in rank for us first because it is the most far reaching, second because it is the deepest, and finally because it is the most fundamental of all questions.

It is the widest of all questions. It confines itself to no particular essent of whatever kind. The question takes in everything, and this means not only everything that is present in the broadest sense but also everything that ever was or will be. The range of this question finds its limit only in nothing, in that which simply is not and never was. Everything that is not nothing is covered by this question, and ultimately even nothing itself; not because it is *something*, since after all we speak of it, but because it *is* nothing. Our question reaches out so far that we can never go further. We do not inquire into this and that, or into each essent in turn, but from the very outset into the essent as a whole, or, as we say for reasons to be discussed below: into the essent as such in its entirety.

This broadest of questions is also the deepest: Why are there essents . . . ? Why, that is to say, on what ground? from what source does the essent derive? on what ground does it stand? The question is not concerned with particulars, with what essents are and of what nature at any time, here and there, with how they can be changed, what they can be used for, and so on. The question aims at the ground of what is insofar as it is. To seek the ground is to try to get to the bottom; what is put in question is thus related to the ground. However, since the question is a question, it remains to be seen whether the ground arrived at is really a ground, that is, whether it provides a foundation; whether it is a primal ground ⟨Ur-grund⟩; or whether it fails to provide a foundation and is an abyss ⟨Ab-grund⟩; or whether the ground is neither one nor the other but presents only a perhaps necessary appearance of foundation—in other words, it is a nonground ⟨Un-grund⟩. Be that as it may, the ground in question must account for the being of the essent as such. This ques-

1. "Essents" = "existents," "things that are."

Reprinted from Martin Heidegger's *Introduction to Metaphysics,* translated by Ralph Mannheim (1959) by permission from Yale University Press.

tion "why" does not look for causes that are of the same kind and on the same level as the essent itself. This "why" does not move on any one plane but penetrates to the "underlying" ⟨"zu-grunde" liegend⟩ realms and indeed to the very last of them, to the limit; turning away from the surface, from all shallowness, it strives toward the depths; this broadest of all questions is also the deepest.

Finally, this broadest and deepest question is also the most fundamental. What do we mean by this? If we take the question in its full scope, namely the essent as such in its entirety, it readily follows that in asking this question we keep our distance from every particular and individual essent, from every this and that. For we mean the essent as a whole, without any special preference. Still, it is noteworthy that in this questioning *one* kind of essent persists in coming to the fore, namely the men who ask the question. But the question should not concern itself with any particular essent. In the spirit of its unrestricted scope, all essents are of equal value. An elephant in an Indian jungle "is" just as much as some chemical combustion process at work on the planet Mars, and so on.

Accordingly, if our question "Why are there essents rather than nothing?" is taken in its fullest sense, we must avoid singling out any special, particular essent, including man. For what indeed is man? Consider the earth within the endless darkness of space in the universe. By way of comparison it is a tiny grain of sand; between it and the next grain of its own size there extends a mile or more of emptiness; on the surface of this grain of sand there lives a crawling, bewildered swarm of supposedly intelligent animals, who for a moment have discovered knowledge.[2] And what is the temporal extension of a human life amid all the millions of years? Scarcely a move of the second hand, a breath. Within the essent as a whole there is no legitimate ground for singling out this essent which is called mankind and to which we ourselves happen to belong.

But whenever the essent as a whole enters into this question, a privileged, unique relation arises between it and the act of questioning. For through this questioning the essent as a whole is for the first time opened up *as such* with a view to its possible ground, and in the act of questioning it is kept open. In relation to the essent as such in its entirety the asking of the question is not just any occurrence within the realm of the essent, like the falling of raindrops for example. The question "why" may be said to confront the essent as a whole, to break out of it, though never completely. But that is exactly why the act of questioning is privileged. Because it confronts the essent as a whole, but does not break loose from it, the content of the question reacts upon the questioning itself. Why the why? What is the ground of this question "why" which presumes to ask after the ground of the essent as a whole? Is the ground asked for in *this* why not merely a foreground—which would imply that the sought-for ground is again an essent? Does not the "first" question nevertheless come first in view of the intrinsic rank of the question of being and its modulations?

To be sure, the things in the world, the essents, are in no way affected by our asking of the question "Why are there essents rather than nothing?" Whether we ask it or not, the planets move in their orbits, the sap of life flows through plant and animal.

But *if* this question is asked and if the act of questioning is really carried out, the content and the object of the question react inevitably on the act of questioning. Accordingly this questioning is not just any occurrence but a privileged happening that we call an *event*.

This question and all the questions immediately rooted in it, the questions in which this one question unfolds—this question "why" is incommensurable with any other. It encounters the search for its own why. At first sight the question "Why the why?" looks like a frivolous repetition and infinitum of the same interrogative formulation, like an empty and unwarranted brooding over words. Yes, beyond a doubt, that is how it looks. The question is only whether we wish to be taken in by this superficial look and so regard the whole matter as settled, or whether we are capable of finding a significant event in this recoil of the question "why" upon itself.

But if we decline to be taken in by surface appearances we shall see that this question "why," this question as to the essent as such in its entirety, goes beyond any mere playing with words, provided we possess sufficient intellectual energy to make the question actually recoil into its "why"—for it will not do so of its own accord. In so doing we find out that this privileged question "why" has its ground in a leap through which man thrusts away all the previous security, whether real or imagined, of his

2. Cf. Nietzsche, *Über Wahrheit und Lüge im aussermoralischen Sinne.* 1873 *Nachlass.*

life. The question is asked only in this leap; it *is* the leap; without it there is no asking. What "leap" means here will be elucidated later. Our questioning is not yet the leap; for this it must undergo a transformation; it still stands perplexed in the face of the essent. Here it may suffice to say that the leap in this questioning opens up its own source—with this leap the question arrives at its own ground. We call such a leap, which opens up its own source, the original source or origin ⟨Ur-sprung⟩, the finding of one's own ground. It is because the question "Why are there essents rather than nothing?" breaks open the ground for all authentic questions and is thus at the origin ⟨Ursprung⟩ of them all that we must recognize it as the most fundamental of all questions.

It is the most fundamental of questions because it is the broadest and deepest, and conversely.

In this threefold sense the question is the first in rank—first, that is, in the order of questioning within the domain which this first question opens, defining its scope and thus founding it. Our question is the *question* of all authentic questions, i.e. of all self-questioning questions, and whether consciously or not it is necessarily implicit in every question. No questioning and accordingly no single scientific "problem" can be fully intelligible if it does not include, i.e. ask, the question of all questions. Let us be clear about this from the start: it can never be objectively determined whether anyone, whether we, really ask this question, that is whether we make the leap, or never get beyond a verbal formula. In a historical setting that does not recognize questioning as a fundamental human force, the question immediately loses its rank.

Anyone for whom the Bible is divine revelation and truth has the answer to the question "Why are there essents rather than nothing?" even before it is asked: everything that is, except God himself, has been created by Him. God himself, the increate creator, "is." One who holds to such faith can in a way participate in the asking of our question, but he cannot really question without ceasing to be a believer and taking all the consequences of such a step. He will only be able to act "as if" . . . On the other hand a faith that does not perpetually expose itself to the possibility of unfaith is no faith but merely a convenience: the believer simply makes up his mind to adhere to the traditional doctrine. This is neither faith nor questioning, but the indifference of those who can busy themselves with everything, sometimes even displaying a keen interest in faith as well as questioning.

What we have said about security in faith as one position in regard to the truth does not imply that the biblical "In the beginning God created heaven and earth" is an answer to our question. Quite aside from whether these words from the Bible are true or false for faith, they can supply no answer to our question because they are in no way related to it. Indeed, they cannot even be brought into relation with our question. From the standpoint of faith our question is "foolishness."

Philosophy is this very foolishness. A "Christian philosophy" is a round square and a misunderstanding. There is, to be sure, a thinking and questioning elaboration of the world of Christian experience, i.e. of faith. That is theology. Only epochs which no longer fully believe in the true greatness of the task of theology arrive at the disastrous notion that philosophy can help to provide a refurbished theology if not a substitute for theology, which will satisfy the needs and tastes of the time. For the original Christian faith philosophy is foolishness. To philosophize is to ask "Why are there essents rather than nothing?" Really to ask the question signifies: a daring attempt to fathom this unfathomable question by disclosing what it summons us to ask, to push our questioning to the very end. Where such an attempt occurs there is philosophy.

It would not serve our purpose to begin our discussion with a detailed report on philosophy. But there are a few things that all must know who wish to concern themselves with philosophy. They can be briefly stated.

All essential philosophical questioning is necessarily untimely. This is so because philosophy is always projected far in advance of its time, or because it connects the present with its antecedent, with what *initially* was. Philosophy always remains a knowledge which not only cannot be adjusted to a given epoch but on the contrary imposes its measure upon its epoch.

Philosophy is essentially untimely because it is one of those few things that can never find an immediate echo in the present. When such an echo seems to occur, when a philosophy becomes fashionable, either it is no real philosophy or it has been misinterpreted and misused for ephemeral and extraneous purposes.

Accordingly, philosophy cannot be directly learned like manual and technical skills; it cannot be directly applied, or judged by its usefulness in the manner of economic or other professional knowledge.

But what is useless can still be a force, perhaps the only real force. What has no immediate echo in everyday life can be intimately bound up with a nation's profound historical development, and can even anticipate it. What is untimely will have its own times. This is true of philosophy. Consequently there is no way of determining once and for all what the task of philosophy is, and accordingly what must be expected of it. Every state and every beginning of its development bears within it its own law. All that can be said is what philosophy cannot be and cannot accomplish.

A question has been stated: "Why are there essents rather than nothing?" We have claimed first place for this question and explained in what sense it is regarded as first.

We have not even begun to ask the question itself, but have digressed into a discussion about it. Such a digression is indispensable. For this question has nothing in common with our habitual concerns. There is no way of familiarizing ourselves with this question by a gradual transition from the things to which we are accustomed. Hence it must, as it were, be singled out in advance, presented. Yet in introducing the question and speaking of it, we must not postpone, let alone forget, the questioning itself.

Here then let us conclude our preliminary remarks.

Every essential form of spiritual life is marked by ambiguity. The less commensurate it is with other forms, the more it is misinterpreted.

Philosophy is one of the few autonomous creative possibilities and at times necessities of man's historical being-there.[3] The current misinterpretations of philosophy, all of which have some truth about them, are legion. Here we shall mention only two, which are important because of the light they throw on the present and future situation of philosophy. The first misinterpretation asks too much of philosophy. The second distorts its function.

Roughly speaking, philosophy always aims at the first and last grounds of the essent, with particular emphasis on man himself and on the meaning and goals of human being-there. This might suggest that philosophy can and must provide a foundation on which a nation will build its historical life and culture. But this is beyond the power of philosophy. As a rule such excessive demands take the form of a belittling of philosophy. It is said, for example: Because metaphysics did nothing to pave the way for the revolution it should be rejected. This is no cleverer than saying that because the carpenter's bench is useless for flying it should be abolished. Philosophy can never *directly* supply the energies and create the opportunities and methods that bring about a historical change; for one thing, because philosophy is always the concern of the few. Which few? The creators, those who initiate profound transformations. It spreads only indirectly, by devious paths that can never be laid out in advance, until at last, at some future date, it sinks to the level of a commonplace; but by then it has long been forgotten as original philosophy.

What philosophy essentially can and must be is this: a thinking that breaks the paths and opens the perspectives of the knowledge that sets the norms and hierarchies, of the knowledge in which and by which a people fulfills itself historically and culturally, the knowledge that kindles and necessitates all inquiries and thereby threatens all values.

The second misinterpretation involves a distortion of the function of philosophy. Even if philosophy can provide no foundation for a culture, the argument goes, it is nevertheless a cultural force, whether because it gives us an over-all, systematic view of what is, supplying a useful chart by which we may find our way amid the various possible things and realms of things, or because it relieves the sciences of their work by reflecting on their premises, basic concepts, and principles. Philosophy is expected to promote and even to accelerate—to make easier as it were—the practical and technical business of culture.

But—it is in the very nature of philosophy never to make things easier but only more difficult. And this not merely because its language strikes the everyday understanding as strange if not insane. Rather, it is the authentic function of philosophy to challenge historical being-there and hence, in the last analysis, being pure and simple. It restores to things, to the essents, their weight (being). How so? Be-

3. The word "Dasein" is ordinarily translated as "existence." It is used in "normal," popular discourse. But Heidegger breaks it into its components "Da" "there" and "Sein" "being," and puts his own definition on it. In general he means man's conscious, historical existence in the world, which is always projected into a there beyond its here. The German word Dasein has often been carried over into translations; the English strikes me as preferable.

cause the challenge is one of the essential prerequisites for the birth of all greatness, and in speaking of greatness we are referring primarily to the works and destinies of nations. We can speak of historical destiny only where an authentic knowledge of things dominates man's being-there. And it is philosophy that opens up the paths and perspectives of such knowledge.

The misinterpretations with which philosophy is perpetually beset are promoted most of all by people of our kind, that is, by professors of philosophy. It is our customary business—which may be said to be justified and even useful—to transmit a certain knowledge of the philosophy of the past, as part of a general education. Many people suppose that this is philosophy itself, whereas at best it is the technique of philosophy.

In correcting these two misinterpretations I cannot hope to give you at one stroke a clear conception of philosophy. But I do hope that you will be on your guard when the most current judgments and even supposed observations assail you unawares. Such judgments are often disarming, precisely because they seem so natural. You hear remarks such as "Philosophy leads to nothing," "You can't do anything with philosophy," and readily imagine that they confirm an experience of your own. There is no denying the soundness of these two phrases, particularly common among scientists and teachers of science. Any attempt to refute them by proving that after all it does "lead to something" merely strengthens the prevailing misinterpretation to the effect that the everyday standards by which we judge bicycles or sulphur baths are applicable to philosophy.

It is absolutely correct and proper to say that "You can't do anything with philosophy." It is only wrong to suppose that this is the last word on philosophy. For the rejoinder imposes itself: granted that *we* cannot do anything with philosophy, might not philosophy, if we concern ourselves with it, do something *with us*? So much for what philosophy is not.

At the outset we stated a question: "Why are there essents rather than nothing?" We have maintained that to ask this question is to philosophize. When in our thinking we open our minds to this question, we first of all cease to dwell in any of the familiar realms. We set aside everything that is on the order of the day. Our question goes beyond the familiar and the things that have their place in everyday life. Nietzsche once said (*Werke, 7,* 269): "A philosopher is a man who never ceases to experience, see, hear, suspect, hope, and dream extraordinary things. . . ."

To philosophize is to inquire into the *extra*-ordinary. But because, as we have just suggested, this questioning recoils upon itself, not only what is asked after is extraordinary but also the asking itself. In other words: this questioning does not lie along the way so that we bump into it one day unexpectedly. Nor is it part of everyday life: there is no requirement or regulation that forces us into it; it gratifies no urgent or prevailing need. The questioning itself is "out of order." It is entirely voluntary, based wholly and uniquely on the mystery of freedom, on what we have called the leap. The same Nietzsche said: "Philosophy . . . is a voluntary living amid ice and mountain heights" (*Werke, 15,* 2). To philosophize, we may now say, is an extraordinary inquiry into the extra-ordinary.

In the age of the earliest and crucial unfolding of Western philosophy among the Greeks, who first raised the authentic question of the essent as such in its entirety, the essent was called *physis*. This basic Greek word for the essent is customarily translated as "nature." This derives from the Latin translation, *natura*, which properly means "to be born," "birth." But with this Latin translation the original meaning of the Greek word *physis* is thrust aside, the actual philosophical force of the Greek word is destroyed. This is true not only of the Latin translation of *this* word but of all other Roman translations of the Greek philosophical language. What happened in this translation from the Greek into the Latin is not accidental and harmless; it marks the first stage in the process by which we cut ourselves off and alienated ourselves from the original essence of Greek philosophy. The Roman translation was later taken over by Christianity and the Christian Middle Ages. And the Christian Middle Ages were prolonged in modern philosophy, which, moving in the conceptual world of the Middle Ages, coined those representations and terms by means of which we still try to understand the beginnings of Western philosophy. These beginnings are regarded as something that present-day philosophers have supposedly transcended and long since left behind them.

But now let us skip over this whole process of deformation and decay and attempt to regain the unimpaired strength of language and words; for words and language are not wrappings in which things are packed for the commerce of those who write and speak. It is in words and language that things first come into being and are. For this reason the misuse of language in idle talk, in slogans and phrases, destroys our authentic relation to things. What does the word *physis* denote? It denotes self-blossoming emergence (e.g. the blossoming of a rose), opening up, unfolding, that which manifests itself in such unfolding and perseveres and endures in it; in short, the realm of things that emerge and linger on. According to the dictionary *phyein* means to grow or make to grow. But what does growing mean? Does it imply only to increase quantitatively, to become more and larger?

Physis as emergence can be observed everywhere, e.g. in celestial phenomena (the rising of the sun), in the rolling of the sea, in the growth of plants, in the coming forth of man and animal from the womb. But *physis*, the realm of that which arises, is not synonymous with these phenomena, which today we regard as part of "nature." This opening up and inward-jutting-beyond-itself ⟨in-sich-aus-sich-hinausstehen⟩ must not be taken as a process among other processes that we observe in the realm of the essent. *Physis* is being itself, by virtue of which essents become and remain observable.

The Greeks did not learn what *physis* is through natural phenomena, but the other way around: it was through a fundamental poetic and intellectual experience of being that they discovered what they had to call *physis*. It was this discovery that enabled them to gain a glimpse into nature in the restricted sense. Hence *physis* originally encompassed heaven as well as earth, the stone as well as the plant, the animal as well as man, and it encompassed human history as a work of men and the gods; and ultimately and first of all, it meant the gods themselves as subordinated to destiny. *Physis* means the power that emerges and the enduring realm under its sway. This power of emerging and enduring includes "becoming" as well as "being" in the restricted sense of inert duration. *Physis* is the process of a-rising, of emerging from the hidden, whereby the hidden is first made to stand.

But if, as is usually done, *physis* is taken not in the original sense of the power to emerge and endure, but in the later and present signification of nature; and if moreover the motion of material things, of the atoms and electrons, of what modern physics investigates as *physis*, is taken to be the fundamental manifestation of nature, then the first philosophy of the Greeks becomes a nature philosophy, in which all things are held to be of a material nature. In this case the beginning of Greek philosophy, as is perfectly proper for a beginning according to the common-sense view, gives the impression of what we, once again in Latin, designate as primitive. Thus the Greeks become essentially a higher type of Hottentot, whom modern science has left far behind. Disregarding the lesser absurdities involved in this view of the beginning of Western philosophy as something primitive, we need only say this: those who put forward such an interpretation forget that what is under discussion is philosophy, one of man's few great achievements. But what is great can only begin great. Its beginning is in fact that greatest thing of all. A small beginning belongs only to the small, whose dubious greatness it is to diminish all things; small are the beginnings of decay, though it may later become great in the sense of the enormity of total annihilation.

The great begins great, maintains itself only through the free recurrence of greatness within it, and if it is great ends also in greatness. So it is with the philosophy of the Greeks. It ended in greatness with Aristotle. Only prosaic common sense and the little man imagine that the great must endure forever, and equate this duration with eternity.

The Greeks called the essent as a whole *physis*. But it should be said in passing that even within Greek philosophy a narrowing of the word set in forthwith, although the original meaning did not vanish from the experience, knowledge, and orientation of Greek philosophy. Knowledge of its original meaning still lives on in Aristotle, when he speaks of the grounds of the essent as such (see *Metaphysics,* I, 1003 a 27).

But this narrowing of *physis* in the direction of "physics" did not occur in the way that we imagine today. We oppose the psychic, the animated, the living, to the "physical." But for the Greeks all this belonged to *physis* and continued to do so even after Aristotle. They contrasted it with what they called *thesis*, thesis, ordinance, or *nomos*, law, rule in the sense of *ethos*. This, however, denotes not mere norms but mores, based on freely accepted obligations and traditions; it is that which concerns free behavior and attitudes, the shaping of man's historical being, the *ethos* which under the influence of morality was later degraded to the ethical.

In Greek, "beyond something" is expressed by the word *meta.* Philosophical inquiry into the realm of being as such is *meta ta physika*; this inquiry goes beyond the essent, it is metaphysics. Here it is not important to follow the genesis and history of this term in detail.

Accordingly, the question to which we have given first rank, "Why are there essents rather than nothing?," is the fundamental question of metaphysics. Metaphysics is a name for the pivotal point and core of all philosophy. . . .

But the inquiry into being as such is of a different nature and origin.

Within the purview of metaphysics and thinking on its level, we can, to be sure, consider the question about being as such as merely a mechanical repetition of the question about the essent as such. In this case the question about being as such is just another transcendental question, though one of a higher order. But this reinterpretation of the question about being as such bars the road to its appropriate unfolding.

However, this new interpretation comes readily to mind; it is bound to suggest itself, particularly as we have spoken in *Sein und Zeit* of a "transcendental horizon." But the "transcendental" there intended is not that of the subjective consciousness; rather, it defines itself in terms of the existential-ecstatic temporality of human being-there. Yet the reinterpretation of the question of being as such tends to take the same form as the question of the essent as such, chiefly because the essential origin of the question of the existent as such and with it the essence of metaphysics remain obscure. And this draws all questions that are in any way concerned with being into the indeterminate.

In the present attempt at an "introduction to metaphysics" I shall keep this confused state of affairs in mind.

In the current interpretation the "question of being" signifies the inquiry into the essent as such (metaphysics). But from the standpoint of *Sein und Zeit*, the "question of being" means the inquiry into being as such. This signification of the title is also the appropriate one from the standpoint of the subject matter and of linguistics; for the "question of being" in the sense of the metaphysical question regarding the essent as such does *not inquire* thematically into being. In this way of asking, being remains forgotten.

But just as ambiguous as the "question of being" referred to in the title is what is said about "forgetfulness of being." It is pointed out—quite correctly—that metaphysics inquires into the being of the essent and that it is therefore an obvious absurdity to impute a forgetfulness of being to metaphysics.

But if we consider the question of being in the sense of an inquiry into being as such, it becomes clear to anyone who follows our thinking that being *as such* is precisely hidden from metaphysics, and remains forgotten—and so radically that the forgetfulness of being, which itself falls into forgetfulness, is the unknown but enduring impetus to metaphysical questioning.

If for the treatment of the "question of being" in the indeterminate sense we choose the name "metaphysics," then the title of the present work is ambiguous. For at first sight the questioning seems to remain within the sphere of the assent as such, yet at the very first sentence it strives to depart from this sphere in order to consider and inquire into another realm. Actually the title of the work is deliberately ambiguous.

The fundamental question of this work is of a different kind from the leading question of metaphysics. Taking what was said in *Sein und Zeit* (pp. 21 f. and 37 f.) as a starting point, we inquired into the *"disclosure of being."* "Disclosure of being" means the unlocking of what forgetfulness of being closes and hides. And it is through this questioning that a light first falls on the *essence* of metaphysics that had hitherto also been hidden.

"Introduction to metaphysics" means accordingly: an introduction to the asking of the fundamental question. But questions and particularly fundamental questions do not just occur like stones and water. Questions are not found ready-made like shoes and clothes and books. Questions *are*, and are only as they are actually asked. A leading into the asking of the fundamental questions is consequently not a going to something that lies and stands somewhere; no, this leading-to must first awaken and create the questioning. The leading is itself a questioning advance, a preliminary questioning. It is a leading for which in the very nature of things there can be no following. When we hear of disciples, "followers," as in a school of philosophy for example, it means that the nature of questioning is misunderstood. Such schools can exist only in the domain of scientific and technical work. Here everything has its definite hierarchical order. This work is also an indispensable part of philosophy and has today been lost. But the best technical ability can never replace the actual power of seeing and inquiring and speaking.

"Why are there essents rather than nothing?" That is the question. To state the interrogative sentence, even in a tone of questioning, is not yet to question. To repeat the interrogative sentence several times in succession does not necessarily breathe life into the questioning; on the contrary, saying the sentence over and over may well dull the questioning.

But even though the interrogative sentence is not the question and not the questioning, it must not be taken as a mere linguistic form of communication, as though, for example, the interrogative sentence were only a statement "about" a question. When I say to you "Why are these essents rather than nothing?" the purpose of my speaking and questioning is not to communicate to you the fact that a process of questioning is now at work within me. The spoken interrogative sentence can of course be interpreted in this way, but this means precisely that the questioning has not been heard. In this case you do not join me in questioning, nor do you question yourself. No sign of a questioning attitude or state of mind is awakened. Such a state of mind consists in a *willing* to know. Willing—that is no mere wishing or striving. Those who wish to know also seem to question; but they do not go beyond the stating of the question; they stop precisely where the question begins. To question is to will to know. He who wills, he who puts his whole existence into a will, *is* resolved. Resolve does not shift about; it does not shirk, but acts from out of the moment and never stops. Re-solve is no mere decision to act, but the crucial beginning of action that anticipates and reaches through all action. To will is to be resolved. The essence of willing is here carried back to determination ⟨Ent-schlossen-heit, unclosedness⟩. But the essence of resolve lies in the opening, the coming-out-of-cover ⟨Ent-borgenheit⟩ of human being-there into the clearing of being, and not in a storing up of energy for "action.". . .

But to know means: to be able to stand in the truth. Truth is the manifestness of the essent. To know is accordingly the ability to stand ⟨stehen⟩ in the manifestness of the essent, to endure ⟨bestehen⟩ it. Merely to have information, however abundant, is not to know. Even if curricula and examination requirements concentrate this information into what is of the greatest practical importance, it still does not amount to knowledge. Even if this information, pruned down to the most indispensable needs, is "close to life," its possession is not knowledge. The man who possesses such information and has learned a few practical tricks, will still be perplexed in the presence of real reality, which is always different from what the philistine means by down-to-earth; he will always be a bungler. Why? Because he has no knowledge, for to know means *to be able to learn.*

In the common-sense view, to be sure, knowledge belongs to the man who has no further need to learn because he has finished learning. No, only that man is knowing who understands that he must keep learning over and over again and who above all, on the basis of this understanding, has attained to the point where he is always *able to learn.* This is much more difficult than to possess information.

Ability to learn presupposes ability to inquire. Inquiry is the willing-to-know analyzed above: the resolve to be able to stand in the openness of the essent. Since we are concerned with the asking of the question that is first in rank, clearly the willing as well as the knowing is of a very special kind. So much the less will the interrogative sentence, even if it is uttered in an authentically questioning tone and even if the listener joins in the questioning, exhaustively reproduce the question. The questioning, which indeed is sounded in the interrogative sentence but which is still enclosed, wrapped up in the words, remains to be unwrapped. The questioning attitude must clarify and secure itself in this process, it must be consolidated by training.

Our next task lies in the development of the question "Why are there essents rather than nothing?" In what direction can it be asked? First of all the question is accessible in the interrogative sentence, which gives a kind of approximation of it. Hence its linguistic formulation must be correspondingly broad and loose. Let us consider our sentence in this respect. "Why are there essents rather than nothing?" The sentence has a caesura. "Why are there essents?" With these words the question is actually asked. The formulation of the question includes: 1) a definite indication of what is put into question, of what is *questioned*: 2) an indication of what the question is about, of what is asked. For it is clearly indicated what the question is about, namely the essent. What is asked after, that which is asked, is the why, i.e. the ground. What follows in the interrogative sentence, "rather than nothing," is only an appendage, which may be said to turn up of its own accord if for purposes of introduction we permit ourselves to speak loosely, a turn of phrase that says nothing further about the question or the object of questioning, an ornamental flourish. Actually the question is far more unambiguous and definite without such an appendage, which springs only from the prolixity of loose discourse. "Why are there essents?" The addition "rather than nothing" is dropped not only because we are striving for a strict formulation of the question but even more because it says nothing. For why should we go on to ask about nothing? Nothing is simply nothing. Here there is nothing more to inquire about. And above all, in talking about nothing or nothingness, we are not making the slightest advance toward the knowledge of the essent.

He who speaks of nothing does not know what he is doing. In speaking of nothing he makes it into a something. In speaking he speaks against what he intended. He contradicts himself. But discourse that contradicts itself offends against the fundamental rule of discourse (*logos*), against "logic." To speak of nothing is illogical. He who speaks and thinks illogically is unscientific. But he who goes so far as to speak of nothing in the realm of philosophy, where logic has its very home, exposes himself most particularly to the accusation of offending against the fundamental rule of all thinking. Such a speaking about nothing consists entirely of meaningless propositions. Moreover: he who takes the nothing seriously is allying himself with nothingness. He is patently promoting the spirit of negation and serving the cause of disintegration. Not only is speaking of nothing utterly repellent to thought; it also undermines all culture and all faith. What disregards the fundamental law of thought and also destroys faith and the will to build is pure nihilism.

On the basis of such considerations we shall do well, in our interrogative sentence, to cross out the superfluous words "rather than nothing" and limit the sentence to the simple and strict form: "Why are there essents?"

To this there would be no objection if . . . if in formulating our question, if altogether, in the asking of this question, we were as free as it may have seemed to us up to this point. But in asking this question we stand in a tradition. For philosophy has always, from time immemorial, asked about the ground of what is. With this question it began and with this question it will end, provided that it ends in greatness and not in an impotent decline. Ever since the question about the essent began, the question about the nonessent, about nothing, has gone side by side with it. And not only outwardly, in the manner of a by-product. Rather, the question about nothing has been asked with the same breadth, depth, and originality as the question about the essent. The manner of asking about nothing may be regarded as a gauge and hallmark for the manner of asking about the essent.

If we bear this in mind, the interrogative sentence uttered in the beginning, "Why are there essents rather than nothing?" seems to express the question about the essent far more adequately than the abbreviated version. It is not looseness of speech or prolixity that leads us to mention nothing. Nor is it an invention of ours; no, it is only strict observance of the original tradition regarding the meaning of the fundamental question.

Still, this speaking of nothing remains in general repellent to thought and in particular demoralizing. But what if both our concern for the fundamental rules of thought and our fear of nihilism, which both seem to counsel against speaking of nothing, should be based on a misunderstanding? And this indeed is the case. True, this misunderstanding is not accidental. It is rooted in long years of failure to understand the question about the essent. And this failure to understand arises from an increasingly hardened forgetfulness of being.

For it cannot be decided out of hand whether logic and its fundamental rules can, altogether, provide a standard for dealing with the question about the essent as such. It might be the other way around. Perhaps the whole body of logic as it is known to us, perhaps all the logic that we treat as a gift from heaven, is grounded in a very definite answer to the question about the essent; perhaps, in consequence, all thinking which solely follows the laws of thought prescribed by traditional logic is incapable from the very start of even understanding the question about the essent by its own resources, let alone actually unfolding the question and guiding it toward an answer. Actually it is only an appearance of strict, scientific method when we invoke the principle of contradiction and logic in general, in order to prove that all thinking and speaking about nothing are contradictory and therefore meaningless. In such a contention "logic" is regarded as a court of justice, established for all eternity, whose rights as first and last authority no rational man will impugn. Anyone who speaks against logic is therefore tacitly or explicitly accused of irresponsibility. And the mere accusation is taken as a proof and an argument relieving one of the need for any further, genuine reflection.

It is perfectly true that we cannot talk about nothing, as though it were a thing like the rain outside or a mountain or any object whatsoever. In principle, nothingness remains inaccessible to science. The man who wishes truly to speak about nothing must of necessity become unscientific. But this is a misfortune only so long as one supposes that scientific thinking is the only authentic rigorous thought, and that it alone can and must be made into the standard of philosophical thinking. But the reverse is true. All scientific thought is merely a derived form of philosophical thinking, which proceeded to freeze into its scientific cast. Philosophy never arises out of science or through science and it can never be accorded equal rank with the sciences. No, it is prior in rank, and not only "logically" or in a table representing the system of the sciences. Philosophy stands in a totally different realm and order. Only poetry stands in the same order as philosophy and its thinking, though poetry and thought are not the same thing. To speak of nothing will always remain a horror and an absurdity for science. But aside from the philosopher, the poet can do so—and not because, as common sense supposes, poetry is without strict rules, but because the spirit of poetry (only authentic and great poetry is meant) is essentially superior to the spirit that prevails in all mere science. By virtue of this superiority the poet always speaks as though the essent were being expressed and invoked for the first time. Poetry, like the thinking of the philosopher, has always so much world space to spare that in it each thing—a tree, a mountain, a house, the cry of a bird—loses all indifference and commonplaceness.

Authentic speaking about nothing always remains extraordinary. It cannot be vulgarized. It dissolves if it is placed in the cheap acid of a merely logical intelligence. Consequently true discourse about nothing can never be immediate like the description of a picture for example. Here I should like to cite a passage from one of Knut Hamsun's last works, *The Road Leads On.* The work forms a whole with *Vagabonds* and *August.* It describes the last years and end of this August, who embodies the uprooted modern man who can do everything equally well yet who cannot lose his ties with the extraordinary, because even in his weakness and despair he remains authentic and superior. In his last days August is alone in the high mountains. And the poet says: "Here he sits between his ears and all he hears is emptiness. An amusing conception, indeed. On the sea there were both motion and sound, something for the ear to feed upon, a chorus of waters. Here nothingness meets nothingness and the result is zero, not even a hole. Enough to make one shake one's head, utterly at a loss."[4]

We see that there is something very interesting about nothing. Let us then go back to our interrogative sentence; let us ask it through, and see whether this "rather than nothing" is merely a meaningless appendage or whether it does not have an essential meaning even in our provisional statement of the question.

Let us begin with the abbreviated, seemingly simpler, and ostensibly stricter form of the question: "Why are there essents?" When we inquire in this way, we start from the essent. The essent *is.* It is given, it confronts us; accordingly, it is to be found at any time, and it is, in certain realms, known to us. Now this essent, from which we start, is immediately questioned as to its ground. The questioning advances immediately toward a ground. Such a method is only an extension and enlargement, so to speak, of a method practiced in everyday life. Somewhere in the vineyard, for example, the vine-disease occurs; something incontestably present. We ask: where does it come from, where and what is the reason for it, the ground? Similarly the essent as a whole is present. We ask: where and what is the ground? This manner of questioning is represented in the simple formula: Why are there essents? Where and what is their ground? Tacitly we are asking after another and higher kind of essent. But here the question is not by any means concerned with the essent as such and as a whole.

But if we put the question in the form of our original interrogative sentence: "Why are there essents rather than nothing?" this addition prevents us in our questioning from beginning directly with an unquestionably given essent and, having scarcely begun, from continuing on to another expected essent as a ground. Instead this essent, through questioning, is held out into the possibility of nonbeing. Thereby the why takes on a very different power and penetration. Why is the essent torn away from the possibility of nonbeing? Why does it not simply keep falling back into nonbeing? Now the essent is no longer that which just happens to be present; it begins to waver and oscillate, regardless of whether

4. Knut Hamsun, *The Road Leads On* (Coward-McCann, 1934), p. 508. Trans. Eugene Gay-Tifft.

or not we recognize the essent in all certainty, regardless of whether or not we apprehend it in its full scope. Henceforth the essent as such oscillates, insofar as we draw it into the question. The swing of the pendulum extends to the extreme and sharpest contrary possibility, to nonbeing and nothingness. And the search for the why undergoes a parallel change. It does not aim simply at providing an also present ground and explanation for what is present; now a ground is sought which will explain the emergence of the essent as an overcoming of nothingness. The ground that is now asked after is the ground of the decision for the essent over against nothingness, or more precisely, the ground for the oscillation of the essent, which sustains and unbinds us, half being, half not being, which is also why we can belong entirely to no thing, not even to ourselves; yet being-there ⟨Dasein⟩ is in every case mine. . . .

We suddenly find ourselves speaking of the nonbeing and being of the essent, without saying how this being or nonbeing is related to the essent. Are the two terms the same? The essent and its being? What, for example, is "the essent" in this piece of chalk? The very question is ambiguous, because the word "the essent" can be understood in two respects, like the Greek *to on.* The essent means first *that* which is at any time, in particular this grayish white, so-and-so-shaped, light, brittle mass. But "the essent" also means that which "brings it about," so to speak, that this thing is an essent rather than a nonessent, that which constitutes its being if it *is*. In accordance with this twofold meaning of the word "the essent," the Greek *to on* often has the second significance, not the essent itself, not that which is, but "is-ness," essentness, being. Over against this, "the essent" in the first sense signifies all or particular essent things themselves, in respect to themselves and not to their is-ness, their *ousia.*

The first meaning of *to on* refers to *ta onta* (entia), the second to *to einai* (esse). We have listed what the essent is in the piece of chalk. This was relatively easy to do. It was also easy to see that the object named can also *not* be, that this chalk need ultimately not be here and not be. What then is being in distinction to what can stand in being or fall back into nonbeing—what is being in distinction to the essent? Is it the same as the essent? We ask the question once again. But in the foregoing we did not list being; we listed only material mass, grayish-white light, so-and-so-shaped, brittle. But where is the being situated? It must belong to the chalk, for this chalk *is.*

We encounter the essent everywhere; it sustains and drives us, enhances and fills us, elevates and disappoints us; but with all this, where is, and wherein consists, the being of the essent? One might reply: this distinction between the essent and its being may occasionally have an importance from the standpoint of language and even of meaning; this distinction can be effected in mere thought, i.e. in ideas and opinions, but is it certain that anything essent in the essent corresponds to the distinction? And even this merely cogitated distinction is questionable; for it remains unclear *what* is to be thought under the name of "being." Meanwhile it suffices to know the essent and secure our mastery over it. To go further and introduce being as distinct from it is artificial and leads to nothing.

We have already said a certain amount about this frequent question: What comes of such distinctions? Here we are going to concentrate on our undertaking. We ask: "Why are there essents rather than nothing?" And in this question we seemingly stick to the essent and avoid all empty brooding about being. But what really are we asking? Why the essent as such is. We are asking for the ground of the essent: that it is and is what it is, and that there is not rather nothing. Fundamentally we are asking about being. But how? We are asking about the being of the essent. We are questioning the essent in regard to its being.

But if we persevere in our questioning we shall actually be questioning forward, asking about being in respect to its ground, even if this question remains undeveloped and it remains undecided whether being itself is not in itself a ground and a sufficient ground. If we regard this question of being as the first question in order of rank, should we ask it without knowing how it stands with being and how being stands in its distinction to the essent? How shall we inquire into, not to say find, the ground for the being of the essent, if we have not adequately considered and understood being itself? This undertaking would be just as hopeless as if someone were to try to bring out the cause and ground of a fire, and yet claim that he need not worry about the actual course of the fire or examine the scene of it.

Thus it transpires that the question "Why are there essents rather than nothing?" compels us to ask the preliminary question: "How does it stand with being?"

Here we are asking about something which we barely grasp, which is scarcely more than the sound of a word for us, and which puts us in danger of serving a mere word idol when we proceed with our questioning. Hence it is all the more indispensable that we make it clear from the very outset how it stands at present with being and with our understanding of being. And in this connection the main thing is to impress it on our experience that we cannot immediately grasp the being of the essent itself, either through the essent or in the essent—or anywhere else.

A few examples may be helpful. Over there, across the street, stands the high school building. An essent. We can look over the building from all sides, we can go in and explore it from cellar to attic, and note everything we encounter in that building: corridors, staircases, schoolrooms, and their equipment. Everywhere we find essents and we even find them in a very definite arrangement. Now where is the being of this high school? For after all it *is*. The building *is*. If anything belongs to this essent, it is its being; yet we do not find the being inside it.

Nor does the being consist in the fact that we look at the essent. The building stands there even if we do not look at it. We can find it only because it already *is*. Moreover, this building's being does not by any means seem to be the same for everyone. For us, who look at it or ride by, it is different than for the pupils who sit in it; not because they see it only from within but because for them this building really is what it is and as it is. You can, as it were, smell the being of this building in your nostrils. The smell communicates the being of this essent far more immediately and truly than any description or inspection could ever do. But on the other hand the building's being is not based on this odor that is somewhere in the air.

How does it stand with being? Can you see being? We see essents; this chalk for example. But do we see being as we see color and light and shade? Or do we hear, smell, taste, feel being? We hear the motorcycle racing through the street. We hear the grouse gliding through the forest. But actually we hear only the whirring of the motor, the sound the grouse makes. As a matter of fact it is difficult to describe even the pure sound, and we do not ordinarily do so, because it is *not* what we commonly hear. [From the standpoint of sheer sound] we always hear *more*. We hear the flying bird, even though strictly speaking we should say: a grouse is nothing audible, it is no manner of tone that fits into a scale. And so it is with the other senses. We touch velvet, silk; we see them directly as this and that kind of essent, the one different from the other. Wherein lies and wherein consists being?

But we must take a wider look around us and consider the lesser and greater circle within which we spend our days and hours, wittingly and wittingly, a circle whose limits shift continuously and which is suddenly broken through.

A heavy storm coming up in the mountains "is," or what here amounts to the same thing, "was" during the night. Wherein consists its being?

A distant mountain range under a broad sky . . . It "is." Wherein consists the being? When and to whom does it reveal itself? To the traveler who enjoys the landscape, or to the peasant who makes his living in it and from it, or to the meteorologist who is preparing a weather report? Who of these apprehends being? All and none. Or is what these men apprehend of the mountain range under the great sky only certain aspects of it, not the mountain range itself as it "is" as such, not that wherein its actual being consists? Who may be expected to apprehend this being? Or is it a non-sense, contrary to the sense of being, to inquire after what is in itself, behind those aspects? Does the being lie in the aspects?

The door of an early romanesque church is an essent. How and to whom is its being revealed? To the connoisseur of art, who examines it and photographs it on an excursion, or to the abbot who on a holiday passes through this door with his monks, or to the children who play in its shadow on a summer's day? How does it stand with the being of this essent?

A state—*is*. By virtue of the fact that the state police arrest a suspect, or that so-and-so-many typewriters are clattering in a government building, taking down the words of ministers and state secretaries? Or "is" the state in a conversation between the chancellor and the British foreign minister? The state *is*. But where is being situated? Is it situated anywhere at all?

A painting by Van Gogh. A pair of rough peasant shoes, nothing else. Actually the painting represents nothing. But as to what *is* in that picture, you are immediately alone with it as though you yourself were making your way wearily homeward with your hoe on an evening in late fall after the last potato fires have died down. What *is* here? The canvas? The brush strokes? The spots of color?

What in all these things we have just mentioned is the being of the essent? We run (or stand) around in the world with our silly subtleties and conceit. But where in all this is being?

All the things we have named *are* and yet—when we wish to apprehend being, it is always as though we were reaching into the void. The being after which we inquire is almost like nothing, and yet we have always rejected the contention that the essent in its entirety *is not.*

But being remains unfindable, almost like nothing, or ultimately *quite* so. Then, in the end, the word "being" is no more than an empty word. It means nothing real, tangible, material. Its meaning is an unreal vapor. Thus in the last analysis Nietzsche was perfectly right in calling such "highest concepts" as being "the last cloudy streak of evaporating reality." Who would want to chase after such a vapor, when the very term is merely a name for a great fallacy! "Nothing indeed has exercised a more simple power of persuasion hitherto than the error of Being . . ."[5]

"Being"—a vapor and a fallacy? What Nietzsche says here of being is no random remark thrown out in the frenzy of preparation for his central, never finished work. No, this was his guiding view of being from the earliest days of his philosophical effort. It is the fundamental support and determinant of his philosophy. Yet even now this philosophy holds its ground against all the crude importunities of the scribblers who cluster round him more numerous with each passing day. And so far there seems to be no end in sight to this abuse of Nietzche's work. In speaking here of Nietzsche, we mean to have nothing to do with all that—or with blind hero worship for that matter. The task in hand is too crucial and at the same time too sobering. It consists first of all, if we are to gain a true grasp of Nietzsche, in bringing his accomplishment to a full unfolding. Being a vapor, a fallacy? If this were so, the only possible consequence would be to abandon the question "Why are there essents as such and as a whole, rather than nothing?" For what good is the question if what it inquires into is only a vapor and a fallacy?

Does Nietzsche speak the truth? Or was he himself only the last victim of a long process of error and neglect, but as such the unrecognized witness to a new necessity?

Is it the fault of being that it is so involved? is it the fault of the word that it remains so empty? or are we to blame that with all our effort, with all our chasing after the essent, we have fallen out of being? And should we not say that the fault did not begin with us, or with our immediate or more remote ancestors, but lies in something that runs through Western history from the very beginning, a happening which the eyes of all the historians in the world will never perceive, but which nevertheless happens, which happened in the past and will happen in the future? What if it were possible that man, that nations in their greatest movements and traditions, are linked to being and yet had long fallen out of being, without knowing it, and that this was the most powerful and most central cause of their decline?

. . . The spiritual decline of the earth is so far advanced that the nations are in danger of losing the last bit of spiritual energy that makes it possible to see the decline (taken in relation to the history of "being"), and to appraise it as such. This simple observation has nothing to do with *Kulturpessimismus,* and of course it has nothing to do with any sort of optimism either; for the darkening of the world, the flight of the gods, the destruction of the earth, the transformation of men into a mass, the hatred and suspicion of everything free and creative, have assumed such proportions throughout the earth that such childish categories as pessimism and optimism have long since become absurd.

We are caught in a pincers. Situated in the center, our nation incurs the severest pressure. It is the nation with the most neighbors and hence the most endangered. With all this, it is the most metaphysical of nations. We are certain of this vocation, but our people will only be able to wrest a destiny from it if *within itself* it creates a resonance, a possibility of resonance for this vocation, and takes a creative view of its tradition. All this implies that this nation, as a historical nation, must move itself and thereby the history of the West beyond the center of their future "happening" and into the primordial realm of the powers of being. If the great decision regarding Europe is not to bring annihilation, that decision must be made in terms of new spiritual energies unfolding historically from out of the center.

To ask "How does it stand with being"? means nothing less than to recapture, to repeat ⟨wiederholen⟩, the beginning of our historical-spiritual existence, in order to transform it into a new begin-

5. *The Twilight of Idols,* Nietzsche's Complete Works, Edinburgh and London, *16* (1911), 19, 22.

ning. This is possible. It is indeed the crucial form of history, because it begins in the fundamental event. But we do not repeat a beginning by reducing it to something past and now known, which need merely be imitated; no, the beginning must be begun again, more radically, with all the strangeness, darkness, insecurity that attend a true beginning. Repetition as we understand it is anything but an improved continuation with the old methods of what has been up to now.

The question "How is it with being?" is included as a preliminary question in our central question "Why are there essents rather than nothing?" If we now begin to look into that which is questioned in our preliminary question, namely being, the full truth of Nietzsche's dictum is at once apparent. For if we look closely, what more is "being" to us than a mere word, an indeterminate meaning, intangible as a vapor? Nietzsche's judgment, to be sure, was meant in a purely disparaging sense. For him "being" is a delusion that should never have come about. Is "being," then, indeterminate, vague as a vapor? It is indeed. But we do not mean to sidestep this fact. On the contrary, we must see how much of a fact it is if we are to perceive its full implication.

Our questioning brings us into the landscape we must inhabit as a basic prerequisite, if we are to win back our roots in history. We shall have to ask why this fact, that for us "being" is no more than a word and a vapor, should have arisen precisely today, or whether and why it has existed for a long time. We must learn to see that this fact is not as harmless as it seems at first sight. For ultimately what matters is not that the word "being" remains a mere sound and its meaning a vapor, but that we have fallen away from what this word says and for the moment cannot find our way back; that it is for this and no other reason that the word "being" no longer applies to anything, that everything, if we merely take hold of it, dissolves like a tatter of cloud in the sunlight. Because this is so—that is why we ask about being. And we *ask* because we know that truths have never fallen into any nation's lap. The fact that people still cannot and do not wish to understand this question, even if it is asked in a still more fundamental form, deprives the question of none of its cogency.

Of course we can, seemingly with great astuteness and perspicacity, revive the old familiar argument to the effect that "being" is the most universal of concepts, that it covers anything and everything, even the nothing which also, in the sense that it is thought or spoken, "is" something. Beyond the domain of this most universal concept "being," there is, in the strictest sense of the word, nothing more, on the basis of which being itself could be more closely determined. The concept of being is an ultimate. Moreover, there is a law of logic that says: the more comprehensive a concept is—and what could be more comprehensive than the concept of "being"?—the more indeterminate and empty is its content.

For every normally thinking man—and we all should like to be normal men—this reasoning is immediately and wholly convincing. But the question now arises: does the designation of being as the most universal concept strike the essence of being, or is it not from the very outset such a misinterpretation that all questioning becomes hopeless? This then is the question: can being be regarded only as the most universal concept which inevitably occurs in all special concepts, or is being of an entirely different essence, and hence anything but an object of "ontology," provided we take this word in its traditional sense?

The word "ontology" was first coined in the seventeenth century. It marks the development of the traditional doctrine of the essent into a discipline of philosophy and a branch of the philosophical system. But the traditional doctrine was an academic classification and ordering of what for Plato and Aristotle and again for Kant was a question, though no longer to be sure a primordial one. And it is in this sense that the word "ontology" is used today. Under this title each school of philosophy has set up and described a branch within its system. But we can also take the word "ontology" in the "broadest sense," "without reference to ontological directions and tendencies" (cf. *Sein und Zeit*, p. 11 top). In this case "ontology" signifies the endeavor to make being manifest itself, and to do so by way of the question "how does it stand with being?" (and not only with the essent as such). But since thus far this question has not even been heard, let alone echoed; since it has been expressly rejected by the various schools of academic philosophy, which strive for an "ontology" in the traditional sense, it may be preferable to dispense in the future with the terms "ontology" and "ontological." Two modes of questioning which, as we now see clearly, are worlds apart, should not bear the same name.

We ask the questions "How does it stand with being?" "What is the meaning of being?" *not* in order to set up an ontology on the traditional style, much less to criticize the past mistakes of ontology. We are concerned with something totally different: to restore man's historical being-there—and that always includes our own future being-there in the totality of the history allotted to us—to the domain of being, which it was originally incumbent on man to open up for himself. All this, to be sure, in the limits within which philosophy can accomplish anything.

Out of the fundamental question of metaphysics, "Why are there essents rather than nothing?" we have separated the preliminary question, "How does it stand with being?" The relation between the two questions requires clarification, for it is of a special kind. Ordinarily a preliminary question is dealt with before and outside the main question, though in reference to it. But, in principle, philosophical questions are never dealt with as though we might some day cast them aside. Here the preliminary question is not by any means outside of the main question; rather, it is the flame which burns as it were in the asking of the fundamental question; it is the flaming center of all questioning. That is to say: it is crucial for the first asking of the fundamental question that in asking its *preliminary* question we derive the decisive fundamental attitude that is here essential. That is why we have related the question of being to the destiny of Europe, where the destiny of the earth is being decided—while our own historic being there proves to be the center for Europe itself.

The question is:

Is being a mere word and its meaning a vapor, or does what is designated by the word "being" hold within it the historical destiny of the West?

To many ears the question may sound violent and exaggerated: for one might in a pinch suppose that a discussion of the question of being might be related in some very remote and indirect way to the decisive historical question of the earth, but assuredly not that the basic position and attitude of our questioning might be directly determined by the history of the human spirit on earth. And yet this relationship exists. Since our purpose is to set in motion the asking of the preliminary question, we must now show that, and to what extent, the asking of this question is an immediate and fundamental factor in the crucial historical question. For this demonstration it is necessary to anticipate an essential insight in the form of an assertion.

We maintain that this preliminary question and with it the fundamental question of metaphysics are historical questions through and through. But do not metaphysics and philosophy thereby become a historical science? Historical science after all investigates the temporal, while philosophy investigates the timeless. Philosophy is historical only insofar as it—like every work of the spirit—realizes itself in time. But in this sense the designation of metaphysical questioning as historical cannot characterize metaphysics, but merely expresses something obvious. Accordingly, the assertion is either meaningless and superfluous or else impossible, because it creates an amalgam of two fundamentally different kinds of science: philosophy and historical science.

In answer to this it must be said:

1. Metaphysics and philosophy are not sciences at all, and the fact that their questioning is basically historical cannot make them so.

2. Historical science does not determine a fundamental relation to history, but always presupposes such a relation. It is only for this reason that historical science can distort men's relation to history, which itself is always historical; or misinterpret it and degrade it to a mere knowledge of antiquities; or else deal with crucial fields in the light of this once established relation to history, and so produce cogent history. A historical relation between our historical being-there and history may become an object of knowledge and mark an advanced state of knowledge; but it need not. Moreover, all relations to history cannot be scientifically objectified and given a place in science, and it is precisely the essential ones that cannot. Historical science can never produce the historical relation to history. It can only illuminate a relation once supplied, ground it in knowledge, which is indeed an absolute necessity for the historical being-there of a wise people, and not either an "advantage" or a "disadvantage." Because it is only in philosophy—*as distinguished from all science*—that essential relations to the realm of what is take shape, this relation *can*, indeed *must*, for us today be a fundamentally historical one.

But for an understanding of our assertion that the "metaphysical" asking of the preliminary question is historical through and through, it is above all necessary to consider this: for us history is not synonymous with the past; for the past is precisely what is no longer happening. And much less is history the merely contemporary, which never happens but merely "passes," comes and goes by. History as happening is an acting and being acted upon which pass through the *present*, which are determined from out of the future, and which take over the past. It is precisely the present that vanishes in happening.

Our asking of the fundamental question of metaphysics is historical because it opens up the process of human being-there in its essential relations—i.e. its relations to the essent as such and as a whole—opens it up to unasked possibilities, futures, and at the same time binds it back to its past beginning, so sharpening it and giving it weight in its present. In this questioning our being-there is summoned to its history in the full sense of the word, called to history and to a decision in history. And this not after the fact, in the sense that we draw ethical, ideological lessons from it. No, the basic attitude of the questioning is in itself historical; it stands and maintains itself in happening, inquiring out of happening for the sake of happening.

But we have not yet come to the essential reason why this inherently historical asking of the question about being is actually an integral part of history on earth. We have said that the world is darkening. The essential episodes of this darkening are: the flight of the gods, the destruction of the earth, the standardization of man, the pre-eminence of the mediocre.

What do we mean by world when we speak of a darkening of the world? World is always world of the *spirit*. The animal has no world nor any environment ⟨Umwelt⟩. Darkening of the world means emasculation of the spirit, the disintegration, wasting away, repression, and misinterpretation of the spirit. We shall attempt to explain the emasculation of the spirit in one respect, that of misinterpretation. We have said: Europe lies in a pincers between Russia and America, which are metaphysically the same, namely in regard to their world character and their relation to the spirit. What makes the situation of Europe all the more catastrophic is that this enfeeblement of the spirit originated in Europe itself and—though prepared by earlier factors—was definitively determined by its own spiritual situation in the first half of the nineteenth century. It was then that occurred what is popularly and succinctly called the "collapse of German idealism." This formula is a kind of shield behind which the already dawning spiritlessness, the dissolution of the spiritual energies, the rejection of all original inquiry into grounds and men's bond with the grounds, are hidden and masked. It was not German idealism that collapsed; rather, the age was no longer strong enough to stand up to the greatness, breadth, and originality of that spiritual world, i.e. truly to realize it, for to realize a philosophy means something very different from applying theorems and insights. The lives of men began to slide into a world which lacked that depth from out of which the essential always comes to man and comes back to man, so compelling him to become superior and making him act in conformity to a rank. All things sank to the same level, a surface resembling a blind mirror that no longer reflects, that casts nothing back. The prevailing dimension became that of extension and number. Intelligence no longer meant a wealth of talent, lavishly spent, and the command of energies, but only what could be learned by everyone, the practice of a routine, always associated with a certain amount of sweat and a certain amount of show. In America and in Russia this development grew into a boundless etcetera of indifference and always-the-sameness—so much so that the quantity took on a quality of its own. Since then the domination in those countries of a cross section of the indifferent mass has become something more than a dreary accident. It has become an active onslaught that destroys all rank and every world-creating impulse of the spirit, and calls it a lie. This is the onslaught of what we call the demonic (in the sense of destructive evil). There are many indications of the emergence of this demonism, identical with the increasing helplessness and uncertainty of Europe against it and within itself. One of these signs is the emasculation of the spirit through misinterpretation; we are still in the midst of this process. This misinterpretation of the spirit may be described briefly in four aspects.

1. The crux of the matter is the reinterpretation of the spirit as *intelligence*, or mere cleverness in examining and calculating given things and the possibility of changing them and complementing them to make new things. This cleverness is a matter of mere talent and practice and mass division of labor. The cleverness itself is subject to the possibility of organization, which is never true of the spirit. The attitude of the littérateur and esthete is merely a late consequence and variation of the spirit falsified into intelligence. Mere intelligence is a semblance of spirit, masking its absence.

2. The spirit falsified into intelligence thus falls to the level of a tool in the service of others, a tool the manipulation of which can be taught and learned. Whether this use of intelligence relates to the regulation and domination of the material conditions of production (as in Marxism) or in general to the intelligent ordering and explanation of everything that

is present and already posited at any time (as in positivism), or whether it is applied to the organization and regulation of a nation's vital resources and race—in any case the spirit as intelligence becomes the impotent superstructure of something else, which, because it is without spirit or even opposed to the spirit, is taken for the actual reality. If the spirit is taken as intelligence, as is done in the most extreme form of Marxism, then it is perfectly correct to say, in defense against it, that in the order of the effective forces of human being-there, the spirit, i.e. intelligence, must always be ranked below healthy physical activity and character. But this order becomes false once we understand the true essence of the spirit. For all true power and beauty of the body, all sureness and boldness in combat, all authenticity and inventiveness of the understanding, are grounded in the spirit and rise or fall only through the power or impotence of the spirit. The spirit is the sustaining, dominating principle, the first and the last, not merely an indispensable third factor.

3. As soon as the misinterpretation sets in that degrades the spirit to a tool, the energies of the spiritual process, poetry and art, statesmanship and religion, become subject to *conscious* cultivation and planning. They are split into branches. The spiritual world becomes culture and the individual strives to perfect himself in the creation and preservation of this culture. These branches become fields of free endeavor, which sets its own standards and barely manages to live up to them. These standards of production and consumption are called values. The cultural values preserve their meaning only by restricting themselves to an autonomous field: poetry for the sake of poetry, art for the sake of art, science for the sake of science.

Let us consider the example of science, which is of particular concern to us here at the university. The state of science since the turn of the century—it has remained unchanged despite a certain amount of house cleaning—is easy to see. Though today two seemingly different conceptions of science seem to combat one another—science as technical, practical, professional knowledge and science as cultural value per se—both are moving along the same downgrade of misinterpretation and emasculation of the spirit. They differ only in this: in the present situation the technical, practical conception of science as specialization can at least lay claim to frank and clear consistency, while the reactionary interpretation of science as a culture value, now making its reappearance, seeks to conceal the impotence of the spirit behind an unconscious lie. The confusion of spiritlessness can even go so far as to lead the upholders of the technical, practical view of science to profess their belief in science as a cultural value; then the two understand each other perfectly in the same spiritlessness. We may choose to call the institution where the specialized sciences are grouped together for purposes of teaching and research a university, but this is no more than a name; the "university" has ceased to be a fundamental force for unity and responsibility. What I said here in 1929, in my inaugural address, is still true of the German university: "The scientific fields are still far apart. Their subjects are treated in fundamentally different ways. Today this hodgepodge of disciplines is held together only by the technical organization of the universities and faculties and preserves what meaning it has only through the practical aims of the different branches. The sciences have lost their roots in their essential ground." (*Was ist Metaphysik*? 1929, p. 8.) Science today in all its branches is a technical, practical business of gaining and transmitting information. An awakening of the spirit cannot take its departure from such science. It is itself in need of an awakening.

4. The last misinterpretation of the spirit is based on the above-mentioned falsifications which represent the spirit as intelligence, and intelligence as a serviceable tool which, along with its product, is situated in the realm of culture. In the end the spirit as utilitarian intelligence and the spirit as culture become holiday ornaments cultivated along with many other things. They are brought out and exhibited as a proof that there is *no* intention to combat culture or favor barbarism. In the beginning Russian Communism took a purely negative attitude but soon went over to propagandist tactics of this kind.

In opposition to this multiple misinterpretation of the spirit, we define the essence of the spirit briefly as follows (I shall quote from the address I delivered on the occasion of my appointment as rector, because of its succinct formulation): "Spirit is neither empty cleverness nor the irresponsible play of the wit, nor the boundless work of dismemberment carried on by the practical intelligence; much less is it world-reason; no, spirit is a fundamental, knowing resolve toward the essence of being." (Rektoratsrede, p. 13.) Spirit is the mobilization of the powers of the essent as such and as a whole. Where spirit prevails, the essent as such becomes always and at all times more essent. Thus the inquiry into the essent as such and as a whole, the asking of the question of being, is one of the essential and fundamental conditions for an awakening of the spirit and hence for an original world of historical being-there. It is indispensable if the peril of world darkening is to be forestalled and if our nation in the center of the Western world is to take on its historical mission. Here we can explain only in these broad outlines why the asking of the question of being is in itself through and through historical, and why, accordingly, our question as to whether being will remain a mere vapor for us or become the destiny of the West is anything but an exaggeration and a rhetorical figure.

But if our question about being has this essential and decisive character, we must above all take an absolutely serious view of *the fact* that gives the question its immediate necessity, the fact that for us being has become little more than a mere word and its meaning an evanescent vapor. This is not the kind of fact which merely confronts us as something alien and other, which we need merely note as an occurrence. It is a fact in which we stand. It is a state of our being-there. And by state, of course, I do not mean a quality that can be demonstrated only psychologically. Here state means our entire constitution, the way in which we ourselves are constituted in regard to being. Here we are not concerned with psychology but with our history in an essential respect. When we call it a "fact" that being for us is a mere word and vapor, we are speaking very provisionally. We are merely holding fast, establishing something which has not yet been thought through, for which we still have no locus, even if it looks as though this something were an occurrence among us, here and now, or "in" us, as we like to say.

One would like to integrate the individual fact that for us being remains no more than an empty word and an evanescent vapor with the more general fact that many words, and precisely the essential ones, are in the same situation; that the language in general is worn out and used up—an indispensable but masterless means of communication that may be used as one pleases, as indifferent as a means of public transport, as a street car which everyone rides in. Everyone speaks and writes away in the language, without hindrance and above all *without danger.* That is certainly true. And only a very few are capable of thinking through the full implications of this misrelation and unrelation of present-day being-there to language.

But the emptiness of the word "being," the total disappearance of its appellative force, is not merely a particular instance of the general exhaustion of language; rather, the destroyed relation to being as such is the actual reason for the general misrelation to language.

The organizations for the purification of the language and defense against its progressive barbarization are deserving of respect. But such efforts merely demonstrate all the more clearly that we no longer know what is at stake in language. Because the destiny of language is grounded in a nation's *relation* to *being*, the question of being will involve us deeply in the question of language. It is more than an outward accident that now, as we prepare to set forth, in all its implication, the fact of the evaporation of being, we find ourselves compelled to take linguistic considerations as our starting point.

Chapter 34

Jean-Paul Sartre

Jean-Paul Sartre (1905–1980) was born in Paris and was a teacher in a French high school. He served in the French army during World War II, was captured by the Germans, and spent time in a prison camp reading German philosophers (especially Hegel, Husserl, and Heidegger). After the war, Sartre's plays, novels, and philosophical work, especially *Being and Nothingness* (1943), set him apart as Europe's premier existentialist. Later he combined existentialism with Marxism, though he never joined the Communist party.

Here is Paul Johnson's description of the impact of Sartre and the following selection on French society:

> [On October 29, 1945, shortly after the end of the war], at the Club Maintenant, Jean-Paul Sartre delivered a lecture, "Existentialism Is a Humanism." Here was the new Paris. This occasion . . . was packed. Men and women fainted, fought for chairs, smashing thirty of them, shouted and barracked. It coincided with the launching of Sartre's new review, *Les Temps Modernes,* in which he argued that literary culture, plus the haute couture of the fashion shops, were the only things France now had left—a symbol of Europe, really—and he produced Existentialism to give people a bit of dignity and to preserve their individuality in the midst of degradation and absurdity. The response was overwhelming. As his consort, Simone de Beauvoir, put it, "We were astounded by the furore we caused." Existentialism was remarkably un-Gallic; hence perhaps, its attractiveness. Sartre was half-Alsacian (Albert Schweitzer was his cousin) and he was brought up in the house of his grandfather, Karl Schweitzer. His culture was as much German as French. He was essentially a product of the Berlin school and especially Heidegger, from whom most of his ideas derived. . . . Thus Existentialism was a French cultural import, which Paris then reexported to Germany, its country of origin, in a sophisticated and vastly more attractive guise. (Paul Johnson, *Modern Times,* Harper & Row, 1983, p. 575f)

In our first selection, "Bad Faith," from *Being and Nothingness,* Sartre contrasts "bad faith" with authenticity (good faith). He argues that any attempt to deny our freedom, to identify ourselves with our roles in society, our gender, race, or religion, is to act in bad faith. Authenticity is to acknowledge one's freedom at every moment of existence.

In our second selection, "Existentialism and Humanism," Sartre sets forth the broader principles of atheistic existentialism: that we are completely free; that since there is no God to give us an essence, we must create our own essence; that we are completely responsible for our actions, and are responsible for everyone else too; that because of the death of God and the human predicament, which leaves us totally free to create our values and our world, we must exist in anguish, forlornness, and despair. Yet there is a certain celebration and optimism in knowing that we are creators of our own values.

In this essay you will come across Sartre's notion that "existence precedes essence." This is a difficult idea, but he seems to mean something like the following. If you have an idea of something in your mind first and then create it, we would say that the idea (essence) of the thing precedes the actuality or existence of it. But if the thing existed before any idea of it, then its existence precedes its essence. If there were a God who created us, who had us in mind, we would have an essence (in terms of a function or purpose) and our existence would succeed our essence, but since, according to Sartre, there is no God to create us, we simply find ourselves existing and must create our own essence (i.e., give ourselves a function or purpose).

FOR FURTHER READING

Barrett, William. *Irrational Man* (Doubleday, 1958).
Caws, Peter. *Sartre* (Routledge, Chapman and Hall, 1984).
Kaufmann, Walter, ed. *Existentialism from Dostoevsky to Sartre* (New American Library, 1975).
Murdoch, Iris. *Sartre, Romantic Rationalist* (Viking Penguin, 1987).
Sartre, Jean Paul. *Being and Nothingness,* trans. H. Barnes (Philosophical Library, 1956).
———. *Existentialism and Human Emotions*, trans. B. Frechtman (Philosophical Library, 1947).
Schilpp, P. A. *The Philosophy of Jean-Paul Sartre* (Open Court, 1981).
Silverman, Hugh and Frederick Elliston, eds. *Jean-Paul Sartre: Contemporary Approaches to His Philosophy* (Duquesne University Press, 1980).

Bad Faith

I. BAD FAITH AND FALSEHOOD

The human being is not only the being by whom *négatítés* are disclosed in the world; he is also the one who can take negative attitudes with respect to himself. In our Introduction we defined consciousness as "a being such that in its being, its being is in question in so far as this being implies a being other than itself." But now that we have examined the meaning of "the question," we can at present also write the formula thus: "Consciousness is a being, the nature of which is to be conscious of the nothingness of its being." In a prohibition or a veto, for example, the human being denies a future transcendence. But this negation is not explicative. My consciousness is not restricted to *envisioning a négatité*. It constitutes itself in its own flesh as the nihilation of a possibility. For that reason it must arise in the world as a *No*; it is as a No that the slave first apprehends the master, or that the prisoner who is trying to escape sees the guard who is watching him. There are even men (*e.g.*, caretakers, overseers, gaolers), whose social reality is uniquely that of the No, who will live and die, having forever been only a No upon the earth. Others, so as to make the No a part of their very subjectivity, establish their human personality as a perpetual negation. This is the meaning and function of what Scheler calls "the man of resentment"—in reality, the No. But there exist more subtle behaviors, the description of which will lead us further into the inwardness of consciousness. Irony is one of these. In irony a man annihilates what he posits within one and the same act; he leads us to believe in order not to be believed; he affirms to deny and denies to affirm; he creates a positive object but it has no being other than its nothingness.

Reprinted from Jean Paul Sartre, *Being and Nothingness.* Trans. Hazel Barnes (Philosophical Library, 1956) by permission.

Thus attitudes of negation toward the self permit us to raise a new question: What are we to say is the being of man who has the possibility of denying himself? But it is out of the question to discuss the attitude of "self-negation" in its universality. The kinds of behavior which can be ranked under this heading are too diverse; we risk retaining only the abstract form of them. It is best to choose and to examine one determined attitude which is essential to human reality and which is such that consciousness instead of directing its negation outward turns it toward itself. This attitude, it seems to me, is *bad faith* (*mauvaise foi*).

Frequently this is identified with falsehood. We say indifferently of a person that he shows signs of bad faith or that he lies to himself. We shall willingly grant that bad faith is a lie to oneself, on condition that we distinguish the lie to oneself from lying in general. Lying is a negative attitude, we will agree to that. But this negation does not bear on consciousness itself; it aims only at the transcendent. The essence of the lie implies in fact that the liar actually is in complete possession of the truth which he is hiding. A man does not lie about what he is ignorant of; he does not lie when he spreads an error of which he himself is the dupe; he does not lie when he is mistaken. The ideal description of the liar would be a cynical consciousness, affirming truth within himself, denying it in his words, and denying that negation as such. Now this double negative attitude rests on the transcendent; the fact expressed is transcendent since it does not exist, and the original negation rests on a *truth*; that is, on a particular type of transcendence. As for the inner negation which I effect correlatively with the affirmation for myself of the truth, this rests on *words*; that is, on an event in the world. Furthermore the inner disposition of the liar is positive; it could be the object of an affirmative judgment. The liar intends to deceive and he does not seek to hide this intention from himself nor to disguise the translucency of consciousness; on the contrary, he has recourse to it when there is a question of deciding secondary behavior. It explicitly exercises a regulatory control over all attitudes. As for his flaunted intention of telling the truth ("I'd never want to deceive you! This is true! I swear it!")—all this, of course, is the object of an inner negation, but also it is not recognized by the liar as *his* intention. It is played, imitated, it is the intention of the character which he plays in the eyes of his questioner, but this character, precisely because he *does not exist*, is a transcendent. Thus the lie does not put into the play the inner structure of present consciousness; all the negations which constitute it bear on objects which by this fact are removed from consciousness. The lie then does not require special ontological foundation, and the explanations which the existence of negation in general requires are valid without change in the case of deceit. Of course we have described the ideal lie; doubtless it happens often enough that the liar is more or less the victim of his lie, that he half persuades himself of it. But these common, popular forms of the lie are also degenerate aspects of it; they represent intermediaries between falsehood and bad faith. The lie is a behavior of transcendence.

The lie is also a normal phenomenon of what Heidegger calls the "*mit-sein*."[1] It presupposes my existence, the existence of the *Other*, my existence *for* the Other, and the existence of the Other *for* me. Thus there is no difficulty in holding that the liar must make the project of the lie in entire clarity and that he must possess a complete comprehension of the lie and of the truth which he is altering. It is sufficient that an overall opacity hide his intentions from the *Other*; it is sufficient that the Other can take the lie for truth. By the lie consciousness affirms that it exists by nature as *hidden from the Other*; it utilizes for its own profit the ontological duality of myself and myself in the eyes of the Other.

The situation can not be the same for bad faith if this, as we have said, is indeed a lie to oneself. To be sure, the one who practices bad faith is hiding a displeasing truth or presenting as truth a pleasing untruth. Bad faith then has in appearance the structure of falsehood. Only what changes everything is the fact that in bad faith it is from myself that I am hiding the truth. Thus the duality of the deceiver and the deceived does not exist here. Bad faith on the contrary implies in essence the unity of a *single* consciousness. This does not mean that it can not be conditioned by the *mit-sein* like all other phenomena of human reality, but the *mit-sein* can call forth bad faith only by presenting itself as *a situation* which bad faith permits surpassing; bad faith does not come from outside to human reality. One does not undergo his bad faith; one is not infected with it; it is not a *state*. But consciousness affects itself with bad faith. There must be an original intention and a project of bad faith; this project implies a com-

1. Tr. A "being-with" others in the world.

prehension of bad faith as such and a pre-reflective apprehension (of) consciousness as affecting itself with bad faith. It follows first that the one to whom the lie is told and the one who lies are one and the same person, which means that I must know in my capacity as deceiver the truth which is hidden from me in my capacity as the one deceived. Better yet I must know the truth very exactly *in order* to conceal it more carefully—and this not at two different moments, which at a pinch would allow us to re-establish a semblance of duality—but in the unitary structure of a single project. How then can the lie subsist if the duality which conditions it is suppressed?

To this difficulty is added another which is derived from the total translucency of consciousness. That which affects itself with bad faith must be conscious (of) its bad faith since the being of consciousness is consciousness of being. It appears then that I must be in good faith, at least to the extent that I am conscious of my bad faith. But then this whole psychic system is annihilated. We must agree in fact that if I deliberately and cynically attempt to lie to myself, I fail completely in this undertaking; the lie falls back and collapses beneath my look; it is ruined *from behind* by the very consciousness of lying to myself which pitilessly constitutes itself well within my project as its very condition. We have here an *evanescent* phenomenon which exists only in and through its own differentiation. To be sure, these phenomena are frequent and we shall see that there is in fact an "evanescence" of bad faith, which, it is evident, vacillates continually between good faith and cynicism: Even though the existence of bad faith is very precarious, and though it belongs to the kind of psychic structures which we might call *metastable,* it presents nonetheless an autonomous and durable form. It can even be the normal aspect of life for a very great number of people. A person can *live* in bad faith, which does not mean that he does not have abrupt awakenings to cynicism or to good faith, but which implies a constant and particular style of life. Our embarrassment then appears extreme since we can neither reject nor comprehend bad faith.

II. PATTERNS OF BAD FAITH

If we wish to get out of this difficulty, we should examine more closely the patterns of bad faith and attempt a description of them. This description will permit us perhaps to fix more exactly the conditions for the possibility of bad faith; that is, to reply to the questions we raised at the outset: "What must be the being of man if he is to be capable of bad faith?"

Take the example of a woman who has consented to go out with a particular man for the first time. She knows very well the intentions which the man who is speaking to her cherishes regarding her. She knows also that it will be necessary sooner or later for her to make a decision. But she does not want to realize the urgency; she concerns herself only with what is respectful and discreet in the attitude of her companion. She does not apprehend this conduct as an attempt to achieve what we call "the first approach"; that is, she does not want to see possibilities of temporal development which his conduct presents. She restricts this behavior to what is in the present; she does not wish to read in the phrases which he addresses to her anything other than their explicit meaning. If he says to her, "I find you so attractive!" she disarms this phrase of its sexual background; she attaches to the conversation and to the behavior of the speaker, the immediate meanings, which she images as objective qualities. The man who is speaking to her appears to her sincere and respectful as the table is round or square, as the wall coloring is blue or gray. The qualities thus attached to the person she is listening to are in this way fixed in a permanence like that of things, which is no other than the projection of the strict present of the qualities into the temporal flux. This is because she does not quite know what she wants. She is profoundly aware of the desire which she inspires, but the desire cruel and naked would humiliate and horrify her. Yet she would find no charm in a respect which would be only respect. In order to satisfy her, there must be a feeling which is addressed wholly to her *personality—i.e.,* to her full freedom—and which would be a recognition of her freedom. But at the same time this feeling must be wholly desire; that is, it must address itself to her body as object. This time then she refuses to apprehend the desire for what it is; she does not even give it a name; she recognizes it only to the extent that it transcends itself toward admiration, esteem, respect and that it is wholly absorbed in the more refined forms which it produces, to the extent of no longer figuring anymore as a sort of warmth and density. But then suppose he takes her hand. This act of her companion risks changing the situation by calling for an immediate decision. To leave the hand there is to consent in herself to flirt, to engage herself. To withdraw it is to break the troubled and unstable harmony which gives the hour its charm. The aim is to postpone the moment of decision as long as possible. We know what happens next; the young woman leaves her hand there, but she *does not notice* that she is leaving it. She does not notice because it happens by chance that she is at this moment all intellect. She draws her companion up to the most lofty regions of sentimental speculation; she speaks of Life, of her life, she shows herself in her essential aspect—a personality, a consciousness. And during this time the divorce of the body from the soul is accomplished; the hand rests inert between the warm hands of her companion—neither consenting nor resisting—a thing.

We shall say that this woman is in bad faith. But we see immediately that she uses various procedures in order to maintain herself in this bad faith. She has disarmed the actions of her companion by reducing them to being only what they are; that is, to existing in the mode of the in-itself. But she permits herself to enjoy his desire, to the extent that she will apprehend it as not being what it is, will recognize its transcendence. Finally while sensing profoundly the presence of her own body—to the point of being aroused, perhaps—she realized herself as *not being* her own body, and she contemplates it as though from above as a passive object to which events can *happen* but which can neither provoke them nor avoid them because all its possibilities are outside of it. What unity do we find in these various aspects of bad faith? It is a certain art of forming contradictory concepts which unite in themselves both an idea and the negation of that idea. The basic concept which is thus engendered utilizes the double property of the human being, who is at once a *facticity* and a *transcendence.* These two aspects of human reality are and ought to be capable of a valid coordination. But bad faith does not wish either to coordinate them or to surmount them in a synthesis. Bad faith seeks to affirm their identity while preserving their differences. It must affirm facticity as *being* transcendence and transcendence as *being* facticity, in such a way that at the instant when a person apprehends the one, he can find himself abruptly faced with the other.

We can find the prototype of formulae of bad faith in certain famous expressions which have been rightly conceived to produce their whole effect in a spirit of bad faith. Take for example the title of a work by Jacques Chardonne, *Love Is Much More than Love.* We see here how unity is established between *present* love in its facticity—"the contact of two skins," sensuality, egoism, Proust's mechanism of jealousy, Adler's battle of the *sexes, etc.*—and love as transcendence—Mauriac's "river of fire," the longing for the infinite, Plato's *eros*, Lawrence's deep cosmic intuition, *etc.* Here we leave facticity to find ourselves suddenly beyond the present and the factual condition of man, beyond the psychological, in the heart of metaphysics. On the other hand, the title of a play by Sarment, *I Am too Great for Myself,* which also presents characters in bad faith, throws us first into full transcendence in order suddenly to imprison us within the narrow limits of our factual essence. We will discover this structure again in the famous sentence: "He has become what he was" or in its no less famous opposite: "Eternity at last changes each man into himself." It is well understood that these various formulae have only the appearance of bad faith; they have been conceived in this paradoxical form explicitly to shock the mind and discountenance it by an enigma. But it is precisely this appearance which is of concern to us. What counts here is that the formulae do not constitute new, solidly structured ideas; on the contrary, they are formed so as to remain in perpetual disintegration and so that we may slide at any time from naturalistic present to transcendence and *vice versa.*

We can see the use which bad faith can make of these judgments which all aim at establishing that I am not what I am. If I were only what I *am*, I could, for example, seriously consider an adverse criticism which someone makes of me, question myself scrupulously, and perhaps be compelled to recognize the truth in it. But thanks to transcendence, I am not subject to all that I am. I do not even have to discuss the justice of the reproach. As Suzanne says to Figaro, "To prove that I am right would be to recognize that I can be wrong." I am on a plane where no reproach can touch me since what I really am is my transcendence. I flee from myself, I escape myself, I leave my tattered garment in the hands of the fault-finder. But the ambiguity necessary for bad faith comes from the fact that I affirm here that I *am* my transcendence in the mode of being of a thing. It is only thus, in fact, that I can feel that I escape all reproaches. It is in the sense that our young woman purifies the desire of anything humiliating by being willing to consider it only as pure transcendence, which she avoids even naming. But inversely "I Am too Great for Myself," while showing our transcendence changed into facticity, is the source of an infinity of excuses for our failures or our weaknesses. Similarly the young coquette maintains transcendence to the extent that the respect, the esteem manifested by the actions of her admirer are already on the plane of the transcendent. But she arrests this transcendence, she glues it down with all the facticity of the present; respect is nothing other than respect, it is an arrested surpassing which no longer surpasses itself toward anything.

But although this *metastable* concept of "transcendence-facticity" is one of the most basic instruments of bad faith, it is not the only one of its kind. We can equally well use another kind of duplicity derived from human reality which we will express roughly by saying that its being-for-itself implies complementarily a being-for-others. Upon any one of my conducts it is always possible to converge two looks, mine and that of the Other. The conduct will not present exactly the same structure in each case. But as we shall see later, as each look perceives it, there is between these two aspects of my being, no difference between appearance and being—as if I were to my self the truth of myself and as if the Other possessed only a deformed image of me. The equal dignity of being, possessed by my being-for-others and by my being-for-myself, permits a perpetually disintegrating synthesis and a perpetual game of escape from the for-itself to the for-others and from the for-others to the for-itself. We have seen also the use which our young lady made of our being-in-the-midst-of-the-world—*i.e.,* of our inert presence as a passive object among other objects—in order to relieve herself suddenly from the functions of her being-in-the-world—that is, from the being which causes there to be a world by projecting itself beyond the world towards its own possibilities. Let us note finally the confusing syntheses which play on the nihilating ambiguity of these temporal ekstases, affirming at once that I am what I have been (the man who deliberately *arrests himself* at one period in his life and refuses to take into consideration the later changes) and that I am not what I have been (the man who in the face of reproaches or rancor dissociates himself from his past by insisting on his freedom and on his perpetual re-creation). In all these concepts, which have only a transitive role in the reasoning and which are eliminated from the conclusion (like the imaginaries in the computations of physicists), we find again the same structure. We have to deal with human reality as a being which is what it is not and which is not what it is.

But what exactly is necessary in order for these concepts of disintegration to be able to receive even a pretence of existence, in order for them to be able to appear for an instant to consciousness, even in a process of evanescence? A quick examination of the idea of sincerity, the antithesis of bad faith, will be very instructive in this connection. Actually sincerity presents itself as a demand and consequently is not a *state*. Now what is the ideal to be attained in this case? It is necessary that a man be *for himself* only what he *is*. But is this not precisely the definition of the in-itself—or if you prefer—the principle of identity? To posit as an ideal the being of things, is this not to assert by the same stroke that this being does not belong to human reality and that the principle of identity, far from being a universal axiom universally applied, is only a synthetic principle enjoying a merely regional universality? Thus in order that the concepts of bad faith can put us under illusion at least for an instant, in order that the candor of "pure hearts" (*cf.* Gide, Kessel) can have validity for human reality as an ideal, the principle of identity must not represent a constitutive principle of human reality and human reality must not be necessarily what it is but must be able to be what it is not. What does this mean?

If man is what he is, bad faith is forever impossible and candor ceases to be his ideal and becomes instead his being. But is man what he is? And more generally, how can he *be* what he is when he exists as consciousness of being? If candor or sincerity is a universal value, it is evident that the maxim "one must be what one is" does not serve solely as a regulating principle for judgments and concepts by which I express what I am. It posits not merely an ideal of knowing but an ideal of *being*; it proposes for us an absolute equivalent of being with itself as a prototype of being. In this sense it is necessary that we *make ourselves* what we are. But what *are we* then if we have the constant obligations to make ourselves what we are, if our mode of being is having the obligation to be what we are?

Let us consider this waiter in the café. His movement is quick and forward, a little too precise, a little too rapid. He comes toward the patrons with a step a little too quick. He bends forward a little too eagerly; his voice, his eyes express an interest a little too solicitous for the order of the customer. Finally there he returns, trying to imitate in his walk the inflexible stiffness of some kind of automaton while carrying his tray with the recklessness of a tight-rope-walker by putting it in a perpetually unstable, perpetually broken equilibrium which he perpetually re-establishes by a light movement of the arm and hand. All his behavior seems to us a game. He applies himself to chaining his movements as if they were mechanisms, the one regulating the other; his gestures and even his voice seem to be mechanisms; he gives himself the quickness and pitiless rapidity of things. He is playing, he is amusing himself. But what is he playing? We need not watch long before we can explain it: he is playing at *being* a waiter in a café. There is nothing there to surprise us. The game is a kind of marking out and investigation. The child plays with his body in order to explore it, to take inventory of it; the waiter in the café plays with his condition in order to *realize* it. This obligation is not different from that which is imposed on all tradesmen. Their condition is wholly one of ceremony. The public demands of them that they realize it as a ceremony; there is the dance of the grocer, of the tailor, of the auctioneer, by which they endeavor to persuade their clientele that they are nothing but a grocer, an auctioneer, a tailor. A grocer who dreams is offensive to the buyer, because such a grocer is not wholly a grocer. Society demands that he limit himself to his function as a grocer, just as the soldier at attention makes himself into a soldier-thing with a direct regard which does not see at all, which is no longer meant to see, since it is the rule and not the interest of the moment which determines the point he must fix his eyes on (the sight "fixed at ten paces"). There are indeed many precautions to imprison a man in what he is, as if we lived in perpetual fear that he might escape from it, that he might break away and suddenly elude his condition.

In a parallel situation, from within, the waiter in the café can not be immediately a café waiter in the sense that this inkwell *is* an inkwell, or the glass is a glass. It is by no means that he can not form reflective judgments or concepts concerning his condition. He knows well what it "means": the obligation of getting up at five o'clock, of sweeping the floor of the shop before the restaurant opens, of starting the coffee pot going, *etc*. He knows the rights which it allows: the right to the tips, the right to belong to a union, *etc*. But all these concepts, all these judgments refer to the transcendent. It is a matter of abstract possibilities, of rights and duties conferred on a "person possessing rights." And it is precisely this person *who I have to be* (if I am the waiter in question) and who I am not. I is not that I do not wish to be this person or that I want this person to be different. But rather there is no common measure between his being and mine. It is a "representation" for others and for myself, which means that I can be he only in *representation.* But if I represent myself as him, I am not he; I am separated from him as the object from the subject, separated *by nothing,* but this nothing isolates me from him. I can not be he, I can only play *at being* him; that is, imagine to myself that I am he. And thereby I affect him with nothingness. In vain do I fulfill the functions of a café waiter. I can be he only in the neutralized mode, as the actor is Hamlet, by mechanically making the *typical gestures* of my state and by aiming at myself as an imaginary café waiter through those gestures taken as an "analogue." What I attempt to realize is a being-in-itself of the café waiter, as if it were not just in my power to confer their value and their urgency upon my duties and the rights of my position, as if it were not my free choice to get up each morning at five o'clock or to remain in bed, even though it meant getting fired. As if from the very fact that I sustain this role in existence I did not transcend it on every side, as if I did not constitute myself as one *beyond* my condition. Yet there is no doubt that I *am* in a sense a café waiter—otherwise could I not just as well call myself a diplomat or a reporter? But if I am one, this can not be in the mode of being in-itself. I am a waiter in the mode of *being what I am not.*

Furthermore we are dealing with more than mere social positions; I am never any one of my attitudes, any one of my actions. The good speaker is the one who *plays* at speaking, because he can not *be speaking.* The attentive pupil who wishes to *be* attentive, his eyes riveted on the teacher, his ears wide open, so exhausts himself in playing the attentive role that he ends up by no longer hearing anything. Perpetually absent to my body, to my acts, I am despite myself that "divine absence" of which Valéry speaks. I can not say either that I *am* here or that I *am* not here, in the sense that we say "that box of matches *is* on the table"; this would be to confuse my "being-in-the-world" with a "being-in-the-midst-of-the-world." Nor that I *am* standing, nor that I *am* seated; this would be to confuse my body with the idiosyncratic totality of which it is only one of the structures. On all sides I escape being and yet—I am. . . .

Consciousness of the Other is what it is not.

Furthermore the being of my own consciousness does not appear to be as the consciousness of the Other. It *is* because it makes itself, since its being is consciousness of being. But this means that making sustains being; consciousness has to be its own being, it is never sustained by being; it sustains being in the heart of subjectivity, which means once again that it is inhabited by being but that it is not being: *consciousness is not what it is.*

Under these conditions what can be the significance of the ideal of sincerity except as a task impossible to achieve, of which the very meaning is in contradiction with the structure of my consciousness. To be sincere, we said, is to be what one is. That supposes that I am not originally what I am. But here naturally Kant's "You ought, therefore you can" is implicitly understood. I can *become* sincere; this is what my duty and my effort to achieve sincerity imply. But we definitely establish that the original structure of "not being what one is" renders impossible in advance all movement toward being in itself or "being what one is." And this impossibility is not hidden from consciousness; on the contrary, it is the very stuff of consciousness; it is the embarrassing constraint which we constantly experience; it is our very incapacity to recognize ourselves, to constitute ourselves as being what we are. It is this necessity which means that, as soon as we posit ourselves as a certain being, by a legitimate judgment, based on inner experience or correctly deduced from a *priori* or empirical premises, then by that very positing we surpass this being—and that not toward another being but toward emptiness, toward *nothing*.

How then can we blame another for not being sincere or rejoice in our own sincerity since this sincerity appears to us at the same time to be impossible? How can we in conversation, in confession, in introspection, even attempt sincerity since the effort will be by its very nature be doomed to failure and since at the very time when we announce it we have a prejudicative comprehension of its futility? In introspection I try to determine exactly what I am, to make up my mind to be my true self without delay—even though it means consequently to set about searching for ways to change myself. But what does this mean if not that I am constituting myself as a thing? Shall I determine the ensemble of purposes and motivations which have pushed me to do this or that action? But this is already to postulate a causal determinism which constitutes the flow of my states of consciousness as a succession of physical states. Shall I uncover in myself "drives," even though it be to affirm them in shame? But is this not deliberately to forget that these drives are realized with my consent, that they are not forces of nature but that I lend them their efficacy by a perpetually renewed decision concerning their value. Shall I pass judgment on my character, on my nature? Is this not to veil from myself at that moment what I know only too well, that I thus judge a past to which by definition my present is not subject? The proof of this is that the same man who in sincerity posits that he is what in actuality he was, is indignant at the reproach of another and tries to disarm it by asserting that he can no longer be what he was. We are readily astonished and upset when the penalties of the court affect a man who in his new freedom *is no longer* the guilty person he was. But at the same time we require of this man that he recognize himself as *being* this guilty one. What then is sincerity except precisely a phenomenon of bad faith? Have we not shown indeed that in bad faith human reality is constituted as a being which is what it is not and which is not what it is?

Let us take an example: A homosexual frequently has an intolerable feeling of guilt, and his whole existence is determined in relation to this feeling. One will readily foresee that he is in bad faith. In fact it frequently happens that this man, while recognizing his homosexual inclination, while avowing each and every particular misdeed which he has committed, refuses with all his strength to consider himself "*a paederast.*" His case is always "different," peculiar; there enters into it something of a game, of chance, of bad luck; the mistakes are all in the past; they are explained by a certain conception of the beautiful which women can not satisfy; we should see in them the results of a restless search, rather than the manifestations of a deeply rooted tendency, etc., etc. Here is assuredly a man in bad faith who borders on the comic since, acknowledging all the facts which are imputed to him, he refuses to draw from them the conclusion which they impose. His friend, who is his most severe critic, becomes irritated with this duplicity. The critic asks only one thing—and perhaps then he will show himself indulgent: that the guilty one recognize himself as guilty, that the homosexual declare frankly—whether humbly or boastfully matters little—"I am a paederast." We ask here: Who is in bad faith? The homosexual or the champion of sincerity?

The homosexual recognizes his faults, but he struggles with all his strength against the crushing view that his mistakes constitute for him a *destiny.* He does not wish to let himself be considered as a thing. He has an obscure but strong feeling that an homosexual is not an homosexual as this table is a table or as this red-haired man is red-haired. It seems to him that he has escaped from each mistake as soon as he has posited it and recognized it; he even feels that the psychic duration by itself cleanses him from each misdeed, constitutes for him an undetermined future, causes him to be born anew. Is he wrong? Does he not recognize in himself the peculiar, irreducible character of human reality? His attitude includes then an undeniable comprehension of truth. But at the same time he needs this perpetual rebirth, this constant escape in order to live; he must constantly put himself beyond reach in order to avoid the terrible judgment of collectivity. Thus he plays on the word *being*. He would be right actually if he understood the phrase, "I am not a paederast" in the sense of "I am not what I am." That is, if he declared to himself, "To the extent that a pattern of conduct is defined as the conduct of a paederast and to the extent that I have adopted this conduct, I am a paederast. But to the extent that human reality can not be finally defined by patterns of conduct, I am not one." But instead he slides surreptitiously towards a different connotation of the word "being." He understands "not being" in the sense of "not-being-in-itself." He lays claim to "not being a paederast" in the sense in which this table *is not* an inkwell.He is in bad faith.

But the champion of sincerity is not ignorant of the transcendence of human reality, and he knows how at need to appeal to it for his own advantage. He makes use of it even and brings it up in the present argument. Does he not wish, first in the name of sincerity, then of freedom, that the homosexual reflect on himself and acknowledge himself as an homosexual? Does he not let the other understand that such a confession will win indulgence for him? What does this mean if not that the man who will acknowledge himself as an homosexual will no longer be the same as the homosexual whom he acknowledges being and that he will escape into the region of freedom and of good will? The critic asks the man then to be what he is in order no longer to be what he is. It is the profound meaning of the saying, "A sin confessed is half pardoned." The critic demands of the guilty one that he constitute himself as a thing, precisely in order no longer to treat him as a thing. And this contradiction is constitutive of the demand of sincerity. Who can not see how offensive to the Other and how reassuring for me is a statement such as, "He's just a paederast," which removes a disturbing freedom from a trait and which aims at henceforth constituting all the acts of the Other as consequences following strictly from his essence. That is actually what the critic is demanding of his victim—that he constitute himself as a thing, that he should entrust his freedom to his friend as a fief, in order that the friend should return it to him subsequently—like a suzerain to his vassal. The champion of sincerity is in bad faith to the degree that in order to reassure himself, he pretends to judge, to the extent that he demands that freedom as freedom constitute itself as a thing. We have here only one episode in that battle to the death of consciousnesses which Hegel calls "the relation of the master and the slave." A person appeals to another and demands that in the name of his nature as consciousness he should radically destroy himself as consciousness, but while making this appeal he leads the other to hope for a rebirth beyond this destruction.

Very well, someone will say, but our man is abusing sincerity, playing one side against the other. We should not look for sincerity in the relation of the *Mit-sein* but rather where it is pure—in the relations of a person with himself. But who can not see that objective sincerity is constituted in the same way? Who can not see that the sincere man constitutes himself as a thing in order to escape the condition of a thing by the same act of sincerity? The man who confesses that he is evil has exchanged his disturbing "freedom-for-evil" for an inanimate character of evil; he *is* evil, he clings to himself, he is what he is. But by the same stroke, he escapes from that *thing*, since it is he who contemplates it, since it depends on him to maintain it under his glance or to let it collapse in an infinity of particular acts. He derives a *merit* from his sincerity, and the deserving man is not the evil man as he is evil but as he is beyond his evilness. At the same time the evil is disarmed since it is nothing, save on the plane of determinism, and since in confessing it, I posit my freedom in respect to it; my future is virgin; everything is allowed to me.

Thus the essential structure of sincerity does not differ from that of bad faith since the sincere man constitutes himself as what he is *in order not to be it.* This explains the truth recognized by all that one can fall into bad faith through being sincere. As Valéry pointed out, this is the case with Stendhal. Total, constant sincerity as a constant effort to adhere to oneself is by nature a constant effort to dissociate oneself from oneself. A person frees himself from himself by the very act by which he makes himself an object for himself. To draw up a perpetual inventory of what one is means constantly to redeny oneself and to take refuge in a sphere where one is no longer anything but a pure, free regard. The goal of bad faith, as we said, is to put oneself out of reach; it is an escape. Now we see that we must use the same terms to define sincerity. What does this mean?

In the final analysis the goal of sincerity and the goal of bad faith are not so different. To be sure, there is a sincerity which bears on the past and which does not concern us here; I am sincere if I confess *having had* this pleasure or that intention. We shall see that if this sincerity is possible, it is because in his fall into the past, the being of man is constituted as a being-in-itself. But here our concern is only with the sincerity which aims at itself in present immanence. What is its goal? To bring me to confess to myself what I am in order that I may finally coincide with my being; in a word, to cause myself to be, in the mode of the in-itself, what I am in the mode of "not being what I am." Its assumption is that fundamentally I am already, in the mode of the in-itself, what I have to be. Thus we find at the base of sincerity a continual game of mirror and reflection, a perpetual passage from the being which is what it is, to the being which is not what it is and inversely from the being which is not what it is to the being which is what it is. And what is the goal of bad faith? To cause me to be what I am, in the mode of "not being what one is," or not to be what I am in the mode of "being what one is." We find here the same game of mirrors. In fact in order for me to have an intention of sincerity, I must at the outset simultaneously be and not be what I am. Sincerity does not assign to me a mode of being or a particular quality, but in relation to that quality it aims at making me pass from one mode of being to another mode of being. This second mode of being, the ideal of sincerity, I am prevented by nature from attaining; and at the very moment when I struggle to attain it, I have a vague prejudicative comprehension that I shall not attain it. But all the same, in order for me to be able to conceive an intention in bad faith, I must have such a nature that within my being I escape from my being. If I were sad or cowardly in the way in which this inkwell is an inkwell, the possibility of bad faith could not even be conceived. Not only should I be unable to escape from my being; I could not even imagine that I could escape from it. But if bad faith is possible by virtue of a simple project, it is because so far as my being is concerned, there is no difference between being and non-being if I am cut off from my project.

Bad faith is possible only because sincerity is conscious of missing its goal inevitably, due to its very nature. I can try to apprehend myself as "*not being cowardly,*" when I am so, only on condition that the "being cowardly" is itself "in question" at the very moment when it exists, on condition that it is itself *one* question, that at the very moment when I wish to apprehend it, it escapes me on all sides and annihilates itself. The condition under which I can attempt an effort in bad faith is that in one sense, I am not this coward which I do not wish to be. But if I were not cowardly in the simple mode of not-being-what-one-is-not, I would be "in good faith" by declaring that I am not cowardly. Thus this inapprehensible coward is evanescent; in order for me not to be cowardly, I must in some way also be cowardly. That does not mean that I must be "a little" cowardly, in the sense that "a little" signifies "to a certain degree cowardly—and not cowardly to a certain degree." No. I must at once both be and not be totally and in all respects a coward. Thus in this case bad faith requires that I should not be what I am; that is, that there be an imponderable difference separating being from non-being in the mode of being of human reality.

But bad faith is not restricted to denying the qualities which I possess, to not seeing the being which I am. It attempts also to constitute myself as being what I am not. It apprehends me positively as courageous when I am not so. And that is possible, once again, only if I am what I am not; that is, if non-being in me does not have being even as non-being. Of course necessarily I *am not* courageous; otherwise bad faith would not be *bad* faith. But in addition my effort in bad faith must include the ontological comprehension that even in my usual being what I *am*, I am not it really and that there is no such difference between the being of "being-sad," for example—which I am in the mode of not being what I am—and the "non-being" of not-being-courageous which I wish to hide from myself. Moreover it is particularly requisite that the very negation of being should be itself the object of a perpetual nihilation, that the very meaning of "non-being" be perpetually in question in human reality. If I were not courageous in the way in which this inkwell is not a table; that is, if I were isolated in my cowardice, propped firmly against it, incapable of putting it in relation to its opposite, if I were not capable of *determining* myself as cowardly—that is, to deny courage to myself and thereby to escape my cowardice in the very moment that I posit it—if it were not on principle *impossible* for me to coincide with my *not-being-courageous* as well as with my being-courageous—then any project of bad faith would be prohibited me. Thus in order for bad faith to be possible, sincerity itself must be in bad faith. The condition of the possibility for bad faith is that human reality, in its most immediate being, in the intrastructure of the pre-reflective *cogito,* must be what it is not and not be what it is.

III. THE "FAITH" OF BAD FAITH

We have indicated for the moment only those conditions which render bad faith conceivable, the structures of being which permit us to form concepts of bad faith. We can not limit ourselves to these considerations; we have not yet distinguished bad faith from falsehood. The two-faced concepts which we have described would without a doubt be utilized by a liar to discountenance his questioner, although their two-faced quality being established on the being of a man and not on some empirical circumstance, can and ought to be evident to all. The true problem of bad faith stems evidently from the fact that bad faith is *faith.* It can not be either a cynical lie or certainty—if certainty is the intuitive possession of the object. But if we take belief as meaning the adherence of being to its object when the object is not given or is given indistinctly, then bad faith is belief; and the essential problem of bad faith is a problem of belief.

How can we believe by bad faith in the concepts which we forge expressly to persuade ourselves? We must note in fact that the project of bad faith must be itself in bad faith. I am not only in bad faith at the end of my effort when I have constructed my two-faced concepts and when I have persuaded myself. In truth, I have not persuaded myself; to the extent that I could be so persuaded, I have always been so. And at the very moment when I was disposed to put myself in bad faith, I of necessity was in bad faith with respect to this same disposition. For me to have represented it to myself as bad faith would have been cynicism; to believe it sincerely innocent would have been in good faith. The decision to be in bad faith does not dare to speak its name; it believes itself and does not believe itself in bad faith; it believes itself and does not believe itself in good faith. It is this which from the upsurge of bad faith, determines the later attitude and, as it were, the *Weltanschauung* of bad faith.

Bad faith does not hold the norms and criteria of truth as they are accepted by the critical thought of good faith. What it decides first, in fact, is the nature of truth. With bad faith a truth appears, a method of thinking, a type of being which is like that of objects; the ontological characteristic of the world of bad faith with which the subject suddenly surrounds himself is this: that here being is what it is not, and is not what it is. Consequently a peculiar type of evidence appears; *non-persuasive* evidence. Bad faith apprehends evidence but it is resigned in advance to not being fulfilled by this evidence, to not being persuaded and transformed into good faith. It makes itself humble and modest; it is not ignorant, it says, that faith is decision and that after each intuition, it must decide and *will what it is.* Thus bad faith in its primitive project and in its coming into the world decides on the exact nature of its requirement. It stands forth in the firm resolution *not to demand too much,* to count itself satisfied when it is barely persuaded, to force itself in decisions to adhere to uncertain truths. This original project of bad faith is a decision in bad faith on the nature of faith. Let us understand clearly that there is no question of a reflective, voluntary decision, but of a spontaneous determination of our being. One *puts oneself* in bad faith as one goes to sleep and one is in bad faith as one dreams. Once this mode of being has been realized, it is as difficult to get out of it as to wake oneself up; bad faith is a type of being in the world, like waking or dreaming, which by itself tends to perpetuate itself, although its structure is of the *metastable* type. But bad faith is conscious of its structure, and it has taken precautions by deciding that the metastable structure is the structure of being and that non-persuasion is the structure of all convictions. It follows that if bad faith is faith and if it includes in its original project its own negation (it determines itself to be not quite convinced in order to convince itself that I am what I am not), then to start with, a faith which wishes itself to be not quite convinced must be possible. What are the conditions for the possibility of such a faith?

I believe that my friend Pierre feels friendship for me. I believe it in *good faith.* I believe it but I do not have for it any self-evident intuition, for the nature of the object does not lend itself to intuition. I *believe it*; that is, I allow myself to give into all impulses to trust it; I decide to believe in it, and to maintain myself in this decision; I conduct myself, finally, as if I were certain of it—and all this in the synthetic unity of one and the same attitude. This which I define as good faith is what Hegel would call the *immediate.* It is simple faith. Hegel would demonstrate at once that the immediate calls for mediation and that belief by becoming *belief for itself,* passes to the state of non-belief. If I *believe* that my friend Pierre likes me, this means that his friendship appears to me as the meaning of all his acts. Belief is a particular consciousness of *the meaning* of Pierre's acts. But if I know that I believe, the belief appears to me as pure subjective determination without external correlative. This is what makes the very word "to believe" a term utilized indifferently to indicate the unwavering firmness of belief ("My God, I believe in you") and its character as disarmed and strictly subjective ("Is Pierre my friend? I do not know; I believe so.") But the nature of consciousness is such that in it the mediate and the immediate are one and the same being. To believe is to know that one believes, and to know that one believes is no longer to believe. Thus to believe is not to believe any longer because that is only to believe—this in the unity of one and the same non-thetic self-consciousness. To be sure, we have here forced the description of the phenomenon by designating it with the word to *know*; non-thetic consciousness is not to *know.* But it is in its very translucency at the origin of all knowing. Thus the non-thetic consciousness (of) believing is destructive of belief. But at the same time the very law of the pre-reflective *cogito* implies that the being of believing ought to be the consciousness of believing.

Thus belief is a being which questions its own being, which can realize itself only in its destruction, which can manifest itself to itself only by denying itself. It is a being for which to be is to appear and to appear is to deny itself. To believe is not-to-believe. We see that reason for it; the being of consciousness is to exist by itself, then to make itself be and thereby to pass beyond itself. In this sense consciousness is perpetually escaping itself, belief becomes non-belief, the immediate becomes mediation, the absolute becomes relative, and the relative becomes absolute. The ideal of good faith (to believe what one believes) is, like that of sincerity (to be what one is), an ideal of being-in-itself. Every belief is a belief that falls short; one never wholly believes what one believes. Consequently the primitive project of bad faith is only the utilization of this self-destruction of the fact or consciousness. If every belief in good faith is an impossible belief, then there is a place for every impossible belief. My inability to *believe* that I am courageous will not discourage me since every belief involves not quite believing. I shall define this impossible belief as *my* belief. To be sure, I shall not be able to hide from myself that I believe in order not to believe and that I do not believe *in order to* believe. But the subtle, total annihilation of bad faith by itself can not surprise me; it exists at the basis of all faith. What is it then? At the moment when I wish to believe myself courageous I *know* that I am a coward. And this certainly would come to destroy my belief. But *first*, I *am* not any more courageous than cowardly, if we are to understand this in the mode of being of the-in-itself. In the second place, I do not *know* that I am courageous; such a view of myself can be accompanied only by *belief,* for it surpasses pure reflective certitude. In the third place, it is very true that bad faith does not succeed in believing what it wishes to believe. But it is precisely as the acceptance of not believing what it believes that it is bad faith. Good faith wishes to flee the "not-believing-what-one-believes" by finding refuge in being. Bad faith flees being by taking refuse in "not-believing-what-one-believes." It has disarmed all beliefs in advance—those which it would like to take hold of and, by the same stroke, the others, those which it wishes to flee. In *willing* this self-destruction of belief, from which science escapes by searching for evidence, it ruins the beliefs which are opposed to it, which reveal themselves as *being only* belief. Thus we can better understand the original phenomenon of bad faith.

In bad faith there is no cynical lie nor knowing preparation for deceitful concepts. But the first act of bad faith is to flee what it can not flee, to flee what it is. The very project of flight reveals to bad faith an inner disintegration in the heart of being, and it is this disintegration which bad faith wishes to be. In truth, the two immediate attitudes which we can take in the face of our being are conditioned by the very nature of this being and its immediate relation with the in-itself. Good faith seeks to flee the inner disintegration of my being in the direction of the in-itself which it should be and is not. Bad faith seeks to flee the in-itself by means of the inner disintegration of my being. But it denies this very disintegration as it denies that it is itself bad faith. Bad faith seeks by means of "not-being-what-one is" to escape from the in-itself which I am not in the mode of being what one is not. It denies itself as bad faith and aims at the in-itself which I am not in the mode of "not-being-what-one-is not."[2] If bad faith is possible, it is because it is an immediate, permanent threat to every project of the human being; it is because consciousness conceals in its being a permanent risk of bad faith. The origin of this risk is the fact that the nature of conscious simultaneously is to be what it is not and not to be what it is. In the light of these remarks we can now approach the ontological study of consciousness, not as the totality of the human being, but as the instantaneous nucleus of this being.

Existentialism and Humanism

What is meant by the term *existentialism*?

Most people who use the word would be rather embarrassed if they had to explain it, since, now that the word is all the rage, even the work of a musician or painter is being called existentialist. . . . It seems that for want of an advance-guard doctrine analogous to surrealism, the kind of people who are eager for scandal and flurry turn to this philosophy which in other respects does not at all serve their purposes in this sphere.

Actually, it is the least scandalous, the most austere of doctrines. It is intended strictly for specialists and philosophers. Yet it can be defined easily. What complicates matters is that there are two kinds of existentialists; first, those who are Christian, among whom I would include Jaspers and Gabriel Marcel, both Catholic; and on the other hand, the atheistic existentialists, among whom I class Heidegger, and then the French existentialists and myself. What they have in common is that they think that existence precedes essence, or, if you prefer, that subjectivity must be the starting point.

Just what does that mean? Let us consider some object that is manufactured, for example, a book or paper-cutter: here is an object which has been made by an artisan whose inspiration came from a concept. He referred to the concept of what a paper-cutter is and likewise to a known method of production, which is part of the concept, something which is, by and large, a routine. Thus, the paper-cutter is at once an object produced in a certain way and, on the other hand, one having a specific use; and one cannot postulate a man who produces a paper-cutter but does not know what it is used for. Therefore, let us say that, for the paper-cutter, essence—that is, the ensemble of both the production routines and the properties which enable it to be both produced and defined—precedes existence. Thus, the presence of the paper-cutter or book in front of me is determined. Therefore, we have here a technical view of the world whereby it can be said that production precedes existence.

When we conceive God as the Creator, He is generally thought of as a superior sort of artisan. Whatever doctrine we may be considering, whether one like that of Descartes or that of Leibnitz, we always grant that will more or less follows understanding or, at the very least, accompanies it, and that when God creates He knows exactly what He is creating. Thus, the concept of man in the mind of God is comparable to the concept of paper-cutter in the mind of the manufacturer, and, following certain techniques and a conception, God produces man, just as the artisan, following a definition and a technique, makes a paper-cutter. Thus, the individual man is the realization of a certain concept in the divine intelligence.

Reprinted from Jean Paul Sartre, *Existentialism.* Trans. Bernard Frechtman (Philosophical Library, 1947) by permission.

In the eighteenth century, the atheism of the *philosophes* discarded the idea of God, but not so much for the notion that essence precedes existence. To a certain extent, this idea is found everywhere; we find it in Diderot, in Voltaire, and even in Kant. Man has a human nature; this human nature, which is the concept of the human, is found in all men, which means that each man is a particular example of a universal concept, man. In Kant, the result of this universality is that the wild-man, the natural man, as well as the bourgeois, are circumscribed by the same definition and have the same basic qualities. Thus, here too the essence of man precedes the historical existence that we find in nature.

Atheistic existentialism, which I represent, is more coherent. It states that if God does not exist, there is at least one being in whom existence precedes essence, a being who exists before he can be defined by any concept, and that this being is man, or, as Heidegger says, human reality. What is meant here by saying that existence precedes essence? It means that, first of all, man exists, turns up, appears on the scene, and, only afterwards, defines himself. If man, as the existentialist conceives him, is indefinable, it is because at first he is nothing. Only afterward will he be something, and he himself will have made what he will be. Thus, there is no human nature, since there is no God to conceive it. Not only is man what he conceives himself to be, but he is also only what he wills himself to be after this thrust toward existence.

Man is nothing else but what he makes of himself. Such is the first principle of existentialism. It is also what is called subjectivity, the name we are labeled with when charges are brought against us. But what do we mean by this, if not that man has a greater dignity than a stone or table? For we mean that man first exists, that is, that man first of all is the being in the future. Man is at the start a plan which is aware of itself, rather than a patch of moss, a piece of garbage, or a cauliflower; nothing exists prior to this plan; there is nothing in heaven; man will be what he will have planned to be. Not what he will want to be. Because by the word "will" we generally mean a conscious decision, which is subsequent to what we have already made of ourselves. I may want to belong to a political party, write a book, get married; but all that is only a manifestation of an earlier, more spontaneous choice that is called "will." But if existence really does precede essence, man is responsible for what he is. Thus, existentialism's first move is to make every man aware of what he is and to make the full responsibility of his existence rest on him. And when we say that a man is responsible for himself, we do not only mean that he is responsible for his own individuality, but that he is responsible for all men.

The word subjectivism has two meanings, and our opponents play on the two. Subjectivism means, on the one hand, that an individual chooses and makes himself; and, on the other, that it is impossible for man to transcend human subjectivity. The second of these is the essential meaning of existentialism. When we say that man chooses his own self, we mean that every one of us does likewise; but we also mean by that that in making this choice he also chooses all men. In fact, in creating the man that we want to be, there is not a single one of our acts which does not at the same time create an image of man as we think he ought to be. To choose to be this or that is to affirm at the same time the value of what we choose, because we can never choose evil. We always choose the good, and nothing can be good for us without being good for all.

If, on the other hand, existence precedes essence, and if we grant that we exist and fashion our image at one and the same time, the image is valid for everybody and for our whole age. Thus, our responsibility is much greater than we might have supposed, because it involves all mankind. If I am a workingman and choose to join a Christian trade-union rather than be a communist, and if by being a member I want to show that the best thing for man is resignation, that the kingdom of man is not of this world, I am not only involving my own case—I want to be resigned for everyone. As a result, my action has involved all humanity. To take a more individual matter, if I want to marry, to have children; even if this marriage depends solely on my own circumstances or passion or wish, I am involving all humanity in monogamy and not merely myself. Therefore, I am responsible for myself and for everyone else. I am creating a certain image of man of my own choosing. In choosing myself, I choose man.

This helps us understand what the actual content is of such rather grandiloquent words as anguish, forlornness, despair. As you will see, it's all quite simple.

First, what is meant by anguish? The existentialists say at once that man is anguish. What that means is this: the man who involves himself and who realizes that he is not only the person he chooses to be, but also a law-maker who is, at the same time, choosing all mankind as well as himself, cannot help escape the feeling of his total and deep responsibility. Of course, there are many people who are not anxious; but we claim that they are hiding their anxiety, that they are fleeing from it. Certainly, many people believe that when they do something, they themselves are the only ones involved, and when someone says to them, "What if everyone acted that way?," they shrug their shoulders and answer, "Everyone doesn't act that way." But really, one should always ask himself, "What would happen if everybody looked at things that way?" There is no escaping this disturbing thought except by a kind of double-dealing. A man who lies and makes excuses for himself by saying "not everybody does that," is someone with an uneasy conscience, because the act of lying implies that a universal value is conferred upon the lie.

Anguish is evident even when it conceals itself. This is the anguish that Kierkegaard called the anguish of Abraham. You know the story: an angel has ordered Abraham to sacrifice his son; if it really were an angel who has come and said, "You are Abraham, you shall sacrifice your son," everything would be all right. But everyone might first wonder, "Is it really an angel, and am I really Abraham? What proof do I have?" . . .

Now, I'm not being singled out as an Abraham, and yet at every moment I'm obliged to perform exemplary acts. For every man, everything happens as if all mankind had its eyes fixed on him and were guiding itself by what he does. And every man ought to say to himself, "Am I really the kind of man who has the right to act in such a way that humanity might guide itself by my actions?" And if he does not say that to himself, he is masking his anguish.

There is no question here of the kind of anguish which would lead to quietism, to inaction. It is a matter of a simple sort of anguish that anybody who has had responsibilities is familiar with. For example, when a military officer takes the responsibility for an attack and sends a certain number of men to death, he chooses to do so, and in the main he alone makes the choice. Doubtless, orders come from above, but they are too broad; he interprets them, and on this interpretation depend the lives of ten or fourteen or twenty men. In making a decision he cannot help having a certain anguish. All leaders know this anguish. That doesn't keep them from acting; on the contrary, it is the very condition of their action. For it implies that they envisage a number of possibilities, and when they choose one, they realize that it has value only because it is chosen. We shall see that this kind of anguish, which is the kind that existentialism describes, is explained, in addition, by a direct responsibility to the other men whom it involves. It is not a curtain separating us from action, but is part of action itself.

When we speak of forlornness, a term Heidegger was fond of, we mean only that God does not exist and that we have to face all the consequences of this. The existentialist is strongly opposed to a certain kind of secular ethics which would like to abolish God with the least possible expense. About 1880, some French teachers tried to set up a secular ethics which went something like this: God is a useless and costly hypothesis; we are discarding it, but meanwhile, in order for there to be an ethics, a society, a civilization, it is essential that certain values be taken seriously and that they be considered as having an *a priori* existence. It must be obligatory, *a priori,* to be honest, not to lie, not to beat your wife, to have children, etc., etc. So we're going to try a little device which will make it possible to show that values exist all the same, inscribed in a heaven of ideas, though otherwise God does not exist. In other words—and this, I believe, is the tendency of everything called reformism in France—nothing will be changed if God does not exist. We shall find ourselves with the same norms of honesty, progress, and humanism, and we shall have made of God an outdated hypothesis which will peacefully die off by itself.

The existentialist, on the contrary, thinks it very distressing that God does not exist, because all possibility of finding values in a heaven of ideas disappears along with Him; there can be no longer an *a priori* Good, since there is no infinite and perfect consciousness to think it. Nowhere is it written that the Good exists, that we must be honest, that we must not lie; because the fact is we are on a plane where there are only men. Dostoievsky said, "If God didn't exist, everything would be possible." That is the very starting point of existentialism. Indeed, everything is permissible if God does not exist, and as a result man is forlorn, because neither within him nor without does he find anything to cling to. He can't start making excuses for himself.

If existence really does precede essence, there is no explaining things away by reference to a fixed and given human nature. In other words, there is no determinism, man is free, man is freedom. On the other hand, if God does not exist, we find no values or commands to turn to which legitimize our conduct. So, in the bright realm of values, we have no excuse behind us, no justification before us. We are alone, with no excuses.

That is the idea I shall try to convey when I say that man is condemned to be free. Condemned, because he did not create himself, yet, in other respects is free; because, once thrown into the world, he is responsible for everything he does. The existentialist does not believe in the power of passion. He will never agree that a sweeping passion is a ravaging torrent which fatally leads a man to certain acts and is therefore an excuse. He thinks that man is responsible for his passion.

The existentialist does not think that man is going to help himself by finding in the world some omen by which to orient himself. Because he thinks that man will interpret the omen to suit himself. Therefore, he thinks that man, with no support and no aid, is condemned every moment to invent man. Ponge, in a very fine article, has said, "Man is the future of man." That's exactly it. But if it is taken to mean that this future is recorded in heaven, that God sees it, then it is false, because it would really no longer be a future. If it is taken to mean that, whatever a man may be, there is a future to be forged, a virgin future before him, then this remark is sound. But then we are forlorn.

To give you an example which will enable you to understand forlornness better, I shall cite the case of one of my students who came to see me under the following circumstances: his father was on bad terms with his mother, and, moreover, was inclined to be a collaborationist; his older brother had been killed in the German offensive of 1940, and the young man, with somewhat immature but generous feelings, wanted to avenge him. His mother lived alone with him, very much upset by the half-treason of her husband and the death of her older son; the boy was her only consolation.

The boy was faced with the choice of leaving for England and joining the Free French Forces—that is, leaving his mother behind—or remaining with his mother and helping her to carry on. He was fully aware that the woman lived only for him and that his going-off—and perhaps his death—would plunge her into despair. He was also aware that every act that he did for his mother's sake was a sure thing, in the sense that it was helping her to carry on, whereas every effort he made toward going off and fighting was an uncertain move which might run aground and prove completely useless; for example, on his way to England he might, while passing though Spain, be detained indefinitely in a Spanish camp; he might reach England or Algiers and be stuck in an office at a desk job. As a result, he was faced with two very different kinds of action: one, concrete, immediate, but concerning only one individual; the other concerned an incomparably vaster group, a national collectivity, but for that very reason was dubious, and might be interrupted en route. And, at the same time, he was wavering between two kinds of ethics. On the one hand, an ethics of sympathy, of personal devotion; on the other, a broader ethics, but one whose efficacy was more dubious. He had to choose between the two.

Who could help him choose? Christian doctrine? No. Christian doctrine says, "Be charitable, love your neighbor, take the more rugged path, etc., etc." But which is the more rugged path? Whom should he love as a brother? The fighting man or his mother? Which does the greater good, the vague act of fighting in a group, or the concrete one of helping a particular human being to go on living? Who can decide *a priori*? Nobody. No book of ethics can tell him. The Kantian ethics says, "Never treat any person as a means, but as an end." Very well, if I stay with my mother, I'll treat her as an end and not as a means; but by virtue of this very fact, I'm running the risk of treating the people around me who are fighting, as a means; and, conversely, if I go to join those who are fighting, I'll be treating them as an end, and, by doing that, I run the risk of treating my mother as a means.

If values are vague, and if they are always too broad for the concrete and specific case that we are considering, the only thing left for us is to trust our instincts. That's what this young man tried to do; and when I saw him, he said, "In the end, feeling is what counts. I ought to choose whichever pushes me in one direction. If I feel that I love my mother enough to sacrifice everything else for her—my desire for vengeance, for action, for adventure—then I'll stay with her. If, on the contrary, I feel that my love for my mother isn't enough, I'll leave."

But how is the value of a feeling determined? What gives his feeling for his mother value? Precisely the fact that he remained with her. I may say that I like so-and-so well enough to sacrifice a certain amount of money for him, but I may say so only if I've done it. I may say, "I love my mother well enough to remain with her" if I have remained with her. The only way to determine the value of this affection is, precisely, to perform an act which confirms and defines it. But, since I require this affection to justify my act, I find myself caught in a vicious circle. . . .

As for despair, the term has a very simple meaning. It means that we shall confine ourselves to reckoning only with what depends upon our will, or on the ensemble of probabilities which make our action possible. When we want something, we always have to reckon with probabilities. I may be counting on the arrival of a friend. The friend is coming by rail or street-car; this supposes that the train will arrive on schedule, or that the street-car will not jump the track. I am left in the realm of possibility; but possibilities are to be reckoned with only to the point where my action comports with the ensemble of these possibilities, and no further. The moment the possibilities I am considering are not rigorously involved by my action, I ought to disengage myself from them, because no God, no scheme, can adapt the world and its possibilities to my will. When Descartes said, "Conquer yourself rather than the world," he meant essentially the same thing.

The Marxists to whom I have spoken reply, "You can rely on the support of others in your action, which obviously has certain limits because you're not going to live forever. That means: rely on both what others are doing elsewhere to help you, in China, in Russia, and what they will do later on, after your death, to carry on the action and lead it to its fulfillment, which will be the revolution. You even *have* to rely upon that, otherwise you're immortal." I reply at once that I will always rely on fellow fighters insofar as these comrades are involved with me in a common struggle, in the unity of a party or a group in which I can more or less make my weight felt; that is, one whose ranks I am in as a fighter and whose movements I am aware of at every moment. In such a situation, relying on the unity and will of the party is exactly like counting on the fact that the train will arrive on time or that the car won't jump the track. But, given that man is free and that there is no human nature for me to depend on, I cannot count on men whom I do not know by relying on human goodness or man's concern for the good of society. I don't know what will become of the Russian revolution; I may make an example of it to the extent that at the present time it is apparent that the proletariat plays a part in Russia that it plays in no other nation. But I can't swear that this will inevitably lead to a triumph of the proletariat. I've got to limit myself to what I see.

Given that men are free, and that tomorrow they will freely decide what man will be, I cannot be sure that, after my death, fellow fighters will carry on my work to bring it to its maximum perfection. Tomorrow, after my death, some men may decide to set up Fascism, and the others may be cowardly and muddled enough to let them do it. Fascism will then be the human reality, so much the worse for us.

Actually, things will be as man will have decided they are to be. Does that mean that I should abandon myself to quietism? No. First, I should involve myself; then, act on the old saying, "Nothing ventured, nothing gained." Nor does it mean that I shouldn't belong to a party, but rather that I shall have no illusions and shall do what I can. For example, suppose I ask myself, "Will socialization, as such, ever come about?" I know nothing about it. All I know is that I'm going to do everything in my power to bring it about. Beyond that, I can't count on anything. Quietism is the attitude of people who say, "Let others do what I can't do." The doctrine I am presenting is the very opposite of quietism, since it declares, "There is no reality except in action." Moreover, it goes further, since it adds, "Man is nothing else than his plan; he exists only to the extent that he fulfills himself; he is, therefore, nothing else than the ensemble of his acts, nothing else than his life."

Chapter 35

Michel Foucault

Michel Foucault (1926–1984) was one of the most influential thinkers in the Western world. He was born in Poitier, France, was educated in Paris, and taught at the prestigious Collège de France. Influenced by Nietzsche's perspectivalism (i.e., "truth is a metaphor connected with will to power"), Foucault sought to uncover the relationship between power and what we consider truth. He called himself an *archeologist of knowledge* who has explored how society or the powers in charge define madness, medicine, illness, law, and sexuality. Regarding the promotion of domination, he wrote:

> Let us not ask, why certain people want to dominate, what they seek, what is their overall strategy. Let us ask, instead, how things work at the level of on-going, at the level of those continuous and uninterrupted processes which subject our bodies, govern our gestures, dictate our behaviors, etc. In other words, rather than ask ourselves how the sovereign appears to us in lofty isolation, we should try to discover how it is that subjects are gradually, progressively, really, and materially constituted through a multiplicity of organisms, forces, energies, material desires, thoughts, etc.

He aimed at uncovering even the rules of discourse that govern science, showing how even these "objective criteria" are culture-power bound. Part of Foucault's program seems to be to reassert the validity of the Sophists with their cognitive relativism (e.g., Protagoras's "Man is the measure of all things, both those which are, that they are, and those which are not, that they are not,"—only Foucault would substitute "those who rule" for "man" in the formula) over against Socrates and Plato who promoted a "mythical" objective and absolutist cognitive framework.

> "Truth" is to be understood as a system of ordered procedures for the production, regulation, distribution, circulation, and operation of statements. "Truth" is linked in a circular relation with systems of power which produce and sustain it, and to effects of power which it induces and which extend it. A "regime" of truth.

It is not that Foucault thought we can break the power relation in order to find an independent, objective truth. Rather we should strive to break the totalitarian domination of truth so that a plurality of groups work out their own truth.

FOR FURTHER READING

Foucault, M. *Madness and Civilization: A History of Insanity in the Age of Reason* (Pantheon, 1965).

———. *The Order of Things: An Archaeology of the Human Sciences* (Pantheon, 1970).

———. *The Archaeology of Knowledge* (Pantheon, 1972).

———. *The Birth of the Clinic: An Archaeology of Medical Perception* (Random House, 1975).
———. *I, Pierre Rivière* (Pantheon, 1975).
———. *Language, Counter-Memory, Practice* (Blackwell, 1977).
———. *The History of Sexuality, Volume 1: An Introduction* (Pantheon, 1978).
———. *Discipline and Punish: The Birth of the Prison* (Random House, 1979).
———. *Power/Knowledge: Selected Interviews and Other Writings 1972–1977* (Pantheon, 1980).
———. "The Subject and Power," afterword to *Michel Foucault: Beyond Structuralism and Hermeneutics*, H. Dreyfus and P. Rabinow (University of Chicago Press, 1983).
———. *The History of Sexuality, Volume 2: The Uses of Pleasure* (Pantheon, 1985).
———. *Death and the Labyrinth: The World of Raymond Roussel* (Doubleday, 1986).
———. *The History of Sexuality, Volume 3: The Care of the Self* (Pantheon, 1986).
———. *Mental Illness and Psychology* (University of California Press, 1987).
Rabinow, P., ed. *The Foucault Reader* (Pantheon, 1985).
Sheridan, Alan. *Michel Foucault: The Will to Truth* (Tavistock, 1980).

The Discourse on Language

I would really like to have slipped imperceptibly into this lecture, as into all the others I shall be delivering, perhaps over the years ahead. I would have preferred to be enveloped in words, borne way beyond all possible beginnings. At the moment of speaking, I would like to have perceived a nameless voice, long preceding me, leaving me merely to enmesh myself in it, taking up its cadence, and to lodge myself, when no one was looking, in its interstices as if it had paused an instant, in suspense, to beckon to me. There would have been no beginnings: instead, speech would proceed from me, while I stood in its path—a slender gap—the point of its possible disappearance.

Behind me, I should like to have heard (having been at it long enough already, repeating in advance what I am about to tell you) the voice of Molloy, beginning to speak thus: 'I must go on; I can't go on; I must go on; I must say words as long as there are words, I must say them until they find me, until they say me—heavy burden, heavy sin; I must go on; maybe it's been done already; maybe they've already said me; maybe they've already borne me to the threshold of my story, right to the door opening onto my story; I'd be surprised if it opened.'

A good many people, I imagine, harbour a similar desire to be freed from the obligation to begin, a similar desire to find themselves, right from the outside, on the other side of discourse, without having to stand outside it, pondering its particular, fearsome, and even devilish features. To this all too common feeling, institutions have an ironic reply, for they solemnise beginnings, surrounding them with a circle of silent attention; in order that they can be distinguished from far off, they impose ritual forms upon them.

Inclination speaks out: 'I don't want to have to enter this risky world of discourse; I want nothing to do with it insofar as it is decisive and final; I would like to feel it all around me, calm and transparent, profound, infinitely open, with others responding to my expectations, and truth emerging, one by one. All I want is to allow myself to be borne along, within it, and by it, a happy wreck.' Institutions reply: 'But you have nothing to fear from launching out; we're here to show you discourse is within the established order of things, that we've waited a long time for its arrival, that a place has been set aside for it—a place which both honours and disarms it; and if it should happen to have a certain power, then it is we, and we alone, who give it that power.'

Yet, maybe this institution and this inclination are but two converse responses to the same anxiety: anxiety as to just what discourse is, when it is manifested materially, as a written or spoken object; but also, uncertainty faced with a transitory existence, destined for oblivion—at any rate, not belonging to us; uncertainty at the suggestion of barely imaginable powers and dangers behind this activity, however humdrum and grey it may seem; uncertainty when we suspect the conflicts, triumphs, injuries, dominations and enslavements that lie behind these words, even when long use has chipped away their rough edges.

What is so perilous, then, in the fact that people speak, and that their speech proliferates? Where is the danger in that?

Here then is the hypothesis I want to advance, tonight, in order to fix the terrain—or perhaps the very provisional theatre—within which I shall be working. I am supposing that in every society the production of discourse is at once controlled, selected, organised and redistributed according to a certain number of procedures, whose role is to avert its powers and its dangers, to cope with chance events, to evade its ponderous, awesome materiality.

In a society such as our own we all know the rules of *exclusion*. The most obvious and familiar of these concerns what is *prohibited*. We know perfectly well that we are not free to say just anything, that we cannot simply speak of anything, when we like or where we like; not just anyone, finally, may speak of just anything. We have three types of prohibition, covering objects, ritual with its surrounding circumstances, the privileged or exclusive right to speak of a particular subject; these prohibitions interrelate, reinforce and complement each other, forming a complex web, continually subject to modification. I will note simply that the areas where this web is most tightly woven today, where the danger spots are most numerous, are those dealing with politics and sexuality. It is as though discussion, far from being a transparent, neutral element, allowing us to disarm sexuality and to pacify politics, were one of those privileged areas in which they exercised some of their more awesome powers. In appearance, speech may well be of little account, but the prohibitions surrounding it soon reveal its links with desire and power. This should not be very surprising, for psychoanalysis has already shown us that speech is not merely the medium which manifests—or dissembles—desire; it is also the object of desire. Similarly, historians have constantly impressed upon us that speech is no mere verbalisation of conflicts and system of domination, but that it is the very object of man's conflicts.

But our society possesses yet another principle of exclusion; not another prohibition, but a division and a rejection. I have in mind the opposition: reason and folly. From the depths of the Middle Ages, a man was mad if his speech could not be said to form part of the common discourse of men. His words were considered null and void, without truth or significance, worthless as evidence, inadmissible in the authentification of acts of contracts, incapable even of bringing about transubstantiation—the transformation of bread into flesh—at Mass. And yet, in contrast to all others, his words were credited with strange powers, of revealing some hidden truth, of predicting the future, of revealing, in all their naiveté, what the wise were unable to perceive. It is curious to note that for centuries, in Europe, the words of a madman were either totally ignored or else were taken as words of truth. They either fell into a void—rejected the moment they were proffered—or else men deciphered in them a naive or cunning reason, rationality more rational than that of a rational man. At all events, whether excluded or secretly invested with reason, the madman's speech did not strictly exist. It was through his words that one recognised the madness of the madman; but they were certainly the medium within which this division became active; they were neither heard nor remembered. No doctor before the end of the eighteenth century had ever thought of listening to the content—how it was said and why—of these words; and yet it was these which signalled the difference between reason and madness. Whatever a madman said, it was taken for mere noise; he was credited with words only in a symbolic sense, in the theatre, in which he stepped forward, unarmed and reconclied, playing his role: that of masked truth.

Of course people are going to say all that is over and done with, or that it is in the process of being finished with, today; that the madman's words are no longer on the other side of this division; that they are no longer null and void, that, on the contrary, they alert us to the need to look for a sense behind them, for the attempt at, or the ruins of some '*oeuvre*'; we have even come to notice these words of madmen in our own speech, in those tiny pauses when we forget what we are talking about. But all this is no proof that the old vision is not just as active as before; we have only to think of the systems by which we decipher this speech; we have only to think of the network of institutions established to permit doctors and psychoanalysts to listen to the mad and, at the same time, enabling the mad to come and speak, or, in desperation, to withhold their meagre words; we have only to bear all this in mind to suspect that the old division is just as active as ever, even if it is proceeding along different lines and, via new institutions, producing rather different effects. Even when the role of the doctor consists of lending an ear to this finally liberated speech, this procedure still takes place in the context of a hiatus between listener and speaker. For he is listening to speech invested with desire, crediting itself—for its greater exultation or for its greater anguish—with terrible powers. If we truly require silence to cure monsters, then it must be an attentive silence, and it is in this that the division lingers.

It is perhaps a little risky to speak of the opposition between true and false as a third system of exclusion, along with those I have mentioned already. How could one reasonably compare the constraints of truth with those other divisions, arbitrary in origin if not developing out of historical contingency—not merely modifiable but in a state of continual flux, supported by a system of institutions imposing and manipulating them, acting not without constraint, nor without an element, at least, of violence?

Certainly, as a proposition, the division between true and false is neither arbitrary, nor modifiable, nor institutional, nor violent. Putting the question in different terms, however—asking what has been, what still is, throughout our discourse, this will to truth which has survived throughout so many centuries of our history; of if we ask what is, in its very general form, the kind of division governing our will to knowledge—then we may well discern something like a system of exclusion (historical, modifiable, institutionally constraining) in the process of development.

It is, undoubtedly, a historically constituted division. For, even with the sixth-century Greek poets, true discourse—in the meaningful sense—inspiring respect and terror, to which all were obliged to submit, because it held sway over all and was pronounced by men who spoke as of right, according to ritual, meted out justice and attributed to each his rightful share; it prophesied the future, not merely announcing what was going to occur, but contributing to its actual event, carrying men along with it and thus weaving itself into the fabric of fate. And yet, a century later, the highest truth no longer resided in what discourse *was*, nor in what it *did*: it lay in what was *said*. The day dawned when truth moved over from the ritualised act—potent and just—of enunciation to settle on what was enunciated itself: its meaning, its form, its object and its relation to what it referred to. A division emerged between Hesiod and Plato, separating true discourse from false; it was a new division for, henceforth, true discourse was no longer considered precious and desirable, since it had ceased to be discourse linked to the exercise of power. And so the Sophists were routed.

This historical division has doubtless lent its general form to our will to knowledge. Yet it has never ceased shifting: the great mutations of science may well sometimes be seen to flow from some discovery, but they may equally be viewed as the appearance of new forms of the will to truth. In the nineteenth century there was undoubtedly a will to truth having nothing to do, in terms of the forms examined, of the fields to which it addressed itself, nor the techniques upon which it was based, with the will to knowledge which characterised classical culture. Going back a little in time, to the turn of the sixteenth and seventeenth centuries—and particularly in England—a will to knowledge emerged which, anticipating its persent content, sketched out a schema of possible, observable, measurable and classifiable objects; a will to knowledge which imposed upon the knowing subject—in some ways taking precedence over all experience—a certain position, a certain viewpoint, and a certain function (look rather than read, verify rather than comment), a will to knowledge which prescribed (and, more generally speaking, all instruments determined) the technological level at which knowledge could be employed in order to be verifiable and useful (navigation, mining, pharmacopoeia). Everything seems to have occurred as though, from the time of the great Platonic division onwards, the will to truth had its own history, which is not at all that of the constraining truths: the history of a range of subjects to be learned, the history of the functions of the knowing subject, the history of material, technical and instrumental investment in knowledge.

But this will to truth, like the other systems of exclusion, relies on institutional support: it is both reinforced and accompanied by whole strata of practices such as pedagogy—naturally—the book-system, publishing, libraries, such as the learned societies in the past, and laboratories today. But it is probably even more profoundly accompanied by the manner in which knowledge is employed in a society, the way in which it is exploited, divided and, in some ways, attributed. It is worth recalling at this point, if only symbolically, the old Greek adage, that arithmetic should be taught in democracies, for it teaches relations of equality, but that geometry alone should be reserved for oligarchies, as it demonstrates the proportions within inequality.

Finally, I believe that this will to knowledge, thus reliant upon institutional support and distribution, tends to exercise a sort of pressure, a power of constraint upon other forms of discourse—I am speaking of our own society. I am thinking of the way Western literature has, for centuries, sought to base itself in nature, in the plausible, upon sincerity and science—in short, upon true discourse. I am thinkings, too, of the way economic practices, codified into precepts and recipes—as morality, too—have sought since the eighteenth century, to found themselves, to rationalise and justify their currency, in a theory of wealth and production; I am thinking, again, of the manner in which such prescriptive ensembles as the Penal Code have sought their bases or justifications. For example, the Penal Code started out as a theory of Right; then, from the time of the nineteenth century, people looked for its validation in sociological, psychological, medical and psychiatric knowledge. It is as though the very words of the law had no authority in our society, except insofar as they are derived from true discourse. Of the three great systems of exclusion governing discourse—prohibited words, the division of madness and the will to truth—I have spoken at greatest length concerning the third. With good reason: for centuries, the former have continually tended towards the latter; because this last has, gradually, been attempting to assimilate the others in order both to modify them and to provide them with a firm foundation. Because, if the two former are continually growing more fragile and less certain to the extent that they are now invaded by the will to truth, the latter, in contrast, daily grows in strength, in depth and implacability.

And yet we speak of it least. As though the will to truth and its vicissitudes were masked by truth itself and its necessary unfolding. The reason is perhaps this: if, since the time of the Greeks, true discourse no longer responds to desire or to that which exercises power in the will to truth, in the will to speak out in true discourse, what, then, is at work, if not desire and power? True discourse, liberated by the nature of its form from desire and power, is incapable of recognising the will to truth which pervades it; and the will to truth, having imposed itself upon us for so long, is such that the truth it seeks to reveal cannot fail to mask it.

Thus, only one truth appears before our eyes: wealth, fertility and sweet strength in all its insidious universality. In contrast, we are unaware of the prodigious machinery of the will to truth, with its vocation of exclusion. All those who, at one moment or another in our history, have attempted to remould this will to truth and to turn it against truth at that very point where truth undertakes to justify the taboo, and to define madness; all those, from Nietzsche to Artaud and Tabaille, must now stand as (probably haughty) signposts for all our future work.

There are, of course, many other systems for the control and delimitation of discourse. Those I have spoken of up to now are, to some extent, active on the exterior; they function as systems of exclusion; they concern that part of discourse which deals with power and desire.

I believe we can isolate another group: internal rules, where discourse exercises its own control; rules concerned with the principles of classification, ordering and distribution. It is as though we were now involved in the mastery of another dimension of discourse: that of events and chance.

In the first place, commentary. I suppose, though I am not altogether sure, there is barely a society without its major narratives, told, retold and varied; formulae, texts, ritualised texts to be spoken in well-defined circumstances; things said once, and conserved because people suspect some hidden secret or wealth lies buried within. In short, I suspect one could find a king of gradation between different types of discourse within most societies: discourse 'uttered' in the course of the day and in causal meetings, and which disappears with the very act which gave rise to it; and those forms of discourse that lie at the origins of a certain number of new verbal acts, which are reiterated, transformed or discussed; in short, discourse which *is spoken* and remains spoken, indefinitely, beyond its formulation, and which remains to be spoken. We know them in our own cultural system: religious or judicial texts, as well as some curious texts, from the point of view of their status, which we term 'literary'; to a certain extent, scientific texts also.

What is clear is that this gap is neither stable, nor constant, nor absolute. There is no question of there being one category, fixed for all time, reserved for fundamental or creative discourse, and another for those which reiterate, expound and comment. Not a few major texts become blurred and disappear, and commentaries sometimes come to occupy the former position. But while the details of application may well change, the function remains the same, and the principle of hierarchy remains at work. The radical denial of this gradation can never be anything but play, utopia or anguish. Play, as Borges uses the term, in the form of commentary that is nothing more than the reappearance, word for word (though this time it is solemn and anticipated) of the text commented on; or again, the play of a work of criticism talking endlessly about a work that does not exist. It is a lyrical dream of talk reborn, utterly afresh and innocent, at each point; continually reborn in all its vigour, stimulated by things, feelings or thoughts. Anguish, such as that of Janet when sick, for whom the least utterance sounded as the 'word of the Evangelist', concealing an inexhaustible wealth of meaning, worthy to be broadcast, rebegun, commented upon indefinitely: 'When I think', he said on reading or listening; 'When I think of this phrase, continuing its journey through eternity, while I, perhaps, have only incompletely understood it . . .'

But who can fail to see that this would be to annul one of the terms of the relationship each time, and not to suppress the relationship itself? A relationship in continual process of modification; a relationship taking multiple and diverse forms in a given epoch: juridical exegesis is very different—and has been for a long time—from religious commentary; a single work of literature can give rise, simultaneously, to several distinct types of discourse. The *Odyssey*, as a primary text, is repeated in the same epoch, in Berand's translation, in infinite textual explanations and in Joyce's *Ulysses*.

For the time being, I would like to limit myself to pointing out that, in what we generally refer to as commentary, the difference between primary text and secondary text plays two interdependent roles. On the one hand, it permits us to create new discourses ad infinitum: the top-heaviness of the original text, its permanence, its status as discourse ever capable of being brought up to date, the multiple or hidden meanings with which it is credited, the reticence and wealth it is believed to contain, all this creates an open possibility for discussion. On the other hand, whatever the techniques employed, commentary's only role is to say *finally*, what has silently been articulated *deep down*. It must—and the paradox is ever-changing yet inescapable—say, for the first time, what has already been said, and repeat tirelessly what was, nevertheless, never said. The infinite rippling of commentary is agitated from within by the dream of masked repetition: in the distance there is, perhaps, nothing other than what was there at the point of departure: simple recitation. Commentary averts the chance element of discourse by giving it its due: it gives us the opportunity to say something other than the text itself, but on condition that it is the text itself which is uttered and, in some ways, finalised. The open multiplicity, the fortuitousness, is transferred, by the principle of commentary, from what is liable to be said to the number, the form, the makes and the circumstances of repetition. The novelty lies no longer in what is said, but in its reappearance.

I believe there is another principle of rarefaction, complementary to the first: the author. Not, of course, the author in the sense of the individual who delivered the speech or wrote the text in question, but the author as the unifying principle in a particular group of writings or statements, lying at the origins of their significance, as the seat of their coherence. This principle is not constant at all times. All around us, there are sayings and texts whose meaning or effectiveness has nothing to do with any author to whom they might be attributed: mundane remarks, quickly forgotten; orders and contacts that are signed, but have no recognisable author; technical prescriptions anonymously transmitted. But even in those fields where it is normal to attribute a work to an author—literature, philosophy, science—the principle does not always play the same role; in the order of scientific discourse, it was, during the Middle Ages, indispensable that a scientific text be attributed to an author, for the author was the index of the work's truthfulness. A proposition was held to derive its scientific value from its author. But since the seventeenth century this function has been steadily declining; it barely survives now, save to give a name to a theorem, an effect, an example or a syndrome. In literature, however, and from about the same period, the author's function has become steadily more important. Now, we demand of all those narratives, poems, dramas and comedies which circulated relatively anonymously throughout the Middle Ages, whence they come, and we virtually insist they tell us who wrote them. We ask authors to answer for the unity of the works published in their names; we ask that they reveal, or at least display the hidden sense pervading their work; we ask them to reveal their personal lives, to account for their experiences and the real story that gave birth to their writings. The author is he who implants, into the troublesome language of fiction, its unities, its coherence, its links with reality.

I know what people are going to say: 'But there you are speaking of the author in the same way as the critic reinvents him after he is dead and buried, when we are left with no more than a tangled mass of scrawlings. Of course, then you have to put a little order into what is left, you have to imagine a structure, a cohesion, the sort of theme you might expect to arise out of an author's consciousness or his life, even if it is a little fictitious. But all that cannot get away from the fact that the author existed, irrupting into the midst of all the words employed, infusing them with his genius, or his chaos.'

Of course, it would be ridiculous to deny the existence of individuals who write, and invent. But I think that, for some time, at least, the individual who sits down to write a text, at the edge of which lurks a possible *oevure*, resumes the functions of the author. What he writes and does not write, what he sketches out, even preliminary sketches for the work, and what he drops as simple mundane remarks, all this interplay of differences is prescribed by the author-function. It is from his new position, as an author, that he will fashion—from all he might have said, from all he says daily, at any time—the still shaky profile of his *oeuvre*.

Commentary limited the hazards of discourse through the action of and *identity* taking the form of *repetition* and *sameness*. The author principle limits this same chance element through the action of an *identity* whose form is that of *individuality* and the *I*.

But we have to recognise another principle of limitation in what we call, not sciences, but 'disciplines'. Here is yet another relative, mobile principle, one which enables us to construct, but within a narrow framework.

The organisation of disciplines is just as much opposed to the commentary principle as it is to that of the author. Opposed to that of the author, because disciplines are defined by groups of objects, methods, their corpus of propositions considered to be true, the interplay of rules and definitions, of techniques and tools: all these constitute a sort of anonymous system, freely available to whoever wishes, or whoever is able to make use of them, without there being any question of their meaning or their validity being derived from whoever happened to invent them. But the principles involved in the formation of disciplines are equally opposed to that of commentary. In a discipline, unlike in commentary, what is supposed at the point of departure is not some meaning which must be rediscovered, nor an identity to be reiterated; it is that which is required for the construction of new statements. For a discipline to exist there must be the possibility of formulating—and of doing so ad infinitum—fresh propositions.

But there is more, and there is more, probably, in order that there may be less. A discipline is not the sum total of all the truths that may be uttered concerning something; it is not even the total of all that may be accepted, by virtue of some principle of coherence and systematisation, concerning some given fact or proposition. Medicine does not consist of all that may be truly said about disease; botany cannot be defined by the sum total of the truths one could say about plants. There are two reasons for this, the first being that botany and medicine, like other disciplines, consist of errors as well as truths, errors that are in no way residuals, or foreign bodies, but have their own positive functions and their own valid history, such that their roles are often indissociable from that of the truths. The other reason is that, for a proposition to belong to botany or pathology, it must fulfil certain conditions, in a stricter and more complex sense than that of pure and simple truth: at any rate, other conditions. The proposition must refer to a specific range of objects; from the end of the seventeenth century, for example, a proposition, to be 'botanical', had to be concerned with the visible structure of plants, with its system of close and not so close resemblances, or with the behaviour of its fluids; (but it could no longer retain, as had still been the case in the sixteenth century, references to its symbolic value or to the virtues and properties accorded it in antiquity). But without belonging to any discipline, a proposition is obliged to utilise conceptual instruments and techniques of a well-defined type; from the nineteenth century onwards, a proposition was no longer medical—it became 'non-medical', becoming more of an individual fantasy or item of popular imagery—if it employed metaphorical or qualitative terms or notions of essence (congestion, fermented liquids, dessicated solids); in return, it could—it had to—appeal to equally metaphorical notions, though constructed according to a different functional and physiological model (concerning irritation, inflammation or the decay of tissue). But there is more still, for in order to belong to a discipline, a proposition must fit into a certain type of theoretical field. Suffice it to recall that the quest for primitive language, a perfectly acceptable theme up to the eighteenth century, was enough, in the second half of the nineteenth century, to throw any discourse into, I hesitate to say error, but into a world of chimera and reverie—into pure and simple linguistic monstrosity.

Within its own limits, every discipline recognises true and false propositions, but it repulses a whole teratology of learning. The exterior of a science is both more, and less, populated than one might think: certainly, there is immediate experience, imaginary themes bearing on and continually accompanying immemorial beliefs; but perhaps there are no errors in the strict sense of the term, for error can only emerge and be identified within a well-defined process; there are monsters on the prowl, however, whose forms alter with the history of knowledge. In short, a proposition must fulfil some onerous and complex conditions before it can be admitted within a discipline; before it can be pronounced true or false it must be, as Monsieur Canguilhem might say, 'within the true'.

People have often wondered how on earth nineteenth-century botanists and biologists managed not to see the truth of Mendel's statements. But it was precisely because Mendel spoke of objects, employed methods and placed himself within a theoretical perspective totally alien to the biology of his time. But then, Naudin had suggested that hereditary traits constituted a separate element before him; and yet, however novel or unfamiliar the principle may have been, it was nevertheless reconciable, if only as an enigma, with biological discourse. Mendel, on the other hand, announced that hereditary traits constituted an absolutely new biological object, thanks to a hiteherto untried system of filtrage: he detached them from species, from the sex transmitting them, the field in which he observed being that infinitely open series of generations in which hereditary traits appear and disappear with statistical regularity. Here was a new object, calling for new conceptual tools, and fresh theoretical foundations. Mendel spoke the truth, but he was not *dans le vrai* (within the true) of contemporary biological discourse: it simply was not along such lines that objects and biological concepts were formed. A whole change in scale, the deployment of a totally new range of objects in biology was required before Mendel could enter into the true and his propositions appear, for the most part, exact. Mendel was a true monster, so much so that science could not even properly speak of him. And yet Schleiden, for example, thirty years earlier, denying, at the height of the nineteenth century, vegetable sexuality, was committing no more than a disciplined error.

It is always possible one could speak the truth in a void; one would only be in the true, however, if one obeyed the rules of some discursive 'policy' which would have to be reactivated every time one spoke.

Disciplines constitute a system of control in the production of discourse, fixing its limits through the action of an identity taking the form of a permanent reactivation of the rules.

We tend to see, in an author's fertility, in the multiplicity of commentaries and in the development of a discipline so many infinite resources available for the creation of discourse. Perhaps so, but they are nonetheless principles of constraint, and it is probably impossible to appreciate their positive, multiplicatory role without first taking into consideration their restrictive, constraining role.

There is, I believe, a third group of rules serving to control discourse. Here, we are no longer dealing with the mastery of the powers contained within discourse, nor with averting the hazards of its appearance; it is more a question of determining the conditions under which it may be employed, of imposing a certain number of rules upon those individuals who employ it, thus denying access to everyone else. This amounts to a rarefaction among speaking subjects: none may enter into discourse on a specific subject unless he has satisfied certain conditions or if he is not, from the outset, qualified to do so. More exactly, not all areas of discourse are equally open and penetrable; some are forbidden territory (differentiated and differentiating) while others are virtually open to the winds and stand, without any prior restrictions, open to all.

Here, I would like to recount a little story so beautiful I fear it may well be true. It encompasses all the constraints of discourse: those limiting its powers, those controlling its chance appearances and those which select from among speaking subjects. At the beginning of the seventeenth century, the Shogun heard tell of European superiority in navigation, commerce, politics and the military arts, and that this was due to their knowledge of mathematics. He wanted to obtain this precious knowledge. When someone told him of an English sailor possessed of this marvellous discourse, he summoned him to his palace and kept him there. The Shogun took lessons from the mariner in private and familiarised himself with mathematics, after which he retained power and lived to a very old age. It was not until the nineteenth century that there were *Japanese* mathematicians. But that is not the end of the anecdote, for it has its European aspect as well. The story has it that the English sailor, Will Adams, was a carpenter and an autodidact. Having worked in a shipyard he had learnt geometry. Can we see in this narrative the expression of one of the great myths of European culture? To the monopolistic, secret knowledge of oriental tyranny, Europe opposed the universal communication of knowledge and the infinitely free exchange of discourse.

This notion does not, in fact, stand up to close examination. Exchange and communication are positive forces at play within complex but restrictive systems; it is probable that they cannot operate independently of these. The most superficial and obvious of these restrictive systems is constituted by what we collectively refer to as ritual; ritual defines the qualifications required of the speaker (of who in dialogue, interrogation or recitation, should occupy which position and formulate which type of utterance); it lays down gestures to be made, behaviour, circumstances and the whole range of signs that must accompany discourse; finally, it lays down the supposed, or imposed significance of the words used, their effect upon those to whom they are addressed, the limitations of their constraining validity. Religious discourse, juridical and therapeutic as well as, in some ways, political discourse are all barely dissociable from the functioning of a ritual that determines the individual properties and agreed roles of the speakers.

A rather different function is filled by 'fellowships of discourse', whose function is to preserve or to reproduce discourse, but in order that it should circulate within a closed community, according to strict regulations, without those in possession being dispossessed by this very distribution. An archaic model of this would be those groups of Rhapsodists, possessing knowledge of poems to recite or, even, upon which to work variations and transformations. But though the ultimate object of this knowledge was ritual recitation, it was protected and preserved within a determinate group, by the, often extremely complex, exercises of memory implied by such a process. Apprenticeship gained access both to a group and to a secret which recitation made manifest, but did not divulge. The roles of speaking and listening were not interchangeable.

Few such 'fellowships of discourse' remain, with their ambiguous interplay of secrecy and disclosure. But do not be deceived; even in true discourse, even in the order of published discourse, free from all ritual, we still find secret-appropriation and non-interchangeability at work. It could even be that the act of writing, as it is institutionalised today, with its books, its publishing system and the personality of the writer, occurs within a diffuse, yet constraining, 'fellowship of discourse'. The separteness of the writer, continually opposed to the activity of all other writing and speaking subjects, the intransitive character he lends to his discourse, the fundamental singularity he has long accorded to 'writing', the affirmed dissymmetry between 'creation' and any use of linguistic system—all this manifests in its formulation (and tends moreover to accompany the interplay of these factors in practice) the existence of a certain 'fellowship of discourse'. But there are many others, functioning according to entirely different schemas of exclusivity and disclosure: one has only to think of technical and scientific secrets, of the forms of diffusion and circulation in medical discourse, of those who have appropriated economic or political discourse.

At first sight, 'doctrine' (religious, political, philosophical) would seem to constitute the very reverse of a 'fellowship of discourse'; for among the latter, the number of speakers were, if not fixed, at least limited, and it was among this number that discourse was allowed to circulate and be transmitted. Doctrine, on the other hand, tends to diffusion: in the holding in common of a single ensemble of discourse that individuals, as many as you wish, could define their reciprocal allegiance. In appearance, the sole requisite is the recognition of the same truths and the acceptance of a certain rule—more or less flexible—of conformity with validated discourse. If it were a question of just that, doctrines would barely be any different from scientific disciplines, and discursive control would bear merely on the form or content of what was uttered, and not on the speaker. Doctrinal adherence, however, involves both speaker and the spoken, the one through the other. The speaking subject is involved through, and as a result of, the spoken, as is demonstrated by the rules of exclusion and the rejection mechanism brought into play when a speaker formulates one, or many, inassimilable utterances; questions of heresy and unorthodoxy in no way arise out of fanatical exaggeration of doctrinal mechanisms; they are a fundamental part of them. But conversely, doctrine involves the utterances of speakers in the sense that doctrine is, permanently, the sign, the manifestation and the instrument of a prior adherence—adherence to a class, to a social or racial status, to a nationality or an interest, to a struggle, a revolt, resistance or acceptance. Doctrine links individuals to certain types of utterance while consequently barring them from all others. Doctrine effects a dual subjection, that of speaking subjects to discourse, and that of discourse to the group, at least virtually, of speakers.

Finally, on a much broader scale, we have to recognise the great cleavages in what one might call the social appropriation of discourse. Education may well be, as of right, the instrument whereby every individual, in a society like our own, can gain access to any kind of discourse. But we well know that in its distribution, in what it permits and in what it prevents, it follows the well-trodden battle-lines of social conflict. Every educational system is a political means of maintaining or of modifying the appropriation of discourse, with the knowledge and the powers it carries with it.

I am well aware of the abstraction I am performing when I separate, as I have just done, verbal rituals, 'fellowships of discourse', doctrinal groups and social appropriation. Most of the time they are linked together, constituting great edifices that distribute speakers among the different types of discourse, and which appropriate those types of discourse to certain categories of subject. In a word, let us say that these are the main rules for the subjection of discourse. What is an educational system, after all, if not a ritualisation of the word; if not a qualification of some fixing of roles for speakers; if not the constitution of a (diffuse) doctrinal group; if not a distribution and an appropriation of discourse, with all its learning and its powers? What is 'writing' (that of 'writers') if not a similar form of subjection, perhaps taking rather different forms, but whose main stresses are nonetheless analogous? May we not also say that the judicial system, as well as institutionalised medicine, constitute similar systems for the subjection of discourse?

I wonder whether a certain number of philosophical themes have not come to conform to this activity of limitation and exclusion and perhaps even to reinforce it.

They conform, first of all, by proposing an ideal truth as a law of discourse, and an immanent rationality as the principle of their behaviour. They accompany, too, an ethic of knowledge, promising truth only to the desire for truth itself and the power to think it.

They then go on to reinforce this activity by denying the specific reality of discourse in general.

Ever since the exclusion of the activity and commerce of the Sophists, ever since their paradoxes were muzzled, more or less securely, it would seem that Western thought has seen to it that discourse be permitted as little room as possible between thought and words. It would appear to have ensured that to *discourse* should appear merely as a certain interjection between speaking and thinking; that it should constitute thought, clad in its signs and rendered visible by words or, conversely, that the structures of language themselves should be brought into play, producing a certain effect of meaning.

This very ancient elision of the reality of discourse in philosophical thought has taken many forms in the course of history. We have seen it quite recently in the guise of many themes now familiar to us.

It seems to me that the theme of the founding subject permits us to elide the reality of discourse. The task of the founding subject is to animate the empty forms of language with his objectives; through the thickness and inertia of empty things, he grasps intuitively the meanings lying within them. Beyond time, he indicates the field of meanings—leaving history to make them explicit—in which propositions, sciences, and deductive ensembles ultimately find their foundation. In this relationship with meaning, the founding subject has signs, marks, tracks, letters at his disposal. But he does not need to demonstrate these passing through the singular instance of discourse.

The opposing theme, that of originating experience, plays an analogous role. This asserts, in the case of experience, that even before it could be grasped in the form of a *cogito*, prior significations, in some ways already spoken, were circulating in the world, scattering it all about us, and from the outset made possible a sort of primitive recognition. Thus, a primary complicity with the world founds, for us, a possibility of speaking of experience, in it, to designate and name it, to judge it and, finally, to know it in the form of truth. If there is discourse, what could it legitimately be if not a discrete reading? Things murmur meanings our language has merely to extract; from its most primitive beginnings, this language was already whispering to us of a being of which it forms the skeleton.

The theme of universal mediation is, I believe, yet another manner of eliding the reality of discourse. And this despite appearances. At first sight it would seem that, to discover the movement of a logos everywhere elevating singularities into concepts, finally enabling immediate consciousness to deploy all the rationality in the world, is certainly to place discourse at the centre of speculation. But, in truth, this logos is really only another discourse already in operation, or rather, it is things and events themselves which *insensibly* become discourse in the unfolding of the essential secrets. Discourse is no longer much more than the shimmering of a truth about to be born in its own eyes; and when all things come eventually to take the form of discourse, when everything may be said and when anything becomes an excuse for pronouncing a discourse, it will be because all things having manifested and exchanged meanings, they will then all be able to return to the silent interiority of self-consciousness.

Whether it is the philosophy of a founding subject, a philosophy of originating experience or a philosophy of universal mediation, discourse is really only an activity, of writing in the first case, of reading in the second and exchange in the third. This exchange, this writing, this reading never involve anything but signs. Discourse thus nullifies itself, in reality, in placing itself at the disposal of the signifier.

What civilisation, in appearance, has shown more respect towards discourse than our own? Where has it been more and better honoured? Where have men depended more radically, apparently, upon its constraints and its universal character? But, it seems to me, a certain fear hides behind this apparent supremacy accorded, this apparent logophilia. It is as though these taboos, these barriers, thresholds and limits were deliberately disposed in order, at least partly, to master and control the great proliferation of discourse, in such a way as to relieve its richness of its most dangerous elements; to organise its disorder so as to skate round its most uncontrollable aspects. It is as though people had wanted to efface all trace of its irruption into the activity of our thought and language. There is undoubtedly in our society, and I would not be surprised to see it in others, though taking different forms and modes, a profound logophobia, a sort of dumb fear of these events, of this mass of spoken things, of everything that could possibly be violent, discontinuous, querulous, disordered even and perilous in it, of the incessant, disorderly buzzing of discourse.

If we wish—I will not say to efface this fear—but to analyse it in its conditions, its activity and its effects, I believe we must resolve ourselves to accept three decisions which our current thinking rather tends to resist, and which belong to the three groups of function I have just mentioned: to question our will to truth; to restore to discourse its character as an event; to abolish the sovereignty of the signifier.

These are the tasks, or rather, some of the themes which will govern my work in the years ahead. One can straight away distinguish some of the methodological demands they imply.

A principle of *reversal*, first of all. Where, according to tradition, we think we recognise the source of discourse, the principles behind its flourishing and continuity, in those factors which seem to play a positive role, such as the author discipline, will to truth, we must rather recognise the negative activity of the cutting-out and rarefaction of discourse.

But, once we have distinguished these principles of rarefaction, once we have ceased considering them as a fundamental and creative action, what do we discover behind them? Should we affirm that a world of uninterrupted discourse would be virtually complete? This is where we have to bring other methodological principles into play.

Next, then, the principle of *discontinuity*. The existence of systems of rarefaction does not imply that, over and beyond them lie great vistas of limitless discourse, continuous and silent, repressed and driven back by them, making it our task to abolish them and at last to restore it to speech. Whether talking in terms of speaking or thinking, we must not imagine some unsaid thing, or an unthought, floating about the world, interlacing with all its forms and events. Discourse must be treated as a discontinuous activity, its different manifestations sometimes coming together, but just as easily unaware of, or excluding each other.

The principle of *specificity* declares that a particular discourse cannot be resolved by a prior system of significations; that we should not imagine that the world presents us with a legible face, leaving us merely to decipher it; it does not work hand in glove with what we already know; there is no prediscursive fate disposing the word in our favour. We must conceive discourse as a violence that we do to things, or at all events, as a practice we impose upon them; it is in this practice that the events of discourse find the principle of their regularity.

The fourth principle, that of *exteriority*, holds that we are not to burrow to the hidden core of discourse, to the heart of the thought or meaning manifested in it; instead, taking the discourse itself, its appearance and its regularity, that we should look for its external conditions of existence, for that which gives rise to the chance series of these events and fixes its limits.

As the regulatory principles of analysis, then, we have four notions: event series, regularity and the possible conditions of existence. Term for term we find the notion of event opposed to that of creation, the possible conditions of existence opposing signification. These four notions (signification, originality, unity, creation) have, in a fairly general way, dominated the traditional history of ideas; by general agreement one sought the point of creation, the unity of a work, of a period or a theme, one looked also for the mark of individual originality and the infinite wealth of hidden meanings.

I would like to add just two remarks, the first of which concerns history. We frequently credit contemporary history with having removed the individual event from its privileged position and with having revealed the more enduring structures of history. That is so. I am not sure, however, that historians have been working in this direction alone. Or, rather, I do not think one can oppose the identification of the individual event to the analysis of long term trends quite so neatly. On the contrary, it seems to me that it is in squeezing the individual event, in directing the resolving power of historical analysis onto official price-lists (*mercuriales*), title deeds, parish registers, to harbour archives analysed year by year and week by week, what we gradually perceive—beyond battles, decisions, dynasties and assemblies—the emergence of those massive phenomena of secular or multi-secular importance. History, as it is practised today, does not turn its back on events; on the contrary, it is continually enlarging the field of events, constantly discovering new layers—more superficial as well as more profound—incessantly isolating new ensembles—events, numerous, dense and interchangeable or rare and decisive: from daily price fluctuations to secular inflations. What is significant is that history does not consider an event without defining the series to which it belongs, without specifying the method of analysis used, without seeking out the regularity of phenomena and the probable limits of their occurrence, without enquiring about variations, inflexions and the slope of the curve, without desiring to know the conditions on which these depend. History has long since abandoned its attempts to understand events in terms of cause and effect in the formless unity of some great evolutionary process, whether vaguely homogeneous or rigidly hierarchised. It did not do this in order to seek out structures anterior to, alien or hostile to the event. It was rather in order to establish those diverse converging, and sometimes divergent, but never autonomous series that enable us to circumscribe the 'locus' of an event, the limits to its fluidity and the conditions of its emergence.

The fundamental notions now imposed upon us are no longer those of consciousness and continuity (with their correlative problems of liberty and causality), nor are they those of sign and structure. They are notions, rather, of events and of series, with the groups of notions linked to these; it is around such an ensemble that this analysis of discourse I am thinking of is articulated, certainly not upon those traditional themes which the philosophers of the past took for 'living' history, but on the effective work of historians.

But it is also here that this analysis poses some, probably awesome philosophical or theoretical problems. If discourses are to be treated first as ensembles of discursive events, what status are we to accord this notion of event, so rarely taken into consideration by philosophers? Of course, an event is neither substance, nor accident, nor quality nor process; events are not corporeal. And yet, an event is certainly not immaterial; it takes effect, becomes effect, always on the level of materiality. Events have their place; they consist in relation to, coexistence with, dispersion of, the cross checking accumulation and the selection of material elements; it occurs as an effect of, and in, material dispersion. Let us say that the philosophy of event should advance in the direction, at first sight paradoxical, of an incorporeal materialism. If, on the other hand, discursive events are to be dealt with as homogeneous, but discontinuous series, what status are we to accord this discontinuity? Here we are not dealing with a succession of instants in time, nor with the plurality of thinking subjects; what is concerned are those caesurae breaking the instant and dispersing the subject in a multiplicity of possible positions and functions. Such a discontinuity strikes and invalidates the smallest units, traditionally recognised and the least contested: the instant and the subject. Beyond them, independent of them, we must conceive—between these discontinuous series of relations which are not in any order of succession (or simultaneity) within any (or several) consciousnesses—and we must elaborate—outside of philosophies of time and subject—a theory of discontinuous systematisation. Finally, if it is true that these discursive, discontinuous series have their regularity, within certain limits, it is clearly no longer possible to establish mechanically causal links or an ideal necessity among their constitutive elements. We must accept the introduction of chance as a category in the production of events. There again, we feel the absence of a theory enabling us to conceive the links between chance and thought.

In the sense that this slender wedge I intend to slip into the history of ideas consists in dealing not with meanings possibly lying behind this or that discourse, but with discourse as regular series and distinct events, I fear I recognise in this wedge a tiny (odious, too, perhaps) device permitting the introduction, into the roots of thought, of notions of *chance, discontinuity* and *materiality*. This represents a triple peril which one particular form of history attempts to avert by recounting the continuous unfolding of some ideal necessity. But they are three notions which ought to permit us to link the history of systems of thought to the practical work of historians; three directions to be followed in the work of theoretical elaboration.

Following these principles, and referring to this overall view, the analyses I intend to undertake fall into two groups. One the one hand, the 'critical' group which sets the reversal principle to work. I shall attempt to distinguish the forms of exclusion, limitation and appropriation of which I was speaking earlier; I shall try to show how they are formed, in answer to which needs, how they are modified and displaced, which constraints they have effectively exercised, to what extent they have been worked on. On the other hand, the 'genealogical' group, which brings the three other principles into play: how series of discourse are formed, through, in spite of, or with the aid of these systems of constraint: what were the specific norms for each, and what were their conditions of appearance, growth and variation.

Taking the critical group first, a preliminary group of investigations could bear on what I have designated functions of exclusion. I have already examined one of these for a determinate period: the disjunction of reason and madness in the classical age. Latter, we could attempt an investigation of a taboo system in language, that concerning sexuality from the sixteenth to the nineteenth century. In this, we would not be concerned with the manner in which this has progressively—and happily—disappeared, but with the way it has been altered and rearticulated, from the practice of confession, with its forbidden conduct, named, clarified, hierarchised down to the smallest detail, to the belated, timid appearance of the treatment of sexuality in nineteenth-century psychiatry and medicine. Of course, these only amount to somewhat symbolic guidelines, but one can already be pretty sure that the tree will not fall where we expect, and that taboos are not always to be found where we imagine them to be.

For the time being, I would like to address myself to the third system of exclusion. I will envisage it in two ways. Firstly, I would like to try to visualise the manner in which this truth within which we are caught, but which we constantly renew, was selected, but at the same time, was repeated, extended and displaced. I will take first of all the age of the Sophists and its beginning with Socrates, or at least with Platonic philosophy, and I shall try to see how effective, ritual discourse, charged with power and peril, gradually arranged itself into a disjunction between true and false discourse. I shall next take the turn of the sixteenth and seventeenth centuries and the age which, above all in England, saw the emergence of an observational, affirmative science, a certain natural philosophy inseparable, too, from religious ideology—for this certainly constituted a new form of the will to knowledge. In the third place, I shall turn to the begining of the nineteenth century and the great founding acts of modern science, as well as the formation of industrial society and the accompanying positivist ideology. Three slices out of the morphology of our will to knowledge; three staging posts in our philistinism.

I would also like to consider the same question from quite another angle. I would like to measure the effect of a discourse claiming to be scientific—medical, psychiatric or socological—on the ensemble of practices and prescriptive discourse of which the penal code consists. The study of psychiatric skills and their role in the penal system will serve as a point of departure and as basic material for this analysis.

It is within this critical perspective, but on a different level, that the analysis of the rules for the limitation of discourse should take place, of those among which I earlier designated the author principle, that of commentary and that of discipline. One can envisage a certain number of studies in this field. I am thinking, for example, of the history of medicine in the sixteenth to nineteenth centuries; not so much an account of discoveries made and concepts developed, but of grasping—from the construction of medical discourse, from all its supporting institutions, from its transmission and its reinforcement—how the principles of author commentary and discipline worked in practice; of seeking to know how the great author principle, whether Hippocrates, Galen, Paracelsus and Sydenham, or Boerhaave, became a principle of limitation in medical discourse; how, even late into the nineteenth century, the practice of aphorism and commentary retained its currency and how it was gradually replaced by the emphasis on case histories and clinical training on actual cases; according to which model medicine sought to constitute itself as a discipline, basing itself at first on natural history and, later, on anatomy and biology.

One could also envisage the way in which eighteenth- and nineteenth-century literary criticism and history have constituted the character of the author and the form of the work, utilising, modifying and altering the procedures of religious exegesis, biblical criticism, hagiography, the 'lives' of historical or legendary figures, of autobiography and memoirs. One day, too, we must take a look at Freud's role in psychoanalytical knowledge, so different from that of Newton in physics, or from that an author might play in the field of philosophy (Kant, for example, who originated a totally new way of philosophising).

These, then, are some of the projects falling within the critical aspect of the task, for the analysis of instances of discursive control. The generalogical aspect concerns the effective formation of discourse, whether within the limits of control, or outside of them, or as is most frequent, on both sides of delimitation. Criticism analyses the processes of rarefaction, consolidation and unification in discourse; genealogy studies their formation, at once scattered, discontinuous and regular. To tell the truth, these two tasks are not always exactly complementary. We do not find, on the one hand, forms of rejection, exclusion, consolidation or attribution, and, on a more profound level, the spontaneous pouring forth of discourse, which immediately before or after its manifestation, finds itself submitted to selection and control. The regular formation of discourse may, in certain conditions and up to a certain point, integrate control procedures (this is what happens, for example, when a discipline takes on the form and status of scientific discourse). Conversely, modes of control may take on life within a discursive formation (such as literary criticism as the author's constitutive discourse) even though any critical task calling instances of control into play must, at the same time, analyse the discursive regularities through which these instances are formed. Any genealogical description must take into account the limits at play within real formations. The difference between the critical and generalogical enterprise is not one of object or field, but of point of attack, perspective and delimination.

Earlier on I mentioned one possible study, that of the taboos in discourse on sexuality. It would be difficult, and in any case abstract, to try to carry out this study, without at the same time analysing literary, religious and ethical, biological and medical, as well as juridical discursive ensembles: wherever sexuality is discussed, wherever it is named or described, metaphorised, explained or judged. We are a very long way from having constituted a unitary, regular discourse concerning sexuality; it may be that we never will, and that we are not even travelling in that direction. No mater. Taboos are homogeneous neither in their forms nor their behaviour whether in literary or medical discourse, in that of psychiatry or of the direction of consciousness. Conversely, these different discursive regularities do not divert or alter taboos in the same manner. It will only be possible to undertake this study, therefore, if we take into account the plurality of series within which the taboos, each one to some extent different from all the others, are at work.

We could also consider those series of discourse which, in the sixteenth and seventeenth centuries, dealt with wealth and poverty, money, production and trade. Here, we would be dealing with some pretty heterogeneous ensembles of enunications, formulated by rich and poor, the wise and the ignorant, protestants and catholics, royal officials, merchants or moralists. Each one has its forms of regularity and, equally, its systems of constraint. None of them precisely prefigures that other form of regularity that was to acquire the momentum of a discipline and which was later to be known, first as 'the study of wealth' and, subsequently, 'political economy'. And yet, it was from the foregoing that a new regularity was formed, retrieving or excluding, justifying or rejecting, this or that utterance from these old forms.

One could also conceive a study of discourse concerning heredity, such as it can be gleaned, dispersed as it was until the beginning of the twentieth century, among a variety of disciplines, observations, techniques and formulae; we would be concerned to show the process whereby these series eventually became subsumed under the single system, now recognised as epistemologically coherent, known as genetics. This is the work Francois Jacob has just completed, with unequalled brilliance and scholarship.

It is thus that critical and genealogical descriptions are to alternate, support and complete each other. The critical side of the analysis deals with the systems enveloping discourse; attempting to mark out and distinguish the principles of ordering, exclusion and rarity in discourse. We might, to play with our words, say it practises a kind of studied casualness. The genealogical side of discourse, by way of contrast, deals with series of effective formation of discourse: it attempts to grasp it in its power of affirmation, by which I do not mean a power opposed to that of negation, but the power of constituting domains of objects, in relation to which one can affirm or deny true or false propositions. Let us call these domains of objects positivist and, to play on words yet again, let us say that, if the critical style is one of studied casualness, then the genealogical mood is one of felicitous positivism.

At all events, one thing must be emphasised here: that the analysis of discourse thus understood, does not reveal the universality of a meaning, but brings to light the action of imposed rarity, with a fundamental power of affirmation. Rarity and affirmation; rarity, in the last resort of affirmation—certainly not any continuous outpouring of meaning, and certainly not any monarchy of the signifier.

And now, let those who are weak on vocabulary, let those with little comprehension of theory call all this—if its appeal is stronger than its meaning for them—structuralism. . . .

Chapter 36

JACQUES DERRIDA

Jacques Derrida (1930–   ) was born into a Jewish family in Algeria, educated in Paris, and deeply influenced by the phenomenology of Edmund Husserl (see Chapter 32). Derrida has concentrated on the phenomenology of literature, in the 1960s developing a theory called *deconstruction*, which although undefined, seems to be related to Heidegger's destruction of Western philosophy. He attacks *logocentricism*, the thesis that reason is sufficient to determine meaning. On the contrary, even for philosophy, there is no privileged position. We cannot get at the meaning of a text without inventing it by use of metaphors and indirection. Derrida's idea of deconstruction also involves the idea that a text contains its own self-destruction. Texts, if viewed closely enough, reveal self-contradictions. Some critics maintain that this makes Derrida's own work self-refuting.

Derrida emphasizes metaphor, pun, and playfulness in his work. He is the author of numerous works, including *Of Grammatology, Post Card*, and *Speech and Phenomena*. In the selection included here Derrida uses Plato's comments on writing in the *Phaedrus* as a point of departure as he distinguishes the reading of a text from the writing of one, subjecting the text to a phenomenologically deconstructive analysis. A text has no final or essential meaning, but must be interpreted by each person afresh. The passage from Plato's *Phaedrus* on which Derrida's reflections concentrate is the following, in which Socrates is speaking:

> Very well, I heard then, that at Naucratis in Egypt there lived one of the old gods of that country, the one whose sacred bird is called the ibis; and the name of the divinity was Theuth. It was he who first invented numbers and calculation, geometry and astronomy, not to speak of draughts and dice and above all writing (*grammata*). Now the King of Egypt at that time was Thamus who lived in the great city of the upper region which the Greeks call the Egyptian Thebes; the god himself they call Ammon. Theuth came to him and exhibited his arts and declared that they ought to be imparted to the other Egyptians. And Thamus questioned him about the usefulness of each one; and as Theuth enumerated, the King blamed or praised what he thought were the good or bad points in the explanation. Now Thamus is said to have had a good deal to remark on both sides of the question about every single art (it would take too long to repeat here); but when it came to writing, Theuth said, "This discipline, my king, will makes the Egyptians wiser and will improve their memories: my invention is a recipe (*pharmakon*) for both memory and wisdom." (*Phaedrus* 274c–e)

FOR FURTHER READING

Derrida, Jacques. *Speech and Other Essays on Husserl's Theory of Signs* (Northwestern University Press, 1973).

———. *Grammatology* (Johns Hopkins University Press, 1975).
———. *Dissemination* (University of Chicago Press, 1981).
———. *Glas* (University of Nebraska Press, 1986).
Sallis, J. *Deconstruction and Philosophy: The Texts of Jacques Derrida* (University of Chicago Press, 1987).
Norris, Christopher. *Derrida* (Harvard University Press, 1987).
Wood, David, ed. *Derrida: A Critical Reader* (Blackwell, 1992).

Plato's Pharmacy

A text is not a text unless it hides from the first comer, from the first glance, the law of its composition and the rules of its game. A text remains, moreover, forever imperceptible. Its laws and its rules are not, however, harbored in the inaccessibility of a secret: it is simply that they can never be called a perception.

And hence, perpetually and essentially, they run the risk of being definitively lost. Who will ever know of such disappearances?

The dissimulation of the woven text can in any case take centuries to undo its web: a web that envelops a web, undoing the web for centuries; reconstituting it too as an organism, indefinitely regenerating its own tissue behind the cutting trace, the decision of each reading. There is always a surprise in store for the anatomy or physiology of any criticism that might think it had mastered the game, surveyed all the threads at once, deluding itself, too, in wanting to look at the text without touching it, without laying hands on the "object," without risking—which is the only chance of entering into the game, by getting a few fingers caught—the addition of some new thread. Adding, here, is nothing other than giving to read. One must manage to think this out: that it is not a question of embroidering upon a text, unless one considers that to know how to embroider still means to have the ability to follow the given thread. That is, if you follow me, the hidden thread. If reading and writing are one, it is easily thought these days, if reading is writing, this oneness designates neither undifferentiated (con)fusion nor identity at perfect rest; the *is* that couples reading with writing must rip apart.

One must then, in a single gesture, but doubled, read and write. And that person would have understood nothing of the game who, at this [*du coup*], would feel himself authorized merely to add on; that is, to add any old thing. He would add nothing: the seam wouldn't hold. Reciprocally, he who through "methodological prudence," "norms of objectivity," or "safeguards of knowledge" would refrain from committing anything of himself, would not read at all. The same foolishness, the same sterility, obtains in the "not serious" as in the "serious." The reading or writing supplement must be rigorously prescribed, but by the necessities of a *game*, by the logic of *play*, signs to which the system of all textual powers must be accorded and attuned. . . . To a considerable degree, we have already said all we *meant to say*. Our lexicon at any rate is not far from being exhausted. With the exception of this or that supplement, our questions will have nothing more to name but the texture of the text, reading and writing, mastery and play, the paradoxes of supplementarity, and the graphic relations between the living and the dead: within the textual, the textile, and the histological. We will keep within the limits of this *issue*: between the metaphor of the *histos* and the question of the *histos* of metaphor.

Since we have already said everything, the reader must bear with us if we continue on awhile. If we extend ourselves by force of play. If we then *write* a bit: on Plato, who already said in the *Phaedrus*

Reprinted from *Dissemination*, translated by Barbara Johnson (University of Chicago Press, 1981), by permission.

that writing can only repeat (itself), that it "always signifies (*sēmainei*) the same" and that it is a "game" (*paidia*).

1. PHARMACIA

Let us begin again. Therefore the dissimulation of the woven texture can in any case take centuries to undo its web. The example we shall propose of this will not, seeing that we are dealing with Plato, be the *Statesman*, which will have come to mind first, no doubt because of the paradigm of the weaver, and especially because of the paradigm of the paradigm, the example of the example—writing—which immediately precedes it. We will come back to that only after a long detour.

We will take off here from the *Phaedrus*. We are speaking of the *Phaedrus* that was obliged to wait almost twenty-five centuries before anyone gave up the idea that it was a badly composed dialogue. It was at first believed that Plato was too young to do the thing right, to construct a well-made object. Diogenes Laertius records this "they say" (*logos* [sc. *esti*], *legetai*) according to which the *Phaedrus* was Plato's first attempt and thus manifested a certain juvenile quality (*meirakïōdēs ti*). Schleiermacher thinks this legend can be corroborated by means of a ludicrous argument: an aging writer would not have condemned writing as Plato does in the *Phaedrus*. This argument is not merely suspect in itself: it lends credit to the Laertian legend by basing itself on a second legend. Only a blind or grossly insensitive reading could indeed have spread the rumor that Plato was *simply* condemning the writer's activity. Nothing here is of a single piece and the *Phaedrus* also, in its own writing, plays at saving writing—which also means causing it to be lost—as the best, the noblest game. As for the stunning hand Plato has thus dealt himself, we will be able to follow its incidence and its payoff later on.

In 1905, the tradition of Diogenes Laertius was reversed, not in order to bring about a recognition of the excellent composition of the *Phaedrus* but in order to attribute its faults this time to the senile impotence of the author: "The *Phaedrus* is badly composed. This defect is all the more surprising since it is precisely there that Socrates defines the work of art as a living being. But the inability to accomplish what has been well conceived is precisely a proof of old age."

We are no longer at that point. The hypothesis of a rigorous, sure, and subtle form is naturally more fertile. It discovers new chords, new concordances; it surprises them in minutely fashioned counterpoint, within a more secret organization of themes, of names, of words. It unties a whole *sumplokē* patiently interlacing the arguments. What is magisterial about the demonstration affirms itself and effaces itself at once, with suppleness, irony, and discretion.

This is, in particular, the case—and this will be our supplementary thread—with the whole last section (274*b* ff.), devoted, as everyone knows, to the origin, history, and value of writing. That entire hearing of the *trial of writing* should some day cease to appear as an extraneous mythological fantasy, an appendix the organism could easily, with no loss, have done without. In truth, it is rigorously called for from one end of the *Phaedrus* to the other.

Always with irony. But what can be said of irony here? What is its major sign? The dialogue contains the only "rigorously original Platonic myths: the fable of the cicadas in the *Phaedrus*, and the story of Theuth in the same dialogue." Interestingly, Socrates' first words, in the opening lines of the conversation, had concerned "not bothering about" mythologemes (229*c*–230*a*). Not in order to reject them absolutely, but, on the one hand, not bothering them, leaving them alone, making room for them, in order to free them from the heavy serious naïveté of the scientific "rationalists," and on the other, not bothering *with* them, in order to free *onself* for the relation with oneself and the pursuit of self-knowledge.

To give myths a send-off: a salute, a vacation, a dismissal; this fine resolution of the *khairein*, which means all that at once, will be twice interrupted in order to welcome these "two Platonic myths," so "rigorously original." Both of these myths arise, moreover, in the opening of a question about the status of writing. This is undoubtedly less obvious—has anyone ever picked up on it?—in the case of the cicada story. But it is no less certain. Both myths follow upon the same question, and they are only separated by a short space, just time enough for a detour. The first, of course, does not answer the question; on the contrary, it leaves it hanging, marks time for a rest, and makes us wait for the reprise that will lead us to the second.

Let us read this more closely. At the precisely calculated center of the dialogue—the reader can count the lines—the question of *logography* is raised

(257 *c*). Phaedrus reminds Socrates that the citizens of greatest influence and dignity, the men who are the most free, feel ashamed (*aiskhunontai*) at "speechwriting" and at leaving *sungrammata* behind them. They fear the judgment of posterity, which might consider them "sophists" (257*d*). The logographer, in the strict sense, is a *ghost writer* who composes speeches for use by litigants, speeches which he himself does not pronounce, which he does not attend, so to speak, in person, and which produce their effects in his absence. In writing what he does not speak, what he would never say and, in truth, would probably never even think, the author of the written speech is already entrenched in the posture of the sophist: the man of non-presence and of non-truth. Writing is thus already on the scene. The incompatibility between the *written* and the *true* is clearly announced at the moment Socrates starts to recount the way in which men are carried out of themselves by pleasure, become absent from themselves, forget themselves and die in the thrill of song (259*c*).

But the issue is delayed. Socrates still has a neutral attitude: writing is not in itself a shameful, indecent, infamous (*aiskhron*) activity. One is dishonored only if one writes in a dishonorable manner. But what does it mean to write in a dishonorable manner? and, Phaedrus also wants to know, what does it mean to write beautifully (*kalōs*)? This question sketches out the central nervure, the great fold that divides the dialogue. Between this question and the answer that takes up its terms in the last section ("But there remains the question of propriety and impropriety in writing, that is to say the conditions which make it proper or improper. Isn't that so?" 274*b*), the thread remains solid, if not easily visible, all through the fable of the cicadas and the themes of psychagogy, rhetoric, and dialectics.

Thus Socrates begins by sending myths off; and then, twice stopped before the question of writing, he invents two of them—not, as we shall see, entirely from scratch, but more freely and spontaneously than anywhere else in his work. Now, the *khairein*, in the *Phaedrus*' opening pages, *takes place in the name of truth*. We will reflect upon the fact that the myths come back from vacation at the time and in the name of writing.

The *khairein* takes place *in the name of truth*: that is, in the name of knowledge of truth and, more precisely, of truth in the knowledge of the self. This is what Socrates explains (230*a*). But this imperative of self-knowledge is not first felt or dictated by any transparent immediacy of self-presence. It is not perceived. Only interpreted, read, deciphered. A hermeneutics *assigns* intuition. An inscription, the *Delphikon gramma*, which is anything but an oracle, prescribes through its silent cipher; it signifies as one signifies an order—autoscopy and autognosis. The very activities that Socrates thinks can be contrasted to the hermeneutic adventure of myths, which he leaves to the sophists (229*d*).

And the *khairein* takes *place* in the name of truth. The *topoi* of the dialogue are never indifferent. The themes, the topics, the (common-)places, in a rhetorical sense, are strictly inscribed, comprehended each time within a significant site. They are dramatically staged, and in this theatrical geography, unity of place corresponds to an infallible calculation or necessity. For example, the fable of the cicadas would not have taken place, would not have been recounted, Socrates would not have been incited to tell it, if the heat, which weighs over the whole dialogue, had not driven the two friends out of the city, into the countryside, along the river Ilissus. Well before detailing the genealogy of the genus cicada, Socrates had exclaimed, "How welcome and sweet the fresh air is, resounding with the summer chirping of the cicada chorus" (230*c*). But this is not the only counterpoint-effect required by the space of the dialogue. The myth that serves as a pretext for the *khairein* and for the retreat into autoscopy can itself only arise, during the first steps of this excursion, at the sight of the Ilissus. Isn't this the spot, asks Phaedrus, where Boreas, according to tradition, carried off Orithyia? This riverbank, the diaphanous purity of these waters, must have welcomed the young virgins, or even drawn them like a spell, inciting them to play here. Socrates then mockingly proposes a learned explanation of the myth in the rationalistic, physicalist style of the *sophoi*: it was while she was playing with Pharmacia (*sun Pharmakeiai paizousan*) that the boreal wind (*pneuma Boreou*) caught Orithyia up and blew her into the abyss, "down from the rocks hard by," "and having thus met her death was said to have been seized by Boreas. . . . For my part, Phaedrus, I regard such theories as attractive no doubt, but as the invention of clever, industrious people who are not exactly to be envied" (229*d*).

This brief evocation of Pharmacia at the beginning of the *Phaedrus*—is it an accident? An hors d'oeuvre? A fountain, "perhaps with curative powers," notes Robin, was dedicated to Pharmacia near the Ilissus. Let us in any case retain this: that a little spot, a little stitch or mesh (*macula*) woven into the back of the canvas, marks out for the entire dialogue the scene where that *virgin* was cast into the abyss, surprised by death *while playing with Pharmacia*. Pharmacia (*Pharmakeia*) is also a common noun signifying the administration of the *pharmakon*, the drug: the medicine and/or poison. "Poisoning" was not the least usual meaning of "pharmacia." Antiphon has left us the logogram of an "accusation of poisoning against a mother-in-law" (*Pharmakeias kata tēs mētryias*). Through her games, Pharmacia has dragged down to death a virginal purity and an unpenetrated interior.

Only a little further on, Socrates compares the written texts Phaedrus has brought along to a drug (*pharmakon*). This *pharmakon*, this "medicine," this philter, which acts as both remedy and poison, already introduces itself into the body of the discourse with all its ambivalence. This charm, this spellbinding virtue, this power of fascination, can be—alternately or simultaneously—beneficent or maleficent. The *pharmakon* would be a *substance*—with all that that word can connote in terms of matter with occult virtues, cryptic depths refusing to submit their ambivalence to analysis, already paving the way for alchemy—if we didn't have eventually to come to recognize it as antisubstance itself: that which resists any philosopheme, indefinitely exceeding its bounds as nonidentity, nonessence, nonsubstance; granting philosophy by that very fact the inexhaustible adversity of what funds it and the infinite absence of what founds it.

Operating through seduction, the *pharmakon* makes one stray from one's general, natural, habitual paths and laws. Here, it takes Socrates out of his proper place and off his customary track. The latter had always kept him inside the city. The leaves of writing act as a *pharmakon* to push or attract out of the city the one who never wanted to get out, even at the end, to escape the hemlock. They take him out of himself and draw him onto a path that is properly an *exodus*:

PHAEDRUS: Anyone would take you, as you say, for a foreigner being shown the country by a guide, and not a native—you never leave town to cross the frontier nor even, I believe, so much as set foot outside the walls.

SOCRATES: You must forgive me, dear friend; I'm a lover of learning, and trees and open country won't teach me anything, whereas men in the town do. Yet you seem to have discovered a drug[1] for getting me out (*dokeis moi tēs emēs exocou to pharmakon hēurēkenai*). A hungry animal can be driven by dangling a carrot or a bit of greenstuff in front of it; similarly if you proffer me speeches bound in books (*en bibliois*) I don't doubt you can cart me all round Attica, and anywhere else you please. Anyhow, now that we've got here I propose for the time being to lie down, and you can choose whatever posture you think most convenient for reading, and proceed (230*d–e*).

It is at this point, when Socrates has finally stretched out on the ground and Phaedrus has taken the most comfortable position for handling the text or, if you will, the *pharmakon*, that the discussion actually gets off the ground. A spoken speech—whether by Lysias or by Phaedrus in person—a speech proffered *in the present, in the presence* of Socrates, would not have had the same effect. Only the *logoi en bibliois*, only words that are deferred, reserved, enveloped, rolled up, words that force one to wait for them in the form and under cover of a solid object, letting themselves be desired for the space of a walk, only hidden letters can thus get Socrates moving. If a *speech* could be purely present, unveiled, naked, offered up in person in its truth, without the detours of a signifier foreign to it, if at the limit an undeferred *logos* were possible, it would not seduce anyone. It would not draw Socrates, as if under the effects of a *pharmakon*, out of his way. Let us get ahead of ourselves. Already: writing, the *pharmakon*, the going or leading astray.

In our discussion of this text we have been using an authoritative French translation of Plato, the one published by Guillaume Budé. In the case of the *Phaedrus*, the translation is by Léon Robin. We will continue to refer to it, inserting the Greek text in parentheses, however, whenever it seems opportune or pertinent to our point. Hence, for example, the word *pharmakon*. In this way we hope to display in the most striking manner the regular, ordered polysemy that has, through skewing, indetermination, or overdetermination, but without mistranslation, permitted the rendering of the same word by "remedy," "recipe," "poison," "drug," "philter," etc. It will also be seen to what extent the malleable unity of this concept, or rather its rules and the strange logic that links it with its signifier, has been dispersed,

1. TN. Hackforth translates "recipe"; Helmbold & Rabinowitz, "remedy."

masked, obliterated, and rendered almost unreadable not only by the imprudence or empiricism of the translators, but first and foremost by the redoubtable, irreducible difficulty of translation. It is a difficulty inherent in its very principle, situated less in the passage from one language to another, from one philosophical language to another, than already, as we shall see, in the tradition between Greek and Greek; a violent difficulty in the transference of a non-philosopheme into a philosopheme. With this problem of translation we will thus be dealing with nothing less than the problem of the very passage into philosophy.

The *biblia* that will draw Socrates out of his reserve and out of the space in which he is wont to learn, to teach, to speak, to dialogue—the sheltered enclosure of the city—these *biblia* contain a text written by "the ablest writer of our day" (*deinotatos ōn tōn nun graphein*). His name is Lysias. Phaedrus is keeping the text or, if you will, the *pharmakon*, hidden under his cloak. He needs it because he has not learned the speech by heart. This point is important for what follows, the problem of writing being closely linked to the problem of "knowing by heart." Before Socrates had stretched out on the ground and invited Phaedrus to take the most comfortable position, the latter had offered to reconstitute, without the help of the text, the reasoning, argument, and design of Lysias' speech, its *dianoia*. Socrates stops him short: "Very well, my dear fellow, but you must first show me what it is that you have in your left hand under your cloak, for I surmise that it is the actual discourse (*ton logon auton*)" (228*d*). Between the invitation and the start of the reading, while the *pharmakon* is wandering about under Phaedrus' cloak, there occurs the evocation of Pharmacia and the send-off of myths.

It it after all by chance or by harmonics that, even before the overt presentation of writing as a *pharmakon* arises in the middle of the myth of Theuth, the connection between *biblia* and *pharmaka* should already be mentioned in a malevolent or suspicious vein? As opposed to the true practice of medicine, founded on science, we find indeed, listed in a single stroke, empirical practice, treatments based on recipes learned by heart, mere bookish knowledge, and the blind usage of drugs. All that, we are told, springs out of *mania*: "I expect they would say, 'the man is mad; he thinks he has made himself a doctor by picking up something out of a book (*ek bibliou*), or coming across a couple of ordinary drugs (*pharmakiois*), without any real knowledge of medicine'" (268*c*).

This association between writing and the *pharmakon* still seems external; it could be judged artificial or purely coincidental. But the intention and intonation are recognizably the same: one and the same suspicion envelops in a single embrace the book and the drug, writing and whatever works in an occult, ambiguous manner open to empiricism and chance, governed by the ways of magic and not the laws of necessity. Books, the dead and rigid knowledge shut up in *biblia*, piles of histories, nomenclatures, recipes and formulas learned by heart, all this is as foreign to living knowledge and dialectics as the *pharmakon* is to medical science. And myth to true knowledge. In dealing with Plato, who knew so well on occasion how to treat myth in its archeo-logical or paleo-logical capacity, one can glimpse the immensity and difficulty of this last opposition. The extent of the difficulty is marked out—this is, among a hundred others, the example that retains us here—in that the truth—the original truth—about writing as a *pharmakon* will at first be left up to a myth. The myth of Theuth, to which we now turn.

Up to this point in the dialogue, one can say that the *pharmakon* and the grapheme have been beckoning to each other from afar, indirectly sending back to each other, and, as if by chance, appearing and disappearing together on the same line, for yet uncertain reasons, with an effectiveness that is quite discrete and perhaps after all unintentional. But in order to lift this doubt and on the supposition that the categories of the voluntary and the involuntary still have some absolute pertinence in a reading—which we don't for a minute believe, at least not on the textual level on which we are now advancing—let us proceed to the last phase of the dialogue, to the point where Theuth appears on the scene.

This time it is without indirection, without hidden mediation, without secret argumentation, that writing is proposed, presented, and asserted as a *pharmakon* (274*e*).

In a certain sense, one can see how this section could have been set apart as an appendix, a super-added supplement. And despite all that calls for it in the preceding steps, it is true that Plato offers it somewhat as an amusement, an hors d'oéuvre or rather a dessert. All the subjects of the dialogue, both themes and speakers, seem exhausted at the moment the supplement, writing, or the *pharmakon*, are introduced: "Then we may feel that we have said enough both about the art of speaking and about the lack of art (*to men tekhnēs te kai atekhnias logōn*)" [2](274*b*). And yet it is *at this moment of general* exhaustion that the question of writing is set out.[3] And, as was foreshadowed earlier by the use of the word *aiskhron* (or the adverb *aiskhrōs*), the question of writing opens as a question of morality. It is truly *morality* that is at stake, both in the sense of the opposition between good and evil, or good and bad, and in the sense of mores, public morals and social conventions. It is a question of knowing what is done and what is not done. This moral disquiet is in no way to be distinguished from questions of truth, memory, and dialectics. This latter question, which will quickly be engaged as *the* question of writing, is closely associated with the morality theme, and indeed develops it by affinity of essence and not by superimposition. But within a debate rendered very real by the political development of the city, the propagation of writing and the activity of the sophists and speechwriters, the primary accent is naturally placed upon political and social proprieties. The type of arbitration proposed by Socrates plays within the opposition between the values of seemliness and unseemliness (*euprepeial aprepeia*): "But there remains the question of propriety and impropriety in writing, that is to say the conditions which make it proper or improper. Isn't that so?" (274*b*).

Is writing seemly? Does the writer cut a respectable figure? Is it proper to write? Is it done?

Of course not. But the answer is not so simple, and Socrates does not immediately offer it on his own account in a rational discourse or *logos*. He lets it be heard by delegating it to an *akoē*, to a well-known rumor, to hearsay evidence, to a fable transmitted from ear to ear: "I can tell you what our fathers have said about it, but the truth of it is only known by tradition. However, if we could discover that truth for ourselves, should we still be concerned with the fancies of mankind?" (274*c*).

The truth of writing, that is, as we shall see, (the) nontruth, cannot be discovered in ourselves by ourselves. And it is not the object of a science, only of a history that is recited, a fable that is repeated. The link between writing and myth becomes clearer, as does its opposition to knowledge, notably the knowledge one seeks in oneself, by oneself. And at the same time, (through writing or through myth, the genealogical break and the estrangement from the origin are sounded). One should note most especially that what writing will later be accused of—repeating without knowing—here defines the very approach that leads to the statement and determination of its status. One thus begins by repeating without knowing—through a myth—the definition of writing, which is to repeat without knowing. This kinship of writing and myth, both of them distinguished from *logos* and dialectics, will only become more precise as the text concludes. Having just repeated without knowing that writing consists of repeating without knowing, Socrates goes on to base the demonstration of his indictment, of his *logos*, upon the premises of the *akoē*, upon structures that are readable through a fabulous genealogy of writing. As soon as the myth has struck the first blow, the *logos* of Socrates will demolish the accused.

2. THE FATHER OF LOGOS

The story begins like this:

SOCRATES: Very well. I heard, then, that at Naucratis in Egypt there lived one of the old gods of that country, the one whose sacred bird is called the ibis; and the name of the divinity was Theuth. It was he who first invented numbers and calculation, geometry and astronomy, not to speak of draughts and dice, and above all writing (*grammata*). Now the King of all Egypt at that time was Thamus who lived in the great city of the upper region which the Greeks call the Egyptian Thebes; the god himself they call Ammon. Theuth came to him and exhibited his arts and declared that they ought to be imparted to the other Egyptians. And Thamus questioned him about the usefulness of each one; and as Theuth enumerated, the King blamed or praised what he throught were the good or bad points in the explanation. Now

2. Here, when it is a question of *logos*, Robin translates *tekhnē* by "art." Later, in the course of the indictment, the same word, this time pertaining to writing, will be rendered by "technical knowledge" [*connaissance technique*].

3. While Saussure, in his *Course in General Linguistics*, excludes or settles the question of writing in a sort of preliminary excursus or hors d'oeuvre, the chapter Rousseau devotes to writing in the *Essay on the Origin of Languages* is also presented, despite its actual importance, as a sort of somewhat contingent supplement, a makeup criterion, "another means of comparing languages and of judging their relative antiquity." The same operation is found in Hegel's *Encyclopedia*; cf. "Le Puits et la pyramide," (1–1968) in *Hegel et la pensée moderne*, (Paris: Presses Universitaires de France, 1970, coll. "Epiméthée.").

Thamus is said to have had a good deal to remark on both sides of the question about every single art (it would take too long to repeat it here); but when it came to writing, Theuth said, "This discipline (*to mathēma*), my King, will make the Egyptians wiser and will improve their memories (*sophōterous kai mnēmonikōterous*): my invention is a recipe (*pharmakon*) for both memory and wisdom." But the King said . . . (274*c–e*).

Let us cut the King off here. He is faced with the *pharmakon*. His reply will be incisive.

Let us freeze the scene and the characters and take a look at them. Writing (or, if you will, the *pharmakon*) is thus presented to the King. Presented: like a kind of present offered up in homage by a vassal to his lord (Theuth is a demigod speaking to the king of the gods), but above all as a finished work submitted to his appreciation. And this work is itself an art, a capacity for work, a power of operation. This artefactum is an art. But the value of this gift is still uncertain. The value of writing—or of the *pharmakon*—has of course been spelled out to the King, but it is the King who will give it its value, who will set the price of what, in the act of receiving, he constitutes or institutes. The king or god (Thamus represents[4] Ammon, the king of the gods, the king of kings, the god of gods. Theuth says to him: *Ō basileu*) is thus the other name for the origin of value. The value of writing will not be itself, writing will have no value, unless and to the extent that god-the-king approves of it. But god-the-king nonetheless experiences the *pharmakon* as a product, an *ergon*, which is not his own, which comes to him from outside but also from below, and which awaits his condescending judgment in order to be consecrated in its being and value. God the king does not know how to write, but that ignorance or incapacity only testifies to his sovereign independence. He has no need to write. He speaks, he says, he dictates, and his word suffices. Whether a scribe from his secretarial staff then adds the supplement of a transcription or not, that consignment is always in essence secondary.

From this position, without rejecting the homage, the god-king will depreciate it, pointing out not only its uselessness but its menace and its mischief. Another way of not receiving the offering of writing. In so doing, god-the-king-that-speaks is acting like a father. The *pharmakon* is here presented to the father and is by him rejected, belittled, abandoned, disparaged. (The father is always suspicious and watchful toward writing.)

Even if we did not want to give in here to the easy passage uniting the figures of the king, the god, and the father, it would suffice to pay systematic attention—which to our knowledge has never been done—to the (permanence of a Platonic schema that assigns the origin and power of speech, precisely of *logos*, to the paternal position), not that this happens especially and exclusively in Plato. Everyone knows this or can easily imagine it. But the fact that "Platonism," which sets up the whole of Western metaphysics in its conceptuality, should not escape the generality of this structural constraint, and even illustrates it with incomparable subtlety and force, stands out as all the more significant.

Not that logos *is* the father, either. But the origin of logos is *its father*. One could say anachronously that the "speaking subject" is the *father* of his speech. And one would quickly realize that this is no metaphor, at least not in the sense of any common, conventional effect of rhetoric. Logos is a son, then, a son that would be destroyed in his very *presence* without the present *attendance of his father*. His father who answers. His father who speaks for him and answers for him. Without his father, he would be nothing but, in fact, writing. At least that is what is said by the one who says: it is the father's thesis. The specificity of writing would thus be intimately bound to the absence of the father. Such an absence can of course exist along very diverse modalities, distinctly or confusedly, successively or simultaneously: to have lost one's father, through natural or violent death, through random violence or patricide; and then to solicit the aid and attendance, possible or impossible, of the paternal presence, to solicit it directly or to claim to be getting along without it, etc. The reader will have noted Socrates' insistence on the misery, whether pitiful or arrogant, of a *logos* committed to writing: ". . . It always needs its father to attend to it, being quite unable to defend itself or attend to its own needs" (275*e*).

4. For Plato, Thamus is doubtless another name for Ammon, whose figure (that of the sun king and of the father of the gods) we shall sketch out later for its own sake. On this question and the debate to which it has given rise, see Frutiger, *Mythes*, p. 233, n. 2, and notably Eisler, "Platon und das ägyptische Alphabet," *Archiv für Geschichte der Philosophie*, 1922; Pauly-Wissowa, *Real-Encyclopädie der classischen Altertumswissenschaft* (art. Ammon); Roscher, *Lexikon der griechischen und römischen Mythologie* (art. Thamus).

This misery is ambiguous: it is the distress of the orphan, of course, who needs not only an attending presence but also a presence that will attend to its needs; but in pitying the orphan, one also makes an accusation against him, along with writing, for claiming to do away with the father, for achieving emancipation with complacent self-sufficiency. (From the position of the holder of the scepter, the desire of writing is indicated, designated, and denounced as a desire for orphanhood and patricidal subversion. Isn't this *pharmakon* then a criminal thing, a poisoned present?)

The status of this orphan, whose welfare cannot be assured by any attendance or assistance, coincides with that of a *graphein* which, being nobody's son at the instant it reaches inscription, scarcely remains a son at all and no longer *recognizes* its origins, whether legally or morally. In contrast to writing, living *logos* is alive in that it has a living father (whereas the orphan is already half dead), a father that is *present, standing* near it, behind it, within it, sustaining it with his rectitude, attending it in person in his own name. Living *logos*, for its part, recognizes its debt, lives off that recognition, and forbids itself, thinks it can forbid itself patricide. But prohibition and patricide, like the relations between speech and writing, are structures surprising enough to require us later on to articulate Plato's text between a patricide prohibited and a patricide proclaimed. The deferred murder of the father and rector.

Just as Socrates supplements and replaces the father, as we have seen, dialectics supplements and replaces the impossible *noēsis*, the forbidden intuition of the face of the father (good-sun-capital). The withdrawal of that face both opens and limits the exercise of dialectics. It welds it irremediably to its "inferiors," the mimetic arts, play, grammar, writing, etc. The disappearance of that face is the movement of differance which violently opens writing or, if one prefers, which opens itself to writing and which writing opens for itself. All these "movements," in all these "senses," belong to the same "system." Also belonging to that same system are the proposition in the *Republic*, describing in nonviolent terms the inaccessibility of the father *epekeina tēs ousias*, and the patricidal proposal which, proffered by the Stranger, threatens the paternal *logos*. And which by the same token threatens the domestic, hierarchical interiority of the pharmacy, the proper order and healthy movement of goods, the lawful prescription of its controlled, classed, measured, labeled products, rigorously divided into remedies and poisons, seeds of life and seeds of death, good and bad traces, the unity of metaphysics, of technology, of well computed binarism. This philosophical, dialectical mastery of the *pharmaka* that should be handed down from legitimate father to well-born son is constantly put in question by a family scene that constitutes and undermines at once the passage between the pharmacy and the house. "Platonism" is both the general *rehearsal* of this family scene and the most powerful effort to master it, to prevent anyone's ever hearing of it, to conceal it by drawing the curtains over the dawning of the West. How can we set off in search of a different guard, if the pharmaceutical "system" contains not only, in a single stranglehold, the scene in the *Phaedrus*, the scene in the *Republic*, the scene in the *Sophist*, and the dialectics, logic, and mythology of Plato, but also, it seems, certain non-Greek structures of mythology? And if it is not certain that there are such things as non-Greek "mythologies"—the opposition *mythos/logos* being only authorized *following* Plato—into what general, unnamable necessity are we thrown? In other words, what does Platonism signify as repetition?

To repeat: the disappearance of the good-father-capital-sun is thus the precondition of discourse, taken this time as a moment and not as a principle of *generalized* writing. That writing (is) *epekeina tēs ousias*. The disappearance of truth as presence, the withdrawal of the present origin of presence, is the condition of all (manifestation of) truth. Nontruth is the truth. Nonpresence is presence. Differance, the disappearance of any originary presence, is *at once* the condition of possibility *and* the condition of impossibility of truth. At once. "At once" means that the being-present (*on*) in its truth, in the presence of its identity and in the identity of its presence, *is doubled* as soon as it appears, as soon as it presents itself. *It appears, in its essence, as* the possibility of its own most proper non-truth, of its pseudo-truth reflected in the icon, the phantasm, or the simulacrum. What is is not what it is, identical and identical to itself, unique, unless it *adds to itself* the possibility of being *repeated* as such. And its identity is hollowed out by that addition, withdraws itself in the supplement that presents it.

The disappearance of the Face or the structure of repetition can thus no longer be dominated by the value of truth. On the contrary, the opposition between the true and the untrue is entirely comprehended, *inscribed*, within this structure or this generalized writing. The true and the untrue are both species of repetition. And there is no repetition possible without the *graphics of supplementarity*, which supplies, for the lack of a full unity, another unit that comes to relieve it, being enough the same and enough other so that it can replace by addition. Thus, on the one hand, repetition is that without which there would be no truth: the truth of being in the intelligible form of ideality discovers in the *eidos* that which can be repeated, being the same, the clear, the stable, the identifiable in its equality with itself. And only the *eidos* can give rise to repetition as anamnesis or maieutics, dialectics or didactics. Here repetition gives itself out to be a repetition of life. Tautology is life only going out of itself to come home to itself. Keeping close to itself through *mnēmē, logos*, and *phōnē*. But on the other hand, repetition is the very movement of non-truth: the presence of what is gets lost, disperses itself, multiplies itself through mimemes, icons, phantasms, simulacra, etc. Through phenomena, already. And this type of repetition is the possibility of becoming-perceptible-to-the-senses: nonideality. This is on the side of non-philosophy, bad memory, hypomnesia, writing. Here, tautology is life going out of itself beyond return. Death rehearsal. Unreserved spending. The irreducible excess, through the play of the supplement, of any self-intimacy of the living, the good, the true.

These two types of repetition relate to each other according to the graphics of supplementarity. Which means that one can no more "separate" them from each other, think of either one apart from the other, "label" them, than one can in *the pharmacy* distinguish the medicine from the poison, the good from the evil, the true from the false, the inside from the outside, the vital from the mortal, the first from the second, etc. Conceived within this original reversibility, the *pharmakon* is the *same* precisely because it has no identity. And the same (is) as supplement. Or in difference. In writing. If he had *meant* to say something, such would have been the speech of Theuth making of writing as a *pharmakon* a singular present to the King.

But Theuth, it should be noted, spoke not another word.

The great god's sentence went unanswered.

. . . .

After closing the pharmacy, Plato went to retire, to get out of the sun. He took a few steps in the darkness toward the back of his reserves, found himself leaning over the *pharmakon*, decided to analyze.

Within the thick, cloudy liquid, trembling deep inside the drug, the whole pharmacy stood reflected, repeating the abyss of the Platonic phantasm.

The analyst cocks his ears, tries to distinguish between two repetitions.

He would like to isolate the good from the bad, the true from the false.

He leans over further: they repeat each other.

Holding the *pharmakon* in one hand, the calamus in the other, Plato mutters as he transcribes the play of formulas. In the enclosed space of the pharmacy, the reverberations of the monologue are immeasurably amplified. The walled-in voice strikes against the rafters, the words come apart, bits and pieces of sentences are separated, disarticulated parts begin to circulate through the corridors, become fixed for a round or two, translate each other, become rejoined, bounce off each other, contradict each other, make trouble, tell on each other, come back like answers, organize their exchanges, protect each other, institute an internal commerce, take themselves for a dialogue. Full of meaning. A whole story. An entire history. All of philosophy.

"*hē ēkhē toutōn tōn logōn* . . . the sound of these arguments rings so loudly in my head that I cannot hear the other side."

In this stammering buzz of voices, as some philological sequence or other floats by, one can sort of make this out, but it is hard to hear: *logos* beds itself [*le logos s' aime lui-même* = logos loves itself; *s' aime* is a homonym for *sème*: to sow, as in a flower bed.—Trans.] . . . *pharmakon* means *coup* . . . "so that *pharmakon* will have meant: that which pertains to an attack of demoniac possession [*un coup démoniaque*] or is used as a curative *against* such an attack" . . . an armed enforcement of order [*un coup de force*] . . . a shot fired [*un coup tiré*] . . . a planned overthrow [*un coup monté*] . . . but to no avail [*un coup pour rien*] . . . like cutting through water [*un coup dans l'eau*] . . . *en udati grapsei* . . . and a stroke of fate [*un coup du sort*] . . . Theuth who invented writing . . . the calendar . . . dice . . . *kubeia* . . . the calendar trick [*le coup du calendrier*] . . . the unexpected dramatic effect [*le coup de théâtre*] . . . the writing trick [*le coup de l'écriture*] . . . the dice-throw [*le coup de dés*] . . . two in one blow [*le coup double*] . . . *kolaphos* . . . *gluph* . . . *colpus* . . . *coup* . . . glyph . . . scalpel . . . scalp . . . *khrusos* . . . *chrysolite* . . . *chrysology* . . .

Plato gags his ears the better to hear-himself-speak, the better to see, the better to analyze.

He listens, means to distinguish, between two repetitions.

He is searching for gold. *Pollakis de legomena kai aei akouomena* . . . "Often repeated and constantly attended to for many years, it is at last with great effort freed from all alloy, like gold . . ." and the philosopher's stone. The "golden rule."

One ought to distinguish, between two repetitions.

—But they repeat each other, still; they substitute for each other . . .

—Nonsense: they don't replace each other, since they are added . . .

—Precisely . . .

One still has to take note of this. And to finish that Second Letter: ". . . Consider these facts and take care lest you sometime come to repent of having now unwisely published your views. It is a very great safeguard to learn by heart instead of writing . . . *to mē graphein all'ekmanthanein*. . . . It is impossible for what is written not to be disclosed. That is the reason why I have never written anything about these things . . . *oud'estin sungramma Platōnos ouden oud'estai*, and why there is not and will not be any written work of Plato's own. What are now called his . . . *Sōkratous estin kalou kai neou gegonotos* . . . are the work of a Socrates embellished and modernized. Farewell and believe. Read this letter now at once many times and burn it. . . ."

—I hope this one won't get lost. Quick, a duplicate . . . graphite . . . carbon . . . reread this letter . . . burn it. *Il y a là cendre*. And now, to distinguish, between two repetitions . . .

The night passes. In the morning, knocks are heard at the door. They seem to be coming from outside, this time . . .

Two knocks . . . four . . .

—But maybe it's just a residue, a dream, a bit of dream left over, an echo of the night . . . that other theater, those knocks from without . . .

Chapter 37

Richard Rorty

Richard Rorty has taught at Princeton University and the University of Virginia and is now a Professor at UCLA. He is the author of several works, including *Philosophy and the Mirror of Nature* (1979), from which the first part of this selection is taken.

In Part I of this selection, "Epistemological Pragmatism," Rorty argues that truth means, not what corresponds to the facts, as is the dominant definition of truth in Western philosophy, but what it is *better* for us to believe. He describes truth as "what you can defend against all comers . . . what our peers will [all things considered] let us get away with saying." He defends the thesis that we should give up metaphysical and epistemological notions of reality and truth in favor of those built on ethnocentric solidarity.

In Part II, "Solidarity Versus Objectivity," Rorty attacks the distinction between objectivity and subjectivity as well as the correspondence theory of truth. He sides with Thomas Kuhn in arguing that we can have no theory-independent notion of reality and proposes to erase the essential difference between science, on the one hand, and the humanities and art, on the other. Embracing the title of "the new fuzzies," Rorty further develops his thesis that a notion of social solidarity replace the enlightenment notion of objective truth.

FOR FURTHER READING

Alcoff, Linda and Elizabeth Potter, eds. *Feminist Epistemologies* (Routledge, 1993).

Anderson, Elisabeth. "Feminist Epistemology: An Interpretation and a Defense." *Hypathia 10*, no. 3 (1995).

Birke, Linda. *Women, Feminism, and Biology: The Feminist Challenge* (Methuen, 1986).

Bloor, David. *Knowledge and Social Imagery* (Routledge, 1991).

Cartwright, Nancy. "The Truth Doesn't Explain Much." In *How the Laws of Physics Lie* (Oxford University Press, 1983).

Code, Lorraine. *What Can She Know?* (Cornell University Press, 1991).

———. *Gendered Species* (Routledge, 1995).

Grandy, Richard. "Information-based Epistemology, Ecological Epistemology and Epistomology Naturalized." *Synthese 70* (1987).

Haraway, D. *Primate Visions: Gender, Race and Nature in the World of Modern Science* (Routledge, 1989).

Rorty, Richard. *Philosophy and the Mirror of Nature* (Princeton University Press, 1979).

———. *Objectivity, Relativism and Truth* (Cambridge University Press, 1991).

———. *Consequences of Pragmatism* (University of Minnesota Press, 1982).

Dismantling Truth: Solidarity Versus Objectivity

PART I

Epistemological Pragmatism

Quine asks how an anthropologist is to discriminate the sentences to which natives invariably and wholeheartedly assent into contingent empirical platitudes on the one hand and necessary conceptual truths on the other. Sellars asks how the authority of first-person reports of, for example, how things appear to us, the pains from which we suffer, and the thoughts that drift before our minds differ from the authority of expert reports on, for example, metal stress, the mating behavior of birds, or the colors of physical objects. We can lump both questions together and simply ask, "How do our peers know which of our assertions to take our word for and which to look for further confirmation of?" It would seem enough for our peers to believe there to be no better way of finding out our inner states than from our reports, without their knowing what "lies behind" our making them. It would also seem enough for us to know that our peers have this acquiescent attitude. That alone seems sufficient for that inner certainty about our inner states which the tradition has explained by "immediate presence to consciousness," "sense of evidence," and other expressions of the assumption that reflections in the Mirror of Nature are intrinsically better known than nature itself. For Sellars, the certainty of "I have a pain" is a reflection of the fact that nobody cares to question it, not conversely. Just so, for Quine, the certainty of "All men are animals," and of "There have been some black dogs." Quine thinks that the "meanings" drop out as wheels that are not part of the mechanisms, and Sellars thinks the same of "self-authenticating non-verbal episodes." More broadly, if assertions are justified by society rather than by the character of the inner representations they express, then there is no point in attempting to isolate *privileged* representation.

Explaining rationality and epistemic authority by reference to what society lets us say, rather than the latter by the former, is the essence of what I call "epistemic behaviorism," an attitude common to Dewey and Wittgenstein. This sort of behaviorism can best be seen as a species of holism—but one which requires no idealist metaphysical underpinnings. It claims that if we understand the rules of a language-game, we understand all that there is to understand about why moves in that language-game are made . . . If we are behaviorists in this sense, then it will not occur to us to invoke either of the traditional Kantian distinctions. But can we just go ahead and be behaviorists? Or, as Quine's and Sellar's critics suggest, doesn't behaviorism simply beg the question? Is there any reason to think that fundamental epistemic notions *should* be explicated in behavioral terms?

The last question comes down to: Can we treat the study of "the nature of human knowledge" just as the study of certain ways in which human beings interact, or does it require an ontological foundation (involving some specific philosophical way of describing human beings)? Shall we take "S knows that p" (or "S knows noninferentially that p," or "S believes incorrigibly that p," or "S's knowledge that p is certain") as a remark about the status of S's reports among his peers, or shall we take it as a remark about the relation between subject and object, between nature and its mirror? The first alternative leads to a pragmatic view of truth and a therapeutic approach to ontology (in which philosophy can straighten out pointless quarrels between common sense and science, but not contribute any arguments of its own for the existence or [non]existence of something). Thus for Quine, a necessary truth is just a statement such that nobody has given us any interesting alternatives which would lead us to question it. For Sellars, to say that a report of a passing thought is incorrigible is to say that nobody has yet suggested a good way of predicting and controlling human behavior which does not take sincere first-person contemporary reports of thoughts at face-value. The second alternative leads to "ontological" explanations of the relations between minds and meanings, minds and immediate data of awareness, universals and particulars, thought and language, consciousness and brains, and so on. For philosophers like Chisholm and Bergmann, such explanations *must* be attempted if the realism of common sense is to be preserved. The aim of all such explanations is to make truth something more than what Dewey called "warranted assertability": more than what our peers will, *ceteris paribus*, let us get away with saying. Such explanations, when ontological, usually take the form of a redescription of the object of knowledge so as to "bridge the gap" between it and the knowing subject. To choose between these approaches is to choose between truth as "what it is good for us to believe" and truth as "contact with reality."

PART II

Solidarity Versus Objectivity

In our culture, the notions of "science," "rationality," "objectivity" and "truth" are bound up with one another. Science is thought of as offering "hard," "objective" truth—truth as correspondence to reality, the only sort of truth worthy of the name. Humanists—philosophers, theologians, historians, literary critics—have to worry about whether they are being "scientific"—whether they are entitled to think of their conclusions, no matter how carefully argued, as worthy of the term "true." We tend to identify seeking "objective truth" with "using reason," and so we think of the natural sciences as paradigms of rationality. We also think of rationality as a matter of following procedures laid down in advance, of being "methodical." So we tend to use "methodical," "rational," "scientific" and "objective" as synonyms.

Worries about "cognitive status" and "objectivity" are characteristic of a secularized culture in which the scientist replaces the priest. The scientist is now seen as the person who keeps humanity in touch with something beyond itself. As the universe was depersonalized, beauty (and, in time, even moral goodness) came to be thought of as "subjective." So truth is now thought of as the only point at which human beings are responsible to something non-human. A commitment to "rationality" and to "method" is thought to be a recognition of this responsibility. The scientist becomes a moral exemplar, one who selflessly exposes himself again and again to the hardness of facts.

One result of this way of thinking is that any academic discipline which wants a place at the trough, but is unable to offer the predictions and the technology provided by the natural sciences, must either pretend to imitate science of find some way of obtaining "cognitive status" without the necessity of discovering facts. Practitioners of these disciplines must either affiliate themselves with this quasi-priestly order by using terms like "behavioral sciences" or else find something other than "fact" to be concerned with. People in the humanities typically choose the latter strategy. They describe themselves either as concerned with "values" as opposed to facts, or as developing and inculcating habits of "critical reflection."

Neither sort of rhetoric is very satisfactory. No matter how much humanists talk about "objective values," the phrase always sounds vaguely confused. It gives with one hand what it takes back with the other. The distinction between the objective and the subjective was designed to parallel that between fact and value, so an objective value sounds vaguely mythological as a winged horse. Talk about the humanists' special skill at critical reflection fares no better. Nobody really believes that philosophers or literary critics are better at critical thinking, or at taking big broad views of things, than theoretical physicists or microbiologists. So society tends to ignore both these kinds of rhetoric. It treats humanities as on a par with the arts, and thinks of both as providing pleasure rather than truth. Both are, to be sure, thought of as providing "high" rather than "low" pleasure. But an elevated and spiritual sort of pleasure is still a long way from the grasp of a truth.

These distinctions between hard facts and soft values, truth and pleasure, and objectivity and subjectivity are awkward and clumsy instruments. They are not suited to divide up culture; they create more difficulties than they resolve. It would be best to find another vocabulary, to start afresh. But in order to do so we first have to find a new way of describing the natural sciences. It is not a question of debunking or downgrading the natural sciences, but simply of ceasing to see them on the model of the priest. We need to stop thinking of science as the place where the human mind confronts the world. We need a way of explaining why scientists are, and deserve to be, moral exemplars which does not depend on a distinction between objective fact and something softer, squishier and more dubious.

To get to such a way of thinking we can start by distinguishing two senses of the term "rationality." In one sense, the one I have already discussed, to be rational is to be methodical: that is, to have criteria for success laid down in advance. We think of poets and painters as using some other faculty than "reason" in their work because, by their own confession, they are not sure of what they want to do before they have done it. They make up new standards of achievement as they go along. By contrast, we think of judges as knowing in advance what criteria a brief will have to satisfy in order to invoke a favorable decision, and of businessmen as setting well-defined goals and being judged by their success in achieving them. Law and business are good examples of rationality, but the scientist, knowing in advance what would count as disconfirming his hypothesis and prepared to abandon that hypothesis as a result of the unfavorable outcome of a single experiment, seems a truly heroic example. Further, we seem to have a clear criterion of the success of a scientific theory—namely, its ability to predict, and thereby to enable us to control some portion of the world. If to be rational means to be able to lay down criteria in advance, then it is plausible to take natural science as the paradigm of rationality.

The trouble is that in this sense of "rational" the humanities are never going to qualify as rational activities. If the humanities are concerned with ends rather than means, then there is no way to evaluate their success in terms of antecedently specified criteria. If we already knew what criteria we wanted to satisfy, we would not worry about whether we were pursuing the right ends. If we thought we knew the goals of culture and society in advance, we would have no use for the humanities—as totalitarian societies in fact do not. It is characteristic of democracies and pluralistic societies to redefine their goals continually. But if to be rational means to satisfy criteria, then this process of redefinition will be bound to be nonrational. So if the humanities are to be viewed as rational activities, rationality will have to be thought of as something other than the satisfaction of criteria which are statable in advance.

[The second] meaning of "rational" is, in fact, available. In this sense, the word means something like "sane" or "reasonable" rather than "methodical." It names a set of moral virtues: tolerance, respect for the opinion of those around one, willingness to listen, reliance on persuasion rather than force. These are the virtues which members of a civilized society must possess if the society is to endure. In this sense of "rational," the word means something more like "civilized" than like "methodical." When so construed, the distinction between the rational and the irrational has nothing in particular to do with the difference between the arts and the sciences. On this construction, to be rational is simply to discuss any topic—religious, literary, or scientific—in a way which eschews dogmatism, defensiveness, and righteous indignation.

There is no problem about whether, in this latter, weaker sense the humanities are "rational disciplines." Usually humanists display the moral virtues in question. Sometimes they do not, but then sometimes scientists don't either. Yet these moral virtues are felt to be not enough. Both humanists and the public hanker after rationality in the first, stronger sense of the term: a sense which is associated with objective truth, correspondence to reality, method and criteria.

We should not try to satisfy this hankering, but rather try to eradicate it. No matter what one's opinion of the secularization of culture, it was a mistake to try to make the natural scientist into a new sort of priest, a link between the human and the non-human. So was the idea that some sorts of truths are "objective" whereas others are merely "subjective" or "relative"—the attempt to divide up the set of true sentences into "genuine knowledge" and "mere opinion," or into the "factual" and the "judgmental." So was the idea that the scientist has a special method which, if only the humanists would apply it to ultimate values, would give us the same kind of self-confidence about moral ends as we now have about technological means. I think that we should content ourselves with the second, "weaker" conception of rationality and avoid the first, "stronger" conception. We should avoid the idea that there is some special virtue in knowing in advance what criteria you are going to satisfy, in having standards by which to measure progress.

[Is Science Rational?]

One can make these issues somewhat more concrete by taking up the current controversy among philosophers about the "rationality of science." For some twenty years, ever since the publication of Thomas Kuhn's book *The Structure of Scientific Revolutions*, philosophers have been debating the question of "whether science is rational." Attacks on Kuhn for being "irrational" are now as frequent and urgent as, in the 1930s and 1940s, were attacks on the logical positivists for saying that moral judgments were "meaningless." We are constantly being warned of the danger of "relativism" which will beset us if we give up our attachment to objectivity and to the idea of rationality as obedience to criteria.

Whereas Kuhn's enemies routinely accuse him of reducing science to "mob psychology," and pride themselves on having (by a new theory of meaning or reference or verisimilitude) vindicated the "rationality of science," his pragmatic friends (such as myself) routinely congratulate him on having softened the distinction between science and nonscience. . . . [H]e has said that "there is no theory-independent way to reconstruct phrases like 'really there.'" He has asked whether it really helps "to imagine that there is some one full, objective, true account of nature and that the proper measure of scientific achievement is the extent to which it brings us closer to the ultimate goal." We pragmatists quote these passages incessantly in the course of our effort to enlist Kuhn in our campaign to drop the objective-subjective distinction altogether.

What I am calling "pragmatism" might also be called "left-wing Kuhnianism." It has also been rather endearingly called (by one of its critics, Clark Glymour) "the new fuzziness," because it is an attempt to blur just those distinctions between the objective and the subjective and between fact and value which the criterial conception of rationality has developed. We fuzzies would like to substitute the idea of "unforced agreement" for that of "objectivity." We should like to put all culture on an epistemological level (or get rid of the idea of "epistemological level"). . . . On our view, "truth" is a univocal term. It applies equally to the judgments of lawyers, anthropologists, physicists, philologists and literary critics. There is point in assigning degrees of "objectivity" or "hardness" to such disciplines. For the presence of unforced agreement in all of them gives us everything in the way of "objective truth" which one could possibly want: namely, intersubjective agreement.

As soon as one says that all there is to objectivity is intersubjectivity, one is likely to be accused of being a relativist. That is the epithet traditionally applied to pragmatists. But this epithet is ambiguous. It can name any of three different views:

1. the silly and self-refuting view that every belief is as good as every other.
2. the wrong-headed view that "true" is an equivocal term, having as many meanings as there are contexts of justification.
3. the ethnocentric view that there is nothing to be said about either truth or rationality apart from descriptions of the familiar procedures of justification which a given society—*ours*—uses in one or another area of inquiry.

The pragmatist does hold this third, ethnocentric view. But he does not hold the first or the second view of relativism.

But "relativism" is not an appropriate term to describe this sort of ethnocentrism. For we pragmatists are not holding a positive theory which says that something is relative to something else. Instead, we are making the purely *negative* point that we would be better off without the traditional distinctions between knowledge and opinion, construed as the distinction between truth as correspondence to reality and truth as a commendatory term for well-justified beliefs. Our opponents call this negative claim "relativistic" because they cannot imagine that anybody would seriously deny that truth has an intrinsic nature. So when we say that there is nothing to be said about truth save that each of us will commened as true those beliefs which he or she finds good to believe, the realist is inclined to interpret this as one more positive theory about the nature of truth: a theory according to which truth is simply the contemporary opinion of a chosen individual or group. Such a theory would, of course, be self-refuting. But we pragmatists do not have a theory of truth, much less a relativistic one. As partisans of solidarity, our account of the value of cooperative human enquiry has only an ethical base, not an epistemological or metaphysical one.

To say that we must be ethnocentric may sound suspicious, but this will only happen if we identify ethnocentricism with pigheaded refusal to talk to representatives of other communities. In my sense of ethnocentricism, to be ethnocentric is simply to work by our own lights. The defense of ethnocentrism is simply that there are no other lights to work by. Beliefs suggested by another individual or another culture must be tested by trying to weave them together with beliefs which we already have. . . .

This way of thinking runs counter to the attempts, familiar since the eighteenth century, to think of political liberalism as based on a conception of the nature of man. To most thinkers of the Enlightenment, it seemed clear that the access to Nature which physical science had provided should now be followed by the establishment of social, political and economic institutions which were "in accordance with Nature." Ever since, liberal social thought has centered around social reform as made possible by objective knowledge of what human beings are like—not knowledge of what Greeks or Frenchmen or Chinese are like, but of humanity as such. This tradition dreams of a universal human community which will exhibit a non-parochial solidarity because it is the expression of an ahistorical human nature.

Philosophers who belong to this tradition, who wish to ground solidarity in objectivity, have to construe truth as correspondence to reality. So they must construct an epistemology which has room for a kind of justification which is not merely social but natural, springing from human nature itself, and made possible by a link between that part of nature and the rest of nature. By contrast we pragmatists, who wish to reduce objectivity to solidarity, do not require either a metaphysics or an epistemology. . . . We see the gap between truth and justification not as something to be bridged by isolating a natural and trans-cultural sort of rationality which can be used to criticize certain cultures and praise others, but simply as the gap between the actual good and the possible better. From a pragmatist point of view, to say that what is rational for us now to believe may not be *true*, is simply to say that somebody may come up with a better idea. . . .

Another reason for describing us as "relativistic" is that we pragmatists drop the idea that enquiry is destined to converge to a single point—that Truth is "out there" waiting for human beings to arrive at it. This idea seems to us an unfortunate attempt to carry a religious conception over into a secular culture. All that is worth preserving of the claim that rational inquiry will converge to a single point is the claim that we must be able to explain why past false views were held in the past, and thus explain how we go about re-educating our benighted ancestors. To say that we think we're heading in the right direction is just to say, with Kuhn, that we can, by hindsight, tell the story of the past as a story of progress.

But the fact that we can trace such a direction and tell such a story does not mean that we have come closer to a goal which is out there waiting for us. We cannot, I think, imagine a moment at which the human race could settle back and say, "Well, now that we've finally arrived at the Truth we can relax." Paul Feyerabend is right in suggesting that we should discard the metaphor of inquiry, and human activity generally, as converging rather than proliferating, becoming more unified rather than more diverse. On the contrary, we should *relish* that thought that the sciences as well as the arts will *always* provide a spectacle of fierce competition between alternative theories, movements and schools. The end of human activity is not rest, but rather richer and better human activity. We should think of human progress as making it possible for human beings to do more interesting things and be more interesting people, not as heading toward a place which has somehow been prepared for us in advance. To drop the criterial conception of rationality in favor of the pragmatist conception would be to give up the idea of Truth as something to which we were responsible. Instead we should think of "true" as a word which applies to those beliefs upon which we are able to agree, as roughly synonymous with "justified.". . .

. . . Pragmatists would like to replace the desire for objectivity—the desire to be in touch with a reality which is more than some community with which we identify ourselves—with the desire for solidarity with that community. They think that the habits of relying on persuasion rather than force, of respect for opinions of colleagues, of curiosity and eagerness for new data and ideas, are the *only* virtues which scientists have. They do not think that there is an intellectual virtue called "rationality" over and above these moral virtues. . . .

Pragmatists interpret the goal of inquiry (in any sphere of culture) as the attainment of an appropriate mixture of unforced agreement with tolerant disagreement (where what counts as appropriate is determined, within that sphere, by trial and error). Such a reinterpretation of our sense of responsibility would, if carried through, gradually make unintelligible the subject-object model of enquiry, the child-parent model of moral obligation, and the correspondence theory of truth. A world in which those models, and that theory, no longer had any intuitive appeal would be a pragmatist's paradise.

When Dewey urged that we try to create such a paradise he was said to be irresponsible. For, it was said, he left us bereft of weapons to use against our enemies; he gave us nothing with which to "answer the Nazis." When we new fuzzies try to revise Dewey's repudiation of criteriology we are said to be "relativistic." We must, people say, believe that every coherent view is as good as every other, since we have no "outside" touchstone for choice among such views. We are said to leave the general public defenseless against the witch doctor, the defender of creationism, or anyone else who is clever and patient enough to deduce a consistent and wide-ranging set of theorems from his "alternative first principles."

Nobody is convinced when we fuzzies say that we can be just as morally indignant as the next philosopher. We are suspected of being contritely fallibilist when righteous fury is called for. Even when we actually display appropriate emotions we get nowhere, for we are told that we have no *right* to these emotions. When we suggest that one of the few things we know (or need to know) about truth is that it is what wins in a free and open encounter, we are told that we have defined "true" as "satisfies the standards of our community." But we pragmatists do not hold this relativist view. We do not infer from "There is no way to step outside communities to a neutral standpoint" to "There is no rational way to justify liberal communities over totalitarian communities." For that inference involves just the notion of "rationality" as a set of ahistorical principles which pragmatists abjure. What we in fact infer is that there is no way to beat totalitarians in argument by appealing to shared common premises, and no point in pretending that a common human nature makes the totalitarians unconsciously hold such premises.

The claim that we fuzzies have no right to be furious at moral evil, no right to commend our views as true unless we simultaneously refute ourselves by claiming that there are objects out there which *make* those views true, begs all the theoretical questions. But it gets to the practical and moral heart of the matter. This is the question of whether notions like "unforced agreement" and "free and open encounter"—descriptions of social situations—can take the place in our moral lives of notions like "the world," "the will of God," "the moral law," "what our beliefs are trying to represent accurately" and "what makes our beliefs true." All the philosophical presuppositions which make Hume's fork seem inevitable are ways of suggesting that human communities must justify their existence by striving to attain a non-human goal. To suggest that we can forget about Hume's fork [the radical separation of facts from values], forget about being responsible to what is "out there," is to suggest that human communities can justify their existence only by comparisons with other actual and possible human communities. . . .

Imagine . . . that a few years from now you open your copy of the *New York Times* and read that the philosophers, in convention assembled, have unanimously agreed that values are objective, science rational, with a matter of correspondence to reality, etc. Recent breakthroughs in semantics and metaethics, the report goes on, have caused the last remaining non-cognitivists in ethics to recant. Similarly breakthroughs in the philosophy of science have led Kuhn formally to abjure his claim that there is no theory-independent way to reconstruct statements about what is "really there." All the new fuzzies have repudiated all their former views. By way of making amends for the intellectual confusion which the philosophical profession has recently caused, the philosophers have adopted a short, crisp set of standards of rationality and morality. Next year the convention is expected to adopt the report of the committee charged with formulating a standard of aesthetic taste.

Surely the public reaction to this would not be "Saved!" but rather "Who on earth do these philosophers think they *are*?" It is one of the best things about the form of intellectual life we Western liberals lead that this *would* be our reaction. No matter how much we moan about the disorder and confusion of the current philosophical scene, about the treason of the clerks, we do not really want things any other way. What prevents us from relaxing and enjoying the new fuzziness is perhaps no more than cultural lag, the fact that the rhetoric of the Englightenment praised the emerging natural sciences in a vocabulary which was left over from a less liberal and tolerant era. This rhetoric enshrined all the old philosophical opposition between mind and world, appearance and reality, subject and object, truth and pleasure. Dewey thought that it was the continued prevalence of such opposition which prevented us from seeing that modern science was a new and promising invention, a way of life which had not existed before and which ought to be encouraged and imitated, something which required a new rhetoric rather than justification by an old one.

Suppose that Dewey were right about this, and that eventually we learn to find the fuzziness which results from breaking down such opposition spiritually comforting rather than morally offensive. What would the rhetoric of the culture, and in particular of the humanities, sound like? Presumably it would be more Kuhnian, in the sense that it would mention particular concrete achievements—paradigms—more, and "method" less. There would be less talk about rigor and more about originality. The image of the great scientist would not be of somebody who got it right but of somebody who made it new. The new rhetoric would draw more on the vocabulary of Romantic poetry and socialist politics, and less on that of Greek metaphysics, religious morality or Englightenment scientism. A scientist would rely on a sense of solidarity with the rest of her profession, rather than a picture of herself as battling through the veils of illusion, guided by the light of reason.

If all this happened, the term "science," and thus the opposition between the humanities, the arts and the sciences might gradually fade away. Once "science" was deprived of an honorific sense, we might not need it for taxonomy. . . . The people now called "scientists" would no longer think of themselves as members of a quasi-priestly order nor would the public think of themselves as in the care of such an order.

In this situation, the "humanities" would no longer think of themselves as such, nor would they share a common rhetoric. Each of the disciplines which now fall under that rubric would worry as little about its method, cognitive status or "philosophical foundations" as do mathematics, civil engineering or sculpture. For terms which denoted disciplines would not be thought to divide "subject matter," chunks of the world which had "interfaces" with each other. Rather, they would be thought to denote communities whose boundaries were as fluid as the interests of their members. In this heyday of the fuzzies, there would be as little reason to be self-conscious about the nature and status of one's discipline as, in the ideal democratic community, about the nature and status of one's race or sex. For one's ultimate loyalty would be to the larger community which permitted and encouraged this kind of freedom and insouciance. This community would serve no higher end than its own preservation and self-improvement, the preservation and enhancement of civilization. It would identify rationality with that effort, rather than with the desire for objectivity. So it would feel no need for a foundation more solid than reciprocal loyalty.

Chapter 38

Margarita Rosa Levin

Margarita Rosa Levin received her Ph.D. from the University of Minnesota and teaches philosophy at Stern College. She is the author of several articles on the philosophy of science and environmental ethics. In the selection that follows, she defends the notion of objective knowledge against contemporary critics such as Richard Rorty, radical feminists, Marxists, Jacques Derrida, and others. After defining *objectivity* as "intersubjectively accessible knowledge . . . independent of anyone's biases, traditions, wishes, or other influences," she examines (1) the general philosophical arguments against the possibility of objectivity, (2) those grounded in the history and sociology of science, and (3) those specifically grounded in the social sciences. Levin argues that the antirationalist arguments not only fail but also presuppose objectivity even in their attempt to undermine it.

FOR FURTHER READING

See "For Further Reading" in Chapter 37.

A Defense of Objectivity

UPHOLDING TRUTH: OBJECTIVITY VERSUS SKEPTICISM AND NIHILISM

It is a paradox that the twentieth century, which has witnessed the greatest triumphs of science and technology, should also be the century in which the ideal of objectivity has been subjected to the most severe challenges. By *objectivity* I mean inter-subjectively accessible knowledge, by definition truly independent of anyone's biases, traditions, wishes, or other influences. The idea that objectivity is not only possible but also regularly realized continues to underpin modern natural science. This same objectivity was a goal that initially inspired the social sciences.

Just *why* the denial of objectivity is so alluring to modern thinkers is perhaps best left to future psychologists and historians. I confine myself to classifying, analyzing, and replying to the various arguments purporting to establish nihilism—the thesis that there is no fixed reality—or skepticism—the thesis that we can't know what that reality is. I claim no great originality or completeness. What follows

This article was commissioned for *The Theory of Knowledge*, edited by L. Pojman (Wadsworth Publishing Co., 1998) and is reprinted by permission of the author.

is meant as a representative sample of current positions.

The order I have chosen sorts arguments against objectivity into four (somewhat artificial) categories that descend in degree of generality. I begin by examining *general* philosophical arguments against the possibility of objectivity in the construction of theories. Then I turn to arguments with similar conclusions but which are grounded in the *history and sociology of science*. Since the social sciences seem particularly vulnerable to charges of bias, I next focus on arguments that single them out. I conclude with arguments against objectivity based on specific claims about *the nature of society and communication*.

GENERAL SKEPTICAL AND NIHILIST ARGUMENTS

One hallmark of objective theory-making is testability. A theory must be tested; if it fails its test, if its predictions turn out false, or it is somehow incompatible with the evidence, it must be rejected. But W. V. O. Quine and Pierre Duhem have separately pointed out that it is never *logically* necessary to discard a hypothesis or theory because of disconfirming evidence. Their position, generally referred to as the Quine–Duhem thesis, is that one can always consistently alter one's "auxiliary assumptions" to accommodate the new evidence. Such assumptions are inevitable: The factors mentioned in one's hypotheses always connect with other factors. There is no getting around this; you can't test everything at once. But it does mean that the seeming failure of a hypothesis to pass its test could, *in principle*, be attributed to an erroneous auxiliary assumption. For example, when testing whether a new medicine will lower high fevers, we must make certain assumptions about how thermometers work. If after administering the medicine we find thermometers inserted in treated patients continue to register high fevers, we *could* argue that the medicine has impaired the ability of the thermometers to record body temperature. There is no logical absurdity in this. If *A* and *B* together imply *C* but *C* turns out to be false, all that follows is that *either A* or *B* (or possibly both) is false.

The relevance of this point to objectivity is that, if we can always save any theory in the face of conflicting evidence, then we can never know any theory to be true. If you *know A*, you can not believe or reasonably assert not-*A*, no matter what the evidence. Since, given the Quine–Duhem thesis, you can *always* believe or assert not-*A*, you can never know *A*. To put the point intuitively, the world never forces acceptance or rejection of theories. Within very wide limits we can believe what we want.

This argument contains two themes that will recur. The first is the implicit use of mathematical certainty as a paradigm: If the data do not *entail* some one theory, then either there is no objective "fact of the matter" or (a weaker conclusion) we can never know what that fact is. The second theme is revealed when it is asked how the theorizer, or the Quinean himself, *knows* that an experiment requires some adjustment to his theory. The situation is evidently one in which it must be assumed to be *objectively true* that evidence and theory conflict. Hence, the second theme: appeal to the concept of objective knowledge in arguments that purport to dispose of it. Even the enemies of objectivity rely on it.

This latter point might be blunted if one could strongly distinguish theory from data—perhaps we can know the *data* are true, for example that the mercury in a thermometer has reached a certain level, but we cannot know that any *theory* is true. But even if this distinction is drawn, surely the knowledge that data conflict with theory would be located on the *theoretical* side of such a line.

However that may be, and whatever the merits of the Quine–Duhem thesis as such, it cannot justify doubts about objectivity. Quine's point, it must be remembered, is a *logical* one—that it is always logically possible to preserve any theory. Another way of saying this is that the language of theories is not definable in terms of the data language. But this observation does not show that there are no objective truths beyond the data; it does not even address that question. Nor does Quine's thesis entail that we cannot *know* that one interpretation of the data is right—unless, again, it is assumed that knowledge requires mathematical certainty. Just because you can *believe* not-*A* doesn't mean you can *rationally* believe it. When you look at any concrete case, you realize how irrational it is, after a certain point, to continue to "make changes elsewhere" rather than accept the failure of hypothesis. For example, we were not compelled to accept Copernicus's heliocentric account of planetary motion. We could have kept Ptolemy's geocentric model by assuming the other planets of followed strange orbits that circled back on themselves (epicycles) and that would have accounted for the observations of their motion in the night skies. But that would have required assuming far more complexity than expected and only for the purpose of saving a particular theory, not for any independent reason. The accepted position since Copernicus has been that heliocentrism is the simplest theory that fits the data. Data need not entail a theory to compel acceptance.

As noted, skepticism based on Quine's thesis works best with a sharp line between theory and data. The next argument rests on the opposite claim: "Theory informs observation." This is the view that theory influences observation to such an extent that the two cannot be distinguished. Two observers with different theories will allegedly disagree on what is supposed to be a common database. Furthermore, on this view, it is impossible to even experience data without uncounsciously interpreting them according to some theory. It is therefore impossible to achieve a neutral perspective from which to judge competing theories.

The *locus classicus* of this position is a passage from *Patterns of Discovery* in which Norwood Hanson imagines the dawn as viewed by Tycho Brahe, a Ptolemaic, and Johannes Kepler, a Copernican:

> Tycho sees the sun beginning its journey from horizon to horizon. He sees that from some celestial vantage point the sun . . . could be watched circling our fixed earth. . . . Kepler will see the horizon dipping, or turning away, from our local fixed star. The shift from sunrise to horizon-turn is . . . occasioned by differences between what Tycho and Kepler think they know.

We are supposed to conclude that two observers with different theories *see* differently and therefore lack common ground. Fortunately, this thought experiment is one we can all perform ourselves. Modern Americans have assimilated more thoroughly than Kepler the idea that Earth goes around the Sun, yet we do not summon our children to view the data by saying "come see this beautiful Earth-turn." Sunrise looks to us just as it did to Brahe. The difference between ourselves and him is that we know that the Sun's apparent motion is deceptive.

So the argument in this particular case fails because one of its premises is false. Despite holding different theories, observers will see the same thing. Nor is the fault in the example. Consider the series of experiments in which several people around a table were asked to compare two objects that were clearly of different lengths. All but one person had been secretly instructed to insist that the objects were the same length. The test subject was therefore under social pressure to deny the evidence of his senses and quite often succumbed and agreed with the rest. This experiment makes no sense and establishes nothing about the influence of nonperceptual factors on perception unless there is an objective fact of the matter as to how the objects appeared to the participants and what their true lengths were. Furthermore, critics of objectivity can get no mileage from this example unless they claim that it actually happened. Once again the critics of objectivity must rely on it for their arguments.

A different version of nihilism is encapsulated in the phrase "we make the world." Many distinguished contemporary philosophers—Nelson Goodman, Richard Rorty, Hillary Putnam—defend some version of it. I will first discuss the fairly accessible version presented by Robert Schwartz in "Let Me Make You a Star." Schwartz argues that human beings, through the order they impose by their thinking, somehow determine what the world is. (What they impose the order *on* is not made clear.) This is reminiscent of Kant's theory of knowledge, but it differs in that the mind's categories are not seen as fixed and a priori. Here is Schwartz:

> Whether there are stars, and what they are like, are facts that can *emerge* only in our attempts to describe and organize the world. The world is not given to us ready-made with stars . . . [T]he property of being a star would lack definitive character and boundaries until fashioned in the course of describing the heavens and accounting for its doings.

To the natural objection that surely people don't *literally* make stars, he responds "Of course they don't! . . . We never compressed huge quantities of gas and set them aglow in the heavens above . . . *It*, the sun, was in the ready-made world all along. Yet, independent of our fashioning the relevant properties and kinds, questions about what *it* is really like *have neither any force nor any answers*" (pp. 437–438).

Schwartz seems to be confusing our freedom to *talk* about something—we can call the Missouri River a separate river or an arm of the Mississippi—with our inability to change the facts of what we're talking about; for example, the Missouri is wet and cold. However much we theorize about it, if we fall in it and can't swim, we will drown.

Schwartz does grant that "there are constraints on our scientific schemes of classification and organization," although these are not spelled out. They are *not* a function of an independently existing world because the idea of "[an] external ready-made version of the world—untinged by our cognitive efforts—is not a notion we can have much confidence in making sense of."

Well, if someone insists that he doesn't understand an idea, you can't force him to admit he does. The most you can do is compare it to another idea that he does understand. So consider a newborn baby lying in his crib, lacking a theoretical framework to make sense of those enduring entities we know to be mother, light, walls, and so on. It hardly makes sense to speak of his knowledge of them, yet the world contains those things anyway. Everything Schwartz says about us can be said of the baby, and that is quite consistent with a definite world existing independently of our knowledge.

Schwartz's promise to "make" a star is most plausible when seen as a promise to remake classification schemes. Most would say that Jupiter is not a star because, unlike our Sun, it is not a burning globe of gas. But one could classify Jupiter as a star because it is a gas giant and just say it is non-burning. In this sense, we "make" Jupiter a star when we so classify it. But it is trivial to switch from one scheme to the other. There is no real disagreement between someone who says there are nine planets and someone who says there are eight planets and one non-burning star, just alternate ways of describing the same facts. So Schwartz's point is the triviality that the world can be described in several ways, not that there is no fixed world until we get around to describing it.

Another opponent of objectivity with a preference for words over facts is Richard Rorty. In *Philosophy and the Mirror of Nature*, he rejects all metaphors about knowledge that suggest that true statements about the world accurately reflect an independent reality, that reality needs to be uncovered or illuminated. He also repudiates any sharp distinction between the sciences and the humanities, between knowledge and opinion, between fact and value. Adopting the term "fuzziness" for his position, he writes:

> We fuzzies would like to substitute the idea of "unforced agreement" for that of "objectivity." We should like to put all culture on an epistemological level . . . [Truth] applies equally to the judgments of lawyers, anthropologists, physicists, philologists and literary critics. There is no point in assigning degrees of "objectivity" or "hardness" to such disciplines. For the presence of unforced agreement in all of them gives us everything in the way of "objective truth" which one could possibly want: namely, intersubjective agreement.

Rorty gives no specific examples of *how* people arrive at "unforced agreement" other than by pointing to evidence. We can certainly imagine fashions in literary criticism as arising from "unforced agreement." If there are several incompatible theories about whether Hamlet's madness is real or feigned, no one will much care. But how do we handle the case of a significant fraction of our population coming to "unforced agreement" to give up the germ theory of disease and adopt the view that illness is due to negative thoughts? Suppose they act on their agreement and refuse immunizations, knowingly sell contaminated meat, and let animals foul the water supply. Does Rorty really think there's no objective truth here, that agreement is the end of the matter? Won't *reality* force them to change their minds?

He does anticipate that critics will misread him:

> [W]hen we say that there is nothing to be said about truth save that each of us will commend as true those beliefs which he or she finds good to believe, the realist is inclined to interpret this as one more positive theory about the nature of truth: a theory according to which truth is simply the contemporary opinion of a chosen individual's group. Such a theory would, of course, be self-refuting. But pragmatists do not have a theory of truth, much less a relativistic one. As partisans of solidarity, our account of the value of cooperative human enquiry has only an ethical base, not an epistemological or metaphysical one.

Well, Rorty can *say* he doesn't have a theory—but if you declare that talk of *X* is meaningless, that opposing views of *X* are wrong, that *X* does not exist, then you certainly *do* have a theory of *X*.

Rorty keeps mocking the picture of human knowledge as seeking to come *closer* to the truth, of progress in reaching "a place which has somehow been prepared in advance." Michael Devitt has an apt response: Belief in objective truth, realism about the world, is *not* the thesis that people *will* know everything. Realism has nothing to do with human activity. To say that there is life on planets in other solar systems is not to say that we will ever contact them, that they have ever visited here, or that some other group is responsible for seeding life both here and there. It is to say that there is life on other planets, period.

Finally, when Rorty says that "from a pragmatist point of view, to say that what is rational for us now to believe may not be *true*, is simply to say that somebody *may come up with a better* idea," one has to ask how it can be better if it isn't true or truer. How does one sort out the unpleasant truth from the delightful delusion? This is an old objection to pragmatism, and Rorty does not avoid it.

MORE SPECIFIC SKEPTICAL AND NIHILISTIC ARGUMENTS

Even if unbiased investigation is theoretically possible, it is sometimes argued, in practice, investigators are human. They have blindspots, preconceptions, and unconscious motives. You cannot expect objectivity from an investigator even if he sincerely believes he has rid himself of bias.

This is an argument that feminists stress: Because of their male gender and their socialization, men are unreliable about any area where gender plays a role. (Feminists are inconsistent—sometimes they attack objectivity *in toto*; at other times they only question the possibility of male objectivity.) At a minimum this includes research in animal and human behavior; more extreme feminists extend this claim to the physical sciences. Feminists cite as an example the work of early male entomologists who erroneously assumed that the large insects that seemed to dominate hives and anthills were "kings."

Now this example clearly has no force unless one can go on to say that further research showed that the "ruling" insects were more properly labeled "queens." Speaking generally, one cannot present an example of investigator bias without also presenting the objective fact that the investigator has missed. So it is unnecessary to examine in detail any instances of bias from the history of science that are produced to support skepticism or nihilism. All such instances self-destruct in the same way.

Let us now consider a more sophisticated argument from the history and sociology of science, namely, that the concept of truth is *unnecessary* for describing what scientists do. On this view, first proposed by Thomas Kuhn in *The Structure of Scientific Revolutions* and adopted by many others, the history of science is significantly like the history of fashion. Just as hemlines go up or down, and different parts of the body are exaggerated or hidden, so too do scientific theories change through time. Experiments are performed, some problems are solved, others go unsolved, new theories are proposed—the old guard defends its views, the young rebels take over. But, just as there is no "correct" dress, there is no "true" theory. We need make no reference to external reality in explaining why scientists believe their theories.

I would make three points about this view. First, not just science but any activity whatever can be redescribed in terms (technically known as "metalinguistic") that make no apparent reference to an external reality. Consider traffic control. The Department of Transportation could be said to be concerned not with actual collisions and traffic jams but with written reports. The department is not out to reduce pedestrian deaths at intersections but to solve the pedestrian-death problem by reducing the number of pedestrian-death-at-intersection reports (the sort of "success" bureaucracies are said to pursue). The history of traffic technology, of the introduction of parking meters and traffic lights, could be told "internally" in terms of decisions taken to install such devices, of satisfaction with their effect on traffic reports, and possibly physical descriptions of the apparatus—all in language that made no commitment to the existence of actual automobiles. Such recasting into metalinguistic form hardly proves that cars are needless conceptual baggage.

It should also be stressed that Kuhn's view is not one scientists take of their own activity. Most scientists believe they are coming ever closer to the truth about how nature works. They may well be mistaken about whether they are succeeding, but it is arrogance for philosophers to claim to know better than scientists what scientists are trying to do.

The third and strongest point is that the nihilist account makes the success of science inexplicable. This is an old problem nihilists have never resolved. Even if they deny any predictive power or explanatory success to the social sciences, they must acknowledge the success of the physical sciences, especially in applications such as engineering. Yet if there is no objective truth, if scientists are merely playing games with each other, this success is a miracle.

Perhaps the most promising response to the success of science is to hark back to the Quine–Duhem thesis and argue that the success of a scientific theory does not logically entail its truth. This is correct. It is also true that many theories can be consistent with a narrow set of observations. But as a theory is tested, refined, and reconfirmed under many different circumstances, it becomes less and less likely that a wildly different theory will do a better job. It is safe to say that we know that certain diseases are caused by germs even though the data do not *entail* this, and many questions about germs remain open. To demand that knowledge have the certainty of mathematics is to use the word *knowledge* in a nonstandard way. You *know* you are reading this article even though it is theoretically possible that you are under a hypnotically induced illusion. Indeed, the demand for absolute certainty is unsatisfiable even in mathematics, since it is always possible that we are systematically confused about some basic rule of inference.

It appears to be rhetorically effective to label the position just stated "naive" realism. One is evidently expected to retract one's views rather than admit to naiveté, but I, for one, will not back off. I won't buy the Brooklyn Bridge, but I will buy the idea that the simplest explanation is the likeliest and the simplest explanation for the success of science is that we are indeed coming nearer to understanding some external reality. Rather than calling my opponents names ("decadent"?), let me challenge them to provide a positive alternative account of the success of science, one that scientists themselves will accept

GENERAL ARGUMENTS FOR SKEPTICISM AND NIHILISM IN THE SOCIAL SCIENCES

The arguments in this category are variations on a single theme: You cannot be objective about what is subjective in nature. The social sciences involve people, and people attach values to their activities, so the social sciences have a normative dimension. Far from seeing it as a problem for social science, some see it as an inevitable, even welcome, aspect of dealing with human beings. Thus, William Outhwaite notes:

> The fact that we are ourselves human beings makes it possible for us to understand what it is like to be another human being, what it is (probably) like to hold the beliefs which other human beings hold, and so on. But this also means that we cannot simply record, in an objective and value-free way, the practices and beliefs of other human beings. The social scientist does not go out into the field as a *tabula rasa* and return with an account of what it is like to be a European car-worker or an African peasant; it is precisely the encounter between the social scientist's own belief and practices and those of the people he . . . is studying which makes up whatever understanding we can have of another social reality.

Indeed, as Outhwaite observes, people and their values are involved on both sides of any inquiry in social science. It is therefore convenient to divide the arguments in this section into those that focus on the values of the human *objects* of social inquiry and those that focus on the values of the inquirer himself.

So let us first ask whether values can be neutrally identified and neturally attributed to others. It seems to me that such attribution is indeed posible. Wittgenstein's celebrated attacks on private languages apply with full force to a private language of values. If evaluating were a private act, people could not learn—as they obviously do learn—what someone means when he says that he "admires" something or "despises" it. There are public indicators of valuing; most clearly, what a culture encourages and discourages—which it is possible to determine at least in principle—is a good sign of what it values. Of course, the values an individual will publicly assent to may not be the values he secretly holds, and ferreting out his true preferences may require considerable ingenuity, but again this is not *in principle* impossible. On the whole, determining values poses no less but no more difficulty than detecting the presence of a shy noctural animal.

But people aren't raccoons, it will be said; detecting guilt is not like detecting leaf eaters in your garden. Two equally remorseful individuals may differ in how much of their feelings they let show and how they show them. There is surely something here inaccessible to ordinary observation. In reply, we must focus again on how we ordinarily spot, for example, guilt. Regret over some past action or inaction typically leads to reluctance to discuss it, expressions of desire that it not be generally known, and possibly the wish that it had never been committed, as well as a desire to be punished for it. These are the sorts of clues that lead me to conclude that a person is experiencing guilt.

To be sure, establishing the same fact about a subject from a different culture requires certain preliminaries, such as acquiring a working knowledge of his language. Aha, says the skeptic, a working knowledge of another language means being able to translate such terms as *guilt* in the first place, and how do we know on the basis of sheer behavior that we are correctly translating such words? Once again, it must be insisted that observable behavior is, in the end, all we *ever* have to go on. No child at his mother's knee has access to his mother's inner states. He knows only what she says and does when she corrects his speech and if this is sufficient to allow the child to learn his mother's words for emotions, it suffices for penetrating an alien language.

However—the skeptic now urges—the problem isn't as simple as just finding the alien's word for "guilt." Correctly identifying his values means, in addition, finding out the sorts of things his culture thinks *ought* to be regretted, the ways in which his culture understands personal responsibility, the culturally approved forms of public displays of emotion—a whole "system of meanings" that must be grasped before guilt can be properly understood. The Irish at a wake behave differently than Jews sitting shiva, yet both are presumably "distressed." In fact, the whole issue of judging foreign values is a special case of *verstehen*. This phrase encapsulates the view that at least some types of behavior are incomprehensible without a certain sympathetic understanding ("verstehen") from the inside of what the behavior means to the participants. Peter Winch had this requirement in mind when he wrote: "A historian or sociologist of religion must himself have some religious feeling if he is to make sense of the religious movement he is studying and understand the considerations which govern the lives of its participants."

Thus, Winch might say, you cannot understand why a born-again Christian might quit his job unless you yourself have experienced a comparable spiritual rebirth. Only then will you realize how even the most pressing material concerns might come to seem unimportant.

Plausible as this may seem, it is simply not true. One need not oneself believe in a world to come to reason that someone who does believe might well lose interest in this world. One need not know what it feels like to have such a belief to make and test predictions about his actions. A great many people understand *Othello* without having endured irrational jealousy. We would do well to remember a quip by Albert Einstein, often cited in this context: It is not the job of science "to *give* the taste of the soup." It *is* the job of science to describe and account for the taste of the soup. Similarly, it is not the job of social science to give the feeling of guilt or "reproduce" the feeling of someone acting within a normative tradition. Its job is to describe the mental state of the agent by the behavior it evokes and its relation to other phenomena.

What do we expect of a social science? Is it information, lawlike statements, predictions, correlations, and unification of seemingly disparate data? Or are social scientists expected to be professional empaths who feel and act like the people they study? Social science should not be conceived so narrowly that one questions whether there has ever been a successful study of human behavior.

The fact is that we *do* understand certain alien "forms of life." Consider the treaties between the various Native American tribes and European settlers. Native Americans did not have the concept of land ownership or, consequently, any idea of the significance that the signing of treaties had for the Europeans. Many of us, accustomed to talk of selling air rights, buying lots, and the distinction between public and private land, find it hard to put ourselves in the natives' frame of mind. Yet we can grasp their system of meanings enough to see how its conflict with that of the European system would have led to trouble on the frontier. You might say that it is not difficult to see the natives' point of view (many environmentalists do say this) and that is why we think we understand them. Well then, consider the focus of the ancient Egyptians on the afterlife, their custom of preserving the body through mummification, filling the tomb with actual goods (food) and representations of goods (statuettes of slaves) needed in the next world. Today's theology is not so literal-minded, and those who expect an afterlife imagine that they will take purely spiritual forms. We can nonetheless discuss and interpret ancient Egyptian finds and even make predictions about future discoveries.

Indeed, it is possible to predict and even influence the behavior of beings whose view of the world we cannot experience, namely, non-humans. None of us, except possibly the blind, have an inking of what it is like to navigate by echolocation as bats do. Scientists have nevertheless analyzed echolocation thoroughly enough to convince bats to try to land on a ledge that isn't there by sending the sort of signals the bat would receive from a genuine ledge.

Having considered the values of the investigated, let us consider the values of the investigator. Neutrally describing behavior to which one is indifferent is hard enough, runs the argument; it is impossible to do justice to practices one considers inhumane, depraved, or unjust. Well, that all depends on what is meant by "doing justice." It certainly seems possible in actual practice to separate fact from values and establish the concrete facts about such institutions as slavery in the antebellum South and Nazi concentration camps. One can deplore these institutions yet ask how they were run and what beliefs sustained them. Did different kinds of plantation workers enjoy different social status? Did German farmers think they would gain anything from the elimination of the Jews?

Let us remember that facts normally *precede* judgments of value, and changes in awareness of facts can and do lead to changes in evaluations. Two recent controversies show at least an intuitive awareness of this on the part of partisans of what might seem like purely normative positions. Opponents of the death penalty, even those who say their opposition is not based on questions of deterrance, almost always deny that capital punishment deters. They thus recognize that how people assess capital punishment depends in large part on what they believe to be its empirical effects. Similarly, those who criticize Harry Truman for dropping the atomic bomb on Japan commonly argue that Japan was on the point of surrender, and they often try to produce documentary evidence for this factual claim. Revisionist historians realize that it is difficult to dispute the decision once it is admitted that it saved millions of lives.

"But," the skeptic asks, "what about the 'big picture'? What caused the Civil War? Did the New Deal hasten the end of the Depression? The facts may not be in dispute, little facts anyway—it's the interpretation of the facts that allows personal values to enter. Values may wait upon facts, but this only tempts historians to shade the facts to reinforce their own values."

The quick answer to this is, "Speak for yourself." A more careful answer begins by admitting that, indeed, we may never have enough data to definitely establish what factors caused the Civil War or even to rank several possible causes in order of importance. And since (for instance) we may never know all of Lincoln's motives for declaring war on the Confederacy, those who approve Lincoln's decision are free to believe that he was acting as he thought his oath of office required, while his critics are free to attribute less flattering motives. The sensible response to the selectivity forced on us by the gaps in the record is not that we can't know *anything* but that there is a difference between uncovering some truths and uncovering them *all*. That we can't know the whole truth does not mean that we can't know any of it. What is more, our inability to find out about something in the past doesn't imply that nothing definite ever happened. Unavoidable ignorance does not justify nihilism, and it is worth noting that ignorance can never be known to be irremediable. A Lincoln diary might turn up tomorrow in some forgotten closet that would help us determine what Lincoln was thinking.

The skeptic is apt to retreat another step and claim that it is the choice of problems and interests that is dictated by values. While true to some extent—although it ignores the contribution of pure curiosity—this is logically irrelevant to the issue of objectivity. Why you become interested in something has no bearing on the quality or validity of your research. A study of driving habits sponsored by General Motors may have merit; a study commissioned by Kelloggs that determines that women prefer Rice Krispies while men prefer Corn Flakes can be as trustworthy as any other study of cereal preferences. To think otherwise is to commit a particularly blatant form of the genetic fallacy. Indeed, a commercially sponsored survey might be *more* reliable, since Kelloggs needs accurate data and doesn't want to be lied to.

It is an *empirical* question whether choice of a topic implies a desire for certain conclusions and, more significantly, whether that desire will blind the investigator to contrary evidence. A relevant experiment involved the submission of papers with identical protocols but different results to social work journals. The version reporting social work intervention in children's environment to be ineffective was rejected significantly more often than the version reporting such intervention to be effective. Interestingly, the negative paper was criticized on methodological grounds when it was identical in that respect to the positive paper. Yet, while this experiment does show something—that social work journals are biased toward reports of the effectiveness of environmental intervention—it *cannot* show that the evaluation of research is always subject to bias. Anyone accepting that strong conclusion would have to think that he accepted it because he was biased (in favor of finding bias everywhere) and not because the conclusion was supported by the evidence. As usual, skepticism defeats itself. There *can't* be evidence that all investigation is biased.

Social scientists are quite aware of the problem of wishes and commitments swaying the critical eye. It is precisely to neutralize such factors that "double-blind" experiments are routinely deployed in experiments. This is especially true for such emotionally charged subjects as beauty and intelligence, or any placebo effect. For instance, a psychologist studying the connection between attractiveness and perceived intelligence would not rely on his own opinion of who was attractive. He—or, better, an assistant unaware of the purpose of the experiment—would show an assortment of photos to a panel of respondents to establish which were generally seen as attractive. Another panel would then be asked for estimates of intelligence based on the photos.

Because investigators, like anyone else, sometimes let their emotions or predilections cloud their judgments, science must be not done in a vacuum. This is why results must be replicable, why raw data must be published so that others may evaluate the arguments and the statistical analyses. It is why people should not be discouraged from engaging in research about those whose background is significantly different from theirs. Failure to appreciate this is *the* error in the often-heard remarks that only blacks should study blacks, only women should study women, and the like. Far from its being the case that you need to be an *X* to study *X*s, non-*X*s are needed to check and correct blindspots that *X*s may have about their own group.

The final objection in this group concerns the reality of social constructs. Personality traits, social forces and institutions, and morale have no obvious physical embodiments. Hence, they might seem more like the impositions of our minds on reality than are the constructs of physics. Proponents of such skepticism generally view the constructs of social theory as vehicles for prejudices and hidden values.

Is there really a problem here? As long as talk about social forces and institutions can be appropriately anchored in talk about observable traits of individuals, there is no *new* objectivity problem. Thus, "socioeconomic status" is epistemologically acceptable because it can be measured in terms of individuals' income, health, and occupation. A more interesting example is the concept of general intelligence, a theoretical construct that is applied to individuals rather than groups but that has drawn criticism for allegedly being arbitrary and value-laden. "Intelligent" is sometimes said to be no more than a label for the middle-class cognitive style or for members of an economic elite that wishes to preserve itself. In fact, although neither a structure nor a process in the brain has been identified as "intelligence," a number of tests of information processing are found to correlate highly with each other, with independent indicators such as academic achievement, and with what people have in mind when they use the word *intelligent*. So talk of intelligence can be anchored in such observables as reaction speed and memorization ability. It is no more suspect than talk of magnetism.

DECONSTRUCTIONIST SKEPTICISM AND NIHILISM

I have not yet addressed doubts concerning objective knowledge of society stemming from Marxism and its currently popular offshoot, deconstuctionism.

Classical Marxism is determinedly iconoclastic and puts great stress on "tensions" and "contradictions" in extant social institutions. Marriage, school, and the legal system supposedly serve the pursuit of power by some economic class. People are unaware of this because they are brainwashed from infancy to see social artifacts as objective and universal. Such institutions need to be "demystified" so people can see what interests they really serve. For example, Marxists claim the family is an economic unit raising future workers for those who control the means of production. The supposed absolute obligation of parents to their children is part of the "false consciousness" induced by capitalism. The way to raise people's consciousness about the function of institutions is to analyze the "contradictions." Television under capitalism, for instance, sells merchandise and keeps workers docile, but by presenting a glamorous world beyond their grasp, it also sows resentment, weakening the capitalist structure.

Michel Foucault stretches this analysis to include language and concepts. Whoever controls discourse controls the categories of thought and hence has "power/knowledge." Categories of description purporting to be objectively correct are merely weapons for seizing control. Thus, psychologists get the power to define what is mentally abnormal and needs treatment, and physicians get to define physical abnormality.

It should be clear that Marxism and all its variations get into trouble when applied to themselves. If all ideas are believed simply because they serve the interests of some class, presumably a Marxist's belief in Marxism is caused by its effectiveness in helping him seize power. On the Marxist's own theory, it is impossible to attain the neutral perspective required to see that his theory is true. The same goes for Foucault, of course; why not label (and dismiss) him as someone seeking to control discourse with his own arbitrary inventions?

An even more extreme position is taken by Jacques Derrida, perhaps the most widely known deconstructionist. His original field was literary criticism, his theme that an author has no privileged knowledge of the meaning of his own work. There is "no transcendental signified," no independent meaning; each reader brings his own interpretation to a text. But Derrida has extended his reach to encompass virtually all human activity: "any apparently coherent system of thought can be shown to have underlying, unresolvable antinomies . . . multiple and conflicting readings that must be held simultaneously." Everything, even nature itself, becomes a "text" open to interpretation. If that seems too bizarre, then certainly *theories* about nature can be treated as text. Science and philosophy are just other fictional genres.

To the extent that there can be an argument for a view like Derrida's, it rests on identifying the meaning of a word with every association the word calls up in anyone's mind. If meaning is so understood, it follows immediately that no word has a stable intersubjective meaning, or a stable intrasubjective meaning across time, and that mutual understanding is impossible. The word *elephant* reminds me of Dumbo but reminds you of Republicans. If both associations partly define the word, we are asking the zookeeper different questions when we each inquire the way to the elephant house. But all this shows is the silliness of defining "meaning" so broadly. It is clearly preferable to restrict the meaning of a word to a core of associations shared by all its users, so that "elephant" means "big gray mammal with floppy ears and a trunk." Our expectation that everyone means *that* by "elephant" is what makes communication possible. It is revealing that deconstructionists commonly support their view of communication by analyzing passages from literature, which of course depend for their effect on the myriad resonances of words. Their view loses all plausibility when applied to literal or technical language. What "unresolvable antinomies" is one likely to find in instructions for changing a fuse?

CONCLUSION

We have found that virtually all critics of objectivity say something like the following:

1. It is an objective fact that there are no objective facts.
2. It is absolutely true that everything is relative to a framework.
3. No one can divorce himself from his social milieu to examine his society with a critical eye, and that conclusion is the result of my having done so.
4. There is evidence for the position that there is no such thing as evidence.

In each case, the skeptic states a position that cannot possibly be substantiated or rationally believed. In each case he is in effect asking that you not apply his assertion to his own position, without giving any reason for exempting his words from his own general claim. His position is futile and self-refuting; it can be stated, but it cannot convince anyone who recognizes its implications.

It might be argued that, strictly speaking, these arguments are not literally contradictory. Consider "theory always influences perception; therefore, there is no objective verification of any claim." The conclusion of this argument (being about theories) does not contradict its premise (which is about observation). To defend skepticism this way, however, overlooks the point of presenting an argument. If we are supposed to accept a conclusion on the basis of a premise, then there must be a reason for accepting the premise. The skeptic must be claiming that we can verify his premise that theory influences perception if he thinks his argument proves that there is no such thing as verification. Merely observing that a premise entails a conclusion accomplishes nothing; I display valid but unsound arguments in logic class every semester. The skeptic must claim that there is some reason to accept his premise as true, in which case his argument really does lead him to contradict himself. If it is replied that the skeptic does not think that his premises are rationally compelling, but only "relatively compelling" to those who share his biases, then his argument loses any point. It can only persuade those who already accept its conclusion and cannot persuade nonskeptics.

Ironically, what the skeptic is attempting is one of the few instances in which inherent contradiction a la Derrida does make a hash out of the whole enterprise. You can't use reason to attack the very idea of reason, and you can't use arguments to convince anyone that arguments are useless. In fact, the ultimate source of Derrida's theory may lie here. Having grasped at some level that the skeptical project is doomed, undermined from within, he may have unconsciously sought to disguise the futility of his own argument by asserting that *all* argument, *all* writing, *all* thinking suffers from this instability, so skeptics are no more misguided than anyone else.

That the self-refuting character of skepticism and nihilism has long been noted makes the persistence of arguments against objectivity curious—like influenza they reappear periodically in slightly different forms and must be attacked with adjusted medications. I suspect that nihilism survives because it resembles a somewhat more benign claim—not that there are no truths or that there is no knowledge, but that we can never be certain which of our beliefs amount to knowledge. The idea that we might know things but not know which ones we know is reminiscent of a paradox about belief. Each of us will grant that, being fallible, not everything we believe is true. But of no particular belief p can we say both that p is false and that we believe p. From this it does not follow that we really are infallible, anymore than the impossibility of being aware that we are dreamlessly asleep shows that we are always awake. Similarly, those of us who hold out for objective knowledge will argue that we can come to know some truths but, alas, may never be in a position to state positively of any given belief that it is one that we know.

Chapter 39

JURGEN HABERMAS

Jurgen Habermas was born in Dusseldorf, Germany, in 1929 and attended universities in Göttingen, Bonn, and Zurich. He became Professor of Philosophy at Frankfurt University in 1983. He now holds a joint appointment at the New School of Social Research in New York City.

Habermas has sought to reconcile Continental Philosophy with the Anglo-American tradition. He has opposed Logical Positivism and naturalistic philosophies in general as promoting *scientism*, the idea that all truth can be reduced to scientific explanation. He argues that all knowledge is guided by cognitive self-interest and that there is no algorithmic process to ensure arriving at objective truth. The best we can do is form ideal conversational situations (*ideal speech situations*) where people can dialogue within community, until "the force of the better argument" leads to understanding and agreement. Critics, especially feminists, have accused Habermas of still holding on to the Enlightenment Project, contending that there are no such things as *ideal speech situations*. They contend that all speech situations are dominated by power structures, which define truth.

In our selection Habermas argues that the traditional view of philosophy as assessor and judge of science and all knowledge claims is bankrupt, but that philosophy can still play the role of guardian of rationality—not in a rigid, absolute sense, but as the fallibilist pragmatist, seeking to arrive at consensus via reasoned discourse in suitable contexts. He acknowledges the pragmatic insights of Rorty (see Chapter 37), but thinks that Rorty fails to appreciate the strength of rational, philosophical discourse in working out our world views.

FOR FURTHER READING

Habermas, J. *Towards a Rational Society* (including "Technology and science as ideology") (Beacon Press, 1971).

———. *Knowledge and Human Interests* (Beacon Press, 1972).

———. *Legitimation Crisis* (Beacon Press, 1973).

———. *Theory and Practice* (Beacon Press, 1973).

———. *Communication and the Evolution of Society* (Beacon Press, 1979).

———. *Theory of Communicative Action*, 2 vols. (Beacon Press, 1984, 1987).

———. *Autonomy and Solidarity* (interviews) (Verso, 1986).

———. *The Philosophical Discourse of Modernity* (MIT Press, 1987).

———. *On the Logic of the Social Sciences* (MIT Press, 1988).

———. *The New Conservativism* (MIT Press, 1989).

———. *The Structural Transformation of the Public Sphere* (MIT Press, 1989).

———. *Moral Consciousness and Communicative Action* (MIT Press, 1990).

———. *Postmetaphysical Thinking* (MIT Press, 1992).

———. *Justification and Application* (MIT Press, 1993).

Philosophy as Stand-in and Interpreter

Master thinkers have fallen on hard times. This has been true of Hegel ever since Popper unmasked him in the forties as an enemy of the open society. It has also been intermittently true of Marx. The last to denounce Marx as a false prophet were the New Philosophers in the seventies. Today even Kant is affected by this decline. If I am correct, he is being viewed for the first time as a *maître penseur*, that is, as the magician of a false paradigm from the intellectual constraints of which we have to escape. Though among a philosophical audience there may still be a majority of scholars whose image of Kant has stayed the same, in the world outside his reputation is being eclipsed, and not for the first time, by Nietzsche.

Historically, Kantian philosophy marks the birth of a new mode of justification. Kant felt that the physics of his time and the growth of knowledge brought by it were important developments to which the philosopher had to respond. For Kant, the new science represented not some philosophically indifferent fact of life but proof of man's capacity to know. Specifically, the challenge Newtonian physics posed for philosophy was to explain how empirical knowledge is at all possible, an explanation that could not itself be empirical but had to be transcendental. What Kant calls 'transcendental' is an inquiry into the a priori conditions of what makes experience possible. The specific upshot of Kant's transcendental inquiry is that those conditions are identical with the conditions of possible objects of experience. The first job for the philosopher, then, is to analyze the concepts of objects as we 'always already' intuitively use them. Transcendental analysis is a nonempirical reconstruction of the a priori achievements of the cognizing subject, achievements for which there is no alternative: No experience shall be thought possible under *different* conditions. Transcendental justification has nothing to do with deduction from first principles. Rather, the hallmark of the transcendental justification is the notion that we can prove the nonsubstitutability of certain mental operations that we always already (intuitively) perform in accordance with rules.

As a master thinker, Kant fell into disfavor because he used transcendental justification to found the new discipline of epistemology. In so doing, he redefined the task, or vocation if you like, of philosophy in a more demanding way. There are two principal reasons why the Kantian view of philosophy's vocation has a dubious ring today.

The first reason has directly to do with the foundationalism of epistemology. In championing the idea of a cognition *before* cognition, Kantian philosophy sets up a domain between itself and the sciences, arrogating authority to itself. It wants to clarify the foundations of the sciences once and for all, defining the limits of what can and cannot be experienced. This is tantamount to an act of showing the sciences their proper place. I think philosophy cannot and should not try to play the role of usher.

The second reason lies in the fact that transcendental philosophy refuses to be confined to epistemology. Above and beyond analyzing the bases of cognition, the critique of pure reason is also supposed to enable us to criticize the abuses of this cognitive faculty, which is limited to phenomena. Kant replaces the substantive concept of reason found in traditional metaphysics with a concept of reason the moments of which have undergone differentiation to the point where their unity is merely formal. He sets up practical reason, judgment, and theoretical cognition in isolation from each other, giving each a foundation unto itself, with the result that philosophy is cast in the role of the highest arbiter for all matters, including culture as a whole. Kantian philosophy differentiates what Weber was to call the 'value spheres of culture' (science and technology, law and morality, art and art criticism), while at the same time legitimating them within their respective limits. Thus Kant's philosophy poses as the highest court of appeal *vis-à-vis* the sciences and culture as a whole.

There is a necessary link between the Kantian foundationalism in epistemology, which nets philosophy the unenviable role of usher, and the ahistoricity of the conceptual system Kant superimposes on culture, which nets philosophy the equally unde-

From *Moral Consciousness and Communicative Action*, Cambridge, Mass.: MIT Press, 1990. Endnotes deleted.

sirable role of a judge parceling out separate areas of jurisdiction to science, morality, and art.

> Without the Kantian assumption that the philosopher can decide *questiones juris* concerning the rest of culture, this self-image collapses. . . . To drop the notion of the philosopher as knowing something about knowing which nobody else knows so well would be to drop the notion that his voice always has an overriding claim on the attention of the other participants in the conversation. It would also be to drop the notion that there is something called "philosophical method" or "philosophical technique" or "the philosophical point of view" which enables the professional philosopher, *ex officio*, to have interesting views about, say, the respectability of psychoanalysis, the legitimacy of certain dubious laws, the resolution of moral dilemmas, the soundness of schools of historiography or literary criticism, and the like.

Richard Rorty's impressive critique of philosophy assembles compelling metaphilosophical arguments in support of the view that the roles Kant the master thinker had envisaged for philosophy, namely those of usher and judge, are too big for it. While I find myself in agreement with much of what Rorty says, I have trouble accepting his conclusion, which is that if philosophy forswears these two roles, it must also surrender the function of being the 'guardian of rationality'. If I understand Rorty, he is saying that the new modesty of philosophy involves the abandonment of any claim to reason—the very claim that has marked philosophical thought since its inception. Rorty not only argues for the demise of philosophy; he also unflinchingly accepts the end of the belief that ideas like truth or the unconditional with their transcending power are a necessary condition of humane forms of collective life.

Implied by Kant's conception of formal, differentiated reason is a theory of modernity. Modernity is characterized by a rejection of the substantive rationality typical of religious and metaphysical worldviews and by a belief in procedural rationality and its ability to give credence to our views in the three areas of objective knowledge, moral-practical insight, and aesthetic judgment. What I am asking myself is this: Is it true that this (or a similar) concept of modernity becomes untenable when you dismiss the claims of a foundationalist theory of knowledge?

What follows is an attempt to narrate a story that might help put Rorty's criticism of philosophy in perspective. Granted, by going this route I cannot settle the controversy. What I can do is throw light on some of its presuppositions. At the outset (section 1 below) I will look at Hegel's critique of Kantian foundationalism and the substitution of a dialectical mode of justification for Kant's transcendental one. Next (section 2) I will retrace some of the lines of criticism and self-criticism that have emerged in the Kantian and Hegelian traditions. In section 3 I will dwell on a more radical form of criticism originating in pragmatist and hermeneuticist quarters, a form of attack that repudiates Kant and Hegel simultaneously. Section 4 deals with thinkers, respectable ones no less, who respond to this situation by annulling philosophy's long-standing claim to reason. In conclusion (section 5) I will argue that philosophy, while well advised to withdraw from the problematic roles of usher (*Platzanweiser*) and judge, can and ought to retain its claim to reason, provided it is content to play the more modest roles of stand-in (*Platzhalter*) and interpreter.

1

Hegel fashioned his dialectical mode of justification in deliberate opposition to the transcendental one of Kant. Hegel—and I can only hint at this here—agrees with those who charge that in the end Kant failed to justify or ground the pure concepts of the understanding, for he merely culled them from the table of forms of judgment, unaware of their historical specificity. Thus he failed, in Hegel's eyes, to prove that the *a priori* conditions of what makes experience possible are truly necessary. In his *Phenomenology of Spirit* Hegel proposes to correct this flaw by taking a genetic approach. What Kant regarded as a unique (Copernican) turn to transcendental reflection becomes in Hegel a general mechanism for turning consciousness back upon itself. This mechanism has been switched on and off time and time again in the development of spirit. As the subject becomes conscious of itself, it destroys one form of consciousness after another. This process epitomizes the subjective experience that what initially appears to the subject as a being in itself can become content only in the forms imparted to it by the subject. The transcendental philosopher's experience is thus, according to Hegel, reenacted naively whenever an in-itself becomes a for-the-subject. What Hegel calls 'dialectical' is the reconstruction of this recurrent experience and of its assimilation by the subject, which gives rise to ever more complex structures. Hegel goes beyond the particular manifestation of consciousness that Kant analyzed, attaining in the end knowledge that has become autonomous, that is, absolute knowledge. This highest vantage point enables Hegel, the phenomenologist, to witness the genesis of structures of consciousness that Kant had assumed to be timeless.

Hegel, it should be noted, exposes himself to a criticism similar to the one he levels against Kant. Reconstructing successive forms of consciousness is one thing. Proving the necessity of their succession is quite another. Hegel is not unaware of this gap, and he tries to close it by logical means, thereby laying the basis for a philosophical absolutism that claims an even grander role for philosophy than did Kant. In Hegel's *Logic* philosophy's role is to effect an encyclopedic conceptual synthesis of the diffuse chunks of content thrown up by the sciences. In addition, Hegel picks up Kant's latent theory of modernity, making it explicit and developing it into a critique of the dirremptive, self-contradictory features of modernity. It is this peculiar twist that gave philosophy a new world-historical relevance in relation to culture as a whole. And this is the stuff of which the suspect image of Hegel as a master thinker is made.

The metaphilosophical attack on the *maîtres penseurs*, whether its target be Hegel's absolutism or Kant's foundationalism, is a recent phenomenon. Antecedents of it can be found in the strands of self-criticism that have run through Kantianism and Hegelianism for quite some time. I shall comment briefly on two lines of self-criticism that I think complement each other in an interesting way.

2

In reference to Kant's transcendental philosophy there are today three distinct critical positions: the analytic one of Strawson, the constructivist one of Lorenzen, and the critical-rationalist one of Popper.

Analytic philosophy appropriates Kant by jettisoning any claim to ultimate justification (*Letztbegründung*). From the very outset it drops the objective Kant had in mind when he deduced the pure concepts of the understanding from the unity of self-consciousness. The analytic reception of Kant is confined to comprehending those concepts and rules that underlie experience insofar as it can be couched in elementary propositions. The analysis focuses on general, indispensable, conceptual preconditions that make experience possible. Unable to prove the objective validity of its basic concepts and presuppositions, this analysis nevertheless makes a universalistic claim. Redeeming it involves changing Kant's transcendental strategy of justification into a testing procedure. If the hypothetically reconstructed conceptual system underlying experience as such is valid, not a single intelligible alternative to it can possibly exist. This means any alternative proposal will be scrutinized with a view to proving its derivative character, that is, with a view to showing that the alleged alternative inevitably utilizes portions of the very hypothesis it seeks to supplant. A strategy of argumentation like this tries to prove that the concepts and presuppositions it singles out as fundamental cannot be dispensed with. Turned modest, the transcendental philosopher of the analytic variety takes on the role of the skeptic who keeps trying to find counterexamples that might invalidate his theories. In short, he acts like a hypothesis-testing scientist.

The *constructivist position* tried to compensate for the justificatory shortfall that has now opened up from the perspective of transcendental philosophy in the following way. It concedes from the start that the basic conceptual organization of experience is conventional while at the same time putting a constructivist critique of language in the service of epistemology. Those conventions are considered valid that are generated methodically and therefore transparently. It should be clear that this approach lays, rather than uncovers, the foundations of cognition.

On the face of it, the *critical-rationalist position* breaks completely with transcendentalism. It holds that the three horns of the "Munchhausen trilemma"—logical circularity, infinite regress, and recourse to absolute certitude—can only be avoided if one gives up any hope of grounding or justifying whatsoever. Here the notion of justification is being dislodged in favor of the concept of critical testing, which becomes the critical rationalist's equivalent for justification. In this connection I would argue that criticism is itself a procedure whose employment is never presuppositionless. That is why I think that critical rationalism, by clinging to the idea of irrefutable rules of criticism, allows a weak version of the Kantian justificatory mode to sneak into its inner precincts through the back door.

Self-criticism in the Hegelian tradition has developed along lines parallel to the self-criticism among Kantians. Again, three distinct positions might be said to be represented by the young Lukács and his materialist critique of epistemology, which restricts the claim to justification of dialectics to the man-made world and excludes nature; by K. Korsch's and H. Freyer's practicism, wherein the classical relation of theory and practice is stood on its head and the 'interested' perspective of creating a society of the future informs the theoretical reconstruction of social development; and finally by the negativism of Adorno, who finds in comprehensive logic of development only the proof that it is impossible to break the spell of an instrumental reason gone mad.

I cannot examine these positions here. All I shall do is to point out certain interesting parallels between the Hegelian and Kantian strands of self-criticism. The self-criticism that begins by doubting the Kantian transcendental deduction and the self-criticism that begins by doubting Hegel's passage to absolute knowledge have this in common: they reject the claim that the categorial makeup and the pattern of development of the human spirit can be proved to be necessary. With regard to constructivism and practicism a similar convergence occurs: both are involved in a shift from rational reconstruction to creative praxis, which is to make possible a theoretical recapitualation of this praxis. Critical rationalism and negativism, for their part, share something too, which is that they reject transcendental and dialectical means of cognition while at the same time using them in a paradoxical way. One may also view these two attempts at radical negation as showing that these two modes of justification cannot be abolished except on penalty of self-contradiction.

My comparison between parallel self-critical strategies to restrict the justificatory claims of transcendental and dialectical philosophies gives rise to the following question: Do these self-limiting tendencies merely reinforce each other, encouraging the skeptic to reject justification all the more roundly? Or does the retrenchment on either side to a position of diminished justificatory objectives and strategies represent a precondition for viewing them not as opposites but as supplementing each other? I think the second possibility deserves serious consideration. The genetic structuralism of Jean Piaget provides an instructive model along these lines, instructive for all philosophers, I think, but particularly those who want to remain philosophers. Piaget conceives "reflective abstraction" as that learning mechanism which explains the transition between cognitive stages in ontogenetic development. The end point of this development is a decentered understanding of the world. Reflective abstraction is similar to transcendental reflection in that it brings out the formal elements hidden in the cognitive content, identifies them as the schemata that underlie the knowing subject's action, differentiates them, and reconstructs them at the next highest stage of reflection. Seen from a different perspective, the same learning mechanism has a function similar to Hegel's power of negation, which dialectically supersedes self-contradictory forms of consciousness.

3

The aforementioned six positions in the tradition of Kant and Hegel stick to a claim to reason, however small in scope, however cautious in formulation. It is this final intention that sets off Popper and Lakatos from a Feyerabend and Horkheimer and Adorno from a Foucault. They still say *something* about the indispensable conditions of claims to the validity of those beliefs we hold to be justified, claims that transcend all restrictions of time and place. Now any attack on the master thinkers questions this residual claim to reason and thus in essence makes a plea for the abolition of philosophy. I can explain this radical turn by talking briefly about a wholly different criticism, one that has been raised against both Kant *and* Hegel.

Its proponents can be found in *pragmatism* and *hermeneutic philosophy*. Their doubts concerning the justificatory and self-justificatory potential of philosophy operate at a more profound level than do the self-criticisms within the Kantian and Hegelian traditions. They step resolutely outside the parameters set by the philosophy of consciousness and its cognitive paradigm, which stresses the perception and representation of objects. Pragmatism and hermeneutics oust the traditional notion of the solitary subject that confronts objects and becomes reflective only by turning itself into an object. In its place they put an idea of cognition that is mediated by language and linked to action. Moreover, they emphasize the web of everyday life and communication surrounding 'our' cognitive achievements.

The latter are intrinsically intersubjective and cooperative. It is unimportant just how this web is conceptualized, whether as 'form of life', 'lifeworld', 'practice', 'linguistically mediated interaction', a 'language game', 'convention', 'cultural background', a 'tradition', 'effective history', or what have you. The important thing is that these commonsensical ideas, though they may function quite differently, attain a status that used to be reserved for the basic concepts of epistemology. Pragmatism and hermeneutics, then, accord a higher position to acting and speaking than to knowing. But there is more to it than that. Purposive action and linguistic communication play a qualitatively different role from that of self-reflection in the philosophy of consciousness. They have no justificatory function any more save one: to expose the need for foundational knowledge as unjustified.

Charles S. Peirce doubted that radical doubt is possible. His intentions were the same as those of Dilthey, who doubted that neutrality in interpretive understanding is possible. For Peirce problems always arise in a specific situation. They come to us, as it were. We do not go to them, for we do not fully control the totality of our practical existence. In a similar vein Dilthey argues that we cannot grasp a symbolic expression unless we have an intuitive preunderstanding of its context, for we do not have unlimited freedom to convert the unproblematic background knowledge of our own culture into explicit knowledge. Every instance of problem solving and every interpretation depend on a web of myriad presuppositions. Since this web is holistic and particularistic at the same time, it can never be grasped by an abstract, general analysis. It is from this standpoint that the myth of the given—that is, the distinctions between sensibility and understanding, intuition and concept, form and content—can be debunked, along with the distinctions between analytic and synthetic judgments, between *a priori* and *a posteriori*. These Kantian dualisms are all being dissolved, a fact that is vaguely reminiscent of Hegel's metacritique. Of course, a full-fledged return to Hegel is made impossible by the contextualism and historicism to which the pragmatist and hermeneutic approaches subscribe.

There is no denying that pragmatism and hermeneutics represent a gain. Instead of focusing introspectively on consciousness, these two points of view look outside at objectifications of action and language. Gone is the fixation on the cognitive function of consciousness. Gone too is the emphasis on the representational function of language and the visual metaphor of the 'mirror of nature'. What takes their place is the notion of justified belief spanning the whole spectrum of what can be said—of what Wittgenstein and Austin call illocutionary force—rather than just the contents of fact-stating discourses. 'Saying things is not always saying how things are'.

Do these considerations strengthen Rorty's interpretation of pragmatism and hermeneutics, which argues for the abnegation by philosophical thought of any claim to rationality and indeed for the abnegation of philosophy *per se*? Or do they mark the beginning of a new paradigm that, while discarding the mentalistic language game of the philosophy of consciousness, retains the justificatory modes of that philosophy in the modest, self-critical form in which I have presented them? I cannot answer this question directly for want of compelling and simple arguments. Once again, the answer I will give is a narrative one.

4

Marx wanted to supersede (*aufheben*) philosophy by realizing it—so convinced was he of the truth of Hegelian philosophy, whose only fault was that concept and reality cleaved unbearably, a fault that Hegel studiously overlooked. The corresponding, though fundamentally different, present-day attitude toward philosophy is the dismissive goodbye and good riddance. These farewells take many forms, three of which are currently in vogue. For simplicity's sake I will call them the therapeutic, the heroic, and the salvaging farewell.

Wittgenstein championed the notion of a *therapeutic* philosophy, therapeutic in the specific sense of self-healing, for philosophy was sick to the core. Wittgenstein's diagnosis was that philosophy had disarrayed language games that function perfectly well in everyday life. The weakness of this particular farewell to philosophy is that it leaves the world as it is. For the standards by which philosophy is being critized are taken straight from the self-sufficient, routinized forms of life in which philosophy happens to survive for now. And what about possible successors? Field research in cultural anthropology seems to be the strongest candidate to succeed philosophy after its demise. Surely the history of philosophy will henceforth be interpreted as the unintelligible doings of some outlandish tribe that today is fortunately extinct. (Perhaps Rorty will one day be celebrated as the path-breaking Thucydides of this new approach, which incidentally could only get under way after Wittgenstein's medicine had proved effective.)

There is a sharp contrast between the soft-spoken farewell of the therapeutic philosopher and the noisy demolition undertaken by someone like Georges Bataille or Heidegger. Their goodbye is *heroic*. From their perspective too, false habits of living and thinking are concentrated in elevated forms of philosophical reflection. But instead of accusing philosophy of homely category mistakes or simple disruptions of everyday life, their deconstruction of metaphysics and objectivating thought has a more incisive, epochal quality. This more dramatic farewell to philosophy does not promise a cure. Rather, it resembles Hölderlin's pathos-laden idea of a rescue attempt *in extremis*. The devalued and discredited philosophical tradition, rather than being replaced by something even more valueless than itself, is supposed to give way to a *different* medium that makes possible a return to the immemorial—to Bataille's sovereignty or Heidegger's Being.

Least conspicuous, finally, is the *salvaging* type of farewell to philosophy. Contemporary neo-Aristotelians best exemplify this type insofar as they do exegeses that are informed by hermeneutics. Some of their work is unquestionably significant. But all too often it departs from pure interpretation in an effort to salvage some old truth or other. At any rate, this farewell to philosophy has a disingenuous ring: While the salvager keeps invoking the need to preserve philosophy, he wants to have nothing to do with its systematic claims. He does not try to make the ancients relevant to the discussion of some subject matter. Nor does he present the classics as a cultural treasure prepared by philosophy and history. What he does is to appropriate by assimilation texts that were once thought to embody knowledge, treating them instead as sources of illumination and edification.

Let us return for a moment to the critique of Kant, the master thinker, and in particular to his foundationalism in epistemology. Clearly, present-day philosophies of the sort just described wisely sidestep the Kantian trap. The last thing they think they can do is show the natural sciences to their proper place. Contemporary poststructuralist, late-pragmatist, and neohistoricist tendencies share a narrow objectivistic conception of science. Over against scientific cognition they carve out a sphere where thought can be illuminating or awakening instead of being objective. These tendencies prefer to sever all links with general, criticizable claims to validity. They would rather make do without notions like consensus, incontrovertible results, and justified beliefs. Paradoxically enough, whereas they make these (unnecessary) sacrifices, they somehow keep believing in the authority and superiority of philosophical insights: their own. In terms of their views on science, the philosophers of the definitive farewell agree with the existentialist proposal (Jaspers, Sartre, Kolakowski) for a division of labor that puts science on one side and philosophical faith, life, existential freedom, myth, cultivation, or what have you, on the other. All these juxtapositions are identical in structure. Where they differ is in their assessment of what Max Weber termed the cultural relevance of science, which may range from negative to neutral to positive. As is well known, Continental philosophy has a penchant for dramatizing the dangers of objectivism and instrumental reason, whereas Anglo-American philosophy takes a more relaxed view of them.

With his distinction between normal and abnormal discourse, Richard Rorty has come up with an interesting variation on the above theme. In times of widely acknowledged theoretical progress, normality takes hold of the established sciences. This means methods become available that make problem solving and dispute settling possible. What Rorty calls commensurable discourses are those discourses that operate with reliable criteria of consensus building. In contrast, discourses are incommensurable or abnormal when basic orientations are contested. Generally, abnormal conversations tend to pass over into normal ones, their ultimate purpose being to annul themselves and to bring about universal agreement. Occasionally, however, abnormal discourses stop short of taking this self-transcending step and are content with 'interesting and fruitful disagreement'. That is, they become *sufficient unto themselves*. It is at this point that abnormal discourses take on the quality that Rorty calls 'edifying'. According to him, philosophy as a whole verges on edifying conversation once it has sloughed off all pretensions to problem solving. Such philosophical edification enjoys the benefits of all three types of farewell: therapeutic relief, heroic overcoming, and hermeneutic reawaking. It combines the inconspicuously subversive force of leisure with an elitist notion of creative linguistic imagination and with the wisdom of the ages. The desire for edification, however, works to the detriment of the desire for truth: 'Edifying philosophers can never end philosophy, but they can help prevent it from attaining the secure path of a science'.

I am partly sympathetic to Rorty's allocation of roles, for I agree that philosophy has no business playing the part of the highest arbiter in matters of science and culture. I find his argument unconvincing all the same. For even a philosophy that has been taught its limits by pragmatism and hermeneuticism will not be able to find a resting place in edifying conservation *outside* the sciences without immediately being drawn back into argumentation, that is, justificatory discourse.

The existentialist or, if you like, exclusive division of labor between philosophy and science is untenable. This is borne out by the particular version of discourse theory Rorty proposes. Ultimately, there is only one criterion by which beliefs can be judged valid, and that is that they are based on agreement reached by argumentation. This means that *everything* whose validity is at all disputable rests on shaky foundations. It matters little if the ground underfoot shakes a bit less for those who debate problems of physics than for those who debate problems of morals and aesthetics. The difference is a matter of degree only, as the postempiricist philosophy of science has shown. Normalization of discourse is not a sufficiently trenchant criterion for distinguishing science from edifying philosophical conversation.

5

To those who advocate a cut-and-dried division of labor, research traditions representing a blend of philosophy and science have always been particularly offensive. Marxism and psychoanalysis are cases in point. They cannot, on this view, help being pseudosciences because they straddle normal and abnormal discourse, refusing to fall on either side of the dividing line. On this point Rorty speaks the same language as Jaspers. What I know about the history of the social sciences and psychology leads me to believe that hybrid discourses such as Marxism and psychoanalysis are by no means atypical. To the contrary, they may well stand for a type of approach that marks the beginning of new research traditions.

What holds for Freud applies to all seminal theories in these disciplines, for instance, those of Durkheim, Mead, Max Weber, Piaget, and Chomsky. Each inserted a genuinely philosophical idea like a detonator into a particular context of research. Symptom formation through repression, the creation of solidarity through the sacred, the identity-forming function of role taking, modernization as rationalization of society, decentration as an outgrowth of reflective abstraction from action, language acquisition as an activity of hypothesis testing—these key phrases stand for so many paradigms in which a philosophical idea is present in embryo while at the same time empirical, yet universal, questions are being posed. It is no coincidence that theoretical approaches of this kind are the favorite target of empiricist counterattacks. Such cyclical movements in the history of science, incidentally, do not point to a convergence of these disciplines in one unified science. It makes better sense to view them as stages on the road to the philosophization of the sciences of man (*Philosophischwerden der Humanwissenschaften*) than as stages in the triumphal march toward objectivist approaches, such as neurophysiology, that quaint favorite child of the analytic philosophers.

What I have said lies mainly in the realm of speculative conjecture. But unless I am completely mistaken, it makes sense to suggest that philosophy, instead of just dropping the usher role and being left with nothing, ought to exchange it for the part of stand-in (*Platzhalter*). Whose seat would philosophy be keeping; what would it be standing in for? Empirical theories with strong universalistic claims. As I have indicated, there have surfaced and will continue to surface in nonphilosophical disciplines fertile minds who will give such theories a try. The chance for their emergence is greatest in the reconstructive sciences. Starting primarily from the intuitive knowledge of competent subjects—competent in terms of judgment, action, and language—and secondarily from systematic knowledge handed down by culture, the reconstructive sciences explain the presumably universal bases of rational experience and judgment, as well as of action and linguistic communication. Marked down in price, the venerable transcendental and dialectical modes of justification may still come in handy. All they can fairly be expected to furnish, however, is reconstructive hypotheses for use in empirical settings. Telling examples of a successful cooperative integration of philosophy and science can be seen in the development of a theory of rationality. This is an area where philosophers work as suppliers of ideas without raising foundationalist or absolutist claims à la Kant or Hegel. Fallibilistic in orientation, they reject the dubious faith in philosophy's ability to do things single-handedly, hoping instead that the success that has for so long eluded it might come from an auspicious matching of different theoretical fragments. From the vantage point of my own research interests, I see such a cooperation taking shape between philosophy of science and history of science, between speech act theory and empirical approaches to pragmatics of language, between a theory of informal argumentation and empirical approaches to natural argumentation, between cognitivist ethics and a psychology of moral development, between philosophical theories of action and the ontogenetic study of action competences.

If it is true that philosophy has entered upon a phase of cooperation with the human sciences, does it not run the risk of losing its identity? There is some justification in Spaemann's warning 'that every philosophy makes a practical and a theoretical claim to totality and that not to make such a twofold claim is to be doing something which does not qualify as philosophy'. In defense, one might argue that a philosophy that contributes something important to an analysis of the rational foundations of knowing, acting, and speaking does retain at least a thematic connection with the whole. But is this enough? What becomes of the theory of modernity, what of the window on the totality of culture that Kant and Hegel opened with their foundational and hypostatizing concepts of reason? Down to Husserl's *Crisis of the European Sciences*, philosophy not only usurped the part of supreme judge, it also played a directing role. Again, what happens when it surrenders the role of judge in matters of science as well as culture? Does this mean philosophy's relation to the totality is severed? Does this mean it can no longer be the guardian of rationality?

The situation of culture as a whole is no different from the situation of science as a whole. As totalities, neither needs to be grounded or justified or given a place by philosophy. Since the dawn of modernity in the eighteenth century, culture has generated those structures of rationality that Max Weber and Emil Lask conceptualized as cultural value spheres. Their existence calls for description and analysis, not philosophical justification.

Reason has split into three movements—modern science, positive law and posttraditional ethics, and autonomous art and institutionalized art criticism—but philosophy had precious little to do with this disjunction. Ignorant of sophisticated critiques of reason, the sons and daughters of modernity have progressively learned to differentiate their cultural tradition in terms of these three aspects of rationality such that they deal with issues of truth, justice, and taste discretely rather than simulataneously. At a different level, this shift toward differentiation produces the following phenomena: (1) The sciences disgorge more and more elements of religion, thus renouncing their former claim to being able to interpret nature and history as one whole. (2) Cognitivist moral theories disgorge issues of the good life, focusing instead strictly on deontological, generalizable aspects of ethics, so that all that remains of 'the good' is the just. (3) With art it is likewise. Since the turn to autonomy, art has striven mightily to mirror one basic aesthetic experience, the increasing decentralization of subjectivity. It occurs as the subject leaves the spatiotemporal structures of everyday life behind, freeing itself from the conventions of everyday perception, of purposive behavior, and of the imperatives of work and utility.

I repeat, these eminent trends toward compartmentalization, constituting as they do the hallmark of modernity, can do very well without philosophical justification. But they do pose problems of mediation. First, how can reason, once it has been thus sundered, go on being a unity on the level of culture? And second, how can expert cultures, which are being pushed more and more to the level of rarefied, esoteric forms, be made to stay in touch with everyday communication? To the extent to which philosophy keeps at least one eye trained on the topic of rationality, that is, to the extent to which it keeps inquiring into the conditions of the unconditional, to that extent it will not dodge the demand for these two kinds of efforts at mediation.

The first type of problem of mediation arises within the spheres of science, morals, and art. In this area we witness the rise of counter-movements. For example, in human sciences nonobjectivist approaches bring moral and aesthetic criticism into play without undermining the primacy of issues of truth. Another example is the way in which the discussion of ethics of responsibility and ethics of conviction and the expanded role of utilitarian considerations within universalist ethics have brought the calculation of consequences and the interpretation of needs into play—and these are perspectives situated rather in the domains of the cognitive and the expressive. Let us finally look at postmodern art as the third example. It is characterized by a strange simultaneity of realistic, politically committed schools on the one hand and authentic followers of the classical modernism to which we owe the crystallization of the specific meaning of the aesthetic on the other. In realistic and politically committed art, elements of the cognitive and the moral-practical come into play once again, but at the level of the wealth of forms unloosed by the avant-grade. To that extent they act as agents of mediation. Counterdevelopments like these, it seems, mitigate the radical differentiation of reason and point to its unity. Everyday life, however, is a more promising medium for regaining the lost unity of reason than are today's expert cultures or yesteryear's classical philosophy of reason.

In everyday communication, cognitive interpretations, moral expectations, expressions, and evaluations cannot help overlapping and interpenetrating. Reaching understanding in the lifeworld requires a cultural tradition that ranges across *the whole spectrum*, not just the fruits of science and technology. As far as philosophy is concerned, it might do well to refurbish its link with the totality by taking on the role of interpreter on behalf of the lifeworld. It might then be able to help set in motion the interplay between the cognitive-instrumental, moral-practical, and aesthetic-expressive dimensions that has come to a standstill today like a tangled mobile. This simile at least helps identify the issue philosophy will face when it stops playing the part of the arbiter that inspects culture and instead starts playing the part of a mediating interpreter. That issue is how to overcome the isolation of science, morals, and art and their respective expert cultures. How can they be joined to the impoverished traditions of the lifeworld, and how can this be done without detriment to their regional rationality? How can a new balance between the separated moments of reason be established in communicative everyday life?

The critic of the master thinkers will likely express his alarm one more time. What in the world, he will ask, gives the philosopher the right to offer his services as a translator mediating between the everyday world and cultural modernity with its autonomous sectors when he is already more than busy trying to hold open a place for ambitious theoretical strategies within the system of the sciences? I think pragmatism and hermeneutics have joined forces to answer this question by attributing epistemic authority to the community of those who cooperate and speak with one another. Everyday communication makes possible a kind of understanding that is based on claims to validity and then furnishes the only real alternative to exerting influence on one another in more or less coercive ways. The validity claims that we raise in conversation—that is, when we say something with conviction—transcend this specific conversational context, pointing to something beyond the spatiotemporal ambit of the occasion. Every agreement, whether produced for the first time or reaffirmed, is based on (controvertible) grounds or reasons. Grounds have a special property: they force us into yes or no positions. Thus, built into the structure of action oriented toward reaching understanding is an element of unconditionality. And it is this unconditional element that makes the validity (*Gültigkeit*) that we claim for our views different from the mere de facto acceptance (*Geltung*) of habitual practices. From the perspective of first persons, what we consider justified is not a function of custom but a question of justification or grounding. That is why philosophy is 'rooted in the urge to see social practices of justification as more than just such practices'. The same urge is at work when people like me stubbornly cling to the notion that philosophy is the guardian of rationality.